—THE—
Good Food Guide 1995

—THE—
Good Food Guide® 1995

Edited by Jim Ainsworth

Consumers' Association

Which? Books are commissioned and researched by
The Association for Consumer Research and published by
Consumers' Association,
2 Marylebone Road, London NW1 4DF

Copyright © 1994 Consumers' Association Ltd

The Good Food Guide is a registered trade mark of
Consumers' Association Ltd.

Cover photograph by Johanna Fernihough
Cover design by Paul Saunders
Typographic design by Tim Higgins
Maps by Bartholomew, a division of
HarperCollins Publishers

British Library Cataloguing-in-Publication Data
A catalogue record for this book is available
from the British Library.

ISBN 0 85202 509 2

Photoset in Linotron Meridien Medium
by Tradespools Ltd, Frome, Somerset
Printed and bound in The Netherlands
by Rotatie Boekendruk B.V., Krommenie

Contents

The Editor

A former restaurateur, Jim Ainsworth owned The Vineyard in Northampton in the early 1980s, wrote the drinks column in *Punch* for eight years, was the restaurant critic for *Wine* magazine and more recently the wine columnist for *Elle* and *Taste*, and has written books on wine.

How to use this *Guide*

All the entries in this year's *Guide* have been rewritten between April and August 1994. The information on which they are based is from reports sent in by readers over the past year and confirmed by anonymous inspection. No entry is based on a single nomination. In every case, readers and inspectors have been prepared to endorse the quality of the cooking, the dining-room and the value for money.

The rating system grades restaurants, on the basis of their cooking, from 1 to 5. This is not based on elegance, ambience, service and value but on food and cooking. The marks reflect the perception of the *Guide* and its reporters, and signify the following:

1 **Competent cooking** Restaurants that achieve a satisfactory standard, endorsed by readers as worthy of the *Guide*.

2 **Good cooking** Restaurants that produce good food in most departments, though some inconsistencies may have been noted. They please most readers much of the time.

3 **Very good cooking** The kitchen achieves consistent quality, rarely disappointing in any department. Seldom faulted by *Guide* reporters.

4 **Excellent cooking** Restaurants with a high level of ambition and achievement. Generally, they delight.

5 **The best** These may excite debate, not as to whether the cooking is good, but whether it is better than their peers'.

* An asterisk next to a mark signifies that the *Guide* and its readers are of the opinion that the restaurant is a particularly fine example within its numeric classification.

The *Guide* office is reliant on proprietors for price information. Each year owners are asked to mark on a questionnaire the cost, for autumn of that year, of any set meals, and also the lowest and highest à la carte prices for each course. We then calculate the lowest and highest prices for a three-course meal per person, including the cost of coffee, service and half a bottle of house wine. The lowest price forms the first figure that you see in the cost line above an entry. In practice, some people may have drinks before the meal and drink a more expensive wine;

also, prices are likely to rise during the currency of the *Guide*. To reflect this, the second price in the cost line is the highest price we have calculated for a three-course meal (sometimes four or five courses if it is a set meal) inflated by 20 per cent to bring some realism to bear on the likely upper limit. In essence, the cost line shows the least and the most you are likely to pay, with most meals falling somewhere in-between.

How to read a *Guide* entry

CANTERBURY Kent [1]   map 3 [2]

▲ *Mary's Kitchen* [3] ♆ ▮ [4] ✻ [5] £ [6] | **NEW ENTRY** | [7]

16 Elwood Avenue, Canterbury CT41 4RX [8]
CANTERBURY (0227) 7770666 [9]   COOKING 2* [11]
on B2068, 2m S of Canterbury [10]   COST £19–£24 [12]

(main text) [13]   CELLARMAN'S CHOICE [14]

CHEF: Mary Smith   PROPRIETORS: Mary and David Smith [15]   OPEN: Mon to Sat; 12 to 2, 7 to 9 [16]   CLOSED: Aug [17]   MEALS: alc (main courses £6 to £12). Set L £12, Set D £25. [18] Cover £1. Minimum £5 L. Unlicensed, but bring your own: corkage £1 [19]   SERVICE: net prices, card slips closed [20]   CARDS: Access, Amex, Diners, Visa [21]   DETAILS: 72 seats. 4 tables outside. Private parties: 26 main room, 10 private room. [22]   Car park. Vegetarian meals. [23] Healthy eating options. [24]   Children's helpings. No children under 10. [25]   Jacket and tie. [26]   No-smoking in dining-room. [27]   Wheelchair access (2 steps; also WC). [28]   No music. [29]   Air-conditioned   ACCOMMODATION: 14 rooms, all with bath/shower. TV. Phone. Air-conditioned. B&B £20 to £40. [30]   Deposit: £50. [31]   Rooms for disabled. [32]   Children welcome. [33]   Baby facilities. [34]   Pets welcome. [35]   Afternoon teas. [36]   Garden. Swimming-pool. Sauna. Tennis. Doors close at 11.30. Confirm by 6. Fax: (0227) 7770666 [37] (*The Which? Hotel Guide*) [38]

---

1 The town and county. The *Guide*'s main entries are divided into eight sections: London, England, Scotland, Wales, Isle of Man, Channel Islands, Northern Ireland and Republic of Ireland. In the London section, restaurants are listed alphabetically by name; in all other sections, they are listed under town. The maps (at the back of the book) can be used as a starting point to locate areas of interest; then look up the entries under the town name. The London maps locate restaurants by name.

2 The map number. The maps are at the end of the *Guide*.

3 The name of the restaurant. ▲ in front of the name denotes that it offers accommodation too.

4 ♆ denotes a wine list that is good, well above the ordinary. The symbol ▮ indicates a truly outstanding wine list.

5 ✻ indicates that smoking (cigarettes, pipes and cigars) is either banned altogether or that one dining-room is maintained for non-smokers. The

symbol does not appear if a restaurant simply has a no-smoking area, or bans smoking at one mealtime only, although these features will be mentioned in the details at the end of an entry. Establishments that do not allow smoking in a dining-room may allow it elsewhere on the premises, such as in the bar or lounge. If you are a smoker, it is always worth checking beforehand.

6 £ indicates that it is possible to have a three-course meal, including coffee, a half-bottle of house wine and service, at *any* time the restaurant is open (i.e. at dinner as well as at lunch, unless a place is only open for dinner), for £20 or less per person. Meals may often cost much more than this, but, by choosing carefully, you should find £20 achievable.

7 If a restaurant is new to the *Guide* this year (it did not appear as a main entry in the last edition), NEW ENTRY appears opposite its name.

8 The restaurant's address and post code.

9 The restaurant's telephone number, including its exchange name and STD code. Note that national dialing codes will change in spring 1995 – see box on page 11 for details.

10 Any special directions in case the restaurant is difficult to find.

11 The *Guide*'s mark, out of five, for cooking quality, ranging from 1 for competent cooking to 5 for the best. See page 7 or the inside front cover for a full explanation. NEW CHEF is indicated instead of a cooking mark for restaurants which had a change of chef as we went to press. These are not the only places (listed) that have new chefs, but are those where the change was too late for our inspection.

12 This is the price range for three-course meals (lunch and/or dinner) for one person, including coffee, wine and service, according to minimum and maximum prices provided by the proprietor for set meals and à la carte dishes. The first figure shows what is probably the least you would have to pay for a three-course meal (often at lunch only), while the second figure indicates a likely maximum amount. The second figure has been inflated by 20 per cent to reflect (i) that some readers will order extra drinks and some top-range dishes, and (ii) likely price rises that will come into play during the life of the *Guide*.

13 The text is based on reports sent in by readers during the last *Guide* year, confirmed by commissioned, anonymous inspections.

14 Some entries conclude with a CELLARMAN'S CHOICE. These are wines, usually more expensive than the house wine, that the restaurant assures us will be in stock during 1995, and recommends as suitable for the kind of food served.

15 The names of the chef(s) and owner(s), so that any change in management will be instantly detectable.

16 The days of the week the restaurant is open, and the times of first and last orders for meals. It is always advisable to book before going to a restaurant. If you book and then cannot go, please remember to telephone the restaurant to cancel.

17 Annual closures.

18 The types of meals that are available, with any variations for lunch (L) or dinner (D). The letters alc denote an à la carte menu. This is followed by a range of main course prices (rounded up to the nearest 50p). Set L and/or Set D denote set lunches and set dinners, and include the basic charge for those meals. Set meals consist usually of three courses, but can cover anything from two to six courses. If a set meal has only two courses, this is stated. Coffee is often included in set meals, wine very occasionally. Special menus, such as a cheaper bar menu or vegetarian menu, may be mentioned in this line. The meal information will be followed by details of any cover charge and minimum charge. (Note that set meals or special menus may not be available at all times – it is always best to check.)

19 A restaurant is unlicensed but customers may bring their own alcoholic drinks on to the premises. Any corkage charge is indicated.

20 Net prices indicates that the prices given on a menu and on a bill are inclusive of VAT and service charge, and that this practice is clearly stated on menu and bill. Card slips closed indicates that the total on the slips of credit cards is closed when handed over for signature. When a fixed service charge is added to the bill, the percentage is specified. When not inc is stated, service is at the discretion of the customer.

21 The credit cards accepted by the restaurant.

22 Not all restaurants will take private parties. The maximum number of people in a party is given for both main and private rooms.

23 This means a vegetarian dish should always be available. If a vegetarian meal is available only with prior notice, we indicate that here. It is always advisable to explain, when booking, if you do not eat meat or fish.

24 Healthy eating options indicates that a restaurant marks on its menu, in words and/or using symbols, low-fat dishes or other healthy eating choices.

25 Some restaurants and hotels are not keen on children in the dining-room. Where it says children welcome or children's helpings, this indicates that they don't mind, although children must be well behaved. Any limitations on age are specified.

26 Jackets and ties are compulsory in very few restaurants and this is specified; otherwise, it is indicated if smart dress is preferred.

27 Any no-smoking arrangements as given to us by the restaurants. See also point 5.

28 Wheelchair access means that the proprietor has confirmed that the entrance is at least 80cm wide and passages at least 120cm across – The Royal Association for Disability and Rehabilitation (RADAR) recommendations. This does not guarantee access to all areas of an establishment. Where there are steps, it will say so. If there are more than three steps, wheelchair access is not stated. If it says 'also WC', then the owner has told us that the toilet facilities are suitable for disabled people.

The *Guide* relies on proprietors giving accurate information on wheelchair access. If you find the details in the *Guide* are inaccurate, please tell us. It is always important to ring first and inform the restaurant of any special requirements.

29 Dining-rooms where live or recorded music is never played. Where a restaurant has told us that music may be played, we indicate this.

30 Room details and the price for rooms and breakfast as given to us by hotels. The first price is for one person in a single room or single occupancy of a double, the second is the upper price for two people in a double room or suite. When a price is for dinner, bed and breakfast, it is indicated as D,B&B.

31 The deposit required to secure accommodation. It may also be expressed as a percentage.

32 There are rooms suitable for wheelchair users.

33 Children are welcome in the accommodation. Any age limitations are specified.

34 At least some facilities, such as cots and high chairs, are available for those guests with babies. It is important to inform the proprietors of any special requirements.

35 Pets are welcome in the hotel, although they may be restricted to certain rooms.

36 Teas are served to non-residents.

37 Other general details about the establishment.

38 (*The Which? Hotel Guide*) denotes that this establishment is also listed in the 1995 edition of our sister guide to over 1,000 hotels in Britain.

Changes to national dialling codes

National dialling codes will change throughout the UK in April 1995. In most cases, the change will involve inserting a 1 after the initial 0; for example, London 071 will become 0171, York 0904 will become 01904. However, for five cities the national codes will change completely, as follows: for Bristol, 0272 becomes 01179; Leeds, 0532 becomes 01132; Leicester, 0533 becomes 01162; Nottingham, 0602 becomes 01159; Sheffield, 0742 becomes 01142. In addition, the international dialling code 010 will change to 00; for example, to reach the Republic of Ireland, you will need to preface the telephone number with 00 353 instead of 010 353.

The top-rated restaurants

Mark 5 for cooking

London
Chez Nico at Ninety
   Park Lane, W1
La Tante Claire, SW3

England
Le Manoir aux Quat'Saisons,
   Great Milton

Scotland
Altnaharrie Inn, Ullapool

Mark 4* for cooking

London
Bibendum, SW3
Le Gavroche, W1
Hyde Park Hotel,
   The Restaurant, SW1

England
L'Ortolan, Shinfield
Paul Heathcote's, Longridge
Waterside Inn, Bray
Winteringham Fields,
   Winteringham

Mark 4 for cooking

London
The Capital, SW3
Clarke's, W8
Connaught, W1
Inter-Continental Hotel,
   Le Soufflé, W1
Le Meridien Hotel,
   Oak Room, W1
Les Saveurs, W1
Turner's, SW3

England
Adlard's, Norwich
Carved Angel, Dartmouth
Castle Hotel, Taunton
Chester Grosvenor Hotel,
   Arkle, Chester
Croque-en-Bouche,
   Malvern Wells
Gidleigh Park, Chagford

Hambleton Hall, Hambleton
Lettonie, Bristol
Lucknam Park, Colerne
Mr Underhill's, Stonham
Morels, Haslemere
Normandie, Birtle
Old Vicarage, Ridgeway
Restaurant Nineteen, Bradford

Scotland
Airds Hotel, Port Appin
Braeval Old Mill, Aberfoyle
Kinnaird, Dunkeld
Peat Inn, Peat Inn
La Potinière, Gullane

Wales
Plas Bodegroes, Pwllheli
Walnut Tree Inn, Llandewi
   Skirrid

Restaurants with outstanding wine cellars

marked in the text with a ▪

London
Au Jardin des Gourmets, W1
Bibendum, SW3
Boyd's, W8
Clarke's, W8
Fifth Floor, SW1
Gilbert's, SW7
Leith's, W11
Mijanou, SW1
Odettes, NW1
Le Pont de la Tour, SE1
RSJ, SE1

England
Adlard's, Norwich
Angel Inn, Hetton
Beetle & Wedge, Moulsford
Carved Angel, Dartmouth
Cherwell Boathouse, Oxford
Chewton Glen, Marryat Restaurant,
    New Milton
Cobwebs, Leck
Corse Lawn House Hotel, Corse Lawn
Croque-en-Bouche, Malvern Wells
Crown, Southwold
Epworth Tap, Epworth
Fountain House, Dedham
Fox and Goose, Fressingfield
French Partridge, Horton
George Hotel, Stamford
Gidleigh Park, Chagford
Gravetye Manor, East Grinstead
Hambleton Hall, Hambleton
Hartwell House, Aylesbury
Harveys, Bristol
Hollington House, Woolton Hill
Le Manoir aux Quat'Saisons,
    Great Milton
Manor, Chadlington
Markwicks, Bristol
Morels, Haslemere
Normandie, Birtle
Old Beams, Waterhouses

Old Manor House, Romsey
Old Vicarage, Ridgeway
Old Vicarage, Witherslack
Pheasants, Ross-on-Wye
Porthole Eating House,
    Bowness-on-Windermere
Priory Hotel, Wareham
Read's, Faversham
Riverside, Helford
Rösers, Hastings
Seafood Restaurant, Padstow
Sir Charles Napier Inn, Chinnor
Sous le Nez en Ville, Leeds
Summer Lodge, Evershot
Le Talbooth, Dedham
Three Lions, Stuckton
Village Restaurant, Ramsbottom
White Moss House, Grasmere
White Horse Inn, Chilgrove
White House Hotel, Williton

Scotland
Airds Hotel, Port Appin
Altnaharrie Inn, Ullapool
Ard-Na-Coille, Newtonmore
Braeval Old Mill, Aberfoyle
Cellar, Anstruther
Champany Inn, Linlithgow
Clifton House, Nairn
The Cross, Kingussie
Inverlochy Castle, Fort William
Knipoch Hotel, Oban
Peat Inn, Peat Inn
La Potinière, Gullane
Summer Isles, Achiltibuie
Ubiquitous Chip, Glasgow

Wales
Old Rectory, Llansanffraid
    Glan Conwy
Penhelig Arms Hotel, Aberdovey
Plas Bodegroes, Pwllheli
Walnut Tree Inn, Llandewi Skirrid

Restaurants of the year

This award – like county restaurants of the year in previous editions of the *Guides* – does not go to the restaurants with the highest mark for cooking, but rather to ones which have shown particular merit or achievement during the year, whether as all-rounders or in some particular field. It may go to an old favourite or to a new entry, but in either case all the places listed below are worth visiting in their own right, and have enhanced the eating-out experience in some way.

London
Aubergine SW10
Sabras NW10

England
Asenby Crab & Lobster
Barnet Mims
Barnsley Restaurant Peano
Birmingham Chung Ying Garden
Bishop's Tachbrook Mallory Court
Cartmel Uplands
Cheltenham Epicurean
Colchester Warehouse Brasserie
Corse Lawn Corse Lawn House Hotel
Eastbourne Grand Hotel, Mirabelle
Goring Leatherne Bottel
Great Missenden La Petite Auberge
Hinton Charterhouse Homewood Park Hotel
Honley Mustards & Punch
Kirkham Cromwellian
Langho Northcote Manor
Leeds Brasserie Forty Four
Leicester Welford Place

Maiden Newton Le Petit Canard
Manchester Yang Sing
Morston Morston Hall
Newcastle upon Tyne 21 Queen Street
Oxford Whites
Plymouth Yang Cheng
Rowde George & Dragon
St Keyne Well House
Southwold Crown
Storrington Manleys
Torquay Table
Walkington Manor House
Woolton Hill Hollington House Hotel

Scotland
Anstruther Cellar
Auchmithie But'n'Ben
Edinburgh Atrium
Ullapool Altnaharrie Inn

Wales
Llanwrtyd Wells Carlton House
Mathry Ann FitzGerald's Farmhouse Kitchen
Penmaenpool Penmaenuchaf Hall

The *Guide*'s longest-serving restaurants

The *Guide* has seen many restaurants come and go. Some, however, have stayed the course with tenacity. (Qualification for this list is that the restaurant has been in each edition of the *Guide* subsequent to its first entry.)

Connaught, W1	42 years
Gay Hussar, W1	38 years
Porth Tocyn Hotel, Abersoch, Gwynedd	38 years
Gravetye Manor, East Grinstead, West Sussex	34 years
Sharrow Bay, Ullswater, Cumbria	34 years
Dundas Arms, Kintbury, Berkshire	32 years
French Partridge, Horton, Northamptonshire	30 years
Walnut Tree Inn, Llandewi Skirrid, Gwent	30 years
Black Bull Inn, Moulton, North Yorkshire	28 years
Rothay Manor, Ambleside, Cumbria	26 years
Sundial, Herstmonceux, East Sussex	26 years
Chez Moi, W11	24 years
Le Gavroche, W1	24 years
Summer Isles Hotel, Achiltibuie, Highland	24 years
The Capital, SW3	23 years
Miller Howe, Windermere, Cumbria	23 years
Cringletie House, Peebles, Borders	22 years
Old Fire Engine House, Ely, Cambridgeshire	22 years
Ubiquitous Chip, Glasgow, Strathclyde	22 years
White Moss House, Grasmere, Cumbria	22 years

Bogus guides

Unfortunately, the past year has once again seen the peddling of bogus 'Good Food Guide' certificates and 'shadowy' guides. Some months ago, Consumers' Association started to receive reports of a company calling itself Consumers Good Food Guide Limited, whose agents visited unsuspecting licensees and restaurateurs and told them they had been nominated for inclusion in the forthcoming issue of *The Good Food Guide*; the bogus company's agent then proceeded to offer a framed certificate bearing the legend 'Consumers Good Food Guide' at a price of around £30. Activities were, it seems, centred in Staffordshire, although there appears to have been the occasional foray into Cheshire and Derbyshire too.

Concerned that people were being duped into parting with money for a meaningless and deceptive certificate, and that the public would believe eating places displaying the certificates had been inspected in the same independent way and to the same high standard as the restaurants in our *Guide*, Consumers' Association wrote to the company requesting that the activities cease and that the company change its name. We stated that the use of the words 'The Good Food Guide', or any words that could be confused with them, amounted to an infringement of our registered trade mark. As our request was ignored, we issued proceedings in the High Court seeking an injunction. At this point, Consumers Good Food Guide Limited, realising it was up against the wall, agreed to give the undertakings we sought.

The Good Food Guide, of course, does not issue certificates, nor does it permit establishments that feature in it to advertise the fact. Despite our best efforts, it is difficult to eradicate all bogus certificates and claims to *Guide* recommendations, and indeed to prevent the emergence of further enterprises attempting to cash in on the *Guide*'s distinguished reputation. Readers, though, can help: if you are a restaurant owner and are contacted by someone purporting to be from *The Good Food Guide* – or something similar – please let us have details so that we can take action to prevent further confusion. If you happen to see a certificate on display, please tell us where so that we can pursue the matter with the proprietor.

■ As we went to press, we obtained an injunction against another bogus operator, which had been sending a circular to restaurateurs, headed 'Good Food Guide (Great Britain)', inviting them to pay £68 for inclusion in a forthcoming 'edition'.

Introduction

The Good Food Guide is *your* guide, and not just in the sense that you have been good enough to buy a copy. Firstly I believe it will increase your pleasure, by helping you find the kinds of restaurants you want to eat in. Secondly, I hope you will feel moved to drop us a line now and again to let us know how you get on. I would like to say a special thank-you to all of you who have contributed in any way to this edition, and hope that regular correspondents, occasional reporters and first-timers alike will keep us informed during the coming year.

We live by the postbag. When you write to us about a restaurant (use the freepost address and it won't cost you a bean), your letter comes direct to the *Good Food Guide* office, where it is read, noted and put into the restaurant's file, along with other people's letters and all the rest of the information we have about it, to be retrieved when the time comes to write an entry for the next edition. Every edition of the *Guide* is written completely from scratch every year.

We are essentially a clearing house. I am an editor, not a guru. The *Guide* is a handbook, not a bible. It should become dog-eared and battered over the course of a year, not kept in pristine condition. It has a shelf-life of 12 months – we want to sell you a fresh copy next year – and its purpose is to be useful and to be used. In essence, it is a way in which you can benefit from other people's experiences, good and bad. We are the medium, not the message, although we are aware that the two are inextricably linked.

Your opinion counts

It only works if you write to us. Call it participatory democracy if you will, or call it shared interactive resource monitoring (I daresay there are some who might). We just call them letters, and are grateful for every single one of them. The *Guide* cannot be better than the information it receives; we only hope it is as good. The reason your letters are important is that this is a people's guide, not, as some try to label it, a foodies' guide.

It is the task of the editor to consider the views expressed, to try to assess from reports whether a meal was 'simply wonderful' because it was the occasion of a successful first date, or whether the décor impressed and the atmosphere buzzed, or whether what appeared on the plate was indeed up to scratch. There are clues from reports – and the more you tell us about the meal, the more useful it is – but hitting the right note in the restaurant entry will always remain tricky. Some reporters may genuinely not have enjoyed the food because they were kept waiting too long before the menu was brought, even though what they ate was of a high standard. Every opinion is legitimate – it is not necessary to be a professional chef to know whether or not you have eaten well – but it is our job to tease out the mood from the food and produce what we believe is a fair assessment.

It is every chef's nightmare to be judged in print by somebody who has no idea about how the food is put together, what skills have been deployed, what subtleties are involved, what the difficulties are of operating to break-neck timetables or an unexpected deluge of customers, and so on. But the argument that restaurants should be judged only by professionals is bogus. Restaurants sell food to anybody who walks through the door and is willing to pay for it. To claim that the food was great although the customer didn't enjoy it is like the old chestnut about the operation being a success although the patient died. The *Guide* does not employ professionals, but we do have a team of some 100 inspectors – unpaid volunteers – who cover most of the country on our behalf.

Who are the inspectors?

They come from all walks of life, with varying degrees of experience and different skills and competencies. Some have been professionally involved in catering, others are dedicated amateurs, most have been sending in reports to the *Guide* for some years. They usually pass on details of their local restaurants as a matter of course, and send us a batch of reports whenever they travel around Britain. All restaurant visits are anonymous. Anybody who claims in a restaurant to be a *Good Food Guide* inspector is, by definition, not one. Where there are few or conflicting reports on a given restaurant, inspectors go in as judge and jury.

Their experience generally enables them to see through the surface gloss to what is really going on in the kitchen – to say, for example, whether faults are superficial or serious. But inspectors are, like everybody else, subject to good and bad performances from the kitchen, and if, as happened in one case this year, an inspector recommends that a restaurant be dropped from the *Guide*, but enough reporters weigh in with accounts of meals they have enjoyed, then the inspector can be overruled. We cherish the contact with ordinary everyday eaters who take the trouble to write to us. Inspectors are there to give an opinion in usually difficult circumstances, to help unscramble some of the conflicting information we receive.

Two sides to every meal

Outside observers worry that our reports are sometimes inconsistent, and assume our reporters are unreliable. But there is another possibility – that kitchens are inconsistent. Chefs understandably judge themselves by their best dishes, by what they are capable of, while reporters simply judge what they eat. What they actually receive on their plate may, for whatever reason, be below the kitchen's best, but it is what they are paying for, so it is of course what they are judging. Therefore, it should not be surprising if reporters' perceptions of the food sometimes differ from those of chefs; nor should it be surprising that reporters may have quite different experiences from each other.

It is our view that neither reporting on nor eating well in restaurants should be the prerogative of a select few. Everybody who eats out has the right to expect fair value for money, to get the best-quality food that their £10, £20 or £50 a head will buy. That is why we are here: to help you get the best deal for whatever amount of money you wish to lay out, based on the experiences of fellow diners.

Good food is worth paying for

The economics of eating in restaurants are not easy to come to grips with. To think of it as a simple tussle between rapacious restaurateurs, out for every penny they can get, and poor customers who are constantly being ripped off, is naive. There is much of that about, of course, and we deplore it absolutely. Restaurants that charge the earth for mediocre food have no place in the *Guide*.

At the same time, good ingredients and good staff cost money, and we the customers have to pay for it. If we don't, then some of the best restaurants will go out of business, leaving the field open to those who merely take short cuts, buying frozen food and microwaving it, which is much cheaper than buying real food and cooking it well. Let us be quite clear about this. If a good restaurant is worth supporting, then we should do it wholeheartedly, and not expect it to dish up brilliant food for a price it cannot sustain. Nobody gains that way. Having run a restaurant, I know that it is not the licence to print money that some may imagine.

The search for value

This is not to say that we should pay whatever sum is asked without question. Far from it. Restaurateurs get up to all kinds of fiddles behind the scenes. We only have to look at the simple and more visible tricks – charging exorbitant rates for bottled water, adding a 15 per cent 'optional' service charge which we all know is, in practical terms, not optional at all, or leaving credit card slips open when service has already been charged for – to see that greed is alive and well in the restaurant trade.

The *Guide* cannot do anything about this directly, but we can, and do, calculate what we believe is the true cost of a meal, taking all the hidden items into account. Circumstances vary, but we give the approximate upper and lower limits per head, wide as these sometimes are, for each entry, as well as the prices of set meals and average main-course items from the menu, based on the information supplied to us by the restaurant. 'How to read a *Guide* entry' on pages 8–11 gives details. The £ sign is a handy symbol indicating restaurants that serve a three-course meal (including coffee, half a bottle of wine and service), any time they are open, for £20 a head or less.

'Good value' is a slippery notion, and we can adopt no more than a rule of thumb approach to it. But we are encouraged by reporters who, after spending £20 a head in one restaurant and feeling ripped off, have then paid £50 a head somewhere else and felt they received good value for money. Elusive and subjective as it is, some indication of value can be gained by comparing a restaurant's cooking mark with the prices charged.

Flexibility breeds content

When we make this comparison, the fixed-price lunch at some of London's top restaurants, which has long been a bargain, emerges as a continuing delight. Indeed, lunchtime customers can generally choose between the set menu or the full menu, while at dinner there is no choice but the expensive one. This discrepancy between lunch and dinner probably matters more outside London, where restaurateurs often complain that people only come for dinner, and then only for special occasions, usually of the anniversarial kind, and generally on Friday or Saturday. Well, of course they do. They don't just pop in because they are hungry, as they might well do for the less expensive lunch. They are spending significantly more money, so they eat there significantly less often. Restaurants in general have failed to recognise that people today demand greater flexibility in their lives. We do not all stick to a rigid lunch and dinner timetable as rigidly as restaurants think we do.

We are a becoming a 24-hour society, and many service-providers have arranged their businesses to reflect this, by introducing more flexible shop-opening and working hours. We can telephone the bank in the middle of the night and talk to somebody about our overdraft. But can we, outside the major cities, get a good meal at a reasonable price when we want it, when we have come home from a hard day's work and can't be bothered to cook? No, only for two hours in the middle of the day – or perhaps dim-sum in the afternoon – but not in the evenings. Many restaurants are missing an opportunity here.

The good news is that some have woken up to what is happening. The rise of the converted pub, especially in London, although not as widespread as some might have hoped or predicted, has been welcome. No frills mean lower bills, and informality is part of the appeal. If you talk to half a dozen restaurateurs in town or village, at least three of them will admit that their new brasserie is doing quite well, especially mid-week when the restaurant is normally dead.

One way out of the gloom, for restaurateurs who can afford some restructuring, is probably to have a bar with snacks and a few good beers, plus a sort of informal bistro-brasserie with good wine by the glass, and finally the restaurant proper. Flexible operations have more chance of survival, because they take account of what customers want. Anything that persuades us to eat out more often, even if we spend less on these casual meals, must surely be in the restaurant's interest.

What's on the menu?

Eating out more often is in the customer's interest too, because the restaurant scene has never been so exciting. Many restaurants, as ever, specialise in a particular style of cooking or a national cuisine (London ones are listed at the back of the *Guide*). But just look at what else is happening. Hundreds of dishes, in scores of restaurants, do not fit easily into any single national framework. Tagliolini with ceps and crème fraîche, steamed mussels with curry spices and coriander, roast quail with wild mushrooms and polenta, and lamb steaks with parsley pesto and Spanish butter-beans: those are all from just one menu in one restaurant. What a glorious mix.

And this particular brew could only happen here. No other country has quite the same blend of British, French, Italian, Spanish, Indian, Chinese, Thai and other cultures to call on. In that sense, diverse as it all is, it is very British, full of real invention and the sheer exuberance of let's-have-a-go cookery, rather like Californian cuisine. Any single item might come from any repertoire. Place your bets on chargrilled asparagus with orange and chervil hollandaise. Is that from San Francisco? No, it is from Leeds. Never mind. It is the ensemble that matters, and the common denominator is that all these bits and bobs from Japan, India and Algeria come together here, in our restaurants. It is British in the sense that Britain is the melting pot. British cooking is no longer defined by just what we grow here, or by traditional recipes and techniques. It is the sum total of what we cook here.

British restaurateurs, and their customers, have been receptive to all this, perhaps, because Britain's food culture is less sharply drawn than some others – a state of affairs seen as something of a handicap until now – and it provides a gap waiting to be filled with whatever ideas can be pinched from elsewhere. As one restaurateur wrote: 'Styles are becoming more blurred as rapid cross-pollination of ideas from widely diverse cuisines [creates] a constant state of evolution. This we find healthy and full of surprises, stimulating for both provider and receiver.'

Cooking skills

The realisation that 'anything goes' is a great liberator, although some may worry that cooking could degenerate into mere assembly, with random pairing of any old ingredients. How about salmon served with Cajun spices and wasabi butter, or salad of scallops and red mullet with Thai-spiced vinaigrette, or grilled duck breast with goats' cheese polenta, again all from one menu? If there are no rules, and if a cook can earn good money by doing no more than chargrilling and arranging, then the danger is that he or she will not bother acquiring any skills. And cooking is a discipline, surely, not just a free-for-all.

Anyone who has suffered badly from quasi-French food in the past may well be grateful that simple chargrilling has become the technique of the moment. It can be applied to pigeon breast, chump of lamb, vegetables or whatever. Fortunately, it is not difficult to do, and is within the grasp of most cooks: because there is little to go wrong, the results can be palatable, even from a novice. Anybody who can throw a few vegetables on the barbie, open a bottle of extra virgin olive oil, and shave a block of Parmesan is well on the way to culinary success in the 1990s. Being able to make pasta, foccaccia, ciabatta and so on may be a bonus, but commercial availability makes it unnecessary in most cases.

One of the other benefits of the 'new wave' free style of cooking is the variety provided by different cooking techniques. There is no one 'correct' way to cook an item. With most 'schools' of cookery up to and including nouvelle, there did seem to be a correct and incorrect way, which was rather inhibiting. Now a pigeon can be lightly casseroled; or the breast grilled and the legs served confit-style; it might appear as a first or main course, perhaps as a salad, with couscous, or in a stock-based sauce and lentils; or it might be chopped up and made into ravioli; and so on. There is a range of options open, some of which are light and summery, enhanced by resonant accompaniments of Mediterranean vegetables, while others may be rich and warming, hearty, earthy, with casseroled root vegetables. This all seems to give menus much more variety than previously, which is all to the good.

Many kitchens are also tending towards a 'dedicated vegetable' served on the same plate as the main course, rather than a selection of inappropriate ones left to go cold on a half-moon side dish. Most reporters who mention this welcome the development, and if the practice helps to concentrate the minds of some chefs, allowing them to think more carefully about the partnership they are planning, then it will have been worthwhile.

Is local food the best?

The fundamental principle remains, however, that the end result can never be better than the ingredients that went into it: a point which, we have already noted, applies to the *Guide* too. Emphasis on local foods, which many restaurants claim, implies a response to the seasons – a response that has been much diminished by our reliance on the global marketplace. The plus-points about local supplies are that they are generally fresher (fish, for example); that provenance (of, say, beef cattle) can be assured – a good restaurant will know about the breed, slaughter, butchering and hanging of its meat; and that the local economy will benefit, which is in the restaurant's own long-term interests. Staying close to home also encourages individuality: samphire grows here, a particular breed of pig is reared there. Given a choice between strawberries picked from the garden, or punnets imported from Israel, there is a strong argument in favour of the former. But since Scottish gardens do not produce lime leaves or red peppers, then it is naive to insist on a doctrinaire approach.

One restaurateur queried what 'out of season' means now that we are in the Common Market, and wondered why anybody should get hung up about using foreign vegetables and fruit 'when everyone is happy to see French cheeses on the board. Should we stop putting on melon and grapefruit at breakfast time?' It would be silly for cooks to ignore what is available, yet one of the pleasures of eating is the variety provided by the changing seasons. There is no right or wrong, just a plea that we don't lose individuality and variety. The same is true of mushrooms, many tame varieties of which are now called 'wild'. Even the genuine article is often dried, imparting a particular and not always appropriate character to a dish.

One silver lining to the recessionary cloud is the cutback in prime cuts of meat. We have nothing against them, but there are lots of under-used, under-appreciated and frankly much more interesting and flavoursome cuts: tongue, neck of lamb, trotters, shoulders, bellies, muzzles, ears, gizzards, even brains and sweetbreads, although the sad news for many diners is the continuing BSE saga, which now makes the use of some items of offal questionable. Pronouncements, findings, rumours and embargoes change by the week, but we fervently pray that some of the tastiest cuts and most versatile bits of food that a chef can lay his or her hands on will not disappear from our kitchens.

Wine: still a way to go

Readers continue to deplore the standard of many house wines, and object to high mark-ups. Most customers are now very familiar with a wide range of excellent wines available at reasonable prices from high street shops and supermarkets, and cannot understand why so many restaurants are behind the times. Customers know to look to vins de pays and Australians in the quest for value, to the Rhône for quality, and to Italy for excitement, and are often bemused by long lists of conservative and unimaginative clarets that make the whole restaurant seem dated. Reporters are going beyond Chardonnay and Cabernet Sauvignon to ask for Syrah, affordable and drinkable Pinot Noir, Marsanne, Barbera and the like.

The bottle and glass symbols are retained as a guide to the best cellars, although some of these list very expensive wines indeed, and are arrogant enough to assume that anything under £20 is unworthy, while most readers feel that anything over £20 is too expensive. We have taken this, admittedly somewhat arbitrary, sum as a guideline when considering the usefulness of lists. Any restaurateur who disdains wines that sell for less than £20 might do well to visit Wales, where whole lists are compiled without ever straying above £15. And some of them are very good indeed. Any wine list that cannot field a good Australian selection, or one from the south of France, for less than £20 is just not trying hard enough.

On a more positive note, many lists are now offering a short house selection of about half a dozen wines by the glass, a simple expedient made possible by technology that is easily and cheaply available. Gadgets will keep half-empty bottles fresh for a few days, if it takes that long to sell the remainder. There is no excuse for not offering a decent selection.

Cooking marks

Cooking is the basis for inclusion in the *Guide*, and for the rating. Unlike other guides, we rate the cooking in every restaurant in the main sections with just a handful of exceptions. This lumps some unlikely bedfellows together. Common sense tells us that the range of talent and quality within each point will vary enormously. To say that the food in restaurant A is better than that in B may be valid, but to say that A should therefore have a higher score does not necessarily follow. An alternative would be to score out of a larger number, say 20, as the *Guide* did for a while in the '80s, but two disadvantages accrue from this. Firstly, such scales tend to begin somewhere in the middle, because to give a restaurant a score of 1 out of 20 makes it seem more a failure than a success. This immediately renders half the scale redundant, making it somewhat pointless, if you will forgive the pun. Secondly, adhering to such a system can degenerate into hair-splitting arguments about fine differences between chefs, which is not what a handbook like this is about. In any case, any marking system will still be subject to the charge that restaurants of differing standards will be lumped together. Only if we had a 1000-point scale would we remove that objection.

The five points of the present system are stretched by asterisks (*) to indicate particularly good performance within a category. In order for these to retain significance, they should be limited to a small number. To that end, we have tried to tidy them up a bit. For a restaurant to lose an asterisk is not necessarily a demotion, more a rationalisation. It is easy to mask uncertainty with a half-score, and we have tried to remove that uncertainty wherever possible. We hope this makes sense, but once again your comments are very welcome.

Disappearing restaurants

Unfortunately for us, chefs do not always move at the right moment. Those who change stoves shortly before the *Guide* goes to press cause particular difficulties. Because we have no feedback on their performance, we have nothing to say about their food, and cannot award a mark for cooking. In such circumstances, we might decide to drop the restaurant from the *Guide* for the current year. The problem is that we are then left with no way of explaining why the restaurant has disappeared. The cooking may or may not have deteriorated – or improved – with the arrival of a new chef, and readers have no way of knowing what has happened.

One restaurant in Cardiff was dropped from the 1994 *Guide* and readers wrote to ask why. Had it changed hands? Closed? Was the new chef so bad that we could not endorse the cooking? No, nothing of the kind. He just arrived at an inconvenient moment. Readers wrote to say that they would have found it more helpful if we had simply said, 'The chef has changed, but the restaurant still exists. Please let us have reports.' We appreciate the sentiments expressed in a number of letters complaining about this state of affairs, and have tried to address the problem.

And finally . . .

This year, therefore, a few restaurants that might normally have been dropped still have an entry, albeit shortened, and without a cooking mark. The text makes the situation clear. For readers who are not prepared to eat in a restaurant without knowing the mark, these are made obvious and are therefore easy to avoid. For those who prefer the adventure of finding out first-hand and reporting to us, nominal inclusion provides an opportunity to do that. Not every case is the same – a new chef may not have been appointed, and if appointed he or she may be unknown to us, or may come from another restaurant in the *Guide* – so we have judged each on its particular circumstances. In this way we can be fair to restaurants, which might otherwise be victims of unfortunate timing, and to readers, who want to know what is going on.

Remember that we are dependent on your observations, so please keep them coming. They symbolise the fact that enjoyment is the key factor. Eating out should be a pleasure, sometimes a celebration, always driven by that happy anticipation that we call hunger. The restaurants featuring in this issue of the *Guide* should enhance that pleasure more than ones that don't appear. Whether they have or not, please tell us about it.

The roots of good food

Derek Cooper – author, broadcaster and journalist

When Raymond Postgate launched the Society for the Prevention of Cruelty to Food in 1949, he had two targets in mind: pretentiousness and the excessive use of processed rubbish. Pretentiousness may never be eliminated, but 45 years on, how are we doing on the rubbish front? In the early days of *The Good Food Guide*, Postgate campaigned against bottled mayonnaise masquerading as the real thing, powdered soup presented as *potage du jour*, tinned fruit in high summer, packet custard, coffee made from liquid essence, *pâté maison* with the indentation of the tin still visible, and rubbery cheeses wrapped in cellophane.

Despite the predilection the British have always shown for things out of packets and tins, Postgate was able to report lyrically on 'the many inns in the countryside at which one will be offered venison, hare, game, trout and salmon from the river admirably prepared'. He enthused about our native strawberries, tomatoes, apples, asparagus, lowland beef and mountain mutton.

When Postgate was writing, all trout and salmon were what we now have to call 'wild'; asparagus came from Norfolk and the Vale of Evesham, not Spain and California; apples were picked in Kent, not Belgium and Holland; strawberries were grown in Hampshire, not Patagonia; and the best raspberries came in due season from Perthshire.

Now, thanks to wide-bodied jets, new growing techniques and hi-tech chill-chains, we can have just about everything all the time. We can buy salmon out of the cages all year round and, for those who can stomach battery, boneless turkeys, every day can be Christmas day. Choice and high profit margins are what food is about; quality, taste and flavour are less important.

The rise of the ready meal

And when it comes to menus, even the smallest restaurant can buy in 'gourmet' dishes ready to be microwaved from frozen in a trice. The chef-free kitchen has become a lucrative reality. Huge catering companies provide a full range of meals at remarkably little cost to the caterer. In 1992 it was estimated by market analysts that the ready-meals industry was turning over around £6 million a day. By 1994 caterers were buying an estimated 2700 tonnes of dehydrated sauces a year plus a substantial tonnage of unseasoned pouch-sealed wet

27

sauces. Unseasoned? One catering brand manager explained that quirk quite simply: 'It allows chefs to add their own signature.'

The widespread and skilful de-skilling of the hotel and restaurant industry is seldom acknowledged by the catering suppliers, who talk glibly about the opportunities presented to chefs. Relieved of the drudgery of cooking, they can add their own creative touch to a frozen ready meal with a sprig of parsley here or a dab of aerosol cream there.

Garnishing, of course, cannot conceal the monotony of mass-produced food. At any one time in Britain these days, thousands of people will be eating identical fillets of prime Atlantic salmon (which is brochure-speak for farmed fish) cooked with the identical gooey sauce; the same pâté de campagne ('presented well, pâté forms a tempting and eye-catching display', says the brochure); and the same chocolate shortcake dessert ('tastes and looks deliciously home-made').

The expectations aroused by the prose are seldom fulfilled in the mouth. When *Caterer & Hotelkeeper*, much of whose revenue comes from advertising catering products, organised a blind tasting of 19 ready soups in early 1994, the panel of chefs was not overimpressed. Although some of the panel found that not all of the soups were as bad as they had expected, words like 'atrocious', 'artificial', 'no real flavour', 'greasy' hung in the air. But what do you expect from products which can sell for as little as 5p a portion? Catering products formulated to a budget frequently use the cheapest possible ingredients. They are held together with a motley cocktail of emulsifiers, stabilisers and gelling agents, cosmetically coloured, protected with preservatives and generally engineered to survive the rigours of a long life on the shelf or in the freezer.

The accessibility and the convenience of ready foods have polarised the catering industry. On the one hand you have a small number of establishments where real cooking of fresh raw materials takes place, and on the other the vast majority of eateries where everything from the soup and prawn cocktail to the peach melba comes off a lorry.

Raw materials: how 'real'?

It is not only how and where the food is prepared which merits attention, but also how the raw materials are produced. Intensive farming and cultivation, the adding of excess water to ham and bacon, broiler production, the unnecessary use of drugs in animal husbandry, the use of 'mechanically recovered meat' (or 'slurry', derived by flushing everything edible from an animal carcass with powerful jets of water) in pies, burgers, pâtés and sausages, and the general adulteration of food have created both anxiety among consumers and a grass-roots revolt against what are seen as unacceptable practices.

Supermarkets and 'heritage' food

Perhaps to a certain extent, however, we are coming to accept a two-tier supply – awful slurry sausages and 'real' sausages, ice-cream made with hydrogenated vegetable fat and 'real' ice-cream, chemical beer and 'real' ale, battery eggs and free-range eggs, intensively reared meat and 'real meat', oversugared jam and 'real' jam, processed cheeses and 'real' cheese.

So wide is the gulf between second-rate food and real food that supermarkets are now offering alternatives. Thus you will find taramasalata with not much smoked roe in it dyed a vile boiled-sweet shade of pink alongside a tub of something slightly more authentic labelled 'luxury' taramasalata. How Postgate would have shuddered at the shabby concept that the real thing, or at least some attempt to duplicate the real thing, was in some way a luxury!

In 1990 Tesco introduced a range of products (initially 17; the number had grown to over 40 by 1994) 'designed to revive old-fashioned speciality fare and preserve the best of British culinary heritage'. For those shoppers who could afford it there was now to be added choice – hand-filled pork pies from Leicestershire, ale brewed in traditionally fired copper vats in Edinburgh, muffins and crumpets with old-fashioned yeast flavours – all preserving 'the high standards, natural ingredients and fine flavours of yesteryear'. Other super-markets with image-building in mind have leapt on to this heritage bandwagon – the aisles now glisten with flashes drawing attention to products claimed to be 'real', 'natural', 'farmhouse', 'country style', 'old-fashioned' and full, of course, of 'heritage' and dear old 'yesteryear'.

The multiples have also been quick to realise that some of their shoppers now wish to make ethical and moral choices. Organic produce, vegetables grown with sustainable farming in mind, and environmentally friendly fruits are appearing on the shelves. Fair Trade produce is there too, grown in the Third World under conditions that are less scandalously exploitative than before.

What menus won't tell you

While consumers are beginning to question how their food is produced, the catering industry is still preoccupied with how it is cooked and presented. Waiters will tell you at great length about how chef has prepared the dish, but there seems to be little concern about the raw materials themselves.

It is good to know how the fish has been marinated, but how was it farmed? What was in the pellets on which it was fed? And the chicken: was it reared with antibiotics? Diners have a right to know whether their food has been irradiated or whether the milk, cream, butter and cheese have come from dairy herds injected with the milk-boosting hormone BST. These are not peripheral or indeed neurotic obsessions. They are central to the future of honest food. If a chef does not know how his vegetables have been grown, his poultry reared or his fish farmed, he cannot cook with any sense of confidence or pride.

Happily chefs are becoming increasingly aware of the vital need to involve themselves in the fight against adulteration and debasement of food. The 'chefs in the school' movement pioneered in France has spread to Britain. Schemes to involve chefs in a closer relationship with growers are springing up in all parts of Britain.

In June 1994 a group of the most influential cooks in the USA gathered in California for a conference at the Fetzer Organic Food & Wine Center to discuss ways in which the raw materials of their menus could be improved. The message that emerged was unanimous: unless chefs campaign for better food, it will become increasingly difficult to find anything worth cooking.

John Ash, chef and culinary director of the Center, summed up the feeling of the conference in this way: 'A lot of people believe that a great cook can do wonders with any piece of junk. Absolutely not! The mark of a great cook is one who spends more time choosing ingredients than cooking them.'

Chunnel vision

Patricia Fenn – travel and food writer

Around the exit of the Tunnel at Sangatte, speculation is rife. Will fortunes be assured from the expected influx? Is there room for more hotels and restaurants? Where will the British head? How many?

The waiting is tough. Times are hard in northern France, and for many a disillusioned restaurateur it is too late. Boulogne in particular has suffered from the ferry withdrawal. Calais is finding that the splendid new autoroute whisks passengers off and away; nowadays the punters are at St Omer by the time they used to be struggling with the Calais suburbs. Rumours of who will be next to go under abound, and survivors are trying extra hard to please. Those with heavy overheads are worst hit, and luxury restaurants are encouraging new customers by setting rock-bottom prices for mid-week lunch menus. It is possible to find Michelin-starred restaurants offering three sublime courses for under £15. Perhaps there has never been a better time to venture across.

It is hard to make cross-Channel comparisons because few French restaurants have an equivalent in Britain. The British are usually thrilled with the most modest group – the rural café/bar restaurants – not only because of the prices, but also because of the Frenchness. (The nearest we have, arguably, are pubs, but they would have to be family-run with everything home-cooked, to compare.) You will not find them listed in smart guides, and only word-of-mouth will reveal which are to be commended, because the menus all look the same. Typical would be: 'Pâté, côte de porc, tarte aux pommes – 55FF'. Boring, you might say. Not only boring, but downright bad if you do not appreciate that this can mean a slice of supermarket terrine, a meagre dry pork chop with canned beans and chips, and cardboard-thin pastry topped with shrivelled apple flakes. On the other hand, with a bit of local knowledge you could expect a bowl of home-made pâté left on the table on a help- yourself basis, with home-pickled gherkins, a juicy pink chop (kidney intact) from a pig bred with fat on it, unlimited home-grown veg, then green salad sprinkled with chervil (but watch out for the dressing – cheap vinegar makes the eyes water), and finally a deep tart with glazed apples reposing on an eggy custard base. Total with half a carafe of rough red wine thrown in – about £6 a head.

These rustic anachronisms are to be found in the time-warped villages of the Boulonnais, so near the ports in distance, so far in spirit.

Anyone who doubts that the 'flat, boring, industrialised' north of France could contain substantial hills, forests, river valleys and photogenic hamlets where tourism has made little impact on agricultural lives should be dragged to the area and made to repent. Predictably, food here will be hearty, simple and cheap.

At Questrecques, for example, 11km south-east of Boulogne, in the remarkably unspoiled rolling country threaded by the little river Liane, is the **Auberge de la Liane**. For 60FF you get thick home-made soup, entrée (could be boudin blanc cooked in port), 'plat' (could be guinea-fowl or skate au beurre noir), cheese or pud. Not so rustic, but in a very unusual landscape, latticed with canals, is the **Restaurant de la Gare** at Les Attaques, 8km south-east of Calais. You can actually drive the whole way alongside the canals. Patron Francis Rambaut was a butcher/traiteur, so go for the meat here – rillettes, terrines, steak. My recent 55FF menu du jour was seafood gratin, sauté of rabbit and good cheese, washed down with house wine at 8FF a pichet.

The next category is the one many of us long for back home – the brasserie. Whenever someone attempts to open an English version, it turns out either expensive or seedy, and the character has never been the same. In France this is the place to head for, without booking, when the kids want a pizza, Mum fancies a salad, Dad a three-course binge and Auntie a small glass of port. Imagine turning up at Quaglino's and asking for just a coffee!

Every French town has a brasserie. Sometimes they are smoke-befuddled, deafening, plastic-menued. But in Boulogne there is the very model of a perfect brasserie: **Chez Jules** in the market square (markets Wednesday and Saturday) – cheerful, bustling, noisy, authentic and producing very good food. The fish is excellent, whether you have a great bowl of mussels or a sophisticated brochette of seafood, along with regional vegetables (leeks, cabbage with caraway, creamed chicory) served in earthenware pots with a hunk of potato galette. Menu at 90FF.

Then come the restaurants which the French call 'correct': no fireworks, but honest week-in, week-out reliability. One example is **Le Channel** in Calais, which has never allowed its long-term popularity to go to its head. If you are looking for one absolutely safe, inexpensive restaurant near Sangatte, it would be this one, where the 85FF menu must be the bargain of the year (snails, salmon with sorrel and beurre blanc, local cheeseboard and unsoggy pear flan). Invest 135FF and you will get langoustines and grilled bass. Calais, always behind Boulogne in matters gastronomic, now scores highly with three good fish restaurants: **Aquar'Aile**, **Au Côte d'Argent** and the smaller, cheaper **Le Grand Bleu**.

At the top end of the gastro-scale are the Michelin rosettes – three around Boulogne – and the 'wanabees'. There are, for example, Tony Lestienne's **La Matelôte**, with an offshoot at the miraculous Nausicaa marine centre; and **La Liégoise**, just as good but without a star; and the **Hostellerie de la Rivière** at nearby Pont-de-Briques. But you might want to make for Wimille, where the delightful little **Relais de la Brocante** would arguably merit a 3 in the GFG scale. Jean-François Laurent's 110FF menu (mid-week evenings too!) produced a crab sandwich like no other: two rounds of rich sablé pastry enclosing crab chunks and chopped leeks, surrounded by a langoustine sauce, then a revelatory rabbit enriched with prunes, and a warm lemon cream flavoured with gin from the nearby village of Houlle. A meal here in the old presbytery would certainly justify a crossing of its own.

It is always a challenge to try to spot the up-and-coming, those who are ambitious and striving for that vital rosette. Two to tip at Wimereux might be the born-again **L'Atlantic** and the minuscule newcomer **L'Epicure**, and, at Marquise, **Le Grand Cerf**, currently in top form. There are plenty to choose from within the half-hour drive from the Tunnel, but add on another 15 minutes or so, to Montreuil, and you could eat at what some might name as simply number one in the north of France – **La Grenouillère**. Roland Gauthier's superb mid-week lunch costs an incredible 130FF. He now has four comfortable rooms – so, even better, make a night of it.

Where to go

To telephone from England, first dial 010 33 (00 33 from April 1995) and then the French numbers given below.

Les Attaques: Restaurant de la Gare, Tel 21 82 22 28 (closed Mon).

Boulogne-sur-Mer: Chez Jules, place Dalton, Tel 21 31 54 12 (open all hours); La Liégoise, 10 rue A. Monsigny, Tel 21 31 61 15 (closed Sun pm, Mon); La Matelôte, 80 bd Ste Beuve, Tel 21 30 17 97 (closed Sun pm); Restaurant de Nausicaa, bd Ste Beuve, Tel 21 33 24 24

Calais: Aquar'Aile, 255 rue J. Moulin, Tel 21 34 00 00; Le Channel, 3 bd Résistance, Tel 21 34 42 30 (closed Sun pm, Tue); Au Côte d'Argent, 1 digue G. Berthe, Tel 21 34 68 07 (closed Sun pm, Mon); Le Grand Bleu, 8 rue J.P. Avron, Tel 21 97 97 98 (closed Sat L and Sun)

La Madelaine-sous-Montreuil: Auberge La Grenouillère, Tel 21 06 07 22 (closed Tue, Wed)

Marquise: Le Grand Cerf, 34 ave Ferber, Tel 21 87 55 05 (closed Sun pm, Mon)

Pont-de-Briques: Hostellerie de la Rivière, 17 rue Gare, Tel 21 32 22 81 (closed Sun pm and Mon)

Questrecques: Auberge de la Liane, Tel 21 33 51 96

Wimereux: L'Atlantic, digue de mer, Tel 21 32 41 01 (closed Sun pm, Mon); L'Epicure, 1 rue Gare, Tel 21 83 21 83 (closed Sun pm)

Wimille: Le Relais de la Brocante, 2 rue Ledinghem, Tel 21 83 19 31 (closed Sun pm and Mon)

Food and wine: the mating game

David Natt – teacher, freelance wine and food writer

How do we get the best out of wine in a restaurant? Choosing a bottle can be daunting, especially if the list is long, eccentrically arranged, and with alarming prices. 'Order whatever you enjoy drinking,' says one school of thought. But this is tantamount to ordering custard with your kippers (if you happen to like both) and completely ignores the fact that food and wine react together. What is liked separately will not necessarily be liked in combination.

What we need is an understanding of the simple chemistry of wine and food, which will help us predict how particular wines and foods are likely to react together. If we can do that, we can make sensible choices. Tim Hanni, a Master of Wine who also trained as a chef, and who now works for Beringer Vineyards in California, has been developing just such a system. It is blissfully simple to understand and operate, and puts the consumer firmly back in the driving seat when it comes to ordering wine. It engenders the sort of confidence that should enable anybody to tackle a restaurant wine list with a spirit of adventure.

Acidity

The key to matching white wines with food is knowing how their acidity reacts. A simple home experiment will confirm what we need to know.

Get hold of a fairly acidic unoaked white – a Touraine Sauvignon Blanc would do nicely – and take a mouthful. It should feel lively, and leave the tongue with a slight smarting sensation on its very edges. That's acidity. Now slice yourself some lemon and take a quick lick. Don't overdo it. You just want the sensation of tartness without a mouthful of lingering flavour. Now take another mouthful of wine. Surprised? Common sense would suggest that piling acidic wine on top of acidic lemon should be mouth-puckering. But it is not at all: the wine is softened, it seems smoother. Take a heftier dose of lemon and the wine will die completely and seem simply watery.

Repeat the experiment with an oaked Australian Chardonnay. The amount of lemon you take is critical. With the Chardonnay, even a tiny quantity of lemon is likely to reduce the wine to tasting of stale cardboard – the effect of stripping out all the fruit acid in the wine, just leaving the oak: not pleasant at all. Rule number one in matching food and wine, then, is:

Acid in food reduces the perception of acid in wine.

So it seems clear that we need to gauge the acidity of the dish we shall be eating. If a sauce is involved, make sure to ask the waiter how it has been made. And don't forget the part played by garnishes.

Take oysters, for instance. The classic partnership is with Champagne, Chablis or a similarly acidic white. Why so? It has little to do with the oyster; as Tim Hanni points out, 'It's just there for the slide.' It has everything to do with the lemon it is normally doused with. Wines with less acidity would die, and that means we positively need something that starts life on the sharp side.

The same is true of salads. Acidic dressings can blunt wines to the point of blandness. We need something with more acidity than we might care to take by itself.

The startling acidity of Chenin Blanc in Vouvray Sec, for instance, is not in the least user-friendly for most drinkers. But partner such a wine, as it might be in the Loire, with a platter of salad vegetables *au vinaigrette* (salade tourangelle), and it comes right into line, revealing its charming appley fruit. Fashionable Mediterranean chargrilled vegetables might have a similarly acidulated dressing. Again, a wine with marked acidity is called for, but perhaps one with not too assertive a character or aroma to jar with the riot of flavours already present in the dish. The lemony acidity and subtle nuttiness of many an Italian white – a Lugana, a Soave or a Gavi – fit the bill perfectly.

Body

Another function of acidity in wine is to counteract the richness of cream, oil or fat. Acidity will certainly cut rich foods, but whether or not the effect is refreshing will depend on how well the weight of the wine balances the food. A light wine will seem simply tart, its acidity thrown into even greater prominence by the richness of the dish. A buttery Chardonnay will better complement a creamy fish dish than will a zingy Sauvignon Blanc. The second principle to apply, therefore, is that:

Body should match body; weight should balance weight.

In the same way, a glass of Muscadet will work excellently with a simple dish of crab-claw meat; treat the crab differently, however – enrich it with mayonnaise, add some of the brown meat and make it into crab cakes – and the same Muscadet will simply taste like acidulated water. A dry rosé or rich Chardonnay will supply the sort of weight required.

The current trend for salad of duck confit as a first course poses similar challenges of wine choice. The combination of rich texture and at least suggested fattiness demands a wine with tremendous presence, good acidity to cut the fat and match the dressing, and yet an overall weight that will allow us to progress to more substantial wines with later courses. The white wines of Alsace excel in such a context – a rich, spicy Tokay-Pinot Gris, for example, would be ideal. A top-flight, off-dry German Riesling would also provide an interesting complement, its residual sugar lending the weight, the inherent acidity cutting the richness. Chicken liver mousse? The sample principles and wine choices apply.

Tannin

When it comes to red wines, it is the level of tannin that we need to consider most closely. Tannin has an astringent effect in the mouth, attacking tongue and gums, leaving them feeling dry and rasping: just like stewed tea. It is a property of many young wines, and understanding how tannin works can help us manipulate it.

There is nothing that a tannin wants more than to find some protein to grab. It is, after all, used to tan leather – i.e. to preserve and strengthen skin protein. In the mouth, wine tannins will latch on to whatever proteins are available, and in the absence of the right food that will mean the muco-proteins of saliva which coat the soft, tender flesh of tongue and gums; no wonder young red wine can appear as tough as old boots.

The art to taming tannin lies in making sure the food does one of two things: it must provide a decoy protein so that the tannin latches on to it rather than us, or it must act as a 'barrier cream' between our flesh and the rampant tannin.

Decoy protein first. No prizes for guessing why rare steak is a classic partner to red wine. In any lightly cooked meat, there is plenty of uncombined protein available for bonding with the wine's tannin. As a result, the wine seems silkier, smoother, and its fruit characteristics are the more appreciable by a palate that has not been traumatised by tannin. Note that word 'uncombined', though: a well-cooked steak will not perform anything like the same function, because when proteins are cooked they combine with one another, and what has been joined together no tannin will put asunder. If you prefer your meat well done, then complement it with a red wine low in tannin and marked for its juicy fruit. A good Beaujolais, for example, would work very well, or an easy-drinking Crozes-Hermitage. The rich berry fruit of many Australian wines will also deliver the sort of mouth-watering flavours that are needed. An oldish wine that has shed its tannin but still has plenty of fruit may provide a classier combination.

A simple home test with both rare and incinerated steaks along with a tannic wine – a just-released claret will do nicely – will confirm the rule:

Free protein tames tannin.

What then of the 'barrier cream' effect? Cream, butter, oil and fat will act as a physical shield to the effects of tannin. Lightly cooked meat in a creamy sauce will lend an air of maturity to many a wine that swaggers with the raw edge of youth. Thus the rule:

Fat and cream protect the palate.

Bear in mind, however, what we said earlier about the need to balance the weights of wine and food. A youthful Chianti will not just lose its tannic edge and acidic shock in the face of steak in a blue cheese sauce; it will be overwhelmed and seem feeble – tamed but emasculated – whereas a full-bodied claret or Rhone Syrah will not be.

Paying attention to the weight or richness of the food is always important. The sticky richness of oxtail stew, for example, demands a belting wine with rich, ripe fruit to balance it. Australian Shiraz, Rhone Syrah or Châteauneuf du Pape are the wines to go for. But do not fall into the trap of thinking that the stronger the dish, the stronger the wine needed to accompany it. Indeed, where that strength is a function of hot spice, we are dealing with something quite particular.

Spice

Any dish with a fair whack of pepper or chilli, for instance, is likely to seem pretty macho, and we could be forgiven for thinking that we would need a pretty gutsy wine to stand up to it. Not so. Wine- and food-matching is not a contest: we need something that is complementary. The rule to remember:

Hot spices sensitise the palate.

They bring out depths of flavour and subtlety of fruit we might not have thought possible, but they also make the palate sensitive to attack from the aggressive elements of alcohol, tannin and acid.

Wines that are light in tannin, not too alcoholic and have plenty of fruit are what we should consider to accompany spicy food: white wines, rosés or light reds such as Beaujolais are just the thing, depending on the weight of the dish. Oddly enough, old wines that need a bit of pepping up can work well too, provided the tannin does not wreak vengeance.

To familiarise yourself with the reaction, try a little young claret at home in the wake of some peppery salami. At first, the claret will seem very fruity, but watch out for the cumulative furnace effect that builds up as the palate becomes more and more sensitised to every element of the wine – not just to the fruit, but to the alcohol and tannin as well.

Sweetness

Sugar in wine behaves rather in the same way as acidity; thus:

Sweetness in food reduces the perception of sweetness in wine.

As long as the wine is sweeter than the food, it will work, although the balance of weights will be critical. A classy Sauternes will seem clumsy alongside a delicate feuilleté of strawberries, while a light, delicious, but desperately unfashionable sparkling Muscat from Italy not only forms a refreshingly light partnership with the dessert but also peps up the system at the end of a meal. Moscato d'Asti or Asti Spumante excels with a wide range of desserts. The beauty of these wines is their balance of sherbet acidity and grapey sweetness, and their clean-cut flavours, which allow them to blend with a variety of other tastes. Try them also with crème brûlée and other creamy, custardy sweets. Again, the wine has just the right profile of weight, acidity and sweetness.

Surprisingly, sweet Astis also have what it takes to complement all but the sweetest of chocolate desserts. There must be enough sweetness to 'out-sweet' the chocolate and enough piercing acidity to reverse the tendency that chocolate has to cling to and smother the palate. In these circumstances, Sauternes and Barsac die, losing both their complexity of flavour and their acid/sweetness balance. They will seem thin and tart, and a waste of money.

Sweet red wines also complement chocolate: Recioto della Valpolicella (amabile, not amarone), for instance, or Banyuls from south-west France, or Mavrodaphne from Greece. They work in the same sort of way that cherry and chocolate do as a flavour combination. Structurally, these wines have significant weight of fruit and alcohol not to be overwhelmed by the smothering effects of chocolate. Unfortunately, they are not as widely available as they deserve to be.

The last option is for those with a very high sweet tolerance: fortified Muscat or Moscatel from Jerez or Malaga in Spain, or the liqueur Muscats of Australia. The darker these are, the better. The best have a burnt caramel twist to the flavour, which functions similarly to acidity in cutting the richness of the dish. The combination is, however, an extremely heavy one and will seem over-the-top to many.

These fortified Muscats are the best bet for two other great stand-bys of the British restaurant repertoire: sticky toffee pudding and ice-cream. The affinity of the wines with toffee is obvious, and the need for extreme sweetness and rich weight in the wine readily apparent. Watch out once again for overload, however. The combination with ice-cream (especially plain vanilla) is more interesting. The extreme coldness of ice-cream numbs the palate, so only wines with enormous reserves of flavour will survive the 'cold shoulder'. The wine's stickiness means that it functions rather like a sauce for the ice-cream; indeed, you might be tempted to pour it over!

To conclude

Those, briefly, are a few ways in which we can help ourselves get more out of wine in a restaurant. But restaurants could help too, particularly if they thought a little more carefully about how they organised their wine lists. Menus are not arranged by country of origin. Why should wine lists be? It should not be too much trouble to produce two types of list: a long one organised by country, and a short one organised by wine style. Many restaurants already have full and short lists; this would be a useful refinement to such a system, allowing less-confident customers to find their way more easily to the sort of wine that will match their food.

There is a lot to be said for organising wines by style: unoaked dry white wines, arranged from lightest to fullest, the same for oaked wines, and a similar list in ascending order of sweetness for off-dry and dessert wines. Reds might be arranged from light to full. These ideas are, after all, increasingly familiar to customers who browse super-market and high-street-multiple wine shelves. A wine list should not be a test of memory, an arcane shibboleth designed to intimidate the customer. It should be an invitation for informed experiment, enabling customers to get more enjoyment from their visit to the restaurant. It should, in short, be the go-between that brings partners together in the mating game of food and wine.

Scoff and you scoff alone

Alan Coren – writer and broadcaster

'These *filets de thon marinés à la coriandre*,' said my daughter, in an accent so impeccable I could scarce forbear a surge of paternal pride at the thought of how much I had paid for it – 'are the fish...?'

'Fresh?' interrupted the waiter, smugly alert.

'...caught with a line?'

The waiter looked at her.

'I know nothing!' he muttered, with a really rather convincing Teuton lilt. 'I am only taking orders.'

Not a bad joke at all. Just the sort of joke you get in recessionary times, when most English waiters have firsts. Even the washers-up have decent seconds. My daughter, however, did not laugh.

'It was a serious question,' she snapped. 'If the tuna were trawled, how do you know dolphin weren't trapped in the nets?'

'I catch your drift,' I intervened. 'You wouldn't want to order tuna and get dolphin. Nobody should eat anything smarter than they are.'

'Why do you *do* this?' cried my daughter. 'Don't you *care*? I'll have,' she said 'the *poulet de Bresse*, if it's really free-range.'

'It won the Paris marathon,' said the waiter, scribbling.

'And I'll have some spinach,' said my sister-in-law.

'With?' inquired the waiter, not unreasonably.

'Just the spinach. But as much as you like.'

'It's her iron-only day,' explained her husband. 'She is realigning her trace elements. I'd like the cassoulet,' he said to the waiter.

'But as it would kill him,' said his wife, 'he'll have a plain grilled sole. And one boiled potato. Small.'

'My cholesterol is nudging 8.4,' said my brother-in-law, glumly. 'One fried egg and I could be looking at a triple bypass.'

'Why don't you have the gnocchi with olive oil, tomatoes and basil?' said my son. 'Very Mediterranean. They all live to be 100, on that.'

'Unless, of course,' said his girlfriend, 'this place doesn't stone-grind its own gnocchi flour...'

'...press its own south-slope olives...'

'...sun-dry its own *pomodori di Puglia*...'

'By the way, did you know that Columbus could tell when he was nearing Genoa from ten miles out, just by the scent from the pesto fields blowing off-shore?'

'Are you winding me up?' said the waiter.

'*Au contraire*, we take our tucker bloody seriously,' replied my son, 'don't we darling?'

'Put it this way,' said his girlfriend, to the waiter. 'I was about to order your *perdreau sauté au feuilles de laitue* when I happened to see one going by and noticed that the meat wasn't wrapped in Cos, it was wrapped in Iceberg. Don't try to deny it.'

'See how pale she's gone?' said my son. 'That's what the wrong sort of lettuce can do to a true gourmet. Take a swig of Badoit, darling.'

'Don't they have any Orkney *pétillant*?' said my sister-in-law, testily. 'Something without much zinc.'

'God help us when we get to the *tisanes*,' said my brother-in-law to me, *sotto voce*. 'We had to walk out of a place last week due to their inability to front up an authoritive camomile.'

His mother, who is 86, lit a Capstan Full Strength.

'I'm terribly sorry,' said the waiter, 'but we try to discourage our guests from smoking,'

'Well, how very thoughtful of you,' said my mother-in-law, each word emerging in its own little blue cloud. 'Thank you for trying. But it's hopeless, I'm afraid. I've been trying myself for 60 years.'

'Are they all wags?' murmured the waiter, to me.

'Just an average family,' I said.

'I'd like a nice rump steak, well done,' my mother-in-law went on, 'with lots of chips.'

'There's only fillet or sirloin,' said the waiter, 'and I don't think Chef would be happy overcooking either of them.'

'Don't be silly,' said my mother-in-law. '*I'm* the one who's supposed to be happy. And may I have a Guinness?'

'I'm sorry, we don't have any.'

'There's a Thresher's down the road,' she said. 'And while you're out,' she added, 'you might get a Wonderloaf. Well, it doesn't have to be a Wonderloaf, just something that hasn't got olives or walnuts or stuff in it. Or this dreadful whole grain –' here she waved it '– where the hard bits get wedged under your upper plate.'

The waiter assured her, somewhat faintly, that he would do what he could, and turned to me.

'I think I'll have the *langue de boeuf bouillie à la ciboulette*,' I said, 'provided it wasn't cut too near the tonsils.'

'Are you sure?' said my wife. 'Don't expect it to be as good as the one you had at that little place in the Ardèche. I bet they only use a commercial *fromage blanc* to thicken the stock here – you know what Battersea can be like when they think nobody's looking.'

I pondered upon this, and – while the waiter staggered off in search of a sommelier sidekick to whom the baton might now thankfully be passed, and while my small niece and nephew wailed themselves into a frenzy over the fact that there was nothing on the menu which even remotely approximated to the Deep Pan Kentucky Fried Fillet o'Whopper McNuggets which form their sole sustenance – upon yet deeper and more unsettling truths.

For back in the sweet langsyne before food became Food, my father was much given to taking his enormous family out to lunch by the rotating dozen, usually to great, gaunt, echoing country hotels where all his guests, from the just-weaned to the imminently dead, had their meal ordered for them, willy-nilly, by the old man, and therefore found themselves invariably tucking into bean soup, smoked trout, rare roast beef with all its fat-soaked life-threatening accoutrements, spotted dick and thick-skinned custard, and sweaty English cheese which left the mouth unroofed, all washed down with umpteen bottles of Beaune, and stickies or firewater to follow, according to gender.

Quite wonderful. Unvarious, true, but that was its strength: here was fare to unite a family, rather than offer it the illimitable opportunities for division which wait to ensnare my own attempts, today, to emulate my departed role model. In 1994, faced with a hundred options on each of a hundred menus from as many gastro- cultures, it is well-nigh impossible to find a convivial spot where the lunchtime bib may be tied on with equal success for all involved, irrespective of age, sex, weight, diet, fashion, politics, past experience or present fad. Furthermore, not only can it take an hour to order, these days, but it can also take the rest of the meal to talk about what one has ordered before, read about, heard about, and, increasingly, had a bash at knocking up oneself.

Is it any wonder that the family is tottering? There are, God knows, enough threats to this embattled institution without its having to cope with bitter divisions over dried dill or rain-forest claret. Could this have been what Prime Minister John Major meant when imploring the nation to return to basics? Coming from a man famously unashamed to praise the processed pea, it would not surprise me at all. Indeed, I might even go along with it.

London

Adams Café £

map 10

77 Askew Road, W12 9AH
081-743 0572

COOKING 1*
COST £16–£23

Frances and Abdel Boukraa's unusual café keeps moving on. Recent refurbishment has given the place a more pleasant, colourful atmosphere, and an extra room at the back provides more space. The glossy bright green walls are covered with Tunisian travel posters, while Art Nouveau plastic cloths cover the tables. Service is generally friendly and intelligent. The short menu centres on Tunisian specialities, plus a few Mediterranean dishes for good measure. Couscous, done four ways, is the star of the show: each ingredient holds its identity – there is no 'falling apart' here. As an alternative, try gargoulette – a lamb casserole tinged with an 'aromatic cloud' of fresh mint – or grilled red mullet. Starters, such as fish soup and authentic brik (filled filo pastries), have been recommended, although sweets may fade into mediocrity. The cover charge pays for bread, olives, harissa and baby meatballs: an extra 55p is added if you bring your own wine. Otherwise the short list has some gutsy North African bottles at rock-bottom prices. House French is £5.95.

CHEFS/PROPRIETORS: Frances and Abdel Boukraa OPEN: Mon to Sat, D only; 7 to 11 CLOSED: bank hols MEALS: alc (main courses £5.50 to £7.50). Cover 95p SERVICE: not inc DETAILS: 60 seats. Private parties: 36 main room, 24 private room. Vegetarian meals. Children welcome. Wheelchair access. Music

Ajimura ✦

map 15

51-53 Shelton Street, WC2H 9HE
071-240 0178

COOKING 2*
COST £14–£53

Opened by Susumu and Harumi Okada in 1972, Ajimura has established a place as one of London's most distinctive Japanese restaurants. Its philosophy is simple: it buys local supplies, employs local staff and nourishes the local community – a service that includes good-value pre-theatre dinners. The place reminds some people of a streetwise wholefood café, and the menu is strong on vegetarian dishes; Ajimura is also one of the few Japanese restaurants offering brown rice cooked with konbu seaweed. 'Sparklingly fresh' sushi topped with enormous slabs of fish are one of the highlights: the sushi vinegar is made to an Okada family recipe dating back to the 1920s. The technique of salting fish for sashimi is also an in-house tradition. Set lunches are a bargain, and the full menu straddles zenzai appetisers (including creamy deep-fried aubergine), tempura, teriyaki, omelettes and hotpots, as well as the essential back-up of soup, rice and pickles. Monthly specials are worth exploring: in May you might find maguro natto (tuna with fermented soya beans), hiya yakko (cold bean curd with bonito flakes) and ume chazuke (salt plum, seaweed and rice in soup). To finish, try yokan (tiny squares of red bean jelly). Drink green tea or saké. House wine is £7.50.

CHEFS: Susumu Okada and Tora Tanizawa PROPRIETORS: Susumu and Harumi Okada OPEN: Mon to Sat, exc Sat L; 12 to 3, 6 to 11 CLOSED: bank hols MEALS: alc (main courses £8 to £15.50). Set L £8 to £8.90, Set pre-theatre D £13 to £14.50, Set D £19.50 to £35 SERVICE: 10% CARDS: Access, Amex, Diners, Visa DETAILS: 56 seats. Private parties: 25 main room, 18 private room. Vegetarian meals. Children welcome. No smoking in 1 dining-room. Music. Air-conditioned. Fax: 071-497 2240

Alastair Little

map 15

49 Frith Street, W1V 5TE
071-734 5183

COOKING 3
COST £25–£74

'Mr Little was away in Italy on the date of our visit,' wrote one reporter, going straight to the heart of the restaurant's difficulties. It has other problems too. The décor, once avant-garde, is now 'becoming tackier by the day' and needs reviving. But the food is what exercises reporters most. Alastair Little never cooks every single dish himself when he is there, but his presence matters. It is he who has set the tone, done the homework, evolved the repertoire and come up with a style that embodies all that is best about contemporary cooking: oysters with shallot relish and spicy sausages, fillet of lamb with couscous salad, or a dish of pancetta loin, rocket, Parmesan, grilled artichokes and truffle oil. It is hardly surprising if Italy is an inspiration, for that is where Mr Little's heart is, and his body too for part of the year.

When he takes off to summer cookery school in the Umbrian hills, leaving the brigade to fend for themselves, then control slips. It is a good team, no doubt, but the performance is not the same. Nevertheless, ingredients remain good, and an inspector enjoyed an expertly roasted Bresse pigeon, meltingly soft, that appeared on a simple puréed pea soup given depth by a lovely ham hock stock, and an equally tender saddle of mildly gamey rabbit. Another reporter enjoyed roast partridge with braised cabbage and 'succulent lamb with unbelievably tasty haricot beans'. Tarte fine of apples contrasts a thin layer of crisp and buttery puff pastry with a thin layer of soft apple segments.

Many more reporters, however, leave with an impression of having eaten 'nothing special'. What irks them most is that prices make no concessions. Even supporters find difficulty with the bill. 'I feel so disappointed that a hero of mine has fallen by the wayside. If I said everything was delicious but should have been exactly half the price, I think that sums it up.'

When the cooking was on form, readers were tolerant of informality, but once it loses its edge then the grumpies win. The restaurant was never comfortable, never quiet, never looked more than a jumped-up café, and it never mattered. But now it does. As other restaurants not only imitate but increasingly catch up, Alastair Little struggles to make the grade on originality and invention. The clever combinations of food and punchy flavours can now be had at more realistic prices in more appealing settings. It has not moved with the times. First courses continue to generate most excitement, while puddings tend to tread water. Cheeses are ordinary, and service does nothing to improve them. In fact, service has come in for as much flak as everything else. There is no problem with a short wine list when the quality is as good as this, although mark-ups are high and half-bottles are few. House wine is £12 (£3.50 per glass).

CHEF: Alastair Little   PROPRIETORS: Mercedes Andre-Vega, Kirsten Pedersen and Alastair Little   OPEN: Mon to Sat, exc Sat L; 12 to 3, 6 to 11.30   CLOSED: Christmas, Easter and bank hols   MEALS: alc (main courses £16 to £24). Set L £10 (2 courses, bar only) to £25   SERVICE: not inc   CARDS: Access, Amex, Visa   DETAILS: restaurant 40 seats, bar 16 seats. Private parties: 16 private room. Vegetarian meals. Children's helpings. Wheelchair access (1 step). No music. Air-conditioned

Alba
map 11

107 Whitecross Street, EC1Y 8JH
071-588 1798

COOKING 1
COST £21–£42

City workers at lunch-time and theatre-goers at dinner are the main beneficiaries of Alba, a modern-looking Italian restaurant just round the corner from the Barbican. The light and pretty pink wash on the walls, grey floor tiles and awkwardly shaped chairs suggest it might be new-wave; flowers and a colourful display of fruit give it a lift.

The menu reads convincingly: bagna cauda is a Torinese speciality, and the sliced raw veal (with rucola leaves and a shave of Parmesan) comes with truffle oil. Other dishes range beyond northern Italy, taking in mussels in white wine, and fillet steak with green peppercorn sauce. Cooking is of the old school. Rabbit, for example, is casseroled with red peppers and served with wedges of polenta, but without due care on one visit for rabbit's tendency to become dry. Vegetables succeed, whether as an accompaniment to main courses or by themselves: asparagus is scraped and served with melted butter. The best time to eat here is probably autumn, when porcini mushrooms and white truffles are in season. Bread can vary from superb to soggy; and a trolley is trundled round, full of chocolatey and fruit creamy puddings. Wines include some good names, although most are over £15. House wine is £8.50.

CHEF: Armando Liboi   PROPRIETOR: Rudi Venerandi   OPEN: Mon to Fri; 12 to 3, 6 to 11   MEALS: alc (main courses £6.50 to £13)   SERVICE: 12.5%, card slips closed   CARDS: Access, Amex, Diners, Visa   DETAILS: 45 seats. Private parties: 60 main room. Vegetarian meals. Children's helpings. Wheelchair access (1 step). Music

Albero & Grana
map 13

Chelsea Cloisters,
89 Sloane Avenue, SW3 3DX
071-225 1048 and 1049

COOKING 2
COST £35–£60

This vibrant Chelsea rendezvous is all about the fusion of art, design and food. The tapas bar throbs with legions of suited young bloods making noise and drinking bottles of Spanish beer 'by the neck'. Beyond is the restaurant with its strikingly bold colours – red walls, mustard columns, black ceilings, check tablecloths. 'Techno-flamenco' music wings through the air. 'It goes all out for the style vote,' observed one visitor.

Angel Garcia has conjured up a version of modern Spanish cooking that can make you sit up and take notice. It challenges and comforts. Mostly the results are finely executed: stuffed squid with black-ink sauce (a favourite starter), 'absolutely magnificent' roast baby leg of lamb with small roasted potatoes, 'beautifully firm grainy cheese' with quince paste and apples served geometrically on a black plate. Against this have been comments about 'cloying' lasagne of black pudding, pig's trotter overwhelmed by butter-beans, and monkfish with an 'overseasoned' sauce. Sherries, riojas and florid descriptions dominate the wine list; 16 bottles are served by the glass. House wine is £9.

CHEF: Angel Garcia   PROPRIETOR: County Supplies Ltd   OPEN: all week (tapas in bar only Sun D); bar 12.30 to midnight, restaurant 12 to 3, 7.30 to 11   CLOSED: some bank hols   MEALS: alc D (main courses £13.50 to £19). Tapas menu (£2.50 to £15)   SERVICE: not inc (12.5% for 7 or more)   CARDS: Access, Amex, Diners, Visa   DETAILS: bar 70 seats, restaurant 50 seats. Private parties: 100 main room, 25 private room. Vegetarian meals. Children's helpings. Smart dress preferred. Music. Air-conditioned. Fax: 071-581 3259

Al Bustan   map 13

| 27 Motcomb Street, SW1X 8JU | COOKING 2 |
| 071-235 8277 | COST £30–£49 |

Mrs Atalla cooks while her husband runs the front-of-house in this rather plush restaurant with lots of trelliswork and stylishly laid tables. The cooking is authentically Lebanese and its great strengths are elegance and integrity. Raw materials – including fish from the market – are first-rate, spicing is accurate and the pastry work is reckoned to be exceptional. The menu eschews flights of fancy in favour of a well-tried repertoire dominated by meze. Reporters have singled out many items, including makanek (lamb sausages with pine-nuts), 'wonderful, non-greasy' Lebanese samosas, a moussaka of aubergine and tomatoes served cold, and rich, sour labneh (strained yogurt drizzled with olive oil). High-protein kebabs feature heavily among the main courses and there are a few raw meat dishes for the brave. The cover charge pays for a cornucopia of raw vegetables with a fierce dip and bread. Service is formal, but unstuffy. The short, mainly French wine list is topped up with a few Lebanese offerings, although prices are in keeping with the Belgravia location. House wine is £12.

CHEF: Mrs Ina'am Atalla   PROPRIETORS: Mr and Mrs Atalla   OPEN: all week; noon to 11 CLOSED: 25 Dec, 1 Jan   MEALS: alc (main courses £7 to £10.50). Cover £2.50. Minimum £12 SERVICE: not inc   CARDS: Access, Amex, Diners, Visa   DETAILS: 65 seats. 6 tables outside. Vegetarian meals. Children's helpings. Smart dress preferred. Wheelchair access. Music. Air-conditioned

All details are as accurate as possible at the time of going to press, but chefs and owners often change, and it is wise to check by telephone before making a special journey. Many readers have been disappointed when set-price bargain meals are no longer available. Ask when booking.

Alexandra

map 10

507 Kingston Road, SW20 8SF

081-542 4838

COOKING 1

COST £19–£37

The small scale of this converted house near Raynes Park station makes for intimate gatherings, so Eric Lecras does not need to tie himself down to a fixed menu or even a fixed wine list. A blackboard lists around seven items per course and the cooking is firmly anchored in the provincial France of duck confit with ceps, fish soup with rouille and boeuf bourguignonne.

'The only thing banned is nouvelle cuisine,' says M. Lecras, somewhat unnecessarily in view of some of the cream-laden items on offer. Mussels with cider and cream, and crêpe dieppoise generously stuffed with salmon, mussels, shrimps and cream, served gratiné with cheese, show the direction Alexandra is heading. Specialities tend to be either rich or ambitious – breast of corn-fed chicken with lobster mousse in a wine and shellfish sauce, or apple tart with fine puff pastry flamed in calvados with an apple caramel sauce, for example – yet the cooking is sensitive, accurately timed, enticingly flavoured and uses high-quality ingredients. Service is discreet but friendly, while the wine list is short and changeable, with house wine at £7.85 (£1.95 per glass).

CHEF/PROPRIETOR: Eric Lecras   OPEN: Mon to Sat, D only, and Sun L; 12 to 1.30, 7 to 10
MEALS: Set L Sun £12.80, Set D Mon to Thur £12.80, Fri and Sat £16.95   SERVICE: 12.5%
CARDS: Access, Visa   DETAILS: 55 seats. 5 tables outside. Private parties: 30 main room, 30 private room. Vegetarian meals with prior notice. Children welcome. Smart dress preferred. No cigars/pipes in dining-room. Music

Al Hamra

map 14

31–33 Shepherd Market, W1Y 7RJ

071-493 1954 and 6934

COOKING 2

COST £30–£44

Al Hamra is the smartest place to eat in Shepherd Market, and windows on three sides make street-watching inevitable. Most of the Middle Eastern clientele exude an air of wealth and power, and although it may be disconcerting to see prawn cocktail on the same menu as lamb's testicles and raw liver, it shows how broad the customer base must be. Table decorations are both colourful and edible. Each is laid with a generous bowl of mixed olives, raw carrot, red radishes, big Cos-type lettuce and chilli peppers. A dedicated vegetarian could make a meal of them, indeed might as well because they come with a £2.50 cover charge.

The repertoire is not quite on a Cantonese scale, but with almost 100 dishes, most of them listed as hors d'oeuvre, nobody can accuse the place of restricting choice. It is sound, evocative Middle Eastern cooking, and lamb is the main meat, minced, ground, grilled or not even cooked at all, some dishes hot, some cold. Much of the food, however, is vegetarian: not because Al Hamra is chasing a trend, but because that is just the way things are in the Middle East. Pulses and beans abound in hummus, falafel and foul medames. Main courses are largely charcoal grills, but a meal of hors d'oeuvre gives more scope and keeps the cost within reason. Arab bread is freshly baked, service can be haphazard, and the wine list is due for a revamp. House wine is £11, or £2.75 per glass. Arak starts at £37 a bottle.

CHEF: Mahir Abboud   PROPRIETORS: Rind Nabulsi and Hassan Fansa   OPEN: all week; noon to midnight   CLOSED: 25 Dec, 1 Jan   MEALS: alc (main courses £8 to £9). Cover £2.50. Minimum £10   SERVICE: not inc   CARDS: Access, Amex, Diners, Visa   DETAILS: 75 seats. 6 tables outside. Private parties: 85 main room. Vegetarian meals. Children's helpings. Smart dress preferred. Wheelchair access. Music. Air-conditioned

All Saints
map 12

12 All Saints Road, W11 1HH
071-243 2808

COOKING 1
COST £25–£36

'Soul food' in downtown Portobello sums up this lively neighbourhood restaurant, where flavour and atmosphere matter more than comfort. The furnishings are functional, the music is 'cool'. Breakfast is served from 10 to 12.30, and the place is open all day for drinks and coffee. Chef Leigh Codyre-Benson and his team hail from New Zealand, and the cooking has a global outlook: Thai fish-cakes with cucumber salad, and crispy duck pancakes with plum chutney, co-exist happily alongside Moroccan-style braised lamb shanks with couscous, and Tuscan chicken with grilled polenta. Vegetarians will not be disappointed by the prospect of chargrilled asparagus with balsamic vinegar and shaved Parmesan, or roast butternut, baby leek and chive risotto. Desserts are the likes of baked lemon tart and crème caramel. The wine list is short, sharp and affordable. House wine is £8.50.

CHEF: Leigh Codyre-Benson   PROPRIETOR: Rupert Smith   OPEN: all week, exc Mon L and Sun D; 12.30 to 3, 7.30 to 11   CLOSED: Christmas, bank hols   MEALS: alc (main courses £8 to £10.50)   SERVICE: not inc, card slips closed   CARDS: Access, Visa   DETAILS: 50 seats. Private parties: 20 main room, 25 private room. Vegetarian meals. Children welcome. Wheelchair access (3 steps). Music

Al San Vincenzo
map 11

30 Connaught Street, W2 2AF
071-262 9623

COOKING 3
COST £32–£52

From outside, the eye is drawn first to the smart red door, then to the black Venetian blinds and finally to the sticker on the window announcing that this is a 'Michael Winner-free zone', a fact that reassured two reporters. The dining-room – hung with old graphics, modern prints, and atmospheric black and white photographs – is small but not cramped. The cooking is southern Italian – mainly from Campania – which means it is plain and occasionally rustic, but never tricksy: not a sun-dried tomato in sight.

The Borgonzolos have been doing this for longer than the current Mediterranean bandwagon has been running. They don't (like some) throw a lot of fashionable ingredients together and hope to conjure a palatable dish out of thin air. They make a simple stew of salt cod and potato. They roast a rabbit (leg and saddle) with herbs and potatoes. And they combine chopped artichoke heart with stoned black olives, in a watery cooking medium, to make a delicate and enjoyable first course that highlights the unshowy everyday ingenuity of real Italian cooking. It can be uneven – overcooked chicken and broccoli in a soup here, an undercooked slice of tongue there – but the taste overcomes doubts: a dark red puddle of crushed berries, pips and all, has just the right amount of acidity to balance the richness of two scoops of dark chocolate mousse. Bread-and-butter pudding, made from panettone, has almonds and bits of orange and lemon rind in it. Excellent coffee, assured service by Signora Borgonzolo, and two dozen wines complete the package. House wine is £10.

CHEF: Vincenzo Borgonzolo   PROPRIETORS: Elaine and Vincenzo Borgonzolo   OPEN: Mon to Sat, exc Sat L; 12.30 to 2, 7 to 10.15   CLOSED: 2 weeks Christmas   MEALS: alc (main courses £11 to £18)   SERVICE: not inc, 10% for 5 or more   CARDS: Access, Visa   DETAILS: 22 seats. Children's helpings by arrangement. No cigars/pipes in dining-room. Music

L'Altro

NEW ENTRY   map 12

210 Kensington Park Road, W11 1NR   COOKING 1
071-792 1066 and 1077   COST £20–£53

Situated in a row of shops close to Portobello Road, L'Altro is the sister restaurant of Cibo, near Olympia. The décor is as rustic as can be, with wrought ironwork, tiled floors and distressed plaster walls. Tables are undressed and chairs may be found wanting for comfort. The vibrant Italian cooking centres on daily deliveries of fresh fish, featured on frequently changing antipasti lunch menus, with more traditional, and more expensive, offerings in the evening. A regular reporter enthusiastically recommends mussels and clams in tomato sauce, a 'delicious' signature dish of aubergine slices rolled with mozzarella, duck and chicken livers with grapes, and deep-fried squid and cuttlefish in 'fine, light batter' among the antipasti. Spaghetti with clams is a reliable, 'beautifully simple' pasta dish containing chillis and whole garlic cloves; skate is combed off the bone and mixed with oil, lemon and capers 'in casual disarray' for a 'splendid' starter. Tiramisù and panna cotta are good desserts, and the ciabatta is usually 'excellent'. House wine is £7.95.

CHEFS: Massimo Bianchi and Ottavio Rizzo   PROPRIETORS: Cibo UK Ltd   OPEN: all week, exc Sun D; 12 to 3, 7 to 11 (11.30 Fri and Sat)   CLOSED: 4 days Christmas   MEALS: alc (main courses L £6.50, D £9.50 to £18.50)   SERVICE: not inc (12.5%, card slips closed, for 5 or more)   CARDS: Access, Amex, Diners, Visa   DETAILS: 45 seats. 3 tables outside. Private parties: 44 main room. Vegetarian meals. Children's helpings. Wheelchair access. Music. Air-conditioned

Anna's Place

map 11

90 Mildmay Park, N1 4PR   COOKING 2
071-249 9379   COST £21–£33

Reporters tend to focus on the glow of Nordic warmth that emanates not just from the cooking here, but from Anna herself. Although she is Swedish, the food is not exclusively so. That said, it is the national dishes of that country which occasion the most enthusiastic praise. The amicability makes up for any lack of elbow room: 'This is a supremely friendly place.' It is as well to be aware that credit cards are not taken, but one couple, caught short on the money front, were astonished, on asking for the nearest cash machine, to be invited to put a cheque in the post when they got home.

The simplicity of the cooking allows the quality of raw materials to shine forth, as in the impeccably fresh fish and the conservation-grade meats. Creamy fish soup has 'silky texture' and a good assortment of pieces of fish, while the house speciality, biff Strindberg, is 'meltingly tender' diced beef fillet marinated in Swedish mustard and served with a toothsome cucumber salad. A vegetarian pasta dish of tagliatelle with mushrooms and courgettes in a cheese sauce showed that non-carnivores are not neglected. Waffles with blueberry compote and cream are a traditional pudding, or there is properly made apple pie, chocolate truffle cake or a citrus and olive oil sponge. The marinated herrings to start can be a revelation for yielding texture and piquancy. Ice-cold Absolut vodka is the best aperitif. The Bruno Paillard champagne is the only item on the wine list to exceed £20, and most bottles are substantially below. House selections from France and California are £7.10.

CHEFS: Beth Diadone and Richard Wells   PROPRIETOR: Anna Hegarty   OPEN: Tue to Sat; 12.15 to 2.15, 7.15 to 10.30   CLOSED: 2 weeks Christmas and Easter, 4 weeks Aug   MEALS: alc (main courses £7 to £10.50)   SERVICE: 10%   DETAILS: 42 seats. 5 tables outside. Private parties: 12 main room. Vegetarian meals. Children's helpings. Wheelchair access (1 step). Music

Arcadia
NEW ENTRY   map 12

Kensington Court,
35 Kensington High Street, W8 5EB
071-937 4294

COOKING 2
COST £24–£37

The Barracloughs bought these premises in the summer of 1993. Once the Ark, sister to a similarly named Notting Hill eatery, Arcadia is now reborn in terms of both name and style. Nicky Barraclough comes to the stoves from the Carved Angel (see entry, Dartmouth) and nearby Clarke's (see entry, London). The setting is a difficult-to-find cobbled passageway off Kensington High Street. A small ground-floor dining-room has been done in shades of buttermilk and green, mirrored to create an impression of space, and decorated with diverting watercolours of recreations on the Thames. Downstairs is in similar vein.

At lunch, set-price meals are the pattern, while a longer *carte* operates in the evening. A good balance is struck between fresh fish and properly hung meats, with Mediterranean or American borrowings worked in thoughtfully rather than being extraneous additions. At a meal in June, 'juicily fresh' calamari were breaded, deep-fried and squeezed with much lemon, and came with a chopped anchovy mayonnaise. More lemon had been used on roast guinea-fowl, again to very good effect as it seemed to lighten the density of the meat, and Puy lentils in a reduction made a fine support. Angus beef sirloin was 'superbly succulent, lean, tender meat', chargrilled and given a red wine sauce containing caramelised ('well-gunged') shallots that offered a 'rich and sweet' contrast both to the meat and to the refreshingly plain vegetable selection, ordered separately. Vanilla-speckled crème brûlée and lemon tart with 'thick zippy filling' showed a sure hand with desserts. Cafetière coffee is hearteningly strong, and breads are various and good. Some dishes – particularly specials – drop off the menu as the evening wears on. Arcadia has done well in building up such a press of business in such a relatively short period. The wine list is a fairly sound and reasonably priced collection with a few stars, such as Vacheron's Sancerre and the rare single-domaine René Manuel red Meursault from Labouré-Roi. House wines start at £9.

CHEF: Nicky Barraclough   PROPRIETORS: Nicky and Stephen Barraclough   OPEN: all week, exc Sat and Sun L; 12 to 2.30, 7 (6.30 Sun) to 11.15   CLOSED: Sun Christmas to Easter   MEALS: alc D (main courses £7.50 to £13). Set L £13.50 (2 courses) to £16   SERVICE: not inc   CARDS: Access, Amex, Visa   DETAILS: 80 seats. 6 tables outside. Private parties: 50 main room, 20 private room. Vegetarian meals. Children's helpings. Smart dress preferred. No cigars/pipes in dining-room. No-smoking area. No music. Air-conditioned

Argyll
map 13

316 King's Road, SW3 5UH   COOKING 2
071-352 0025   COST £24–£48

The much-vaunted change of direction at the Argyll has wrought a mighty transformation in its ambience as well as its food. Erstwhile chef Anand Sastry left on amicable terms and was replaced in April 1994 by Tony Carey from Le Caprice (see entry, London). The tone of the menu is now very much in today's metropolitan mainstream (Caesar salad, tomato and basil galette, and grilled rabbit with olives and polenta), and seating has been carefully maximised. Even when full, though, the place avoids feeling cramped and the pace of service on a busy night fairly motors.

The menu is long on content and modishness: for example, smoked ham knuckle with parsley and lentils, chargrilled cuttlefish in ink, grilled ribeye with salsa verde, and Thai-spiced sausage with cucumber and peanuts. An inspection meal just after Tony Carey had hit the stoves took in fairly gentle Thai-spiced shrimp broth, tender roast foie gras on toasted sourdough, and 'densely satisfying' Toulouse sausages with a salad of potato and (not much) onion. Chargrilled neck of lamb in thick slices of variable quality came with 'very d-i-y' accompaniments of a pot of aïoli and half a lemon. Desserts – passion-fruit crème caramel and chocolate marquise – were fine, but might have been better if the respective garnishes of kumquats and caramelised apricots had been switched. Coffee could improve. The wine list is concise and modern, grouped largely by grape variety, with prices that feel just slightly over the odds for the context. International house wines start at £9.75.

CHEF: Tony Carey   PROPRIETORS: Christian Arden and Elizabeth Mortimer   OPEN: Mon to Sat, exc Mon L; 12 to 2.30, 6.30 to 12   MEALS: alc (main courses £7.50 to £13.50). Set L £12 (2 courses) to £15   SERVICE: not inc   CARDS: Access, Amex, Diners, Visa   DETAILS: 80 seats. Private parties: 80 main room. Vegetarian meals. Children's helpings on request. No pipes in dining-room. Wheelchair access. Music. Air-conditioned. Fax: 071-352 1652

Arisugawa
map 14

27 Percy Street, W1P 9FF   COOKING 3
071-636 8913   COST £16–£68

The basement dining-room at this elegant Japanese restaurant is one of the most striking in London. In addition to the sushi counter and private rooms, there is a platform eating area at the back, about two feet off the floor. Shoes must be removed to gain access and, by means of ingenious technology, sections of it slide about, so that tables can be combined or separated. A number of set-price menus include an illustrated one at lunch-time. The speciality menu appears inscribed in Japanese calligraphy on a fan.

Cooking and presentation are of uniformly high standard. Sushi is excellent and may comprise eel with pickled mooli or toro – the fattiest cut of tuna. Grilled salted quail's eggs or chicken wings are 'remarkable value'. The salted mackerel is 'screamingly fresh', the assorted pickles (including turnip and plum) are exquisitely sharp-tasting, but Japanese experts may find some of the flavours slightly more delicate than they are used to. Chawan-mushi in particular seems to use a very light stock. On the other hand, a dish called stamina-tofu, which includes chopped fermented soy beans, mountain-yam and raw quail's egg, is most definitely not for the uninitiated. Service, from kimonoed waitresses, is skilful and charming, if not invariably Anglophone. House wine is £10, but it would be wiser to stick to saké or Japanese beer.

CHEF: Akira Takeuchi PROPRIETOR: Ms Masako Yamamoto OPEN: Mon to Sat, exc Sat L; 12.30 to 2.30, 6 to 10 (9.30 Sat) CLOSED: bank hols MEALS: alc (main courses £5 to £15). Set L £7 to £14, Set D £25 to £40. Cover £1 D SERVICE: 15%, card slips closed CARDS: Access, Amex, Diners, Visa DETAILS: 100 seats. Private parties: 100 main room, 20 private room. Vegetarian meals. Children's helpings. Smart dress preferred. Music. Air-conditioned. Fax: 071-323 4237

Les Associés

map 10

172 Park Road, N8 8JY
081-348 8944

COOKING 1*
COST £23–£52

'A French restaurant run by French people' is the associates' epigrammatic summing up of their Crouch End rendezvous. It is a place that continues to please. Little quibbles like 'irritatingly slow service' and high smoke levels do not detract from the atmosphere of the place or the quality of the food. Gilles Charvet offers a short, regularly changing menu that promises the likes of meaty venison terrine with chutney, salmon tartare topped with crème fraîche, lightly cooked scallops with langoustine sauce, and pork with apples and an 'unctuous' calvados sauce. It is also worth asking about the specials, which often have a seasonal theme, such as wild mushrooms. The mixed plate of desserts shows off the skills of a kitchen that can produce good tarte Tatin, and chocolate and pear mousse, as well as home-made ice-creams. Around 30 French regional wines appear on the handwritten list; serious drinking starts at £15. House wine is £9.80.

CHEF: Gilles Charvet PROPRIETORS: Gilles Charvet, Dominique Chéhere and Didier Bertran OPEN: Wed to Fri L, 12.30 to 2; Tue to Sat D, 7.30 to 10 CLOSED: Aug MEALS: alc (main courses £12 to £15). Set L £15.95 SERVICE: not inc, card slips closed CARDS: Access, Visa DETAILS: 37 seats. Private parties: 37 main room. Vegetarian meals. Children's helpings. No pipes in dining-room. Wheelchair access. Music

'The proprietor seemed to be a bit disorganised, but eventually he got us a drink and put some yukky music on. The atmosphere was a bit frosty, almost as though we'd disappointed him by turning up.' (On eating in County Durham)

Aubergine

NEW ENTRY map 13

11 Park Walk, SW10 0AJ
071-352 3449

COOKING 3*
COST £29–54

This stylish, exuberant newcomer deals in contemporary French food. The small room is inviting, open and airy: a pale, creamy sunny yellow, with striking flowers and large tables generously spaced. Even on a weekday evening Aubergine can have an electric atmosphere. It is significant that many reporters refer to the chefs with whom Gordon Ramsay has worked – Marco Pierre White and Albert Roux in London, Joël Robuchon and Guy Savoy in Paris – spotting dishes that make reference to his mentors. But Ramsay is now beginning to develop a style of his own.

'It isn't cuisine du terroir but it keeps its feet on the ground' was one punning comment. Freshness and flavour appear centre stage, and Ramsay avoids the fanciful posing gestures that bedevil many of today's prima donna chefs. People go to enjoy his food, and they report favourably on a long list of dishes that include parfait of duck foie gras with toasted brioche, a standard of the repertoire perhaps, but done with consummate skill, fine-textured and full of flavour. The lightness of touch is appreciated in, for example, a raviolo of salmon mousse: floating in a fine asparagus bouillon on one occasion, served with a five-spice vinaigrette on another – 'a dish of glad, confident vivacity and real invention'. Indeed, fish is the strongest suit, brimming with delights in a 'delicately delectable mousse' (described on the menu as 'a tian') of leeks and scallops, or in squares of roasted red mullet set on slices of fried artichoke around dressed leaves, with depth and interest coming from diced black olives and tomatoes. Any imbalances are due mostly to heavy-handed seasoning.

Desserts do not quite scale the same heights, but mille-feuille of red fruits with thin layers of crisp pastry, and crème brûlée, unmoulded with an exactly brittle burnt top and spiked with apple crisps, have won support. The value is good (especially at lunch-time), which is why the place is always busy. Waits of several weeks in order to eat at a reasonable hour have exasperated ('booking is a bore'), although 'the food is worth waiting for'. Staff are French, friendly, helpful, charming, well briefed, knowledgeable, and deliver an intricate and passionate description of the menu. Problems in service seem largely to have stemmed from the press of numbers. The exciting thing is that Ramsay has plenty more potential packed away waiting to reveal itself. Aubergine has the makings of a real star. A sound wine list allows scope for drinking well under £20, especially from the New World, but some of the French wines are so good it is tempting to spend more. House wine is £10.50 (£3 per glass).

CHEF/PROPRIETOR: Gordon Ramsay OPEN: Mon to Sat, exc Sat L; 12 to 2.30, 7 to 11 MEALS: Set L £18, Set D £28 SERVICE: not inc CARDS: Access, Amex, Diners, Visa DETAILS: 45 seats. Private parties: 45 main room. Vegetarian meals with prior notice. Children welcome. Smart dress preferred. No music. Air-conditioned. Fax: 071-351 1770

The Guide *relies on feedback from its readers. Especially welcome are reports on new restaurants appearing in the book for the first time. All letters to the* Guide *are acknowledged.*

Au Jardin des Gourmets ▮ ⁵✳

map 15

5 Greek Street, W1V 6NA	COOKING 2
071-437 1816	COST £20–£52

Rumours that this might change to a Russian restaurant under the new owners so far remain unfounded. For the moment at least, it continues as one of Soho's longest-serving French-style restaurants, 'a haven away from the yapping trendy taco and lager joints'. The calm first-floor dining-room may be a bit staid for some, but has its advantages. 'There are not many restaurants where single women feel able to go and eat,' writes one who, laden with shopping, was grateful for the courteous and understanding welcome and proceeded to enjoy smoked duck salad, a plate of steamed salmon, cod, scallops and king prawns arranged around a mound of spinach with new potatoes, finishing with pear tarte Tatin with clotted cream and a caramel sauce.

Regulars endorse the consistency. 'For the third year in succession we have continued to be delighted by this restaurant.' The food may not excite but it certainly pleases, with fresh crab salad, snails in red wine sauce, roast rack of lamb with lyonnaise potatoes, baked Alaska and a parade of excellent cheeses, including Epoisses, Roquefort and Tomme de Savoie. Coffee comes with lots of dark chocolates, and bread and butter is up to scratch. The ground-floor brasserie is more informal, serving up pasta with pesto, Toulouse sausage with flageolet beans, onglet (flank of beef) with shallots, and Cotswold trifle, although its prices have shot up since last year.

The wine list is not entirely French. Long runs in Burgundy and Bordeaux shift the balance significantly in favour of red, but interest is sustained throughout and prices are fair, even for grand wines. One couple who asked for advice were pointed towards a vin de pays which they considered to be extremely good value. There is a decent selection of half-bottles, and house Duboeuf is £8.75 (£2.20 per glass). CELLARMAN'S CHOICE: Pouilly-Fumé 1993, Dom. Chatelain, £18.50; Auxey-Duresses 1988, J-P. Diconne, £24.50.

CHEF: Denis Loubry   PROPRIETOR: Novoport Group Ltd   OPEN: Mon to Sat, exc Sat L; restaurant 12.15 to 2.30, 6 to 11.15; brasserie 12 to 2.45, 6 to 11.15   CLOSED: 25 and 26 Dec, Easter, bank hol L   MEALS: alc (main courses £11 to £16.50). Restaurant Set L and D £13.50 to £21.50, brasserie Set L and D £10.95 (2 courses) to £14.50. Cover £1.50   SERVICE: restaurant 15%, brasserie net prices, card slips closed   CARDS: Access, Amex, Diners, Visa   DETAILS: restaurant 88 seats; brasserie 75 seats. Private parties: 55 restaurant, 30 brasserie. Vegetarian meals. Children's helpings. Jacket and tie restaurant; smart dress preferred brasserie. No smoking in 1 dining-room. No pipes in restaurant or brasserie. Wheelchair access. Music. Air-conditioned. Fax: 071-437 0043

L'Aventure

map 11

3 Blenheim Terrace, NW8 0EH	COOKING 1
071-624 6232	COST £29–£44

L'Aventure hides behind layers of foliage in a tranquil cul-de-sac in St John's Wood. The foliage is dotted with fairy lights, and a glassed-in terrace at the front manages to look pretty in summer, cosy in winter. The formula is as before: fixed-price menus at lunch and dinner, with four choices per course, plus recited specials. When the food pleases, this place is valued for its solid commitment to the honest cause of cuisine bourgeoise. Thus, crisped scallops with spinach and a cream sauce, and tenderly pink duck livers with mushrooms in a wine reduction, were major-league starters that quite surprised for their quality. One reporter regretted that a perfectly well-cooked turbot fillet was accompanied by a strongly salty anchovy sauce, but better balance was found in carré d'agneau with roast garlic or chicken leg stuffed with duck liver mousse in puff pastry. Chocolate truffle on white chocolate sauce ('extremely good') is appreciated, though tarte Tatin could do with a little more caramelising. Contentment is thrown into relief by doubts expressed by some about indifferent service and value. It is not that the kitchen does not try hard, but coffee is not included, and the cheapest bottle of wine is £13.50.

CHEF: Alain Perdrix   PROPRIETORS: Catherine Parisot and Chris Mitas   OPEN: all week, exc Sat L; 12.30 to 2.30, 7.30 to 11   MEALS: Set L £18.50, Set D Mon to Sat £25, Sun £18.50 SERVICE: not inc   CARDS: Access, Amex, Diners, Visa   DETAILS: 50 seats. 5 tables outside. Private parties: 48 main room. Vegetarian meals with prior notice. Children's helpings. Smart dress preferred. No cigars before 11pm. Music

Bahn Thai

map 15

21A Frith Street, W1V 5TS
071-437 8504

COOKING 2
COST £22–£46

'Easily the most interesting and challenging Thai food in central London,' observes a reporter who is familiar with the scene. Englishman Philip Harris is a champion of the culture and cuisine of Thailand, and his restaurant pleads the cause convincingly. The ground floor has been attractively transformed into a café/bistro, with tables spilling out on to the street. This is an ideal setting for light lunches and snacks culled from the vast, authentic menu: 'wonderfully fragrant' satays, 'brilliant' khanom jeep (steamed dumplings served on a pool of 'extraordinarily good' warm soy and garlic sauce), and yum hoi chell (hot-and-sour scallop salad) have been first-rate. Tom yum soup is a benchmark dish: 'balanced, with a rich flavour of chilli and citrus and coconut'. Other high points from recent meals have included green chicken curry, and crispy fried pomfret with tamarind sauce.

Even desserts draw ecstatic praise: durian ice-cream 'with a true flavour slowly emerging as you spooned it down' and a slab of hot cake made with caramelised onions that was 'oozily rich' are two winners. Upstairs is less inspiring as a backdrop for such dazzlingly good food; the Thai staff mean well, but may struggle with the English language. Chrysanthemum tea or Singha Thai beer are suitable accompaniments. Some effort has gone into assembling a list of wines 'which are not overawed by Thai spicing' and the selection is a good one, with plenty of bright young Sauvignons and Chardonnays. Wines by the glass to suit particular dishes might be a further improvement.

CHEF: Penn Squires   PROPRIETORS: Bahn Thai plc/Philip Harris   OPEN: all week; 12 to 2.45, 6 to 11.15 (12.30 to 2.30, 6.30 to 10.30 Sun)   CLOSED: Christmas, Easter, bank hols   MEALS: alc (main courses £4.95 to £19.95)   SERVICE: 12.5%, card slips closed   CARDS: Access, Amex, Diners, Visa   DETAILS: 100 seats. 4 tables outside. Private parties: 50 main room, 20 to 30 private rooms. Vegetarian meals. Children welcome. Smart dress preferred. No cigars/pipes in dining-room. Wheelchair access (also WC). Music. Air-conditioned. Fax: 071-439 0340

Bedlington Café £

map 10

24 Fauconberg Road, W4 3JY
081-994 1965

COOKING 1
COST £16–£22

'This is comfortably the best Thai in the area,' comments an expert, although 'comfort' isn't a word that really applies to this buzzy, cramped café. By day it is a greasy spoon, by night it serves up vivid and full-frontal dishes from a simple menu that takes in satays, squid salad, jungle curry, chilli fish and chicken with sweet basil. A small selection of Laotian specialities such as salty beef, bamboo salad and spicy mincemeat add variety, and a few pseudo-Cantonese dishes are included for those who like to play it safe. The place is unlicensed, but you can bring your own wine (50p corkage).

CHEF: Mrs P. Priyanu PROPRIETORS: Mr and Mrs C. Priyanu OPEN: all week; 9 to 2, 6.30 to 10 MEALS: alc (main courses £3 to £5). Set L and D £10 to £12. Unlicensed, but bring your own: corkage 50p SERVICE: not inc DETAILS: 35 seats. Vegetarian meals. Children welcome. Wheelchair access. No music

Belgo ⁵⁄₊✱ £

map 11

72 Chalk Farm Road, NW1 8AN
071-267 0718

COOKING 1
COST £15–£44

This noisy refectory serves Belgium's classic snack, mussels and chips, with gusto and lots of good beers. Some readers are disturbed, when they book, to learn that they can only have the table for two hours. But it can be two hours of Rabelaisian fun: 'The fish names embedded into the walls are a constant delight, as are the see-through toilets.' The short, snappy menus include Lunch for a Fiver (with wild boar sausage), Franco-Belgo (steak and waffle) – and Belgo Complet with salade liègeoise, pot of moules-frites and Hoegaarden beer, all for 10 quid. Mussels (Belgo gets through two tons a week) are cooked in anything from pastis to a sauce of coconut, coriander and lemon grass, and there are lobster, asparagus and a clutch of other classics from waterzoï to carbonade flamande. Waffles are 'utterly scrummy'. Waiters dress as monks, service is friendly, and beer is the thing to drink – white, wheat, Trappist, Kriek and Gueuze – and there is flavoured schnapps if the two-hour meter hasn't run out. The new air-conditioning should please non-smokers. House wines are £8.75.

CHEF: Phillipe Blaise PROPRIETORS: André Pllsnier and Denis Blais OPEN: all week; 12 to 3, 6 to 11.30 (noon to 11.30 Sat, noon to 10.30 Sun) MEALS: alc (main courses £5.50 to £16). Set L and D £8.95 to £10 (2 courses) SERVICE: 15% (optional), card slips closed CARDS: Access, Amex, Diners, Visa DETAILS: 120 seats. Private parties: 10 main room. Vegetarian meals. Children's helpings. No music. Air-conditioned

---

⁵⁄₊✱ *indicates that smoking is either banned altogether or that a dining-room is maintained for non-smokers. The symbol does not apply to restaurants that simply have no-smoking areas.*

£ *indicates that it is possible to have a three-course meal, including coffee, a half-bottle of house wine and service, at any time the restaurant is open (i.e. at dinner as well as at lunch, unless a place is open only for dinner), for £20 or less per person.*

Belvedere

Holland House, off Abbotsbury Road,
Holland Park, W8 6LU
071-602 1238

COOKING 1
COST £25–£47

The setting is 'stylish, exclusive and discreet', the building an impressive orangery with high ceilings, arched windows, stained-glass panels and an airy Victorian feel. It attracts the sort of clientele 'who probably know more about Armani and Klein than food and wine'. Duncan Wallace took his place at the stove in the spring of 1994 and cooks a shortish *carte* that runs from parfait of duck liver with port jelly and toasted brioche to fish and chips with mushy peas and a 'Wally' pickle. Some of the food is very tasty, but it lacks consistency. For an inspector, a tartare of scallops 'could have been cod or cotton wool', although tartlet of caramelised onions reassured him that someone could cook very well – thin pastry filled with jammy, caramelly onions in their juice, helped by a contrasting vinegary lollo rosso salad. Hunky, crispy-coated fish-cakes are well partnered by a caper and tarragon sauce, while rosette of beef 'could not be challenged for flavour, seasoning, or the most juicy texture'. A trio of mango was 'perfect for mangophiles', with a light and creamy bavarois, not-too-sweet sorbet and just-ripe macerated slices. Service is a bit stop-and-go, the wine list perfunctory with split vintages. House wine is £10.50 (£2.20 per glass).

CHEF: Duncan Wallace PROPRIETORS: John Gold and William Z. Ofner OPEN: all week, exc Sun D; 12.30 to 3, 7 (6 June to Aug) to 11 CLOSED: 25 Dec MEALS: alc (main courses £7.50 to £13.50) SERVICE: not inc CARDS: Access, Amex, Diners, Visa DETAILS: 140 seats. 5 tables outside. Private parties: 150 main room. Car park. Vegetarian meals. Children welcome. Wheelchair access (3 steps). Music. Air-conditioned

Bertorelli's

map 15

44A Floral Street, WC2E 9DA
071-836 3969

COOKING 1
COST £22–£43

Opposite the stage door of the Royal Opera House, Bertorelli's is equally popular as a bolt-hole for theatre-goers planning forays to less exalted venues. The ground-floor dining-room is all Art Deco, glass and chrome; the mood is lively and urbane. Maddalena Bonino cooks a modern Italian menu: for example, ricotta and aubergine terrine with roasted pepper salsa, and griddled scallops on fennel couscous with saffron dressing. Roast guinea-fowl comes with sage polenta and marinated red onions, and the creditable pasta has interesting sauces. The results are sound and colourful. Downstairs is a bar for pizzas and snacks. The cover charge pays for good breads plus olives and gherkins. Fair-priced bottles from reputable Italian growers dominate the wine list, and 20 wines are served by the glass. House wines are £8.25.

CHEF: Maddalena Bonino PROPRIETORS: Groupe Chez Gérard Ltd OPEN: Mon to Sat (café menu Sat L restaurant); 12 to 3, 5.30 to 11.30 CLOSED: 25 and 26 Dec MEALS: alc (main courses £7 to £14). Cover £1.50 SERVICE: 12.5% (optional), card slips closed CARDS: Access, Amex, Diners, Visa DETAILS: 90 seats. Private parties: 35 main room. Vegetarian meals. Children's helpings. Smart dress preferred. No-smoking area. No cigars/pipes in dining-room. Wheelchair access (1 step). No music. Air-conditioned. Fax: 071-836 1868

Bibendum ▮

map 13

Michelin House,
81 Fulham Road, SW3 6RD
071-581 5817

COOKING 4*
COST £22–£84

This is one of the most attractive dining-rooms in London, a one-off with individuality and personality which are matched by the bold flavours of Simon Hopkinson's food. The room has its moods, ever-changing like a seascape: light and airily fresh above the charivari at lunch-time, more serious and formal at night, austere in winter, expansive in summer. Seat covers move through the colours with the seasons, from light green in spring through bright yellow and red to winter blue. The constant is an ability to charm and excite whatever the occasion. We may flinch at the prices, we may rail against the 15 per cent service charge, but we must also be thankful that it was Sir Terence Conran who sympathetically restored the place without making it seem like a tawdry themed restaurant.

Subtlety is not the main commodity that Simon Hopkinson peddles. The attraction is big flavours that are easy to like, whether they originate in the Mediterranean, the Far East or nearer home. He reminds his audience of native English ingredients such as smoked haddock, fruit crumbles and good old-fashioned Cheddar cheese. Flavours are strong – rock oysters covered with a robust curry-flavoured hollandaise and warmed under the grill, for instance – but rarely so powerful as to defeat their object. Apple tart with ice-cream is a perfect example of its kind, and chocolate pithiviers is delightfully rich and intense.

Prices invite the view that lapses, however small, are unforgiveable. If salt overwhelms the food or timing goes completely awry (as they can), then perceived value diminishes. In this context the set lunch beckons. One reporter enjoyed grilled squid dressed with parsley, olive oil and lemon juice, then marinated oriental chicken with Thai spicing, plus a cool green salad and three separate small plates of vegetables, and finally four thin slivers of Caerphilly cheese. 'I thought every penny well spent.' The bits and bobs are good also, from brilliant black olives to excellent chocolate truffles.

Portions can be large. Some people just come in for a first course, a pudding and a smoke – a restaurant that sells ashtrays (a Conran sideline shared with Quaglino's) is hardly likely to have a no-smoking policy. Niggles include 'the hordes of businessmen who overwhelm the place', and occasional blips in service. The Oyster Bar downstairs is not built for comfort, especially on winter evenings, but the rest of the time it entertains with light lunches, an enormous seafood platter (£45 for two) and an array of simple, strong flavours that echo those in the restaurant.

The wine list is undoubtedly one of the finest in the country, paying due regard to the glories of Italy, the villages of Burgundy, the maturity of claret and anybody looking for a sweet wine. Historic bottles include Barsac as old as the Michelin building itself. Prices (many in three figures), however, are frightening. Not a single Burgundy, Alsace or Bordeaux can be had for £20, allowing for the 15 per cent service charge; indeed the service charge alone on a bottle of Hermitage La Chapelle 1961 amounts to over £80. There are just enough bottles under £20 to satisfy, although it would be helpful if they were collected together on to a single page. House wines begin at £9.50 (£2.99 per glass). CELLARMAN'S CHOICE: Mercurey Blanc, premier cru, Les Champs Martins 1992, Juillot, £46.50; Gevrey Chambertin 1991, Dom. Denis Mortet, £46.50.

CHEFS: Simon Hopkinson and Matthew Harris PROPRIETORS: Simon Hopkinson, Paul Hamlyn and Sir Terence Conran OPEN: all week; restaurant 12.30 to 2.30 (3 Sat and Sun), 7 to 11.30 (10.30 Sun); Oyster Bar noon to 11 (noon to 3.30, 7 to 10 Sun) CLOSED: 24 to 28 Dec, Easter Mon MEALS: alc (main courses restaurant £12 to £21, Oyster Bar £6.50 to £18.50). Set L £25 SERVICE: 15%, card slips closed CARDS: Access, Amex, Visa DETAILS: restaurant 72 seats, Oyster Bar 40 seats. Vegetarian meals. Children's helpings. No children inside Oyster Bar. Wheelchair access. No music restaurant. Air-conditioned restaurant. Fax: 071-823 7925

Billboard Café £ map 11

222 Kilburn High Road, NW6 4JP COOKING 1
071-328 1374 COST £15–£39

'Still a reliable oasis,' confirm regulars who like to start the evening by sitting at the bar, drinking 'highly recommendable' margaritas and nibbling pesto toasts. Others have different, but equally pleasurable memories: 'It was rather strange to eat a delightful Sunday lunch with people at the next table having breakfast surrounded by their Sunday supplements.' All are happily accommodated in this lively warehouse conversion. The cooking is a mix of Italian old and new, with lots of fish, chargrilling and home-made pasta dominating a menu that roams through bruschetta, tortelloni with fresh sage and butter, and spicy Italian sausages on a bed of sauté spinach. Daily additions offer even wider choice in the shape of black-bean soup, spinach and chicken salad with passion-fruit, and pasta with veal and grappa. Puddings sounded the only note of disappointment for one reporter. To drink, try steamed milk laced with calvados, or explore the short, largely Italian wine list. House wine is £6.95.

CHEF: Nasser Nateghi PROPRIETORS: Nasser Nateghi and Lindsay Smith OPEN: Mon to Sat D, Sat and Sun L; 12 to 2.45, 6.30 to 12 (12.30 Fri and Sat) MEALS: alc (main courses £5 to £12.50). Sat and Sun brunch £6.25. Set D £10 to £15 SERVICE: 10%, card slips closed CARDS: Access, Visa DETAILS: 65 seats. Private parties: 65 main room. Vegetarian meals. Children's helpings. Smart dress preferred. Wheelchair access. Music. Air-conditioned. Fax: 071-625 1550

Bistrot Bruno map 15

63 Frith Street, W1V 5TA COOKING 3*
071-734 4545 COST £27–£47

When Bruno Loubet left the Four Seasons Hotel in 1993, he assumed full responsibility at the stoves in Soho. That put the standard of the food on a sharp upward trajectory so that, while prices remained stable, Bistrot Bruno became one of the smartest venues in the area. Even so, the décor has a spartan minimalism, and tables are packed so closely together that murmured confidentialities will be known the length of Frith Street by the time you're perusing the dessert menu.

Superlatives spill forth from readers' reports for cooking that is not just considered exemplary value, but is also full of sheer, undiluted excitement. Every dish speaks of a desire for maximum impact. Ingredients are very much in line with the current hunger for strength and simplicity: chicken livers, snails, calves' brains, sardines, salt cod, mustard dressings and garlic confit. Lobster tortellini with an orange and tomato vinaigrette were 'delicate in texture yet full of flavour', duck livers on a sweetcorn pancake with garlic sauce provided a memorable starter for one seasoned eater-out, while another thought her summer vegetable risotto 'utterly brilliant'. Enthusiastic notices have also been received for roast stuffed rabbit leg with lime-pickled new potato, guinea-fowl with olives and spiced fennel, cod wrapped in Parma ham, grilled grey mullet with capers, 'fabulous' crispy-skinned duck on a bed of prunes, and assiette d'agneau – an imposing plate of fried neck, stuffed trotter and a baked potato filled with tripe. Desserts have been pronounced 'interesting and adult' by over-18s who have enjoyed invigorating anise and lime parfait, îles flottantes flavoured with Pernod, and apple mille-feuille with cinnamon ice-cream. Incidentals such as lemon-marinated succulent green olives, powerful espresso and the legendary chocolate-coated sorbet petits fours on cocktail sticks all keep up the pace. Pierre Condou writes that Loubet's 'involvement here will remain, his menus executed by chefs he has trained', after he moves on to pastures new. It is to be hoped that the exacting standards he has set will remain as well.

Wines are a fairly small, carefully selected bunch, arranged in an international jumble in ascending order of price. There are some excellent modern classics, such as Chateau Lastours oak-aged Corbières and the Jurançon sec of Dom. Cauhapé. House wines from south-west France start at £8.75.

CHEFS: Bruno Loubet and Jason Hornbuckle   PROPRIETORS: Pierre and Kathleen Condou OPEN: Mon to Sat, exc Sat L; 12.15 to 2.30, 6.15 to 11.30   MEALS: alc (main courses £11 to £16)   SERVICE: not inc, card slips closed   CARDS: Access, Amex, Diners, Visa   DETAILS: 42 seats. Private parties: 20 main room. Vegetarian meals. Children's helpings. No cigars/pipes in dining-room. Wheelchair access (2 steps). Music. Air-conditioned. Fax: 071-287 1037

Bistrot 190 £

map 13

189 Queen's Gate, SW7 5EU   COOKING 1*
071-581 5666   COST £20–£40

'Awash with people on a springtime Sunday afternoon' was the observation of an out-of-towner who turned up for brunch. The bistro on the ground floor of the Gore Hotel has all the trademarks of Antony Worrall-Thompson – from the waiters' jazzy waistcoats right down to the décor, which is all big, bold gestures, prints and artefacts. Bare tables and noise suit the place. The policy of 'no bookings unless you are a member' still causes confusion, frayed tempers and long queues. The food is a decent example of high-volume modern cooking, built around vivid assemblies culled from all sorts of places, from Tuscany to Thailand. Patchiness is almost inevitable. Creamy risottos, pasta, warm salads, chargrilling and salsas are the mainstays. Linguini with walnuts and Gorgonzola cream, and chargrilled chicken with roast garlic and tomato sauce have hit the button. England also has its say with salmon fish-cakes and chips, sausage hotpot with wild parsley mash, and rhubarb crumble with custard. The sharp wine list varies depending on the supplier, and the selection of trendy world beers is worth a try. House wines start at £8.50. We have received mixed reports this year on Downstairs at One Ninety, the basement fish restaurant also run by Antony Worrall-Thompson.

CHEFS: Antony Worrall-Thompson and Harry Greenhalgh   PROPRIETOR: 190 Queensgate plc
OPEN: all week; 7am to 11am, noon to 5pm, 6pm to 12.30am (11.30pm Sun)   CLOSED: 3 days
Christmas   MEALS: alc (main courses £5.50 to £11). Set breakfast £6.95 to £8.95, Set L Sun
£12.50   SERVICE: not inc (10%, card slips closed, for 6 or more)   CARDS: Access, Amex,
Diners, Visa   DETAILS: 55 seats. Private parties: 70 main room, 28 private room. Vegetarian
meals. Children's helpings on request. Music. Fax: 071-581 8172

▲ Blakes

| NEW ENTRY | map 13

33 Roland Gardens, SW7 3PF   COOKING 2*
071-370 6701   COST £46–£122

Blakes has been a long-runner in the *Guide*, with odd years out as chefs have
come and gone. The hotel is a conglomeration of tall Victorian town houses in a
quiet South Kensington street, but 'with the impression of having been set down
somewhere in South-east Asia'. If that gives a clue to the cooking, then some clue
about prices may be gleaned from the fact that this is where rich and glossy folk
stay during international meanderings. The best way to remain exclusive is to
charge the earth. Nearly £10 for a bowl of soup or a salad of cucumber and dill is
the sort of thing. A black metal staircase leads down from the entrance hall,
where a single lovebird fills the space with whistles and whoops, to the
dining-room, bar and lounge. Anybody dressed entirely in black with white
shoes will be more or less invisible among the black walls and white-tiled floor
of the dining-room.

It is the sort of place where you expect to find blinis with beluga caviare, and
indeed (for a staggering £44) they share the billing with foie gras, truffles and
other luxuries. There is more interest, however, in lamb carpaccio served with
cracked wheat flavoured with lime and mint, or inkfish risotto, or any of the
Eastern-inspired dishes such as chicken tikka with a raita of cucumber, mint and
chilli, or Szechuan duck with roasted salt and pepper. The duck flesh is tender,
the skin crispy, and it comes with a small white dumpling filled with sweet-sour
paste, and a piquant salsa of spring onion and ginger, the latter a favourite
spicing. The ginger ravioli served with roast scallops were 'very sexy' according
to a ginger fetishist. Soufflé suissesse is puffball size, with a silver jug of Gruyère
sauce to pour in, and the most exciting pudding is probably a circular mould of
cinder toffee ice-cream with a 'delicious and satisfyingly brittle and crunchy
croquant' made of wild rice and, of course, ginger. Air-conditioning is good
enough to remove cigar smoke efficiently, service is polite, prices include
unlimited mineral water, and the wine list is short and just as expensive as
everything else. The only thing under £20 is house wine at £15 (£4 per glass).

CHEF: Peter Thornley   PROPRIETOR: Anouska Hempel   OPEN: all week; 12.30 to 2.45, 7.30 to
11.45   MEALS: alc (main courses £22.50 to £24.50). Set L £26 (2 courses) to £32, Set
post-theatre D £32   SERVICE: 15%, card slips closed   CARDS: Access, Amex, Diners, Visa
DETAILS: 40 seats. Private parties: 60 main room, 15 and 22 private rooms. Vegetarian meals on
request. Children's helpings on request. Music. Air-conditioned   ACCOMMODATION: 52 rooms,
all with bath/shower. TV. Phone. Air-conditioned (some rooms). B&B £137 to £623. Lift. Children
welcome. Baby facilities on request. Afternoon teas. Fax: 071-373 0442 (*The Which? Hotel
Guide*)

'Having drunk all these wines, we offer them with confidence.' (From a wine list)

Blue Elephant

map 10

4–6 Fulham Broadway, SW6 1AA
071-385 6595

COOKING 1*
COST £28–£63

The décor is breathtakingly lush, with its waterfalls, jungle vines and Koi carp swimming in pools. This is the international face of 'Royal Thai cuisine' from a mini-chain of restaurants with branches in a number of European cities. The effusively written menu promises a great deal: 'an awakening of citrus fruits', grilled rainbow trout with 'a green sauce fiery as a volcano' and a brown sauce 'sweet as a first kiss'. Presentation is beautiful and the kitchen can deliver the goods: 'seashells' (grilled, marinated scallops with a spicy sauce), 'emerald chicken' wrapped in toey leaves, and whole grey mullet 'swimming' in a sea of vegetables have been highly rated. The separate vegetarian menu relies heavily on yod phaeng (a light, chewy soya-based ingredient that appears in soups, salads and curries). Prices are steep and reporters have criticised the practice of leaving credit card slips open when 15 per cent service charge has been levied. The short wine list has some bottles that suit the food. House wine is £8.95.

CHEF: Rungsan Mulijan   PROPRIETOR: Blue Elephant International plc   OPEN: all week, exc Sat L; 12 to 2.30, 7 to 12.30 (10.30 Sun)   MEALS: alc (main courses £6.50 to £14.50). Set L and D £25 to £28 (minimum 2). Cover £1.50   SERVICE: 15%   CARDS: Access, Amex, Diners, Visa   DETAILS: 250 seats. Private parties: 100 main room. Vegetarian meals. Children welcome. Smart dress preferred. Wheelchair access (2 steps; also WC). Music. Air-conditioned. Fax: 071-386 7665

Blueprint Café

map 11

Design Museum, 22 Shad Thames,
Butlers Wharf, SE1 2YD
071-378 7031

COOKING 1
COST £26–£46

The Blueprint has a talent for polarising opinion. Some return and return for the thrilling riverside ambience, with strings of lanterns wafting in the evening breeze, the bright, hard-edged design lines of the interior and the thoroughly modern menu. Others take strenuous issue. It is certainly a lively debate. As well as the expected Caesar salad, grilled goats' cheese and roasted vegetables with Parmesan shavings, the menu essays bolder things. A dinner in May yielded roast duck breast au poivre that had 'tender and tasty' meat that was somewhat overwhelmed by peppercorns and a 'well-cooked' fricassee of monkfish and prawns accompanied by an underwhelming saffron sauce. Chocolate mousse roulade with 'excellent' crème anglaise and 'memorable' coffee parfait have been successful desserts. The wine list is short, not especially distinguished and rather expensive. House white from South Africa and red from Italy are both £9.50.

CHEF: Lucy Crabb   PROPRIETOR: Sir Terence Conran   OPEN: all week, exc Sun D; 12 to 3 (3.30 Sun), 7 to 11   MEALS: alc (main courses £7.50 to £14). Minimum £10   SERVICE: 15%, card slips closed   CARDS: Access, Amex, Diners, Visa   DETAILS: 85 seats. 22 tables outside. Private parties: 80 main room. Vegetarian meals. Children's helpings. Smart dress preferred. No pipes in dining-room. Wheelchair access (also WC). Music

Bombay Brasserie

map 13

Courtfield Close,
Courtfield Road, SW7 4UH   COOKING 1
071-370 4040 and 373 0971   COST £23–£50

'This place has two things going for it,' notes a reporter. He was referring to the splendidly faded colonial atmosphere and the menu, which is a potentially fascinating tour through the regional cuisines of the Sub-continent. Goan fish dishes, snacks from Bombay's Chowpatty beach, Northern tandooris, fiery South Indian specialities and Persian-influenced Parsee dishes. At times the kitchen delivers the goods: sev batata puri was 'a glorious mishmash of flavours on a dry corn paste base, topped with a wig of fried vermicelli', while lamb rogan josh and dalcha murg (chicken casseroled with lentils) were fine versions of mainstream curries. Nan bread is outstanding. Not all is perfection, however, evidenced on one occasion by an 'overcooked' pomfret in a banana leaf and on others by problems with temperatures: 'We had a bottle of white wine and this unfortunately was warmer than the food,' lamented one reporter. All of this comes at prices that some say are 'over the top'. Service is very courteous and attentive. New World wines are popular choices on the wine list. House wine is £9.75.

CHEF: Udit Sarkhel   PROPRIETOR: Taj International Hotels   OPEN: all week; 12.30 to 3, 7.30 to 12   CLOSED: 25 and 26 Dec   MEALS: alc (main courses £11 to £17). Set L £14.95. Cover 50p. Minimum £25 D   SERVICE: not inc   CARDS: Access, Diners, Visa   DETAILS: 175 seats. Private parties: 100 main room, 25 and 100 private rooms. Vegetarian meals. Children's helpings L. Smart dress preferred. No-smoking area. Music. Air-conditioned. Fax: 071-835 1669

Boyd's ▮

map 12

135 Kensington Church Street, W8 7LP   COOKING 2
071-727 5452   COST £24–£57

Boyd's has been redecorated, but lovers of the bright conservatory atmosphere of old need not worry, as the feeling of airiness has been retained. Green-stained tables, cream walls, foliage and fine screening on the arched glass roof all create a sense of measured calm. Over the years, Boyd Gilmour's cooking has settled into a gentle routine. He has not let contemporary developments pass him by, enthusiastically embracing the olive oil, goats' cheese and basil tendency of latter times. There is, however, a danger of lapsing into a certain monotony. At a dinner in June, turbot, John Dory, beef and chicken were all chargrilled, while chargrilled lamb came with chargrilled vegetables – although the touch was sufficiently light for the charcoal to have been elusive in the finished dish. Charred scallops with mange-tout and red pepper and a chive butter sauce had rather fugitive flavours, the whole effect 'slightly too sweet', but faith was partially restored by a chocolate chip and caramel terrine with passion-fruit, actually a rough-textured parfait, with 'flavours, textures, contrasts spot-on'. More than one person has commented that pastry tends to be fairly heavy these days, although one man appreciated the chewiness of a slice of pear tart.

The wine list is a joy. The choices in almost every region are original and stimulating, and prices, while never low, are certainly not ridiculous. The run of vintages of Ch. Boyd-Cantenac, back to 1978, is faithfully maintained, burgundies are by impeccable growers and Georg Breuer's Riesling and Grauer Burgunder (Pinot Gris) are worth a look. Half-bottles are plentiful. The house selection starts at £10. CELLARMAN'S CHOICE: Olivet Lane Russian River Chardonnay 1989, £17; Bordeaux Supérieur, Ch. de Paranchère 1989, £15.50.

CHEFS: Boyd Gilmour and Jake Watkins PROPRIETOR: Boyd Gilmour OPEN: Mon to Sat; 12.30 to 2.30, 7 to 11 CLOSED: 2 weeks Christmas/New Year, bank hols MEALS: alc (main courses £11.50 to £15). Set L £14 SERVICE: not inc CARDS: Access, Amex, Diners, Visa DETAILS: 40 seats. Private parties: 40 main room. Vegetarian meals. Children welcome. Music. Air-conditioned. Fax: 071-221 0615

Brackenbury
map 10

| 129–131 Brackenbury Road, W6 0BQ | COOKING 2* |
| 081-748 0107 | COST £18–£32 |

It speaks volumes about the changing gastro-economic times that many of London's favourite places to eat are those where all the emphasis is on the contents of the plate rather than the surroundings. The Brackenbury has been created out of a pair of knocked-through terraced houses. Inside, attention may be caught by the bare wooden floor, the crumbling paintwork or the hodgepodge of furniture. From the bar area you can get an arresting view of 'illuminated dustbins in the back yard'. Then there are the acoustics: 'Hard surfaces mean it's noisy, and the clientele seem to have built-in amplifiers.' On the other hand: 'It is a buzz of people enjoying themselves.'

Eclecticism rules in the food. Adam Robinson rewrites the menus twice daily, cooking whatever comes his way. Dishes admired this year have been crostini of lamb's brains with salsa verde, salad of pigeon breast with walnuts, bresaola with rocket dressed with truffle oil, grilled red bream with braised fennel, tomatoes and basil, breast of mallard with red cabbage and crab-apple jelly, and 'excellent' prune and armagnac ice-cream. Reports do surface, to be sure, of inaccurate seasoning, inadequate quantity, or dishes that do not seem sufficiently well balanced in flavour. Then again: 'We have not encountered such value for money for a long time.' Bread and coffee are of reliable quality. The succinct wine list is arranged in ascending order of price, and makes the majority of its selections available by the glass – a heartwarming policy. Choices are stimulating, taking in Rolly-Gassmann Gewurztraminer, Basedow Barossa Shiraz and Laurent-Perrier rosé. House wines are £8.50.

CHEF: Adam Robinson PROPRIETORS: Adam and Katie Robinson OPEN: all week, exc L Mon and Sat and Sun D; 12.30 to 2.45, 7 to 10.45 CLOSED: Christmas and New Year, bank hols MEALS: alc (main courses £5 to £10) SERVICE: not inc CARDS: Access, Amex, Diners, Visa DETAILS: 55 seats. 5 tables outside. Private parties: 8 main room. Vegetarian meals. Children's helpings. Wheelchair access. No music

'The only couple in jeans and rugby shirt, with their young daughter tucking into dishes with ease, turned out to be the owners. Everyone else was smartly dressed.'
(On eating in Wales)

Brady's £

map 10

513 Old York Road, SW18 1TF
081-877 9599

COOKING 1
COST £15–£22

'In a street full of restaurants, this one is full,' observes a local, who warns that 'if you don't know it, there is a wicked one-way system'. Luke and Amelia Brady have stuck to their guns and have not deviated from their notion of a fish and chip shop with class. The fish is as fresh as can be, and it is either done in 'excellent' batter or grilled and plated up with proper chips. Tuna and swordfish line up with cod and plaice, and the blackboards also list highly popular crab-cakes and salmon fish-cakes. Finish off with splendid treacle tart tinged with coconut. A bevy of young girls rushes around busily, serving with a smile. You may glimpse the wine list as it whizzes by, but the house wine at £6.50 is fine – although many people opt for beer.

CHEF: Luke Brady   PROPRIETORS: Luke and Amelia Brady   OPEN: Mon to Sat, D only; 7 to 10.45 (10.30 Mon)   MEALS: alc (main courses £4 to £6)   SERVICE: 10%   DETAILS: 38 seats. Private parties: 38 main room. Children's helpings. Wheelchair access (1 step). Music

Buchan's

map 10

62–64 Battersea Bridge Road, SW11 3AG
071-228 0888

COOKING 1
COST £18–£40

Buchan's is a neighbourhood restaurant – has to be in Battersea – with lots of rough edges, but its heart is in the right place. The wood panelling, paintings and prints contrive to give an unpretentious and domestic feel, and it salutes the author with 39 wines and 39 whiskies. Otherwise, only haggis with neeps and tatties, Oban crab and Loch Fyne oysters sound a Scottish note. The rest of the fortnightly changing menu offers ten first and main courses and six puddings, and ranges from curried couscous to braised salt beef and lamb's tongue with parsley dumplings to baked rhubarb and orange cake with custard. Saucing is not a particularly strong point, although the items sauces accompany are decent enough: poached tomatoes stuffed with spinach, Roquefort tart well judged for flavour, and banana and apple tarte Tatin served warm with a light toffee sauce, which was 'a great success'. The range is perhaps too ambitious: an inspector wondered if the solution might be to concentrate on cooking fewer dishes rather better. The same person found the drink much easier to swallow than the optional service charge. All but a couple of the wines stay comfortably under £20, quality is generally high, house Italian is £8.95, and over a dozen wines are available by the glass (mostly £2 to £3). There is also a beer of the month.

CHEF: Alain Jeannon   PROPRIETORS: Jeremy and Denise Bolam   OPEN: all week; 12 to 2.45 (3.15 Sun), 6 to 10.45 (10 Sun)   CLOSED: 25 and 26 Dec   MEALS: alc (main courses £7 to £14). Set L Sun £10.50. Bar menu Mon to Sat   SERVICE: 10% (optional), card slips closed   CARDS: Access, Amex, Diners, Visa   DETAILS: 70 seats. 4 tables outside. Private parties: 50 main room. Vegetarian meals. Children's helpings on request. Wheelchair access (1 step). Music. Air-conditioned. Fax: 071-924 1718

See the back of the Guide *for a listing of all restaurants in the Main Entries sections.*

Bu San £   map 11

43 Holloway Road, N7 8JP   COOKING 1*
071-607 8264   COST £15–£56

The port of Bu San is the second largest city in Korea and it looks across the water to Japan. Appropriately, Young Hyung Lee's menu brings the two cuisines together, the Korean influence in bulgogi, kim-chee (pickled, fermented cabbage), dam chi tang (mussel soup with garlic and white radish) and barbecued chicken marinated in chilli sauce, sharing the bill with sashimi, sunomono and teriyaki. There is a healthy slant to the cooking, and vegetarians are given full consideration. Dramatic displays of carved fruit and vegetables are a feature of the place, although the prospect of 'edible food lost underneath gaping pimentos and sculpted carrots' irritated one party. However, 'the clear definite flavours of tiger prawns, aubergines, seaweed etc. made finding them worthwhile'. Tastes are seldom less than spicy, sometimes fiercely so: 'the devilish hotness of the broccoli' was the enduring memory from one meal. Prices are very reasonable. Saké, Japanese plum wine and ginseng brandy are alternatives to the short list of European wines. House wine is £7.20 (£1.60 per glass).

CHEF: Young Hyung Lee   PROPRIETORS: Young Hyung Lee and K. Lee   OPEN: all week, exc Sat and Sun L; 12 to 2.30, 6 to 11   CLOSED: 25 and 26 Dec, 1 and 2 Jan, bank hols L   MEALS: alc (main courses £3 to £8.90). Set L £5.20 to £6.50 (1 course with rice and coffee/tea), Set D (minimum 2) £13.95 to £17.25   SERVICE: 10%, card slips closed   CARDS: Visa   DETAILS: 47 seats. Private parties: 50 main room. Vegetarian meals. Children's helpings. Smart dress preferred. Wheelchair access (also WC). Music. Air-conditioned

---

Butlers Wharf Chop House ♥   NEW ENTRY   map 11

36E Shad Thames, Butlers Wharf, SE1 2YE   COOKING 2
071-403 3403   COST £22–£49

This may sound odd, but to find the place ignore the signs in Shad Thames saying 'Chop House'. Instead, go through the grey pillars as if entering Le Pont de la Tour, and the Chop House is on the left. Or just follow the noise. It is all part of the Conran waterfront feeding frenzy, with tables outside on warm days overlooking the river and Tower Bridge. Tables inside are set close together, chairs are ergonomically disastrous, and the unadorned new wood of floors and tables flies a somewhat threadbare flag for Britain beside the greater indulgence of its French and Italian neighbours (see Le Pont de la Tour and Cantina del Ponte entries, both London).

'It is full of city businessmen in grey suits, but we did not find this a deterrent.' Nevertheless, a tolerance for people who smoke cigars on adjoining tables while you are eating, send plates crashing to the floor amid gales of laughter, and use mobile phones to tell chauffeurs they are ready to be picked up, comes in handy. This is a peculiarly British form of torture, but for those who can endure it there is good food as a reward. Attention centres on British-inspired dishes, generally more British than inspired: deep-fried plaice and chips with tartare sauce, sausage and mash, steak and kidney pudding with oysters, a daily roast, lambs' kidneys with bubble and squeak and tasty bacon, and simple grilled chops. As a bonus there may be smoked salmon and scrambled eggs, fresh oysters, banana fritters with caramel, and rhubarb fool. Portions can be large.

Waiters, mostly male, service the tables obviously and often, as if the boss were watching. Jugs of claret provide diversion (there are eight to choose from) and wines by the glass are commendable. First-growth claret ensures a steady trickle of City funds across the bridge, no harm in that, but the selection below £20 is extremely good too. Mark-ups are not rapacious, although the 15 per cent service charge on everything diminishes the value. House wines are from £9.75. CELLARMAN'S CHOICE: Graves, Ch. Roquefort 1992, £15.25; Henschke Cabernet Sauvignon 1988, £23.75.

CHEF: Rod Eggleston   PROPRIETORS: Sir Terence Conran and Joel Kissin   OPEN: all week, exc Sun D (Sat L bar only); 12 to 3, 6 to 11   CLOSED: Christmas   MEALS: alc D (main courses £7.50 to £13.50). Set L Mon to Fri £19.50, Sun £16.50 (2 courses) to £19.50. Bar menu (main courses £6.50 to £7.50). Sat and Sun brunch £12.50 (2 courses) to £14.50   SERVICE: 15%, card slips closed   CARDS: Access, Amex, Diners, Visa   DETAILS: restaurant 115 seats, bar 40 seats. 12 tables outside restaurant, 6 outside bar. Private parties: 12 main room. Vegetarian meals. Children welcome. Wheelchair access (also WC). Music (bar). No music (restaurant). Fax: 071-403 3414

Le Cadre

map 10

10 Priory Road, Priory Park, N8 7RD   COOKING 1*
081-348 0606   COST £22–£42

'Good food, good wine and a good time!' the menu promisingly screams at this simply decorated and eminently useful place between Muswell Hill and Crouch End. The food is classic French bistro (the chef is from Normandy) and, on a good night, certain dishes elevate it significantly above its context. On a packed Tuesday night in June, a slab of duck terrine with hazelnuts had genuine textural interest and a port jelly that tasted eloquently of itself, while a dish of salmon baked in pastry with a pale green watercress and champagne sauce delighted both for colour appeal and for the correctly judged balancing of flavours. Even better, 'amazingly good' in fact, was a rich game stew under a pastry lid that included wild boar, pheasant, hare and venison, all coated with a strong gravy sharpened with juniper berries. Determined to test the pastrywork to the utmost, one of the diners ordered tarte Tatin and found an intriguing tartness in the apple slices that was compensated by sticky syrup. Slight disappointments were registered by a thinnish fish soup and a raspberry mousse that was pale pink in both colour and flavour. 'Espresso coffees kept us in the mood.' The short, entirely French wine list has sensible prices, and is supplemented by a list of specials on a blackboard. House wines are £9.

CHEF: Yannick Chuat   PROPRIETORS: David Misselbrook and Marie Fedyk   OPEN: Mon to Sat, exc Sat L; 12 to 2.30, 7 to 11   CLOSED: 25 to 30 Dec, bank hols   MEALS: alc (main courses £10 to £13.50). Set L £11.50 (2 courses) to £13.50, Set D Mon to Thur £13.50, Fri and Sat £15.50   SERVICE: not inc   CARDS: Access, Amex, Diners, Visa   DETAILS: 50 seats. 6 tables outside. Private parties: 50 main room. Vegetarian meals. Children welcome. Music

'We were offered a choice: espresso, cappuccino, de-caff or cafetière. The waitress who brought the latter called it "cafeteria coffee".' (On eating in Avon)

Café des Arts

map 11

82 Hampstead High Street, NW3 1RE
071-435 3608

COOKING 2
COST £23–£38

Not many people know there is a listed seventeenth-century farmhouse in Hampstead village. In the '60s, this was Fagin's Kitchen, a haven of bistro Frenchness. Reborn in 1992 as the Café des Arts, it now has a menu that speaks in many tongues – Italian, Spanish, Chinese, French and English – but all inflected with a Californian accent. Grilled marinated chicken with gazpacho and chilli cornbread or roast mackerel fillets with sweet potato and basil galette, papaya and sweet chilli purée are difficult to locate anywhere other than San Francisco.

The menu is a single list, on which at least five dishes can be either starter or main, depending on how much smoked trout hash with poached egg and dill hollandaise you think you might want. Good reports have come in for grilled squid stuffed with ratatouille with an almond and tarragon pesto, wokked spinach on grilled tapénade crostini full of 'lovely textural contrast', and zucchini and feta blinis with roasted vine tomatoes and avocado and caper salsa. Disappointment is occasioned when the flavours of dishes do not live up to their scintillating menu billings, as in a wild leaf salad with raspberry vinaigrette that turned out to be a pile of lamb's lettuce with raspberry vinegar and not much evidence of oil. Desserts carry some punch in items like poached pear with toffee ice-cream or chocolate brownie with whisky fudge sauce. The wine list is short and adequate. More smart Italian or Californian flavours would boost it no end. House French red and Italian white are £7.95.

CHEF: Sally James   PROPRIETOR: Brian Stein   OPEN: all week; 12 to 4, 6 to 11.30 (11 Sun) CLOSED: 25 and 26 Dec, L 1 Jan   MEALS: alc (main courses £5 to £9)   SERVICE: 12.5%, card slips closed   CARDS: Access, Amex, Diners, Visa   DETAILS: 65 seats. Private parties: 29 main room. Vegetarian meals. Children welcome. No cigars/pipes in dining-room. Wheelchair access (3 steps). Music

Café Fish

map 14

39 Panton Street, SW1Y 4EA
071-930 3999

COOKING 1
COST £21–£42

The chaotic hubbub makes for a lively time in this high-ceilinged dining-room off Haymarket. Pictures of fish and fishing cover every inch of the walls, huge blackboards advertise the food, and waiters whisk briskly between the closely packed tables. The place works best at lunch-time, when the pace is fast; late in the evening it can run out of steam and has been known to offer 'tired' food. Decent fish and vegetarian dishes are the mainstays. Soupe de poisson, grilled Dover sole, plates of fish and chips, baked monkfish with bacon and spinach, and grilled marinated vegetables with couscous are some fixtures. Also seek out the plats du jour. Service may seem impersonal at times, although one reporter was impressed by the customer satisfaction questionnaire that arrives with the bill. The downstairs wine bar is good for drinks, snacks and chat. Reasonably priced whites are the frontrunners on the short wine list. House wine is £8.25.

CHEF: Andrew Magson   PROPRIETOR: Groupe Chez Gérard Ltd   OPEN: Mon to Sat, exc Sat L restaurant; 12 to 3, 5.45 to 11.30; wine bar 11 to 11   MEALS: alc (main courses £6.75 to £15). Cover £1.25   SERVICE: 12.5% (optional), card slips closed   CARDS: Access, Amex, Diners, Visa   DETAILS: 94 seats. 3 tables outside. Vegetarian meals. Children welcome. No-smoking area. Music. Fax: 071-930 7550

Café Royal ⦗map 14⦘

Café Royal ♥   map 14

68 Regent Street, W1R 6EL   COOKING 2
071-437 9090   COST £25–£86

The Grill Room's heyday was around the turn of the century, as suggested by the décor of gilded mirrors, painted ceiling, ornate mouldings and red plush seats. A drinks trolley negotiates the acres of space with ease, and a long menu indicates that the kitchen must be pretty big too. It deals in luxury ingredients and a few of the classic hotel dishes that many might consider out of date, although enough is going on to show that Herbert Berger is not simply treading water. He can turn out carpaccio of tuna with roasted sesame seeds, spices, black radish and lime, alongside more straightforward asparagus in season, chateaubriand and roast rack of lamb with truffled potatoes. Berger is also a dab hand with smoked haddock, which may appear with Savoy cabbage or in puff pastry with quail's egg, in both cases spiked with a mustard sauce.

The usual problems of catering on a large scale, however, can result in dishes that do not always quite live up to intention, as in one inspector's rather chewy veal served with a saffron risotto. But ingredients are sound enough, including very fresh fillets of John Dory and red mullet served with peas and foie gras butter, and combinations can work well: for example, pressed terrine of provençale vegetables served with smoked quail confit. Puddings may be the most successful department, if the iced prune and armagnac soufflé is anything to go by. Bread and appetisers fall some way behind, but espresso coffee is good. The Brasserie is an old-fashioned room encircling a bar and serving informal food along the lines of spinach ravioli, seared mackerel fillet, fish-cakes and oxtail casserole. The Grill Room's wine list, rather like the menu, combines French classics with even more interesting interlopers from Italy and the New World. Bottles under £20 are plentiful.

CHEF: Herbert Berger   PROPRIETOR: Forte plc   OPEN: Grill Room Mon to Sat, exc Sat L; 12 to 2.30, 6 to 11. Brasserie all week; noon to 11 (6 Sun)   CLOSED: some bank hols (telephone to check)   MEALS: Grill Room alc (main courses £18 to £24); Set L £22.50, Set D £36. Brasserie alc (main courses £8 to £13.50); Set L and D £12.50 (2 courses) to £15.50   SERVICE: not inc   CARDS: Access, Amex, Diners, Visa   DETAILS: Grill Room 45 seats, Brasserie 90 seats. Private parties: 80 main room. Vegetarian meals. Children's helpings Sun. Jacket and tie Grill Room. No-smoking area Brasserie. Wheelchair access (also WC). No music Grill Room. Music Brasserie. Air-conditioned. Fax: 071-439 7672

🍾 *denotes an outstanding wine cellar;* ♥ *denotes a good wine list, worth travelling for.*

The text of entries is based on unsolicited reports sent in by readers, backed up by inspections conducted anonymously. The factual details under the text are from questionnaires the Guide *sends to all restaurants that feature in the book.*

Canteen

map 10

Unit G4, Harbour Yard,
Chelsea Harbour, SW10 0XD
071-351 7330

COOKING 3
COST £33–£44

'Although the Chelsea Harbour development remains one of the least unpleasant riverside projects, no amount of publicity has managed to relieve the public areas of a ghost-town feel.' So speaks a trained architect. Fountains splash, yachts bob in the marina, all is unruffled tranquillity and desertion. The Canteen remains perhaps the best reason for coming here. A social anatomiser, surveying the clientele, noted 'older, elegantly dressed jet-set couples (tan and diamonds)' mingling with 'the mobile-phone brigade in Lacoste shirts and Perosel sunglasses', and even 'families with children'. There has been great upheaval in the kitchens over the past year, culminating in Tim Payne (ex-Tante Claire and Harveys – see entries, London) taking over in May. The menu continues as before, offering a generous range of choice at what is effectively a set price, barring the odd supplement. Descriptions sound fairly curt, and presume more than a passing acquaintance with culinary French: artichokes barigoule, roast chicken with sauce bois boudrin.

A summer Sunday lunch contained ups and downs. The ink risotto with roasted squid was on the heavy side with 'undercooked' rice. Entrecôte 'minute' was suitably thin and tender, garnished with little discs of breaded bone marrow of poignant flavour. A grilled fillet of red mullet (always good) came with diced ratatouille vegetables, tapénade and deep-fried battered sage leaves that had been left in the oil too long, but the lemon tart was 'fabulous', with its 'crumbly pastry' just standing up to the 'luxuriously long lemon bite' of the filling. Others write in with tales of bangers and mash 'executed to perfection', 'fantastic' rabbit of rich, earthy taste, 'succulent' roasted sea scallops with sauce vierge, memorable duck confit with potato galette, and 'divine' prune and armagnac tart. Evenings get 'screamingly busy', and service may become correspondingly intermittent. But persevere, the wine list concentrates principally on France, with an international smattering in the lower price range. There are some good bottles, such as Zind-Humbrecht Alsace Riesling and Babich Pinot Noir from New Zealand, but prices rise a bit sharply. House French is £12.

CHEFS: Tim Payne and Peter Reffell   PROPRIETORS: Michael Caine, Marco Pierre White and Claudio Pulze   OPEN: all week; 12 to 3, 7 to 12 (12.30 to 3.30, 7 to 10.30 Sun)   MEALS: alc (main courses £11.50). Cover £1   SERVICE: not inc   CARDS: Access, Visa   DETAILS: 150 seats. Private parties: 12 main room. Vegetarian meals with prior notice. Children welcome. Smart dress preferred. No pipes in dining-room. Wheelchair access (3 steps; also WC). No music. Air-conditioned

Cantina del Ponte

map 11

36C Shad Thames, Butlers Wharf, SE1 2YE
071-403 5403

COOKING 2
COST £23–£49

'Mediterranean food and wine' is what Cantina del Ponte says it offers. The decision to go for it or not depends on whether those Conran shops full of olive oil, herbs, Italian breads and cheeses spell freshness and vibrancy to you, or whether – like one man – you see the whole thing as a gastronomic theme park peopled by the under-25s. Chargrilling is the preferred cooking method, and the style bedrock is ostensibly, although by no means exclusively, Italian. Antipasti and calamari are joined among the starters by salt cod timbale with rocket, anchovy and capers, or lentil and roast duck soup. Pizza toppings may be traditional – margherita – or more unusual, as in prosciutto with radicchio purée. Main courses offer roast quails with polenta and marsala, grilled rib-eye with field mushrooms, and tiger prawns with cannelli beans and piri-piri sauce.

Standards tend to fluctuate, as returning customers attest: one couple had a fine pasta dish with squid, and then 'wonderful' lambs' kidneys with fried parsley, but have been disappointed since. Others had great tomato timbale and minestrone to start, and 'excellent' mascarpone with mixed berries and chocolate mousse with mango sorbet to finish, but found the pizzas in between thinly topped. The almost entirely Italian wine list is short but admirably well chosen. Prices are fairly reasonable, but remember to add 15 per cent for service. House Pinot Grigio and Montepulciano d'Abruzzo are £8.95.

CHEF: Louis Loizia PROPRIETORS: Sir Terence Conran, Joel Kissin and David Burke OPEN: all week, exc Sun D; 12 to 3, 6 to 11 CLOSED: Christmas MEALS: alc (main courses £6.50 to £14.50). Minimum £10 SERVICE: 15%, card slips closed CARDS: Access, Amex, Diners, Visa DETAILS: 140 seats. 13 tables outside. Vegetarian meals. Children welcome. Wheelchair access. Music. Fax: 071-403 0267

▲ *The Capital* 🍷 map 13

22–24 Basil Street, SW3 1AT — COOKING 4
071-589 5171 — COST £28–£69

Basil Street is a handy short-cut between Harrods and Harvey Nichols, and although housed in what looks like a nondescript '60s apartment block, the Capital is a captivating 'grand hotel in miniature'. David Levin is a true veteran of the restaurant scene, and during his years here has cultivated a succession of talented chefs, including Richard Shepherd, Brian Turner and, since 1989, Philip Britten. The restaurant has been a benchmark for quality, unstinting with luxury and supported by a wine list in the grand style. As we go to press the long, thin dining-room with its sumptuous boudoir décor – overdue for a facelift – is undergoing extension, restyling and redecoration.

Although the *carte* concentrates on predictably expensive ingredients, including scallops, asparagus, foie gras and lobster, some of the combinations are innovative. The kitchen works in classic vein, running up lobster beignets, soufflés of smoked salmon and spinach or passion-fruit and ginger (both of these on the set fish menu) and – a highlight of one inspector's entire eating year – a langoustine risotto. It was perfectly cooked in what appeared to be tomato-based stock, with plump and sweet-tasting shelled langoustines, the richness cut by minute dice of tomato, with speckles of caviare dotted throughout, not as a luxury garnish but to introduce saltiness. The ability to buy well, season correctly and balance flavours was also apparent in a light beetroot bouillon that provided an unobtrusive background to the four barely cooked langoustines which accompanied it.

A wide range of cooking techniques and saucing is evident across the menu, and flavours are often carefully considered. But the food can also fail to excite: 'It is immaculate but on the bland side. One could admire the smoothness rather than relish it,' noted one reporter. An inspector found one-dimensional dishes, especially on the fish menu, flabby pasta, overcooked and uninspiring seafood, and heavy-handed sweetness in puddings, all contrasting with superb dishes at the same meal. Service is exemplary – discreet, smooth, swift and efficient – and while the wines are grand, with long runs of single properties, mark-ups are not rapacious. There is a chink in the curtain that lets a few bottles show through for less than £20. House wine is £10.50 (£3.75 per glass).

CHEF: Philip Britten   PROPRIETOR: David Levin   OPEN: all week; 12 to 2.30, 7 to 11.15   MEALS: alc (main courses £18 to £22.50). Set L £22 to £25, Set D £40. Minimum £30 D alc   SERVICE: net prices, card slips closed   CARDS: Access, Amex, Diners, Visa   DETAILS: 35 seats. Private parties: 8 main room, 12 and 24 private rooms. Car park. Vegetarian meals. Children's helpings. Smart dress preferred. No cigars/pipes in dining-room. Wheelchair access (3 steps; also WC). No music. Air-conditioned   ACCOMMODATION: 48 rooms, all with bath/shower. TV. Phone. Air-conditioned. B&B £194 to £336. Rooms for disabled. Lift. Children welcome. Pets by arrangement (not in public rooms). Afternoon teas. Confirm by 6. Fax: 071-225 0011 (*The Which? Hotel Guide*)

Le Caprice

map 14

Arlington House,
Arlington Street, SW1A 1RT
071-629 2239

COOKING 2*
COST £25–£55

Tinted windows and narrow blinds coyly hide a smart, black and white L-shaped room: a modern brasserie with hard surfaces, modern pictures and smart, functional table settings. It is a busy place, and could easily be 10 times as big and still full, generating a compelling atmosphere.

Le Caprice lives up to most expectations. The free-ranging Californian-style menu trots appealingly through the plain and simple (dressed crab), Mediterranean (gazpacho, risotto, pasta), rich (foie gras), classic (eggs Benedict), common (Lincolnshire sausages, deep-fried cod and chips), and exotic (gulls' eggs with celery salt). 'This is simple food, not messed about, very much geared to current fashion but perfect if your need is for something light and refreshing,' sums up one satisfied luncher. An example might be a 'galette' of thin, crisp pastry overlaid with tasty sliced tomato and dribbled with pesto.

In its enthusiasm and drive, the kitchen can appear immune to the idea of balance: piling on mint flavour in a ragoût of lamb sweetbreads with delightful young shelled broad beans; or allowing dried morels to dominate the flavour of fresh ones in a springtime risotto. But fish, vegetables and salads are generally impressive, as in seared scallops with fat Alsace bacon, or an artfully heaped salad with sweet and juicy pumpkin, pancetta and salty Pecorino, dressed in a balsamic vinaigrette. Mild innovation extends to puddings of elderflower jelly with summer berries, and crisp sugar-coated churros with rich and buttery hot chocolate sauce.

With more than one sitting, tables may normally be reserved for a couple of hours, but check first. Sundays find a collection of newspapers on the bar and a particularly high cholesterol count among the eggs, bacon, steak, fudge and chocolate. Smiling service is polite, forthcoming and helpful. The wines don't take risks, yet manage to be interesting, and prices cover a wide range, with a reasonable selection by the glass, starting at £2.50. House wine is £8.50.

CHEFS: Tim Hughes and Mark Hix   PROPRIETORS: Christopher Corbin and Jeremy King   OPEN: all week; 12 to 3 (3.30 Sun), 6 to 12   CLOSED: Christmas to New Year   MEALS: alc (main courses £8 to £17). Cover £1.50 (not at bar)   SERVICE: not inc   CARDS: Access, Amex, Diners, Visa   DETAILS: 70 seats. Vegetarian meals. Children welcome. No cigars in dining-room. Wheelchair access. Music. Air-conditioned. Fax: 071-493 9040

Casale Franco   map 11

134–137 Upper Street, N1 1TQ   COOKING 1
071-226 8994   COST £24–£51

Tucked away down an alley off Islington's Upper Street, this popular venue is a worthy fixture of the local eating scene. The layout is all narrow passages, with eating areas on two levels, and spotlights hung from tangled copper tubing. It pulls in a lively, mixed crowd and the atmosphere earns full marks. The waiters are a warm, friendly bunch, although the front-of-house man has upset more than one reporter. Pizzas and pasta 'every which way' are the mainstays of the menu, but note that pizzas are not available at lunch-time or as a single-dish meal after 8pm. Elsewhere, the kitchen dishes up trattoria stalwarts such as fegato veneziana and frittura di mare as well as more fashionable ideas, including imaginative grilled vegetables and seafood dressed with olive oil, or octopus and celery salad. Home-made ice-creams make a good finish. Portions are hefty. An all-Italian wine list offers fair-priced drinking and better-than-average house wine at £9, or £2.50 per glass.

CHEF: Mario Pensa   PROPRIETORS: Gisella and Franco Pensa   OPEN: Fri to Sun L, Tues to Sun D; 12.30 to 2.30, 6.30 to 11.30 (11 Sun)   MEALS: alc (main courses £6.50 to £17.50). Cover £1. Minimum £6.50   SERVICE: not inc   CARDS: Access, Visa   DETAILS: 135 seats. 10 tables outside. Private parties: 50 main room, 50 private room. Vegetarian meals. Children welcome. Smart dress preferred. No-smoking area. Wheelchair access. Music. Air-conditioned. Fax: 071-359 5569

Cheng-du £   map 11

9 Parkway, NW1 7PG   COOKING 1
071-485 8058   COST £19–£48

This attractive modern brasserie has clean lines, a long bar down one side, a few showy paintings, and elegantly quiet jazz in the background. The menu offers fixed-price 'superiore' and 'classico' menus as well as a *carte* that is more northern and Szechuan than Cantonese. 'West Lake' sour prawns, sizzling lamb slices and hot-and-sour pork are the kind of thing on offer. When dishes stray beyond standard items into more modern interpretations, they can stretch the chef too far, but pork dumplings with garlic dressing (steamed first, then grilled) and powerfully smoked chicken winglets tossed in peppercorn salt are both good. The absence of MSG is welcome. A short but decent wine list begins with house Italian at £8.20 (£2.20 a glass).

'On the second day at the hotel we were asked if we could eat out, or have a salad, so they could have a night off.' (On eating in Cornwall)

CHEF: Mr Lam   PROPRIETOR: Redfern Enterprises Ltd   OPEN: all week; 12 to 2.30, 6.30 to 11.30   MEALS: alc (main courses £4.50 to £18). Set L and D £17.20 (minimum 2)   SERVICE: 12.5%   CARDS: Access, Amex, Visa   DETAILS: 75 seats. Private parties: 75 main room. Vegetarian meals. Children welcome. Smart dress preferred. Wheelchair access (also WC). Music

Chez Liline

map 10

101 Stroud Green Road, N4 3PX   COOKING 1
071-263 6550 and 272 9719   COST £23–£40

The shop front with the name Chez Liline shines out like a beacon in this hinterland between Finsbury Park and Holloway Road. Inside, it is informal – often boisterous – with closely packed tables and pictures of tropical fish on the lime-green walls. The menu is seafood, and 'even the starters dwell 'neath the sea', noted one reporter. Mario Ho Wing Cheong brings to the London scene a taste of Mauritius – an amalgam of Asian, French and African influences. Tomatoes and saffron provide the colour, spices such as chilli, coriander and ginger create the taste. The variety shows in vindaye de poisson (marinated emperor fish in a zingy sauce of saffron, mustard seed and garlic), bourgeois fish in a rich, 'very buttery, olive oily' aïoli sauce, and parrot-fish braised with aubergines. A beautifully concocted warm salmon and lobster salad was the high point of one meal. Tropical fruit and good ice-creams round things off. Service is 'very friendly and helpful'. The wine list, organised by grape, is broadminded and understandably favours whites. House wine is £9.25.

CHEFS: Mario Ho Wing Cheong and Pascal Doudrich   PROPRIETOR: Mario Ho Wing Cheong   OPEN: Mon to Sat; 12.30 to 2.30, 6.30 to 10.30   CLOSED: bank hols   MEALS: alc (main courses £8.50 to £15). Set L and D Mon to Thur £10 to £11.75 (both 2 courses). Minimum £10   SERVICE: not inc   CARDS: Access, Amex, Visa   DETAILS: 44 seats. Private parties: 20 main room. Vegetarian meals with prior notice. Children's helpings. Music

Chez Max

NEW ENTRY   map 11

168 Ifield Road, SW10 9AF   COOKING 3
071-835 0874   COST £25–£45

'It seems almost an accident that they can produce such lovely food.' The Renzlands have always delivered value for money, and an uncertain feeling that they are learning French at night school. 'It all makes you feel as if you've been given a part in a play with no script,' wrote one after a lunchtime performance. The bumble, fuss and occasional ineptitude are quite theatrical, but 'my, my, the food!' This Max runs in tandem with Le Petit Max in Hampton Wick (see entry). Arrive early for lunch and you may wonder if you have the right place: no name on the fascia, no menu in the window until '12.30 precisely'. Limited eating and drinking goes on at ground level, the real action taking place mainly in the long, peppermint-green basement with framed menus on the walls, and tables and chairs that don't match.

French food, mostly from Lyons southwards, is the stock-in-trade of the Renzland repertoire, but the brothers are not above serving un-French deep-fried plaice and chips with tartare sauce. The food is plain, honest and simple, beginning with an oval slipper of bread, which is warm, sliced, salty, oil-flavoured, with a crisp crust: 'I could have lunched off that and the wrinkly provençale olives.' Refinement appears in the likes of rich yet silky-light parfait of foie gras and chicken liver, but the real strength is in getting the simple things right as well: salads with a good mix of fresh and inventive greens, a light dressing based on good oil, and some shaved Parmesan, for example. Gratin dauphinois is 'just as it should be', according to one who referred us to Elizabeth David's no-cheese exemplar. This came with roundels of neck of Devon lamb which was 'deep pink inside, caramelly-grilled outside, tender, garlicky and very lamby', followed by 'thick eggy creamy crème brûlée with a nice touch of vanilla and a crisp top'. The dozen or so French wines are quirky, but you can always bring your own and pay the £3.50 corkage. Alsace Riesling and southern Syrah are £9 per half-litre.

CHEFS: Bruce Poole and Rob Jones PROPRIETORS: Max and Marc Renzland, and Graham Thomson OPEN: Mon to Sat, exc L Mon and Sat; 12.30 to 2.30, 7 to 11 CLOSED: Christmas, Easter, bank hols MEALS: Set L £15.50, Set D £23.50 SERVICE: 10%, card slips closed CARDS: Access, Visa DETAILS: 85 seats. 3 tables outside. Private parties: 8 main room, 15 private room. Vegetarian meals with prior notice. No children under 12. No pipes in dining-room. No music

Chez Moi

map 12

1 Addison Avenue, W11 4QS
071-603 8267

COOKING 3
COST £22–£46

'A nice old-fashioned restaurant' is how one reporter sees Chez Moi. It has sailed along under the same ownership, and with the same chef, since 1967, and has been in the *Guide* for 24 years. Some dishes seem to have appeared on the menu almost as long but, far from being stuck in a rut, the restaurant has simply acquired a gentle confidence in both cooking and service. It is staffed by professionals who are welcoming, polite and make everyone feel pleasantly at ease, and the dark gold and pink colours give the dining-room a warm feel. The only anachronism that grates is the heavy use of French on the menu, which does not appear to serve any useful purpose.

Lamb is the strong suit and the *carte* lists four alternatives: rack done two ways (one with a mustard crust), chargrilled cutlets, and flattened, chargrilled pieces of best end sandwiched between layers of ratatouille. The execution is, after so many years' practice, down to a fine art: well trimmed, tasty, and cooked appropriately. Variety (which the kitchen must need as much as the regulars) comes from vegetarian couscous, or a version of Thai chicken in which cubes of breast are simmered in coconut milk, lemon grass, lime leaf, green curry, fish sauce and half a dozen other flavourings. The fixed-price lunch, considered the bargain, has a choice of four items per course, and might begin with omelette Arnold Bennett or Caesar salad. Main courses of chicken breast (curried, in paprika sauce, or with vegetables), or salmon topped with hollandaise sauce, are accompanied by a generous portion of 'beautifully cooked' vegetables. Puddings, which include a couple of hot pancakes and some Moroccan filo pastries, are rather less inspiring. Most of the wines outside Bordeaux and Burgundy are less than £20, although they don't offer such generous choice as the classic regions. House wine is £8.

CHEF: Richard Walton   PROPRIETORS: Richard Walton and Colin Smith   OPEN: Mon to Sat, exc Sat L; 12.30 to 2, 7 to 11   CLOSED: bank hols   MEALS: alc (main courses £11.50 to £15). Set L £14   SERVICE: not inc   CARDS: Access, Amex, Diners, Visa   DETAILS: 45 seats. Private parties: 16 main room. Vegetarian meals. Children's helpings. Smart dress preferred. No pipes in dining-room. Wheelchair access. No music. Air-conditioned

Chez Nico at Ninety Park Lane

map 14

90 Park Lane, W1A 3AA
071-409 1290

COOKING 5
COST £38–£110

Hop out of the chauffeur-driven limo, duck under the brown awning, ignore the foyer where coats and bags are taken (no numbered tickets here, the staff remember who was wearing and carrying what) and straight into business. The dining-room is large and formal, comfortable but not fussy, with many mirrors, a wall of window, and enough space to allow for privacy between large tables elegantly set. It is also a sea of black and white, like being in a penguin colony with hundreds of waiters – although it is probably only dozens – who wheel, dive and turn but thankfully never flap. The menu arrives pronto and off you go.

One of the things that makes Nico Ladenis stand out from his peers is that his food evolves. 'Nico moves with the times,' writes one reporter. To this extent he is an exciting chef. Food that stands still can soon look outdated. Chefs do not have to be fashionable, far from it, but to grind on for years without looking up to see what everybody else is doing is very boring. Nico is not boring. The food is neither entirely French, despite foie gras, served warm with caramelised orange and salad leaves, nor really Italian, despite a shin of veal with a light but concentrated sauce, that is osso buco in all but name. It is Nico's own, characterised by dishes that may appear simple, but have many layers of flavour. They may even look easy to do, until you try them. Of boudin blanc one reporter asked, 'How can such a simple sausage contain such a multitude of tastes?' A brilliant risotto of ceps at one meal was perfectly judged for timing and flavour. Maize-fed chicken is served with 'tiny, heavenly foie gras pancakes'. A sense of balance and ease of accomplishment run through dishes such as a chunk of salmon, brilliantly fresh, dark from grilling on one side, warm yet delightfully undercooked in the middle, served with a sharp-sweet sauce, with delicate ginger permeating the whole dish. The same applies to superbly textured, iced nougat parfait with crunchy bits and creamy bits, accompanied by a raspberry coulis with a gentle infusion of caraway, and to a simple but beautiful lemon tart.

Two things have irritated some reporters: service and prices. The first is perplexing. Many reporters consider the service beyond reproach, while others seem to have had a bad time. There is no pattern to it, no logic, just different experiences. As for prices, the £25 for lunch is an undisputed bargain, while the *carte* causes a problem for some: £46 for two courses seems a lot. In the restaurant's defence – and it is worth defending – three courses for £54 (which includes service) is less than some other top London restaurants charge, restaurants that are not rated as highly. The cost, of course, is high but it is difficult to see how you could get better cooking than this in London at any price.

Wines contribute to the financial concern. 'The towering prices divert attention,' says one hardened reporter. 'The prices make you wince,' writes another of equally long standing. They start at £18.50 and just never seem to stop. The collection is high on quality, but to list nothing from the south of France or Australia for under £20 takes some doing. Several wines are available by the glass.

CHEFS: Nico Ladenis and Eric Chavot   PROPRIETORS: Nico and Dinah-Jane Ladenis   OPEN: Mon to Sat, exc Sat L; 12 to 2, 7 to 11   MEALS: Set L £25, Set D £46 (2 courses)   SERVICE: net prices, card slips closed   CARDS: Access, Amex, Diners, Visa   DETAILS: 70 seats. Private parties: 20 private room. Vegetarian meals. No children under 6. Smart dress preferred. No pipes in dining-room. Wheelchair access (1 step). No music. Air-conditioned. Fax: 071-355 4877

Chinon   map 12

| 23 Richmond Way, W14 0AS | COOKING 3 |
| 071-602 4082 and 5968 | COST £26–£47 |

Chinon occupies two floors of a house near Shepherd's Bush, among a maze of one-way streets and mini-roundabouts, and has nothing to do with the Loire. The ground floor is bar and restaurant: below is a private dining-room. Jonathan Hayes's food is beyond fashion, although it has a Mediterranean slant. He is a careful cook, and his strength is to think flavours through and mark them out with some precision. There is no sense of dishes being thrown together; rather they are integrated, with just enough going on to provoke interest.

This much we know from his track record, although we have had remarkably little feedback on meals this year. Price may have something to do with it, but the portions are generous and cooking of this quality deserves support. Interpretations are often personal in some small way, as in a fillet of sole with sweet-and-sour aubergine, or the addition of balsamic vinegar to crème fraîche to accompany smoked salmon and asparagus. Puddings tend to come with ice-cream or sorbet: rhubarb in the case of vanilla bavarois with praline, and vanilla in the case of pear tart. Wines, mostly French, are sensibly chosen and priced, with good choice under £20, beginning with Romanian Pinot at £9.50. More reports, please.

CHEF: Jonathan Hayes   PROPRIETORS: Barbara Deane and Jonathan Hayes   OPEN: Mon to Sat; 12.30 to 2, 6.30 to 10.30 (11 Fri and Sat)   MEALS: alc (main courses £8.50 to £13)   SERVICE: 12.5%, card slips closed   CARDS: Access, Amex, Visa   DETAILS: 50 seats. Private parties: 35 main room. Vegetarian meals on request. No children under 10. No cigars/pipes in dining-room. Music. Air-conditioned

Christopher's   map 15

| 18 Wellington Street, WC2E 7DD | COOKING 1 |
| 071-240 4222 | COST £24–£64 |

Noisy throngs pack the downstairs bar, then a strange silence enfolds the winding stairs, and finally London babble is restored as you reach the dimly lit dining-room. 'Classic American East Coast food' say the proprietors, and while some items on the menu seem to stretch that concept a little, the core repertoire of crab-cakes with red pepper mayo, Caesar salad, Maine lobsters and peppered ribeye hits the right note. Lobster guacamole to start has been 'dead straight', if somewhat timidly seasoned, while roast pigeon with port sauce and parsnip mash had impressively gamey meat and a satisfyingly rich reduction. Stuffed chicken leg on lentils with roasted vegetables was too dry for one reporter. Desserts tend be substantial, with large slabs of plain New York cheesecake or properly rich chocolate terrine with coffee sauce. Purists should go for the hot toffee pudding with Jack Daniel's syrup. The wine list has some fine Californian and southern hemisphere wines, and a bunch of snooty clarets and burgundies as well. 'Christopher's Choice' house wines start at £10.

CHEF: Adrian Searing   PROPRIETORS: Christopher Gilmour and Lord Gilmour   OPEN: all week, exc Sun D; 12 to 3, 6 to 11.30 (bar Mon to Sat; 11.30am to 11pm)   CLOSED: Christmas, bank hols   MEALS: alc (main courses £8 to £18.50). Set L Sun £12 (2 courses). Set pre-theatre D £15   SERVICE: not inc   CARDS: Access, Amex, Diners, Visa   DETAILS: 120 seats. Private parties: 100 main room, 32 private room. Vegetarian meals. Children welcome. Smart dress preferred. Music. Fax: 071-240 3357

Chuen Cheng Ku £ | NEW ENTRY | map 15

17 Wardour Street, W1V 6HD   COOKING 1
071-437 1398 and 734 3281/3509   COST £16–£48

This Chinatown warhorse has had mixed fortunes of late, but the consensus is that it is once again a serious contender in Soho. A totem pole marks the entrance to a series of dining-rooms on different levels with enormous chandeliers and colourful murals. Lunchtime dim-sum (served from 11am to 6pm) draw favourable comments: heated trolleys are wheeled around loaded with wrinkly steamed prawn and pork dumplings, chunky pork balls with Chinese mushrooms, curried squid and whelks with chilli ('cut into slices so that they resembled some unidentifiable wild mushroom'). Excellent char siu with noodles in soup is assembled at the table. The full menu is fiercely Cantonese, with a few forays into northern Chinese territory. Seafood is a major suit. Dishes occasionally lack intensity and the cooking is earthy rather than refined, but reporters have been pleased by crispy aromatic duck, steamed eel with chilli and black-bean sauce, and steamed minced pork with salted egg. House wine is £7.30.

CHEF: Mr So   PROPRIETOR: Peter Au   OPEN: all week; 11am to 11.45pm   CLOSED: 24 and 25 Dec   MEALS: alc (main courses £6 to £13). Set L and D £9 to £30 (minimum 2)   SERVICE: not inc   CARDS: Access, Amex, Diners, Visa   DETAILS: 400 seats. Private parties: 180 main room, 60, 100 and 120 private rooms. Vegetarian meals. Children's helpings. Wheelchair access (1 step). Music. Air-conditioned

▲ *Claridge's* ♟   map 14

Brook Street, W1A 2JQ   COOKING 2
071-629 8860   COST £37–£82

Claridge's offers dining in the grand-hotel style, with rather predictable food impeccably served by a cast of thousands, and is one of the few restaurants where the atmosphere starts outside on the pavement. One reporter was thrilled by the police (sirens screaming), the press and a whole menagerie of uniformed minions and flunkies. 'Unfortunately it wasn't for us.' You are met at the door, along with royalty and visiting dignitaries, ushered in and passed smoothly from hand to hand. In the cocktail bar a three-piece orchestra manages to make some headway above the hubbub with Gilbert and Sullivan. Serried ranks of staff murmur good evenings, and everybody is utterly charming.

The set menu for one reporter was soup, salad or fish, then boeuf Stroganov, poached chicken or fish, followed by raspberry and fig tart or sweets from the trolley. A certain amount of comfort food is inevitable, and the *carte* runs to poached egg with spinach and smoked haddock, grilled salmon with braised cucumber, roast rack of lamb, plus game and other roasts and grills according to season and market. What with the gleaming silver, the dome-lifting and the atmosphere, 'you begin to believe that you have had a wonderful meal, when what appears on the plate is rather ordinary'. That is true of asparagus consommé with cheese straws, well-flavoured duck pâté with Sauternes jelly, a mixed plate of wild salmon, lobster and prawns in a seafood sauce, and strawberry flan and banana mousse cake, off a trolley that also offers tiramisù, trifle and fruit salad. The vegetables tell a different story, however: an inspector found the green beans 'some of the nicest I have ever eaten'.

Economy is not the first consideration when dining at Claridge's, yet it is possible to drink well for a modest outlay. Germany, Italy, Australia, South Africa and Chile all offer decent bottles under £20. There is a fair selection of half-bottles, and 10 wines available by the glass start at £3.75. CELLARMAN'S CHOICE: Chardonnay de Vieilles Vignes 1992, Rodet, £20.75; Crozes-Hermitage 1990, Paul Jaboulet, £21.25.

CHEF: Marjan Lesnik PROPRIETOR: The Savoy Group plc OPEN: all week, exc Sat L; 12.30 to 3, 7 to 11.15 MEALS: alc (main courses £17.50 to £26). Set L £21 (2 courses) to £36.50, Set D £28 to £36.50 SERVICE: net prices, card slips closed CARDS: Access, Amex, Diners, Visa DETAILS: 140 seats. Private parties: 40 main room, 4 to 250 private rooms. Vegetarian meals. Children's helpings. Smart dress preferred. No pipes in dining-room. Wheelchair access (also WC). Music. Air-conditioned ACCOMMODATION: 190 rooms, all with bath/shower. TV. Phone. Air-conditioned. B&B £140 to £362. Rooms for disabled. Lift. Children welcome. Baby facilities. Afternoon teas. Doors close at 1am. Confirm by 4. Fax: 071-499 2210

Clarke's ▮   map 12

124 Kensington Church St, W8 4BH   COOKING 4
071-221 9225   COST £30–£50

'I have long wanted to visit this restaurant and was not disappointed,' wrote a first-timer. One who has been before found that it continues to dazzle, with perfect balance and effortless simplicity, yet with flavours that are always vivid and full-frontal. 'The cooking goes straight to the heart and senses, it is heady stuff.' The no-smoking dining-room is below street level, but spacious, light and flowery, and there is two-way traffic between kitchen and shop next door, which has a tempting array of excellent cheese, bread (buy before lunch or it may run out), oils, herbs and wine.

The food has a directness and clarity about it, with emphasis on simple preparation of top-quality ingredients. Chargrilling is the main cooking method, flavours are often spiked with something like coriander or lemon grass to give brightness and lift, and piles of salad items are arranged artfully 'in a neat jumble'. Lunch offers two or three courses with limited choice at each, while dinners are fixed at four courses (one of them cheese) with no choice. Menus for both change daily and both include service. Part of the appeal is the balance: in overall conception (given the lack of choice in the evening), and in individual dishes, where treatment of all the components, including herbs and vegetables, is given equal emphasis. Although the no-choice idea is a great package for ditherers, the margin for misjudging the tastes of customers is minimal, hence a leaning to chicken, lamb or a fairly meaty fish for the main course.

Fish cooking, universally praised, suits the simple treatment as well as anything. One reporter enjoyed the contrast of firm red mullet set against fine-textured swordfish, both chargrilled and offset by a generous bundle of deep green rocket and a shiny mound of finely sliced fennel, with an unctuous and garlicky aïoli. That may sound a lot, but in practice dishes rely on simplicity for effect, flavours combining without any discordant notes. Cheese is two pieces of something like Wigmore or Wellington, already cut on to a plate, served with light, crisp oatmeal biscuits. Puddings may be conservative but they avoid the sticky toffee end of the spectrum. Rhubarb and ginger cream, a tall fluted glass of strawberries and huge tayberries in champagne, and lemon tart with crisp wafer-thin pastry and a plum sauce have all been endorsed.

It has to be said that not all reporters are equally happy. Some feel they could barbecue a piece of chicken just as well at home, and, given the relative predictability of supplies and lack of wastage, wonder if prices, especially at dinner, might not be reduced. After all, the cooking is not built on extravagantly expensive ingredients. Service for most reporters is polite, informative and sharp without forcing the pace. For others, it has been more detached and off-hand. It should be very easy when there are no orders to confuse. Wines hit the bull's eye at every level, from good French country wines through smart Burgundies, and wonderful Italians under £20, to excellent Californians. Prices are designed to encourage good drinking, and around 10 really good wines are normally available by the glass from £2 to £5. CELLARMAN'S CHOICE: Marsanne 1992, Qupé, £19; Bonny Doon 'Le Cigare Volant' 1990, £25.

CHEFS: Sally Clarke and Elizabeth Payne   PROPRIETOR: Sally Clarke   OPEN: Mon to Fri; 12.30 to 2, 7 to 10   CLOSED: 1 week Christmas, 4 days Easter, 2 weeks Aug   MEALS: Set L £22 (2 courses) to £26, Set D £37   SERVICE: net prices, card slips closed   CARDS: Access, Visa   DETAILS: 90 seats. Private parties: 12 main room. Vegetarian meals. Children welcome. No cigars/pipes in dining-room. Wheelchair access. No music. Air-conditioned. Fax: 071-229 4564

Condotti £   map 14

4 Mill Street, W1R 9TE   COOKING 1
071-499 1308   COST £15–£29

'Gives pizza a good name,' remarked a reporter. This lively venue near New Bond Street is a functional, crowded place with a famous collection of prints and artwork on the walls. It has dropped Pizzeria from its name, but is first cousin to Pizza Express and the cooking has all the distinctive trademarks of that chain: free-range eggs, pizzas that have a good doughy base, and vivid but restrained toppings, plus a back-up of baked mushrooms with rocket, useful salads, sorbets, ice-creams and good cappuccino. Peroni beer and freshly squeezed orange juice are listed alongside a handful of workaday Italian wines. House wine is £7.75.

CHEF: Johnny Medina   PROPRIETORS: Enzo Apicella and Peter Boizot   OPEN: Mon to Sat;
11.30am to midnight   CLOSED: bank hols   MEALS: alc (main courses £5 to £6.50)   SERVICE:
not inc   CARDS: Access, Amex, Diners, Visa   DETAILS: 120 seats. Private parties: 70 main
room, 50 private room. Vegetarian meals. Children welcome. Wheelchair access (3 steps). No
music. Air-conditioned

▲ *Connaught*   map 14

Carlos Place, W1Y 6AL   COOKING 4
071-499 7070   COST £38–£126

They don't come more traditional than the Connaught, and they don't often do it
so well. Progress from the entrance, through the lobby, turn right past a cold hors
d'oeuvre display and bowing commis waiters, and into the dining-room with its
acres of polished panels. It is a 'solid, comfortable, somewhat masculine place',
in the old English style and reminded one 'of an officers' mess dining-room from
my RAF service'. Battalions of waiters, each dressed according to station, buzz
and hover around tables, carving, slicing, filleting with surgical efficiency,
flaming, pouring, presenting on silver platters, lifting domes, pushing trolleys
and generally putting in a lot of service. 'I had expected the Connaught to be
stuffy, but the place is friendly and relaxed,' and staff are helpful and faultlessly
professional.

Fashion and the world outside continue to have little effect on the Connaught.
The scale of the menu suggests a brasserie, offering 'something for everyone',
from simple caviare or smoked salmon to some very time-consuming French
classics. Thai spices, for instance, don't get a look-in. This is the world of daily
specials – steak and kidney pie (Monday and Saturday lunch), boiled silverside
(Thursday) – of sausage and bacon and lamb cutlets, of sherry trifle and light,
custardy, crusty-topped and gently wobbling bread-and-butter pudding – how
utterly British! So too, in a way, are 'superb' croustade d'oeufs de caille
Maintenon, salade caprice des années folles, sole meunière and pintadeau en
cocotte grand-mère. It is all rather Edwardian in the mix of Anglo-French
Escoffier food.

The strength is the consistency year after year, although not every dish excels.
Terrine of foie gras for one reporter was a bit grey at the edges, 'slightly too
gamey and overcooked', and when pastry languishes under a silver dome it soon
goes claggy. But the range of dishes is so wide, encompassing just about every
skill in the book, that you feel there is nothing this kitchen cannot do. And yet
the cooking is not showy, but bundles along on a stream of confidence and verve,
and for the most part delivers. Starters have a high strike rate, varying from
kipper pâté, through artichokes or asparagus to simple consommé 'with a
long-drawn-out beef flavour'. Puddings can be a high point too, as in five sorbets
with a tuile basket and thinly sliced exotic fruits 'so clearly distinctive that each
fruit flavour, whether lemon, passion-fruit, orange or raspberry, sang like
different notes on a scale'. It is good value, one reporter felt, in the way that a
Rolls-Royce is worth the money. The wine list is long and expensive and
hoity-toity, with nothing from the New World, although house wine (£15.75 for
a carafe) and dessert wines by the glass are good.

CHEF: Michel Bourdin PROPRIETOR: The Savoy Group plc OPEN: restaurant all week, Grill Room Mon to Fri (Sat and Sun Jan to early Apr, D only Sat and Sun early Apr to July and early Sept to end-Dec); 12.30 to 2.30, 6.30 to 10.30 CLOSED: Grill Room bank hols, Aug to early Sept MEALS: alc (main courses £10 to £38.50). Set L Mon to Sat £25, Sun £30, Set D £35. Minimum £25 SERVICE: 15%, card slips closed CARDS: Access, Amex, Diners, Visa DETAILS: restaurant 75 seats, Grill Room 35 seats. Private parties: 10 and 22 private rooms. Car park. Vegetarian meals. Children welcome. Jacket and tie. Wheelchair access (also men's WC). No music. Air-conditioned ACCOMMODATION: 90 rooms, all with bath/shower. TV. Phone. Room prices on application. Rooms for disabled. Lift. Children welcome. Baby facilities. Afternoon teas. Fax: 071-495 3262 (*The Which? Hotel Guide*)

▲ Conrad London, Brasserie   `NEW ENTRY`   map 10

Chelsea Harbour, SW10 0XG   COOKING 2
071-823 3000   COST £30–£52

Except for those who live there, Chelsea Harbour seems a long way from anywhere, and car parking for one lunchtime reporter cost £4. The modern hotel has an appropriately smart and nautical feel, a big modern dining-room, thick carpet and an air of ease and calm. Peter Brennan used to cook at Turner's (see entry, London) and prefers light, fast cooking methods of stir-frying, flash-frying, grilling and steaming. The set menus are no-choice, and one of them offers an unusual pan-fried gravlax with lemon butter, after salad of deep-fried squid in tempura batter, and before grilled poussin with garlic sauce. Gravlax appears also in shredded form, with a potato pancake and crème fraîche. Jack-the-lad dishes of Cumberland sausages with onion gravy, and cod 'n' chips with a Guinness batter share the billing on a wide-ranging *carte* with French onion soup, and warm salad of baby artichokes and sun-dried tomatoes.

Some dishes work well, including wild mushroom risotto, and two extremely fine-looking, tender fillets of rabbit laid down either side of a plate, with the dark liver at the top, a pile each of thin pasta and spinach, and a delightful variation on the classic mustard sauce, with tiny dice of chopped kidney adding to the enjoyment. Other dishes have been less successful despite first-rate ingredients. Dover sole with potatoes, olives and artichokes sounds like a cheery way of dealing with a flat fish from the Channel, but the bouncy fresh fillets, perfectly timed, were let down by their accompaniments. Portions can be hefty. There is reasonable choice on the annotated wine list, with seven house wines all around £15, or £3 per glass.

CHEF: Peter Brennan PROPRIETOR: Hilton Hotels Corporation of America OPEN: all week; 12 to 2.30, 7 to 10.30 MEALS: alc (main courses L £9 to £15, D £10 to £16.50). Set L Mon to Sat £13.50 (2 courses) to £16.50, Set D £22.50 to £24.50. Sun brunch £28.50 (inc champagne) SERVICE: 10%, card slips closed CARDS: Access, Amex, Diners, Visa DETAILS: 60 seats (200 Sun). 14 tables outside. Private parties: 25 main room, 200 private room. Car park. Vegetarian meals. Children's helpings. Smart dress preferred. Wheelchair access (also WC). Music. Air-conditioned ACCOMMODATION: 160 rooms, all with bath/shower. TV. Phone. Air-conditioned. Rooms for disabled. Lift. Children welcome. Pets welcome. Afternoon teas. Swimming-pool. Sauna. Fax: 071-351 6525

'Every time we saw the chef he had his hand on someone's bottom.'
(On eating in Nottinghamshire)

Cork & Bottle ♥ £

map 15

44-46 Cranbourn Street, WC2H 7AN
071-734 7807

COOKING 1
COST £17–£31

This long-running basement wine bar is so popular it would be cramped however big it was; and it is not large. Don't come here for a leisurely meal. They serve over 400 portions of grilled garlicky Mediterranean prawns a week, never mind anything else. It is lively, cheery, good-humoured, casual – and useful because of the long opening hours and better-than-average bar food. Grab a table if you can, have a squint at the blackboard, line up at the counter and choose from raised ham and cheese pie, Hungarian meat loaf, or pork in a rich casserole sauce of pimentos and almonds. One reporter enjoyed scrambled eggs with smoked salmon, and an unlikely sounding monkfish with jalapeño pepper and coriander pesto with a pineapple coulis. Be warned that 'you can only have chips if you have steak'. Not everybody likes the crush, and there are some who doubt the consistency of the food, but support has been positive enough.

Cork & Bottle's director Don Hewitson has been championing Australian wines since 1977 and doesn't look like giving up now. South Australia is the prime source, but he also backs other parts of the world, from France to California. Prices are reasonable, there is always something of interest, and even the house wines (at £9.95) are splendidly fruity. No fewer than 30 wines are available by the glass from £2.20 to £3.95, with lots from the New World. CELLARMAN'S CHOICE: Te Mata 'Elston' Chardonnay 1993, £21.50; Juliénas 1993, Paquet, £14.95. Don Hewitson has also opened the Hanover Square Wine Bar and Grill at 25 Hanover Square W1, Tel: 071-408 0935. Reports, please.

CHEF: Louis Egham   PROPRIETOR: Cork & Bottle Wines 1991 Ltd   OPEN: all week; 11am to 11.45pm Mon to Sat, noon to 10.15 Sun   CLOSED: 25 Dec, 1 Jan   MEALS: alc (main courses £4.50 to £9)   SERVICE: not inc   CARDS: Access, Amex, Visa   DETAILS: 85 seats. 4 tables outside. Private parties: 20 main room, 20 private room. Vegetarian meals. No pipes/cigars in dining-room. Music. Air-conditioned. Fax: 071-483 2230

Criterion Brasserie

map 14

224 Piccadilly, W1V 9LB
071-925 0909

COOKING 1
COST £25–£42

Possibly the most enviably sited restaurant in London, the Criterion, 'bang next to Eros', commands Piccadilly Circus. Last year's comparison of the interior to a Victorian swimming-pool is supplanted this year for one visitor by memories of the trim, marbled gleam of Soviet railway stations.

The menu is built along equally stolid lines. Certain dishes – Caesar salad, fish and chips, grilled sirloin with fries, sticky toffee pudding – are stalwarts, but room is made for specials and seasonality too. An inspection meal started with grilled goats' cheese salad with ham and pine-nuts that was 'a bit of a mish-mash' but pleasant, and a 'tangy, zesty' dish of linguine with chilli, smoked chicken and artichokes. Honey-roasted hock of ham with beans and lentils had 'lovely, sticky' meat and an enjoyably coarse mustard sauce, but loin of lamb with apricots and balsamic vinaigrette was heavier-going. Amaretto crème brûlée was of the non-crunch variety, but fine, while a lemon tart had hardish pastry and a bracingly tart strawberry coulis. Vegetables, charged extra, will bump up the bill, but the French fries are worth it. The wine list makes a serious effort to deliver flavours worthy of the food, such as Fetzer Sundial Chardonnay and Aglianico del Vulture. House Italian is £8.95 (white) or £9.50 (red).

CHEF: Brian Baker   PROPRIETOR: Forte plc   OPEN: all week, exc Sun D; noon to 11.30 (5.30 Sun)   MEALS: alc (main courses £7.25 to £12). Set L and D £10 (2 courses). Minimum £4 SERVICE: not inc   CARDS: Access, Amex, Diners, Visa   DETAILS: 220 seats. Private parties: 250 main room. Vegetarian meals. Children welcome. No cigars/pipes in dining-room. Wheelchair access (also WC). No music. Air-conditioned. Fax: 071-839 1494

Crowthers
map 10

481 Upper Richmond Road West,
SW14 7PU
081-876 6372

COOKING 2
COST £27–£36

After about a dozen years in East Sheen, the Crowthers have acquired an asset more precious than rubies to restaurateurs – customer loyalty. Regulars won't allow certain dishes to be dropped ('the menu tends to evolve rather than change radically,' says Philip Crowther), but that sterling support is what also accounts for the fretful tone of a couple of February reports that left visitors wondering whether the usual team was away. Reporters use block capitals and much underlining to sing the praises of dishes such as 'superb' sweet potato and garlic soup, 'top-class' shiitake mushroom parcels with wild mushroom sauce, roast guinea-fowl with a marjoram and madeira sauce, and honey and brandy ice-cream in a brandy-snap basket. Incidentals, from home-made brown rolls to good petits fours, are usually enjoyed. Service is for the most part very willing, but can appear flustered if there is plenty to do. Wines are a fairly priced dispassionate selection, with the vast majority well within £20. House wines are £8.50.

CHEFS: Philip Crowther and Justin Gellatly   PROPRIETORS: Philip and Shirley Crowther   OPEN: Tues to Sat, exc Sat L; 12 to 2, 7 to 10.30   CLOSED: 1 week Christmas, 2 weeks summer MEALS: Set L £14.75 (2 courses) to £17.50, Set D £15.85 (2 courses) to £20.50   SERVICE: not inc   CARDS: Access, Visa   DETAILS: 32 seats. Private parties: 32 main room. Vegetarian meals. Children's helpings on request. Smart dress preferred. Wheelchair access (1 step). No music. Air-conditioned

Daphne £
map 11

83 Bayham Street, NW1 0AG
071-267 7322

COOKING 1
COST £17–£30

'More steady than exciting' is the consensus about the food, but there is little doubt about the reliability of this friendly Greek-Cypriot restaurant or its atmosphere of local friendliness and good humour. The menu is in the tried and tested mould of meze and grills plus long-cooked stews and casseroles such as beef stifado and pork afelia. Blackboard specials respond to the mood of the times by emphasising fish and vegetarian dishes: you might find anything from grilled gilt head bream (flown in from Greece) and cuttlefish cooked in its own ink with olive oil and spinach and topped with feta cheese to artichokes with broad beans in their pods. Reporters have endorsed chargrilled octopus tenderised in the oven with olive oil and lemon. Overall, the value for money is reckoned to be 'incredible'. Greek sweetmeats round things off. A handful of Greek and Cypriot wines show up on the short list, although the house wine – at £8.50 – is French.

CHEFS: Lambros Georgiou and Kyriacos Zacharias PROPRIETORS: Panikos and Anna Lymbouri OPEN: Mon to Sat; 12 to 2.30, 6 to 11.30 MEALS: alc (main courses £5.50 to £9.50) SERVICE: not inc CARDS: Access, Visa DETAILS: 85 seats. 10 tables outside. Private parties: 30 main room. Vegetarian meals. Children's helpings. Wheelchair access (1 step; also WC). Music

Daphne's

map 13

112 Draycott Avenue, SW3 3AE
071-589 4257

COOKING 1*
COST £29–£54

Reports almost invariably mention the famous faces spotted during the course of a meal: could that be Joan Collins? Ivana Trump? the Duchess of York's father? It could indeed; Daphne's has become a stargazer's paradise. The décor feels good: an airy, umber-hued, stone-floored front room leads to a conservatory and then a garden room with real plants scaling the walls, and a glass roof that can be retracted (depending on the weather forecast).

The food tends to be quietly commended rather than raved about; the idiom is thorough-going Italian, running the gamut from bruschetta, carpaccio, grilled squid, pasta dishes and risotti to roast sea bass with balsamic salsa, and chargrilled sirloin. One diner thought the practice of battering and deep-frying courgette flowers a 'cunning' conceit without culinary rationale. Seafood risotto is enjoyed, though, for its properly 'gluey' texture. 'Very good' lobster ravioli, 'excellent' calf's liver alla veneziana, linguine with clams, courgette fritters, fig tart with vanilla ice-cream and densely rich pot-au-chocolat all receive endorsements. Some find the service unco-ordinated, some query the portion control on vegetables charged extra, some regret the stench of cigars in the middle of dinner. A New Yorker flying through thought Daphne's 'a friendly place for a companionable meal'. The wine list makes a pretty good job of providing a fair range of style in Italy, France and outside Europe, and there is just enough below £20 to offer genuine choice. House Italian is £9.50.

CHEF: Edward Baines PROPRIETOR: Mogens Tholstrup OPEN: all week; 12 to 3 (to 4 Sun brunch), 7 to 11.30 MEALS: alc (main courses £9.50 to £16.50) SERVICE: 15%, card slips closed CARDS: Access, Amex, Diners, Visa DETAILS: 110 seats. 7 tables outside. Private parties: 8 main room. Vegetarian meals. Children's helpings on request. Smart dress preferred. Wheelchair access (2 steps). No music. Air-conditioned. Fax: 071-581 2232

Del Buongustaio

| NEW ENTRY | map 10

283 Putney Bridge Road, SW15 2PT
081-780 9361

COOKING 1
COST £22–£42

Owned by the same Australo-Italian team that have Osteria Antica Bologna (see entry, London), this unassuming bistro brings a ray of Italian sunshine to Putney. The food specialities are from the region of Emilia-Romagna, the chef's own home territory, and the setting in which they are presented is a tiled, salmon-pink room of considerable cheer.

The à la carte menu of classical dishes is supplemented by a five-course *menu degustazione*. Antipasti are good and varied, and may include chillied clams, puréed squid on crostini, or skewered peppers. An early summer meal took in accurately cooked crostini topped with mozzarella and truffle, artichoke and porcini flan (the two elements puréed together to achieve 'lovely flavour'), and rather heavy Gorgonzola ravioli. A winter meal impressed more for venison sausage on a purée of cannellini beans, calf's liver in balsamic sauce with an accompaniment of chicory wrapped in prosciutto, and tiramisù with a 'very good bitter chocolate sauce'. Wines have been bemusingly classified by somebody with a taste for romantic fiction: 'Wines for the good times', 'Serious but with a smile', 'What good memories are made of'. Perhaps something is lost in the translation. At any rate, the selections are sound, and the dual nationality – Italian and Australian – reflects the ownership. House wines from the Veneto are £7.90.

CHEFS: Aurelio Spagnuolo and Antonio Strillozzi PROPRIETORS: Rochelle Porteus and Aurelio Spagnuolo OPEN: all week, exc Sat L and Sun D; 12 to 3 (12.30 to 3.30 Sun), 6.30 to 11.30 CLOSED: 10 days Christmas and New Year, Sun L July and Aug, Aug bank hol MEALS: alc (main courses £5.90 to £9.50). Set L £9.50 (2 courses), Set D £19.50. Cover 80p SERVICE: not inc (10% for large groups) CARDS: Access, Amex, Visa DETAILS: 50 seats. Private parties: 14 main room. Vegetarian meals. Children's helpings. Smart dress preferred. Wheelchair access (1 step). Music. Air-conditioned. Fax: 081-789 9659

dell'Ugo   map 15

56 Frith Street, W1V 5TA   COOKING 1
071-734 8300   COST £22–£41

'Oil, oil everywhere,' observed a visitor. Bottles of the eponymous stuff (dell'Ugo is a Tuscan olive oil) are on every table, displays fill the windows and the kitchen relies heavily on its deep, green richness. The bistro is on three floors, becoming slightly more formal and quieter as you move upwards. At street level it can be deafening, as the cardiac thud of the music competes with the hubbub of conversation. Warhol-style displays of custard tins and old sauce bottles decorate the room. Antony Worrall-Thompson's amalgam of Mediterranean peasant cooking, oriental and old English can produce vivid results: seafood and corn chowder, warm goats' cheese and red pepper tart, oysters stuffed with crabmeat and bacon, chargrilled squid with roasted vegetables, and pear and almond tart have all been mentioned. Country breads, bruschetta, salads and pasta are mainstays. Most pronounce the place excellent value for money. The short, sharp wine list varies depending on which merchant is supplying the goods. House wine is £8.45.

CHEF: Mark Emberton PROPRIETOR: Simpsons of Cornhill plc OPEN: Mon to Sat, exc Sat L restaurant; 12 to 3, 5.30 to 12.15 (11am to 11pm ground floor) CLOSED: bank hols MEALS: alc (main courses £7 to £11) SERVICE: not inc CARDS: Access, Amex, Diners, Visa DETAILS: 200 seats. 6 tables outside. Private parties: 60 main room, 16 private room. Vegetarian meals. Children welcome. Wheelchair access (1 step). Music. Air-conditioned. Fax: 071-734 8784

The Guide *always appreciates hearing about changes of chef or owner.*

▲ Dorchester ♥

map 14

Park Lane, W1A 2HJ   COOKING 2
071-629 8888   COST £28–£98

The Dorchester contains four restaurants. All are independent, with their own kitchens and chefs. The connection is Willi Elsener, who oversees the lot. The Grill Room – in warm 1930s Spanish style – is the main dining-room and not particularly large, although wheels are considered essential to get around. Indeed it seems to have more trolleys than a supermarket: one for smoked salmon, one for bread, one for salads, one for cheese, one for puddings and so on. More than a hint of traditional British can be found in Morecambe Bay potted shrimps, braised oxtail, and a rotating lunch dish of steak and kidney pie on Wednesday, or fish pie on Friday. And, of course, there are grills of liver and bacon, fish and T-bone steak.

It is questionable, though, how much of the food reflects the skills of Willi Elsener, who, in a place this size, is possibly more of an executive than a chef. Roast beef, trundled round on a chariot, continues to cook in the steam under its dome, with Yorkshire puddings wilting in the muggy humidity. Perhaps the tourists like it, but a lot has happened over the last decade to unstick grand hotels from this mud – look what Bruno Loubet did for the Inn on the Park, never mind Nico and Marco. The cooking on the whole, however, is perfectly adequate, culminating at one meal in an excellent diplomat pudding.

The Terrace goes in for chinoiserie décor and perky flavourings of lemon grass in a dressing for king prawns served with a three pepper terrine, or cardamom that infuses a grapefruit sauce for a vegetable-filled baked salmon parcel. But it is now open only two nights a week for dinner dances, the rest of the time being given over to private parties.

The Oriental is based on big Hong Kong originals, with Cantonese dishes and lots of waiters. Shark's fin and abalone feature, as do deep-fried crispy pigeon with pickled vegetables, and deep-fried soft shell crab in chilli pepper and herbal salt. Simon Yung will happily mix cocktails of ingredients to clients' specifications. Lunchtime dim-sum (more trolleys) might include shredded chicken spring rolls or steamed prawn and shark's fin parcel, while the fixed-price dinner menu is typically seven dishes long.

The Dorchester Bar, meanwhile, with yet another kitchen, serves antipasti at lunch and light Italian dishes all day, including pasta with ragoût of duck, ravioli filled with artichoke, John Dory with fennel, and coffee cream pudding.

The same wine list furnishes all three main restaurants (the Bar has its own short Italian list), and is full of impressive bottles (Bordeaux and Burgundy are naturally strong suits) at high mark-ups. Those with more sense than money will struggle to find much under £20, but it can be done. House wine throughout is £16 (for claret) or £17.50 (Latour's Chardonnay from Ardèche) and nine wines are normally available by the glass from around £4. CELLARMAN'S CHOICE: Riesling 1991, Beyer, £23.50; St-Julien, Connétable Talbot 1984, £21.

See the inside of the front cover for an explanation of the 1 to 5 rating system for cooking standards.

CHEFS: Willi Elsener (Grill and Terrace), Simon Yung (Oriental) and Pado Sari (Dorchester Bar) PROPRIETOR: Dorchester Hotel Ltd OPEN: Grill all week; 12.30 to 2.30, 6 to 11 (7 to 10.30 Sun and bank hols). Terrace Fri and Sat, D only; 7 to 11.30. Oriental Mon to Sat, exc Sat L; 12.30 to 2.30, 7 to 11. Dorchester Bar all week; noon to 11.45 (noon to 3, 7 to 10 Sun) CLOSED: Aug Terrace and Oriental MEALS: alc (main courses Grill £13.50 to £26, Oriental £9.50 to £32, Dorchester Bar £10.50 to £17.50). Grill Set L £23.50, Set D £28; Terrace Set D £38 to £42; Oriental Set L £20 to £22, Set D £28 SERVICE: net prices, card slips closed CARDS: Access, Amex, Diners, Visa DETAILS: Grill 81 seats, Terrace 81 seats, Oriental 77 seats, Dorchester Bar 59 seats. Private parties: 10 and 14 main rooms, 6, 10 and 12 private rooms. Vegetarian meals. Children welcome Grill. No children under 12 Terrace and Oriental. No children under 16 Dorchester Bar. Smart dress preferred. Wheelchair access (2 steps Terrace; also WC). No music Grill and Oriental. Music Terrace and Dorchester Bar. Air-conditioned ACCOMMODATION: 247 rooms, all with bath/shower. TV. Phone. Air-conditioned. B&B £244 to £329. Rooms for disabled. Lift. Children welcome. Baby facilities. Afternoon teas. Sauna. Fax: 071-359 7351 (071-359 1191 Grill)

La Dordogne   map 10

5 Devonshire Road, W4 2EU   COOKING 1
081-747 1836 and 994 7327   COST £25–£43

A cabbie, after authoritatively informing a reporter that Chiswick was now very fashionable for eating out, deposited his fare at the Dordogne with the assurance that it would be 'full of refugees from central London prices'. This tiny restaurant aims to be as 'authentically French' as is achievable in west London. Oysters from Brittany and the Irish Sea, and traditional ways with lobster, are among the specialities for which it is famed.

The *carte* deals in the Gallic classicism of another era, such as salade gourmande (foie gras, quail's eggs and smoked duck), moules marinière, and beef fillet on a potato galette with green peppercorn sauce. Ostentation comes to the fore in the showpiece desserts, a selection of which may be taken by those who can't choose. Sauces, it is noted, are sufficiently well-judged not to overwhelm the principal ingredient, and a 'surprisingly good' dauphinois is the focal point of the vegetable dish. Service can on occasion be more non-committal shrugs than welcoming smiles. Wines are French, with a reasonable showing from the south-west. House wines begin at £8.60 (£2.50 per glass).

CHEF: Giles Companie PROPRIETOR: R. Pouyet OPEN: all week, exc Sat and Sun L; 12 to 2.30, 7 to 11 CLOSED: bank hols MEALS: alc (main courses £8.50 to £12). Cover £1 SERVICE: 10% CARDS: Access, Amex, Diners, Visa DETAILS: 80 seats. 6 tables outside. Private parties: 30 main room, 20 and 35 private rooms. Vegetarian meals with prior notice. Children welcome. Smart dress preferred. Wheelchair access (1 step; also WC). Music. Fax: 081-994 9144

Eagle £   map 11

159 Farringdon Road, EC1R 3AL   COOKING 1*
071-837 1353   COST £20–£32

A silver lining of the recessionary cloud has been a move to simple, inexpensive food served in plain surroundings, where frills and comfort are stripped away, sometimes along with the insides of whole buildings. The Eagle was the first of its breed in London, and the pity is that dozens more have not followed suit. It used to be a pub and still behaves like one: beers are lined up, and there is no obligation to eat. One wall is a bar-cum-kitchen, open to view. If there are any warts, you see them. Place an order, hand over your money, then scramble back to your seat if you can get one, and carry on drinking until the food turns up. Dishes are chalked up and rubbed off a board as the mealtime progresses.

The Mediterranean is the principal source of ingredients, from swordfish, salt cod and grilled sardines to sun-dried tomatoes, pancetta and Parmesan, to pesto, sage, ground cumin and fresh coriander until it is coming out of your ears. Grills include an Italian sausage with lentils, and stews run to shin of veal, or Spanish butter-beans with chorizo, pork, ham and black pudding. In the hurly-burly the cooking may not always hit the mark, but nothing much goes wrong with salads – Lebanese-style, Greek-style, or bonito with borlotti beans – and much use is made of bread: focaccia, bruschetta with anchovies and slow-roast tomatoes, Turkish olive bread with aubergine purée, and the ever-popular marinated rumpsteak sandwich bifeana. A dozen wines are £10 top whack apart from fizz, and all served by the glass for around £2.

CHEF: David Eyre   PROPRIETORS: Michael Belben and David Eyre   OPEN: Mon to Fri; 12.30 to 2.30, 6.30 to 10.30   CLOSED: 2/3 weeks Christmas, bank hols   MEALS: alc (main courses £6 to £9.50)   SERVICE: not inc   DETAILS: 55 seats. 4 tables outside. Private parties: 80 main room. Vegetarian meals. Children's helpings. Wheelchair access (1 step). Music

Efes Kebab House ✳ £

80 Great Titchfield Street, W1P 7AF
071-636 1953

map 14

COOKING 1
COST £17–£30

This kebab house is named after ancient Ephesus near Izmir in Turkey, but service is so swift that there is hardly time to read the potted history on the back of the menu. Photographs of Radio 1 DJs on the walls are not quite as ancient. Lamb in one form or another is the main business: diced, minced, spit-roasted doner, cutlets, liver, grilled kidney and so on, with chicken or steak the alternatives. Portions are generous, the protein a bit unrelenting, and the value certainly good.

One couple who began with meze were so full they could barely eat a main course of yogurt kebab that included large sheets of doner meat, a beefburger, and a piece each of chicken and lamb. Vegetarians can get away with a selection of first courses such as carrots with yogurt, hummus, the aubergine dish imam bayeldi, stuffed vine leaves, and börek pastry filled with soft cheese and egg. Sweet, syrupy, nutty pastries and Turkish coffee are the way to finish. Turkish wine, lager and liqueurs make the rest of the drinks list easy to ignore, though French house wine is £7.60. Another branch, Efes II at 175 Great Portland Street, W1, lays on live music and belly-dancing at weekends until 2am.

CHEFS/PROPRIETORS: Khazim Akkus and Ibrahim Akbas   OPEN: Mon to Sat; noon to 11.30pm   MEALS: alc (main courses £5.50 to £9.50). Set L and D £14 to £15 (minimum 2). Cover 75p. Minimum £5   SERVICE: not inc   CARDS: Access, Amex, Diners, Visa   DETAILS: 190 seats. 20 tables outside. Private parties: 150 main room, 50 private room. Vegetarian meals. Children welcome. Smart dress preferred. No-smoking room. Wheelchair access. Music. Air-conditioned. Fax: 071-323 5082

English Garden

map 13

10 Lincoln Street, SW3 2TS   COOKING 1
071-584 7272   COST £22–£53

Off the King's Road and handy for Sloane Square, the English Garden preserves its horticultural credentials with hanging plants in the Gothic conservatory. It is a Chelsea town house, bright, mirrored and comfortable, and hangs on to its Englishness with grilled Cumberland sausage, bubble and squeak, grilled sirloin of beef with Yorkshire pudding and onion gravy, and roly-poly pudding. But the cooking is not dyed-in-the-wool and runs to some dishes of no particular fixed abode, including grilled sardines with tomato and basil, grilled scallops with coriander salsa, and clementine tart. Reporters speak highly of fish, meat and puddings, less so of vegetables, and are perplexed that it all costs as much as it does. The wine list for some reason cannot rustle up a single bottle of English wine, preferring instead to hop straight over to the classic regions of France, where it finds both quality and fair prices, although not necessarily at the same time. House wines at £9.50 include the decent Ch. Reynier.

CHEF: Brian Turner   PROPRIETOR: Roger Wren   OPEN: all week; 12.30 to 2.30 (2 Sun), 7.30 to 11.30 (10 Sun)   CLOSED: 25 and 26 Dec   MEALS: alc (main courses £9 to £15.50). Set L £14.75   SERVICE: not inc   CARDS: Access, Amex, Diners, Visa   DETAILS: 70 seats. Private parties: 20 main room, 10 and 20 private rooms. Vegetarian meals. Children's helpings. Smart dress preferred. Music. Air-conditioned. Fax: 071-581 2848

L'Escargot

map 15

48 Greek Street, W1V 5LQ   COQKING 2
071-437 2679 and 6828   COST £29–£81

Business at L'Escargot is conducted on three levels: in the ground-floor brasserie, and in the restaurant on the first and second floors. It is as well to be clear about where you want to eat and when, particularly in the case of the restaurant, and to check for closures, which can be frequent. The menus, seemingly set in stone, contain much with which London has become familiar in recent years (best end of lamb 'Reform', moules marinière with pistou, bouillabaisse, duck confit with red cabbage) as well as less obvious ideas such as stewed oysters with a red wine vinaigrette, and duck foie gras roasted with grapes.

A certain monotony of garnishing cropped up in an inspection lunch in the brasserie, at which virtually every dish had a base of mashed something. The Chablis sauce with snails turned out to be 'a thick and delicious gunge' redolent of garlic and lemon crammed into each shell. Oyster beignets with risotto was 'a clever novelty', the shells glued to the plate with mash, filled with lemony rice topped with crisply battered oysters of satisfying freshness. Balance and flavour are not always judged finely, although bavette of beef 'fremoise' (served on a potato and parsnip purée) was enjoyed for its fibrous meat of good flavour and 'rich boozy sauce'. Ice-cream and sorbet torte was 'a large wedge of pink and white' in a thin sponge casing, while the compote of rhubarb came with a thick cream sauce that was 'heavy on the vanilla'. Snail-shaped chocolate truffles are still served with coffee. The wine list is comprehensive in range within France, less so elsewhere, but will prove expensive unless you stick with the south of France or the house selections. The latter start at £10.50.

CHEFS: Garry Hollihead and David Cavalier   PROPRIETOR: Jimmy Lahoud   OPEN: first floor Tue to Sat, exc Sat L; 12.15 to 2.15, 7 to 10.45. Ground floor Mon to Sat, exc Sat L; 12.15 to 2.15, 6 to 11.15   CLOSED: first floor Aug   MEALS: alc (main courses ground floor £10.50 to £18, first floor D £16.50 to £22). First floor Set L £25, Set D £39.50 (2 persons)   SERVICE: not inc   CARDS: Access, Amex, Diners, Visa   DETAILS: ground floor 90 seats, first floor 50 seats. Private parties: 12 main room, 34 and 50 private rooms. Vegetarian meals. Children welcome. No cigars in dining-room. Wheelchair access (3 steps; also men's WC). Music. Air-conditioned. Fax: 071-437 0790

L'Estaminet   map 15

14 Garrick Street, WC2E 9BJ   COOKING 1*
071-379 1432   COST £21–£42

This bright, friendly French restaurant is the closest you will get to an auberge in Covent Garden. The welcome is cheery and the portions are large, the culinary focal point being Provence. Two ladies lunching in November who fled the smoke-filled subterranean wine bar were unprotestingly given the wine bar menu at a table in the ground-floor restaurant. They had steak sandwiches and coffee, but were treated 'as though we had really spent some money'. Fish cookery is highly praised, as in brochette of mussels with saffron rice or a main-course of plentiful mixed grilled fish that included salmon, squid, prawns, mussels and three sorts of white fish; olive oil poured over by the waiter enhanced the overall effect. Another enjoyed a simple toasted goats' cheese salad, followed by fillet steak with sauce poivrade, accompanied by baked tomatoes with garlic breadcrumbs, mange-tout and chips. Nougat glace with a raspberry sauce was more like straight praline ice-cream, but was still good. It is all delightfully old-fashioned and – for many – mightily satisfying. The mainly French wine list, short on producers names, is supplemented by a trio of southern hemisphere bottles. These are almost alone in being dignified with the names of their producers. House wine is £8.

CHEF: Philippe Tamet   PROPRIETOR: Christian Bellone   OPEN: Mon to Sat; 12.30 to 2, 6 to 11.30   CLOSED: bank hols   MEALS: alc (main courses £7.50 to £13.50). Set pre-theatre D £9.99 (2 courses). Cover £1.50   SERVICE: 12.5%, card slips closed   CARDS: Access, Amex, Visa   DETAILS: 70 seats. Private parties: 50 main room, 30 private room. Vegetarian meals. Children's helpings on request. Smart dress preferred. No-smoking area. Wheelchair access (1 step). Music. Fax: 071-831 1829

Faulkner's ⅝ £   map 11

424–426 Kingsland Road, E8 4AA   COOKING 1
071-254 6152   COST £10–£27

While many kitchens dash around with pesto, squid ink and sun-dried tomatoes, throwing coriander leaf over everything, the nation's chippies carry on as they have always done, making a virtue out of a simple formula. To do it well sounds easy, yet few make the grade. Faulkner's uses fresh fish, good batter and groundnut oil, and brings in the kids for their own two-foot menu of scampi and chips, soft drink and ice-cream. Skate, rock salmon and jellied eels ring the changes on cod, haddock, sole and plaice. Drink tea or a fair-priced wine. House white is £5.60 (£1.40 per glass).

CHEFS: Michael Webber and Patrick Gibson   PROPRIETOR: Mark Farrell   OPEN: all week; 12 to 2, 5 to 10 (11.30am to 10.30pm Sat, noon to 9pm Sun)   CLOSED: 2 weeks at Christmas, bank hol Mons   MEALS: alc (main courses £3.50 to £9.50). Minimum £2.50   SERVICE: not inc   DETAILS: 60 seats. Children's helpings. Smart dress preferred. No smoking in 1 dining-room. Music. Air-conditioned. Fax: 071-249 5661

Fifth Floor   🍾

map 13

Harvey Nichols,
109–125 Knightsbridge, SW1X 7RJ   COOKING 2
071-235 5250   COST £29–£74

A lot happens on the fifth floor, where the atmosphere has even bucked up in the evenings thanks to the brilliantly stocked food shop, wine shop, café and busy bar. The large open dining-room, by the same designer who worked on Kensington Place (see entry, London), has the air of a smart canteen. The great advantages of the shop and delicatessen are that you can walk round them first, work up an appetite and see what ingredients the kitchen has to play with. The drawback is that it can backfire if the kitchen chooses to ignore them. 'I was disappointed with the artichokes – baby bottled kind – having noted the big, fresh French ones on sale in the adjoining delicatessen,' wrote one reporter, also irked to be told that 'we don't do cheese', despite 'probably the best cheese in London on display seven yards away'.

The food is fashionable, lively, modern, inventive, and thankfully takes a few risks: sausage and couscous salad, sweetbreads on toast, and braised pig's head with creamed potatoes and fennel, for example. The cooking does not always demand a high degree of skill to bring it off, but relies on assembly of good ingredients. It also has a British vein worthy of Bibendum (see entry, London), where Henry Harris used to work, in smoked haddock fish-cakes with tartare sauce and chips, and Bury black pudding with pease pudding and mustard sauce. Praise has come for carrot and coconut soup, roast grilse with red wine sauce on a bed of celeriac, and warm pecan pie with vanilla ice-cream. Vegetables have disappointed, breads have pleased, especially caraway-flavoured rye.

A short wine list is available during the day. The big one, which only comes out on request, makes the most of the extraordinary variety the British wine market enjoys, giving bags of choice, interesting styles, fascinating bottles, wonderful producers and standard mark-ups. It is toweringly good in France, with some remarkable vintages. On top of that is an impressive choice by the glass and a good range of beers. CELLARMAN'S CHOICE: St-Véran 'Terres Noires' 1992, Dom. des Deux Roches, £17.50; Devil's Lair Pinot Noir 1992, £24.50.

CELLARMAN'S CHOICE: *Wines recommended by the restaurateur, normally more expensive than house wine.*

CHEF: Henry Harris PROPRIETOR: Harvey Nichols and Co Ltd OPEN: Mon to Sat; 12 to 3 (3.30 Sat), 6.30 to 11.30 CLOSED: 25 and 26 Dec MEALS: alc (main courses £8 to £26.50). Set L and D £17.50 (2 courses) to £21.50. Café menu D SERVICE: 12.5%, card slips closed CARDS: Access, Amex, Diners, Visa DETAILS: 110 seats. Private parties: 8 main room. Vegetarian meals. Children's helpings. Smart dress preferred. Wheelchair access (also WC). No music. Air-conditioned. Fax: 071-235 5020

Fire Station £   [NEW ENTRY]   map 11

150 Waterloo Road, SE1 8SB   COOKING 1*
071-620 2226   COST £17–£30

No prizes for guessing the origins of this place. Just in case, the words 'LCC Fire Brigade Station, A.D. 1910' remain as part of the original brick frontage and the eating area is adorned with hose and ladder. Right by Waterloo station and handy for the South Bank, the restaurant is one huge room divided into drinking at the front and eating at the back, plus the exposed kitchen where diners can watch the chefs in action. Menus are chalked on blackboards, the transience of it all elevated to a frenetic art-form. Ingredients are swapped from one dish to another, and certain things disappear altogether, as a woman desirous of fruit crumble ruefully noted halfway through her main course.

Culinary idioms are liberally mixed and matched, so that one dinner took in an impressive chilled Japanese consommé with prawns and two types of seaweed, 'wonderfully rare and tender' chargrilled onglet steak with béarnaise and 'four huge chips', and a very effective espresso granita. Something of the spirit of emergency of the building's fire-fighting days pervades the service: 'Coffee was brought about five seconds after the desserts.' For those in the mood, the Fire Station will be a valued addition to the area. Wines too are chalked on a board, with house selections at £7.25.

CHEF: Dan Evans PROPRIETOR: Regent Inns plc OPEN: Mon to Sat; 12.30 to 2.30 (3 Sat), 6.30 to 11.30 CLOSED: 25 Dec, 1 Jan, bank hols MEALS: alc (main courses £6 to £9) SERVICE: not inc, card slips closed CARDS: Access, Amex, Diners, Visa DETAILS: 95 seats. Private parties: 20 main room, 60 private room. Vegetarian meals. Children welcome. Wheelchair access (1 step; also WC). Music. Air-conditioned

First Floor   map 12

186 Portobello Road, W11 1LA   COOKING 1
071-243 0072   COST £26–£47

This appropriately named restaurant sits above a bar on a central stretch of the Portobello Road. The antiques in the street market closely resemble those inside. Bacchanalian decorations, a profusion of dried leaves and roots, mismatching chairs and tables give an air of genteel decadence. Not unbearably trendy, it made 'an agreeably eccentric place to have lunch' for one reporter. At times the room can be crowded and bustling with stylish folk who come for food that is not just Mediterranean but Atlantic, Pacific and slightly North Sea as well. How about baked Nile perch with palm heart and a dried shrimp and coconut sauce, or salmon fish-cakes with coconut polenta and a splash of sweet-sour-chilli Thai sauce? The chef, incidentally, is a Brazilian who has worked in New York. Had enough? There's more: mini-pizzas, gazpacho heavily laden with the taste of raw onion, and almost-right summer pudding. The kitchen is happy to assemble ingredients into likeable dishes, but stops short of serious cooking. Italian bread comes with spicy olive oil for dipping, service may be laconic, and the shortish wine list has some soothing prices. House Italian is £9.50 (£3.50 per glass).

CHEF: Nilton Campos   PROPRIETOR: Raymond Blundell   OPEN: all week; 12 to 5, 7.30 to 11.30 (12 to 10 Sun)   CLOSED: 25 Dec, 1 Jan   MEALS: alc (main courses £8 to £14). Cover £1.50 D SERVICE: not inc (12% for 10 or more), card slips closed   CARDS: Access, Amex, Diners, Visa DETAILS: 125 seats. Private parties: 60 main room, 28 and 35 private rooms. Vegetarian meals. Children's helpings. Music. Fax: 071-221 9440

▲ Four Seasons Hotel ♥

map 14

Hamilton Place, Park Lane, W1A 1AZ
071-499 0888

COOKING 3*
COST £32–80

Jean-Christophe Novelli is an evolving chef. After cooking at Provence in Lymington, Hampshire to great acclaim, he came to London with a bagful of confidence and stepped into Bruno Loubet's shoes in the poshest part of the West End. It is a big responsibility to impress the pants off people and prove a good investment. Novelli is also, now, part of a larger organisation, one that moves more slowly. The result is that the cooking, so far, is largely technique-led, and not quite as deft or responsive as it might be. He has laid a solid foundation, and now needs to lighten up, relax and let rip. When he is firing on all cylinders, it is presumed he will go like a rocket.

The dining-room aims for classical elegance, but still feels like a hotel dining-room. This is West End cooking at West End prices, but Novelli does not rely on the usual run of expensive ingredients. He revels in seafood – haddock, sea bream and lots of shellfish – and serves them variously between layers of filo pastry, with a vegetable risotto and sea-urchin sauce, or gently braised in beer.

A love of offal comes to a head, so to speak, in a main course of pig's trotter, pig's tail, oxtail, sweetbreads, brains, and poached ox tongue, which very nearly works. It all seemed to one reporter so dark and deeply flavoured as to resemble 'an operatic aria for five basses', and the pigs' tails on this occasion were so lacking in flesh that the reporter could hardly get a note out of them. But mastery of technique is not in question. A lobster mousse wrapped in thin cannelloni, the flavour echoed in a creamy sauce, is a fine example of its kind. The lengths Novelli will go to are shown in a dish of rabbit: the saddle boned and stuffed with a mousse, a cutlet (with tiny bone handle) encased in a soufflé mixture similar in flavour to the mousse, and a confit of the leg. He sure can cook, this dish tells us, but where is the zip, where are the flavour contrasts that have us on the edge of our seats? Probably still wrapped up and waiting to be unleashed.

Puddings sound good – a light rice pudding flavoured with star-anise and cardamom, served with poached pear in sangria, or crispy almond tart with warm mango and a passion-fruit sorbet, for example – although in practice they can be slightly off-beam. Service is what we expect of grand hotels, and the wine waiter deserves special mention for being helpful but not too directive. Wine prices are high, but the list is a good one in the sense that it covers a lot of ground just about everywhere it touches down. Think of a wine: it's probably here. There are stacks of half-bottles and a page of mineral waters. Nearly a dozen house wines (from £14), all available by the glass (from £2.80), are very welcome. CELLARMAN'S CHOICE: Saint-Véran. Vieilles Vignes 1992, Georges Duboeuf, £23.50; Château Lyonnat Cru Classé 1989, £28.

CHEF: Jean-Christophe Novelli   PROPRIETOR: Four Seasons Group   OPEN: all week; 12.30 to 3, 7 to 10.30   MEALS: alc (main courses £18.50 to £28). Set L Mon to Sat £25, Sun £28, Set D £45   SERVICE: net prices, card slips closed   CARDS: Access, Amex, Diners, Visa   DETAILS: 55 seats. Private parties: 8 main room, 12, 14 and 30 private rooms. Car park. Vegetarian meals on request. Healthy eating options. Children's helpings. Smart dress preferred. No pipes in dining-room. Wheelchair access (also WC). No music. Air-conditioned   ACCOMMODATION: 227 rooms, all with bath/shower. TV. Phone. Air-conditioned. B&B £247 to £303. Rooms for disabled. Lift. Children welcome. Baby facilities. Small dogs welcome. Afternoon teas. Fax: 071-493 6629

French House Dining Room

map 15

49 Dean Street, W1V 5HL
071-437 2477

COOKING 2
COST £23–£41

'The French' lives on. The pub on the ground floor is now inhabited by a new generation of Soho bohemians with no memory of the wartime gatherings, champagne and Gauloise cigarettes that turned it into a legend. Up a flight of stairs is the restaurant, a little dining-room enlarged by mirrors that felt very 'old Soho' to one visitor. An open window serves as air-conditioning, picture lights hang over non-existent pictures, and the chairs are hard wood. The place buzzes with conversation, noise and activity.

The menus are changed twice daily, which can stretch a kitchen, but the results on the plate are generally fresh and enterprising. Here are dishes ancient and modern, fashionable and homespun. 'Splendid' grilled lamb's tongue gets a sorrel vinaigrette, venison sausages are served with lentils, and smoked quail is paired with dandelion. Elsewhere, you find roast belly of pork with red cabbage, meatballs with mash, Jerusalem artichokes with fennel and red onions, and sweetbreads with 'healthily' fresh watercress garnished with huge caper berries on stems. Bread is home-made, cheeses are British, and puddings carry on in similar vein. Service can be speedy, but it is well-informed and interested. The short wine list is patriotically French. House wine is £8.95.

CHEFS: Fergus Henderson and Margot Clayton   PROPRIETORS: Jon Spiteri, Fergus Henderson and Margot Clayton   OPEN: all week; 12.30 to 3, 6.30 to 11.30 (10.30 Sun)   MEALS: alc (main courses £7 to £15)   SERVICE: not inc   CARDS: Access, Amex, Diners, Visa   DETAILS: 30 seats. Private parties: 35 main room. Vegetarian meals. Children welcome. No music

Fulham Road

NEW ENTRY   map 13

257–259 Fulham Road, SW3 6HY
071-351 7823

COOKING 3
COST £22–£55

'Stephen Bull is now following in Worrall-Thompson's footsteps as gastronomic empire-builder,' opines one observer, although the cooking is not as off-the-cuff in Bull's empire. This third venture, in the heart of Chelsea, is just the place for a bit of decorative whimsy. Walls are chessboard squares in varying shades of cream, hung with black and white photographs, and the aesthetically clean lines are interrupted by the black and gold animal-print fabric. It is all a shade softer than either Stephen Bull in Blandford Street or Stephen Bull's Bistro and Bar (see entries, London), just bold enough to arouse interest, yet neutral enough as a background for colourful customers to paint themselves a place. A legitimate niggle from one reporter is that, although the restaurant consists of two interconnecting rooms, neither is designated as no-smoking.

The team is a strong one, Richard Corrigan having cooked impressively at Mulligan's and Bentley's. The food is not a committee compromise but a fresh-faced and interesting amalgam of the two: hot buttered oysters with caviare – 'five in a portion and plenty' – from Corrigan, and 'exquisite' banana meringue with butterscotch from Bull. Constant invention and movement mean that ingredients get jiggled round and combined in ever-changing ways to produce, for example, a mousse of broad beans wrapped in Serrano ham with gazpacho cream on an early menu; on the same menu was a risotto of walnuts, celery and Gorgonzola. Later, the beans and ham were turned into a risotto; on another occasion the risotto used crab and peas. It is an enterprising merry-go-round that generally delights.

Despite comments about unbalanced flavourings, many dishes have pleased a wide number, including superbly fresh and perfectly roasted fillets of red mullet 'full of real flavour and succulence', boudin of rabbit and langoustines, and hot chocolate soufflé. Salads abound – crab and crispy pork with black beans and lime, for example – adding to the impression of lightness. Bread is decent, especially the one with cheese and smoked ham. Service has on occasion been up and down, although praise for head of house is unstinting. Reporters in the spring of 1994 felt that the set lunch eclipsed that of many competitors for quality and value. The short wine list is well chosen, varied, up-to-date and moderately priced. House wine is £10.50.

CHEF: Richard Corrigan   PROPRIETOR: Stephen Bull   OPEN: all week; 12 to 2, 6.30 to 11.15   CLOSED: bank hols, 1 week Christmas   MEALS: alc (main courses £10.50 to £16). Set L £14.50 (2 courses) to £17.50   SERVICE: not inc, card slips closed   CARDS: Access, Amex, Visa   DETAILS: 85 seats. Private parties: 12 private room. Vegetarian meals. Children's helpings. Wheelchair access. No music. Air-conditioned. Fax: 071-490 3127

Fung Shing £

map 15

15 Lisle Street, WC2H 7BE
071-437 1539

COOKING 3
COST £19–£57

This elegant restaurant, deep in Soho Chinatown, continues to deliver arguably the finest food of its kind in the capital. The interior is a stylish mix of greenery, paintings and smartly laid tables. Most reporters continue to heap praise on the quality of the food: 'balance and care are evident in every dish', 'hard to fault anything', 'no detectable flaws' are typical comments. What impresses is the care and thoughtfulness that goes into the cooking: here is a kitchen that can balance refinement with strong, traditional flavours. Occasional mishaps, such as, on one occasion, 'tasteless, tough venison' with yellow-bean sauce, are far outweighed by the list of successes.

Diners tend to opt for mainstream dishes such as wun-tun soup, king prawns with garlic, steamed scallops with black-bean sauce, baked crab with chilli, and sweet-and-sour chicken, along with well-handled vegetables, mixed noodles and rice. The mainly Cantonese menu also promises more esoteric specialities, along the lines of carp cooked in 'superior sauce', eel with coriander, crispy fried intestine and sizzling veal. Invest £35 and you can also sample braised whole abalone with oyster sauce. Service veers between 'cursory and slow' and 'too quick, but otherwise 10 out of 10'. The wine list is a classy match for the food, with some notably serious clarets and burgundies as well as New World bottles. House wine is £8.50.

CHEF: Kwan Fu   PROPRIETOR: Forum Restaurant Ltd   OPEN: all week; noon to 11.30   MEALS: alc (main courses £6 to £16). Set L and D £11 to £12. Minimum £8.50 D   SERVICE: not inc, card slips closed   CARDS: Access, Amex, Diners, Visa   DETAILS: 80 seats. Private parties: 50 main room, 30 private room. Vegetarian meals. Children welcome. Smart dress preferred. Music. Air-conditioned. Fax: 071-734 0284

La Gaulette   map 14

53 Cleveland Street, W1P 5PQ   COOKING 1*
071-580 7608 and 323 4210   COST £28–£53

This fish restaurant in the shadow of the Telecom Tower is owned by Mauritian chef and entrepreneur Sylvain Ho Wing Cheong. Making extensive use of the best from the daily markets, it offers an impressive range of tropical fish, shellfish and crustacea in addition to more familiar specimens. The operation runs on two levels, bistro and restaurant, and there are several menus, the *carte* being joined by a series of set-price deals, including 'gastronomique' menus at £26. The diversity of Mauritian culinary culture is reflected in dishes such as lobster grilled with tomatoes, herbs and chilli, or red snapper with ginger and spring onions. Parrot-fish gets the chilli treatment as well, while bourgeois comes with a green peppercorn sauce. Sauces are usually sufficiently well judged not to overpower the various fish. A quartet who signed up for a 'gastronomique' menu, however, were nonplussed to find the sauce with the third-course fish bearing a remarkable similarity to the sauces that had accompanied the first and second courses. House French wines are £8.95.

CHEF/PROPRIETOR: Sylvain Ho Wing Cheong   OPEN: Mon to Sat, exc Sat D; 12 to 3, 6.30 to 11 CLOSED: bank hol Mons, 25 and 26 Dec   MEALS: alc (main courses £11 to £18). Bistro Set L £5 (2 courses), Set D £8 (2 courses); restaurant Set L £13.95 (2 courses), Set D £18.95 to £26 SERVICE: not inc   CARDS: Access, Amex, Diners, Visa   DETAILS: restaurant 30 seats, bistro 40 seats. Private parties: 40 private room. Vegetarian meals. Children welcome. Smart dress preferred. Wheelchair access (1 step). Music. Fax: 081-697 7255

Le Gavroche ❢   map 14

43 Upper Brook Street, W1Y 1PF   COOKING 4*
071-408 0881 and 499 1826   COST £36–£119

'A bargain,' wrote one reporter, and another agreed. They were not referring to the wine list, nor to dinner, but to the set lunch, where there are no hidden extras, bread is replenished, coffee keeps coming, and mineral water and half a bottle of wine are included. It is less of a bargain at dinner when the same menu shoots up to £48 without wine, exposing the limited puddings: cheese, ice-cream or sorbet, or melon surprise. But anything that makes grand cooking more approachable is welcome.

The basement dining-room is 'gentlemen's club' décor, but with English stiffness utterly banished and replaced by French style and efficiency. Ladies are given menus without prices, even when they have made the booking, which is probably meant to seem gallant, although it is now merely anachronistic. The beauty is that the place is serious without being solemn. 'You can eat magnificent food, but you don't have to be high-minded about it.' Even the dome-lifting is not prolonged theatre, and it is a mark of high professionalism, as one reporter observed, for so many staff to remain unobtrusive.

The cooking is classical French, which, almost by definition, does not change. Michel Junior is not likely to develop a sudden interest in bruschetta and sun-dried tomatoes; although he did serve râble de lapin on a round of polenta, an item which the menu could not bring itself to mention. The modifications he undertakes are slight, subtle, gentle, gradual, resulting perhaps in a bit less cream and weight, but not much less. Otherwise the enterprise sails its steady course, unbuffeted by the winds of change whipping up around it. This can make it seem just a little lacking in vitality. But there is no more point in accusing the Gavroche of being conservative than there is in accusing the Queen of being elitist: that is just the way things are. The cooking is absolutely correct, totally impressive in execution, difficult to fault for quality. The excitement resides in the fact that it is all done so well.

Among changes is a different approach to the classic soufflé suissesse, now lighter than before but 'with too much egg white, too much like île flottante', for one reporter who rated Albert's version superior. The prince-and-pauper aspect of French cooking, in which highly refined and earthy foods co-exist, is here exemplified by, on the one hand, mousseline of lobster, or a dish of asparagus, de-veined langoustines and morels in a creamy sauce with a pleasantly sweetish caramel flavour. The other strand shows in daube de boeuf à la bourgeoise, and in an 'absolutely brilliant' saucisse de Lyon with poitrine de porc and long-cooked white haricot beans. The division breaks down with puddings, which are good rather than outstanding: light omelette Rothschild, tartelette tiède of pears, and a praline surprise which comes in a moulded tuile looking like a neat gift-box tied with string, and in which decoration and fiddle were the lasting impressions.

Bread is ordinary, the cheeseboard superlative (and the waiter knowledgeable about them), and wines are as splendid as they are heftily marked up. Still, if you have a million quid's worth tied up, they have to earn their keep. It is largely outside Bordeaux and Burgundy that bottles under £20 are to be found, but the sommelier is very helpful, not at all snooty, and it is perfectly possible to drink well for a reasonable outlay. There is not a thing from Australia, but house wine is £16.50 and nine are available by the glass between £3.50 and £50. CELLARMAN'S CHOICE: Chablis St-Martin 'Cuvée Albert Roux' 1993, Dom. Laroche, £29.50; St-Emilion, Ch.Vieux Sarpe 1985. £29.50.

'The staff had decided that Table 11 was to be ours, and there then followed a short discussion between them as to which table actually was number 11, and who was looking after it.' (On eating in Essex)

CHEF: Michel Roux Junior   PROPRIETOR: Le Gavroche Ltd   OPEN: Mon to Fri; 12 to 2, 7 to 11
CLOSED: 23 Dec to 3 Jan, bank hols   MEALS: alc (main courses £24 to £34). Set L £36, Set D £48
to £75   SERVICE: net prices   CARDS: Access, Amex, Diners, Visa   DETAILS: 60 seats. Private
parties: 10 main room, 20 private room. Vegetarian meals. Children welcome. Jacket and tie. No
cigars in dining-room. No music. Air-conditioned. Fax: 071-491 4387 and 409 0939

Gay Hussar

map 15

2 Greek Street, W1V 6NB   COOKING 2
071-437 0973   COST £25–£48

For 38 of its 40 years in business this great Soho landmark has been in the *Guide*.
The Gay Hussar has a faintly Bohemian air and, perhaps due to the red and gold
décor, betrays a sense that it may once have been a tiny bit grander.

It attracts regulars – 'Our liking for their food is undimmed after 19 years of
dinners there when in London' – but there is no need to pretend to have a
Hungarian relative: everybody gets the same treatment. 'I have never had a bad
dish, let alone a bad meal at any time over many years, and they don't know me
from Adam!' The food responds to fashion like the weather to wishful thinking.
Who else serves Transylvanian stuffed cabbage, chilled cherry soup, quenelles
of carp, or Serbian-style chicken with egg barley? It may all taste a bit less exotic
than it sounds, but the food is full of flavour, and not ashamed of bulk or fat. 'It is
amusing to see tourists stunned by the size of the portions; it must seem to them
the bargain price of a lifetime.' The wine list is so endearingly out of touch it even
lists Bull's Blood. House Hungarian is £9 (£2.50 per glass).

CHEF: Laszlo Holecz   PROPRIETOR: Restaurant Partnership plc   OPEN: Mon to Sat; 12.30 to
2.30, 5.30 to 10.45   CLOSED: bank hols   MEALS: alc (main courses £11 to £15). Set L £16
SERVICE: 12.5%, card slips closed   CARDS: Access, Amex, Diners, Visa   DETAILS: 70 seats.
Private parties: 20 main room, 12 private room. Vegetarian meals. Children's helpings on
request. Smart dress preferred. Wheelchair access. No music. Fax: 071-437 9920

Gilbert's 🍾

map 13

2 Exhibition Road, SW7 2HF   COOKING 1
071-589 8947   COST £23–£41

If you are dining here in the Prom season, you will find it a pleasant walk up or
down Exhibition Road, depending on whether you are eating before or after
your concert. Erstwhile partner Ann Wregg sold her share of the business in
September 1993, but Julia Chalkley cooks on. The homely feel to the interior,
with dishes arriving from the kitchen by dumb waiter, and breads such as
walnut and onion all home-made, has been lovingly preserved.

The occasionally misbegotten experimentalism of recent years has now been
curtailed in favour of tried-and-true favourites such as baked mushrooms stuffed
with goats' cheese and thyme, provençale fish stew with aïoli, and lapin
moutarde and entrecôte béarnaise. Chocolate tipsy cake is a stalwart. There are
still too many supplementary charges for a short prix fixe. One man went home
happy after a lunch of mussels cooked in Pineau des Charentes, brochette de
boeuf, raisin and armagnac ice-cream, and buckets of coffee. The wine list,
arranged by grape variety, has long been an absolute treasure. Half-bottles alone

are superb, and the main list contains so much that is good at such sane prices that choice is a matter of great and lingering difficulty. A wine club has now been inaugurated. House wines start at £8.90 for Côtes du Ventoux.

CHEFS: Julia Chalkley and Gina Mahsoudi   PROPRIETOR: Julia Chalkley   OPEN: Mon to Fri; 12 to 2, 6 to 10 (pre- and post-Promenade concert meals)   MEALS: alc (main courses £5.50 to £10.50). Set L £9.50 to £14.50 (2 courses), Set D £14.50 to £19.50 (2 courses)   SERVICE: 12.5% (not inc for groups of 6 or more)   CARDS: Access, Amex, Diners, Visa   DETAILS: 32 seats. 4 tables outside. Private parties: 30 main room. Vegetarian meals. No babies or toddlers D. Music.

Gopal's of Soho   map 15

12 Bateman St, W1V 5TD	COOKING 1
071-434 1621 and 0840	COST £21–£39

Gopal's, with its modest but pleasingly decorated dining-room, is one of the more consistent and reliable 'new wave' Indian restaurants in the capital. The menu has some noticable regional overtones: Karnataka (in the South) provides 'meenu' (a fish curry), and coconut rice is also prepared in the South Indian style; Goa is represented by mutton xacutti (a fiery speciality made with coconut and vinegar) and Goan murg. Cheemen masala is a Malabar dish of king prawns; dum ka murg is steamed chicken cooked in a sealed pot with Hyderabadi spices and herbs. Thalis are well reported: a party of 25 celebrating the reunion of the tour company of *The Sound of Music* found each dish 'succulent, accurately spiced, delicate or more pungent, depending on what it was'. Rice and nan bread are 'light and tasty'. Service is generally tolerant and friendly. Cobra beer suits the food, but the wine list (put together by consultant David Wolfe) is well worth serious consideration. House wine is £7.90.

CHEF/PROPRIETOR: N.P. Pittal   OPEN: all week; 12 to 2.45, 6 to 11.15   CLOSED: 25 and 26 Dec   MEALS: alc (main courses £5.85 to £10.35). Cover £1   SERVICE: not inc   CARDS: Access, Amex, Visa   DETAILS: 50 seats. Private parties: 50 main room. Vegetarian meals. Children welcome. Smart dress preferred. Wheelchair access (1 step). Music. Air-conditioned. Fax: 071-434 1621

Grahame's Seafare £   map 14

38 Poland Street, W1V 3DA	COOKING 1
071-437 3788 and 0975	COST £20–£45

There is something reassuring and comforting about a regime that seems ageless. As one regular put it: 'They [the staff] have all been here for years. The customers delight in those they meet and thoroughly enjoy the cooking of those they do not.' Fish, as fresh as could be, is grilled, steamed, deep-fried in matzo meal or cooked in milk and butter, and served with hearty helpings of 'excellent' chips. Other specialities are old-school stalwarts such as sole bonne femme and plaice Mornay. The Jewish connection shows in gefilte fish, chopped herring, and cream cheese with smatana, and in the provision of rye bread, and sweet and sour cucumbers. A handful of well-chosen wines offer the prospect of decent drinking without breaking the bank. House wine is £8.25.

The Guide *always appreciates hearing about changes of chef or owner.*

CHEF/PROPRIETOR: Chetin Ismet   OPEN: Mon to Sat; 12 to 2.45, 5.30 to 9 (8 Fri and Sat)   MEALS: alc (main courses £8 to £18)   SERVICE: not inc, card slips closed   CARDS: Access, Amex, Diners, Visa   DETAILS: 84 seats. Private parties: 84 main room. Children's helpings. Smart dress preferred. No music. Air-conditioned. Fax: 081-294 1808

Granita

map 11

127 Upper Street, N1 1QP
071-226 3222

COOKING 2*
COST £21–£35

A pair who value the Almeida Theatre higher than rubies now give thanks to Granita for making an Islington evening even sweeter. It is but a minute's trot from the final curtain to last orders. Some protest that our description last year of the interior was a touch unfeeling. Austere it may be, but for once the simplicity of bare wooden tables, bare floor and pictureless walls is thought a genuine foil to the food. 'There is nothing of minimalist affectation here,' wrote one. 'We found it calming.'

Ahmed Kharshoum's food works well against this backdrop, the clear Mediterranean/West Coast flavours ringing out in dishes such as roasted aubergine with plum tomato and bruschetta, or couscous salad with apricot, or ginger, pine-nuts and watercress. Linguine is served with red onion, olives and capers, chargrilled yellowfin tuna with potato cake, and roasted rack of lamb with puréed flageolets and grilled courgettes. A spring dinner that ranged through bruschetta slathered with aubergine and tahini paste, 'excellent' fettuccine with sun-dried tomatoes, rosemary and garlic ('a simple dish made special') and 'delicious' sweet duck breast sauced with orange and Grand Marnier pleased one couple mightily. They finished with fine pear and almond tart and chocolate chip ice-cream. Peripheral details, such as the onion bread and good cafetière coffee, are also endorsed. Granita is getting it right.

In keeping with the restrained ambience, a short but intelligent selection of wines is offered. France, Italy and the New World get roughly equal billing, and there is red or white Rioja. Easy-going prices help matters too. House French is £8.50.

CHEF: Ahmed Kharshoum   PROPRIETORS: Ahmed Kharshoum and Vicky Leffman   OPEN: Tue to Sun, exc Tue L; 12.30 to 2.30, 6.30 to 10.30 (10 Sun)   CLOSED: 10 days Christmas, 5 days Easter, 2 weeks Aug   MEALS: alc (main courses £6.50 to £11.50). Set L £11.50 (2 courses) to £13.50   SERVICE: not inc   CARDS: Access, Visa   DETAILS: 62 seats. Private parties: 55 main room. Vegetarian meals. Children's helpings. Wheelchair access (1 step). No music. Air-conditioned

Great Nepalese £

map 11

48 Eversholt Street, NW1 1DA
071-388 6737

COOKING 1*
COST £10–£32

This is a family business. 'On my last visit,' observed a devotee, 'the main attraction was Gopal's grandson, a mysterious child with an unnerving godlike aura.' The most amenable of restaurants, the Great Nepalese continues to serve Euston commuters, students and Camden Town locals with unfailing good humour and gutsy food. The menu has its share of standard Indian curries and tandoori dishes, but the Nepalese specialities are better. Masco bara (deep-fried lentil cakes), mamocha (little steamed pastries) and herby bhutuwa chicken are some of the high points. Toriko sag is reckoned to be 'the best Indian spinach dish in London', and it's worth exploring the black dhal, vivid green coriander relish and gundruko achar (made from Tibetan pickled dry vegetables). Excellent boiled basmati rice and good breads are the back-up. Drink lager or spicy masala tea and finish with a shot of devastating Nepalese rum. House wine is £6.55 a litre.

CHEF: Mr Masuk   PROPRIETOR: Gopal Manandhar   OPEN: all week; 12 to 2.45, 6 to 11.45   CLOSED: 25 and 26 Dec   MEALS: alc (main courses £3 to £8.50). Set L £5.75 to £11, Set D £11. Minimum £5   SERVICE: 10%, card slips closed   CARDS: Access, Amex, Diners, Visa   DETAILS: 48 seats. Private parties: 34 main room. Vegetarian meals. Children's helpings. Music

Greek Valley £

map 11

130 Boundary Road, NW8 0HR
071-624 3217

COOKING 1
COST £16–£26

The Bosnics' restaurant is useful in what is a rather barren area off Abbey Road. Plants fill the window space and a large Greek mural is painted on one wall. Service is always polite and welcoming. The menu stays within limits, and the food is generally on target. Grilled red pepper with vinegar and garlic dressing, grilled halloumi cheese and mushrooms in garlic butter have drawn praise from the list of meze. The kitchen also copes well with standards such as moussaka and kleftiko ('I've never eaten better' was one enthusiastic comment) as well as more unusual items like briami (baked mixed vegetables). The midweek special menu (Monday to Thursday) is great value. Workaday Greek Cypriot wines loom large on the list. House wine is £6.50.

CHEF: Petros Bosnic   PROPRIETORS: Petros and Effie Bosnic   OPEN: Mon to Sat, D only (L by arrangement); 6 to 11.45   MEALS: alc (main courses £5.50 to £10). Set D Mon to Thu £7.95   SERVICE: not inc   CARDS: Access, Visa   DETAILS: 75 seats. Private parties: 42 main room, 30 private room. Vegetarian meals. Children's helpings. Smart dress preferred. Wheelchair access (1 step). Music. Air-conditioned (partly)

Greenhouse

map 14

27A Hays Mews, W1X 7RJ
071-499 3331 and 3314

COOKING 3*
COST £28–£62

'Tucked away, yet in the middle of Mayfair' is the setting. The green canopied entrance leads past interesting bits of topiary, sculptures, and wooden effigies that reminded one reporter 'of the pagan images of English folklore and morris dancing'. Well, it takes all sorts. There is no waving of limp hankies by the staff – service is mostly chatty, and on the ball – but the link with traditional British ways is central to the cooking. Gary Rhodes is a champion of the timeless national larder, with a talent for rescuing 'heritage food' from the museum and turning it into lively dishes that suit contemporary tastes. He is a great revitaliser of the past, a get-up-and-go TV cook, and his gestures are full of vigour, youthful enthusiasm and bags of talent.

Tub-thumping chauvinism is not the motive force, however. Rhodes is propelled, very simply, by what works on the plate. Consider beef carpaccio, braised oxtail, and date crunchie with golden syrup ice-cream. What do they all have in common? Nothing except Gary Rhodes. He borrows, combines, transforms and, if all else fails, invents whatever he thinks will work. So do many others, but the strike rate here is exceptionally high, including fillet of smoked haddock with Welsh rarebit on a tomato and chive salad, grilled mackerel on mashed potatoes with fennel, artichokes and a spring onion sauce, and steamed orange sponge with marmalade ice-cream.

Some may counter that braised oxtail – a lauded regular – is a rather safe dish from the standard repertoire, and so it is, but it still dazzles: 'a big bowl of six mighty pieces, topped with English-peasant brunoise of root vegetables. Superb meat, oozing succulence, and around it an elementally sticky gravy that is rich without being cloying, and concentrated without being Marmite. It adhered to the lips, and drops of it solidified on my specs as they lay on the table.' This is seriously sensual food. Even plain chicken breast with grilled mushrooms and braised red onions is 'brilliant'. Reporters have not been enthusiastic about the £2.95 charge for mineral water, but all manage to find a suitable wine from the short list of 21 bottles. House Gamay and Sauvignon Blanc are £10.50.

CHEF: Gary Rhodes   PROPRIETOR: David Levin   OPEN: all week, exc Sat L; 12 to 2.30 (12.30 to 3 Sun), 7 to 11 (6.30 to 10 Sun)   CLOSED: bank hols   MEALS: alc (main courses £6.50 to £18.50). Set L Sun £18.50. Cover £1   SERVICE: not inc   CARDS: Access, Amex, Diners, Visa   DETAILS: 90 seats. Private parties: 14 main room. Vegetarian meals. Children's helpings. No children under 6 Mon to Sat. Smart dress preferred. Wheelchair access (3 steps). Music. Air-conditioned. Fax: 071-225 0011

Grill St Quentin

map 13

3 Yeoman's Row, SW3 2AL   COOKING 1
071-581 8377   COST £25–£50

A 'stunning' floral arrangement in the centre of the room and the attractive mirrored bar provide the setting for heartily traditional, simple French brasserie fare. Only about half the main dishes are grills, while starters stress seafood. Crab mayonnaise was a Breton specimen, 'the best crab I have ever tasted by a long way', and served with a rich, if salty, mayonnaise. Clumsiness was evident on one occasion, however, in the handling of fresh oysters and the over-enthusiastic grilling of a poussin, but gigot d'agneau carved from the trolley proved to be 'good, reasonably tender' meat of 'decent flavour' accompanied by 'excellent' mushy beans. Crisp pommes frites are usually enjoyed, but a dinner visitor who ordered new potatoes in their skins found them unsettlingly black and tasting 'metallic'. Reblochon grilled rarebit-style on thin toast was 'very tasty', while lemon tart, according to one reporter, came with fine lemon sorbet. Wines are exclusively French. Clarets go back to 1970, but prices otherwise are distinctly below what one would expect for Knightsbridge. House wines are £8.60.

'The guinea-fowl proved a bit of a disappointment. It looked as if someone had sat on it.' (On eating in Wales)

CHEF: Eric Bidaut   PROPRIETOR: The Savoy Group plc   OPEN: all week; 12 to 3 (3.30 Sun), 6.30 to 11.30 (10.30 Sun)   MEALS: alc (main courses £9 to £17.50). Set L £8 (2 courses)   SERVICE: 12.5%, card slips closed   CARDS: Access, Amex, Diners, Visa   DETAILS: 140 seats. Private parties: 25 main room. Vegetarian meals. Children welcome. Smart dress preferred. No music. Air-conditioned. Fax: 071-584 6064

▲ Halcyon Hotel NEW ENTRY map 12

129 Holland Park Avenue, W11 3UT   COOKING 1
071-221 5411   COST £31–£60

The heart may sink at the prospect of yet another basement restaurant, especially one attached to a hotel, but the feel of the Room at the Halcyon is light and garden-fresh, 'almost Mediterranean', with tiled floors, whitewashed walls, paintings for sale, mirrors framed in leafy mahogany and 'tortured trees'. The menu is expensive and trendy, including tartare of marinated salmon with lime yogurt and pickled cucumber, and pan-fried chicken livers with horseradish mashed potato. An Asian influence is brought to bear in a dish that involves pan-fried monkfish with curry-spiced chickpeas, a 'blow-away' cream and coriander sauce, plus rice cake and mango chutney.

'If money were no object this would be an OK place,' writes one, and the high prices do come in for comment by reporters. Enough supporters have come forward, however, to sing the Room's praises. Endorsements have come for steamed and fried duck 'cooked more or less Szechuan-style', chargrilled salmon with stir-fried vegetables, and pan-fried scallops with marinated cucumber and less-than-fiery wasabi. Wines begin at £12.50 and go rapidly upwards.

CHEF: Martin Hadden   PROPRIETOR: Halcyon Hotel Corporation Ltd   OPEN: all week, exc Sat L; 12.30 to 2.30, 7 to 10.30 (11 Sat)   CLOSED: bank hols (exc 25 Dec)   MEALS: alc (main courses £12 to £18). Set L £18 (2 courses), Set D £21   SERVICE: not inc, card slips closed   CARDS: Access, Amex, Diners, Visa   DETAILS: 70 seats. 12 tables outside. Private parties: 80 main room, 10 private room. Vegetarian meals. Children's helpings on request. Smart dress preferred. Music. Air-conditioned   ACCOMMODATION: 43 rooms, all with bath/shower. TV. Phone. Air-conditioned. B&B £174 to £578. Rooms for disabled. Lift. Children welcome. Baby facilities. Pets by arrangement. Afternoon teas. Tennis. Confirm by 6. Fax: 071-229 8516

▲ The Halkin   map 13

5 Halkin Street, SW1X 7DJ   COOKING 1
071-333 1234   COST £33–£60

The Halkin is just off Belgrave Square, so smart décor is expected. The cool and comfortable dining-room has good linen, china and glassware, a long-stemmed rose on each table, and the cooking leans towards Italy. At one meal, ravioli enclosed clams and broccoli (from the fixed-price menu) and pleasantly fishy lobster from the *carte*. But saucing can be a let-down, and savoury dishes are left in the shade by desserts. Tiramisù is a proper one with a central core of moist macaroon, lightly boozy and tasting of coffee and chocolate, albeit with a rather flashy net of spun sugar on top. Orange tart is an individual crisp pastry case with a sharp custardy filling, lightly browned on top, with a very sweet and light ginger sauce. Cheeses include Taleggio and coarsely cut Parmesan in good health. Coffee is strong and freshly made. Appetisers and petits fours are not highlights. Ordinary brown and white rolls are superior to the bread offered with cheese. The Italian wines are impressive, although Belgravia prices put many of them beyond reasonable reach. House Bardolino (from Masi, at £14) and Soave (from Pieropan, at £15) are good.

CHEF: Stefano Cavallini   PROPRIETOR: Xuo International   OPEN: all week, exc L Sat and Sun; 12.30 to 2.30, 7.30 to 11 (7 to 10 Sun)   MEALS: alc (main courses £15.50 to £19). Set L £19.50 (2 courses) to £26   SERVICE: net prices, card slips closed   CARDS: Access, Amex, Diners, Visa   DETAILS: 50 seats. Private parties: 40 main room, 26 private room. Car park. Vegetarian meals. Children welcome. Smart dress preferred. No cigars/pipes in dining-room. Wheelchair access (also WC). Music. Air-conditioned   ACCOMMODATION: 41 rooms, all with bath/shower. TV. Phone. Air-conditioned. B&B £233.50 to £302. Deposit: 100%. Rooms for disabled. Lift. Children welcome. Baby facilities. Afternoon teas. Confirm by 6. Fax: 071-333 1100 (*The Which? Hotel Guide*)

Harveys   map 10

2 Bellevue Road, SW17 7EG	COOKING 3
081-672 0114	COST £29–£43

Marco Pierre White has moved on to The Restaurant at the Hyde Park Hotel (see entry, London). Mark Williamson was his sous-chef when Harveys first opened, then went walkabout to Wales, Australia and the Far East, before returning to base. Harveys, too, has returned to its roots. 'This is a serious, stylish local restaurant serving interesting and well-prepared food,' enthused one reporter. Customers are smart, affluent, mostly the wrong side of 35, and bring a certain confidence and stridency to the hardly-changed-at-all dining-room with its creamy yellows, big mirrors and slightly worn chairs. English is not the first language of the staff, which has led to at least one garbled booking: 'We had to peer at all the names to see which one we were.' But when the place is full it fires easily on all cylinders.

The menu is static, therefore deaf and blind to the seasons, but it avoids the usual clichés and so brings an appealing freshness of its own. Half the 10 main courses are fish. If the cooking lacks the whirlwind flair of the old regime, it also lacks the expense, and the innovation and obvious ability win through despite minor shortcomings. The rustic appeal of asparagus bruschetta is muted by the more robust flavours of accompanying sun-dried tomatoes, olives, flaked Parmesan and mushrooms. But it is still an enjoyable dish, as is a light filo pastry in the form of a ravioli 'with a delicious filling of creamed lobster', prettily served in a light and creamy champagne sauce with small dice of skinned tomato and chopped chives. There is praise, too, for duck cassoulet with an excellent sausage of the leg meat, all authentic apart from the pig's trotter. Puddings are not the strongest suit, but an inspector enjoyed pecan nut zucotta, a small dome-shaped cake topped with chocolate and served with a coffee sauce. Espresso coffee is good. The wine list is a simple, reliable, round-the-world affair arranged by price, beginning at £8.50, with about half of it under £20.

'We were handed a large white plate with two small canapés nestling in the middle, like a cartoon face with squinty bloodshot eyes.' (On eating in Yorkshire)

CHEF: Mark Williamson PROPRIETOR: Larkbrace Ltd OPEN: all week, exc L Mon and Sat; 12 to 2.30, 7 to 11 MEALS: alc (main courses £10.50 to £14.50). Cover £1 SERViCE: not inc CARDS: Access, Amex, Diners, Visa DETAILS: 55 seats. Private parties: 20 main room. Vegetarian meals. Children's helpings. Smart dress preferred. Wheelchair access. No music. Air-conditioned

Hilaire ▼

map 13

68 Old Brompton Road, SW7 3LQ

COOKING 3*

071-584 8993

COST £26–£65

Although slap-bang in the middle of cosmopolitan South Kensington, Hilaire epitomises the classic neighbourhood restaurant. It seems to have been here for ever, and the atmosphere 'felt like being at a relative's dinner party' for one reporter, who noted a three-generation family celebration at one table, transatlantic foodies at the next. Expansion and refurbishment are planned as we go to press.

The cooking aspires to more than most dinner parties, and results are often exemplary, partly because they avoid fussiness and allow Bryan Webb to concentrate on essential elements. A simple crab mayonnaise stands out because it is excitingly fresh, the mainly white meat held together with the barest emulsion, spiked only with chopped chives. The food relies on input from Mr Webb's native Wales (laverbread with oysters, for example) as well as from the more usual sources, such as France, Italy, and Thailand. Ideas are put through an inventive mill, coming out with langoustine and carrot salad with Thai seasoning, roast calves' sweetbreads with pea and olive mash, and a passion-fruit and caramelised banana tart.

Flavours are gentle rather than forthright, which some people, perhaps expecting the exuberance typical of much contemporary food, may interpret as blandness. But it is not so. The style shows restraint and discipline without being conservative. Good technique and good saucing are only occasionally let down by clumsy handling, especially the toughness of items such as pigeon or duck. Lamb, however, has been technically close to perfection, cooked pink and well rested, with broad beans and a rich gravy. And carefully cooked red mullet, with crisp skin and firm, moist flesh, comes with positive but light accompaniments of Puy lentils, diced tomato with cumin, and a homely buttery sauce. The food has underlying consistency and quality, making Hilaire a benchmark of its kind: serious and classy. A two course supper is available downstairs, or upstairs after 9.30pm. Arrangement of wines by style is sensible, although prices are high (Cloudy Bay Chardonnay 1992 is three times the retail price). Half a dozen wines by the glass and three dozen half-bottles (including some interesting sweeties) are very welcome. The house selection starts at £9.75. CELLARMAN'S CHOICE: Olivet Lane Russian River Chardonnay 1989, £17.50; Penley Estate Shiraz/Cabernet 1990, £20.50.

CHEF: Bryan Webb PROPRIETORS: Bryan Webb and Dick Pyle OPEN: Mon to Sat, exc Sat L; 12.30 to 2.30, 7 to 11.30 CLOSED: bank hols MEALS: alc (main courses £12 to £18). Set L £12.50 (2 courses), Set D £16 (2 course supper) to £25.50 SERVICE: not inc CARDS: Access, Amex, Diners, Visa DETAILS: 50 seats. Private parties: 35 main room, 20 private room. Vegetarian meals. Children's helpings. No cigars/pipes in dining-room. Wheelchair access. No music. Air-conditioned. Fax: 071-581 2949

▲ *Hyde Park Hotel, The Restaurant*   NEW ENTRY   map 13

66 Knightsbridge, SW1X 7LA
071-259 5380

COOKING 4*
COST £37–£100

The blue awning juts into the street with 'Marco Pierre White' modestly picked out on it in gold. Marco has followed Nico into the grand-hotel setting, although the 'shabby secondary hotel entrance' is somewhat less than grand. It leads to an open-plan room with a sense of space, a small seating area for drinks, bright paintings and lavish disposition of tables. Marco is cooking for a different clientele than he found in Wandsworth or Chelsea. Gone are the youth and vitality of the old customers, unable to keep up with a fixed £65 dinner, to be replaced by the more elderly moneyed classes.

The food can be brilliant. 'Simply the best meal we have ever had,' wrote one who has 'tried most of them from Girardet downwards'. Understandably, lobster, caviare and foie gras abound, but they impress less than the cooking itself. In fish mode, 'outstanding turbot with an excellent herb crust' came with girolles and 'a very intense and complex sauce'. The unctuous richness of saucing delights, particularly rib-sticking in a dish of 'boiled beef'. A wonderful poached pigeon breast 'en vessie' is 'cooked rare, highly flavoured and succulent', with braised cabbage and bacon the like of which reporters have not experienced before, set off by a small turret of excellent liver mousse. 'Nothing was out of place on the plate, everything was there for a reason.' As the menu notes, this dish was first performed in 1989.

The habit of identifying the year of creation is regarded with benevolent curiosity. 'I certainly don't want to eat old favourites, I want the fire and enthusiasm of '93 and beyond,' wrote an early visitor. The *carte* is long, the cooking complex, and meals begin with a soup sampler. Skills range from 'remarkably high' to 'inexcusably careless'. One critic noted 'lots of technique but none of that wonderful passion needed to make food live', although White-watchers have been reassured by desserts. 'They were always one of the high spots of Harveys, and there is no sign of deterioration here,' says a reporter, citing as one of the finest a pyramid of nougat ice-cream topped with passion-fruit sorbet, all encased in wafer-thin slices of caramel, floating on a perfectly judged grapefruit and passion-fruit sauce.

Service, prowly and tense at times, is not always the smooth, oiled machine it might be. There are so many waiters for this and that 'you almost expect a lad to come and water the flowers'. The feel is of one man's kitchen in another man's hotel, rather than an integrated whole. Most reports mention the cost. 'There are cheaper places to eat good food.' If £65 is too much, the set-price three-course lunch at around £25 may be the way in, although the wine list does not help. A fair smattering of New World wines balances the usual list of unaffordable clarets, and although half-bottles are virtually non-existent, a dozen dessert wines by the glass are welcome. Other drinks are pricey too: 'Twelve pounds for a gin and tonic and a tomato juice takes some explaining.'

'I had meringue cake for dessert. This was probably the original for that old Glaswegian joke about ' "Is this a cake or a meringue? Naw, yer not wrang, it's a cake." '
(On eating in South Yorkshire)

CHEF: Marco Pierre White   PROPRIETOR: Marco Pierre White, Michael Caine and Claudio Pulze (The Restaurant), Forte plc (Hyde Park Hotel)   OPEN: Mon to Sat, exc Sat L; 12.30 to 2.30, 7 to 11   MEALS: Set L £25, Set D £65   SERVICE: not inc, card slips closed   CARDS: Access, Amex, Diners, Visa   DETAILS: 50 seats. Private parties: 12 main room. Vegetarian meals. Children welcome. Smart dress preferred. Wheelchair access (also WC). No music. Air-conditioned. ACCOMMODATION: 185 rooms, all with bath/shower. TV. Phone. Air-conditioned. B&B £245 to £1790. Room for disabled. Lift. Children welcome. Baby facilities. Afternoon teas.

Imperial City
map 11

Royal Exchange, Cornhill, EC3V 3LL   COOKING 1
071-626 3437   COST £22–£51

As usual in the City, expect three things. The atmosphere needs people, so lunch is the time to go. The cooking can be good, but it may be Westernised; in this case, since Ken Hom (consultant) is the guru of this school, the adaptation is done reasonably well. And three, prices are a bit on the high side. The menu is short for a Cantonese restaurant, but there is still a fair choice that includes duck in tangy mustard sauce, hot-and-sour soup, crispy lacquered quail and steamed sea bass. Regional dishes may be more token than real, but are still worth eating – for example, crackling northern-style chicken with garlic, braised red pork casserole Shanghai-style, and spicy Szechuan dan-dan noodles. In fact, noodles are among the better dishes, and the lack of MSG throughout is appreciated. Wines are very well chosen, reasonably priced, arranged by style, and help to make the package an attractive one. House wine is £8.50 (£2.20 per glass) and Tsingtao beer is £2.40.

CHEFS: K.L. Tan and Ken Hom (Consultant)   PROPRIETOR: Thai Restaurants plc   OPEN: Mon to Fri; 11.30am to 8.30pm   CLOSED: 24 to 26 Dec, 1 Jan, bank hols   MEALS: alc (main courses £6.50 to £18). Set L and D £13.90 to £24.80 (minimum 2)   SERVICE: 12.5%, card slips closed   CARDS: Access, Amex, Diners, Visa   DETAILS: 180 seats. Private parties: 200 main room, 15 private room. Vegetarian meals. Children welcome. Wheelchair access (also WC). Music. Air-conditioned. Fax: 071-338 0125

Inaho
map 12

4 Hereford Road, Bayswater, W2 4AA   COOKING 2
071-221 8495   COST £15–£37

'Good to find Japanese food at a reasonable price,' enthused a reporter who loved the neighbourhood atmosphere of this tiny Bayswater restaurant. Tables are packed close together, so it's 'not a place for smokers who want to remain popular'. Little wooden signposts on the tables advertise menu supplements. The kitchen delivers a convincing version of Japanese 'home-style' cooking with a familiar range of appetisers, sashimi, tempura, rice and noodles. Nasuden (baked aubergine with garlic sauce) is a 'delicious mush' that manages to preserve the innate sweetness of the eggplant without any accompanying bitterness. Seaweed salad is a colourful collation of four different types, visually composed for full effect. Excellent, assorted sushi is served Wednesday to Saturday evenings. For a novel dessert, try delicate green tea ice-cream. There is a minimal wine list, but saké, Japanese beer and tea are preferable. House wine is £7.

CHEF: S. Otsuka   PROPRIETOR: H. Nakamura   OPEN: Mon to Sat, exc Sat L; 12.30 to 2.30, 7 to 11   CLOSED: 10 days Christmas and New Year, 4 days Easter   MEALS: alc (main courses £6.50 to £12). Set L £8 to £10, Set D £20 to £22   SERVICE: 10%   CARDS: Access, Visa   DETAILS: 20 seats. Private parties: 22 main room. Vegetarian meals. No children under 12. Smart dress preferred. No cigars/pipes in dining-room. No music

L'Incontro

map 13

87 Pimlico Road, SW1W 8PH
071-730 3663 and 6327

COOKING 2
COST £26–£68

Visitors to Venice are often told there isn't a great deal of good eating in the watery city. Perhaps Venetians should come to the Pimlico Road. L'Incontro had a reshuffle in its kitchens early in 1994, and now offers an additional one-plate, weekly-changing lunch menu that may include calf's liver, osso buco, casseroled squid and pasta variations. The evening *carte* draws praise for the quality of the freshly made pasta. An inspector who was dazzled by the brightness of the interior also encountered a healthy sparkle in the food. A simple plate of grilled Mediterranean vegetables, 'doused in good oil by the passing waiter', provided plenty to delight the eye and palate. Poached sea bass in balsamic vinegar married bracing sharpness with richly textured fish, while a delicate suggestion of truffle came through in lightly grilled escalopes of beef. The simplest finales – an Italian cheese platter or fresh figs, for example – may be the best way of concluding. Some people regret the high prices, while not impugning the quality of the food.

The verdict on the wines is unchanged: they are steeply priced and there is no system to the list in terms of style, vintage or price. The mainly Italian bottles are supplemented by a smattering of French. House wines from Sardinia are £12.50.

CHEF: Nicola Celmanti   PROPRIETOR: Gino Santin   OPEN: Mon to Sat; 12.30 to 2.30 (3 Sat), 7 to 11.30   CLOSED: 25 and 26 Dec   MEALS: alc (main courses £14.50 to £21.50). Set L £13.50 (2 courses) to £16.80. Cover £1.50 D   SERVICE: 12% D, not inc L   CARDS: Access, Amex, Diners, Visa   DETAILS: 55 seats. Private parties: 65 main room, 35 private room. Vegetarian meals. Children's helpings on request. Smart dress preferred. No pipes in dining-room. Wheelchair access. Music. Air-conditioned. Fax: 071-730 5062

▲ Inter-Continental Hotel, Le Soufflé ♥

map 13

1 Hamilton Place, W1V 0QY
071-409 3131

COOKING 4
COST £38–£76

The bar is a functional meeting place, no more, while the dining-room is done out in cream and green, perhaps in an effort to compensate for the lack of natural daylight. Shrubs in tubs help the illusion along. Peter Kromberg has been at the stove here, man and boy, since 1975, and while technique and accomplishment remain standard, the flavours and ingredients respond to forces at work elsewhere. It is unlikely, for example, that he would have been serving pumpkin chutney with a pie of goose liver, truffle and chicken 20 years ago, or that he would have served sauté scallops on a light fromage blanc, with a sauce of watercress and lime zest. Some classical chefs stay with the narrowest repertoire, some wander off into sun-dried tomatoland or flirt with every Thai spice in the book. Kromberg does neither. He develops within a circumscribed framework that never loses sight of its classical French origins, and yet moves with the times.

Some dishes are a little involved, like a first course of steamed red mullet in a yellowish pool of vinaigrette surrounded by little heaps of saladings. A trail of heavily marinated, finely diced and skinny aubergine sat along the top, and a couple of large, cheesy grissini lay criss-crossed over the plate, to no great advantage. Yet Kromberg is as capable as the next man of cooking simply, as in a collection of grilled fish with flaked Maldon salt, a seasonal salad and nothing else. The soufflé is a hallmark dish, but one reporter was disappointed by his. It came in a filo pastry base instead of a soufflé dish, and tasted more of egg than apricot. It was good, but by no means distinguished.

Occasionally heavy-handedness knocks a dish off-balance. A saffron risotto was one such, where the asparagus and porcini were completely overwhelmed by unannounced and extremely bitter leaves. Saffron worked better in the mashed potatoes that came with one reporter's baked cod: a large moist chunk on a dab of intense sauce that gave sharpness and depth. That same three-dimensional effect came through in a blackberry tart: a filo pastry case spread with lemon curd, and a dozen large berries standing straight as soldiers on top, soft and yet exuding more flavour than even fresh-picked ones usually do. When it hits the high notes, the cooking is extremely good.

Wines are certainly fine, although there is some ostentation where the selection could be more intelligent. Go to the outer regions of France, or hop out of it altogether, to find much for less than £20. The first-page sommelier's selection is very useful in this respect, and no one will grumble with the quality of wines by the glass: nine of them from £3.50 to £6. House vin de pays is £14.50. CELLARMAN'S CHOICE: Cloudy Bay Sauvignon 1991, £25; Côte de Nuits Villages 1990, Groffier, £19.

CHEF: Peter Kromberg   PROPRIETOR: Inter-Continental Hotels Group   OPEN: Tue to Sun, exc Sat L and Sun D; 12.30 to 3 (12 to 4 Sun), 7 to 10.30 (11.15 Sat)   CLOSED: Aug   MEALS: alc (main courses £13.50 to £23). Set L Tue to Fri £27.50, Sun £26, Set D £37.50 to £43   SERVICE: not inc   CARDS: Access, Amex, Diners, Visa   DETAILS: 80 seats. Private parties: on application. Vegetarian meals. Healthy eating options. Children welcome. Smart dress preferred. No-smoking area. No pipes in dining-room. Music. Air-conditioned   ACCOMMODATION: 469 rooms, all with bath/shower. TV. Phone. Air-conditioned. B&B £195 to £282. Rooms for disabled. Lift. Children welcome. Afternoon teas. Sauna. Fax: 071-491 0926

Isohama £   [NEW ENTRY]   map 11

312 Vauxhall Bridge Road, SW1V 1AA   COOKING 2
071-834 2145   COST £24–£50

A modest frontage opposite the Victoria Apollo theatre gives on to a tiny entrance lobby, then to a single ground-floor room. Large, modern floral watercolours are for sale and the ebonised wooden tables are closely set. Set dinners are at £25 and £28, and the long *carte* contains all the usual sections with a wide choice of appetisers and noodle dishes, including a full range of 'tea soups'. Nabe dishes, cooked at the table, require advance notice. From a long list of cheap lunches, two specials, changed weekly, are particularly good value. A short 'Japanese menu' is available to those who ask.

Among dishes that have been enjoyed are edamame (soya beans in the pod), light, fresh and crisp tempura, and ohitashi (spinach with grated bonino). Indeed, fish and vegetables receive most commendation, including hiya yakko (a huge portion of fine silky bean curd), nameko oroshi (mushrooms on grated mooli), and kurage su (beautifully textured jellyish with cucumber and seaweed in vinegar). One regular visitor 'can vouch for the quality of the huge bowls of noodles in soup, and plaice, fried whole and very crisp, as well as grilled and salted fish of various kinds'. Drink brown tea or saké.

CHEF: Yukio Saito   PROPRIETOR: Senko (UK) Ltd   OPEN: Mon to Sat, exc Sat L; 12 to 2.30, 6 to 10.30   MEALS: alc. Set D £25 to £28   SERVICE: 10%, card slips closed   CARDS: Access, Amex, Diners, Visa   DETAILS: 35 seats. Private parties: 20 main room. Children welcome. No music. Air-conditioned

Ivy
map 15

1 West Street, WC2H 9NE   COOKING 2
071-836 4751   COST £24–£59

Wedge-shaped, like a piece of come-hither cheese, the Ivy sits opposite *The Mousetrap* and snaps up custom before and after the show. Meals are well paced for those with theatre bookings, the place hums with efficiency and control, and service is busy without being hurried. The bar occupies the top triangle of the cheese, leaving a trapezoidal dining-room that feels like a country club fallen on better times, with polished oak panelling, leaded windows and conspicuously commissioned art.

The menu shares dishes with Le Caprice (jointly owned, see entry, London), although the Ivy retains the feel of the younger sib, with more 'brunch' food along the lines of corned beef hash with fried egg, and eggs Benedict. The comfort quotient is high, with an emphasis on food that is easily digestible and in manageable quantity. Basil gnocchi, which sounds like someone who might be playing in a nearby theatre, is 'really yummy, quite childish and terribly satisfying.' Chips are 'like they should be', and risotto nero is 'superb'. Some dishes, such as duck with mashed potatoes, or hake with chips and peas, are self-contained, but the cost of extra vegetables (deep-fried onions, roast carrots with cumin, and bubble and squeak, for example) irks some. Pasta is thin and partnered with anything from an eggy-creamy-cheesy sauce to queen scallops with the right amount of smoked bacon. Americanisms are not confined to corned beef hash. Meaty swordfish (like 'underwater chicken') comes with chargrilled pumpkin and sweetcorn fritters. Desserts cover standard tiramisù, more ambitious hazelnut praline pithiviers, and good bread-and-butter pudding. The wine list is a satisfying assembly of reliable names from around the world, with a fair selection by the glass. House wine is £8.50.

CHEFS: Mark Hix and Desmond McDonald   PROPRIETORS: Jeremy King and Christopher Corbin   OPEN: all week; 12 to 3 (3.30 Sun), 5.30 to 12   CLOSED: 25 and 26 Dec, 1 Jan, L bank hols   MEALS: alc (main courses £6.50 to £19). Set L Sat and Sun £14. Cover £1.50 restaurant   SERVICE: not inc   CARDS: Access, Amex, Diners, Visa   DETAILS: restaurant 110 seats, bar 16 seats. Private parties: 60 private room. Valet parking Sun. Vegetarian meals. Children welcome. Wheelchair access. Music. Air-conditioned. Fax: 071-497 3644

Iznik £

map 11

19 Highbury Park, N5 1QJ   COOKING 1*
071-354 5697   COST £17–£26

'Gets better and better,' eulogises a devotee of this North London restaurant. By day it is a café, while in the evening it serves up authentic Turkish cooking from the Ottoman court in Istanbul. What appeals is the genuine warmth of the place, its leisurely buzz and the personality of Adem Oner. Dangling lights, rugs and artefacts are dotted around the colourful dining-room; the music might be jazz or Turkish 'trad'. The clearly set-out menu caters equally well for carnivores and vegetarians. Reporters have mentioned many favourites from the list of meze: delicately fashioned dolmas, arnavit cigeri (diced liver with paprika and olive oil), and karnibahar kizartma (cauliflower dipped in egg with yogurt dressing). Beykos kebabi (chunks of marinated lamb wrapped in slices of aubergine and served with mild spicy rice) is a typically well-executed main course. To finish, try ekmek kadayifi (bread imported from Turkey drenched in syrup and thick cream), or asure (dried fruit compote). The list of Turkish beverages is worth exploring; otherwise, the wine list has a few cheap and cheerful bottles. House wine is £6.95.

CHEF: Ahmet Poyraz PROPRIETORS: Adem and Pirlanta Oner OPEN: all week; 10 to 4 (9 to 4 Sat and Sun), 6.30 to 11 (7 to 11 Sat and Sun) MEALS: alc (main courses £6 to £9.50) SERVICE: 10% DETAILS: 54 seats. Private parties: 60 main room. Vegetarian meals. Children welcome. Wheelchair access (1 step). Music

Jade Garden £

map 15

15 Wardour Street, W1V 3HA   COOKING 1*
071-437 5065 and 439 7851   COST £15–£46

'My favourite spot is up on the balcony,' observes a devotee of this well-established Chinatown rendezvous. 'There is a little more space and intimacy here, and you can look down on the frenetic throng of Chinese and all comers plundering the dim-sum.' Items are freshly cooked to order and the quality is consistently good. Tasty morsels have included slithery char siu, cheung-fun dressed with soy, stuffed bean curd rolls, steamed beef ball and ginger dumplings pointed up with star-anise, and grease-free paper-wrapped king prawns. The full menu is Cantonese, with a strong showing of fish, barbecued meats and noodles. Look for out-of-the-way dishes such as abalone with bêche-de-mer (sea cucumber), fried shark's fin with scrambled eggs, and stewed mutton with dried bean curd and oyster sauce. Staff are neatly dressed, fast and cheerful. Drink tea, saké or Tsingtao beer. House wine is £7.50.

CHEF: Raymond Lee PROPRIETORS: L.S. and P.W. Man OPEN: all week; noon to 11.30 (11.30am to 10.30pm Sun) MEALS: alc (main courses £5.50 to £12.50). Set L and D £9.50 to £17, (minimum 2) SERVICE: not inc CARDS: Access, Amex, Visa DETAILS: 200 seats. Private parties: 80 private room. Vegetarian meals. Children welcome. Smart dress preferred. Wheelchair access (1 step). No music. Air-conditioned

Report forms are at the back of the book; write a letter if you prefer.

Joe's Cafe

map 13

126 Draycott Avenue, SW3 3AH
071-225 2217

COOKING 1
COST £24–£49

'Chic décor, jazzy food' is how this place is normally seen, although it could as easily be the other way round. Joe's may sound like a truckers' roadside tea stop, but is in fact a smart Sloane address with a buzzing atmosphere, staffed by keen young waiters. The menu hops about from fish soup with rouille to bang-bang chicken, from oxtail stew with celeriac and potato mash to grilled sea bass with salsa verde. More of a restaurant than a café in terms of what it can cook, it is informal enough for folk to drop in for just a couple of dishes. The food is for the grazing classes and can work out as cheap or expensive as you like. Chocolate cake or sticky toffee pudding put on any calories carefully avoided in first-course salads. All-day Sunday brunch begins with a jug of Bloody Mary or Buck's Fizz and runs through the repertoire of eggs Benedict and corned beef hash, with Toulouse sausage and salmon fish-cakes for good measure. Prices on the short wine list are not those of a café. House French is £9.25 (£2.50 per glass).

CHEF: Jerome Laugénie   PROPRIETOR: Joseph Ettedgui   OPEN: all week, exc Sun D; 12 to 4 (11 to 5 Sun), 6 to 11.30   MEALS: alc (main courses £6 to £15). Cover £1   SERVICE: 12.5%   CARDS: Access, Amex, Diners, Visa   DETAILS: 80 seats. 2 tables outside. Private parties: 12 main room. Vegetarian meals. Children welcome. Smart dress preferred. Wheelchair access (1 step). Music. Air-conditioned

Kalamaras £

map 12

76–78 Inverness Mews, W2 3JQ
071-727 9122 and 2564

COOKING 2
COST £16–£33

'A great atmosphere, delightful no-nonsense staff and supremely edible food,' enthuses a regular. Stelios Platonos hails from Paros, which is why his long-standing restaurant is reckoned to deliver some of the most genuine Greek food in London. A tendency to bring dishes to the table at the same time and, according to one reporter, what might be called 'a heavy hand with the salt' do little to detract from the quality of expertly fried kalamarakia (baby squid), salt cod balls, and 'earthy' loukanika sausages on a skewer. Many items, such as garidopites (prawn filo parcels) and melizanes (fried aubergines), come with an intense garlic sauce. Wild greens provide a good sharp foil, and salads are deliciously pointed up with herbs and olives. Lamb dominates the list of main dishes, all of which are served with new potatoes cooked with parsley and lemon. Sakoula thalassini (fillets of hake and salmon baked in filo pastry with rosemary) is a fish speciality. Pastries and fresh fruit complete the picture. Around 20 Greek wines offer gutsy, affordable drinking. Kalamaras (Micro) at 66 Inverness Mews is similar in mood and style – but bring your own wine.

CHEF/PROPRIETOR: Stelios Platonos   OPEN: Mon to Sat, D only; 6 to 12   CLOSED: bank hols   MEALS: alc (main courses £5.50 to £10). Set D £15.50   SERVICE: 10%, card slips closed   CARDS: Access, Amex, Diners, Visa   DETAILS: 88 seats. Private parties: 30 private room. Vegetarian meals. Children's helpings. No cigars/pipes in dining-room. Wheelchair access. Music. Air-conditioned

Kastoori £   map 10

188 Upper Tooting Road, SW17 7EJ   COOKING 1
081-767 7027   COST £13–£26

The Thanki family continue to offer some of the most distinctive Indian vegetarian food south of the river. The heart of their menu concentrates on the cooking of Kathia Wadi (an area of Gujarat where tomatoes, chilli, garlic and coriander are the basic ingredients of the local cuisine). Dishes range from familiar starters such as onion bhajias, dahi vadai and sev puri to assorted vegetable curries, masala dosai and chana bhatura (chickpeas and potatoes with fried bhatura bread). In addition, look for the section devoted to family recipes from Africa, such as matoki (green banana curry) and kasodi (sweetcorn cooked in coconut milk with a ground peanut sauce). Details like the home-made chutneys, rice and breads are up to scratch: rotlo (millet loaf) is served on Sundays. The cleanliness of the place is 'impressive', although service may seem rather vague. Drink lassi, masala tea or Kingfisher beer. House wine is £6.75.

CHEFS: Dinesh Thanki and Manoj Thanki   PROPRIETORS: the Thanki family   OPEN: all week, exc L Mon and Tue; 12.30 to 2.30, 6 to 10.30   CLOSED: 25 Dec, 1 week mid-Jan   MEALS: alc (main courses £3 to £4.50). Set L and D £7.25 to £11.25. Minimum £4   SERVICE: not inc   CARDS: Access, Visa   DETAILS: 84 seats. Private parties: 30 main room. Vegetarian meals. Children's helpings. Smart dress preferred. Wheelchair access (also women's WC). Music. Air-conditioned

Kensington Place ♥   map 12

201 Kensington Church Street, W8 7LX   COOKING 3*
071-727 3184   COST £21–£57

Regulars have become quite attuned to the atmosphere of Kensington Place. It is still worth pointing out to first-timers that, if they are out for a quietly reflective evening within Kensington's leafy bowers, they are in for a fairly clangorous awakening. The acoustics here are among the most dramatic in London: in full cry, on a full night, the hubbub is quite formidable. On the other hand, this was among the first places in the capital to catch the mood of disaffection with the painstaking formality of gastronomic temples as the '80s had defined them. Gaze through the full-length windows at the front, and mark that the popularity of the approach is not one whit diminished. If there is a disadvantage to this, it is that some people feel as if too many tables have been shoehorned in. Staff do their level best, but tales of delay are inevitable. A family who found attention 'rather slow', paid full rate for children's portions and spent their lunch wreathed in cigarette smoke were entitled to be a bit grumpy. Their verdict, however, was: 'We all enjoyed the food very much and will try to go again.'

That Rowley Leigh can win such improbable converts is due to the excellence of much that his kitchen turns out. The Mediterranean mode was adopted here long before others lunged at the speeding bandwagon, and it has been successfully sustained. Game terrine with caponata, pigeon crostini with truffle paste and rocket, roast John Dory with orange and balsamic vinegar, grilled sea bass with lentils and salsa verde, salt duck with potatoes and onions, couscous with rabbit, merguez and harissa – all infuse the sun-soaked Med repertoire with a streak of bold invention that intrigues and delights. Correspondents this year have endorsed griddled scallops with pea purée and mint vinaigrette, hare stew with chestnuts and dumplings, and simple desserts like apple charlotte, lemon tart and 'delicious' passion-fruit pavlova. Finish with high-intensity espresso. The vibrancy of the food is easily matched by the state-of-the-art wine list full of fashionable and dependable names at generally affordable prices. It packs an awful lot into a short space. House wines are £8.75 (white) and £9.75 (red). CELLARMAN'S CHOICE: Jura, L'Etoile 1987, Dom. de Montbourgeau, £20; Crozes Hermitage 1990, Paul Jaboulet, £14.

CHEF: Rowley Leigh PROPRIETORS: Nick Smallwood and Simon Slater OPEN: all week; 12 to 3, 6.30 to 11.45 (10.15 Sun) CLOSED: 3 days Christmas MEALS: alc (main courses £8 to £14.50). Set L £13.50 SERVICE: not inc CARDS: Access, Visa DETAILS: 150 seats. Private parties: 30 main room. Vegetarian meals. Children's helpings. Wheelchair access (1 step; also WC). Music. Air-conditioned. Fax: 071-229 2025

Lahore Kebab House ⁙✳ £   **NEW ENTRY**   map 11

2 Umberston Street, E1 1PY   COOKING 1
071-488 2551   COST £10–£17

If you find yourself in Whitechapel and fancy some good Pakistani cooking, try the Lahore. Don't think of it as a way of killing time; you will be turned around like greased lightning. If you want to drink, pick up a bottle or a couple of cans in the nearest off-licence. Don't expect elegance or noticeable politesse. In these 'seriously basic' surroundings, the food you will eat is a thing of beauty and a joy for 20 minutes. Chicken tikka ('the best in London – bursting with flavour from the marinade'), chicken karai of exquisite tenderness and delicacy, mixed vegetable curry in which all the components – including the freshly ground spices – can be tasted. Dhal of precisely accurate texture and nan hot from the tandoor will persuade many to agree with our inspector, who thought this 'a remarkable establishment'. Add to this the fact that the place seems to be always open, and Lahore seems a clear winner. Other places with similar names are in the vicinity, so mark the address carefully.

CHEFS: M. Din and M. Azeem PROPRIETOR: M. Siddique OPEN: all week; noon to midnight MEALS: alc (main courses £3 to £4). Set L and D £6 to £10. Unlicensed, but bring your own: no corkage SERVICE: not inc DETAILS: 80 seats. 6 tables outside. Private parties: 60 main room. Car park. Vegetarian meals. Children welcome. No smoking in dining-room. Wheelchair access. No music. Air-conditioned

▲ *Lanesborough*   map 13

1 Lanesborough Place, SW1X 7TA   COOKING 3
071-259 5599   COST £30–£72

Walk past (or better still, climb out of) the chauffeur-driven cars that park in front of the former St George's Hospital, proceed along the passageway with its artificial fire, and turn right into the Conservatory. The Dining Room has closed, perhaps a harbinger signalling the beginning of the end for grand West End dining-rooms. The Conservatory evokes comment. 'A mish-mash of Gothic fan vaulting, Moorish lanterns, Italian waterspouts and Chinese statues' is one view. 'A Disney version of the Connaught' is another.

Paul Gayler's championing of vegetarian food remains strong. Wild mushroom risotto or roasted artichoke salad with aïoli are among the offerings. Otherwise the influences are as mixed as the décor, with a Eurasian strand coming to the fore in crispy crab spring roll with sweet soy and ginger, highly praised mussels in Thai cream sauce, and a sweet and very creamy oriental chicken soup with coconut milk and shiitake. Roast duckling on a white-bean brandade with a fricassee of provençale vegetables is a signature dish. Both breast (cooked pink) and leg are crisp-skinned, while the lump of light brown paste that is bean brandade is dry and texturally challenged. But the vegetables and well-reduced sauce bring vitality. Terrine of foie gras and white chicory is 'stunning', and well-matured chargrilled beef fillet with lardons is attractively rich and accomplished.

Plain dishes include grilled Dover sole or salmon, and prawn cocktail. Surely prawn cocktail here must be a pretty sophisticated affair? Nope. 'It is as dull as ditchwater, a bog-standard version complete with iceberg lettuce and "marie rose" sauce. Marks & Spencer sells infinitely better prawns.' It was a joke. Well, two inspectors dining together laughed out loud (but then it wasn't their £8.50). 'The bread and butter, if anything, was worse.' It is difficult to imagine a more cynical cobbling together of second-rate materials in a restaurant with ambition. Unevenness on occasions highlights the difficulties of serving meals all week. Even Paul Gayler has to have time off, and it may be that comments such as 'perhaps it was just a bad night for the kitchen' coincide with his absence. Service charge is included, although service can be at sixes and sevens. Wines are grand, and prices heart-stoppingly high, with precious little under £20. House white is £14.50, red £17.50, and 10 wines are normally available by the glass from £3 upwards.

CHEF: Paul Gayler   PROPRIETOR: Goodwill Nominees   OPEN: all week; 12 to 2.30, 6.30 to 12   MEALS: alc (main courses £7.50 to £26). Set L £22.50, Set D £28.50   SERVICE: net prices, card slips closed   CARDS: Access, Amex, Diners, Visa   DETAILS: 106 seats. Private parties: 100 main room, 30 to 75 private rooms. Car park. Vegetarian meals. Healthy eating options. Children's helpings. Smart dress preferred. Wheelchair access (also WC). Music. Air-conditioned   ACCOMMODATION: 95 rooms, all with bath/shower. TV. Phone. Air-conditioned. Room only £170 to £295. Rooms for disabled. Children welcome. Baby facilities. Small dogs welcome. Afternoon teas. Confirm by 6. Fax: 071-259 5606

Langan's Brasserie

map 14

Stratton Street, W1X 5FD   COOKING 1
071-493 6437   COST £30–£55

It reached the stage of being famous for being famous long ago. Langan's is an 'address' for those with glamour and the clout that goes with it, a bright, sparkling and inviting place with a sense of occasion. It may also have a ghostly gloss from the late Peter Langan himself, and was the Quaglino's of its day two decades ago: big, bold and confident. It is still a wonderful place – charisma downstairs, social black hole upstairs. The brasserie style hasn't changed much, but then brasseries don't. The spinach soufflé and Mrs Langan's chocolate pudding must be the long-running *Mousetraps* of London restaurant dishes. For the rest, grilled calf's liver or bangers and mash are its stock in trade, helped along by halibut with ginger or roast guinea-fowl. One reporter, however, was less than happy with items such as 'nondescript' warm salad with lardons and 'undistinguished' sausage, while another cited dry guinea-fowl in an over-seasoned red wine sauce. The wine list is short. We have not been able to confirm the details below as, again this year, no reply to our questionnaire has been forthcoming.

CHEFS: Richard Shepherd, Dennis Mynott and Roy Smith PROPRIETORS: Michael Caine and Richard Shepherd OPEN: Mon to Sat, exc Sat L; 12.30 to 3, 7 to 11.45 (8 to 12.45 Sat) CLOSED: bank hols MEALS: alc. Cover £1 SERVICE: 12.5% CARDS: Access, Amex, Diners, Visa DETAILS: 200 seats. Private parties: 12 main room. Children welcome. Music. Air-conditioned

Lansdowne £
map 11

90 Gloucester Avenue, NW1 8HX   COOKING 1
071-483 0409   COST £17–£28

The Lansdowne spills on to the pavement in clement weather, opening out what is already just a big gutted space with jumble-sale furniture. The food is a blend of Mediterranean and rejuvenated British. It is a place for black pudding, or chunky chopped steak and chips, as well as bouillabaisse or baked cod with tapénade, and for a lamb sandwich, the meat marinated, the bread hefty and white. What the Lansdowne lacks in refinement – pasta may be heavy, risotto leaden – it more than makes up for in heartiness and bonhomie. The food is fresh and filling and the treatment straightforward, although the kitchen can handle such things as black bream – the whole fish, head and all, nicely grilled and moist – with fennel salad in a light olive oil dressing.

The character changes at different times of the week. A regular rates Sundays highly, with 30-somethings and toddlers at lunch (the only meal for which bookings are taken) and jazz in the evening with West Indian food. Prices ensure popularity: 'Chairs are snatched as soon as they are vacated, and the menu becomes progressively shorter as dishes run out and are wiped off the blackboard. This is not a place to come for a quiet meal.' Note that credit cards are not accepted. Draught cider and Hook Norton ales are good, and house Valdepeñas and vin de pays are £8 (£2 per glass).

CHEFS: Amanda Pritchett and Simon Green PROPRIETORS: Amanda Pritchett, Simon Palmer and Simon Green OPEN: all week, exc Mon L; 12.30 to 2.30 (1 to 2.30 Sun), 7 to 10 CLOSED: 25 Dec, 1 Jan MEALS: alc (main courses £5.50 to £7.50). Set L Sun £15 SERVICE: not inc DETAILS: 70 seats. 6 tables outside. Private parties: 12 main room. Public house rules apply to children. Wheelchair access (1 step). Music

Launceston Place ♥
map 13

1A Launceston Place, W8 5RL   COOKING 2*
071-937 6912   COST £23–£52

The confident feel of a wealthy town house is what pervades this restaurant at the end of a residential street. Grey carpets and soft cream walls coalesce into a simple elegance, everywhere looks immaculate, diffuse lights reflect off dark oil paintings, and deeply cushioned chairs at spacious tables fill the linked series of intimate rooms.

Ingredients on the longish *carte* come straight from central casting: sour dough bread, tapénade, roast or grilled vegetables, goats' cheese, risotto with morels or fresh herbs, woodpigeon, and deep-fried lambs' sweetbreads with caper sauce. Just as the chef could probably put them together in almost any combination to produce a decent menu, so 'almost any random combination of starter and main course would make a sumptuous meal'. Half a roast lobster from 'local waters' (they have their own tank) is lightly flavoured with coriander butter, while lentils and celeriac soak up the juice. Scallops are properly seared, charcoaly, sweet, fresh and juicily tender. Although main courses can be a let-down (small portions, underseasoning and undercooking are among reported problems), first courses and desserts are generally on top form, including griddled foie gras with a confit of shallots on flaky, buttery puff pastry.

Reporters fall over themselves with superlatives for geranium bavarois with summer fruits ('superb, intoxicating to the senses'), for 'unctuous' chocolate parfait with fresh cream quenelle, and 'exquisite' thin pastry under a just-warm lemon tart. Service varies: 'well-timed and discreet' is one view, 'arrogant' is another. Sensible pricing of the largely French wines shows them to good effect. About half the bottles are under £20, and the lucky-dip of grape varieties ensures a wide and appealing diversity of styles. Any wine in a half-bottle is also available by the glass. CELLARMAN'S CHOICE: Pinot d'Alsace 1991, Faller, £18; Madiran 1985, Plaimont, £14.50.

CHEF: Cathy Gradwell PROPRIETORS: Nick Smallwood and Simon Slater OPEN: all week, exc Sat L and Sun D; 12.30 to 2.30 (3 Sun), 7 to 11.30 CLOSED: bank hol Mons MEALS: alc (main courses £10.50 to £15.50). Supper menu 10 to 11pm (main course, £7.50 to £8.50). Set L and D (before 8pm) Mon to Fri £13.50 (2 courses) to £16.50, Set L Sun £16.50 SERVICE: not inc CARDS: Access, Amex, Visa DETAILS: 80 seats. Private parties: 90 main room, 14 and 30 private rooms. Vegetarian meals. Children's helpings on request. No pipes in dining-room. Wheelchair access (1 step). No music. Air-conditioned. Fax: 071-938 2412

Laurent £

map 11

428 Finchley Road, NW2 2HY
071-794 3603

COOKING 1
COST £18–£28

Situated in what seems like the front room of a small house, this restaurant is a genuine family business with 'homely and home-spun' atmosphere. Laurent Farrugia cooks, his daughter works out front and her husband helps in the kitchen. Couscous is the reason for eating here and it now comes five ways, including chicken and fish (halibut steak). Plates are piled high, and the value for money is never in doubt. Any blandness is set off by saucers of fiery harissa sauce and you must not miss out on the excellent home-made merguez sausages served as an extra. To start, there is brique à l'oeuf; to finish, opt for refreshing lemon or blackcurrant sorbet. Mint tea and coffee are alternatives to the handful of quaffable North African wines. House wine is £8.80.

CHEF/PROPRIETOR: Laurent Farrugia OPEN: Mon to Sat; 12 to 2, 6 to 11 CLOSED: first 3 weeks Aug MEALS: alc (main courses £6.50 to £10). Minimum £6.50 SERVICE: not inc CARDS: Access, Amex, Visa DETAILS: 36 seats. Private parties: 50 main room. Vegetarian meals. Children's helpings. Smart dress preferred. Wheelchair access (1 step). No music

Leith's 🍾

map 12

92 Kensington Park Road, W11 2PN
LONDON 071-229 4481

COOKING 3
COST £46–£69

These three Victorian terraced houses were refurbished to celebrate Leith's 25th anniversary. The entrance, down a cobbled passageway at the side, leads through a small bar to four interconnected rooms decorated with bright modern figure paintings. It feels very middle class, hardly exciting or trendy, but is useful for those who want to get away from the hustle and bustle that accompanies so much eating in London. Spotlights shine directly on to tables, making the most of the colour in the food, especially Mediterranean vegetables.

A trolley arrives with a display of hors d'oeuvre, part of the à la carte menu. At this stage of a meal, most people's eyes are bigger than their tummies, so there is a temptation to pile the plate high with Puy lentils and artichoke, glistening peppers and aubergines, and a smoked salmon parcel containing chopped raw salmon, onion and caper. But then it costs £11.75 however much you have, so why not? The set menu, meanwhile, offers ravioli of duck livers and artichokes in a vegetable and tarragon broth, or perhaps a courgette flower filled with delicately flavoured, delightfully textured fish mousseline, served on a warm puddle of translucent liquid tinged with red from the squares of tomato flesh. The kitchen does not want for technique.

Fresh supplies are assured from Leith's farm, and the fixed-price vegetarian menu is as welcome as it is serious, offering feuilleté of roasted plum tomatoes and artichokes with an olive butter sauce, or a casserole of braised vegetables and tarragon with garlic cream. Braising and pot roasting are commonly used methods, and casseroled ox cheek with a well-reduced stock-based sauce brings heartiness to the package. The menu changes seasonally, although duckling and charcoal grilled rib of beef are regulars. Rhubarb soufflé with vanilla ice-cream appeared in spring, while strawberry flummery was on a summer menu.

Leith's is one of the few restaurants with a brigade of more-mature gentlemen of service, who are full of polite 'sirs' and who stick to the clichés like glue. 'A very good choice, sir,' for the food, and 'we sell a lot of that, sir,' for the wine, are expressions we had thought extinct. One way and another, the service is not quite as sharp as the food. But the wines are. Carefully selected, offering a range of quality and price within each major country, they only really let rip in Burgundy and Bordeaux, which is where most of the half-bottles are. Good Spanish wines get more of a look-in than usual, and prices generally encourage adventure. There are five or six house wines around £15 (£3.50 per glass). CELLARMAN'S CHOICE: Stellenbosch Louisvale Chardonnay 1991, £18.50; Pauillac, Dom. de Cartieux 1990, £21.50.

CHEF: Alex Floyd   PROPRIETOR: Prue Leith   OPEN: all week, D only; 7.30 to 11.30   CLOSED: 4 days Christmas, 2 days Aug bank hol   MEALS: alc (main courses £17.50 to £21.50). Set D £25 (2 courses)   SERVICE: 15%, card slips closed   CARDS: Access, Amex, Diners, Visa   DETAILS: 75 seats. Private parties: 24 main room, 40 and 40 private rooms. Vegetarian meals. No children under 7. No music. Air-conditioned

'When I asked the waitress if she could recommend the cheeses, she said, ''If I were you, I'd stick to the sweets.'' ' (On eating in Wiltshire)

Lobster Pot

map 11

3 Kennington Lane, SE11 4RG
071-582 5556

COOKING 1
COST £19–£66

The Régents deserve full marks for trying to get as far away from Kennington Lane as possible without actually moving. All the clichés combine in a self-parody of maritime kitsch, from a trompe-l'oeil harbour view on the first-floor deck (for aperitifs and coffee) through 'underwater' portholes that look into an aquarium, to nets, lines, bobs, ropes, a likeness of Cap'n Birdseye and recorded seagull noises. It is a family-run French restaurant dealing in home-made bouillabaisse, seafood platter, live lobsters and whatever the market coughs up: whiting, perhaps, or marlin grilled with a Creole sauce. More or less any combination of crustacea is here for the asking, the seasons determining exceptions. Garlic, butter and cream account for much of the saucing, with mushrooms and peppers following on behind. Meat, and puddings of profiteroles or tarte Tatin, complete the picture. A short wine list includes house Sauvignon Blanc at £9.50 (£2.70 per glass).

CHEF: Hervé Régent   PROPRIETORS: Hervé and Nathalie Régent   OPEN: Tue to Sat (Sun and Mon parties only, by arrangement); 12 to 2.30, 7 to 10.45   MEALS: alc (main courses £12.50 to £30). Set L £12.50 to £18.50, Set D £18.50. Minimum £15.50 L, £23 D   SERVICE: net prices, card slips closed   CARDS: Access, Amex, Diners, Visa   DETAILS: 24 seats. Private parties: 30 main room. Vegetarian meals with prior notice. Children's helpings. No children under 6. Smart dress preferred. Wheelchair access (1 step). Music. Air-conditioned. Fax: 071-582 9751

▲ London Hilton, Windows Rooftop Restaurant

NEW ENTRY   map 14

22 Park Lane, W1A 2HH
071-493 8000

COOKING 3
COST £42–£93

The 28th floor offers some of the best views of London, all for the price of a drink in the bar. The restaurant hardly seems designed for serious eating, and it is old-fashioned enough to offer ladies a menu without prices. People come to gawp at the skyline, listen to live music and take a turn around the dance floor between courses. 'The staff appeared to be surprised by our interest in the food,' wrote one member of a threesome. 'They had watched us order some of the more interesting dishes and seen us tasting each other's, and apparently this never happens.' Perhaps they will become more used to it as Jacques Rolancy moves into gear. David Chambers (formerly of Le Meridien, see entry, London) went to the Hilton as executive chef early in 1994, while Rolancy, after cooking in a variety of places in France, took over specific responsibility for the Windows Rooftop Restaurant in May 1994.

The simpler dishes – niçoise vegetable salad with quail's eggs and garlic croûtons, for instance – do not show the kitchen to best effect, but fish and shellfish play a big part, and play it well. Jellied seafood consommé with lobster comes looking a bit grey and splodgy on top, but rake away the covering and underneath is a quivering just-set liquid with sensationally good lobster flavour, and a few bits of asparagus providing textural counterpoint. Other riches such as foie gras are dealt with equally skilfully, as in a layered terrine with artichoke, set off by three small scoops of delightful fig marmalade that is not too sweet. Among meats, roast Gressingham duck comes in two parts, neither very wonderful, but veal fillet, cooked as requested, is presented with a stew of dark fresh morels, more asparagus and a deep-flavoured, well-reduced sauce.

Desserts for fixed-price menus are from the trolley, but the *carte* offers a pastry mille-feuille with strawberries and a vanilla-specked crème anglaise, and a dish of apple sorbet spiked with paper-thin apple slices, served with stewed apple slices with syrup and a swirl of cracked pepper to help the flavour along. Service is grand-hotel style – smooth, professional and polite – and some wines are 'horrendously, ludicrously and quite ridiculously marked up'. For example, one wine that can be bought for £4.99 in the high street is on offer at £26. The list needs radical overhaul; otherwise it will deter customers from setting foot in the place.

CHEFS: Jacques Rolancy and David Chambers   PROPRIETOR: Hilton International   OPEN: all week, exc Sat L and Sun D; 12.30 to 2.30, 7 to 11.30 (12.30 Fri and Sat)   MEALS: alc (main courses £13 to £29.50). Set L £30.95 to £34, Set D £33.50 to £44. Cover £5 Fri and Sat   SERVICE: not inc (10% for 8 or more)   CARDS: Access, Amex, Diners, Visa   DETAILS: 120 seats. Private parties: 120 main room, 25 to 120 private rooms. Vegetarian meals. Children welcome. Jacket and tie. Wheelchair access (also women's WC). Music. Air-conditioned   ACCOMMODATION: 448 rooms, all with bath/shower. TV. Phone. Air-conditioned. B&B £159 to £176. Rooms for disabled. Lift. Fax: 071-493 4957

Lou Pescadou map 11

241 Old Brompton Road, SW5 9HP   COOKING 1
071-370 1057   COST £18–£46

The name is, apparently, provençale patois for 'fisherman', and that is the key to this genuinely Gallic fish bistro. Eat in the front café, the long bar or the raised dining-room leading on to a small terrace. Most reporters come here for carefully cooked fish and shellfish, although an occasional dissenting voice can be heard murmuring about average ingredients. The three-course set lunch is a bargain; otherwise choose from fixtures such as oysters, mussels and squid, or explore the list of daily specials, which might include scallops provençale or halibut with tomato and basil. The back-up is pizzas, pasta, salads and steaks; pissaladière is a speciality. Desserts are good. Coffee and herbal infusions ('super verveine tea made with real, fresh leaves') bolster a handful of French wines. House wine is £9.80.

CHEF: Laurent David   PROPRIETORS: Daniel Chobert and Laurent David   OPEN: all week; 12 to 3, 7 to 12   MEALS: alc (main courses £8 to £12.50). Set L £8. Cover £1   SERVICE: 15%, card slips closed   CARDS: Access, Amex, Diners, Visa   DETAILS: 55 seats. 8 tables outside. Private parties: 35 private room. Vegetarian meals. Children's helpings. Wheelchair access (1 step). No music

Net prices *in the details at the end of an entry indicates that the prices given on a menu and on a bill are inclusive of VAT and service charge, and that this practice is clearly stated on menu and bill.*

Magno's Brasserie

map 15

65A Long Acre, WC2E 9JH
071-836 6077

COOKING 1
COST £25–£45

'Our menu has gradually been adapted by the demands of our customers,' say the proprietors. The laudably democratic approach at this Covent Garden bistro is what gives it its habitual buzz of custom, which might comprise office-workers sick of desktop lunching, or theatre patrons in the evening happy to be out by curtain-up. The seasonally-changing *carte* is accompanied by an inclusive menu priced for either two or three courses. The food is unpretentious French cuisine bourgeoise, offering perhaps Roquefort baked in puff pastry, moules marinière with turmeric, a variation of eggs Benedict with smoked salmon instead of ham, rack of lamb with ratatouille, braised pork knuckle with lentils and smoked bacon. Pasta dishes are something of a speciality. For desserts, stalwarts such as lemon tart seem the best bet.

Service is a model of affability to the extent that reporters come to trust the staff: one pair ordering two lots of sauté potatoes were assured that one lot would be enough, and wisely took the advice. The wine list is also reliable and doesn't just stick chauvinistically to French produce. Among the strangers are Wolf Blass from South Australia and Los Vascos, one of the best Cabernet Sauvignons from Chile. House bordeaux is £8.95.

CHEF: Gilbert Rousset   PROPRIETORS: E. Coliadis and A.G. Wastell   OPEN: Mon to Sat, exc Sat L; 12 to 2.30, 5.30 to 11.30   CLOSED: Christmas, New Year and bank hols   MEALS: alc (main courses £8 to £14). Set L £12.50 (2 courses) to £15.50, Set pre-theatre D £9.95 (2 courses), Set D £15.50   SERVICE: 12.5%, card slips closed   CARDS: Access, Amex, Diners, Visa   DETAILS: 70 seats. Private parties: 70 main room. Vegetarian meals. Children's helpings. Smart dress preferred. Wheelchair access. Music. Air-conditioned. Fax: 071-379 6184

Malabar

map 12

27 Uxbridge Street, W8 7TQ
071-727 8800

COOKING 1
COST £14–£41

Most dishes on the short menu plough the familiar furrow of tandoori chicken and lamb tikka, but there are departures in the form of charcoal grilled chicken livers marinated in yogurt and spices. Indeed, the Malabar connection has more to do with spices than with a regional cooking style. Long chicken is cooked with cloves and ginger, sweetcorn kernels are mixed with green chillies and peppers, while banana (with ginger) and pumpkin (with butter and fresh herbs) are among vegetable side dishes. Rice pudding with coconut and raisins is one of the more interesting desserts. A dozen and a half wines are under £15, including the Indian fizz, Omar Khayyam. House wine is £8.50, lassi £1.55, or there is mint tea.

CHEF: A. Hossain   PROPRIETORS: Jo Chalmers and Anil Bist   OPEN: all week; 12 (12.30 Sun) to 2.45, 6 to 11.15   CLOSED: 4 days Christmas, last week Aug   MEALS: alc (main courses £4.50 to £9.50). Set L (Mon to Sat) and D £11.75 and £29.90 (2 persons). Sun buffet £6.95. Cover 80p   SERVICE: net prices   CARDS: Access, Visa   DETAILS: 56 seats. Private parties: 14 main room, 20 private room. Vegetarian meals. Children welcome. No music. Air-conditioned (partial)

Mandarin Kitchen £

map 12

14–16 Queensway, W2 3RX
071-727 9012 and 9468

COOKING 1
COST £16–£62

Queensway has a healthy contingent of Chinese eating-places, with other ethnic establishments providing friendly competition, and this restaurant is an asset to the neighbourhood. Seafood is the main strength. Interesting items such as steamed geoduck (Alaskan king clam) with garlic and soy, carp pot with ginger and spring onion, and sizzling pomfret in mandarin sauce augment king prawns, crab and eel in various guises. Scottish lobsters are served six ways with soft noodles. High points from recent meals have included deep-fried shreds of smoked chicken, fried shredded beef with chilli, Cantonese roast duck and pak choi greens with oyster sauce. Some have found the dining-room 'cavernous and gloomy'. One reporter also had the 'unusual experience of squeezing past a waitress in the men's lavatory putting on her make-up in the mirror'. Service can be variable, despite the legions of staff. Chinese tea, saké and Tsingtao beer suit the food; otherwise choose from the short, reasonably priced wine list. House wine is £7.50.

CHEF: Mr Man   PROPRIETOR: Helen Cheung   OPEN: all week; noon to 11.30   CLOSED: 25 and 26 Dec   MEALS: alc (main courses £5 to £20). Set L and D £8.90 to £10.50   SERVICE: not inc CARDS: Access, Amex, Diners, Visa   DETAILS: 110 seats. Private parties: 20 main room. Vegetarian meals. Children welcome. Smart dress preferred. Wheelchair access. Music. Air-conditioned

▲ Manzi's

map 15

1–2 Leicester Street, WC2H 7BE
071-734 0224

COOKING 1
COST £22–£61

Situated on one side of Leicester Square, this fish restaurant of long standing is often used by theatre or cinema patrons. It remains completely impervious to the march of fashion, serves giant quantities and does the simplest things best. One couple who visit regularly advise avoidance of sauces in favour of plain-grilled or fried items. Chips are a better bet than most other vegetables, and coffee has recently seen a great improvement. Three 'succulent' sardines with a wedge of lemon made a 'thoroughly enjoyable' starter, and a wing and middle cut of accurately cooked skate a filling main course. Most dishes can be Mornayed for those who dare. Service is mainly reliable. Wines are mostly innocent of producers or vintages, so stay with house carafes, from £8.75.

CHEFS/PROPRIETORS: the Manzi family   OPEN: all week, exc Sun L; 12 to 2.45, 5.30 to 11.45 (6 to 10.45 Sun)   CLOSED: 25 and 26 Dec   MEALS: alc (main courses £7 to £25). Set D £17 (from 5.30 to 7.30)   SERVICE: not inc   CARDS: Access, Amex, Diners, Visa   DETAILS: 50 seats upstairs, 70 seats downstairs. Private parties: 20 main room. Vegetarian meals with prior notice. No children under 5. No pipes in dining-room. Wheelchair access (3 steps). Music upstairs ACCOMMODATION: 15 rooms, all with bath/shower. Phone. TV. B&B £40 to £63. Children welcome. Fax: 071-437 4864

▲ *This symbol means accommodation is available.*

Mas Café $\boxed{\text{NEW ENTRY}}$ map 12

6–8 All Saints Road, W11 1HH	COOKING 2
071-243 0969	COST £16–£38

'Mas' is the local word for the carnival in Notting Hill, but you would be wrong to expect Caribbean food here. The chef is from New Zealand, and the style is Pacific Rim with Mediterranean borrowings. A restaurant has been housed in these premises for years, but none has succeeded in creating anything like the frisson that the Mas has. The richly coloured interior and oddly intimate lighting feel good. Enjoyment of an evening here may depend on your taste in music; this is Notting Hill, and the beat goes on.

Phillip Reynolds's cooking shows a determination not to be outdone by its surroundings. First courses offer pasta and gnocchi, pulses and fungi, and items like sauté duck livers with rocket and green beans, or a nage of monkfish, tiger prawns and salmon. Earthiness comes to the fore in main dishes of marinated quails with braised artichokes or roasted loin of pork with white-bean purée. Fish is treated robustly, as in blackened red snapper with tomato and olive oil. A 'mélange' of spring vegetables with chilli oil eaten in May was light but full of fiery flavour, while a starter of duck confit with oyster mushrooms and lentils had plenty of bulk from beans as well, the meat agreeably moist and properly fatty. The kitchen really gets into its stride with seared salmon in a smoked tomato vinaigrette: a large chunk of fish on finely cut leeks with hot oil and 'utterly delicious' roasted smoky cherry tomatoes. Desserts can demonstrate a delicate touch in lavender and rose bavarois with rose syrup, or a childlike wickedness in glazed banana parfait with a light chocolate sauce. Bread is of excellent quality. Mixed vegetables or rosemary potatoes are charged extra and arrive in crazy quantities. The wine list is a terse collection of largely French and Italian bottles with some producers' names missing, but – with the exception of champagne – everything is below £20. House French is £9.

CHEF: Phillip Reynolds   PROPRIETORS: Ian Alexander, Charles Hickey, David Stacey and Michael White   OPEN: all week, exc L Mon and Tue; 12 to 2.45 (11 to 4.45 weekend), 6 to 11.30 (10.30 Sun)   CLOSED: 25 and 26 Dec, bank hols   MEALS: alc (main courses L £3 to £5.50, D £7.50 to £10)   SERVICE: not inc (12.5% for 8 or more), cards slips closed   CARDS: Access, Visa   DETAILS: 70 seats. Private parties: 30 main room, 70 private room. Vegetarian meals. Children's helpings. No-smoking area. Wheelchair access. Music

Mayflower map 15

68–70 Shaftesbury Avenue, W1V 7DF	COOKING 2
071-734 9207	COST £22–£60

This long-standing restaurant on the fringes of Soho Chinatown maintains a high reputation and caters for a mixed crowd of local Chinese and Westerners. The long menu of around 170 dishes makes challenging reading, and it is wise to focus on the hotpots, casseroles and esoteric Cantonese specialities, rather than Westernised sizzling dishes, curries and stir-fries. Reporters have endorsed the quality and satisfying richness of saltfish and chicken with bean curd, and coconut chicken with yams. Here is a kitchen that is at home with fish lips, duck's webs and sea cucumbers, and can deliver deep-fried milk balls, steamed preserved egg with pork, and stewed lamb with dried bean curd. In less demanding territory, you will also find dried scallop and mushroom soup, baked prawns with ginger and spring onion, and grilled duck with lemon sauce. The repertoire also extends to a hefty contingent of one-plate rice and noodle dishes, although these are served only after 11pm. Service is reckoned to be quick, 'with the minimum fuss or elaboration'. Tea flows freely, and orange segments arrive at the end of the meal. House wine is £12.

CHEF: Fook On Chung   PROPRIETOR: Patrick Tsang   OPEN: all week, D only; 5pm to 4am   MEALS: alc (main courses £5 to £12). Set D £12 to £13 (minimum 2 to 4)   SERVICE: not inc   CARDS: Access, Amex, Diners, Visa   DETAILS: 124 seats. Private parties: 40 Main room, 40 private room. Vegetarian meals. Children welcome. Music. Air-conditioned

Melati £ 　　　　　　　　　　　　　　　　　　　　　　　　map 15

21 Great Windmill Street, W1V 7PH 　　　　　　　　　　　COOKING 1
071-734 6964 and 437 2745 　　　　　　　　　　　　　　COST £20–£39

Set in the heart of strip-club Soho, this café is one of the few authentic Indonesian/Malaysian venues in the capital. It consists of narrow, pine-furnished rooms on three floors, with views of the street action from its front windows. The long menu covers a lot of ground, taking in satays, big bowls of laksa soup, a host of noodle dishes and a strong contingent of seafood. Meatless dishes such as pecal longtong (rice cakes with vegetables and peanut sauce) and sambal tauco (fried sliced beans in brown-bean sauce) are attractive options for vegetarians, while composite one-plate meals are useful for a quick snack. Levels of heat and chilli can be unpredictable and occasionally the cooking veers into clumsiness, but there is always relief in desserts such as cendol (an incomparable concoction of jelly strips served with coconut milk and palm syrup). The unasked-for provision of iced water is welcomed; otherwise drink jasmine tea, Bintang or Tiger beer. House wine is £8.45. Melati's sister-restaurant, Minang, serves similar food and can be found at 11 Greek Street, W1V 5LE, Tel: 071-434 1149.

CHEF: Hasyim Damurai   PROPRIETORS: S. Alamsjah and Margaret Ong   OPEN: all week; noon to 11.30 (12.30 Fri and Sat)   CLOSED: 25 Dec   MEALS: alc (main courses £4.50 to £7.50). Set L and D £16.50 (2 courses) to £21.25 (inc wine)   SERVICE: not inc, card slips closed   CARDS: Access, Amex, Diners, Visa   DETAILS: 120 seats. Private parties: 40 main room. Vegetarian meals. Children welcome. Wheelchair access (1 step). Music. Air-conditioned

▲ Le Meridien Hotel, Oak Room 　　　　　　　　　　　map 14

21 Piccadilly, W1V 0BH 　　　　　　　　　　　　　　　COOKING 4
071-734 8000 　　　　　　　　　　　　　　　　　　　COST £31–£75

It doesn't take a genius to work out why the restaurant is called the Oak Room, although the liming of the wood softens and lightens the whole effect, made airier still by a high ceiling. The room is grand but not intimidating, with a few sofas and a piano down one end, and tables spaced widely enough for private conversation. The departure of David Chambers to the London Hilton (see entry, London) could have left a gaping hole in the kitchen, but the world is full of rising stars, one of whom is Alain Marechal, shipped in from Nice. Michel Lorain from Joigny continues to hold the reins by planning the seasonally changing menus, and it all seems to work to advantage.

The cooking is high French, the menu enticing and inventive, even a little playful in its use of Australian yabbies (crayfish) served with girolle mushrooms and French beans in a béarnaise mousseline, or the coffee-flavoured sauce for roast duck. Truffles are used intelligently: sliced and left uncooked for greater aroma around a roast fillet of turbot on a bed of white haricot beans, with wonderful-tasting shallots strewn about.

Regulars will note that some items remain the same – gazpacho with warm langoustines and quenelles of courgette, for example – but variety within and between dishes overcomes any sense of having been here before, and the interplay of flavours and texture contrasts is intriguing. A centrepiece of sweetbreads, nicely crisped but soft inside, partners half a dozen small pieces of slightly gelatinous calf's cheek, each hidden under a small lettuce leaf; a rich sauce with great depth of flavour and a gentle nuttiness is offset by a just-sharp sprinkling of gribiche, the whole thrown into relief by a few threads of finely shredded Belgian endive. There is never too much going on in a dish, yet always enough to intrigue. Only occasionally does it slip over into unnecessary garnishing, as when caviare is scattered over a braised knuckle of veal to no great effect.

Puddings can also employ striking flavours, including lemon grass with vanilla in a dish of crispy sliced apples and pineapple sorbet, and if a little of the whizz seems to have gone out of the cooking by then, the skill certainly does not diminish, as a hot passion-fruit soufflé shows. Bread is a big disappointment, petits fours are good, and service is plentiful and personable enough. The sommelier knows his wines, which are almost entirely claret and burgundy at silly prices. Alsace and the Loire offer a tiny glimpse of sanity. Good house wine is £15.50 (£3.35 per glass).

CHEFS: Alain Marechal and Michel Lorain   PROPRIETOR: Le Meridien Hotel   OPEN: Mon to Sat, exc Sat L; 12 to 2.30, 7 to 10.30   CLOSED: 3 weeks Aug   MEALS: alc (main courses £18 to £25). Set L £24.50, Set D £28 (inc wine) to £46   SERVICE: not inc   CARDS: Access, Amex, Diners, Visa   DETAILS: 50 seats. Vegetarian meals. Children welcome. Jacket and tie. No cigars/pipes in dining-room. Wheelchair access (also WC). Music. Air-conditioned   ACCOMMODATION: 264 rooms, all with bath/shower. TV. Phone. Air-conditioned. Room only £235 to £650. Rooms for disabled. Lift. Children welcome. Baby facilities. Afternoon teas. Swimming-pool. Sauna. Snooker. Fax: 071-437 3574

Le Mesurier
map 11

113 Old Street, EC1V 9JR
071-251 8117

COOKING 1*
COST £28–£42

Gillian Enthoven's formula – lunches only, with the restaurant available for private parties in the evenings as long as there are at least 15 and not more than 26 of you – continues unchanged. In the unlikely setting of a three-storey terraced town house on Old Street, a rather cottagey atmosphere is created, enlivened by some old advertising posters for antique brands of laxative and long-forgotten exhibitions at the Natural History Museum. The doorbell must be rung to gain admittance, and once inside you will be offered a tiny menu of three choices per course. The accent is bistro French, with soufflés and pancakes a particular love. A reporter admired the gentleness of an anchovy cream sauce with spinach soufflé to start, but thought the lime chutney with fried crab-cakes needed to have been sharper. Garlicky rack of lamb with a 'rich, well-balanced' orange sauce worked a treat and came with blackened filo cases of puréed leek. On the deficit side, sea bass needed longer cooking, but had an impressively vibrant red pepper sauce. Cheeses, an unimaginative French selection, disappointed, but an iced coffee soufflé was 'wonderfully rich, creamy and smooth'. Coffee itself is 'dark and powerful'. The wine list, from Corney and Barrow, has sound, if unsurprising, choices. House French is £9.

CHEFS: Gillian Enthoven and Loic le Pape PROPRIETOR: Gillian Enthoven OPEN: Mon to Fri, L only; 12 to 3 (D party bookings only 6 to 9) CLOSED: 10 days Christmas, 3 weeks Aug MEALS: alc (main courses £8.50 to £12) SERVICE: 12.5% (optional), card slips closed CARDS: Access, Amex, Diners, Visa DETAILS: 25 seats. Private parties: 25 main room. Vegetarian meals with prior notice. No children under 10. Smart dress preferred. Wheelchair access. No music. Fax: 071-608 3504

Mijanou ▮ ⅍   map 13

143 Ebury Street, SW1W 9QN   COOKING 2*
071-730 4099   COST £26–£55

'Our restaurant goes against the current,' write the Blechs. It is not large and bare, it is not noisy (although smoke-free upstairs may be jollier than downstairs), and it is neither Italian nor contemporary British in outlook. Sonia Blech describes herself 'as an old Franco-Italian grandma who cooks what she loves in the most honest way she knows'. The result is a menu that responds only minimally to markets and seasons and, in the hurly-burly of London restaurant life, can seem a little old-fashioned.

Fruity and sweet flavours in first courses can produce esoteric combinations – for example, a terrine of oxtail and foie gras on a muscat and passion-fruit jelly, served with an apple and onion relish. Generous quantities are also something of a throwback, as are the 'little bits of this and that' which can fill a plate. Grilled veal escalope comes with batons of courgette, beans, carrot, swede, baby squash filled with spinach and topped with almonds, and small cheese-flavoured rounds of polenta, not to mention a large volume of sauce made from port, red wine and pecan nuts. But the basics are of high quality and, in the case of fillet of beef grilled and stuffed with exotic mushrooms, are cooked exactly as requested. Among puddings there is praise for a light chocolate mousse surrounded by light sponge in a Grand Marnier sauce.

The urbane Mr Blech is knowledgeable about wine and also operates a small retail outlet. Each dish on the menu has a numbered selection of wines that are considered appropriate – a good idea in theory but one that entails much tedious cross-reference. If help is needed, it is easier to ask. His other notion, of listing wines under 20 headings according to type as well as country of origin, is more successful, and the admirably wide-ranging list is on the ball and generally fair-priced. Fifteen wines by the glass (mostly around £3.50) are a lesson to other restaurants. CELLARMAN'S CHOICE: Vin de Pays d'Oc, Les Chemins du Bassac Rosé 1992, £12; Pouilly Fuissé 'Futs de Chêne' 1992, Dom. des Gerbeaux, £22.

CHEF: Sonia Blech PROPRIETORS: Neville and Sonia Blech OPEN: Mon to Fri; 12 to 2, 7 to 10 (11 if booked) CLOSED: 2 weeks Christmas, 10 days Easter, last 3 weeks Aug, bank hols MEALS: alc (main courses £16). Set L £13.50 (2 courses) to £16.50, Set D £35 SERVICE: not inc CARDS: Access, Amex, Diners, Visa DETAILS: 30 seats. 6 tables outside. Private parties: 25 main room. Vegetarian meals. Children welcome. Smart dress preferred. No smoking upstairs. Wheelchair access (3 steps). No music. Air-conditioned. Fax: 071-823 6402

Mirabelle

NEW ENTRY map 14

56 Curzon Street, W1Y 8DL
071-499 4636

COOKING 3*
COST £26–£69

Two Japanese-owned French restaurants inhabit Curzon Street (the other is Les Saveurs, see entry, London), but this one offers Japanese food as well, in the tatami room or teppanyaki bar that share the basement with the main dining-room. The Mirabelle also boasts a garden where pre-prandial business is dealt with. The judicious use of skylights and backlit arched windows creates the impression that you are eating at ground-floor level, thus avoiding the dinginess that can afflict some basement restaurants.

The various set menus, including a six-course *menu surprise*, are bolstered by a fairly long *carte*. Prices indicate that this basement is not for bargains. One man dining in May opted for the surprise package and received a circular piece of pâté de foie gras with diced beetroot and 'incredibly fine tendrils of crisp potato', red mullet on a bed of spinach and salsify with a citrus butter sauce (the acid sharpness of which just prevented the whole from toppling into over-richness), and then a 'quite superb' dish of three griddled scallops, their corals mixed with diced tomato, with watercress purée and a chive butter. So far, so good. The main course was thought somewhat disappointing: good beef tournedos was let down by overly chewy texture and a 'rather insipid' stock. A cheese course that consisted of a piece of Roquefort on toasted brioche with walnuts, apples and grapes used too overbearing a cheese for the delicate accompaniments, but a slice of chocolate marquise sprinkled with more walnuts was appositely rich, with 'excellent texture'. Other dishes that have garnered praise have been celeriac parcels stuffed with truffles and morels, 'very fine' langoustine tails on fresh pasta with tomatoes and courgettes, and dark chocolate soufflé with a warm coffee sauce.

A multiplicity of breads is offered, seemingly throughout the meal; they may contain onions, caraway seeds or sun-dried tomatoes, but all are of high standard. Espresso is 'strong and reviving', and service is friendlier than the surroundings may suggest. There is enough judgement and flair in Michael Croft's cooking to justify the premium prices charged, although wine prices are more difficult to understand. The wines themselves are a pedigree collection of the smartest clarets and burgundies imaginable, with only token showings from elsewhere. If money is no object, it is a fine list. Otherwise the sommelier's recommendations are all helpfully under £20.

'The next table asked "What is tiramisù?" "It's white and kind of sloshy," [explained the waitress].' (On eating in Sussex)

CHEF: Michael Croft PROPRIETOR: Akitada Sekine OPEN: Mon to Sat, exc Sat L; 12 to 2, 6.30 to 10.30 CLOSED: 2 weeks August, bank hols MEALS: alc (main courses £16.50 to £19.50). Set L £15 (2 courses) to £18, Set D £28 to £45 SERVICE: net prices, card slips closed CARDS: Access, Amex, Diners, Visa DETAILS: 120 seats. Private parties: 14 main room, 10 to 34 private rooms. Vegetarian meals with prior notice. Children welcome. Jacket and tie D. Music. Air-conditioned. Fax: 071-499 5449

Mr Kong £ {map 15}

21 Lisle Street, WC2H 7BA   COOKING 2
071-437 7341 and 9679   COST £13–£35

With over 70 restaurants in Chinatown, quality must be high and prices reasonable if you want to 'stand out from the rest', writes Mr Kong. 'We are right in the heart of theatre-land,' he adds, 'so we know what theatre-goers need – fast service and good food.' We cannot grumble at that, although one who had gone for a leisurely dinner become inadvertently caught up in a scramble: 'The main course arrived while I was still eating my soup.' Cooking is mostly Cantonese, with some spicy dishes for good measure, and the long *carte* includes braised duck webs with fish lips and a good line in chicken. What Chinese customers eat most is either emperor or mandarin chicken, but it also comes fried in hot sauce, cold, and paper-wrapped.

Seafood is a strong suit and runs to steamed scallops with garlic, baked lobster with ginger and spring onion on fried noodles, sweet-and-sour fish, and mussels or crab in black bean and chilli. It is worth considering specials such a boiled geoduck with jelly fish, or boneless duck web with baby clam in the pot. Rice is 'good and sticky'. There are no puddings. The atmosphere, especially downstairs, does not get many votes, and credit card slips are left open even though a 10 per cent service charge is included in the prices. Tea or rice wine are alternatives to the 18 European wines; house French is £6.80.

CHEFS: K. Kong and Y.W. Lo PROPRIETORS: K. Kong, Y.W. Lo, M.T. Lee, K.C. Tang and C.Y. Chau OPEN: all week; noon to 1.45am CLOSED: 4 days Christmas MEALS: alc (main courses £5.50 to £12). Set L and D £8.60 to £21 (minimum 2). Minimum £7 after 5pm SERVICE: net prices CARDS: Access, Amex, Diners, Visa DETAILS: 115 seats. Private parties: 40 main room. Vegetarian meals. Children welcome. Smart dress preferred. Wheelchair access (1 step). Music. Air-conditioned

Mitsukoshi {map 14}

Dorland House,
14–20 Regent Street, SW1Y 4PH   COOKING 2*
071-930 0317   COST £36–£85

This basement of a department store makes a convenient lunch stop for Japanese and Westerners alike. Its forte is a series of well-balanced set menus at fixed prices. The shokado lunch box of tempura, grilled or fried fish, boiled vegetables, rice, miso soup and pickles is £25. There are kaiseki banquets, a run of different sushi combinations, and seven-item shabu-shabu and sukiyaki meals as well as a *carte* that includes a variety of seaweeds, squid sashimi with sea urchin, fermented soya beans with tuna, and tempura. Staff are happy to explain anything that is a mystery, although that may not extend to whisky prices: £230 for a bottle of 25-year-old Bowmore, for instance. Wines are a curious mix, with a quota of ostentatious names at three-figure prices, making saké a relatively good buy. House wine is £15.

CHEF: J. Shimada PROPRIETOR: Mitsukoshi (UK) Ltd OPEN: Mon to Sat; 12 to 2, 6 to 9.30 MEALS: alc (courses £4.50 to £27). Set L and D £20 to £50. Cover £1.50 SERVICE: 15%, card slips closed CARDS: Access, Amex, Diners, Visa DETAILS: 80 seats. Private parties: 80 main room, 12 and 24 private rooms. Vegetarian meals with prior notice. No children under 2. Jacket and tie. No music. Air-conditioned. Fax: 071-839 1167

Miyama   map 14

| 38 Clarges Street, W1Y 7PJ | COOKING 3 |
| 071-499 2443 | COST £24–£67 |

Fumio Miyama is 'a rare and distinguished chef-patron' who is capable of producing some of the best Japanese food in London. His Mayfair restaurant is in a side street off the main drag, done out in 'modern international Japanese' style. Austere pictures and sculptures line the walls, the tables are – unusually – laid with white cloths and napkins, and small vases of flowers add a colourful touch. The menu lists the familiar repertoire of set meals – tempura, teriyaki, sushi and teppanyaki – while more unusual dishes can be found on the *carte*. Among the highlights are ohitashi (spinach and flaked bonito in soy sauce), delicate dobin-mushi 'consommé' served in a special Japanese pot, and chawan mushi (egg, vegetables and chicken slowly steamed in a small cup and served with green herbs as garnishes). Even more impressive is unagi kabayaki: two massive pieces of grilled eel, with a wonderful rich oily texture and a delicate glaze which was deemed by one reporter to be 'the epitome of eeldom'. Incidentals and extras such as miso soup, rice and pickles are of a very high order. Saké is offered with a choice of different patterned cups. The wine list is limited to around two dozen familiar European names. House wine is £10. A second branch, City Miyama, is at 17 Godliman Street, EC4, Tel: 071-489 1937.

CHEFS/PROPRIETORS: F. Miyama and T. Miura OPEN: all week, exc L Sat and Sun; 12 to 2.30, 6 to 10.30 MEALS: alc (main courses £8 to £16). Set L £12 to £18, Set D £32 to £40 SERVICE: 15% CARDS: Access, Amex, Diners, Visa DETAILS: 67 seats. Private parties: 28 main room, 6 and 10 private rooms. Vegetarian meals. Children's helpings. Smart dress preferred. Wheelchair access. Music. Air-conditioned. Fax: 071-493 1573

Monkeys   map 13

| 1 Cale Street, Chelsea Green, SW3 3QT | COOKING 2 |
| 071-352 4711 | COST £20–£59 |

An old town house on a quiet Chelsea corner is a pleasing spot for a restaurant. The primate theme – pictures of monkeys everywhere, a stuffed toy surveying the dining-room – may briefly baffle, but the ambience is a cool and relaxing one, even if someone thought it 'a bit Dickensian'. Thomas Benham's cooking is in recognisable Anglo-French idiom, and comes via a *carte* or a pair of fixed-price menus – one of three courses, one of four. A dinner in April suggested that there is some capability in the performance, but some dishes were let down by poor finishing. Terrines, one of sweetbreads and wild mushrooms, the other of brill, salmon and scallops, were both of high quality but were muffled by stridently fruity sauces. Similarly, the chicken that came with pine-nuts on salad leaves had been subjected to a marinating that spoiled the overall effect. Mignons of venison, from the cheaper *prix fixe*, had 'a good rich gamey sauce' and were almost overwhelmingly generous in quantity. The 'respectable' cheese selection may be a better bet than the crème that, on this occasion, was rather too brûlée for its own good. Coffee and petits fours were pronounced 'excellent'. Service, has been found courteous and helpful, although it can get a bit stretched. House wine is £11.

CHEF: Thomas Benham   PROPRIETORS: Thomas and Brigitte Benham   OPEN: Mon to Fri; 12.30 to 2.30, 7.30 to 11   CLOSED: 2 weeks Easter, 3 weeks Aug, 25 Dec, 1 Jan   MEALS: alc (main courses £13 to £19.50). Set L £12.50 to £17.50, Set D £22.50 to £35. Minimum £17.50 D   SERVICE: not inc   CARDS: Access, Visa   DETAILS: 40 seats. Private parties: 50 main room. Vegetarian meals with prior notice. Children welcome. Smart dress preferred. No pipes in dining-room. Wheelchair access (3 steps). No music. Air-conditioned

Museum Street Café ✳

map 14

47 Museum Street, WC1A 1LY   COOKING 2*
071-405 3211   COST £22–£35

Revolutionary upheaval erupted at the Café in April 1994, when it reopened after a six-week lay-off with an open-plan kitchen and 10 more seats. Furthermore, it now takes credit cards and sells wine. Whatever next? Reports suggest that standards remain on target. One pair, taking advantage of the chance to have a good look-in on the kitchen, opined that it must be 'the most placid in London'. The new skylit seating area near the bar will be pleasant indeed at lunch.

Menus continue to be short and to the point and speak an unmistakably contemporary language: chicken liver crostini, leek and goats' cheese tart, and rocket salad with marinated beef, mushrooms and a ginger and orange vinaigrette. It helps to be a devotee of the chargrill when it comes to main courses. On a spring lunch menu, four of the five options – salmon, tuna, chicken and beefburger – had all received the treatment. The tuna, appreciated for its 'succulent' texture, came with lentils, green beans, 'chunky' carrot purée and a 'very green and very fresh' salsa verde. Baking skills are evident in orange poppy seed cake and hazelnut spice cake served with prunes cooked in red wine. Cheeses are from Neal's Yard Dairy. Espresso was 'sharp and bitter' for one, but some people like it that way.

The fledgling wine list is a model of concise intelligence. It contains just two dozen items, but each can be ordered with confidence. More halves would be useful. House wines from the Pays d'Oc are £7.90. Those for whom old habits die hard should note that you can still pitch up with your own bottle, but you will now be charged £4 to have it opened.

CHEFS/PROPRIETORS: Gail Koerber and Mark Nathan   OPEN: Mon to Fri; 12.30 to 2.30, 6.30 to 9.30   CLOSED: bank hols   MEALS: Set L £12 (2 courses) to £15, Set D £17 (2 courses) to £21   SERVICE: not inc (12.5% for 5 or more)   CARDS: Access, Diners, Visa   DETAILS: 34 seats. Vegetarian meals with prior notice. Children welcome. No smoking. Wheelchair access (2 steps; also WC). No music. Air-conditioned

Neal Street Restaurant

map 15

26 Neal Street, WC2H 9PS
071-836 8368

COOKING 2
COST £43–£71

The restaurant arm of Antonio Carluccio's Covent Garden operation does seem to divide opinion: some frankly doubt whether it should be in the *Guide* at all, while others relish the simplicity of most of the food, the quality of raw materials and the 'charming and chatty' service. Almost everyone regrets the high prices charged, including extra for vegetables and 15 per cent service added automatically to the bill. It all goes on in a long, light, mirrored space with cream-painted brick walls and colourful abstract paintings. Antipasti are properly appetising, and may include 'unusual and delicious' items like courgette slices marinated in chilli oil. A straightforward plate of chanterelle, oyster, girolle and button mushrooms makes a great signature starter.

On the other hand, home-made spaghetti with a simple tomato and basil sauce impressed for the precise texture of the pasta. Salmon tagliatelle with a cream sauce used good fish, delicately poached, and medallions of beef with a sauce of ceps achieved 'remarkable depth' through the use of a generous quantity of fungi. Desserts are well-executed too: pear poached in white wine, stuffed with 'soft, slightly sour' stracchino cheese and garnished with rocket, or fine semifreddo with layers of rich flavour – chocolate, almond and coffee. Both espresso and cappuccino are 'good and strong'.

The wine list is predominantly Italian, as is only seemly. Many of the makers are very good, but prices – with the greater part well over £20 – will depress. The reluctance of Italian growers to bottle in halves lessens choice in that department. House selections are £12.50.

CHEF: Nick Melmoth-Coombs   PROPRIETOR: Antonio Carluccio   OPEN: Mon to Sat; 12.30 to 2.30, 7.30 to 11   MEALS: alc (main courses £15.50 to £19)   SERVICE: 15%, card slips closed   CARDS: Access, Amex, Diners, Visa   DETAILS: 65 seats. Private parties: 26 private room. Vegetarian meals. Children welcome. Smart dress preferred. Wheelchair access (1 step). No music. Air-conditioned. Fax: 071-497 1361

New Loon Fung £

map 15

42–44 Gerrard Street, W1V 7LP
071-437 6232

COOKING 1
COST £18–£45

Up a flight of stairs, next door to the Loon Fung supermarket, is the latest incarnation of this Chinatown stalwart. Inside are two large rooms, graciously done out in shades of pink with well-spaced tables and a cool, airy feel that is altogether different from the 'traffic jams' of some similar Soho venues. The well-reported dim-sum menu served from 11.30am to 5pm (from 11 on Sunday) offers a wide selection of morsels, including curried whelks, scallop dumplings and ox tripe with liver. Excellent examples have included 'outstandingly good' prawn and chive dumplings sitting on a cabbage leaf in their steaming basket, crispy wun-tun, Vietnamese spring rolls and slithery char siu cheung-fun. Dishes arrive straight from the kitchen, ingredients are noticeably fresh, and flavours are full-frontal. The main menu is a monster tome of 250 items that are firmly in the Cantonese mould of hotpots, casseroles, heaps of seafood and a mighty contingent of one-plate rice, soup and noodle dishes, with a nod to

Peking and Szechuan along the way. The wine list is creditable and keenly priced. House wine is £8, or £2.10 per glass.

CHEFS: Mr Man and Mr Suen PROPRIETOR: Mr J. Chin OPEN: all week; 11.30am to 11.30pm (midnight Fri and Sat) CLOSED: 2 to 3 days Christmas MEALS: alc (main courses £5 to £16). Set L and D £9 (2 courses, min 2) to £24 (minimum 8) SERVICE: not inc CARDS: Access, Amex, Diners, Visa DETAILS: 400 seats. Private parties: 280 main room, 30 private room. Vegetarian meals. Children's helpings. Music. Air-conditioned. Fax: 071-437 3540

Nico Central
map 14

35 Great Portland Street, W1N 5DD
071-436 8846

COOKING 3
COST £26–£44

This and Simply Nico (see entry, London) are both chips off the old Ladenis block that have gone from being hot-shot marvels under the maestro's regime to a rather more modest and comfortable middle age. Nico Central is calming, light and airy, with tables set close enough for eavesdropping. One couple finds it 'useful' at lunch and 'a nice place for a quiet intimate meal at night'. The menu is a canny mix of dishes that appeal for both luxury and flavour, all attractively packaged at a price that readers consider fair – 'one of London's bargains'. The food is not exploratory, but carefully researched and considered, designed for a market that likes to see confident cooking and copper-bottomed security of technique for its money. That market is satisfied by pink, moist lamb 'expertly cooked', chicken 'soft, tender and full of flavour', 'excellent baked brill', and duck that is 'crispy outside, moist and succulent inside', served with borlotti beans.

The choice of nine or ten options per course is generous, and the style is a satisfying mix of flavours, some classical, some with a bias to south and south-west France, including foie gras and chicken liver pâté on toasted brioche, poached egg with béarnaise sauce in a mushroom tartlet, or baked fillet of brill with provençale vegetables. Everything fits, including crunchy mange-tout and 'just-picked' carrots 'not swimming in butter but glistening', outstanding mashed potatoes and crisp, lightly salted chips. The cheeseboard offers a fair selection in prime condition, and puddings include 'the most delicious mango sorbet I have ever eaten'. A set dinner of this quality for £22 is considered good value for money, and the à la carte has been 'worth every penny'. Reporters noted a loss of sharpness in service with the departure of Marion Scrutton, but a new manager, Robin Bidgood, is now in place. It is possible to drink well and still come away with a reasonable bill thanks to a fair number of bottles under £20, house wine at £11.50 and four other good wines by the glass at £4 each.

CHEF: Andrew Jeffs PROPRIETORS: Nico and Dinah-Jane Ladenis OPEN: Mon to Sat, exc Sat L; 12 to 2, 7 to 11 CLOSED: 11 days Christmas, 4 days Easter, bank hol Mon L MEALS: alc L (main courses £8 to £14). Set D £22 SERVICE: net prices, card slips closed CARDS: Access, Amex, Diners, Visa DETAILS: 55 seats. Private parties: 10 main room, 10 private room. Vegetarian meals. No children under 5. Smart dress preferred. No pipes in dining-room. Wheelchair access (1 step). No music. Air-conditioned. Fax: 071-355 4877

'The white wine was warmer than the iced water, which was warmer than the red wine.' (On eating in Cumbria)

Nosh Brothers

773 Fulham Road, SW6 5HA
COOKING 1*
071-736 7311
COST £25–£41

The framework here is a pair of restaurateurs doing a Blues Brothers comedy routine in bouncer gear and dark glasses. At the Parsons Green end of the Fulham Road, Mick and Nick Nosh have created a two-storey shrine to themselves, with blown-up photographs the only wall adornment and the bill arriving with a picture postcard of the 'brothers' clutching a magnum of Chianti and a naked woman. The heart plummets. The joke, however, has never obscured the culinary flair behind the set-up. The reasonably priced menu offers relatively simple food of the likes of vichyssoise, smoked haddock risotto, salmon with lemon hollandaise, penne with tomato and basil, steak and chips, apple turnover and banoffi pie. It is all served in generous portions to a background of loud rock.

A report of a May dinner from a man left cold by the themed approach mentions 'extremely good' gazpacho full of 'lively' vegetables and pieces of ice, a 'remarkably delicate' tortilla filled with red peppers, potatoes and peas, and a mushroom, leek and Gruyère tart that had fine pastry and came with an unexpected salad of tomatoes, olives and asparagus. The horseradish accompaniment to braised beef onglet was in the mashed potato beneath it (a neat idea). Desserts were top-drawer chocolate mousse with a piece of honeycomb on top and a slice of straightforward carrot cake. Two of the six main courses had run out by 9pm, as had bread. The wine list offers seven whites, nine reds and two champagnes, a few of them served by the glass. House wines from the Languedoc are £8.50.

CHEFS: Mick Nosh and Chris Endeacott PROPRIETORS: Mick and Nick Nosh OPEN: Mon to Sat, D only; 7 to 11 MEALS: alc (main courses £7.50 to £12). SERVICE: 12.5%, card slips closed CARDS: Access, Amex, Visa DETAILS: 65 seats. Private parties: 65 main room. Vegetarian meals. Children welcome. Wheelchair access. Music. Air-conditioned. Fax: 071-736 7311

Noughts 'n' Crosses
map 10

77 The Grove, W5 5LL
COOKING 2
081-840 7568
COST £23–£34

Sheltering behind the Ealing Broadway shopping centre, this neighbourhood restaurant produces reliable food that attracts local support. There are three rooms, including a conservatory at the back overlooking a small, beautifully maintained garden where tables are put out when the sun shines. Anthony Ma hails originally from Hong Kong, and occasionally allows Chinese influences to creep into some of his essentially French cooking.

The seasonally changing fixed-price menu offers a fair deal of choice. In the spring, Italian influences were blossoming among the crêpes and the rouille. Spinach gnocchi with tomatoes in an 'intense' mushroom béchamel were a success, though the bruschetta, despite good grilled aubergine and tomatoes, suffered from bland mozzarella and flabby dressing. The oriental tendency surfaced in fillets of John Dory with a sauce of spring onions and soy that was sufficiently well judged not to overpower the fish. Other bold ideas have included tagliatelle with mussels and leeks in a spiced yellow-bean sauce, and wild rabbit with apricots, rosemary and mustard. Desserts, too, try out new combinations: a 'pleasantly moist' baked almond, coconut and citrus pudding and a more substantial white chocolate and hazelnut cheesecake. Vegetables are plentiful and first-rate, breads offer lots of choice, and filter coffee is strong. Service has been described as 'efficient, but taciturn and cool'. The wine list is perfunctory, but prices are reasonable. House Bergerac is £8.90.

CHEF: Anthony Ma   PROPRIETORS: Jörgen Kunath and Anthony Ma   OPEN: Tue to Sat, D only, and Sun L; 12 to 2, 7 to 10   CLOSED: 26 Dec to 4 Jan, Aug   MEALS: Set L Sun £14.90, Set D £18.90   SERVICE: not inc (10% for 7 or more)   CARDS: Access, Amex, Visa   DETAILS: 55 seats. 5 tables outside. Private parties: 25 main room, 25 private room. Vegetarian meals. Children's helpings Sun L. Smart dress preferred. No-smoking area. Wheelchair access (1 step). Music. Fax: 081-840 1905

Odette's 🍶

map 11

130 Regent's Park Road, NW1 8XL
071-586 5486 and 8766

COOKING 3
COST £20–£51

It is pleasant indeed to sit in the sun in front of Odette's and have lunch brought out to you. It might be pleasanter still if this villagey stretch of Regent's Park Road were not, on some days, a busy jumble of double-parked cars, builders' vans and parping horns. Retreat inside to the calm of Odette's, and a warren of irregularly shaped rooms awaits. Most people like the idiosyncratic character, the informality and liveliness. The conservatory at the back is airy and light, while the dining-room's gilded mirrors and green velvet chairs 'give it the look of a French drawing-room'. The basement wine bar is comfortable and modestly priced, serving up oysters, Caesar salad, crab risotto, rumpsteak burger, or plaice 'n' chips.

The food is a bright modern run of ideas that might have been imported straight from California: creamed salsify and wilted sorrel soup, fillet of red mullet with pesto tagliatelle and gazpacho sauce, or baked halibut with a compote of spicy aubergines and coriander. It crackles with ideas and combinations that can, to some, be startling, such as toasted scallops with salt cod mash and black pudding, or sauté foie gras with soufflé potato pancake, prune and cinnamon. It prompts the comment that 'this is the most individual, the least cliché-ridden English restaurant I have been to for a long time'.

Praise is heaped on a salad of squid and asparagus ('an ambitious melange of strong flavours'), on chorizo sausage and lentils which add depth to beef fillet, and on rhubarb and mascarpone trifle (like an old-fashioned fool) which was 'a triumph of simplicity and felicity'. Another found the selection of Spanish cheeses 'a pleasant surprise'. In the other camp – for Odette's does divide opinion – reporters would generally prefer more and better vegetables. Wild mushroom risotto has been judged 'artless', and some of the marriages – squid with beans, or pork kebab and oysters – are not made in heaven. Although it is good to see innovation, more road-testing of experimental ideas before they left the kitchen would be welcome.

Wines draw heavily from Bibendum just up the road, and are laid out by style and weight rather than by country. They match the food's maverick enthusiasms, yet have an eye for quality. Prices of some might be more enticing, but there is ample choice under £20, and 'wines of the month' promote ad hoc bottles of interest. Half-bottles abound, fine house wines from the pays d'Oc are from £9.95, and 16 wines by the glass range from £3.50 to £5. CELLARMAN'S CHOICE: Cameron Winery Pinot Blanc 1991, £19.55; Bandol 1992, Dom. de la Tour du Bon, £19.55.

CHEF: Paul Holmes PROPRIETOR: Simone Green OPEN: all week, exc Sat L and Sun D; 12.30 to 2.30, 7 to 11 MEALS: alc (main courses restaurant £7 to £14, wine bar £5 to £8). Set L £10 SERVICE: not inc, card slips closed CARDS: Access, Amex, Diners, Visa DETAILS: 55 seats. 4 tables outside. Private parties: 30 main room, 8 private room. Vegetarian meals. Children's helpings. Smart dress preferred. No music. Air-conditioned

O'Keefe's £ map 14

| 19 Dering Street, W1R 9AA | COOKING 1 |
| 071-495 0878 | COST £18–£29 |

'A useful place off Oxford Street for a quick lunch', O'Keefe's has seen a change of chef since the last *Guide*, although the style is not radically different. The room is bright, minimally decorated, with close-packed tables, a take-away counter along one side and a glimpse of the engine room. The canny menu runs well on enthusiasm and some basic skills. Most first courses and puddings are designed for quick assembly – or else prepared beforehand – leaving hands free for grilling main-course fish, chicken or Cumberland sausage. Salad greens are sprinkled about more liberally than the menu indicates, even appearing underneath a risotto of pesto and field mushrooms. Fish varies from salmon ceviche and its Nordic counterpart, sweet cured herring, through fish-cakes to a thin slice of seared tuna enlivened with garlic, red chilli and ginger. Thai chicken and Irish stew indicate the free-for-all scope, although Anglo-Italian ideas form the backbone, and simple Bob's-your-uncle food is the result. Bread is fresh, varied, and offered more than once, and breakfast lasts from 8 to 10.30. Mark-ups on the short wine list are reasonable, with house wine at £7.50 (£1.85 per glass).

CHEFS: Beth Coventry, Sarah Jobson and Eliza Hare PROPRIETOR: Romano Crolla OPEN: Mon to Sat, exc Sat D; 12.30 to 3.30 (4 Sat), 7.30 to 10 CLOSED: 25 and 26 Dec, bank hols MEALS: alc (main courses £5.50 to £8) SERVICE: not inc L, 12.5% D DETAILS: 38 seats. 4 tables outside. Vegetarian meals. Children's helpings on request. No smoking at bar. Wheelchair access. Music. Fax: 071-629 7082

Olivo map 11

| 21 Eccleston Street, SW1W 9LX | COOKING 1 |
| 071-730 2505 | COST £25–£41 |

'A useful find near Victoria station,' said one of this modern trattoria with a leaning towards Sardinian food. The distressed frontage hides a noisy, bare and busy room done out in mustard and blue, into which tables are squeezed. The love affair with extra virgin olive oil is one reason for the cover charge; the others are the basket of mixed bread to dip into it, and a small bowl of fragrant black and green olives. Limpid green oil crops up too on chargrilled vegetables, and in a salad of thin asparagus spears and flaked Parmesan.

There is a full house of other seminal ingredients, from balsamic vinegar and sun-dried tomatoes to particularly good polenta mash (much lighter than it sounds) served with lambs' kidneys. Sardinian specialities include chargrilled stuffed calamari with plum tomatoes, basil and, of course, extra virgin olive oil, and thin spaghetti tossed with grated dried grey mullet roe. Among puddings, mascarpone and lemon tart is creamy and indulgently rich. The head waiter does a good job of greeting, serving and being attentive throughout. From the short Italian wine list, £20 will bring a good bottle and some change. House wine is £8.50 (£2.40 per glass).

CHEF: Giorgio Locatelli PROPRIETORS: Jean-Louis Journade and Mauro Sanna OPEN: Mon to Sat, exc Sat L; 12 to 2.30, 7 to 11 CLOSED: 1 week Christmas, 3 weeks Aug, bank hols MEALS: alc (main courses £8 to £11). Set L £13.50 (2 courses) to £15.50. Cover £1.30 SERVICE: not inc CARDS: Access, Amex, Visa DETAILS: 43 seats. Children's helpings with prior notice. No children under 10. Smart dress preferred. No cigars/pipes in dining-room. Wheelchair access (1 step). Music. Air-conditioned

192 ♥

map 12

192 Kensington Park Road, W11 2ES
071-229 0482

COOKING 2
COST £18–£47

The latest chef at 192 is Albert Clark, son of Ossie Clark and Celia Birtwell, who made a splash in fashion in the swinging '60s. He replaces Josh Hampton, who in turn was successor to Dan Evans. The eras of Maddalena Bonino and Alastair Little are now pre-history. Redecoration has made the interior a little easier on the eye, and the restaurant is now on two levels – ground-floor and basement, though it still caters to a young and happening Notting Hill crowd.

The longish menus change twice a day, which is as often as they could change, but in the opinion of a reporter the food no longer seems to be 'aiming to take the world by storm'. Choices in June included Caesar salad, mozzarella with tomato and basil, Parma ham and melon, and beef carpaccio with shaved Parmesan and truffle oil. Main courses are where the more daring turns are attempted: sea bass steamed with chilli, coriander, ginger and soy; grilled sirloin with baby artichokes and salsa verde; or cold loin of veal with tuna mayonnaise and capers. A salad of baby artichokes, roast peppers, red onion and Gorgonzola was a 'generous plateful', but the dressing was surprisingly 'bland' for one based on blue cheese, and a vegetarian dish of half an aubergine gratinated with mozzarella and wild mushrooms disappointed. Better was a herb-crusted halibut with a 'simple but successful' fennel butter sauce. Puddings offer lots of carbohydrate, but the chocolate brownies with crème fraiche had great textural appeal, and even a bowl of mango sorbet was 'first-rate'. Service is 'not especially communicative, but polite'. The concise and modern wine list displays evidence of sound intelligence in all the regions it covers, and prices are very favourable. For those who want to ring the changes, or just drink modestly, many of the bins are available in two sizes of glass. House French is £8.75.

Remember, if you especially want the set menu, that some restaurants restrict availability, particularly at weekends and on public holidays.

CHEF: Albert Clark   PROPRIETORS: Anthony Mackintosh, John Armit and Tchaik Chassay
OPEN: all week; 12.30 (1 Sun) to 3 (3.30 Sat), 7 to 11.30 (11 Sun)   CLOSED: 25 and 26 Dec, Aug
bank hol   MEALS: alc (main courses £8.50 to £13.50). Set L £8.50 (2 courses)   SERVICE: not
inc   CARDS: Access, Amex, Diners, Visa   DETAILS: 105 seats. 4 tables outside. Private parties:
10 main room. Vegetarian meals. Children's helpings on request. No cigars/pipes in dining-
room. No-smoking area. Wheelchair access. Music. Air-conditioned

Orsino

|NEW ENTRY| map 12

119 Portland Road, W11 4LN   COOKING 1
071-221 3299   COST £20–£40

This sister restaurant to Orso (see entry below) and Joe Allen opened in the
autumn of 1993, marking a move away from the theatreland to which Joe Allen
has stuck since he began naming restaurants after himself and bears, both here
and in New York. To find it, a magnifying glass may be helpful: not to look on the
map but to find the front door. Everybody walks past at least twice. Through the
revolving doors are tall windows, tricksy Venetian blinds, and wall lights that
look as if they want to be something else. Since Anne Kettle has come from
Orso's kitchen, it should be no surprise that the menus are similar. Small pizzas
feature, and main courses are mostly grilled: corn-fed chicken, swordfish and
calf's liver, for example.

Contemporary ingredients – ricotta and buffalo mozzarella, roasted onions
and peppers, and leaves of arugula and dandelion – are assembled in salads,
tossed in with pasta, or thrown together to produce most of the appetisers and
first courses, but always in fairly simple combinations. It all sounds rather
healthy. A lunch might consist of Sicilian vegetables with black olives and
pine-nuts, followed by thin spaghetti with pesto, green beans and new potatoes,
and then ice-cream. Fish is done well, from a hefty portion of 'superb' steamed
mussels cooked with shallots, white wine and herbs, to a roast fillet of John Dory
with wild mushrooms. Treatment of vegetables – celeriac with rosemary, for
example – is just as good, although puddings may sound better than they taste.
Service can be slack on the early-evening shift, perking up later. One reporter
who knows both Orso and Orsino reckons that the food is similar in both, that
the ambience is better here, but service isn't. The Italian wine list clocks up a
good score of top names, and prices are very fair. There are no half-bottles, but
house wine is £9 a litre.

CHEF: Anne Kettle   PROPRIETOR: Orsino Restaurants Ltd   OPEN: all week; noon to 10.45
CLOSED: 24 and 25 Dec   MEALS: alc (main courses £9.50 to £11). Set L £11.50 (2 courses) to
£13.50   SERVICE: not inc   DETAILS: 100 seats. Private parties: 25 private room. Vegetarian
meals. Children welcome. No-smoking area. No music. Air-conditioned. Fax: 071-229 9414

Orso ♥

map 15

27 Wellington Street, WC2E 7DA   COOKING 1
071-240 5269   COST £28–£46

Orso continues to attract a loyal band of regulars for its solid, regional Italian
cooking in basement surroundings that evoke new comparisons every year. The
off-colour white tiles gave one man 'the impression of eating in the changing-

room of the local swimming-pool'. Service can seem a touch 'production-line' for some; others find it perfectly professional. The fairly long menu offers plenty of bright Mediterranean flavour in the appetisers, variously topped small pizzas, a short selection of pasta dishes and a good range of meats. Recommended dishes include saffron spaghetti with scallops and garlic, a generous bowl of penne with broccoli and tomato, 'splendid' spinach and cheese tortellini, and 'excellent' marinated sardines. Many admire the accuracy of cooking in items as diverse as rabbit and monkfish, and the relative lightness of desserts such as panna cotta with strawberries or ricotta cheesecake with raspberry sauce. Vegetables are charged extra but come in fine dressings of olive oil and lemon, and the cappuccino is usually enjoyed. Apart from champagnes, the wine list is exclusively Italian, and boasts many fine producers. Prices run a surprisingly wide gamut, with plenty of choice below £20. Half-bottles are conspicuous by their absence. House wines are £9 a litre.

CHEF: Martin Wilson   PROPRIETOR: Orso Restaurants Ltd   OPEN: all week; noon to midnight   CLOSED: 24 and 25 Dec   MEALS: alc (main courses £9.50 to £11)   SERVICE: not inc   DETAILS: 100 seats. Vegetarian meals. Children welcome. No-smoking area. No music. Air-conditioned. Fax: 071-497 2148

Osteria Antica Bologna ⸙ £   map 10

23 Northcote Road, SW11 1NG   COOKING 1*
071-978 4771   COST £19–£33

Imagine someone running off to Italy, hankering after pub grub, and opening up The Old Manchester Arms in Rome selling steak and kidney pie and chips. Would the Italians go for it? No, it only seems to work the other way round. 'It was born from our love of osteria life in Bologna, where Aurelio grew up and I lived for many years,' writes Rochelle Porteous. Most things in Italy are relaxed, osterias even more so. They peddle simple country food and wine in humble surroundings. This one is so relaxed it opens all day Saturday and Sunday, and is a great place to take a group of friends. There isn't much room, but if you can all squeeze round a table you can try a few different assagi (Italian meze). A whole plateful of any single one of them is, frankly, less than exciting, but taken together they make a splendid prelude to a main course of Sicilian goat cooked in almond and tomato pesto.

The assagi range from simple olives in garlic and oil to a dish of beans, sausage, cabbage, pancetta, potato and corn meal, by way of capunata antica, an early version of caponata 'before the introduction of New World ingredients such as tomato and aubergine'. Some pasta, including raviolotti del sud (stuffed with cauliflower, saffron, garlic, pecorino and walnuts), is made in-house, while orecchiette are bought from Puglia. If goat doesn't appeal, there is always rabbit, lamb meatballs or octopus, in which garlic, herbs, tomato and wine usually feature. Puddings are home-made too and include a rich version of tiramisù. The wine list puts interest and variety before illustrious names, is not afraid of quirks, aims for good producers, and is not marked up more than necessary. It encourages and rewards adventurous drinkers, and does most of it for less than £20 a bottle. House wine is £6.90, and dessert wines by the glass are wonderful. CELLARMAN'S CHOICE: Pagadebit 1992, Celli,£9.90; Lambrusco Grasparossa Secco 1993, Chiarli, £9.50.

CHEFS: Aurelio Spagnuolo and Raffaele Petralia   PROPRIETORS: Rochelle Porteous and Aurelio Spagnuolo   OPEN: all week; weekdays 12 to 3, 6 to 11, Sat noon to 11.30, Sun 12.30 to 10.30   CLOSED: 10 days over Christmas   MEALS: alc (main courses £5.50 to £10.50). Set L £7.50 (2 courses). Cover charge 60p   SERVICE: not inc (10% for large groups)   CARDS: Access, Amex, Visa   DETAILS: 75 seats. 5 tables outside. Private parties: 30 main room. Vegetarian meals. Children's helpings. Wheelchair access. Music. Air-conditioned

Osteria Basilico £

map 12

29 Kensington Park Road, W11 2EU
071-727 9957

COOKING 1
COST £16–£32

Thriving, buzzing, packed and casual in the extreme, the Osteria sails close to the wind. Reports are mixed, at their best enthusing over the atmosphere as much as the food. It is a modest place on two floors, with the feel of a neighbourhood café and décor of dried plants, scrubbed tables and old chairs. Friends drop in to join others at table, adding chairs, ordering beer and food as they go.

A few simple and easily available items from sausage to gnocchi are interwoven to give the impression of much going on, and cooking is mostly boiling pasta, grilling sole and bread, pan-frying sausage and salmon, deep-frying squid and whitebait (yes, still going strong here), and tossing salads. Tomatoes are everywhere, but at least they are tasty, fresh ones. Expensive ingredients are avoided, and at these prices the antipasto buffet is understandably restricted to one visit per person. Service is *allegro con spirito*. The largely under-£10 wine list is basic, with little information. House Sangiovese and Trebbiano are £7.20 (£1.80 per glass).

CHEF: A. Palano   PROPRIETOR: Eurogold Restaurants Ltd   OPEN: all week; 12 to 3, 6.30 to 11 (10.30 Sun)   CLOSED: 25 Dec   MEALS: alc (main courses £4.50 to £8.50)   SERVICE: 10% (optional)   DETAILS: 60 seats. Private parties: 45 main room. Vegetarian meals. Children welcome. No cigars/pipes in dining-room. Wheelchair access (1 step). Music. Fax: 071-229 7980

Panda Si Chuen £

map 15

56 Old Compton Street, W1V 5PA
071-437 2069

COOKING 1
COST £16–£42

Pandas would get a bit of shock if they moved from a diet of bland bamboo to the spiciness of this Szechuan regular, although by all accounts the heat is less than it might be back home. For most of us, that's fine. The place looks as clean as a new pin and service could not be more pleasant or helpful. Plain-sounding dishes of lemon chicken or sweet-and-sour pork are easily traded for more interesting pelmeni (wun-tun) which comes three ways – in red chilli and soy sauce, in consommé soup, or in hot-and-sour soup – at least one of which ought to be tried. But then so should a lot of other dishes from a long menu that takes in tea-smoked duck, stewed croaker fish, sizzling oysters in fish flavour sauce, bean thread with minced meat and dry shrimp, and red-cooked aubergine. It is best to drink tea or lou chiew (Chinese rice wine), but house French wine is £7.

See the back of the Guide *for a listing of all restaurants in the Main Entries sections.*

CHEF: C.K. Liu PROPRIETOR: K.C. Chew OPEN: Mon to Sat; noon to 11.30 MEALS: alc (main courses £4.50 to £7.50). Set L and D £9.50 to £16.50 (minimum 2) SERVICE: not inc CARDS: Access, Amex, Diners, Visa DETAILS: 60 seats. Private parties: 40 main room, 14 private room. Vegetarian meals. Children welcome. Smart dress preferred. Music. Air-conditioned

Pearl of Knightsbridge

map 13

22 Brompton Road, SW1X 7QN
071-225 3888

COOKING 3
COST £19–£90

'The Pearl is aptly named,' says one. Unlike many overpriced places posing as 'up-market' Chinese, 'this shines out as an example of how things should be done.' The black and white décor is simple and smart, and tea is kept warm on a burner and replenished at regular intervals. The long Cantonese menu runs from the familiar to the exotic, including specials of shark's fin, abalone, whole roast suckling pig and bird's nest with coconut juice. A few extras poke their nose in, such as Szechuan hot-and-sour soup, and Peking duck which, like the pig, needs to be ordered in advance. Seafood is a strong suit, with lobster cooked five ways.

The Pearl stands out not just for good handling of expensive ingredients but also for proper treatment of humbler dishes along the way, from mixed hors d'oeuvre (sesame prawn toast, soft shell crab, shrimp ravioli, seafood spring rolls and seaweed) through impressively fresh steamed sea bass, to 'some like it hot' chicken with red chillies. Rice and noodles are up to standard, and puddings include some genuine Cantonese specialities such as sago cream heavily flavoured with coconut. 'Outstanding dishes are no longer let down by carelessness in others,' maintains a regular, noting that consistency has improved and that the Pearl is on an even keel. Outside Bordeaux and Burgundy the wines stay sensibly under £20. House wine is £11 (£2.50 per glass).

CHEF: Hong Cheung PROPRIETORS: the Lam family OPEN: all week; 12 to 2.45, 6 to 11.15 (11.30 Sat, 11 Sun and bank hols) CLOSED: 25 and 26 Dec MEALS: alc (main courses £5.50 to £38). Set L £8.50 (2 courses) to £12.50 (2 courses), Set D £25 (minimum 2) to £55 (minimum 4). Cover £2 after 6pm. Minimum £15 D SERVICE: not inc (10% for 10 or more) CARDS: Access, Amex, Diners, Visa DETAILS: 95 seats. Private parties: 60 main room, 35 private room. Vegetarian meals with prior notice. Children welcome. Smart dress preferred. Music. Air-conditioned

The Peasant

NEW ENTRY map 11

240 St John Street, EC1V 4PH
071-336 7726

COOKING 1
COST £21–£36

This used to be a pub, although that hardly matters. It is simply a knocked-about shell in which to enjoy simple Italian-based food. It would be nice to think that this, the Eagle and the Lansdowne (see entries, London) were the harbingers of a trend towards good, inexpensive food served in humble surroundings. Frills are anathema, as the name suggests. The owners have simply ripped off the wallpaper, freshened up the table tops, and left the floorboards and bar much as before: people still wander in for a drink, because good beers are on draught and in bottles. The place could not feel more casual.

The food is deceptively simple. Without first-class ingredients, and a fine sense of the balance of flavours, it would be easy to screw it up, but Carla Tomasi (formerly of Frith's in Soho) does not. She gets a long way on assemblies: one of artichokes, rocket, potatoes and coppa, another of Pecorino Sardo with sprouting broccoli, parsley and black olive relish, and yet another of creamy Spanish cheese with pear and salad. Cooking centres on baking and grilling (properly done fillet of grey mullet, served with sliced potatoes baked in rosemary) and soups and stews: broad bean and spaghetti broth from Calabria, or trippa alla romana. There is usually a risotto or pasta dish. Service is disconnected, the wine list is short, functional and well priced, and don't forget the beers. House wine is £8.50 (£1.80 per glass).

CHEF: Carla Tomasi PROPRIETORS: Craig Schorn and Michael Kittos OPEN: all week, exc Sat L and Sun D; 12.30 to 2.30 (3 Sun), 6.30 to 11 CLOSED: 23 Dec to 4 Jan, bank hols MEALS: alc (main courses £7 to £9). Set L Sun £11.50 (2 courses) to £13.50 SERVICE: 10%, card slips closed CARDS: Access, Visa DETAILS: 80 seats. Private parties: 70 main room, 40 private room. Vegetarian meals. Children's helpings. No cigars/pipes in dining-room. Wheelchair access (also WC). Music

Le P'tit Normand

map 10

185 Merton Road, Southfields, SW18 5EF
081 871-0233

COOKING 1
COST £17–£33

The atmosphere of Philippe Herrard's likeable French bistro is helped along by service that is absolutely charming, relaxed and free of 'Gallic incivilities'. Ingredients are first-rate, prices are very fair, and the menu is short and to the point: it avoids avant-garde gestures in favour of well-executed mainstream stuff with Normandy as its bedrock. A fixed repertoire of fish soup, 'earthy' boudin noir with Dijon mustard and apples, crêpes dieppoise and duck breast vallée d'Auge is bolstered by blackboard specials that include delicately sauced panaché of monkfish, turbot and salmon. All main dishes are served with potatoes; other vegetables are up to standard. Desserts are the likes of strawberry tart. To drink, there are enticing aperitifs, including mûroise (cider with blackberry cream liqueur), while the vintage calvados is 'an absolute must'. The wine list is a modest collection from the major French growing regions; 'latest discoveries' are chalked on a board. House wine is £7.95.

CHEF/PROPRIETOR: Philippe Herrard OPEN: all week, exc Sat L; 12 to 2, 7 to 10.30 MEALS: alc (main courses £8.75 to £9.25). Set L £9.95, Set L Sun £11.95 SERVICE: 12.5%, card slips closed CARDS: Access, Amex, Diners, Visa DETAILS: 34 seats. Private parties: 50 main room. Vegetarian meals with prior notice. Children's helpings on request. Smart dress preferred. No pipes in dining-room. Wheelchair access. Music

Phuket £

map 10

246 Battersea Park Road, SW11 3BP
071-223 5924

COOKING 1*
COST £16–£33

'A very pleasant surprise,' observed a seasoned reporter about this Thai restaurant opposite the Latchmere pub. The décor is agreeable and unassuming, with mirrors on the walls and vases of flowers on the well-spaced tables.

High-quality food with finely tuned flavours is the hallmark of the kitchen, and the menu is a well-balanced selection of around 50 dishes. Benchmark items such as satays, tom yum soups, roast duck curry and Thai noodles are augmented by a few less common specialities. Look for 'goong hom par' (described as a large prawn in a jacket of crabmeat, wrapped in a thin rice pancake and deep-fried) as well as 'phu and goong ob' (a hotpot loaded with crab claws, king prawns, vermicelli, celery, coriander and soy sauce). Finish with exotic fruit or home-made desserts. Special set menus emphasise the overall value for money. The wine list is clearly annotated, with plenty of appropriate drinking for around £10. House wine is £6.50.

CHEF: Miss O. Mungnatee   PROPRIETOR: P. Vatanawan   OPEN: all week, D only; 6 to 11.30   MEALS: alc (main courses £4.50 to £6). Set D £12.50 to £15 (minimum 2)   SERVICE: 10%   CARDS: Access, Amex, Visa   DETAILS: 60 seats. Private parties: 30 main room, 14 private room. Vegetarian meals. Children welcome. Smart dress preferred. No-smoking area. Music

Pied-à-Terre
map 14

34 Charlotte Street, W1P 1HJ   COOKING 3*
071-636 1178   COST £28–£65   •

The setting does not endear itself to all readers. The décor is rather 'minimalist, stark and cold', and while some modern art provides relief it is not to everybody's liking. Then there are the metal chairs. But at least the place has a pleasantly bustling atmosphere much of the time, and attention is soon diverted by superior amuse-gueules and the pursuit of modern French food that is Richard Neat's occupation.

The cooking is robust with lots of hare, rabbit, venison and pigeon – heavy gamey dishes that come with rich sauces, and quite a bit of potato in one form or another, all looking quite brown. Little greenery appears on the plate, salads are few, and no vegetarian dish can be had without prior notice, which is strange these days. On the other hand, there is no shortage of fish, especially the more luxurious varieties such as turbot or sea bass, and praise washes over brill cooked with oysters and a red wine sauce, John Dory with scallops on stir-fried leeks with watercress sauce, and a first course of smoked whiting fillet on a poached egg on a potato galette on spinach, with good hollandaise. Then the occasional wild card turns up, as in lambs' offal in broad-bean soup.

The less expensive three-course lunchtime menu draws support, although the choice of two items only at each stage restricts its value for some. An example in spring was mille-feuille of duck confit with buttered lentils, or pan-fried red mullet with almond sauce; then brill fillet with deep-fried oysters and baby leeks, or roasted rabbit with foie gras sauce and cabbage; and finally chocolate tart or cheese. Flavours are characterful and 'the food tastes of what it is'. Technical accomplishment runs through to 'a knockout passion-fruit soufflé'. Service is 'delightful, efficient without appearing to be so, and everything is done quietly and professionally'. Wines are French, mostly in classic vein, but with a token showing from elsewhere and a few good bottles under £20. Half a dozen wines are served by the glass from £3.25 to £4.

CHEF: Richard Neat PROPRIETORS: David Moore and Richard Neat OPEN: Mon to Sat, exc Sat L; 12.15 to 2.15, 7.15 to 10.15 MEALS: Set L £19.50 and £38, Set D £38 SERVICE: net prices, card slips closed CARDS: Access, Amex, Diners, Visa DETAILS: 40 seats. Private parties: 10 main room, 8 private room. Vegetarian meals with prior notice. Children's helpings by arrangement. Smart dress preferred. No cigars/pipes in dining-room. Wheelchair access (3 steps). No music. Air-conditioned

Pizzeria Castello £

map 11

20 Walworth Road, SE1 6SP
071-703 2556

COOKING 1
COST £13–£21

Like fish and chip shops, pizzerias work to a simple formula, and once they have it right then the whole thing runs on castors, smooth as you like. A good dough, a proper oven and a varied selection of generous and flavoursome toppings all keep Castello buzzing. The kitchen will normally do you a medium-thick base, but will bake thin ones to order, and you can build your own by adding extras of baby artichoke, pineapple (if you must) or green chilli. If you don't like garlic, stay away. Minestrone and a few pasta dishes turn it into a big meal, bread is good, and Peroni is the lager to drink, although the wines are good of their kind, not expensive and well worth a punt. House wine is £6.30 (£1.50 per glass).

CHEF: F. Arrigoni PROPRIETORS: Renzo Meda and Antonio Proietti OPEN: Mon to Sat, exc Sat L; noon (5pm Sat) to 11pm MEALS: alc (main courses £4 to £6) SERVICE: not inc (10% for 7 or more) CARDS: Access, Amex, Visa DETAILS: 150 seats. Private parties: 30 main room. Vegetarian meals. Children's helpings. Smart dress preferred. Wheelchair access (also WC). Music. Air-conditioned

Le Pont de la Tour ▮

map 11

36D Shad Thames, Butlers Wharf, SE1 2YE
071-403 8403

COOKING 3
COST £26–£70

Conran operations always bring vitality, a particularly welcome commodity south of the river where old warehouses have not quite vanished and new businesses often seem a bit lost. Le Pont de la Tour is bright, friendly and welcoming, with the air of an inner sanctum approached through shops and a bar serving grills, shellfish and salads. A vegetarian menu, Saturday and Sunday brunch, fixed-price lunch and evening *carte* are part of the flexibility that pervades the whole site. A table by the window, or outside on the terrace, naturally makes the most of views over Tower Bridge.

There is broad choice, too, on each menu, from leek and wild mushroom tart through calf's liver and bacon, and duck breast with lentils, to blueberry and almond tart, with a serious look at fish along the way: roast cod with braised fennel, rare grilled tuna with mint, chilli and lime, and smoked haddock risotto. Reporters enjoy the plainness and liveliness of the cooking, be it in simple grilled Dover sole on the bone, or a sauté of squid with pickled ginger and spring onions. And when the kitchen is on form the superlatives flow: 'superb' roast partridge on a bed of creamed cabbage and bacon, 'divine' pear and honey tart, a 'wonderful' tarte Tatin, and a 'superbly rich St-Emilion au chocolat, just as sinful as you'd expect'.

Reporters are divided on the question of value, but those who allow views and atmosphere into the equation are generally more sympathetic. One who lives across the bridge and eats here twice a week reports that price rises do not seem to be justified. The inherent problems of a restaurant open for all but one meal a week mean that a different hand at the stove, and changing front-of-house staff, inevitably produce unevenness. Service is generally very sharp, judged by one reporter as 'probably the most professional, efficient but unobtrusive restaurant service I have ever witnessed. Top marks.' But with a fixed charge of 15 per cent, it ought to be good.

Wines are a high point. 'Fine if you know your regions, producers and vintages, but daunting for a novice,' writes one. 'Do people really pay £850 a bottle?' asks another. A short selection up to £20 is helpful, another up to £55 indicative of the typical custom. Choice is extremely generous, with producers ranging from the established best to the up-and-coming; mark-ups are no worse than average, and quality is very impressive. Half-bottles, except for sweet wines, are a bit thin. House wines begin at £10.75. CELLARMAN'S CHOICE: Chablis premier cru 'Les Vaillons' 1992, Dom. Jean Defaix, £22.50; Devil's Lair Pinot Noir 1991, £22.50.

CHEF: David Burke PROPRIETORS: Sir Terence Conran, Joel Kissin and David Burke OPEN: restaurant all week, exc Sat L; 12 to 3, 6 to 12. Bar and grill all week; noon to midnight (11 Sun) CLOSED: Christmas MEALS: alc D (main courses £15.50 to £18.50). Set L £25, Set pre- and post-theatre D £19.50. Sat brunch £14.95 (2 courses) to £17.95. Sun brunch (main courses £8.50 to £14). Grill menu (main courses £8 to £14.50) SERVICE: 15%, card slips closed CARDS: Access, Amex, Diners, Visa DETAILS: restaurant 105 seats, bar and grill 65 seats. 22 tables outside restaurant, 11 tables outside bar and grill. Private parties: 9 main room, 22 private room. Vegetarian meals. Children welcome. Wheelchair access. No music. Fax: 071-403 0267

Poons £

map 15

4 Leicester Street, WC2H 7BL
071-437 1528

COOKING 1
COST £12–£45

'What a transformation!' exclaimed a fan of this famous Chinese bolt-hole opposite the Swiss Centre. Gone is the 'seedy Formica café'. In its place is a bright new restaurant with fresh aspirations. The interior is gleaming white with colourful prints on the walls, tablecloths and a curved bar at one end. A few devotees have been disappointed, but most reckon that it has been a change for the better. Service is sharp and chatty. The menu is much the same and prices are exceptionally low. The Poon family's renowned wind-dried foods, full-blooded Cantonese one-plate meals, casseroles and hotpots steal the show, while fried stuffed tofu and chicken with dried fungus and tiger lilies have both been notable for their strong, gutsy flavours. It is also worth investigating the intriguing list of specialities, such as deep-fried quail's eggs in crabmeat sauce and steamed Dover sole with tangerine peel. Drink tea or Tsingtao beer. House wine is £6.50.

'The best that could be said of this was that it wasn't quite as revolting as the other dish.' (On eating in Yorkshire)

CHEF: K.W. Lam   PROPRIETOR: W.N. Poon   OPEN: all week; noon to 11.30   CLOSED: 4 days at Christmas   MEALS: alc (main courses £3.90 to £13.50). Set L and D £7 to £17 (minimum 2)   SERVICE: not inc   DETAILS: 130 seats. Private parties: 35 main room, 24, 30 and 35 private rooms. Vegetarian meals. Children welcome. Smart dress preferred. Wheelchair access. No music. Air-conditioned

Quaglino's   map 14

16 Bury Street, SW1Y 6AL   COOKING 2
071-930 6767   COST £29–£50

'Quaglino's was a very glamorous restaurant from the 1930s and had a particular place in the social history of those times,' claims the restaurant. It is still glamorous, a huge bustling place of entertainment with a great sense of occasion: magnificent, impressive, noisy, busy. There is only one way in: down a Hollywood staircase from the bar (which serves cold food) into a basement that reporters have likened to a hotel foyer, a station, and a greenhouse. Large, round tables fill the body of the room, while smaller red-topped tables hug the central spine. Stainless steel, glass and mirrors dominate. Pillars, roughly the size you normally see in cathedrals, are striped with gold and silver, and decorated with swirling multicoloured designs. On a scale of one to ten for glitz, Quaglino's rates eleven.

A brasserie spirit runs through the food, closely matching the Paris and Edwardian originals with its emphasis on fresh oysters, crab, langoustine and lobster, calf's tongue vinaigrette and grilled fish. 'Very fresh, very good, very large,' reckoned one reporter of a plateau de fruits de mer. There is no pig's trotter, no choucroute (and no beer), but there are salads to begin, and a mixed *carte* of roast rabbit, boudin blanc, and shoulder of roast pork with crackling and apple sauce. Mostly the food is very simple and the kitchen copes, but those who take their eyes off the staircase for long enough to consider what is on the plate may find rather ordinary crab and saffron tart ('just a quiche, really') or a bowl (everything comes in a bowl) containing shin of beef with lardons, unevenly cooked and enough to feed a family of four.

To feed upwards of 600 a night (tables are turned over at least twice) is a massive undertaking, and perhaps we should marvel not that it is done well but that it is done at all. However, too many errors are reported for the kitchen to be considered wholly reliable, and after all, this is a restaurant, not just a meeting place. 'More hype than substance,' concludes one reporter, 'though the crowds of beautiful people make it an exciting place to be.' At least people are having fun eating, even if the food is not always the source of that pleasure. The smoking policy consists of a perambulating girl with a tray of cigarettes hanging round her chest. Considering the size of the place, a non-smoking area is possible. It is certainly desirable. Service is fair 'but not worth 15 per cent', which all Conran restaurants add on, especially when complaints are not always met with good grace. The wine list is mostly under £20, with a reasonable choice by the half-bottle or glass. House vin de pays is £10.75.

'Why does bread have to be offered, and wine poured, with the other arm behind the back, I wonder?' (On eating in Manchester)

CHEF: Martin Webb   PROPRIETORS: Sir Terence Conran, Joel Kissin, Keith Hobbs and Tom Conran   OPEN: all week; 12 to 3, 5.30 to 12 (1am Fri and Sat, 11 Sun). Antipasti Bar all week; noon to midnight (11pm Sun)   CLOSED: Christmas   MEALS: alc (main courses £9 to £19.50). Set L Sat and Sun, and pre-theatre £12.95 (2 courses). Antipasti Bar (dishes £4.50 to £19.50)   SERVICE: 15%, card slips closed   CARDS: Access, Amex, Diners, Visa   DETAILS: restaurant 338 seats, Antipasti Bar 90 seats. Private parties: 12 main room, 40 private room. Vegetarian meals. Children welcome. Wheelchair access (also WC). Music. Air-conditioned. Fax: 071-839 2866

Quality Chop House   map 11

94 Farringdon Road, EC1R 3EA   COOKING 2
071-837 5093   COST £21–£45

Charles Fontaine cooks traditional British dishes in French style; the sausages, served with mashed potato and onion gravy, are Toulouse, and the black pudding is French. It is not all old-fashioned – there is warm asparagus with Pecorino, and smoked haddock and lentil salad – but, as one reader pointed out, 'No olive oil or frou-frou vinegars have seeped in here.' Buffalo mozzarella has, and Parma ham with raclette cheese has, but the thrust is still hearty café food.

The sit-up-and-beg bench-seats are original nineteenth-century, and more convivial than comfortable. The frontage – with 'Progressive Working Class Caterers' etched into the glass – dates from the same period. According to a regular, 'Charles Fontaine is still to be seen cooking, though not as much as previously.' What the cooking lacks in refinement it makes up for in no-nonsense simplicity, from eggs, bacon and chips to first-rate grilled ox tongue. It is a good place to go for fried cod and chips, and grilled calf's liver and bacon. There are four wines by the glass and some good English beers. House wine is £9.

CHEF/PROPRIETOR: Charles Fontaine   OPEN: all week, exc Sat L; 12 to 3, 6.30 to 11.30 (7 to 11.30 Sun)   CLOSED: Dec 25 to Jan 2   MEALS: alc (main courses £5.50 to £13)   SERVICE: not inc   DETAILS: 40 seats. Vegetarian meals. Children's helpings. No cigars/pipes in dining-room. Wheelchair access. No music. Air-conditioned

---

Quincy's   NEW ENTRY   map 11

675 Finchley Road, NW2 2JP   COOKING 1
071-794 8499   COST £29–£38

'The impression is of a French local restaurant,' observes a reporter. Window boxes trail flowers in summer, a lace half-curtain hangs from a brass rail, and old prints and photographs crowd the dark-green walls. The floral chintzy effect combines with the small scale to make it seem 'cosy', yet service is very sharp: 'really good professional waiters, intuitive, well informed, respectful without being creepy'. Add to this a short but varied menu that takes in fish boudin, carrot and sweet potato timbale with coriander beurre blanc, and calf's liver with onion marmalade, and it begins to build into an attractive package.

The basic cooking is well managed, the timing accurately judged in a pink rack of lamb with a crisp herb crust, for example. Flavours combine to good effect in a tangy tomato soup tempered by a swirl of courgette cream, and a piece of halibut is not overwhelmed by its mustard sauce and pickled cucumber. Fresh fruit

147

salad with lemon and strawberry granitas may not be all that innovative, but it is 'a delicious dessert'. In all this, appearance is given fair consideration, and incidentals of rough wholemeal bread, unsalted butter and plentiful options at coffee stage, including herbal infusions, fall into line. House wine is £9.

CHEF: David Philpott   PROPRIETOR: David Wardle   OPEN: Tue to Sat, D only; 7 to 11   CLOSED: 22 to 29 Dec   MEALS: Set D £22 to £24   SERVICE: not inc   CARDS: Access, Amex, Visa   DETAILS: 35 seats. Private parties: 8 main room, 12 private room. Vegetarian meals. Children welcome. Music. Air-conditioned

Ragam £
map 14

57 Cleveland Street, W1P 5PQ   COOKING 1*
071-636 9098   COST £12–£39

'Packed, cramped tables, but who cares?' comments a regular who relishes this little restaurant opposite the Middlesex Hospital. Owners and staff are invariably relaxed, chatty and charming to a fault. The cooking is still honestly forthright, flavours are up-front and dishes avoid 'gut-churning greasiness'. South Indian specialities are the main attraction: masala dosais (slit them open and fill them with fiery sambal), uthappam (a potent pizza-style pancake) and dahi vadai are consistently good. Also look for rasam (a hot pepper soup) and kaalan (a curry made with yogurt, coconut and sweet mango). In addition, you will find a full repertoire of curry-house stalwarts such as chicken malabar, keema peas and sag gosht. Vegetables and rice are spot-on; breads are brilliant. It is all 'ridiculously good value for money'. Drink lassi, lager or masala tea. Wines start at £8.

CHEFS: J. Dharmaseelan and G.K.C. Nair   PROPRIETORS: J. Dharmaseelan, T. Haridas and S. Pillai   OPEN: all week; 12 to 3, 6 to 11.15 (11.50 Fri, 11.30 Sat, 10.50 Sun)   CLOSED: 25 and 26 Dec   MEALS: alc (main courses £2.50 to £7). Minimum £6.50   SERVICE: 10%, card slips closed   CARDS: Access, Amex, Diners, Visa   DETAILS: 36 seats. Private parties: 40 main room, 20 private room. Vegetarian meals. Children welcome. Wheelchair access (also WC). Music. Air-conditioned

Rani £
map 10

7 Long Lane, N3 2PR   COOKING 2
081-349 4386 and 2636   COST £14–£31

The décor suggests modish West End brasserie rather than North London vegetarian restaurant, but the Pattnis' converted shop continues to deliver top-flight Gujarati cooking. Glass-topped tables, red and white walls and Venetian blinds at the windows set the tone. An international team of waiters and waitresses in red waistcoats provide chatty, if laid-back, service. Vivid, distinctive flavours are the kitchen's hallmarks, and the commitment to 'home cooking' shows in the first-rate pickles and chutneys that accompany vegetable bhajias, samosas and other starters.

The list of curries is always enterprising, particularly if you opt for the daily specials: Thursday's offering of spinach and sweetcorn has been greatly appreciated. Otherwise, you might find stuffed aubergine and potato, bananas with fenugreek and tomato, and tindora (baby cucumbers) with potato and yogurt sauce. Breads such as fried methi thapla are first-rate, and the fried brown rice with mushrooms and cashews is worth considering. Set meals are excellent value and a buffet is served at lunch and on Monday evening. Tips are not expected or accepted: any money left is donated to charity. To drink, there is lassi, plus lager, a handful of workaday wines and herbal tea. French house wine is £8.40.

CHEFS: Mrs Kundan Pattni and Mrs Sheila Pattni   PROPRIETOR: Jyotindra Pattni   OPEN: all week. exc L Mon and Sat; 12.15 to 3 (4 Sun), 6 to 10.30   CLOSED: 25 Dec   MEALS: alc (main courses £4.50 to £5.50). Set L £8, Set D Mon £10, Tue to Sun £12.70 (2 courses) to £20.90 (minimum 2). Minimum £8 D Sun to Fri, £10 Sat   SERVICE: card slips closed   CARDS: Access, Amex, Visa   DETAILS: 90 seats. Private parties: 60 main room, 23 private room. Vegetarian meals. Healthy eating options. Children's helpings Tue to Sun D. No children under 6 after 8pm. Smart dress preferred. No-smoking area. No smoking in dining-room Mon and Sat. Wheelchair access (1 step). Music

Ransome's Dock ♥

map 10

35-37 Parkgate Road, SW11 4NP

COOKING 2*

071-223 1611 and 924 2462

COST £19–£39

'Seldom have three of us had a more enjoyable meal, beautifully cooked and served in very pleasant surroundings,' begins one report. The dining-room overlooks a narrow waterway and a couple of moored barges. It's hardly Venice, but it is still worth asking for a table by the window. The room looks modern but 'feels cosy' – a rare achievement, although for one reader the wash of ocean blue suggests it is a restaurant that wants to be a swimming-pool. That effect is dispelled by plain wooden tables, plain cutlery, old adverts and a periodic table of fruits on the walls. The paucity of public transport means a taxi ride for many, but the benefit is 'an absence of Soho trendies', in the view of one reporter.

The contemporary menu combines British and Mediterranean ideas to good effect. A parsley pesto gives zing to a lamb steak, and Spanish butter-beans provide the bulk. Fine-flavoured wild salmon, perfectly cooked, combines well with tender and mildly aniseedy fennel; plain new potatoes come with it. 'The mussels served in a sauce of cream, curry and coriander were the best I have ever had,' enthused one reporter. Puddings are in the British tradition of rhubarb fool or lemon tart. Service is friendly and courteous, and there is quiet jazz and blues in the background. Wines are very savvy, and bang up to date with good producers. Pick a price (house wines start at around £9) and choose with total confidence. If in doubt, take the CELLARMAN'S CHOICE: Mount Langi Ghiran Riesling 1993, £13.50; Crozes-Hermitage 1991, A. Graillot, £17.50.

CHEFS/PROPRIETORS: Martin and Vanessa Lam   OPEN: all week, exc Sun D; 12 to 3.30, 6 to 11 (12 Sat)   CLOSED: Christmas   MEALS: alc (main courses £8.50 to £12.50). Set L £11.50 (2 courses)   SERVICE: not inc   CARDS: Access, Amex, Diners, Visa   DETAILS: 65 seats. 9 tables outside. Private parties: 50 main room. Car park D. Vegetarian meals. Children's helpings. Smart dress preferred. No pipes in dining-room. Wheelchair access (1 step; also WC). Music. Air-conditioned. Fax: 071-924 2614

▲ The Regent London

map 11

222 Marylebone Road, NW1 6JQ

071-631 8000

COOKING 3

COST £28–£64

The Great Central, a Victorian railway hotel of monstrous splendour, just in front of Marylebone station, was reborn in 1993. Sharp intakes of breath were occasioned by the grandiose conversion, most notably the central atrium, a deep well of bright, multi-storeyed space where drinks are taken, ivories are tickled and palm trees rustle evocatively in the air-conditioning. The Dining Room has caused a few gasps as well, not so much for the maplewood furnishings and muted puce colour scheme (though the row of huge french windows relieves the slight drabness), as for the undeniable quality of the Italian cooking by Paolo Simioni.

This delivers, in grand hotel surroundings, much of what is going on in the noisy haunts of Chelsea, but the execution and standard of raw materials may be considerably better here. Thus, starters include Valtellina bresaola with marinated mushrooms and artichokes, carpaccio with shaved Parmesan and white truffle oil, or a straight salad of rocket, radicchio and endive with balsamic vinaigrette. Pasta and risotto may be taken as first or second courses, their sauces offering refreshing choice, as in pappardelle with duck and black olives, egg and herb tagliolini with scallops and courgettes, or risotto with crab and leek. A good variety of fish is available, there is a separate list of grilled items, and meats include medallions of veal with morels and asparagus, saddle of rabbit stuffed with olives on a basil sauce, and roast breast and rolled leg of pigeon with a sauce combining aged balsamic vinegar and port.

Only the desserts depress as the trolley is wheeled forth, the creamy concoctions harking back to an earlier era, although orange tart and tiramisù have both been pronounced 'excellent'. Children have their own menu which is extremely good value. Service is impeccably courteous and dignified. A roll-call of Italian quality is present on the wine list, together with some pedigree French stuff and good non-European choices, although not much will be found below £20. House Valpolicella (Bertani) and Soave Classico (Anselmi) are, respectively, £19.50 and £22.

CHEF: Paolo Simioni PROPRIETOR: Regent Four Seasons Hotel Group plc OPEN: all week; 12 (12.30 Sun) to 3, 7 to 11 MEALS: alc (main courses £8.50 to £20.50). Set L £21.50, Set D £28 SERVICE: net prices, card slips closed CARDS: Access, Amex, Diners, Visa DETAILS: 106 seats. Private parties: 28 main room, 60 to 300 private rooms. Car park. Vegetarian meals. Children's helpings. Smart dress preferred. No-smoking area. Wheelchair access (also WC). Music. Air-conditioned ACCOMMODATION: 309 rooms, all with bath/shower. TV. Phone. Air-conditioned. B&B £200 to £360. Rooms for disabled. Lift. Children welcome. Afternoon teas. Swimming-pool. Sauna. Fax: 071-631 8080

Riva

map 10

169 Church Road, SW13 9HR

081-748 0434

COOKING 2

COST £23–£41

The polished wood façade, in a small parade of shops, looks slightly mysterious and therefore inviting. The room is elegantly conceived and exactly executed, with rag-roll paint, steel engravings of porticos, columns and architectural sections, a wall of mirrors, discreet lighting, and flowers that soften the whole effect. Riva has done more than its share to propel real Italian cooking to the top in the '90s, championing regional food, serving up direct and appealing flavours, helping to transform perceptions about Italian food with its inventiveness, freshness and variety.

Unfortunately, however, reports this year have been less than enthusiastic. Some dishes, notably involving fish, have disappointed, as have, on some occasions, vegetables and puddings. Careless timing, poor pastry and weak espresso are among the grumbles. Unresponsive service, widely reported, has not helped matters. But Riva still has its plus side. Grilled baby squids, for example, each about two inches long, are arranged around a pile of fried chives and dill with a dribble of olive oil: simple, well flavoured, forthright. Tomato sauce for spaghetti is light yet intense, resplendent with the taste of mussels, clams and prawns, all cooked as they should be. The short list of interesting Italian wines is sensibly priced, with house wine at £9.50.

CHEF: Francesco Zanchetta   PROPRIETOR: Andrea Riva   OPEN: all week, exc Sat L; 12 to 2.30, 7 to 11 (11.30 Fri and Sat, 9.30 Sun)   CLOSED: Christmas, Easter, bank hols   MEALS: alc (main courses £7 to £11.50)   SERVICE: 10%, card slips closed   CARDS: Access, Visa   DETAILS: 50 seats. 2 tables outside. Private parties: 40 main room. Vegetarian meals. Children's helpings. Smart dress preferred. No cigars/pipes in dining-room. Wheelchair access. Music. Air-conditioned

River Café ♥ map 10

Thames Wharf Studios,
Rainville Road, W6 9HA   COOKING 3
071-381 8824   COST £28–£54

Admirers of the unadorned starkness of the original room should not be disappointed by the minimalist redecoration – bare white walls, a stainless steel serving counter down one side, a hologram wall clock – while others who found the atmosphere too nearly that of a 'works canteen' may be rewarded by softer lines, the plush blue carpet and crisp white table linen. Either constituency will continue to welcome the chance to sit on the terrace for a summer lunch, and note the passage of the sun over Harrods' depository opposite.

The culinary style is located in that California-led appropriation of Italian ingredients and techniques of which the River Café, back in 1987, was one of London's earliest exponents. Although nobody involved in the venture is Italian, all dishes are named in that language. The highly visible and fragrant chargrill works overtime (on one menu, squid, langoustine, scallops and lamb all got the treatment), and the now-familiar repertoire of extra-virgin, balsamic, basil, rocket (buckets of it), Parmesan and chillies is still affectionately rendered. A good balance is struck in the offering of ultra-modern ideas such as seared wild salmon with artichoke hearts, rocket, dandelion and crushed olives alongside classics like osso buco with polenta. Bread-thickened soups have become a passion, with crumbled ciabatta bulking a vine tomato broth. If grumpiness is occasioned, it is nearly always at the service, although robust seasoning comes in for criticism from some. Contrast those niggles with the opinion of a man who enjoyed a 'spectacularly distinguished' meal that concluded with a 'perfectly executed, divine' lemon tart, and that of another who commended the Café's 'nerve to take simple, but best, ingredients and cook them simply but well'.

Genuinely helpful notes are appended to the wine list, which is exclusively Italian, save for Billecart-Salmon and Bollinger champagnes. It will go a long way to explaining what all the buzz over new Italian wines has been about. House red and white from the Veneto are £9.50. CELLARMAN'S CHOICE: Favorita 1993, Deltetto, £16; Chianti Rufina Riserva 1988, Selvapiana, £18.50.

CHEFS: Rose Gray, Ruth Rogers, Theo Randall and Jake Hodges   PROPRIETORS: Richard and Ruth Rogers, and Rose Gray   OPEN: all week, exc Sun D; 12.30 to 2.30 (1 to 2.30 Sun), 7.30 to 9.30   CLOSED: Christmas, New Year, bank hols   MEALS: alc (main courses £10 to £18) SERVICE: 12.5% card slips closed   CARDS: Access, Visa   DETAILS: 100 seats. 10 tables outside. Private parties: 8 main room. Car park D and Sat L. Vegetarian meals. Children's helpings. No cigars/pipes in dining-room. Wheelchair access. No music. Fax: 071-381 6217

Rotisserie

map 12

| 56 Uxbridge Road, W12 8LP | COOKING 1 |
| 081-743 3028 | COST £24–£35 |

'This was our first visit; we had thought it too far. We now wish we had been going for years,' wrote one couple of this griller they had missed. It stands out in the neighbourhood, subjecting Aberdeen Angus beef, calf's liver, Sri Lankan prawns and French poultry to charcoal or rotary grilling. There is usually calamari and a fish of the day as well. Saucing is just as simple, ranging from a spicy piri piri job with chicken wings, to béarnaise for the rib of beef. Frites are the normal accompaniment, so there is not a lot to go wrong. All this is backed up by appetisers of Cornish crab with avocado, or chargrilled chorizos, and salads with grilled or roast vegetables, with crème brûlée or fruit crumble to finish. Two dozen wines take in the New World and keep their prices low. House French is £8.50 (£2.10 per glass).

CHEF: Emmanuel Schandorf   PROPRIETOR: Ian Davies   OPEN: all week, exc Sat and Sun L; 12 to 3, 6.30 to 11   MEALS: alc (main courses £7 to £11). Set L and D £8.95 (2 courses)   SERVICE: not inc   CARDS: Access, Amex, Visa   DETAILS: 70 seats. Private parties: 40 main room. Vegetarian meals. Children welcome. Wheelchair access. Music. Fax: 081-743 6627

Royal China

map 12

| 13 Queensway, W2 4QJ | COOKING 2 |
| 071-221 2535 | COST £21–£66 |

'A great atmosphere of East/West' was how one reporter described the mood of this rather flash Chinese restaurant. The menu is in the Cantonese tradition, although it also ventures into Peking duck, Szechuan prawns with chilli, and chicken satay. Otherwise it offers an enticing mixture of classics, esoteric specialities and fashionable flourishes. Among the more unusual items, you might find dry scallop soup with chives, sliced preserved pork knuckle with jellyfish, steamed minced pork with salted egg, and sizzling veal with honey and black-bean sauce. Those with less adventurous palates could settle for beef with oyster sauce, sweet-and-sour chicken or braised bean curd with vegetables. The kitchen also follows the seasons by offering dishes such as double-steamed melon soup and braised dry oyster with seaweed. Among the sweets, look for the chilled mango pudding – 'a smooth, refreshing mousse'. Dim-sum are served throughout the afternoon (noon to 5pm). Service is pleasant and efficient. The wine list includes some reasonably priced French and Italian bottles as well as saké. House wine is £8.50. A second branch is in Putney (3 Chelverton Road, SW15 1RN, Tel: 081-788 0907).

CHEFS: Simon Man and Wai Hung Law   PROPRIETOR: Playwell Ltd   OPEN: all week; noon to 11.15   CLOSED: 24 and 25 Dec   MEALS: alc (main courses £5 to £15). Set D £20 to £26 (minimum 2)   SERVICE: 12.5%   CARDS: Access, Amex, Diners, Visa   DETAILS: 100 seats. Private parties: 100 main room, 15 private room. Vegetarian meals. Children's helpings. Smart dress preferred. Music. Air-conditioned

RSJ ▮ £ map 11

| 13A Coin Street, SE1 8YQ | COOKING 2 |
| 071-928 4554 | COST £19–£39 |

RSJ is inevitably destined to be considered handy for Waterloo and the National Theatre. But readers go because it puts on its own show. The stage is appealing, with bright pictures and good solid black chairs 'on which you can hang a jumper or jacket without its sliding on to the floor'. Now *that's* sensible. As we write, the downstairs brasserie and upstairs restaurant have edged closer together in style and price, but as you read they will probably have separated again, with the brasserie reverting to its original purpose of serving simpler and less expensive food.

Dishes are well conceived, and aim for deep-down satisfaction, as in pot roast belly of pork, roast rump of lamb with basil mashed potatoes, boudin blanc with potted cabbage, and baked lemon pudding with English custard. There is lightness too: one reporter's lunch took in a terrine of summer vegetables, steamed sea trout, and a Grand Marnier bombe. Most consider the set-price short-choice menu a bargain, with the likes of risotto of preserved tomato, pan-fried salmon, and white wine tart with a grape confit. But one reporter was less convinced by a terrine from the *carte* with '30 per cent rabbit and 70 per cent pulses; the two mouthfuls of rabbit were quite pleasant'.

Service is mostly informal, friendly, efficient and caring, and the wine list is eccentric in its concentration on the Loire to the exclusion of almost everywhere else. Quite what three red burgundies and two clarets are doing among that lot is anybody's guess. Talking of mysteries, some readers have pointed out that more help and information might make the choosing less of a lottery for them. When you hit lucky, though, the wines can be stunning. The brasserie list of wines by the glass extols the virtues of drinking chilled Loire reds, especially suitable for, and we quote, 'a barmy evening'. House Anjou rouge and Saumur blanc are £9.75, and 10 or more wines are normally available by the glass. CELLARMAN'S CHOICE: Savennières 1990, Dom. des Baumard, £16.95; Saumur Champigny 1990, Dom. de Nerleux, £13.75.

'The white wine was warmer than the iced water, which was warmer than the red wine.' (On eating in Cumbria)

LONDON

CHEFS: Ian Stabler and Anthony Demetre PROPRIETOR: Nigel Wilkinson OPEN: Mon to Sat, exc Sat L; 12 to 2, 6 to 11 CLOSED: bank hols MEALS: alc (main courses restaurant £8 to £12, brasserie £6 to £7). Restaurant Set L and D £15.95 SERVICE: 10%, card slips closed CARDS: Access, Amex, Visa DETAILS: restaurant 42 seats, brasserie 40 seats. 6 tables outside. Private parties: 10 main room, 20 private room. Vegetarian meals. Children's helpings. Music. Air-conditioned

Rules

map 15

35 Maiden Lane, WC2E 7LB
071-836 5314

COOKING 2
COST £24–£46

In 1998, Rules will be celebrating 200 years of feeding London, an extraordinary landmark in the life of the capital's oldest restaurant. Meanwhile, it goes on faithfully serving a clientele who flock there for unreconstructed British cooking. The specialities are furred and feathered game in season, fresh fish, potted things and pies. The atmosphere may recall the senior common room, but even those initially wary soon find the welcome warming enough, and the cooking quite sound.

Nor are modern ideas completely eschewed: a metropolitan sophisticate dining with her parents admired the 'hot, melting filling with lots of flavour' in a Stilton and walnut tart. She then had a vegetarian dish of aubergine 'lasagne' with peppers, tomatoes and an 'odd' chilli butter sauce that was doused with 'the most gorgeous olive oil'. Contrast that with an omnivore who had a dry sherry as a prelude to scrambled eggs with smoked salmon, 'superb' herb-crusted rack of lamb with cabbage and potatoes, a piece of mature Cheddar that came with home-made fruit cake and a glass of spiced ginger wine, 'light and digestible' apple suet pudding with syrup cream sauce and a cup of coffee. Rules keeps all sorts of people happy. Only a very few wines are offered, mostly perfectly drinkable, and nearly everything comes in bottle or half. House wines are £8.50. The stout of heart should start with a tankard of Black Velvet at £7.

CHEFS: Neil Pass and Frank Wilkinson PROPRIETOR: John Mayhew OPEN: all week; noon to 11.45 (10.30 Sun) CLOSED: 24 to 26 Dec MEALS: alc (main courses £12 to £15). Set L Sat and Sun £15.95, Set pre-theatre supper (3 to 6pm) £12.95 (2 courses) SERVICE: not inc (12.5% for 7 or more), card slips closed CARDS: Access, Amex, Visa DETAILS: 140 seats. Private parties: 9 main room, 28, 30 and 50 private rooms. Vegetarian meals. Children's helpings on request. No pipes in dining-room. Wheelchair access. No music. Air-conditioned. Fax: 071-497 1081

Sabras £

map 10

263 High Road,
Willesden Green, NW10 2RX
081-459 0340

COOKING 2
COST £12–£23

Over the past year, Hemant and Nalinee Desai have been fighting a rear-guard action against the effects of the recession. They talk of 'lotus blossoms in the mud', but they carry on against the odds. Their spotless Indian vegetarian restaurant shines out among the gloom of the neighbourhood, and they have found all kinds of ways of inducing new trade. Cut-price café lunches (book in advance), outside catering, a drinks club, and even financial incentive schemes are part of their survival strategy.

The food is among the best of its kind currently available in London. Vivid flavours and fresh, 'three-dimensional' spicing are the hallmarks of the cooking; dishes continually challenge and fire the palate. Brilliant farsan snacks such as bulging samosas in filo pastry, and moong dhal vadas (balls of deep-fried lentils, spring onions and yogurt) come with dazzling home-made chutneys. South Indian dosas are massive affairs served up with fiery sambar, coconut chutney and yogurt, while the list of curries includes 'wonderfully sharp' spinach in yogurt sauce and ravaiya (a complex mix of stuffed baby aubergines, bananas and potatoes). The choice of dhals features 'magnificently earthy' udad made from tiny black beans, breads are exquisite, and fried rice is a 'bonanza of tastes'. To finish, explore the cabinet of barfi (colourful home-made sweetmeats). Lassi, milkshakes and a menu of world beers back up the short, sharp wine list. Australian house wine is £7.95.

CHEFS/PROPRIETORS: Hemant and Nalinee Desai OPEN: Tue to Sun; 12 to 3, 6.30 to 10.30 (lunch-time visitors are asked to phone in advance) MEALS: alc (main courses £3.50 to £6). Set L £5.95 to £7.55 (2 courses), Set D £8 to £12 SERVICE: net prices, card slips closed DETAILS: 32 seats. Private parties: 32 main room. Vegetarian meals. Children welcome. Smart dress preferred. Separate smoking area. Wheelchair access. Music

Saga

| NEW ENTRY | map 14

43–44 South Molton Street, W1 1HB   COOKING 2
071-629 3931   COST £17–£87

An expensive restaurant in an expensive street it may be, but the price you pay is considered worth it. The ground-floor sushi bar seats about a dozen, making it one of London's largest, while the rambling restaurant downstairs can cope with around 80. The décor is warm, rustic Japanese, with convoluted vaulting and lots of woodwork. Service is by elegantly dressed waitresses. Set dinners are what would be, in Western terms, a banquet, while the long carte offers the expected range of sashimi, sushi, tempura and sukiyaki. The £17 selection of sushi includes tiny sweet prawns, salmon roe, sea urchin and a form of semi-crisp herring roe, as well as tuna roll and a piece each of salmon, toro, sea bass and squid. Tempura of prawns, white fish, aubergine and green pepper is particularly light, and special sunomono consists of mackerel, crab and tenderised octopus with cucumber and four different seaweeds in an excellent mild, but well-flavoured, vinegar.

The single sheet of special and seasonal dishes (14 on one side in English, 29 on the other in Japanese) offers the most exciting, and indeed the best, food. A knowledgeable reporter in May enjoyed tuna chopped to a thick paste with spring onion and a raw yolk of quail's egg on top, and sashimi using kisu fish or sillago, common in Japanese waters but not found in Western seas. This was sliced thinly and 'the flavour was as delicate as any sashimi I have eaten, and must be recommended to anyone who gets the chance'. It was garnished with fine-flavoured shiso leaf, grated turnip and carrot, and grated ginger instead of wasabi – 'worth every penny'. Tender chicken livers and hearts in broth, with a few slices of poached mooli, make a hearty winter dish. As well as warm and chilled saké there are several types of shochu, the Japanese spirit made from buckwheat, barley and sweet potato. House wine is £12.90.

CHEFS: Mr Kikuchi, Mr Umeda, Mr Hiyoshi and Mr Fusha   PROPRIETOR: Mr Hashimoto   OPEN: all week; 12.30 to 2.30, 6.30 to 10   CLOSED: Christmas and New Year   MEALS: alc (main courses £5.50 to £22). Set L £6.50 to £17, Set D £37 to £55. Cover £1   SERVICE: not inc L, 15% D   CARDS: Access, Amex, Diners, Visa   DETAILS: 98 seats. Private parties: 30 main room, 6, 8 and 10 private rooms. Vegetarian meals. Children welcome. Music. Air-conditioned. Fax: 071-629 7507

St Quentin

| NEW ENTRY | map 13 |

243 Brompton Road, SW3 2EP   COOKING 2
071-581 5131 and 589 8005   COST £18–£46

This is the sister restaurant to the Grill St Quentin in Yeoman's Row (see entry, London), serving comparable food at similar prices, all very reasonable for the area. It has the feel, remarked one evocatively, of 'a Paris brasserie of the '50s or '60s', down to the mirrored dado, chandelier lighting and tables that are 'too close for comfort'. Nigel Davis, executive chef for both establishments, actually cooks at this one, and produces some very creditable classic French dishes. Omelette aux fines herbes was not quite the runny specimen that a purist was hoping for but still had plenty of herb flavour. Bayonne ham with a celeriac rémoulade was 'moist and delicately flavoured', the sauce nicely sharp, while an otherwise straightforward gazpacho was given a 'massive garnish of lobster and crab fragments'. A dish of lambs' kidneys in a red wine sauce was fine. Desserts keep up the standards. 'Deliciously dark and bitter' chocolate pavé had a delicate orange cream and brandy snaps, and pear poached in red wine came with 'excellent' cinnamon ice-cream. High-quality breads and well-cooked, if slightly sparse, vegetables do not let the side down. House wine is £8.60.

CHEF: Nigel Davis   PROPRIETOR: The Savoy Group plc   OPEN: all week; 12 to 3 (3.30 Sun), 7 to 11.30 (6.30 to 11 Sun)   MEALS: alc (main courses £7 to £15). Set L and D (7 to 8) £8 (2 courses) to £10   SERVICE: 12.5% (optional), card slips closed   CARDS: Access, Amex, Diners, Visa   DETAILS: 75 seats. Private parties: 25 private room. Vegetarian meals. Children welcome. Smart dress preferred. No music. Air-conditioned. Fax: 071-584 6064

Salloos

map 13

62–64 Kinnerton Street, SW1X 8ER   COOKING 2
071-235 4444   COST £28–£60

This long-standing Pakistani restaurant just off Knightsbridge is a bit short of space in its upstairs dining-room but deals in fairly refined food with 'no overly stodgy or greasy dishes and some especially good cooking'. The menu revolves around chicken and lamb, with a standard run of tandoori items (the lamb cutlets are good) helped along by specialities of chicken cooked in a soufflé of cheese, eggs and milk, and shredded lamb cooked in a mixture of whole wheat germ, lentils and spices. It is good to see hot carrot halwa as well as standard kulfi to finish.

If there is a wait, that may be because preparation of some dishes only begins after the order is placed, when you may be invited to pop into the kitchen to have a look. A whole young lamb, marinated and stuffed with rice, herbs and raisins, needs 24 hours' notice. Prices may seem high, although perhaps not for the area.

The £1.50 cover charge is for poppadums and chutneys, and the 15 per cent service charge is for lots of helpful suggestions that could result in too much food on the table if you are not careful. Wine mark-ups bump the bill up even further, though there are some interesting bottles on the Corney and Barrow page. House wine is £12.50 (£3 per glass).

CHEFS: Abdul Aziz and Humayun Khan PROPRIETORS: Mr and Mrs Salahuddin OPEN: Mon to Sat; 12 to 2.30, 7 to 11.15 MEALS: alc (main courses £8.50 to £14.50). Set L £16, Set D £25. Cover £1.50 SERVICE: 15%, card slips closed CARDS: Access, Amex, Diners, Visa DETAILS: 65 seats. Private parties: 65 main room. Vegetarian meals. No children under 6 after 8pm. Smart dress preferred. No music. Air-conditioned

Les Saveurs ▼ 　　　　　　　　　　　　　　　　　　 map 14

37A Curzon Street, W1Y 8EY 　　　　　　　　　　　　　　 COOKING 4
071-491 8919 　　　　　　　　　　　　　　　　　　　 COST £32–£62

This high-class French restaurant 'appears to be part of the Curzon cinema', and dining is done in the basement. Light wood panelling gives it an opulent feel – 'featureless' for one reporter but pleasantly devoid of ornate decoration for another. Scalloped shades and candles provide the light, and the feel-good factor is reinforced by comfortable chairs and large tables well spread. The luxury and Art Deco bits make it like 'Paris transported to London', for one reporter.

Enthusiasm for the food is universal. 'Certainly one of London's best,' observes more than one contributor. Apprenticeship in some of the best kitchens in France, where Joël Antunès acquired a sound technical and classical grounding, was time well spent. He has taken the best of this and made it work for him, rather than becoming a prisoner of tradition. The food is inventive yet simple, exciting yet carefully controlled for flavour and texture. A spring menu offered aspic of oysters with sea urchin cream, scallops with white-bean cream and olive oil, and a pyramid of spice bread stuffed with pineapple confit. Originality is helped along by, but by no means dependent on, ideas about spicing picked up from a stint at the Oriental Hotel in Bangkok.

When it is firing on all cylinders, the kitchen can produce exquisite dishes of tender quail on a delightfully dressed salad with diced wild mushrooms, 'stunningly good' terrine of duck foie gras and aubergine. At one summer meal, neat slices of 'very pink, wonderfully tender and delightfully tasty pigeon breasts' were placed on a thin layer of couscous, with pastilia pastry (half-way between filo and samosa) to crunch on. Around the edge of the plate were some very green and very fresh skinned broad beans and a generous amount of very fresh chanterelles. 'A sublime dish,' said the one who ate it. Talent, flair and creativity are the hallmarks of the cooking, and if there are occasional misjudgements – delicate smoked scallops served with an overpoweringly strong horseradish sauce, for example – they amount to no more than simply careless quirks and do not call into question the quality of execution.

Lunch is the bargain, but dinner is still rated as good value: 'Frankly I don't know how they do it – £36 for my meal was a snip.' To the extent that atmosphere is determined by people rather than décor, Les Saveurs succeeds brilliantly with service that is 'quick, friendly (but not too), helpful and unobtrusive'. If the stock of wines was sold and the proceeds donated to the government it would probably wipe out the national debt. Yves Saboua is a mightily impressive sommelier. 'The house wine was served as if I had chosen something much more expensive' was a refreshing comment, and those who choose it (£15 a bottle, £3.50 a glass) are more than satisfied. The wine list is long, distinguished, mainly French and for those who drink mature vintages of top claret the mark-ups are not always high. For the rest of us, 'other wines' offer some prospect of getting away with less than £20, but no compromises are made on quality. CELLARMAN'S CHOICE: Meursault Blagny 1988, Matrot, £43; Pommard Jarollières 1985, Pousse d'Or, £58.

CHEF: Joël Antunès PROPRIETOR: Fujikoshi UK Ltd OPEN: Mon to Fri; 12 to 2.30, 7 to 10.30 CLOSED: 2 weeks Aug, 2 weeks Christmas and New Year MEALS: Set L £21, Set D £32 (2 courses) to £39 SERVICE: not inc CARDS: Access, Amex, Diners, Visa DETAILS: 55 seats. Private parties: 45 main room, 10 private room. Vegetarian meals. Children welcome. Jacket and tie. No music. Air-conditioned. Fax: 071-491 3658

▲ *The Savoy* map 15

Strand, WC2R 0EU   COOKING 2*
071-836 4343   COST £24–£93

The Savoy is as distinguished as they come. Built by Richard D'Oyly Carte in 1884, with César Ritz as the first manager and Auguste Escoffier as the first chef, it is a haven of the old guard. In the grand hotel tradition, there is more than one restaurant: the main River restaurant, the general-purpose Grill and the all-day 'Upstairs' snackery.

The River restaurant is enormous, heavily swagged, multi-draped and crystal-chandeliered, with mirrors everywhere. Tables near the window have a grandstand view of the Embankment and the Thames, while at those further back you 'almost need a torch to read the menu'. The dozens of staff are helpful and attentive, although prices – melon in season at £12.80, for example – can horrify. It is worth noting the £47 seasonal menu with its wine and food partnerships, which ensures ample variety and a good match with each course. To some extent, cooking on this scale is a matter of logistics; dishes are not so much cooked by a single individual as assembled by a small army of chefs, the results wheeled round and carved, spooned or lifted on to the plate. One summer visitor was underwhelmed by seasonal leaves with langoustines and truffles, and rosettes of lamb wrapped in rösti potato with yet more truffles. She got more enjoyment out of stuffed morel mushrooms with 'beautifully timed' asparagus, and 'nicely prepared' John Dory, but was bowled over by 'superb' cherry tart with coconut ice-cream.

Old-fashioned carving and flambéing are alive and well in the Grill, and you can tell what day it is by the lunchtime specials: sausages with creamed potatoes and onions on Mondays, Lancashire hotpot on Thursdays, while roast lamb comes every day of the week.

'Upstairs' overlooks the courtyard entrance and deals in Caesar salad, Irish oysters, fish-cake with parsley sauce, and leg of lamb steak with aubergine and pesto. Seafood has received particularly good reports, and the big shellfish platter is commendably varied. Marble-topped tables, keen staff, positive flavours and surprises like clam chowder in sourdough bread are the currency. Champagne is served by the half-pint in a silver tankard. Elsewhere the wine list is par for the course in an establishment with lofty aspirations. Quality is not stinted, and just enough bottles are under £20 to offer fair choice. Half-bottles are good and house wine is £14.75 (£2.95 per glass).

CHEFS: Anton Edelmann (River Restaurant) and David Sharland (Grill and 'Upstairs') PROPRIETOR: The Savoy Group plc OPEN: River Restaurant all week; 12.30 to 2.30, 6 to 11.30 (7 to 10.30 Sun). Grill Mon to Sat, exc Sat L; 12.30 to 2.30, 6 to 11.15. 'Upstairs' Mon to Sat, exc Sat L; noon to midnight CLOSED: Grill Aug, Grill and 'Upstairs' bank hols MEALS: River Restaurant alc (main courses £20 to £31), Set L Mon to Sat £27, Sun £21.75, Set D £32 to £47 (inc wine). Grill alc (main courses £14.50 to £21), Set pre- and post-theatre D £26.75 (2 courses) to £29.75. 'Upstairs' alc (main courses £7 to £13) SERVICE: River Restaurant net prices, card slips closed. Grill and 'Upstairs' not inc CARDS: Access, Amex, Diners, Visa DETAILS: River Restaurant 200 seats, Grill 100 seats, 'Upstairs' 36 seats. Private parties: 10 and 50 main rooms, 6 to 80 private rooms. Vegetarian meals (with prior notice River Restaurant). Children welcome. Jacket and tie, exc 'Upstairs' (smart dress preferred). No pipes in dining-rooms. Music (exc 'Upstairs'). Air-conditioned ACCOMMODATION: 202 rooms, all with bath/shower. TV. Phone. Air-conditioned. Room only £212 to £323. Rooms for disabled. Lift. Children welcome. Baby facilities by arrangement. Afternoon teas. Swimming-pool. Sauna. Confirm by 6. Fax: 071-240 6040 (The Which? Hotel Guide)

Shaw's ♥ 　　　　　　　　　　　　　　　| NEW ENTRY |　map 13

119 Old Brompton Road, SW7 3RN 　　　　　　　　　　　　COOKING 2
071-373 7774 and 4472 　　　　　　　　　　　　　　　　COST £21–£47

It used to be Chanterelle, then Neil Shaw (chairman of Tate & Lyle) and his sculptress wife Pixie and friends bought it in spring 1994, bringing in a new chef. Frances Atkins is not new to the *Guide*, though. She was at Farleyer House in Aberfeldy, and before that at the Old Plow Inn at Speen in Bucks. Old Chanterelle regulars need have no qualms about the change. The dining-room has been spruced up, big gilded mirrors help the feeling of space, and comfort and crisp linen are the order of the day. It feels prosperous, with colourful paintings to relieve the beige.

Sound ingredients underpin a smart-sounding menu that makes good use of fish and shellfish, rabbit and pigeon, and takes in crab and potato cake with crisp bacon and cabbage, as well as poached guinea-fowl in lemon and garlic served with a sausage of its meat on a bed of crisp potato with asparagus. Some ideas are a bit ambitious, or just don't quite come off – a carrot and coriander sauce for ravioli of langoustine, for example, or a blob of mayonnaise tasting of curry powder that wasn't quite up to the excellent grilled scallops it accompanied. Among desserts such as peach clafoutis and a chilled marmalade pudding with apple cream sauce, one that stood out was a trio of chocolates with a crème de menthe sauce, using cream, mousse, sponge, and dark and white chocolates to good effect.

Service is by Gerald Atkins, full of avuncular charm, helped by a team of young Australian-sounding men. The lads are keen enough, although seem upon occasion to have little understanding of what they are bringing to table: at one meal the waiter blithely offered to grind pepper on to everything, including an already peppered duck breast. Bread can be under par, but wines are extremely well chosen and reasonably marked up. There is lots of interest from Down Under, but Europe and California are mouthwatering too. What it lacks in half-bottles it makes up for in wines by the glass, principally for aperitif and dessert. House wine is around £12. CELLARMAN'S CHOICE: Capel Vale Chardonnay 1990, £15; Chianti Classico 1991, Isole e Olena, £15.

CHEF: Frances Atkins PROPRIETORS: Sir Neil and Lady Shaw, Gerald and Frances Atkins, Torunn Fieldhouse and David Banks OPEN: all week, exc Sat L and Sun D; 12 to 2 (4 Sun); , 7 to 10 CLOSED: Christmas and New Year, last 2 weeks Aug, bank hols MEALS: alc L (main courses £10.50 to £15). Set L £13 (2 courses), Set D £24.50 (2 courses) to £27.50 SERVICE: net prices CARDS: Access, Amex, Diners, Visa DETAILS: 44 seats. 3 tables outside. Private parties: 10 main room. Vegetarian meals. Children welcome. Smart dress preferred. Wheelchair access (1 step). No music. Air-conditioned

Shogun
map 14

| Britannia Hotel, Adams Row, Mayfair, W1 | COOKING 2 |
| 071-493 1255 | COST £23–£52 |

The restaurant is in the basement of a hotel off Grosvenor Square, but independently owned. Waiters wear formal black, waitresses are in kimonos, both sorts are skilful and charming, and there is no difficulty getting English explanations from the owner or maitre d' about anything that is not already clear from the menu. Accommodations to Western tastes might include slightly larger portions of meat, some dilution of flavour, and an absence of shellfish in the sashimi assortment of tuna, salmon, sea bass, yellowtail and turbot. But the raw fish is outstandingly good and there is no compromise in the heat of the accompanying wasabi.

The chef at the small sushi counter is highly professional. 'His dexterity and speed in cutting the fish and shaping the sushi were astonishing,' writes one who has seen a few at it. Tempura batter is crisp, and pickles and sticky rice are good. In addition to the *carte*, half a dozen six-item set dinners – revolving around duck or salmon, for example – include an assortment of hors d'oeuvre, clear soup, sashimi, prawn tempura, fruit and green tea. Prices, as in most London Japanese restaurants, are high, and that goes for wines too. Saké is £4 for a small carafe.

CHEF: S. Daito PROPRIETOR: Miss H. Mitsuka OPEN: Tue to Sun, D only; 6 to 11 CLOSED: 10 days at Christmas MEALS: alc (main courses £8 to £17). Set D £30 to £32 SERVICE: 12.5%, card slips closed CARDS: Access, Amex, Diners, Visa DETAILS: 60 seats. Private parties: 100 main room. Children welcome. Smart dress preferred. Music. Air-conditioned

Simply Nico
map 11

| 48A Rochester Row, SW1P 1JU | COOKING 3 |
| 071-630 8061 | COST £31–£40 |

'This has become a regular venue since reading about it in the *Guide*,' said a reporter who enjoys the well-presented food, relaxed ambience and value for money. The place can seem bare and brightly lit, tables are close together, and the chairs do not fit everybody's backside, but one visitor felt the atmosphere improved with the buzz of conversation, helped along by good service from relaxed and friendly staff. And the price of dinner is not much more than that for lunch, which is as welcome as it is rare.

Nico's restaurants inevitably live out of each other's pockets, so it is not unusual to see similar dishes cropping up on more than one menu. This one certainly reflects the master's keenness for ceps and foie gras, for which some reporters are grateful. Foie gras on toasted brioche with caramelised orange achieved 'perfect balance, perfect execution' for one, and duck terrine with pistachios and cherries was not far behind. But the food here is more laid-back, using the charcoal grill for rib of beef with béarnaise sauce and for grilled lamb cutlets. The food may not excite, but raw materials are of the highest quality, including, for one reporter, superbly fresh brill. The chips are applauded as much as the mashed potatoes with olive oil. Puddings get fewer mentions but might include lemon tart or nougat glace with raspberry sauce. There are no bargains on the short wine list, but one regular reckons it has improved over the last year or two, and wines by the glass (starting at £3.50) have picked up.

CHEF: Andrew Barber   PROPRIETORS: Nico and Dinah-Jane Ladenis   OPEN: Mon to Sat, exc Sat L; 12 to 2, 7 to 11   MEALS: Set L £20 (2 courses) to £23.50, Set D £25   SERVICE: net prices, card slips closed   CARDS: Access, Amex, Diners, Visa   DETAILS: 45 seats. Private parties: 20 main room. Vegetarian meals. No children under 4. Smart dress preferred. No pipes in dining-room. Wheelchair access. No music. Air-conditioned. Fax: 071-355 4877

Singapore Garden Restaurant £

map 11

83–83A Fairfax Road, NW6 4DY
071-328 5314

COOKING 1*
COST £19–£46

Some of the best South-east Asian cooking in north London is to be had at this popular neighbourhood restaurant. The Lim family know their regulars and keep first-timers well pleased with a big menu of polyglot Far Eastern dishes. China, Thailand and Indonesia are all represented, but the serious stuff is in the list of specials and Singaporean and Malaysian dishes. Mrs Lim's cooking is refined, subtle and careful. Classic satays, beef rendang, 'searingly hot' Pacific prawn sambal and fried mee hoon noodles are praised regularly for their clear flavours and authenticity. In more esoteric territory, look for kang kong blachan (dry-cooked Chinese spinach with fermented shrimp paste, chilli and garlic): 'wonderful stuff', enthused an aficionado. Occasional lapses are outweighed by spicy successes. Tiger beer or non-alcoholic grass jelly are the preferred tipples. House wine is £8.50. Another branch, Singapore Garden II, is at 154 Gloucester Place, NW1 6DJ, Tel: 071-723 8233.

CHEF: Mrs S.K. Lim   PROPRIETORS: the Lim family   OPEN: all week; 12 to 2.45, 6 to 10.45 (11.45 Fri and Sat)   CLOSED: 5 days Christmas   MEALS: alc (main courses £5 to £11.50). Set L and D £16. Minimum £10   SERVICE: not inc   CARDS: Access, Amex, Diners, Visa   DETAILS: 100 seats. 3 tables outside. Private parties: 60 main room, 60 private room. Vegetarian meals. Children welcome. Smart dress preferred. No cigars in dining-room. Music. Air-conditioned

London round-ups listing additional restaurants that may be worth a visit can be found after the main London section.

Card slips closed *in the details at the end of an entry indicates that the total on the slips of credit cards is closed when handed over for signature.*

Snows on the Green

map 10

166 Shepherd's Bush Road, W6 7PB
071-603 2142

COOKING 2
COST £22–£40

Lavender abounds – in pictures, on the walls and tables – reminding us that Sebastian Snow takes Provence seriously as a source of inspiration. Italy figures prominently too, but this is not just another bistro with a jar of sun-dried tomatoes and a bowl of polenta waiting for something to happen. They are there, naturally, along with balsamic vinegar and bruschetta, but the cooking goes beyond superficial treatment to get close to the heart of Mediterranean food. The direct style may mean there are few surprises, but at least what you read on the menu is generally what you get on the plate, which might be ravioli of Swiss chard with ricotta and sage, baked egg with ratatouille, or goats' cheese feuilleté with stuffed provençale vegetables.

Another pleasure is the contrast between light, clean tastes – steamed hake with artichoke hearts and tomatoes, or marinated salmon with soured cream – and the earthiness of a daube of oxtail, or lamb roasted with white beans and garlic. Balance of flavours extends to the puddings. Mascarpone and mango tart is 'a perfect combination of tartness and sweetness with a creamy base'. The staff are 'incredibly nice without being unctuous', although some wonder about the silly waistcoats the waitresses are compelled to wear: 'If you dress people in silly clothes, it only encourages them to behave in a silly way.' The wine list is a single page of sound bottles mostly under £20, with house wine from £8.75 (£2.25 per glass).

CHEF/PROPRIETOR: Sebastian Snow   OPEN: all week, exc Sat L and Sun D; 12 to 3, 7 to 11 CLOSED: Christmas, bank hols   MEALS: alc (main courses £9 to £11), Set L £11.50 (2 courses) to £13.50   SERVICE: not inc, card slips closed   CARDS: Access, Visa   DETAILS: 70 seats. Private parties: 24 private room. Vegetarian meals. Children welcome. No pipes in dining-room. Wheelchair access. Music. Air-conditioned. Fax: 071-602 7553

Soho Soho £

map 15

11–13 Frith Street, W1V 8TS
071-494 3491

COOKING 1
COST £19–£46

The downstairs café-bar and rôtisserie have a lively café atmosphere, while upstairs in the dining-room – bright and airy in daylight, candle-lit at night – the approach is more serious. The view of Frith Street is pleasantly diverting. The cooking claims to be provençale, although some dishes – calf's liver, for example, served with asparagus, oyster mushrooms and tarragon sauce – show that it is not crisply focused. Nevertheless, capers, olives and fennel, plus a French accent from the waitress, help to sharpen it. Fish soup, a standard of the provençale repertoire, is good. Daily specials do more than add interest; they are probably the best bet. At an inspection meal a fillet of brill, from the regular, unchanging, laminated menu, was too shrivelled for comfort, while sea bass, one of the daily specials, was perfectly fresh and delightful. Vegetables are subject to similar ups and downs; the same meal produced undercooked potatoes at £1.75 a portion.

The welcome is generally warm and the service friendly, though not invariably so. The cover charge of £1.50 in the restaurant includes olives tossed in oil and herbs, toasted almonds and good bread. The more interesting wines come from a southern swathe of vines that sweep from Italy, across Provence, through the Rhône and Languedoc into Spain. House wines start a £9.50 in the restaurant and £7.95 in the rôtisserie. Car parking is free at the nearby NCP for diners but not lunchers.

CHEF: Laurent Lebeau PROPRIETORS: Neville Abraham and Laurence Isaacson OPEN: Mon to Sat, exc Sat L restaurant; restaurant 12 to 3, 6 to 12; rôtisserie noon to 1am MEALS: restaurant alc (main courses £10 to £13); rôtisserie alc (main courses £6 to £9.50). Cover £1.50 restaurant SERVICE: 12.5% (optional), card slips closed CARDS: Access, Amex, Diners, Visa DETAILS: restaurant 60 seats, rôtisserie 80 seats. 6 tables outside. Private parties: 60 private room. Vegetarian meals. Children welcome. No-smoking area. No cigars/pipes in restaurant. Wheelchair access rôtisserie (1 step). Music rôtisserie. Air-conditioned. Fax: 071-437 3091

Sonny's ✳

map 10

94 Church Road, SW13 0DQ   COOKING 2
081-748 0393   COST £24–£43

A reporter who knew Sonny's of old welcomed the 'real return to form. A new chef has made all the difference and there is much more of an air of confidence about the place.' Others, however, have not been as enthusiastic. On paper it should be easy. Pluck Redmond Hayward from Redmond's at Cleeve Hill, in the *Guide* last year at a score of 3*, and set him down in Barnes. Off he goes and cooks to the same standard, right? Somehow it doesn't quite work like that.

The restaurant is behind the shop and salad-dominated café, a long, narrow room with cream walls and paper tablecloths; chairs are 'the sort you see in a school hall'. It is bright, lively, friendly and relaxed, with a cheerful bustle. Many current enthusiasms are echoed on the menu, from steamed boned skate wing with black butter and capers to calf's liver with a cake of potato, onion and smoked bacon, although one reporter wonders if the kitchen is trying a bit too hard when it comes to monkfish with Thai curry sauce and mango raita. Successes are easy to understand, given Redmond Hayward's evident skill. Soups are well reported: thick, rich, spicy shellfish soup, with a gratifyingly pungent smell and taste, and celery and onion soup made from good stock. Cod, 'cooked correctly', may be topped with crumbs and herbs, with allumette potatoes, while pigeon breast, tender and full of taste from marination, is roasted pink on creamy Savoy cabbage. One reporter's banana crème brûlée and chocolate sauce were both good, although not together.

Tastes at inspection, however, did not stand out as they should. 'Pleasant but unremarkable' was the summing-up. 'There was nothing to lift the cooking above the ordinary.' To the extent that the food disappoints, prices can be considered high, which is a shame because they are actually quite low. Service is up and down – decidedly up when Pippa Hayward is there. Three dozen wines mix Old and New Worlds well, combining excitement and quality in the range of £8 to £30. Choice by the glass is particularly good, beginning with house wine at £1.75.

'I think there were carrots, and that they tasted forgettable.'
(On eating in Worcestershire)

CHEF: Redmond Hayward   PROPRIETOR: Rebecca Mascarenhas   OPEN: all week, exc Sun D; restaurant 12.30 to 2.30 (3 Sun), 7.30 to 11; café all week; 10 to 6   CLOSED: bank hols   MEALS: alc (main courses £7.50 to £14). Set L and D £12.95 (2 courses); Set L Sun £16.50   SERVICE: not inc   CARDS: Access, Amex, Visa   DETAILS: 100 seats. Private parties: 20 private room. Vegetarian meals. Children's helpings Sun L. Smart dress preferred. No-smoking room. Wheelchair access. No music. Air-conditioned. Fax: 081-748 2698

The Square ♥

map 14

32 King Street, SW1Y 6RJ
071-839 8787

COOKING 3
COST £36–£69

The chic modern interior moves some to rhapsodies: 'Opulent crimson, royal blue and shimmering gold abound in squares, cubes protrude from the walls, spangles of gold hang like Egyptian curtains at the window.' Others appreciate the 'roominess and light'. The Square continues to run smoothly. People note that it is expensive, but do not doubt the value in food that achieves a fine balance between the gutsy and the understated. The *carte* offers a surprisingly wide choice of perhaps a dozen or so starters, and five each of fish and meat for mains. The tendency noted last year of simply listing the components of a dish is maintained. If 'roast sea bass, pesto noodles, sauce vierge' sounds a little take-it-or-leave-it to some, it may for others be a refreshing change from the burgeoning inclination to include every last herb leaf in the name of a dish.

Enthusiastic reports have endorsed 'particularly rich' shallot soup with thyme cream, a traditional 'thick, smooth' fish soup with rouille, cheese and croûtons, 'superb' sauté of langoustines with pimentos and garlic leaves, seared scallops with roasted endive in a Sauternes sauce that achieved 'perfect balance' between bitter and sweet elements, and mixed grilled fish with a pungently earthy tomato coulis. The declared aim is lightness, but that does not stop the kitchen delivering in darkest February a dish of 'extremely tender, and very strongly flavoured' beef fillet and oxtail stew. Puddings that have pleased include panacotta with blueberries, pear tarte Tatin, cherry tart with clotted cream, an admirably seasonal pear, blackberry and hazelnut pie, and 'perfect' white chocolate mousse with dark chocolate sauce. Service is generally found to be cheerful and attentive, but can lag when the place fills up.

An apartheid system still rules the wine list. The first half is arranged by classic grape variety, while the remainder of the list concentrates on 'fine wines' (principally clarets and burgundies) with a smattering of non-Europeans. Here the baseline is £25 for 1991 Bourgogne Rouge or Crozes-Hermitage. Choices are inspired and imaginative. The Square Selection offers more democratic drinking from £12.50 the bottle, £8 the half or £3.50 the glass. CELLARMAN'S CHOICE: Menetou-Salon Morogues 1992, Pellé, £18.50; Chorey-lès-Beaune 1990, Cornu, £27.50.

CHEF: Philip Howard   PROPRIETOR: Nigel Platts-Martin   OPEN: all week, exc L Sat and Sun; 12 to 2.45, 6 to 11.45 (7 to 10 Sun)   CLOSED: bank hols, 24 Dec to 4 Jan (exc 31 Dec)   MEALS: alc (main courses £13 to £19.50)   SERVICE: not inc   CARDS: Access, Amex, Diners, Visa   DETAILS: 70 seats. Private parties: 12 main room, 24 private room. Vegetarian meals with prior notice. Children welcome. Smart dress preferred. Wheelchair access (1 step). No music. Air-conditioned. Fax: 071-321 2124

Sree Krishna £

map 10

192–194 Tooting High Street, SW17 0SF
081-672 4250 and 6903

COOKING 1
COST £11–£34

The attraction is simple: south Indian vegetarian food plus a range of standard meat dishes, all at give-away prices. Expect no frills. Most of the vegetarian dishes are £2 or less, most of the meat dishes between £3 and £3.50. Subtlety is not on offer, but a good variety of food certainly is, including much that is wrapped in a dosai pancake (potatoes and fried onions, for example) or made into a rissole, cake or doughnut, and best eaten with sambar (a mild curry) and coconut chutney. Meat dishes run the gamut from korma to vindaloo, with birianis and lots of vegetables for back-up. Drink lassi or lager.

CHEF: Mullath Vijayan PROPRIETORS: T. Haridas and family OPEN: all week; 12 to 3, 6 to 11 (12 Fri and Sat) CLOSED: 25 and 26 Dec MEALS: alc (main courses £2 to £6.50). Minimum £5 SERVICE: 10%, card slips closed CARDS: Access, Amex, Diners, Visa DETAILS: 120 seats. Private parties: 60 main room, 60 private room. Vegetarian meals. Children welcome. Smart dress preferred. Wheelchair access (also WC). Music. Air-conditioned

Sri Siam

map 15

14 Old Compton Street, W1V 5PE
071-434 3544

COOKING 2
COST £17–£37

'The first thing you notice on entering this long, narrow dining-room is the serious perfume and the coolness of the place,' observed a supporter of this premier-league Thai restaurant. The mood is ethnic, with abstract prints, artefacts and dolls adorning the walls, although the Western Muzak can seem oddly out of place. Service is generally careful and pleasant. Set lunch and dinner menus provide a good-value introduction to the cuisine, but it is worth delving into the full repertoire for more adventurous stuff. Flavours are acutely balanced, although chilli ratings can have different effects on different people. While some have found the spicing rather tame, others have suffered more agony than ecstasy: that tauhu (tofu) curry was 'festooned with halved red chillies, seeds and all' was the complaint of one reporter, who sought relief in exotic fresh fruit. Tender satays, fragrant fish-cakes, stuffed chicken wings, roast duck curry, stir-fried beef with chillies and basil, and sweet-and-sour Thai prawns are benchmark dishes that seldom disappoint. A full complement of vegetarian options is also available. The short wine list favours the modern methods of the New World. House wine is £8.50, or £2.10 per glass.

CHEF: K.N. Udom PROPRIETOR: Thai Restaurants plc OPEN: all week, exc Sun L; 12 to 3, 6 to 11.15 (10.30 Sun) CLOSED: 24 to 26 Dec, 1 Jan MEALS: alc (main courses £4 to £8). Set L £9.50, Set D £14.95 (minimum 2) SERVICE: 12.5% CARDS: Access, Amex, Diners, Visa DETAILS: 90 seats. Private parties: 100 main room. Vegetarian meals. Children welcome. Music. Air-conditioned

'Service was chaotic, explained partly by the fact that the village cricket team was celebrating in the other bar and that there was only the poor owner to cope with two bars, take the food orders and deal with a flood in the kitchen.' (On eating in Sussex)

Sri Siam City

map 11

85 London Wall, EC2M 7AD
071-628 5772

COOKING 2
COST £22–£48

Beyond the wine bars, sandwich bars and corporate dining-rooms of the City, only a couple of eating-places stand out, and this Thai restaurant is one of them, a sister to the Soho original (see entry on previous page). Like other venues around, it springs to life at lunch-time, although the Barbican is close enough for evenings to follow suit. The large scale is commuted to manageable size by a division into upper and lower eating areas, and the feeling is of somewhere smart and stylish with a sense of occasion – 'the kind of place you can take someone to impress them', according to one reporter. 'The heat of the food is toned down to suit the conservative bankers who dine here,' whether they eat traditional tom yum kai soup (hot and sour) or green chicken curry. Among beef dishes, sia rong hai is grilled sliced meat served with mint and coriander with a lime and chilli dressing. Meatless dishes are given space, too, including papaya pok pok, which is the fruit tossed with carrots, cabbage, lime juice, peanuts and dried shrimps. Desserts are mostly fruity and refreshing, and kong wan is four tiny banana-leaf baskets filled with layers of green and white custard. Wines are few but well chosen, helpfully arranged by style and fairly priced. House wine is £8.50 (£2.25 per glass).

CHEF: P. Lerdjirakul PROPRIETOR: Thai Restaurants plc OPEN: Mon to Fri; 11.30am to 8pm CLOSED: 25 and 26 Dec, 1 Jan, bank hols MEALS: alc (main courses £6.50 to £10.50). Set L and D £13.90 to £24.80 (minimum 2) SERVICE: 12.5% (optional), card slips closed CARDS: Access, Amex, Diners, Visa DETAILS: 130 seats. Private parties: 180 main room. Vegetarian meals. Children welcome. Wheelchair access (also WC). Lift. Music. Air-conditioned. Fax: 071-628 3395

Stephen Bull ♥

map 14

5–7 Blandford Street, W1H 3AA
071-486 9696

COOKING 2*
COST £30–£48

The simple 'Stephen Bull' signature sets the tone of modish, clean, decorative minimalism. Pure white walls and small modern pictures contrast with charcoal banquettes and comfortable dark chairs. The noise level is surprisingly low given the reflective surfaces, and the atmosphere discreet. A sense of confidence emanates from smart male management who are correct and attentive. If the menu has lots of in-vogue ingredients, this is not so much because Mr Bull is following fashion, more because he has been leading it for some time. Saffron butter, orange salsa, pea purée, grilled zander, and steamed carp with shellfish ravioli are among the items we might see.

New chef Tommy Slowey cooked here for a while a few years back and maintains the style, including an old favourite: twice-cooked goats' cheese soufflé. Flavour is a high priority, as dishes testify: spiced parsnip soup with chilli oil and fresh coriander, mussels in a curry-flavoured sauce with pasta, and crisp Thai spiced crab-cakes with lime hollandaise, black beans and ginger pilaff. But in an effort to pursue it, some of the craft and technique that is a characteristic of Stephen Bull's own cooking has rather gone out of the window, resulting in occasional coarse and inelegant dishes. At inspection, some items were 'poor, showing lack of understanding of ingredients and technique'. The mousse in courgette flower was one example.

The weight of dishes varies with the seasons, although reporters reckon that one portion of anything called an 'assiette' will do two people, be it pork (with belly, crackling, loin chop, spare rib, tenderloin, chorizo sausage, slivers of Parmesan, kidney beans and a raunchy sauce) or dessert, among whose components might be mango parfait, 'date pudding steamed to gungy perfection', and various chocolate delights. 'They keep thinking up new and sinfully delicious puddings,' ranging from panna cotta to old-fashioned steamed puddings. The wine list may be short but is a model of its kind. Wines have been chosen with pin-point accuracy for high quality and variety of taste, and prices further encourage good drinking. House wines are tip-top too (from £10.50), 10 half-bottles are welcome, and there are half a dozen dry wines by the glass, around £3 to £4.

CHEF: Tommy Slowey   PROPRIETOR: Stephen Bull   OPEN: Mon to Sat, exc Sat L; 12 to 2.15, 6.30 to 10.30   CLOSED: 1 week Christmas, bank hols   MEALS: alc (main courses £10.50 to £15)   SERVICE: not inc, card slips closed   CARDS: Access, Amex, Visa   DETAILS: 55 seats. Private parties: 50 main room. Vegetarian meals. Children's helpings. No cigars/pipes in dining-room. Wheelchair access (1 step). No music. Air-conditioned. Fax: 071-490 3128

Stephen Bull's Bistro and Bar ▼   map 11

71 St John Street, EC1M 4AN   COOKING 2*
071-490 3127   COST £22–£39

Depending on your business, the bistro is handy for both the Barbican and Smithfield Market. It opened in 1992 as the second limb of Stephen Bull's Marylebone restaurant (see entry above), and the style is even more pared-down, with splashes of primary colour on the otherwise unadorned walls. Add to that the 'extremely rigid' chairs, and it is clear that the aim is not cocooned luxury.

Cool Mediterranean flavour permeates the menus: escabèche of red mullet with spiced aubergine, deep-fried sardines in chickpea batter with saffron dressing, and lamb chump with niçoise salsa and grilled tomato sauce. Where others have exclusively ploughed the Italian furrow, the kitchen here also uses Spanish things to good effect, such as chorizo sausage, Manchego cheese, Serrano ham, roast hake, and a salsa with hazelnuts (à la romesco) served with tuna. A regular describes it as 'excellent peasant cooking – it does exactly what it sets out to do'. He recommends 'fine soups that stick to your ribs', provençale vegetable tart with pesto, poussin grilled with rosemary and garlic, brown sugar meringue with bananas, among others. 'I should think it might be a very good place for an amorous evening,' he adds, 'at any rate for the young.' Service is generally thought 'first-class'.

Wine prices are generous to a fault. The choices reflect current thinking, with names such as Langi Ghiran in Victoria, Deltetto in Piedmont, Bonny Doon from Santa Cruz and Ostertag in Alsace. A handful of halves is offered. Prices open at £8.95. CELLARMAN'S CHOICE: Bergerac 1992, Ch. Terillon, £10; Corbières 1991, Dom. Bellevue, £10.50.

LONDON

CHEF: Stephen Carter PROPRIETOR: Stephen Bull OPEN: Mon to Sat, exc Sat L; 12 to 2.15, 6.30 (7 Sat) to 10.45 CLOSED: 1 week Christmas, bank hols MEALS: alc (main courses £6.50 to £12) SERVICE: not inc CARDS: Access, Amex, Visa DETAILS: 90 seats. Private parties: 90 main room. Vegetarian meals. Children's helpings. No cigars/pipes in dining-room. Wheelchair access (1 step). Music. Air-conditioned. Fax: 071-490 3128

Suntory
map 14

72–73 St James's Street, SW1A 1PH

COOKING 3*

071-409 0201

COST £40–£137

As befits the area, Suntory has politeness, conservatism and expense written all over it. All is smiles and bows from suited staff, and everything is done with impeccable taste. White walls and carefully placed ceramics come as near as they can to producing a feeling of serenity in the middle of a city, although the downstairs teppanyaki bar is more high-spirited. The target is top-level Japanese executives in London, and it hits the nail on the head. 'The cost is outrageous, but that is why Japanese businessmen entertain here.' The generosity of the host is a tangible indication of the guest's importance, a philosophy which rather militates against the Western idea of value for money, but there we are. Fixed-price dinner meals beginning at around £50 give an indication of what to expect, the only small crumb of comfort being that service is included.

It is encouraging to see that Western diners are offered the same range of dishes as Japanese diners, including some which in the past Westerners might have been considered unable to eat, such as jellyfish with vinegar. Seasonal dishes, too, are an integral part of the menu. One-pot dishes are prepared at table, while among the usual run of items might be lobster onigarayaki, charcoal-grilled in the shell. Take the chef's recommendations for excitement, which might include sea tangle with herring roe and asparagus, sardine and burdock tempura, or beef sushi. Delicacy and lightness are a feature, with interesting textural contrasts, and dishes can be stunning to look at. Cold savoury egg custard with lobster meat combines the lot. Wines and saké subscribe to the same pricing principles as the food. House wine is £14 (£3.50 per glass).

CHEF: K. Kato PROPRIETOR: Suntory Ltd OPEN: Mon to Sat; 12 to 2, 6 to 10 CLOSED: bank hols MEALS: alc (main courses £18 to £44). Set £33.50, Set D £49.80 to £67 SERVICE: net prices, card slips closed CARDS: Access, Amex, Diners, Visa DETAILS: 120 seats. Private parties: 100 main room. Vegetarian meals. Children welcome. Smart dress preferred. Wheelchair access. No music. Air-conditioned. Fax: 071-499 7993

Le Suquet
map 13

104 Draycott Avenue, SW3 3AE

COOKING 1*

071-581 1785

COST £27–£50

Deep in Sloane country, this long-serving French restaurant goes on and on. On fine days there are tables outside, although the crush can be too much for some people: 'This place is small, and feels it,' observed one. Fish is the reason for coming here and the raw material is handled with reasonable skill. Several varieties of oysters (including belons), langoustines and 'splendid' moules marinière in a classic broth line up alongside scallops in saffron sauce, herby, well-garlicked cod provençale, and grilled John Dory accompanied by a tomato and basil sauce. Meagre portions of vegetables disappointed an inspector. Satisfying desserts revolve around tarts, fresh fruit and sorbets. Service has come in for some criticism: 'off-hand, verging on arrogance' and 'slapdash' were the experiences of two reporters. The wine list is Gallic, straightforward and business-like. House wine is £7.50.

CHEFS: Jean-Yves Darcel and Phillipe Moron PROPRIETOR: Pierre Martin OPEN: all week; 12 to 2.30 (3 Sat and Sun), 7 to 11.30 MEALS: alc (main courses £10 to £15). Cover £1 SERVICE: 15% (optional), card slips closed CARDS: Access, Amex, Diners, Visa DETAILS: 70 seats. 5 tables outside. Private parties: 40 main room, 18 private room. Vegetarian meals with prior notice. Children welcome. Smart dress preferred. Music. Fax: 071-225 0838

Surinder's

map 12

109 Westbourne Park Road, W2 5QL
071-229 8968

COOKING 1
COST £21–£31

A diehard constituency still exists in London for old-fangled French bistro cooking, and Surinder Chandwan has been one of its more tenacious purveyors since 1985. Readers are almost invariably supportive of his efforts, often travelling across the capital for the experience. The fixed-price menu of around a half-dozen choices at each stage is written in terse French and includes crab en cocotte, foie gras (with a supplement) and saddle of lamb. Game sausage as a starter was appreciated by one, save for its being 'smothered in warm red cabbage, which I dislike'. Main courses may include venison with prunes and tournedos Rossini, while puddings are good for things like chocolate mousse and strawberry bavarois, perhaps less successful in the case of a 'very odd' French version of bread-and-butter pudding – served cold. Wines are a sound bistro selection, even if there are a few too many alternative vintages for comfort. House wines are £7.95.

CHEF/PROPRIETOR: Surinder Chandwan OPEN: Tues to Sat D only; 7 to 11 MEALS: Set D £14.95 to £18.95 SERVICE: 10%, card slips closed CARDS: Access, Amex, Visa DETAILS: 45 seats. Private parties: 45 main room. Vegetarian meals. Children welcome. Smart dress preferred. No music

La Tante Claire ♥

map 13

68 Royal Hospital Road, SW3 4HP
071-352 6045

COOKING 5
COST £32–£105

'Now I know what grade 5 means: a wonderful meal,' writes one reporter. A 10-minute stroll away from Sloane Square, the pastel blue and yellow dining-room is charming, fresh, elegant, bright with modern paintings. It is light but not frothy, serious but not pompous, a place where people come to enjoy themselves. Staff play a significant part in delivering the feel-good vibes: thoroughly professional, only too happy to help, unsnooty, not to mention well-informed and efficient. It is a restaurant with no sense of showiness or stuffiness, and Pierre Koffmann continues to amaze and delight his customers.

The kitchen's strength is an emphasis on the essential flavour of food, 'recalling the farmyard, the sea, the garden and the slaughterhouse'. Salmis of woodcock is two bloody breasts, two legs, and 'the head and beak split asunder' on a bed of celeriac purée, all full of robust, livery, gamey flavours 'which could be off-putting to the timid'. If the cooking conveys something of the 'terroir' of Koffmann's native south-west France, that does not necessarily mean it is earthy, but simply that it derives from the products of that region: apple croustade, for example, with a deep-flavoured clear caramel sauce and 'terrific caramelised apples'. The food is extremely refined, even when employing ox cheek or the classic pig's trotter. Foie gras, common enough in top restaurants, is particularly sensuous and flavoursome. Refinement is evident too in a dish of seared scallops, the flavour 'outstanding', the timing spot-on and the ink sauce an 'astonishingly dense, creamy, even unctuous charcoal grey accompaniment with a coral-based addition feathered across it'.

'The £25 lunch year in, year out, represents [London's] best bargain,' asserts one reader. 'There is something so reassuring, so civilised, about having lunch in Mr Koffmann's dining-room.' Even those less fulsome in their praise, who manage to pick a few holes, still admit they would much rather spend the money here – on slightly flawed excellence – than anywhere else. Everything, from first-class appetisers and French cheese in beautiful condition, to a good variety of breads, and the petits fours with coffee, helps to sustain enjoyment, although under the heading 'niggles' we might ask for a menu with an English translation to obviate the boring repetition of explanations around the room. And given the trouble Koffmann and his team go to in preparing the food, and the prices we pay for eating it, the cigar smoke is regrettable.

Wines are French, and the south-west section is welcome for its sanity. Elsewhere, affordable bottles may be outnumbered by flash expensive ones, but the fact that service is included helps enormously, and the choice of half-bottles is generous. The sommelier gives good advice, and knows who has ordered what, and therefore how to dispose of the remains of the white wine without asking. Excellent house red (£17.80) and white (£13.90) are £3 per glass. CELLARMAN'S CHOICE: Auxey-Duresses 1989, J.P. Diconne, £34.20; Mercurey 'Clos l'Evêque', premier cru, Chante Flute 1988, H. de Suremain, £32.50.

CHEF/PROPRIETOR: Pierre Koffmann OPEN: Mon to Fri; 12.30 to 2, 7 to 11 CLOSED: 1 week Christmas, 3 weeks Aug MEALS: alc (main courses £24.50 to £35). Set L £25. Minimum £45 D SERVICE: net prices, not inc CARDS: Access, Amex, Diners, Visa DETAILS: 42 seats. Private parties: 45 main room. Vegetarian meals with prior notice. Children welcome. Jacket and tie D. No pipes in dining-room. Wheelchair access (1 step; also WC). No music. Air-conditioned. Fax: 071-352 3257

Tatsuso   NEW ENTRY   map 11

32 Broadgate Circle, EC2M 2QS   COOKING 3
071-638 5863   COST £26–£104

'Without doubt one of the best Japanese restaurants in London' was the opinion of one who has eaten here several times. He returns for the calmly civilised feel of the basement restaurant, the 'charming' service from formally attired waiters and – most importantly – the absolute clarity and precision of the cooking. The ground floor is host to a large teppanyaki room; the more serious business goes on downstairs. Tables are well-spaced, and screens ensure further privacy.

Menus are long and lucidly laid out, but the recited specials may lose something in the translation. Pleasant piquancy is delivered in boiled spinach garnished with smoky grated bonito, deep-fried turbot fins turned 'slightly gelatinous' by a mildly vinegary marinade, and 'superbly done' chawan-mushi (savoury egg-custard garnished with chicken, shrimp and vegetables). Sushi and sashimi are also stylishly presented. Green-tea and sesame-seed ice-creams make fine desserts. The wines are a Japanese investor's collection of classic names from the French regions. Clarets are good, even if burgundies depend heavily on the more familiar négoçiants. Prices will deliver a sharp upward shove to the final bill. House wines are £13.

CHEFS: Mr Maehara and Mr Yamanaka PROPRIETOR: Terriibroadgate Ltd OPEN: Mon to Fri; 11.30 to 2.30, 6.30 to 9.30 MEALS: alc (main courses £6 to £28). Set L £20 to £70, Set D £19 to £70 SERVICE: 13%, card slips closed CARDS: Access, Amex, Diners, Visa DETAILS: 130 seats. Private parties: 80 main room. Vegetarian meals. Children's helpings. Smart dress preferred. Wheelchair access. Music. Air-conditioned. Fax: 071-638 5864

Thai Garden ⚡✳ £   map 10

249 Globe Road, E2 0JD   COOKING 2
081-981 5748   COST £11–£29

Jack and Suthinee Hufton are dedicated to the promotion of Thai food without the use of red meat or poultry, and reports confirm that their little Bethnal Green restaurant is firmly on course. The menu divides equally between vegetarian and seafood, and the cooking is based on freshly bought ingredients. The balance of flavours is all-important. Some items are adapted versions of classics: satay is made from marinated Chinese mushrooms served with wholemeal bread, peanut sauce and pickles; a meatless version of 'larb' consists of chopped mushrooms with fried grains of rice, spices and basil. Others, such as sum-tum (green papaya salad) and tom-yum goong (hot and sour prawn soup) are staples of the repertoire. Popular specialities include keaw-wahn goong (a 'green curry' of prawns and Thai aubergines), goong kratiem (stir-fried prawns with garlic and white pepper) and yum ta-lay (seafood salad with lemon grass and lime). The kitchen has no truck with MSG and uses only 'fragrant' Thai rice. Set meals are a good-value introduction for beginners. Singha Thai beer and jasmine tea suit the food; otherwise there is a minimal wine list. House wine is £5.95 (£1.50 per glass).

CHEFS: Pensri Vichit and Visanu Plapplatong PROPRIETORS: Suthinee and Jack Hufton OPEN: Mon to Sat, exc Sat L; 12 to 2.45, 6 to 10.45 CLOSED: bank hols MEALS: alc (main courses £4 to £6.50). Set L £6.50, Set D £14.50 to £19 SERVICE: 10%, card slips closed CARDS: Access, Visa DETAILS: 32 seats. Private parties: 20 main room, 12 private room. Vegetarian meals. Children's helpings on request. No smoking in 1 dining-room. Wheelchair access (1 step). Music

⚡✳ *indicates that smoking is either banned altogether or that a dining-room is maintained for non-smokers. The symbol does not apply to restaurants that simply have no-smoking areas.*

Thailand

map 10

15 Lewisham Way, SE14 6PP	COOKING 2*
081-691 4040	COST £22–£41

Everybody agrees that this tiny venue in scruffiest Lewisham does some of the best Thai food around. Other establishments have their obeisant service and sumptuous décor, but here the experience is enjoyed for its small-scale sense of domesticity. The minuscule dining-room is such that one reporter wished the proprietor would grasp the nettle and forbid smoking, so that non-addicts may enjoy her food the more. This is offered by way of an admirably clear menu that does not expect you to try out your Thai pronunciation, but provides plenty of stimulating choice.

Aficionados are impressed by the degree of authenticity, evidenced by soups that are white-hot with chilli, or chicken that comes with onions, raisins and assertive coriander. A slate of Lao specialities includes strips of beef cooked over charcoal served with toasted rice, chillies and lime, and a basket of sticky rice to be eaten with the fingers. The single waitress 'handles a full house with disarming ease'. Occupying pride of place on the wall is a platinum disc awarded in the 1970s to the chart-topping Slade. What can this mean? House wine from Sicily at £8.50 leads a short, serviceable list, and there is a page-long selection of fine whiskies, including many cask-strength malts.

CHEF/PROPRIETOR: Khamkhong Kambungoet   OPEN: Tue to Sat, D only; 6 to 11   MEALS: alc (main courses £5.50 to £10.50).   SERVICE: not inc   CARDS: Access, Amex, Visa   DETAILS: 25 seats. Private parties: 25 main room. Vegetarian meals. No children under 5. No music. Air-conditioned

Thistells £

map 10

65 Lordship Lane, SE22 8EP	COOKING 1
081-299 1921	COST £13–£35

'Every expense has been spared in the conversion of this former shop,' writes a reporter of the black-and-white-tiled neighbourhood restaurant in Dulwich. It is a family business that warmly welcomes children and runs on informality. Sami Youssef is from Egypt and cooks some of the things he probably would if he still lived there, including falafel with tahini sauce, foul medames and couscous of lamb or vegetables. Interspersed with these are grilled mackerel with ginger and lime dressing, fried liver with eastern herbs, and banoffi pie. Some of the dishes suit vegetarians and vegans. The short list of wines from around the world is as sympathetically priced as they come, with a few reasonable bottles under £10. House wine is £7 (£1.50 per glass).

CHEF: Sami Youssef   PROPRIETORS: Sami and Anne Youssef   OPEN: all week, exc L Mon and Sat, and Sun D; 12 to 3, 7 to 10.30   MEALS: alc (main courses £5.50 to £10.50). Set L £8   SERVICE: 10%, card slips closed   CARDS: Access, Visa   DETAILS: 40 seats. 4 tables outside. Private parties: 45 main room. Vegetarian meals. Children's helpings. Smart dress preferred. Wheelchair access. Music

Report forms are at the back of the book; write a letter if you prefer.

Tokyo Diner ✦ £   NEW ENTRY   map 15

2 Newport Place, WC2H 7JJ   COOKING 1
071-287 8777   COST £7–£16

Just off Leicester Square, behind the Warner cinema, this no-frills diner has a mission to bring real Japanese food to an audience who might otherwise be intimidated by the technicalities and forbidding price structures found elsewhere. 'Our food,' says proprietor Richard Hills, 'does not try to represent the mystical east.' No bookings, cheques, credit cards or tips are taken. A philosophy of environmental consciousness extends to using only line-caught tuna. The speciality is bento box set meals, containing noodles and prawns, salmon sashimi with potato salad, rice and a fourth element of your own choosing. 'Mixed fry' offers prawn, mackerel and chicken, egged and crumbed, and fried in vegetable oil. There are also classic teriyaki dishes, pork or beef cooked with ginger, and croquettes with pork or vegetables. Bowls of well-flavoured miso soup accompany. Soba (buckwheat) noodles come in a 'deeply and pleasingly flavoured' soya-based broth topped with poached chicken. Good fresh sushi comes with extra wasabi for the heat-seeking diner. Tea is included. Otherwise, drink Kirin or Sapporo beer or saké. Wine is limited to house French at £6.50. 'We do not serve coffee or desserts.'

CHEF: Sueharu Hamaue   PROPRIETOR: Richard Hills   OPEN: all week; noon to midnight MEALS: Set meals £3.45 to £11.90   DETAILS: 90 seats. Vegetarian meals. Children welcome. No smoking in 1 dining-room. Wheelchair access. Music. Air-conditioned

La Truffe Noire ✦   map 11

29 Tooley Street, SE1 2QF   COOKING 2
071-378 0621   COST £20–£76

This particular truffle can be rooted out beneath the concrete walkways around London Bridge station, an unlikely spot to find a corner that is forever France, among the mainly Italian eateries around Tower Bridge. Most of the business takes place in the light, spacious ground-floor room, though a bistro provides lunches in the basement.

The lengthy *carte* is supplemented by a set-price three-course business menu and a shorter *prix fixe* offering simple bourgeois cooking. The main menu, which makes a virtue of identifying the nationalities of principal ingredients, proffers terrine of duck and pistachios with sweet onion compote, turbot with a Sauternes sauce, and Scottish tournedos with shiitake mushrooms. Desserts continue the regional attributions with Washington State apple pancake with red fruit coulis and mango from Mali filled with exotic ice-creams. A June meal took in 'perfectly cooked' sauté foie gras with a light mustard sauce, and 'fairly bland' grilled Hawaiian mahi-mahi on shredded leeks. Fine desserts included raspberry mille-feuille with berry coulis and well-flavoured sorbets in a biscuit cup. Incidentals, such as bread and coffee, are adequate. Service can seem a bit stretched on busy nights. The pre-eminently French wine list represents noticeably better value than it used to. Choices are fairly standard, with a tiny selection from the 'Nouveau Monde'. Halves are thin on the ground (there are none on the page of fine wines), but the digestifs are a tempting selection. Various house wines are £8.

CHEF: Philippe Roth   PROPRIETORS: Mr and Mrs M. Alam-Ahmed   OPEN: Mon to Fri (Sat and Sun by arrangement for parties); 11.45 to 2.30, 6.30 to 10.30   CLOSED: 23 Dec to 1 Jan, bank hols   MEALS: alc (main courses £10 to £25). Set L £8 (2 courses) to £19, Set D £19   SERVICE: 12.5% (optional), card slips closed   CARDS: Access, Amex, Diners, Visa   DETAILS: restaurant 56 seats, bistro 30 seats. 8 tables outside. Private parties: 50 main room, 12 and 30 private rooms. Vegetarian meals. Children's helpings on request. Smart dress preferred. No smoking in 1 dining-room. No cigars/pipes in dining-room. Wheelchair access (1 step). Music. Air-conditioned. Fax: 071-403 0689

Turner's   map 13

| 87–89 Walton Street, SW3 2HP | COOKING 4 |
| 071-584 6711 | COST £23–£62 |

This is a highly personal restaurant. Brian Turner used to be a chef/proprietor, but his natural inclination to play host means that he spends much of his time out front, greeting and chatting in his kitchen whites. Don't worry, somebody else is flying the plane, and with the arrival of Alan Thompson the cooking has shifted up a notch. The double act works to everybody's benefit in this smart blue and gold room, bright and fresh at lunch-time, 'comfortable, cosy and civilised' in the evening.

The food, based on first-class materials, is sophisticated and comforting rather than experimental or challenging. It nourishes, gratifies and cheers with fat turbot, succulent scallops, rib of beef, whole roast calves' kidneys, feather-light sorbet and liquescent Reblochon. Luxury ingredients are kept in check, while fish plays a central role, from a tartlet of salt cod or salad of langoustines and smoked salmon, to perfectly grilled fillet of red mullet. Flavours shine through and work beautifully together. 'This is light, delicious food showing balance and restraint in the kind of meal one dreams of having,' writes an inspector who enjoyed a main course breast of guinea-fowl with assorted mushrooms and a copious, deep, glossy stock reduction.

Menus are at fixed prices for two, three or four courses and contain no hidden extras; even service is included. The set lunch menu is 'outstanding value'. 'This must be one of London's bargains for the standard of food,' writes a regular visitor who, in a later report, boldly changed his assessment to 'the biggest bargain in Britain'. Reporters appreciate that this is one place where, in belt-tightening hard times, corners have not been cut, except perhaps to incorporate more rabbit or cod, which would be welcome whatever the circumstances. The only cloud on the horizon is that the wine list does not match the food for value. It is all good stuff, particularly the Fèvre Chablis, but more wines under £20 would be welcome. Four house wines begin at £13.50, or £4 per glass.

CHEF: Alan Thompson   PROPRIETOR: Brian J. Turner   OPEN: all week, exc Sat L; 12.30 to 2.30, 7.30 to 11.15 (10 Sun)   CLOSED: bank hols, 24 to 30 Dec   MEALS: alc (2 courses £32). Set L £9.95 (2 courses) to £13.50, Set D £23.50 (2 courses) to £29.50   SERVICE: net prices, card slips closed   CARDS: Access, Amex, Diners, Visa   DETAILS: 52 seats. Private parties: 52 main room, 20 and 30 private rooms. Vegetarian meals. Children's helpings. Smart dress preferred. Music. Air-conditioned. Fax: 071-584 4441

Two Brothers £

map 10

297–303 Regent's Park Road, N3 1DP
081-346 0469

COOKING 2
COST £15–£38

The two brothers are Leon and Tony Manzi running a double-fronted shop – half restaurant, half take-away – with no bookings, just a queue. They know fresh fish when they see it, and they see it every day, dip it in good batter, lob it in groundnut oil (changed daily) and dish it up moist and crisp with proper hollandaise, mayonnaise or tartare sauce. Cod, haddock and plaice might be mainstays, but there is skate as well, and maybe more on the blackboard, with thick chips cut from maris piper spuds. It is 'not just another chippy' – because chippies do not normally run to fresh oysters and mussels, or take this much trouble over materials, or go in much for grilling and steaming. Watch out for plump marinated herrings and Tony's Arbroath smokies, and a matching wine list full of youthful fruit. House Côtes de Duras is £8.10 (£1.90 per glass).

CHEFS/PROPRIETORS: Leon and Tony Manzi   OPEN: Tue to Sat; 12 to 2.30, 5.30 to 10.15   CLOSED: last 2 weeks Aug   MEALS: alc (main courses £6 to £14)   SERVICE: not inc, card slips closed   CARDS: Access, Amex, Visa   DETAILS: 90 seats. No babies after 6.30pm. No-smoking area. No cigars/pipes in dining-room. Music. Air-conditioned

Upper Street Fish Shop £

map 11

324 Upper Street, N1 2XQ
071-359 1401

COOKING 1
COST £13–£24

'At last! A really good fish and chip shop,' enthused a traveller who sought refuge in this popular Islington café on a cold Saturday evening. He continued: 'Fleshy, flakey cod in a light, grease-free batter with scrummy chips. The mushy peas were a good balance between mush and pea. The tea must have been some of the strongest in London, although the pot was willingly topped up with hot water by friendly, efficient staff.' The Conways make everything from smoked salmon pâté to ice-cream, their fish is battered, poached or grilled, and they serve Irish rock oysters as well as whole grouper with new potatoes and salad. To finish, try home-made treacle tart, fruit crumble or bread-and-butter pud. Note that there is a minimum charge, which means you have to order a main course rather than just a bowl of fish soup. The place is unlicensed, but you can bring your own wine.

CHEF: Stuart Gamble   PROPRIETORS: Alan and Olga Conway   OPEN: Mon to Sat, exc Mon L; 12 to 2, 5.30 to 10   CLOSED: 1 week after bank hols   MEALS: alc (main courses £6.50 to £9). Minimum £6.30. Unlicensed, but bring your own: no corkage   SERVICE: not inc   DETAILS: 50 seats. Children's helpings. Wheelchair access. No music. Air-conditioned

Vegetarian Cottage £

map 11

91 Haverstock Hill, NW3 4RL
071-586 1257

COOKING 1
COST £13–£36

A pair of well-designed, white-walled rooms with eclectic artwork and Art Deco fan wall lights provides the setting for this restaurant. It is one of the few places devoted to the Buddhist tradition of Chinese vegetarian cooking – a cuisine that draws heavily on the virtues of everything from bean curd and glutens to fungi and lotus leaves. The outcome is a repertoire of dishes that often mimic their carnivorous counterparts: deep-fried layers of soya bean sheets become 'vegetarian duckling', 'sweet-and-sour fish' is made of yams, while 'Buddha's Cushion' is a pile of mixed vegetables sitting on a nest of black moss. Reporters have praised tiny cubes of tofu and vegetables wrapped in lettuce leaves, crisp delicate balls of deep-fried milk, winter melon and bean curd soup ('subtle but not bland') and sweet walnut pudding. A few genuine seafood dishes such as stir-fried fish pieces and steamed scallops with garlic are also competently handled. The value for money is excellent and service is very friendly. The wine list is worth proper consideration. Australian house wine is £6.80.

CHEF: C. Wong   PROPRIETORS: Y.K. Tsui and S.W. Chu   OPEN: all week, D only, and Sun L; 12 to 3.15, 6 to 11.15   CLOSED: 2 to 3 days Christmas   MEALS: alc (main courses £4.50 to £15.50). Set L Sun £8, Set D £11.80 to £13.50. Minimum £8   SERVICE: not inc   CARDS: Access, Visa   DETAILS: 70 seats. Private parties: 30 main room. Vegetarian meals. Children welcome. Smart dress preferred. No-smoking area. Wheelchair access (2 steps). Music. Air-conditioned

Villandry Dining Room £✳

map 14

89 Marylebone High Street, W1M 3DE   COOKING 1
071-224 3799 and 487 3816   COST £22–£36

The heart of this set-up is a zealously Gallic delicatessen, and the restaurant co-exists alongside it. You may find yourself tucked behind a wooden pillar or rubbing shoulders with one of the waiters endlessly slicing charcuterie. A room at the back provides more light and space, but less frenetic fun. Never mind the rickety chairs: what you get is honest food, based on top-notch ingredients, cooked with zing and served up with style. The place opens for breakfast and the occasional dinner, but lunch is the main attraction. Book or arrive early if you want to get the full measure of the daily menu.

A basket of first-rate bread appears when you sit down. Excellent soups, such as provençale trout or parsley ('enough for a family') are regularly endorsed, and the repertoire also takes in salads, vegetarian tarts, good puddings and a scattering of substantial offerings such as chateaubriand with ratatouille, and baked brill with balsamic vinegar sauce. A bevy of waitresses bustles around at a rate of knots, coping cheerily with the influx and crush. Wines are supplied direct by Legrand of Paris, which means some unfamiliar names but intriguing, if slightly pricey, drinking. House wine is £11.90.

CHEFS: Caroline Simmonds and Rosalind Carrarini   PROPRIETORS: Jean-Charles and Rosalind Carrarini   OPEN: Mon to Sat, L only (D third Thur of Month); 12.30 to 3, 7.30   CLOSED: Christmas to New Year, bank hols   MEALS: alc (main courses £6.50 to £12)   SERVICE: net prices, card slips closed   CARDS: Access, Amex, Visa   DETAILS: 50 seats. Private parties: 45 main room. Vegetarian meals. Children welcome. No smoking in dining-room. Wheelchair access. Music. Air-conditioned. Fax: 071-487 1370

£ indicates that it is possible to have a three-course meal, including coffee, a half-bottle of house wine and service, at any time the restaurant is open (i.e. at dinner as well as at lunch, unless a place is open only for dinner), for £20 or less per person.

Wagamama ✶ £

map 14

4 Streatham Street, WC1A 1JB
071-323 9223

COOKING 1
COST £14–£24

'Welcome to Wagamama, positive eating and positive living,' says the menu. Whatever positive eating is, it seems to work. 'A great discovery,' writes a reporter, 'and worth queuing for.' The fast-food Japanese-style noodle bar has a single-minded commitment to doing the right thing. A combination of *kaizen* management, whereby 'everybody in the organisation is actively involved in suggesting and implementing small improvements continuously', plus a good old-fashioned suggestion box, makes it responsive to what customers want, which is good food, low prices and no hanging about. 'Absorbing and refreshing,' wrote one, of the atmosphere, not the hot towel. If you don't mind the wait, it is fun, and very good value.

Meals are organised around one-pot noodle dishes in broth (called ramen) with added chicken, seafood, chilli beef and so on, most of them under a fiver. The most satisfying way to eat is to slurp the noodles noisily, like a wine taster, drawing in air to make the most of taste and smell simultaneously. There are no first courses, but pan-fried noodles and rice dishes bring variety. The menu is helpful – 'squeeze lime into soup and place coriander and bean sprouts on top of noodles' – and waitresses even more so. Orders are punched into a hand-held electronic gizmo, and the food appears soon after. All sorts of drinks, from 'raw juice' to organic wine, from saké to sparkling elderflower, from yogurt to free tea, make a wine list virtually redundant, but there is a brief one all the same, starting at £6.80.

CHEF: Ayumi Meada   PROPRIETOR: Wagamama Ltd   OPEN: Mon to Sat; 12 to 2.30 (12.30 to 3.30 Sat), 6 to 11   CLOSED: Christmas, public holidays   MEALS: alc (main courses £3.50 to £5.50)   SERVICE: not inc   DETAILS: 104 seats. Private parties: 104 main room. Vegetarian meals. Children welcome. No smoking in dining-room. No music. Air-conditioned. Fax: 071-323 9224

Waltons

map 13

121 Walton Street, SW3 2HP
071-584 0204

COOKING 2
COST £22–£68

The outside world is kept at bay. 'Glaring yellow gloss, chromes and mirrors remind you that this restaurant operates in a world of its own.' So spoke one who, dining here in mid-June, echoed the common feeling of encroaching unreality that strikes many people in Waltons. It has plied the British line (ancient and modern) through two decades, succeeding with most of what it does. There isn't much of old England in terrine of truffled foie gras with Sauternes jelly and brioche, but 'ragoo' of scallops and mussels with spinach and a saffron sauce sounds a traditional note. Soups display Lakeland influences; main courses offer Scottish beef, English duck and South Downs lamb. The aforementioned June meal tested the range: a Mediterranean salad was 'neither remarkable nor original' but delivered plenty of sunny flavour in avocado, cucumber, olives and sun-dried tomatoes in a rosemary-scented olive oil dressing, while courgette and Stilton soup was 'delightfully rich and satisfying'. Meats chosen were duck and lamb, both agreeably tender. The duck came garnished with lingonberries, and the sauce was a stock and armagnac reduction that somehow managed to unite fruit and meat; the lamb had wild mushrooms in abundance and infusions of rosemary and thyme. Vegetables centred on the inevitable dauphinois, but were otherwise 'colourful and delicious'. Ice-creams were disappointing, the sorbet was good, and the English burnt cream 'wonderfully dense and rich'.

The wine list opens with a handy selection of highlights from the main run. Pedigree clarets and burgundies are accorded the most prominent exposure, but Rhônes aren't bad and the handful of German Rieslings are very fairly priced. Southern Europe and the New World receive more perfunctory treatment. House French is £9.50.

CHEF: Paul Hodgson   PROPRIETOR: Roger Wren   OPEN: all week; 12.30 to 2.30, 7.30 to 11.30 (12.30 to 2, 7 to 10 Sun and bank hols)   CLOSED: D 25 Dec, 26 Dec   MEALS: alc (main courses £12.50 to £17). Set L Mon to Sat £14.75, Sun £16.50, Set post-theatre D £21 (2 courses) SERVICE: not inc, card slips closed   CARDS: Access, Amex, Diners, Visa   DETAILS: 90 seats. Private parties: 45 main room, 6, 12 and 20 private rooms. Vegetarian meals. Children's helpings on request. Smart dress preferred. Wheelchair access (1 step). Music. Air-conditioned. Fax: 071-581 2848

Wiltons   map 14

55 Jermyn Street, SW1Y 6LX   COOKING 3
071-629 9955   COST £32–£89

This 250-year-old St James's institution is as venerable as any in the *Guide*. Its use by captains of industry, politicians, art dealers and aristocracy explains both the private banquettes and the preponderance of sausage and mash, fish-cakes, kedgeree, and steak and kidney pudding. The food is pure establishment British, a very particular gents' club style that opens with oysters, lobster or beluga caviare and moves through grilled fish, steak, lamb chop and kidneys to sherry trifle or a savoury of Welsh rarebit. Along the way it takes in potted shrimps, real turtle soup and such old-fashioned arrangements as fried whiting en colère, not to mention Britain's most risible pud: spotted dick and custard. Fish is of high quality, with sea bass and turbot singled out, although the best buy doubtless varies with the market. Game is plentiful in winter. 'We found the service eccentric,' wrote one couple, not expecting to have to ask for butter or pour their own wine. Another reporter affirmed that the service is 'excellent, once you are used to the mix of somewhat grand maître d's and matronly ladies'. The wine list is solid and predictable rather than imaginative, though it has 20 half-bottles. House wines are from £13.50.

CHEF: Ross Hayden   PROPRIETORS: Rupert, Richard and James Hambro   OPEN: all week; 12 to 2.30, 6 to 10.30   MEALS: alc (main courses £10 to £26.50). Cover £1. Minimum £12.50 SERVICE: not inc   CARDS: Access, Amex, Diners, Visa   DETAILS: 90 seats. Private parties: 18 private room. Vegetarian meals. No children under 8. Jacket and tie. No smoking at the bar. Wheelchair access. No music. Air-conditioned. Fax: 071-495 6233

Not inc *in the details at the end of an entry indicates that no service charge is made and any tipping is at the discretion of the customer.*

Zen Central

map 14

20 Queen Street, W1X 7PJ
071-629 8089 and 8103

COOKING 1*
COST £31–£91

Like others in the Zen chain, this is no ordinary Chinese restaurant: expect swanky décor, 'serious' prices, small portions and food that aims to be eclectic. Mirrors adorn the white walls in the rectangular dining-room and service is out of the top drawer ('probably the best I have come across in a Chinese restaurant in the UK' was one considered view). The kitchen (an MSG-free zone) is capable of serving up decent versions of Peking ravioli with chilli sauce, steamed dim-sum dumplings, braised bean curd with mushrooms, and veal cutlet in black pepper sauce. Special fried rice is superlative, while baked rice with duck and shrimps in a lotus leaf redeemed an otherwise indifferent meal on another occasion. Elsewhere, spring rolls and crispy Szechuan duck rub shoulders with double-boiled shark's fin and fish-cakes with fresh coriander and ginger. The wine list is a 'majestic' tome with big names and heavyweight prices. House wine is £12.

CHEF: Michael Leung   PROPRIETOR: Tealeaf Ltd   OPEN: all week; 12.15 to 2.30, 6.30 to 11.30 (11 Sun)   MEALS: alc (main courses £9.50 to £35). Set L £28 to £35, Set D £35 to £42. Cover £1. Minimum £20 L.   SERVICE: not inc (10% for 6 or more), card slips closed   CARDS: Access, Amex, Diners, Visa   DETAILS: 100 seats. Private parties: 60 main room. Vegetarian meals. Children welcome. Smart dress preferred. No cigars in dining-room. Wheelchair access. Music. Air-conditioned. Fax: 071-437 0641

Zoe £

map 14

3–5 Barrett Street,
St Christopher's Place, W1M 5HH
071-224 1122

COOKING 2
COST £17–£41

Just a few steps from Oxford Street, Zoe is thought by some to be the most successful outpost of the Antony Worrall-Thompson empire. At ground-floor level is a pillared café-bar of sinuous shape; downstairs is a dimly lit, racket-filled restaurant with clattery wooden floor and lots of space between tables. The menu continues to major on the Mediterranean, but with interesting twists: Taleggio cheese is melted over leeks, potatoes and Serrano ham, baked figs are garnished with pancetta and a runny Gorgonzola sauce, and goats' cheese is bandaged in vine leaves, chargrilled and served with chunky pear chutney. Main courses are less far-fetched than starters. Recommended dishes have included corn- and crab-cakes with poached eggs and hollandaise, Barnsley chump chop with a red pepper and aubergine tart, chicken breast with a Toulouse forcemeat and wild rice, and sticky fig pudding with coffee ice and clotted cream. Service, in the experience of some, can be prone to error. House wine is £8.25.

CHEF: Conrad Melling   PROPRIETOR: Kindexcess Ltd   OPEN: Mon to Sat; 11.30am to 11.30pm   MEALS: alc (main courses £7.50 to £13). Set L and D £7.50 (2 courses) to £10. Café menu (dishes £3 to £12)   SERVICE: not inc   CARDS: Access, Amex, Diners, Visa   DETAILS: 200 seats. 25 tables outside. Private parties: 100 main room. Vegetarian meals. Children's helpings. No-smoking area. Wheelchair access (3 steps). Music. Air-conditioned. Fax: 071-935 5444

London round-ups

This mixed bag of places to eat takes in cafés, bars, bistros and anywhere else that, for one reason or another, does not quite fit the *Guide*'s specifications for main entries. These are places on which we may need more reports, or for which reports may have been contradictory, or where standards over the year may have fluctuated. But they're all worth a visit, and if we get some more feedback from you, the readers of the *Guide*, some of them could become main entries in the future.

Alfred   WC2
245 Shaftesbury Avenue   map 14
071-240 2566
New restaurant wedged between the extreme north of Shaftesbury Avenue and New Oxford Street, with a few outside tables. Décor is modern and very bare, tables are cramped, yet Fred Taylor (ex-owner of the club Fred's) and ex-Belgo chef Robert Gutteridge are presenting good British food and a wide choice of British beers that should earn them a reputation.

Andrew Edmunds   W1
46 Lexington Street   map 14
071-437 5708
Fashionable Soho establishment with an eclectic European menu that offers reasonable value. Wooden floors, exposed wood tables, friendly service and an energetic crowd make for an unpretentious atmosphere. Nice selection of wines.

Aroma   W1
1B Dean Street   map 15
071-287 1633
This small but perfectly conceived café will not be everyone's cup of tea, but is ideal for the Soho crowd seeking a hip and wholesome lunch venue, though the sometimes queue and crush should be noted. Points in favour are the fun crockery, funky background music, speciality sandwiches using breads such as walnut, ciabatta, manoucher and sun-dried tomato, not forgetting coffee every

which way: espresso, café amandine and mocca to name but three. Branches also at: 135 Bishopsgate, EC2, 071-374 2774
West One Centre, 381 Oxford Street, W1, 071-495 6945
168 Piccadilly, W1, 071-495 6995
273 Regent Street, W1, 071-495 4911
Aroma at Books Etc, 120 Charing Cross Road, WC2, 071-240 4030
36A St Martin's Lane, WC2, 071-836 5110.

Arts Theatre Café   WC2
6 Great Newport Street   map 15
071-497 8014
The interior may be dark but the content of the Italian menus is certainly illuminating. In this compact basement below a children's theatre, most people opt for the daily-changing fixed-price one which appears at lunch and dinner and offers good value. Popular dishes have been fish soup, marinated scallops with spiced lentils, and mango tarte Tatin.

Atlantic Bar and Grill   W1
20 Glasshouse Street   map 14
071-734 4888
Cavernous 200-seater restaurant and bar beneath the Regent Palace Hotel in Piccadilly that is home to a hip crowd late at night. The arresting Art Deco staircase, ornamentation and colour scheme are more vibrant than the cooking, although the menu shows ambition and the Far East is represented. A bar menu is available until 3am, making it a useful all-hours venue.

Avenue West Eleven   W11
157 Notting Hill Gate   map 12
071-221 8144
New, appropriately named Notting Hill
bar and restaurant that's not far from
Holland Park. This is Phillip McMullen's
second enterprise (Brasserie du Marché
aux Puces his first) and early signs are
encouraging, even if the kitchen is still
finding its feet: an eclectic menu lists
exotic ingredients, quite a lot of fish and
pretty-sounding desserts. Décor and table
settings are seriously arty and ethnic, so
expect a local, rather fashion-conscious
crowd.

Aziz   W6
116 King Street   map 10
081-748 1826
Hammersmith tandoori with a consistent
kitchen and diligent staff. A good range of
flavours, from hot chillies to mild sauces,
accompanied by fresh paratha and nan
breads. 'Surprisingly good' Cona coffee.

Beotys   WC2
79 St Martin's Lane   map 15
071-836 8768/8548
Greek long-stayer that remains well-
frequented by theatre-goers and those in
search of a calm atmosphere. Stay with
the half of the menu devoted to authentic
dishes rather than straying to the more
pedestrian international section.

Bianco   N8
298 Park Road   map 10
081-348 0470
Long-established Crouch End Italian on a
busy corner at the foot of Muswell Hill.
This trattoria has undergone something of
a new lease of life in recent months: the
cooking displays moments of flair and the
set-price menus are great value for lunch
and cheap for dinner. Typical choices are
black linguini with mussels in saffron
sauce, spicy chicken sausage with onion
marmalade, hake with couscous, and
baked apples with vanilla marscapone.
Minus points for service and a basic
wine list.

Bice   W1
13 Albemarle Street   map 14
071-409 1011
Terrifically expensive Mayfair Italian
unfortunately situated in a basement. The
original Bice opened in Milan in 1926 and
there are branches in Paris, New York,
Chicago and Tokyo. Simple, classic dishes
have been well thought out and service is,
as you'd expect, professional. There is a
fixed-price menu for those wishing to eat
more economically.

Big Night Out   NW1
148 Regent's Park Road   map 11
071-586 5768
Not the theme restaurant its name
suggests but a coolly modern
neighbourhood venue in Primrose Hill.
Competent treatment of quality
ingredients. A fixed-price menu offers
reasonable value for two or three courses
(and not just at night, either). Finish with
decent coffee and petits fours.

Blah Blah Blah   W12
78 Goldhawk Road   map 10
081-746 1337
Fairly chic, far-from-usual vegetarian
restaurant (hippies need not apply) using
fresh ingredients to good effect and
steering clear of the usual clichés. Each
table has a box of crayons and white
paper cloths. Unlicensed, but take your
own wine.

Books for Cooks   W11
4 Blenheim Crescent   map 12
071-221 1992
Miniature café tucked away at the back of
this appropriately named bookshop. It
might be short on space but provides a
cosy lunchtime retreat from shopping in
Portobello Road or the reading of endless
recipes.

Le Braconnier   SW14
467 Upper Richmond Road West   map 10
081-878 2853
Terracotta and green dining-room with
comfortable benches down both sides,
and lots of mirrors. First-class ingredients

and presentation and good cooking, though sometimes in need of more seasoning. Things nevertheless enjoyed have included asparagus tart, noisettes of venison with wild mushrooms, truffe au chocolat, and an unusual 'very almondy' summer pudding.

Brasserie du Marché aux Puces   W10
349 Portobello Road   map 11
081-968 5828
Bare boards-type brasserie at the extreme north end of the Portobello Road, a short distance from the main cluster of Notting Hill restaurants. Geography affords this corner site a loyal neighbourhood clientele who can be the judge of the new chef who joined as we went to press. Reports, please.

Café de Colombia   W1
Museum of Mankind,
6 Burlington Gardens   map 14
071-287 8148
Piccadilly pit-stop within the ever-curious Museum of Mankind (no charge). Opens morning through lunch till late afternoon for well-prepared salads, peerless pastries and cakes, and excellent coffee.

Café dell'Ugo   SE1
56–58 Tooley Street   map 11
071-407 6001
Antony Worrall-Thompson's latest venture is housed in one of the old railway arches a few doors down from the London Dungeon; the unusual layout and interior have met with approval. Opportunities for eating are various: downstairs is a café-bar serving inventive snack food, upstairs a restaurant with a totally diverse menu, dotted with arcane references. A change of chef as we went to press. Reports, please.

Café du Marché   EC1
22 Charterhouse Square   map 11
071-608 1609
Converted warehouse in Smithfield Market that's a French brasserie, decorated with style along rustic lines. Competent enough cooking of quality

ingredients though execution needs refinement. Not cheap (especially for wines) but the set-lunch menu offers the best value. Live piano music in the evenings.

Café Rouge   W8
2 Lancer Square,   map 12
off Kensington Church Street
071-938 4200
Kensington branch of chain producing decent food at economical prices in a Gallic atmosphere. Continental breakfasts to fuel anyone's day, well- presented salads, fresh fish and classic steak sandwiches and fries always feature. Coffee is unanimously good but service can vary from branch to branch.
Branches also at: 140 Fetter Lane, EC4, 071-242 3469
6–7 South Grove, N6, 081-342 9797
19 Hampstead High Street, NW3, 071-433 3404
Hay's Galleria, Tooley Street, SE1, 071-378 0097
29–31 Basil Street, SW3, 071-584 2345
390 King's Road, SW3, 071-352 2226
855 Fulham Road, SW6, 071-371 7600
200 Putney Bridge Road, SW15, 081-788 4257
26 High Street, Wimbledon, SW19, 081-944 5131
15 Frith Street, W1, 071-437 4307
46 James Street, W1, 071-487 4847
Unit 209, Whiteley's, Queensway, W2, 071-221 1509
30 Clifton Road, W9, 071-286 2266
31 Kensington Park Road, W11, 071-221 4449
291 Sandycombe Road, Kew, Richmond, Surrey, 081-332 2882
7A Petersham Road, Richmond, Surrey, 081-332 2423.

Le Champenois   EC2
10 Devonshire Square   map 11
071-283 7888
French basement restaurant following the City pattern of opening for lunch only. Stylish presentation but results do vary as far as seasoning and flavours are concerned. One diner finished up with a

'just right' chocolate mousse in a chocolate cup with coffee sauce.

Chez Gérard W1

8 Charlotte Street map 14
071-636 4975

Stylish site for the Fitzrovia branch of this small restaurant group. A series of booths and high partitions around tables creates privacy when things are in full swing. Steak-frites and chateaubriand are perennial favourites but vegetarians are not ignored: witness goats' cheese salad, mushroom brioche or chargrilled vegetables. Baguette and olives are included in the cover charge. Branches also at: 31 Dover Street, W1, 071-499 8171
119 Chancery Lane, WC2, 071-405 0290.

China China W1

3 Gerrard Street map 15
071-439 7511

Value-for-money Chinatown café recommended for its one-plate meals such as crispy duck on rice. This and the speedy service conspire to form a genuine Hong Kong-style haunt.

Chutney Mary SW10

535 King's Road map 11
071-351 3113

Not Indian, but Anglo-Indian, this restaurant has a menu which will seem half-familiar but yet strangely different. Many influences at work, from the days of the Raj to authentic Sub-continent recipes. Some like to sit in the conservatory, and the Verandah Bar serves drinks and snacks. Expensive, but then this is just around the corner from Chelsea Harbour.

Como Lario SW1

22 Holbein Place map 13
071-730 2954

Busy Italian between Sloane Square and the Pimlico Road where the tables are close together but the atmosphere is jolly and the service keen. Expect such things as black tagliatelle with lobster sauce,

polenta and side orders of roasted fennel and onion. Cheap for the area.

Florians N8

4 Topsfield Parade, Middle Lane map 10
081-348 8348

Crouch End restaurant with a bar addition for lighter meals or just drinks. The modern Italian menu changes every few months and includes such items as bresaola with buffalo ricotta and pistachio nuts, pan-fried Italian sausages with sauté spinach and chilli, grilled polenta, and tiramisù. There has been a change of chef. Reports, please.

Formula Veneta SW10

14 Hollywood Road map 13
071-352 7612

Chic venue in a stretch chock-full of restaurants, this Italian has the benefit of a garden in summer (tables here need booking) and a glossily dressed local clientele. Fresh seafood and fish feature strongly; many other worthwhile dishes include risottos for two people, attractive pastas – for example, tagliolini with speck and rocket – and fair desserts. Decent ciabatta, ditto cappuccino. On occasion, service does get stretched.

Four Seasons W2

84 Queensway map 12
071-229 4320

Economical Bayswater Chinese distinguished by its display of roast meats. There are various Cantonese dishes and one-plate meals, although crispy duck is probably one of the best options.

The Gate W6

Temple Lodge, map 10
51 Queen Caroline Street
081-748 6932

Summer is the time to eat at this Hammersmith vegetarian restaurant which shares premises with a church, as the few courtyard tables make a pleasant alternative to those in the functional-looking dining-room (approached by steep, outside stone steps). That said, the modern menu lists much to interest most and cooking is well-judged, presentation particularly impressive. Confit vegetable tartlet, sweet potato and leek gnocchi, raspberry crème brûlée, and mocha chocolate mousse are the sorts of dishes to expect.

Green Cottage NW3
9 New College Parade, map 11
Finchley Road
071-722 5305 and 7892
Plain neighbourhood Chinese with a standard Cantonese menu boosted by no less than 10 vegetarian main courses; parties of carnivores get the option of several set-dinner menus. Service is abruptly efficient, with chit-chat not an option.

Haandi NW1
161 Drummond Street map 11
071-383 4557
Good-value Drummond Street Indian that's best enjoyed at lunch, when the budget-conscious buffet comes into operation. Wide selection of items including meat and vegetarian curries, rice, nan bread, and chutneys. Arrive early to avoid sitting in the basement.

Harveys Café SW10
358 Fulham Road map 11
071-352 0625
First-floor leaseholder of Fulham Road pub has stripped-wood floors, art on the walls and a youthful mood. Expect home-made bread, choice olives, and such things as celeriac brandade with rosemary crostini, salmon fish-cakes, and spiced lentils with Italian sausages. No credit cards.

Ikkyu W1
67 Tottenham Court Road map 14
071-436 6169 and 636 9280
Basement Japanese that is often busy and a lot cheaper than most, enabling those keeping track of prices to sample fairly freely from the long menu. Sushi, sashimi and yakitori sections feature. Several reports have cited a fall-off in the standards of ingredients this year. Green tea comes free with meals.

Jin W1
16 Bateman Street map 15
071-734 0908 and 0856
Soho Korean restaurant where each table has a small barbecue for grilling things – the recommended approach as these specialities are the stars of the menu. Side dishes of kim-chee (hot pickled cabbage) and noodles are worthy accompaniments.

Joe Allen WC2
13 Exeter Street map 15
071-836 0651
American restaurant with bar that stays open late (last orders 12.30am) and often requires booking. Warning: staff do not let customers keep tables more than two hours. The open-brick basement is not gloomy, owing in part to the jazzy soundtrack and theatreland crowd. Good soups, big salads, burgers and chips, plus several more fashionable things. Service can vary; no credit cards.

Julie's W11
135 Portland Road map 12
071-229 8331
Terribly pretty, unmistakably romantic, definitely discreet restaurant comprising five theatrically decorated dining-rooms, all of which can be reserved for parties. Julie's has been here for over 25 years but the menu today is modern British. There is also a champagne bar and a wine bar (although celebrity customers are more likely to be glimpsed dining).

Kanishka W1
161 Whitfield Street map 14
071-388 0860
A corner spot with two dining-rooms and cushioned cane-backed chairs; tables are close together. The long menu has vegetarian and meat sections and is largely North Indian but with Goan and other regional dishes too. Spicing has a clarity about it, although service is less impressive.

Kaspia W1

18–18A Bruton Place   map 14
071-493 2612

If caviare is to your taste (and pocket),
then this is the place to indulge, both in
the panelled restaurant and with
purchases from the attached shop. Those
feeling a little fazed by the prospect of
high prices can always choose to eat from
one of the set menus, perhaps starting
with bortsch, taking in fish and some
caviare, thus keeping the bill within
affordable limits.

Kettners W1

29 Romilly Street   map 15
071-437 6437

The Champagne Bar is a favourite after-
work meeting point for starting off an
evening; many get no further than the
ornate, *fin de siècle* dining-rooms where
thin-base pizzas are readily devoured.
Pizzas are not the only food option,
although not the best.

King's Road Café SW3

Habitat, 208 King's Road   map 13
071-351 1211

Habitat fans and Chelsea shoppers alike
can now reap the benefits of an in-store
café open seven days a week. The short
Italian menu includes several things for
vegetarians; portions are generous and
flavours well-matched. Equally a good
place to drop in for a proper cappuccino
and cake (the queues move quickly).

Kym's SW1

70–71 Wilton Road   map 11
071-828 8931

Chinese close to Victoria Station that
shows consistency. Peking, Szechuan and
Hunan cuisines are on the menu though
dishes are not organised by region. Peking
duck, turreted fried prawns and baked
fried rice with assorted seafood in a lotus
leaf have been enjoyed. Relaxing
ambience and restrained décor.

Lemonia NW1

89 Regent's Park Road   map 11
071-586 7454

Large, lively Greek Cypriot restaurant in
Primrose Hill. Attractive surroundings
(though often full to bursting come
evenings) and pleasant service. The
selection of meze offers good value for an
interesting meal.

Maroush III W1

62 Seymour Street   map 11
071-724 5024

Smart Lebanese restaurant near Marble
Arch that stays open late. The meze are
worth exploring, and chargrilled things
dominate the main courses. Finish with
sticky pastries and coffee. Branches also
at: 38 Beauchamp Place, SW3,
071-581 5434
21 Edgware Road, W2, 071-723 0773
(music and dancing after 10.30pm;
minimum spend £38 per person).

Meson Don Felipe SE1

53 The Cut   map 11
071-928 3237

Authentic tapas bar just along from
Waterloo Station. Go for the friendly, fun
atmosphere and the good list of Spanish
wines and sherries. Convenient enough
for South Bank and Young Vic visitors.

Mezzanine SE1

National Theatre, South Bank   map 11
071-928 3531

Although this restaurant has a captive
pre-theatre clientele, the kitchen is
turning out well-timed meals from good
ingredients. Hot spinach mousse with
Parmesan sauce, grilled brill with fennel
salad, and creamy rice pudding are
representative. Coffee and bread are
above average, as is service. Booking
advised.

Le Midi SW6

488 Fulham Road   map 11
071-386 0657

Compact French restaurant just along
from Fulham Broadway. Included in the
price of bread are crudités, mayonnaise

185

and olives; for main courses find country dishes such as rabbit casserole, and perhaps finish with chocolate marquise, or pear and almond tart. Well-chosen wines.

Mon Plaisir WC2

21 Monmouth Street   map 15

071-836 7243 and 240 3757

This is a good location for theatreland and the environs have always been appealing. Very simple French things have been mostly superseded by more involved, but not necessarily more successful, dishes. On a happier note, the pre-theatre menu is competitively priced and desserts and coffee are enjoyable. Another branch at: Mon Petit Plaisir, 33 Holland Street, W8, 071-937 3224.

Le Muscadet W1

25 Paddington Street   map 14

071-935 2883

Professionally run French restaurant near Baker Street. A daily-changing menu (in French, on a blackboard) and authentic delivery of traditional dishes, plus good sauces and well-chosen wines. Although desserts are first-class, the cheeseboard is the real strength, with specially imported French country cheeses.

Namaste E1

30 Alie Street   map 11

071-488 9242

East End Indian where the menu is a world away from the high street tandoori, with many Goan specialities. The Namaste special thali enables diners with a curiosity for the exotic to sample two vegetarian and five non-vegetarian dishes of their choice. Careful cooking and a sure touch in the spicing.

New World W1

1 Gerrard Place   map 15

071-434 2508

Cavernous Chinese establishment that's good for dim-sum at lunch, but less good for standard Cantonese choices in the evening (although late opening hours are a plus). Tea comes automatically.

Odin's W1

27 Devonshire Street   map 14

071-935 7296

Elegant, club-like, supremely relaxing restaurant possessing a picture collection by its founder, the late Peter Langan, and a regular clientele. Safe English cooking maintains its standards; fish seems a popular choice.

Le Palais du Jardin WC2

136 Long Acre   map 15

071-379 5353

Big, upbeat (sometimes noisy) brasserie with an exceptionally busy bar and surprisingly good service. Menu choices range from the fashionable to the old-fashioned, and cooking is very creditable: rabbit and quail salad with apple vinaigrette, fish-cakes, Toulouse sausages with decent chips, and tarte Tatin. The mostly French wines are modestly priced.

Il Passetto WC2

230 Shaftesbury Avenue   map 14

071-836 9391

Theatreland Italian of the old school that continues to please with its cheery atmosphere. Competent cooking that occasionally misses the mark; fresh fish specials shown first at the table in their raw state, before cooking, are worth sampling. Service fits in with those rushing to a show.

Patisserie Valerie SW3

215 Brompton Road   map 13

071-823 9971

Perfect for refuelling after a stint at the Victoria & Albert Museum, this elegant café is also popular with Catholics who pour in here after Sunday morning Mass at the Brompton Oratory, opposite. Classic cappuccino, creamy calorie-laden cakes of the best quality, and simple lunch dishes. Take a table in the back room or perch at tall bar stools for the best views. Branches also at: 44 Old Compton Street, W1, 071-437 3466 Patisserie Valerie at Maison Sagne, 105 Marylebone High Street, W1, 071-935 6240.

Pierre Victoire
SW1
9 William Street
map 13
071-823 2070
This company-owned site that's part of Pierre Levicky's empire (the other three London addresses listed below are franchises) offers very easily affordable eating in an expensive part of town. Cheapness is the chief recommendation, and some French dishes, as well as desserts like banoffi pie and bread-and-butter pudding, have been enjoyed. Non-plush surroundings and informal service. Other branches at: 6 Panton Street, Haymarket, SW1, 071-930 6463
136 Upper Richmond Road, Putney, SW15, 081-789 7043
156 Chiswick High Road, Chiswick, W4, 081-995 1656.

Poons
WC2
27 Lisle Street
map 15
071-437 4549
Quintessential Cantonese café turning out gutsy, authentic food at realistic prices. You don't come here for comfort – downstairs is tiny and the upper level chaotic – but for the fun of observing. Find wind-dried ducks and sausages, soups, one-plate rice and noodle dishes based on barbecued meats, a few hotpots plus Westernised offerings for the tourists.

La Poule au Pot
SW1
231 Ebury Street
map 13
071-730 7763
Ever-popular, long-surviving French restaurant with a good – romantic for some – atmosphere. The play-safe, entirely à la carte menu is expensive but portions are enormous and dishes such as coquille St Jacques, goats' cheese salad, suprême of chicken with tarragon, and steak and frites have suited. Charming service.

Ritz Hotel
W1
Piccadilly
map 14
071-493 8181
With its beautiful Louis XVI-style dining-room, and salons and bedrooms awash with gilt and marble, the Ritz maintains a reputation for luxury that's second to none. Although the cooking is not so obviously showy, chef David Nicholls is consistently producing good English food and, these days, the cost of the set-price lunch and dinner menus is raising a cheer. For some, the pianist is 'as marvellous as ever'.

Rodin
SW1
4 Millbank
map 11
071-233 0032
Unexpected location in the basement of a refurbished corner office building far away from mainstream restaurant territory. Tables spill out into a central marble atrium, and greenery and trees in tubs add to the outdoors feel. A conservative menu – possibly pitched at nearby Parliament – is executed with precision. Wines are not cheap. Closed Saturday dinner.

San Remo
SW13
195 Castelnau
map 10
081-741 5909
Good neighbourhood Italian proving popular with the Barnes crowd. Tables are crammed in but the atmosphere and service are jolly. Everyone seems to order off the specials board and the risotto nero and various seafood dishes are recommended.

The Ship
SW18
Jews Row
map 10
081-870 9667
Immensely popular, hugely jolly riverside pub tucked away next to Wandsworth Bridge but drawing crowds from all the SW postcodes. New chef Nick Walton does a dazzling line in barbecues – and as it's the only source of heat, this single cooking technique is augmented with marinades, sauces, salad dressings and all manner of fashionable ingredients. Tables outside and in the conservatory; decent wines.

Sol e Luna WC2

Thomas Neal's Centre, map 15
22 Shorts Gardens
071-379 3336

Last year it was called Mezzaluna New York; this year it is under new management and has a change of chef. The restaurant is within a Covent Garden warehouse conversion, now given over to flats and fashionable shops; the terracotta-tiled dining-room is below ground. No reports yet of the new chef, but the thin-crust pizzas from the wood-fired oven still seem the things to eat.

Soulard N1

113 Mortimer Road map 11
071-254 1314

Small French bistro on the fringes of Islington that's useful for traditional staples and a short, reasonably priced, entirely Gallic wine list. Service is friendly.

Spread Eagle SE10

2 Stockwell Street map 10
081-853 2333

The floors slope noticeably to one end in the upstairs dining-room of this ancient coaching inn. Beams, low ceilings and a relaxed atmosphere enhance the surroundings further. Most of the staff, including the chef, are French and service is charming. The three-course set menu offers good value and the cooking is consistent.

Surya NW6

59–61 Fortune Green Road map 11
071-435 7486

Agreeable, family-run North Indian vegetarian restaurant just off the Finchley Road. Worthy if only mildly flavoured food from a standard range of starters, including bhel pooris and vegetable cutlets, followed by assorted curries; mushroom bhajia is good. Daily specials are worth investigating. Lassi is excellent, otherwise drink lager or reasonably priced house wine.

Tate Gallery Restaurant SW1

Millbank map 11
071-834 6754

This basement restaurant within the gallery only opens for lunch (closed Sunday). Highlights include the Whistler murals, the wine list that majors on clarets, and very sound British cooking. Service is consistently good and provision for seating non-smokers is a conscious thing.

Vasco & Piero's Pavilion W1

15 Poland Street map 14
071-437 8774

Long-established West End Italian convenient for theatre buffs and cinema-goers, among others. Set-price lunch and dinner menus offer competitive prices for this part of town. Freshly made pasta might be spinach and ricotta tortellini, or mushroom ravioli with shiitake mushrooms; calf's liver with fresh sage and grilled stuffed calamari are house specialities. Pleasant service, good coffee.

Versilia NW3

250 Finchley Road map 11
071-794 7640

Finchley Road Italian concentrating on fish. Service can be slow on occasion but the kitchen has provided good fritto misto di mare, charcoal-grilled prawns and seafood pancake.

Wakaba NW3

122A Finchley Road map 11
071-722 3854 and 586 7960

Spartan-looking yet stylish Japanese opposite Finchley Road underground station.There is a sushi bar at the rear of the room, and a broader range of menu for those at tables. Only open for dinner, Monday to Saturday.

White Horse on Parsons Green SW6

1–3 Parsons Green map 10
071-736 2115

Affectionately known by a whole bunch of locals as the 'Sloaney Pony', this Parsons Green pub remains popular owing to its well-kept draught ales (including guest beers), cavernous, comfortable room and above-average bar food. Friendly staff and a lively crowd.

White Tower   W1
1 Percy Street   map 14
071-636 8141

Old-fashioned Greek establishment with the quiet atmosphere of a gentlemen's club and polite, attentive, 'almost nannyish' service from a large collection of staff. The menu is slightly eccentric, warning gently of the dangers of garlic and onions and extolling the virtues of the plainly cooked items. Finish with fresh fruit, good coffee and Turkish delight.

Willoughby's Café-Bar   N1
26 Penton Street   map 11
071-833 1380

Small café-style restaurant within walking distance of the Angel. A short menu boosted by blackboard specials is available weekdays for lunch and dinner and Saturday evenings. Typical offerings are kedgeree, beef casseroled in ale, iced chocolate mousse, and treacle tart. Excellent house wine.

Wilsons   W14
236 Blythe Road   map 12
071-603 7267

Shepherd's Bush restaurant with a Scottish feel about it, which doesn't just apply to the furnishings but extends to the British cooking too. Fair value; friendly and efficient service.

Wódka   W8
12 St Albans Grove   map 13
071-937 6513

This modern Polish restaurant in residential Kensington might have hard seats, but the list of flavoured vodkas and the interesting menu are of interest. Not all dishes are Eastern European in origin, but those that are may prove the most successful.

Ziani   SW3
45–47 Radnor Walk   map 13
071-351 5297 and 352 2698

Smartly kitted-out Italian restaurant in a quiet residential street off the King's Road. Notable cooking and a Venetian style to the menu, though recipes come from all over Italy. Tables are very close together, so you had better not mind being overheard.

England

▲ The Elms, Brooke Room

Stockton Road, Abberley WR6 6AT
GREAT WITLEY (0299) 896666
on A443, between Worcester and Tenbury   COOKING 2*
Wells, 2m W of Great Witley   COST £24–£40

At the time of writing the Elms was up for sale. It is a handsome Queen Anne
mansion that still boasts its original plaster friezes and fireplaces. The décor goes
in for trompe-l'oeil effects with some gusto, one of the dining-rooms having a
mural depicting a balustraded patio. Surroundings, including the formal
gardens, are a model of classical order. Our complaints last year of a vitiating
blandness creeping into the cooking appear to have been addressed and the
kitchen seems to be gaining confidence.

Two set prices obtain, either for 'Dinner' or 'Traditional Dinner'; the only
point of difference between them is the choice of main courses. 'Traditional'
offers mixed grill, chicken and mushroom pie, tomato and herb omelette and the
like, although the concept of tradition may be stretched for vegetarians into
baked apple, raisin and blue cheese strudel. Non-traditional choices bring on
hot-smoked salmon with crab meat and crayfish bisque; medallions of pork with
an apple, pear and brandy sauce; and breast of duckling with honey and pink
peppercorns. A diner in May admired the technique in a mousseline of scallops
wrapped in salmon; the wine-based sauce was speckled with truffles and
caviare, but gained its strongest taste from tomato. The main course of roast
venison was coated rather than stuffed (as advertised) with mushroom duxelles,
but delivered meat of 'excellent supple texture'. Two fine ice-creams – tutti-frutti
and cappuccino (both 'surprisingly intense') – came in a brandy-snap basket for
dessert, garnished with lots of fruit and two sauces. Home-made breads and
coffee also came in for praise. The wine list makes a decent fist of things in
France, but is perfunctory elsewhere. Prices are stiffish, but mitigation is at hand
in the 'Elms Selection', most of which is good. House French is £11.50.

The Guide *relies on feedback from its readers. Especially welcome are reports on new
restaurants appearing in the book for the first time. All letters to the* Guide *are
acknowledged.*

CHEF: Michael Gaunt PROPRIETOR: Queens Moat Houses plc OPEN: all week, D only, and Sun L (Mon to Sat L by arrangement for 6 or more); 12 to 2, 7.30 (7 Fri and Sat) to 9.30 MEALS: Set L Sun £15.95, Set D £18 to £24 SERVICE: not inc, card slips closed CARDS: Access, Amex, Diners, Visa DETAILS: 70 seats. 6 tables outside. Private parties: 70 main room, 20, 26 and 40 private rooms. Car park. Vegetarian meals. Children's helpings. Smart dress preferred. No cigars/pipes in dining-room. Wheelchair access (also WC). Music ACCOMMODATION: 25 rooms, all with bath/shower. TV. Phone. B&B £74.50 to £177. Children welcome. Pets welcome (Coach House rooms only). Afternoon teas. Garden. Tennis. Fax: (0299) 896804

ABINGDON Oxfordshire   map 2

▲ *Thame Lane House* ⚡✳

1 Thame Lane, Culham,
Abingdon OX14 3DS
ABINGDON (0235) 524177   COOKING 2
off A415, Abingdon to Dorchester road   COST £24–£38

'This was the third time we have eaten at this delightful and unassuming establishment,' writes a supporter, who finds the charm of the proprietors matched by the cooking. It is a small restaurant in a private house. Mostly the treatment is warm and natural and puts people at ease. One report concludes that 'Mrs Beech is a gifted and enthusiastic cook'. She keeps everything sensibly under control by offering a choice of three or four first and second courses, and two or three puddings, which reporters find is perfectly balanced and in no way limiting. The clarity and simplicity of the cooking appeal, and show an assured hand dealing with notably fresh ingredients.

Shellfish, including Welsh oysters, 'wonderful' langoustines with courgettes and thyme, and a plate of oysters, mussels and prawns with mayonnaise is a feature. Soufflés come in for consistent praise: for example, 'light and delicious' goats' cheese with a simple salad, or twice-cooked mushroom soufflés in cream with Swiss cheese. This might be followed by roast leg of lamb with sorrel cream, and meringue gâteau with chestnuts and rum. 'The crêpes fourrées aux pommes with sabayon au calvados came high on a list of things for which it is worth putting on weight,' enthused one. A few find the fixed price rather high, but with coffee and service included, most agree on the value. The short French wine list curiously ignores the Rhône and the south. Apart from the £10 house wines (which include the token foreigner, Bulgarian Cabernet Sauvignon), prices are £15 and upwards.

CHEF: Marie-Claude Beech PROPRIETORS: Michael and Marie-Claude Beech OPEN: all week, exc Mon L and Sun D; 12.30 to 1.30, 7.15 to 8.45 CLOSED: 1 week Jan, 2 weeks Aug MEALS: Set L and D £18.50 (residents only) to £26.50 SERVICE: net prices, card slips closed CARDS: Access, Visa DETAILS: 16 seats. Private parties: 18 main room. Car park. Vegetarian meals with prior notice. Children's helpings with prior notice. Smart dress preferred. No smoking. Wheelchair access (1 step). No music ACCOMMODATION: 5 rooms, 1 with bath/shower. TV. B&B £28 to £54. Deposit:15. Children welcome. Garden. Doors close at 11.30. Confirm by 6

Restaurateurs justifiably resent no-shows. If you quote a credit card number when booking, you may be liable for the restaurant's lost profit margin if you don't turn up. Always phone to cancel.

▲ *Austins*

243 High Street, Aldeburgh IP15 5DN
ALDEBURGH (0728) 453932

As the Guide *went to press, changes of chef and management
at this establishment made our review invalid.*

PROPRIETOR: Austins of Aldeburgh Ltd   OPEN: Tue to Sat, D only, and Sun L; 12.30 to 1.45, 7.30
to 9.30   MEALS: Set L Sun £13.75, Set D £19.75   SERVICE: not inc, card slips closed   CARDS:
Access, Visa   DETAILS: 40 seats. Private parties: 22 main room. Vegetarian meals with prior
notice. Children's helpings on request. No children under 12. No cigars/pipes in dining-room.
Music   ACCOMMODATION: 7 rooms, all with bath/shower. TV. Phone. B&B £47.75 to £70. No
children under 12 (exc babies). Baby facilities. Pets welcome (£5 surcharge for dogs). Fax:
(0728) 453668

Regatta

171–173 High Street, Aldeburgh IP15 5AN   COOKING 1
ALDEBURGH (0728) 452011   COST £21–£33

The new-look Regatta set sail in March 1994, when Robert Mabey took off to his
brasserie in Sudbury (see entry), bequeathing control of the kitchen here to
Chris Hyde. There is now a thorough-going feel of life on the ocean wave to the
light, bright dining-room, painted in pastel shades of sunshine and sea and
adorned with nautical maps. A menu of mainly seafood starters acknowledges
the Mediterranean movement, while main courses all include rice, noodles or
chips. Reporters eating here in May found good value in the largely competent
cooking, and although salad of roasted peppers, prawns and olives
disappointed, the Butley-Orford smoked salmon was 'wonderful'. Roast
guinea-fowl with caramelised onions and herb gravy extracted real flavour from
that sometimes bland bird, while sliced lamb chump with a ragoût of lentils was
tender and good. 'Chips' and 'chunky chips' turn out to be of undifferentiated
chunkiness that turned out to be for two. Chocolate marquise was thought 'too
sweet' but was helped by a mint cream sauce, while the brown-bread ice-cream
with caramel sauce lacked for nothing in textural richness. Service is friendly
and obliging. The short wine list keeps considerably within the sub-£20 sector
(apart from Bollinger) but still manages a brisk globetrot. House Australian
is £6.95.

CHEF: Chris Hyde   PROPRIETORS: Robert and Johanna Mabey   OPEN: all week Apr to Sept, Wed to Sun and bank hols Oct to Mar; 12 to 2, 7 to 10   MEALS: alc (main courses £7 to £11.50) SERVICE: not inc   CARDS: Access, Amex, Visa   DETAILS: 80 seats. Private parties: 30 main room, 40 private room. Vegetarian meals. Children's helpings. No-smoking area. Wheelchair access (2 steps; also WC). No music. Fax: (0728) 452011

ALDERHOLT Dorset   map 2

Moonacre

Fordingbridge Road, Alderholt SP6 3BB
FORDINGBRIDGE (0425) 653142
off B3078, between Cranborne and   COOKING 2
Fordingbridge   COST £16–£33

In this simple, whitewashed country cottage with exposed timber-framed ceiling, Barbara Garnsworthy makes it her business to cater for meat-eaters, fish-eaters and vegetable-eaters alike. She also looks after those who favour straightforward chicken or steak and those who prefer more adventurous venison or pike quenelles. 'Balance is probably the key,' she reckons, both to the menus and in the cooking. Her style is simple but by no means boring. The main item is presented plainly, but lifted with a dash of something sweet, salty or spicy: horseradish and chive cream with marinated salmon, honey and ginger dressing with scallops and crab, and spiced damson sauce with terrine of pigeon breast, for instance.

Herbs are home-grown, and other supplies are diligently fostered. Vegetables are simple, fresh and well cooked. Puddings may be as straightforward as a plate of local blueberries (from a pick-your-own farm), as traditional as brown-bread ice-cream, or as interesting as greengage frangipane tart with cinnamon ice-cream. Not all reporters have been happy with the outcome, one feeling short-changed on quantity and expecting more flair in presentation and more flavour in the food. Wines are very sensibly chosen to provide a good variety of styles and flavours, yet the list is kept commendably short. House Valdepeñas red and Côtes de Gascogne white are £7.50 (£2 per glass).

CHEF: Barbara Garnsworthy   PROPRIETORS: Barbara Garnsworthy and Edward Bourke   OPEN: Tue to Sat, D only, and Sun L; 12 to 2, 7 to 10   CLOSED: 2/3 weeks Feb   MEALS: alc (main courses £7.50 to £12). Set L Sun £10, Set D Tue to Thur £9 (2 courses) to £11   SERVICE: not inc, card slips closed   CARDS: Access, Visa   DETAILS: 36 seats. Private parties: 36 main room. Car park. Vegetarian meals. Children's helpings. Wheelchair access (1 step). No music

---

Prices quoted in the Guide *are based on information supplied by restaurateurs. The prices quoted at the top of each entry represent a range, from the lowest meal price to the highest; the latter is inflated by 20 per cent to take account of likely price rises during the year of the* Guide.

🍴✲ *indicates that smoking is either banned altogether or that a dining-room is maintained for non-smokers. The symbol does not apply to restaurants that simply have no-smoking areas.*

ALNWICK Northumberland   map 7

John Blackmore's ⚘✻

1 Dorothy Foster Court, Narrowgate,
Alnwick NE66 1NL   COOKING 2*
ALNWICK (0665) 604465   COST £19–£41

Situated in a row of old stone houses within striking distance of the castle, the
Blackmores' restaurant presents a fairly rugged face to the outside world. The
interior, however, is decorated in soft pastels and frills, and a cosy – some would
say 'cramped' – feel pervades the dining-room. There are suggestions of
trimming this year from people who have eaten here before, as if incidentals are
being reined in a little, but the welcome is as unceremoniously warm as ever.

The à la carte menu offers a wide choice, with starters tending to an almost
main-course substantiality in a smoked chicken and mushroom pancake with
Gruyère sauce, or rough-textured, 'nicely gamey' pheasant mousse with
mushrooms, cabbage and madeira. The substance extends in main dishes to
'succulent, perfectly cooked' mignons of local venison with apples, mushrooms
and cider cream, and breaded pork fillet with a creamy curry sauce and
cashew-nuts. Crème brûlée and lemon cheesecake were both enjoyed. A menu
note offers opponents of the al dente school of vegetable cookery the chance to
specify longer cooking. Wines are a short but adequate selection, listed by colour
only. House French is £7.80.

CHEF: John Blackmore   PROPRIETORS: John and Penny Blackmore   OPEN: Tue to Sat, D only; 7
to 9   CLOSED: Jan   MEALS: alc (main courses £12 to £16). Set D Tue and Wed £16.50 (inc
wine)   SERVICE: not inc, card slips closed   CARDS: Access, Amex, Diners, Visa   DETAILS: 28
seats. Private parties: 28 main room. Vegetarian meals. No children under 5. Smart dress
preferred. No smoking in dining-room. Wheelchair access (2 steps). Music

---

AMBERLEY West Sussex   map 3

▲ Amberley Castle, Queen's Room ⚘✻

Amberley BN18 9ND
BURY (0798) 831992
on B2139, between Storrington and   COOKING 2
Bury Hill   COST £25–£71

The only medieval castle hotel in England, is the claim. The castle itself is early
twelfth-century, the dining-room thirteenth. Dark panelling, candlelight,
squashy sofas, fresh flowers and an air of luxury make it 'a place to dress up for'.
Forget New British Cooking, Modern European and all the rest; this is Castle
Cuisine, forged by Nigel Boschetti – not medieval gruel or haunch of venison
roasting over an open fire, not wenches and banquets, but some attempt to link
past and present. That is the theory, although quite how baked seafood sausage
with glazed onions, or figs poached in red wine with an almond ice-cream, fit in
is anybody's guess. Dinner of five courses (no choice, and one of which is coffee)
comes to 23,570 groats (call it forty quid).

The less expensive three-course fixed-price dinner has three items at each
stage, along the lines of delicately flavoured trout timbale (with an unlikely but

unctuous sauce of leeks and port), boned and reassembled sole with anchovies, and rhubarb bavarois. Not everybody has been happy with the food and service, but at inspection all went well. The wine list recommends bottles for each dish, although since they are not available by the glass (except for dessert wine), it would need a large party to take advantage. But it is a good start. Quality is high, prices are higher. Notes, and a short selection of bottles under £20, are helpful, as are eight wines by the glass from £3.50 upwards. House wine is £11.95.

CHEF: Nigel Boschetti   PROPRIETORS: Joy and Martin Cummings   OPEN: all week; 12 to 2, 7 to 9.30   MEALS: alc (main courses £19.50 to £22.50). Set L Mon to Sat £13.50 (2 courses) to £16.50, Sun £21.50, Set D £25.50 to £40   SERVICE: not inc, card slips closed   CARDS: Access, Amex, Diners, Visa   DETAILS: 70 seats. Private parties: 40 main room, 12, 14 and 48 private rooms. Car park. Vegetarian meals. Children's helpings. Jacket and tie. No smoking in dining-room. No music   ACCOMMODATION: 14 rooms, all with bath/shower. TV. Phone. Air-conditioned. B&B £80 to £225. Deposit: 50%. Rooms for disabled. Children welcome. Baby facilities. Pets welcome by arrangement. Afternoon teas. Garden. Doors close at midnight. Fax: (0798) 831998

AMBLESIDE Cumbria   map 7

▲ *Rothay Manor* ♥ ⅝✳

Rothay Bridge, Ambleside LA22 0EH
AMBLESIDE (053 94) 33605   COOKING 2
off A593 to Coniston, ¼m W of Ambleside   COST £17–£42

Over the years, the Nixons have turned this Regency hotel into one of the most favoured retreats in the Lake District. Undoubtedly, one of its great strengths is the caring attitude of the staff, who are eminently obliging, friendly and 'appropriate in their manner, whatever the hour'. Attentiveness extends also to the kitchen and the dining-room. The short dinner menu is priced according to the number of courses taken, and most reckon that it offers good value.

Jane Binns's cooking retains an English undercurrent, with well-hung game, roasts (including leg of lamb strewn with fresh mint) and an abundance of exactly cooked vegetables, not to mention the presence of treacle tart and Cumberland rum nicky on the sweets trolley. But the repertoire also embraces melon with a 'delicious' raspberry coulis, mimosa salad, Basque chicken and strawberry savarin. A full menu is available for vegetarians. The popular lunch buffet now features more hot dishes, along the lines of chicken and leek pie and beef bourguignonne. Good drinking under £20 is not just a sideline but a main thrust of the wide-ranging and carefully chosen wine list. There are some half-bottles, but more useful still is the offer to serve half a whole bottle at three-fifths of the full bottle price; not for every wine, of course, but enough to make it a genuinely generous gesture. Four house wines are £9. CELLARMAN'S CHOICE: Coteaux du Languedoc, La Serre Chardonnay 1992, £9.20; McWilliams Cabernet Sauvignon/Merlot 1992, £10.60.

'I do dislike restaurants where you cannot wipe your mouth without getting a new napkin.' (On eating in London)

CHEFS: Jane Binns and Colette Nixon PROPRIETORS: Nigel and Stephen Nixon OPEN: all week; 12.30 to 2 (12.45 to 1.30 Sun), 8 to 9 CLOSED: 2 Jan to 12 Feb MEALS: alc L (main courses £6.50). Set L Mon to Sat £11, Sun £14.50, Set D £21 (2 courses) to £27 SERVICE: not inc, card slips closed CARDS: Access, Amex, Diners, Visa DETAILS: 70 seats. Private parties: 12 main room, 32 private room. Car park. Vegetarian meals. Children's helpings. Smart dress preferred. No smoking in dining-room. Wheelchair access (1 step; also WC). No music. Air-conditioned ACCOMMODATION: 18 rooms, all with bath/shower. TV. Phone. B&B £69 to £150. Deposit: £60. Rooms for disabled. Children welcome. Baby facilities. Afternoon teas. Garden. Doors close at 11. Confirm by 6. Fax: (053 94) 33607 (*The Which? Hotel Guide*)

AMERSHAM Buckinghamshire map 3

King's Arms

30 High Street, Old Amersham HP7 0DJ COOKING 1*
AMERSHAM (0494) 726333 COST £19–£41

This redoubtable Tudor inn retains much of its original character, especially in the popular bar, while the dining-room has benefited from a recent face-lift. Visitors reckon it can still feel 'cramped', with tables packed closely together and little chance of privacy. 'People having an affair or talking about one should definitely dine elsewhere,' observed one reporter. The commitment and enthusiasm of the place are clear, and Gary Munday's cooking draws appreciative comments. His monthly-changing dinner menu is backed up by occasional special events and 'plateaux de fruits de mer'. Terrines, such as salmon and dill or chicken and pistachio, are regularly endorsed. Other good dishes have included poached salmon with a light ginger sauce and brochette of liver and bacon with an intense sage sauce. To finish, date and fig pudding with sticky toffee sauce is 'everything an Englishman would expect of this dish'. Set lunches are excellent value. The list of around 70 wines features plenty of well-respected names. Chilean house wine is £7.75.

CHEF: Gary Munday PROPRIETOR: John Jennison OPEN: Tue to Sun, exc Sun D; 12 to 2, 7 to 10 MEALS: alc (main courses £13 to £15.50). Set L Tue to Sat £8.50 (2 courses) to £11.50, Sun £14.50, Set D Tue to Fri £17, Sat £23. Minimum £8.50 L, £13 D SERVICE: not inc CARDS: Access, Amex, Diners, Visa DETAILS: 30 seats. Private parties: 48 main room, 12 private room. Car park. Vegetarian meals. Children welcome. Smart dress preferred. No cigars/pipes in dining-room. No music. Fax: (0494) 433480

APPLETHWAITE Cumbria map 7

▲ *Underscar Manor*

Applethwaite, nr Keswick CA12 4PH
KESWICK (076 87) 75000 COOKING 2*
off A66, 1½m N of Keswick COST £26–£45

Appearances matter at Underscar. The beautiful Italianate house is set high on the hills overlooking the fells and Derwentwater, with terrific views. Who else but the Victorians would have built it? The 40 acres of land include both natural woods and formal gardens with terraces, manicured lawns, shrubberies and a well-stocked herb garden of lovage, thyme, angelica and sage. The house is comfortable, the decoration truly, madly, deeply ornate: chandeliers, heavily gilded cornices, festoons of ruching, long, pink diaphanous drapes, cut-glass decanters and engraved glasses.

The three-course dinner menu (plus mid-meal soup, and coffee) has six options per course. First-rate consommé is full of meaty goodness, dotted with minute squares of tomato flesh and snippets of chives. Well-hung steak, an enormous portion, is cooked very rare as requested, and topped with a tiny sliver of precisely cooked foie gras. Pear poached in red wine, served with honey ice-cream, is attractively sweet and tart at the same time. The cooking, like the décor, can sometimes run into the baroque. Flavours may be obscured by good intentions, although the basics are sound. Excellent gamey duck, slightly undercooked, has a crisp skin and celeriac mousse, but a reporter felt there was no need for three slices of very sweet and rather soft '50s-style pineapple. There can be imbalances, approximate timing of some items, and too many conflicting tastes on a plate, as if the kitchen wants to make something appear even more impressive than it already is. Dinner is, however, considered good value.

Service seems to have slipped a bit since last year. It is all very well being able to lift domes, but an inspector would have preferred somebody who could provide useful information about the food and wine. The predominantly French list shows choice for under £20 a bottle, but excitement is the preserve of the pricier fine wine section. House French is £10.50.

CHEFS: Robert Thornton and Stephen Yare PROPRIETORS: Pauline and Derek Harrison, and Gordon Evans OPEN: all week; 12 to 1.30, 7 to 8.30 (9 Sat) MEALS: Set L £18.50, Set D £25 to £28.50 SERVICE: not inc, card slips closed CARDS: Access, Amex, Visa DETAILS: 60 seats. 6 tables outside. Private parties: 40 main room, 30 private room. Car park. Vegetarian meals. No children under 12. Smart dress preferred. No smoking in dining-room. No music ACCOMMODATION: 11 rooms, all with bath/shower. TV. Phone. D,B&B £75 to £250. No children under 12. Afternoon teas. Garden. Doors close at midnight. Fax: (076 87) 74904 (*The Which? Hotel Guide*)

ASENBY North Yorkshire map 7

Crab & Lobster

Asenby, nr Thirsk YO7 3QL
THIRSK (0845) 577286 COOKING 2
off A168, between A19 and A1 COST £21–£51

A breathless report sums the place up: 'Just off the A1. Pub with large car park. Warm welcome. Good beer, real ale. Crisps, nuts, small chipolata sausages to nibble while you choose from a good menu. Dishes written up on beams and blackboards. Individual and different. Atmosphere terrific on a wet and miserable evening. Try it, you'll love it.' Admired dishes have included warm salad of sea bass and scallops, crab and lobster bisque, fresh pasta with turbot, crab-crusted salmon, cold seafood platter, a pint of prawns in a jug and fish-pie. Four different kinds of bread are offered. Rose petal ice-cream with raspberries and strawberries in a biscuit bowl is a good dessert. Excellent service keeps everyone happy. The short wine list includes house Duboeuf at £7.95.

CHEFS: David Barnard and Michael Pickard PROPRIETORS: David and Jackie Barnard OPEN: all week, exc Sun D; 12 to 2.30, 7 to 10 CLOSED: 25 Dec MEALS: alc (main courses brasserie £8 to £11.50, restaurant £11 to £21). Set L £12.95 SERVICE: not inc CARDS: Access, Amex, Visa DETAILS: restaurant 75 seats, brasserie 35 seats. 15 tables outside. Private parties: 65 main room. Car park. Vegetarian meals. Children's helpings L. Smart dress preferred. Music. Fax: (0845) 577109

ASHBOURNE Derbyshire   map 5

▲ *Callow Hall* ⚡✳

Mappleton Road, Ashbourne DE6 2AA
ASHBOURNE (0335) 343403
¾m NW of Ashbourne, turn left off A515 at
crossroads with Bowling Green pub on left,   COOKING 1*
Mappleton Road first on right   COST £20–£52

The waterway that runs by Callow Hall is mentioned in Izaak Walton's *The Compleat Angler*. Residents in search of trout or grayling may fish for them to their heart's content in the stretch of Bentley Brook that belongs to the Hall. The house itself is a grey-stone Victorian edifice of some grandeur, the dining-room decorated in a striking colour scheme of rich reds. David and Anthony Spencer cook a longish *carte* in the evenings, together with a prix fixe of five or six courses, and a set-price Sunday lunch menu.

The style is fairly straightforward English country-house, with occasional florid excursions. One reporter, for example, doubted the wisdom of chicken stuffed with king prawns and salmon on a tomato sauce. An inspection meal turned up some good things, however. Accurately seasoned starters such as poached king scallops on the half-shell with a Noilly Prat cream sauce, or sliced monkfish tail on tomato fondue with olive oil and herbs, showed an encouragingly light touch, while a dish of sauté pork medallions with port and Stilton sauce and a timbale of celery was, if anything, almost too heavy. Main courses come with a multiplicity of vegetables. Desserts tend to be classically creamy and rich, but the quality of prune and armagnac ice-cream in a brandy-snap basket – 'perfect texture and not too sweet' – with an 'intense' raspberry coulis won over its consumer. The British and French cheeses are worth a look. 'Mrs Spencer's concerned and personal management of the dining-room is an added bonus.' The wine list makes fairly exhaustive sallies into the big French regions, although the listing could do with tidying into either vintage or price order. Sift through for the bargains. House wines are £8.95.

CHEFS: David Spencer and Anthony Spencer PROPRIETOR: David and Dorothy Spencer, and Anthony Spencer OPEN: Tue and Sun L (other days by arrangement), Mon to Sat D; 12.30 to 1.30, 7 to 9.30 CLOSED: 25 and 26 Dec MEALS: alc D (main courses £13 to £17). Set L £13.50, Set D £27.50 to £29.50 SERVICE: not inc CARDS: Access, Amex, Diners, Visa DETAILS: 60 seats. Private parties: 40 main room, 30 and 40 private rooms. Car park. Vegetarian meals. Children's helpings. Smart dress preferred. No smoking in dining-room. No music ACCOMMODATION: 16 rooms, all with bath/shower. TV. Phone. B&B £65 to £120. Rooms for disabled. Children welcome. Baby facilities. Dogs by arrangement (not in public rooms). Garden. Fishing. Doors close at midnight. Fax: (0335) 343624 (*The Which? Hotel Guide*)

ASTON CLINTON Buckinghamshire   map 3

▲ Bell Inn ♥ ⅝✳

Aston Clinton HP22 5HP
AYLESBURY (0296) 630252   COOKING 1
on A41, between Tring and Aylesbury   COST £27–£75

Giles Stonehouse arrived in summer 1994 following the departure of Jean-
Claude MacFarlane. Our inspector visited soon after, as Mr Stonehouse was still
settling in and endeavouring to make his mark on the kitchen. The dining-room
remains the same, though, and the 'sad air about it' has rung true for more than
one reporter over the year. Bell Inn smokies are still here, too, along with Mr
Waller's Aylesbury duck, British cheeses and cherry tart plus coffee on a
£36-a-head menu for two. Other set menus and the *carte* offer a fairly wide choice
between them, taking in mushroom and tarragon soup, shin of lamb, and rum
and banana soufflé. At our inspector's meal, which included foie gras terrine,
grilled lobster and gratin of red fruits, it was the turbot in lemon butter sauce that
stood out for freshness. Prices are still hefty, as they are on the wine list 'of epic
War and Peace proportions'. It is largely an assembly of French classics of
estimable quality, dotted with some gems and curiosities for the inquisitive.
Mark-ups are variable, but some are painful. House recommendations offer a
quick way of finding something under £20. House wine is £12.95 (£2.50 per
glass). CELLARMAN'S CHOICE: Hawkes Bay Sauvignon Blanc 1992, £18.75;
Margaux Private Reserve 1989, £29.50.

CHEF: Giles Stonehouse   PROPRIETOR: Michael Harris   OPEN: all week; 12.30 to 1.45, 7.30 to
9.45   MEALS: alc (main courses £12.50 to £22). Set L Mon to Sat £13.50 (2 courses) to £17.50,
Sun £25, Set D £25, Set L and D £36. Bistro menu   SERVICE: not inc, card slips closed   CARDS:
Access, Amex, Visa   DETAILS: 130 seats. Private parties: 250 main room, 20 private room. Car
park. Vegetarian meals. Children's helpings. Smart dress preferred. No smoking in dining-room.
Wheelchair access (also WC). No music   ACCOMMODATION: 21 rooms, all with bath/shower. TV.
Phone. B&B £79 to £150. Deposit 100%. Rooms for disabled. Children welcome. Baby facilities.
Pets welcome. Afternoon teas. Garden. Confirm 1 day ahead. Fax: (0296) 631250 (*The Which?
Hotel Guide*)

AYLESBURY Buckinghamshire   map 2

▲ Hartwell House ▮ ⅝✳

Oxford Road, Aylesbury HP17 8NL
AYLESBURY (0296) 747444
on A418, 2m from Aylesbury   COOKING 2
towards Oxford   COST £29–£69

Like Middlethorpe Hall in York and Bodysgallen Hall in Llandudno (see
entries), Hartwell is part of the Historic House Hotels group, an organisation that
rescues stately homes (this is no mere country house), renovates them, gardens
included, and sets up a kind of self-supporting commercial venture to recoup the
money. Refurbishment at Hartwell is immaculate, and whatever was good
enough for Louis XVIII, who lived here for five years from 1809, is probably
good enough for the rest of us.

With surroundings like this, the food has much to emulate. Whole roast lobster salad, terrine of goose liver with Sauternes jelly, and poached corn-fed chicken in a champagne sauce with truffle-flavoured risotto all suggest that Louis XVIII would feel quite at home if he were suddenly to come back. If you miss the ravioli of crab and leek with a lobster cream sauce, never mind, just catch the roast medallion of turbot with a cassoulet of beans and a coriander sauce, which is about as close as the smooth, reassuring cooking gets to earthiness and exotic flavouring. The luxury-mobile finally comes to rest with baked banana with a chocolate toffee sauce, or caramelised pear cream with a caramel sauce.

Wines are as aristocratic as they come, marred only by some high mark-ups. The saving grace is that quality is not compromised, even at the bottom end, so those with less than £20 to spend can still drink well. It would help if such bottles were laid out in a single page. House wines begin at £11.90, and sticky Australian Liqueur Muscat by the glass is just the thing to go with the rich puds. CELLARMAN'S CHOICE: Pinot Grigio 1991, Lageder, £19.70; Ch. Gressier Grand Poujeaux 1983, £31.

CHEF: Alan Maw   PROPRIETOR: Historic House Hotels Ltd   OPEN: all week; 12.30 to 2, 7.30 to 9.45   MEALS: Set L £16.50 (2 courses) to £22.40, Set D £38   SERVICE: net prices, card slips closed   CARDS: Access, Amex, Diners, Visa   DETAILS: 80 seats. Private parties: 60 main room, 18, 30 and 60 private rooms. Car park. Vegetarian meals. No children under 8. Jacket and tie D. No smoking in dining-room. Wheelchair access (also WC). Music. Air-conditioned   ACCOMMODATION: 47 rooms, all with bath/shower. TV. Phone. B&B £103.50 to £375. Rooms for disabled. Lift. No children under 8. Pets welcome (in Hartwell Court). Afternoon teas. Garden. Swimming-pool. Sauna. Tennis. Fishing. Confirm by 4. Fax: (0296) 747450 (*The Which? Hotel Guide*)

BARNARD CASTLE Co Durham   map 7

Blagraves House ⁵⁕ | NEW ENTRY |

30–32 The Bank, Barnard Castle DL12 8PN   COOKING 2*
STAINDROP (0833) 37668   COST £21–£36

Oliver Cromwell, that indefatigable seventeenth-century restaurant inspector, ate at Blagraves in 1648, partaking of oatcakes and burnt wine. The building has some fine plaster crests and imposing stone fireplaces dating from that time, though the structure itself is 200 years older than that. There is nothing artificial about the décor: 'huge oak ceiling beams are there to hold the place up, not for decoration.' The view of rolling hills and sheep is an agreeable one.

The Marleys have been running their restaurant here since 1988, and have built up a steady local following for their confidently cooked, seasonal menus of exemplary value. Two dinner menus are offered, a *carte* supplemented by daily specials and a three-course midweek prix fixe. They are built on a solid foundation of self-sufficiency, with breads, chutneys, herbs and truffles all being produced on the premises. The style is a gentle version of modern British that none the less delivers plenty of flavour in dishes like duck liver parfait scented with thyme, chicken and leek ravioli with a marjoram sauce, and sauté rabbit with real ale and mustard. A meal in late May produced fine wild mushrooms in filo pastry and nicely mature breast of chicken with a sauce of sherry and hazelnuts. Desserts can include dark chocolate terrine with coffee bean sauce, or 'terrific' pear and almond tart with good frangipane base and fine pastry. Trimmings, such as the aperitif nibble (perhaps a mini-quiche of Stilton and spring onion), the unfussy but well-timed vegetables, and coffee, have all been praised. Service may be 'diffident' but not inattentive. The wine list is shortish and just adequate to the task, comprising fairly priced and mostly rather youthful bottles. House Bordeaux is £7.95.

CHEFS/PROPRIETORS: Kenneth and Elizabeth Marley   OPEN: Tue to Sat, D only; 7 to 9.30 MEALS: alc (main courses £8 to £13.50). Set D Tue to Thur £12.95   SERVICE: not inc, card slips closed   CARDS: Access, Visa   DETAILS: 26 seats. Private parties: 26 main room, 40 private room. Vegetarian meals. Children's helpings. Smart dress preferred. No smoking in dining-room. Music

---

BARNET Hertfordshire   map 3

Mims

63 East Barnet Road, New Barnet EN4 8RN   COOKING 2
081-449 2974   COST £22–£48

The prospect of sampling seared tuna with pickled vegetable noodles for Sunday lunch in Barnet is one good reason why this out-of-town restaurant is an asset. Mr Al-Sersy learned his trade with the Roux brothers, but has gone his own way. His cooking has plenty of zing and modern Mediterranean flourishes, although most visitors confirm that the place operates at a leisurely pace. Vivid ideas abound. Squid is stuffed with salsa and anchovy mousse; grilled sweetbreads are paired with Jerusalem artichoke purée; pan-roast hake is served with grilled courgette salad. Main dishes are served with appropriate selections of vegetables. Regulars note that the chocolate assortment is an 'absolutely marvellous' finale; also look for tarte Tatin or charlotte of mascarpone cheese with banana ice-cream. Menus are changed twice daily: lunch is fixed price for two courses (desserts are extra); dinner is à la carte. Around three dozen carefully chosen wines appear on the well-spread list, plus a welcome and generous clutch of half-bottles. House wine is £8.95.

CHEF: Mr I. Al-Sersy   PROPRIETORS: Mr M. Abouzahrah and Mr I. Al-Sersy   OPEN: Tue to Sun, exc Sat L; 12 to 2.30 (5 Sun), 6.30 to 11 (10.30 Sun)   CLOSED: 1 week Sept, 1 week Dec   MEALS: alc D (main courses £10.50 to £16). Set L £9.50 (2 courses) to £14   SERVICE: not inc   CARDS: Access, Visa   DETAILS: 40 seats. Private parties: 40 main room. Car park. Vegetarian meals with prior notice. No children under 6. Smart dress preferred. No cigars/pipes in dining-room. Wheelchair access (1 step). No music

---

BARNSLEY South Yorkshire   map 5

Armstrongs ▼

6 Shambles Street, Barnsley S70 2SQ   COOKING 1
BARNSLEY (0226) 240113   COST £20–£39

Although it may not look particularly interesting from the outside, Armstrongs is 'well-decorated, spacious and makes you feel welcome as soon as you walk through the door'. Nick Pound's food is self-styled 'eclectic', with Thai,

Moroccan and soul food all getting a look-in from time to time. Chillies, limes, coriander, Indian spices and salsa add to the heat, while coconut sometimes takes it away. One reporter who enjoyed melted blue cheese on toasted brioche with crisp lettuce, pear, cherry tomato and a tangy balsamic vinegar dressing found all the flavours 'well realised, the consistencies right and the combination working well'. Praise, too, has focused on cheese soufflé with cream and chives, lamb with light Indian spicing, and traditional apple crumble and custard. When flavours are less than forthright, they fail to impress. The roving wine list stays obligingly under £20 for much of the way. House French is £8.85 (£1.85 per glass).

CHEF/PROPRIETOR: Nick Pound OPEN: Tue to Sat, exc Sat L; 12 to 2, 7 to 9.30 MEALS: alc (main courses £8 to £15). Set D £12.95 (7 to 8, Tue to Fri) SERVICE: not inc CARDS: Access, Amex, Visa DETAILS: 60 seats. Private parties: 40 main room, 20 private room. Vegetarian meals. Children's helpings on request. Wheelchair access (1 step). Music

Restaurant Peano ♟

102 Dodworth Road, Barnsley S70 6HL
BARNSLEY (0226) 244990

COOKING 2*
COST £19–£42

The Peanos have been in this three-storey detached Victorian stone house since 1990. It was once a vicarage, and a private garden at the back supplies some of the herbs. The cooking is serious, and Michael Peano's credentials are very sound. His culinary centre of gravity is in France and Italy, but occasionally he takes a flyer, normally with chicken, to produce a Moroccan version or an oriental chicken salad. For the most part, though, the repertoire deals in pasta, Mediterranean vegetables, and some hefty meat jobs. This is Barnsley, so don't expect much in the way of light, fish main courses, rather guinea-fowl with sarladaise potatoes, saddle of lamb with white beans, sirloin of beef and calf's liver.

This year the price for the table d'hôte menu has been reduced, a sensible response in a difficult economic climate. Michael Peano does not want his to become just a 'special occasion' restaurant and there is much sense in being the kind of place to which people can return without having to think twice. Cheaper cuts of meat, more steak and kidney pie, oxtail, Lancashire hotpot and so on do the trick well. The food is fresh, generally flavoursome, almost always interesting and occasionally surprising. Wines are few, largely Franco-Italian, and extremely well chosen and very fairly priced. House wine is £9.50.
CELLARMAN'S CHOICE: Soave Classico Vigneto Calvarinho 1992, Pieropan, £15; Rocca Rubia 1989, Santadi, £15.50.

CHEF: Michael Peano PROPRIETORS: Michael and Tracey Peano OPEN: Tue to Sat, exc Sat L; 12 to 1.30, 7 to 9.30 CLOSED: first week Jan, 1 week June MEALS: alc (main courses £9.50 to £11.50). Set L and D Tue to Fri £11.95 SERVICE: not inc, card slips closed CARDS: Access, Amex, Visa DETAILS: 40 seats. Private parties: 50 main room. Car park. Vegetarian meals with prior notice. Children's helpings. Smart dress preferred. No cigars/pipes in dining-room. Wheelchair access (1 step). Music

♦ denotes an outstanding wine cellar; ♟ denotes a good wine list, worth travelling for.

BARNSTAPLE Devon map 1

▲ *Lynwood House* ⁵✕ £

Bishops Tawton Road,
Barnstaple EX32 9DZ
BARNSTAPLE (0271) 43695
1m S of town centre, before A377   COOKING 1
roundabout   COST £20–£56

Four members of the Roberts family (plus four dogs) are the incumbents of this Victorian house just off the Exeter Road out of Barnstaple. Ruth and son Matthew run the kitchen and manage to please all comers with light meals, vegetarian options, good-value fixed-price lunches and special gourmet evenings. The full evening *carte* shows a preference for fresh fish: the pot of mixed seafood cooked in wine, cream and cheese sauce is a perennial favourite. Otherwise you might be tempted by grilled Dover sole, poached skate with capers and brown butter, roast duckling and medallions of fillet steak with tomatoes, mushrooms and red wine. Salads are lighter alternatives. Sweets are typically old-school stalwarts such as cream caramel or ice-cream with raspberry sauce. The wide-ranging wine list has enough variety and half-bottles to keep most diners contented. House wines start at £8.75.

CHEFS: Ruth Roberts and Matthew Roberts   PROPRIETORS: John, Ruth, Matthew and Christian Roberts   OPEN: Mon to Sat (Sun residents only); 12 to 2, 7 to 9.30   MEALS: alc (main courses £11 to £18.50). Set L £11.95 (2 courses) to £13.95. Light meal menu, exc Sun (courses £4 to £7)   SERVICE: not inc   CARDS: Access, Amex, Visa   DETAILS: 50 seats. Private parties: 60 main room, 20 private room. Car park. Vegetarian meals. Children's helpings. Smart dress preferred. No smoking in dining-room. Wheelchair access (also WC). Music   ACCOMMODATION: 5 rooms, all with bath/shower. TV. Phone. B&B £40.50 to £60.50. Children welcome. Pets welcome (not in public rooms). Fax: (0271) 79340 (*The Which? Hotel Guide*)

BARTON-UPON-HUMBER Humberside map 6

Elio's £

---

11 Market Place,
Barton-upon-Humber DN18 5DA   COOKING 1
BARTON-UPON-HUMBER (0652) 635147   COST £17–£38

Elio Grossi's 'cramped but friendly' trattoria sits on the north bank of the Humber, on the opposite side of the bridge to Hull, nestling in the corner of a small market square. The proprietor assures us that the menu and wine list have not changed one whit since last year's entry, so regulars will have benefited from inflation-proofed eating this past year. Classic Italian dishes of the old school such as home-made minestrone, stuffed mushrooms with garlic butter, five ways with spaghetti, braised squid and veal saltimbocca are bolstered by fresh fish of the day and a slate of vegetarian dishes that includes spicy rigatoni all'arrabbiata ('pasta with an enraged sauce,' according to the menu). A couple who enjoyed properly dressed crab and aubergines topped with Parmesan to start then ordered baby halibut from the blackboard, and were gratified to find that they were eating the only two bought that day. Desserts are limited to the old standards and can be 'disappointing'. Litre carafes of Tokai or Sangiovese are £7.50.

CHEF/PROPRIETOR: E.M. Grossi   OPEN: Mon to Sat, D only; 6 to 10.30 (11 Fri and Sat)   MEALS: alc (main courses £6 to £14). Set D £24.50 (for 2, inc wine)   SERVICE: 10%   CARDS: Access, Amex, Visa   DETAILS: 42 seats. Private parties: 40 main room, 15 and 20 private rooms. Vegetarian meals. Children's helpings on request. Smart dress preferred. Wheelchair access (1 step). Music

---

BARWICK Somerset   map 2

▲ *Little Barwick House* ✼✸

Barwick, nr Yeovil BA22 9TD
YEOVIL (0935) 23902
off A37, take second left opposite   COOKING 3
Red House pub   COST £32–£41

Barwick Park is full of follies; if you glance from the upper windows of Little Barwick House, a white-fronted Georgian dower house, with trim, sloping lawns dominated by a large cedar, you may chance to see one. The house itself was once full of the Colley family, but the daughters have now flown the nest, one of them to cook for Sally Clarke in London. The dining-room is smartly decorated, but without unseemly elaboration, in a warm rust-red with Persian carpets. Veronica Colley cooks a fixed-price, four-course menu, the tariff dropping if only two courses are taken. Dishes are in the uncomplicated Anglo-French mould, emphasising local ingredients with 'honest, substantial' treatments.

A spring meal consisted of a salad of sauté chicken livers that were well herbed and accompanied by plenty of crunch from croûtons and leaves, another of chicken tikka and avocado with yogurt and lime sauce that proved 'more pleasing to the palate than to the eye', rack of lamb with rosemary twigs and garlicky cooking juices, and medallions of venison with a port and blackcurrant sauce that was 'light and intense, but not in any way cloying'. Cheeses were a good selection, amaretto ice-cream was 'very creamy', while apple and almond tart was an object lesson – 'crisp, sweet pastry, spongy almond base, smooth and thinly sliced caramelised apple'. Trimmings, from creamed leek and Parmesan nibbles to start, through the unfussy vegetables to the good cafetière coffee with truffles, are all well done. The 'congenial and informal' approach is readily understood and appreciated. The wine list's geography is pleasingly wide-ranging, and it does not stray into prohibitive price regions. The notes are helpful, and there is a healthy sprinkling of halves. House wines are £8.90.

CHEF: Veronica Colley   PROPRIETORS: Christopher and Veronica Colley   OPEN: Mon to Sat, D only (Sun D residents only); 7 to 9 (9.30 Sat)   MEALS: Set D £22.90 to £24.90   SERVICE: not inc, card slips closed   CARDS: Access, Amex, Visa   DETAILS: 40 seats. Private parties: 40 main room, 20 private room. Car park. Vegetarian meals. Children's helpings. No smoking in dining-room. Wheelchair access (1 step). No music. Air-conditioned   ACCOMMODATION: 6 rooms, all with bath/shower. TV. Phone. B&B £46 to £76. Deposit: £20. Children welcome. Baby facilities. Pets welcome (not in public rooms). Garden. Doors close at 11. Fax: (0935) 20908 (*The Which? Hotel Guide*)

▲ *Fischer's Baslow Hall* ♥ ✳

Calver Road, Baslow DE45 1RR   COOKING 3
CHESTERFIELD (0246) 583259   COST £21–£54

Fischer's is well placed: not far from Chatsworth, within easy reach of the Peak District, and close enough to Sheffield to keep the wheels turning. It is a warm Edwardian stone house, tastefully refurbished and with efficient, friendly and obliging service.

The restaurant succeeds partly because it uses first-class, fresh ingredients. The menu is imaginative without being fussy, and Max Fischer integrates the various strands – British, French, Italian and Far Eastern – into a short but varied menu. Among dishes likely to appear are escalope of salmon with oriental spices, ravioli filled with soft English goats' cheese, paupiette of oxtail, and nougat glacé on hazelnut meringue. Timing is accurate and cooking is accomplished. Reporters have enjoyed a first course of lamb's kidney and liver in red wine sauce, roast saddle of lamb, and individual rhubarb (locally grown in spring) crumble that comes with a jug of custard. Introductory savouries are much appreciated. Café Max offers a cheaper menu in another room, along the lines of Alsace onion tart, bangers and mash (with caramelised apple), and lemon tart.

The varied wine list spans a range of styles and prices, and quality is high. There may be no bargains, but very good and characterful drinking can be had for around £20. Good-quality house wine is £9.50 (£2.45 to £3 per glass). CELLARMAN'S CHOICE: Chablis 1991, Louis Michel, £15.50; Crozes-Hermitage Thalabert, 1990, Jaboulet, £21.

CHEF: Max Fischer   PROPRIETORS: Max and Susan Fischer   OPEN: all week, exc Sun D (residents only) and Sun L Café Max; 12 to 2, 7 to 9.30   CLOSED: 25 and 26 Dec   MEALS: restaurant Set L Mon to Sat £14.50 (2 courses) to £16.50, Sun £18.50, Set D £36. Café Max alc (main courses £7.50 to £12.50)   SERVICE: not inc, card slips closed   CARDS: Access, Amex, Diners, Visa   DETAILS: restaurant 40 seats, Café Max 25 seats. 4 tables outside. Private parties: 40 main room, 12 and 24 private rooms. Car park. Vegetarian meals with prior notice. Children's helpings on request L. No children D restaurant. Children welcome Café Max. Smart dress preferred. No smoking in main dining-room. Wheelchair access (3 steps; also WC). No music restaurant. Music Café Max   ACCOMMODATION: 6 rooms, all with bath/shower. TV. Phone. B&B £70 to £120. Deposit: £50. Children welcome. Baby facilities. Afternoon teas. Garden. Doors close at midnight. Fax: (0246) 583818 (*The Which? Hotel Guide*)

▲ *Bath Spa Hotel, Vellore Restaurant*

Sydney Road, Bath BA2 6JF   COOKING 3
BATH (0225) 444424   COST £26–£67

The high-vaulted Vellore restaurant used to be a ballroom. Dining here is on a grand scale with prices to match, although some quirky touches help to break the ice. 'The approach appears initially to be formal, but we do try not to be stuffy,' writes the general manager. You will find pastry mice dotted around the room and even two teddy bears sitting at a table reading the menu. The kitchen unearths some old favourites of swanky hotel catering with chateaubriand steak and Dover sole meunière. Anything more up to date is considered 'food art', and priced accordingly. A choice of onion soup or crab and prawn salad, then salmon in orange butter or breast of chicken wrapped in bacon, followed by exotic fruit with yogurt ice-cream, or chocolate soufflé with vanilla ice-cream, were the choices on one set menu.

Perky flavours appear in wok-fried scallops stir-fried with ginger and lime, the Mediterranean sun shines through in a ratatouille of aubergine and olives with smoked garlic jus that is served with lamb fillet, and the trencherman tendency is well satisfied by cassoulet of broad beans and lardons that comes with peppered duck breast. Salads, dressings, pasta and sauces are up to the mark. As we went to press, a new *carte* was planned, to add to the set menu. House wine is a staggering £17.50. The less expensive, plant-filled and mural-covered Alfresco Brasserie serves up Caesar salad, Rich Man's cod and chips, Thai chicken and tiger prawn curry, and chocolate burger.

CHEFS: Jonathan Fraser and Ben Davis   PROPRIETOR: Forte plc   OPEN: all week, D only, and Sun L; 12.30 to 2, 7 to 10   MEALS: Set L Sun £14.95, Set D £34   SERVICE: not inc, card slips closed   CARDS: Access, Amex, Diners, Visa   DETAILS: 100 seats. Private parties: 60 and 200 private rooms. Car park. Vegetarian meals. Children's helpings. Smart dress preferred. No-smoking area. Wheelchair access (also WC). Music. Air-conditioned   ACCOMMODATION: 98 rooms, all with bath/shower. TV. Phone. B&B £109 to £198. Deposit: 1 night. Rooms for disabled. Lift. Children welcome. Baby facilities. Pets welcome (ground floor only). Afternoon teas. Garden. Swimming-pool. Sauna. Tennis. Confirm by 4. Fax: (0225) 444006

Clos du Roy   NEW ENTRY

1 Seven Dials, Saw Close, Bath BA1 1EN   COOKING 2*
BATH (0225) 444450   COST £20–£48

Philippe Roy moved back into the centre of Bath in 1992 after a period in a nearby country house. His current location is in Seven Dials – a Georgian repro development just next to the Theatre Royal. Although the reception area may make you feel you have stepped into an office, everything has been done to give the dining-room its own idiosyncratic character. The theme is musical: instruments adorn the walls, windows are surrounded by fabric prints of squiggly staves, screens between tables are decorated with musical notation. A pianist provides the real thing from a white baby grand, offering competent renditions of popular classics leavened with foot-tapping stuff like 'The Girl from Ipanema'.

The format is a long *carte* and a three-course prix fixe in the evenings, as well as a *menu du jour* for lunch-times, or pre- or post-theatre. The style is intensely French, with roots in the days of nouvelle in terms of both conception and presentation. A spring meal turned up a roulade of salmon and fennel wrapped in nori with a sweet dill vinaigrette that had 'excellent consistency' and only left the diner wishing there were more of it. The other starter of fried cod on mashed potato with a sherry sauce had 'good flaky cod, crisp on the outside, and a strong meaty sauce' but was rather clumsily garnished with raw spring onion. Main-course meats – duck breast with roasted turnips and a brace of boned quails with leek mousse and port sauce – were both good, though the leek was more shredded than moussed and, again, quantities were not exactly generous.

Those who can't choose between desserts such as nougat parfait with red fruit coulis, mango charlotte or *croquant aux deux chocolats* may opt for the chef's selection instead. The predominantly French wine list is arranged according to style. It has some good growers, prices are eminently fair for the location, and the provision of halves seems proportionate to the scale. House wines are £8.95.

CHEFS: Philippe Roy and Nigel Treble   PROPRIETORS: Philippe and Emma Roy   OPEN: all week; 12 to 2.30, 6 to 11   MEALS: alc (main courses £11.50 to £15.50). Set L £8.95 (2 courses) to £11.95, Set D £18.50 to £22.50. Pre- and post-theatre menu   SERVICE: not inc, card slips closed   CARDS: Access, Amex, Diners, Visa   DETAILS: 82 seats. 5 tables outside. Private parties: 100 main room. Vegetarian meals. Children's helpings. Smart dress preferred. No cigars/pipes in dining-room. Wheelchair access (also WC). Music. Fax: (0225) 460218

Garlands

7 Edgar Buildings, George Street,
Bath BA1 2EE   COOKING 1
BATH (0225) 442283   COST £22–£35

'Smart' is the word that best describes this intimate restaurant with its elegantly draped curtains, ornate curlicued pelmets and mirrors. Tom Bridgeman's cooking is in tune with the times, although he is equally at home with classic Anglo/French ideas. His fixed-price menus (two or three courses) take in the likes of warm pigeon breast with pickled beetroot, chicory and balsamic vinegar, breast of duck with green peppercorns and cognac, and cutlet of salmon with a Thai-style crust. Fish is from Newlyn market. A five-course 'gourmet menu' is served on Friday nights, and highlights from one meal included asparagus salad with rocket and Parmesan, and 'excellent' strawberries glazed with Grand Marnier sabayon. Most reporters are quite happy with the service. The café-bar at the back deals in light meals and snacks such as kedgeree and Toulouse sausages with mash. A decent selection of reasonably priced wines is arranged by grape type. House wine is £9.95.

CHEF: Tom Bridgeman   PROPRIETORS: Tom and Jo Bridgeman   OPEN: Tue to Sun; 12 to 2.15, 7 to 10.30   MEALS: Set L £10.95 (2 courses) to £13.95, Set D £16.95 (2 courses) to £19.50, Set gourmet D Fri £15. Café-bar menu (main courses £5.50 to £9)   SERVICE: not inc   CARDS: Access, Amex, Diners, Visa   DETAILS: 28 seats. 4 tables outside. Private parties: 12 main room, 40 private room. Vegetarian meals. Children's helpings. Music

Hole in the Wall ♥   NEW ENTRY

16 George Street, Bath BA1 2EH   COOKING 3
BATH (0225) 425242   COST £21–£33

The Hole in the Wall is a venue that rightfully deserves blue-plaque status. It was here that George Perry-Smith – one of the seminal British restaurant figures of the last 50 years – opened up when post-war rationing was still in force and Elizabeth David was beginning to be published. It is fitting that, after many years of languishing in mediocrity, it is now reborn under the aegis of Chris Chown of Plas Bodegroes (see entry Wales, Pwllheli). The basement restaurant is 'womb-like but not claustrophobic', a sense of space created by glass partitions engraved with large depictions of cooking utensils. Adrian Walton, formerly of Partners West Street in Dorking (see entry), joined the kitchen team in April 1994, and a pleasing mix of old and new permeates a menu that will change with the seasons.

A quartet who ate in May reported an exciting start by the new regime. Parsleyed ham with beetroot chutney had 'sensuous, melting parsleyed vinous jelly and generous chunks of ham', 'intensely offally' lambs' tongues with mustard dressing was a 'very simple and quite delicious' starter, while the brandade on French beans with olive and tomato had all its flavours and textures working to perfection. Main courses are characterised by unabashed substantiality. Braised lamb shank with garlic and lemon had a crust of garlicky rosemary that 'had worked its way through to the bone in varying degrees so that every mouthful had a different balance of flavours', although the accompanying flageolets needed a little longer to attain the hoped-for 'oozy degree of internal collapse'. All the essence of long cooking was present in the 'intense and smoky' sauce. A cassoulet that included neck of duck made into a sausage was thought formidably good, and a gentler dish of salmon in puff pastry with a Pwllhelian garnish of leeks and laverbread and chive cream sauce also worked extremely well. Vegetables, said one tired of miniature things, 'had at least been given a chance to grow up'. The British farmhouse cheeses are of the best. St-Emilion au chocolat with spiced pears, crème brûlée or sherry trifle are dessert possibilities. Coffee is fine, and the staff are 'friendly and knowledgeable'. Now that dignity has been restored to this pillar of our culinary heritage, the Hole in the Wall looks set fair to produce great things.

The well-thought-out and attractively priced wine list more than matches the menu for eclecticism. Most of the wines are fairly youthful, but there are many good names, such as Rolly-Gassmann in Alsace, Fèvre in Chablis and Newton Vineyards in the Napa Valley. Halves abound, and much is available by the glass. House wines from southern France are £9. CELLARMAN'S CHOICE: Graves, Ch. Beauregard Ducasse 1990, £16; Arneis 1991, Damonte, £14.

CHEFS: Christopher Chown and Adrian Walton PROPRIETORS: Christopher and Gunna á Trødni OPEN: Mon to Sat; 12 to 2, 6 to 11 CLOSED: Christmas MEALS: alc (main courses £10). Set L Mon to Fri £9.50 (2 courses) SERVICE: not inc, card slips closed CARDS: Access, Visa DETAILS: 72 seats. Private parties: 18 main room. Vegetarian meals. Children welcome. No-smoking area. No music. Air-conditioned

▲ Queensberry Hotel, Olive Tree ⅋✳

Russel Street, Bath BA1 2QF	COOKING 2
BATH (0225) 447928	COST £19–£41

The Rosses' aim with the Olive Tree was to create a venue that would be used as a neighbourhood bistro in its own right, and thus avoid the stultification that can attend so many hotel dining-rooms. They certainly seem to have got the ambience right. Situated in the basement of the Queensberry, it is an agreeable room with pink-washed walls, tiled floor and angular black chairs. Menus change frequently, and – led by the market – fish is more prominently featured on Thursdays.

A French accent comes across in dishes such as provençale fish soup with rouille and croûtons, scallops grilled with apples in a sauce of their corals and cider, and roast guinea-fowl with lentils and smoked bacon. Hot chocolate pudding and custard, rice pudding blobbed with black cherry purée and apple feuilleté with cinnamon ice-cream are typical desserts. A man who dined on aubergine fritters with tomato coulis, rack of lamb and warm apple tart thought every dish 'stunningly good', while another pair enjoyed crab and saffron terrine with spiced tomato sauce and a 'very refreshing' grapefruit and Campari sorbet. Some have found flavours a bit stretched, as in a fish soup one night that had too much tomato and not enough fish, and one or two have complained of overcooked lamb. The wine list is sourced from good West Country suppliers such as Reid Wines and Yapp Brothers. It is concise and fairly priced, with nearly everything under £20. 'Wines of the month' are £10.50.

CHEFS: Stephen Ross, Rupert Pitt and Janice Wilmot   PROPRIETORS: Stephen and Penny Ross   OPEN: Mon to Sat; 12 to 2, 7 to 10 (post-theatre by arrangement)   CLOSED: 1 week Christmas   MEALS: alc (main courses £7.50 to £13). Set L £10.50, Set D Mon to Fri £17 SERVICE: not inc, card slips closed   CARDS: Access, Amex, Visa   DETAILS: 45 seats. Private parties: 25 main room, 16 private room. Vegetarian meals. Children's helpings. No smoking in dining-room. Wheelchair access (3 steps; also WC). Music   ACCOMMODATION: 22 rooms, all with bath/shower. TV. Phone. B&B £89 to £160. Lift. Children welcome. Baby facilities. Afternoon teas. Fax: (0225) 446065 (*The Which? Hotel Guide*)

▲ Royal Crescent Hotel, Dower House

15–16 Royal Crescent, Bath BA1 2LS   COOKING 2
BATH (0225) 319090   COST £27–£65

The setting is famously wonderful. The beautifully weathered building in an elegant crescent has a comfortable dining-room, spacious rather than intimate, with silver candlesticks and huge plates. Fixed-price menus with a choice of three or four items per course, and a *carte* twice that size, offer welcome flexibility. The cooking still has an opulent edge in its use of langoustines, lobster, foie gras and language: 'flowers of turbot', and a tranche of salmon 'cushioned on mange-tout with Jacqueline liquor', which on enquiry turned out to be a light sauce. 'Why not call it a light sauce then?' asked a down-to-earth reporter.

Praise has come for quail with tortellini bound in a red shallot dressing, langoustine brochette ('like a fishy doner kebab') with shredded leeks and a cream sauce, and rare breast of pigeon with foie gras and a truffle essence gravy. But some of the execution on occasion may appear to lose its way, with overcooking of that flowery turbot and, for one reporter, scallops served without their coral. Two completely different sauces at an inspection meal appeared very similar: one of 'spinach and cabbage liquor', the other made from vin jaune. 'Why do they taste the same?' 'Because they are the same,' came the reply. Is that uninformed service, or brutal honesty? The wine list majors on classic French, with token input from elsewhere, and mark-ups can be high. Half a dozen house wines from £11.75 are available also by the glass.

Several sharp operators have tried to extort money from restaurateurs on the promise of an entry in a guidebook that has never appeared. The Good Food Guide makes no charge for inclusion and does not offer certificates of any kind.

CHEF: Steven Blake   PROPRIETOR: Queens Moat Houses plc   OPEN: all week; 12.30 to 2, 7 to 9.30 (10 Fri and Sat)   MEALS: alc (main courses £18 to £20). Set L £14.50 (2 courses) to £18.50, Set D £30   SERVICE: not inc, card slips closed   CARDS: Access, Amex, Diners, Visa   DETAILS: 65 seats. 5 tables outside. Private parties: 80 main room, 45 private room. Car park. Vegetarian meals. Children's helpings. No children under 7 D. Smart dress preferred. No cigars/pipes in dining-room. Wheelchair access (1 step; also WC). Music   ACCOMMODATION: 42 rooms, all with bath/shower. TV. Phone. Air-conditioned (some rooms). B&B £108 to £381.50. Rooms for disabled. Lift. Children welcome. Pets welcome (not in public rooms). Afternoon teas. Garden. Confirm by noon. Fax: (0225) 339401 (*The Which? Hotel Guide*)

Woods

9–13 Alfred Street, Bath BA1 2QX   COOKING 1
BATH (0225) 314812   COST £17–£34

David Price's well-established restaurant adjacent to the Assembly Rooms continues to offer good value in Georgian Bath. Racing prints line the hessian walls and extra tables have been squeezed into the bar area. The atmosphere hums and a bevy of young waitresses keeps things moving at a pace. Kirk Vincent's cooking is inventive, colourful and nicely judged. He can turn his hand to anything from thick fish soup with rouille, and Thai squid with Japanese pickled vegetables, to roast Gressingham duckling with spiced pears on a maple syrup sauce. Sweets (from 'Cholesterol corner') might include a combination of filo parcels of dried fruits marinated in calvados and orange with a hot butterscotch sauce. On Sundays, children under eight eat at half-price in the brasserie and have the chance to meet Kooky the Clown. The wine list takes in classic clarets as well as some decent bottles from the New World. House wines start at £9.50.

CHEF: Kirk Vincent   PROPRIETORS: David and Claude Price   OPEN: all week, exc Sun D restaurant; restaurant 12 to 2.30, 6 to 11; brasserie 11am to 11pm (3 Sat, 7 Sun)   CLOSED: 24 to 26 Dec   MEALS: alc (main courses L £4 to £7, D £11). Set L Sun £10, Set D Mon to Fri £10.95, Sat £18.95   SERVICE: not inc, card slips closed   CARDS: Access, Amex, Visa   DETAILS: 120 seats. 6 tables outside. Private parties: 80 main room, 40 private room. Vegetarian meals. Children's helpings. Smart dress preferred. No cigars/pipes in dining-room. Wheelchair access (2 steps; also WC). Music. Fax: (0225) 443146

BEAMINSTER Dorset   map 2

▲ Bridge House 🔆

3 Prout Bridge, Beaminster DT8 3AY   COOKING 1
BRIDPORT (0308) 862200   COST £17–£38

Watch out for the Lady in Blue! A friendly ghost is said to float through the oldest parts of this converted thirteenth-century clergy house deep in Hardy's Wessex. Books by the man himself and baskets of dried flowers add to the 'delightful' mood of the place. No music plays. Lindsay Wakeman cooks capably and rings the changes with her *carte* and table d'hôte menus. Fish gets a good airing with dishes such as baked red mullet with tomato and basil, or poached skate with prawn and saffron sauce. New ideas appear from time to time, although staunch regulars often settle for roast best end of lamb and fillet of Aberdeen Angus beef.

Framing the main dishes you might find first-rate mussels, 'faultless' filo pastry cases filled with bacon and mushrooms, chocolate bavarois and créme brûlée. Excellent walnut bread is a bonus. The wine list will undoubtedly benefit from the change to main suppliers Reynier/Eldridge Pope. House wines start at £7.50.

CHEFS: Lindsay Wakeman and Peter Pinkster PROPRIETOR: Peter Pinkster OPEN: all week; 12.30 to 1.45, 7 to 8.30 (9 Sat and all days summer) CLOSED: 25 and 26 Dec MEALS: alc (main courses £11 to £14). Set L £9.95 (2 courses), Set D £16.50 (Set L and D not available Christmas) SERVICE: not inc, card slips closed CARDS: Access, Amex, Diners, Visa DETAILS: 36 seats. 3 tables outside. Private parties: 48 main room, 14 private room. Car park. Vegetarian meals. Children's helpings on request. Smart dress preferred. No smoking in dining-room. No music ACCOMMODATION: 14 rooms, all with bath/shower. TV. Phone. B&B £35 to £92. Deposit: £25. Children welcome. Pets welcome (not in public rooms or unattended in bedrooms). Afternoon teas. Garden. Doors close at 11.30. Confirm by 6. Fax: (0308) 863700 (*The Which? Hotel Guide*)

BECKINGHAM Lincolnshire   map 6

Black Swan 🍴✳

Hillside, Beckingham LN5 0RF
NEWARK (0636) 626474   COOKING 2
off A17 to Sleaford, 6m E of Newark   COST £18–£37

The Swan has made its home in a whitewashed seventeenth-century coaching-inn by the River Witham in this sleepy old village. Drive boldly down the no-through road to reach it. Inside is very small, even congested at busy mealtimes. The fixed-price menus usually include a choice of three starters and mains and four desserts. Extras of sorbet, cheese and coffee can then be slotted in. At Sunday lunch, children under 11 ('one child per adult') may eat for nothing.

The food is on the gentle side of modern British, resists forcing ingredients into unwilling combinations, but brings off tricks like saucing fish with a chicken stock. At a Sunday lunch in April, fish soup with lemon and saffron in which floated quenelles of fish mousse with tarragon was 'light and refreshing' and balanced its flavours well, while a tartlet of chicken, spinach and bacon came with a well-dressed salad but also an inappropriate stock-based sauce. Breast of pheasant topped with a layer of minced mushrooms and herbs baked in filo was a good main course and came with a 'rich and very stocky' brown ale sauce – an unusual idea that worked. Grilled sirloin was on the tough side, but the chicken stock sauce really lifted a dish of turbot fillets on spinach. Hot soufflés such as rum and raisin prove popular with regulars, but apple tart with vanilla ice-cream is also 'perfectly fine'. Service – resplendent in white gloves – can be a little bit awkward when under duress. The wine list is an honest attempt to provide some good drinking at generally reasonable prices. There is much under £20 but still a lack of producers' names. House French is £7.90.

CHEFS: Anton Indans and Claire Rogers PROPRIETORS: Mr and Mrs Anton Indans OPEN: Tue to Sun, D only, and Sun L (Tue to Sat L by arrangement); 12 to 2, 7 to 10 CLOSED: 25 and 26 Dec MEALS: Set L Tue to Sat £14.75, Sun £12.50, Set D £14.75 to £19.90 SERVICE: not inc CARDS: Access, Visa DETAILS: 36 seats. 4 tables outside. Private parties: 26 main room, 12 and 26 private rooms. Car park. Vegetarian meals. Children welcome. Smart dress preferred. No smoking in dining-room. Wheelchair access (also WC). No music

BERWICK-UPON-TWEED Northumberland   map 7

▲ *Funnywayt'mekalivin*

41 Bridge Street,
Berwick-upon-Tweed TD15 1ES   COOKING **2***
BERWICK-UPON-TWEED (0289) 308827   COST £13–£32

There is no stopping Elizabeth Middlemiss. In addition to dinners and buffet
lunches, she now offers bed and breakfast in rooms above her converted
plumber's shop. The food continues to delight: one visitor felt that it compared
very favourably with the best of its kind in provincial France. 'Impeccable' was
the verdict on a four-course evening meal that included carrot and orange soup
with roughly hewn home-baked bread, spongey salmon and prawn roulade,
pork steak with a delicate sauce of cider, mushrooms and cream plus a helping of
perfectly cooked vegetables, followed by a slice of bramble, pear and almond tart
that had 'a magical flavour'. On other occasions, reporters have enjoyed
cauliflower mousse, crêpes florentine, apricot parfait and cranachan (raspberries
with cream, toasted oatmeal and Drambuie). The home-made ice-creams are
reckoned to be out of this world and the option of ripe cheese with oatcakes is
worth following up. Meals kick off with an aperitif of kir and canapés and end
with good coffee and home-made truffles. Service is attentive without being
over-familiar. The wine list is very keenly priced and the New World contingent
is especially good. House wines are £7.95 and £8.25.

CHEF: Elizabeth Middlemiss   PROPRIETORS: Mr and Mrs Middlemiss   OPEN: Mon to Sat L, Wed
to Sat D; 11.30 to 2.30, 7.30 for 8   CLOSED: 25 and 26 Dec, 1 Jan   MEALS: alc L (main courses
£4 to £5). Set D £22.50   SERVICE: net prices, card slips closed   CARDS: Access, Visa   DETAILS:
38 seats. 4 tables outside. Private parties: 26 main room, 8 private room. Vegetarian meals.
Children's helpings. Smart dress preferred. No smoking L, no smoking during meal D. Music
ACCOMMODATION: 3 rooms. TV. B&B £20 to £40. Deposit: £10. Children welcome. Baby facilities

---

BEXHILL East Sussex   map 3

Lychgates

5A Church Street, Old Town,
Bexhill TN40 2HE   COOKING **2**
BEXHILL (0424) 212193   COST £18–£32

Deep in Bexhill's old town, next to St Peter's church and a mile away from the
sea, this small restaurant of modest ambitions has found the going a little tough
in the last couple of recessionary years. It is a shame because visitors usually
come away feeling well and capably fed by John Tyson's sensitive French
cooking. The homely dining-room is the setting for a very cheap three-course
lunch menu with coffee, and alternative three- and five-course offerings in the
evening. A lot of boning and stuffing goes on, and sauces tend to the old-school
richness of cream and alcohol. Squid provençale had tender, sweet squid stewed
with tomatoes and anchovy, and was greatly enjoyed. A ballottine of chicken
was a highly flavoured leg of the bird stuffed with pear and ginger on a madeira
sauce. The pear contributed moistness rather than taste, but there was enough
going on to make the dish a success. Cream, Stilton and cider formed the 'superb'

213

sauce for strips of sauté pork fillet. Chocolate truffle gâteau is as boozy as everything else, and the crème brûlée has its adherents. The Tysons deserve more support when Bexhill feels ready again to venture out to restaurants. The wine list is still spread a little thinly around the classic French regions, although a scattering of New World wines does help. House French is £8.75.

CHEF: John Tyson   PROPRIETORS: John and Sue Tyson   OPEN: Tue to Sun, exc Sun D (L bookings only); 12.30 to 2, 7 to 10.30   CLOSED: 25 Dec, 2 weeks summer   MEALS: Set L £10 (2 courses) to £12.95, Set D £18.50 to £21.95   SERVICE: card slips closed   CARDS: Access, Visa   DETAILS: 28 seats. Private parties: 18 main room. Vegetarian meals (vegans with prior notice). Children's helpings. No cigars/pipes in dining-room. Wheelchair access. No music

---

BIBURY Gloucestershire   map 2

▲ Swan Hotel ⁵⁄ₓ | NEW ENTRY |

Bibury GL7 5NW   COOKING 3*
CIRENCESTER (0285) 740695   COST £23–£56

The long, creeper-covered building is an ancient inn opposite the bridge over the trout-filled River Coln. 'The reception hall boasts an automatic piano that drones out anonymous noise whenever the staff remember to switch it on', while the dining-room is large, high-ceilinged like a ballroom, and bedecked with ornate plaster cornices. Red and gold are the colours, most surfaces bearing a circular emblem of a swan.

The menu offers a generous, indeed ambitious, selection of items, some of them quite involved: for instance, boneless chicken winglets filled with herb mousse, pan-fried with shallots and smoked bacon, and served around a tartlet of quail's eggs with sherry vinegar juices. The fixed-price multi-choice pattern is three courses plus a taster of Bibury trout to begin, and a mid-meal soup or sorbet. It is a mark of the kitchen's commitment that these incidentals are smartly handled, the first a small square, fresh, grilled, with an intense accompanying smear of creamy deep-brown stock. The sorbet of summer fruits was as good as our inspector had ever eaten, freshly made with 'a perfect consistency and temperature'.

Ingredients, flavours, textures and combinations were all impressive in an inspection meal that began with well-integrated ratatouille (using good olive oil) to accompany chunks of fresh black bream, and went on to a main course of roast woodpigeon – 'a pyramid of overlapping rough slices of superb quality, superbly timed'. Also on the plate was a boudin of foie gras and chicken – 'very soft, very luscious, very decadent'. Vegetables were up to standard, and the dessert combined white chocolate and red fruits in a many-layered construction, crunch provided by chopped roasted hazelnuts mixed with cream. The sense of excitement, and of some brilliant cooking, was sustained to the end.

The cooking score indicates the level of talent the kitchen delivered at this inspection, although we have also received reports of food that is well below par. Coffee is better than the petits fours, while service has involved some very long waits. Staff are 'exceptionally nice' and 'give the impression that they really care', although they are not always clued up. Although the wine list is long, 'several bottles we tried to order were not available'. House wines are from £13.

Jankowski's, in the same building, is an informal brasserie open all day every day for coffee, afternoon tea, snacks, salads and more substantial meals of couscous or chargrilled blue shark.

CHEF: Guy Bossom PROPRIETORS: Mrs E.A. Hayles and Mr J.A. Furtek OPEN: all week, D only, and Sun L; 12.30 to 2, 7.30 to 9.30 MEALS: Set L Sun £15.95, Set D £35 SERVICE: net prices, card slips closed CARDS: Access, Amex, Diners, Visa DETAILS: 60 seats. Private parties: 80 main room, 10 private room. Car park. Vegetarian meals. Children's helpings. Jacket and tie D. No smoking in dining-room. Wheelchair access (also WC). No music ACCOMMODATION: 18 rooms, all with bath/shower. TV. Phone. Room only £97 to £210. Deposit: £50. Children welcome. Baby facilities. Afternoon teas. Garden. Fishing. Doors close at 11.30. Confirm by noon. Fax: (0285) 740473 (*The Which? Hotel Guide*)

BILLESLEY Warwickshire   map 2

▲ Billesley Manor ♈

Billesley B49 6NF
STRATFORD-UPON-AVON (0789) 400888   COOKING 2*
off A46, 3m W of Stratford-upon-Avon   COST £25–£55

Since road numbers were changed, this sixteenth-century country hotel is now to be found about half a mile off the A46. It is worth the detour. Outside are fine gardens and topiary; inside, all is grand and impeccably laid out. Mark Naylor's cooking is in the modern mould of medallions of venison with rhubarb chutney, John Dory with saffron and fennel, and Gressingham duck with parsnip and honey purée plus gin and juniper sauce, backed up by fish specials and roasts carved from the trolley. The good-value fixed-price lunch has pleased reporters, who have mentioned a crisp salad of smoked duck and bacon strips, herby rack of lamb with caramelised onions, an 'odd combination' of 'excellent' salmon with sun-dried tomatoes, and warm Bakewell tart with raspberry coulis. Details such as dainty sweetmeats have also found favour with visitors. Service is youthful and attentive, without being fussy. The wine list is a sound selection with good quality across the board, a fair spread of vintages where appropriate, and a helpful star system to highlight particularly good value. House wine is £10.50 (£2.25 per glass). CELLARMAN'S CHOICE: Menetou-Salon 1992, Dom. Clément, £18.75; Pinot Noir Herrenweg 1990, Zind-Humbrecht, £25.50.

CHEF: Mark Naylor PROPRIETOR: Queens Moat Houses plc OPEN: all week; 12.30 to 2, 7.30 to 9.30 (10pm Fri and Sat) MEALS: alc (main courses £15 to £19). Set L £17, Set D £27 SERVICE: not inc, card slips closed CARDS: Access, Amex, Diners, Visa DETAILS: 80 seats. 6 tables outside. Private parties: 100 main room, 14 to 40 private rooms. Car park. Vegetarian meals. Children's helpings. Jacket and tie D. No cigars/pipes in dining-room. No music ACCOMMODATION: 41 rooms, all with bath/shower. TV. Phone. B&B £99 to £160. Children welcome. Pets welcome. Afternoon teas. Garden. Swimming-pool. Tennis. Doors close at 1am. Confirm by 6. Fax: (0789) 764145

'The intermittent background music was not intrusive, but it was notably half-hearted. Do they want us to hear it or not? (I'd prefer not, especially as one track featured that dreadful cliché, the French accordion.)' (On eating in London)

BIRCH VALE Derbyshire

map 5

▲ *Waltzing Weasel*

New Mills Road, Birch Vale SK12 5BT
NEW MILLS (0663) 743402
on A6015, ½m W of Hayfield

COOKING 1
COST £26–£36

'People still come here for a pint or two and a chat, and are treated with exactly the same courtesy as if they were high spenders in the restaurant,' writes one who has enjoyed doing both. The view is a big attraction too, across to Kinder Scout. Lunch is a carvery, a lavish spread that includes a huge salmon, game pie, a couple of flans and some interesting salads, as well as pink roast rib of beef, 'juicy, tasty, with a nice rim of crisp fat'.

George Benham's cooking is in the solidly satisfying British mould of Barnsley chop, venison in puff pastry, and beef cooked in beer and served with dumplings, all based on sound ingredients that deliver freshness and flavour. 'A lovely thick piece of halibut, perfectly cooked' is the kind of result that reporters appreciate. Vegetables are plain, fresh, well cooked, 'salads are as good as they look', and the cheese selection includes Stilton, Shropshire Blue, Lancashire, Cheddar and Yarg. Among puddings, a rich dark chocolate mousse has been singled out for praise. Service is happy and professional, and the moderately priced wine list is just right for the job. House French is £8.25 (£1.75 per glass).

CHEF: George Benham   PROPRIETORS: Linda and Michael Atkinson   OPEN: all week; 12 to 2, 7 to 9   CLOSED: 25 Dec   MEALS: Set D £19.50 (2 courses) to £23.50. Bar menu L   SERVICE: not inc, card slips closed   CARDS: Access, Amex, Visa   DETAILS: 30 seats. 2 tables outside. Private parties: 32 main room. Car park. Vegetarian meals. Children's helpings. No children under 5. Smart dress preferred. Wheelchair access (1 step). No music. Air-conditioned ACCOMMODATION: 8 rooms, all with bath/shower. TV. Phone. Air-conditioned. B&B £45 to £95. Deposit: £20. No children under 12. Pets by arrangement. Garden. Fishing. Doors close at 12.30am. Confirm by 4. Fax: (0663) 743402 (*The Which? Hotel Guide*)

BIRDLIP Gloucestershire

map 2

▲ *Kingshead House* ▼

Birdlip GL4 8JH
GLOUCESTER (0452) 862299
½m off A417 between Gloucester and
Cirencester, on B4070 towards Stroud

COOKING 1*
COST £22–£43

Warren and Judy Knock's restaurant with room (for there is only one) was once a coaching-inn. Intimations of a bygone era are preserved in the green and white dining-room with its shiny floorboards, old stone fireplace and classical music. Judy Knock's menus have a slightly revivalist feel to them as well; although she is constantly trying out new ideas, the tone is recognisably early modern British. When things go well, her cooking delivers bold, fresh flavours, but an inspection meal revealed some unevenness of production.

From the fixed-price dinner menu (of three or four courses, as you wish, plus coffee) a summer salad of monkfish and prawns had 'excellent ingredients and attractive presentation' and good walnut oil dressing, but a second-course salad of marinated vegetables with garlic-topped focaccia seemed clumsier. Lamb's liver with orange and Dubonnet sauce showed faltering judgement with overcooked liver and a too-sweet sauce, but an apricot and almond tart to finish had good pastry and an 'interesting, intense' amaretto ice-cream. Others have enjoyed mushroom blini, grilled beef fillet with a 'sharp' caper sauce and 'memorably good' rhubarb and gingerbread tart. Vegetables come in profusion, fine home-made chocolate truffles arrive with coffee and service is 'amiable'. The handwritten wine list, replete with Warren Knock's extensive notes, provides a generous spread of choice from around the world, with the vast majority of bottles under £20. Half-bottles are plentiful. House wines are from £9.80. CELLARMAN'S CHOICE: Pinot Bianco 'Alla Pergole' 1991, Longariva, £13.50; Bourgogne Pinot Noir 1990, Dom. Parent, £16.50.

CHEF: Judy Knock   PROPRIETORS: Judy and Warren Knock   OPEN: Tue to Sun, exc Sat L and Sun D; 12.30 to 1.45, 7.30 to 9.45   CLOSED: 26 and 27 Dec, 1 Jan   MEALS: alc L Tue to Fri (main courses £7 to £10). Set L Sun £15.50, Set D £22.50 to £24.50   SERVICE: not inc (10% for 6 or more)   CARDS: Access, Amex, Diners, Visa   DETAILS: 34 seats. 3 tables outside. Private parties: 34 main room. Car park. Vegetarian meals. Children's helpings. Smart dress preferred. No smoking while others eat. Wheelchair access (also WC). Music   ACCOMMODATION: 1 room with bath/shower. TV. B&B £32 to £52. Deposit: £10. Children welcome. Pets by arrangement. Garden. Doors close at midnight. Confirm by 6

BIRKENHEAD Merseyside   map 5

Beadles

15 Rosemount, Oxton, Birkenhead L43 5SG   COOKING 1
051-653 9010   COST £23–£31

The building in the centre of Oxton village dates from 1847, and the double-shop front is original. Bea Gott's cooking is not old-fashioned, though. The strengths are good fresh fish posted up daily and simply cooked, and a short but wide-ranging menu that starts lively, moves to satisfying main courses and ends on a positively comforting note with hot cardamom bananas and crème fraîche, tiramisù, or dark and white chocolate marquise. High points among the flavours come with lovage soup, mussels in cumin sauce, Thai-style seared beef salad, or else a red onion and coriander salsa served with roast breast of chicken. Many dishes are 'the sort one could eat every day without tiring of', including perhaps gnocchi with pesto, roast red peppers stuffed with anchovies and parmesan, or confit of duck leg with butter-beans. That is the essence of a good neighbourhood restaurant: to be able to keep the regulars happy, week in, week out, and to field a sensible wine list that takes £15 as its ceiling (apart from Champagne). House French is £6.50.

CHEF: Bea Gott   PROPRIETORS: Roy and Bea Gott   OPEN: Tue to Sat, D only; 7.30 to 9 CLOSED: 2 weeks Aug and Sept   MEALS: alc (main courses £9 to £10.50)   SERVICE: not inc (10% for 6 or more), card slips closed   CARDS: Access, Visa   DETAILS: 34 seats. Private parties: 34 main room. Vegetarian meals with prior notice. No children under 7. Smart dress preferred. Wheelchair access (1 step). Music

---

Not inc *in the details at the end of an entry indicates that no service charge is made and any tipping is at the discretion of the customer.*

BIRMINGHAM West Midlands — map 5

Chung Ying £

16–18 Wrottesley Street, B5 4RT
021-622 5669

COOKING 1
COST £16–£43

Competition is hotting up in Birmingham's Chinese quarter, and this well-established Cantonese restaurant is now being challenged by bullish young neighbours. However, it still has the power to excite, as a man of the cloth was able to testify: 'How can they have such a huge variety of food (nearly 300 dishes!) ready for almost instant service. At 6.45 on a Saturday evening the place was thriving with families: I can only imagine what the kitchen was like!' He chose what his wife 'would not have allowed on the table' and was delighted with shark's fin and sweetcorn soup, ox-tripe with ginger, and a massive mixed-meat chow mein 'stuffed with at least a dozen chunks of meat, prawns and unidentified objects'. Other reporters have endorsed items from the vast list of dim-sum – especially stuffed green pepper and Shanghai dumplings. The menu is strong on seafood, casseroles, roast meats and one-plate meals, although there have also been comments relating to 'rubbery' deep-fried squid, and 'dry' spare ribs. The atmosphere is one of 'controlled bustle' and service is generally 'electric'. House wine is £8.50.

CHEF/PROPRIETOR: Siu Chung Wong OPEN: all week; noon to 11.30pm (Sun 10.30) CLOSED: 25 Dec MEALS: alc (main courses £5 to £12). Set L and D £8.50 to £10.60 (minimum 2 to 6) SERVICE: not inc CARDS: Access, Amex, Diners, Visa DETAILS: 200 seats. Private parties: 120 main room, 120 private room. Vegetarian meals. Children welcome. Smart dress preferred. Wheelchair access (2 steps). Music. Air-conditioned. Fax: 021-666 7051

Chung Ying Garden

17 Thorp Street, B5 4AT
021-666 6622

COOKING 2
COST £21–£38

Crowds are returning to this glitzy restaurant on the fringe of Birmingham's Chinese quarter, and the kitchen is responding with arguably the best Cantonese food in the city. Enter through smoked-glass doors, go up stairs lit by fairy lights into a spacious dining-room defined by massive marbled pillars, huge murals and a mini-canopy billowing from the ceiling.

The menu is a gargantuan tome running to over 300 dishes. Forty dim-sum, including steamed spare ribs with plum sauce, and crispy wun-tun and green pepper stuffed with minced prawn, are impeccable examples of the genre; elsewhere, you will find scores of one-plate rice and noodle dishes, plus authentic hotpots and casseroles. The strong, earthy flavours of stewed duck with yams, braised fish-head with belly pork, spicy squid stuffed with minced prawn, and stuffed beancurd with aubergines are balanced by more delicate, Western-sounding specialities, including fried fillet of halibut in cream sauce and deep-fried chicken stuffed with banana. Dishes are handled with care and thoroughness, presentation is neat, and portions are generous. Service gets a clean bill of health: the waiters are generally sharp, quick and knowledgeable. House wine is £8.95.

CHEF/PROPRIETOR: Siu Chung Wong   OPEN: all week, exc Sun D; noon to midnight (11 Sun)
MEALS: alc (main courses £4.50 to £10.50). Set L and D £12.90 to £16   SERVICE: not inc
CARDS: Access, Amex, Diners, Visa   DETAILS: 350 seats. Private parties: 200 main room, 40, 60
and 70 private rooms. Vegetarian meals. Children welcome. Wheelchair access (also WC).
Music. Air-conditioned. Fax: 021-622 5860

Henrys £

27 St Pauls Square, B3 1RB   COOKING 1
021-200 1136   COST £20–£46

Henry Wong's restaurant in Birmingham's newly fashionable jewellery quarter
offers the prospect of civilised Chinese food in a rather elegant setting of striking
prints and murals. The cooking is sound, although some reporters feel it lacks
the authentic 'edge' of some other comparable restaurants in the city. Peking and
Cantonese dishes rub shoulders on the menu, which offers around 100 mostly
familiar specialities, including crispy aromatic duck, deep-fried squid, chicken
with lemon sauce and bean curd in black-bean sauce. Sizzling is applied to
everything from oysters and grilled salmon to loin of lamb and vegetarian
wun-tun. The short wine list has several bottles that suit the food admirably.
House wine is £8.

CHEF: William Choi   PROPRIETOR: Henry Wong   OPEN: Mon to Sat; 12 to 2, 6 to 11 (11.30 Fri
and Sat)   MEALS: alc (main courses £6 to £9). Set L and D £13 (minimum 2)   SERVICE: not inc
CARDS: Access, Amex, Diners, Visa   DETAILS: 140 seats. Private parties: 140 main room, 40
private room. Vegetarian meals. Children's helpings. Smart dress preferred. Music. Air-
conditioned

Maharaja £

23–25 Hurst Street, B5 4AS   COOKING 1*
021-622 2641   COST £14–£30

'It is one of the most cultured curry houses I know,' observed a reporter about
this unchanging, civilised restaurant not far from the Hippodrome. The modest
dining areas (one in the basement) are done out in pinks and blues and the walls
are festooned with mystical paintings, scenes of courtly life and prints of Indian
textile art; the music is classical ragas of uncompromising duration and
complexity. Service is discreet, ever courteous and as carefully paced as you
could wish for. The menu eschews new-wave trickery and fashionable baltis in
favour of a short repertoire of north Indian and Punjabi dishes. Flavours are
distinctive, spicing is vivid and the kitchen does not hold back on the green
chillies: they liven up excellent aloo tikkian (deep-fried potato rissoles), give a
final flourish to chana masaladar, and add fire to masala kulcha bread. The
kitchen can also deliver tandooris, chicken sagwala (with finely prepared
spinach), lamb pasanda and prawn biriani. The wine list has plenty of creditable
drinking for under £10. House wine is £6.80.

An asterisk (*) after the 1 to 5 cooking mark at the top of an entry signifies that the Guide
and its readers think that the restaurant is a particularly fine example within its rating.

CHEF: Bhupinder Waraich   PROPRIETOR: N.S. Batt   OPEN: Mon to Sat; 12 to 2.30, 6 to 11.30
MEALS: alc (main courses £5.50 to £7.50). Set L £7.50 (2 courses), Set D £10.75. Minimum £7
SERVICE: 10%, card slips closed   CARDS: Access, Amex, Diners, Visa   DETAILS: 62 seats.
Private parties: 30 main room. Vegetarian meals. Children welcome. Smart dress preferred.
Wheelchair access (also WC). Music. Air-conditioned

Sloans ﹢�֍ ♟

27–29 Chad Square, Hawthorne Road,	
Edgbaston, B15 3TQ	COOKING 2
021-455 6697	COST £22–£51

The location is suburban, close to the Botanical Gardens, and the food European,
although of no particular national persuasion. Lunch is the more interesting
option, with a choice of four, four and three items per course respectively,
beginning, for example, with cabbage and smoked bacon soup with savoury
dumplings, or a scallop and oyster chowder, and ending with pecan pie with hot
chocolate sauce, or treacle pudding with vanilla ice-cream.

Invention thrives best in fish dishes: fillets of grey mullet are pan-fried in
sesame oil with bean sprouts, spring onions, black beans and coriander, while
fillets of mackerel come with pasta and pesto. Salmon may be topped with a
celeriac soubise, and served with trompette mushrooms and flageolet beans.
Presentation is good, so is pastry, and 'saucing is much above average'. Whole
breast of wood pigeon, and fillets of rabbit (marinated with thyme, served on
fondant potato with sweet chestnut and armagnac) add interest to a *carte* of lamb,
rib of beef, duck and roast chicken. Vegetables and salads are extra. Wines are
predominantly French and varied in style. Although some prices are high (only
half a dozen clarets out of 44 are under £20), so is the quality. A page of French
country wines and a fair selection of half-bottles are helpful. House wine is
£8.75. CELLARMAN'S CHOICE Haute Garonne Chardonnay 1991, £15.25; Côtes
du Jura Pinot Noir 1988, £14.25.

CHEF: Simon Booth   PROPRIETORS: Roger Narbett and John Narbett   OPEN: Mon to Sat, exc
Sat L; 12 to 2.15, 7 to 10 (10.30 Sat)   MEALS: alc (main courses £10.50 to £14.50). Set L £11 (2
courses) to £14   SERVICE: not inc (10% for parties of 8 or more)   CARDS: Access, Amex, Diners,
Visa   DETAILS: 68 seats. Private parties: 80 main room. Car park. Vegetarian meals. Children
welcome. Smart dress preferred. No-smoking room. Wheelchair access (1 step; also WC).
Music. Air-conditioned. Fax: 021-454 4335

BIRTLE Greater Manchester   map 5

▲ *Normandie* ▮

Elbut Lane, Birtle BL9 6UT	
061-764 3869 and 1170	COOKING 4
off B6222, 3m NE of Bury	COST £20–£52

'The building is no beauty, and hasn't been since the Champeau family extended
the old inn.' That was some time ago, and although the Moussas are stuck with
the structure they have at least made the inside welcoming and comfortable. It

has the smack of a Mediterranean villa, an illusion easily dispelled by looking out of the window across to Manchester.

Pascal Pommier's cooking is impressive, his timing and seasoning spot on. While the food may not be at the front of the field for creativity and innovation, neither does it rely on flash ingredients or fussy embellishments to make an impact. Lengthy and finicky preparation may be involved, but the result on the plate is effective. A dish of squab pigeon includes not just the tender breasts but a puff pastry parcel attached to a handle (one of the leg bones) containing leg meat, mushrooms and herbs. Overall the cooking has a confidence based on sound technique and an understanding of how flavours and textures work together.

Fish is first-class, very fresh and well handled: light treatment invariably brings out the best, and pastrywork is good. An inspector enjoyed both aspects together in a fricassee of seafood in a large vol-au-vent, with a creamy shellfish sauce scattered with seafood and pea-sized vegetables. Among many dishes that reporters have endorsed are mussels with blinis which are 'a cross between Yorkshire pudding and an oven-baked omelette'.

Dishes on the *carte* are self-contained, prices are not greedy, and the three-course lunch (with a choice of two items at each stage) is considered good value; the chef throws in 'an additional something' at the start which can fairly be considered a part of the meal, and coffee and petits fours are included. One reporter enjoyed a lunch of tomato soup, salmon on a bed of samphire with a well-judged sorrel sauce, and a pudding involving a roast pear, cinnamon, honey, a pastry basket and ice-cream. Indeed, puddings have received as much praise as anything, including 'unbelievably good' pears with caramelised pastry layers, and a chocolate tart with a rich melting inside on a good short-crust pastry base, with a domed top that looked like a soufflé, and a zesty orange sauce all around.

Good raisin and nut bread comes with cheese, and the fact that a charge for the business-like service is neither included nor expected adds greatly to reporters' enjoyment. Wines make a real effort to cater for all tastes and pockets without sacrificing quality. The list provides security and predictability among the big names, but adds a bit of spice in, for example, the all-too-short Italian section. It even sticks up for Asti Spumante. Mark-ups are reasonable, and good house wines begin at £12.25 (£2.50 per glass). CELLARMAN'S CHOICE: Sylvaner d'Alsace 1992, Sipp, £16.96; Côte de Beaune 'Maranges' 1988, Dom. Chevrot, £26.50.

CHEF: Pascal Pommier PROPRIETORS: Gillian and Max Moussa OPEN: Mon to Sat, exc L mon and Sat; 12 to 2, 7 to 9.30 CLOSED: 2 weeks from 26 Dec, 1 week Easter, bank hols (exc 25 Dec) MEALS: alc (main courses £10.50 to £21.50). Set L £12.50 (2 courses) to £15, Set D £18.95 SERVICE: card slips closed CARDS: Access, Amex, Diners, Visa DETAILS: 60 seats. Private parties: 50 main room. Car park. Vegetarian meals. Children's helpings on request. Smart dress preferred. No cigars/pipes in dining-room. Wheelchair access (1 step; also WC). Music ACCOMMODATION: 23 rooms, all with bath/shower. TV. Phone. B&B £49 to £79. Rooms for disabled. Lift. Children welcome. Baby facilities. Garden. Confirm by noon. Fax: 061-764 4866

Card slips closed *in the details at the end of an entry indicates that the total on the slips of credit cards is closed when handed over for signature.*

BISHOP'S TACHBROOK Warwickshire map 2

▲ *Mallory Court* ♥

Harbury Lane,
Bishop's Tachbrook CV33 9QB
LEAMINGTON SPA (0926) 330214
off B4087, 2m S of Leamington Spa

COOKING 3
COST £32–£84

Near Bishop's Tachbrook, not in it, is the location, so watch carefully for Mallory Court signs on trees. The manor is less imposing than many, although the door is opened on arrival by observant staff. The well-kept garden is restful, the floral wallpaper in the lounge less so, while tables in the oak-panelled dining-room are grandly disposed. 'A hotel of supreme charm,' noted one reporter, 'although knowing it was a hotel almost caused us to avoid it.' The poor reputation of hotel catering lingers – not the fault of Mallory Court, which does its best to remove the blemish.

The menus afford two crumbs of financial comfort. The 'Gourmet' menu at £60 is quite possibly a bargain compared with à la carte prices for the same dishes, and 'no service charge is made or expected', which is welcome news. Even so, a saddle of rabbit for two at £47 is one expensive bunny. The menu reassures with its strong classical vein and modern, sometimes quite light, treatments. Fish stands out for freshness: scallops and braised fillet of turbot at one meal, both accurately timed and brilliantly successful. The coral mousse accompanying the chargrilled white scallop muscle just missed the mark for texture and flavour, and 'wild' mushrooms with the turbot amounted to buttons, shiitake and oysters, but the fish itself was good enough to rise above all that. Saucing impresses, from a delicately gingery emulsion with the scallops, and sieved tomato flesh flecked with torn basil leaves for ravioli of spinach and ricotta, to a sensitive reduction for a dish of Gressingham duck, marred only by excessive reliance on orange for flavouring.

Vegetables are individually tailored for each main course, although they may be more approximately cooked than anything else on the menu. Desserts are a sensation, including a large wedge of glazed lemon tart with a rich curdy filling, good pastry and perfectly judged glaze. Passion-fruit soufflé (with sorbet) is impeccable and technically perfect. Service by a young team keeps the atmosphere light. Wines range from classic Bordeaux to new-wave Californian by way of short but good selections from Alsace, Rhône, Italy, Spain and the Antipodes. Prices are on the high side. House wine begins at £8.95. CELLARMAN'S CHOICE: Wairau River Sauvignon Blanc 1992; Corbières Ch. les Ollieux Romanis 1990, £13.25.

CHEF: Alan Holland PROPRIETORS: Alan Holland and Jeremy Mort OPEN: all week; 12.30 to 2, 7 to 9.45 CLOSED: 3 to 12 Jan MEALS: alc (main courses £23 to £27.50). Set L £19.50 (2 courses) to £23.50, Set D £30, Set gourmet L and D £60 SERVICE: card slips closed CARDS: Access, Amex, Visa DETAILS: 50 seats. Private parties: 50 main room. Car park. Vegetarian meals. No children under 9. Smart dress preferred. No cigars/pipes in dining-room. Wheelchair access (2 steps). No music ACCOMMODATION: 10 rooms, all with bath/shower. TV. Phone. B&B £98 to £210. No children under 9. Afternoon teas. Garden. Swimming-pool. Tennis. Doors close at midnight. Fax: (0926) 451714

BLACKPOOL Lancashire   map 5

September Brasserie

15–17 Queen Street, Blackpool FY1 1PU	COOKING 2
BLACKPOOL (0253) 23282	COST £19–£42

It is an unlikely combination: Pat Wood (hairdresser) and Michael Golowicz (cook) joined forces in 1989 to open a brasserie above a hair studio. Much is packed into a small space, so it may feel a bit cramped, and front window seats are coveted. Lunch-times are more café-like and better value, with bare-topped tables and less expensive main courses.

The cooking is robust and often approximate, and some of the flavour combinations seem to have escaped the drawing board prematurely: chunky jellied rabbit terrine with rhubarb, for example. The oddball flavours excite some but disappoint others. Ingredients inspire confidence – fresh langoustines, red mullet, veal kidney, venison – although saucing may do little to enhance them. Side-plated vegetables are good: creamy mashed potato, parsnip, squash, broccoli and green beans. Puddings are a high point, with summer fruit crumble, poached peach in a caramel basket, and banana baked in puff pastry which 'arrives with the pastry cleverly cut to resemble a banana skin'.

Bread is heavy white cob with flavourings of fried onion or black pudding, and service has sometimes been below par. When the conference mobs ride in, ordinary diners may feel pushed out, with long waits between courses. More direction and organisation are called for. But despite all that, September is still one of the best things that has happened to Blackpool for a long time. The wine list is short, bottles are well chosen, and prices are sympathetic. House wines are around £10.

CHEF: Michael Golowicz   PROPRIETORS: Michael Golowicz and Pat Wood   OPEN: Tue to Sat; 12 to 2, 7 to 9.30 (pre- and post-theatre by arrangement)   CLOSED: 2 weeks summer, 2 weeks winter   MEALS: alc (main courses L £5.50 to £7.50, D £10 to £14). Set D £15.95   SERVICE: not inc, card slips closed   CARDS: Access, Amex, Diners, Visa   DETAILS: 44 seats. Private parties: 44 main room. Vegetarian meals. Children's helpings. Smart dress preferred. Music

---

BLACKWATER Cornwall   map 1

Pennypots

Blackwater TR4 8EY	
ST DAY (0209) 820347	COOKING 3
off A30, 3/4m W of village centre	COST £30–£39

The whitewashed house used to be called Blackbird Cottage, but a scrapbook in the bar tells how Jane Viner began to put a penny in a pot for every customer they served, and the name changed. The white and pink dining room is attractively cottagey, the atmosphere relaxed, homely, warm and welcoming, the pace leisurely. Jane Viner and a couple of helpers are attentive, helpful and quietly professional. This is a modest operation with a high degree of skill at all levels. Ken Viner spent five or six years at the Aldershot Army School of Catering, but it doesn't show. The food is inventive without being restlessly up-to-the-minute, taking in fillet of smoked salmon lightly grilled, on a lime and hazelnut vinaigrette, and cinnamon soufflé with plums sautéd in brandy and an apricot ice-cream.

The *carte* is a generous spread of half a dozen items at each stage. 'Our general style of cooking is light and direct,' write the Viners, and it suits fish particularly well. Curled fillets of steamed turbot and Dover sole, at a summer inspection, were surrounded by a generous scattering of fresh-tasting, grit-free mussels in their shells, all in a simple but carefully done butter sauce. At the same meal, very fresh and lightly pan-fried scallops came on a bed of crisp, deep-fried cucumber strips interspersed with shreds of seaweed. 'Over the last two years we have been using more oils and vinegars to produce sauces,' say the Viners, and home-grown herbs add lift to a number of dishes: grilled red mullet is served with sesame-seed oil and a light soy sauce flavoured with fresh coriander and ginger.

Lightness comes through, too, in ravioli of lobster with asparagus in an olive oil and basil dressing – yet when dishes need weight and depth, they get it: in a rich and properly reduced port wine sauce for tender and tasty lamb fillet, for example. Bread, ice-creams, petits fours and other incidentals are all made in-house, and wines are sensibly chosen and considerately priced. Many are under £15, yet not chosen simply on price, and the New World is decently represented. House French is £7.50 (£1.75 per glass).

CHEF: Kevin Viner   PROPRIETORS: Kevin and Jane Viner   OPEN: Tue to Sat, D only; 7 to 10
CLOSED: 4 weeks winter   MEALS: alc (main courses £12.50 to £14)   SERVICE: not inc, card slips
closed   CARDS: Access, Visa   DETAILS: 30 seats. Private parties: 20 main room, 10 private
room. Car park. Vegetarian meals with prior notice. Children's helpings. No smoking before
10pm. Wheelchair access (1 step). Music

BLANDFORD FORUM Dorset   map 2

▲ *La Belle Alliance* ⁵✳

White Cliff Mill Street,
Blandford Forum DT11 7BP   COOKING 2
BLANDFORD (0258) 452842   COST £24–£35

The Davisons' restaurant-with-rooms is in a late Victorian building on the edge of town. A couple who honeymooned here in 1989 have returned regularly since, as much for the 'great warmth and charm' of the place as to relive that first flush. The food, they reckon, is always 'superbly prepared and imaginatively served', and Lauren Davison is a 'perfect hostess, showing a real interest in customers'. Two fixed-price dinner options are available: a 'bistro' menu of two or three courses, and a four-course seasonal 'gourmet' menu.

The level of technique is pretty ambitious in dishes such as a hot-smoked cheese soufflé served on salad leaves with apples and celery, strips of duck breast in a puff pastry case with orange and hazelnut sauce, and steamed fillets of brill stuffed with bacon and spinach with a white wine and chive sauce. Philip Davison's skill in execution is such that most things work. Intermediate courses, of the likes of avocado and apple salad or mixed berry sorbet, 'surprise and delight'. Fish is particularly enjoyed, as in smoked trout with a mixture of shellfish in a sauce of champagne vinegar and cucumber, and salmon marinated in yogurt and lemon juice, then grilled and served on a creamy basil-flavoured sauce. The multi-layering continues into dessert stage in items like rich chocolate mousse in a dark chocolate cup with white chocolate ice-cream and a raspberry coulis. The wine list makes a creditable attempt to source good-value bottles from around the world. Choices are sound and prices are fair. Four French house wines come at £8.95.

CHEFS: Philip Davison and Richard Morris   PROPRIETORS: Philip and Lauren Davison   OPEN: Tue to Sat (and bank hol Sun), D only (L by arrangement for parties); 7 to 9.30 (6.45 to 10 Fri and Sat)   CLOSED: first 2 weeks Jan   MEALS: Set D £13.95 (2 courses) to £19.95   SERVICE: not inc, card slips closed   CARDS: Access, Amex, Visa   DETAILS: 32 seats. Private parties: 38 main room. Car park. Vegetarian meals with prior notice. Children's helpings by arrangement. No smoking in dining-room. Wheelchair access (1 step). Music   ACCOMMODATION: 6 rooms, all with bath/shower. TV. Phone. B&B £48 to £66. Room for disabled. Children by arrangement. Baby facilities. Pets by arrangement. Doors close at midnight. Confirm by 6. Fax: (0258) 480053

BOLLINGTON Cheshire   map 5

Mauro's £

88 Palmerston Street, Bollington SK10 5PW   COOKING 1*
MACCLESFIELD (0625) 573898   COST £20–£41

Strange things can happen in a north of England trattoria: on Christmas Eve the local brass band trooped into Mauro's and started playing carols. 'It was a jolly event,' reflected one witness to the scene, 'and lo and behold, big fat snowflakes started to fall outside right on cue – a white Christmas.' The refurbishment is now complete, with a proper bar/reception area helping to take some of the pressure off the service although it still needs to be sharper. It feels relaxed without drifting into homely informality. The tremendous antipasti trolley earns full marks: hot king prawns in butter, stuffed aubergines and artichoke hearts have been applauded. There has been praise for home-made pasta, and for sauces with the main dishes. Fresh fish and daily specials, such as salmon-filled ravioli topped with raddichio, are also worth noting. Desserts are creamy. Interesting drinking is provided by 50 wines from the Italian regions, and the restaurant also has a daunting array of grappas. House wine is £8.30.

CHEF/PROPRIETOR: Vincenzo Mauro   OPEN: Tue to Sat, exc Sat L (Sun L first Sun of month); 12 to 2, 7 to 10   MEALS: alc (main courses £8.30 to £15.50)   SERVICE: not inc (10% for 6 or more)   CARDS: Access, Amex, Visa   DETAILS: 50 seats. Private parties: 60 main room. Vegetarian meals. Children's helpings. Smart dress preferred. No cigars. Wheelchair access (also WC). Music

---

BOLTON ABBEY North Yorkshire   map 5

▲ Devonshire Arms, Burlington Restaurant ⅝✳

Bolton Abbey BD23 6AJ
BOLTON ABBEY (0756) 710441   COOKING 2
at junction of A59 and B6160, 5m NW of Ilkey   COST £26–£68

Luxury abounds at this lavishly refurbished seventeenth-century coaching inn, complete with helipad, set in 12 acres of land in the Yorkshire Dales National Park. The Burlington Restaurant is an airy, spacious room done out in shades of green with a Georgian-style conservatory offering views of the lawned gardens and nearby hills. Gavin Beedham makes good use of local ingredients, including moorland grouse, venison and herbs from the hotel's own plot for a dinner menu that changes every few weeks. Meals are fixed price for five courses, although many dishes carry a surcharge. Ideas from the Mediterranean and the Far East are grafted on to a bedrock of modern French cuisine: layers of foie gras, mango and duck are given a dressing of sun-dried tomatoes and pistachio nuts; fillet of beef is topped with oyster mousse on a black-bean sauce; collops of monkfish are laid on a bed of water-chestnuts and mango with a tomato and lemon balm dressing. Service is beyond reproach. The range of wines is broad, the quality high in France for those with the money to pay for it, and the New World section as welcome as the 19 half-bottles. House wine is £10.95.

CHEF: Gavin Beedham PROPRIETORS: Duke and Duchess of Devonshire OPEN: all week; 12 to 2, 7 to 10 (9.30 Sun) MEALS: alc (main courses £14.50 to £18). Set L £17.95 to £21.50, Set D £28.95 SERVICE: 10%, card slips closed CARDS: Access, Amex, Diners, Visa DETAILS: 75 seats. Private parties: 12 main room, 10, 16 and 26 private rooms. Car park. Vegetarian meals. Children's helpings. No children under 12. Jacket and tie. No smoking in dining-room. Wheelchair access (also WC). No music ACCOMMODATION: 40 rooms, all with bath/shower. TV. Phone. B&B £90 to £145. Rooms for disabled. Children welcome. Baby facilities. Pets welcome. Afternoon teas. Garden. Swimming-pool. Sauna. Tennis. Fishing. Doors close at 1am. Confirm by 6. Fax: (0756) 710564 (*The Which? Hotel Guide*)

BOTLEY Hampshire   map 2

Cobbett's

15 The Square, Botley SO3 2EA   COOKING 1
BOTLEY (0489) 782068   COST £34–£48

Botley is on a navigable part of the Hamble, so those with small boats are able to arrive by water, Venetian-style. The Skipwiths have been in this half-timbered Tudor house for over 20 years, serving up food with a fairly traditional French bias that has been passed through their own mill, so to speak. Alongside poultry liver terrine and marinated haunch of venison are a mousseline of broccoli and Brie on a leek and herb coulis with roasted almonds, and boned spring chicken with ginger and pineapple. Ingredients are good – for example, a half-lobster with fresh tomatoes in the sauce – and one reporter enjoyed a ragoût with artichoke hearts, asparagus and a perfectly poached egg in the centre as a starter, and a variation on strawberries and cream to finish. Main courses are served with a pastry cup of vegetables. The French cheeses are mostly in good condition, and the wine list is due for expansion. House wine is £9.85.

CHEFS: Lucie Skipwith and Giles Hester PROPRIETORS: Charles and Lucie Skipwith OPEN: Mon to Sat, exc L Mon to Sat; 12 to 2, 7.30 (7 Sat) to 10 CLOSED: 2 weeks winter, 2 weeks summer, bank hols MEALS: Set L and D £18.50 (2 courses) to £23 SERVICE: not inc CARDS: Access, Visa DETAILS: 40 seats. Private parties: 50 main room, 8 and 14 private rooms. Car park. Vegetarian meals. No children under 13 D. Smart dress preferred. No cigars/pipes in dining-room. No music. Fax: (0489) 799641

The Good Food Guide *is a registered trade mark of Consumers' Association Ltd.*

BOTTESFORD Leicestershire   map 5

La Petite Maison

1 Market Street, Bottesford NG13 0BW
BOTTESFORD (0949) 842375   COOKING 1
just off A52 Nottingham to Grantham road   COST £24–£41

Andrew and Beverley Goodson describe their 'English Continental' bistro as 'more like a private dining-room than a restaurant'. The old building has its own cottage garden, while inside is a mix of beams, woodwork and warm burgundy tones. The owners look to their home patch for supplies, procuring game from Belvoir Castle, picking soft fruit from local farms and buying Scalford Stilton direct from the creamery. This translates into a repertoire that blends old favourites like confit of duck, braised oxtail and coq au vin with more modern ideas along the lines of chicken and chive ravioli. Soups and home-baked brown bread draw notes of approval. Sticky toffee pudding is the best-selling sweet and petits fours are 'handcrafted' on the premises. The short, sensibly chosen wine list has plenty of decent drinking for around £10. House wine is £8.95.

CHEF: Adrian Hutchinson   PROPRIETORS: Andrew and Beverley Goodson   OPEN: Tue to Sun, exc Sun D; 12 to 2, 7 to 10   CLOSED: 26 to 30 Dec, first 2 weeks Jan   MEALS: alc (main courses £10 to £15). Set L Sun £10.95, Set D £14.95   SERVICE: not inc   CARDS: Access, Amex, Visa DETAILS: 38 seats. 3 tables outside. Car park. Vegetarian meals. Children's helpings. Wheelchair access. Music

---

BOUGHTON LEES Kent   map 3

▲ *Eastwell Manor* ⁵⅄✳

Eastwell Park, Boughton Lees TN25 4HR
ASHFORD (0233) 635751   COOKING 2
on A251, 3m N of Ashford   COST £23–£65

Eastwell is grand: the gardens cover 62 acres, the estate 3000. Despite 11 'sleeping policemen' in the drive, 'the approach certainly makes you think good things lie ahead'. A stone-flagged courtyard, heavy oak door, dark wood panelling and leather chairs all lend gravitas, but fresh flowers and the blue and white dining-room rescue the place from sinking under its own weight.

New chefs bring enthusiasm, and Ian Mansfield has it coming out of his ears. Food echoes the contrasting décor, with fireworks among the more expensive menus, and everyday cooking of standard fare. An appetiser of diced raw salmon makes a promising start. It is not alone in having a pesto sauce 'They must have a pesto factory lurking in the grounds.' Among other popular items are a slightly sweet soup of butternut squash topped with a fluffy melting sabayon dusted with nutmeg, and crisp-skinned roasted baby chicken, split in half and flattened, served with parsley-flecked slippery noodles. Praise comes too for beef fillet and for duck breast 'cooked to perfection', but a dish of red mullet with tapénade produced on one occasion 'stunned silence followed by hoots of laughter', as the dome-lifting ceremony revealed two tiny fillets and no sign of tapénade, just a purée of tomatoes. Ideas, nevertherless, are appealing: a cardamom-scented juice for ravioli of crab and ginger; a polenta and olive sandwich for lamb; rhubarb pithiviers with blackcurrant sauce and almond ice-cream. Ian Mansfield is certainly going places.

The hotel is well reported, and staff are young and eager to please. The wine waiter is a patient and knowledgeable guardian of 200 round-the-world bins with a fair selection (including vins de pays) under £20. One rosé, six red and six white wines are served by the glass. House wines start at £12.

CHEF: Ian Mansfield   PROPRIETOR: Queens Moat Houses plc   OPEN: all week; 12.30 to 2, 7 to 9.30 (10 Fri and Sat)   MEALS: Set L £14.50 to £36.50, Set D £24.50 to £42   SERVICE: not inc, card slips closed   CARDS: Access, Amex, Diners, Visa   DETAILS: 80 seats. Private parties: 95 main room, 40 and 65 private rooms. Car park. Vegetarian meals. Children's helpings. Jacket and tie. No smoking in dining-room. Wheelchair access (2 steps). Music   ACCOMMODATION: 23 rooms, all with bath/shower. TV. Phone. B&B £100 to £255. Deposit: £50. Rooms for disabled. Lift. Children welcome. Baby facilities. Pets welcome. Afternoon teas. Garden. Tennis. Snooker. Doors close at midnight. Fax: (0233) 635530 (*The Which? Hotel Guide*)

BOURNEMOUTH Dorset   map 2

Sophisticats

43 Charminster Road,
Bournemouth BH8 8UE   COOKING 2
BOURNEMOUTH (0202) 291019   COST £27–£39

'It was the find of the holiday,' wrote one reporter, 'thanks to the *Guide*.' 'It is the best part of Bournemouth,' enthused another. John Knight and Bernard Calligan have been running this small, unpretentious restaurant in a row of shops on an unprepossessing street since 1980, weathering more than one recession.

Menus change in circular fashion, each one a sample from a large repertoire of standard dishes that the kitchen does well and confidently. Visitors get plenty of choice, regulars re-order their favourites, the service is discreet and friendly, and everyone is happy. Steak is a feature: sirloin or fillet plainly grilled, or baked in foil with tomatoes, mushrooms, cheese and herbs, or marinated in soy sauce, wine and spices. Some dishes seem a little more elaborate than necessary – crabmeat with onion and mayonnaise served on toast with grilled cheese, for example – which may be why the simpler ones, such as rolls of smoked salmon stuffed with prawns, come in for most praise. The freshness of fish makes an impact: Dover sole, halibut, and monkfish tails in whole grain mustard sauce have all been recommended. Alcohol and cream trickle through the puddings, from a pancake filled with cherries and chocolate, flamed with kirsch and served with cream, to a more refreshing ice-cream of Bacardi and coconut with a lime syrup. A basic wine list backs up the food, with most bottles under £20. House wine is £7.95.

CHEF: Bernard Calligan   PROPRIETORS: John Knight and Bernard Calligan   OPEN: Mon to Sat, D only; 7 to 9.30   CLOSED: 2 weeks Feb, 1 week July, 2 weeks Nov   MEALS: alc (main courses £11 to £13)   SERVICE: not inc   DETAILS: 34 seats. Private parties: 16 main room. Vegetarian meals. Children welcome. Wheelchair access (also WC). Music

---

See the back of the Guide *for a listing of all restaurants in the Main Entries sections.*

BOWNESS-ON-WINDERMERE Cumbria   map 7

Porthole Eating House ▮

3 Ash Street,
Bowness-on-Windermere LA23 3EB   COOKING 2
WINDERMERE (053 94) 42793   COST £25–£52

The restaurant, a seventeenth-century cottage and one of the oldest in Bowness, has been a fixture for over 20 years. 'Pavarotti sang, the log fire burned,' for one reporter and the welcome is always warm. Nobody stands on ceremony, tables are bare wood, and some of the dishes hark back a long way, for example scampi Mornay and sirloin steak Diane. The basics are Italian but make no attempt to jump on the colourful contemporary bandwagon. People do not go for exciting cooking. Spaghetti bolognese, breast of chicken saltimbocca, and orange Positano are the sort of dishes that thousands of high street Italian restaurants have peddled for over a generation. The difference here is partly that the Porthole does them better than most, and partly that it does personalise some dishes on a rather more interesting weekly-changing menu to produce mushrooms stuffed with crab, or a fillet of salmon coated with herbs and white fish mousseline.

Bread is baked in-house, sweets are standard, and 'service is not impeccable, but I like a little human fallibility'. Wines are uniformly excellent, many from top producers whether well known or not. Like most good lists it cannot resist enthusiasms, for example, a clutch of gems from Giuseppe Quintarelli (price on application), and a decent showing of German wines. Mark-ups are extremely reasonable, and the sense is of a list that has been put together by a devoted fan over a number of years. It has a welcome generosity that makes good drinking such a pleasure.

CHEF: Michael Metcalfe   PROPRIETORS: Judy and Gianni Berton   OPEN: Wed to Mon, D only; 6 to 11   CLOSED: mid-Dec to end Feb   MEALS: alc (main courses £8.50 to £16)   SERVICE: not inc, card slips closed   CARDS: Access, Amex, Diners, Visa   DETAILS: 40 seats. 11 tables outside. Private parties: 40 main room. Vegetarian meals. Children's helpings. Music. Fax: (053 94) 88675

BRADFIELD COMBUST Suffolk   map 3

▲ Bradfield House ⚖✳

Bradfield Combust IP30 0LR
SICKLESMERE (0284) 386301
on A134 Sudbury Road, 4m S of   COOKING 2
Bury St Edmunds   COST £22–£36

Roy and Sally Ghijben's half-timbered, pink-painted, seventeenth-century country house is a restaurant with rooms, some antique furnishings, and vases of fresh flowers. Frills are few, table settings are basic, and at busy times there may be a press on space in the small dining-room; but charming service brings warmth to it all.

The menu is a homely mix of English and French dishes, simply cooked; among them are hotpot of mushrooms with a puff-pastry lid, and breast of chicken with a pea and spinach sauce. Braised endive is baked in a ramekin dish, with a very cheesy sauce and a crumbly bacon topping. The venison pie uses fallow deer from the Denham Estate, and port in the gravy; and pan-fried fillet of beef, pink and tender, is highly rated. Herbs from the well-kept garden give a lift. Among the desserts, exceptional stem ginger ice-cream, and the pungent freshness and tang of real fruit in sorbets stand out. The sound collection of wines strays rarely over £20 a bottle, and offers a varied choice including two-dozen half-bottles. House wine is £7.50.

CHEF: Roy Ghijben   PROPRIETORS: Roy and Sally Ghijben   OPEN: Tue to Sat, D only; 7 to 8.45 (9 Sat)   MEALS: alc (main courses £11 to £14.50). Set D £16.50 (not Sat)   SERVICE: net prices, card slips closed   CARDS: Access, Visa   DETAILS: 36 seats. Private parties: 26 main room, 14 private room. Car park. Vegetarian meals with prior notice. Children's helpings on request (not Sat). No children under 8. Smart dress preferred. No smoking in dining-room. Wheelchair access (1 step; also WC). No music   ACCOMMODATION: 4 rooms, all with bath/shower. TV. Phone. B&B £45 to £85. Deposit: £20. Children welcome. Baby facilities. Garden. Doors close at midnight. Confirm by 6. Fax: (0284) 386301 (*The Which? Hotel Guide*)

BRADFORD West Yorkshire   map 5

▲ *Restaurant Nineteen* ☕

North Park Road, Heaton,
Bradford BD9 4NT   COOKING 4
BRADFORD (0274) 492559   COST £35–£43

The nineteenth-century end-of-terrace house in a tree-lined street on the edge of Lister Park is grander than it sounds. As we went to press, a refurbishment was under way to mark 10 years in business – an achievement, all the more so in perilous economic times. A vestibule opens into a fine hall and staircase, with two generously proportioned dining-rooms leading off, with well-spaced tables. Four-course set dinners offer just enough choices: four or five to begin, followed by either soup or a dish of rice or pasta, then four main courses. Dishes are described simply and accurately, value for money is a frequent theme of reports, and menus are built from a rolling repertoire.

Stephen Smith spins different accompaniments around core items such as roast breast and casseroled leg of duck: blueberries and balsamic vinegar on one occasion, sage and onion tart on another. Mustard puddings, and dumplings of horseradish or rosemary and thyme, bring texture and flavour to braises of beef or ham hock. Mostly the cooking is accurate, although occasional lapses are reported. Vegetables, all served in bowls instead of on plates, are incorporated into each main course. This is a kitchen that pays full attention to fine ingredients, and brings well-developed skills to bear: mousses are light, sauces properly emulsified, jellies firm. If there is a fault, it is that the cooking tries too hard to impress, and complication can set in – as when rhubarb is presented three ways: a rather basic jelly, a ginger flavoured crème brûlée, and a blob of rhubarb ice-cream in a tulip biscuit. The effort to put more 'work' on the plate is understandable, if unnecessary. Greater clarity and simplicity have been appreciated in a superior bread-and-butter pudding (incorporating prunes soaked in armagnac) and a starkly uncluttered lemon tart with 'an excellent flavour, soft custardy texture, good pastry and well-brûléed top'.

Staff are friendly and helpful, service is excellent, and wines do not bump up the bill disproportionately. New-look Australian, Italian and southern French wines balance the weight of the classics, in style as well as in price. Good drinking among the less expensive wines is particularly welcome. CELLARMAN'S CHOICE: Le Volte 1991, Antinori, £16.50; Bianco 1992, Avignonesi, £12.

CHEF: Stephen Smith PROPRIETORS: Stephen Smith and Robert Barbour OPEN: Mon to Sat, D only; 7 to 9.30 (10 Fri and Sat) CLOSED: 2 weeks Christmas to New Year, 2 weeks Aug to Sept MEALS: Set D £26 SERVICE: not inc, card slips closed CARDS: Access, Amex, Diners, Visa DETAILS: 36 seats. Private parties: 36 main room. Car park. Vegetarian meals with prior notice. No children under 8. Smart dress preferred. No cigars/pipes in dining-room. Music ACCOMMODATION: 4 rooms, all with bath/shower. TV. Phone. B&B £60 to £70. No children under 8. Doors close at 11.30. Confirm 1 day ahead. Fax: (0274) 483827 (*The Which? Hotel Guide*)

BRADFORD-ON-AVON Wiltshire   map 2

▲ *Woolley Grange* ♥ ⚡✳

Woolley Green,
Bradford-on-Avon BA15 1TX
BRADFORD-ON-AVON (0225) 864705 | NEW CHEF |
on B3105, 1m NE of Bradford-on-Avon   COST £22–£40

The Woolley of the name is no accident. This handsome Jacobean house of Bath stone was built with seventeenth-century wool money for one of the city's wealthy clothiers. For 200 years it was owned by the Baskervilles, but the only hound you are likely to encounter now is Birdie, the Chapmans' springer spaniel. Children are as welcome as their parents, and there cannot be many country houses that advertise pinball and table-football among the facilities.

As we go to press, Colin White is scheduled to move to Gannets Bistro (see entry Newark) and a new chef has not yet been appointed here. White's cooking was sympathetic to the civilised setting, acknowledging the Mediterranean upheaval in metropolitan circles, without pitching headlong into it and alienating the natural constituency of Woolley. The Terrace menu offers lighter, cheaper snacks such as omelette Arnold Bennett, toasted goats' cheese and real hamburgers.

On the wine list Masson Blondelet Pouilly Fumé, a trio of German Rieslings, Givry from Mouton, Filliatreau's Saumur-Champigny and Capel Vale Shiraz give a flavour of confident selection. A curiosity of the list is that it contains no dry whites from outside Europe, with the sole exception of Taltarni Sauvignon Blanc in halves. House wines from Duboeuf are £9.85. CELLARMAN'S CHOICE: Sauvignon Blanc 1992, Ch. la Jaubertie, £13.50; Morgon 'Les Versauds' 1992, Dom. Perrachon, £16.

PROPRIETORS: Nigel and Heather Chapman OPEN: all week; 12.15 to 2, 7.15 to 10 MEALS: alc L (main courses £9 to £15). Set L Sun £17, Set D £28. Terrace menu SERVICE: net prices, card slips closed CARDS: Access, Amex, Diners, Visa DETAILS: 75 seats. 6 tables outside. Private parties: 30 main room, 12 and 22 private rooms. Car park. Vegetarian meals. Children's helpings. No smoking in dining-room. Wheelchair access (1 step; also WC). No music ACCOMMODATION: 20 rooms, all with bath/shower. TV. Phone. B&B £80 to £165. Rooms for disabled. Children welcome. Baby facilities. Pets welcome. Afternoon teas. Garden. Swimming-pool. Tennis. Doors close at midnight. Fax: (0225) 864059 (*The Which? Hotel Guide*)

▲ *Ivy House* ♥ ⁵⁄✳

Braithwaite, nr Keswick CA12 5SY
KESWICK (076 87) 78338
turn into Braithwaite off A66,   COOKING 1
then left down small road at Royal Oak pub   COST £25–£31

The house is a combination of three, the oldest dating back to 1630, one circa 1790 'and another we cannot identify'. It is painted green all over, with no trace of ivy, just a rambling rose round the entrance. Comfortable three-piece suites and open log fires in the lounge make it a room to relax in after a day on the fells.

Dishes served in the upstairs dining-room revolve around a small repertoire that has pleased regulars. Good first courses have included chunks of pork served satay-style with a pleasantly spicy and chutney-like peanut sauce and a refreshing cucumber relish, carrot and apricot pâté with peach chutney, and avocado with prawns. Fish has been enjoyed – a 'generous piece of fresh, firm and delicate lemon sole', for instance – even when poached for longer than necessary. Gressingham duck with fruit, roast rack of lamb, banoffi pie and sticky toffee pudding are other fixtures. Tiramisù is enjoyable if not exactly authentic. The wine list is concise, well put together, well annotated and very keenly priced, with only one bottle (outside champagne) over £20. House vin de pays is £6.95. CELLARMAN'S CHOICE: St-Aubin Blanc 1990, Prudhon, £17,25; Basedows Shiraz 1991, £11.25.

CHEFS: Wendy Shill and Peter Holton PROPRIETORS: Nick and Wendy Shill OPEN: all week, D only; 7 for 7.30 CLOSED: Jan MEALS: Set D £18.95 SERVICE: not inc, card slips closed CARDS: Access, Amex, Diners, Visa DETAILS: 32 seats. Private parties: 10 main room. Car park. Vegetarian meals. Children's helpings. Smart dress preferred. No smoking in dining-room. Music ACCOMMODATION: 12 rooms, all with bath/shower. TV. Phone. B&B £34 to £68. Deposit: £20. Children welcome. Baby facilities. Dogs by arrangement, not in public rooms. Doors close at 11.30. Fax: (076 87) 78113 (*The Which? Hotel Guide*)

▲ *Farlam Hall*

Brampton CA8 2NG
HALLBANKGATE (069 77) 46234
on A689, 2½m SE of Brampton (not at   COOKING 2*
Farlam village)   COST £37–£46

Six members of the Quinion and Stevenson families are in residence at this country house on the road between Brampton and Alston. The building dates back to the seventeenth century, although it was enlarged during Victorian times: both John Wesley and George Stephenson were visitors. Outside are four acres of mature gardens complete with a stream and ornamental lake; the interior is a graceful mix of antiques and tasteful furnishings. Dinner is fixed price for four courses plus coffee. Chef Barry Quinion might offer confit of Gressingham duckling with a dressing of raspberry vinegar and walnut oil or hot spinach and prawn pancakes, before escalope of salmon with creamed leeks and hollandaise or stir-fried fillet of beef with peppers. English cheeses and desserts bring up the rear. The list of around 40 wines is a well-spread choice and prices are fair across the range. House wine is £9.95.

CHEF: Barry Quinion   PROPRIETORS: the Quinion and Stevenson families   OPEN: all week, D only; 8 for 8.30   CLOSED: Christmas to New Year   MEALS: Set D Sun to Fri £28.50 Sat £29.50 SERVICE: not inc, card slips closed   CARDS: Access, Amex, Visa   DETAILS: 45 seats. Private parties: 25 main room. Car park. Vegetarian meals with prior notice. No children under 5. Smart dress preferred. No cigars/pipes in dining-room. Wheelchair access (2 steps). No music ACCOMMODATION: 12 rooms, all with bath/shower. TV. Phone. D,B&B £92 to £200. No children under 5. Afternoon teas. Garden. Doors close at 11. Confirm by 4. Fax: (069 77) 46683 (*The Which? Hotel Guide*)

BRAY Berkshire   map 2

▲ *Waterside Inn* ♥

Ferry Road, Bray SL6 2AT
MAIDENHEAD (0628) 20691   COOKING 4*
off A308 Maidenhead to Windsor road   COST £38–£128

'A wonderful place to enjoy good food, where people come to have a good time,' reckons a reporter who has eaten at the Waterside for a dozen years. The inn is a black and white pebble-dashed building with a modern extension (the dining-room) bolted on to make the most of the 'magical' Thames-side location. A sunny day is a wonderful time to go, shade provided by an ancient weeping willow which must have more rings than Elizabeth Taylor. Service pops in and out of the small summer-house to bring canapés and menus and take orders.

Heaven knows what the Japanese and Americans, never mind the British, make of the old-fashioned menu-French. What is a Douillet Dubarry for instance? A tasting menu of four courses plus sorbet and coffee works out at around £60 a head (minimum two people) which, when you see the *carte* prices, doesn't seem so bad. This is the place to come for absolutely classic French food done properly. It is modern in the sense that it has taken on board the more positive messages which have influenced restaurant food since the '80s. Meals are now much lighter here and depend less on animal fats than they did a decade ago. Otherwise, fashion seems to have passed the place by. 'It is difficult to fault the cooking,' wrote one, 'although I missed an edge, a passion.'

Correct execution of dishes that can look quite simple on the plate, and yet demand a high degree of skill to produce, is what keeps the Waterside on top. Accurately poached eggs in a fresh and buttery puff-pastry basket with well-timed asparagus and a light, eggy, buttery mousseline sauce may not excite, but the dish pleases because it is so well done. The foundation on classical techniques means that food is unlikely to suffer unevenness, much less meet with disaster. The distinct flavours of chicken, artichoke and foie gras work well together in a layered terrine, which comes with a quenelle of intense, creamed cauliflower (that's the Douillet Dubarry): an unlikely accompaniment perhaps, but a brilliant match. At another meal a fairly ordinary-sounding crème brûlée with pistachio was a highlight, the delicate greenish cream a wonderful variation on a standard of the repertoire – a joy.

Even when quiet, the Waterside must look busy, with all those waiters buzzing around. It is like being centre stage during a ballet, as everybody is swept through effortlessly and seamlessly from beginning to end. A regular notes that 'people still often laugh ruefully when presented with the bill, acknowledging that they have had a good time, and that it was worth it after all'. The wine list is as French as the Eiffel Tower, although prices are a little higher, but sensible advice is forthcoming. House Duboeuf Beaujolais is £17.50. CELLARMAN'S CHOICE: St-Julien, Ch. Talbot 1987, £29; Sélection des Frères Roux 1989, Dom. Defaix, £27.

CHEFS: Michel Roux and Mark Dodson   PROPRIETOR: Michel Roux   OPEN: Tue to Sun, exc Tue L (Sun D Apr to Oct only); 12 to 1.30 (2.30 Sat and Sun), 7 to 10   CLOSED: 5 weeks from 26 Dec   MEALS: alc (main courses £24.50 to £36). Set L £28.50 to £36, Set D £48 (mid-Oct to Apr) to £62   SERVICE: net prices   CARDS: Access, Diners, Visa   DETAILS: 75 seats. Private parties: 80 main room, 8 private room. Car park. Vegetarian meals. No children under 12. Smart dress preferred. No cigars in dining-room. Wheelchair access. No music. Air-conditioned   ACCOMMODATION: 7 rooms, all with bath/shower. TV. Phone. B&B £120 to £210. Deposit: £60. No children under 12. Confirm 1 day ahead. Fax: (0628) 784710

BRIGHOUSE West Yorkshire   map 5

Brook's ✹✸

6 Bradford Road, Brighouse HD6 1RW   COOKING 1*
HUDDERSFIELD (0484) 715284   COST £20–£38

In the white-walled, floorboarded dining-room, customers are handed wax crayons at dinner's end with which to decorate the tablecloths. Some may view it as occupational therapy; the more competitively minded may see their work exhibited at the next visit. Meanwhile, the fixed-price menus should provide plenty to divert the attention before the artwork gets under way. In March, diners could choose from salmon mousseline with celeriac salad and mussels, rosemary-scented grilled shark on salad, and a cassoulet made with rabbit as starters. Mains offered monkfish with lentils and a ginger and coriander cream sauce, chicken breast stuffed with spinach on an orange sauce, and grilled fillet steak with king prawns and sauce Café de Paris. At dessert stage, old favourites, such as apple and berry strudel with custard or the much-supported bread-and-butter pudding, have their say. The cumulative effect may be a little heavy, but the originality of approach deserves support. Breads are 'excellent'. The fairly short wine list contains some good bottles at prices that will not break the bank. House French is £7.50.

CHEF: Richard Ullah   PROPRIETOR: Darrell Brook   OPEN: Mon to Sat, D only (some Sundays); 6 (7 Sat) to 11   MEALS: Set D £15.50 (2 courses) to £18.95, 'early bird' menu £12.95 (6 to 7pm)   SERVICE: not inc   CARDS: Access, Visa   DETAILS: 55 seats. Private parties: 70 main room, 20 private room. Vegetarian meals. Children's helpings on request. Smart dress preferred. No smoking in dining-room. Wheelchair access (1 step). Music

---

The text of entries is based on unsolicited reports sent in by readers, backed up by inspections conducted anonymously. The factual details under the text are from questionnaires the Guide *sends to all restaurants that feature in the book.*

Black Chapati

12 Circus Parade, New England Road,
Brighton BN1 4GW
BRIGHTON (0273) 699011

COOKING 2
COST £16–£36

The setting is a monochromatic 'cabin' of a dining-room a few minutes' drive from the centre of town. Black-topped tables, white walls and a blackboard advertising rare beers and ciders are the extent of the décor.

The point of the place is its brilliantly risky food. Stephen Funnell has moved far beyond conventional Indian cooking into something that is 'maverick Asian', pulling in strands from Japan, Thailand and elsewhere. The result is a menu that might offer salmon teriyaki with soy-dressed greens and pickled ginger as well as rump of lamb with chickpeas and masala cabbage. What impresses is the fact that the inventiveness does actually work. Breast of woodpigeon with udon noodles, and an intense coriander pesto and smoked duck breast with lentil salad and sweet mustard sauce, are complex, distinctive and impressively put together – although 'glorious' crispy roast duck served with an exotically fruity ginger and tamarind sauce was the high point of a star meal for one party. Classic vegetarian thalis and genuine Indian dishes are in a class of their own: Funnell's version of bhel poori is 'a bomb of flavours firing off unexpectedly, but never losing balance'. Sweets include not only exotic ice-creams but also a 'near perfect' crème brûlée. Sunday lunch buffets are well-reported. A handful of wines offer fairly priced, interesting drinking. House wine is £8.50.

CHEFS/PROPRIETORS: Stephen Funnell and Lauren Alker OPEN: Tue to Sat D, and Sun L; 1 to 3, 7 to 10.30 MEALS: alc (main courses £9.50 to £12.50). Sun L buffet £8.95 SERVICE: 10%, card slips closed CARDS: Access, Amex, Visa DETAILS: 30 seats. 2 tables outside. Private parties: 30 main room. Vegetarian meals. No children under 6. Wheelchair access. Music

Langan's Bistro

1 Paston Place, Brighton BN2 1HA
BRIGHTON (0273) 606933

COOKING 1*
COST £21–£42

A blustery walk along the sea-front should stir the appetite for the hearty food on offer at the Langan empire's southernmost outpost in smart Kemptown. The atmosphere is not dissimilar to that of the Mayfair Langan's (see entry, London) – 'Dressed to the nines or verging on the scruffy, no one would feel uncomfortable.' The *carte* offers around half a dozen choices at each stage and is joined at lunch-time by a *prix fixe* that has just two alternatives per course. Recommendations come in for a mussel and saffron tart with hair-fine leeks, 'splendid, generously proportioned' panaché of fish, a pair of skilfully presented quails on vegetable compote, apple and date crumble, and orange crème brûlée. The short, handwritten wine list is an entirely French selection that confines itself to basic choices from the main regions. House Duboeuf is £7.70.

Report forms are at the back of the book; write a letter if you prefer.

CHEF: Mark Emmerson PROPRIETORS: Michael Caine and Richard Shepherd OPEN: Tue to Sun, exc Sat L and Sun D; 12.30 to 2.15, 7.30 to 10.15 MEALS: alc (main courses £13.50 to £15). Set L £12.50 (2 courses) to £14.50. Cover 75p SERVICE: 10% CARDS: Access, Amex, Diners, Visa DETAILS: 48 seats. Children's helpings on request. Music. Air-conditioned. Fax: (0273) 675686

Whytes

33 Western Street, Brighton BN1 2PG COOKING 1*
BRIGHTON (0273) 776618 COST £26–£34

Set in a converted fisherman's cottage in the hinterland between Brighton and Hove, Whytes is reckoned to be 'one of the few grown-up restaurants' in town. Ian and Jane Whyte run it as a family business: he cooks, she serves. Fixed-price menus change every few weeks, and the kitchen makes good use of local fish: monkfish and salmon terrine with tomato and basil coulis, and ragoût of brill and sole with scallops and mussels are typical examples. Among the starters, leek and Roquefort filo parcels, and roast red onion, Parmesan and spinach salad receive regular endorsements. The repertoire of main dishes features good meat and game enlivened with colourful sauces: roast crispy duckling with pears (or with caramelised grapefruit and pink peppercorns), fillet of lamb with garlic and cumin, or medallions of fillet steak with stout and mushrooms. Puddings are mostly traditional favourites such as crème brûlée, and pancakes with orange and Grand Marnier. The good-value French wine list is topped up with a few more expensive 'connoisseur' bins. House wines start at £7.50.

CHEF: Ian Whyte PROPRIETOR: Ian and Jane Whyte OPEN: Mon to Sat, D only; 7 to 9.30 MEALS: Set D £14.50 (2 courses) to £17.95. SERVICE: not inc CARDS: Access, Amex, Visa DETAILS: 40 seats. Private parties: 28 main room, 14 private room. Vegetarian meals. Children welcome. Smart dress preferred. Music

---

BRIMFIELD Hereford & Worcester map 2

▲ Poppies ♼ ✸

The Roebuck, Brimfield SY8 4NE
BRIMFIELD (0584) 711230 COOKING 3*
on A49, 4m S of Ludlow COST £38–£58

Standing in the bar area of this village pub, a reporter reflected that 'you would never guess you were in the ante-room of a gastronomic experience', but Carole Evans's food – which may be had in either bar or adjacent dining-room – tends to win instant converts. The dining-room is in muted good taste, with damask tablecloths, dark blue glassware for water, rattan chairs and flowers. Carole Evans works terribly hard: a soup plate stands on no fewer than three plates 'for the look of the thing', sorbets come in an ice bowl in which are set ferns and flowers.

All of this would be to no avail unless the cooking itself merited it. The overwhelming consensus is that it does. A three-course, fixed-price menu is offered at lunch, and a longer *carte* in the evening. There is a palpable passion for bringing out the best in whatever is seasonal and good. So in spring asparagus cropped up in two different ways among the starters, with a red and yellow pepper bavarois and in a ragoût with wild mushrooms on tagliatelle, the 'superb flavours' in the latter supported by a 'rich, subtle and perfumed sauce'. Other good things from the same meal included a cold soup of pea, lettuce and mint in which the flavours of all three components registered clearly, and 'large frilly round' ravioli filled with lobster on a lemon grass sauce. Fillet of Herefordshire beef on a purée of peas and walnuts (the nuts providing a 'delicious complementary flavour'), and bread-and-butter pudding in an individual ramekin with an apricot coulis are also rated highly. The cooking gives a deceptive impression of effortlessness, being – in the words of one – 'neither inaccessibly arty nor ostentatiously trendy'.

A large range of British and Irish cheeses is informatively presented. Pre-prandial nibbles, bread, cafetière coffee and petits fours all receive good notices. Service divides readers: one person's 'unhurried and soothing' is another's unacceptable delay. A woman who spoke affectionately of 'comely Renoiresque local girls in black and white' found them unendingly helpful. The wine list is the product of an enquiring mind, rather than a lazy trawl through the obvious great names of each region. Prices are not that low, but there are pages of halves (from £9) to consider. CELLARMAN'S CHOICE: Bourgogne Aligoté Bouzeron 1992, de Villaine, £16.50; Chianti Classico Terrabianca 1990, Scassino, £17.50.

CHEF/PROPRIETOR: Carole Evans   OPEN: Tue to Sat; 12 to 2, 7 to 10   MEALS: alc (main courses bar £6 to £13.50, restaurant £16.50 to £18.50). Set L £18   SERVICE: not inc, card slips closed   CARDS: Access, Amex, Visa   DETAILS: 36 seats. Private parties: 40 main room, 18 private room. Car park. Vegetarian meals. Children's helpings. On request. Smart dress preferred. No smoking in 1 dining-room. No music   ACCOMMODATION: 3 rooms, all with bath/shower. TV. Phone. B&B £45 to £60. Deposit: £30. Children welcome. Pets by arrangement. Doors close at 12.30am. Confirm by 6.30. Fax: (0584) 711654 (*The Which? Hotel Guide*)

BRINKWORTH Wiltshire   map 2

Three Crowns £

Brinkworth SN15 5AF
MALMESBURY (0666) 510366
on B4042 Malmesbury to   COOKING 1
Wootton Bassett road   COST £18–£31

The pub is on the main road through the village, with a conservatory bolted on one end, a garden for the family, window boxes of bright flowers and a great atmosphere. The bar is for lunchtime snacks of ploughman's and cold roast beef, and, of course, for drinking, while the flagged conservatory is set aside for more substantial eating. But it remains an informal pub at heart, with no booking. There are no first courses either, but a heck of a choice for everything else, all the balls kept in the air by high turnover. Protein is the main pursuit, with T-bone, sirloin, rump and fillet steaks, chicken, duck and venison, plus pies of steak and kidney or seafood. But vegetarian dishes, and fish particularly, give the place all-round appeal. Whole fresh sea bass is baked, and halibut or sea trout are poached, served with garlic butter or cream sauce. Pork tenderloin is served with a sweet sauce of cider and Stilton, and locally smoked chicken with a sauce of sherry, cream and mustard. If supplies of cream or alcohol dried up the kitchen would be completely at sea. It becomes obvious why there are no first courses when the plate of six different vegetables arrives with the main course. Sweet fruit pancakes, interesting ice-creams (including Christmas pudding) and cheeses bring up the rear. The wine list was being overhauled at the time of writing. House wine is £8.25.

CHEFS: Anthony Windle and Anthony Gale PROPRIETORS: Mr and Mrs Anthony Windle OPEN: all week; 12 to 2, 6.30 (7 Sun) to 9.30 MEALS: alc D (main courses £8.50 to £14). Light L menu SERVICE: not inc CARDS: Access, Amex, Visa DETAILS: 90 seats. 8 tables outside. Car park. Vegetarian meals. Children's helpings. Smart dress preferred. Wheelchair access. Music

---

BRISTOL Avon   map 2

Bell's Diner ✶ £

1 York Road, Montpelier, Bristol BS6 5QB
BRISTOL (0272) 240357
take Picton Street off Cheltenham Road   COOKING 2
(A38) – runs into York Road   COST £17–£36

Montpelier is either 'one of Bristol's less salubrious areas' or a 'colourful' part of town, depending on which way you look at it. Progress at Bell's Diner over the last year has been steady, and the informality of approach is readily understood and appreciated by most. When the atmosphere is right, lack of cushions can easily be forgiven. The food is also on target. Menus change two or three times a week and brim with sound, modern ideas. The Cornish haul of fish is put to optimum use, and Mediterranean and even Far Eastern treatments are boldly tried. This brings on to the menu items like sauté squid with noodles and a sauce of coconut, chilli and coriander, or grilled scallops with a mooli julienne and hoisin sauce. Warm tartlet of smoked salmon, capers and cream cheese was adjudged 'absolutely superb' by one couple, who went on to enjoy butterflied leg of lamb with minted flageolets, and guinea-fowl done Normandy-style with apples, calvados and cream. A gratinated vegetarian dish of goats' cheese gnocchi with pesto and mascarpone had 'wonderful' contrasts of richness and sharpness. Sticky toffee pudding does not cloy, while mango and lime mousse with a fresh mango coulis and chocolate roulade with sauces of coffee cream and raspberry have both been commended.

Incidentals are good, and service is amiably informal, with even chef pitching in as the evening draws to a close. Plenty of modern, challenging flavours have been tracked down for the wine list, and prices are agreeably level-headed. House selections start at £7.75.

CHEFS: Peter Taylor and Shirley Ann Bell PROPRIETORS: Shirley Ann Bell, Peter Taylor and Mark Hall OPEN: Tue to Sat, D only, and Sun L; 12.30 to 3, 6.45 to 10 (10.30 Sat) CLOSED: 30 Aug to 8 Sept, Sun L May to Sept MEALS: alc D (main courses £7.50 to £10). Set L Sun £10, Set D £12 SERVICE: not inc (10% for 8 or more) CARDS: Access, Visa DETAILS: 55 seats. Private parties: 28 main room, 18 private room. Vegetarian meals. Children's helpings. No smoking in dining-room. Music. Fax: (0272) 244280

Harveys 🍾

12 Denmark Street, Bristol BS1 5DQ
BRISTOL (0272) 275034

COOKING 3
COST £23–£56

History is laid on with a trowel in this stylish basement dining-room. Harveys the wine merchant was founded in these medieval cellars in 1796, and if the brick walls, arches, tunnels, barrels and dark stained wood are not sufficiently atmospheric, the wine museum is: well worth a visit for the glassware alone. The wares of the modern menu are laid out at length, and include a good choice of fish from hot chowder of smoked haddock, through sea bass, to John Dory with a mousse of crab and Jerusalem artichoke.

Accompaniments can be elaborate, perhaps to impress the corporate entertainers: home-cured bresaola of beef is sliced on to crisp parsnip, has a salad of French beans, apple and baby capers, and is 'finished' with twirls of fresh Parmesan. And what are we to make of fillet of red mullet with marinated vegetables, caramelised orange, wild mushrooms and a thyme butter sauce? No wonder the main item can sometimes get lost – a pity when first-class pink lamb, tender calf's liver, and wonderful pigeon breast topped with lightly cooked goose liver are available. Bacon is difficult to avoid – it featured in all four savoury dishes eaten at one meal – while vegetables may combinine carrot with orange, and green bean with onion. High-rise constructions are popular, not least the hot orange soufflé with Drambuie and chocolate cream.

Pastries and chocolates (with the rather disappointing coffee) are good. Service is polite and accurate, if slightly aloof, and there is live music some nights. Sherry is well kept and fresh, and goes well with introductory tapas of chorizo, and olives with toasted almonds. Port, Château Latour (and its kid brother Les Forts) also reflect the wine merchant's interests. Clarets are particularly impressive, with good value among the humbler bottles. House wines are £12. CELLARMAN'S CHOICE: Pauillac, Les Forts de Latour 1978, £60; Carneros Acacia Chardonnay 1989, £19.

CHEF: Ramon Farthing   PROPRIETORS: John Harvey and Sons   OPEN: Mon to Sat, exc Sat L; 12 to 1.45, 7 to 10.45   CLOSED: bank hols   MEALS: alc (main courses L £13 to £17.50, D £16.50 to £19.50). Set L £16.50, Set D £28   SERVICE: net prices, card slips closed   CARDS: Access, Amex, Diners, Visa   DETAILS: 120 seats. Private parties: 70 main room, 50 private room. Valet parking D. Car park. Vegetarian meals. Healthy eating options. No children under 8. Smart dress preferred. No-smoking area. Music. Air-conditioned. Fax: (0272) 275003

Howards

1A–2A Avon Crescent, Hotwells,
Bristol BS1 6XQ
BRISTOL (0272) 262921

COOKING 1
COST £20–£40

A Georgian builder bagged a good dockside spot not far from the city centre. Along came Brunel, and now the house looks out on to Clifton Suspension Bridge, with walkways and Victorian lock gates everywhere, and SS *Great Britain* just round the corner. Along came the Howards and David Roast, and it became a friendly, efficient bistro with a mission to serve simple, tasty food. The *carte* is seasonal, while the blackboard lists fish and anything else on offer that day, such as deep-fried American soft-shell crabs. The mix has evolved to take in smooth chicken liver pâté with olive and onion bread (all breads are made in-house) and Thai chicken wrapped in filo leaves on a red pepper sauce, as well as home-made ravioli of goats' cheese, calf's liver with onion compote and bacon, and baked Alaska. The cooking is no more ambitious than it needs to be and gets the basics right. Good quantities of vegetables include dauphinois potatoes, and the shortish list of well-chosen wines offers most bottles for less than £20, including burgundy. A separate fine wine list extends the scope, while house wine is £7.50. A sister restaurant, Howards Bistro, is situated a few miles south in Nailsea at 2 Kings Hill, Nailsea, Tel: (0275) 858348; reports please.

CHEF: David Roast   PROPRIETORS: Christopher and Gillian Howard   OPEN: Mon to Sat, exc Sat L (other times by arrangement); 12 to 2.30, 7 to 11.30   CLOSED: 25 and 26 Dec   MEALS: alc (main courses £10.50 to £15.50). Set L £13, Set D Mon to Fri £15   SERVICE: not inc (10% for 8 or more)   CARDS: Access, Amex, Diners, Visa   DETAILS: 65 seats. Private parties: 40 main room. Vegetarian meals. Children's helpings on request. No-smoking area. Wheelchair access. Music

Hunt's

26 Broad Street, Bristol BS1 2HG	COOKING 3
BRISTOL (0272) 265580	COST £19–£43

The premises used to be a tea and coffee merchant's in the heart of the old commercial centre, now surrounded by financial institutions and the law courts. The shop-window frontage opens into a small ante-room with a polished wooden bar counter and a few tables, with just enough room for a drink before moving to large, well-spaced tables in the adjoining room. The Hunts take sound ingredients as their starting point – vegetables from a nearby farm, game from a local man who shoots and hangs it – and subject them to largely French recipes, trimmed to their own likes and preferences, producing charcuterie, sorrel soup, guinea-fowl with apples and calvados, and calves' kidneys with black pudding. Half a dozen first courses and five mains are supplemented by a fish menu that might use Cornish crab in a salad or put Scottish scallops with bacon and thyme.

'It is like the best kind of informal French restaurant,' claims one reporter, who ate there for the first time shortly after the last *Guide* appeared and now makes it a regular fortnightly stop for the 'extraordinary value' set lunch. His first meal consisted of grilled fillet of plaice with béarnaise sauce and boiled potatoes, followed by a trio of chocolate mousses – two courses with coffee and a glass of wine for £13.70. No wonder he went back. Another reporter enjoyed a meal of baked goats' cheese with buttered baby leeks and a sweet-sour hot onion marmalade, fresh turbot in a cream sauce, and a properly cooked cardamom-flavoured crème brûlée served with a small dish of sharp stewed rhubarb and strawberries.

The bill holds no surprises – vegetables and service are included – nor do the wines, a sensibly priced collection of young bottles with helpful tasting notes. The house selection of half a dozen wines between £10 and £15 includes four by the glass from £2.25.

See inside the front cover for an explanation of the symbols used at the tops of entries.

CHEFS: Andrew Hunt and Haydn Neal   PROPRIETOR: Andrew and Anne Hunt   OPEN: Tue to Sat, exc Sat L; 12 to 2, 7 to 10 (10.30 Sat), and pre- or post-theatre by arrangement   CLOSED: 10 days Christmas, 1 week Easter, 2 weeks summer   MEALS: alc (main courses £13.50 to £16). Set L £10.50 (2 courses) to £12.50   SERVICE: net prices, card slips closed   CARDS: Access, Amex, Visa   DETAILS: 40 seats. Private parties: 26 main room, 26 private room. Vegetarian meals with prior notice. Children's helpings. Smart dress preferred. Wheelchair access (1 step). Music. Fax: (0272) 265580

Lettonie ♥

9 Druid Hill, Stoke Bishop,
Bristol BS9 1EW   COOKING 4
BRISTOL (0272) 686456   COST £26–£57

Lettonie concentrates more on essentials than peripherals. This ordinary house in an unassuming suburban terrace of shops accommodates cooking of a high order. The fittings have been refined over the years, so the dining-room is now quite comfortable and more in keeping with the kitchen's aspirations. Large tables decorated with one-off porcelain plates promote a sense of well-being, while silver coffee-pots add distinction.

'You wouldn't think the owner-chef was Hungarian,' wrote one reporter, impressed by the fine cosmopolitan blending of new and classic ideas, although the signature dish of scrambled duck egg with Sevruga caviare strikes an Eastern European note. It is served in a pool of flaming vodka – 'you have to blow it out quickly or the egg overcooks' – with blinis and a choice of pepper, lemon or straight vodkas to drink. Tortellini are a useful form of packaging, most notably containing langoustine, or pike and squat lobster, or even (as a savoury) goats' cheese with a tomato and olive sauce. Transformations and re-assemblies also figure, sometimes giving a trompe l'oeil effect: what looks like an intact quail thigh is actually a mousse of quail fashioned around the bare bone, served with a breast wrapped in more mousse and Parma ham. 'Triumphant' pig's trotter is adorned with 'fine, crisp, hair-like pork scratchings concealing a light filling of pork and chicken', surrounded by shallots and 'flavour-crammed strips of parsnip and green beans'. Fish is well treated too. Salmon, soft inside and just beginning to caramelise and crisp on the outside, is served with asparagus and capers in a warm olive oil dressing.

The cheeseboard might offer 'lovely Epoisses and an interesting hard cows' cheese from Spain'. It must be the sun that makes the cows hard. Puddings are generally soft and indulgent. Banana fritters come with honey ice-cream, ginger sponge is 'explosively tasty', and a 'magnificent dense, intense chocolate marquise' has the sponge on the inside. An extra charge is made for water and coffee, but one reporter felt compensated by a complimentary starter of sweetbreads wrapped in smoked bacon and cabbage leaf. Service, either by Siân Blunos or a bright young French maître d', is well-informed, friendly and efficient. The predominantly French wine list balances well-known names against lesser ones of good quality, with fair choice under £20, and vintages show some maturity. There is a reasonable number of half-bottles, and house wines (from £10.50) are well worth a look. CELLARMAN'S CHOICE: Margaux, Ch. Martinens 1985, £20.10; St-Véran Cuvée Prestige 1991, Lasserat, £22.85.

CHEF: Martin Blunos   PROPRIETORS: Martin Blunos and Siân Blunos   OPEN: Tue to Sat; 12.30 to 2, 7 to 9   CLOSED: 2 weeks Christmas, 2 weeks Aug, bank hols   MEALS: Set L £15.95 to £29.95, Set D £19.50 (Tue to Thur) to £29.95   SERVICE: not inc   CARDS: Access, Amex, Visa   DETAILS: 24 seats. Private parties: 24 main room. Vegetarian meals with prior notice. Children welcome. Smart dress preferred. Wheelchair access (1 step). Music. Fax: (0272) 686943

Markwicks 🍾

43 Corn Street, Bristol BS1 1HT	COOKING 3*
BRISTOL (0272) 262658	COST £24–£56

'Bristol is a maze to those unfamiliar with it.' To find Markwicks, just look for the banks. It is in the basement of former commercial rooms in the old business centre of the city, surrounded by money. When Judy Markwick is there (which, fortunately, is most of the time) customers get 'a most pleasant and immediate welcome' and service cannot be faulted. The personal involvement of husband and wife brings about an integration of food and service that reporters appreciate. It results in a feeling of being 'exceedingly well looked after'.

If soup is on the menu, the advice is to take it, whether it be 'splendid curried parsnip soup with that pleasant sweetness of the vegetable', or rocket soup which has 'plenty of flavour'. Many dishes have a Mediterranean impetus, from fish soup with aïoli, rouille and garlic croûtons, to scallops and prawns with a couscous salad. Other items help the theme along: a pesto crust for baked cod, crisp aubergine fritters, grilled peppers with rack of lamb, and wide use of balsamic vinegar. You may find also smoked haddock soufflé, good salads – with hot slivers of duck, or maybe sweetbreads, for example – as well as prune and armagnac tart and queen of puddings. Lunch is praised for value.

House wines (from £10) are so good that the remainder of the list could be safely ignored, were it not so chock-full of interest and value. It is selective (no long strings of vintages or producers to plough through) and bang up to date, balancing excitement and quality in a way that inspires confidence. CELLARMAN'S CHOICE: Pacherenc du Vic-Bilh, Ch. Bouscassé 1992, Brumont, £14.50; Ochoa Tempranillo 1990, £14.50.

CHEFS: Stephen Markwick and Sara Ody   PROPRIETORS: Stephen and Judy Markwick   OPEN: Mon to Sat, exc Sat L; 12 to 2, 7 to 10.30   CLOSED: 1 week Christmas, 1 week Easter, 2 weeks Aug, bank hol Mons   MEALS: alc (main courses £15 to £16.50). Set L £12.50 (2 courses) to £15, Set D £19.50   SERVICE: not inc, card slips closed   CARDS: Access, Amex, Visa   DETAILS: 40 seats. Private parties: 8 main room, 6 and 16 private rooms. Vegetarian meals. Children's helpings on request. Smart dress preferred. No music

Melbournes

74 Park Street, Bristol BS1 5JX	COOKING 1*
BRISTOL (0272) 226996	COST £15–£27

This buzzy, cosmopolitan place continues to pack them in. Regular full houses and two sittings in the evening prove that the owners have hit on a successful formula. Whirling fans, bright lights and walls festooned with work by modern Australian artists are the style of the place. Customers are encouraged to bring their own wine – Australian style – and the food hits the button. This is a no-frills set-up – no nibbles, no fancy breads – but it offers honest cooking that is fresh and 'full of lovely flavours'. The fixed-price dinner menu is excellent value, while the set lunches are cheaper still. Mainstays such as warm profiteroles with smoked mackerel mousse and anchovy sauce, roast fillet of lamb spiked with fresh rosemary, and brandy-snap basket filled with chocolate ice-cream are supplemented by specials of tuna steak with Cajun sauce or breast of pheasant in pastry. Service is 'proper, pleasant and leisurely', but seldom sluggish. The list of around 50 wines favours the antipodes and offers some very decent drinking. House wine is £6.25.

CHEF: C.J. Cowpe   PROPRIETORS: A.P. Wilshaw, N.J. Hennessy and C.J. Cowpe   OPEN: all week, exc L Mon and Sat and Sun D; 12 to 2 (3 Sun), 7 to 10.30   CLOSED: 24 to 30 Dec   MEALS: alc L (main courses £6.50 to £12). Set L £7.50 (2 courses) to £9, Set D £13.25 (2 courses) to £15   SERVICE: 10%, card slips closed   CARDS: Access, Amex, Diners, Visa   DETAILS: 100 seats. Private parties: 30 main room. Vegetarian meals. Children's helpings Sun L. No cigars/pipes in dining-room. Wheelchair access (1 step). Music

Muset

16 Clifton Rd, Clifton, Bristol BS8 1AF	COOKING 1*
BRISTOL (0272) 732920	COST £23–£32

Muset, which occupies three levels in the 'vast catacombs of a nineteenth-century building', brought big-scale eating to Bristol when the new Quaglino's was scarcely a gleam in Sir Terence Conran's bank account. It is noisily packed most nights, and has stayed that way through the slump. The proximity of the sprawling students' union building probably helps, but the place has built a firm bedrock of regular support for food that ventures beyond the usual brasserie confines. Mushrooms marinated with lemon grass and 'sweet and crumbly' duck confit were satisfying starters, while steak chasseur, rare pigeon breasts on a strong stock sauce and lamb with a wine and redcurrant sauce are all competently rendered main courses. Vegetables can be under par. Bakewell tart of rich solidity, 'nicely egged' crème brûlée and chocolate roulade have all received recommendations. Almost inevitably in a place of this scale some things go wrong, but what everyone loves is the chance to bring their own wine, which will be opened without charge. If you arrive after the off-licence has closed, the wine list is more than adequate. It draws inspiration from around the world, with plenty of stylish names. House wines are £7.95.

CHEFS: David Wheadon and Paul Baker   PROPRIETOR: The Muset Partnership   OPEN: all week, D only; 7 to 10.30   MEALS: Set D £13.50 (2 courses) to £15.50. Minimum £13.50   SERVICE: not inc (10% for 6 or more, card slips closed)   CARDS: Access, Amex, Visa   DETAILS: 150 seats. Private parties: up to 130 private rooms. Vegetarian meals. Children's helpings by arrangement early D. Smart dress preferred. Wheelchair access (1 step). Music. Air-conditioned. Fax: (0272) 732920

Several sharp operators have tried to extort money from restaurateurs on the promise of an entry in a guidebook that has never appeared. The Good Food Guide *makes no charge for inclusion and does not offer certificates of any kind.*

Rocinante's £

85 Whiteladies Road, Bristol BS8 4NT	COOKING 1
BRISTOL (0272) 734482	COST £17–£28

If you consider deep-fried whitebait, falafel and gooseberry fool to be tapas, then this is a tapas bar. It matters not from where the stuff originates; more significantly it is all divided into small, medium-sized and large dishes on the short and friendly menu. This youthful, light-hearted, up-beat, boisterous café enjoys a good laugh as much as good food and wine. Fresh organic produce is the foundation, all fish is wild not farmed – 'but not from over-trawled waters' – and certainly fresh. Eggs are free-range, and there is no microwave. The Mediterranean badge is worn with pride, while other dishes are picked up without a second's thought: chickpeas with cumin, tortilla, big prawns with aïoli, squid deep-fried in beer batter, home-made sausages with onion marmalade, and salmon and cod marinated in lime juice with garlic, chillies and coriander leaf. Parties that buy a few dishes and share probably get the best deal. House Spanish is £7.75 (£1.75 a glass).

CHEFS: Barny Haughton and Heather Statten PROPRIETORS: Barny Haughton and Matthew Pruen OPEN: all week; 12 (10 Sun) to 3, 6 to 11 MEALS: alc (main courses £5.50 to £10) SERVICE: not inc (10% for 6 or more) CARDS: Access, Visa DETAILS: 100 seats. 6 tables outside. Private parties: 70 main room, 30 private room. Vegetarian meals. Children welcome. Music

---

BROADHEMBURY Devon	map 1

Drewe Arms

Broadhembury EX14 0NF	
BROADHEMBURY (0404) 841267	
off A373, between Cullompton	COOKING 2*
and Honiton	COST £25–£29

'What a gorgeous place!' raved two travellers who made a detour to this remarkable hostelry. The 'estate' village hasn't changed in years and the thirteenth-century thatched pub next to the church epitomises everyone's idea of Arcadian rural England. A huge log fire burns in a 'roast-an-ox-size' fireplace, carved walking sticks bedeck the walls, an eel trap hangs from the ceiling. The combination of fine locally brewed beers, infectious friendliness and spot-on cooking adds up to big crowds, so booking is essential. Broadhembury is miles from the sea, but sparkling fresh fish is the star attraction on the blackboard menus. The seafood selection is a marvellous assortment of piscine delights with a fruity sauce. Other approved dishes have included fillet of brill with prawns and mushrooms, poached turbot with herby hollandaise, and lobster salad. Kerstin Burge also woos the customers with 'amazingly good' warm chicken and bacon salad, and venison in mushroom sauce. Sweets are out of the top drawer: treacle tart, 'masterly' mango sorbet, gargantuan wedges of 'wonderfully brittle, nut-packed' hazelnut meringue. Bar snacks are always available. The short, keenly priced wine list is a neat selection. House wine is £6.95.

CHEF: Kerstin Burge   PROPRIETOR: Kerstin and Nigel Burge   OPEN: all week, exc Sun D; 12 to 2, 7 to 10   MEALS: alc (main courses £12). Set L and D £16.95   SERVICE: not inc   DETAILS: 40 seats. 10 tables outside (limited garden menu). Private parties: 25 main room. Car park. Vegetarian meals with prior notice. Children's helpings. Wheelchair access (1 step; also WC). No music

---

BROADWAY Hereford & Worcester   map 2

▲ Collin House

Collin Lane, Broadway WR12 7PB	
BROADWAY (0386) 858354	COOKING 2
on A44, 1m NW of Broadway	COST £18–£37

'Faded gentility' was one reporter's view of this sixteenth-century Cotswold stone house, but comfort and 'solicitous, welcoming service' can cause visitors to linger: 'We arrived for 6 – and, leaving after 10, still felt reluctant' to go. The cooking resides in the world of benign country-house food, with an emphasis on bulk and richness. A wide-ranging *carte*, priced on the main course, offers the likes of pan-fried croquettes of salmon on a tomato sauce, a 'vast' dish of wild rabbit delicately set off by prunes and light herb dumplings, and 'superb' home-made ginger ice-cream. Other dishes might include baked breast of guinea-fowl with caramelised citrus sauce, sea bass with tomato and basil vinaigrette, and venison with gin and mulberry sauce. Some reports would welcome greater concentration on incidentals such as bread, vegetables and coffee. Light lunches are served in the seventeenth-century bar or in the garden (weather permitting): expect anything from steak and kidney pie to pan-fried prawns with Mediterranean sauce. The list of around 60 wines is a realistically priced, catholic selection. House wine is £9.75.

CHEFS: Mark Brookes and Anthony Ike   PROPRIETOR: John Mills   OPEN: all week; 12 to 1.30, 7 to 9   MEALS: alc bar L (main courses £4.50 to £7). Set L £14.50, Set D £15 to £23   SERVICE: not inc, card slips closed   CARDS: Access, Visa   DETAILS: 30 seats. 5 tables outside. Private parties: 32 main room. Car park. Vegetarian meals. Children's helpings at L. No children under 7 D. Smart dress preferred. No cigars/pipes in dining-room. Wheelchair access (1 step; also WC). No music   ACCOMMODATION: 7 rooms, all with bath/shower. B&B £45 to £96. Deposit: £40. Children welcome. Baby facilities. Garden. Swimming-pool. Doors close at midnight (*The Which? Hotel Guide*)

▲ Dormy House ✸✕

Willersey Hill, Broadway WR12 7LF	COOKING 1*
BROADWAY (0386) 852711	COST £23–£55

Set on a windy Cotswold hilltop close by the golf course that gives the hotel its name, Dormy House is a seventeenth-century farmhouse with twentieth-century facilities. Oak beams, rafters and mellow stone walls are still to be seen in the bar, while the airy, conservatory-style dining-room is done out with lots of tapestry work, long drapes and a billowing tented ceiling. Having taken over the mantle of head chef, Alan Cutler has moved the cooking into a more elaborate version of hotel cuisine, complete with luxury ingredients and mid-course sorbets. Specialities such as tagliatelle of scallops in a light Noilly Prat and fish stock consommé, and baked fillet of pork with glazed apples and green Chartreuse sauce show the range. The cooking is competent, although flavours may be swamped by complexity, as in roast loin of lamb wrapped in a potato galette with an aubergine and courgette timbale. Desserts such as hot Tia Maria and walnut soufflé are capably handled. Service is attentive and observant. The weighty wine list focuses on big champagnes, clarets and burgundies, but prices are fair and halves show up well. House wine is £9.95.

CHEF: Alan Cutler   PROPRIETOR: Jorgen Philip-Sorensen   OPEN: all week, exc Sat L; 12.30 to 2 (2.30 Sun), 7.30 to 9 (7 to 9.30 Sat)   CLOSED: 25 and 26 Dec   MEALS: alc (main courses £18 to £20). Set L £14 (2 courses) to £16, Set D £25.50   SERVICE: not inc   CARDS: Access, Amex, Diners, Visa   DETAILS: 80 seats. Private parties: 40 main room, 8 and 14 private rooms. Car park. Vegetarian meals. Children's helpings L, and D 5 to 7.30. Smart dress preferred. No smoking in 1 dining-room. Music   ACCOMMODATION: 49 rooms, all with bath/shower. TV. Phone. B&B £58 to £116. Rooms for disabled. Children welcome. Baby facilities. Pets welcome (not in public rooms). Afternoon teas. Garden. Sauna. Doors close at 12.30am. Confirm by 6. Fax: (0386) 858636 (The Which? Hotel Guide)

Hunters Lodge

High Street, Broadway WR12 7DT   COOKING 1
BROADWAY (0386) 853247   COST £20–£44

The creeper-covered lodge stands far enough back from the road to feel detached from the tourists who pile through the village. Log fires, ticking clocks, cats and family snapshots evoke a domestic feel, and candlelight is all that illuminates the heavy beams, mullioned windows, dark-varnished bare tables, and old framed diplomas and awards. Hunters may not move much with the times but appeals for its relaxed 'no rules' approach, which goes for everything from dress to minimum spend. An inspector who visited five years after her previous encounter noted that the food is now less ambitious and more prosaic. The fixed-price menu might offer soup or local asparagus with hollandaise, rump steak with a red wine sauce, and sweet or cheese, while choice on the *carte* runs to crispy crabmeat croquettes, roast best end of lamb with a herb crust, and meringue nest with butterscotch sauce and cream. Nibbles and coffee are below par, while the predominantly French wine list is sound and reasonably priced with a good selection of half-bottles. House wine is £7.70 (£1.65 per glass).

CHEF: Kurt Friedli   PROPRIETORS: Kurt and Dottie Friedli   OPEN: Wed to Sat D, Sat and Sun L; 12.30 to 1.45, 7.30 to 9.45   MEALS: alc (main courses £9.50 to £14.50). Set L Sat £14, Sun £15, Set D £18.50   SERVICE: not inc, card slips closed   CARDS: Access, Amex, Diners, Visa   DETAILS: 45 seats. Private parties: 36 main room, 20 private room. Car park. Vegetarian meals. Children's helpings. No children under 8. Wheelchair access (2 steps; also WC). Music

▲ Lygon Arms

High Street, Broadway WR12 7DU   NEW CHEF
BROADWAY (0386) 852255   COST £31–£67

The Lygon Arms is part of picture-postcard village England, with all the luxurious appointments typical of the Savoy Group, including a health spa. The dining-room wows visitors with its barrel-vaulted ceiling, heraldic frieze and seventeenth-century minstrels' gallery. Amidst all the trappings of internationalism it still manages to exude a friendly atmosphere, which is what endears it to readers: 'The ambience was quite delightful,' affirms one.

Former chef Clive Howe developed a rather personalised branch of the English cooking movement that suited it well, re-working ideas from old cookery books and using local and seasonal produce in a repertoire that included broths, fish in oatmeal crust, braised oxtail, rhubarb compote, old-fashioned blancmange and the like. He is moving on as we go to press, and Roger Narbett is scheduled to head up the team after two years with Willi Elsener at the Dorchester. In his spare time he is also chef to the England football team, which has nothing whatsoever to do with the fact that the cooking has no score this year. Reports please.

The wine list is good, but mark-ups are generally too high for comfort. The Loire and vins de pays will afford some relief, and most other countries help to even things out a bit; there is a good selection of half-bottles. The two 'everyday' house wines are £12, with the 'Superior House Selection' coming in at about £20 a bottle.

CHEF: Roger Narbett   PROPRIETOR: The Savoy Group plc   OPEN: all week; 12.30 to 2, 7.30 to 9.15 (9.30 Sat)   MEALS: alc (main courses £15.50 to £21.50). Set L £19.50 to £38, Set D £29.75 to £38   SERVICE: not inc, card slips closed   CARDS: Access, Amex, Diners, Visa   DETAILS: 120 seats. 10 tables outside. Private parties: 95 main room, 12, 40, 60 and 95 private rooms. Car park. Vegetarian meals. Children's helpings. No children under 3 D. Jacket and tie D. Wheelchair access (also WC). Music   ACCOMMODATION: 65 rooms, all with bath/shower. TV. Phone. B&B £103 to £182. Rooms for disabled. Children welcome. Baby facilities. Pets welcome. Afternoon teas. Garden. Swimming-pool. Sauna. Tennis. Snooker. Fax: (0386) 858611 (*The Which? Hotel Guide*)

BROCKENHURST Hampshire   map 2

Le Poussin ⅝✶

The Courtyard, Brookley Road,
Brockenhurst SO42 7RB   COOKING 3*
LYMINGTON (0590) 23063   COST £24–£47

Between Bestsellers (the bookshop) and Robert Bruce (the hairdresser) is a narrow archway. Through that is a tiny, rather scruffy courtyard, and the much smarter restaurant, with ceiling spots to highlight the tables, already laid with black and green olives and sticks of cheese pastry. Alex Aitken is a New Forest man. He lives in a natural larder, and makes full use of it. Rarely does a combination of first-class raw materials, and the talent to convert them into fine dishes, co-exist as happily. Pigs roam the forest, rooting and snaffling, venison is on the hoof, and the New Forest is a prime spot for wild mushrooms – what bounty! In spring the free-range pork might appear with fresh morels and home-made pasta. Fillet of venison is seared, blood-red inside, 'with a glorious gamey taste, and the most heavenly creamy mashed potatoes'.

Menus are flexible, listing four courses (with a choice of two items at each) but allowing the freedom to eat only two or three if preferred. Sausage 'with the texture of a perfect quenelle' is a favourite device for packaging seafood or chicken: the first with a saffron sauce, the latter with wild rice. Trios are popular too: fillet of pork, beef and lamb in a reduced red wine sauce, or of salmon, skate and plaice in a light fish and herb sauce. Rustic salads of cured meats, and game and pork terrines, emphasise Le Poussin's roots. Not everybody is happy, however. Some flavours have lacked vitality, some cooking times have been approximate. Service is well paced, efficient and professional, if sometimes lacking in warmth.

Advice on wine is worth taking – 'We had the best Spanish red I have ever tasted' – although another imbiber found that inexpert decanting 'ensured that all the sediment entered the decanter'. There are some impressive names on the predominantly French wine list, although vintages yo-yo from extreme maturity to extreme youth, without any notes for guidance. Australia looks like a developing interest. The house wine selection has around 10 bottles from £10 upwards.

CHEF: Alex Aitken PROPRIETORS: Alex and Caroline Aitken OPEN: Wed to Sun, exc Sun D (booking advisable); 12 to 2, 7 to 10 MEALS: Set L Wed to Sat £10 (2 courses) to £15, Sun £12.50 (2 courses) to £17, Set D £20 (2 courses) to £25 SERVICE: not inc CARDS: Access, Visa DETAILS: 24 seats. 3 tables outside. Private parties: 24 main room. Car park. Vegetarian meals with prior notice. Children welcome. No smoking in dining-room. Wheelchair access (1 step; also WC). No music. Fax: (0590) 22912

BROMSGROVE Hereford & Worcester   map 5

▲ Grafton Manor

Grafton Lane, Bromsgrove B61 7HA
BROMSGROVE (0527) 579007   COOKING 1*
1½m SW of Bromsgrove, off B4091   COST £27–£50

The fabric of the manor scores a rare success: 'It is baronial but not imposing', with ample grounds, a large lawn at the front, and a large herb garden at the rear which serves the kitchen well. Arrivals are whisked upstairs to the bar: a huge sitting area 'with a few Gothic quirks'. Grafton is not a place that reporters pop into casually for an impromptu meal. 'They know their market,' observed one who was celebrating a special occasion, surrounded by well-to-do businessmen and women.

Simon Morris likes to inject Indian influences into his cooking, producing fillet of cod marinated in yogurt with aromatic spices, and a dish of aubergine and apple with lamb kofta. But he has not entirely 'gone native'. Some of the results are cross-cultural – tomato and bergamot terrine, for instance – while some have moved as far away from the Indian sub-continent as pasta with mushrooms and olives in pesto sauce, or the spring nettle sauce that accompanies grilled fillet of salmon. What matters is that the flavours work. Roast pheasant with puréed turnip, and bread and clove stuffing is 'brilliant', according to one report, and parsnip and ginger soup is impressively 'creamy, tangy and earthy'. Wine prices are for special occasions and business customers, but house wines (from £10.55) and those from Australia and New Zealand help to redress the balance.

▲ *This symbol means accommodation is available.*

CHEFS: Simon and Nicola Morris PROPRIETORS: the Morris family OPEN: all week, exc Sat L; 12.30 to 1.30, 7.30 to 9 CLOSED: 3 days Jan MEALS: Set L Sun £16.95, Mon to Fri £20.50, Set D £19.95 to £28.50 SERVICE: not inc, card slips closed CARDS: Access, Amex, Diners, Visa DETAILS: 45 seats. Private parties: 42 main room, 18 private room. Car park. Vegetarian meals. Children welcome. Smart dress preferred. Wheelchair access (2 steps). No music ACCOMMODATION: 9 rooms, all with bath/shower. TV. Phone. B&B £85 to £150. Children welcome. Baby facilities. Garden. Fishing. Doors close at midnight. Confirm 2 days ahead. Fax: (0527) 575221 (*The Which? Hotel Guide*)

BROXTED Essex   map 3

▲ *Whitehall*

Church End, Broxted CM6 2BZ
BISHOP'S STORTFORD (0279) 850603   COOKING 2
off B1051, 3m SW of Thaxted   COST £32–£64

What twentieth-century buildings will future generations use to house their restaurants? Elizabethan manor houses like this – and few come prettier – are made for the job, as if some sixteenth-century builder could see the restaurant potential in the original designs. Wooden beams and galleries are straight out of the history books, while renovation has produced a fine and tasteful contrast. Conference delegates and travellers using Stansted Airport appear to constitute a fair part of the business, but Whitehall still feels agreeable and congenial for diners (we have no reports of lunch).

Paul Flavell's menu throws up a generous choice of modern dishes helped along by flourishes of raspberry vinaigrette, nutmeg croûtons, or potato and ginger rösti. Despite occasional excursions into exotica – roast breast of chicken with carrots and scallops in a Thai cardamom sauce, for example – invention is generally kept in check. Centrepieces are stylishly done, and range from hot haddock soufflé or home-made sausages to duck marinated in honey and thyme, and steamed fillet of sea bass with potato and crab pancakes. Extra vegetables offer a better-than-average selection of chips, mushroom risotto, and tempura of aubergine, among others. Puddings are accomplished too, taking in hot raspberries in puff pastry on a tarragon anglaise, and a white chocolate and pistachio nut parfait on a butterscotch sauce. A short New World selection adds interest to the mainly French wine list, although there are few bargains. House French is £14, house Australian £16.

CHEF: Paul Flavell PROPRIETORS: the Keane family OPEN: all week; 12.30 to 2, 7.30 to 9.30 MEALS: Set L £19.50, Set D £34 to £37.50 SERVICE: not inc, card slips closed CARDS: Access, Amex, Diners, Visa DETAILS: 60 seats. Private parties: 120 main room, 16 and 120 private rooms. Car park. Vegetarian meals. Children welcome. Smart dress preferred. No cigars/pipes in dining-room. Wheelchair access (also WC). No music ACCOMMODATION: 25 rooms, all with bath/shower. TV. Phone. B&B £75 to £155. Rooms for disabled. Children welcome. Afternoon teas. Garden. Swimming-pool. Tennis. Doors close at midnight. Fax: (0279) 850385 (*The Which? Hotel Guide*)

'This remains a place where one can not only eat headless chickens, but be served by them too.' (On eating in London)

BRUTON Somerset

map 2

Truffles

95 The High Street, Bruton BA10 0AR	COOKING 2
BRUTON (0749) 812255	COST £21–£38

'The proprietors told us that they recently visited Turkey and brought back some culinary ideas. This sort of thing should be encouraged,' notes a reader convinced of the mind-broadening powers of travel. The Bottrills do have itchy feet. They have been to the Far East, India and Africa in recent years, and their gleanings crop up on the monthly-changing menus that Martin Bottrill cooks. On cold nights the fire roars, as it must have once for the weavers whose home this originally was, and the three-course, set-price menu provides plenty to divert the attention.

In March, offerings included leek and Roquefort mousse with a raita-style yogurt dressing of cucumber and mint, mussels baked in Goan fashion with coconut, ginger and chilli, braised lamb sweetbreads with spinach and morels, and duck breast with fig and orange sauce. Desserts mobilise vivid flavours such as lime yogurt parfait with orange sauce or white chocolate mousse with carrot marmalade. Even crème brûlée contains apricot. The eponymous truffles are the chocolate sort that come in a brandy-snap basket with coffee. The reporter who described this as a 'very pleasant, personal restaurant with an obviously happy clientele' got it right.

The wine list makes a determined attempt to furnish the diner with both choice and value. It shows a real fondness for New World wines, but the French selections are sound as well, even if a native of that country would cringe at some of the spelling. Basic house French is £7.95, but is supplemented by an award-winning oaked Chardonnay from the Aude at £13.95 that is well worth a punt.

CHEF: Martin Bottrill   PROPRIETOR: Denise and Martin Bottrill   OPEN: Tue to Sat, D only, and Sun L (weekday L and Sun D by arrangement); 12 to 2, 7 to 10   MEALS: Set L Sun £12.95, Set D £12.50 to £19.95   SERVICE: not inc, card slips closed   CARDS: Access, Visa   DETAILS: 22 seats. Private parties: 25 main room. Vegetarian meals. Children's helpings Sun L. No children under 7. Smart dress preferred. Wheelchair access (1 step). No music

BUCKLAND Gloucestershire

map 2

▲ *Buckland Manor* ▾ ⁕

Buckland WR12 7LY	
BROADWAY (0386) 852626	COOKING 2
on B4632, 2m SW of Broadway	COST £29–£73

The heavy wood panelling of the hall and bar lounge of this Cotswold manor is lightened in the dining-room, although tasselled velvet curtains, varnished antique tables, William Morris prints for the chair fabric and cut glass all speak of a dignified reserve. Add to this a formal dress code, domed main courses, high prices and impeccably trained French service, and there is hardly a chink of mitigating frivolity to be seen through the serious intent.

The menu does its best to rejig tried and tested ideas without straying too far into novelty: roast duckling with orange and jasmine tea sauce for instance, or sauté fillet of lamb with *two* mint sauces. But the luxuries get piled on too: poached Cornish lobster with caviare, or ballottine of quail with foie gras, truffle and pistachio. Puddings plough a familiar furrow of crêpes suzette and apple tart with cinnamon ice-cream. Handling of these ideas varies from successful (warmed Teign oysters, served with tagliatelle flavoured with tomato and basil) to, on one occasion, over-peppered beef fillet, and a hot chocolate soufflé whose hot chocolate sauce precluded any stab at flavour contrast. Vegetables, according to an inspector's report, were poor.

A fistful of house wines and French country wines, reasonably priced and all available by the glass, head up a list that not only roams the world but keeps 17 different wine merchants on their toes. Extensively annotated, the list takes some getting through, but the lively and up-to-date New World section alone makes it worth the effort, and there are nearly a hundred half-bottles. CELLARMAN'S CHOICE: Wairau River Sauvignon Blanc 1993, £14.30; Normans Winery Shiraz 1991, £12.30.

CHEF: Martyn Pearn   PROPRIETORS: Roy and Daphne Vaughan   OPEN: all week; 12 to 2, 7.30 to 9   MEALS: alc (main courses £19 to £25.50). Set Mon to Sat L £18.50, Set L Sun £20.50 SERVICE: not inc   CARDS: Access, Amex, Visa   DETAILS: 40 seats. Car park. Vegetarian meals. No children under 8. Jacket and tie. No smoking in dining-room. Wheelchair access. No music ACCOMMODATION: 14 rooms, all with bath/shower. TV. Phone. B&B £145 to £290. No children under 12. Afternoon teas. Garden. Swimming-pool. Tennis. Fax: (0386) 853557 (*The Which? Hotel Guide*)

BURFORD Oxfordshire   map 2

▲ *Lamb Inn* ⁵⁄✳

Sheep Street, Burford OX18 4LR   COOKING 1
WITNEY (0993) 823155   COST £18–£48

'The perfect English idyll in a wild, quiet garden in bloom,' mused reporters who enjoyed an al fresco lunch outside this picture-postcard Cotswold inn with honeysuckle and roses entwined around its grey stonework. In bad weather, it is worth seeking solace around the log fires that burn in the three lounges. Bar lunches are light dishes along the lines of asparagus with garlic, and warm avocado salad, and Wadworth beers are on handpump. Dinner in the restaurant is a different matter. Pascal Clavaud works to a menu that inhabits the realms of smoked chicken and shiitake mushroom ravioli with spring onion sauce, medallions of monkfish with buttered leeks and saffron sauce, and tangerine brioche on an orange crème anglaise. Seasonal game is a major theme. Sunday lunch kicks off with Buck's Fizz, and a buffet is laid out later in the day. The well-spread list of 70 wines has plenty of decent drinking to suit all palates and pockets. House wine is £8.50.

'The computer-generated bill identified one main dish as ''Food'', which made me wonder what the others were considered to be.' (On eating in London)

CHEF: Pascal Clavaud PROPRIETORS: Mr and Mrs R. de Wolf OPEN: restaurant all week, D only, and Sun L; 12.30 to 1.45, 7.30 to 9. Bar Mon to Sat, L only; 12 to 2 CLOSED: 25 and 26 Dec MEALS: alc Mon to Sat (main courses £12.50 to £17.50). Set L Sun £16, Set D Mon to Sat £20, Sun buffet £16.50. Bar menu L SERVICE: not inc CARDS: Access, Visa DETAILS: 55 seats. Private parties: 16 main room. Car park. Vegetarian meals. Children's helpings. Smart dress preferred. No smoking in dining-room. Wheelchair access (2 steps; also men's WC). No music ACCOMMODATION: 15 rooms, 12 with bath/shower. TV. Phone. B&B £35 to £90. Children welcome. Baby facilities. Dogs welcome (£5 charge). Garden. Doors close at 11. Fax: (0993) 822228 (*The Which? Hotel Guide*)

BURNHAM MARKET Norfolk   map 6

Fishes' £

Market Place, Burnham Market PE31 8HE	COOKING 1*
FAKENHAM (0328) 738588	COST £19–£45

'This is a fish restaurant!' insists Gillian Cape, although she is happy to knock up something for vegetarians or buy a steak from the butcher opposite if given warning. Support for her friendly place continues unabated: 'I have been going to Fishes' twice a year for the 20 years since it opened,' commented a reporter who was happily accommodated along with spouse, two 8-year old children, and the 70-year-old nanny of one of them. The catch from the local boats and the output of the smokehouse are the mainstays for a menu that includes crab soup, gravlax, salmon fish-cakes, skate wings with capers, home-baked ham with smoked turkey and goose breast, and much more besides. Reporters have also endorsed potted shrimps 'from the Wash', and baked oysters with mussels. Set-price weekday lunches are particularly good value. Service is generally friendly, although the leisurely pace does not suit everyone. The short, reasonably priced wine list includes an example from the local Elmham Winery. House wine is £7.50.

CHEFS: Gillian Cape, Paula Ayres and Carole Bird PROPRIETOR: Gillian Cape OPEN: Tue to Sun, exc Sun D; 12 to 2 (2.15 Sun), 6.45 to 9.30 (9 weekdays off-season) CLOSED: 24 to 26 Dec, 27 Dec L, 3 weeks Jan to Feb MEALS: alc (main courses £5.50 to £12.75). Set L £8.95 (2 courses) to £12.25 SERVICE: not inc, card slips closed CARDS: Access, Amex, Diners, Visa DETAILS: 48 seats. Private parties: 14 main room. Vegetarian meals with prior notice. Children's helpings. No children under 5 after 9. No smoking while others eat. Wheelchair access. No music

---

BURPHAM West Sussex   map 3

George and Dragon

Burpham BN18 9RR	
ARUNDEL (0903) 883131	
off A27, 1m E of Arundel, signed	COOKING 1
Warningcamp	COST £21–£30

The pub is two-and-a-half miles up a single-track road high up on the downs. This is serious walking and hiking country. Well-liked owners Marianne and George Walker have left and chef Kate Holle is now co-proprietor, along with

James Rose. Little else has changed. The restaurant menu majors in fulsome, fancy-free dishes such as pork en croûte, fillet of lamb with marsala sauce and vegetarian strudel. A Swiss influence shows up in butterleberli (strips of calf's liver pan-fried in butter) and in the rösti potatoes. A trolley of fine home-made sweets might include 'the best tiramisù I have ever tasted'. Reporters have enjoyed high-class bar food along the lines of crab and avocado salad, and filo pastry filled with chicken, mango and Brie. Real ales are chalked up on a blackboard, and the place has a creditable, fairly priced wine list spanning the globe. House French is £7.80.

CHEFS: Kate Holle, David Futcher and Gary Scutt   PROPRIETORS: Kate Holle and James Rose
OPEN: restaurant Mon to Sat, D only, and Sun L; 12 to 1.30, 7.15 to 9.30. Bar meals all week, exc
Sun D; 12 to 1.45 (2 Sun), 7.15 to 9.45   CLOSED: 25 Dec   MEALS: Set L Sun £14.50, Set D
£15.50 (2 courses) to £18.50   SERVICE: 10% for restaurant, card slips closed; not inc for bar
CARDS: Access, Visa   DETAILS: 40 seats. 8 tables outside (bar food only). Private parties: 40
main room. Vegetarian meals. No babies. Smart dress preferred. Wheelchair access (also WC).
No music. Air-conditioned (partly)

BURTON UPON TRENT Staffordshire   map 5

▲ *Dovecliff Hall*

Dovecliff Road, Stretton, Burton upon Trent
DE13 0DJ
BURTON UPON TRENT (0283) 31818
¾m off A38, between Stretton   COOKING 2
and Rolleston   COST £20–£48

This elegantly restored Georgian country-house overlooking the River Dove imparts a sense of calm in an area known more for the hustle and bustle of industry and commerce. The gardens are formal, the dining-room high-ceilinged and the cooking is successful country-house led by Hilary Hine.

The *carte* is priced according to the choice of main course, and there are fixed-price menus as well. A respect for tradition (recent as well as age-old) comes across in baked filo parcels of Brie with cranberry sauce, brochette of scallops wrapped in bacon, and versions of moules marinière, gravad lax and duck liver pâté with brioche. Other culinary cultures than British and French are acknowledged in a first course of chicken curry served in a poppadum basket with saffron rice, or the Chinese spicing in a main course of grilled duck breast. Puddings offer what is expected today: bread-and-butter, crème brûlée, treacle tart, for example. A tranquil evening may take on a different character when the pianist is giving it plenty, and service on one occasion, while efficient, was 'lacking in warmth'.

The wine list kicks off in imposing fashion, with some fine and expensive clarets. Burgundies are nowhere near as good, but those in search of price relief will be driven outside France anyway to the reasonable selections from Spain, Italy and Germany. The international house wines start at £10.

See the back of the Guide *for a listing of all restaurants in the Main Entries sections.*

CHEFS: Hilary Hine and I. Johnson PROPRIETORS2: Mr and Mrs N.O. Hine OPEN: Tue to Sun, exc Sat L and Sun D; 12 to 1.45, 7 to 9.30 CLOSED: 1 week Christmas, 1 week spring, 2 weeks summer MEALS: Set L £9.50 (2 courses) to £11.50, Set L Sun £13.95, Set D £17.50 to £29 SERVICE: not inc CARDS: Access, Visa DETAILS: 85 seats. 3 tables outside. Private parties: 85 main room, 16 and 60 private rooms. Car park. Vegetarian meals. Children's helpings. Smart dress preferred. No cigars/pipes in dining-room. Wheelchair access (also WC). Music ACCOMMODATION: 7 rooms, all with bath/shower. TV. Phone. B&B £55 to £95. Children welcome. Garden. Fishing. Doors close at midnight. Confirm by 10am. Fax: (0283) 516546

BURY ST EDMUNDS Suffolk   map 3

Mortimer's £

31 Churchgate Street,
Bury St Edmunds IP33 1RG   COOKING 1
BURY ST EDMUNDS (0284) 760623   COST £19–£42

This branch of Mortimer's (the other is at Ipswich, see entry) has clocked up 10 years' service to the seafood lovers of Suffolk. The formula remains unchanged: a giant menu that spans the range from the honest simplicity of prawn cocktails, taramasalata and smoked eel with horseradish to classically sauced main courses such as lemon sole dieppoise (mussels, prawns, mushrooms, white wine and cream) and monkfish provençale (tomatoes, onions, herbs and garlic). The fish is always of the freshest, and many enjoy it plainly cooked. One couple reported the previously generous portions now somewhat reduced. Doubts may creep in when the mark is missed, as in plum sorbet and potted shrimps both short on flavour for one reporter. Service has, on occasion, been found 'rushed'. The list of mainly white wines does justice to the food, the Alsace section in particular looking more than ample. House French is £7.25.

CHEFS: Kenneth Ambler and Hannah Jolly PROPRIETORS: Kenneth Ambler and Michael Gooding OPEN: Mon to Sat, exc Sat L; 12 to 2, 7 to 9 (6.30 to 8.15 Mon) CLOSED: 23 Dec to 6 Jan, last 2 weeks Aug, bank hols MEALS: alc (main courses £7.50 to £17) SERVICE: not inc CARDS: Access, Amex, Diners, Visa DETAILS: 60 seats. Private parties: 12 main room. Vegetarian meals. Children's helpings. Smart dress preferred. No-smoking area. Wheelchair access (1 step; also WC). No music. Fax: (0284) 752561

CALSTOCK Cornwall   map 1

▲ Danescombe Valley Hotel ▼ ✴

Lower Valley, Calstock PL18 9RY
TAVISTOCK (0822) 832414   COOKING 2*
1m W of Calstock on riverside road   COST £32–£40

'This is now our favourite place in England at which to stay-and-eat-and-drink,' enthused a couple from Oxfordshire who relish the prospect of a visit to Martin and Anna Smith's idiosyncratic house overlooking the Tamar. Their 'husband and wife' efforts are supported by a housekeeper and a loyal band of local suppliers. Vegetables are grown 'along the lane' by a gardener famed for his 'early growing techniques', salmon is netted from the river just outside the hotel door, soft fruits are from the Tamar Valley, and a marvellous array of unpasteurised cheeses fly the flag for the West Country. The accent is firmly on flavour. 'This is helped by reducing the chain from producer to the plate of raw ingredients,' explains Martin. Anna Smith's cooking shows something of her Italian roots in dishes such as baked peppers, Calstock asparagus baked with Parmesan, and guinea-fowl stuffed with fennel and potatoes then roasted with olives and garlic. The fixed-price dinner menu offers no choice for four courses, but variety is the key. A typical day's offering might be roast tomato soup, then rack of lamb with mustard and honey, then cheese, and finally apple crumble tart with honey ice-cream.

You can tell wine is a hobby for the Smiths. The list has a high ratio of comment to wine, and some interesting bottles and obscure grape varieties. It also has that other hallmark of the enthusiast: prices that say 'go on, try this'.

CHEF: Anna Smith PROPRIETORS: Martin and Anna Smith OPEN: Fri to Tue, D only; 7.30 for 8 CLOSED: 30 Oct to 7 Apr (exc 4 days Christmas) MEALS: Set D £27.50 SERVICE: net prices, card slips closed CARDS: Access, Amex, Diners, Visa DETAILS: 12 seats. Private parties: 12 main room. Car park. Vegetarian meals with prior notice. No children under 12. No smoking in dining-room. No music ACCOMMODATION: 5 rooms, all with bath/shower, and 1 cottage. D,B&B £97.50 to £175. Deposit: £50. No children under 12. Garden. Doors close at 1am. Confirm by 5. Fax: (0822) 832414 (*The Which? Hotel Guide*)

CAMBRIDGE Cambridgeshire   map 3

Midsummer House ♀

Midsummer Common,
Cambridge CB1 1HA   COOKING 2*
CAMBRIDGE (0223) 69299   COST £35–£70

The Victorian brick house on the edge of the common is as small as its sign is discreet. Park in Pretoria Road and walk over the footbridge, or ask for directions. The entrance is like that of a private house, except for the greeter. Narrow stairs lead up to a small and intimate dining-room, while the airy conservatory looks out on to the gardens. The place is designed to induce a feeling of well-being before the business of eating begins.

The fixed-price meals offer half a dozen choices per course, usually with something for vegetarians, although simplicity is not always the watchword. In winter a first course of snails with garlic, thyme and parsley was served on rösti potatoes with a red wine sauce, each gastropod sitting on half a baby turnip. In summer they came baked in filo pastry, a common device here for parcelling and packaging. Ingredients are good and carefully handled, although the kitchen sometimes does not quite know when to stop when it comes to garnishes and combinations of flavours.

Heartiness appears, in a bean cassoulet with braised salmon, young leeks and mashed potato, or in a dish of calf's liver, sweetbreads and ox tongue on a bed of spinach with a red Sancerre butter sauce. The big plates hold lots of food, and that goes for puddings as well, in which chocolate and cream play a significant role. Consider a 'wonderful cake consisting of layers of light ganache with a sliver of sponge, liqueur-flavoured raspberry purée and a rich dark layer of chocolate truffle'. Despite all this 'the chef's touch is lighter than it might appear'.

Not so the accountant's. Prices are considered high. The tenor of reports is less prettiness please, more directness of flavour, and smaller bills.

France dominates the wine list, but the whole thing keeps its ear to the ground in order to pick good producers just about everywhere. Mark-ups can be on the high side, but there is stacks available by the glass, including a dozen from California, all mostly £2 to £4. Wines are suggested to partner food, and help is available from the wine waiter.

CHEF: Hans Schweitzer PROPRIETORS: Chris Kelly and Hans Schweitzer OPEN: Tue to Sun, exc Sat L and Sun D; 12.15 to 2, 7.15 to 10 CLOSED: 26 Dec to 2 Jan MEALS: Set L Tue to Fri £17 (2 courses) to £23, Sun £25, Set D Tue to Fri £24 (2 courses) to £36, Sat £30 to £36 SERVICE: not inc CARDS: Access, Amex, Visa DETAILS: 60 seats. 15 tables outside. Private parties: 60 main room, 16 private rooms. Vegetarian meals. Children's helpings. No Music. Fax: (0223) 302672

Twenty Two ♥

22 Chesterton Road, Cambridge CB4 3AX   COOKING 2
CAMBRIDGE (0223) 351880   COST £28–£39

Candle-lit tables add to the homely atmosphere in this small Victorian terraced house owned by two lecturers from the local catering college. The form is a monthly-changing menu of three courses, with a mixed leaf salad tossed in before the main and a £3.50 supplement for extra fish or cheese.

Ideas are interesting without being flashy: smoked chicken ravioli has a coriander dressing, leek and basil tart takes a red pepper dressing, while the polenta served with chicken breast is flavoured with herbs and bacon. Soups set a tasty precedent, adding celeriac to carrot, or curry to lentils. Sauces to accompany rabbit, tuna or roast pigeon are often a reduction, perhaps flavoured with a herb such as basil or tarragon. For variety, some dishes are processed a little more. Timbale is a favoured form (applied to fish, pork, and fruit puddings), and chicken might be made into sausages, served with creamed potatoes and a shallot sauce. There is a sense of climax at the end. 'Poached pears with raspberry coulis and an ice-cream was the highlight of the meal,' and tiramisù has impressed with its lightness. Service is warm, courteous and attentive. The free-ranging wine list keeps up to date with developments, concentrating on moderately priced bottles chosen for flavour and character. House wines (including Gyöngyös Sauvignon Blanc, and Domaine de Limbardie red) start at £8.50. CELLARMAN'S CHOICE: Jackson Estate Sauvignon Blanc 1993, £15.50; Valdepeñas Gran Reserva 1984, Viña Albali, £11.95.

CHEF: Chris Gorham PROPRIETORS: David Carter and Louise Crompton OPEN: Tue to Sat, D only (L by arrangement); 7.15 to 9.45 CLOSED: 1 week at Christmas MEALS: Set D £19.50 to £23. SERVICE: not inc CARDS: Access, Visa DETAILS: 30 seats. Private parties: 34 main room, 12 private room. Vegetarian meals. Children's helpings on request. No children under 11. Smart dress preferred. Music

The Guide is totally independent, accepts no free hospitality, and survives on the number of copies sold each year.

CAMPSEA ASH Suffolk   map 3

▲ Old Rectory ▼ ⚡✳

Campsea Ash IP13 0PU
WICKHAM MARKET (0728) 746524   COOKING 2
on B1078, 1m E of A12   COST £23–£29

The Rectory might be 'suitable for a Victorian parson with eight children',
observed one visitor who ate in Stewart Bassett's 'idiosyncratic' country-house
hotel. He runs the place, cooks and seems to know most of his guests' likes and
dislikes. The original dining-room has been converted into a sitting-room, and
meals are now served in the 'barn-like' conservatory with its royal blue and
mustard colour schemes, stripped pine tables and wicker chairs.

Dinner now consists of three courses, with cheese as an optional extra. The
considered view of one inspector is that Stewart Bassett is 'capable of producing
masterpieces', but that his cooking can be 'patchy'. Marvellous dishes such as
'classic' tagliatelle with wild mushrooms, grilled poussin with a herb crust and a
'superb winey reduction sauce', and moist apple and orange sponge show what
can be done. Vegetables are first-rate and cheeses are kept in good order. Sunday
lunch is a welcome addition to the set-up. An extensive wine list includes some
very mature claret and eight vintages of Lebanon's Ch. Musar. Prices are
extremely favourable, making for affordable as well as interesting drinking. A
generous spread of half-bottles is welcome. House French is £9.

CHEF/PROPRIETOR: Stewart Bassett   OPEN: Mon to Sat, D only, and Sun L; 12.30 to 1.45, 7.30 to
8.30 (8.45 Sat) (residents only Mon D and Sun L)   CLOSED: 25 and 26 Dec   MEALS: Set L Sun £8
to £10 (2 courses), Set D £16 to £17.50   SERVICE: not inc   CARDS: Access, Amex, Diners, Visa
DETAILS: 40 seats. Private parties: 34 main room, 8 and 18 private rooms. Car park. Vegetarian
meals with prior notice. Children's welcome. Smart dress preferred. No smoking in dining-room.
Music   ACCOMMODATION: 9 rooms, all with bath/shower. B&B £30 to £60. Deposit: £10.
Children welcome. Dogs welcome. Garden. Doors close at midnight. Confirm by 7.30 (The
Which? Hotel Guide)

CANTERBURY Kent   map 3

▲ Sully's

County Hotel, High Street,
Canterbury CT1 2RX   COOKING 2
CANTERBURY (0227) 766266   COST £23–£48

'Excellent food and service, no Muzak, perfect for impressing new arrivals from
abroad,' sums up one reporter. Access to the car park is via Stour Street, since the
High Street is now pedestrianised. The hotel is opposite the post office, and the
restaurant is 'in an early 1970s time capsule', complete with bare bricks, alcoves,
a loud carpet and 'garage-standard glassware'.

Pan-fried duck foie gras arrives on a galette of celeriac, while asparagus salad
comes with a confit of chicken gizzard. Roast veal kidney is served with beef
marrow, as French as you like, but the flourishes indicate that Eric Marin-
Gavignet doesn't just go by the book. Braised halibut has a rhubarb and white
wine sauce, for example, and among more striking flavours are a creamed ginger
sauce with coriander (for roast poussin) and liquorice ice-cream, served with

sautéd bananas and spicy cake. There is a fondness for butter (vegetables are 'swimming in it') and for hollandaise sauce, ladled, for example, over a warm tartlet of quail's eggs and asparagus, or a brandade of smoked haddock on a bed of green beans. Pastry work is good, extending to thin puff pastry for a pineapple and mango tart. A few Italian and Australian wines pad out the predominantly French list, which includes some classic bottles from the classic regions. House vin de pays is £10.50 (£2 per glass).

CHEF: Eric Marin-Gavignet   PROPRIETOR: Laughing Water Hotels Ltd   OPEN: all week; 12.30 to 2.30, 7 to 10   MEALS: alc (main courses £13 to £16). Set L £12.50 (2 courses) to £15, Set D £15.50 (2 courses) to £18   SERVICE: not inc   CARDS: Access, Amex, Diners, Visa   DETAILS: 50 seats. Private parties: 18 main room, 30, 100 and 130 private rooms. Car park. Vegetarian meals. Children's helpings. Smart dress preferred. No pipe smoking in dining-room. Wheelchair access (also female WC). No music. Air-conditioned   ACCOMMODATION: 73 rooms, all with bath/shower. TV. Phone. B&B £74.50 to £110. Rooms for disabled. Children welcome. Baby facilities. Afternoon teas. Confirm by 6. Fax: (0227) 451512

CARLTON North Yorkshire   map 7

▲ Foresters Arms £   NEW ENTRY

Carlton, nr Leyburn DL8 2BB
CARLTON (0969) 40272   COOKING 1
off A684, 4½m SW of Leyburn   COST £17–£33

Set in a sprawling Wensleydale village not far from Middleham Castle, this seventeenth-century sandstone inn has been given a new lease of life with the arrival of Messrs Higginbotham and Thornalley. The interior has been modernised, but the flagstone floors, polished beams and splendid stone fireplace remain. Outstanding bar meals show the capabilities of the kitchen: one typically good lunch consisted of Wensleydale cheese with pork sausages in a salad bowl of 'chamberpot proportions', perfectly executed roast sea bass followed by baked chocolate cake with crème anglaise. Dinner in the restaurant is a more flamboyant five-course affair. Elaboration is everywhere and menu descriptions are full of flourishes such as 'sauté king scallops presented with a summer salad lacquered by a lemon and saffron vinaigrette' or 'breast of Lunsedale duckling accompanied by a garlic confit bordered by a rosemary and claret jus'. The overall artistry has greatly impressed reporters, who also approve of the knowledgeable, welcoming service. The short wine list is dominated by France, but prices are fair across the range. House wine is £8.95.

CHEF: B.K. Higginbotham   PROPRIETORS: B.K. Higginbotham and S.J. Thornalley   OPEN: Tue to Sun, exc Sat L restaurant and Sun D; 12 to 2, 7 to 9.30   MEALS: bar alc (main courses £5.50 to £10.50). Set L and D £19.95   SERVICE: not inc, card slips closed   CARDS: Access, Visa   DETAILS: 30 seats. Private parties: 35 main room. Car park. Vegetarian meals. No children under 12. Smart dress preferred. No-smoking area. Wheelchair access. Music   ACCOMMODATION: 3 rooms, all with bath/shower. TV. Phone. B&B £30 to £55. Deposit: £20. Children welcome. Baby facilities. Pets welcome (1 room only). Afternoon teas

---

▲ *This symbol means accommodation is available.*

CARTERWAY HEADS Northumberland   map 7

▲ *Manor House Inn* ✤ £

Carterway Heads, Shotley Bridge DH8 9LX
CONSETT (0207) 55268   COOKING 1
on A68, 3m W of Consett   COST £13–£26

Ladies rub shoulders with the farm lads in this lively pub on the moors. The owners make good use of local produce, procuring everything from Craster kippers to venison and hare for a repertoire that moves happily between the homespun and the fashionable. Home-cured gravlax and chicken casseroled with tomato, mint and garlic have pleased lunch-time visitors; you might also find Alsatian onion tart, asparagus and Parmesan gratin and wild salmon with basil butter. Regulars are always 'seduced' by the pudding list – sticky toffee, and hot chocolate and walnut have both made pleasurable finales. Service is reckoned to be 'excellent'. Real ales and ciders supplement the modest wine list, which is an intriguing, ever-changing selection from around the world. House wine is £7.

CHEFS: Jane Pelly, Elizabeth Fielding and Gordon Graves   PROPRIETORS: Anthony and Jane Pelly, and Elizabeth Fielding   OPEN: all week; 12 to 2.30, 7 to 9.30 (9 Sun)   CLOSED: 25 Dec   MEALS: alc (main courses £3.50 to £9). Set L and D £15.50   SERVICE: not inc, card slips closed   CARDS: Access, Visa   DETAILS: 100 seats. 6 tables outside. Private parties: 50 main room. Car park. Vegetarian meals. Children's helpings. Smart dress preferred. No smoking in 1 dining-room. Wheelchair access (2 steps). Music   ACCOMMODATION: 4 rooms. TV. B&B £20 to £35. Children welcome. Baby facilities. Doors close at 11.30

CARTMEL Cumbria   map 7

▲ *Uplands* ✤

Haggs Lane, Cartmel LA11 6HD
CARTMEL (053 95) 36248
2½m SW of A590, 1m up road opposite Pig   COOKING 3*
and Whistle   COST £20–£38

Since 1985, the partnership of Tom and Diana Peter (with John Tovey as a founding father) has made this one of the Lake District's most enticing country hotels. The views out towards Morecambe Bay are wonderful, and all is peace in house and garden. The kitchen draws supplies from a thriving local network: game from Holker Hall, sea bass from the Furness Peninsula, char from Windermere, organic vegetables from a gardener in the area.

The short lunch menu is outstanding value, although it stays with a tried and tested repertoire of dishes, such as poached fillet of salmon with chive and vermouth sauce, and breast of chicken stuffed with apricots, hazelnuts and tarragon. However, familiarity can be comforting, and even regular visitors are never disappointed. 'We must come more often,' remarked one couple, who singled out the quality of the raw materials, the exactness of Tom Peter's cooking and his 'mouthwatering' presentation. The Tovey influence shows in the marvellous tureens of soup (mushroom and apple, courgette and rosemary, parsnip and ginger) served with a warm wholemeal loaf suffused with black treacle and the elaborate vegetables (deep-fried leek rings, mashed swede and turnip with horseradish, celeriac purée with pine-nuts). The four-course dinner menu focuses on specialities such as fillets of Dover sole with asparagus and hollandaise, and roast guinea-fowl with brandied apricots. Desserts – another Tovey forte – might include raspberry and apple pie, 'decadent' poached peach with butterscotch sauce, and that Lakeland classic, sticky toffee pudding. Good value extends to the short wine list, which is noted for its New World selection. House wine is £7.50.

CHEF: Tom Peter   PROPRIETORS: John Tovey, and Tom and Diana Peter   OPEN: Tue to Sun; 12.30 to 1, 7.30 for 8   CLOSED: 1 Jan to 25 Feb   MEALS: Set L £14, Set D £25   SERVICE: not inc, card slips closed   CARDS: Access, Amex, Visa   DETAILS: 28 seats. Private parties: 12 main room. Car park. Vegetarian meals with prior notice. No children under 8. Smart dress preferred. No smoking in dining-room. Wheelchair access (1 step; also WC). Music   ACCOMMODATION: 5 rooms, all with bath/shower. TV. B&B £47 to £80. No children under 8. Pets welcome (not in public rooms). Garden. Doors close at midnight. Confirm by 6. Fax: (053 95) 36248 (*The Which? Hotel Guide*)

CASTLE CARY Somerset   map 2

▲ Bond's |NEW ENTRY|

Ansford Hill, Castle Cary BA7 7JP
CASTLE CARY (0963) 350464
on A371, 400yds past station towards   COOKING 1*
Wincanton   COST £20–£39

Bond's is a listed Georgian building run as a small country-house hotel. Rooms are simply but tastefully furnished, and housekeeping is impeccable. Although the dining-room might feel more like that of a guesthouse rather than a hotel, Yvonne Bond's cooking is very sound and covers a reasonably wide repertoire. The combination of daily and monthly menus results in a flexible choice that might take in lightly creamy, but fiery, hot Thai fish soup, with a mound of bean sprouts and king-size prawns in the middle, guinea-fowl legs wrapped in cabbage leaves, and rice pudding with a thin cinnamon-flavoured custard. The wok is used for lamb's liver (sliced and marinated in oil, wine and lovage), and wild rabbit and bacon. Salmon may be marinated with stem ginger, or with lime and dry sherry, and black pudding has been served with grilled confit of goose and a pear compote for a main course, and with sweet caramelised onion marmalade and a mustard sauce as a first course. There is some wrapping of meat in pastry, which works well. Bread and canapés (a cross between ratatouille and chutney on a croûton, perhaps) provide good back-up, and the short wine list is reasonably priced. House wine is £8.50.

CHEF: Yvonne Bond   PROPRIETORS: Yvonne and Kevin Bond   OPEN: all week, D only; 7 to 9.30 (7.30 Sun and Mon)   CLOSED: 1 week Christmas   MEALS: Set D £12.50 to £23.25   SERVICE: not inc, card slips closed   CARDS: Access, Visa   DETAILS: 20 seats. 2 tables outside. Private parties: 16 main room. Car park. Vegetarian meals. Children welcome. No music   ACCOMMODATION: 7 rooms, all with bath/shower. TV. Phone. B&B £38 to £80. Deposit: £40. Babies welcome. No children under 8. Afternoon teas. Garden. Doors close at 11.30

The Good Food Guide *is a registered trade mark of Consumers' Association Ltd.*

CASTLE COMBE Wiltshire · map 2

▲ *Manor House Hotel* 🍴✳

Castle Combe, nr Chippenham SN14 7HR
CASTLE COMBE (0249) 782206   COOKING 2
on B4039, 3M NW of junction with A420   COST £27–£75

The first Manor of Castle Combe existed before the Norman Conquest and
pre-dates the castle itself. History looms large hereabouts. Parts of the original
fourteenth-century house remain, and antique touches such as the beautiful
Italian frieze in the lounge help to give the place its character. Twenty-six acres of
parkland and gardens complete with walks, stone statues and specimen trees are
outdoor attractions. In contrast to the unashamed Englishness of the setting,
Mark Taylor's cooking is international, drawing inspiration from around the
globe. Samosas of sweet peppers and tomatoes with basil leaves, soufflé of goats'
cheese with ground pine-kernels and tomato salsa, and fillet of brill cooked 'in
paper' with ceps and home-made tagliatelle are typical of his approach. Desserts
range from iced tiramisù soufflé to hot apple fritters with caramel syrup and
apple sorbet. The fascinating list of English farmhouse cheeses includes rare
names such as Little Rydings from Timsbury and Golden Cross from East
Sussex. Wines are extensive, the list is full of good things, but prices are
uncomfortably high. House white is £16.50, house red £17.50, both £2.95
per glass.

CHEF: Mark Taylor PROPRIETOR: Manor House Hotel Ltd OPEN: all week; 12 to 2, 7 to 10
MEALS: alc (main courses £18.50 to £22). Set L £16.95, Set D £32 SERVICE: not inc, card slips
closed CARDS: Access, Amex, Diners, Visa DETAILS: 70 seats. 12 tables outside. Private
parties: 10 main room, 10, 12 and 20 private rooms. Car park. Vegetarian meals. Children's
helpings. Smart dress preferred. No smoking in dining-room. Wheelchair access (3 steps; also
WC). Music ACCOMMODATION: 36 rooms, all with bath/shower. TV. Phone. B&B £110 to £315.
Rooms for disabled. Children welcome. Baby facilities. Dogs welcome (£10 per night).
Afternoon teas. Garden. Swimming-pool. Tennis. Fishing. Doors close at 2am. Confirm by noon.
Fax: (0249) 782159 (*The Which? Hotel Guide*)

CHADDESLEY CORBETT Hereford & Worcester · map 5

▲ *Brockencote Hall* 🍴✳

Chaddesley Corbett DY10 4PY
CHADDESLEY CORBETT (0562) 777876
on A448, Kidderminster to Bromsgrove   COOKING 1*
road, just outside village   COST £21–£54

'An aura of relaxed opulence' is how one reporter describes the atmosphere of
this classical house set in 70 acres of grounds. The new extension is
'sympathetically linked to the original building', and friendly, efficient staff –
plus log fires when appropriate – are welcoming.

   Eric Bouchet's cooking revolves around fixed-price menus of three or four
choices per course, more for pudding, and 'is consistently good, and beautifully
presented with an artistic flourish,' according to one fan. For those who thought
snails and frogs' legs had disappeared from the repertoire, the news is they are
alive and well, or rather they were, until served (respectively) in filo pastry with

gnocchi, and poached in a chicken and cucumber bouillon with baby carrots. Some of the seafood is of Scottish origin, including hot-smoked salmon, and Gigha oysters wrapped in courgette, served with shredded chicory, smoked salmon and saffron cream. The robust French vein, however, runs through everything, from a pastry pouch of langoustine tails flavoured with fennel and Pernod, to quail's eggs in aspic served with a warm quail confit, and pan-fried foie gras with a Sauternes butter sauce. There is more than a touch of opulence to the wine list, but a short house selection (from £9.40) makes good use of lesser-known and interesting French regions.

CHEF: Eric Bouchet   PROPRIETORS: Alison and Joseph Petitjean   OPEN: all week, exc Sat L; 12 to 1.30, 7 to 9.30   MEALS: Set L £16.50 to £28.80, Set D £21.50 to £35.50   SERVICE: net prices, card slips closed   CARDS: Access, Amex, Diners, Visa   DETAILS: 60 seats. Private parties: 45 main room, 18 and 28 private rooms. Car park. Vegetarian meals with prior notice. Children's helpings. Smart dress preferred. No smoking in dining-room. Wheelchair access (also WC). No music   ACCOMMODATION: 17 rooms, all with bath/shower. TV. Phone. B&B £79 to £120. Rooms for disabled. Children welcome. Baby facilities. Afternoon teas. Garden. Doors close at midnight. Confirm by 6. Fax: (0562) 777872

CHADLINGTON Oxfordshire   map 2

▲ *Manor* ▮ ⸙

Chadlington OX7 3LX   COOKING 1
CHADLINGTON (0608) 676711   COST £32–£40

The Grants run an organised yet relaxed regime, enhanced by 'the aesthetic pleasure of taking meals in that splendid dining-room' with its high ceiling and ornate fireplace. The building has the gravitas typical of Cotswold mansions, as well as reassuring views of safely grazing sheep. 'The cooking satisfied without everything quite coming off,' wrote one reporter prepared to overlook minor blemishes in a meal that went from chicken and almond soup, via pigeon breasts with crab apple and wine sauce, to bread-and-butter pudding. Chris Grant's cooking has a homely appeal but is not above tackling something out of the ordinary once in a while, such as turkey with gin and lime sauce. Meals are five courses, beginning with a set soup (lettuce and lovage, for instance) and ending with cheese. In between is a modest choice that might take in grapefruit soufflé, chicken breasts with smoked bacon and Stilton, and chocolate pavé with praline cream.

The wine list succeeds without straying much outside France, although the Germans are good too. It stays mostly with the classics, plus a few others from the regions, including Jura for curiosity. Even the prestigious bottles are not outrageously expensive – first-growth clarets back to the 1950s are still only in double figures – but even more unusual are red and white burgundy, and even a handful of Sauternes and Barsacs, under £20. A generous selection of half-bottles completes the rosy picture. House Duboeuf is £8.50.

CHEF: Chris Grant   PROPRIETORS: Chris and David Grant   OPEN: all week, D only; 7 to 8.30   MEALS: Set D £25.50   SERVICE: net prices, card slips closed   CARDS: Access, Visa   DETAILS: 20 seats. Car park. Vegetarian meals with prior notice. Children's helpings on request. No smoking in dining-room. Music   ACCOMMODATION: 7 rooms, all with bath/shower. TV. Phone. B&B £60 to £110. Children welcome. Garden. Doors close at 11. Fax: (0608) 676674

CHAGFORD Devon | map 1

▲ *Gidleigh Park* ▮ ⁵✳

Chagford TQ13 8HH
CHAGFORD (0647) 432367
from Chagford Square turn right at Lloyds
Bank into Mill Street, take right fork after
150 yards, follow lane for 1½m

COOKING 4
COST £47–£80

Shaun Hill is a difficult act to follow. He went off in the middle of 1994 to do other things after nine years at Gidleigh. When he arrived in 1985, John Webber must have been a difficult act to follow too, but the Hendersons have a knack of knowing where to look for new blood. Michael Caines is an Exeter lad who has cooked around – for Raymond Blanc and Joël Robuchon among others – so he knows one end of a lobster from another. He arrived just in time for an inspector to pop along and take a look. 'He is an innovative chef, and if the dinner we had after only a few weeks of his being at Gidleigh Park is anything to go by, he will very soon be established as one of the country's top chefs.'

Caines's style is less robust than that of his predecessor, although no less imaginative or flavourful. A few flash ingredients appear, including truffle vinaigrette for a salad of scallops and potatoes, and a sprinkling of caviare on warmed Rossmore oysters, but the cooking is not gimmicky. 'The dishes we tasted demonstrated sure-handed cooking with not too much gastro-display, yet with clarity, balance and freshness of ideas.' One of these was crab ravioli, generously filled with intensely flavoured crab meat, aromatised with lemon grass and ginger, the sauce gentle and soothing, and just enough to whet the plate.

First-rate ingredients are the foundation, and Caines's sound classical technique turns them into impressive dishes. Pigeon breasts, sweet and pink with a hint of muskiness, are served as a salad and dressed with a gentle pigeon stock, which is gamey and pungent without being overwhelming. Seasoning is spot-on. Polish shows in precisely cooked lamb sweetbreads, the crusty surface contrasting with a delicately yielding inside, and in a dish of sweet, tender rabbit, beautifully textured and full of flavour, with a generous scattering of chanterelle, girolle and oyster mushrooms.

Caines cooks with enthusiasm, flair and attention to detail, nowhere more apparent than in a plate of caramel desserts that makes 'a pleasant change from the more usual chocolate selections', and includes a miniature soufflé cooked 'in an oversized thimble', a tiny crème caramel, and a caramel-flavoured rice pudding topped with caramelised apricot. Cheese and breads are as good as before.

Wines are as before too, ready to drink, with mark-ups progressively reduced the higher up the scale you go. The Alsace section is bolstered by a clutch of Trimbach's Riesling Clos Ste Hune this year, Italian and American wines are excellent, and other regions and countries producing fine wine are well represented. Wines by the glass are well above average (from £4), and Paul Henderson has discovered the pleasures of beer, prompting a good run of bottles, including Chimay, Lambic and some English ales. CELLARMAN'S CHOICE: Jurançon Sec 1990, Dom. Cauhapé, £23; Ch. Routas, Cuvée La Truffière 1992, Bieler, £20.

CHEF: Michael Caines PROPRIETORS: Paul and Kay Henderson OPEN: all week; 12.30 to 2, 7 to 9 MEALS: Set L £37.50 to £47.50, Set D £47.50 to £55 SERVICE: net prices, card slips closed CARDS: Access, Amex, Diners, Visa DETAILS: 40 seats. Private parties: 8 main room, 30 private room. Car park. Vegetarian meals with prior notice. Children's helpings. Smart dress preferred. No smoking in dining-room. No music ACCOMMODATION: 15 rooms, all with bath/shower. TV. Phone. D,B&B £190 to £365. Children welcome. Baby facilities. Pets welcome (not in public rooms). Afternoon teas. Garden. Tennis. Fishing. Fax: (0647) 432574

CHARINGWORTH Gloucestershire   map 2

▲ *Charingworth Manor* ♟ ✳

Charingworth,
nr Chipping Campden GL55 6NS
EVESHAM (0386) 593555   COOKING 2*
on B4035, 2½m E of Chipping Campden   COST £26–£47

Yes, here is another gorgeous Cotswold stone manor house with gables, mullioned windows, nooks, crannies, low ceilings, ancient beams, four-poster beds, and a spa that could have come straight from a Roman emperor's villa. Unlike antiques, on sale in every town and village for miles around, manor houses are bolted to the floor and cannot easily be shipped off to Milwaukee or Honshu. That is why there are so many of them still around, although, as we go to press, we learn that this one is for sale. We don't know whether William Marmion will be cooking as you read this, but in case he is, here is what we were going to say anyway.

His style is contemporary, which is to say it relies on some traditional ideas but brightens them up with a dash of orange chutney here, to accompany a game terrine, or a green salsa there, beside the tournedos of beef. The choice of half a dozen items for each of the three courses might produce a meal of grilled goats' cheese with roasted bell peppers, ragoût of sea bass with mussels and asparagus, and mango and passion-fruit parfait. Fish is given due prominence among main courses, the quality is high and flavours are impressive. It is the distinction in flavour across the board, and concentration on the main business of a dish rather than on unnecessary garnishing, that appeal about the cooking. Service is of the formal dome-lifting variety. The impressively aristocratic wine list struggles to provide much under £20. It deals fairly thoroughly with the main regions of France, and has some good vintages, yet completely ignores anything south of the Rhône. Half-bottles are reasonably well distributed. House wine begins at £11 and there is a short but welcome selection by the glass. CELLARMAN'S CHOICE: Pinot Grigio 'Collio' 1992, Puiatti, £19.50; Bannockburn Cabernet Sauvignon 1988, £21.75.

CHEF: William Marmion PROPRIETOR: Blandy Brothers & Co Ltd OPEN: all week; 12.30 to 2, 7 to 9.30 MEALS: Set L £17.50, Set D £29.50 SERVICE: not inc, card slips closed CARDS: Access, Amex, Diners, Visa DETAILS: 48 seats. Private parties: 40 main room, 36 private room. Car park. Vegetarian meals. No children under 10 D. Smart dress preferred. No smoking in dining-room. No music. Air-conditioned ACCOMMODATION: 24 rooms, all with bath/shower. TV. Phone. B&B £90 to £195. Deposit: £50. Children welcome. Baby facilities. Pets welcome (not in public rooms). Afternoon teas. Garden. Swimming-pool. Sauna. Tennis. Snooker. Doors close at 12am. Confirm by 9. Fax: (0386) 593353 (*The Which? Hotel Guide*)

CHEDINGTON Dorset   map 2

▲ *Chedington Court* ♀

Chedington DT8 3HY
CORSCOMBE (0935) 891265   COOKING 2
off A356, 4½m SE of Crewkerne   COST £31–£42

Chedington bills itself a 'hotel and golf club', but the course is a mile away, so don't worry about awakening to the sound of five-irons hacking stray balls out of the rough. Birdsong is a more likely alarm. The house itself is a dignified mid-nineteenth-century pile, its interiors discreetly done, all old gold and burnished wood. In the evenings, a fixed-price, five-course menu that changes daily offers a choice of four starters, a set fish course, four main courses (with usually one vegetarian), a dessert trolley and cheeses, plus coffee. Against the grain of country-house style, the menus read fairly simply: 'The food', says a reporter, 'is reliable rather than exciting – and none the worse for that.' A mid-May menu included terrine of avocado and prawns, glazed onion tartlet with a thyme sauce, and tomato and basil gâteau with aubergine and pesto among the starters, followed by steamed fillet of turbot with vegetables and herbs. Main courses offered beef sirloin with pink peppercorns, stuffed quail pot-roasted in port and shallots, and a madeira-flamed spinach and cream cheese pancake. Service is 'unobtrusively civilised'.

An extravagantly lengthy wine list tours the world for pedigree wines, and prices are relentlessly reasonable. Choices outside Europe look a bit staid, but the roll-call of clarets, burgundies and Rhônes, and the exhaustive list of fine German wines, will make for long and happy contemplation. Halves are available in heartening profusion. House French starts at £7.50. CELLARMAN'S CHOICE: Mercurey 1992, Ch. de Chamirey, £19.50; Brouilly, Ch. des Tours 1992, £14.50.

CHEFS: Hilary Chapman and James West   PROPRIETORS: Philip and Hilary Chapman   OPEN: all week, D only; 7 to 9   CLOSED: 2 Jan to 2 Feb   MEALS: Set D £27.50   SERVICE: net prices, card slips closed   CARDS: Access, Amex, Visa   DETAILS: 30 seats. Private parties: 30 main room, 22 private room. Car park. Vegetarian meals. Children's helpings (at 6.30). No children under 10. Smart dress preferred. No cigars/pipes in dining-room. Wheelchair access (2 steps; also WC). Music   ACCOMMODATION: 10 rooms, all with bath/shower. TV. Phone. D,B&B £80 to £176. Deposit: £30. Children welcome. Baby facilities. Pets welcome (not in public rooms). Afternoon teas. Garden. Golf. Snooker. Doors close at midnight. Fax: (0935) 891442 (*The Which? Hotel Guide*)

CHELTENHAM Gloucestershire   map 2

Le Champignon Sauvage ♀

24–26 Suffolk Road,
Cheltenham GL50 2AQ   COOKING 3*
CHELTENHAM (0242) 573449   COST £24–£48

David Everitt-Matthias has worked in the past with the great Pierre Koffmann, and the influence shows up not least in the earthy southern French inspiration of many of his dishes. There is, remarked an inspector, 'tremendous attention to detail' in such items as an amuse-gueule that consisted of a tiny piece of pigeon on a pearl barley 'risotto' with beetroot in a blob of sauce containing fragments of chocolate. This 'restaurant français' is housed in a pair of terraced cottages knocked together, with an understated grey colour scheme within that provides a soberly neutral backdrop for the food. The Frenchness extends to a large collection of aperitifs and digestifs on view behind the bar, and also – alas – to the laborious menu descriptions that contain nonsenses like 'glace ripple au chocolat' and will be ignored anyway by non-linguists.

Once past that, it is clear that there is serious talent at work in the execution of dishes such as belly pork braised with Chinese spices and served on salad leaves with sauté potatoes and onions, hake fillet on that signature barley risotto, this time with leeks and a red wine and veal stock sauce, or herb-crusted chicken breast with flageolets, tapénade and 'a roundel of delicately scented chicken mousse'. Desserts are similarly fine, as in a powerful chocolate and prune terrine with bitter orange syrup. The French cheeses are a wide, and quite unusual, selection in prime condition. Despite the restaurant's name, wild mushrooms are not invariably present on the menus. Occasional slips do occur: one couple gruffly reported overdone ribeye steak and unsatisfactory coffee. When it's on form, though – which it mostly is – few would disagree with the 'really excellent' verdict proclaimed by an inspector.

California, Australia and New Zealand join forces on the wine list to rival the pedigree French selections. There are some very fine bottles, although if you only have £20 to spend, you will not find much available in the way of claret or burgundy. The Rhône and Alsace afford some relief. House wines start at £8.50.

CHEF: David Everitt-Matthias   PROPRIETORS: David and Helen Everitt-Matthias   OPEN: Mon to Sat, exc Sat L; 12.30 to 1.30, 7.30 to 9.15   MEALS: Set L £17.50, Set D £18.50 to £32   SERVICE: not inc   CARDS: Access, Amex, Diners, Visa   DETAILS: 30 seats. Private parties: 30 main room. Vegetarian meals with prior notice. Children welcome. Smart dress preferred. Wheelchair access (1 step; also WC). No music. Air-conditioned

Epicurean

81 The Promenade, Cheltenham GL51 1PJ
CHELTENHAM (0242) 222466

COOKING 3*
COST £21–£55

Patrick McDonald has moved like a hermit crab from one shell to another: still the same creature inside, still the same cooking, but in a new home at the downtown end of the elegant Promenade. He has taken over the entire Edwardian terraced house and, in what is rapidly becoming standard practice, filled it full of possibilities. The basement is a tapas bar, with newspapers on sticks, beers, interesting wines by the glass, and 'London pseudo-tapas' of mussels with tomato and garlic, and treacle tart. The ground floor is a bistro, with rag-rolled walls, wrought iron post-modern furniture and bold modern paintings, which serves soups, salads, pasta, grills, roasts, stews, casseroles and spotted dick – and of course treacle tart.

Up the grey carpeted stairs in the new restaurant dining-room, tables gleam and sparkle amid grey and white floral wallpaper, pale wood panelling and heavy ruched curtains. 'Luxuriously austere' was how an early visitor saw it. Service is formal, smart and efficient, and the food is quite different from that served downstairs: no treacle tart, for one thing, although chocolate tart and lemon tart appear on all three floors. A strand of luxury runs from lobster and langoustine ravioli to a prince-and-pauper terrine of foie gras and pork knuckle.

'Simple and expertly done' is how our inspector described the food he ate, impressed by a roundel of finely chopped raw salmon with chives, shallots and black pepper, topped with neatly pebble-dashed caviare set in a smear of crème fraîche. A big slab of salmon – crisped on the outside, barely cooked within – and a creamy risotto full of chopped girolles, trompettes de mort and shiitake mushrooms with a generous shaving of summer truffle, both indicate sureness of touch. Desserts include caramelised apple on rich buttery pastry, or a visually more arresting pyramid of vanilla parfait studded with liqueur-macerated prunes and draped with spun sugar, surrounded by crème anglaise with a border of dark chocolate. Expensive, yes, but the place delivers the goods. The performance was all the more impressive for being within a week or two of the move. High prices appear to dominate the wine list, but enough bottles under £20 (although not always tops for quality) make the package tempting. House wine is £9.75.

CHEF: Patrick McDonald PROPRIETORS: Patrick and Claire McDonald OPEN: Mon to Sat; 12 to 2, 7 to 10 MEALS: alc bistro (main courses £7.50 to £8.75). Restaurant Set L £14.50 (2 courses) to £17.50, Set D £25 (2 courses) to £35 SERVICE: not inc CARDS: Access, Amex, Diners, Visa DETAILS: 30 seats. Private parties: 30 main room, 18 private room. Vegetarian meals with prior notice. Children's helpings on request. No children under 8. Smart dress preferred. No cigars/pipes in dining-room. No music

Mayflower

32–34 Clarence Street,
Cheltenham GL50 3NX
CHELTENHAM (0242) 522426 and 511580

COOKING 1*
COST £14–£47

'One of the better Cantonese/Pekinese restaurants we have visited' was the verdict of a seasoned traveller after a Sunday visit to this spruce, Regency-style venue. Prices are not cheap, but the food is fresh and accurately cooked, although some of the spicy fire is toned down for local palates. The menu covers a lot of familiar territory, with a few idiosyncratic ideas such as sauté chicken with mango and pickled ginger. Recommended dishes have included spiced fish slices, spring rolls, aromatic crispy duck, and sizzling fillet steak. Szechuan seafood hotpot is a popular speciality. The wine list is a serious selection of about 120 well-spread bins; descriptions are knowledgeable, mark-ups reasonable. Australian house wine is £8.25.

CHEFS: Mr C.F. Kong and Mrs M.M. Kong PROPRIETORS: the Kong family OPEN: all week, exc Sun L; 12 to 1.45, 5.45 to 10.45 (11.15 Fri and Sat) CLOSED: 25 to 27 Dec MEALS: alc (main courses £6 to £9.50). Set L £6.50, Set D £15 to £27.50 SERVICE: not inc CARDS: Access, Amex, Diners, Visa DETAILS: 130 seats. Private parties: 80 main room, 50 private room. Vegetarian meals. Children welcome. Smart dress preferred. Wheelchair access (1 step). Music. Air-conditioned. Fax: (0242) 251667

An asterisk (*) after the 1 to 5 cooking mark at the top of an entry signifies that the Guide and its readers think that the restaurant is a particularly fine example within its rating.

Staithes Restaurant 🍴✻

12 Suffolk Road, Cheltenham GL50 2AQ
CHELTENHAM (0242) 260666
on A40, S of town centre at junction with
Bath Road

COOKING 1*
COST £23–£42

Formerly Bonnets Bistro – and before that Bonnets Bistro at Staithes (named after the North Yorkshire village from whence their bonnet logo comes) – the renamed restaurant remains small and family run. He cooks, she serves at a measured pace. Seasonality is the key to a menu that might offer 'very tomatoey' tomato soup with basil, chicken in madeira sauce, and baked Alaska with a fruit coulis. Paul Lucas is also capable of delivering poached fillet of smoked haddock with curry and mango sauce, Barbary duck breast garnished with marinated blackcurrants, and peach crème brûlée. Most popular of all is caramelised bacon salad cut by the sharpness of sherry vinegar. Twenty-one wines, listed on one side of the printed menu, are short on detail but high on quality. House wine is £9.95.

CHEF: Paul Lucas   PROPRIETORS: R.E. Lucas and P.R. Lucas   OPEN: Mon to Sat D only; 7 to 10 (L by reservation only)   CLOSED: 1 week Christmas, 2 weeks summer, bank hols   MEALS: alc (main courses £7 to £14)   SERVICE: net prices, card slips closed   CARDS: Access, Amex, Diners, Visa   DETAILS: 30 seats. Private parties: 24 main room, 10 private room. Vegetarian meals (prior notice preferred). Children's helpings on request. No children under 8. Smart dress preferred. No smoking in dining-room. Wheelchair access. Music

---

CHESTER Cheshire   map 5

▲ Chester Grosvenor Hotel, Arkle 🍷

Eastgate Street, Chester CH1 1LT   COOKING 4
CHESTER (0244) 324024   COST £35–£73

After two 'flawed' experiences at Arkle, an inspector writes: 'The room is still ugly but everything else seems to have come together.' In particular, 'people seemed to be eating there for pleasure, the bill was within reason and, most important of all, the food has got its priorities straight in going for taste above all else'.

Action proceeds seamlessly from canapés in the mahogany bar, with book-filled shelves and deep armchairs, to the dining-room – 'one of the least satisfactory temples of gastronomy that I have ever seen'. Windows look on to a hotel corridor through which passing hotel guests stare at diners, and false stone walls and uninspiring horsey prints don't help, though well-spaced tables and sympathetic lighting make amends and the painting of Arkle, the racehorse, isn't bad.

Luxury ingredients are trotted out as a matter of course, lobster and foie gras among them, but so are insides and extremities. A whole roasted veal kidney with shredded tongues demonstrates a brave divergence from customary hotel fare, and a house speciality assembles sweetbreads, trotter, foie gras and tongues on a single plate. The rich-and-poor combination works to good effect in a dish of thick fillet steak served on a bed of chopped-up oxtail, with deep, intense flavours; accompanying root vegetables are roasted until wrinkly, which concentrates their taste. Fish is a success too. 'A salad of scallops and tuna was a triumph,' along with its complement of grilled and braised vegetables. Cooking techniques embrace a wide range, bringing admirable variety to the short *carte*. Presentation is a delight, and portions are very generous: nine cutlets of very pink, well flavoured lamb served in three chunks (and that's just one portion). If some dishes appear to combine a bewildering number of ingredients, the only reply is that it works. The brasserie serves much simpler food.

Cheese is a well-kept selection of unpasteurised French and British, and puddings confirm the kitchen's high-octane performance. 'My trio of caramel desserts looked and tasted wonderful: a caramel sponge, a light crème caramel, and best of all a box formed by squares of caramel, the lid half removed, with an iced parfait inside. A nest of spun sugar gilded the lily, while a caramel 'fruit' with stalks resting on the box lid added wit.' The wine list has 900 bottles to choose from. Silly prices abound, but there are bottles under £20, even under £10, and a good selection of halves. House vin de pays is £10.50. CELLARMAN'S CHOICE: Viognier, Dom. St. Hilaire 1992, £19; Santenay 'Gravières' 1989, Nouveau, £24.50.

CHEFS: Paul Reed and Simon Radley   PROPRIETOR: Grosvenor Estate Holdings   OPEN: all week, exc Mon L and Sun D; 12.30 to 2.30, 7.30 to 10.30   CLOSED: 25 and 26 Dec, bank hols   MEALS: alc (main courses £17 to £25). Set L £18 (2 courses) to £22.50, Set D £37   SERVICE: not inc   CARDS: Access, Amex, Diners, Visa   DETAILS: 45 seats. Vegetarian meals. Children's helpings. Jacket and tie. No cigars/pipes in dining-room. Wheelchair access (also WC). Music. Air-conditioned   ACCOMMODATION: 86 rooms, all with bath/shower. TV. Phone. Air-conditioned. B&B £146 to £244. Rooms for disabled. Children welcome. Baby facilities. Afternoon teas. Sauna. Confirm by 12. Fax: (0244) 313246

CHICHESTER West Sussex   map 3

Droveway £✳

30A Southgate, Chichester PO19 1DR   COOKING 1
CHICHESTER (0243) 528832   COST £23–£45

The name conjures up images of 'a long, lush driveway and sulky-riding' in the minds of some visitors, when the reality is a modest first-floor establishment in the centre of town. Inside is 'a potentially cavernous' dining-room, but the choice of lighting, colour schemes and pictures makes it 'romantically grand as daylight fades'.

Jonas Tester's cooking has a modern Anglo-French accent and reports confirm that the kitchen is well in control. Good ingredients – particularly fish – and sharp technique are its hallmarks. Leek and asparagus charlotte in yogurt sauce, darne of salmon with sorrel sauce, and calf's liver with celeriac and balsamic vinegar are typically successful dishes. From the short pudding list, the brûlée infused with strands of saffron has been a winner. Service is informed and attentive. A page of half-bottles kicks off the reasonably priced wine list. House wine is £10.

Not inc in the details at the end of an entry indicates that no service charge is made and any tipping is at the discretion of the customer.

CHEF: Jonas Tester PROPRIETORS: Elly and Jonas Tester OPEN: Tue to Sat; 12.30 to 2, 7 to 10 (post-theatre by arrangement) CLOSED: first 2 weeks Jan MEALS: alc (main courses £10 to £15). Set L £11.50 (2 courses) to £14, Set D £19.50 SERVICE: not inc, card slips closed CARDS: Access, Amex, Visa DETAILS: 38 seats. Private parties: 28 main room. Vegetarian meals. Children's helpings. Smart dress preferred. No smoking in 1 dining-room. Music

---

CHILGROVE West Sussex
map 3

White Horse Inn 🍾

High Street, Chilgrove PO18 9HX
EAST MARDEN (0243) 535219
on B2141, between Chichester and   COOKING 1*
Petersfield   COST £21–£46

Barry Phillips and family have run this eighteenth-century country inn since the late '60s, and it remains one of the most favoured establishments of its kind around the South Downs. Bar lunches and suppers are ever popular with the local crowd and visitors to Goodwood, but most interest centres on the restaurant. Fish gets plenty of endorsements: sea bass with sweet-and-sour sauce, monkfish in mustard sauce and brill stuffed with salmon mousse in a herb sauce have all been good. Neil Rusbridger can also deliver fillet of lamb with aubergine gâteau, honey-roast duck with caramelised turnips and confit of garlic, as well as roast pork. Desserts such as chocolate roulade, cherry tart and lemon soufflé are recited verbally. Service is happy and cheerful. The Phillipses plan to offer bed and breakfast in an old cottage adjacent to the inn by the end of 1994. Wine has always been as powerful a draw as the food. The list is a monster, but quite simple to use. This is what you do. Think of a wine, decide which vintage you would like, then ask for it. There is no need to look in the tome because it is almost bound to be there, especially if it is a claret. There are half-bottles galore and enough curiosities to kill a cat: botrytis Sauvignon Blanc from Israel, for example. House wine changes monthly. CELLARMAN'S CHOICE: Muscadet, Cuvée de Millenaire 1992, Marquis de Goulaine, £12.95.

CHEF: Neil Rusbridger PROPRIETORS: Dorothea and Barry Phillips, and Neil Rusbridger OPEN: Tue to Sun, exc Sun D; 12 to 2, 7 (6 bar) to 9.30 (10.30 summer) CLOSED: last week Oct, 3 weeks Feb MEALS: alc (main courses L £10.50 to £13.50, D £13.50 to £18.50). Set L £17.50, Set D £23. Bar supper 6 to 10 £12.50 SERVICE: 10%, card slips closed CARDS: Access, Diners, Visa DETAILS: 70 seats. 3 tables outside. Private parties: 34 main room, 10 to 34 private rooms. Car park. Vegetarian meals. No children under 14. No cigars/pipes in dining-room. Wheelchair access. Music. Air-conditioned. Fax: (0243) 535301

Prices quoted in the Guide *are based on information supplied by restaurateurs. The prices quoted at the top of each entry represent a range, from the lowest meal price to the highest; the latter is inflated by 20 per cent to take account of likely price rises during the year of the* Guide.

Restaurateurs justifiably resent no-shows. If you quote a credit card number when booking, you may be liable for the restaurant's lost profit margin if you don't turn up. Always phone to cancel.

CHINNOR Oxfordshire   map 2

Sir Charles Napier 🍴

Sprigg's Alley, nr Chinnor OX9 4BX
HIGH WYCOMBE (0494) 483011
off B4009, take Bledlow Ridge turn from   COOKING 2
Chinnor, 2m up hill   COST £26–£49

Sculptures and champagne on tap are just two features of Julie Griffiths'
idiosyncratic pub/restaurant surrounded by Chiltern beechwoods. The place is
enchanting in summer, when you can sit on the terrace shaded by vines and
wistaria and look out on to the lawns and herb gardens. Inside, the mood is
eccentrically atmospheric: the balancing weight on the door is a frying pan on a
rope; a surrealist sculpture of a woman's torso occupies one corner of the
dining-room; the furniture consists of unmatching tables and chairs. The venue
attracts a lively, animated crowd. The innovative and up-to-the-minute menu
offers sharp, light and accurate cooking. Batiste Tolu can deliver 'real American-
style' crab-cakes with lime and coriander, and crostini of pigeon and mushrooms
with truffle oil, as well as old favourites like roast Gressingham duck with sage,
apple and onion or salmon in pastry with ginger and currants. Puddings are the
likes of lemon tart and banana and caramel ice-cream. Weekly set menus are
good value. Service is deliberately 'jeans and sweater' casual.

The wine list is delightful, dedicated to sheer enjoyment at prices that
encourage exploration. There is a good variety of styles and enthusiasms – and
occasionally a brilliant star (and that's just the Loire Valley). If all else fails, the
house wines, from £10.75, offer a good safety net.

CHEF: Batiste Tolu   PROPRIETOR: Mrs Julie Griffiths   OPEN: Tue to Sun, exc Sun D, and L bank
hol Mon; 12 to 2.30 (12.30 to 3.30 Sun), 7 to 10   MEALS: alc (main courses £9.50 to £14). Set L
Tue to Sat £12.50, Set D Tue to Fri £14   SERVICE: 12.5% (optional), card slips closed   CARDS:
Access, Visa   DETAILS: 80 seats. 10 tables outside. Private parties: 50 main room, 30 and 50
private rooms. Car park. Vegetarian meals. Children's helpings L. No children under 7 D. No
cigars/pipes in dining-room. Wheelchair access. Music

CHOBHAM Surrey   map 3

Quails

1 Bagshot Road, Chobham GU24 8BP   COOKING 1
CHOBHAM (0276) 858491   COST £20–£42

Surrey has always supported traditional French cuisine, and the prix fixe menu
that supplements the *carte* at Quails during weekdays features a different region
of France each month. 'Gastronomie du Val de Loire' in the spring offered
mouclade, salmon with cabbage and fennel, and chicken fricasseed in St Nicolas
de Bourgueil wine. Otherwise, invention is let rip for goats' cheese tartlet with
toasted almonds and gooseberries, filo parcel of monkfish with smoked bacon,
grain mustard and seaweed, ocean perch with samphire and clams, and pork
tenderloin with a tapénade crust and red pepper coulis. One reader commented
that filo parcels of one thing or another crop up rather monotonously through the
first and second courses; but, by and large, the ideas are sound, and the sultanas

in the bread-and-butter pudding are soaked in calvados. A birthday outing suffered occasional long waits, but others have found the service 'pleasantly restful'. The wine list has many excellent names (especially within France), but prices are top-heavy with most sections galloping over the £20 hurdle very quickly. House wines from south-west France are £9.50.

CHEF: Christopher Wale PROPRIETORS: the Wale family OPEN: Tue to Sun, exc Sat L and Sun D; 12.30 to 2, 7 to 10 MEALS: alc (main courses £9.75 to £12.75). Set L and D Tue to Fri £12.95 SERVICE: not inc CARDS: Access, Amex, Diners, Visa DETAILS: 40 seats. Private parties: 40 main room. Car park. Vegetarian meals. Children welcome. Smart dress preferred. Wheelchair access. Music. Air-conditioned

---

CHRISTCHURCH Dorset map 2

Splinters

12 Church Street, Christchurch BH23 1BW | NEW CHEF
CHRISTCHURCH (0202) 483454 | COST £20–£39

Splinters is a grade II listed building, in the oldest part of Christchurch, just along from the priory. The bar is all wood and Laura Ashley, and meals often finish with coffee in the upstairs drawing-room with its view of the castle. The atmosphere is relaxed: 'It is refreshing to find quality in such informal surroundings.' Shortly before going to press, we learned that Eamonn Redden, formerly at the Cavendish Hotel in Baslow in Derbyshire, has taken over as head chef from Robert Rees. Dishes from Eamonn Redden's summer menu included a monkfish sausage starter with lemon and a fresh dill sauce, potted rabbit with ale and apple chutney, main courses of roast breast of duck stuffed with sage noodles, with honey sauce and melon, and goats' cheese and almond Wellington with a sweet pepper hollandaise sauce. Wines on the whole are sensibly chosen and priced, and half a dozen house wines begin at £9 (£2 per glass). Splinters has also launched 'Number 11 Brasserie' right next door. Reports on both, please.

CHEFS: Eamonn Redden and Kerry Oliver PROPRIETORS: Robert Wilson and Timothy Lloyd OPEN: all week; 12 to 2.30, 7 to 10.30 CLOSED: 2 weeks from 10 Jan MEALS: alc (main courses L £4.50 to £11.50, D £10 to £15). Set L £8.60 (2 courses), Set L Sun £12.50 SERVICE: not inc CARDS: Access, Amex, Diners, Visa DETAILS: 40 seats. Private parties: 22 main room, 8 and 22 private rooms. Vegetarian meals. Children's helpings. Smart dress preferred. Music. Fax: (0202) 483454

CLAYGATE Surrey map 3

Le Petit Pierrot

4 The Parade, Claygate KT10 0NU | COOKING 1*
ESHER (0372) 465105 | COST £26–£39

One reporter (who has known Claygate for 20 years) found this French restaurant in a parade of shops just by the station a little difficult to locate. Local residents and business folk, who use it most, have already surmounted that hurdle. Inside, mirrors abound, reflecting the green and beige curtain material and maximising the low wattage of the lamps. The menu changes every six weeks, the style is largely French (as is the wine list), and the choice is six or seven items per course.

Jean-Pierre Brichot does not stray far from the standard French repertoire. Navarin d'agneau with winter root vegetables, or sauté calf's liver with sage and lime, cover familiar territory, although watercress soup may be enlivened with goats' cheese quenelles, and boneless skate wing might come with lentils and vinaigrette. Tastes are sometimes disappointingly muted, but cream of split-pea soup with bacon, home-marinated salmon served with quail's eggs, and the sorbets receive positive reports. The frills are up to scratch: presentation is pretty, a bouchée of haddock and mushrooms starts the ball rolling, and coffee and petits fours are very good. House wine is Bouches du Rhône – Grenache or Sémillon – at £8.95.

CHEF: Jean-Pierre Brichot   PROPRIETORS: Jean-Pierre and Annie Brichot   OPEN: Mon to Sat, exc Sat L; 12.15 to 2.30, 7.15 to 10.30   MEALS: Set L £9.95 (2 courses) to £16.85, Set D £18.95   SERVICE: not inc   CARDS: Access, Amex, Diners, Visa   DETAILS: 32 seats. Private parties: 35 main room. Vegetarian meals with prior notice. No children under 9. Smart dress preferred. No pipes in dining-room. Wheelchair access (1 step). Music. Air-conditioned. Fax: (0372) 467642

CLITHEROE Lancashire   map 5

Auctioneer

New Market Street, Clitheroe BB7 2JW   COOKING 2
CLITHEROE (0200) 27153   COST £19–£34

There is always something going on at the Auctioneer. Themed dinner menus crop up more or less every month, and celebrations this year have included Valentine weekend, the cuisine of South Africa, the Paris restaurant scene, an Easter feast of fish and the *cucina rustica* of Tuscany – not bad going for a converted pub in Clitheroe. When the service is led by Frances Van Heumen, her 'calm and informative' presence settles everyone down. The fortnightly changing menus are set-price in the evenings, à la carte at lunch. Although the style is mostly modern British, the odd cliché creeps in. Prawns and avocado with marie rose sauce is a bit old-hat, but parsnip, apple and tarragon soup, crab wrapped in smoked salmon on a watercress sauce, or sauté turbot with prawns, walnuts and grapes should more than compensate in the creativity department. One regular pair find standards do fluctuate somewhat, but there are always at least a couple of dishes to enjoy. Fillet of fried shark was 'meaty but tender', sliced sucking pig had an 'excellent' stuffing of Parma ham and sage and came with a sauce enriched with Chianti, while chocolate marquise was appropriately invigorating. Farmhouse cheeses are usually good – Lancashire is the real thing – and the coffee is decently strong. Wine choices are solid rather than exciting but prices are eminently reasonable, with most items below £20. Great provision of half-bottles is made for the size of the list. House burgundy is £9.75.

CHEFS: Henk Van Heumen   PROPRIETORS: Henk and Frances Van Heumen   OPEN: Tue to Sun; 12 to 1.30, 7 to 9 (9.30 Fri and Sat)   MEALS: alc L (main courses £6.50 to £9). Set L Sun £13.50, Set D £15.75 (2 courses) to £20.75. Minimum £6.25 L   SERVICE: not inc   CARDS: Access, Amex, Visa   DETAILS: 48 seats. Private parties: 24 main room, 24 private room. Vegetarian meals. Children's helpings L. No babies. Smart dress preferred. Music

COCKERMOUTH Cumbria   map 7

Quince & Medlar ✻ £

13 Castlegate, Cockermouth CA13 9EU   COOKING 1
COCKERMOUTH (0900) 823579   COST £18–£24

'The strange house' on the sloping corner of a tree-lined street next to the castle is as comfortable as you could wish for: even the loos are worth a mention. Colin and Louisa Le Voi live and work here, serving up enterprising vegetarian food for anyone who cares to explore what they have to offer. Dishes often have a familiar ring to them, but there is none of the stodgy cliché associated with old-style meatless cooking. Reporters have heaped praise on the 'beautiful bread', carrot and apricot pâté, 'wonderfully light' spinach roulade filled with herby cheese, and a Chinese vegetable stir-fry with wild rice that was a veritable 'mountain of flavours'. Desserts are enticing offerings, including armagnac ice-cream, iced passion fruit soufflé and koshaf (mixed dried fruits in 'blossom water'). A few organic wines show up on the short, intelligently chosen list. House wine is £6.80.

CHEFS/PROPRIETORS: Colin and Louisa Le Voi OPEN: Tue to Sun, D only; 7 (6.30 Sat) to 9.30 CLOSED: 3 weeks Jan, Sun and Mon Nov to Easter MEALS: alc (main courses £6.50 to £7.50) SERVICE: not inc, card slips closed CARDS: Access, Visa DETAILS: 26 seats. Private parties: 16 main room. Vegetarian meals. No children under 6. Smart dress preferred. No smoking in dining-room. Music

---

COGGESHALL Essex   map 3

Baumann's Brasserie

4–6 Stoneham Street, Coggeshall CO6 1TT   COOKING 1
COLCHESTER (0376) 561453   COST £16–£39

Baumann's is bang in the middle of Coggeshall, not far from the clock tower. With its polished wood floors, low ceilings, crisp white tablecloths, handsome split-level extension, jazz music and the late Peter Langan's idea of an agreeable collection of pictures crammed together on the walls, it is a congenial setting for a restaurant. On offer are laid-back dishes such as grilled red snapper, marinated chicken with jalapeño corn fritters, and pecan pie with banana bread. The food has been found on occasion to be less good than it might be, perhaps because the place fills up just as well without making a special effort. An inspector found overcooked fish, insipid stock for soup and large variations in seasonings and temperatures, but praised basic ingredients, a salad of pork scratchings with bits of liver, decent lamb steak and fine chocolate mousse. 'Every dish we had was heavy with cream,' noted another. Service is not always a strong point, while wines are decent and reasonably priced with house Australian at £8.50 (£1.80 per glass).

See inside the front cover for an explanation of the symbols used at the tops of entries.

CHEFS: Mark Baumann and Douglas Wright   PROPRIETOR: Baumann's Brasserie Ltd   OPEN: Tue to Sun, exc Sat L and Sun D; 12.30 to 2, 7.30 to 10   CLOSED: 2 weeks Jan   MEALS: alc (main courses £10 to £13.50). Set L Tue to Sat £9.95, Sun £14.95   SERVICE: not inc, card slips closed   CARDS: Access, Amex, Visa   DETAILS: 80 seats. Private parties: 50 main room. Vegetarian meals with prior notice. Children's helpings. Smart dress preferred. No cigars/pipes in dining-room. Wheelchair access (also WC). Music. Fax: (0376) 563762

COLCHESTER Essex   map 3

Warehouse Brasserie £

12A Chapel Street North,
Colchester CO2 7AT   COOKING 2
COLCHESTER (0206) 765656   COST £18–£34

The Warehouse remains on top form, and its popularity now extends to a lively session on Sunday lunch-time. 'If only every town had an efficient, reliable, reasonable and busy restaurant like this, what a different country this would be,' commented one of its loyal followers, who 'arrives early, leaves late and always eats well'. Flexibility is the name of the game: have a single dish or three courses, order from the main menu or pick one of the daily specials. The kitchen delivers exemplary modern brasserie cooking based on carefully sourced ingredients: salad of queen scallops is enlivened with al dente mange-tout and a spring onion and lemon vinaigrette, deep-fried filo parcels filled with roast duck are 'deliciously crisp, not soggy', and pan-fried cod in olive oil is served with crisp shredded celeriac. By contrast, rump steak topped with a chunk of maître d' butter struck one reporter as a throwback to the '70s. Sweets are the likes of warm lemon tart and brown bread ice-cream. Bottles from the New World feature heavily on the keenly priced wine list; also look for wines of the month. House French is £7.50.

CHEFS: Anthony Brooks, Stuart Mott and Mark Burley   PROPRIETORS: Mel Burley and Anthony Brooks   OPEN: all week, exc Sun D; 12 to 2, 7 to 10 (pre- and post-theatre D by arrangement)   CLOSED: 25 and 26 Dec, Good Fri L   MEALS: alc (main courses £6 to £12.50)   SERVICE: not inc   CARDS: Access, Visa   DETAILS: 80 seats. Private parties: 100 main room. Vegetarian meals. Children's helpings. No smoking downstairs. Wheelchair access (1 step). No music. Air-conditioned

---

COLERNE Wiltshire   map 2

▲ Lucknam Park

Colerne SN14 8AZ
BATH (0225) 742777   COOKING 4
off A420 at Ford, 6m W of Chippenham   COST £33–£70

The house, at the end of an imposing drive, is a long, low and rambling Georgian Palladian mansion set in 280 acres of parkland. Views are of gardens and a majestic double avenue of trees, sofas are squashy, and pampering is allowed free rein in the leisure spa. It is, for one respondent, a 'corporate variant' of the more traditional country-house hotel; for another, 'luxury with a large slice of humanity and enthusiasm'. Everybody – telephonist, housekeepers, waiters –

joins in the welcome. It all costs money, of course, but reporters feel they have had fair value because they have enjoyed it all so much: 'As the dinner was so good, we stayed for lunch and had another outstanding meal.'

The food commands attention, so much so that for one reporter there could have been 'herds of cows wearing pink tutus dancing Swan Lake on the patio' and she would not have noticed. 'There is real emphasis on excellence, and great confidence,' writes our inspector. 'It is all very gleeful cooking from someone who finds the creative process really exciting.' Organic duck, seasonal game, Cornish fish and Hereford beef are organised into a menu of estimable variety, from unusual confit of duck leg with rhubarb purée, to intriguing tortellini of lamb in a mutton broth with lime leaves, and rich warm terrine of potato, sweetbreads and foie gras, or hot chocolate pudding with clotted cream.

One trademark is 'to take a bird or animal and present various bits of it cooked in a different fashion', hence pigeon breast ('intense and very tender') with a confit of the legs. Puddings are subject to similar treatment: exotic fruits cooked three different ways, for example. Accuracy and timing are not in doubt. 'My Trelough duck was rare, exactly as I understand rare to mean', and this came with a generous piece of foie gras caramelised on the outside and meltingly pink inside. Intricacy and detail worked to good effect in a first course of five variations on a theme of salmon that included tasty mouthfuls of gravlax, salmon eggs and smoked salmon. Involved? Yes. Fussy? No. And the cooking is accomplished and inventive enough to shrug off any cavils about minor imperfections.

Staff range from probationers to masters of their craft. One reporter wondered why, if even Raymond Blanc doesn't demand it, a tie should be a necessary accompaniment to a meal here. 'However, the request is made with great charm so as to suggest that one is a feisty Bohemian rather than socially inept.' The wine waiter is 'totally charming and encyclopaedic. He had been to practically every vineyard we mentioned.' The list is a giant and prices are high, but then so is the standard. Value for money exists, and if it is not immediately apparent, ask for the wine waiter's help. The choice of half-bottles is welcome, and house wine is £15. CELLARMAN'S CHOICE: Bourgogne Chardonnay 1990, Dom. Boussey, £26; Madiran 1989, Dom. du Crampilh, £19.

CHEF: Michael Womersley PROPRIETOR: Lucknam Park Hotels Ltd OPEN: all week; 12.30 to 2.30, 7.30 to 9.30 (9.45 Sat) MEALS: Set L £19.50 (2 courses) to £22.50, Set D £39.50 SERVICE: not inc, card slips closed CARDS: Access, Amex, Diners, Visa DETAILS: 85 seats. 2 tables outside. Private parties: 85 main room, 10 to 28 private rooms. Car park. Vegetarian meals. Children's helpings. No children under 8 D. Jacket and tie D. No smoking in dining-room. Wheelchair access (also WC). No music ACCOMMODATION: 42 rooms, all with bath/shower. TV. Phone. B&B £100 to £400. Rooms for disabled. Children welcome. Baby facilities. Afternoon teas. Garden. Swimming-pool. Sauna. Tennis. Snooker. Fax: (0225) 743843 (*The Which? Hotel Guide*)

'*It has been smartened up since my last visit, with the ghastly formica tables now having been replaced by plain wooden ones, and the cheap benches with stuffing hanging out replaced by cheap benches without stuffing hanging out. I was a bit disconcerted until I saw the cardboard on the floor – for a moment I thought they had gone nouvelle.*'
(On eating in London)

COOKHAM Berkshire map 2

Alfonso's

19–21 Station Hill Parade,
Cookham SL6 9BR COOKING 1
BOURNE END (062 85) 25775 COST £20–£35

Enthusiasm is infectious. 'The welcome the whole family gives to visitors is unequalled,' writes one, eagerly returning the tribute on behalf of just about every reporter. The Baenas run a simple, small but elegant restaurant that is both enjoyable and value for money. Tables are close enough to be cosy but not crowded, and the whole dining-room appears to be wrapped in a blanket of goodwill.

The Spanish thread running through the menu is more than just a nod to fashion, and takes in flavourings of sherry (with lambs' kidneys) and sherry vinegar (with a smoked fish salad) as well as salt-cured, air-dried Serrano ham served with a pear poached in Galician wine. Beef with a shallot and green peppercorn sauce, and lamb with a tomato and garlic sauce are praised. Crisp stir-fried vegetables accompany. 'Wonderful' bread-and-butter pudding is fruity and alcoholic. Southern French house wine is £8.25, and little above £20 will be found on the 40-bottle list.

CHEFS: Richard Manzano and Simon Hall PROPRIETORS: Mr and Mrs Alfonso Baena OPEN: Mon to Sat, exc Sat L; 12.30 to 2, 7 to 10 (10.30 Fri and Sat) CLOSED: 2 weeks Aug MEALS: Set L £12.50, Set D £16.50 SERVICE: not inc CARDS: Access, Amex, Diners, Visa DETAILS: 34 seats. Private parties: 34 main room. Car park. Vegetarian meals. Children's helpings. Smart dress preferred. No pipes in dining-room. Wheelchair access (also women's WC). Music

COPPULL MOOR Lancashire map 5

Coppull Moor 🍴✳

311 Preston Road, Coppull Moor PR7 5DU COOKING 2
CHORLEY (0257) 792222 COST £22–£36

This converted pub has a small 'parlour' for drinks furnished with 'overstuffed' armchairs and settees, and two dining-rooms. Barry Rea circulates and chats as well as cooks, and he is keen for people to sample as many different tastes at one meal as possible. An idea of the substance involved in the set meals can be gained from beef in puff pastry, or medallions of venison (marinated first) served with the liver and sweetbreads in a sauce of port, blackberry and orange. Cooking times and seasoning are carefully attended to. It should come as no surprise that a man as keen to share as many tastes as this is equally at home with sweet-and-sour sauce (served with poached breast and baked leg of poussin) as with more homely apple and mint sauce with saddle of local lamb. Five or more vegetables help things along: runner beans with a shallot and smoked bacon dressing, potatoes roasted in duck dripping, beetroot glazed with cream sherry, deep-fried savoury courgettes, to name just four.

'Taster plates are provided to encourage guests to sample each other's choices', and a selection of five desserts on one plate is offered to those who find it difficult to make a decision. A spring array included a meringue swan, steamed layered chocolate pudding, mango mousse, and a caramelised blueberry and blackberry crumble. The menu commendably states that no gratuities are expected, and booking is essential. The extensive wine list cops out a little by gathering from négoçiants, but prices are very fair. House Hungarian is £9 and, note this: 'All wines on the list can be served by the glass.' That must be a record.

CHEF/PROPRIETOR: Barry Rea   OPEN: Tue to Sun; 12.30, 8 for 8.30   CLOSED: last week Jan, first week Feb   MEALS: Set L Tue to Sat and Sun brunch £17.50, Set D Tue to Thur £21.50, Fri to Sun £25.50   SERVICE: card slips closed   CARD: Amex   DETAILS: 26 seats. Private parties: 26 main room, 12 and 12 private rooms. Car park. Vegetarian meals. No children under 14. Smart dress preferred. No smoking in dining-rooms. Music

---

CORBRIDGE Northumberland   map 7

Valley 🍴✳ £

Old Station House, Station Road,
Corbridge NE45 5AY
HEXHAM (0434) 633434 and 633923
off B6321 S of Corbridge towards   COOKING 1
Riding Mill   COST £18–£37

The building is the Old Station House outside Corbridge, and a 'unique train service' operates along the line: a waiter meets parties from Newcastle Station, escorts them and takes their orders. The menu has a long run of curry-house favourites – bhunas, dopiazas, dhansaks, vindaloos and the like – but the interesting stuff is in the list of chef's recommendations. Mangsho pesta ke shadi is topside of beef cooked with spices and pistachio nuts; murgh-e-khazana is chicken breast with a mild sauce sweetened with honey; salmon is fried with garlic, ginger and raw onion. Vegetables and vegetarian dishes show up well: look for dhai baigun (grilled aubergine stuffed with spices and topped with yogurt) or crisp cabbage bhaji. The wine list is a respectable choice of around 40 good-value bins. House wine is £6.95.

CHEFS: Abdul Khalick and Titu Ahad   PROPRIETOR: S.N. Aziz   OPEN: Mon to Sat, D only; 6 to 11 (L by arrangement for parties)   CLOSED: 25 Dec   MEALS: alc (main courses £4.50 to £9.50). Set D £40 (2 people) to £75 (4 people)   SERVICE: not inc   CARDS: Access, Amex, Diners, Visa   DETAILS: 70 seats. Private parties: 40 main room, 10 and 20 private rooms. Car park. Vegetarian meals. Children's helpings. Smart dress preferred. No smoking in 1 dining-room. Wheelchair access. Music

---

CORSE LAWN Gloucestershire   map 2

▲ Corse Lawn House Hotel 🍾 £

Corse Lawn GL19 4LZ
GLOUCESTER (0452) 780771   COOKING 3
on B4211, 5m SW of Tewkesbury   COST £20–£57

The recession has found the Hines re-examining the operation in a way that other country-house hotels might emulate. Instead of allowing the conference and banqueting trade to take over, and putting themselves on the international circuit, they have dug deeper into the local community. The place is a commendable cross between a country-house hotel and a popular pub. 'People need cheering up,' claims Baba Hine, and she sets to with a will. The Queen Anne coaching-inn is beside the village green, and the original 'coach wash' in front has long been an ornamental pond. Recent additions fit well with the original, pictures abound, and rooms are coloured with rosy pinks, soft beiges and pale blues.

Food flavours are vivid, portions large enough, and elements are orchestrated into pleasing dishes with genuine freshness of thought. Those with a Gallic background seem to be brought off with most gusto, among them Mediterranean fish soup in a large silver tureen: dark orange, deeply scented, full flavoured and creamy, with a very garlicky rouille. 'Flavour' is the word that runs through reports of so many dishes, including sweet crayfish on firm, light-textured noodles, and a grilled saddle and roast leg of rabbit. Puddings are indulgent, and hot butterscotch sponge, cooked to order, is 'comfort food at its best: light and fluffy sponge on a wickedly rich dark toffee sauce, with a crescent of vanilla sauce'. Details are applauded too: 'The best bread-stick in the UK,' eulogised one reporter.

Staff seem able to turn their hand to anything: 'The young man who served us had made some of the desserts, and was on breakfast-cooking duty in the morning.' Breakfasts, apparently, are well worth staying for. The bistro's keen prices make it justly popular. Wines explore France in some detail, with a good variety of producers, which makes up for the cursory New World section. Mark-ups are standard and half-bottles good. House wines are £9.75. CELLARMAN'S CHOICE: Sauvignon Blanc 1990, Ch. la Jaubertie, £16.60; Minervois 1990, Ch. Gourgazaud, £11.50.

CHEF: Baba Hine PROPRIETORS: Baba, Denis and Giles Hine OPEN: all week; 12 to 2, 7 to 10 MEALS: alc (main courses bistro £6 to £10, restaurant £13 to £25.50). Set L £15.95, Set D £23.50 SERVICE: not inc, card slips closed CARDS: Access, Amex, Diners, Visa DETAILS: restaurant 50 seats, bistro 22 seats. 6 tables outside. Private parties: 75 main room, 15 and 25 private rooms. Car park. Vegetarian meals. Children's helpings. Smart dress preferred. No smoking while others eat. Wheelchair access (also WC). No music ACCOMMODATION: 19 rooms, all with bath/shower. TV. Phone. B&B £70 to £90. Rooms for disabled. Children welcome. Baby facilities. Pets welcome. Afternoon teas. Garden. Swimming-pool. Tennis. Doors close at midnight. Confirm by 6. Fax: (0452) 780840 (The Which? Hotel Guide)

CRANLEIGH Surrey   map 3

La Barbe Encore

High Street, Cranleigh GU6 8AE   COOKING 1*
CRANLEIGH (0483) 273889   COST £20–£38

This little French bistro on Cranleigh's main thoroughfare is not a particularly pretty sight inside, with its net curtains, orange colour scheme and drab bric-à-brac, but the welcome is warm and Jean-Pierre Bonnet's cooking should reconcile most to its arcane charm. The fixed-price bilingual menus change seasonally and offer a mix of the traditional – snails with garlic butter, or squid rings cooked in white wine with tomatoes and cream, for example – and the innovative. The latter tendency has brought on to the menu dishes like a salad of fried pigeon breast with diced artichoke heart dressed with warm balsamic vinegar. That balance of styles is carried through to dessert stage, so that you can choose between tarte fine aux pommes with cinnamon ice-cream and caramel sauce, or chocolate tart with espresso sauce. A good range of teas and tisanes is available, in addition to coffee. Service is commended as 'helpful and intelligent', even if it may not always be fluent in English. The short wine list is serviceable enough. House French is £9.30.

CHEF: Jean-Pierre Bonnet   PROPRIETORS: Ann and Jean-Pierre Bonnet   OPEN: Tue to Sun, exc Sat L and Sun D; 12 to 1.45, 7 to 9.45   MEALS: Set L £7.95 to £14.95, Set D £10 (Tue and Wed) to £17.95 (all 2 courses)   SERVICE: not inc   CARDS: Access, Amex, Visa   DETAILS: 65 seats. Private parties: 75 main room. Vegetarian meals. Children welcome. Smart dress preferred. No-smoking area. Wheelchair access (1 step). Music. Fax: (0483) 273889

CROYDE Devon   map 1

▲ Whiteleaf at Croyde 🍴✳

Croyde, nr Braunton EX33 1PN   COOKING 2
CROYDE (0271) 890266   COST £22–£39

Croyde is an attractive seaside village on the edge of Exmoor National Park and the Whiteleaf is first and foremost a guesthouse, dating from the 1930s. The Wallingtons are immediately on first-name terms with guests, and the tendency to fuss is more a virtue than a fault. If the place has a faint air of eccentricity about it, that too is a virtue. David Wallington, a busy and obviously dedicated man, lays down the ground rules: orders for dinner need to be in by 6.30pm for an 8.15pm start. He cooks a long menu, seven days a week, and is up early to bake the breakfast bread.

The Wallingtons' travels show up in the repertoire. Items from south-west France (cassoulet, confit) and Italy (bruschetta, polenta, pasta), tempered with an occasional dip into a favoured cookery book, produce a sizeable menu that many a brasserie would have difficulty holding together. Deep-fried Gorgonzola tartlets with spiced quince, and a savoury vegetable bread-and-butter pudding (for main course), show the level of invention. But most dishes show a simpler approach, from fish-cakes to steak and kidney pie with a suet crust, and mixed fruit crumble. The wine list has been trimmed this year, with bin-ends sold off at bargain prices. Value is still very good, and Italy provides much of the interest. House Côtes du Roussillon is £7.80.

CHEF: David Wallington   PROPRIETORS: David and Florence Wallington   OPEN: all week, D only; 6.30 to 8.15   MEALS: Set D £17.50 to £21.75   SERVICE: net prices, card slips closed   CARDS: Access, Visa   DETAILS: 16 seats. 2 tables outside. Private parties: 16 main room. Car park. Vegetarian meals. Children welcome. Smart dress preferred. No smoking in dining-room. No music   ACCOMMODATION: 3 rooms, all with bath/shower. TV. Phone. B&B £37 to £54. Deposit: £25. Children welcome. Baby facilities. Pets welcome (not in public rooms). Garden. Doors close at midnight. Confirm by 7 (The Which? Hotel Guide)

Card slips closed *in the details at the end of an entry indicates that the total on the slips of credit cards is closed when handed over for signature.*

CRUDWELL Wiltshire	map 2

▲ *Crudwell Court* ♥ ⁵✳

Crudwell, nr Malmesbury SN16 9EP
MALMESBURY (0666) 577194   COOKING 1*
on A429, 3m N of Malmesbury   COST £18–£41

'The setting is one of the loveliest I've met, and one of the most English,' writes a regular visitor – 'quite gloriously Cotswold'. At this one-time rectory silence reigns inside and out, except for the church clock striking occasionally.

While owners and chefs have come and gone (the present team has been here since 1991), the style of cooking has changed little. Soft herring roes poached in wine with cream and tarragon has been a regular, and deep-fried Brie with cranberry sauce harks back a while. There is enough convincing professionalism in the kitchen to turn out a small and flavoursome cone of sole mousseline in a moat of light stock-based sauce, and one diner found that a dish of pork cooked with an apple and cider sauce was so competently done as to lay the ghost of previous unhappy experiences with this combination elsewhere. An inspector found on one occasion a slight roughness in execution, but sauces saved the day. That went for the puddings too: an excellent, intense strawberry coulis surrounding a very large portion of lemon and honey roulade. Bread and butter could be improved. The wine list is reasonably on the ball, put together by a Master of Wine, with some good-value bottles, not least from the New World. CELLARMAN'S CHOICE: Haut-Médoc, Ch. Sénéjac 1989, £17.00; Crozes-Hermitage Mule Blanche 1991, Jaboulet £14.25.

CHEF: Chris Amor PROPRIETORS: Nick Bristow and Iain MacLaren OPEN: all week; 12 to 2, 7.30 to 9.30 MEALS: Set L Sun £11.50, Set L Mon to Sat £14.50, Set D £19.50 to £26 SERVICE: not inc, card slips closed CARDS: Access, Amex, Diners, Visa DETAILS: 80 seats. Private parties: 80 main room, 50 and 30 private rooms. Car park. Vegetarian meals. Children's helpings. Smart dress preferred. No smoking in dining-room. Wheelchair access (1 step; also WC). No music ACCOMMODATION: 15 rooms, all with bath/shower. TV. Phone. B&B £50 to £88. Deposit: £20. Children welcome. Baby facilities. Pets welcome (not in public rooms). Afternoon teas. Garden. Swimming-pool. Confirm by 6. Fax: (0666) 577853 (*The Which? Hotel Guide*)

DARLINGTON Co Durham	map 7

Cottage Thai

94–96 Parkgate, Darlington DL1 1RX   COOKING 1
DURHAM (0325) 361717   COST £20–£40

Cottage Thai is a couple of hundred yards from the railway station, its brown-painted shop-front cheered up by the artfully floodlit Civic Theatre opposite. The high-ceilinged dining-room has painted oriental screens and an abundance of green plants to overcome its rather basic nature. A full spread of 70 dishes covers the repertoire from spring rolls and chicken soup with coconut milk, through red and green curries, fried chicken and beef, to specials of duck. Along the way come vegetables – either stir-fried or deep-fried in batter – while 'son-in-law' egg may be so called because it is hard-boiled, or perhaps because the treatment it receives is both sweet and sour.

Flavours pack a real punch. 'The beauty of it was, the more you ate the more happened in your mouth,' according to a reporter who enjoyed a spicy prawn hot-and-sour soup with lemon grass and herbs. Rice and noodles are properly done, and portions are not large for the price. Spicing is generally well handled for length and depth of flavour, textures are varied and can easily be organised to deliver contrasts with help from the all-female, all-charming front-of-house staff. They are careful to adjust recommendations to individual tolerance for heat and spice, and concerned to get things just right. Drink tea or Singha beer. House wine is £7.50.

CHEF/PROPRIETOR: Malinee Burachati OPEN: Mon to Sat; 12 to 1.30, 6.30 to 10.15 CLOSED: 2 weeks Aug MEALS: alc (main courses £4 to £9). Set L and D (minimum 2) £15 to £26 SERVICE: not inc CARDS: Access, Amex, Visa DETAILS: 50 seats. Private parties: 50 main room. Vegetarian meals. Children's helpings. Smart dress preferred. No-smoking area. Wheelchair access (also WC). Music

Victor's

84 Victoria Road, Darlington DL1 5JW	COOKING 2*
DARLINGTON (0325) 480818	COST £14–£32

In the surroundings of Victoria Road, a variety of trades is plied: second-hand vacuum cleaners, chips, erotica. The walk from the railway station may induce despondency, but a welcome awaits in the form of the Robinsons' enterprise, pleasing many for its unswerving dedication to value and its celebration of good seasonal produce, albeit in slightly scruffy, though comfortable enough, surroundings. Excitement mounts as meals progress, and the final bill always amazes for its modesty. Three courses plus coffee are offered at an inclusive price, with an additional soup or sorbet choice at dinner.

Jayne Robinson seems to do most of the cooking, and shows a skilful hand in marshalling flavours and seasonings to their best advantage. Recommendations include vegetable tempura in 'airy light batter', boudin of scallops with a raspberry vinaigrette, grilled sea bass enlivened with a tomato and chilli sauce, and meltingly tender paupiettes of venison in a strong red wine reduction. Desserts maintain the pace with profiteroles accompanied by an admirably bitter chocolate sauce, and fresh pear with shortcake and whipped cream – 'quite simply the best I've eaten'. Appetisers, breads and petits fours are all sound. The wine list is short and to the point. It will not set the pulse racing, and some burgundy producers' names need filling in, but everything save champagne is under £14. House wines from California are £8.

CHEFS: Peter and Jayne Robinson, and Trudy Neave PROPRIETORS: Peter and Jayne Robinson OPEN: Tue to Sat; 12 to 2, 7.30 to 10.30 CLOSED: 1 week Christmas MEALS: Set L £8.50, Set D £20 SERVICE: not inc, card slips closed CARDS: Access, Amex, Diners, Visa DETAILS: 32 seats. Private parties: 32 main room. Vegetarian meals. Children's helpings. Wheelchair access (2 steps). Music

The text of entries is based on unsolicited reports sent in by readers, backed up by inspections conducted anonymously. The factual details under the text are from questionnaires the Guide *sends to all restaurants that feature in the book.*

DARTMOUTH Devon   map 1

Billy Budd's

7 Foss Street, Dartmouth TQ6 9DW   COOKING 1
DARTMOUTH (0803) 834842   COST £15–£34

Most visitors love the atmosphere of this bistro: its friendliness, efficiency and happy mood are infectious, despite the pressure of popularity. Honest fish cookery is the main attraction, which means seafood crêpes, wild salmon with béarnaise sauce, Dover sole and grilled John Dory. Reporters have also enthused about lamb cooked with chilli, ginger and honey on a bed of home-made noodles, and duck with plum sauce. Home-made ginger ice-cream is a star among the sweets. Crêpes, omelettes, pasta and bangers define the simpler menu at lunch when the ambience is also more low-key. The wine list keeps to sound, basic drinking. House wine is £8.45.

CHEF: Keith Belt   PROPRIETORS: Keith Belt and Lynne Carnell   OPEN: Tue to Sat; 12 to 2, 7.30 to 9.30   CLOSED: 1 week Nov, 3 weeks Feb to Mar (telephone to check)   MEALS: alc (main courses L £4 to £6, D £11 to £13). Minimum £10.95 D   SERVICE: not inc, card slips closed   CARDS: Access, Visa   DETAILS: 35 seats. Private parties: 25 main room. Vegetarian meals. Children's helpings. No children under 11 D. Smart dress preferred. Wheelchair access (1 step). Music

Carved Angel ▌

2 South Embankment, Dartmouth TQ6 9BH   COOKING 4
DARTMOUTH (0803) 832465   COST £36–£68

The restaurant stands on the quay like a culinary beacon. Beyond the simple Tudor frontage, the single dining-room is light and airy: bobbing yachts can be viewed one way, the kitchen the other. It may not be customary to watch what is going on in the engine-room when cruising along, but the Carved Angel does not stand on ceremony and has nothing to hide. Nor does it revere food in hushed, awe-struck tones, rather it respects good ingredients and treats them sensibly. 'The food is simple, not tarted up or prettified; it relies on freshness and quality, coaxed along by herbs,' writes one. 'The quality of ingredients and cooking standards are consistently excellent. What it does it does superbly,' attests another.

What the place has done for ages is to take the principles and ideas that underpin the best of French cooking and apply them to its own circumstances. Sometimes the ingredients and recipes are direct translations, as in the long-running provençale fish soup with rouille and croûtons, a wonderful rich colour, aromatic and served in a deep tureen, which is both delicate and full of flavour. But traditional French recipes say nothing of soy and lemon grass, or cornbreads and pineapple pickle, all of which are served with braised duck, and nothing of coconut and kaffir lime leaves, which here add zest to lobster. The restaurant's position allows for brilliantly fresh fish and shellfish, none better than a simple crab salad for some or, for others, sweet, firm and lightly cooked brill, and 'a superb piece' of Dover sole, done simply with sorrel and herbs. More than most, the Carved Angel takes its local supplies seriously, from year-round vegetables and fruit to seasonal game. Supporters praise everything from the excellent olives to 'a simple bowl of fresh raspberries with clotted cream', and an outstanding basil ice-cream. 'I ate it once here years ago and have dreamt of it ever since,' wrote one, whose dreams were not shattered by a second encounter.

The practice of including everything – mineral water, coffee and service – in set-price meals is to be applauded. Apart from wine, there are no hidden extras; what you see is what you pay. Curiously, not all readers understand this. One reporter avoided pudding to try to save money, not realising it was already included. Even so, niggles about the food have led others to observe that the all-in figure is only a bargain if everything goes swimmingly, and not all reporters are charmed, remarking variously on poor bread, tired salad, 'dry chewy partridge', and a number of other things that have left them less than impressed. If service were up to scratch it might help matters, but there have been long waits recorded for this and that. It is friendly enough, it just drifts. Expectations are high, and while there is no doubt about what the kitchen can do, the question some reporters are asking is why it does not do it every time. Other expectations surface too – why no credit cards, and why is smoking allowed? – perhaps suggesting that even the best places need to move with the times.

Wines target quality throughout but keep the ordinary drinker in mind. Mark-ups are not greedy, and there is much to enjoy under £20 as well as bags of good stuff not far above it. The list is arranged with the New World up front and encourages exploration. It takes sherry, madeira, spirits and the like just as seriously. Three house wines and two dessert wines are £14 (£3 per glass). CELLARMAN'S CHOICE: Meursault 'Les Charmes' 1990, Drouhin, £31.50; Cornas 1985, Clape, £26.

CHEFS: Joyce Molyneux and Nick Coiley PROPRIETORS: Joyce Molyneux and Meriel Matthews OPEN: Tue to Sun, exc Sun D; 12.30 to 2, 7.30 to 9.30 CLOSED: 6 weeks from 2 Jan MEALS: alc (main courses £15 to £24). Set L Tue to Sat £24 to £29, Sun £30, Set D £40 (2 courses) to £45 SERVICE: net prices DETAILS: 48 seats. Private parties: 40 main room, 12 and 20 private rooms. Vegetarian meals. Children's helpings. Smart dress preferred. Wheelchair access. No music. Fax: (0863) 835141

DEDHAM Essex   map 3

▲ *Fountain House* ▮ ⅝✳

Dedham Hall, Brook Street,
Dedham CO7 6AD   COOKING 1
COLCHESTER (0206) 323027   COST £23–£29

Set in six acres of fields and gardens in the heart of Constable country, the Sartons' aptly named guest house is extremely popular with artists who come to paint in the studio and grounds. The ambience is 'of the best'. Wendy Sarton's cooking is plain and fresh: scrambled eggs with smoked salmon, devilled lamb's kidneys, baked trout with orange and walnut stuffing, beef Wellington ('red in the middle as it ought to be and crusty on the outside ditto'). Menus change every week, although chocolate fondue is a permanent fixture among the sweets.

France is treated seriously, but not given undue prominence on the wine list. Excellent bottles from Australasia, Italy, America and Germany are on offer at encouragingly low prices, allowing access to a wide range of high-quality styles for less than £20. There is a generous offering of half-bottles, and a spread of eight house wines under £10. CELLARMAN'S CHOICE: Gewurztraminer 1990, Schleret, £16; Bourgogne Rouge, Les Charmes au Chatelain 1988, Dom. Mortet.

CHEF: Wendy Sarton   PROPRIETORS: James and Wendy Sarton   OPEN: Tue to Sat, D only, and Sun L; 12.30 to 2, 7.30 to 9.30   MEALS: Set L £16.50, Set D £18.50   SERVICE: not inc, card slips closed   CARDS: Access, Visa   DETAILS: 35 seats. Private parties: 50 main room. Car park. Vegetarian meals. Children's helpings. Smart dress preferred. No smoking in dining-room. Wheelchair access. Music   ACCOMMODATION: 6 rooms, all with bath/shower. TV. B&B £34 to £57. Children welcome. Baby facilities. Garden. Doors close at midnight. Confirm by 6 (*The Which? Hotel Guide*)

▲ *Le Talbooth* ▮

Gun Hill, Dedham CO7 6HP
COLCHESTER (0206) 323150   COOKING 2
on B1029, off A12, 6m NE of Colchester   COST £23–£60

The pastoral setting by the River Stour is 'outstandingly peaceful, provided there are not too many revellers and not too much traffic pounding down the A12,' commented one visitor. Gerald Milsom's gabled, half-timbered house has been a *Guide* regular for many years and in its latest guise continues to offer high standards of comfort and cooking. Chef Henrik Iversen eschews the heady world of haute cuisine in favour of traditional realism: chateaubriand is now the most regularly endorsed dish. Other commendable items have included pan-fried red mullet, steak and kidney pudding, and an orange parfait that had a 'wonderful combination of tangy and sweet'. For those wanting more modern invention, the kitchen can also deliver stir-fried lamb fillet with lemon grass, ginger and coconut or medallions of pork with spinach, shiitake mushrooms and walnut sauce. Cut-price lunches centre on roasts, cottage pie and poached salmon with hollandaise. Service is ever-attentive.

The wine list garners a collection of top producers and has a wide but fair spread of prices. There is relief for those with £20 or less to spend and balanced coverage of the New World as well as some mouthwateringly mature clarets, and a decent spread of half-bottles. House red is £9.25 (£2.25 a glass), house white is £12.95 (£2.75 a glass). CELLARMAN'S CHOICE: Pinot Blanc, St-Helena 1991, £16.50; Crozes-Hermitage, Les Jalets 1989, Jaboulet, £16.25.

CHEF: Henrik Iversen   PROPRIETOR: Gerald Milsom   OPEN: all week; 12 to 2, 7 to 9.30   MEALS: alc (main courses £11 to £18.50). Set L Mon to Fri £12.50 (2 courses) to £15, Sat £16.50 (2 courses) to £19.50, Sun £19.95, Set D £16.50 (2 courses) to £19.50   SERVICE: 10%, card slips closed   CARDS: Access, Amex, Visa   DETAILS: 75 seats. 10 tables outside. Private parties: 85 main room, 24 private room. Car park. Vegetarian meals. Children's helpings. Smart dress preferred. Music   ACCOMMODATION: 10 rooms, all with bath/shower. TV. Phone. B&B £85 to £140. Children welcome. Garden. Fax: (0206) 322309 (*The Which? Hotel Guide*)

▮ *denotes an outstanding wine cellar;* ▮ *denotes a good wine list, worth travelling for.*

The Guide *office can quickly spot when a restaurateur is encouraging customers to write recommending inclusion – and sadly, several restaurants have been doing this in 1994. Such reports do not further a restaurant's cause. Please tell us if a restaurateur invites you to write to the* Guide.

DENMEAD Hampshire   map 2

Barnards £

Hambledon Road, Denmead PO7 6NU
PORTSMOUTH (0705) 257788   COOKING 2
on B2150, 2m NW of Waterlooville   COST £20–£38

The Barnards have been on the move in 1994. Having felt they had outgrown their previous address in Cosham, they have moved to Denmead. The new premises are fairly simply furnished in a similar style to the old ones. Their aim is still to present classic French cooking within the framework of a monthly-changing *carte* and a simpler fixed-price menu.

First impressions following the move agree that David Barnard's standards are as consistent as ever. Savoury soufflés are a particular favourite, and a twice-cooked Swiss cheese soufflé on saladings with a celery vinaigrette had good, strong flavour. The fixed-price menu in June offered moules marinière that pleased a shellfish devotee and grilled, fanned sirloin with a garlic and herb butter. Fruit tends to be present at all stages, so crab may come with pink grapefruit and be followed by duck breast with caramelised lime sauce and a compote of 'peppery pineapple'. The latter dish was found too sweet by one reporter, although the meat itself was 'nicely rare' and enjoyed. Home-made ice-creams such as honey or brown bread show a deft touch, and chocolate mousse laced with brandy impressed a chocoholic. The short, fairly-priced wine list is adequate to the task in hand. House French is from £8.25.

CHEF: David Barnard   PROPRIETORS: David and Sandie Barnard   OPEN: Tue to Sat, D only (L parties by arrangement); 7.30 to 10   MEALS: alc (main courses £12.50 to £16). Set D £13.50   SERVICE: net prices, card slips closed   CARDS: Access, Amex, Visa   DETAILS: 30 seats. Private parties: 30 main room. Vegetarian meals. Children's helpings. No-smoking area. Wheelchair access (2 steps). Music

DENT Cumbria   map 7

▲ Stone Close ⁑✳ £

Main Street, Dent LA10 5QL   COOKING 1
DENT (053 96) 25231   COST £12–£19

Patricia Barber and Graham Hudson are dedicated to providing daytime sustenance for walkers and tourists trekking their way through the Yorkshire Dales National Park. Their admirable pit-stop is a converted seventeenth-century cottage with low beams, flagged floors and bare wooden tables. Open fires burn in two original cast-iron ranges. The kitchen delivers exactly what is needed: robust, hearty food and plenty of it. Fixtures such as salads, baked potatoes, rolls and some good old-fashioned puddings are backed up by daily specials of tomato and basil soup, spicy lamb and lentils, and leek and mushroom pie. The wine list is tiny; otherwise opt for one of the speciality teas, non alcoholic Sheffield Stout or refreshing elderflower cordial. House wine is £7.80 a litre.

CHEF: Patricia Barber   PROPRIETORS: Graham Hudson and Patricia Barber   OPEN: all week; 10.30am to 5.30pm   CLOSED: Jan and Feb, mid-week Nov to Mar   MEALS: alc (main courses £3 to £4.50)   SERVICE: not inc   DETAILS: 45 seats. Private parties: 25 main room. Vegetarian meals. Children's helpings. No smoking in dining-room. Wheelchair access. Music ACCOMMODATION: 3 rooms. B&B £16.50 to £29. Deposit: £10. Children welcome. Baby facilities. Dogs welcome. Afternoon teas (*The Which? Hotel Guide*)

DINTON Buckinghamshire   map 3

La Chouette £

Westlington Green, Dinton HP17 8UW
AYLESBURY (0296) 747422   COOKING 1
off A418, 4m SW of Aylesbury   COST £19–£57

Belgian restaurants in Britain are a rare animal – a pity, really, because the country's tradition of fine food and excellent beers deserves attention. This one is set in a former pub, in a quiet village off the A418 where thatching is alive and well. Pictures of birds, and the hook-beaked, large-eyed nocturnal bird of prey that constitutes the logo, reflect the proprietor's pastime. 'The owl has landed,' writes a reporter, delighted with his first visit.

The restaurant is largely a one-man band, and Frédéric Desmette is friendly, articulate, enthusiastic and talented. The talent shows through in scallop salad with a first-class vinaigrette; in good (and properly seasoned) beurre blanc with a fillet of turbot; in flavoursome breast of pheasant; and in light zabaglione made with white wine. 'Dishes of poultry, fish and seafood tend to use a lot of cream, so there is less variety of taste than we would have preferred' was the opinion of one reporter, though the result was still 'delicious'. The £10 lunch menu is three courses of whatever Mr Desmette feels like. Wines are good but pocket-draining; house wines are £10. Beers are interesting, with a small selection of about a dozen (including five Trappist) displayed in the bar.

CHEF/PROPRIETOR: Frédéric Desmette   OPEN: all week, exc Sat L and Sun D; 12 to 2, 7 to 9 (Sun L with reservation one day ahead)   MEALS: alc (main courses £9 to £12.50). Set L and D £10 to £35   SERVICE: 12.5%, card slips closed   CARDS: Access, Visa   DETAILS: 40 seats. 4 tables outside. Private parties: 45 main room. Car park. Vegetarian meals. Children's helpings. Smart dress preferred. No cigars/pipes in dining-room. Wheelchair access (1 step; also WC). Music

---

DISS Norfolk   map 6

▲ Salisbury House ⁙✳

84 Victoria Road, Diss IP22 3JG   COOKING 1*
DISS (0379) 644738   COST £29–£43

Barry and Sue Davies keep house and home in this Victorian residence just out of town. Outside it has attractions aplenty, including a walled patio, a croquet lawn with its own summer house, and a duck pond graced with weeping willows. The interior manages to combine homeliness and intimacy with a touch of luxury. Service is first-class. Reporters like the inventiveness of Barry Davies's cooking and his way with fish: 'divine' skate en croûte with watercress sauce, and 'exquisite' monkfish in leek, coriander and saffron sauce have been highlights. Elsewhere, it is a matter of modern British flourish folded into creamy French classic – as in salad of warm sweetbreads with mange-tout, salmon roulade with chive sauce, slow-roasted shoulder of lamb with couscous, and warm winter tart with spiced apple and calvados sabayon. Menus change monthly and the price varies according to the number of courses taken. The extensive wine list is notable for its bin-ends and impressive collection of half-bottles: big names from Burgundy and Bordeaux are the main attractions. House wines start at £7.50.

CHEF: Barry Davies   PROPRIETORS: Barry and Sue Davies   OPEN: Tue to Sat, D only (Tue to Fri L by arrangement, 12.15 to 1.45); 7.30 to 9.15   CLOSED: 1 week Christmas, 2 weeks Aug   MEALS: Set L and D £18.50 (2 courses) to £27   SERVICE: not inc   CARDS: Access, Visa   DETAILS: 36 seats. 3 tables outside. Private parties: 20 main room, 14 and 20 private rooms. Car park. Vegetarian meals. Children's helpings. Smart dress preferred. No smoking in dining-room. Wheelchair access (1 step; also WC). Music   ACCOMMODATION: 4 rooms, all with bath/shower. TV. B&B £39 to £70. Deposit: £10 per night. Children welcome. Garden. Doors close at 11.30. Confirm by 7 (*The Which? Hotel Guide*)

Weaver's Wine Bar

Market Hill, Diss IP22 3JZ	COOKING 1
DISS (0379) 642411	COST £17–£32

Set in a heavily timbered fifteenth-century building that was once a chapel, Weaver's is the hub of the town. A bevy of good-humoured local ladies welcomes all comers, who stream in for decent home-cooked lunches listed on a blackboard by the door. The menu is a mixed bag, taking in home-made venison sausages with pickled red cabbage, turkey enchiladas, stir-fried chicken tikka masala and braised oxtail, as well as fresh fish from the East Coast ports. Dinners are more ambitious, but the style is similar: salmon is steamed on a bed of spring onions and ginger; breast of Barbary duck is roasted and served with a Muscat sauce. Vegetarians have their own menu. The creditable wine list includes a trio from English vineyards, as well as plenty from the New World. House wine is £7.95.

CHEF: William Bavin   PROPRIETORS: William and Wilma Bavin   OPEN: Mon to Sat, exc Sat L; 12 to 2, 7 to 9.30   CLOSED: Christmas, bank hol Mons   MEALS: alc (main courses £8 to £12). Set D Mon to Fri £10   SERVICE: not inc, card slips closed   CARDS: Access, Diners, Visa   DETAILS: 80 seats. Private parties: 50 main room, 50 private room. Children's helpings. No smoking L 12 to 2, D 7 to 9.30. Music

DORCHESTER Dorset	map 2

Mock Turtle

34 High West Street, Dorchester DT1 1UP	COOKING 1
DORCHESTER (0305) 264011	COST £19–£40

'We arrived for lunch on spec, just as they were turning the sign to 'closed', but they let us in warmly and treated us with admirable good humour,' commented holiday makers who made a pit-stop at this popular local eating house. Mid-week lunches (Tuesday to Friday) are excellent value and fresh fish is a strong suit: powerful prawn bisque 'redolent of shell and stock', and grilled halibut with herb sauce have been singled out. In the evening the kitchen moves into the realms of Lunesdale duck breast in puff pastry, and délice of cod with mussels and white wine sauce. Vegetables are abundant and sweets are the likes of summer fruit tart with whipped kirsch cream. Dorchester's own brewery and wine merchant, Eldridge Pope, supplies the wines, which provide decent drinking at fair prices. House wines start at £7.95.

CHEF: Raymond Hodder PROPRIETORS: Raymond, Alan and Vivien Hodder OPEN: Mon to Sat, exc L Mon and Sat, and bank hol Sun D; 12 to 2, 7 to 9.30 MEALS: Set L £10 (2 courses) to £12.50, Set D £15.95 (2 courses) to £18.95 SERVICE: not inc CARDS: Access, Visa DETAILS: 60 seats. Private parties: 20 main room. Vegetarian meals. Children's helpings. No cigars or pipes in dining-room. Wheelchair access (1 step). Music

---

DORKING Surrey   map 3

Partners West Street £※

2, 3 and 4 West Street, Dorking RH4 1BL   COOKING 2
DORKING (0306) 882826   COST £20–£43

West Street is lined with antique shops, and the restaurant is genuine Tudor half-timbered, with seating on two floors (both rooms are now no-smoking). Changes in the summer of 1994 mean that Tim McEntire now oversees both this and the Brasserie (see entry, North Cheam), leaving a new team in charge of day-to-day cooking in Dorking. Dinner is now à la carte, while lunch (except on Sunday) offers both *carte* and fixed- price menus. The new style reads well and sounds light, making much of vegetables and fish. On the inaugural summer *carte*, a dish of lamb sweetbreads was the only first-course meat option, leaving the field clear for the likes of smoked haddock brandade, charred salmon terrine, and gazpacho with marinated chargrilled vegetables. Bright flavours give the whole thing zest: a lime and chive sauce with the smoked haddock, coriander in a ravioli of goats' cheese, or citrus couscous and vegetable vinaigrette with roast sea bass. Salt cod and black olive mash keep the Mediterranean flag flying.

Early reports, however, indicate that the food is rather heavier than it sounds, with first courses 'swimming in butter', and a rather 'oily and greasy' effect in main courses. Puddings include glazed lemon tart with raspberry sorbet, and chocolate and hazelnut torte with hot cherries. Cheeses are British. Good black olives arrive with the menu, bread is a choice of sun-dried tomato, oatmeal rolls or brown ciabatta, and coffee is plentiful. Service is friendly, attentive and efficient, even when the house is full. Local Denbies wines rightly feature on the bit-of-everything list, which is careful to target a range of pockets. House French is £10.95 (£2.25 per glass).

CHEF: Tim McEntire, Anthony Robinson, Paul Boyland and Nathan Darling PROPRIETOR: Partners Restaurants plc OPEN: all week, exc Sat L and Sun D; 12.30 to 2, 7.30 to 9.30 MEALS: alc (main courses £12.95). Set L Mon to Fri £11.95, Set L Sun £11.95 to £14.95 SERVICE: net prices, card slips closed CARDS: Access, Amex, Diners, Visa DETAILS: 45 seats. Private parties: 18 and 30 private rooms. Vegetarian meals. Children's helpings. No smoking in 1 dining-room. Wheelchair access (1 step). No music

---

Report forms are at the back of the book; write a letter if you prefer.

DORRINGTON Shropshire
map 4

▲ Country Friends

Dorrington SY5 7JD
DORRINGTON (0743) 718707
on A49, 5m S of Shrewsbury

COOKING 3
COST £32–£40

This husband-and-wife operation flows along amiably, although one party felt that it was not quite as matey as the name suggests, and found themselves speaking in hushed tones. The main change this year is that the set dinner and à la carte have both been scrapped. In comes a new two- or three-course meal for a fixed price. The advantages are simplicity and a what-you-see-is-what-you-get all-in price, the same at lunch as at dinner. The cooking remains reliable, the dishes interesting, and the style is a gentle country adaptation of the middle English repertoire, including calf's liver with citrus fruit, Trelough duck breast with a spiced plum and ginger sauce, and queen of puddings (with a gin and lime ice-cream) or Welsh rarebit to finish.

Menus allow enough choice between the lightness of twice-baked courgette soufflé and the weight of chocolate truffle cake, and it is good to see beans adding depth to some dishes: butter beans with confit of duck, and a tartlet of flageolet beans with baby onions and bacon that comes with lamb. Bread is a Whittaker passion that brings appreciative murmurs. The wine list contains a good smattering of old and new – Worlds, styles and vintages. Half-bottles are reasonable in scope, and house wines (French or Australian) are good, as well as good value at £9.50 and £10.50.

CHEF: Charles Whittaker   PROPRIETORS: Charles and Pauline Whittaker   OPEN: Tue to Sat; 12 to 2, 7 to 9 (9.30 Sat)   CLOSED: last 2 weeks July, 1 week end Oct, Christmas   MEALS: Set L and D £20.50 (2 courses) to £24.50   SERVICE: not inc   CARDS: Access, Amex, Visa   DETAILS: 45 seats. Private parties: 45 main room. Car park. Vegetarian meals. Children welcome. No smoking while others eat. Wheelchair access (1 step). No music   ACCOMMODATION: 3 rooms, 1 with bath/shower. D,B&B £60 to £98. Deposit: £20. Children welcome

DREWSTEIGNTON Devon
map 1

▲ Hunts Tor House ⁵✳

Drewsteignton EX6 6QW
DREWSTEIGNTON (0647) 281228

COOKING 2*
COST £24–£32

In a tiny village west of Exeter, Chris and Sue Harrison have created a little monument to Devon produce. 'Little' is the operative concept: there are just eight places for dinner. If each of the four guest rooms is occupied by two, then non-residents will be ruefully turned away. In any case, outsiders should allow 24 hours' notice of a booking.

Sue Harrison cooks a frequently changing no-choice menu of three courses plus cheese (after the dessert) as an extra. The style is confidently simple, avoiding the insane combinations encountered at some country houses, and diners will be asked beforehand whether there is anything they don't want to eat. Broccoli timbale with a tomato coulis and olive oil is a starter that has impressed for its 'heavenly' freshness, chicken breast may be sensitively sauced with ginger and soy, while praline parfait with blackcurrant coulis was an unusual idea that worked well. Others have delighted in smoked pigeon with lentils, monkfish with a tomato and basil sauce, salmon in filo with ginger and currants, duck breast with a white bean sauce, madeira syllabub and chocolate marquise with strawberries. Support the Devon cheeses – they are always good. Coffee is 'good and strong'. On quiet nights, the atmosphere may be thought a trifle sombre, but that is hardly a unique problem. Bills include a small donation to the Devon Wildlife Trust. The short wine list is largely French, buttressed by a half-dozen others, including Teruzzi & Puthod's delightful Vernaccia di San Gimignano. House wines are £8.60 (Cotes de Duras Sauvignon) or £9.50 (Errazuriz Chilean Merlot).

CHEF: Sue Harrison   PROPRIETORS: Sue and Chris Harrison   OPEN: all week, D only; 7.30 (book 1 day ahead)   CLOSED: end Oct to end Feb   MEALS: Set D £17 to £19   SERVICE: not inc DETAILS: 8 seats. Private parties: 8 main room. Vegetarian meals with prior notice. No children under 14. Smart dress preferred. No smoking in dining-room. Music   ACCOMMODATION: 4 rooms, all with bath/shower. B&B £27 to £55. Deposit: £10. No children under 14. Pets welcome (not in public rooms). Doors close at midnight. Confirm by 3

DRYBROOK Gloucestershire   map 2

Cider Press 🍴✳

The Cross, Drybrook GL17 9EB   COOKING 2
DEAN (0594) 544472   COST £22–£40

On the edge of the Forest of Dean, Bernadette Fitzpatrick's tiny country restaurant works to a philosophy of fresh flavours and informality. Customers are encouraged to stay all evening. The kitchen makes use of local ingredients, including naturally reared meat, and fish is delivered direct from Cornwall. Chef Christopher Challener is keen to explain the short menu in detail and will often bring out the catch of the day before it is cooked. His repertoire shows influences from far and wide: loin of lamb dusted with coriander and black pepper has an Indian feel; sea bass steamed in a parcel with spring onions, ginger, shiitake mushrooms, lime juice and sesame oil has Chinese echoes; while fresh tagliolini with wild mushrooms, and chicken stuffed with pesto and pine-nuts show a liking for the Mediterranean. Main courses come with nouvelle-style steamed vegetables and the menu lists recommended wines for particular dishes. English and French cheeses go well with a glass of Vinoix, made from organic red Côtes du Rhône enriched with organic walnuts. Tiramisù is a well-reported sweet. The short wine list has a serious bias towards organic production. House wine is £7.50.

CHEF: Christopher Challener   PROPRIETOR: Bernadette Fitzpatrick   OPEN: Wed to Sat, D only (L Wed to Sun, and D Mon and Sun, by arrangement); 7 to 10.30   CLOSED: first 2 weeks Jan MEALS: alc (main courses £10 to £15)   SERVICE: not inc   CARDS: Access, Amex, Visa   DETAILS: 26 seats. 2 tables outside. Private parties: 30 main room. Vegetarian meals with prior notice. Children welcome. Smart dress preferred. No smoking in dining-room. Wheelchair access (1 step; also WC). Music

Forsters

2 St Bedes, Station Road,
East Boldon NE36 0LE
091-519 0929   COOKING **2**
on main Newcastle to Sunderland road   COST £21–£40

The Forsters opened in 1990 with an ambitious menu and cooking to match; now their intentions seem more modest. They aspire to no more (and no less) than that elusive grail: the sort of restaurant to be found in any village in France – family-run, serving simple fresh food in a relaxing atmosphere. It is a laudable aim, and they get it right.

The menu inclines to popular classics such as moules marinière, pork and chicken liver pâté enlivened with home-made apricot chutney, and snails in garlic butter. There are occasional excursions into the likes of a Cheddar and chive soufflé, or grilled king prawns Thai-style, but the thrust is what one man can comfortably take on in the kitchen. That includes a beautifully presented, perfectly poached egg, topped with sliced avocado, smoked salmon and hollandaise sauce, sitting on a toasted featherlight muffin. Main courses are typically a prime cut of meat with a reduced sauce founded on stock – roast lamb with basil, tomato and lamb gravy, or a slab of pork tenderloin cut in half-inch slices, the meat juices laced with calvados – while fish depends on availability. Everything, including chips, arrives on one plate. Puddings might do with more zip. Service is first-rate: willing, courteous and pleasant. The modest, round-the-world wine list combines quality with reasonable pricing, entirely suited to the task in hand. House wine is £7.65.

CHEF: Barry Forster   PROPRIETORS: Barry and Sue Forster   OPEN: Tue to Sat, D only; 7 to 10 (11 Sat)   CLOSED: bank hols   MEALS: alc (main courses £12 to £13.50). Set D Tue to Fri £15   SERVICE: not inc   CARDS: Access, Amex, Diners, Visa   DETAILS: 28 seats. Private parties: 30 main room. Car park. Vegetarian meals with prior notice. Children's helpings. No children under 8. Smart dress preferred. No cigars/pipes in dining-room. Music

▲ Grand Hotel, Mirabelle

Jevington Gardens, Eastbourne BN21 4EQ   COOKING **3***
EASTBOURNE (0323) 412345   COST £28–£62

The Grand is Eastbourne's last gesture before the South Downs rise steeply to the west. It faces the Channel, protected from its full force by the garden and drive. The restaurant is separate from the hotel, and the discreet entrance, down a short flight of steps tucked round the side, is not designed to bring in casual passers-by. The deep bay windows, each large enough to accommodate a table of six, are quite something. Drapery apart, the room is plain, and tables are generously sized and spaced.

'The food is extraordinarily good value,' notes an inspector who dined off the fixed-price dinner menu. Main courses vary from aubergine lasagne with curry spices to braised veal sweetbreads wrapped in Parma ham with a madeira jus, and the set price covers everything, including excellent canapés served in the bar, a complimentary warm soufflé of goats' cheese at table, a mid-meal sorbet, as well as coffee with petits fours. What also impresses is the menu-planning, with a sensible balance of fish, white meats, red meat and game.

Keith Mitchell adopts, in his own words, 'a serious modern approach to classical methods', perhaps exemplified by a warm, wobbly chicken liver mousse, very fine-textured, and served with small slices of toasted olive bread; or perhaps a medley of red mullet, sea bass, brill, salmon, scallop and an oyster arranged around a small mound of finely chopped spinach, in a rich, firmly flavoured red wine sauce, the fish in top condition, carefully prepared and correctly cooked. Warm 'English breakfast salad' is a lunchtime novelty of poached eggs, bacon lardons, black pudding and sauté potatoes that might catch on.

Throughout is a steady hand on flavouring, and little or no resort to pyrotechnics, expensive ingredients or elaboration for the sake of it, even with the usual temptation for chefs: puddings. Lemon tart consists of a smooth, light-textured and clear-flavoured filling on a delicate thin pastry, flashed under the grill and scattered with soft fruits. Service is well drilled, confident, efficient but friendly. Sadly the wine list does not match the cooking, rather lacking in serious intent, with some big mark-ups and a rather high 'entry price' for anything decent. Half a dozen house wines begin at £14 or £2.80 per glass.

CHEFS: Keith Mitchell and Neil Wiggins PROPRIETOR: De Vere Hotels OPEN: Tue to Sat; 12.30 to 2.30, 7 to 10 CLOSED: first week Jan MEALS: alc (main courses £16 to £22). Set L £18.50, Set D £22.50 to £28.50 SERVICE: not inc, card slips closed CARDS: Access, Amex, Diners, Visa DETAILS: 56 seats. Private parties: 50 main room, 10 to 400 private rooms. Car park. Vegetarian meals. Children's helpings. Smart dress preferred. No smoking before 2pm or 9pm. No cigars/pipes in dining-room. Wheelchair access (also WC). Music. Air-conditioned ACCOMMODATION: 161 rooms, all with bath/shower. TV. Phone. B&B £40 to £180. Rooms for disabled. Lift. Children welcome. Afternoon teas. Garden. Swimming-pool. Sauna. Snooker. Confirm by 6. Fax: (0323) 412233

EAST BUCKLAND Devon   map 1

▲ *Lower Pitt* £✻

East Buckland EX32 0TD
FILLEIGH (0598) 760243   COOKING 1*
2m N of A361, 4m NW of South Molton   COST £23–£33

The Lyonses do everything themselves in their sixteenth-century longhouse, except on busy nights. 'We are the business,' they explain, and have been since 1978. It is an environmentally conscious operation, in which bottles, paper and kitchen waste are all rigorously given a second lease of life. The Lyonses take supplies equally seriously, shopping around for the best local game, fish, meat and any herbs or seasonal vegetables not already poking up through the compost.

The setting is a quiet hamlet on the edge of Exmoor. Farm buildings and old ploughs add to the rustic feel, but the interior is very much twentieth- century. The long, narrow, whitewashed dining-room is partly divided by high-backed settles, making for intimacy rather than conviviality, while the green-carpeted conservatory with its flowering plants is the place to be in fine weather. The style is country cooking with flair, off a seasonally changing menu, and with occasional exotic borrowings. Diced leg of lamb may be served Kashmiri-style with coriander, mild garam masala, dried apricots and flaked almonds, while prawns are stir-fried with Thai seasonings.

Most flavours, however, are more gentle. Twice-baked cheese soufflé (made with double Gloucester and dotted with chives) is light, and pieces of smoked salmon are served in nothing more than a warm custard cream. Light, creamy, herby sauces are the norm. Chocolate roulade is a flour-free sponge, and apple strudel served with clotted cream is better than the normal run of its kind. A dozen house wines (from £8.50), half of them available by the glass (£1.50), are much appreciated. The rest of the list is a sensible selection, almost entirely under £20 a bottle, with a generous choice of halves.

CHEF: Suzanne Lyons   PROPRIETORS: Jerome and Suzanne Lyons   OPEN: Tue to Sat, D only (L by arrangement for 6 or more); 7 to 9   MEALS: alc (main courses £9 to £10)   SERVICE: not inc, card slips closed   CARDS: Access, Amex, Visa   DETAILS: 32 seats. 3 tables outside. Private parties: 16 main room, 16 private room. Car park. Vegetarian meals. No children under 12. Smart dress preferred. No smoking in dining-room. No music   ACCOMMODATION: 3 rooms, all with bath/shower. DB&B £55 to £110. Deposit: 10%. No children under 10. Garden. Doors close at 11. Confirm by 6. Fax: (0598) 760243 (*The Which? Hotel Guide*)

EAST GRINSTEAD West Sussex   map 3

▲ *Gravetye Manor* ▮ ✳

Vowels Lane, East Grinstead RH19 4LJ
SHARPTHORNE (0342) 810567   COOKING 3
off B2028, 2m SW of East Grinstead   COST £35–£68

Gravetye sits on a Sussex hilltop, master of all it surveys. Enlargements to this imposing stone-built Elizabethan mansion have continued through the centuries, the most recent being the extension of the north wing painstakingly overseen by Peter Herbert in 1992. Its 30 acres of landscaped grounds are the splendid bequest of the horticultural pioneer William Robinson, who lived at the manor for 51 years. The thousand acres of natural forest that form the wider setting extend to guests the free-range franchise that Gravetye's hens enjoy. Scramble with your tackle down a steep valley to the lake, and wait for the trout to bite. The interior of the house, with its comfortable antique furnishings and log fires, provides restful surroundings.

Stephen Morey's cooking has passionate advocates. It is presented within the framework of a classical *carte*, supplemented by a *prix fixe* of three courses plus coffee. Menu descriptions have a refreshing straightforwardness. A November lunch took in 'smooth and delicate' chicken boudin on a bed of creamy leeks, 'perfect' game terrine with mushrooms and leeks surrounded by vegetable crisps, 'best-quality' roast beef with the trimmings (including fine Yorkshire pudding), and densely rich chocolate and chestnut torte. That couple were mesmerised by 'the mixing and the turning' of a bespoke salad being made up at the next table from the diners' own choice of oil and vinegar. Other recommended dishes have been coarse-textured quail pâté with pistachios, a salad of braised ham hock with lentils, tortellini of scallops and crab, and a vegetarian dish of warm artichoke heart with mushrooms, quail's eggs and hollandaise. Grand Marnier soufflé omelette to finish shows confident dash in the pudding department. Despite the fact that the menu invites you to ask for plainer food if you wish, it proved difficult on one occasion to obtain unadorned melon. Bread and petits fours come in for wholehearted praise, and the staff are 'impeccable and charming'. The habit of giving prices only to the host continues, though, admittedly, the practice finds some support among readers. Less acceptable is the absence of VAT on menu prices: the 17.5 per cent is then added to the bill.

The wine list is a thoroughly exhaustive tome. Alsaces alone are a joy, a range of good Chablis producers is offered, and lovers of serious German wine are well looked after. Prices are inevitably pretty stiff, and it is easy to forget that VAT has not yet been levied on them, but those with a will (and a wallet) can partake of some of the world's great wines. House burgundy from Latour and Drouhin is £15.50 plus VAT. CELLARMAN'S CHOICE: Niersteiner Kranzberg 1976, Gustav Gessert, £42; Chardonnay 'Il Marzocco' 1989, Avignonesi, £33.

CHEF: Stephen Morey   PROPRIETORS: Peter Herbert and Leigh Stone-Herbert   OPEN: all week; 12.30 to 2, 7.30 to 9.30 (9.00 Sun)   MEALS: alc (main courses £13 to £20 – plus VAT). Set L £22, Set L Sun £28, Set D £28 (all plus VAT)   SERVICE: inc (but VAT added), card slips closed   CARDS: Access, Visa   DETAILS: 50 seats. Private parties: 8 main room, 20 private room. Car park. Vegetarian meals. Children's helpings. No children under 7. Smart dress preferred. No smoking in dining-room. Wheelchair access. No music   ACCOMMODATION: 18 rooms, all with bath/shower. TV. Phone. B&B £98 to £240 – plus VAT. Deposit: 1 nights accommodation. No children under 7 (exc 'babes in arms'). Baby facilities (cots only). Garden. Fishing. Doors close at midnight. Confirm by 9. Fax: (0342) 810080 (*The Which? Hotel Guide*)

EDENBRIDGE Kent   map 3

Honours Mill

87 High Street, Edenbridge TN8 5AU   COOKING 3
EDENBRIDGE (0732) 866757   COST £20–£45

The Goodhews have made their small restaurant at the end of the High Street into a place of relaxed comfort. You may need to dodge the threateningly low beams in the bar with its simple wicker furniture and floor of bare brick, but people immediately feel at home in the 'charming, warm and friendly' dining-room. The main evening menu, of three courses plus coffee at a fixed price, is supplemented by a cheaper weekday dinner menu that includes half a bottle of house wine. Lunch is a particularly good deal.

The cooking is nothing if not ambitious, essaying combinations that may sound a little wild: a sausage of lamb sweetbreads with pear liqueur sauce stands out from a March menu. For some unfathomable reason, dishes are listed bilingually; perhaps in anticipation of a flood of Chunnel visitors. The simpler, classic dishes work best. So a warm salad of duck confit with bacon and croûtons was 'thoroughly enjoyed – almost too generous'. Entrecôte of beef with red wine and a potato rösti was similarly generous, with carefully timed meat and well-flavoured sauce. Discordant notes were struck by a dish of best end of lamb with hard French beans and a rather inappropriate sauce. Desserts keep up the creativity with *bisquit glace*, full of crunchy meringue, nuts and caramel on a raspberry coulis, and light chocolate torte with a crème anglaise flavoured with mint and coffee. Incidentals all receive proper attention, and service is described as 'friendly, efficient and knowledgeable'. Not surprisingly, France is the country most enthusiastically represented on the wine list, with some good names and some dull. A small New World section rounds it off, and there is a thoroughly commendable range of half-bottles. House wines are £9.95.

CHEFS: Martin Radmall and Neville Goodhew PROPRIETORS: Neville, Duncan and Giles Goodhew OPEN: Tue to Sun, exc Sat L and Sun D; 12.15 to 2, 7.15 to 10 CLOSED: 2 weeks after Christmas MEALS: Set L Tue to Fri £14.50 to £31.75, Sun £22.50, Set D Tue to Fri £25 (inc wine) to £31.75, Sat £31.75 SERVICE: net prices CARDS: Access, Amex, Visa DETAILS: 40 seats. Private parties: 40 main room. Vegetarian meals with prior notice. Children's helpings Sun L. Smart dress preferred. No music

---

ELY Cambridgeshire   map 6

Old Fire Engine House ♀ ✠

25 St Mary's Street, Ely CB7 4ER   COOKING 1
ELY (0353) 662582   COST £24–£37

A promenade around Ely Cathedral may be the preamble to eating at the Old Fire Engine House. You will find it at the end of the Palace Green, west of the cathedral's main doors. It really did once house Ely's fire engine; as you pass through the bar, be sure not to miss the 1912 photograph of that majestic vehicle, attended by its proud brigade. Terri Kindred's menus change every day and offer homely British cooking based on fine Fenland produce, peppered with intriguing historical references. Mitoon of pork is thick chunks wrapped in bacon – a substantial starter. Otherwise, hearty soups, smoked fish, steak and kidney pie, beef braised in Guinness and port, syllabubs, Cambridge burnt cream, and home-made yogurt with honey and almonds are typical offerings. Readers like the comforting domesticity of the set-up and the 'lack of fuss'. Smoked salmon pâté, pork and rabbit stew, duck with a sauce of orange, onion and brandy, and sherry trifle all receive commendations.

Michael Jarman has put together a peach of a wine list, predominantly French but providing an imaginative spread of choice at reasonable prices. The list of bin-ends at the back is worth a look for some lovely old antiques at comparatively modest mark-ups. House wines are from £6.50. CELLARMAN'S CHOICE: Marqués de Casa Concha 1991, Concha y Toro, £10.50; Chianti Classico 1988, Isole e Olena, £16.

CHEF: Terri Kindred PROPRIETORS: Ann Ford and Michael Jarman OPEN: all week, exc Sun D; 12.30 to 2, 7.30 to 9 CLOSED: 24 Dec to 5 Jan, bank hols MEALS: alc (main courses £11 to £13.50) SERVICE: not inc CARDS: Access, Visa DETAILS: 55 seats. 8 tables outside. Private parties: 36 main room, 22 private room. Car park. Vegetarian meals. Children's helpings. No smoking in 1 dining-room. No music

---

Several sharp operators have tried to extort money from restaurateurs on the promise of an entry in a guidebook that has never appeared. The Good Food Guide makes no charge for inclusion and does not offer certificates of any kind.

EMSWORTH Hampshire map 2

Spencers

36 North Street, Emsworth PO10 7DG
EMSWORTH (0243) 372744

COOKING 2
COST £20–£43

The dining-room is gas-lit, but in other respects the Spencers move with the times. The menu changes monthly, 'to keep both customers and staff interested in their cuisine'. Smoked venison served with sloe-gin sauce and a cinnamon-poached pear should keep everybody on their toes. A few exotic Eastern touches, including Java chicken and Chinese fish parcel, weave in and out of more familiar Western dishes of duck and port terrine or sirloin steak with mustard sauce. 'Vegetables were cooked perfectly with our main courses,' wrote one who lunched on cold avocado soup, chicken in Thai sweet sauce, and rhubarb mousse in pastry.

Plain grills of beef, lamb or fish solve the problem of what to do if excitement isn't your bag, while puddings show a bit of flair. One is layers of blackberry purée, pear custard and lightly poached meringue, topped with toasted almond and caramel, another is a blend of cream cheese, apple and calvados piped into an almond tulip, accompanied by an apple and maple syrup bake. Wines have a conservative streak, but mark-ups make some of them unbelievably good value. How about Cloudy Bay Sauvignon Blanc for £15? Australian house wines at £8.25 (£1.65 per glass) emphasise the generosity.

CHEF: Denis Spencer PROPRIETORS: Denis and Lesley Spencer OPEN: Tue to Sat, exc Sat L; 12 to 2, 7.15 to 10.30 CLOSED: 25 and 26 Dec MEALS: alc L (main courses £7.50 to £10). Set D £17.50 (2 courses – not Fri and Sat) to £23.50, Set 'midweek special' D Tue to Fri £12.50 (2 courses) to £14.50 SERVICE: not inc, card slips closed CARDS: Access, Amex, Visa DETAILS: 44 seats. Private parties: 26 main room, 12 private room. Vegetarian meals. Children welcome. No cigars/pipes in dining-room before 10pm. Music. Air-conditioned

---

EPWORTH Humberside map 5

Epworth Tap ▮ £

9–11 Market Place, Epworth DN9 1EU
EPWORTH (0427) 873333
3m S of M180, junction 2

COOKING 2
COST £17–£27

Although John Wynne is not quite as involved from day to day as he used to be, the Tap continues to run as smoothly as ever, a measure of the steadily increasing confidence of Helen Wynne's cooking, which has made an unpretentious wine bar and bistro into one of Humberside's few gastronomic hotspots. Thoughtfulness radiates through the whole operation, from the conscientious sourcing of local supplies, including fish from Doncaster market, to the splendour of the wine list. Certain things remain constant on the menu and are done well because of long practice. Chicken liver pâté made with oloroso sherry has 'distinctive, intense flavour', comes with a salad dressed with walnut oil, and is hugely popular. Ham in a Riesling jelly – Helen Wynne's rendition of jambon persillé – and vegetable-based soups are long-stayers among the first courses. Tastes remain clearly defined in main courses such as an escalope of salmon lightly steamed and sauced with fish stock and saffron or 'slightly fatty, richly flavoured and tender' roast lamb with a honey- and mint-scented stock. Rhubarb gratinée and chocolate and orange charlotte have joined old favourites on the pudding list.

The wine list is a paragon. Customers overwhelmed by its range are often grateful for John Wynne's unpompous and sound advice. The clarets alone would shame many a London restaurant, burgundies are the superb, with many mature vintages, and Rhônes too are first-class. Turn the page and the list strides confidently out of France for Ridge Zinfandels, Henschke's Hill of Grace Shiraz, Gaja's magisterial Barbarescos, and so on. Prices throughout are generous to the point of self-denial. House wines are £7.95. CELLARMAN'S CHOICE: Henschke Chardonnay-Semillon 1992, £13.95; Côte Rôtie 'Les Jumelles' 1983, Jaboulet, £20.

CHEF/PROPRIETOR: Helen Wynne   OPEN: Wed to Sat, D only; 7.30 to 9.30   CLOSED: 2 weeks after Christmas   MEALS: alc (main courses £5.50 to £9). Set D Sat £15.95   SERVICE: not inc, card slips closed   CARDS: Access, Amex, Visa   DETAILS: 70 seats. Private parties: 40 main room, 24 private room. Vegetarian meals with prior notice. Children's helpings. No smoking in dining-room Sat. Music

ERPINGHAM Norfolk   map 6

▲ *Ark* ♥ ⅝

The Street, Erpingham NR11 7QB
CROMER (0263) 761535   COOKING 2
off A140 Cromer road, 4m N of Aylsham   COST £18–£36

Erpingham isn't much to write home about, but this brick cottage has charm and a long garden extending from french windows. Well-spaced tables are laid with linen cloths. The Kidds dance to a traditional British theme, with Italian and French variations, and slow cooking is often the tempo. It is a 'simple country style' maintains one, 'homely' writes another, with a choice of four or five dishes per course. Aubergines are well used: stuffed with pine-kernels and raisins as part of a vegetarian main course (along with stuffed courgette and green pepper), or served three ways – a smooth purée and two pickled versions – as a first course. A salad of sun-dried tomatoes and quartered, hard-boiled bantam eggs with shavings of Parmesan comes perilously close to being a cliché, but is much enjoyed all the same. The home-grown vegetables are highly acclaimed. Gravlax is classically well made, and reporters have also enjoyed Parmesan soufflé, sea bass with sorrel sauce, and iced orange soufflé with candied peel.

Sunday lunch is a simpler affair, dominated by roast beef or leg of lamb and a couple of vegetarian dishes. The beef itself has been disappointing, but accompaniments are outstanding: crispy roast potatoes, Yorkshire pudding, and 'proper old-fashioned vegetables cut in the domestic way', including sprouting broccoli, buttered cabbage and roast parsnips. Bed and breakfast rates a favourable mention in most reports. Ten varied house wines at £8 get the wide-ranging, considerably priced list off to a good start. Those who have asked for advice are glad they did. CELLARMAN'S CHOICE: Sauvignon de Touraine, Dom. de Clay, 1992, £9.75; Bordeaux Sec, Ch. de l'Hurbe 1992, £10.50.

CHEFS: Sheila and Becky Kidd PROPRIETORS: Mike and Sheila Kidd OPEN: Tue to Sun D only (telephone to check first), and Sun L (midweek L for 6 or more by arrangement); 12.30 to 2, 7 to 9.30 (10 Sat) MEALS: Set L Sun £12.50, Set D £16.75 (2 courses) to £21.25 SERVICE: not inc DETAILS: 36 seats. Private parties: 36 main room, 20 private room. Car park. Vegetarian meals. Children's helpings. Smart dress preferred. No smoking in dining-room. Wheelchair access (also WC). No music ACCOMMODATION: 3 rooms, 2 with bath/shower. TV. D,B&B £50 to £100. Deposit: £25. Rooms for disabled. Children welcome. Baby facilities. Garden. Confirm by noon

---

EVERSHOT Dorset   map 2

▲ *Summer Lodge* ▮

Evershot DT2 0JR   COOKING 3
EVERSHOT (0935) 83424   COST £26–£70

Edward Denny (ex-Box Tree, Ilkley – see entry) arrived at Summer Lodge just as last year's *Guide* was going to press. The chopping and changing in the kitchens prior to his arrival made it difficult to gain a consistent picture, but the past year has seen stability once more established. A reporter dining in May found the whole Georgian package 'entrancing – the rambling roses, the low-built house, the labrador'. The approach is full of courteous concern, to the extent that a bewildering number of staff may visit your table in the course of an evening. Children are treated with the same care as is shown to their elders.

The *carte* is supplemented by shorter fixed-price menus at lunch and dinner, showcasing Edward Denny's gentle country-house style. Luxuries abound but are not forced into anything other than fairly classic contexts. Smoked salmon blinis come with caviare and a horseradish sauce, terrine of duck and foie gras is studded with pistachios, and sea bass is accompanied by scallops and sauced with a velouté of champagne and more caviare. Soups impressed an inspection party; the mushroom looked a touch grey but 'the flavours came singing through', while the seafood version came in a shallow bowl with generous helpings of scallops, lobster and sea fish. What dishes may lack in terms of proportion, they tend to make up for in richness. Puddings were a 'delightful' hot raspberry soufflé with raspberry sorbet, and a hunk of chocolate tart that could not be finished and was courteously doggy-bagged. Vegetables are 'lightly cooked'. Breads offer a good range and are served with painstakingly sculpted butter.

Pains have also been taken with the wine list. The first sign of its serious intent is the opening page of 14 sherries by the glass. Alsaces are extremely fine, German Rieslings are from the best recent vintages, California producers are top-notch and a majestic flight of clarets goes back to 1961. Halves are exceedingly plentiful, and those in search of a fine digestif are offered a run of landed cognacs from local boy Thomas Hine. House wines are a white Bergerac (£11.75) and a red Minervois (£11.50). CELLARMAN'S CHOICE: Margaux, Ch. Labégorce Zédé 1985, £26.45; Ca' del Solo Il Pescatore 1991, Grahm, £22.

Not inc in the details at the end of an entry indicates that no service charge is made and any tipping is at the discretion of the customer.

CHEFS: Edward Denny and Leslie Rennie   PROPRIETORS: Nigel and Margaret Corbett   OPEN: all week; 12.30 to 1.45, 7.30 to 9   MEALS: alc (main courses £17.50 to £25). Set L Mon to Sat £17.50 (2 courses) to £19.50, Set L Sun £17.50, Set D £27.50   SERVICE: not inc, card slips closed   CARDS: Access, Amex, Visa   DETAILS: 50 seats. 6 tables outside. Private parties: 20 main room, 8 private room. Car park. Vegetarian meals. Children's helpings on request. Smart dress preferred. No-smoking while others eat. Wheelchair access (also WC). No music ACCOMMODATION: 17 rooms, all with bath/shower. TV. Phone. B&B £100 to £235. Deposit: £50. Rooms for disabled. Children under 8 by arrangement. Pets welcome (not in public rooms). Afternoon teas. Garden. Swimming-pool. Tennis. Doors close at midnight. Fax: (0935) 83005 (*The Which? Hotel Guide*)

EVESHAM Hereford & Worcester   map 2

▲ *Evesham Hotel, Cedar Restaurant* ▼

Cooper's Lane, off Waterside,
Evesham WR11 6DA   COOKING 1
EVESHAM (0386) 765566   COST £17–£40

'We have a lousy location,' writes John Jenkinson, of this sixteenth-century Georgian updated building 'up an unmarked side street'. The family is proud of its eccentricity, which is immediately manifest in the wine list. Every country you can think of, bar France and Germany, is represented, including Ireland, the Netherlands, Sweden, Zimbabwe, Hawaii (among other states of the USA) and Brazil, with particularly good showings from Australia and California.

The menu, like the list of cocktails and alcohols, is a jokey attempt to demonstrate how informal the whole enterprise is. It roams the world picking up such items as a cashew-nut sauce in which to drop sautéed chicken livers, the better to set them on toast with orange segments. Sometimes the clashes can be heard miles away, as when pork fillet is marinated in soy sauce, sherry and sesame oil with ginger and sugar, served on a peanut and star-anise sauce. A lot of it sounds way over the top, but in practice the flavours may not be as bold as they appear: goats' cheese on a julienne of celeriac pleases rather than excites, and the bean sprouts on to which roast leg of lamb is sliced could do with a punchier flavour. But there is good tangy lemon pudding to finish. House Chilean is £9. CELLARMAN'S CHOICE: Backsberg Sauvignon Blanc 1992, £10.20; Wolf Blass Red Label 1991, £12.70.

CHEF: Ian Mann   PROPRIETORS: the Jenkinson family   OPEN: all week; 12.30 to 2, 7 to 9.30 CLOSED: 25 and 26 Dec   MEALS: alc (main courses £8.50 to £16.50)   SERVICE: net prices, card slips closed   CARDS: Access, Amex, Diners, Visa   DETAILS: 55 seats. Private parties: 12 private room. Car park. Vegetarian meals. Children's helpings. No cigars/pipes in dining-room. No music   ACCOMMODATION: 40 rooms, all with bath/shower. TV. Phone. B&B £53 to £105. Children welcome. Baby facilities. Pets welcome (not in public rooms). Afternoon teas. Garden. Swimming-pool. Confirm by 5. Fax: (0386) 765443 (*The Which? Hotel Guide*)

The 1996 Guide will be published before Christmas 1995. Reports on meals are most welcome at any time of the year, but are particularly valuable in the spring. Send them to **The Good Food Guide**, *FREEPOST, 2 Marylebone Road, London NW1 1YN. No stamp is needed if posted in the UK.*

map 1

Lamb's ❦✳

15 Lower North Street, Exeter EX4 3ET COOKING 1
EXETER (0392) 54269 COST £20–£43

'A well-deserved and welcome new entry,' wrote one after reading last year's
Guide. 'I wish we had known about it before now.' Lamb's is a well-placed
addition to eating in Exeter, near the Victorian Iron Bridge, a couple of hundred
yards from Cathedral Square. The building is a five-storey eighteenth-century
terraced house with dining-rooms on two floors, and the young team running it –
now headed by the former sous-chef – is high on enthusiasm and vigour. The
claim is that everything apart from cheese is made in-house, on a seasonally
changing *carte* that gives fish and vegetables equal billing with meat. There is
welcome invention, and the freshness in the repertoire comes from not saluting
all the flags currently fluttering in the wind. Tagliatelle with salmon and citrus,
salmon marinated in Chablis and lime, and hot-smoked prawns are the kind of
dishes that draw in the crowds, along with duck liver parfait with a fried quail
egg, tarte Tatin of root vegetables, and pear and almond tart. Wines are bright
and perky, attractively priced, with over a dozen available by the glass. House
wine is £8.50.

CHEF: Paul George Bending   PROPRIETORS: Ian and Alison Aldridge   OPEN: all week, exc Sat L;
12 to 2, 6 to 10   CLOSED: bank hols   MEALS: alc (main courses £8.50 to £14). Set L and D (until
7) £9 (2 courses)   SERVICE: not inc, card slips closed   CARDS: Access, Amex, Visa   DETAILS:
42 seats. 2 tables outside. Private parties: 24 main room, 30 private room. Vegetarian meals.
Children's helpings. Smart dress preferred. No smoking on 1 floor. Wheelchair access (1 step).
Music. Partially air-conditioned. Fax: (0392) 431145

▲ St Olaves Court Hotel

Mary Arches Street, Exeter EX4 3AZ COOKING 2*
EXETER (0392) 217736 COST £23–£44

The Georgian building stands in its own walled garden, just 400 yards from
Exeter Cathedral. The 'soothingly decorated' dining-room lends itself to
relaxing meals where the service is swift and helpful and the atmosphere is
'unpretentious', fun and thoroughly conducive to enjoyment. The new team in
the kitchen seems to have its collective finger on the culinary pulse, making
judicious use of herbs and spices. Coriander, lemon grass and curry (the last in a
dressing for quenelles of smoked haddock) are just the sort of thing to add zest to
first courses and make a lively start. 'Add-ons', as one reporter noted, are
'imaginative but unfussy, and serve to emphasise the original taste of the
ingredients'. The kitchen's ability runs to 'a delicious concoction of poached
mussels with a thatch of shredded leeks under a saffron tomato mousseline,
served with rouille and croûtons'.

It is good to see a selection of light dishes – fillets of Torbay dab with glazed
leeks and basil butter sauce, or a warm salad of lamb's liver with a shallot and
thyme dressing – available as a less expensive alternative to lunch or dinner.
Heartier appetites will welcome the optional intermediate course at dinner, as
well as dishes such as oxtail wrapped in a Savoy cabbage leaf on a purée of

spiced parsnips, or fillet steak, accurately timed, served with a ravioli of wild mushrooms in a thyme-flavoured red wine sauce.

Desserts have had a fillip, with pastry and ice-creams much in evidence, often to good effect in the same dish. The contrast in tastes and textures of a tulip of peeled pear with a blob of hazelnut ice-cream, sitting in a butterscotch sauce on a thin crisp sweet pastry case, made it 'a memorable dish'. Wines are wide-ranging, with reasonable choice under £20; and although short on half-bottles they are happy to open a full bottle and sell what remains by the glass, which is jolly useful all round. House wine is £10.50.

CHEFS: Jason Horn, Colin Liddy and Jos Davey   PROPRIETORS: Raymond and Ute Wyatt, and Peter Collier   OPEN: all week, exc Sat and Sun L; 12 to 1.45, 6.30 to 9.30   CLOSED: 26 Dec to 4 Jan   MEALS: alc (main courses L £11.50, D £13 to £16.50). Set L £13.50 to £20.50, Set D £13.50   SERVICE: not inc, card slips closed   CARDS: Access, Amex, Diners, Visa   DETAILS: 63 seats. 5 tables outside. Private parties: 45 main room, 18 private room. Car park. Vegetarian meals. Children's helpings on request. Smart dress preferred. No cigars/pipes in dining-room. Wheelchair access (3 steps). No music   ACCOMMODATION: 15 rooms, all with bath/shower. TV. Phone. B&B £60 to £90. Rooms for disabled. Children welcome. Baby facilities. Pets welcome (not in public areas). Afternoon teas. Garden. Confirm by 5. Fax: (0392) 413054 (*The Which? Hotel Guide*)

EXMOUTH Devon   map 1

Barnaby's Restaurant

9 Tower Street, Exmouth EX8 1NT   COOKING 1*
EXMOUTH (0395) 269459   COST £23–£33

Cushions have now softened the rickety chairs in the Aylwards' personable restaurant. The owners take care and put effort into creating an atmosphere that is friendly and without pretension. James Aylward loves 'real flavours': lemon grass, fresh ginger, elderflowers. His philosophy extends to the pursuit of wild, rather than factory-farmed, produce: veal and foie gras, for example, have no place in his kitchen. The result is a menu that might feature scallop mousse with laverbread sauce and toasted brioche, mustard-glazed rack of lamb with rosemary, fillet of turbot with samphire, and bread-and-butter pudding infused with citrus zest and vanilla pods. The option of settling for a fixed price based on the main course, or treating the repertoire as a *carte* is a neat and flexible notion. Service gets the thumbs-up. Monthly wine evenings are an attraction for interested customers, and the list offers 25 wines by the glass; like the cooking, the emphasis is on individuality and distinctiveness.

CHEF: James Aylward   PROPRIETORS: James and Sally Aylward   OPEN: Tue to Sat, D only; 7 to 9.30 (L for parties of 6 or more by arrangement)   MEALS: alc (main courses £10 to £13). Set D £15.95 to £18.95   SERVICE: not inc, card slips closed   CARDS: Access, Visa   DETAILS: 35 seats. Private parties: 27 main room. Vegetarian meals. Children welcome. Wheelchair access (1 step). Music

---

The Guide *is totally independent, accepts no free hospitality, and survives on the number of copies sold each year.*

EYTON Hereford & Worcester   map 2

▲ Marsh ┊✳

Eyton HR6 0AG
LEOMINSTER (0568) 613952   COOKING 1
off B4361, 2m NW of Leominster   COST £27–£38

Set in a beautiful garden, this fourteenth-century house, calm to the point of
silence, is heavily beamed and flag-floored, with a particularly impressive
medieval hall for a lounge. Since last year the price of a three-course meal has
come down by a substantial £9, making it much better value. Dishes have
become a bit more complicated, a main course vegetarian option appears, and
pastry work remains the strength. There can be imbalances, as when two
first-courses out of four involved smoked fish. At inspection, a goats' cheese
soufflé was well risen, although the leeks and hazelnuts were felt not to add
anything worthwhile. Main courses – roast Herefordshire duck or saddle of lamb
stuffed with apricots, for example – come with customised vegetables.
Incidentals are made in-house, with good cheese pastry to start, and a sticky
square of something nutty and chocolatey to accompany first-rate coffee. The
40-strong wine list has improved, mark-ups are about average, and the choice of
half-bottles is good. House wines start at £7.50 and include local Bodenham
Reichensteiner 1990 at £9.75, or £5 per half-bottle.

CHEF/PROPRIETOR: J.A. Gilleland   OPEN: all week, D only, and Sun L; 12.30 to 2, 7.30 to 9
MEALS: Set L Sun £18.50, Set D £18.50   SERVICE: not inc, card slips closed   CARDS: Access,
Amex, Diners, Visa   DETAILS: 24 seats. Private parties: 24 main room, 16 private room. Car
park. Vegetarian meals. Children welcome. Smart dress preferred. No smoking in dining-room.
No music   ACCOMMODATION: 5 rooms, all with bath/shower. TV. Phone. B&B £45 to £100.
Deposit: £25. Children welcome. Baby facilities. Garden. Doors close at 11. Confirm by 6 (The
Which? Hotel Guide)

FAVERSHAM Kent   map 3

Read's ▮

Painter's Forstal, Faversham ME13 0EE
FAVERSHAM (0795) 535344   COOKING 3*
on Eastling road, 1m S of Faversham   COST £24–£53

People don't exactly go into raptures in describing the outward aspect of Read's –
'an unprepossessing 'block' of architecture' in the view of one. The interior has
been described by more than one reader as 'clinical', though others appreciate
the crispness of table napery and the atmosphere of relaxed civility. A garden
room extension has been added to the restaurant, so that views of the Belmont
Valley can be enjoyed, and the area for eating outdoors has grown. What does
evoke consensus is the quality and assurance of David Pitchford's cooking.
Within a framework of fixed-priced menus – with four choices per course at
lunch, seven at dinner – his food strikes chords because it relies on methods of
preparation established over time, so people understand it. Read's is not the
place for strident, experimental combination. Menus change daily for variation,
not because yesterday's bright idea didn't work. Children are encouraged to try

their own version of the lunch menu, but are warned, 'No fish-fingers or burgers'.

A spring evening menu included new season's salmon tartare with cucumber and dill, fillet of pink trout grilled with courgettes and a lobster sauce, and roast chump of new lamb with a mille-feuille of aubergine and rosemary jus. There is no shyness in offering straight classics such as gazpacho, Caesar salad or coq au vin. Visitors, praising intensity of flavours in these dishes, wonder how it is done. The answer lies in top-quality ingredients, and also in careful timing. Even a chicken parfait, an hors-d'oeuvre that can be vapid and pointless in the wrong hands, is pronounced 'very refined but with dense flavour', arriving with coarse-textured toast and a lightly dressed winter salad. Desserts such as a chocolate cup filled with coffee mousse that avoids over-sweetness, or crème brûlée accompanied by sharp fruits (orange segments, perhaps, or raspberries, depending on the time of year), round things off well. Trimmings are up to the mark, plaudits flowing in for the home-made fudge with coffee.

Wine comes in for exactly the same treatment. The main list, quite a weighty tome, is stuffed with classics, and includes some 1940s burgundies for the intrepid. For those who do not feel at home leafing through so serious a catalogue, the list is prefaced by a shorter collection of good-value bottles. There are also plenty of halves. House wines are £12. CELLARMAN'S CHOICE: Sancerre 1991, Comte Lafond, £16; Cape Mentelle Cabernet Sauvignon 1990, £16.

CHEF: David Pitchford   PROPRIETORS: David and Rona Pitchford   OPEN: Tue to Sat; 12 to 2, 7 to 10   MEALS: Set L £14.50, Set D £23.50 to £32   SERVICE: not inc, card slips closed   CARDS: Access, Amex, Diners, Visa   DETAILS: 45 seats. 3 tables outside. Private parties: 60 main room, 18 private room. Car park. Vegetarian meals. Children's helpings. Smart dress preferred. Wheelchair access (1 step). Music. Fax: (0795) 591200

FELSTED Essex   map 3

Rumbles Cottage

Braintree Road, Felsted CM6 3DJ
GREAT DUNMOW (0371) 820996   COOKING 1
on B1417, between A130 and A120   COST £20–£36

Named after Rumboldes, a previous owner of this sixteenth-century cottage, Rumbles operates successfully as an idiosyncratic country restaurant. Joy Hadley is an inventive cook who likes to take risks and experiment with ideas: her monthly 'guinea-pig menus' are a way of testing out new creations on a willing band of regular customers. If a dish gets the seal of approval, it will graduate to the regular *carte*, which changes every few weeks. Joy uses local supplies, and has a green-fingered touch, growing everything from white aubergines to purple-top turnips. Her eclectic output might embrace Spanish chickpea soup, Caribbean escovitch (pickled fish), pork fillet with a creamy Dijon mustard sauce and twice-baked soufflés with tomato and pesto. In addition, a pasta menu appears on Fridays. Recently reported successes have included pears stuffed with blue cheese pâté, paupiettes of trout with bacon, and orange water and coriander custard. Service is 'perfectly OK'. The 50-strong wine list is a collection of eminently affordable bottles. House wines start at £7.60.

CHEF/PROPRIETOR: E. Joy Hadley   OPEN: Tue to Sat, D only, and Sun L; 12 to 2, 7 to 9   MEALS: alc (main courses £10.50 to £12.50). Set L Sun £12.50, Set D Tue to Thur £12.50, Fri D 'pasta' meal £10 (2 courses)   SERVICE: not inc   CARDS: Access, Visa   DETAILS: 50 seats. Private parties: 22 main room, 8 to 22 private rooms. Vegetarian meals. Children's helpings. No-smoking area. Wheelchair access (1 step). No music

---

FLITWICK Bedfordshire   map 3

▲ *Flitwick Manor* 🌟

Church Road, Flitwick MK45 1AE
FLITWICK (0525) 712242
on A5120, S of Flitwick, 2m N of M1   COOKING 2
junction 12   COST £27–£54

'We had a perfect day, with drinks under cool umbrellas on the terrace,' mused reporters after an August visit to this eighteenth-century house set in lovely grounds complete with a croquet lawn, grotto and castellated walled garden. A change of ownership occurred in February 1994, but chef Duncan Poyser is still in residence. Dinner is an ambitious fixed-price affair that promises such things as hot mussel soufflé basted with saffron, grilled chump of lamb with white-bean cassoulet, steamed fillet of sole with fennel and lobster vinaigrette, and warm compote of cranberries topped with a clementine soufflé spiked with bitter chocolate. Lunchtime visitors have spoken well of velouté of wild mushrooms, grilled leg of lamb with rosemary and olives, and hot banana soufflé, although salting was thought to be heavy-handed on one occasion. Vegetables may be little more than an elaborate nouvelle garnish. Service can be 'slow': 'lunch took two hours and we were the only people in,' reported a couple who ate only two courses. House wine is £10.50.

CHEF: Duncan Poyser   PROPRIETOR: West Register (Hotels) Ltd   OPEN: all week; 12.30 to 2, 7 to 9.30   MEALS: Set L £16.50 (2 courses) to £19.50, Set D £35.50   SERVICE: not inc   CARDS: Access, Amex, Diners, Visa   DETAILS: 50 seats. 5 tables outside. Private parties: 60 main room, 10, 20 and 30 private rooms. Car park. Vegetarian meals with prior notice. Children's helpings. Smart dress preferred. No smoking in dining-room. Wheelchair access. No music   ACCOMMODATION: 15 rooms, all with bath/shower. TV. Phone. Air-conditioned (3 rooms). B&B £88 to £190. Children welcome. Pets welcome. Afternoon teas. Garden. Tennis. Doors close at 11.30. Confirm by 6. Fax: (0525) 718753

FOLKESTONE Kent   map 3

Paul's

2A Bouverie Road West,
Folkestone CT20 2RX   COOKING 1
FOLKESTONE (0303) 259697   COST £23–£30

Easily found opposite Sainsbury's, Paul and Penny Hagger's bright, well-lit restaurant serves hot fresh food at reasonable prices. The menu, like the room, is long, thanks partly to a reluctance to cut out old favourites when newer dishes come along. Local fish and decent butchery (tender fillet of lamb is highly praised) underpin the cooking. Cream sauces – variously herby, winey, cheesy or mildly spicy – and some flavoured butters are applied to fillets of black sea bream stuffed with smoked salmon, calf's liver or strips of turkey breast. Out-of-the-ordinary first courses include haggis samosa. Food comes sizzling hot and vegetarians are offered the likes of baby beetroot baked with black mushrooms and ginger. Almond and apricot mousse is one of the more interesting puddings. Many of the wines are under £15, and bin-ends repay inspection. House vin de table is £6.95.

CHEFS/PROPRIETORS: Penny and Paul Hagger   OPEN: all week; 12 to 2.30, 7.30 (7 Sat) to 9.30   CLOSED: 25 and 26 Dec   MEALS: alc (main courses £10)   SERVICE: not inc   CARDS: Access, Visa   DETAILS: 100 seats. 10 tables outside. Private parties: 100 main room. Car park D and weekends. Vegetarian meals. Children's helpings on request. Wheelchair access (2 steps; also women's WC). No music

---

FORTON Lancashire   map 5

El Nido

Whinney Brow Lane, Forton PR3 0AE
FORTON (0524) 791254   COOKING 1
on A6, 1m S of M6 junction 33   COST £18–£40

At first sight it looks much like a stone-built Lancashire pub, but pictures of bullfights give a clue to El Nido's real provenance. Fans dangle from the wall, Spanish Muzak plays, and the menu arrives with the promise of avocado flamenca and cerdo hijo (fillet of pork with bacon and apricots in a honey, red wine and sherry sauce). Vegetable Stroganov indicates that the cooking is not entirely 'pure', but a certain amount of garlic – with mushrooms, snails or prawns – shows willing, and squid (stuffed or fried), baked eggs and paella might make a matador feel at home. Puddings are from a trolley, and not as sweet and eggy as they might be in Jerez or Granada. Spanish wines are the ones to go for, mostly under £15. House wine is £7.95.

CHEFS: Lloyd Kenny and Tony Pool   PROPRIETORS: René and Tracey Mollinga   OPEN: Tue to Sun, exc L Tue and Sat (L Wed to Fri May to Sept only); 12 to 2, 7 to 10.15   MEALS: alc (main courses £7.50 to £14.50). Set L £8.95, Set D £15.50   SERVICE: not inc   CARDS: Access, Visa   DETAILS: 50 seats. 3 tables outside. Private parties: 50 main room. Car park. Vegetarian meals. Children's helpings. Smart dress preferred. Wheelchair access (also WC). Music. Air-conditioned

---

FOWEY Cornwall   map 1

Food for Thought

Town Quay, Fowey PL23 1AT   COOKING 2
FOWEY (0726) 832221   COST £22–£40

The Billingsleys' restaurant stands right on Fowey Quay, so it isn't surprising that fish looms large in the kitchen. Martin's fixed-price menus are dotted with piscine dishes such as scallops griddled on salsa verde, sea bass with hollandaise or orange butter sauce, turbot with a brioche herb crust and saffron sauce, and rendezvous of seafood with langoustine and light lobster sauce. Carnivores' eyes might focus on other offerings such as fillet of Cornish lamb baked in pastry with madeira sauce or roast breast of Barbary duck with armagnac cream sauce. Good-quality vegetables might include a nicely produced broccoli mousse. Lovers of rich clotted cream will revel in the list of desserts: it adorns everything from sticky toffee pudding to lemon tart. The mood of the place is too 'fussy' for some and service is not always as cheerful as it might be. Around 70 wines offer a safe, sound selection at realistic prices. House wines start at £6.95.

CHEF: Martin Billingsley   PROPRIETORS: Martin and Caroline Billingsley   OPEN: Mon to Sat, D only; 7 to 9   CLOSED: Jan and Feb   MEALS: Set D £15.95 to £24.95   SERVICE: not inc, card slips closed   CARDS: Access, Visa   DETAILS: 38 seats. Private parties: 30 main room. No children under 12. No music. Fax: (0726) 832060

FRAMPTON ON SEVERN Gloucestershire   map 2

Saverys

The Green, Frampton on Severn GL2 7EA
GLOUCESTER (0452) 740077   COOKING 2*
2½m NW of M5 junction 13   COST £30–£36

This is England at its most English. Cricket is played on the green (so ducks are not the only ones to waddle across it) and the whole place looks pretty as a picture. Inside the small brick-built house are pot plants, ruffled pink curtains, spindle-back chairs and candle-lit tables. Saverys seems to survive on a diet of regulars, who are instrumental in keeping the format as it is: three courses of five or six choices covering well-trodden ground. Change this and you might as well turn the green into a baseball field.

Soup, chicken liver parfait and smoked salmon may be enlivened by a tart of wild mushrooms with baked egg and Parmesan cheese, or a crab mousse with a lime and ginger dressing. Main courses rotate around duck breast, loin of lamb and roast fillet of beef, with fish varying by the day. Alcohol finds its way into sauces but, like everything else here, a sense of scale keeps it all in balance. Beef is well-hung, timing is right, the repertoire well practised, and puddings are comforting: white chocolate marquise on a coffee and Tia Maria custard, or raspberry and strawberry meringue with vanilla ice-cream. The package is further helped by an unhurried approach, and a very short wine list that largely sticks to a £20 ceiling. House wine is £7.95.

CHEF: John Savery   PROPRIETORS: John Savery and Patricia Carpenter   OPEN: Tue to Sat, D only; 7 to 9   MEALS: Set D £22.95 to £25.90   SERVICE: not inc, card slips closed   CARDS: Access, Visa   DETAILS: 26 seats. Private parties: 28 main room. Vegetarian meals with prior notice. No children under 14. Smart dress preferred. No pipes in dining-room. Wheelchair access. Music

---

Dining-rooms where music, either live or recorded, is never played are signalled by No music in the details at the end of an entry.

The Guide relies on feedback from its readers. Especially welcome are reports on new restaurants appearing in the book for the first time. All letters to the Guide are acknowledged.

FRESSINGFIELD Suffolk map 6

Fox and Goose ▮

Fressingfield IP21 5PB
FRESSINGFIELD (0379) 586247   COOKING 3
on B1116, 3½m S of Harleston   COST £21–£46

Ruth Watson's career has in many ways been emblematic of where British cooking has gone in the last few years. From country-house hotel (Hintlesham Hall) to country pub is a remarkable trajectory, but one that has been accomplished with consummate ease and good sense. Located just by the church in this little village not far from the border with Norfolk, the Fox and Goose is certainly off most people's idea of the beaten track. Nothing daunted, an impressively loyal customer base has been built up, which appreciates the informal approach, the good-humoured surroundings and the reliable cooking that none the less shows a willingness to experiment. On high days and holidays, bar snacks may include 30 grams of oscietra caviare on rye toast.

Although the backbone of the kitchen is favourite British dishes like salmon and smoked haddock fish-cakes, toad-in-the-hole and steak pie, there is a broad international sweep to the menus as well. An April lunch took in spicy chicken wings with garlic sauce, grilled halloumi with lemon oil and pitta, and Thai-style red curry of chicken, coconut and basil. Dishes may be intriguingly difficult to place. One couple recalled a prawn soup in 'vaguely Thai style, but served with croûtons and a pesto-like accompaniment'. The bemusement did not preclude the judgement that it was 'as good a soup as we have had anywhere'. The Oriental forays are not invariably successful: one or two have found the batter in the tempura not sufficiently crisp. Recommendations, though, flow freely for dishes such as warm salmon with salad niçoise, fried mushrooms on toast with creamy cep sauce, grilled squid with coriander masala, lamb rump with broad beans and mint, and sticky toffee pudding with pecans. All the incidentals are rated highly, and coffee comes with 'a rather trendy assortment of chocolates'. Why can't more pubs be like this?

The wines speak eloquently of true enthusiasm in the buying department. A vast, authoritative list is offered to those who have the time and passion to browse through it. Clarets go back to 1955, burgundies to 1953. Otherwise the commendable policy is adopted of listing easy-drinking, good-value selections on a separate sheet. Not that exemplary value isn't evident throughout. This is a list that wants everyone to join in the fun. House red, from the Watsons' own Côtes de Provence vineyard is £8.50. The white, currently a vin de pays from Gascony, is £9.80.

CHEFS: Ruth Watson, Brendan Ansbro, James Perry and Max Dougall PROPRIETOR: Ruth Watson OPEN: Wed to Sun; 12 to 2.15, 7 to 9.30 CLOSED: 2 weeks Nov, Christmas MEALS: alc (main courses £7.50 to £15.50). Set L Wed to Sat £9.95 (2 courses) to £13.50. Bar snacks SERVICE: not inc DETAILS: 50 seats. 4 tables outside. Private parties: 24 main room, 24 private room. Car park. Vegetarian meals. Children's helpings. No cigars/pipes in dining-room. No music. Fax: (0379) 588107

▮ denotes an outstanding wine cellar; ▼ denotes a good wine list, worth travelling for.

FROME Somerset · · · map 2

Croft's ✸

NEW ENTRY

21 Fromefield, Frome BA11 2HE
FROME (0373) 472149
on B3090, ½m NE of Frome

COOKING 1*
COST £22–£26

Margaret Graham's cottagey little restaurant is in a seventeenth-century whitewashed building on the outskirts of town. Inside are two pleasant beamed dining-rooms with pot plants, pictures and old-fashioned 'school-type' chairs. It feels like a mixture of bistro and farmhouse rolled into one. What impresses about the place is that it never overreaches itself: limited covers and a short repertoire ensure that every detail is right. No high-flown fancies or trendiness get in the way of freshness and genuine flavour.

The three-course dinner menu is truly outstanding value for dishes such as courgette ravioli with prawn sauce, braised beef in Guinness and orange, and steamed almond sponge with cherry sauce. Fish of the day might be 'excellent' skate wing in cider, and there is always something for vegetarians. The quality of the ingredients shows through in perfectly timed sirloin steak and grilled sole; reports have also mentioned spiced prawns au gratin, smoked salmon tart, and hot chocolate fondant cake with clotted cream on the side. The short wine list shows the same commitment to value and quality. House wine is £7.50.

CHEF/PROPRIETOR: Margaret Graham OPEN: Tue to Sat, D only; 7 to 9.30 (10 Sat) MEALS: Set D £13.95 SERVICE: not inc (10% for parties of 10 or more, on food only), card slips closed CARDS: Access, Visa DETAILS: 28 seats. Private parties: 20 main room, 10 private room. Vegetarian meals. Children welcome. Smart dress preferred. No smoking in dining-room. No music

---

GATESHEAD Tyne & Wear · · · map 7

▲ Eslington Villa Hotel ✸

8 Station Road, Low Fell,
Gateshead NE9 6DR
091-487 6017
on A6127, 2m S of Newcastle city centre

COOKING 2
COST £21–£51

'A country-house hotel in an urban location' may sound an unlikely prospect, but Eslington Villa, with its steeply sloping lawn, gilt-framed pictures and conservatory, makes the most of available resources. A strong local following has accumulated, so that weekends tend to be particularly busy. Ian Lowrey's cooking is not the least part of the attraction. The fixed-price menu of three courses plus coffee offers reasonable choice, but greater elaboration comes into play on the fairly lengthy *carte*. Beef with red onion salsa, steamed monkfish with red peppers and a white wine sauce, and beef fillet with wild mushrooms and Meaux mustard appeared on an early spring menu. Underpinning it all is an inclination towards the tried-and-true rather than the innovative. Puddings bring on lots of chocolate, toffee, butterscotch and cream (sticky toffee *and* banoffi on the same menu is going it a bit), and cheeses are of good quality and come with apple, grapes and salad. Coffee is fine, and the approach to customers brims with confident cheer. The serviceable wine list strays above £20 only for champagne and a couple of white burgundies. The choice is thoroughly international. House French and Australian are £8.95.

CHEF: Ian Lowrey   PROPRIETORS: Mr N. and Mrs M. Tulip   OPEN: all week, exc Sat L and Sun D; 12 to 2, 7 to 10   CLOSED: 1 week Christmas, bank hols   MEALS: alc (main courses £16 to £18). Set L £9.95 (2 courses) to £13.95, Set D £21.95   SERVICE: not inc   CARDS: Access, Amex, Diners, Visa   DETAILS: 60 seats. Private parties: 45 main room, 16 private room. Car park. Vegetarian meals with prior notice. Children's helpings. Smart dress preferred. No smoking in dining-room. Wheelchair access (2 steps; also WC). Music   ACCOMMODATION: 12 rooms, all with bath/shower. TV. Phone. B&B £34.50 to £74.50. Rooms for disabled. Children welcome. Pets welcome. Afternoon teas. Garden. Doors close at 1am. Confirm by 5. Fax: 091-482 2359

GEDNEY DYKE Lincolnshire   map 6

Chequers ⅝✳ £

Main Street, Gedney Dyke PE12 0AJ
HOLBEACH (0406) 362666
just off B1359, from Gedney roundabout on   COOKING 1
A17, 3m E of Holbeach   COST £16–£32

This 'warm and comfortable pub' in the tiny village of Gedney Dyke provides a hearty mix of standard items and interesting blackboard specials in the uncluttered dining-room, with fish as a strong suit. Cajun chicken with limes, roast Gressingham duck and grilled steak coated with a Stilton sauce share the stage with deep-fried scallops wrapped in bacon, fillet of lemon sole on fresh papaya purée and cod with stir-fried vegetables. One reporter had 'excellent' South African bobotie along with 'lovely' vegetables, which are served separately. Desserts are amorous-sounding offerings – at least they were on a 'Valentine's Day' menu – such as passion-fruit Pavlova and chocolate 'heavenly bliss'. The short wine list is from Adnams, so quality and value are assured. House wine is £6.50.

CHEFS: Judith Marshall and Sarah Tindale   PROPRIETORS: Judith and Rob Marshall   OPEN: all week, exc Sat L; 12 to 1.45, 7 to 9 (9.30 Fri and Sat, 8.30 Sun)   CLOSED: 25 to 27 Dec; Sun D Nov to end-Mar   MEALS: alc (main courses £6 to £11.50)   SERVICE: not inc, card slips closed   CARDS: Access, Amex, Diners, Visa   DETAILS: 32 seats. Private parties: 30 main room. Car park. Vegetarian meals. Children's helpings. Smart dress preferred. No smoking in conservatory. Music

---

GILLINGHAM Dorset   map 2

▲ Stock Hill ⅝✳

Gillingham SP8 5NR
GILLINGHAM (0747) 823626 and 822741
off B3081, 1½m W of Gillingham   COOKING 2*
                                                                     COST £26–£44

The lions of Longleat are but 20 minutes' drive from the Hausers' country house near Gillingham, but then you will not exactly lack for the company of beasts at Stock Hill itself. Indian wooden horses rear gracefully in the entrance hall; Egyptian bronze cats prepare to leap from windowsills; a cockerel perches on a coffee table. The building is a welcoming late Victorian pile in rough-cast grey stone sitting in 10 mature acres, and approached beneath ancient beeches. Within its smart confines, Peter Hauser cooks a fixed-price dinner menu of four courses plus coffee, a choice of soups appearing after the starters. He is Austrian by birth, and there are strong central European accents in some of the dishes – very strong in cevapoici with Bosnian rice, or Esterhazy torte mit Beerensaft.

A dinner in June unearthed a distinct inconsistency of standard. Braised Cornish octopus on spinach noodles was 'hard and tough' and beaten for flavour by a 'heavily over-spiced' sauce, but there was a flavour of fine stock in the carrot and parsley soup, and poached beef sirloin with horseradish cream offered good meat in a thin sauce. Vegetables were lots of bits and bobs. Mint and vanilla parfait lacked flavour, and coffee was weak, but to balance the account, others have found the cooking 'of an extremely high standard'; the food on an Austrian evening was also fulsomely praised. The wine list majors in France, but travels pretty widely beyond those shores, not omitting Austria, of course. Halves offer fair choice. House French is £9.95.

CHEFS: Peter Hauser and Lorna Connor   PROPRIETORS: Peter and Nita Hauser   OPEN: all week, D only, and Sun L; 12.30 to 1.45, 7.30 to 8.45   MEALS: Set L Sun £18.50, Set D £28   SERVICE: not inc, card slips closed   CARDS: Access, Diners, Visa   DETAILS: 24 seats. Private parties: 24 main room, 12 private room. Car park. Vegetarian meals. Children's helpings L. No children under 7. Smart dress preferred. No smoking in dining-room. Wheelchair access. No music   ACCOMMODATION: 9 rooms, all with bath/shower. TV. Phone. D,B&B £90 to £210. Deposit: £50. No children under 7. Garden. Sauna. Tennis. Doors close at midnight. Confirm by 5. Fax: (0747) 825628 (The Which? Hotel Guide)

GLASTONBURY Somerset   map 2

▲ *No.3* 🍴

3 Magdalene Street, Glastonbury BA6 9EW
GLASTONBURY (0458) 832129   COOKING 1
on A39 Wells to Bridgwater road   COST £38–£46

Glastonbury, harbinger of the New Age, is an apt setting for John and Ann Tynan's restaurant-with-rooms, and they are tuned in to the mood of the place. Their Georgian house stands close by the Abbey gardens and they now offer guests additional services, including beauty consultancy, massage and aromatherapy. In addition, they are aware of the nutritional implications of good cooking: allergy patients are referred to them by local specialists. Dinners are now limited to residents and their friends, although others are accommodated if there is space. The menu is fixed price for four courses (including a sorbet midway) and may include charlotte poireaux made from locally grown leeks and walnuts from the Tynans' own trees, and Cornish scallops poached and served with shrimp sauce. Typical main dishes might be fillet of brill, 'Aga-grilled' with lemon butter and prawns, salmis of game, and breast of chicken stuffed with avocado mousse served with Dubonnet sauce. The wine list runs to more than 100 bins, with plenty of choice and variety across the range. House wine is £9.50.

▲ *This symbol means accommodation is available.*

CHEF: Ann Tynan   PROPRIETORS: John and Ann Tynan   OPEN: Wed to Sat, D only; 7.30 to 9 (residents only, exc by arrangement)   MEALS: Set D £28   SERVICE: not inc   CARDS: Access, Visa   DETAILS: 18 seats. 2 tables outside. Private parties: 12 main room. Car park. Vegetarian meals. Smart dress preferred. No smoking. Wheelchair access (3 steps). No music ACCOMMODATION: 6 rooms, all with bath/shower. TV. Phone. B&B £50 to £75. Room for disabled. Children welcome. Garden. Doors close at 11.30. Confirm by 6 (*The Which? Hotel Guide*)

GOLCAR West Yorkshire	map 5

Weavers Shed

Acre Mill, Knowl Road, Golcar HD7 4AN
HUDDERSFIELD (0484) 654284
on B6111, 2½m W of Huddersfield   COOKING 2
from A62   COST £17–£42

Stephen Jackson has redecorated the bar and gallery room, and put up new curtains, but the original bare stone floors and walls of this country restaurant in a converted woollen mill remain. Value for money and an astute use of local ingredients mark out the cooking. Lunch is a robust set-price menu of Yorkshire pudding with wholegrain mustard gravy, chicken and leek pie, sirloin steak and other hearty offerings for North Country appetites. Dinner brings more ambitious stuff in the shape of hot celeriac terrine with spiced carrot purée, guinea-fowl with grapes and Sauternes, and breast of pigeon with vegetables and lentil purée. Desserts include 'spot-on' apple pie with acacia honey sauce and ginger ice-cream as well as ever-popular sticky toffee pudding. Reporters have particularly liked veal with peanut sauce, Lunesdale duckling with caramelised mango sauce and perfectly cooked fillet of beef with tarragon and garlic. Service is excellent and long-serving Shirley Bramald (who once worked in the mill) is a much-loved fixture of the place. The wine list is as keenly priced as the food and offers a well-spread choice from around the globe. House wine is £8.95.

CHEFS: Ian McGunnigle and Stephen Jackson   PROPRIETOR: Stephen Jackson   OPEN: Tue to Sat, exc Sat L; 12 to 1.45, 7 to 9.15   CLOSED: first 2 weeks Jan, last 2 weeks July   MEALS: alc D (main courses £9.50 to £14). Set L £10.95   SERVICE: not inc   CARDS: Access, Amex, Visa DETAILS: 70 seats. Private parties: 40 main room, 30 private room. Car park. Vegetarian meals (vegan with prior notice). Children welcome. Smart dress preferred. Wheelchair access (2 steps; also WC). Music

---

All details are as accurate as possible at the time of going to press, but chefs and owners often change, and it is wise to check by telephone before making a special journey. Many readers have been disappointed when set-price bargain meals are no longer available. Ask when booking.

Several sharp operators have tried to extort money from restaurateurs on the promise of an entry in a guidebook that has never appeared. The Good Food Guide *makes no charge for inclusion and does not offer certificates of any kind.*

GORING Oxfordshire

map 2

Leatherne Bottel

Goring RG8 0HS
GORING-ON-THAMES (0491) 872667
on B4009 out of Goring, 5m S of
Wallingford

COOKING 2*
COST £32–£51

This has a magical, tranquil setting, especially on a warm evening. The owners walk around in jeans and T-shirts, staff are easy-going, and the river engenders a leisurely feel: 'We sat outside and watched a dinghy from the local sailing club sink.' Inside are small dining-rooms with a few tables in each. Victorian settees, old settles and wild flowers in informal arrangements lend character.

It is a short step from garden to kitchen: salad leaves, herbs, nettle tops, chickweed, vegetables and summer berries are within easy reach and liberally used. 'Goats' cheese is made locally for us,' say the owners. Game dominates winter menus, fish the summer ones: chargrilled monkfish with an olive oil and balsamic vinegar dressing, grilled John Dory with broad beans. This is light, responsive cooking, imaginative and informed, yet with an assertive style. There is nothing half-hearted about smoked haddock with fresh horseradish, black olive oil dressing, parmesan and shrimp toast.

The clean, pin-sharp flavours are helped by Eastern spicing: chilli, miso, lemon grass and lemon leaves in a dish of mussels, or coriander in crab-cakes. Shoulder of lamb is slow-braised with white beans, tomatoes, rosemary and garlic, and served with roast black pudding. Texture contrasts are good. Stir-fried sweetbreads appear with slices of Jerusalem artichoke and crunchy water-chestnuts. Vegetables are plain, barely seasoned, lightly cooked, and rolls are baked on the premises and flavoured with tomatoes, olives, spinach and walnuts. One reporter summed up an early summer visit: 'a delightful, friendly place with excellent imaginative food but high prices. Except for the dessert, everything was delicious'. The short wine list, mostly youthful, is high on flavour and mark-ups. House wine is £10.50.

CHEFS: Keith Read and Clive O'Conner PROPRIETORS: Keith Read and Annie Bonnet OPEN: all week; 12.15 to 2 (2.30 Sat and Sun), 7.15 to 9 (9.30 Sat) CLOSED: 25 Dec MEALS: alc (main courses £12.50 to £16) SERVICE: not inc CARDS: Access, Amex, Visa DETAILS: 60 seats. 20 tables outside. Private parties: 20 main room, 12 private room. Car park. Vegetarian meals. Smart dress preferred. Wheelchair access. No music. Air-conditioned

---

GRAMPOUND Cornwall

map 1

Eastern Promise ⅝✴ £

1 Moor View, Grampound TR2 4RT
ST AUSTELL (0726) 883033

COOKING 1
COST £20–£36

'A compound of country restaurant and Chinese corner café' is how one reporter summed up this enterprising establishment in a historic Cornish village. It is also one of the few Chinese places with a female chef. Lisa Tse produces dishes that are full of fresh, bright flavours, and her menu cuts a path through a familiar Peking/Szechuan repertoire of crispy wun-tun, hot-and-sour soup, aromatic

313

crispy duck and stir-fried beef with oyster sauce. Cornish fish also shows up well, along with sizzling scallops, 'magnificent' squid with garlic and chilli, and braised crab with ginger and spring onion. Visitors have praised the quality of the rice, and the monk's vegetables with bean curd and thread noodles. Philip Tse is a charming host, and service is punctual and unobtrusive. Prices are on the high side, but no tips are accepted. Saké and Tsingtao beer are alternatives to the modest list of acceptable wines. House wine is £7.

CHEF: Lisa Tse   PROPRIETOR: Philip Tse   OPEN: all week, exc Wed, D only; 6 to 11   MEALS: alc (main courses £7 to £12). Set D (minimum 2) £17.50 to £20   SERVICE: card slips closed   CARDS: Access, Amex, Diners, Visa   DETAILS: 70 seats. Private parties: 40 main room, 30 private room. Car park. Vegetarian meals. No children under 3. Smart dress preferred. No smoking in dining-room. Wheelchair access. Music. Air-conditioned

---

GRASMERE Cumbria　　　　　　　　　　　　　　　　　　　　　　　map 7

▲ Michael's Nook ♼ ⚹

Grasmere LA22 9RP　　　　　　　　　　　　　　　　　COOKING 3*
GRASMERE (059 34) 35496　　　　　　　　　　　　　　COST £37–£58

Many places in the Lake District close in winter, but Michael's Nook carries on considerably without a break, as it has carried on pleasing readers for a generation. Dinner is a little less expensive than last year, a small but welcome concession to hard times. Built in 1859, less than a mile from Dove Cottage, the house was named after the shepherd in Wordsworth's poem 'Michael'. The Giffords arrived in 1969 and have carved out a place for themselves as purveyors of comfort, on a scale somewhere between domestic and grand (the antiques reflect Reg Gifford's other interest), and of consistently good food.

The cooking has roots in the Franco-British repertoire yet does not hesitate to call on support from elsewhere to add zest and variety. Indeed, the range of dishes is impressive, from ravioli of sweetbread or pressed leek terrine, to tartlet of poached egg glazed with a coriander sabayon, and braised boneless oxtail, topped with foie gras, with root vegetables and a madeira sauce. Menus always make room for soups – creamed swede and bacon or crab bisque, for example – and warm salads, perhaps of pan-fried skate wing, or of quail and foie gras. Birds, game or otherwise, are another constant feature whose simple and sometimes classic treatment brings out the best from roast pigeon, guinea-fowl cooked in a pot au feu, or roast breast of poussin served on a chickpea purée with a ballottine of the leg.

Vegetables have included 'the best pommes dauphinois' that one reporter had tasted. A trio of chocolate desserts on a crème de menthe sauce may be the most memorable dessert from among hazelnut nougat with a sauce of passion-fruit and orange, or a warm apple croustade with calvados ice-cream and cinnamon sauce. Cheeses are varied and served at the right stage of maturity, bread and petits fours are first-rate, and service manages to temper formality with warmth. Quality at the realistic end of the wine list is fair, with Alsace, the French regions, Spain, Italy and the New World holding out the best prospects. The quartet of English wines is welcome. House wine is £11.70 (£3.50 per glass). CELLARMAN'S CHOICE: St-Aubin premier cru 'Les Perriers' 1991, Prudhon, £19.50; Mercurey 1989, Jacqueson, £19.50.

CHEF: Kevin Mangeolles   PROPRIETORS: Mr and Mrs R.S.E. Gifford   OPEN: all week; 12.30 to 1, 7.30 to 8.30   MEALS: Set L £27.50, Set D £38   SERVICE: not inc   CARDS: Access, Amex, Diners, Visa   DETAILS: 50 seats. Private parties: 28 main room, 40 private room. Car park. Vegetarian meals with prior notice. No children under 10. Jacket and tie. No smoking in dining-room. Wheelchair access (1 step). No music   ACCOMMODATION: 14 rooms, all with bath/shower. TV. Phone. D,B&B £108 to £370. Deposit: £50. Children welcome (high tea). Garden. Fishing. Doors close at 11.45. Fax: (059 34) 35765

▲ *White Moss House* ▮ ⁵⚓

Rydal Water, Grasmere LA22 9SE
GRASMERE (053 94) 35295   COOKING 3*
on A591, at N end of Rydal Water   COST £36–£48

Touring in Cumbria may leave you with the impression that every last edifice in the region was visited, stayed in or just gazed on by William Wordsworth, but this Lakeland stone house at the north end of Rydal Water was actually owned by him. People come to the Lakes for rest and comfort, but the Dixons have opted to avoid the frills-and-furbelows philosophy of other places in favour of a simpler, less obtrusive but still comfortable style. When Peter Dixon says of his own cooking, 'Presentation is of a high order, but not stupidly fussy', the sentiment rings true of the whole place.

The proven formula is a nightly-changing set dinner of soup, fish, meat with a plethora of vegetables, a choice of (usually) three desserts, cheeses and coffee. Local suppliers are chosen for what they do best, and the provenance of materials proudly announced on menus. Dishes are described in exhaustive detail, not out of a misplaced desire to pile on the style, but simply because Peter Dixon wants you to know about all the good things that will appear on your plate. On an April menu, Argyll salmon is poached with champagne and souffléd, 'married' to Wastwater sea trout smoked over oak and bracken, and accompanied by smoked Westmorland cheese. Soups range from the delicate (fennel and almond) to the positively aggressive (morel, marjoram and marsala) which have been 'much enjoyed'. The nerveless production of soufflés in a full house continues to astonish – 'The bombe of brill was superb...we would happily have enjoyed a bigger serving of this as a main course' – and the quality of local meats and game is excellent. Herdwick spring lamb is 'pink and tender' and comes with a Scarborough fair of a herb crust (parsley, sage, rosemary and thyme). A historical slant is often evident in puddings such as 'Huntsman's' or 'Guardsman's', supplemented by wine-based sorbets of pink champagne or Gewürztraminer. Cheese celebrates the best British farmhouse producers.

To complete the picture of contentment, a formidably good wine list has been put together. Clarets are a roll-call of classed growths, backed up by Cabernets and Merlots from all over, cru Beaujolais have some maturity for once, burgundies display fine pedigree, and Spain and Italy get a fair hearing, as do fine German Rieslings. Many wines are available in halves, and the list is prefaced with a selection of personal choices to assist the bewildered, starting at £9.95.

▮ *denotes an outstanding wine cellar;* ⍦ *denotes a good wine list, worth travelling for.*

CHEFS: Peter Dixon and Colin Percival PROPRIETORS: Susan and Peter Dixon OPEN: Mon to Sat, D only; 7.30 for 8 CLOSED: Dec to Feb MEALS: Set D £27.50 SERVICE: not inc, card slips closed CARDS: Access, Visa DETAILS: 18 seats. Car park. Vegetarian meals with prior notice. Older children welcome. No smoking in dining-room. Wheelchair access. No music ACCOMMODATION: 6 rooms, all with bath/shower. TV. Phone. D,B&B £83 to £194. Older children welcome. Garden. Fishing. Doors close at 11. Confirm by 5 (*The Which? Hotel Guide*)

GRAYSHOTT Hampshire   map 2

Woods Place

Headley Road, Grayshott GU26 6LB   COOKING 1
HINDHEAD (0428) 605555   COST £26–£37

Ice-cold aquavit and Swedish beer as aperitifs should give notice that the accent here is Scandinavian. One pair who take regular Saturday lunches at Woods appreciate the 'friendly welcome, jolly music, excellent food' and the opportunity for a walk in the real woods afterwards. The gravad lax, commented the writer, was 'the best I have ever tasted', while brioche topped with melted Brie and smoked salmon also sharpened the appetite well. Piquancy is forthcoming in main courses such as turbot fillet with an accompaniment of aubergines marinated in honey and vinegar and served with a fresh tomato sauce, or saddle of hare in a juniper-scented cream. Mocha bavarois with apricot coulis, poached pears with lime and caramel sauce, or pancakes with blueberry ice-cream round things off in style. Within its tiny compass, the wine list contains some decent bottles, and the prices won't shock. House wines are £7.90.

CHEF: Eric Norrgren PROPRIETORS: Dana and Eric Norrgren OPEN: Tue to Sat; 12 to 2, 7 to 12 MEALS: alc (main courses £9.30 to £13) SERVICE: 10% CARDS: Access, Amex, Diners, Visa DETAILS: 36 seats. Private parties: 16 main room. Vegetarian meals with prior notice. Children's helpings. Smart dress preferred. Wheelchair access (also WC). Music. Fax: (0428) 605555

GREAT DUNMOW Essex   map 3

▲ *The Starr* ▼ ⅝✳

Market Place, Great Dunmow CM6 1AX
GREAT DUNMOW (0371) 874321   COOKING 2
off A120, 9m E of Bishop's Stortford   COST £23–£54

An old coaching inn with a Georgian façade, The Starr has a forest of beams within, but the dining-room feels airy and light. 'We butcher our own meat, and bake our own bread freshly each day,' writes Brian Jones, justly proud of his all-round professionalism. Regulars love it, which is why they are regulars of course; 'An excellent meal, very well cooked and presented' was one conclusion. There is an air of comfort and, sometimes, a feeling of best-behaviour formality. Eating out at The Starr is an occasion worthy of some effort, which is rewarded with food that has one foot in the traditional camp of quail wrapped in pastry with port wine and mushrooms, and one that makes the leap to baked fillet of red mullet with roasted vegetables.

The tradition may be British (venison pie) or French (quenelles of pike mousse) but it usually wins. Well-trodden paths are what please: scallops with bacon, or skate with butter and capers. Hot puddings are usually sticky and served with custard. Savouries include herring roe and Welsh rarebit. Lunch from the *carte* may be light, but dinner is a weightier three- or four-course affair. Service is quick and considerate. Wines are sound and reliable, with good choice under £15, a bit of a splash from Australia and New Zealand, but with room for burgundy-lovers to indulge. There are two-dozen half-bottles, and house wines start at £10.95. CELLARMAN'S CHOICE: Margaux, Ch. d'Angludet 1989, £20.95; Auxey-Duresses 1991, Leflaive, £19.95.

CHEF: Mark Fisher   PROPRIETORS: Brian and Vanessa Jones   OPEN: all week, exc Sat L and Sun D; 12 to 1.30, 7 to 9.30   CLOSED: 1 week after New Year   MEALS: alc weekday L (main courses £8 to £15). Set L Sun £21.50, Set D £21.50 to £35   SERVICE: not inc, 10% and card slips closed for 8 or more and residents   CARDS: Access, Amex, Visa   DETAILS: 50 seats. Private parties: 50 main room, 12 and 36 private rooms. Car park. Vegetarian meals. Children's helpings. Smart dress preferred. No smoking in dining-room. Wheelchair access (also WC). Music   ACCOMMODATION: 8 rooms, all with bath/shower. TV. Phone. B&B £30 to £100. Rooms for disabled. Children welcome. Baby facilities. Dogs by arrangement. Fax: (0371) 876337 (*The Which? Hotel Guide*)

GREAT GONERBY Lincolnshire   map 6

Harry's Place 🍴✳

17 High Street, Great Gonerby NG31 8JS
GRANTHAM (0476) 61780   COOKING 3*
on B1174, 2m NW of Grantham   COST £41–£69

The Hallams' idiosyncratic restaurant in a little village near Grantham is a true cottage industry. Ten people will fill it, but the doors open just as readily if there are only two of you. This gives it the comfortably laid-back feel of a domestic dinner party. But do not be deceived. The dedication to self-sufficiency is of such single-mindedness that, by the time you take your seats of an evening, Harry Hallam will have baked two lots of bread, made a quantity of ice-cream, simmered batches of fish and meat stock, and – depending on the time of year – cleaned and filleted wild salmon from the River Dee or boned and trimmed a loin of roe deer.

The menus are kept sensibly short, with just a pair of alternatives at each course and a good selection of British and French cheeses. Prices are undoubtedly high, particularly for main courses, but people do not doubt the palpable quality of it all. Starters may be as simple as a poached egg with sweetcorn in a pastry case with hollandaise, or as elaborate as sauté chicken livers served cold with a sherry and black-pepper jelly, Cumberland sauce and mixed salad leaves. Great pains are taken over the stocks, so that a reduction of fish stock with Noilly Prat and chives gives the right degree of support to salmon, and the roe deer gains depth of flavour from its own stock enriched with tarragon, white wine and madeira. Boldness is evinced in a breast of corn-fed chicken cooked in red wine and cassis with bacon, blackcurrants and shallots. Hot dessert soufflés (such as apricot, or plum with cognac) are enjoyed, as are old favourites like lemon tart or bread-and-butter pudding with vanilla ice-cream.

'The food lived up to our expectations and beyond,' said one couple who ate an evocative dinner of fish soup, partridge, Bramley apple and calvados soufflé, and shortbread with strawberries. While Caroline Hallam sees to everything out front, Harry usually emerges to universal approbation at the end of the meal. All is satiety and contentment. The tiny wine selection reads like a heavily condensed version of some grand hotel list. It is all terribly serious and there is just one half-bottle and no house wine as such. The choices are certainly very good, but only three out of the dozen bottles are below £20.

CHEF: Harry Hallam   PROPRIETORS: Harry and Caroline Hallam   OPEN: Tue to Sat (Sun and Mon by arrangement); 12.30 to 2, 7 to 9.30   CLOSED: 25 and 26 Dec, bank hols   MEALS: alc (main courses £15 to £22.50)   SERVICE: not inc   CARDS: Access, Visa   DETAILS: 10 seats. Private parties: 10 main room. Car park. Vegetarian meals with prior notice. Children's helpings. No children under 5. No smoking in dining-room. Wheelchair access (1 step). No music

GREAT MILTON Oxfordshire   map 2

▲ *Le Manoir aux Quat'Saisons* ▮ ✳

Church Road, Great Milton OX44 7PD
GREAT MILTON (0844) 278881
from M40 south, off A329 1m from
junction 7; from M40 north, off at
junction 8, then A418 right after ¼m,   COOKING 5
right again after 1½m on to A329   COST £42–£113

The tranquil and expansive garden is 'a lovely setting for a summer celebration'. In winter a warm lounge beckons with a fire and comfortable chairs. Whatever the season, 'a thoroughly grand and enjoyable and gracious experience' is on the cards. The manor must have been quite something when it went up in the fifteenth century, and has become no less impressive as creepers and Raymond Blanc have taken hold. By all accounts the conservatory is the place to eat in, but the yellow dining-room (the Loxton) had 'improved beyond recognition' for a reporter who had not visited for a while. The bold, bright, cheerfully Mediter-ranean paintings are by no means at odds with the old house; rather, they are a harbinger of the vitality of the food.

Blanc's menu jumps with invention and excitement, from marinated red mullet in a purée of salt cod to an elaborate fishy construction divided into three parts: slices of raw scallop with shiso leaves; a big moneybags parcel made of seaweed and filled with crab; deep-fried oyster with lime leaves. The style is essentially light, so fish plays a significant part, the treatment always resourceful: cardamom in the sauce for sea bass, or crushed mint-flavoured peas under a 'divine' fillet of marinated and lightly cooked wild salmon. Meat can be exquisite too, as in a bulging corn-fed squab stuffed with boudin blanc, surrounded by an artful scattering of peas and chanterelles, the whole dish greater than the sum of its parts – 'It tasted brilliant.'

Blanc avoids the mistake of being too reverent about the food. His ideas are not textbook ones and he has a gentle sense of humour, poking fun at himself perhaps by running that archetypal French item, the frog's leg, past us, scraped to the bone 'to make a kind of nugget on a stick', and served with juicy, succulent chanterelles that were 'the best ever' for a seasoned reporter. He is, however, deadly serious about the food, its freshness, supplies, technique and all the rest, yet turns it into entertainment for his audience. That is a rare skill, and one to be cherished. Café crème, 'either humorous or naff, depending on your viewpoint', is a coffee cup and saucer made from dark bitter chocolate, the cappuccino froth hiding a brilliantly flavoured coffee ice-cream. It is not 'naff', because flavour comes first.

Hiccups seem to be associated with special rates and packages, to which folk are understandably attracted because they are frightened by the normal tariff. But the deals appear to be no substitute for paying full whack for the real thing. Service is unremarkable: a shame for those who like to be surrounded by theatre, but a plus-point for others who prefer to get on with the business of eating and enjoying themselves. The wines are sensational, but prices, for many of our reporters, are intimidating. With Côtes de Provence at over £40, it takes a steady hand to persevere. There are under-£20 needles in the predominantly French haystack, although, strangely, none of them comes from Italy or the New World.

CHEFS: Raymond Blanc and Clive Fretwell PROPRIETOR: Raymond Blanc OPEN: all week; 12.15 to 2.15 (2.30 Sun), 7.15 to 10.15 MEALS: alc (main courses £28 to £33). Set L Mon to Sat £29.50, Set L and D £65 SERVICE: net prices CARDS: Access, Amex, Diners, Visa DETAILS: 100 seats. Private parties: 46 main room, 24, 46 and 62 private rooms. Car park. Vegetarian meals. Children's helpings. Smart dress preferred. No smoking in 2 dining-rooms. Wheelchair access (also WC). No music. Air-conditioned (some areas) ACCOMMODATION: 19 rooms, all with bath/shower. TV. Phone. B&B £165 to £375. Deposit: £150. Rooms for disabled. Children welcome. Baby facilities. Pets welcome (in grounds and kennels). Garden. Swimming-pool. Tennis. Fax: (0844) 278847 (*The Which? Hotel Guide*)

GREAT MISSENDEN Buckinghamshire   map 3

La Petite Auberge

107 High Street,
Great Missenden HP16 0BB   COOKING 1*
GREAT MISSENDEN (0494) 865370   COST £31–£47

Small, discreet and quiet, the Auberge produces 'unpretentious but consistently good cuisine which is utterly French. It is good for a relaxed tête-à-tête.' A meal for two might consist of leek terrine with herb vinaigrette, and hot scallop mousse with coral sauce; roast squab with cabbage and lardons, and fillet of beef with marrow; then chocolate crème de menthe gâteau, and caramelised lemon tart. Many of the dishes are widely encountered and freely adapted, but they cohere into a simple and convincing French provincial style at the hands of Hubert Martel. Light cooking makes the most of good ingredients, whether vegetables, 'tender and juicy sea bass', or tasty veal kidney in a Dijon mustard sauce. 'There is no vegetarian meal on the menu, but we warned them in advance about the vegetarian in our party and they came up with pleasing results.' Service is low key, homely and efficient. The short French wine list has bottles from £9.50 (there is no house wine) and also includes dessert wines by the glass.

Report forms are at the back of the book; write a letter if you prefer.

CHEF: Hubert Martel   PROPRIETORS: Mr and Mrs Hubert Martel   OPEN: Mon to Sat, D only; 7.30 to 10.30   CLOSED: 3 weeks Christmas, bank hols   MEALS: alc (main courses £13.50 to £15.50)   SERVICE: not inc   CARDS: Access, Visa   DETAILS: 30 seats. Private parties: 30 main room. Vegetarian meals with prior notice. Children welcome. Smart dress preferred. Wheelchair access (also WC). Music

---

GRIMSTON Norfolk   map 6

▲ *Congham Hall* ⁵✳

Grimston PE32 1AH
HILLINGTON (0485) 600250   ┌─────────────┐
                                                  │ *NEW CHEF* │
off A148 or B1153, 7m E of King's Lynn   └─────────────┘
                                                    COST £23–£67

The Georgian manor house – a delight in summer and in winter – is set in 40 acres of parkland a few miles from King's Lynn and makes the most of its garden by growing 300 different varieties of herb: jolly useful for Jonathan Nicholson, who took over as head chef in spring 1994. His menus suggest a light, modern touch, producing various risottos and ravioli dishes, as well as confit of rabbit with grilled aubergine and pesto, among other Mediterranean-type dishes. More homespun classics, including braised oxtail and hot steamed sponge pudding with raspberries, add their weight. Pleasant, welcoming, smiling service has always been a feature of Congham and puts everybody at ease. House wine is £11.50. A lack of feedback on the new regime means we are unable to award a cooking mark. More reports, please.

CHEF: Jonathan Nicholson   PROPRIETORS: Christine and Trevor Forecast   OPEN: all week, exc Sat L; 12.30 to 2, 7.30 to 9.30   MEALS: Set L £13.50 (2 courses) to £15, Set D £21.50 to £36   SERVICE: not inc, card slips closed   CARDS: Access, Amex, Diners, Visa   DETAILS: 50 seats. 4 tables outside. Private parties: 50 main room, 18 private room. Car park. Vegetarian meals. No children under 12. Jacket and tie. No smoking in dining-room. Wheelchair access (2 steps; also WC). No music   ACCOMMODATION: 14 rooms, all with bath/shower. TV. Phone. B&B £65 to £180. No children under 12. Afternoon teas. Garden. Swimming-pool. Tennis. Doors close at 11.30. Confirm by 6. Fax: (0485) 601191 (*The Which? Hotel Guide*)

HALFORD Warwickshire   map 2

Sykes House ⁵✳

Halford CV36 5BT   COOKING 2
STRATFORD-UPON-AVON (0789) 740976   COST £37–£46

This sixteenth-century Cotswold-stone house is a quarter of a mile from the Fosse Way in the tiny village of Halford and still feels like the private home it was until 1990. The form is to book (minimum 24 hours' notice), check that the menu suits, and turn up between 7.30 and 8.15. The entrance is via a modern patio door, and the dining-room is through the kitchen, which is 'immaculate and spotless at 8pm!' It is, of course, dining on the Cunliffes' terms, and the whole idea struck one reporter as rather precious, but the arrangements allow the cooking to show at its best.

'Welcoming appetisers' of smoked salmon curls or quail's eggs on olive tapénade toast set the ball rolling. A meal in June then went on to carrot vichyssoise (other days it might be cep soup or nettle broth), before steamed Cornish turbot in a buttery sauce, then mint-glazed lamb steak (a double eye of the chop, boned out), which came with second helpings of creamy gratin potatoes and crunchy Evesham asparagus. A highly scented and refreshing elderflower sorbet followed a creamy goats' cheese and rocket salad dressed with white truffle oil, and the meal finished with strawberry and white chocolate terrine, capped by home-made chocolate truffles, Cape gooseberries and unlimited coffee. The price is all-in, with no service charge made or expected. Wines are arranged by style, not heavily marked up, and include some interesting and attractive bottles. Three dry wines and three sweet ones are available by the glass for around £3.

CHEF: David Cunliffe   PROPRIETORS: David and Peggy Cunliffe   OPEN: Wed to Sat, D (reservations only at least 24 hrs ahead), D Mon and Tue and L Mon to Sat by arrangement for 8 or more; 7.30 to 8.15   MEALS: Set D £32.50   SERVICE: card slips closed   CARDS: Visa DETAILS: 24 seats. Private parties: 12 main room, 12 private rooms. Car park. Vegetarian meals with prior notice. Children welcome. Smart dress preferred. No smoking in dining-room. No music

---

HAMBLETON Leicestershire   map 6

▲ *Hambleton Hall* ▮

Hambleton LE15 8TH
OAKHAM (0572) 756991   COOKING 4
off A606, 3m SE of Oakham   COST £37–£86

'The setting is magnificent, especially on a fine evening', when the terrace affords expansive views across Rutland Water and rolling countryside. The house, like the village, is solid and Victorian; an enormous display of flowers in the sitting-room nearly reaches the high ceiling, a harbinger of decorative flourishes to come. Classical oils and fox-hunting prints in the formal dining-room add gravitas. The menu is a long, free-ranging *carte* of some two dozen items set against a fixed-price menu with absolutely no choice at all, prompting one visitor to wonder if the function of the set menu was to encourage a move to more expensive options. Reporters expect some concession to straitened economic circumstances, and don't see much evidence of it. Extras mount inexorably, making Hambleton's perceived value for money problematic. On the other hand, luxuries are never far away: crab, lobster, asparagus, morels everywhere, langoustines, scallops, foie gras and truffles.

The cooking is highly elaborate in conception, design and execution. Very finely diced courgettes, tomatoes and aubergines may turn up in several guises. Deep-fried vegetables – shaved, thinly sliced or shredded, according to circumstance – are a standard decoration, and it can all look very attractive. At one summer meal a stockade of baby leeks was erected around tomatoes and langoustines, with a tomato jelly on top, into which were poked bits of deep-fried vegetable up to six inches high. Underneath the intricate designs, a lot of good cooking goes on. A crazy-paving terrine makes the most of its components – chicken breast, hardly-cooked-at-all lamb, foie gras and tongue – while breast of chicken with morel sauce and baby vegetables is first-rate. The Sunday staple of roast beef and Yorkshire pudding, although not typical of

Hambleton fare, is as good a version as any. Passion-fruit soufflé was a standard that one whose birthday treat it was 'almost cried with pleasure'.

Service can sometimes lack joie de vivre. The Harts take their training responsibilities seriously, and although the top players come in for praise the general awkwardness can mean that not everybody finds the whole experience fun. The sensibly chosen wine list explores the classics without resorting to three-figure bottles, California is well represented, and careful selection outside France generally makes for some delightful drinking. Price-banded 'wines of the moment' simplify the search for those with an upper cash limit, and specially selected wines by the glass for some set meals 'is a highly commendable practice'. CELLARMAN'S CHOICE: Leeuwin Estate Cabernet Sauvignon 'Prelude' 1992, £22; Bonny Doon 'Clos de Gilroy 1992, £18.

CHEF: Aaron Patterson PROPRIETORS: Tim and Stefa Hart OPEN: all week; 12 to 2, 7 to 9.30 MEALS: alc (main courses £16 to £30). Set L and D £29.50 SERVICE: not inc, card slips closed CARDS: Access, Amex, Visa DETAILS: 60 seats. 4 tables outside. Private parties: 60 main room, 15 and 20 private rooms. Car park. Vegetarian meals. Children's helpings. Smart dress preferred. No cigars/pipes in dining-room. Wheelchair access (also WC). No music ACCOMMODATION: 15 rooms, all with bath/shower. TV. Phone. Air-conditioned (2 rooms). B&B £120 to £265. Rooms for disabled. Lift. Children welcome. Baby facilities. Pets by arrangement (not in public rooms). Afternoon teas. Garden. Swimming-pool. Tennis. Doors close at 1am. Fax: (0572) 724721 *(The Which? Hotel Guide)*

HAMPTON WICK Greater London　　　　　　　　　　　　　map 3

Dijonnais

35 High Street, Hampton Wick,
Kingston upon Thames KT1 4DA　　　　　　　　　　COOKING 2
081-977 4895　　　　　　　　　　　　　　　　　　COST £19–£42

The special appeal of this neat little restaurant owes much to the character of its owners, Lionel and Jan Jolivet. He cooks, she serves. Everything pleases here, from the Gallic atmosphere and the 'really delightful music – some typically French songs followed by Mozart' – to the generous helpings of robust food. The style is pure French provincial, with no frippery or frills: fish soup, snails, omelettes, beef tongue with madeira sauce, duck with cider and apples. Mussels with copious, soupy sauces earn plenty of endorsements, as do the fruit tarts – although some have found them rather filling after two hearty courses. Reporters have also praised a gougère with quail's eggs and spinach purée, chicken in cheese and white wine sauce, and lamb with pepper sauce and couscous. The all-French wine list stretches only to around 20 bottles, consisting of well-known names from reputable growers. House wine is £9.

CHEF: Lionel Jolivet PROPRIETOR: Lionel and Jan Jolivet OPEN: Mon to Sat, exc Sat L; 12 to 2.30, 6 to 10 (7.00 Fri and Sat) CLOSED: Easter and bank hols MEALS: alc (main courses £7.50 to £13.50). Set L £10 to £10.95, Set D £17.50. Cover £1 SERVICE: not inc CARDS: Access, Amex, Visa DETAILS: 28 seats. 1 table outside. Private parties: 25 main room. Vegetarian meals. Children's helpings on request. Smart dress preferred. Wheelchair access (1 step). Music

Le Petit Max

97A High Street, Hampton Wick KT2 5NB	COOKING 3
081-977 0236	COST £26–£46

This Max (see also Chez Max, London) is small, just by the station and doesn't sell wine, but is conveniently next door to an off-licence. Corkage is £2. By day it is Bonzo's café and by night a good French restaurant. No money is wasted on peripherals. Good-value food is the stock-in-trade, which means bare brick walls and dark blue paint relieved only by a display of French menus and red and white gingham tablecloths. It may mean cramped seating too, but folk have been prepared to queue at 10 o'clock at night for a second sitting, so what's a numb bum if the price is right?

The no-frills approach applies to the food as well as the décor. Crab cocktail has a slice of lemon perched on the edge and a generous splash of marie rose sauce added at the last minute (you can see the kitchen). But Marc Renzland has never skirted round luxury items on his menus: lobster has a supplementary charge, but salad of duck with foie gras is a standard item consisting of roast breast, smoked breast and foie gras, with a large mound of salad leaves under a good dressing. Corners are not cut either, except perhaps to serve things up in soup bowls rather than on plates. One summer evening the plat du chef was four trimmed lamb cutlets, cooked pink and served with good French beans, gratin dauphinois and a rich red wine sauce. Olives and varied breads are part of the package, and if the menu is occasionally more approximate than accurate in its descriptions, the food itself turns out fine. Puddings have included a rich chocolate pot (rather low on the advertised praline) and an excellent caramelised pear tart on very thin pastry. Note that credit cards are not accepted.

CHEF: Marc Renzland   PROPRIETOR: Le Petit Max Ltd   OPEN: Tue to Sun, D only, and Sun L; 12.30 to 4, 7 to 10.30 (6.45 to 11.15 Fri and Sat, 8 to 9.30 Sun)   CLOSED: 1 week Christmas, 2 weeks summer, 1 week autumn   MEALS: Set L and D £22.50. Unlicensed, but bring your own: corkage £2   SERVICE: 10% (optional)   DETAILS: 34 seats. Private parties: 32 main room. Vegetarian meals with prior notice. Children's helpings Sun L. No children under 8. No music

---

HARROGATE North Yorkshire   map 5

La Bergerie

11–13 Mount Parade, Harrogate HG1 1BX	COOKING 1
HARROGATE (0423) 500089	COST £23–£30

Jacques and Juliet Giron run their modest restaurant as a family business. He cooks, she oversees front-of-house. The food is 'traditional French', with the emphasis on the cuisine of the south-west, and specialities have an authentic ring: pâté de pays de Luchon (duck and armagnac pâté), and perdrix a l'etuvée de choux au porto are typical. Other dishes might include saddle of venison served on a bed of leeks with a juniper, red wine and cognac sauce, and roast best end of lamb with provençale sauce. Cassoulet toulousain is a permanent fixture. Desserts include orange and lemon tart, and white chocolate mousse with caramel topping. The wine list is staunchly Gallic and prices are realistic across the range. House wine is £7.90.

CHEF: Jacques Giron PROPRIETORS: Jacques and Juliet Giron OPEN: Mon to Sat, D only; 7 to 11 (L and Sun by arrangement) MEALS: Set D £14.50 to £16.50 SERVICE: not inc CARDS: Access, Visa DETAILS: 32 seats. Private parties: 10 and 20 private rooms. Vegetarian meals. Children's helpings. Wheelchair access (1 step; also WC). Music

Drum and Monkey £

5 Montpellier Gardens, Harrogate HG1 2TF	COOKING 2
HARROGATE (0423) 502650	COST £14–£43

Originally a pub, this wine bar-cum-restaurant has had years of practice at offering seafood to well-heeled Harrogate residents and visitors alike. Bookings have to be made way ahead for dinner in either the plainly furnished upstairs restaurant or in the bar, although casual visitors can be fitted in downstairs at lunch-time, when it is first come, first served. The atmosphere has been described as one of 'studied smugness' on the part of the staff, but they do work hard and efficiently. Spankingly fresh fish and shellfish are the order of the day (no meat is served). Grilling, baking and steaming are the main cooking techniques: nothing is fried. Smoked salmon pâté, lobster cocktail and seafood roulade with sweet-and-sour sauce are good choices as starters, before grilled Dover sole, whiting stuffed with crabmeat and hollandaise sauce or sea trout salad. The seafood pie was 'a revelation' for one visitor. To finish, try fresh fruit or raisins in madeira with ice-cream. The short wine list favours whites and is excellent value. House wine is £6.55.

CHEF: Keith Penny PROPRIETOR: William Fuller OPEN: Mon to Sat; 12 to 2.30, 7 to 10.15 CLOSED: 24 Dec to 2 Jan MEALS: alc (main courses L £4 to £15, D £7 to £15.50) SERVICE: not inc CARDS: Access, Visa DETAILS: 50 seats. Private parties: 8 main room. Children welcome. Wheelchair access (also WC). No music

Grundy's   NEW ENTRY

21 Cheltenham Crescent, Harrogate HG1 1DH	COOKING 1
HARROGATE (0423) 502610	COST £21–£37

The green façade of the Grundys' Victorian terraced house may look inauspicious but things are different inside. Shades of pink colour the modern dining-room with its alcoves, well-spaced tables and comfortable chairs. Val Grundy is a self-taught cook who offers a choice of fixed-price menus and a *carte* with some intriguing, up-to-the-minute touches. Asparagus, pesto and roast pepper salad is a typical starter, while main courses might include roast Barbary duckling with a well-balanced kumquat and lime sauce. Other offerings are fillet of lamb with honey and sherry sauce and marinated breast of chicken with hazelnut and carrot cream. Steaks also draw favourable reports. 'Unforgettable' sticky toffee pudding is served with ice-cream. Chris Grundy and his staff provide impeccable service. The well-described wine list is arranged according to style and character rather than grape or region. House wine is £8.50.

The Good Food Guide *is a registered trade mark of Consumers' Association Ltd.*

CHEF: Val Grundy   PROPRIETORS: Chris and Val Grundy   OPEN: Mon to Sat, D only; 6.30 to 10
CLOSED: 2 weeks Jan to Feb, 2 weeks July to Aug, bank hols   MEALS: alc (main courses £9 to
£13.50). Set D £10.95 (2 courses) to £12.95   SERVICE: 10% (optional), card slips closed
CARDS: Access, Amex, Visa   DETAILS: 40 seats. Private parties: 32 main room. Vegetarian
meals. Children's helpings. No pipes in dining-room. Music

Millers, The Bistro

1 Montpellier Mews, Harrogate HG1 2TG	COOKING 2
HARROGATE (0423) 530708	COST £22–£34

'I have nothing but praise for the food and service,' wrote one who nevertheless
had problems with the close proximity of smokers. Millers is a small place, and
packs more in than when it was a restaurant. The other response to economy is a
simple *carte* of £5 starters and £9.50 main courses in a largely Franco-Italian
mould. The cooking is a notch above the boys who pile grilled vegetables on to a
piece of bread and call it bruschetta: there is some skill to turning out a good
risotto, whether saffron yellow, or inky black with roast calamari.

Flavours are kept straightforward. Terrine of pressed duck and foie gras gets a
tangy sauce gribiche, while trout, asparagus and sirloin of beef go a long way on
hollandaise or béarnaise sauces. As well as instant grilling, there are some
slow-cooked dishes such as pot-roast guinea-fowl. The cover charge brings
tapénade 'and an ample provision of good bread upon which to spread it while
waiting for the first course to appear'. Around 40 wines are young, good of their
type and mostly under £20, beginning with vin de pays at £8.95 (£1.60
per glass).

CHEF: Simon Gueller   PROPRIETORS: Simon and Rena Gueller   OPEN: Tue to Sat; 12 to 2.30, 7
to 10.30   CLOSED: bank hols   MEALS: alc (main courses £9.50). Set L £9.50 (2 courses). Cover
£1   SERVICE: not inc   CARDS: Access, Amex, Visa   DETAILS: 40 seats. Private parties: 40 main
room. Vegetarian meals. Children welcome. Wheelchair access (1 step; also WC). Music

---

HARROW Greater London   map 3

Percy's ✦

NEW ENTRY

66–68 Station Road, Harrow HA2 7SJ	COOKING 1*
081-427 2021	COST £28–£45

An agreeably eccentric air pervades Percy's. It looks improbably jaunty in the
unprepossessing environs of North Harrow. Much of the fresh produce used
comes in shipments from a Devon farm. The interior of the restaurant is white
and light, with '30s adornments, the approach to customers is garrulous and
friendly, and Tina Bricknell-Webb's cooking mines a rich seam of eclecticism.
This last brings on to the menu items like monkfish and prawn terrine with
daikon radish and beetroot spaghetti, sea bass baked with smoked-garlic butter,
and breast of guinea-fowl stuffed with buckwheat, mushrooms, sage and
onions, and roasted with garlic and honey.

In the event, dishes may be less complicated to taste than their menu
specifications imply. At an inspection, a terrine of John Dory, monkfish, eel,
prawns, mussels and asparagus had finely worked flavour and texture, and came

with powerfully aromatic saffron mayonnaise. Thai-spiced chicken breast with curry leaves and a coconut cream sauce scored for balance as well as inventiveness. On the other hand, a starter of chargrilled red peppers with feta was short of either charring or seasoning, and roast haunch of venison with a rosemary and juniper jus needed more seasoning or marinating. Chocolate and rum pithiviers was as rich as required, while the lemon tart came with 'intensely weird, but lovely' rosemary ice-cream. Vegetables are profuse, and coffee is 'pretty strong'. The shortish wine list is well-chosen, moderately priced and filled out with expansive notes. House wines start at £9.80.

CHEF: Tina Bricknell-Webb   PROPRIETORS: Tony and Tina Bricknell-Webb   OPEN: Tue to Sat; 12 to 2.30, 6.30 to 10.30   MEALS: alc (main courses £12 to £16)   SERVICE: 10% (optional), card slips closed   CARDS: Access, Amex, Diners, Visa   DETAILS: 80 seats. Private parties: 40 main room, 40 private room. Car park. Vegetarian meals. No children under 8. Smart dress preferred. No smoking. Wheelchair access. Music

---

HARVINGTON Hereford & Worcester   map 2

▲ Mill at Harvington ▾ ⁙✗

Anchor Lane, Harvington WR11 5NR
EVESHAM (0386) 870688
S of B439 Evesham to Bidford-on-Avon   COOKING 2
road, avoid village   COST £17–£45

The Georgian mansion and eighteenth-century red brick malting mill stand in eight acres of woods and parkland. Gradual refurbishment does nothing to disturb the tranquillity that the River Avon, flowing gently past, bestows. The dining-room opens on to the lawn and gardens, and the kitchen on to Evesham produce and its own herbs.

Meals are priced according to choice of main course, and the food has an old-fashioned streak to it, with steak, kidney and oyster pudding (in suet pastry with a rich gravy) and calf's liver with Dubonnet and orange. Good textured rack of lamb, a velvety sauce lifted by the tang of lemon for a blanquette of pork, and simple fruit parfait with a creamy texture are some of the things the kitchen does well. 'Duck breast with chicken livers was a surprisingly good combination,' according to one, who also found that cheesy sauces may be ladled over potatoes or seafood pancake with more enthusiasm than judgement. But 'one feels that there is understanding of, and feeling for, good food', which shows up in hot seafood sausage baked and served with a white wine sauce, as well as chocolate brandy-cake and pecan pie. The approach to wine is unstuffy, bottles are arranged by style, and there are copious notes on grape varieties. Only two wines (apart from sweeties) are available by the glass at any given time, but they change frequently and vary from simple blended French table wine through Cloudy Bay Sauvignon Blanc to Ch. Lascombes 1981. CELLARMAN'S CHOICE: Tatachilla Hill Chenin NV, £9; Corbières 1990, Dom. du Trillol, £10.50.

'The bean job resembled something that you slap between two bricks to build a wall. What a lost opportunity.' (On eating in London)

CHEFS: Jane Greenhalgh, Bill Downing and John Hunter PROPRIETORS: Simon and Jane Greenhalgh OPEN: all week; 11.45 to 1.45, 7 to 8.45 CLOSED: 24 to 29 Dec MEALS: alc light L (main courses £4 to £7), Set L £10.95 (2 courses) to £13.95, Set D £19.50 to £28 SERVICE: not inc, card slips closed CARDS: Access, Amex, Diners, Visa DETAILS: 45 seats. 12 tables outside. Private parties: 40 main room, 14 private room. Car park. Vegetarian meals. Children's helpings on request. No children under 10. Smart dress preferred. No smoking in dining-room. Wheelchair access (1 step; also WC). No music ACCOMMODATION: 15 rooms, all with bath/shower. TV. Phone. B&B £54 to £85. Rooms for disabled. No children under 10. Garden. Swimming-pool. Tennis. Fishing. Fax: (0386) 870688 (The Which? Hotel Guide)

HARWICH Essex   map 3

▲ Pier at Harwich ♥

| The Quay, Harwich CO12 3HH | COOKING 1 |
| HARWICH (0255) 241212 | COST £20–£51 |

Nautically themed, the Pier does simple fish and chips best. Big boats pass, en route for the Continent, and everybody turns to watch. The heavy motifs – wooden rails and brass instrument cowls – do not detract unduly from the food, which makes much of the local catch. The closer the cooking stays to fish (choose from cod, haddock or plaice) and chips ('they glisten without being greasy'), the more effective it becomes, although moderate success accrues to plump local mussels cooked in white wine and cream, and fat scallops are quickly fried in butter and served with strips of bacon. Fish pie contains salmon and scallops as well as the regulation cod. Steak and chicken provide variety, and the dozen puddings include butterscotch pie, and gin and lavender ice-cream. The house selection of two dozen wines, starting at £8.95, is perfectly adequate for the cooking, but Lay & Wheeler supplies good-value, interesting bottles, including over 20 half-bottles, and perfectly sound drinking throughout the list. CELLARMAN'S CHOICE: Allan Scott Sauvignon Blanc 1993, £18.50; Backsberg Pinotage 1990, £12.95.

CHEF: C.E. Oakley PROPRIETOR: Milsom Hotels (Dedham) Ltd OPEN: all week; 12 to 2, 6 to 9.30 CLOSED: 25 and 26 Dec MEALS: alc (main courses £7 to £17). Set L Mon to Fri £11.75, Sun £14.25, Set D Mon to Sat £16 SERVICE: 10% card slips closed CARDS: Access, Amex, Diners, Visa DETAILS: 80 seats. Private parties: 100 main room, 60 private room. Car park. Vegetarian meals. Children's helpings. No cigars/pipes in dining-room. Wheelchair access (2 steps). Music ACCOMMODATION: 6 rooms, all with bath/shower. TV. Phone. B&B £45 to £72.50. Children welcome. Doors close at midnight. Fax: (0255) 551922 (The Which? Hotel Guide)

HASLEMERE Surrey   map 3

Morels ▮ ⁵✳

| 23–27 Lower Street, Haslemere GU27 2NY | COOKING 4 |
| HASLEMERE (0428) 651462 | COST £28–£53 |

The walk from the public car park, hidden across the road, is short. The linked cottages on the raised pavement that form the restaurant have the pleasant effect of dividing it into separate rooms. Bright cool blue is the colour scheme, set off smartly by crisp white linen and fresh flowers. The style of cooking is modern French, tipped towards the sunny south. Mediterranean fish soup, for instance, has a pungent aroma, smooth texture and is full of flavour, the strength deriving simply from the generous amount of fish used. An accompanying rouille is stingingly hot, and for one reporter 'the croûtons started off looking like communion wafers, but within seconds of being popped into the soup they trebled in size. Very satisfying.'

The cooking is unquestionably polished and technically accomplished, although reporters have praised it more because it lacks faults than because it excites. The shorter and cheaper fixed-price menus are good value, particularly as some dishes overlap with the more expensive *carte*. Textures are an integral part of each dish, and flavours remain identifiable, as in a much-enjoyed, gentle-tasting, firmish but creamy goats' cheese that was spread with a layer of pesto and neatly parcelled in light filo; crunch came from a small tangle of assorted leaves, lightly dressed in a good olive oil-based dressing. Richness is generally kept in check, although a dish of earthy, tender, boned oxtail in a sauce of the braising liquor and port 'sticks to your lips like cling-film'. Earthiness is welcome, too, in a dish of gamey pigeon that is rosy pink, moist and firm.

Desserts, for one reporter, are 'where you actually do get the feeling that here is a very good chef at work'. Crème brûlée is 'a superb, creamy-textured custard of perfect consistency, served in a flat dish. The light brûlée fractured into 100 pieces with a gentle tap.' Assiette du chef is a large plate with a tiny version of all the desserts listed that day, 'designed to encourage the Billy Bunters among us to indulge'. Service has been known to let the side down by its lack of attention to the finer points. 'Formal in attire and attitude' was how one reporter put it, and more than one has remarked on the solemnity and reserve of the place, on the lack of sheer festive enjoyment that food of this quality deserves.

Wines are predominantly French, and quality comes before price. This is a laudable approach with the one disadvantage that those with less than £20 to spend have a restricted choice: Beaujolais and Chardonnay both start at £20. Nevertheless, there are good and mature vintages, and excellent runs of claret and white burgundy. House wines are unsatisfactory: difficult to locate on the list, with no price given per glass, and judged 'mean' and 'stewed' by an inspector, who paid £2 a glass. All those faults should be easy to put right. CELLARMAN'S CHOICE: Bourgogne Rouge 1989, Barthod, £18; St Véran 'Vieilles Vignes' 1992, Dom. Saumaize, £22.

CHEF: Jean-Yves Morel   PROPRIETORS: Jean-Yves and Mary-Anne Morel   OPEN: Tue to Sat, exc Sat L; 12.30 to 2, 7 to 10   CLOSED: 3 weeks end Sept   MEALS: alc (2 courses £25). Set L £17, Set D Tue to Fri £19.50   SERVICE: not inc   CARDS: Access, Amex, Diners, Visa   DETAILS: 50 seats. Private parties: 50 main room. Vegetarian meals with prior notice. Children's helpings. No smoking in dining-room. Wheelchair access (1 step). No music

---

The Guide *office can quickly spot when a restaurateur is encouraging customers to write recommending inclusion – and sadly, several restaurants have been doing this in 1994. Such reports do not further a restaurant's cause. Please tell us if a restaurateur invites you to write to the* Guide.

HASLINGDEN Lancashire map 5

Hazel Tree

32 Manchester Road, Haslingden BB4 5ST
ROSSENDALE (0706) 211530   COOKING 1
on A56, 7m SE of Blackburn   COST £17–£31

Andrew Lyzniak and Noel Scarry plan to move to larger premises but, as we went to press, were still in residence at their converted shop and pleasing customers with their idiosyncratic brand of bistro cooking. 'We are new English pirates,' they admit 'and will steal an idea from anywhere.' Regularly changing blackboard menus testify to their Jolly Rogering instinct and their forthright use of fresh local ingredients. Danish herrings with rye bread, Cajun halibut with lime and dill sauce, parrot-fish cooked in a paper bag with ginger and leeks, and roast guinea-fowl with calvados are typical of their output. Some reporters have detected a heavy hand in the kitchen, but most applaud dishes such as filo parcels of Brie and Stilton, sole with spicy tomato sauce, and roast leg of lamb with mint and garlic. Desserts span everything from home-made gâteaux to tarte Tatin. Service is easygoing. The wine list – also on a blackboard – is a short slate of good-value bottles in the £10 bracket. House wine is £8.50.

CHEFS/PROPRIETORS: Andrew Lyzniak and Noel Scarry OPEN: Tue to Sun, exc Tue D; 10.30 to 1.30 (1 Sun), 7 to 9 (5.30 to 9 Sun) MEALS: alc (main courses £9.50 to £11). Set D £9.95 (exc Sat) SERVICE: not inc, card slips closed CARDS: Access, Visa DETAILS: 40 seats. Private parties: 30 main room. Vegetarian meals. Children's helpings. Smart dress preferred. Wheelchair access (1 step). Music

HASTINGS East Sussex map 3

Rösers 🍾

64 Eversfield Place, St Leonards,
Hastings TN37 6DB   COOKING 3*
HASTINGS (0424) 712218   COST £23–£46

As President Reagan is reputed to have asked, when first hearing of political stirrings in Poland, 'First off, where is it?' Rösers appeared in the last *Guide* under St Leonards. It has not moved, but Gerald Röser points out that, although its postal address is St Leonards, his restaurant is directly opposite Hastings pier. Since we assume that readers will want to visit, rather than just write to him, we have relocated this entry under Hastings. It is a small and comfortable 'esplanade' house, quiet and 'beautifully run'. 'The décor is still a bit behind the times but the food certainly isn't.'

The cooking adapts as it goes. Although Belgian chocolate mousse with a coffee cream sauce ('fantastic!') is a regular, one reporter, who had not visited for a while, felt that the menu had been simplified and streamlined in his absence. Updated classical techniques underpin the cooking, and the menu balances lightness against weight, roast seafood on a light fish sauce against fillet of beef with foie gras parfait in madeira sauce. Good supplies of fish are well handled – 'Röser must be one of the best cooks of scallops.' Even the lighter dishes have good depth of flavour, and marinating adds to the taste of others. Rack of

Romney Marsh lamb, for instance, is doused in olive oil and seasoned with garlic, ginger, rosemary and coriander before being roasted. A dish of mushrooms sauté with garlic and herbs and sandwiched between layers of rösti potatoes shows that vegetarians are not neglected, and an unusual item such as cauliflower terrine with langoustines (on a spring menu) crops up now and again. Good chargrilled vegetables and 'a salad of wonderful leaves' indicate that all departments are working well.

Normally wine lists of this length, and with such prestigious bottles as these, are marked up dramatically to pay for the bank loan. It is greatly to Rösers' credit that the quality is here and the accountant kept at bay. The safe route has been taken with regard to many producers (although, curiously, Germans are largely absent) rather than opting for excitement, but many will be grateful for that. Post-prandial spirits are worth considering too. House wine is from £8.95 but there are more interesting bottles for a few pounds extra. CELLARMAN'S CHOICE: Lindemans Chardonnay Bin 65 1993, £13.95; Châteauneuf-du-Pape 1986, Dom. du Vieux Télégraphe, £24.80.

CHEF: Gerald Röser   PROPRIETORS: Gerald and Jenny Röser   OPEN: Tue to Sat, exc Sat L; 12 to 2, 7 to 10   CLOSED: 1 week Jan, 1 week Aug   MEALS: alc (main courses £11 to £14). Set L £10.95 (2 courses) to £15.95, Set D Tue to Fri £18.95   SERVICE: net prices, card slips closed   CARDS: Access, Amex, Diners, Visa   DETAILS: 40 seats. Private parties: 16 main room, 30 private room. Vegetarian meals. Children welcome. No cigars/pipes in dining-room. Wheelchair access (2 steps). Music

---

HAWORTH West Yorkshire   map 5

▲ Weavers ⅚✳

15 West Lane, Haworth BD22 8DU
HAWORTH (0535) 643822
beside car park for Brontë Parsonage   COOKING 1
Museum   COST £18–£37

The ante-room is rather cluttered, cramped and 1950-ish, but the dining-room at the back is modern, stylish, candle-lit, with attentive and professional staff. The kitchen offers a mixed bag of dishes, from deep-fried potato skins to cow pie, from 'Yorkshire pudding wi' onion gravy', (with the most un-Yorkshire option of vegetarian gravy) to kofta meatballs with mint sauce. 'The ingredients are superb,' writes an inspector, 'but I think the restaurant is confused about where it wants to be.' Perhaps the effort of coping with clashing cultures (or preparing too many dishes ahead) takes its toll in the cooking. It tends to dryness in meats and blandness in sauces, although the natural juices served with roast fillet of pork (with stuffing and crackling) at one meal were a creditable exception. At the same meal, 'old school pud of the day' was very good bread and butter with custard sauce. Wines are cleverly chosen and reasonably priced, although there are a lot of split vintages. Seven house wines are available by the glass from £1.60.

▲ *This symbol means accommodation is available.*

CHEFS: Colin and Jane Rushworth PROPRIETOR: the Rushworth family OPEN: Tue to Sat D, and Sun L (winter only); 12 to 1.30, 7 to 9.15 CLOSED: 2 weeks summer MEALS: alc (main courses £8 to £14). Set D £9.95 (2 courses) and £11.95, Set L Sun £9.95 SERVICE: not inc CARDS: Access, Amex, Diners, Visa DETAILS: 45 seats. Private parties: 16 main room. Vegetarian meals. Children's helpings on request. Smart dress preferred. No smoking in dining-room. Music. Air-conditioned ACCOMMODATION: 4 rooms, all with bath/shower. TV. Phone. B&B £47.50 to £67.50. Deposit: 10%. No children under 5. Doors close at midnight. Confirm by 6 (The Which? Hotel Guide)

HAYDON BRIDGE Northumberland map 7

General Havelock Inn £

Ratcliffe Road, Haydon Bridge NE47 6ER   COOKING 1
HEXHAM (0434) 684376   COST £19–£34

'A real honest place,' enthused one reporter after a meal at Ian and Angela Clyde's popular establishment close to the river. The green-painted building looks like a pub, but the interior is something very different. A small bar caters for the drinking needs of locals, but most of the action takes place in the two-storey restaurant with its exposed roof timbers and French doors opening on to the lawn. The place soon warms up as it fills with customers, and Ian Clyde's personable, easy-going manner adds to the atmosphere. Dinner revolves around a four-course menu that never strays into the realms of high art, but offers 'simple stuff, superbly done'. Crab tartlet has drawn rave reviews; elsewhere there have been good reports of seafood pancake, perfect crisp-skinned duck with redcurrant sauce, and salmon with lemon and dill sauce. Big platefuls of properly cooked vegetables also receive the thumbs-up. The wine list is well spread and prices are 'lenient'. House wine is £9.50.

CHEF: Angela Clyde PROPRIETORS: Ian and Angela Clyde OPEN: Wed to Sun, exc Sun D; 12 to 1.30, 7.30 to 8.30 CLOSED: first 2 weeks Jan, first 2 weeks Sept MEALS: alc (main courses £5.80 to £6). Set L £11, Set D £19 SERVICE: not inc DETAILS: 28 seats. 1 table outside. Private parties: 30 main room. Vegetarian meals. Children's helpings. Smart dress preferred. Wheelchair access (1 step). No music

---

HAYFIELD Derbyshire map 5

▲ Bridge End

7 Church Street, Hayfield SK12 5JE   COOKING 2
NEW MILLS (0663) 747321   COST £22–£43

For those undertaking the Pennine Way walk from north to south, reward as evening draws nigh may be found at this nineteenth-century stone building, opened by the Tiers as a restaurant and guesthouse several years ago. The weekly-changing menu cooked by Jonathan Holmes and Joanne Winch offers six to eight choices at each stage and, although descriptions of dishes may be thought a shade long-winded, there is plenty to tempt the adventurous.

This is ambitious British cooking, not afraid to give an everyday fish like plaice the Japanese treatment – tempura batter, pickled ginger and dipping sauces. That ambition may outstrip co-ordination upon occasion, however: one couple found two fish dishes conflated into one rather crowded soup-plate of Arbroath smokies, sea bream, monkfish, prawns and smoked salmon. Simpler is often better, as in a 'sweet and creamy' tomato and lentil soup, 'generous, tender' roast beef with good Yorkshire pudding, sinew-stiffening casseroled hare with beetroot and mustard, or an apple crumble that combines sharp and soft flavours and comes with a real vanilla custard. British cheeses are dealt with admirably, with taste descriptions and even a map provided to aid the unfamiliar. Home-made bread is usually approved, and cafetière coffee is smooth and strong. Niggles about service have surfaced this year, with some complaining of excessive waits. Wines are sound with a modest ambition that fits the food, yet with interest and quality built in. Mark-ups reduce as the price rises, making better bottles more affordable. House wine is £9.50 (£2.30 per glass).

CHEFS: Jonathan Holmes and Joanne Winch PROPRIETORS: Geoffrey and Barbara Tier OPEN: Tue to Sat D, and Sun L; 12 to 3, 7.30 to 10 MEALS: alc (main courses £9 to £14.50). Set L Sun £13 SERVICE: not inc CARDS: Access, Amex, Diners, Visa DETAILS: 52 seats. Private parties: 32 main room, 20 private room. Car park. Vegetarian meals. Children's helpings. Smart dress preferred. Wheelchair access (2 steps). Music ACCOMMODATION: 4 rooms, all with bath/shower. TV. B&B £28 to £45. Children welcome. Baby facilities. Fax: (0663) 742121 (*The Which? Hotel Guide*)

HELFORD Cornwall

map 1

▲ *Riverside* ▮

Helford TR12 6JU
MANACCAN (0326) 231443
off B3293, 6m E of Helston

COOKING 2
COST £35–£42

For quietness, the Riverside takes some beating. Whitewashed cottages stand in a well-tended hillside garden overlooking the picturesque Helford Estuary. Brightly coloured shrubs and flowers poke out of terracotta pots. There are log fires when it's cold, and tables and chairs on the terrace when it's warm. The kitchen has had a long love affair with provincial France; no particular region, just a simple, restrained and careful way with seafood, which is abundant, and a few meat dishes for variety. Pan-fried scallops with baby asparagus and spinach might be followed by roast monkfish wrapped in Parma ham on creamed leeks, and crème brûlée. Four or five choices are offered per course, and after fish, lamb is a favourite: best end in puff pastry with a rosemary and red wine sauce, or as a trio along with sweetbreads and kidney, for example. The hotel receives as much favourable mention as the food, although reporters who stay a few days may find the same vegetables cropping up with each meal. Service can be charm itself, or, for one reporter, 'rather combative and too loud'.

The wine list takes maturity seriously, in particular offering some venerable claret vintages. The range is extensive, good properties and producers abound, prices are fair, South Africa has blossomed, and a star system helps to pick out priorities. The half-bottle selection is amazing, and 10 good wines by the glass cost between £2.50 and £3.50. CELLARMAN'S CHOICE: Cloudy Bay Sauvignon Blanc 1992, £21.50; Glen Carlou Merlot 1992, £21.80.

CHEF: Susie Darrell PROPRIETORS: Edward and Susie Darrell OPEN: all week, D only; 7.30 to 9 CLOSED: Nov to early Mar MEALS: Set D £30 SERVICE: net prices DETAILS: 35 seats. 4 tables outside. Private parties: 12 main room. Car park. Vegetarian meals with prior notice. Children's helpings on request. No children under 10. Smart dress preferred. Wheelchair access (1 step; also WC). No music ACCOMMODATION: 6 rooms, all with bath/shower. TV. B&B £75 to £95. Deposit: £75. Rooms for disabled. Children welcome. Garden. Confirm by 6. Fax: (0326) 231103 (*The Which? Hotel Guide*)

HERSTMONCEUX East Sussex   map 3

Sundial ※

Gardner Street, Herstmonceux BN27 4LA	COOKING 2
HERSTMONCEUX (0323) 832217	COST £26–£71

The Bertolis' cottage restaurant is perched on the Weald, the sandstone ridge that runs down to Hastings, and enjoys an extensive view to the north. Visitors find the interior a softly lit, low-ceilinged haven, in which the necessarily limited space has been intelligently used. Some may take the view that the place 'is all a little out of date', but for others that is its charm. Two set-price lunch menus are offered, which change twice weekly, while the long *carte* is refreshed fortnightly. In addition to those, a five-course *menu surprise* can be had for a minimum of two diners.

The cooking is French, the style deeply classical. Typical dishes might be terrine of leeks and smoked salmon, baked sea bass with mussels and fennel in a white wine sauce, and duck breast with red wine and redcurrants. At a spring dinner, a mousseline of three fish had good flavour, while moules marinière was fine textbook stuff. Pigeon breast with lambs' kidneys showed that meat cookery is also sound, the 'juicily moist' texture supported well by the richness of the sauce. A charlotte royale was set very firm, but a lime syllabub was admirably intense and had a raspberry sauce floating on top of it. The wine list is as classic as the food. Its strongest suit is old clarets and younger but fine burgundies, with prices on the high side. Relief can be sought in the Loire or the Rhône. House wines start at £10.75 for pichets of Soave or Valpolicella.

CHEF: Giuseppe Bertoli PROPRIETORS: Giuseppe and Laure Bertoli OPEN: Tue to Sun; 12 to 2 (2.30 Sun), 7 to 9.30 CLOSED: Christmas to 20 Jan, last 3 weeks Aug MEALS: alc (main courses £17.50 to £22.50). Set L £15.50 to £19.50, Set D £24.50 SERVICE: 10%, card slips closed CARDS: Access, Amex, Diners, Visa DETAILS: 50 seats. 8 tables outside. Private parties: 60 main room, 22 private room. Car park. Vegetarian meals. Healthy eating options. Children's helpings. No smoking in dining-room. Wheelchair access (1 step; also WC). Music

---

The text of entries is based on unsolicited reports sent in by readers, backed up by inspections conducted anonymously. The factual details under the text are from questionnaires the Guide *sends to all restaurants that feature in the book.*

Restaurateurs justifiably resent no-shows. If you quote a credit card number when booking, you may be liable for the restaurant's lost profit margin if you don't turn up. Always phone to cancel.

HETTON North Yorkshire   map 5

Angel Inn ▮ ⚘ £

Hetton BD23 6LT
SKIPTON (0756) 730263   COOKING 3
off B6265, 5m N of Skipton   COST £18–£35

Customers eating in the bar, brasserie or restaurant, secure among wheel-backed
chairs and old beams, may have been blissfully unaware of the major
refurbishment going on in the kitchens. What is clear is that for the Angel,
standards have not wavered one iota. In the bar and brasserie, where the
approach is informal, choice abounds in the form of scallops baked with garlic
and Gruyère, warm goats' cheese crostini, calf's liver on Parmesan polenta, and
the famed 'little moneybags' of seafood with lobster sauce. A reporter was full of
admiration for a Saturday lunch that took in 'substantial' fish soup with 'two
blobs of excellent aïoli' and fine granary bread, sliced breast of 'very gamey'
pigeon with wild mushrooms and button onions and an 'intensely reduced
stock', and sticky toffee pudding with butterscotch sauce.

At dinner and Sunday lunch in the restaurant, a fixed-price menu of three
courses plus coffee comes into play, the food acquiring a greater complexity from
a broader range of influences. Confit of duck leg served with vegetables à la
grecque, breast of corn-fed chicken stuffed with foie gras and sauced with a
truffle jus, or roast leg of rabbit filled with tarragon butter and wrapped in
pancetta with mustard sauce indicate that ambition does not flag. Nor is there
any misplaced reverence about the cooking: a terrine of ham shank and foie gras
with a smear of Cumberland sauce achieved for one 'an intriguing mixture of the
humble and the haute'. Vegetables are usually sound, cheeses are fine (although
one reporter found the staff unable to identify some of them), and breads are
always good. Regulars have noticed traces of greater formality creeping into the
restaurant service of late, but this is still a deservedly popular place – so much so,
that at peak times Hetton must find the press of traffic a little wearying.

The wine list continues to astonish for its breadth and a pricing policy of
exemplary fairness. Its main business is still in France and Italy, but the more
clipped treatment of the Americas and the southern hemisphere still shows a
knowledgeable mind at work. Note that Krug champagne is offered at no more
than the average retail price. Halves are hearteningly plentiful. House wines are
£8.95. CELLARMAN'S CHOICE: Pauillac, Ch. Lynch-Bages 1983, £27.50; Chorey-
lès-Beaune 1990, Ch. de Chorey-lès-Beaune, £15.60.

CHEFS: John Topham and Denis Watkins   PROPRIETORS: Denis and Juliet Watkins, and John
Topham   OPEN: restaurant Mon to Sat, D only, and Sun L; 12 to 2, 7 to 9.30. Bar/brasserie all
week; 12 to 2, 6 to 10 (9.30 Sun)   MEALS: bar/brasserie alc (main courses £5 to £11.50).
Restaurant Set L Sun £16.75, Set D £21.95   SERVICE: not inc   CARDS: Access, Visa   DETAILS:
restaurant 56 seats, bar/brasserie 63 seats. Private parties: 40 main room, 36 private room. Car
park. Vegetarian meals. Children welcome; children's helpings at Sun L only. Smart dress
preferred in restaurant. No smoking in 1 dining-room. Wheelchair access (1 step). No music.
One room air-conditioned. Fax: (0756) 730363

See the back of the Guide *for a listing of all restaurants in the Main Entries sections.*

HEXHAM Northumberland   map 7

Black House 🍴✻

Dipton Mill Road, Hexham NE46 1RZ
HEXHAM (0434) 604744   COOKING 2*
on Whitley Chapel road, S of Hexham   COST £25–£47

There can't be many restaurants reached by passing through a vast stable door,
but the Black House is set in the auxiliary buildings of an old Northumberland
farmhouse. Any austerity imparted by the bare stone walls and beams of the
dining area is more than offset by luxuriant festoons of dried flowers, and the
split-level design contributes a certain quirky character.

Hazel Pittock's cooking mobilises many different ingredients and flavours in a
labour-intensive but seemingly effortless style. A February menu offered a
three-fish feuilleté of smoked haddock, cod and oysters, as well as mushroom
and basil tartlet, Caesar salad (with or without anchovies), and main courses of
sufficient elaboration – as in pork fillet rolled in crushed peppercorns and sea
salt, served on a mustard cream sauce with crisp galettes of parsnip – to be
thought worthy of the silver-dome treatment. Desserts allow spices a say in pear
and ginger upside-down pudding, or spiced apple strudel with cinnamon
ice-cream. Trimmings like the very good canapés and the coffee elicit high
marks. If you bear in mind that wines are listed in vintage order, from oldest to
youngest, your path through the list will be made the easier. It is all French, with
the exception of a trio of Germans, and the choices are mostly very appealing.
There is a generous helping of halves, and prices are level-headed. House French
is £8.75.

CHEF: Hazel Pittock   PROPRIETORS: Chris and Hazel Pittock   OPEN: Tue to Sat, D only, and Sun
L before bank hols and on Mothering Sunday by arrangement; 12 to 1.30, 7 to 9.30   MEALS: alc
(main courses £8.50 to £16.50)   SERVICE: not inc, card slips closed   CARDS: Access, Visa
DETAILS: 28 seats. Private parties: 28 main room. Car park. Vegetarian meals. No children under
12. Smart dress preferred. No smoking in dining-room. Wheelchair access. Music

HIGH ONGAR Essex   map 3

The Shoes

The Street, High Ongar CM5 9ND
ONGAR (0277) 363350   COOKING 1*
off A414, between Harlow and Chelmsford   COST £23–£54

The building, a seventeenth-century former coaching-inn, is half-timbered,
with black beams and shoes everywhere: different types adorn every bit of shelf
space, mainly ceramic and painted, all single – 'I didn't check to see if they were
left or right feet.' The kitchen tries hard with ideas, although some of them may
suffer from what one reporter described as 'new-age trendiness', citing a goats'
cheese and kiwi-fruit terrine as the sort of thing that does not quite work. Some
flavours fail to reach threshold, while others are positively enthusiastic.

The kitchen is certainly high on zeal, turning out a first course of pan-fried
rabbit, stacked skywards on gaufrette potatoes, with a sauce of cream and pan
juices, followed by a refreshing grapefruit sorbet, then fillet of beef on a bed of

lentils and chickpeas, with bacon and a red wine jus. Sweets in general are very sweet. Caramel soufflé is creamy and well risen, accompanied by a rum-flavoured ice-cream with chopped prunes, while a small chocolate soufflé with a very sweet apricot sauce is one of several offerings, including 'a great mousse' and an orange chocolate tart, on the plate of chocolate desserts. Wines are a sensible collection from the major producing countries, and although some mark-ups are high there is good drinking under £20 and a fair selection of half-bottles. House wine is £9.95.

CHEF: Sue Kesseck   PROPRIETORS: Lyndon Wootton, and Peter and Doreen Gowan   OPEN: Tue to Sun, exc Sat L and Sun D; 12 to 2.30, 7 to 9.45   CLOSED: 1 week after Christmas   MEALS: alc (main courses £15 to £20). Set L £16   SERVICE: not inc, card slips closed   CARDS: Access, Visa   DETAILS: 58 seats. 4 tables outside. Private parties: 50 main room, 20 private room. Vegetarian meals. Children's helpings Sun L. Smart dress preferred. Wheelchair access (2 steps). Music

---

HINTLESHAM Suffolk   map 3

▲ *Hintlesham Hall* ♥ ⁵⁄✳

Hintlesham IP8 3NS
HINTLESHAM (0473) 652268   COOKING 3
on the A1071, 4½m W of Ipswich   COST £28–£60

Hintlesham is one of the more enticing country hotels, a Georgian-fronted Elizabethan house in extensive and well-kept grounds, with a legacy of sophisticated but unhackneyed décor. There are several dining-rooms – 'the one we were shown to was large, with acres of space between tables' – and luxuries abound, but any formality is compensated for by staff who are 'keen as mustard and nice with it'. The cooking is very creditable, raw materials are spot on, the food is technically excellent, presentation is wonderful and details are practically flawless, from salad dressings to the endless stream of varied canapés and appetisers that runs through reports: scallop on cucumber, vegetables in filo pastry, gravlax with dill mayonnaise, Welsh rarebits, mini pizzas, chicken liver parfait on croûtons.

The quarterly-changing *carte* is full of choice but, by its nature, lacks spontaneity and market sensitivity. Individual dishes score highly, from exquisite game pâté ('moist, well-flavoured and multiple-textured'), to well-hung steak correctly cooked, and bread-and-butter pudding 'as good as I have known'. Combinations can work well too, such as red pepper terrine served with a ratatouille-like sauce and pastry boats filled with truffled scrambled egg, or the flavour of moist guinea-fowl pointed up by braised and slightly bitter chicory. Yet somehow meals may lack impact as a whole and the 'bloat factor' can be high, as in a first course of sauté foie gras on a bed of polenta with ceps. Flavours can disappear before they reach the plate, leaving reporters upon occasion bemused about their absence and confused by food that does not appear to live up to the promise of the menu.

Superbly kept and served French and British unpasteurised cheeses are served with raisin and walnut breads. Wines cover a lot of ground (although their service can be under par), so choice is extensive and quality is high. Mark-ups are on the greedy side, but house French is £12.50. CELLARMAN'S CHOICE: Vins de Pays d'Oc, James Herrick Chardonnay 1992, £13.75; Rioja Gran Reserva 1975, Berberana, £26.40.

CHEF: Alan Ford   PROPRIETOR: Hintlesham Hall Ltd   OPEN: all week, exc Sat L; 12 to 1.45, 7 to 9.30   MEALS: alc (main courses £15.50 to £22). Set L weekdays £18.50, Sun £19.50, Set D Sun to Thur £23   SERVICE: net prices, card slips closed   CARDS: Access, Amex, Diners, Visa DETAILS: 120 seats. Private parties: 81 main room, 14 and 42 private rooms. Car park. Vegetarian meals. Children's helpings L. No children under 10 D. Smart dress preferred. No smoking in dining-room. Wheelchair access (1 step; also WC). Music   ACCOMMODATION: 33 rooms, all with bath/shower. TV. Phone. B&B £85 to £300. Children welcome. Pets welcome (not in public areas). Garden. Swimming-pool. Sauna. Tennis. Fishing. Golf. Snooker. Doors close at midnight. Confirm 1 day ahead. Fax: (0473) 652463 (*The Which? Hotel Guide*)

HINTON CHARTERHOUSE Avon   map 2

▲ *Homewood Park Hotel* 🏃✳

Hinton Charterhouse BA3 6BB
BATH (0225) 723731   COOKING 3
off A36, 6m SE of Bath   COST £29–£59

The large, mainly Georgian, ivy-covered country house of Bath stone is set in 10 acres of pretty grounds. Bay windows in the newly decorated and elegant dining-room look out on to a garden of flowers and mature trees, and rolling countryside. Well-spaced tables contribute to the sense of comfort and well-being. Swiss training ensures that the reception is welcoming and helpful, and service throughout is attentive, friendly, professional and discreet. What matters most is that 'the whole place lacks pretension and pomposity', for which the entire staff must take credit.

'We stayed three nights and worked through the menu' makes it sound hard graft for these reporters, yet the visit drew unstinting praise, underlining the consistency of the kitchen. Lightness is a characteristic of the cooking, as witnessed in a sausage of sole, salmon and sorrel with home-made spinach noodles and a spicy saffron infusion. Saucing, too, is on the gentle side, and pastry work is highly praised, both sweet and savoury. Puff pastry is a vehicle for spinach (to accompany pan-fried monkfish and asparagus) and for a first course of pink roasted wood pigeon, served with braised lentils. Lunch is a bargain, and dinner is lunch with knobs on. Thus roasted breast of corn-fed chicken with flageolet beans at lunch becomes pan-fried with oyster mushrooms as well, in a chervil sauce with truffles, for dinner. Some dishes, though, seem over-described. 'Imaginative and memorable' puddings include butterscotch cream tart with banana fritters and banana ice-cream. Presentation is regularly praised: 'From canapé to coffee it was a delight to the eye.'

Wines are intelligently selected in each region, and the list is brief enough to present a manageable choice. Comparison with the previous year (always an illuminating exercise) shows that prices have remained largely stable – some have even dropped slightly, making it even better value than before. There are 20 half-bottles. House wine is £12.50.

▲ *This symbol means accommodation is available.*

CHEF: Tim Ford   PROPRIETORS: Frank and Sara Gueuning   OPEN: all week; 12 to 1.30, 7 to 9.30   MEALS: alc (main courses £14.50 to £18.50). Set L £16 (2 courses) to £20, Set D £27.50   SERVICE: not inc   CARDS: Access, Amex, Diners, Visa   DETAILS: 50 seats. Private parties: 40 main room, 15 private room. Car park. Vegetarian meals. Children's helpings D (early sitting). Smart dress preferred. No smoking in dining-room. Wheelchair access (also WC). No music   ACCOMMODATION: 15 rooms, all with bath/shower. TV. Phone. B&B £80 to £140. Rooms for disabled. Children welcome (some bedrooms). Baby facilities. Afternoon teas. Garden. Tennis. Doors close at 11. Fax: (0225) 723820 (*The Which? Hotel Guide*)

HOLDENBY Northamptonshire   map 3

▲ *Lynton House* ⚡✶

Holdenby NN6 8DJ
NORTHAMPTON (0604) 770777
between A50 and A428, E of Holdenby   COOKING 2
towards Church Brampton   COST £21–£46

The Bertozzis have knocked through and added another extension – a small conservatory for drinks – to their old rectory. The views of rolling middle-England countryside close to Althorp are as restful as any. Italian cooking may have polarised into high street trattorias (three meats plus three shapes of pasta, times three sauces, equals a menu of 18 dishes) and the new-wave Mediterranean exponents, but Lynton House has had little to do with either. Sure, Carlo's background is Italian, hence the brodetto, ravioli and all the rest, but Carol is English, and the style that has developed combines family cooking with what the garden can provide.

Antipasti and pasta are the main strengths, from baby artichokes marinated in oil and herbs to zampone with olives, from gnocchi alla romana to the best ravioli, filled with spinach and ricotta, that one reporter had tasted. Mackerel fillets with lemon, sea bass with fennel and chargrilled squid are among an increasing range of fish options. Fillet of beef is a regular in some form – 'cooked exactly as I requested' – and other meats range from pigeon breast with wild mushrooms to pig's trotter with polenta. Puddings embrace strawberries with ricotta cream, crème brûlée and trifle (or zuppa inglese as it is called in the tussle for ownership), as well as the inevitable tiramisù. Italian wines are the natural accompaniment (consider Aglianico from the south or Bricco dei Manzoni from the north) with house wine at £9.75.

CHEF: Carol Bertozzi   PROPRIETORS: Carol and Carlo Bertozzi   OPEN: Mon to Sat, exc L Mon and Sat; 12.30 to 1.45, 7.30 to 9.45   CLOSED: Christmas, Easter, 2 weeks summer   MEALS: alc (main courses £12 to £17). Set L £11.50 (2 courses) to £16.75, Set D £19.75   SERVICE: not inc, card slips closed   CARDS: Access, Amex, Visa   DETAILS: 45 seats. 4 tables outside. Private parties: 60 main room, 20 private room. Car park. Vegetarian meals. Children's helpings. No children under 6. Smart dress preferred. No smoking in 1 dining-room. No cigars/pipes in dining-rooms. Wheelchair access (also men's WC). No music   ACCOMMODATION: 5 rooms, all with shower. TV. Phone. B&B £49 to £55. No children under 6. Garden. Doors close at midnight. Confirm by 9am (*The Which? Hotel Guide*)

Report forms are at the back of the book; write a letter if you prefer.

HOLT Norfolk   map 6

Yetman's ♈ ⚒

37 Norwich Road, Holt NR25 6SA   COOKING 2
HOLT (0263) 713320   COST £27–£46

'We were greeted enthusiastically by a gentleman with jeans and wild hair.'
Peter Yetman is not one to adopt the formal mode, and does not expect anybody
else to do so either. Some mistake the place for a pub, and are surprised to find a
smart, polished dining-room and accomplished food within. The frequently
changing menus are priced according to the number of courses taken (up to four)
and are kept within sensible bounds. Dishes tend to the simple and are all the
more enjoyed for that. An April evening menu took in twice-baked cheese
soufflé with salad, gravlax, sauté chicken livers with pancetta on brioche,
poached turbot with a white wine and mushroom sauce 'of high quality', and
chargrilled fillet of lamb with leeks and redcurrant jelly. Recommendations also
come for 'truly wonderful' moules marinière full of 'plumptious' specimens
from the Stiffkey boats, basil pancakes stuffed with spinach and ricotta in a
cream sauce with Parmesan, and 'beautifully made' chocolate roulade with
raspberries.

The wine list is very intelligently put together. It leads with the USA, New
Zealand and Australia before concluding its business with a brisk but clever
trawl through France. There is a formidable choice below £20. Prices open at
£9.25. CELLARMAN'S CHOICE: Oyster Bay Chardonnay 1993, £14.25; Margaux,
Ch. Labégorce Zédé 1989, £19.50.

CHEF: Alison Yetman   PROPRIETORS: Alison and Peter Yetman   OPEN: Sat and Sun L (bookings
only Oct to Apr), Wed to Sun D (Mon D summer), L and D Good Fri and bank hol Mons; 12.30 to 2,
7.30 to 9 (7 to 9.30 summer)   MEALS: Set L Sat £14.95 (2 courses) to £22.25, Set L Sun £19.75 (2
courses) to £27. Set D £19.75 (2 courses) to £27   SERVICE: not inc   DETAILS: 32 seats. Private
parties: 20 main room, 12 private room. Vegetarian meals. Children's helpings on request. No
smoking in dining-room. Wheelchair access (1 step). No music

HONLEY West Yorkshire   map 5

Mustards & Punch   NEW ENTRY

6 Westgate, Honley HD7 2AA   COOKING 2
HUDDERSFIELD (0484) 662066   COST £21–£41

Those puzzled by the name of this shop-turned-eatery will find clarification
dawning as they enter. Display cabinets are filled with pots of mustard, and
framed cartoons from *Punch* adorn the walls. Scott Hessel's new bistro, with its
clutter of potted palms, Chinese lanterns, bookcases and sewing-machines may
make you feel you have wandered on to a set of *The Caretaker*, but any Pinteresque
intimations are quickly dispelled by booming jazz and the arrival of the menu.
Scott Hessel is a Roux-trained high-flyer who has done short stints with
London megachefs, and also worked at the Crab & Lobster (see entry, Asenby).
Habitués of the latter will recognise the style as much in the food as in the décor.
The man can cook. Menus are changed so frequently they are simply chalked on
blackboards. The style is a faithful rendition of what might almost be the

quintessential '90s style: vigorous modernism in the starters (goats' cheese 'tarte Tatin' with sun-dried tomatoes and pesto, warm salad of lobster and tapénade, Thai prawn salad) shading to brasserie classicism in the main dishes (côte de boeuf grillé, plateau de fruits de mer, rack of lamb with tarragon and tomato) and atavistic nostalgia in the puddings (sticky toffee, spotted dick). At an inspection meal, good judgement was shown in a dish of grilled scallops with a light, saffroned curry sauce, and shoulder of lamb with garlic and shallots was 'sweet and tender' meat in a 'well-reduced tasty gravy'. The sticky toffee pudding and a lemon and passion-fruit tart finished things well. Cheeses have been properly matured. Service is 'cheerful and pleasant', and does its faltering best when both basement and ground-floor rooms are full. Here we have a neighbourhood favourite in the making.

The Bateman cartoons on the wine list may detain the attention for longer than the brief list itself, but the selections are sound, pleasingly eclectic and made with an eye to value. Nearly everything is under £20. House wines from La Chaumière are £7.95.

CHEF/PROPRIETOR: Scott Hessel   OPEN: Tue to Sat, exc Sat L; 12 to 2.30, 7 to 10 (11 Sat)
MEALS: alc (main courses £8 to £15)   SERVICE: not inc, card slips closed   CARDS: Access,
Visa   DETAILS: 60 seats. Private parties: 34 main room. Car park. Vegetarian meals. Children
welcome. No cigars/pipes in dining-room. Wheelchair access (1 step). Music. Air-conditioned

---

HORNCASTLE Lincolnshire   map 6

Magpies £✸

73–75 East Street, Horncastle LN9 6AA   COOKING 1
HORNCASTLE (0507) 527004   COST £15–£36

Things run smoothly at this well-oiled restaurant, the pace is relaxed and the welcome pleasantly familiar. Matthew Lee and family have succeeded in nurturing a loyal band of customers, many of whom are now friends. They are committed to using local produce, including naturally reared beef, although luxury ingredients are normally reserved for occasional gourmet evenings. This translates into a short menu that has strong modern French overtones and a few touches of individual flair. One very satisfactory meal took in feuilletine of oyster mushrooms with a salad of asparagus, ragoût of oysters and scallops, and roast guinea-fowl with coriander, orange and thyme jus. Vegetables are handled capably and desserts such as 'divine' lemon tart with pear ice-cream round things off well. The wine list continues to grow; France dominates, although other countries are represented. Eight house wines are all priced at £7.50.

CHEFS: Matthew and Simon Lee   PROPRIETORS: the Lee family   OPEN: Tue to Sat, D only, and
Sun L; 12.30 to 1.45, 7.30 to 10   CLOSED: 2 weeks Sept   MEALS: alc D Sat (main courses
£10.50 to £12.50). Set L Sun £9.50, Set D Tue to Fri £14.95. Minimum £12.50 D   SERVICE: not
inc   CARDS: Access, Visa   DETAILS: 40 seats. Private parties: 40 main room. Vegetarian meals
with prior notice. Children's helpings Sun L. No children under 4. Smart dress preferred. No
smoking in dining-room. Wheelchair access. Music

The Guide always appreciates hearing about changes of chef or owner.

HORSHAM West Sussex   map 3

Cole's 🍴✗

Worthing Road, Southwater,	
Horsham RH13 7BS	COOKING 2
HORSHAM (0403) 730456	COST £27–£40

NEW ENTRY

'No frills, high quality' was the succinct conclusion of one reporter of this family business that began in 1991. Mr and Mrs Cole run front-of-house while daughter Elizabeth cooks. The long, low, sixteenth-century house, very pretty, very rustic, is in a picture-postcard setting behind a large pond 'with plastic ducks. But they fooled me!' Inside it looks 'exactly what you would expect from a home counties barn: lofty ceiling, dark beams, cream walls'.

Menus don't change much, and success is judged on the basis of good-quality meats – Scottish beef or roast rack of spring lamb – cooked as requested and 'full of flavour'. Traditional flavourings and partnerships of liver and sage, pork fillet with apple and cider, skate with black butter, and boned roast duck with orange and ginger, form the basis of a sound repertoire. 'I suspect Miss Cole must be a pâtissier first and foremost,' guessed one reporter after sampling a circle of sablé pastry with fanned apple slices glazed on top. Otherwise there might be sticky toffee pudding or raspberry vacherin. Service is smiling, helpful and efficient. The wines, two dozen French and a handful of others, span a reasonable range of prices. House wine is £9.25 (£1.60 per glass).

CHEF: Elizabeth Cole   PROPRIETORS: the Cole family   OPEN: Tue to Sun; 12 to 2, 7 to 9 (Sun D by arrangement only)   MEALS: alc (main courses £10 to £15). Set L £12.95 (2 courses) to £15 SERVICE: not inc   CARDS: Access, Amex, Diners, Visa   DETAILS: 36 seats. Private parties: 36 main room. Car park. Vegetarian meals. Children's helpings. Smart dress preferred. No smoking in dining-room. Wheelchair access (2 steps; also WC). Music

---

HORTON Northamptonshire   map 3

French Partridge 🍷 🍴✗

Horton NN7 2AP	
NORTHAMPTON (0604) 870033	COOKING 3
on B526, 5m SE of Northampton	COST £28–£36

Thirty years is a long life for a restaurant, let alone a partridge, but that is how long this family-run establishment on the Northampton to Newport Pagnell road has been going. Whole eras of fashion have come and gone, and the Partridges have drawn what they like best from it all, and let history deal with the rest. The setting is an old coaching-inn, modestly decorated and comfortable. Menus change with the seasons, and offer four courses plus coffee for a fixed price that rises by £1 on Saturdays.

The aim, says the kitchen, is 'consistency rather than shock tactics', but that does not mean the food stays permanently in France. A winter menu offered Bermuda fish chowder, blinis filled with sour cream and smoked salmon, Moroccan-style lamb meatballs in a tomato sauce seasoned with cumin, allspice and mint, and key lime pie. The second course is usually an alternative of fish or a vegetable-based dish, often richly done with fortified wines, such as grilled halibut with banana and sherry sauce or mushrooms in a crisp bread case with madeira sauce. Puddings bring on crème brûlée with apricots, or iced pear soufflé with raspberry sauce. It is all precisely weighted so that, in the words of one man, 'this is no place for boisterous over-indulgence'. If doubts creep in, the fault may seem to lie in sauces that overwhelm the main ingredient, as in that banana and sherry potion that seemed 'far too sweet' for one. Others appreciate the 'friendly and congenial' approach, and the adaptability readily forthcoming for somebody who wanted to expand a first-course dish into a main.

If further evidence of the Partridges' friendly intentions is required, cast a wondering eye over the wine list. It is an enterprising collection of top-quality bottles at virtual giveaway prices. Burgundy growers include Gagnard, Clerget, Lespinasse and Forest, Rhônes take in Graillot's Crozes-Hermitage and Chante Cigale Chateauneuf, and there are fine German Rieslings and good New Zealand Sauvignons, as well as a slate of house selections that travels from the Ardèche to Woughton Park table wine from Milton Keynes. Halves are generously provided. House wines start at £9. CELLARMAN'S CHOICE: Chablis Grand Cru 1992, Fèvre, £16.50; Haut-Médoc, Ch. Cissac 1985, £21.

CHEFS: David Partridge and Justin Partridge   PROPRIETORS: David and Mary Partridge   OPEN: Tue to Sat, D only; 7.30 to 9   CLOSED: 2 weeks Christmas, 2 weeks Easter, first 3 weeks Aug   MEALS: Set D weekdays £23, Set D Sat £24   SERVICE: net prices   DETAILS: 50 seats. Private parties: 16 main room. Car park. Vegetarian meals. Children welcome. No smoking in dining-room. No smoking room. Wheelchair access. No music. Fax: (0604) 870032

HUDDERSFIELD West Yorkshire   map 5

Bradley's £   NEW ENTRY

84 Fitzwilliam Street,
Huddersfield HD1 5BB   COOKING 1*
HUDDERSFIELD (0484) 516773   COST £14–£36

Andrew Bradley (ex-head waiter at the Box Tree, Ilkley) has teamed up with his friend Johnathan Nichols to open this restaurant in a stone building once occupied by Paris 2. Inside is a split-level dining area with dim lights, parquet floors and brown anaglypta walls. Andrew runs the front-of-house with chatty confidence and is supported by a well-trained team. Most interest centres on the excellent-value 'early bird menu' (the fixed price includes half a bottle of wine), which runs along the lines of devilled lambs' kidneys in a filo basket, creamy fish stew and hot strawberries in a puff-pastry parcel with rosewater sauce. Ingredients and technique – especially with sauces – are impressively good. The full *carte*, plus a list of blackboard specials, treads a similar path: poached salmon and chive sausage, sauté king prawns with garlic and coriander, excellent pink duck breast with a confit of its leg and madeira sauce, bangers and mash. Cheeses are English. The wine list is an adequate mix of mainly New World and second-division French offerings with plenty of decent drinking for around £12. House wines start at £6.95.

See inside the front cover for an explanation of the symbols used at the tops of entries.

CHEFS: Jonathan Nichols and Kyle Hopkin   PROPRIETORS: Jonathan Nichols and Andrew Bradley   OPEN: Mon to Sat, exc Sat L; 12 to 2, 6 to 10.30   CLOSED: bank hol Mons   MEALS: alc (main courses £6.50 to £13). Set L £9.95, Set D £11.95 (6 to 7.30 Tue to Fri, 6 to 7 Sat, 6 to 9 Mon)   SERVICE: not inc   CARDS: Access, Visa   DETAILS: 65 seats. Private parties: 65 main room. Car park. Vegetarian meals. Children's helpings on request. No cigars/pipes in dining-room. Wheelchair access (also WC). Music. Air-conditioned

---

▲ *Lodge Hotel* ⚡✳

48 Birkby Lodge Road, Birkby,
Huddersfield HD2 2BG   COOKING 1*
HUDDERSFIELD (0484) 431001   COST £20–£38

A couple enjoyed contemplating the view of 'summer rhododendrons and glinting evening sunlight' from the lounge, and found the dining-room 'a pleasant place to dine'. Dinner is a fixed-price four-course affair, with a daily changing soup or sorbet after the starter. Dishes move with the seasons and reflect a modern British temperament. A man who frequently dives for eels was impressed by a warm salad of smoked eel with button mushrooms, bacon and caramelised shallots and a blackberry vinegar dressing, while another warm salad, this time from the extensive vegetarian menu, brought together wild mushrooms, aubergine and pine-nuts in an orange dressing and was pronounced 'absolutely delicious'. The soup – a Toveyesque blend of watercress, pea and pear – 'worked a treat'. Chicken breast came with lobster tail and was 'brilliantly offset' by a sauce of crayfish and dill. The cheeseboard is an international selection and desserts offer richnesses like chocolate mousse, a cake of apple, prune and armagnac, and banoffi pie. Coffee comes with good home-made chocolate truffles. The wine list shows a determination to seek out decent growers at fair prices across the geographical spectrum. Highlights include Crochet's Sancerre, white burgundies from Leflaive and Sanford Pinot Noir from Santa Barbara. Nine house recommendations start at £9.50.

CHEFS: Richard Hanson, Kevin Birley and Garry Birley   PROPRIETORS: Kevin Birley and Garry Birley   OPEN: all week, exc Sat L and Sun D; 12 to 2, 7.30 to 9.45   CLOSED: 26 Dec, Easter Mon   MEALS: alc L Mon to Fri (main courses £6.50 to £9). Set L Sun £11.95, Set D £21.95. Minimum £6.95 L   SERVICE: not inc, card slips closed   CARDS: Access, Amex, Visa   DETAILS: 50 seats. 4 tables outside. Private parties: 62 main room, 10 to 22 private rooms. Car park. Vegetarian meals. Children's helpings. No children under 5 D. Smart dress preferred. No smoking in dining-room. Wheelchair access (1 step; also WC). Music   ACCOMMODATION: 11 rooms, all with bath/shower. TV. Phone. B&B £45 to £70. Rooms for disabled. Children welcome. Baby facilities. Pets welcome (not in public rooms). Afternoon teas. Garden. Snooker. Doors close at 1am. Fax: (0484) 421590 (*The Which? Hotel Guide*)

The Guide office can quickly spot when a restaurateur is encouraging customers to write recommending inclusion – and sadly, several restaurants have been doing this in 1994. Such reports do not further a restaurant's cause. Please tell us if a restaurateur invites you to write to the Guide.

The Guide is totally independent, accepts no free hospitality, and survives on the number of copies sold each year.

HUNSTRETE Avon map 2

▲ *Hunstrete House* ⁵⅟✳

Hunstrete, Chelwood BS18 4NS
CHEWTON MENDIP (0761) 490490 COOKING 2
off A368, 4m S of Keynsham COST £23–£56

This seventeenth-century Georgian manor house was acquired by Arcadian International plc at the end of 1993. The previous chef went to Australia, and has been replaced by former sous-chef Robert Clayton. People enjoy the 'utter magic' of the setting. A pair who lingered on a 'rustic bench' in the garden after lunch, watching others lost in concentration over the croquet mallets, found it 'very relaxing'. The aim, says the management, is 'an honest depiction of grand country living, not Chelsea-on-Avon'.

The dining-room is decorated in a restfully cool peach shade, and menus demonstrate good judgement in the conception of dishes, so that nothing sounds as if it has too many layers. Among the offerings on a spring dinner menu were roast foie gras with olive and morel brioche and glazed orange, grilled red mullet with basil creamed potato and sauce vierge, and herb-crusted fillet of lamb with potato rösti and a tomato jus. At an inspection lunch a smoked salmon and cream cheese mousse wrapped in smoked salmon gained point from a lemony vinaigrette, while a terrine of salmon and monkfish with fennel came with an upstanding accompaniment of mustard sauce. Steamed guinea-fowl – a kind of sausage – had a gelatinous burgundy sauce that was gratefully mopped up with bread. Good sorbets of mango, coconut and strawberry came with a 'brandy-snap frisbee', but the cheese selection seemed a bit tired. An admirable range of coffees is offered, along with plentiful petits fours. If you have less than £20 to spend on wine, you will find your choice within France severely curtailed, while selections outside are perfunctory. Otherwise the handsomely resourced will enjoy poring over the glories of Bordeaux and Burgundy. House wine is £10.50.

CHEF: Robert Clayton PROPRIETOR: Arcadian International plc OPEN: all week; 12.30 to 2, 7.30 to 9.30 MEALS: alc (main courses £12 to £19). Set L Mon to Sat £15, Sun £19.50, Set D £23.50 SERVICE: not inc, card slips closed CARDS: Access, Amex, Visa DETAILS: 50 seats. 6 tables outside. Private parties: 50 main room, 30 private room. Car park. Vegetarian meals. Children by arrangement. Jacket and tie. No smoking in dining-room. Wheelchair access (also WC). Music ACCOMMODATION: 24 rooms, all with bath/shower. TV. Phone. B&B £95 to £115. Children by arrangement. Pets welcome (not in public rooms). Afternoon teas. Garden. Swimming-pool. Tennis. Confirm by 6. Fax: (0761) 490732

All details are as accurate as possible at the time of going to press, but chefs and owners often change, and it is wise to check by telephone before making a special journey. Many readers have been disappointed when set-price bargain meals are no longer available. Ask when booking.

Several sharp operators have tried to extort money from restaurateurs on the promise of an entry in a guidebook that has never appeared. The Good Food Guide makes no charge for inclusion and does not offer certificates of any kind.

HURSTBOURNE TARRANT Hampshire   map 2

▲ *Esseborne Manor* ♟

Hurstbourne Tarrant SP11 0ER
HURSTBOURNE TARRANT (0264) 736444   COOKING 2
on the A343, 1½m N of Hurstbourne Tarrant   COST £20–£49

This well-decorated manor house dates from the late Victorian era and once
served as the farmhouse for the surrounding estate. At lunch-time, a prix fixe
menu is offered, which may be taken either as three courses or as a two-course
'quickie', as well as a bargain three-course no-choice option; a slightly longer
carte is the routine for dinner. The food has an earthy, countrified feel to it. A
spring dinner menu included curly endive salad with Swiss cheese and smoked
ham in a Dijon mustard dressing served in 'enormous' quantity, salmon
marinated in tomato and coriander with toasted olive bread, and lamb's liver
with smoked bacon and caramelised onions and a mustard gravy.

Reporters at an April lunch approved 'delicious' leek and potato soup with
toasted almonds, a duo of sauté salmon and plaice with ratatouille, and
good-quality roast beef and Yorkshire pudding, but found a vegetable
mousseline 'bland' although enlivened with a 'piquant' dressing of diced
peppers and yogurt. Chocolate mousse was enjoyed by a dessert agnostic.
Service is commended as 'excellently timed and good-humoured'. Equally
commendable is the intelligent and wide-ranging wine list. It is extremely
reliable in the classic regions of France, including representatives of nine of the
ten cru villages of Beaujolais, a short but good Rhône selection and Alsaces from
Trimbach. Australia and New Zealand are well served. House Australian is £12.
CELLARMAN'S CHOICE: Cloudy Bay Sauvignon 1993, £16; Mercurey premier cru
'Les Velay' 1990, Dom. de la Monette, £23.40.

CHEF: Andrew Norman PROPRIETORS: Michael and Frieda Yeo, and Simon Richardson OPEN:
all week; 12.30 to 2, 7.30 to 9.30 MEALS: alc D (main courses £11 to £17.50). Set L £9.95 to
£17.50, Set D £17.50 to £27.50 SERVICE: not inc, card slips closed CARDS: Access, Amex,
Diners, Visa DETAILS: 36 seats. Private parties: 36 main room. Car park. Vegetarian meals. No
children under 12. Smart dress preferred. Wheelchair access (also WC). No music
ACCOMMODATION: 12 rooms, all with bath/shower. TV. Phone. B&B £84 to £125. Rooms for
disabled. No children under 12. Afternoon teas. Tennis. Fax: (0264) 736473 (*The Which? Hotel
Guide*)

HUXHAM Devon   map 1

▲ *Barton Cross*

Huxham, Stoke Canon EX5 4EJ
EXETER (0392) 841245
½m from A396 Exeter to Tiverton road at   COOKING 1*
Stoke Canon, 5m N of Exeter   COST £32–£39

Set in the Exe Valley, but only 10 minutes' drive from Exeter, this country hotel
is a pleasing conversion of three seventeenth-century thatched cottages,
complete with exposed beams and inglenooks. Bedrooms, by contrast, are
thoroughly modern. Meals are served in an unusual galleried restaurant, and the
owners draw supplies from helpful neighbourhood sources. Fish comes from a

345

local trawlerman, potatoes from the farm next door and soft fruit from a lady in the village. Menus are fixed-price for two or three courses (plus a sorbet) and the style shows in dishes such as pan-fried sardines with fiery piri-piri sauce, honey-glazed breast of duckling with spiced plum sauce, and local venison steaks with parsnip purée and a sauce of sloe gin and peppercorns. Home-made sweets come with clotted cream, and cheeses are English. The wine list is a keenly priced, knowledgeably chosen collection of the classic and the new. House wine is around £10.50.

CHEF: Stuart Fowles   PROPRIETORS: Mr and Mrs R.V.J. Ball   OPEN: Mon to Sat; 12.30 to 1.45, 7 to 9.30   MEALS: Set L and D £18.50 (2 courses) to £22.50   SERVICE: not inc, card slips closed   CARDS: Access, Amex, Diners, Visa   DETAILS: 32 seats. 4 tables outside. Private parties: 38 main room, 10 private room. Car park. Vegetarian meals. Children's helpings. Smart dress preferred. Wheelchair access. Music   ACCOMMODATION: 7 rooms, all with bath/shower. TV. Phone. B&B £63.50 to £85. Children welcome. Baby facilities. Pets welcome. Afternoon teas. Garden. Confirm by 6. Fax: (0392) 841942

ILKLEY West Yorkshire   map 5

Box Tree

35–37 Church Street, Ilkley LS29 9DR   COOKING 3*
ILKLEY (0943) 608484   COST £35–£51

It looks much the same as it always has: an eighteenth-century building, once a farmhouse, that has been 'furnished eccentrically', although some of the more flashy and sentimental items have gone, to be replaced by works with more credibility and artistic interest. 'The general mix of classiness and cottageyness remains.' Another change is the arrival of Thierry Leprêtre-Granet from White-chapel Manor (see entry, South Molton) just as the *Guide* was going to press last year. He impresses not only for his technical accomplishment but also for the signs of an individual identity. The more classical side of the quarterly-changing menu shows in foie gras 'properly seized on the outside, pink and sweet inside, served with pickled artichoke hearts and some well-dressed salad leaves', while more contemporary notes are struck in fillet of cod with a white port and balsamic vinegar sauce, and turbot with spices, celeriac purée and veal jus.

Dinner, which begins with an impressive batch of canapés, is three courses plus an appetiser: at one meal a cylinder of smoked salmon filled with aubergine purée. A first course proper of pig's trotter stuffed with mushrooms and duck liver sounds a bit Desperate Dannish, even for Yorkshire, but in fact it is served cold, 'a few slices carefully crafted', arranged on a base of cauliflower florets, button onions and mushrooms à la greque. Warmth and depth of flavour pervade the cooking, from rich roast loin of hare with a red wine and game sauce to a 'masterful' osso buco which was 'two meltingly tender slices of veal shin, the bone filled with marrow, served with root and green vegetables cut in tiny dice'. Taste was enhanced by a sauce of madeira, stock and orange juice, and accurately cooked wild rice replaced the customary risotto; an elegant version of the traditional dish.

'Speaking as one who can take desserts or leave them, I have to declare that my lemon tart was brilliant: a crisp wafer-thin pastry case filled with de-pithed segments of lemon coated in a sweet glaze which masked all suggestion of tartness while retaining the juice and freshness of the fruit.' Throughout, flavours are mostly well-judged, only occasionally let down by extremes of over- or under-seasoning. Good coffee – a choice of strengths and blends – comes with more excellent pastrywork. Service is accomplished, although no harm would come if it relaxed a bit more. Wines jump through the usual hoops, although some producers are unusual. Mark-ups are about standard, half-bottles are good, house wine is £13, and several wines are available by the glass to suit the menu.

CHEF: Thierry Leprêtre-Granet PROPRIETOR: The Box Tree Restaurant Ilkley Ltd OPEN: Tue to Sat, exc Sat L and Sun D (Sat L by arrangement); 12 to 2.30, 7 to 10.30 CLOSED: last 2 weeks Jan MEALS: Set L £22.50, Set D £29.50 SERVICE: not inc, card slips closed CARDS: Access, Amex, Visa DETAILS: 60 seats. Private parties: 32 main room, 14 private room. Vegetarian meals. Children's helpings. Smart dress preferred. No-smoking area. No cigars/pipes in dining-room. Wheelchair access. No music. Fax: (0943) 607186

IPSWICH Suffolk   map 3

Kwok's Rendezvous £

23 St Nicholas Street, Ipswich IP1 1TW   COOKING 1
IPSWICH (0473) 256833   COST £18–£32

A seventeenth-century town house with a Georgian front is an unlikely setting for a provincial Chinese restaurant, but Ipswich is lucky to have such a place. Thomas Kwok's 70-dish menu is a mixture of Peking and Szechuan, with a repertoire that takes in sesame prawn toasts, bang-bang chicken, piquant Ganshaw prawns, double-cooked pork and sauté lotus root with hot bean paste. Peking duck and aromatic crispy duck are perennial favourites. Regulars confirm that the food is 'consistently excellent'. House wine is £7.30.

CHEF: Thomas Kwok PROPRIETORS: Lucia and Thomas Kwok OPEN: Mon to Sat (Sat L by arrangement only); 12 to 2, 7.15 to 10.30 CLOSED: 2 weeks spring MEALS: alc (main courses £4.50 to £6). Set L and D £13.95 to £15.95 (minimum 2). Minimum £9.95 SERVICE: not inc CARDS: Access, Amex, Visa DETAILS: 50 seats. Private parties: 50 main room. Vegetarian meals. Children welcome. Smart dress preferred. Wheelchair access (2 steps; also WC). Music

Mortimer's on the Quay £

Wherry Quay, Ipswich IP4 1AS   COOKING 1
IPSWICH (0473) 230225   COST £19–£42

This warehouse conversion, on the water-front at Ipswich docks, is the partner of the original Mortimer's in Bury St Edmunds (see entry). Although the culinary purpose is exactly the same – the freshest fish and seafood, classically prepared – the cooking here tends to be slightly more elaborate. Starters such as rollmops in sherry, crab pâté with toast and gravlax may be straightforward enough, but main courses let fly with a variety of well-constructed sauces and accompaniments. John Dory comes with a prawn and dill butter, salmon with shrimps and hollandaise, brill with béarnaise, and monkfish with a mild curry cream sauce and rice. For a resonant finale, try the chocolate pot spiked with

Pusser's Navy rum. Fish-shaped Belgian chocolates accompany coffee. The wine list offers a generous choice. House French is £7.25.

CHEFS: Kenneth Ambler and Carol Theobald   PROPRIETORS: Kenneth Ambler and Michael Gooding   OPEN: Mon to Sat, exc Sat L; 12 to 2, 7 to 9 (6.30 to 8.15 Mon)   CLOSED: 23 Dec to 6 Jan, last 2 weeks Aug, bank hols   MEALS: alc (main courses £7.50 to £17)   SERVICE: not inc CARDS: Access, Amex, Diners, Visa   DETAILS: 80 seats. Private parties: 12 main room, 20 private room. Vegetarian meals. Children's helpings. Smart dress preferred. No-smoking area. Wheelchair access (1 step; also WC). No music. Fax: (0284) 752561

IXWORTH Suffolk   map 6

Theobalds ♥ ⁵⭑

68 High Street, Ixworth IP31 2HJ	COOKING 2
PAKENHAM (0359) 231707	COST £24–£46

The Theobald family have been going well over a decade in their intimate and well-supported restaurant in this quiet Suffolk village north of Bury St Edmunds. Pre- and post-dinner business is conducted before a large brick inglenook fireplace in winter, on the patio in summer. Everybody seems to know everybody else, which makes for a relaxed atmosphere. Menus are priced by choice of main course and change seasonally. Tiny home-made bread rolls are plentiful and 'greeted everywhere with delight'. A winter menu offered chicken and leek soup with chicken dumplings, salad of smoked ham, Gruyère, mushrooms and croûtons with a mustard dressing, noisettes of hare wrapped in bacon with a blackcurrant-flavoured game stock and fillet of sea bass with roast fennel and a white port and mustard sauce. Twice-baked cheese soufflé with a brittle top is a good stalwart. An inspector felt that desserts let the side down a bit, and coffee, too, fails to impress.

A cosmopolitan wine list affords lots of choice from good producers at manageable prices. There is a profusion of halves, and if a caveat should be entered, it is that the classic French bottles tend to be predominantly on the youthful side. Country wines start at £10.30. CELLARMAN'S CHOICE: Bourgogne Chardonnay, Les Champs Perriers 1990, Henri Clerc, £17.95; Hollick Coonawarra Shiraz 1990, £18.70.

CHEF: Simon Theobald   PROPRIETORS: Simon and Geraldine Theobald   OPEN: Tue to Sun, exc Sat L and Sun D; 12 to 1.30, 7 to 9.30   CLOSED: bank hols   MEALS: Set L £12.95 (2 courses) to £15.95, Set D £20.50 (vegetarian) to £28.50, Set 'fish supper' Fri 29.50 (inc wine)   SERVICE: not inc   CARDS: Access, Visa   DETAILS: 36 seats. Private parties: 40 main room. Vegetarian meals. Children's helpings. No children under 7 D. Smart dress preferred. No smoking in dining-room. No music

---

⁵⭑ *indicates that smoking is either banned altogether or that a dining-room is maintained for non-smokers. The symbol does not apply to restaurants that simply have no-smoking areas.*

The 1996 Guide will be published before Christmas 1995. Reports on meals are most welcome at any time of the year, but are particularly valuable in the spring. Send them to The Good Food Guide, *FREEPOST, 2 Marylebone Road, London NW1 1YN. No stamp is needed if posted in the UK.*

JEVINGTON East Sussex   map 3

Hungry Monk ✸

Jevington BN26 5QF
POLEGATE (0323) 482178
off A22/A259, between Polegate   COOKING 1*
and Friston   COST £30–£48

The setting is an 'outrageously picturesque village' in a South Downs valley. The house is fifteenth-century, a terrace of cottages 'knocked with reasonable sensitivity' into one building with a string of small sitting-rooms, each with a log fire in winter. The restaurant has been around since the late '60s and still packs in the crowds; it is a carefully managed operation in which it is possible to feel processed.

Some of the food harks back a long way – chicken liver pâté en croûte or marinated loin of pork with juniper berries and cream, for instance. This is also the original home of banoffi pie, but sun-dried tomatoes in a vegetarian risotto show a response to changing times. Nevertheless, an inspector felt that the kitchen is being led by a rather safe formula, endlessly repeated without much enthusiasm or vitality, yet 'just sophisticated enough to tempt the Volvos out of Lewes'. Some dishes at that meal were good, including calf's liver with green peppercorn sauce, fillets of brill and salmon with scallops, and a warm tart of orange, ginger and almond with crème fraîche. Five vegetables are served with the main course, and coffee comes with a glass of house ruby port. The press of custom may explain why service has been 'without warmth or interest', and 'very uninvolved'. The slightly conservative range of wines has a decent run of bourgeois clarets and a quartet of English wines, including one from the justly celebrated Breaky Bottom.

CHEFS: Claire Burgess and Thai La Roche PROPRIETORS: Sue and Nigel Mackenzie OPEN: all week, D only, and Sun L; 12 to 2.45, 7 to 10.30 MEALS: Set L and D £20.90 SERVICE: not inc (12.5% for 8 or more) CARDS: Amex DETAILS: 40 seats. Private parties: 40 main room, 6, 10 and 16 private rooms. Car park. Vegetarian meals. Children's helpings. No children under 3. Smart dress preferred. No smoking in dining-room. Music

---

KELSALE Suffolk   map 3

Hedgehog Hall ✸

Main Road, Kelsale IP17 2RF
SAXMUNDHAM (0728) 602420 and 604499   COOKING 1
on W side of A12, 1m N of Saxmundham   COST £17–£36

Visitors to the Aldeburgh Festival or the Proms at Snape may like to know a late dinner can be had at the Hedgehog, a timbered building with thatched roof and, according to one man, 'charming ambience'. Boards with different menus abound, but you can mix and match between them, and there is masses of choice. Dishes are homely and comforting and may include black pudding with apple and ginger relish, grilled sirloin with garlic mushrooms, or 'wicked bread-and-butter pudding' with a slug of Scotch. Approval has been signalled for locally made spicy sausages, trout fillet with a herbed sauce, and strong-tasting lemon tart with 'a large dab of clotted cream'. Dissatisfaction was reported by one group who waited and waited for food one Sunday lunch-time, and found the Hedgehog at its prickliest when they spoke up. Others have experienced just the opposite temperament and go on to praise the 'excellent value for money'. The wine list contains some good bottles, but is one of those stream-of-consciousness types that has no presentational logic other than colour. A range of house wines, including a Navarra red cheerfully described as 'Spanish plonk', is £7.95.

CHEF: Sara Fox   PROPRIETORS: Sara Fox and Peter Hill   OPEN: Tue to Sun; 12 to 2.30, 7 to 10 (later during Aldeburgh Festival and Snape Proms)   MEALS: alc L Tue to Sat (main courses £5 to £11.50). Set L Sun £10.75, Set D £13.50 (2 courses) to £15.75   SERVICE: not inc   CARDS: Access, Visa   DETAILS: 60 seats. 6 tables outside. Private parties: 30 main room, 40 private room. Car park. Vegetarian meals. Children's helpings. No smoking in dining-room. Wheelchair access (1 step; also WC). Music. Fax: (0728) 602420

KENDAL Cumbria

map 7

Moon ⅙✳ £

129 Highgate, Kendal LA9 4EN   COOKING 1
KENDAL (0539) 729254   COST £18–£27

Valerie Macconnell closed her popular bistro-restaurant for a month early in 1994 to refurbish the place, research recipes and re-plan her kitchen. A new butcher and fishmonger have helped to broaden the repertoire, which is a mixed bag with a marked vegetarian presence. Menus change each month and dishes sound colourfully enticing. Mango and Brie strudel with tomato and ginger coulis or prawn kebabs with satay sauce are typical starters. Main dishes are in similar vein: Mexican pork tortillas, spiced lamb and apricot bobotie, mushroom and broad-bean korma. Sweets have included spotted dick with 'really good custard' and splendid home-made ice-creams. A monthly 'starter club' is planned in addition to the popular 'pudding club'. Informality, excellent value and pleasant service outweigh any lack of refinement in the cooking. European bottled beers supplement the short list of reasonably priced wines. House wine is £7.55 a litre.

CHEFS: Sharon Moreton and Valerie Macconnell   PROPRIETOR: Valerie Macconnell   OPEN: all week, D only; 6.30 (6 Sat) to 10   MEALS: alc (main courses £7 to £8.50)   SERVICE: not inc, card slips closed   CARDS: Access, Visa   DETAILS: 38 seats. Private parties: 40 main room, 28 private room. Vegetarian meals. Children's helpings. No smoking downstairs. Wheelchair access. Music

---

KENILWORTH Warwickshire

map 5

Restaurant Bosquet ♥

97A Warwick Road, Kenilworth CV8 1HP   COOKING 3*
KENILWORTH (0926) 52463   COST £30–£50

'This has to be the best restaurant for miles around...a rare treat in the often barren Midland setting,' enthused one. There is no sitting-room or bar, just a dusky pink dining-room in a Victorian semi that invites serious eating. Meals may begin with fat, juicy green olives and a sweet onion tart. The food is serious French stuff with rich glossy sauces and plenty of fish: red mullet with saffron, perhaps, or a generous slab of warm sea bass terrine – light, delicate and bouncy – wrapped around with leek, sitting in a beurre blanc sauce flecked with chives. Good use is made of seasonal produce: in spring, asparagus with a piquant orange sauce, morel mushrooms with loin of veal, and a top-drawer mix of mushrooms (including girolles and trompettes-de-mort) to partner a sandwich tower of veal sweetbreads and puff pastry.

Sauces are well judged and add considerably to the pleasure. They are typically slightly thicker than a simple jus, but not heavily reduced, and alcohol and cream are used in moderation. When these sauces are coupled with good textural contrasts and careful cooking of prime ingredients, the result is dishes that hang together beautifully. Young, tasty squab pigeon is cut neatly into component parts and placed around a Savoy cabbage leaf folded over a dark and creamy splodge that has a vibrant livery taste, a tantalising burst of something alcoholic, and lovely depth of flavour. Reports of lamb have varied from 'disappointing' to 'the best lamb I've tasted in years; and I come from Wales!' Vegetables are so good that the occasional hiccup (perfectly good spinach obscured by pieces of sweet candied orange zest) stands out, so to speak, like a sore thumb. Come to that, main courses could probably stand by themselves without a side-plate of vegetables. The totally French wine list is an example of an increasingly rare bird, although thousands of restaurants in France seem to manage perfectly well without Chile and Bulgaria. Wines from the Rhône and south-west are well worth exploring on this compact list, and prices are generally favourable, with a good spread in Bordeaux. House wine is around £11. CELLARMAN'S CHOICE: Jurançon Cuvée Marie Hours 1992, £17; Madiran Bouscassé 'Vieilles Vignes' Brumont 1987, £20.

CHEF: Bernard Lignier   PROPRIETORS: Bernard and Jane Lignier   OPEN: Tue to Sat, D only (L by arrangement); 7 to 9.30   CLOSED: 1 week Christmas, 3 weeks Aug   MEALS: alc (main courses £14.50 to £15). Set D Tue to Fri £19.80   SERVICE: not inc   CARDS: Access, Amex, Visa   DETAILS: 26 seats. Private parties: 32 main room. Vegetarian meals on request. Children's helpings. Smart dress preferred. Wheelchair access (2 steps). No music

---

KESWICK Cumbria   map 7

▲ *Swinside Lodge* ⁵✗

Newlands, Keswick CA12 5UE
KESWICK (076 87) 72948
off A66 Penrith to Cockermouth road,
turn left at Portinscale and follow Grange | NEW CHEF |
road for 2m   COST £30–£41

Graham Taylor runs this Victorian house beside Derwentwater as an informal country hotel, and caters for fell-walkers and lazybones alike, of any age from teens to 90. But it is no spartan hostel, rather a comfortable spread with a pleasantly informal atmosphere. Into this haven stepped Chris Astley (formerly at Mallory Court – see entry, Bishop's Tachbrook) and supporting team during 1994. A lack of feedback on the new regime has meant that we are unable to award a cooking score this year.

The pattern has been a five-course dinner with no choice before pudding, which puts an onus on the kitchen to come up with a balanced meal. First courses are generally hot – a soufflé, mousse or savoury tart, for example – then after a soup the main course may be a roast. A late spring example shows the style: a parcel of lamb with feta cheese, sun-dried tomatoes and basil, followed by watercress and lime soup, and then chicken breast with truffle and tarragon sauce. Vegetables have included a root, a green, potatoes and one other, while puddings might offer a choice of passion-fruit soufflé, glazed lemon tart, or coffee and walnut ice-cream. Cheeses are an interesting collection of nine northern varieties – Cotherstone, Coverdale, Redesdale and Swaledale among them – plus Stilton. There is no licence and no corkage charge. Reports, please.

CHEFS: Chris Astley, Scott Merrick and Graham Taylor PROPRIETOR: Graham Taylor OPEN: all week, D only; 7 for 7.30 CLOSED: mid-Dec to mid-Feb MEALS: Set D £24 to £27.50. Unlicensed, but bring your own: no corkage SERVICE: not inc DETAILS: 18 seats. Car park. Vegetarian meals with prior notice. No children under 12. Smart dress preferred. No smoking in dining-room. No music ACCOMMODATION: 9 rooms, all with bath/shower. TV. DB&B £60 to £135. Deposit: £20. No children under 12. Doors close at 11. Confirm by 4 (*The Which? Hotel Guide*)

KEYSTON Cambridgeshire   map 6

Pheasant Inn ♥ ⅝✳ £

Keyston PE18 0RE
BYTHORN (0832) 710241   COOKING 2*
on B663, 1m S of junction with A14   COST £19–£49

The Pheasant is an old, thatched, beamed, white-painted pub in a picturesque and sprawling village. The same menu and prices operate throughout, although the Red Room is slightly more formal, bookable, and has a no-smoking policy. Flexible menus ('eat whatever you like') change every two weeks and offer a modern line-up with Mediterranean and Far Eastern influences to the fore: Tuscan bean soup, Parma ham with artichoke hearts and salsa verde, and chicken with a hot Thai curry sauce, for example. A satisfying traditional British vein also shows through in deep-fried cod in a beer and chive batter with chips, and a tasty lamb and vegetable suet pudding with mashed potato.

Roger Jones (ex-Summer Lodge in Evershot, see entry) uses fish from his old Dorset supplier – and it is very fresh. At inspection a fillet of turbot was perfectly steamed and tasty, served with roasted red peppers on a warm 'salad' of boiled potatoes with a blob of pesto on top. What counts here is energy and enthusiasm. Supplies and cooking are basically sound, although a few corners are cut and some dishes can be rather approximate. 'Wild' mushroom risotto is made with Paris browns and lacks the integration of a proper risotto, as if the kitchen has not quite got on the inside of it. A tall cylinder of delightfully rich yet light coffee parfait on a circle of biscuit pastry would have been fine without the large mortar board of inferior dark chocolate perched on top. Service is capable, and what it doesn't know it finds out. The backing of Poste Hotels ensures a first-rate wine list of interesting, bang up-to-date bottles, very sympathetically priced. It is helpfully divided into sections by style, and quality is uniformly high. House wines begin at £7.95 with around a dozen available by the generous glass from

£1.75. CELLARMAN'S CHOICE: Vin de Pays d'Oc, La Serre Sauvignon Blanc 1993, £9.45; Henschke Shiraz-Cabernet 1991, £14.75.

CHEF: Roger Jones   PROPRIETOR: Poste Hotels   OPEN: all week; 12 to 2, 6.30 to 10 (7 to 9.30 Sun)   CLOSED: D 25 and 26 Dec   MEALS: alc (main courses £6 to £14)   SERVICE: not inc, card slips closed   CARDS: Access, Amex, Diners, Visa   DETAILS: 100 seats. 4 tables outside. Private parties: 18 main room, 40 private room. Car park. Vegetarian meals. Children's helpings on request. No smoking in dining-room. Wheelchair access (1 step). No music. Fax: (0832) 710241

KINGSBRIDGE Devon   map 1

▲ Buckland-Tout-Saints Hotel, Queen Anne ☆✳

Goveton, Kingsbridge TQ7 2DS
KINGSBRIDGE (0548) 853055   COOKING 2*
1½m off A381, 2m NE of Kingsbridge   COST £23–£43

The house is one of the most handsome in the area: Queen Anne, mellowing stone, six acres of well-manicured, terraced gardens sloping down to ancient trees, and a croquet lawn adding to the perfect English country house impression. Less traditional is the helipad, 'for stressed execs nipping down for dinner'. The bar, to which diners are shepherded, is a Victorian afterthought, with less-than-inspiring panelling and leather upholstery, but the dining-room makes up for it with original pine panelling in prime nick.

A new team has been cooking here since October 1993. Jeremy Medley came from Ston Easton Park and retains the dinner format of three courses with four choices at each stage, as well as the general tilt of Anglo-French ideas. Just enough invention provokes interest, without compromising the basic conservatism, all based on sound ingredients. Dishes are described with admirable restraint, allowing diners an element of surprise, usually pleasant. A cannelloni of Devon scallops and leeks consisted of three home-made horn-shaped pasta shells enclosing a mousse of scallops, with a buttery sauce based on fish stock. On the other hand, the 'fresh winter berries' in a tiramisù at an inspection meal turned out to be two strawberries.

When the balance is right – a good, well-reduced sauce with rare beef sirloin, enriched with pork belly and flavoured with thyme, for instance – the cooking is hard to fault. Vegetables are integral to the dish. Pastry is not the strongest department: 'Petits fours were boring, but not as bad as the appetisers with drinks' was one comment. The eight 'House selection' wines (from £8.75) are adequate, but it is better to choose from the interesting, mostly French list, which has plenty of inexpensive options to first growth claret and a fair selection of half-bottles.

CHEF: Jeremy Medley   PROPRIETORS: John and Tove Taylor   OPEN: all week; 12.30 to 1.45, 7.30 to 9.30   MEALS: Set L £14.50, Set D £25   SERVICE: not inc, card slips closed   CARDS: Access, Amex, Diners, Visa   DETAILS: 48 seats. 5 tables outside. Private parties: 30 main room, 16 private room. Car park. Vegetarian meals. Children's helpings. Smart dress preferred. No smoking in dining-room. No music   ACCOMMODATION: 13 rooms, all with bath/shower. TV. Phone. D,B&B £75 to £190. Children welcome. Baby facilities. Pets welcome by arrangement. Afternoon teas. Garden. Doors close at midnight. Confirm by 6. Fax: (0548) 856261

map 6

Riverside

27 King Street, King's Lynn PE30 1HA   COOKING 1
KING'S LYNN (0553) 773134   COST £16–£40

In 1994 Michael and Sylvia Savage celebrated 10 years in residence at their 'delightful' oak-beamed restaurant by the banks of the River Ouse. The setting is a joy in fine weather, and the place is often open in summer from 10 in the morning for coffee, tea and salads on the terrace overlooking the water. A pianist tickles the ivories in the evening. Light lunches of fisherman's pie, moussaka, filled pancakes and the like are excellent value; otherwise choose something more substantial such as medallions of pork with Stilton sauce. Dinner is more ambitious and might include hot calabrese mousse, baked monkfish with roasted peppers and garlic, and loin of lamb on a bed of creamed leeks, as well as steaks. Home-made sweets are from the trolley, or there are locally made ice-creams and sorbets from Prospero of Wiveton. The modest wine list has plenty of good drinking from reliable makers. House wine is £7.95.

CHEFS: Dennis Taylor and Pat Isbill   PROPRIETORS: Michael and Sylvia Savage   OPEN: Mon to Sat; 12 to 2, 7 to 10   CLOSED: 25 to 30 Dec   MEALS: alc (main courses L £5 to £11, D £12 to £16). Set D £15.95   SERVICE: not inc, card slips closed   CARDS: Access, Visa   DETAILS: 70 seats. 12 tables outside. Private parties: 80 main room. Car park. Vegetarian meals. Children's helpings. Smart dress preferred. Music

Rococo 🍸

11 Saturday Market Place,
King's Lynn PE30 5DQ   COOKING 2
KING'S LYNN (0553) 771483   COST £20–£42

'Please may King's Lynn keep this special place, and may as many *Guide* readers as possible avail themselves of its charms' is the plea of one, among many, who want Rococo to succeed. The cheery front room, strewn with wine books and magazines, is welcoming. The paint is bright green (a Norfolk speciality), while the dining-room is a light primrose yellow. Big oil paintings add a freshness, boldness and vigour to the restaurant that make it appear sunny, even in winter.

The cooking uses local ingredients, and captures something of that same vigour. Juicy Norfolk shrimps are served by themselves, or incorporated into a sauce with home-preserved tomatoes to accompany a seared fillet of salmon. Chicken tastes 'like it used to', and duck is reared specially for the restaurant. Ideas come from far and wide, but often have a local link: sweet roasted peppers with marinated local goats' cheese; or crab, spiced Caribbean-style and layered with crisp pastry leaves. Vegetables – high-quality gratin dauphinois, celeriac and crunchy sugar-snap peas, for example – are praised as a relief from the usual boring group of over-cooked and inappropriate piles of mush; nor are they blanched to fork-defying semi-rawness. For dessert there may be creamy rice pudding with rum-soaked sultanas, a steamed sponge, or 'splendid' raspberry pie. The wine list is put together by a serious enthusiast, with interesting bottles from all over the place at reasonable prices. CELLARMAN'S CHOICE: Sancerre 1991, Dom. Roger, £22; Hollick Chardonnay 1991, £17.50.

CHEF: Nicholas Anderson PROPRIETORS: Anne and Nicholas Anderson OPEN: Mon to Sat, exc Mon L (Sun L and D, and Mon L by arrangement); 12 to 2.30, 7.30 to 10 MEALS: Set L £9 (2 courses) to £12, Set D £19.50 (2 courses) to £24.50 SERVICE: not inc CARDS: Access, Amex, Visa DETAILS: 40 seats. Private parties: 40 main room. Vegetarian meals. Children's helpings. Smart dress preferred. No smoking while others eat. No cigars/pipes in dining-room. Wheelchair access (also WC). Music

---

KINGSTON UPON THAMES Surrey map 3

Ayudhya

14 Kingston Hill,
Kingston upon Thames KT2 7NH
081-549 5984 and 546 5878

COOKING 1*
COST £21–£41

Since 1984 this attractively decorated restaurant has provided a good service for the citizens of Kingston and beyond. Chef and proprietor Somjai Thanpho offers a menu of around 80 dishes that spans the full range of accessible Thai cuisine from soups and salads to curries of various 'colours', stir-fries and noodles. Look for the more unusual items such as kai bai toey (deep-fried chicken wrapped in a screw pine leaf), yam makeua (a salad made with roasted green Thai aubergines), and haw mok talay (curried seafood mousse steamed on a bed of Chinese leaves). Vegetarians are well catered for. Desserts bring a choice of exotic fruit or delicacies such as sankhaya (steamed egg custard made with coconut milk, pumpkin and palm sugar). Singha Thai beer suits the food, but the extended wine list is also worth serious consideration. It is a wide-ranging compilation of interesting bottles from well-respected growers, with the balance tilted towards suitable whites. House wines start at £6.95.

CHEF/PROPRIETOR: Ms Somjai Thanpho OPEN: all week, exc Mon L; 12 to 2.30, 6.30 to 11 (11.30 Fri and Sat, 12.30 to 3 and 6 to 11 Sun) CLOSED: 25 Dec, 1 Jan, Easter Sun MEALS: alc (main courses £5 to £9) SERVICE: not inc CARDS: Access, Amex, Diners, Visa DETAILS: 80 seats. Private parties: 42 main room, 30 private rooms. Vegetarian meals. Children's helpings on request. Smart dress preferred. No-smoking area. Wheelchair access (1 step). Music

---

KINGTON Hereford & Worcester map 4

▲ *Penrhos Court* ¾

Kington HR5 3LH
KINGTON (0544) 230720
on A44, 1m E of Kington

COOKING 1*
COST £34–£41

One of the main reasons for eating here, muses a reporter, 'is to savour being in a medieval building, toasting your toes on a chilly evening before a vast log fire in a gargantuan chimney through which you can see the last daylight glimmering, staring up at the blackened oak-plank ceilings and admiring the cruck beams that hold up the ancient barn'. Parts of this old house date back to 1280, and Martin Griffiths has spent the last 20 years bringing the place back to life. The restaurant is in the hands of Daphne Lambert, whose scholarly interest in medieval cookery results in some intriguing seasonal feasts and banquets. Elsewhere the emphasis is on simple modern dishes based around local, organic and additive-free produce. Occasional signs of a heavy hand in the kitchen are outweighed by sharp, subtle cooking, as in marinated sea trout with lime and dill, couscous salad with sun-dried tomatoes and coriander and chargrilled lamb steak with spinach and thyme. To finish, lemon and mint sorbet is a better bet than substantial chocolate and orange cake. Much of the wine list is from Bibendum and it offers a well-spread selection at fair prices. House wines are from £10.50.

CHEF: Daphne Lambert   PROPRIETORS: Daphne Lambert and Martin Griffiths   OPEN: all week, D only; 7.30 to 10   CLOSED: Feb   MEALS: Set D £23.50   SERVICE: not inc, card slips closed CARDS: Access, Amex, Diners, Visa (all with 4% surcharge)   DETAILS: 70 seats. Private parties: 70 main room, 20, 40 and 70 private rooms. Car park. Vegetarian meals. Children's helpings. No smoking in dining-room. Music   ACCOMMODATION: 11 rooms, all with bath/shower. TV. Phone. B&B £50 to £120. Deposit: 50%. Rooms for disabled. Children welcome. Baby facilities. Garden. Doors close at midnight. Confirm 1 day ahead. Fax: (0544) 230754

KINTBURY Berkshire   map 2

▲ *Dundas Arms* ♟

53 Station Road, Kintbury RG15 0UT
KINTBURY (0488) 58263, changes to
(01488) 658263 autumn 1994
1m S of A4, between Newbury and   COOKING 1
Hungerford   COST £23–£46

Enjoy the setting and explore the wine list at the Dalzell-Pipers' well-known Berkshire rendezvous. The pub stands on a strip of territory between the River Kennet and the Kennet and Avon Canal; on fine days it is a most agreeable spot, with tables on the jetty overlooking the water. Snacks are served in the bar, while the restaurant menu offers a comfortable selection of dishes old and new. Smoked haddock rarebit, calf's liver and bacon, and roast rib of beef share the bill with fillet of red mullet with saffron onions and fried scallops with tomato and coriander. Vegetables and cheeses receive good reports. Sweets, such as chocolate mousse and iced orange soufflé, also draw favourable comments. Reporters reckon that flavour matters more than presentation on the plate.

The wine list is unbalanced. France is the only European country listed, and most of the bottles are from Bordeaux and Burgundy. The result is a massive amount of red and not much white. But given those restrictions, there is a lot of pleasure to be had. Claret is the strongest suit, mixing venerable bottles with very good affordable ones. Burgundy prices are not off the end of the scale, despite the good names, and quality in the token New World section is high. CELLARMAN'S CHOICE: Madfish Bay Chardonnay 1993, £13.50; Pomerol, Ch. la Croix des Moines 1990, £19.

'The two quail were not so much rare as raw. Dismembering them with the fingers was a bloodbath: napkins hideously stained, blood dripping down our arms. It was like an operating theatre; no wonder the table next to us asked to be moved.'
(On eating in London)

CHEFS: David Dalzell-Piper, Sue Bright and Stuart Hall   PROPRIETORS: D.A. and W.E. Dalzell-Piper   OPEN: Mon to Sat, exc Mon D; 12 to 1.30 (2 bar), 7.30 to 9.15   MEALS: alc (main courses £12 to £16). Set L £16.50. Bar menu   SERVICE: not inc   CARDS: Access, Amex, Visa   DETAILS: 40 seats. 15 tables outside. Private parties: 24 main room. Car park. Vegetarian meals. Children's helpings. Smart dress preferred. No cigars/pipes in dining-room. No-smoking area. Wheelchair access (2 steps). No music   ACCOMMODATION: 5 rooms, all with bath/shower. TV. Phone. B&B £40 to £65. Rooms for disabled. Children welcome. Pets by arrangement. Doors close at 11. Confirm by 6. Fax: (0488) 58568, changes to (01488) 658568 autumn 1994 (*The Which? Hotel Guide*)

KIRKHAM Lancashire   map 5

Cromwellian ♥

16 Poulton Street, Kirkham PR4 2AB   COOKING 3
KIRKHAM (0772) 685680   COST £27–£37

'It continues to outshine all others in our district by sheer consistency and imagination,' reports one reader. 'It grows on you,' says an inspector, adding that it has improved over the years and now has style and a self-confidence that, along with the personalities of Peter and Josie Fawcett, put it among the front-runners in the region. 'Each room is no bigger than the lounge in a medium-sized semi; this, together with the friendliness of the proprietor, makes you feel instantly at home.'

'After eight years, so many of the dishes have become favourites of our customers that innovation has become slightly more muted,' confesses Peter Fawcett. Yet small variations on well-known themes add interest to the three-course menu of limited but perfectly acceptable choice. The coleslaw accompanying a generous first-course fillet of lightly poached salmon is made from fennel ('fennelslaw', they call it), while noisettes of lamb come with a vol-au-vent 'pie' of fennel and basil, and a minted pea sauce.

The potato dish still reigns supreme, says a reporter, who calls it 'one of life's dependables': King Edwards, thinly sliced then oven-baked with cream and onions, served brown and crisp on top, yet soft and creamy below'. Cheeses too 'deserve the same recognition'. Shropshire blue is served with apple chutney, and all cheeses come with 'home-baked bread which is hot, grainy and fruity'. Hot upside-down apple and caramel pudding with a butterscotch sauce benefits from a dollop of thick cream. The wine list offers a good spread of styles and prices, with vins de pays, Alsace, Italy and the New World offering, as ever, some of the best drinking under £20. Over 20 half-bottles are welcome. House wines begin at £8.95. CELLARMAN'S CHOICE: Haut-Médoc, Ch. St. Saturnin 1986, £17.50; Muscadet des Coteaux de la Loire 1990, Guindon, £10.50.

CHEFS: Josie Fawcett and Diane Rowe   PROPRIETORS: Peter and Josie Fawcett   OPEN: Tue to Sat D; 7 to 9   CLOSED: first week Jan, 2 weeks Aug   MEALS: Set D £19.50 to £22.50   SERVICE: not inc, card slips closed   CARDS: Access, Amex, Visa   DETAILS: 16 seats. Private parties: 12 main room, 8 private room. Vegetarian meals. Children's helpings. Smart dress preferred. Wheelchair access. Music

---

♦ *denotes an outstanding wine cellar;* ♥ *denotes a good wine list, worth travelling for.*

▲ *Langar Hall*

Langar NG13 9HG
HARBY (0949) 60559, changes to
(0949) 860559 autumn 1994   COOKING 1
between A46 and A52, 4m S of Bingham   COST £23–£57

'All looked rural and idyllic as we drove up the long drive to the hotel: rolling countryside, lambs, croquet lawn, tables outside.' Langar Hall, built in 1830 just behind the church, successfully straddles the divide between private home and antique-filled country-house hotel, with silver candelabra, large oil paintings, comfortable furniture and old family photograph albums. One dining-room is open, spacious and light with classical overtones, the other is 'warmer and cosier', while a third room is opened up for small parties.

There have been changes in the kitchen. Imogen Skirving runs front-of-house, plans the menus and cooks 'for fun and emergencies'. Many of the ideas remain from the kitchen's previous regime (Dan Evans has moved to the Fire Station, Waterloo, see entry, London). Watercress and nettle soup shows the seasonal focus, while braised lamb with tabbouleh, and warm black cherry clafoutis with cassis ice-cream, indicate the lack of restriction on ideas. Highlights have included a salad of blue cheese and walnuts (Stilton is made not far away), and gravlax served with a soft and creamy potato 'pancake', crisp on the outside. Although enthusiasm remains high, there is a feeling that some dishes have been handed down from one chef to another without the commensurate level of skill being passed on. The singing butler has gone (Chichester Theatre Company's gain), but the quality of help and service is still extremely high. The 40-bottle wine list with standard mark-ups concentrates on France, but house Australian is £8.50.

CHEFS: Toby Garratt and Stephen Cass   PROPRIETOR: Imogen Skirving   OPEN: Mon to Sat (Sun L by arrangement); 12.30 to 2, 7.30 to 9.30 (7 to 10 Fri and Sat)   MEALS: alc (main courses £8.50 to £18). Set L £15 to £20, Set D £25   SERVICE: not inc   CARDS: Access, Amex, Visa   DETAILS: 48 seats. 4 tables outside. Private parties: 50 main room, 8 and 18 private rooms. Car park. Vegetarian meals with prior notice. Children's helpings by arrangement. No children under 10. No-smoking area. Music   ACCOMMODATION: 12 rooms, all with bath/shower. TV. Phone. B&B £60 to £125. Deposit: £25. Children welcome. Pets by arrangement. Afternoon teas. Garden. Fishing. Doors close at 12.30am. Confirm by 4. Fax: (0949) 61045, changes to (0949) 861045 in autumn 1994 (*The Which? Hotel Guide*)

▲ *Northcote Manor*

LANCS
1995
STICKY PUD

Northcote Road, Langho BB6 9BE
BLACKBURN (0254) 240555   COOKING 2*
on A59, 9m E of M6 exit 31   COST £24–£49

The Manor is an old house, not a sealed isothermic bubble. 'Tables are well-spaced. We were lucky to have one pressed against a radiator,' reported a winter visitor. 'The cooking is as good as ever,' said another, whose fears – that business customers attracted by the new extension might lower the tone – were not realised. Over a decade together has brought Craig Bancroft and Nigel Haworth to a working combination of traditional Lancashire food and modern, broadly European, cooking.

Local produce is much appreciated here, some of it coming together in a single plate that combines Fleetwood smoked salmon with Morecambe Bay potted shrimps, 'delicious' Bury black puddings and good old-fashioned brawn. There is a variant on Hindle Wakes (with rhubarb and basil stuffing); and Goosnargh duckling is well done in both senses. This is not a fusty old backwater, though. Modern dishes get equal billing, from croquettes of celeriac and spinach on a spiced pepper sauce, to seared escalope of tuna on a salade niçoise. Flexibility of choice is much appreciated: items on the fixed-price 'Market Menu' are helpfully interchangeable with those on the *carte*. Among sticky toffee pudding aficionados, of whom there must be a fair number now, Northcote Manor is rated extremely highly: 'I've had sticky toffee pudding in many restaurants out of the GFG (and made it myself) and this was the best.' Wines (including half bottles) are extensive, styles (and mark-ups) are varied, and house wine is £8.80 (£1.85 per glass).

CHEF: Nigel Haworth   PROPRIETORS: Craig J. Bancroft and Nigel Haworth   OPEN: all week; 12 to 1.30 (2 Sun), 7 to 9.30 (10 Sat)   CLOSED: 1 and 2 Jan   MEALS: alc (main courses L £9.50, D £10.50 to £17). Set D £25   SERVICE: 10% (optional), card slips closed   CARDS: Access, Amex, Diners, Visa   DETAILS: 100 seats. Private parties: 100 main room, 35 private room. Car park. Vegetarian meals. Children's helpings. Smart dress preferred. Wheelchair access (2 steps; also WC). Music   ACCOMMODATION: 14 rooms, all with bath/shower. TV. Phone. B&B £64 to £80. Room for disabled. Children welcome. Baby facilities. Afternoon teas. Garden.. Fax: (0254) 246568 (*The Which? Hotel Guide*)

LANGLEY MARSH Somerset   map 2

▲ *Langley House Hotel* ♟ ✸

Langley Marsh TA4 2UF
WIVELISCOMBE (0984) 623318   COOKING 3
½m N of Wiveliscombe   COST £34–£47

Although the original house is sixteenth-century, its character was altered significantly in the early eighteenth, and a plain Georgian face is now presented to the world. Most of the guest rooms have views over the handsomely manicured gardens, and the setting is as tranquil as can be. Décor is on the frilly side, and Peter Wilson's food draws many plaudits.

The format is a four-course, fixed-price dinner menu (though the price may change from night to night, depending on what is being cooked). The only choice comes at dessert stage. A summer meal that began with a good warm salad of quail breast dressed with walnut oil went on to a fillet of 'creamy, fleshy' turbot grilled with a crab crust and sauced with a herby tomato coulis. Meat was rosettes of lamb accompanied by a little tartlet of onion purée 'zapped with cassis', served with organically grown vegetables from the Wilsons' own kitchen garden. Cranachan to finish had plenty of whisky and cream and the raspberries had been 'picked that afternoon'. Other menus have tried breadcrumbed fillet of sea bass with leeks and a beurre blanc, steamed red mullet with spring onions and basil in a warm vinaigrette, veal fillet with apricot, coriander and walnuts, and roast breast of guinea-fowl with wild mushrooms and leeks and a bearnaise sauce. Elderflower syllabub is a favourite, as is 'icky sticky pudding with toffee sauce'. On a more adult note, unpasteurised Stilton from the Long Clawson dairy appears regularly on the menu.

The French-dominated wine list has many excellent bottles, together with a sheet of bin-ends for the high rollers. Clarets are a dream, Burgundy is represented by fine growers and a smaller Rhône selection includes mature Guigals. Other European countries get shorter shrift. Halves are available in healthy quantity. Although a few wines below £20 are offered in each region, mark-ups soon get into their stride. House French is from £8.75.

CHEF: Peter Wilson   PROPRIETORS: Peter and Anne Wilson   OPEN: all week, D only; 7.30 to 8.30   MEALS: Set D £24.50 to £28.50   SERVICE: not inc, card slips closed   CARDS: Access, Amex, Visa   DETAILS: 20 seats. Private parties: 6 main room, 20 private room. Car park. Vegetarian meals. Children's helpings. No very young children D. Smart dress preferred. No smoking in dining-room. Wheelchair access (1 step; also WC). No music   ACCOMMODATION: 8 rooms, all with bath/shower. TV. Phone. B&B £58.50 to £104.50. Children welcome. Baby facilities. Pets welcome (not in public rooms). Afternoon teas. Garden. Doors close at midnight. Confirm by 6. Fax: (0984) 624573 (The Which? Hotel Guide)

LAUNCESTON Cornwall   map 1

Randells

Prospect House, 11 Western Road,
Launceston PL15 7AS   COOKING 1
LAUNCESTON (0566) 776484   COST £21–£32

This converted Victorian town house is draped in hanging baskets, with window boxes in summer, open fires in winter and an air of homely comfort all year round. It must be handy when you can both cook and serve, as Patrick Randell and Debbie Hutchings do, swapping over whenever they fancy a change. The menu rolls on a two-month cycle, dipping back into the archives for brie rolled in breadcrumbs and deep-fried with a cranberry sauce, but keeping regulars happy with peppered steak and chocolate terrine. Game is plentiful and popular – Dartmouth pie uses venison, dried fruit and spices – and fish turns up in salmon and cod quenelles with a watercress sauce, or as sole mille-feuille. The plate of south-west cheese is a popular alternative to banoffi pie or warm lemon tart. The few wines are made more attractive by being mostly under £10, and available in a small carafe and by the glass as well. House Australian is £8.90 (£1.80 per glass).

CHEFS/PROPRIETORS: Patrick Randell and Debbie Hutchings   OPEN: Tue to Sat, D only; 7 to 9 (9.30 Sat)   CLOSED: 2 weeks Jan   MEALS: alc (main courses £7.50 to £12)   SERVICE: not inc   CARDS: Access, Amex, Visa   DETAILS: 32 seats. Private parties: 22 main room. Vegetarian meals. Children's helpings. Wheelchair access (3 steps). Music

---

The Guide *is totally independent, accepts no free hospitality, and survives on the number of copies sold each year.*

LAVENHAM Suffolk   map 3

▲ Great House 👫

Market Place, Lavenham CO10 9QZ   COOKING 2
LAVENHAM (0787) 247431   COST £16–£54

'A pleasant French interlude in the heart of the English countryside' is one
woman's view of the Great House, which overlooks the medieval Guildhall. The
architecture may be straight out of the English Middle Ages but, in the kitchen,
Regis Crépy keeps faith with his Gallic roots. He turns his hand to anything from
coq au vin to ravioli of langoustines, with skilful and thoroughly enjoyable
results. M. Crépy knows his sauces: finely tuned hollandaise with asparagus,
wild mushroom with calf's liver, butterscotch with home-made almond and
nougat ice-cream. Other high points have included salmon and spinach quiche
with tomato coulis, best end of lamb with creamy mint sauce, and skate wing
with black butter. The 'stupendous' French cheeseboard is worth exploring. In
all, the food is reckoned to be excellent value. Reporters also endorse the
courteous, caring attitude of the staff, which is perfectly in tune with the
atmosphere of the place. The extensive, mainly French wine list covers a lot of
ground in terms of price. House wines (not the cheapest on the list) are £15.

CHEF/PROPRIETOR: Regis Crépy   OPEN: Tue to Sun, exc Sun D; 12 to 2.30, 7 to 9.30 (10.30 Sat)
MEALS: alc (main courses Tue to Sat L £4 to £9, D £13 to £17). Set L Sun £15.95, Set D Tue to Fri
£11.95   SERVICE: not inc   CARDS: Access, Amex, Visa   DETAILS: 45 seats. 7 tables outside.
Private parties: 50 main room. Vegetarian meals. Children's helpings. Smart dress preferred. No
smoking in dining-room. Wheelchair access (2 steps; also WC). Music   ACCOMMODATION: 4
rooms, all with bath/shower. TV. Phone. B&B £50 to £88. Deposit: £25. Children welcome. Baby
facilities. Pets by arrangement. Afternoon teas. Garden. Doors close at midnight. Fax: (0787)
248080 (The Which? Hotel Guide)

LEAMINGTON SPA Warwickshire   map 2

Les Plantagenêts 👫

15 Dormer Place,
Leamington Spa CV32 5AA   COOKING 2
LEAMINGTON SPA (0926) 451792   COST £22–£44

Rémy Loth is a knowledgeable, all-round French restaurateur with bags of
ebullient personality. His good manners and helpful descriptions of the menu
and daily specials please most visitors, and the atmosphere improves the more
there are. The setting is the cellar of one of Leamington's Regency terraces, across
the park from the Pump Rooms. Gothic-style decorations along with assorted
copper and blackened iron cooking utensils line the walls in the comfortably
upholstered dining-room. French accordion music plays in the background. The
cooking is classic French with a generous dollop of cream and butter. One
family, who called in for lunch, were greatly impressed by the good-value
fixed-price menu which offered elegantly wrought dishes, including salad of
squid and avocado, a duo of salmon and monkfish with a simple velouté sauce,
and excellent fillets of lamb with garlic and baby onions. Fine desserts such as
'beautiful' individual French apple tarts and 'sublime' floating islands make a

good finish, although one visitor found fault with the French cheeseboard. House wines are £10.50, or £2 per glass.

CHEF/PROPRIETOR: Rémy Loth   OPEN: Mon to Sat, exc Sat L; 12 to 2.15, 7.15 to 10.15   MEALS: alc (main courses £14 to £16). Set L £12.50, Set D £18.50   SERVICE: not inc   CARDS: Access, Amex, Visa   DETAILS: 40 seats. Private parties: 45 main room. Vegetarian meals with prior notice. Children's helpings. Smart dress preferred. No smoking in 1 dining-room. Music

---

LECK Lancashire   map 7

▲ Cobwebs ▮ ⅝✳

Leck, Cowan Bridge LA6 2HZ
KIRKBY LONSDALE (052 42) 72141
2m SE of Kirkby Lonsdale on A65, turn left   COOKING 3
at Cowan Bridge   COST £32–£41

Paul Kelly and Yvonne Thompson continue to run Cobwebs, although, as we went to press, the place was on the market. It is a pleasant, if rather isolated, house with a light, spacious extension forming the dining-room. Wide windows allow uninterrupted views of lambs and rabbits romping in the fields. It is a two-handed operation: Yvonne Thompson cooks and Paul Kelly does everything else. He is one of the great hosts, by turns garrulous and provocative, and has the enviable knack of getting strangers to talk to each other over drinks and nibbles.

An evening menu offers a choice of soup or another starter, then a single main course, dessert, a selection of regional cheeses and coffee. Sometimes a sorbet is inserted, the guests invited to guess its founding ingredient. The trick of serving two soups in one bowl is clever enough, though people tend not to like it when one is hot and the other cold. At a dinner in May, both were hot: a thick, creamy cauliflower and Parmesan broth, and a deep tomato given lift with plenty of fresh herbs. The alternative was a fine mixture of salmon, monkfish and prawns with roasted peppers and a warm balsamic vinaigrette. Main courses have grown more substantial over the years, as evidenced by thickly sliced beef fillet with shallots and chanterelles in a rich red wine reduction. Pudding was a chocolate and hazelnut cheesecake ('like a melted slab of whole-nut chocolate') that achieved 'lightness' and was sharply counterpointed by an orange sauce. A separate card explains about the cheeses, and Paul Kelly is keenly evangelistic about them. He still serves unassisted, with the 'grim determination of Daley Thompson in the midst of a decathlon'.

The wine list is an absolute gem, radiant with enthusiasm at every turn, with prices that invite enjoyment. Advice is willingly dispensed, and great care taken in serving. Burgundies, Alsaces, Rhônes and Australians are all superb, and those who love old vintage champagne will be sorely tempted. Malts and cognacs proliferate too, and the chances are that your choice of liqueur will be there as well. This is a drinker's paradise. Prices open at £8. CELLARMAN'S CHOICE: Martinborough Riesling 1993, £13; Nine Popes Shiraz 1991, £18.

▲ *This symbol means accommodation is available.*

CHEF: Yvonne Thompson PROPRIETORS: Paul Kelly and Yvonne Thompson OPEN: Wed to Sat, D only; 7.30 for 8 CLOSED: Jan to mid-Mar MEALS: Set D £25 SERVICE: not inc, card slips closed CARDS: Access, Visa DETAILS: 25 seats. Private parties: 25 main room. Car park. Vegetarian meals. No children under 12. Smart dress preferred. No smoking in dining-room. Wheelchair access (1 step). Music ACCOMMODATION: 5 rooms, all with bath/shower. TV. Phone. B&B £45 to £60. Deposit: 10%. No children under 12. Garden. Snooker. Doors close at 11.30. Confirm by 6. Fax: (052 42) 72141 (*The Which? Hotel Guide*)

LEDBURY Hereford & Worcester   map 2

▲ *Hope End* ▼ ⅍

Hope End, Ledbury HR8 1JQ
LEDBURY (0531) 633613
2m N of Ledbury, just beyond   COOKING 3
Wellington Heath   COST £34–£46

Elizabeth Barrett Browning spent part of her childhood here, among the Malvern Hills and tracts of eighteenth-century parkland that are no less tranquil today. People appreciate the setting and are impressed by the handsome exterior of the house with a minaret at one end. The dining-room, however, is thought rather bleak. It is comfortable, but descriptions like 'dreary and cold', and 'brown and gloomy' reflect the fact that country-house flounce is not the chosen mode.

What is well worth the experience is the Hegartys' avid horticulturalism. The walled garden spills its cornucopia into the kitchen: old apple varieties, artichokes, kale, seven sorts of pumpkin, baskets of fruit and fistfuls of herbs form the outline of the short, fixed-price dinner menus that Patricia Hegarty changes frequently. There is an earthiness about the food, which may start with a tomato and oatmeal tart with walnut oil and parsley, or egg stuffed with tapénade served with anchovies and saladings, and then proceed to roast best end of lamb with perry gravy and medlar jelly, or breast of Trelough duck with gooseberry sauce. An inspection meal in May yielded 'very rough, strong, gamey' duck confit with a good salad of chicory and orange, and shredded rump steak with a 'brilliant' mustard and savory sauce 'bursting with interesting flavours'. Three vegetables are the norm, and may include 'perfect' steamed new potatoes, strips of buttery courgette and roughly chopped chard. A wholemeal treacle tart filled with crystallised peel had good filling, helped along by creamy, full-flavoured lemon ice-cream. Bread has been thought underseasoned, but coffee strong and superb. The wine list is a roll-call of the great and the good, with fine pedigree evident in Bordeaux, Rhônes and white burgundies, and a healthy sprinkling of non-European bottles. Prices are by no means excessive. House burgundy is £8.

CHEF: Patricia Hegarty PROPRIETORS: John and Patricia Hegarty OPEN: all week, D only; 7.30 to 8.30 CLOSED: mid-Dec to first week Feb MEALS: Set D £30 SERVICE: card slips closed CARDS: Access, Visa DETAILS: 24 seats. Private parties: 8 main room. Car park. Vegetarian meals. No children under 12. Smart dress preferred. No smoking in dining-room. No music ACCOMMODATION: 9 rooms, all with bath/shower. Phone. B&B £85 to £140. Deposit: £60. No children under 12. Garden. Doors close at 11.30. Fax: (0531) 636366 (*The Which? Hotel Guide*)

The Guide *always appreciates hearing about changes of chef or owner.*

LEEDS West Yorkshire   map 5

▲ *Brasserie Forty Four* £

44 The Calls, Leeds LS2 8AQ   COOKING 2*
LEEDS (0532) 343232   COST £18–£47

Jeff Baker has taken the kitchen by the scruff of its neck at this trendy Leeds hot-spot, and reports suggest a concomitant upswing in standards. It is a converted cornmill, part of a waterside development that encompasses swish accommodation next door at 42 The Calls. The interior is big and bustly, with wooden floors and plain white walls and a balcony overlooking the river. A fashionable brasserie *carte* is underscored with weekly-changing specials, a fixed-price lunch menu of two or three courses plus coffee, and discount deals for those prepared to eat before 7.15 or after 10 in the evenings.

Influences are eclectic, with the main menu offering tuna with provençale vegetables, Toulouse sausage with lentils, or blackened rib of beef with Cajun spices. An inspector was impressed by the lightness of a chicken boudin with fennel and saffron – 'a delicate and creditable dish' – and the sureness of touch in a just-warmed (rather than fully cooked) marinated fillet of salmon with lime, ginger and coriander salsa. Main courses kept up the pace with 'sweet and tender' rack of lamb on a red pepper and olive compote, and roast guinea-fowl with mushroom and truffle risotto that had 'very earthy' meat and 'moist, rich' risotto. Vegetables, charged extra, were thought rather uninspiring, but then a slice of 'brilliant, intense' lemon tart and good crêpes suzette finished things fittingly. The wine list kicks off, fashionably, with 21 house wines, before offering a well-chosen, up-to-the-minute international selection. There are some interesting bin-ends, but it is probably wiser to stick to the house list, which opens with red and white Bergerac at £8.95.

CHEF: Jeff Baker   PROPRIETORS: Jonathan Wix and Michael Gill   OPEN: all week, exc Sat L and Sun D; 12 to 2.30 (3 Sun), 6.30 to 10.30 (11 Sat)   CLOSED: 5 days Christmas   MEALS: alc (main courses £5 to £13). Set L Mon to Fri £7.50 (2 courses) to £11.75, Sun £14.70   SERVICE: not inc (10% for 10 or more)   CARDS: Access, Amex, Visa   DETAILS: 125 seats. 20 tables outside. Private parties: 50 main room, 60 private room. Vegetarian meals. Children's helpings. No cigars/pipes in dining-room. Wheelchair access (also WC). Music. Air-conditioned ACCOMMODATION: 41 rooms, all with bath/shower. TV. Phone. B&B £60 to £130. Rooms for disabled. Lift. Children welcome. Baby facilities. Pets by arrangement. Afternoon teas. Doors close at 11. Confirm by 10. Fax: (0532) 343332 (*The Which? Hotel Guide*)

▲ *Haley's*

Shire Oak Road, Headingley,
Leeds LS6 2DE   COOKING 2
LEEDS (0532) 784446   COST £28–£52

'A bit like a country-house hotel in the city' is an apt description of this elegant Victorian house named after a master stonemason who worked in Leeds at the turn of the century. It stands in a quiet cul-de-sac, a couple of miles from the city centre and not far from the university. Inside, the mood is restful and the staff try hard to please. Choose between the short *menu du chef* or the effusively described Anglo-French *carte*, which promises anything from a trio of salmon (poached, baked and smoked) with two mustard sauces to marinated lamb kebab with coriander relish and Persian nan bread. Timing is spot-on and presentation is of a high order. Marinated salmon with tiny pieces of raw scallop and a lemon oil dressing succeeds as a perfect balancing act, fillet steak is cooked precisely to the point where it turns 'from purple to pink', while cherry and kirsch soufflé accompanied by a brandy-snap basket containing a black cherry sorbet is reckoned to be a 'mouth-wateringly good' finish. English and French 'country' cheeses come with home-made biscuits and walnut bread. The 50 wines are largely French, including house Bergerac at £11.95 and eight wines by the glass.

CHEF: Chris Baxter PROPRIETOR: John Appleyard OPEN: Mon to Sat D; 7.15 to 9.45 MEALS: alc (main courses £15 to £18.50). Set D £18.95 to £23.95 SERVICE: not inc, card slips closed CARDS: Access, Amex, Diners, Visa DETAILS: 45 seats. Private parties: 45 main room, 14 and 25 private rooms. Car park. Vegetarian meals. Children's helpings by arrangement. No cigars/ pipes in dining-room. Music. Air-conditioned ACCOMMODATION: 22 rooms, all with bath/ shower. TV. Phone. B&B £85 to £102. Children welcome. Baby facilities. Afternoon teas. Confirm by 6 on day before arrival. Fax: (0532) 753342 (*The Which? Hotel Guide*)

Leodis 🍷 £

Victoria Mill, Sovereign Street,
Leeds LS1 4BJ — COOKING 2
LEEDS (0532) 421010 — COST £18–£44

In a former mill in the regenerated waterfront area of the city centre, this huge brasserie has taken well to conversion. The original brick walls and cast-iron pillars remain, while the vaulted ceilings catch the noise and throw it back. The place buzzes, and the longish menu crackles with '90s food, that strange mixture of British nursery favourites (bangers and mash) and modern European (scallops with roast pepper salad) that culminates in dishes as unlikely as pithiviers of oxtail. Here is a restaurant that's not afraid to call a faggot a faggot; they are braised and served with peas and pasta.

It is a big operation, but timing is good: calf's liver is cooked spot-on, and served with bubble and squeak and smoked bacon. The movement that has lifted food of the poor to new heights in Europe is at work here too: why else would they serve black pudding with mashed swede and carrot? The wine list is enthusiastic, and makes a real effort to find good bottles that sell for less than £15 or £16. The world is successfully plundered for tastes that have wide appeal. Expensive wines have their own pages, and there are 20 half-bottles. House wines start at £7.95 and are also available by the glass. CELLARMAN'S CHOICE: Molina Sauvignon Blanc 1992, Viña Echeveria, £11.95; Hamilton Russell, Pinot Noir 1991, £13.95.

CHEF: Steven Kendell PROPRIETORS: Martin Spalding and Steven Kendell OPEN: Mon to Sat, exc Sat L; 12 to 2, 6 to 10 (11 Fri and Sat) CLOSED: 24 and 25 Dec, 1 Jan MEALS: alc (main courses £6 to £16). Set L and D (to 7.30pm) £10.95 SERVICE: not inc CARDS: Access, Amex, Visa DETAILS: 180 seats. 12 tables outside. Private parties: 180 main room. Car park. Vegetarian meals. Children welcome. Smart dress preferred. Wheelchair access (also WC). Music. Air-conditioned. Fax: (0532) 430432

Report forms are at the back of the book; write a letter if you prefer.

Paris ♥

36A Town Street, Horsforth,
Leeds LS18 4RJ   COOKING 1
LEEDS (0532) 581885   COST £16–£41

The interior is a brilliant contrast to a rather drab exterior, on a rather dreary
main street in a prosperous Leeds suburb. Poor acoustics and clouds of smoke
may restrict the appeal of the large, lofty upstairs room with wooden tables, but
there is a genuinely kind welcome, even to late arrivals who get lost. The menu is
long and easy-going, and the operation appeals equally to delicate appetites and
hungry students. It is canny with ingredients, serving up wild mushrooms, roast
tomatoes, basil pasta and creamed morels, and the kitchen does not fall down in
any of the basic departments. Salmon and coriander potage, beneath a bird's nest
weave of fried onion, is chunky, rich, oily and lemon-fresh, and monkfish (on a
rather dainty filigree rösti base) scores for both taste and texture.

The attractively priced 'early bird' menu has been known to stay up well past
its 7.30 bedtime. Specials are usually fishy, and a limited number of vegetarian
options are listed. Satisfying puddings include a chocolate terrine and fresh fruit
salad with bilberries, raspberries, cherries, figs and passion-fruit. Service is
friendly and smiling. Wines are well chosen, varied in style and sympathetically
priced: plenty of good stuff around £10 to £15, with headroom for those who
want something special. Ten wines 'in a glass of their own' (from around £2.25)
encourage vinous promiscuity. House wines are from £7.95. CELLARMAN'S
CHOICE: Chardonnay de l'Ardèche 1992, £12.25; Rioja 1989, Don Jacobo,
£11.95.

CHEFS: Thomas Mulkerrin and Louis Dutton   PROPRIETORS: Martin Spalding and Steven
Kendell   OPEN: all week, D only; 6 to 10.30 (11 Fri and Sat)   MEALS: alc (main courses £6 to
£13). Set D (to 7.30pm) £12.95 (inc wine)   SERVICE: not inc   CARDS: Access, Amex, Visa
DETAILS: 86 seats. Private parties: 86 main room. Vegetarian meals. Children's helpings. Smart
dress preferred. Music

Sous le Nez en Ville ▮ £

The Basement, Quebec House,
Quebec Street, Leeds LS1 2HA   COOKING 1*
LEEDS (0532) 440108   COST £16–£46

A reporter who, in 1993, was delighted to be attended to by 'a hunky French
waiter with a gorgeous accent' has this year commended the ' very sexy accents' of
the staff once again. Despite this distraction, she managed to focus her attention
on the food long enough to endorse it wholeheartedly. 'We'll be going back for
more,' she gasps. Everybody has been excited this year by the performance of
this bustling basement bistro in the business centre of Leeds. The choice on the
menu is staggering, supplemented by a long list of fresh fish chalked on a
blackboard, and yet Andrew Carter has very sensibly not tried to over-reach
himself in terms of elaboration. Most dishes succeed. Moules marinière
compared with the best of France for one diner – 'fresh, sweet and succulent' –
and braised mallard in madeira sauce offered meat of high flavour, while a thin
apple tart with caramel ice-cream had good crisp pastry and nice sharpness in the

fruit. Others have enjoyed calf's liver with caramelised onions and 'baby' black pudding, chicken breast with a pesto crust, pork with prunes, and pear and almond tart with cinnamon ice-cream. Incidentals all pass muster. Service is very willing and everybody is happy.

The wine list is a treasure trove of goodies, dealing confidently with the French regions (Alsace could do with a brush-up, however), before branching out into the rest of the world. Spain and Italy are well covered, as are New Zealand and Australia, California more uncertainly, and dessert wines splendidly. House Australian is £7.95. CELLARMAN'S CHOICE: Oyster Bay Sauvignon Blanc 1993, £12.50; Crozes-Hermitage 1991, Graillot, £17.95.

CHEF: Andrew Carter   PROPRIETOR: C.R.C.R. Partnership   OPEN: Mon to Sat, exc Sat L; 12 to 2.30, 6 to 10.30 (11 Fri and Sat)   CLOSED: bank hols   MEALS: alc (main courses £6 to £13.50). Set D (6 to 7.30pm) £12.95 (inc wine). Bar menu   SERVICE: not inc, card slips closed   CARDS: Access, Amex, Visa   DETAILS: 70 seats. Private parties: 70 main room, 20 private room. Vegetarian meals. Children welcome. No pipes in dining-room. No-smoking area. Music D. Fax: (0532) 450240

LEICESTER Leicestershire   map 5

Welford Place £

9 Welford Place, Leicester LE1 6ZH   COOKING 1
LEICESTER (0533) 470758   COST £17–£41

This is just what every city and large town needs: somewhere that opens all day from breakfast onwards, hotting up for midday meals ('the set lunch remains the best value for money for many miles around'), idling through afternoon tea, and perking up for dinner, only fizzling out just before midnight. The endeavour, enterprise and sheer flexibility impress, backed up by a reasonable standard of food. The location ensures a steady supply of business and legal folk, and the building retains the feel of a gentlemen's club without the stuffiness. The same team also runs the Wig & Mitre in Lincoln (see entry).

Menus change hourly, daily or periodically, depending on what they are offering, and an Anglo-Italian vein runs through mixed bean soup with roasted squid, shin of veal with saffron potatoes, and tiramisù. But there are also warm dill-cured salmon with lemon vinaigrette, braised shoulder of lamb, cottage pie, and steamed chocolate pudding with white chocolate sauce. Staff are as accommodating as the opening hours, and service is next to impeccable. 'Children, dogs, smoking vegetarians, vegans and minorities of all descriptions are all welcome providing there is a reasonable consideration for other people,' say the owners. The vast majority of wines are under £20 and full of interest. Four house wines (£9.50 a bottle) plus one fizz and five pudding wines are available by the variably sized glass from £2.55.

CHEFS: Lino Poli and Jamie Matts   PROPRIETORS: Michael and Valerie Hope   OPEN: all week; 8am to midnight   MEALS: alc (main courses £8.50 to £14.50). Set L £8 (2 courses) to £9.50, Set D £10 (2 courses) to £12.75   SERVICE: not inc, card slips closed   CARDS: Access, Amex, Diners, Visa   DETAILS: 216 seats. Private parties: 60 main room, 16 to 50 private rooms. Vegetarian meals. Children's helpings. Wheelchair access. No music. Fax: (0533) 471843

LEWDOWN Devon   map 1

▲ *Lewtrenchard Manor* ♟ ⁵⁄✳

Lewdown EX20 4PN
LEWDOWN (0556) 783256
off A30 Okehampton to Launceston road,   COOKING 2
turn left at Lewdown for ¾m   COST £23–£48

Once the home of the Reverend Sabine Baring-Gould, hymnist, this old stone manor house not far from the Cornish border once more has Patrick Salvadori at the stoves. A couple who spent a night there in June found the ambience as authentically domestic and welcoming as the Murrays intend. From the first tour of the grounds, ably conducted by Doomer the labrador, to the final lingering over toast in a 'beautiful' breakfast room, Lewtrenchard represented a haven that they found difficult to leave.

Despite the changes of chef, the menus – fixed-price for three courses plus coffee, or the four-course gourmet version – have stayed true to a gentle country-house idiom that pleases for its avoidance of silly elaboration. Steamed Tamar salmon with a watercress cream sauce, fried cod fillet with parsley butter, and roast breast of guinea-fowl with a thyme-scented stuffing and lemon butter sauce announce the style. Roast loin of lamb is generally tender and tasty, and beef fillet refreshingly accompanied by modern things like goats' cheese, red peppers and olive oil instead of the usual booze-and-cream option. Properly made ice-creams and sorbets impress, as did a dark chocolate box filled with lemon mousse and sauced with a Grand Marnier-spiked custard.

The wine list casts its net widely to haul in bottles from the southern hemisphere as plentifully as it does from France. Selections are commendable throughout, South Africa yielding a particularly rich harvest. Prices, especially for the non-European wines, are very reasonable. House wines are mostly £8.50. CELLARMAN'S CHOICE: Thelema Chardonnay 1991, £17.50; Kanonkop Pinotage 1990, £13.50.

CHEF: Patrick Salvadori   PROPRIETORS: James and Sue Murray   OPEN: all week, D only, and Sun L (Mon to Sat L by arrangement); 12.15 to 1.45, 7.15 to 9.30   MEALS: alc (main courses £16 to £18). Set L £16, Set D £25   SERVICE: not inc, card slips closed   CARDS: Access, Amex, Diners, Visa   DETAILS: 30 seats. Private parties: 8 main room, 16 private room. Car park. Vegetarian meals with prior notice. Children's helpings L. Children under 8 by arrangement. Smart dress preferred. No smoking in dining-room. Wheelchair access.   ACCOMMODATION: 8 rooms, all with bath/shower. TV. Phone. B&B £75 to £135. Children under 8 by arrangement. Baby facilities. Pets welcome (not in public rooms). Afternoon teas. Garden. Fishing. Doors close at midnight. Confirm by 6. Fax: (0556) 783332 (*The Which? Hotel Guide*)

All details are as accurate as possible at the time of going to press, but chefs and owners often change, and it is wise to check by telephone before making a special journey. Many readers have been disappointed when set-price bargain meals are no longer available. Ask when booking.

The Guide relies on feedback from its readers. Especially welcome are reports on new restaurants appearing in the book for the first time. All letters to the Guide are acknowledged.

LIFTON Devon   map 1

▲ *Arundell Arms* ⁵⅝✗ £

Lifton PL16 0AA
LIFTON (0566) 784666   COOKING 1*
just off A30, 3m E of Launceston   COST £19–£46

Now that the village of Lifton has been bypassed, the Arundell Arms is a haven
of peace and quiet. This is a sporting inn with a vengeance, set in a valley of five
rivers, with 20 miles of fishing rights on the Tamar and its tributaries. The
kitchen now works to two regularly changing fixed-price menus featuring
seasonal and local produce. Devon beef may appear as tournedos with roasted
shallots and onion sauce or as a roast rib with Yorkshire pudding. Salmon and
sea trout are from the hotel's own waters, game comes from its organised shoots.
Philip Burgess is equally at home with staunchly traditional braised oxtail, or a
fancy fricassee of turbot, scallops, Cornish potatoes and a nutmeg cream. Sweets
are the likes of chocolate pancake with dark chocolate and walnut sauce; cheeses
fly the flag for West Country producers. Popular bar snacks are served at
lunch-time and in the evening. The wine list is a sound selection, drawn mainly
from France; a decent number are served by the glass. House wines start at £9.50.

CHEF: Philip Burgess PROPRIETOR: Anne Voss-Bark OPEN: all week; restaurant 12.30 to 2,
7.30 to 9.30; bar 12 to 2.30, 6 to 10 MEALS: Set L £12.75 (2 courses) to £27.50, Set D £21.50 to
£27.50. Bar menu SERVICE: not inc CARDS: Access, Amex, Diners, Visa DETAILS: 70 seats.
Private parties: 80 main room, 30 private room. Car park. Vegetarian meals. Children's helpings
on request. No smoking in dining-room. Wheelchair access (2 steps). Music ACCOMMODATION:
29 rooms, all with bath/shower. TV. Phone. B&B £37.50 to £90. Children welcome. Baby
facilities. Pets welcome. Afternoon teas. Garden. Fishing. Doors close at 11.30. Fax: (0566)
784494 (*The Which? Hotel Guide*)

LINCOLN Lincolnshire   map 6

Jew's House

15 The Strait, Lincoln LN2 1JD   COOKING 2
LINCOLN (0522) 524851   COST £25–£45

Tottering down Steep Hill after a visit to the cathedral is the sensible order to do
things in; labouring upwards after lunch may be rather a challenge. Chef
Richard Gibbs worked in south-west France in the 1970s, and did a stint with
Rick Stein at the Seafood Restaurant (see entry, Padstow) before opening in this
ancient house four years ago. The southern French influence is still very much in
evidence in dishes such as warm duck breast salad with a sesame dressing,
niçoise vegetables en croûte with a Roquefort and chive sauce, and a pairing of
venison and duck with a sauce of armagnac and shallots. It is modulated,
however, by the contemporary British accent in smoked haddock mousse with
smoked salmon and a chive cream sauce, rolled fillet of pork with apple and
sage, or roast guinea-fowl with smoked pork and rosemary. Vegetables,
including a choice of potatoes or salads, cost extra; fish specials are chalked on a
blackboard. Pastrywork comes to the fore in apple, lemon or almond tarts, or, for
those prepared to wait 20 minutes, a soufflé Grand Marnier. Coffee arrives with
hand-made chocolates. Richard Gibbs's cooking has a consistency and flair that

pleases many. Wine selections are sound and prices fair, though halves are a bit thin and the list itself is in a bit of a jumble. House wines start at £8.50.

CHEF: Richard Gibbs   PROPRIETORS: Richard and Sally Gibbs   OPEN: Mon to Sat, exc Mon L; 12 to 1.30, 7 to 9.30   CLOSED: bank hol Mons   MEALS: alc (main courses £10 to £14). Set L and D £18.50   SERVICE: not inc   CARDS: Access, Amex, Diners, Visa   DETAILS: 28 seats. Private parties: 30 main room. Vegetarian meals. Children's helpings. No pipes in dining-room. Music

Wig & Mitre

29 Steep Hill, Lincoln LN2 1LU	COOKING 2
LINCOLN (0522) 535190 and 523705	COST £22–£39

'When in Lincoln, the Wig & Mitre is really the place to go,' confirms a local supporter of this all-purpose restaurant at the top of Steep Hill. The ancient building plays host to a happy gathering of faithful followers – clergy, lawyers, ladies shopping and passing tourists. The secret of its success is its flexibility: menus that change twice daily, all-day opening and cheery informality. Part of the first floor is still a pub; the rest is given over to eating. The full *carte* lists an array of modern-sounding dishes such as confit of duck with celeriac purée and balsamic vinegar, and rack of lamb with mint and butter-beans. Many customers opt for the blackboard with its range of pub-style offerings, including potted rabbit, and chicken liver parfait with home-made chutney. Fish gets a good airing (curried mussel and saffron soup has been 'excellent'), and up-market sandwiches are also available. Occasional patchiness is perhaps a result of extreme popularity. Service usually copes well under pressure. The wine list shows a preference for big names from Bordeaux and Burgundy, although some more modest regional wines are also on offer. House wine is £9.40.

CHEFS: Paul Vidic and Peter Dodd   PROPRIETORS: Valerie and Michael Hope   OPEN: all week; 8am to 11.30pm   CLOSED: 25 Dec   MEALS: alc (main courses £7.50 to £13.95)   SERVICE: not inc, card slips closed   CARDS: Access, Amex, Diners, Visa   DETAILS: 120 seats. 6 tables outside. Private parties: 60 main room, 40 private room. Vegetarian meals. Children's helpings. Wheelchair access (1 step; also WC). No music. Fax: (0522) 532402

LINTON West Yorkshire   map 5

▲ Wood Hall ⁙✳   NEW ENTRY

Trip Lane, Linton, nr Wetherby LS22 4AJ	
WETHERBY (0937) 587271	
from Wetherby take A661 N for ½m, turn	
left to Sicklinghall and Linton, then left to	
Linton and Wood Hall, turn right in Linton	COOKING 2
opposite Windmill pub	COST £33–£52

This magnificent Georgian hall is set in 100 acres of parkland overlooking the River Wharfe. Inside, all is chic and elegant. A warm glow pervades the Georgian Restaurant, which is stylish to a fault, from the heavy drapes to the floral displays on the immaculately laid tables. Service is astutely polite and professional. Chef Andrew Mitchell pleases the crowds with French onion soup, sirloin steak with all the trimmings and peach melba, but the main thrust of his regularly changing menu is modern English with a French undercurrent. His skill and technique are evident in warm tartlet of smoked haddock, beautifully layered terrine of seafood with baby leeks and saffron vinaigrette, and fillet of beef glazed with Stilton sabayon surrounded by a rich, reduced port sauce. Desserts are showpieces such as chocolate torte on coffee-bean sauce with chantilly cream; also look for the 'taste of apples' (a witty assemblage of cider cheesecake, Cox mousse and calvados sorbet with vanilla sauce). The wine list was being revised as we went to press, but it promises good value and a catholic choice. House wine is £10.

CHEF: Andrew Mitchell   PROPRIETOR: Country Mansion Hotels   OPEN: all week, exc Sat L; 12.30 to 2 (2.30 Sun), 7 to 10   MEALS: alc D (main courses £14 to £18.50). Set L £15.95, Set D £22.95   SERVICE: not inc, card slips closed   CARDS: Access, Amex, Diners, Visa   DETAILS: 70 seats. 5 tables outside. Private parties: 40 main room, 20 to 120 private rooms. Car park. Vegetarian meals. No children under 8. Jacket and tie. No smoking in dining-room. Wheelchair access (3 steps; also WC). Music   ACCOMMODATION: 43 rooms, all with bath/shower. TV. Phone. B&B £90 to £250. Lift. Children welcome. Baby facilities. Pets welcome (some rooms). Afternoon teas. Garden. Swimming-pool. Sauna. Fishing. Snooker. Doors close at 11. Confirm by 6. Fax: (0937) 584353

LITTLE SHELFORD Cambridgeshire   map 3

Sycamore House ▼ ✸   NEW ENTRY

1 Church Street, Little Shelford CB2 5HG   COOKING 2
CAMBRIDGE (0223) 843396   COST £27–£33

The Sharpes used to own Twenty Two in Cambridge (see entry), but sold up towards the end of 1992, and forsook the city for the gentle embrace of Little Shelford. Sycamore House is actually a former pub where the refurbishment has been kept simple and informality produces a 'happy atmosphere'. The formula is as it was in Cambridge: a fixed-price, four-course menu with around four choices at each stage, a salad intervening between starter and main. Chilled soups are favoured in summer (melon and ginger, perhaps, or 'refreshing' cucumber and mint), or there may be twice-baked goats' cheese soufflé, or salmon marinated in Sauternes, lime juice and green peppercorns and served with avocado salsa. Main courses may be calf's liver with a mustard sauce, or sauté guinea-fowl with lentils and coriander. A dinner in June took in 'simple, fresh, perfectly seasoned' pork terrine with red onion marmalade, 'nicely browned' boned quail with a 'restrained' sauce of grapes and madeira, and monkfish fried in butter, lemon and coriander that evoked comparisons with Breton fish restaurants. Puddings of crêpes suzette, and strawberry tart garnished with a 'sparkling cluster of redcurrants', were both enjoyed. The Sharpes appear to have taken the move in their stride.

A wide-ranging international wine list has been put together, with a keen eye to quality/price ratios. Most of the list is well under £20. Halves are a bit limited, but the house red is Guigal's Côtes du Rhône at £8.95. The white, a Bordeaux, is £7.95. CELLARMAN'S CHOICE: Wairau River Sauvignon 1993, £12.95; Rockford 'Basket Press' Shiraz 1990, £15.

CHEF: Michael Sharpe   PROPRIETORS: Michael and Susan Sharpe   OPEN: Tue to Sat, D only; 7.30 to 9.30 (L by arrangement)   CLOSED: Christmas   MEALS: Set D £19.50   SERVICE: not inc, card slips closed   CARDS: Access, Visa   DETAILS: 24 seats. Private parties: 25 main room. Car park. Vegetarian meals. No children under 12. Smart dress preferred. No smoking in dining-room. No music

---

LITTLE WALSINGHAM Norfolk   map 6

▲ Old Bakehouse ⅚✳ | NEW ENTRY |

33 High Street,
Little Walsingham NR22 6BZ
WALSINGHAM (0328) 820454   COOKING 1
on the B1105, 4½m N of Fakenham   COST £18–£38

Little Walsingham has been a place of pilgrimage for centuries, although not for its food. At one time it was second only to Canterbury in the ecclesiastical hierarchy. Nowadays tourists come as well (it is less than five miles from the sea), and the Old Bakehouse, dating from Tudor times, was once the village bakery. The former grain store is now the cellar bar, and the dining-room is Georgian. 'It's a lovely big old barn of a place,' observed a visitor, 'all kitted out in pink and pine.'

Despite the proximity of the sea, fish is not given centre stage. Local crab is cooked in filo pastry (served with a yogurt and saffron sauce) and sea bream is baked with garlic, tomatoes and parsley; but these take their place alongside fillet steak, pork fillet with an unctuously creamy prune sauce, and a chicken breast that positively pops with exotica, including ginger, mango and coriander. That apart, the food is untrendy, which comes as a relief to many. Green pea and smoked bacon soup is thick and comforting, the beef in beef Wellington is pink, and the temptation to put on rich puddings, such as banoffi pie, sticky toffee pudding and spotted dick with custard, is not resisted. Service is friendly and unfussy, and the wines are varied and well priced. House wine is £8.35.

CHEF: Christopher Padley   PROPRIETORS: Christopher and Helen Padley   OPEN: Tue to Sat, D only, and Sun L once a month; 12.30 to 2, 7 to 8.45   CLOSED: 1 week Nov, 2 weeks Jan to Feb, 1 week June, Tue Nov to Easter   MEALS: alc (main courses £13.50 to £15). Set L Sun £11.50   SERVICE: not inc, card slips closed   CARDS: Access, Visa   DETAILS: 36 seats. Private parties: 28 main room. Vegetarian meals. Children's helpings Sun L. Smart dress preferred. No smoking in dining-room. Wheelchair access (2 steps; also WC). Music   ACCOMMODATION: 3 rooms, 1 with shower. TV. B&B £22.50 to £40. Deposit: £5. Children welcome. Pets by arrangement. Confirm by 6 (The Which? Hotel Guide)

LIVERPOOL Merseyside   map 5

Armadillo ⅄

20–22 Mathew Street, L2 6RE   COOKING 2*
051-236 4123   COST £16–£38

New owners have taken over since last year but the chefs have stayed on to cook the same kind of food. Redecoration and possible expansion were imminent as we went to press, which will divide regulars, who would be happy to see a refurbishment but sad to lose the character of this long-running and immensely likeable city-centre attraction in a former warehouse close to the Cavern. A natural informality reigns, helped by enthusiastic service that disarms criticism – 'The wine service was gorgeously atrocious: a girl clasping two bottles like they were skittles, unsure what to do with them, or which was which, but very pleasantly served.' It is pure Scouse and irresistible.

The cooking runs too fast to be tied down to a description, but a few dishes give the feel: poached skate served with potato salad and anchovy vinaigrette, scrambled egg with asparagus on brioche, and crisp duck leg with mango chutney. 'The single most outstanding feature of the food is the saucing and dressing, deliciously varied and subtle,' writes one. Vegetarian dishes are considered 'inventive, imaginative and flavoursome' by a stalwart supporter who has enjoyed braised leeks à la grecque, pesto dumplings, bean burgers, and twice-baked cheese soufflé. Meanwhile goats' cheese on vine leaves, aubergine in a light wine and olive oil dressing, and red mullet on a brunoise of vegetables have all received endorsement. Puddings might be strawberry mousse or apple crumble. Early suppers include the likes of stuffed vine leaves, king prawns and the daily fish cooked in spicy coconut broth. The wine list has an eye for both quality and excitement. What is more, except for champagne and a couple of burgundies, it does it all for less than £20 a bottle. House wine is £7.50 (£1.50 per glass). CELLARMAN'S CHOICE: St Hallett Old Block Shiraz 1991, £17.50; Gewurztraminer 1989, Rolly-Gassman, £14.95.

CHEFS: John Scotland, Stewart St John and Edward Sweeney PROPRIETORS: Frank and John Kenny OPEN: Tue to Sat; 12 to 3, 7.30 to 10.30 (5 to 6.45 early supper Mon to Fri) MEALS: alc (main courses L and early supper £5 to £6.50, D £10 to £15) SERVICE: not inc (10% for 10 or more), card slips closed CARDS: Access, Amex, Visa DETAILS: 70 seats. Private parties: 50 main room. Vegetarian meals. Children's helpings on request. Smart dress preferred. Wheelchair access (3 steps). Music

---

LIVERSEDGE West Yorkshire   map 5

▲ Lillibet's

64 Leeds Road, Liversedge WF15 6HX   COOKING 1*
HECKMONDWIKE (0924) 404911   COST £17–£38

A feeling of tranquillity surrounds this neatly maintained stone house. Outside are well-tended lawns and shrubs; inside, everything looks spick and span. Dinner is three courses with several choices at each stage. The main thrust of Liz Roberts's cooking is modern British – salad of beef fillet with mustard mayonnaise, and roast duckling with raspberry and orange sauce, for example – but she also handles spicily exotic ideas such as crispy prawn balls and Thai salmon in filo parcels. Flavours are clear and accompaniments such as tomato coulis with prawn terrine, and rhubarb and ginger compote with well-timed fillet of venison, have plenty of zing. Vegetables are generous, but not overwhelming. Apple and calvados tart has been a highly enjoyable finale. Light weekday lunches span everything from sandwiches to roasts and pasta. The list of around 100 wines is a well-spread, thoughtfully chosen selection that promises a good deal of sound drinking for under £15. House wines start at £9.25.

CHEF: Liz Roberts   PROPRIETORS: Martin and Liz Roberts   OPEN: Mon to Sat, exc L Mon and Sat; 12 to 1.45, 7 to 9.30   CLOSED: 25 Dec for 9 days   MEALS: alc L (main courses £5 to £8). Set L £9.25, Set D £17.25 to £21.95   SERVICE: not inc   CARDS: Access, Amex, Visa   DETAILS: 60 seats. Private parties: 70 main room. Car park. Vegetarian meals. Children's helpings. Smart dress preferred. No cigars/pipes in dining-room. Wheelchair access (3 steps). Music ACCOMMODATION: 13 rooms, all with bath/shower. TV. Phone. B&B £49 to £65. Children welcome. Garden. Doors close at midnight. Fax: (0924) 404912 (*The Which? Hotel Guide*)

LOCKINGTON Humberside   map 6

Rockingham Arms   NEW ENTRY

52 Front Street, Lockington YO25 9SH
MARKET WEIGHTON (0430) 810607   COOKING 1
off A164, between Beverley and Driffield   COST £26–£41

Despite the name, this is more of a country restaurant than a country pub. The dining-room is in converted stables, and meals are served in a setting of open fires, provençale fabrics and candlelight. David Barker is a well-known local figure and has created a most agreeable establishment with the help of exceedingly pleasant, professional staff. The menu (fixed-price for two or three courses) is backed up by a few specials and daily fish dishes. Ingredients are above-average, as in a dish of lamb cutlets and fillet cooked pink with a creamy tarragon sauce. Otherwise, you might find parfait of chicken livers with toasted brioche, a hotpot of mushroom, smoked haddock and cider in a filo basket, and escalopes of pork with spiced apricot, orange and coriander sauce. Puddings are not always so successful, although a lacy biscuit cup filled with ice-cream and fresh fruit has been endorsed. The creditable list of around 60 wines offers plenty of reasonably priced drinking. Australian house wine is £7.95.

CHEFS/PROPRIETORS: David and Susan Barker   OPEN: Tue to Sat, D only; 7 to 10   CLOSED: 25 and 26 Dec, bank hols   MEALS: Set D £17 (2 courses) to £20   SERVICE: not inc   CARDS: Access, Visa   DETAILS: 60 seats. Private parties: 20 main room. Car park. Vegetarian meals. Children welcome. Smart dress preferred. Music

---

LONG CRENDON Buckinghamshire   map 2

▲ Angel Inn 🍸✳

Bicester Road, Long Crendon HP18 9EE
LONG CRENDON (0844) 208268   COOKING 1
on B4011, 2m NW of Thame   COST £21–£39

'The best pub meal I have had for over 40 years,' enthused a reporter who ate at this renovated coaching-inn. Its attractions are obvious: a warm fire by the bar with comfortable sofas, a maze of appealing rooms and eating areas, and food that is reliably on-the-ball. A monthly-changing printed menu of up-market pub/brasserie dishes is bolstered by a blackboard of specials, with fish as the main attraction. Many items have received endorsements: for example, bream roasted with Cajun spices; chargrilled squid with roasted peppers; baked cod with tempura king prawns and spinach; halibut with tomato fondue. Salads of crispy duck or chargrilled lamb are abundantly embellished with all manner of ingredients. Desserts are the likes of treacle tart or nougat and honey ice-cream. Portions are generous and prices are fair. Staff mean well, although they may find difficulty in coping. The ever-improving wine list has a useful contingent from the New World (you can also bring your own, with a corkage charge of only £1). House wines are under £10.

CHEFS: M.E. Jones and Wendy Showler   PROPRIETORS: Mr and Mrs M.E. Jones   OPEN: all week, exc Sun D; 12 to 2.30, 6.30 to 10   CLOSED: all day Sun 1 May to 30 Aug   MEALS: alc (main courses £6.50 to £12.50)   SERVICE: not inc   CARDS: Access, Visa   DETAILS: 100 seats. 5 tables outside. Private parties: 50 main room, 10, 20 and 50 private rooms. Car park. Vegetarian meals. Children's helpings by arrangement. No smoking in conservatory. No cigars/pipes in dining-room. Wheelchair access. Music   ACCOMMODATION: 4 rooms, all with bath/shower. TV. Phone. B&B £35 to £54. Children welcome. Baby facilities. Afternoon teas

---

LONG MELFORD Suffolk   map 3

Scutchers Bistro ▼

Westgate Street, Long Melford CO10 9DP   COOKING 1*
SUDBURY (0787) 310200 and 310620   COST £21–£32

Situated on the road to Sudbury, the Barretts' pub conversion has brought attractive modernity to an old timbered building opposite Melford Hall. Parking on the steep forecourt can be a little tricky: don't forget the handbrake. The à la carte menu offers a fair range of choice, augmented by daily blackboard specials, for food that is modern British with occasional touches of the Far East. Warm duck salad with cucumber, spring onions and hoisin sauce is Peking duck without the pancakes, while steamed crab wun-tuns with coriander come with soy for dipping. Otherwise, choices include spicy gratinated smoked haddock, chicken liver and bacon salad with a raspberry dressing, or roast pork stuffed with ham and Gruyère on a tomato sauce. Noodles with leeks, bacon and cheese, ravioli of salmon mousse, and skate with caper butter all receive endorsements. Afters can include items such as ice-cream sundaes, steamed chocolate pudding or tuile baskets of raspberries. A surprisingly wide range of wines is offered, arranged by grape variety. Makers are mostly very good (Henschke, Prunotto, Wairau River, Guigal), prices are encouraging, and notes are thoughtfully written. House wines start at £8.50. CELLARMAN'S CHOICE: Martinborough Sauvignon Blanc 1993, £14.50; Keyneton Estate Shiraz/Cabernet 1991, £14.

CHEF/PROPRIETOR: Nicholas Barrett   OPEN: Mon to Sat; 12 to 2, 7 to 9.30   CLOSED: bank hols   MEALS: alc (main courses £7 to £10.50)   SERVICE: not inc, card slips closed   CARDS: Access, Amex, Visa   DETAILS: 75 seats. 6 tables outside. Private parties: 75 main room. Car park. Vegetarian meals. Children's helpings. Smart dress preferred. Wheelchair access (also WC). Music

---

Prices quoted in the Guide are based on information supplied by restaurateurs. The prices quoted at the top of each entry represent a range, from the lowest meal price to the highest; the latter is inflated by 20 per cent to take account of likely price rises during the year of the Guide.

Paul Heathcote's ✤

104–106 Higher Road, Longridge PR3 3SY   COOKING 4*
PRESTON (0772) 784969   COST £33–£64

This stone cottage, on the bend of a road leading out of a workaday Lancashire village (follow signs for Jeffery Hill and the golf club), has been extended, and the dining area now comes closer to fulfilling the aspirations of the kitchen than hitherto. The old contradiction between homely surroundings and formal service has thus been resolved, both sides coming together to produce a cottagey but comfortable environment with relaxed and friendly, but still correct and competent, service. Tables are quite large and reasonably well spaced, in three interlinked dining-rooms; cutlery, glassware, crockery and flowers enhance the simple appeal.

Although quite prepared to deal in olives, red and yellow peppers, sun-dried tomatoes and balsamic vinegar (most notably in a first course with pink lamb fillet), Paul Heathcote does not hesitate to bang the British drum at every opportunity. He is not doctrinaire, which gives him the freedom to improvise, but he does steer some of the cooking towards the black pudding end of the spectrum, although some of these items have been pushed off the menu by the BSE scare, but a robust dish of pig's trotter is filled with ham hock and sage, served with a tartlet of shredded potato and pea purée, and an onion sauce: 'an inspired mix of peasant and haute cooking', according to a reporter. Those opposing characteristics appear in more than one dish. A light, juicy undercooked rack of lamb (on a dark stock reduction with small brown lentils) comes with a selection of sliced, humble vegetables such as Savoy cabbage, carrot, swede, salsify and turnip, all cooked accurately and tasting powerfully of themselves. Overall, though, the 'haute' side of Heathcote's wins out. Morel and shiitake mushrooms, and crisp asparagus tips, are scattered over a breast of corn-fed Goosnargh chicken, which is poached and served in a broth scented with truffle oil: 'another inspired dish full of flavour'. It is the kitchen's high technical standards, and its insistence on putting flavour first, that give it drive and conviction.

The *carte* is an interesting read, with most dishes promising just enough complexity. Occasionally the language irritates with 'symphonies' that 'nestle', but prices please, which is more important. Mid-meal sorbets are the least satisfactory item. Cheeses (unpasteurised cows' and goats') dance to the British beat, sometimes working themselves up into a savoury such as deep-fried Stilton beignets with a herb salad. Ice-creams – 'intense and technically impeccable' – sometimes accompany puddings: honey ice-cream with glazed rice pudding, or vanilla with hot banana soufflé, for example. The wine list is admirably extensive, there are some wonderful bottles, and the wine waiter knows his stuff, but mark-ups are just too high for comfort. House wine is £14.

CHEFS: Paul Heathcote and Andrew Barnes   PROPRIETOR: Paul Heathcote   OPEN: Tue to Sun D, Fri and Sun L; 12 to 2.15, 7 to 9.30   MEALS: alc (main courses £17 to £19). Set L £22.50, Set D £32.50   SERVICE: 10% (optional – £15 max.), card slips closed   CARDS: Access, Amex, Visa DETAILS: 55 seats. Private parties: 60 main room, 18 private room. Car park. Vegetarian meals. No children under 5. Smart dress preferred. No smoking in dining-room. Wheelchair access. Music. Fax: (0772) 785713

map 2

Peat Spade Inn

Longstock, nr Stockbridge SO20 6DR
ANDOVER (0264) 810612   COOKING 1*
off A3057, 1m N of Stockbridge   COST £22–£37

Julie Tuckett is now the sole owner of this tidy Victorian country pub near the River Test – in addition to running the bar, chatting to customers and cooking. This is fishing country, and the talk is all of flies and spinners. Meals can be eaten in bar or dining-room and the style is flexible: mix and match dishes, order a couple of starters, or go for the full three-course set menu. Proper cooking takes time, so do not come here for a quick snack, chips or a microwaved re-heat. Julie's way of doing things is sure and direct: meat and game are chargrilled or roasted, vegetables are steamed, puddings are mostly hot. Her repertoire is short, seasonal and well-tried: rich shellfish soup, home-made rillettes of pork, local sausages, roast fillet of salmon, guinea-fowl with calvados, cider and cream. Decent bread, 'divine' butter and draught beers from the nearby Hampshire Brewery are added attractions. The wine list is good and varied with plenty available by the glass. Fourteen house wines range from £9.25 to £12.

CHEF/PROPRIETOR: Julie T. Tuckett   OPEN: all week, exc Sun D; 12 to 2, 7.15 to 10   CLOSED: 25 and 26 Dec, 3 weeks Jan to Feb   MEALS: alc (main courses £7.50 to £12). Set L and D £11.85 (2 courses) to £16.50   SERVICE: not inc, card slips closed   CARDS: Amex, Diners   DETAILS: 30 seats. 6 tables outside. Private parties: 24 main room, 14 private room. Car park. Vegetarian meals. Children's helpings. Wheelchair access (also WC). No music

map 3

Jeremy's at The Crabtree ✠✳

Brighton Road, Lower Beeding RH13 6PT
HORSHAM (0403) 891257   COOKING 2
on A281 4m S of Horsham   COST £16–£36

The Crabtree – an imposing Georgian building – is a pub of two halves. To the right, as you go in, is the cosy no-smoking dining-room decorated with watercolours and bottles of oils and vinegars. The rest is a maze of eating and drinking areas with big oak settles, massive flagstones and low beams. It is pleasantly atmospheric and fairly buzzes.

Jeremy Ashpool's cooking is all about excitement, vitality and taking risks with new ideas. This shows up in the dinner menu, which might feature the likes of new season's lamb with bulgar wheat, marrow purée and roasted garlic; turbot in coriander and lime sauce; or seared venison fillet with wild rabbit and mushroom mousseline, and red onion compote. Lunch is simpler and cheaper, and there is plenty of support for mussel soup with dill, Sicilian rabbit stew, baked gammon with apricot sauce and lamb casserole with flageolet beans. The home-baked bread is spectacular. Service is very friendly but may be slow at peak times. King & Barnes real ales supplement the short, sharp wine list. House wine is £9.

CHEF: Jeremy Ashpool PROPRIETOR: Jeremy's Restaurant Ltd OPEN: all week, exc Sun D; 12.30 to 2, 7.30 to 9.45 MEALS: alc L (main courses £6 to £9). Set L Mon to Sat £8.50, Sun £14.50, Set D £9.50 (Tue to Thur) to £21.50 SERVICE: not inc L, 10% D and Set L Sun, card slips closed CARDS: Access, Visa DETAILS: 40 seats. Private parties: 25 main room, 25 private room. Car park. Vegetarian meals. Children's helpings on request. No smoking in 1 dining-room. Wheelchair access. Music. Fax: (0403) 891606

▲ South Lodge 🍴✳

Brighton Road, Lower Beeding RH13 6PS
LOWER BEEDING (0403) 891711   COOKING 2
on A281, 6m S of Horsham   COST £28–£69

Visitors to South Lodge either delight in the imposing grandeur of this nineteenth-century grey-stone mansion, or else find its Victorian severity weighing heavy on the soul. It is just as well perhaps that most find the service pleasantly informal, displaying 'involvement and a genuine wish to please'.

Tony Tobin left the kitchens at the end of 1993, and was replaced by John Elliott in March 1994. First reports suggest a period of settling in will be required. An inspection meal in May found a menu full of good ideas, but rather nervously executed. Crab and salmon tortellini seemed 'heavy rather than subtle', a chicken sausage on spinach was felt to have 'excellent texture and firm flavour' but was paired with a mustard-dominated tarragon cream sauce. Crispy aromatic duck on olive oil mash with lentils was enjoyed, and roast fillet of sea bass had a tomato and basil fondue that was good in itself though the basil tended to mask the delicacy of the fish. Sorbets and ice-creams were well presented and a hot raspberry soufflé with vanilla ice-cream was 'a highlight'. Home-made rolls, cafetière coffee and mini-frangipane tarts as petits fours are all thought fine. With closer attention to balance of flavours, there is no reason why John Elliott should not succeed in keeping South Lodge on track. Wines, though pricey, are fairly classical and offer a good spread. House Bordeaux is £13.50.

CHEF: John Elliott PROPRIETOR: Laura Hotels Ltd OPEN: all week; 12.30 to 2.30 (3 Sun), 7.30 to 10 (11 Fri and Sat) MEALS: alc (main courses £18 to £23). Set L £15, Set D £25 to £32 SERVICE: not inc, card slips closed CARDS: Access, Amex, Diners, Visa DETAILS: 40 seats. 4 tables outside. Private parties: 80 main room, 10 to 80 private rooms. Car park. Vegetarian meals. Children's helpings. Jacket and tie. No smoking in dining-room. Wheelchair access (1 step; also WC). No music ACCOMMODATION: 39 rooms, all with bath/shower. TV. Phone. B&B £90 to £255. Rooms for disabled. Children welcome. Baby facilities. Afternoon teas. Garden. Tennis. Fishing. Snooker. Confirm by 6. Fax: (0403) 891766 (The Which? Hotel Guide)

LOWER SLAUGHTER Gloucestershire   map 2

▲ Lower Slaughter Manor 🍴✳

Lower Slaughter, GL54 2HP
COTSWOLD (0451) 820456   COOKING 3
off A429, at sign 'The Slaughters'   COST £31–£59

The neighbouring villages of Upper and Lower Slaughter are among the most attractive in the Cotswolds, which is saying something. The Manor, built in 1658, is a listed building that retains a period feel, albeit that of a slightly later period. The fifteenth-century six-gabled dovecote in the walled garden is just as it was, while the house has gained wood panelling and some fine ornate plasterwork, as well as four-poster beds and a heated pool and sauna. 'An oasis of comfortable elegance,' one called it.

'Modern classical' may be an overworked term to describe the food here, but it fits like a glove. The kitchen is comfortable with luxuries, yet does not scatter them around willy-nilly, and is equally at home with quick, light cooking of fish (roast turbot, grilled Dover sole) as with long, slow roasts and braises such as shank of lamb or pig's trotter. Among the pleasingly novel ideas are a Thai pancake and Cabernet Sauvignon butter sauce that come with seared scallops, the white haricot beans and sherry vinaigrette that accompany a warm confit of salmon, and the 'first-class' layered terrine of foie gras and chicken on a Californian Muscat jelly. There has been praise, too, for parsley and shallot ravioli with pan-fried langoustines, and for a salad of marinated quail with vegetable terrine.

The food reassures and comforts while retaining a strong sense of individuality, and flavours hold attention. One regular reporter who stayed two days reckoned the cooking was well up to standard throughout. British and Irish cheeses receive plaudits, and two puddings stand out for excellence: a honey and lime soufflé served with a small citrus fruit salad and an orange sorbet, and a mixture of apple slices and blackcurrants steamed en papillote, accompanied by cinnamon ice-cream and palmier biscuits. A long list of French bottles (some ordinary, some classic, some swanky) is bolstered by an interesting Californian selection. More Australian and New Zealand wines are on the way. House French is £15.50 (£3.75 per glass).

CHEF: Julian Ehlers PROPRIETORS: Audrey and Peter Marks OPEN: all week; 12 to 2 (2.30 Sun), 7 to 9.45 (10 Sat) CLOSED: 2 weeks Jan MEALS: Set L £17.95, Set D £29.50 SERVICE: not inc, card slips closed CARDS: Access, Amex, Visa DETAILS: 36 seats. Private parties: 30 main room, 14 private room. Car park. Vegetarian meals. No children under 10. Jacket and tie D. No smoking in dining-room. No music ACCOMMODATION: 14 rooms, all with bath/shower. TV. Phone. D,B&B £140 to £290. Rooms for disabled. No children under 10. Afternoon teas. Garden. Swimming-pool. Sauna. Tennis. Doors close at midnight. Fax: (0451) 822150 (*The Which? Hotel Guide*)

LOW LAITHE North Yorkshire   map 7

Dusty Miller

Low Laithe, Summerbridge HG3 4BU
HARROGATE (0423) 780837   COOKING 3
on B6165, 2m SE of Pately Bridge   COST £29–£52

The Dusty Miller 'continues to be excellent in all respects', says one reporter. 'Although expensive, for a special occasion it cannot be bettered.' With wonderful views of the Nidd Valley, lots of flowers, starched linen and gleaming glassware, this stone-built house makes an appealing setting for some accomplished cooking. The Dennisons put their effort where it matters, into sourcing first-class ingredients, buying well and taking proper care with stocks and sauces. Pretence is absent, and the food is both direct and unfussy.

Dinner may be a simple set meal of ravioli of lobster, chicken breast with polenta and roasted pimento, and then either tropical fruit salad or cheese. The *carte* offers half a dozen choices that make good use of local lamb and of seafood: a plate of Irish oysters, perhaps, or a tartlet of leeks and scallops, or whatever arrives on the van from Scarborough. Dressings can be simple – hollandaise for asparagus, béarnaise for beef – and seasonings are accurate. One reporter who went through his meal with a fine toothcomb, trying to find fault, ended up being all the more impressed with the detail. House wine is £12.90 (£3 per glass for white, £3.60 for red).

CHEFS: Brian Dennison and Ben South   PROPRIETORS: Mr and Mrs Brian Dennison   OPEN: Tue to Sat, D only (L, Sun and Mon D by arrangement); 6.30 to 11   CLOSED: 25 Dec, 1 Jan, 2 weeks early Aug   MEALS: alc (main courses £10 to £18). Set D £24   SERVICE: not inc, card slips closed   CARDS: Access, Amex, Visa   DETAILS: 35 seats. Private parties: 32 main room, 14 private room. Car park. Vegetarian meals. Children's helpings. No children under 9. Smart dress preferred. Music. Fax: (0423) 780065

LYMINGTON Hampshire   map 2

▲ *Gordleton Mill Hotel, Provence* ⁑✳   NEW ENTRY

Silver Street, Hordle,
nr Lymington SO41 6DJ
LYMINGTON (0590) 682219
off A337, 1½m W of Lymington   COOKING 1
towards Hordle   COST £26–£72

This is where Jean-Christophe Novelli cooked before high-tailing it to the bright city lights (see Four Seasons Hotel, London). Didier Heyl took over as the *Guide* went to press last year, which is why Provence appeared in the round-up section. The setting is an old watermill on the edge of the New Forest, with white-painted bridges, lawns, weeping willows and a kitchen garden that supplies herbs and vegetables. The hotel is lavishly decorated, with an airily pink dining-room and a warm and welcoming atmosphere. Staff are very accommodating.

The kitchen's heart is firmly in France, and the long menus, from the £15 lunch through to the full *carte*, are a good read, taking in John Dory with chickpeas and sour cream, guinea-fowl with couscous, and an iced Grand Marnier parfait in a nougatine shell served with a passion-fruit coulis. The food is attractively presented. Chicken livers and croûtons of goats' cheese come on a gigantic plate arranged around a pile of mixed leaves, with a raspberry vinaigrette – 'a fantastic combination, perfectly executed' – and one reporter enjoyed poached peach with raspberry and peach coulis on ice-cream with a spun-sugar dome. But not all departments are working to the same standard, as an inspector discovered with a disappointing cassoulet the individual components of which were indistinguishable in taste. Rather a lot of work goes into some dishes, including wrapping lamb in basil and pastry, but the resulting flavour does not always justify the effort, which is a pity given the range and calibre of ingredients. The wine list has a solid French backbone, a penchant for quality, and mark-ups mostly just tantalisingly too much for comfort. House wines begin at £12 (£2.50 per glass).

CHEF: Didier Heyl   PROPRIETOR: William F. Stone   OPEN: all week (exc Sun D and Mon low season); 12 to 2.30, 7 to 9.30   CLOSED: first 2 weeks Jan   MEALS: alc (main courses £10.50 to £21). Set L Mon to Sat £15, Sun £19.50, Set D (exc Fri and Sat) £21.50 (inc wine)   SERVICE: not inc   CARDS: Access, Amex, Diners, Visa   DETAILS: 50 seats. 6 tables outside. Private parties: 70 main room, 25 private room. Car park. Vegetarian meals. Children's helpings. No children under 7 D. Smart dress preferred. No smoking in dining-room. Wheelchair access (also WC). Music. Air-conditioned   ACCOMMODATION: 7 rooms, all with bath/shower. TV. Phone. B&B £60 to £100. Deposit: 50%. Children welcome. Small dogs by arrangement. Afternoon teas. Garden. Fishing. Doors close at 1am. Confirm by 6. Fax: (0590) 683073 (*The Which? Hotel Guide*)

LYMPSTONE Devon   map 1

▲ *River House* ⁵✳

The Strand, Lympstone EX8 5EY   COOKING 1*
EXMOUTH (0395) 265147   COST £21–£58

'Lovely place, warm welcome, and what a view!' exclaimed an enthusiastic reporter, unprepared for the panorama of the Exe estuary and distant Dartmoor, 'on which you can feast your eyes both while drinking downstairs and eating upstairs'. Colours – pale yellow and apricot – are restful, tables well spaced, and the menus full of fish.

The fixed price of £26.50 is for three courses, but options for one more or one less exist, and at lunch an alternative *carte* is provided: such flexibility is welcome. Ideas come from round the globe (Moroccan tagine of lamb or Indonesian chicken, for example), but the foundation is a local abundance of fish and vegetables. One couple enjoyed a plain grilled Dover sole 'about 24 inches long and perfectly cooked', and an 'enormous, hot gratin of aubergine, peppers and courgettes' for main course, followed by vanilla ice-cream, and rhubarb fool with double cream and a raspberry coulis. Michael Wilkes does front-of-house virtually single-handed, and can be 'very good company'. Vins de pays, some under £10, offer good drinking, from a list with a fair range of prices. House French is £8.95 and eight wines are available by the glass from £2.50.

CHEF: Shirley Wilkes   PROPRIETORS: Shirley and Michael Wilkes   OPEN: Tue to Sun, exc Sun D; 12 to 1.30, 7 to 9.30 (10.30 Sat)   CLOSED: 25, 26 and 28 Dec, 1 Jan   MEALS: alc L (main courses £5 to £10). Set L Sun £16 (2 courses) to £20, Set L Tue to Sat and D £22.95 (2 courses) to £30.75   SERVICE: not inc   CARDS: Access, Amex, Visa   DETAILS: 34 seats. Private parties: 60 main room, 14 private room. Vegetarian meals. Children's helpings. No children under 6. Smart dress preferred. No smoking in dining-room. No music   ACCOMMODATION: 2 rooms, both with bath/shower. TV. Phone. B&B £55 to £74. Children welcome

---

The text of entries is based on unsolicited reports sent in by readers, backed up by inspections conducted anonymously. The factual details under the text are from questionnaires the Guide *sends to all restaurants that feature in the book.*

⁵✳ *indicates that smoking is either banned altogether or that a dining-room is maintained for non-smokers. The symbol does not apply to restaurants that simply have no-smoking areas.*

MAIDEN NEWTON Dorset

map 2

Le Petit Canard

Dorchester Road, Maiden Newton DT2 0BE
MAIDEN NEWTON (0300) 320536

COOKING 2*
COST £30–£39

The hinterland of Dorset seems an unlikely place to find chargrilled kangaroo, but Geoff and Lin Chapman are restaurateurs with a mission. In their small village restaurant, lit with fairy lights and candles, they offer a thoroughly challenging and well-executed modern menu where classical French, Far Eastern and Mediterranean influences are all clearly visible. Despite the eclecticism, fervent use is made of local produce: Piddle Valley black-faced lamb, game from nearby estates, West Country cheeses, and herbs and vegetables from the neighbouring village are all rhapsodised.

Starters may take in a warm salad, a stir-fry, a brochette, a soup and a soufflé. Reports differ as to the effectiveness of some treatments, but all commend the boldness. The breadth of style is shown by scallops and bacon in filo pastry parcels, rabbit stir-fried with peppers and mange-tout and dressed with 'ginger-chilli-orange oil', and duck slow-roasted with black beans and cracked pepper. A reporter who appreciated a 'meaty and hearty' wild mushroom and venison soup went on to enjoy slices of salty chicken breast on a fine satay sauce with 'spot-on' vegetables. Raspberry mascarpone dacquoise turned out to be layers of circular meringue, squashed raspberries, bland mascarpone and 'very sweet crushed hazelnut gunge – very satisfying'. More fish would be nice, as would a restraining hand on the meteorological metaphors ('strawberry drizzles' and 'a caramel puddle' appeared on one menu), but the Chapmans are justifiably proud of encouraging Dorset diners into adventurous habits. The wine list has some excellent French choices at fair prices, and bin-ends are worth a look, but the style of the cooking seems to call for a more enterprising range outside Europe. House wines are from £10.

CHEF: Geoff Chapman   PROPRIETORS: Geoff and Lin Chapman   OPEN: Tue to Sat, D only; 7 to 9   MEALS: Set D £20 to £21   SERVICE: not inc   CARDS: Access, Visa   DETAILS: 28 seats. Private parties: 34 main room. Vegetarian meals. No children under 7. No cigars/pipes in dining-room. Wheelchair access (2 steps). Music

---

MALVERN WELLS Hereford & Worcester

map 2

Croque-en-Bouche

221 Wells Road, Malvern Wells WR14 4HF
MALVERN (0684) 565612
on A449, 2m S of Great Malvern

COOKING 4
COST £40–£53

'Our high expectations of the Croque-en-Bouche were fully met during an evening of superb eating.' This is a true test of anywhere with a high reputation, and the Joneses come up with the goods time after time. 'We grow as much as possible ourselves, cook everything ourselves, and serve dinner ourselves,' they write. This requires dedication, and if Robin Jones appears a mite more serious than jovial customers would like, then we just have to accept him the way he is: well practised, perfectly polite and correct, just not matey. The terraced Victorian house is built on a steep slope. You go in at ordinary pavement level, walk through to the lounge, and stare out as if from a clifftop over the Bredon Hills. The dining-room is plain and square, with little to distract attention from the business of eating.

Meals begin with soup, proceed to an intermediate and then a main course, after which comes salad as a separate item, then cheese and dessert. The price includes service but not coffee. The repertoire is varied, but strong preferences surface, especially among fish and lamb. Salmon is 'smoked by the restaurant with applewood and fennel', and fish terrine crams tiger prawns, crab and skate into a tight space. The Japanese selection is impressive, pointing up how comfortable the kitchen feels with exotica, always properly done. It makes sense to apply Middle Eastern and North African ideas to lamb, and Marion Jones's versions – stuffed with couscous or cracked wheat, sometimes red peppers too, flavoured with lemon and mint, or cumin – convert a rustic one-pot dish of the souk into a more genteel English format. But the rich, full flavours work.

Novelties have included Cornish porbeagle shark with tapénade and grilled pimento – 'a very distinguished dish'. Soup, often with a vegetable component and served with home-made bread, is brought to table in a big tureen from which you help yourself, while main courses come with excellent potato gratin, the only extra vegetable on offer. Salads could not be better dressed if they went to Savile Row. English cheeses have included 'superb' cheddar, a ewes' milk and a particularly interesting local blue cheese, while sorbets of pineapple, passion-fruit, and even kiwi fruit have intense flavour. Wine, like the soup, is left on the table for you to deal with. Because Robin Jones understands wine he does not go in for the sort of window dressing and fancy footwork that others, who know less about it, mistakenly think is important. He has two lists, one red, one white, both 'absurdly long', as he puts it, inviting us to suggest a style and price and let him find something to suit. Trust him, he is really good, and it will save hours. What's more, the prices are sensational, and it is impossible to get ripped off. There are 'house wines' galore, wines by the glass from £2.50, and the chance to buy a case to take away. CELLARMAN'S CHOICE: Wairau River Sauvignon 1993, £14.50; Chianti Classico 1990, Felsina Berardenga, £17.50.

CHEF: Marion Jones PROPRIETORS: Robin and Marion Jones OPEN: Wed to Sat, D only; 7.30 to 9 (9.30 Sat) CLOSED: Christmas, New Year, 2 weeks Sept MEALS: Set D £33.50 SERVICE: net prices, card slips closed CARDS: Access, Visa DETAILS: 24 seats. Private parties: 6 main room, 6 private room. Children welcome. No smoking in dining-room. Wheelchair access (1 step). No music

Planters

191–193 Wells Road,
Malvern Wells WR14 9HB
MALVERN (0684) 575065
on A449, 3m S of Great Malvern

COOKING 2
COST £22–£36

Snazzy South-east Asian food in the conventional heartlands of old Worcestershire is an unlikely prospect, but this family-run restaurant succeeds in breaking the mould. The menu spans Sri Lanka, Thailand and Indonesia, with a range of dishes that takes in satays, nasi goreng, pork in mustard and chilli sauce, stir-fried turkey with sweet peppers and lemon grass, achar (pickled vegetables), and stir-fried jak-fruit with fresh coconut. A fixed-price 'feast menu' covers much of the repertoire, while one-plate meals (available every evening except Saturday) are great value. The owners lay on special gourmet events, and staff and customers have banded together to organise cricket matches, and jazz on a river boat. Service is speedy without seeming frantic. The short wine list is strong on flavour, with plenty of halves. House wines are from £7.25.

CHEF: Chandra de Alwis   PROPRIETOR: Sandra Pegg   OPEN: Tue to Sat, D only; 7 to 9.30 (post-theatre bookings by arrangement)   MEALS: alc (main courses £7 to £8). Set D £18.95 (minimum 2)   SERVICE: not inc, card slips closed   CARDS: Access, Visa   DETAILS: 40 seats. Private parties: 40 main room. Vegetarian meals. Children welcome. No cigars/pipes in dining-room. Wheelchair access (1 step). No music

---

MANCHESTER Greater Manchester	map 5

Gaylord £

Amethyst House, Spring Gardens, M2 1EA	COOKING 1*
061-832 4866	COST £13–£37

The Gaylord empire stretches from London and Manchester to Chicago and Hong Kong, its restaurants stylish bastions of old-style north Indian cooking. The Manchester branch, on the first floor of a modern terrace, holds its own among the city's richly cosmopolitan ethnic competition by working to a menu that inhabits the world of karahi chicken, sag gosht and prawn biriani, backed up by breads and an array of vegetarian dishes: look for paneer makhani (home-made cheese cooked tandoori-style with tomatoes and cream), tinda masala and sag kamal kakri (lotus roots with spinach). Set lunches are good value. House wine is £7.95.

CHEF: V.K. Wadhera   PROPRIETORS: P.K. Chadha and R. Kapoor   OPEN: all week; 12 to 2.30, 6 to 11.30   CLOSED: 25 Dec, 1 Jan   MEALS: alc (main courses £5 to £9). Set L Mon to Sat £5.95 (2 courses), Set L and D £11.95 to £14.95   SERVICE: 10%   CARDS: Access, Amex, Diners, Visa   DETAILS: 90 seats. Private parties: 90 main room. Vegetarian meals. Children welcome. Smart dress preferred. No-smoking area. Music. Air-conditioned. Fax: 061-832 6037

Koreana £

40A King Street West, M3 2WY	COOKING 1
061-832 4330	COST £11–£33

'Koreana appears to have opted for broadening the appeal by introducing European-type additions,' observes one who has watched it develop over the years. The good news is that £12.50 buys any starter, main course and sweet, and that Korean dishes remain very much at the core, with sesame, garlic, ginger, chilli and spring onions providing much of the seasoning. Dishes range from delicate items such as yonner gui (grilled salmon steaks with lemon sauce) to more vivid ones, including dweji gogi bokum (stir-fried sliced pork and vegetables in a spicy, garlicky sauce).

Gu jul pan – a lacquered box containing a mixture of deep-fried chicken, crabmeat parcels, prawns, pork galantine and a small spicy beefburger – makes a good first course, while beef bulgogi (sweetly marinated strips of meat cooked at the table) is a classic of the repertoire. Five-course banquets centre on meat, seafood or vegetables, and staff are ready with advice for anybody unfamiliar with Korean food. The choice of drink runs through tea (ginseng or green) to saké or wine from the short list. House wine is £7.50 (£1.70 per glass).

CHEF: Hyun-Suk Shin PROPRIETOR: Koreana Ltd OPEN: Mon to Sat, exc Sat L; 12 to 2.30, 6.30 (5.30 Sat) to 11 (11.30 Fri and Sat) MEALS: Set L £4.95 to £7.30, Set L and D £12.50 to £19.50 SERVICE: not inc, card slips closed CARDS: Access, Amex, Diners, Visa DETAILS: 60 seats. Private parties: 60 main room. Vegetarian meals. Children welcome. Smart dress preferred. Music. Fax: 061-832 2293

Kosmos Taverna £

| 248 Wilmslow Road, M14 6LD | COOKING 1 |
| 061-225 9106 | COST £20–£31 |

'The atmosphere is exactly as it was,' claimed one who had not visited for a long time: full of 'noisy Greek types and friendly waiters. It is hectic and good fun', with close-packed tables in small, busy rooms. The long menu covers the Greek Cypriot standards and a few more besides, from soups, salads, and dips of hummus or skordalia, through stuffed vine leaves to stifado, afelia, and kebabs of lamb or chicken. Meat-eaters and vegetarians can tuck in happily side by side to generous gung-ho helpings, but the food can vary in quality: from excellent grilled baby squid to, for one reporter, tasteless king prawns and tough stifado. Everything is made in-house, though, and chocolate fudge cake takes its place alongside halva, Greek delight and galatoboureko, a filo pastry roll of custard and honey. Nothing is very expensive, and that goes for the selection of largely Cypriot wines too, which start at £8.

CHEF: Loulla Astin PROPRIETORS: Stewart and Loulla Astin OPEN: all week, D only, and Sun L; 6.30 (1 Sun) to 11.30 (12.30 Fri and Sat) MEALS: alc (main courses £5.50 to £11). Set L and D £11 to £14 (minimum 2) SERVICE: not inc CARDS: Access, Visa DETAILS: 90 seats. Private parties: 40 main room. Vegetarian meals. Children's helpings. Smart dress preferred. No cigars/pipes in dining-room. Wheelchair access. Music. Air-conditioned. Fax: 061-256 4442

Lime Tree

| 8 Lapwing Lane, West Didsbury, M20 8WS | COOKING 1 |
| 061-445 1217 | COST £17–£34 |

The restaurant is a converted shop at the end of a terrace in an upwardly mobile enclave on the fringes of Didsbury. It functions capably as a neighbourhood bistro. The décor sticks to a formula of green and cream colour schemes, polished wooden floors and candles in wine bottles. The mood of noisy, cheerful buzz pulls in the crowds. The cooking follows suit. It is competent, without taking itself too seriously or trying to ape in-vogue Mediterranean minimalism. Mussels with pesto, game terrine with 'jammy' Cumberland sauce, and monkfish tails with red pepper purée are handled with confidence. Vegetables are accurately timed, and the coffee is strong. The modest wine list is slanted towards interesting bottles at the lower end of the price spectrum. House wine is £8.50.

CHEFS: Simon Haywood, Lee Cross and Damien Kay PROPRIETORS: Patrick Hannity and Robert Williams OPEN: all week, D only, and Sun L; 12 to 2.30, 6.30 to 10.30 CLOSED: 25 and 26 Dec, 1 Jan, bank hol Mons MEALS: alc (main courses £7.50 to £12.50). Set L Sun £10.50 SERVICE: not inc CARDS: Access, Amex, Visa DETAILS: 80 seats. Private parties: 45 main room, 40 private room. Vegetarian meals. Children's helpings Sun L. Wheelchair access. Music

Little Yang Sing

17 George Street, M1 4HE   COOKING 2
061-228 7722   COST £15–£51

Situated behind the Piccadilly Plaza, this premier-league Chinese restaurant sustains its reputation as one of the best Cantonese venues in the city. The setting is a basement in the heart of Chinatown with minimalist décor and closely packed tables. What the kitchen delivers is authentic stuff, although it is also capable of innovation. The list of dim-sum is shorter than in some other places, but it offers high quality and some intriguing items such as deep-fried king prawn dumplings with 'mayonnaise sauce' and minced beef curried samosas. The full menu has a strong contingent of one-plate rice and noodle dishes as well as baked king prawns with salt and pepper, steamed chicken with Chinese sausages, and duck with green pepper and black-bean sauce ('always an excellent combination', according to one reporter). A full vegetarian menu is also on offer and it is worth exploring the Cantonese banquets, which often feature unusual specialities such as deep-fried fillet of grouper topped with ham and prawn paste or asparagus with glazed walnuts. Service is very efficient and the staff smile. The short wine list makes familiar reading, but prices are fair. House wine is £8.95.

CHEF: Au Ting Chung PROPRIETOR: Miss O.K. Yeung OPEN: all week; 12 to 4, 6.30 to 11.10 MEALS: alc (main courses £5 to £12). Set L £8.95, Set D £14 to £30 SERVICE: 10% CARDS: Access, Amex, Visa DETAILS: 90 seats. Private parties: 90 main room. Vegetarian meals. Children's helpings L. Smart dress preferred. No music. Air-conditioned. Fax: 061-237 9257

▲ Moss Nook

Ringway Road, M22 5NA
061-437 4778
on B5166, 1m from Manchester Airport,   COOKING 3
M56 junction 5   COST £24–£62

'The food was good, the service better, but when the bill arrived we still gulped at the huge total,' wrote one reporter after eating from the à la carte menu. That may be so, but it is still considered good value for money. The surroundings are not particularly pretty – although no worse than those of most other Manchester restaurants – but in any case are soon forgotten once the opulent swags and drapes, and the red velvet walls, begin to take effect. Large tables, synchronised dome-lifting and an indulgent larder gesture expansively towards the lavish end of the market. A first course of lobster with salad leaves and raspberry dressing might cost in the region of 'twelve pounds ninety-five pence', which is how they write the prices.

The cooking is hot on presentation, and steers a comfortable course through fillet steak studded with garlic and served with a creamed green peppercorn sauce, or duck breast with apple and calvados sauce. Ingredients are good, and although the cooking may lack the ingenuity and excitement demanded by more cosmopolitan diners, it rarely disappoints. Asparagus spears are wrapped in a slice of fresh salmon and eaten with béarnaise sauce; big goujons of chicken breast are served with a spicy and honey-sweet sauce and a pot of yogurt dressing. A small portion of soup arrives mid-meal. Vegetables are dainty.

The 'grand selection' of desserts is recommended, and might incorporate a tiny steamed suet pudding, a chocolate box of cream and fruit, and a nut and rum paste in pastry, among others. The Menu Surprise runs to seven courses, counting pre-meal nibbles and coffee as two of them. A few modest clarets and vins de pays, plus an all-Rosemount selection from Australia, balance price and quality quite well, and there is a page or two of heart-stopping French classics. House wine starts at £9.50.

CHEF: Kevin Lofthouse PROPRIETORS: Pauline and Derek Harrison OPEN: Tue to Sat, exc Sat L; 12 to 1.30, 7 to 9.30 MEALS: alc (main courses £18 to £19). Set L £16.50, Set D £28 SERVICE: not inc, card slips closed CARDS: Access, Amex, Diners, Visa DETAILS: 70 seats. 5 tables outside. Private parties: 50 main room. Car park. Vegetarian meals with prior notice. No children under 8. Smart dress preferred. No music ACCOMMODATION: 1 room in cottage, with bath/shower. TV. Phone. D,B&B £140. No children under 8. Garden. Fax: 061-498 8089

Pearl City £

33 George Street, M1 4PH
061-228 7683

COOKING 1*
COST £15–£45

This is a bastion of old-style Cantonese cooking in the heart of Manchester's Chinatown. Its strength lies in the range of around 30 dim-sum and a plethora of roast meats and one-plate meals. Among the dim-sum you will find whelks marinated in satay sauce, turnip and dried meat cake, and sweet lotus cream bun, as well as steamed beef balls, roast pork bun and deep-fried prawn dumplings. As an alternative, the Westernised set lunch is reckoned to be excellent value. The menu of more than 250 dishes covers a lot of ground, taking in shredded duck with pickled cabbage soup, fried chicken with ginger and spring onion, sliced beef with green pepper, and pork with oyster sauce, not to mention a handful of specialities from Peking and Szechuan. Seafood is a major suit: ask for the 'best of the day'. The restaurant is on two floors above a rather 'scruffy' stairway and the upkeep of the place has cast doubts in the minds of some visitors. House wine is £7.90.

CHEF/PROPRIETOR: Mr Cheung OPEN: all week; noon to 2am (4am Sat, midnight Sun) MEALS: alc (main courses £6 to £14). Set L £4.50 (2 courses) to £19.50 (minimum 2). Set D (minimum 2) £15.50 to £19.50 SERVICE: 10% CARDS: Access, Amex, Visa DETAILS: 200 seats. Private parties: 200 main room. Vegetarian meals. Children welcome. Smart dress preferred. Music. Air-conditioned. Fax: 061-237 9173

'Some of the waiters were so old I feared they would not see the evening out.'
(On eating in a grand hotel in London)

Siam Orchid £

54 Portland Street, M1 4QU   COOKING 1
061-236 1388 and 9757   COST £14–£41

Not all the food in Manchester's Chinatown is Chinese: this small Thai
restaurant provides a justifiably popular alternative. A reporter who had been
before noted that 'the pictures of kick boxers have been replaced by views of
Thailand'. This altogether more friendly feel extends to the menu, which has an
informative preface for the inexperienced and still runs to nearly 100 dishes,
including rice and noodles, and is now supplemented by a vegetarian menu
offering formidable choice. Dipping sauces are praised for being 'splendidly
lethal', even if on occasion they may be spicing up a fairly bland main ingredient.
Garlic-fried spare ribs, pork toasties (a Thai version of sesame prawn toasts), and
steamed fish with gingery plum sauce are all recommended. Wines are very
reasonably priced, though in most cases producers and vintages are not listed.
Thai beer is a good alternative. House French wine is £8.

CHEF: C. Sirisompan   PROPRIETORS: C. Sirisompan and K. Sirisambhand   OPEN: all week,
weekdays 11.30 to 2.30, 6.30 (6 Fri) to 11.30; Sat and Sun noon to 11.30pm (11pm Sun)
CLOSED: 25 Dec, 1 Jan, bank hols L   MEALS: alc (main courses £4.50 to £8.50). Set L £5 to £7
(both 2 courses), Set D £16 to £27   SERVICE: 10% (not inc Set L)   CARDS: Access, Visa
DETAILS: 60 seats. Private parties: 60 main room. Vegetarian meals. Children welcome. Music.
Air-conditioned. Fax: 061-236 8830

That Café

1031–1033 Stockport Road,
Levenshulme, M19 2TB   COOKING 1
061-432 4672   COST £18–£35

Stockport Road extends drearily on and on through Levenshulme but in its
upper reaches is That Café – 'worth the effort to get there,' says a reader. A
pleasing air of characterful decrepitude pervades the interior, with its clutter of
old furniture, fire-irons and plants, and people appreciate the warmth of their
reception. Joseph Quinn's cooking is more firmly rooted in the present, and is
especially treasured in an area not over-endowed with good restaurants. A
monthly-changing dinner menu is the main business, with a shorter and much
simpler prix fixe midweek. Starters emblematically span the last three decades
of restaurant fashion with mushrooms in port and Stilton, goats' cheese timbale
with raspberry vinaigrette, and bruschetta with peppers, aubergines,
mozzarella, extra-virgin olive oil and basil. Breast of turkey in a Drambuie cream
sauce with hazelnuts pleased a pre-Christmas trio mightily, while others have
singled out salmon with quail's eggs and spinach mayonnaise, and a
'particularly delicious' banana cheesecake with toffee sauce. Vegetarians have
plenty of choice. Wines are virtually a one-bottle-per-region selection, most
quite acceptable without being exciting. Three English fruit wines are served
with the same care as the grape variety. House Portuguese is £7.95.

The Guide *always appreciates hearing about changes of chef or owner.*

CHEF: Joseph Quinn PROPRIETORS: Joseph Quinn and Stephen King OPEN: Tue to Sun, D only, and Sun L; 12 to 3.30, 7 to 10.30 (11 Sat) MEALS: alc (main courses £9 to £13). Set L Sun £10.95, Set D Tue to Thur £12.95 SERVICE: not inc, card slips closed CARDS: Access, Amex, Visa DETAILS: 80 seats. Private parties: 50 main room, 30 private room. Vegetarian meals. Children's helpings. No-smoking area. Wheelchair access (1 step). Music

▲ Woodlands

33 Shepley Road, Audenshaw, M34 5DJ
061-336 4241

COOKING 2
COST £24–£41

The setting is a Victorian villa on the suburban fringe of Manchester. Inside, it boasts high ceilings, lots of lamps and comfortable furnishings; the bar area is one of the front rooms. Staff are hard-working and chatty without being obtrusive. William Jackson's cooking generally meets with approval, although an occasional note of dissent can mar the overall picture. The midweek table d'hôte (Tuesday to Friday) provides good value but few culinary surprises. A better bet is the *carte*, which promises big portions of French-style dishes with light, carefully crafted sauces. Mushrooms in a filo basket with paprika, fresh scallops with spring onions and chive cream sauce, and medallions of lamb – cooked pink – with two tarragon sauces have been singled out. Side plates of abundant vegetables generally succeed, although on one occasion they were reckoned to be a 'shiny, greasy mess' and remained uneaten. Baked Alaska with chocolate sauce is a typical dessert. Bread is warm and fresh, coffee can be weak. The wine list is tilted in favour of France at the expense of the New World, but prices are fair. House wine is £8.25.

CHEF: William Jackson PROPRIETORS: Mr and Mrs Dennis Crank OPEN: Tue to Sat, exc Sat L (Sun L last Sun of month only); 12 to 2, 7 to 9.30 (10 Sat) CLOSED: first week Jan, 1 week Easter, 2 weeks mid-Aug MEALS: alc (main courses £12.50 to £13.50). Set L and D £15.65 (exc Sat) SERVICE: not inc, card slips closed CARDS: Access, Visa DETAILS: 40 seats. Private parties: 24 main room, 17 private room. Car park. Vegetarian meals with prior notice. Children's helpings on request. Smart dress preferred. No cigars/pipes in dining-room. Wheelchair access (3 steps; also WC). Music ACCOMMODATION: 3 rooms, all with shower. TV. Phone. B&B £40 to £60. Children welcome. Garden

Yang Sing £

34 Princess Street, M1 4JY
061-236 2200

COOKING 3
COST £18–£45

After a few lapses and inconsistencies, Yang Sing is back on form. Without doubt, it is capable of producing some of the finest Chinese food in the land. The kitchen scores highly because Harry Yeung cares about freshness and quality; there is a precision and clarity about the cooking that few similar restaurants can match. Daytime dim-sum are outstanding: reporters have praised many items, including spicy meat and nut dumplings, prawn and crabmeat dumplings, innovative 'beef olives' stuffed with vegetables, coriander and garlic, and deep-fried prawns served Western-style with a pot of mayonnaise. Yeung's loyalty to his Cantonese roots shows in the hotpots, casseroles, roast meats and one-plate dishes that dominate much of the vast menu: this is the world of fish lips, goose webs, ox tripe and chicken gizzard. Scallops are steamed and served in the shell, braised duck sits on a bed of pak choi greens, sizzling beef is 'impeccable'. The restaurant's reputation also hinges on inventive specialities such as casserole of wild boar with watercress, marinated pigeon and stir-fried squid in cheesy batter. Staff are knowledgeable and noticeably good-humoured. The short wine list offers a reasonably priced selection of decent bottles. House wine is from £8.60.

CHEF: Harry Yeung   PROPRIETOR: Yang Sing Restaurant Ltd   OPEN: all week; noon to 11.15
CLOSED: 25 Dec   MEALS: alc (main courses £6.50 to £9.50). Set L and D £14 (minimum 2)
SERVICE: 10%   CARDS: Access, Amex, Visa   DETAILS: 150 seats. Private parties: 220 main
room, 36, 72 and 110 private rooms. Vegetarian meals. Children welcome. Smart dress
preferred. Wheelchair access (via goods lift). Music. Air-conditioned. Fax: 061-236 5934

MANNINGTREE Essex   map 3

Stour Bay Café ✸

39–43 High Street, Manningtree CO11 1AH   COOKING 1
COLCHESTER (0206) 396687   COST £20–£39

A refreshing breath of Californian air blows through this town-centre restaurant, and gives Sherri Singleton's menu an enviable lightness of touch. The seasonings are zingily upbeat: coriander leaf, fresh lime, mint, lemon grass, ginger, coconut, and wasabi butter. The colours (if sometimes by implication) are bright: roasted red peppers, yellow-fin tuna, and a 'custard' of ricotta, pine-nut and basil to accompany wild mushrooms. It all speaks of lively West Coast invention, and of tastes that excite. Fish is given prominence. Grilled sea bass comes with arugula, pesto and lime, while the brown butter for wing of skate uses macadamia nuts. Not all the excitement transfers to the plate, but reporters have enjoyed fresh bread dunked into carrot and coriander soup, oysters Rockefeller, and salmon fillet wrapped in oak-smoked salmon in a saffron basil butter. Among puddings of pecan waffle and Key lime pie are some good ice-creams, notably the brown-bread version. The 40-bottle wine list is predominantly New World, the bulk of it laudably below £15. House wine from Fetzer is £8.55.

CHEF: Sherri Singleton   PROPRIETORS: David McKay and Sherri Singleton   OPEN: Tue to Sun,
exc Tue to Thur L and Sun D; 12 to 2.30 (3 Sun), 7 to 10   CLOSED: 2 weeks Jan, 2 weeks Sept
MEALS: alc (main courses £7.50 to £14)   SERVICE: not inc   CARDS: Access, Amex, Visa
DETAILS: 65 seats. Private parties: 65 main room, 20 private room. Vegetarian meals. Children's
helpings. No smoking in dining-room. Wheelchair access. No music. Air-conditioned. Fax:
(0206) 395462

The 1996 Guide will be published before Christmas 1995. Reports on meals are most welcome at any time of the year, but are particularly valuable in the spring. Send them to The Good Food Guide, *FREEPOST, 2 Marylebone Road, London NW1 1YN. No stamp is needed if posted in the UK.*

The Guide is totally independent, accepts no free hospitality, and survives on the number of copies sold each year.

MARY TAVY Devon   map 1

▲ *Stannary* ✳※

Mary Tavy PL19 9QB
MARY TAVY (0822) 810897
on A386 Tavistock to Okehampton road,   COOKING 1
4m NE of Tavistock   COST £39–£53

'Dining here is quite an experience!' exclaimed a visitor, who marvelled at the amazing collection of Carlton Ware pottery and at the 'evangelical zeal' with which this elegant restaurant is run. Michael Cook and Alison Fife are champions of vegetarianism, organic production and self-sufficiency. Their sixteenth-century-cum-Victorian house on the edge of Dartmoor is a hive of activity, although it can exude an almost monastic atmosphere. Alison Fife offers a surprisingly elaborate – and far from cheap – fixed-price menu that is full of thoroughly 'worked' ideas and mixed flavours. Wild foods, fungi, seaweeds and oriental vegetables all appear in dishes such as mushrooms stuffed with bulgar wheat on a blue cheese sauce, parsley 'spears' (actually more like rissoles) with a 'chunky' sweet-and-sour sauce, and 'nests' of hazelnuts and leeks surrounded by a 'wonderfully dark madeira-type gravy'. Fried yams and beans in comfrey sauce might feature as accompanying vegetables. 'Divine' ice-creams are alternatives to the list of substantial puddings. A huge array of coffees, teas, infusions and non-alcoholic cordials support the substantial, well-considered wine list. Organic and vegetarian bottles show up strongly. House wine is £9.20.

CHEF: Alison Fife   PROPRIETORS: Michael Cook and Alison Fife   OPEN: Tue to Sat, D only; 7 to 9 (later if pre-arranged)   CLOSED: Tue and Wed in winter   MEALS: Set D £24 (2 courses) to £35   SERVICE: not inc, card slips closed   CARDS: Access, Amex, Visa   DETAILS: 20 seats. 3 tables outside. Private parties: 30 main room. Car park. Vegetarian meals. No children under 12. Smart dress preferred. No smoking in dining-room. Music   ACCOMMODATION: 3 rooms, 1 with bath/shower. TV. D, B&B £70 to £120. Deposit: £20. No children under 12. Garden. Doors close at midnight. Confirm by 6. Fax: (0822) 810898

MASHAM North Yorkshire   map 7

Floodlite

---

7 Silver Street, Masham HG4 4DX
RIPON (0765) 689000   COOKING 3
off A6108, 9m NW of Ripon   COST £16–£43

'Here, someone of real calibre is at work, and it shows,' commented reporters about Charles and Christine Flood's restaurant. One evening, however, did not start well: 'Nobody to greet us. We found our way downstairs and helped ourselves to wine lists and menus.' But from then on, all was fine. King prawns and squid with ginger and garlic, fillet steak with mushroom purée and hollandaise sauce, good hot vegetables, and apple and almond tart with caramel sauce and praline ice-cream were all to our reporters' liking. Charles Flood has a fondness for roasting game: loin of roe deer is paired with wild mushrooms, widgeon is pointed up with ginger and spring onions, and saddle of hare is accompanied by turnips and red wine sauce. Fish shows up in the form of 'very good' salmon and pike terrine with dill sauce, grilled lobster and baked salmon with mustard seeds. The fixed-price Sunday lunch is reckoned to be 'the bargain of the north'. The wine list runs to around 80 bins, the range is well-spread, and plenty of decent drinking can be had for under £15. House wines are £7.50 and £7.95.

CHEF: Charles Flood   PROPRIETORS: Charles and Christine Flood   OPEN: Fri to Sun L, Tue to Sun D; 12 to 2, 7 to 9.30   MEALS: alc (main courses £8 to £16.50). Set L Sun £10.50   SERVICE: not inc, card slips closed   CARDS: Access, Amex, Visa   DETAILS: 38 seats. Private parties: 28 main room. Vegetarian meals. Children's helpings. Smart dress preferred. Wheelchair access (2 steps). Music

---

MATLOCK Derbyshire

map 5

▲ *Riber Hall*

Matlock DE4 5JU
MATLOCK (0629) 582795
1m off A615 at Tansley

COOKING 2
COST £25–£46

The hotel is a slice of Tudor history, built in true Derbyshire style from local sandstone. Everywhere are echoes of the past. A superb walled garden has an ancient flagged walkway, while the interior boasts some marvellous touches, including an ornately carved mantlepiece. 'There is a genuine lived-in feel – as if the squire was still in residence,' noted one visitor. The restaurant has been moved to a handsome upstairs room with mullioned windows and gold drapes; like the lounge, it is now no-smoking.

Chef Jeremy Brazelle's capabilities show up well in the fixed-price lunch menu: his style is pure country-house, with the emphasis on fine technique, accurate sauces and deliberate presentation. Monkfish and salmon terrine is set off by a duo of sauces – one pink, one yellow – while fanned breast of chicken receives a sherry and red pepper sauce tinged with basil. Sweets, such as white and dark chocolate terrine with lime-flavoured crème anglaise, are showpieces. The full *carte* inhabits similar territory: grilled turbot with baby vegetables and dill butter sauce, calf's liver and kidney with leek purée and grain mustard sauce, or sauté fillet of beef with chanterelles. Service is discreet and 'serious'. The wine list is substantial, with a catholic choice of makers and prices to match. Chilean house wine is £10.90.

CHEF: Jeremy Brazelle   PROPRIETOR: Alex Biggin   OPEN: all week; 12 to 1.30, 7 to 9.30   MEALS: alc (main courses £12.50 to £17). Set L £11.50 (2 courses) to £18.50   SERVICE: not inc, card slips closed   CARDS: Access, Amex, Diners, Visa   DETAILS: 60 seats. Private parties: 40 main room, 16 and 35 private rooms. Car park. Vegetarian meals. Children's helpings. No children under 10. Smart dress preferred. No smoking in dining-room. No music   ACCOMMODATION: 11 rooms, all with bath/shower. TV. Phone. B&B £79.50 to £137. Deposit: £35. No children under 10. Afternoon teas. Garden. Tennis. Doors close at 11. Fax: (0629) 580475 (*The Which? Hotel Guide*)

All entries in the Guide *are rewritten every year, not least because restaurant standards fluctuate. Don't trust an out-of-date* Guide.

MAWGAN Cornwall map 1

Yard Bistro £

Trelowarren, Mawgan TR12 6AF
MAWGAN (0326) 221595
off B3293, 3m SE of Helston

COOKING 1
COST £13–£35

You may need a spot of persistence to find the Yard Bistro. Trelowarren Manor is easy to locate; thereafter, look for the door marked 'Tackroom Loos' and you have it. The bistro is in the old carriage house. Inside are plain dark green walls and cane chairs, and a 'thoroughly jolly' approach. The cooking at lunch is based on old-fashioned hearty fare like Cumberland sausages, seafood broth and lamb cobbler; in the evening, greater invention comes into play. An inspection in May turned up 'sharp-tasting' asparagus and watercress mousse with hazelnuts, a 'plump and tender' pigeon breast on brioche with a herb butter sauce and well-nigh faultless crab soufflé that was 'sinfully rich'. Sauces tend to be strong. Iced chocolate and honey terrine was an enjoyable pudding, while strawberry mille-feuille was overwhelmed by a blackcurrant coulis and not exactly seasonal. Vegetables included some unusual but good casseroled roots. Service is 'affable'. The wine list offers a standard choice at fair prices. House red and white are £7.50.

CHEF: Trevor Bayfield   PROPRIETOR: R.F. Vyvyan   OPEN: Tue to Sat, exc D Tue and Sun; 12 to 2, 7 to 9   CLOSED: Christmas to Easter (exc private parties)   MEALS: alc (main courses £9 to £11.50). Light L menu   SERVICE: not inc   DETAILS: 55 seats. 5 tables outside. Private parties: 70 main room. Car park. Vegetarian meals. Children's helpings. Wheelchair access (also WC). Music

---

MAWNAN SMITH Cornwall map 1

▲ Nansidwell Country House

Mawnan Smith TR11 5HU
FALMOUTH (0326) 250340
off A494 Helston road, take left fork at
Red Lion in village

COOKING 2
COST £20–£52

The house was built in 1902 for a local judge, and the aspect it presents to visitors coming up the drive may well be one of juridical severity. A couple who arrived on a misty May midday gulped at the imposing façade – all 'massive mullions and transoms and no fancy bits' – but were given a window table looking out to sea. The garden was a riot of azaleas and magnolias, something to lift the spirits.

The Robertsons' declared aim is to create a warmly domestic atmosphere, and they seem to succeed. Fixed-price menus offer two or three choices at lunch and five at dinner for starter and main, with a choice of puddings or cheese to follow. The abiding impression left by Tony Allcott's cooking is one of lightness and delicacy. This can of course be a virtue for those who hate being overwhelmed; the drawback is that it can mean a certain blandness creeping into dishes that sound richer. Reporters who enjoyed a platter of home-smoked fish with creamed horseradish thought the balance of flavours was spot-on. Chicken mousse on an artichoke heart with a raspberry vinegar sauce was brought off

393

with aplomb, achieving a genuine, if unlikely, marriage of flavours. Good apple and almond pudding with vanilla custard was appreciated, and a white chocolate mousse with blackcurrant coulis garnished with fruity exotica was pronounced 'entirely delectable'. Home-made granary bread is given the nod as well. Wines are stolid rather than exciting, but an attempt is made to offer a good geographical range at indisputably fair prices. A slate of house selections starts at £10 for Spanish red and white.

CHEF: Tony Allcott   PROPRIETORS: Jamie and Felicity Robertson   OPEN: all week; 12.30 to 1.30, 7 to 9   CLOSED: Jan   MEALS: Set L £12.75, Set D £23 to £31.50   SERVICE: not inc, card slips closed   CARDS: Access, Visa   DETAILS: 35 seats. 2 tables outside. Private parties: 45 main room. Car park. Vegetarian meals. Children's helpings. No children under 7 D (exc by prior arrangement). Smart dress preferred. No cigars/pipes in dining-room. Wheelchair access. No music   ACCOMMODATION: 12 rooms, all with bath/shower. TV. Phone. B&B £35 to £140. Deposit: £100. Rooms for disabled. Children welcome. Baby facilities. Pets welcome (not in public rooms). Garden. Tennis. Fax: (0326) 250440 (*The Which? Hotel Guide*)

MELBOURN Cambridgeshire
map 3

Pink Geranium ⁵✳

Station Road, Melbourn,
nr Royston SG8 6DX
ROYSTON (0763) 260215
just off A10, 2m N of Royston

COOKING 2
COST £29–£70

The thatched cottage opposite the church was built around 1500, and restored after a fire in 1991, which is presumably when the conservatory was added. Anybody who does not like pink should stay well away. The small open-plan rooms on different floors help to preserve a sense of calm and order. Comfortably casual furnishings and fabrics suit the cottage style. It feels well looked after, the welcome is warm, and service has everything under control.

The cooking tends to play safe, with a pastry tartlet of creamed leek, smoked haddock and hollandaise to begin, followed by breast of chicken in a mushroom cream sauce, or saddle of venison with caramelised red cabbage and a calvados jus. But that is all to the good because the basics are right. The kitchen shows obvious mastery of technique, and ingredients (fish from Cornwall daily, for example) and timing are both good. The wide-ranging wine list is on the ball and reasonably priced, with a fair choice of half-bottles. Those who wish to avoid driving may avail themselves of the door-to-door Bentley and Jaguar service. House French begins at £10.95, and 10 or more wines are normally available by the glass from £3.50.

CHEFS: Steven Saunders and Philip Guest   PROPRIETORS: Steven and Sally Saunders   OPEN: Tue to Sun, exc Sat L and Sun D; 12 to 2.30, 7 to 10.30   MEALS: alc (main courses £19 to £25). Set L £14.95 (2 courses) to £17.95, Set D £29.95   SERVICE: not inc, card slips closed   CARDS: Access, Amex, Visa   DETAILS: 70 seats. Private parties: 55 main room, 18 and 55 private rooms. Car park. Vegetarian meals. Children's helpings. Smart dress preferred. No smoking in dining-room. Wheelchair access (also women's WC). No music. Fax: (0763) 262110

See the back of the Guide *for a listing of all restaurants in the Main Entries sections.*

MELKSHAM Wiltshire   map 2

▲ Toxique ⚡✳

| 187 Woodrow Road, Melksham SN12 7AY | COOKING 2 |
| MELKSHAM (0225) 702129 | COST £23–£48 |

Helen Bartlett is not one to be hidebound by a solitary culinary style. In this intimate country restaurant, her cooking is aiming deliberately for a polyglot complexity that she seems to be bringing off. This must be virtually the only place in this year's *Guide* that boasts of catering for *fewer* covers than last year (a contraction by no less than a quarter). The change is motivated, admirably, by the desire to keep things running smoothly rather than shoehorning tables in and then panicking when they fill up. The fixed-price dinner menu of three courses plus coffee and mineral water, inclusive of service, is one of the great deals of the region.

An indication of the eclecticism may be gained from a spring menu that took in chestnut and almond soup with lemon grass, salad of smoked duck and pancetta on baby spinach and rocket dressed with walnut oil, and spring lamb with charred red peppers, tomatoes, aubergine and sauté potatoes. There is a distinct love of using perfumed seasonings to extend the flavour range of a dish, as in seared monkfish infused with garlic and coriander accompanied by a lime and chilli vinaigrette. A correspondent who does not eat meat wrote to praise the genuine range of choice available to a vegetarian. The wine list continues to improve, but principally in the classic French areas, with prices quickly moving above £20. A handful of French provincial wines provides relief. Elsewhere, the selections are briefer but the prices easier. House French is £9.75.

CHEF: Helen Bartlett   PROPRIETORS: Peter Jewkes and Helen Bartlett   OPEN: Wed to Sat, D only, and Sun L (Wed to Fri L by arrangement); 12.30 to 2, 7 to 10   MEALS: Set L Sun £14 (2 courses) to £17.50, Set D £26.50 to £35   SERVICE: net prices, card slips closed   CARDS: Access, Amex, Visa   DETAILS: 30 seats. Private parties: 20 main room. Car park. Vegetarian meals. Children's helpings. Smart dress preferred. No smoking in dining-room. Wheelchair access (1 step). Music   ACCOMMODATION: 4 rooms, all with bath. D,B&B £70 to £120. Children welcome. Baby facilities. Garden (*The Which? Hotel Guide*)

MELMERBY Cumbria   map 7

Village Bakery ⚡✳ £

Melmerby CA10 1HE	
LANGWATHBY (0768) 881515	COOKING 1
on A686, between Penrith and Alston	COST £16–£23

The brick-built, wood-fired ovens where organic breads are baked form the spiritual centre of the Bakery, in a little Pennine village that plies the arts-and-crafts trade. Breakfasts, lunches and teas are offered for an appreciative tourist crowd. Breakfast goes on until 11am and will fill you up with raspberry porridge, Waberthwaite's bacon and new-laid eggs with wholemeal toast. Vegetarians have their own fry-up that includes an aduki bean pattie. A couple lunching at Easter found rather mild flavours in leek and potato soup of fortifying thickness, and in a seafood gratin. Cumberland sausage comes with its traditional local accompaniment of apple sauce or there is Canadian-style pork chop casseroled with apples, apple juice and maple syrup. Gluten-free chocolate almond cake will satiate any remaining hunger pangs. Newquay steam bitter, Aspall's organic 'cyder' and Dunkerton's perry supplement a handful of organic wines. House wines are £6.40.

CHEF: Diane Richter   PROPRIETORS: Lis and Andrew Whitley   OPEN: all week, daytime only; 8.30am (9.30 Sun) to 5pm   CLOSED: Christmas   MEALS: alc (main courses £5.50 to £7.50)   SERVICE: not inc, card slips closed   CARDS: Access, Diners, Visa   DETAILS: 40 seats. Private parties: 25 main room. Car park. Vegetarian meals. Children's helpings. No smoking in dining-room. Wheelchair access (1 step). No music. Fax: (0768) 881848

MERLEY Dorset   map 2

Les Bouviers ⅝✳

Oakley Hill, Merley,
nr Wimborne BH21 1RJ   COOKING 1
WIMBORNE (0202) 889555   COST £18–£48

'It is easily missed, on the main road for Bournemouth', but enough reporters who have found it have sung the praises of Les Bouviers. Some find the menus (written in both English and French) bewildering: two fixed-price ones at lunch, with extra dishes and fish options, plus a large *carte*. Classical and regional French ideas constitute the backbone, and vary from clear oxtail soup with vegetables and chickpeas, through poached egg with smoked salmon and hollandaise to venison with a sauce of bitter chocolate and juniper. Our reports applaud lightly cooked chicken livers in a salad, 'astonishingly memorable grilled sole fillets with slightly salty beurre blanc', and pink, tender, boned roast pigeon, as well as ice-creams and sorbets. Wines are mostly French. House wine is £8.75.

CHEF/PROPRIETOR: James Coward   OPEN: all week, exc Sat L and Sun D; 12 to 2, 7 to 10   MEALS: alc (main courses £14 to £18). Set L Mon to Fri £8.95 (2 courses) to £18.95, Set L Sun £16.75, Set D £21.95 to £34.95 (inc wine)   SERVICE: not inc, card slips closed   CARDS: Access, Amex, Diners, Visa   DETAILS: 60 seats. Private parties: 60 main room. Car park. Vegetarian meals. Children's helpings. Smart dress preferred. No smoking in 1 dining-room. Wheelchair access. Music

---

MIDDLE WALLOP Hampshire   map 2

▲ Fifehead Manor

Middle Wallop SO20 8EG   COOKING 2*
ANDOVER (0264) 781565   COST £24–£40

Fifehead Manor is almost as old as the hills, and travellers find it handy for Salisbury, Winchester and the south coast. Mark Robertson's menu changes half a dozen times a year, and the cooking leans heavily on French and English dishes during winter, while influences from the Mediterranean and further afield are more apparent in summer and autumn. Home-smoking seems to go on all year: eel on one occasion, trout on another, and duck breast with a pear and peppercorn vinaigrette on a spring menu.

Borrowings are generally straightforward, and pesto is a favourite: in minestrone soup, or around a terrine of brill with provençale vegetables. Far Eastern spices and the tang of citrus fruit give a refreshing lift to other dishes: pan-fried calf's liver is spiked with gin and lime, crisp breast of duck comes in an orange and grapefruit sauce, while chicken breast is cooked with Balinese spices. Steaks are particularly liked: large, succulent and tender, with sauces varying from béarnaise to mustard and caper, and always well judged. Service is attentive but unobtrusive. 'We were the only lunchers but the waitress did not, thank goodness, stay and watch every mouthful.' Wines are almost exclusively French, covering the safe and reliable middle ground, with reasonable choice under £20. Southern French house wine is around £10.

CHEF: Mark Robertson   PROPRIETOR: Margaret Van Veelen   OPEN: all week; 12 to 2, 7.30 to 9.30 (10 summer)   MEALS: Set L £17.50 to £25, Set D £25   SERVICE: not inc   CARDS: Access, Visa   DETAILS: 75 seats. 8 tables outside. Private parties: 40 main room, 16 and 20 private rooms. Car park. Vegetarian meals. Children's helpings. Wheelchair access (also men's WC). Music   ACCOMMODATION: 16 rooms, all with bath/shower. TV. Phone. B&B £50 to £105. Rooms for disabled. Children welcome. Baby facilities. Pets welcome. Afternoon teas. Garden. Doors close at 11. Fax: (0264) 781400 (*The Which? Hotel Guide*)

MIDHURST West Sussex   map 3

▲ *Angel Hotel* ♥

North Street, Midhurst GU29 9DN   COOKING 2*
MIDHURST (0730) 812421   COST £20–£45

The Angel was once a watering-hole for coaches clattering across the Downs into Midhurst. Converted in 1992 by Peter Crawford-Rolt, it still refreshes the weary traveller on the way to Arundel Castle, perhaps, or Goodwood. The eating takes place in two rooms: a brasserie and a more formal restaurant. Reports have surfaced this year of an operation running at full stretch, with staff numbers looking a bit low for the press of weekend business particularly. Once both menus are taken into account, an awful lot of food is being prepared.

The cooking is very much in the modern British camp in dishes such as roe deer terrine with beetroot relish and a kumquat and orange confit, crab and ricotta parcel with Thai cucumber salad, and pork cutlet with sage mash and sweet mustard sauce. Recommended dishes this year have included a mixture of red and grey mullet with Mediterranean vegetables and couscous ('fresh, light, tasty and attractively presented'), stuffed lamb noisettes with a tomato and basil sauce, and poached pear in puff pastry with warm butterscotch sauce. Desserts tend to be rich and sticky – flamed banana tart with rum and cinnamon sauce, dark chocolate marquise with pineapple marmalade, and white chocolate and Grand Marnier torte, for example – but are generally enjoyed. It all comes at a surprisingly moderate price for this part of the world. Wines are arranged largely by grape variety and the list has many good producers, though the easier prices tend to be concentrated outside the classic French regions. House French is £9.50. CELLARMAN'S CHOICE: Bianco 1992, Avignonesi, £18.50; Madiran Dom. Meinjarre 1990, Brumont, £17.

CHEFS: Peter Crawford-Rolt and Andrew Stephenson   PROPRIETORS: Peter Crawford-Rolt and Nicholas Davies   OPEN: all week; 12 to 2.30, 6 to 10 (9 Sun)   MEALS: alc (main courses restaurant £9.50 to £15, brasserie £8 to £12.50). Set L Mon to Sat £11.50 (2 courses) to £13.50, Set L Sun restaurant £15.95, brasserie £13.95, Set D brasserie £16   SERVICE: not inc, card slips closed   CARDS: Access, Amex, Diners, Visa   DETAILS: 120 seats. 8 tables outside. Private parties: 100 main room, 40 and 80 private rooms. Car park. Vegetarian meals. Children's helpings. Smart dress preferred. Wheelchair access (1 step; also WC). No music
ACCOMMODATION: 21 rooms, all with bath/shower. TV. Phone. B&B £55 to £130. Deposit: 50%. Rooms for disabled. Children welcome. Baby facilities. Afternoon teas. Garden. Fax: (0730) 815928 (*The Which? Hotel Guide*)

Maxine's ⁵✳

Elizabeth House, Red Lion Street,
Midhurst GU29 9PB
MIDHURST (0730) 816271

COOKING 2*
COST £18–£35

'If Midhurst were Normandy, this would definitely be our neighbourhood restaurant,' comments a reporter who now resides across the Channel. Others from closer to home also endorse the virtues of this charming, heavily timbered restaurant. Customers are mostly regulars and the mood is informal: sweaters are more *de rigueur* than jackets. The décor is a happy jumble of plastic geraniums, lace curtains and copper jelly moulds. 'Phallic saucissons' hang from the beams. The set menu (not available Saturday night) is exceptional value, but everything is reasonably priced. Robert de Jager's cooking is unfussy and draws the best out of good, honest ingredients: fish soup is a rich, 'wonderfully fishy' brew, crispy duck with raspberry sauce is half a bird cooked to a tee, sirloin steak is well-hung and perfectly timed. The standard repertoire is fleshed out with specials such as monkfish with ginger. Vegetables show touches of invention, while sticky toffee pudding is the best-selling sweet. Sunday lunch gets mixed reports. Marti de Jager runs the front-of-house with modesty and single-minded efficiency. France dominates the keenly priced wine list and halves are plentiful. House wine is from £7.25.

CHEF: Robert de Jager   PROPRIETORS: Robert and Marti de Jager   OPEN: Wed to Sun, exc Sun D; 12 to 1.30, 7 to 9.30   CLOSED: 2 weeks Jan   MEALS: alc (main courses £8.50 to £14). Set L and D (exc Sat) £12.95   SERVICE: net prices, card slips closed   CARDS: Access, Visa   DETAILS: 24 seats. Private parties: 30 main room. Vegetarian meals with prior notice. Children's helpings. No smoking in dining-room. Wheelchair access (3 steps). No music

---

MILFORD ON SEA Hampshire   map 2

Rocher's

69–71 High Street,
Milford on Sea SO41 0QG
LYMINGTON (0590) 642340
on B3058, 3m SW of Lymington

COOKING 2*
COST £20–£41

A small restaurant with mullioned windows and an old lamppost outside, in a pretty New Forest village, is the setting for classical French cooking very soundly based on careful buying. A spring inspection suggested that Alain

Rocher's food would shine the more brightly if he would exercise a restraining hand on sauces. Central ingredients of impeccable quality – 'fine, juicy, chewy scallops' – can sometimes get lost in the sauce, although braised sweetbreads with mushrooms had a sauce that was 'sympathetic' to the tenderness of the offal. A puff-pastry case filled with spinach and shallots might have done with some aromatic herb to lift it. Nougat glace with a mango sauce was light, and another reporter had praise for a 'very good' crème brûlée with summer fruits. The service is welcoming and conscientious ('An intensely serious young French waiter carried each plate to the table as if it were the crown jewels'), and the intention is to make people feel at home. Alain Rocher is from the Loire and accords that region due precedence on the wine list. The selections are patriotic, and you will need to look outside Bordeaux and Burgundy for price relief, but there are many good bottles. Halves are generously provided. House wines start at £8.50.

CHEF: Alain Rocher PROPRIETORS: Alain and Rebecca Rocher OPEN: Wed to Sat (Sun bank hols), D only, and Sun L; 12.30 to 1.45, 7.15 to 9.45 CLOSED: 2 weeks June MEALS: Set L Sun £13.50, Set D £16.50 (exc Sat) to £22.90 SERVICE: not inc, card slips closed CARDS: Access, Amex, Diners, Visa DETAILS: 30 seats. Private parties: 30 main room. Vegetarian meals with prior notice. No children under 10 L, 13 D. Smart dress preferred. No cigars/pipes in dining-room. Wheelchair access. No music

---

MINCHINHAMPTON Gloucestershire map 2

Markey's ❋

	NEW ENTRY

The Old Ram, Market Square,
Minchinhampton GL6 9BW COOKING 1
BRIMSCOMBE (0453) 882287 COST £12–£32

The Markeys have refurbished this 300-year-old semi-derelict stone-built village pub by the church, installing flower prints, soft greens, pale yellows and ruched cushions set against walls of rough Cotswold stone, all of which give it a genteel air. The aim is to be affordable on a regular basis, yet special enough to keep customers interested, and the owners have a successful track record, having appeared in the *Guide* in other restaurants over the years. Some readers may remember them at Markey's Stone Cottage in Nailsworth.

The food is plainer here. Changing customer demands and dietary considerations mean that Ian Markey keeps an eye on gluten and animal fats, and generally tones down the richness and seasoning of sauces, which may explain the fact that flavour has been conspicuous by its absence in some of the dishes reported on. Nevertheless, much pleases, including good-quality venison steak and very fresh fish: a piece of pan-fried halibut served with a shortcrust pastry tartlet of ratatouille for one reporter. Savoury dishes occasionally incorporate some sweetness – peaches with duck breast, for instance. Service by Ann Markey is more than friendly: it is kind, really helpful and well-informed. The wine list is an assembly of three dozen varied and well-chosen bottles, sympathetically priced. House wine is £7.50, and eight wines are available by the glass, starting at £1.50.

CHEF: Ian Markey PROPRIETORS: Ian and Ann Markey OPEN: Tue to Sun, exc D Tue and Sun; 12 to 1.30, 7 to 9.15 CLOSED: 1 week after 31 Dec, 1 week June/July MEALS: alc D (main courses £9 to £11). Set L Tue to Sat £5.25 (2 courses) to £6.50, Sun £7.50 (2 courses) to £9.25 SERVICE: not inc, card slips closed CARDS: Access, Amex, Visa DETAILS: 30 seats. Private parties: 30 main room. Vegetarian meals. Children's helpings L. No babies D. Smart dress preferred D. No smoking in dining-room. Wheelchair access (1 step; also WC). No music

---

MINSTER LOVELL Oxfordshire map 2

▲ *Lovells at Windrush Farm* ✝ | NEW ENTRY |

Old Minster Lovell OX8 5RN
WITNEY (0993) 779802
off B4047, 3m NW of Witney, on S bank of
River Windrush

COOKING 1*
COST £22–£45

The honey-coloured stone farmhouse, in 80 acres of pasture and woodland, dates from the sixteenth century. Accommodation is in converted barns, and a mile stretch of the River Windrush offers guests the chance to walk, fish and picnic. On the opposite bank is Minster Lovell Hall. The dining-room is small, with large windows, in rather formal blue, grey and cream – more like a London hotel than a Cotswold farmhouse.

Lunch, a modest three fixed courses, is seemingly simple but full of flavour: in spring, a creamy vegetable soup with blobs of pesto, then maize-fed chicken wrapped in bacon and sliced, and a frangipane pear tart surrounded by crème anglaise with a hint of orange. The seven-course dinner can be something of a challenge. The pattern is usually an appetiser or two, then soup, fish, main course, French cheese, something icy, then pudding and coffee. Interest is maintained with oak-smoked fillet of beef on Savoy cabbage, and lamb cutlet with a pastry case of stewed neck and shoulder. Fresh truffles pop up from time to time. Vegetables are cooked al dente and plain. Service is warm. Wines are mostly French, clarets have some maturity without being museum pieces, and there are nearly 20 half-bottles. House wine is from £12.

CHEF: Robert Marshall-Slater PROPRIETOR: Lovells Windrush Farm Ltd OPEN: Tue to Sun, exc Sat L and Sun D; 12.30 to 2, 7.45 to 9 CLOSED: Jan MEALS: Set L Tue to Fri £13.50, Sun £16.50, Set D £27.50 SERVICE: not inc CARDS: Access, Amex, Visa DETAILS: 18 seats. Private parties: 18 main room. Car park. Vegetarian meals with prior notice. Children's helpings. Smart dress preferred. No smoking in dining-room. Wheelchair access (1 step). No music ACCOMMODATION: 2 rooms, both with bath/shower. TV. Phone. D,B&B £75 to £160. Children welcome. Baby facilities. Pets welcome. Garden. Swimming-pool. Sauna. Fishing. Snooker. Doors close at midnight. Confirm by 6

Prices quoted in the Guide *are based on information supplied by restaurateurs. The prices quoted at the top of each entry represent a range, from the lowest meal price to the highest; the latter is inflated by 20 per cent to take account of likely price rises during the year of the* Guide.

✝ *indicates that smoking is either banned altogether or that a dining-room is maintained for non-smokers. The symbol does not apply to restaurants that simply have no-smoking areas.*

MOLLINGTON Cheshire map 5

▲ *Crabwall Manor*

Parkgate Road, Mollington CH1 6NE
CHESTER (0244) 851666 COOKING 3
off A540, 3m N of Chester COST £23–£62

'Nothing that Kubla Khan decreed in Xanadu could compare with what was decreed at Crabwall Manor,' reckons one reporter of the turreted red-brick building and extensions. Monday to Friday it runs on corporate business; weekends are for leisure breaks. Whatever conference hotels do for delegates, they certainly strike ordinary reporters as very odd places: 'The ambience is Hollywood-meets-English-country-house.' A manager accosts customers in the bar, presses hands and enquires if this is their first visit: 'It was our umpteenth and he didn't recognise us, so it's all a bit formulaic.' The Manor is certainly plush and comfortable, and in the conservatory-style dining-room extension table spacing and settings are well above the norm.

Michael Truelove's abilities (he was at the Box Tree in Ilkley for a while) are now beginning to surmount the demands of corporate catering. 'Bread and vegetables are much improved,' reports a regular, who noted a general return to form. The kitchen is technically accomplished and food of high quality emanates from it, happily without reliance on luxury ingredients. The foundation is good animal protein. Boudin of pheasant is an ethereally light 'sausage' tasting gently of game bird. Two plump roast breasts of widgeon are served pink, on a bed of chopped leek and cream. Sauces are a strong point and accompaniments are sensitively produced: a 'tarte Tatin' of shallots to go with grilled salmon; lentils and smoked bacon with braised lamb shank. Fillet of John Dory is served with crab jus, Japanese noodles and salmon caviare. 'The service has black holes before and after the meal', which begins with good canapés of smoked salmon pâté on toast, and deep-fried prawn dim-sum. Sorbets appear mid-meal, and puddings include rich and moist chocolate marquise, chilled caramelised rice pudding, and hot lemon soufflé.

The monster wine list takes a crack at everything, although the very fact that the hotel needs to finance such a large stock may account for some of the high prices. Trimmed and sharpened, it could be a terrific list. Martini's Asti Spumante is not méthode champenoise (as claimed), and not worth £17.50. But there are excellent bottles. The choice under £20 is good, and half-bottles are generous to a fault. House wines are from £12.

CHEF: Michael Truelove PROPRIETOR: Carl Lewis OPEN: all week, exc Sat L; 12 to 2, 7 to 9.30 MEALS: alc (main courses £9 to £22). Set L Sun £14.75 SERVICE: not inc, card slips closed CARDS: Access, Amex, Diners, Visa DETAILS: 90 seats. Private parties: 90 main room, 100 private room. Car park. Vegetarian meals. Children's helpings on request. Jacket and tie. No smoking in dining-room. Wheelchair access (3 steps; also WC). Music. Air-conditioned ACCOMMODATION: 48 rooms, all with bath/shower. TV. Phone. Rooms for disabled. Children welcome. Garden. Snooker. Doors close at 1am. Confirm 1 day ahead. Fax: (0244) 851400 (*The Which? Hotel Guide*)

▲ *This symbol means accommodation is available.*

MONTACUTE Somerset	map 2

▲ *Milk House* ✠

On-the-Borough, Montacute TA15 6XB	COOKING 1
YEOVIL (0935) 823823	COST £19–£38

The Duftons' fifteenth-century gold-stone house stands at the heart of one of Somerset's classic villages, and it is greatly liked for the relaxing atmosphere, civilised mood and personable service. Recent reports have been unanimous in their enthusiasm for Lee Dufton's cooking. Her style is a convincing version of French provincial with a few influences from the Middle East and Africa. This is an enterprise with a strong allegiance to 'natural' ingredients and organic produce: meat dishes favour game, fish is wild, cheeses are local, and soya milk and dairy-free spreads are available for special diets. Menus evolve with the seasons: warm goats' cheese salad, spiced mushrooms with nut topping, breast of duck with walnut and onion sauce, and guinea-fowl with herb sauce have all been praised. Home-baked celery-seed bread and garden-fresh vegetables also draw favourable comments. Desserts range from sticky toffee pudding to liqueured berries with meringues. The wine list offers plenty of reasonably priced drinking and an impressively chosen organic contingent. House wine is around £9.

CHEF: Lee Dufton PROPRIETORS: Lee and Bill Dufton OPEN: Wed to Sat, D only, and Sun L; 12.30 to 2, 7.30 to 9 CLOSED: 24 to 28 Dec MEALS: alc D (main courses £9.50 to £12.50). Set L Sun £12.50, Set D £19.80 SERVICE: not inc, card slips closed CARDS: Access, Visa DETAILS: 24 seats. 3 tables outside. Private parties: 36 main room, 24 private room. Vegetarian meals. Children's helpings. Smart dress preferred. No smoking in dining-room. Wheelchair access. No music ACCOMMODATION: 2 rooms, all with bath/shower. B&B £35 to £58. Deposit: £20. Garden. Confirm by 5

MORETON-IN-MARSH Gloucestershire	map 2

Annie's

3 Oxford Street,	
Moreton-in-Marsh GL56 0LA	COOKING 1
MORETON-IN-MARSH (0608) 651981	COST £25–£48

Just off the main street, Annie's has a long, narrow dining-room, with warm stone walls, flagstone floors and three fireplaces. It is comfortable, decked out with dried flowers, chintz, country-style chairs and white linen tablecloths.

'English and French country cooking' is how Anne Ellis describes the style, 'with some international influences'. The norm is half a dozen choices per course, fewer at Sunday lunch. Simply roasted whole poussin, served with a lemon and mustard sauce, is typical of the fare. Herbs, spices and alcohol all play a part in saucing, along with pan juices, and all are well controlled. Roast leg of lamb with rosemary and garlic comes with a pot of extra gravy. Tiger prawns wrapped in filo pastry, and fried with garlic, chilli and spring onions, mark the most exotic limit of the menu. Apple and blackberry crumble with real custard is much more Cotswold. Service is 'efficient, friendly and charming'. Fifty or so well-chosen wines, mostly French, are moderately priced. House Merlot and Chardonnay are £9.50 (£2.25 per glass).

CHEFS: David Ellis   PROPRIETORS: David and Anne Ellis   OPEN: Mon to Sat, D only, and Sun L; 12 to 2, 7 to 10   CLOSED: 16 Jan to 10 Feb   MEALS: alc (main courses £13.50 to £17.50). Set L Sun £17.50, Set D £19   SERVICE: not inc, card slips closed   CARDS: Access, Amex, Diners, Visa   DETAILS: 30 seats. Private parties: 30 main room, 10 private room. Vegetarian meals with prior notice. Children's helpings. Smart dress preferred. No smoking while others eat. Wheelchair access. Music

Marsh Goose ⁑✳

High Street, Moreton-in-Marsh GL56 0AX   COOKING 3
MORETON-IN-MARSH (0608) 652111   COST £21–£47

The Marsh Goose is an easy-going restaurant with a constantly changing menu that makes the most of seasonal produce. The hype and skin-deep glamour that pervade much of the Cotswolds are mercifully absent. Here are small rooms, on different levels, that feel intimate. Lunch is a laid-back affair, eaten off bare tables; apart from Sundays, a single course may suffice. In the evening the cloths come out, the log fire burns and a sense of occasion pervades the establishment.

Some restaurants complain that they cannot take a dish off the menu because customers object: 'I came especially for the Dover sole, and it isn't on!' The Marsh Goose gets round this by having so many favourites that regulars are bound to find something they enjoyed last time or the time before. The menu changes for every meal and takes its lead from the market: 'We buy the ingredients and then decide how to combine them,' writes Leo Brooke-Little, 'as opposed to writing a menu and buying accordingly.' This is the way to do things. It shows in carefully considered soups – onion with caraway, or cauliflower with thyme – and in other partnerships: a lime and fresh ginger sauce successfully cuts the richness of wild duck; and marinated red peppers contrast well with goats' cheese in filo pastry. There is mild invention (rather than wild experiment), along with a sense of balance. The common thread to endorsements is that flavour is paramount, right to the end: black coffee jelly comes in a brandy-snap biscuit together with clotted cream, caramelised walnuts and butterscotch sauce; 'lime parfait is absolutely sublime'.

The ostensibly fixed-price dinner menu niggles with its supplements – £3 for this, £4 for that – and, despite the number of waiting staff, service sometimes lacks sharpness. On the other hand, for one couple, 'the enjoyment of our meal was enhanced by the ban on smoking in the dining-room.' House wines for £9 from Navarra, and dessert wines by the glass and half-bottle, are useful additions to the wide-ranging list.

CHEF: Sonya Kidney   PROPRIETORS: Sonya Kidney, Leo Brooke-Little and Gordon Campbell-Gray   OPEN: Tue to Sun, exc Sun D; 12.30 to 2.30, 7.30 to 9.45   MEALS: alc L Tue to Sat (main courses £10.50 to £13). Set L Tue to Sat £13.50, Set L Sun £18, Set D £23   SERVICE: not inc   CARDS: Access, Amex, Visa   DETAILS: 60 seats. Private parties: 20 main room, 16 private room. Vegetarian meals. Children's helpings on request. Smart dress preferred. No smoking in dining-room. Wheelchair access (also WC). No music

▲ Morston Hall

Morston NR25 7AA
CLEY (0263) 741041
2m W of Blakeney, on A149

COOKING 2*
COST £19–£33

Galton Blackiston hiked across country in 1991 from Lake Windermere, where he was one of John Tovey's chefs at Miller Howe (see entry, Windermere), back to the Norfolk of his childhood and this modestly proportioned but comfortable seventeenth-century country house. The setting is a sleepy coastal village close by the seal sanctuary at Blakeney Point. Visiting ornithologists should take binoculars down to the salt flats of Cley next the Sea.

Under its current management, Morston has become a hive of industry, producing its own breads, biscuits for cheese, and chocolate truffles, and pickling and bottling through the winter weeks of closure. The Lakeland format has travelled well. Dinner menus change every day, offering four courses plus coffee at an inclusive price, with the only choice coming at dessert stage. Influences have grown more disparate over the years: a March dinner opened with a 'sandwich' of roasted aubergine and red peppers with goats' cheese and a tomato vinaigrette, and then proceeded to baked cod with a herb crust and salsa verde, followed by roast pork fillet stuffed with prunes and sauced with Marsala. A few days before, it had been chicken liver parfait with Cumberland sauce and tomato chutney, mussel soup with almonds and chives, then rack of lamb with couscous, hummus, redcurrants and capers. Vegetables are usually three or four, in individual styles, and puddings are of the likes of chocolate torte with white chocolate sauce or roasted pears with vanilla ice-cream. Our postbag is single-minded testimony to the popularity of this formula. 'Flavours do show a certainty and lightness of touch,' writes one. All appreciate the consistency of standard, the 'friendly and professional' service and the undoubted value. Morston is becoming quite a magnet.

The wine list is fairly comprehensive as to geography. It is arranged by grape variety, with helpful notes, and prices are certainly not over the odds. One criticism could be that many of its choices look rather safe, even a little dull. The supply of halves is adequate, and wines available by the glass are listed on a separate sheet. House French is £8.50.

CHEF: Galton Blackiston   PROPRIETORS: Tracy and Galton Blackiston, and Justin Fraser   OPEN: all week, D only, and Sun L; 12.30 for 1, 7.30 for 8   CLOSED: 1 Jan to late Feb   MEALS: Set L £13, Set D £21   SERVICE: not inc, card slips closed   CARDS: Access, Amex, Visa   DETAILS: 40 seats. Private parties: 40 main room. Car park. Vegetarian meals. Children's helpings. Smart dress preferred. No smoking during meals. Wheelchair access (1 step; also WC). No music   ACCOMMODATION: 4 rooms, all with bath/shower. TV. Phone. D,B&B £80 to £130. Children welcome. Baby facilities. Pets welcome (not in public rooms). Afternoon teas. Garden. Confirm by 6. Fax: (0263) 741041 (The Which? Hotel Guide)

Several sharp operators have tried to extort money from restaurateurs on the promise of an entry in a guidebook that has never appeared. The Good Food Guide *makes no charge for inclusion and does not offer certificates of any kind.*

MOULSFORD Oxfordshire   map 2

▲ *Beetle & Wedge* ▮ ✳

Moulsford OX10 9JF
CHOLSEY (0491) 651381   COOKING 3
off A329, down Ferry Lane to river   COST £25–£70

Take your pick from a number of settings for eating and drinking. The old
beamed Boathouse has walls of bare brick, a tiled floor and an open charcoal fire
for grilling. When the sun beats down, the Watergarden opens for al fresco
eating; an awning is pulled across in case of sudden downpour. At the most
formal level, the newly refurbished Dining Room has been equipped with a
barrel-vaulted roof of glass, terracotta and marble flooring, and Persian rugs.
Civility reigns throughout.

Richard and Kate Smith have taken the Beetle & Wedge from strength to
strength since they opened it in 1988. The various à la carte menus brim over
with freshness, seasonality and inspiration, and draw effusive praise. Nor are
they stuck in an English country time-warp, but offer us black noodles with
sauté squid and seared scallops, poached pheasant eggs with smoked haddock,
spinach and hollandaise, and roast monkfish with spring onions, garlic and
ginger. 'I can hardly praise it too highly,' said a seasoned eater-out and wine
expert, who also approved of the 'magnificent quantities' in which fino sherry
was served. While some have professed themselves 'startled' or 'astonished' at
the standard of the food, others have encountered greasiness in a salad of duck or
in the potato rösti, and undercooking of monkfish. Rhubarb crumble, lemon tart
with lemon ice-cream, hot Cointreau soufflé with raspberry sauce, and lemon
curd beignets soufflés ('each the size of a tennis ball') indicate the style of
desserts. Service, even on a 'sunny bank holiday when the place was jumping', is
generally considered 'excellent'.

A 'dipstick' policy applies to some wines on the extensive list, enabling the
curious to be charged for the proportion drunk, plus a small supplement. The
greater part is French, prices tending to reflect the impeccable pedigree of the
selections from the classic regions. For everyday drinking, go for the Rhône,
Loire or Alsace ranges, where prices are keenest. House wines are £10.75.
CELLARMAN'S CHOICE: Côtes du Vivarais, Mas de la Bégude 1990, £14.50;
Cornas, Les Collines de Laure 1991, Colombo, £17.50.

CHEF: Richard Smith   PROPRIETORS: Richard and Kate Smith   OPEN: Dining Room Tue to Sun,
exc Sun D; Boathouse all week; 12.30 to 2, 7.30 to 10   MEALS: alc (main courses Dining Room
£19.50 to £24.50, Boathouse £8 to £16). Set L Dining Room Tue to Sat £17.50, Sun £27.50
SERVICE: not inc   CARDS: Access, Amex, Diners, Visa   DETAILS: Dining Room 50 seats,
Boathouse 60 seats. 18 tables outside. Private parties: 50 main room, 60 private room. Car park.
Vegetarian meals. Children's helpings. Smart dress preferred in Dining Room. No smoking in
Dining Room. Wheelchair access (also WC). No music   ACCOMMODATION: 10 rooms, all with
bath/shower. TV. Phone. B&B £75 to £125. Rooms for disabled. Children welcome. Baby
facilities. Pets by arrangement. Garden. Doors close at midnight. Fax: (0491) 651376
(*The Which? Hotel Guide*)

▮ *denotes an outstanding wine cellar;* ▼ *denotes a good wine list, worth travelling for.*

MOULTON North Yorkshire   map 7

Black Bull Inn

Moulton DL10 6QJ
DARLINGTON (0325) 377289   COOKING 2*
1m SE of Scotch Corner, 1m from A1   COST £21–£58

'For my money the guiding light in the area' is a typically glowing verdict on the
Pagendams' North Yorkshire pub/restaurant. The place is divided into several
eating areas: an informal beamed bar for lunchtime snacks, a panelled seafood
restaurant (no bookings), a conservatory and 'Hazel' – a renovated Pullman
carriage – for more formal dining. Some reporters have commented on the 'lovely
atmosphere' and the sheer professionalism of the set-up, while others have
mentioned 'flavour' and 'value' as the main attractions. The long menu divides
up equally between fish and meat, taking in grilled Dover sole and roast rack of
lamb, as well as roast fillet of monkfish with Bayonne ham, and pigeon breasts in
filo pastry with wild mushrooms and madeira sauce. A ramekin of Arbroath
smokies in a cream sauce followed by pan-fried scallops with spinach and chive
butter sauce were reckoned to be 'simple and excellent'. Georges Duboeuf
figures heavily on the well-spread wine list, which offers plenty of choice and
fair prices. House wines start at £7.25.

CHEF: Stuart Birkett PROPRIETORS: G.H. and A.M.C. Pagendam OPEN: all week, exc Sun D;
12 to 2, 6.45 to 10.15 CLOSED: 24 to 27 Dec MEALS: alc (main courses £11.50 to £19.50). Set L
Mon to Sat £13.75, Set L Sun £15 SERVICE: not inc, card slips closed CARDS: Access, Amex,
Visa DETAILS: 100 seats. 4 tables outside. Private parties: 10 main room, 12 and 30 private
rooms. Car park. Vegetarian meals. No children under 7. No music. Fax: (0325) 377422

NAILSWORTH Gloucestershire   map 2

William's Bistro

3 Fountain Street, Nailsworth GL6 0BL   COOKING 2
STROUD (0453) 835507   COST £21–£53

William Beeston has succeeded in pulling off a highly successful and
enterprising double-act. First of all, he has a first-rate delicatessen. Second, up
the stairs behind the shop, is his bistro – a cottagey dining-room with roller
blinds at the windows and paintings on the walls. 'Just the sort of place one is
pleased to have nearby for popping out in the evening,' noted a local reporter,
who appreciated the excellent value, friendly welcome and lack of fuss that are
the Bistro's hallmarks. The menu changes each day to reflect supplies, but
consistently good and 'beautifully cooked' fish is the undoubted star of the
show: a choice of four or five is always on offer in the shape of, for example,
salmon with green salsa, red mullet with saffron sauce, or sea bass with oysters.
Fisherman's stew is a fixture. Meat-eaters might be offered anything from
braised oxtail to breast of chicken with spring onions and ginger. Big helpings of
perfectly timed vegetables deserve a special mention. The wine list avoids
ridiculous mark-ups, and it advertises a modest selection of very drinkable stuff.
House wine, made in Nailsworth, is £7.

CHEFS: Clive Gawlick and William Beeston PROPRIETORS: William and Rae Beeston OPEN: Tue to Sat, D only; 7 to 9.30 CLOSED: Christmas to New Year, bank hols MEALS: alc (main courses £8.50 to £20) SERVICE: not inc, card slips closed CARDS: Access, Visa DETAILS: 45 seats. Vegetarian meals. Children's helpings. No music. Fax: (0453) 835950

NANTWICH Cheshire   map 5

Churche's Mansion ✹✗

Hospital Street, Nantwich CW5 0RY   COOKING 2*
NANTWICH (0270) 625933   COST £19–£49

Mr Churche was a wealthy Elizabethan merchant. The green fields that must once have hedged his mansion about are now replaced by a roundabout and one-way system, but the house retains its character. The attitude of the Lathams is as accommodating as could be: 'If guests wish to sit in front of the fire and fall asleep, that's fine with us.' If they did, though, they might miss Graham Tucker's vivacious, confident cooking. The menus are fixed-price according to the number of courses taken, and there is an à la carte menu for light lunches only.

An Easter dinner delivered plenty of food for thought. Mussels in a fish-based nage offered generous quantity and were accompanied by 'sweet but fierce' rouille. Warm asparagus tart with red onions and Gruyère had 'decent pastry' but could have done with a tad more cheese, while a hungry diner enjoyed a starter of home-made black pudding with foie gras, served with poached egg, lardons and mash on a sauce of truffles, madeira and red wine. After 'sharp, reviving' kumquat sorbet, both pesto-crusted lamb with creamed parsnips and rosemary sauce, and Gressingham duck breast wrapped in rösti with an apple and sultana ragoût and sage sauce, demonstrated very capable handling of top-quality meat. Vegetarian offerings, such as risotto of Jerusalem artichokes, tomatoes and spinach flavoured with thyme, come on their own menu. Vegetables may be a trifle dull, but then invention soars again in desserts like nougat glace with caramel ice-cream and a cappuccino sauce, or gratinated strawberries with rhubarb and Pernod ice-cream and rhubarb coulis. 'Everything was calm and unhurried and totally lovely,' said a woman whose birthday it was. Bibendum is the major supplier of wines, and the choices are adventurous and wide-ranging. There is an enterprising showing of halves. House wines start at £9.25.

CHEF: Graham Tucker PROPRIETORS: Robin Latham and Amanda Latham OPEN: Tue to Sun, exc Sun D; 12 to 2.30, 7 to 9.30 CLOSED: second week Jan MEALS: light L (courses £3.50 to £7.50). Set L £11.50 (2 courses) to £14, Set D £22 SERVICE: not inc, card slips closed CARDS: Access, Diners, Visa DETAILS: 50 seats. 4 tables outside. Private parties: 48 main room, 24 and 48 private rooms. Car park. Vegetarian meals. Children's helpings. No children under 10 D. Smart dress preferred. No smoking in dining-room. Wheelchair access. Music. Fax: (0270) 74256

The 1996 Guide will be published before Christmas 1995. Reports on meals are most welcome at any time of the year, but are particularly valuable in the spring. Send them to The Good Food Guide, *FREEPOST, 2 Marylebone Road, London NW1 1YN. No stamp is needed if posted in the UK.*

NAYLAND Suffolk   map 3

Martha's Vineyard ▼ 🌟

18 High Street, Nayland CO6 4JF
COLCHESTER (0206) 262888   COOKING 3
off A134, 6½m N of Colchester   COST £25–£32

Set in the lovely village of Nayland, this restaurant not only looks small – it *is*
small. Tables are closely packed upstairs and down, the chairs are functional
wood, the napkins are paper and the fabric place-mats come in all colours. Frills
are out. Do not expect candles, nibbles or petits fours. Instead, Larkin Rogers
bakes bread, cooks high-quality ingredients in an up-to-the-minute fashion and
keeps her prices in check. The restaurant is now only open for dinner on Friday
and Saturday.

   Much of her inspiration is from the southern states of the USA (her home
territory), but is matched by almost evangelical support for local producers.
'Serve it when it is in season' might be her motto. Her short fixed-price menus
change regularly, and are full of ideas with unexpected twists. Chesapeake
crab-cakes spiked with chilli and coriander have been praised. Otherwise, the
repertoire might take in open pumpkin ravioli with smoked chicken and spiced
pecans in bourbon cream, chilled fillet of beef with rocket and shaved Parmesan,
and pan-roasted chicken marinated in lime juice and Jamaica pepper. Spicing
and seasoning have on occasion been overdone, and one or two reporters have
wondered about the appropriateness of the vegetables served with each dish,
but this is impressive cooking that jangles the tastebuds. Puddings are the likes
of chocolate semi-freddo with Cointreau-soaked biscotti; British cheeses are
served with oat biscuits. Christopher Warren runs the front-of-house with
exuberant cheerfulness. The wine list is short, but not short of good wine. It is
sharply bought, packs a wide variety of interesting styles and tastes into a small
space, looks to California for a lot of reds, and is decently priced with a good
selection of half-bottles. House wine begins at £8.95 (£2.50 per glass).
CELLARMAN'S CHOICE: Chassagne-Montrachet 1990, Colin-Deléger, £30;
Beaune, Blanche Fleur 1990, Tollot-Beaut, £27.50.

CHEFS: Larkin Rogers and Denise Woolsey   PROPRIETORS: Christopher Warren and Larkin
Rogers   OPEN: Fri and Sat, D only; 7 to 9.30   CLOSED: 2 weeks winter, 2 weeks summer
MEALS: Set D £15 (2 courses) to £17.50   SERVICE: not inc (10% for 6 or more)   CARDS: Access,
Visa   DETAILS: 41 seats. Private parties: 8 main room. Vegetarian meals. Children's helpings.
No smoking in dining-room. Wheelchair access. No music

NEAR SAWREY Cumbria   map 7

▲ Ees Wyke 🌟

Near Sawrey, Ambleside LA22 0JZ
HAWKSHEAD (053 94) 36393   COOKING 2
on B5286 road from Hawkshead   COST £25–£30

'Salad Beatrix' often appears on the menu at this likeable country hotel, in
honour of Beatrix Potter, who used to spend her summers in this late-Georgian
house. Five-course fixed-price dinners are exceptional value, particularly for

residents, and each day brings something different. John Williams's cooking mirrors his classical training: he is not one for culinary fireworks, but can deliver safe and sound dishes in the mould of roast leg of lamb with apricot and lemon stuffing, suprême of guinea-fowl with redcurrants and pink peppercorns, and fricassee of scampi and scallops in ginger and dry vermouth sauce. High points from recent meals have included sauté chicken livers, open fish tart with dill sauce, kidneys in red wine sauce, and an 'unusually sticky, melt-in-the-mouth' sticky toffee meringue. The short wine list has a few bottles from most major wine-producing countries, and prices are kept in check. House wine is £9.

CHEF: John Williams   PROPRIETORS: Margaret and John Williams   OPEN: all week, D only; 7 for 7.30   CLOSED: Jan and Feb   MEALS: Set D £18 (non-residents)   SERVICE: not inc   DETAILS: 24 seats. Private parties: 24 main room. Car park. Vegetarian meals. Children's helpings. No children under 8. Smart dress preferred. No smoking in dining-room. Wheelchair access (1 step). No music   ACCOMMODATION: 8 rooms, all with bath/shower. TV. B&B £36 to £76. Deposit: £25. No children under 8. Pets welcome (not in public rooms). Garden. Doors close at midnight (*The Which? Hotel Guide*)

NETHERFIELD East Sussex   map 3

▲ *Netherfield Place*

Netherfield TN33 9PP
BATTLE (0424) 774455   COOKING 2*
off B2096, 2m W of Battle   COST £18–£45

This 1920s country house near the site of the Battle of Hastings is set in 30 acres, including a walled kitchen garden. The interior is unshowy, with simple wood panelling and a granite fireplace in the dining-room, and feels warm and convivial. Michael Collier cooks a varied *carte* with reasonably priced set menus and a decent vegetarian selection to back it up. Fish is well handled, be it local trout, Dover sole or Loch Fyne salmon, the latter topped with grated potato and roasted. Game is a strong suit too, and might appear as a venison and wild mushroom gâteau. Guinea-fowl is poached and stuffed with a plum and grape mousse, while strips of local pigeon and rabbit have appeared to good effect in a lightly dressed salad. The kitchen does not attempt to be avant-garde and more often than not is as British as potted shrimps, calf's liver and bacon, or Sussex loin of pork. Puddings range from a light apple and peppermint parfait to a more substantial mascarpone cheesecake. A short New World section on the wine list complements a reasonable spread from France. House wine is £8.95.

CHEF: Michael Collier   PROPRIETORS: Michael and Helen Collier   OPEN: all week; 12.30 to 2, 7 to 9.30 (9 Sun)   CLOSED: last week Dec, first 2 weeks Jan   MEALS: alc (main courses £15 to £16.50). Set L Sun £14.95, Mon to Fri £15.95 (inc wine), Sat £15.50, Set D £22.50   SERVICE: not inc   CARDS: Access, Amex, Diners, Visa   DETAILS: 60 seats. 6 tables outside. Private parties: 75 main room, 16 and 30 private rooms. Car park. Vegetarian meals. Children's helpings. Smart dress preferred. No cigars in dining-room. Wheelchair access (also WC). Music   ACCOMMODATION: 14 rooms, all with bath/shower. TV. Phone. B&B £56 to £125. Children welcome. Baby facilities. Afternoon teas. Garden. Tennis. Doors close at 11. Fax: (0424) 774024 (*The Which? Hotel Guide*)

NEW ALRESFORD Hampshire   map 2

▲ *Hunters*

32 Broad Street, New Alresford S024 9AQ   COOKING 2
WINCHESTER (0962) 732468   COST £21–£42

The setting is a pretty Georgian building in a town close to the Watercress Line
and the River Itchen. Enter through a small courtyard. The dining-room is done
out with masses of hunting prints and memorabilia on the walls, and endless
shelves loaded with china. It makes a comfortable backdrop for Michael
Greenhalgh's impressive cooking. His style is modern Anglo-French, with many
nods to current fashion in exciting-sounding dishes such as smoked wood
pigeon with lentil and artichoke salad, grilled slices of salmon with olive oil,
shallots, dill and chives, and passion-fruit soufflé with peach schnapps sauce.
The *carte* changes every three months; cheaper and simpler offerings – wild boar
sausages with creamed potatoes or confit of duck with rosemary sauce, for
instance – can be found on the nightly fixed-price menu. This is a set-up with
great potential, although regulars have noted a few lapses of late. The wine list is
shared with the sister restaurant in Winchester (see entry). It offers a well-spread
selection, mostly from France and the New World. House wines start at £8.95.

CHEF: Michael Greenhalgh   PROPRIETORS: David and Martin Birmingham   OPEN: all week, exc
Sun D; 12 to 2, 7 to 10   CLOSED: 25 to 30 Dec, Sun May to Sept   MEALS: alc (main courses £8 to
£16). Set D Mon to Fri £11.95 (2 courses) to £13.95   SERVICE: not inc   CARDS: Access, Amex,
Diners, Visa   DETAILS: 110 seats. 8 tables outside. Private parties: 30 main room, 80 private
room. Vegetarian meals. Children's helpings. Wheelchair access (also WC). Music
ACCOMMODATION: 3 rooms, all with bath/shower. TV. B&B £37.50 to £47.50. Deposit: £10.
Children allowed. Afternoon teas. Garden. Doors close at 11pm. Confirm by 11am

---

NEWARK Nottinghamshire   map 5

Gannets Bistrot ✳ £

35 Castlegate, Newark NG24 1AZ   │NEW CHEF│
NEWARK (0636) 702066 and 610018   COST £20–£32

Hilary and David Bower have recently revamped their popular establishment
hard by the castle – in particular, they have extended the ground-floor café (open
all week, 10am to 4.30pm) to include a new garden room. The bistrot is upstairs,
where all is calm and 'the welcoming smiles put one immediately at ease'. Colin
White, ex-Woolley Grange (see entry, Bradford-on-Avon), is scheduled to cook
here by the time the *Guide* appears and the aim will be to serve plain, simple food
at around £25 a head. The wine list is short, affordable and sprinkled with good
names. House wine is £8.95 a litre.

CHEF: Colin White   PROPRIETORS: Hilary and David Bower   OPEN: Tue to Sat; 12 to 2, 6.30 to
9.30   CLOSED: 25 and 26 Dec   MEALS: alc (main courses £7 to £10)   SERVICE: 10%, card slips
closed   CARDS: Access, Visa   DETAILS: 40 seats. Private parties: 40 main room. Vegetarian
meals. Children's helpings. No smoking in dining-room. Music

The Guide *always appreciates hearing about changes of chef or owner.*

Courtney's

5–7 The Side, NE1 3JE   COOKING 2*
091-232 5537   COST £22–£41

'As a single diner, I was offered a choice of glossy magazines to read while waiting for a table and between courses,' noted a first-time visitor who appreciated the good humour of Michael and Kerensa Carr's restaurant near the Quayside. It is brasserie through and through. Here is a kitchen that relishes salsas, blackened chicken, colourful terrines and vinaigrettes. Grilled calf's liver with bacon prompted one reporter to admit that he was 'hooked' and that it would take a seriously good item from the blackboard to tempt him away from his beloved offal. What the board offers from day to day is generally exotic fish plus, perhaps, venison and veal. Vegetarians are kept happy with the likes of vegetable and aubergine gâteau or baked avocado and radicchio with tomato sauce.

Set lunches (priced for two or three courses) still draw the crowds with halibut and salmon terrine, eggs Benedict, hearty pheasant casserole topped with a huge mound of crisp onion strips, and fillet of salmon in caviare sauce. To finish, try chocolate marquise or raspberry crème brûlée. California and Australia provide the most lively drinking on the short, jazzy wine list. House wines from Salisbury Estate are £10.

CHEF: Michael Carr   PROPRIETORS: Michael and Kerensa Carr   OPEN: Mon to Sat, exc Sat L; 12 to 2, 7 to 10.30   CLOSED: 1 week Christmas, 2 weeks May, bank hols   MEALS: alc (main courses £10.50 to £15). Set L £12.50 (2 courses) to £14.50   SERVICE: not inc   CARDS: Access, Amex, Visa   DETAILS: 26 seats. Private parties: 26 main room. Vegetarian meals. Children's helpings on request. Smart dress preferred. No cigars/pipes in dining-room. Wheelchair access. Music. Air-conditioned

Fisherman's Lodge 🍴✳

Jesmond Dene, Jesmond, NE7 7BQ   COOKING 3
091-281 3281   COST £25–£73

Sitting right in the middle of Jesmond Dene Park, this restaurant was once the town residence of Lord Armstrong, inventor, engineer and one of Newcastle's benefactors. The substantial building, with its solid stonework and high-pitched roofs, impresses visitors, although some have found the atmosphere inside a bit on the 'stiff' side.

Steven Jobson heads the kitchen team, and he is a cook of considerable skill and flair. He offers 'chef's classics' such as braised turbot with leeks and champagne sauce, chargrilled fillet of beef with mushrooms and peppercorn sauce, and a 'medley' of Northumbrian lamb (roast shoulder, a herb-crusted cutlet, and sliced fillet with madeira sauce), as well as a wide choice of daily specialities. A modern thread runs through many of his ideas: sea bass and red mullet are chargrilled with slivers of garlic, olive oil and chives, lamb shank is braised with cabbage, and halibut is steamed with ginger, spring onions, lime and soy. Desserts are elaborate concoctions such as gratinated tropical fruits with coconut sorbet. A separate vegetarian menu offers the likes of pithiviers of

411

vegetables 'scented' with curry and herbs, with light cardamom sauce. Starter-sized snacks are also available at lunch-time. The wine list is a big slate of about 150 bins with plenty of acceptable drinking for around £15. House wine is £10.

CHEFS: Steven Jobson and Poul Amer   PROPRIETORS: Franco and Pamela Cetoloni   OPEN: Mon to Sat, exc Sat L; 12 to 2, 7 to 11   CLOSED: bank hols   MEALS: alc (main courses £16 to £26). Set L Mon to Fri £17, Set D Mon to Fri £25   SERVICE: not inc   CARDS: Access, Amex, Diners, Visa   DETAILS: 65 seats. 10 tables outside. Private parties: 14 main room, 14 and 40 private rooms. Car park. Vegetarian meals. Children's helpings on request. No children under 10. Smart dress preferred. No smoking in dining-room. Wheelchair access (1 step). Music. Fax: 091-281 6410

Leela's ✳ £

20 Dean Street, NE1 1PG   COOKING 1
091-230 1261   COST £16–£41

Leela Paul was originally renowned for dinner parties before she set up her restaurant not far from the Theatre Royal. Reporters confirm that her south Indian food tastes 'home-made' and that the freshness of the ingredients shines through. A healthy vegetarian bias cuts across the menu. Meat-eaters are also well catered for, although portions are not geared to Geordie trencherman appetites. Familiar names such as bhel pooris, masala dosai and vegetable biriani share the bill with more esoteric-sounding specialities; marinating and restrained spicing are the hallmarks of the kitchen. King prawn pappas ('in fish tamarind sauce') have been accompanied by 'the best basmati rice I've had in a restaurant'. Vegetables and side dishes are worth investigation. The wine list is promising, although some feel that it does not really match the food. Otherwise drink lager, lassi or a non-alcoholic cocktail. House wine is £8.95.

CHEF: Kuriakose Paul   PROPRIETORS: Kuriakose and Leela Paul   OPEN: Mon to Sat; 12 to 2.30, 6 to 11.30   MEALS: alc (main courses £8 to £13). Set L and D £9.95 to £16.95   SERVICE: not inc CARDS: Access, Amex, Diners, Visa   DETAILS: 50 seats. Private parties: 30 main room. Vegetarian meals. Children's helpings. Smart dress preferred. No smoking in dining-room. Music

21 Queen Street ▼

19–21 Queen Street, Princes Wharf,
Quayside, NE1 3UG   COOKING 3*
091-222 0755   COST £22–£59

Number 21, in an otherwise deserted street one block back from the river, is virtually under the Tyne Bridge. The sleek modern interior, domestic in scale, offers comfort, not hard surfaces. Blond wood fittings, cool cream walls, a bar with high stools, and a calm, cleanly elegant dining-room with shot-silk curtains and discreet lighting are an appropriate setting for Terence Laybourne's cooking. It is complex and highly wrought food, not at all the currently favoured style of whack-it-on-the-chargrill-and-Bob's-your-uncle. Yet it is accessible to anyone with the price of a meal: high perhaps, but the carte does offer some room for manoeuvre, and by way of confirmation all seem to be enjoying themselves rather than transacting business. 'The combination of stylish informal atmosphere and seriously good food produces a winning formula.'

The advice is to arrive early to choose from the whole menu because some items disappear fast. The *carte* revels in potatoes and pulses, at least in first courses: warm potato pancake with smoked salmon, pommes à l'huile with marinated salmon, soup of haricot beans, salad of broad beans and Parmesan. Another characteristic is to contrast cheaper humble, earthy ingredients with posh expensive ones, as in a warm salad of Jersey potatoes with roast lobster and truffle, or a terrine of 'fibrous ham knuckle surrounding a melting sweet heart of foie gras, with an inspired garnish of lightly acidulated pease pudding'. All these items, incidentally, were on the same menu.

Duck exemplifies the sort of work involved, cooked not two ways but five: the breast sliced on rösti potato, confit of the leg on a spiral of linguine, a sage-flavoured sausage on small green lentils, and the liver grilled (crisp outside, melting within) on braised spring onions and mushrooms. 'Even the massive plates provided here had to concede defeat at this stage.' The thigh, marinated and braised in red wine, was served on an endive salad dressed in a fruity olive oil vinaigrette on a side plate. Here endeth the duck.

Classic tournedos Rossini is a staple, as is Kielder venison served with a compote of lentils, while fish has included stuffed courgette flowers with stir-fried scallops. Oxtail – rich, tender and fatty – is boned and stuffed with braised tongue and cabbage leaves, and is very filling. 'Sorry, but I couldn't face a sweet,' said one satisfied diner. Not many can, although invention and richness are undiminished in a warm minestrone of red fruits with mascarpone sorbet, black pepper and basil, or a chocolate extravaganza. Coffee comes with a cake stand of petits fours. Although mark-ups are variable, wine prices are generally fair, quality is high across the board, at all price levels, and there is a reasonable selection of half-bottles. Half a dozen wines are available by the glass. House wine starts at £9.60. CELLARMAN'S CHOICE: Sauvignon Blanc, Poggio Alle Gazze 1991, £21; Viña Ardanza Reserva 1985, La Rioja Alta, £18.95.

CHEF: Terence Laybourne   PROPRIETORS: Susan and Terence Laybourne   OPEN: Mon to Sat, exc Sat L; 12 to 2, 7 to 10.45   MEALS: alc (main courses £18 to £19.50). Set L £15 to £17   SERVICE: not inc   CARDS: Access, Amex, Diners, Visa   DETAILS: 50 seats. Private parties: 50 main room. Vegetarian meals with prior notice. Children's helpings on request. Smart dress preferred. No pipes in dining-room. Wheelchair access. No music. Fax: 091-221 0761

NEW HAW Surrey   map 3

L'Ecluse £

---

10 Woodham Lane, New Haw KT15 3NA   COOKING 1
WEYBRIDGE (0932) 858709   COST £16–£34

Next to a barber's shop, L'Ecluse looks 'very French', feels like a bistro, with simple furniture, prints and paintings, and goes in for robust china and paper napkins. The style is good, plain cooking with no frills, and the set menu is as typical as a striped jersey and a string of garlic: mussels, onion soup or duck pâté; steak au poivre, trout with almonds or chicken with tarragon; then cheese, crème brûlée or crêpes. The *carte* offers more choice, and reporters have enjoyed the really intense garlic in the moules marinière, served with good chips; the salad of quail's eggs and lardons; sausage flavoured with fennel seeds and served with mashed potato in a tomato and onion sauce; and prune and armagnac ice-cream. 'Value for money it most certainly is,' said one reporter who recommended it as a venue for a birthday party. A savoury buckwheat galette or sweet pancakes and a glass of wine make a cheap and simple lunch. Wines are French and reasonably priced. House wine is £7.50.

CHEF: Bernard Dumonteil   PROPRIETOR: Francesca Duval   OPEN: Tue to Sat, exc L Tue and Sat; 1.20 to 2, 7 to 10.30   MEALS: alc (main courses £8.50 to £12.50). Set D Mon to Fri £13.50 to £15.50. Menu express £9.50   SERVICE: not inc   CARDS: Access, Visa   DETAILS: 35 seats. 2 tables outside. Private parties: 30 main room. Vegetarian meals. Children's helpings. Wheelchair access. Music

---

NEW MILTON Hampshire   map 2

▲ Chewton Glen, Marryat Restaurant 🍾 ✻

Christchurch Road, New Milton BH25 6QS
HIGHCLIFFE (0425) 275341
from A35 follow signs to Walkford and
Highcliffe, take second turning on left after   COOKING 3
Walkford down Chewton Farm road   COST £29–£66

Chewton reclines amid 70 acres of parkland on the edge of the New Forest and only a few miles from the Channel. Plenty goes on within its confines: golf, tennis, pumping serious iron – the lot, including serious eating and drinking. It is a low-slung, red-brick building of Georgian origin, once the home of swashbuckling author Captain Marryat, in whose honour the dining-room is named. The next-door tented conservatory restaurant with its 'hanging balls of greenery' and 'diffusing light' is pleasing to the eye. A pair of May diners felt it was like sitting in a wedding marquee.

Pierre Chevillard's cooking is substantial, with the accent on seasonality, and a keen concern for textural impact (the word 'crispy' is applied liberally throughout a spring menu, even to salmon). The *carte* offers a welter of choice, while the fixed-price menus afford some financial relief. The country-house style is seen in full flow in shiitake mushroom consommé, roasted salmon with grilled celeriac and onion jam, medallions of local venison with black pepper sauce and winter fruits, and Valrhona chocolate tart with pistachio sauce. At an inspection, a first course of red mullet had an 'inspired' accompaniment of hollowed-out potatoes stuffed with olives, the plate garnished with sun-dried tomatoes and rocket in 'rich green' olive oil. Scallops and langoustines were roasted and dressed in a hazelnut oil that served to sweeten the charred surfaces of the shellfish. The flavour in a roast leg of milk-fed lamb was buttressed by tasty fat, a strongly flavoured wild thyme jus and 'a soft unctuous mass' of flageolet beans with bags of garlic. Beef fillet with a horseradish crust needed more bite, the meat 'very tender' but not rare as requested. Lemon gratin with poached cherries had properly crusted mousse of good density on a biscuit base, while the (now expected) extra flavouring in otherwise traditional crème brûlée was mandarin. Good espresso was served with sugary petits fours 'better suited to a children's tea party'.

The wine list has many venerable clarets (though it would be a brave diner indeed who would risk £340 on 1937 Latour), superb burgundies, top-class modern Italian wines and impeccable American and antipodean bottles. Champagne is treated with thorough reverence. If only, comes the inevitable sigh, there were more choice at the realistic end of the budgetary range. House wine is from £12.50.

CHEF: Pierre Chevillard PROPRIETORS: Martin and Brigitte Skan OPEN: all week; 12.30 to 2, 7.30 to 9.30 MEALS: alc (main courses £15 to £21.50). Set L £18 (2 courses) to £23, Set D £39.50 SERVICE: net prices, card slips closed CARDS: Access, Amex, Diners, Visa DETAILS: 180 seats. 10 tables outside. Private parties: 70 and 120 private rooms. Car park. Vegetarian meals. No children under 7. Jacket and tie. No smoking in dining-room. Wheelchair access (2 steps; also WC). Music ACCOMMODATION: 58 rooms, all with bath/shower. TV. Phone. B&B £192 to £378. Rooms for disabled. No children under 7. Afternoon teas. Garden. Swimming-pool. Sauna. Tennis. Golf. Snooker. Fax: (0425) 272310 (The Which? Hotel Guide)

NORTH CHEAM Surrey   map 3

Partners Brasserie £

23 Stonecot Hill, North Cheam,
nr Sutton SM3 9HB
081-644 7743
on A24, 1m SW of Morden   COOKING 1
(nr Woodstock pub)   COST £17–£33

'Funny place,' sums up one reporter, 'but wonderful value for money.' It is the bargain version of Partners West Street, Dorking (see entry), and looks like a shop from the outside, in a row of other shops. Inside, it is 'bedecked in primary shades, but tastefully and cheerfully done'. Reporters mostly feel comfortable with the informal atmosphere and friendly staff, and are uniformly impressed by the food: simple maybe, but accurately cooked and tasty. Main courses of brill, Welsh lamb, rabbit and beef sirloin are variously chargrilled, braised, poached, roasted and casseroled, and rarely stray above £10. Reporters have also praised potato soup made from good stock, toasted muffin with a perfectly poached egg in chive sauce, strawberry shortbread, and dense chocolate marquise. Service is tiptop, and the wine list is short and to the point, with house burgundy at £7.95 (£1.95 per glass).

CHEF: Timothy Franklin PROPRIETOR: Partners Restaurants plc OPEN: Tue to Sat, exc Sat L; 12 to 2, 7 to 9.30 MEALS: alc (main courses £7 to £12). Set L and D £9.95 SERVICE: 10%, card slips closed CARDS: Access, Amex, Diners, Visa DETAILS: 30 seats. Private parties: 32 main room. Vegetarian meals. Children's helpings. Wheelchair access (1 step). No music. Air-conditioned

---

The Guide office can quickly spot when a restaurateur is encouraging customers to write recommending inclusion – and sadly, several restaurants have been doing this in 1994. Such reports do not further a restaurant's cause. Please tell us if a restaurateur invites you to write to the Guide.

Old Woolhouse

Market Place, Northleach GL54 3EE   COOKING 3
COTSWOLD (0451) 860366   COST £47–£56

Jacques Astic's cooking is French because he is, and it is broadly classical in style. One couple enjoyed a tartlet of mussels with a 'wonderful perfume of cumin'. The good-sized mussels were tender and came in a cream sauce garnished with shreds of orange and fennel, all in a wafer-light pastry case. Then followed a generous portion of roast pheasant with red wine sauce served with rings of baked apple, sauté chestnuts and cranberries. 'Pommes dauphinoise seemed more than usually good', while a hazelnut meringue, slightly caramelised, was 'a perfect consistency', dribbled with apricot sauce. Another reporter enjoyed crab tartlet followed by kidneys in a mustard sauce, then raspberry tarte. We have just enough information to persuade us that the cooking is as good as before, although we are a little short of detail, having received neither menu nor wine list from the restaurant, and can only confirm that the wines are all French. Reports, please.

CHEF: Jacques Astic   PROPRIETORS: Jacques and Jenny Astic   OPEN: Tue to Sat, D only (other times by arrangement); 8 to 10   CLOSED: 1 week Christmas, 2 weeks Oct   MEALS: Set D £35 SERVICE: not inc   DETAILS: 18 seats. Private parties: 18 main room. Vegetarian meals with prior notice. Children welcome. Smart dress preferred. No music

Wickens ♥ ⁵✷

Market Place, Northleach GL54 3EJ   COOKING 3
COTSWOLD (0451) 860421   COST £19–£42

Comparisons between Wickens and the Old Woolhouse (see previous entry) are inevitable, because they face each other across the Market Place, yet they could hardly be more different in style. 'An English restaurant in an English village' is how the Wickenses describe their Cotswold stone house, not so much stating the obvious as making the operation sound easier and simpler than it really is. Christopher cooks, Joanna does the puddings and front-of-house, and they work to a natural pace and scale: as much as they can handle, and no more. They have spent many years building supply lines, integrating the kitchen into a network in which local meat, game and vegetables work to the benefit of producers and customers alike, and it shows in the quality of hare (the leg braised in Shiraz, the saddle sliced and pan-fried), roast leg of locally bred Cotswold lamb, and chargrilled pork cutlet.

The repertoire has evolved over the years, although puddings remain traditional. 'There is not a boring dish in sight.' Nor are there needless flourishes on the menu or on the plate, and value for money remains extremely good. Although restraint is a feature, when there is a real opportunity to do something with a dish, they take it. A wedge of onion tart, with light, fragile pastry and a luscious chunky creamy filling of onion (roughly cut and sweated in an indecent amount of butter) comes with a salad of scorzonera, alfalfa and ribbons of raw carrot in a grainy mustard vinaigrette. 'Pity there wasn't more of it.' Clean, fresh tastes are the norm, whether in a lightly spiced chowder of mussels, prawns, corn and potatoes, or even a light version of the ubiquitous sticky toffee pudding. The light lunch menu offers salads, soups, sausages, pasta and more.

In keeping with the style, English (particularly Gloucestershire) wines are prominent. America, Australia and New Zealand are the other strengths. France (apart from champagne) doesn't get a look-in. Good value runs throughout, and the bottled beers are welcome. House wine is £8.25 (£1.75 per glass). CELLARMAN'S CHOICE: Crickley Windward Bacchus/Seyval Blanc 1992, £9.75; Beenleigh Vineyard Cabernet Sauvignon/Merlot 1992, £18.75.

CHEFS/PROPRIETORS: Christopher and Joanna Wickens   OPEN: Tue to Sat (L Nov to Apr by arrangement); 12.15 to 1.30, 7.20 to 9   MEALS: alc D (main courses £11.50 to £15). Set D £19.50. Light L menu   SERVICE: net prices, card slips closed   CARDS: Access, Amex, Visa DETAILS: 36 seats. Private parties: 22 main room. Vegetarian meals. Children welcome. No smoking in dining-room. Music

---

NORWICH Norfolk   map 6

Adlard's ▮

79 Upper St Giles Street, Norwich NR2 1AB   COOKING 4
NORWICH (0603) 633522   COST £22–£52

Perhaps the most extraordinary thing about Adlard's is how ordinary it looks: just another business in a row of shops. But that epitomises the style. We should delight that a talent like David Adlard's is still operating on a small and unpretentious scale. He has not been swallowed up by a giant organisation with more money than taste; he has not disappeared into the bowels of a Park Lane hotel; he does not have a TV show. He just turns out food of a very high order, potters around the place, makes phone calls, serves beer, then goes back into the kitchen for the next order. It is all very reassuring.

The dining-room is a small split-level monument to green, but doesn't oppress. People come in for amazing-value lunches – mussels with curry butter sauce (served with spinach and toasted brioche), followed by boeuf à la bourguignonne, or roast wild pigeon with apple chutney and herb salad for £10 – or to spin out a starter and sweet at dinner: there is no obligation to eat like a horse. The restaurant understands different needs, from birthday parties to business dinners to non-meat-eaters. It adapts, and so does the food.

Adlard's training is French, so he uses classical techniques. Breast of Lunesdale duck, cooked pink and thickly sliced on to the plate, is accompanied by a frilly hat of evenly cooked ravioli containing the minced leg meat, with a dark sauce, reduced but barely sweet. The sauce has great depth and length of flavour, holds the whole dish together, yet doesn't dominate the bird; nor do the small cubes of fresh beetroot and the pile of glistening spinach. There is no overt flaunting of fashionable credentials in this, just sound technique and understated excellence. Flavours are refined, yet direct; they don't shout, they persuade.

Nevertheless, some dishes have a modernity about them – salad of chargrilled vegetables with balsamic vinegar, for example – and a sense of indulgence is apparent, without dipping into an ostentatious bucket of fancy and expensive trimmings. Sliced potatoes are cooked with cream and a rich cheesy topping. Locally smoked salmon is chargrilled on one side (the heat barely reaches the

417

other) and served with a crunchy short pastry tartlet of meltingly soft-boiled quail's egg and a beurre blanc; only the slightly excessive vinegary bite prevents it from being totally wonderful. Ice-creams, parfaits and mousses take their place among bread-and-butter pudding and pedigree cheeses to finish.

In keeping with the unintimidating ethos, the wine list is organised back to front, from bin beginnings, through a generous choice of half-bottles and a classy New World section, to French heavyweights. Notes are commendably short and helpful. CELLARMAN'S CHOICE: James Herrick Chardonnay 1993, £11; Barbera d'Asti 1990, Ceppi Storici, £12.50.

CHEF: David Adlard   PROPRIETORS: David and Mary Adlard   OPEN: Tue to Sat; 12.30 to 1.45, 7.30 to 10.30   MEALS: alc D (main courses £17). Set L (2 courses) £10 to £13, Set D £29 to £32   SERVICE: not inc, card slips closed   CARDS: Access, Amex, Visa   DETAILS: 40 seats. Private parties: 18 main room. Vegetarian meals with prior notice. Children's helpings on request. No smoking until after main course. Wheelchair access. Music

Brasted's

NEW ENTRY

8–10 St Andrews Hill, Norwich NR2 1AD   COOKING 1
NORWICH (0603) 625949   COST £21–£50

Norwich has more than its fair share of churches, and streets named after them. Brasted's, on a corner near St Andrew's church on the edge of the pedestrianised city centre, has the air of an old building fallen on better times. The small dining-room is covered in tent-like swathes of red and white stripy material, wrapping everybody in an informal cocoon. Wooden dressers support glasses, cups, saucers, bottles and copies of the menu – a *carte* of around seven items per course. Regulars can plug into a light, fixed-price Club Lunch, of two to four courses, which helps to bring the price down.

Ideas are simple and effective. Smoked haddock is poached in milk and made into a savoury custard. Fresh tomato pudding is 'like an individual summer pudding' filled with diced tomato, spring onion, basil, thyme and garlic. Beef Stroganov is made from fillet, while navarin of lamb (more like a tasty casserole) uses chunks of lean leg meat. Flavours are well judged in puddings – a winter compote of pear, walnuts, prunes and orange marinated in red wine and cinnamon, for instance – and savouries offer an alternative finish. Service is easy and personable. Standard mark-ups on a largely French wine list tilt the balance firmly over £20 a bottle, halves are reasonable, and half a dozen house wines begin at £10.50.

CHEF: Adrian Clarke   PROPRIETOR: John Brasted   OPEN: Mon to Sat, exc Sat L; 12 to 2, 7 to 10   CLOSED: bank hols   MEALS: alc (main courses £9.50 to £18). Set L (2 courses) £8.50 to £15   SERVICE: not inc, card slips closed   CARDS: Access, Amex, Diners, Visa   DETAILS: 22 seats. Private parties: 24 main room. Vegetarian meals. Children's helpings. Smart dress preferred. Music. Fax: (0603) 766445

If a restaurant is new to the Guide *this year (did not appear as a main entry in the last edition),* NEW ENTRY *appears opposite its name.*

By Appointment ✱

27–29 St Georges Street, Norwich NR3 1AB	COOKING 2
NORWICH (0603) 630730	COST £27–£43

In the old part of the city, close to the river and the cathedral, this intimate restaurant is in a converted fifteenth-century merchant's house. Antique furniture, Victorian silverware and fine porcelain are its embellishments. Timothy Brown says his style of cooking is that of his mother and grandmother; he specialises in variations on a theme. He can turn his hand to steak and kidney pudding or spotted dick, although his repertoire also takes in elaborate ideas such as fillets of sole lined with lobster mousse and partnered by champagne and lobster sauce garnished with grapes. Roasting meat, poultry and game is a favourite device, as in loin of lamb with apricot and pistachio stuffing accompanied by a sauce of tomatoes, honey, rosemary and thyme. Norfolk mussels are cooked with a touch of Pernod, and wild salmon is marinated on the premises. The wine list, from Lay & Wheeler, is a good slate of bottles from most major growing countries; prices are not sky-high. House wine is from £9.95.

CHEF: Timothy Brown PROPRIETORS: Timothy Brown and Robert Culyer OPEN: Mon to Sat, D only; 7 to 9.30 MEALS: alc (main courses £12 to £15) SERVICE: not inc CARDS: Access, Visa DETAILS: 36 seats. Private parties: 36 main room, 6 to 36 private rooms. Car park. Vegetarian meals. No children under 12. Smart dress preferred. No smoking in dining-room. Wheelchair access (also WC). Music

Green's Seafood

[NEW ENTRY]

82 Upper St Giles Street, Norwich NR2 1LT	COOKING 1
NORWICH (0603) 623733	COST £22–£42

Entry to this predominantly fish restaurant is gained down the side of the building, almost opposite Adlard's (see entry). Sit in the bar and order from the menu, or better still off the blackboard, or even better by having a squint in the cold counter to see what appeals. A visitor in spring enjoyed tempura of red pepper, broccoli, spring onion, white fish, squid and king prawn with a couple of spicy dips, and a main course of sea bass on mashed potatoes with a black olive and tomato sauce. Others have endorsed crab and avocado mousse, grilled lemon sole and halibut. Puddings are recited (without prices) and seem to consist of pastry, cream and fruit in varying combinations. Sticky toffee pudding is a light sponge dome well impregnated with dark toffee, served with a caramel sauce and a scoop of vanilla ice-cream. A pianist livens up the dining-room some nights. Wines touch on the New World, and half-bottles are conspicuous by their absence. House wine is from £8.

CHEF/PROPRIETOR: Dennis Crompton OPEN: Tue to Sat, exc Sat L; 12 to 2.30, 7 to 11 CLOSED: 1 week Christmas, 1 Jan, bank hols MEALS: alc (main courses £9 to £16). Set L £12.50 (2 courses) to £15, Set D £21 (2 courses) to £24 SERVICE: not inc CARDS: Access, Visa DETAILS: 50 seats. Private parties: 60 main room, 40 private room. Car park D. Vegetarian meals. No children under 8. Smart dress preferred. No cigars/pipes in dining-room. Wheelchair access (1 step; also WC). Music. Air-conditioned

Marco's ▼ ※

17 Pottergate, Norwich NR2 1DS	COOKING 1*
NORWICH (0603) 624044	COST £32–£47

There is ambition in Marco Vessalio's smartly refurbished Italian restaurant. Ring the bell to get in off the street, and flop into a big comfortable sofa in the bar. The dining-room, decked out in lemony primrose yellows, is so smart that one reporter wondered if he was paying for it through the food prices. We all are, in whichever restaurant we eat. Despite saddle of lamb with redcurrant sauce, or chicken with prawn and ginger, the general thrust is as Italian as zabaglione, or rice terrine with sole fillet and pesto. First-rate gnocchi – soft, light and melting – are made on the premises, and sauced with mushrooms, fresh tomato and cream. Bread is made in-house too. Vegetables include a skewer of roasted aubergine pieces and sliced red pepper, presumably so as not to interfere with the saucing of the main dish. Italian bread pudding, cake-like and full of raisins, is served with a slightly bitter orange sauce and a glass of Prosecco. Service is charming. The wine list explores the diversity of Italy and latches on to some good producers. Mark-ups are about average. House Sicilian is £9. CELLARMAN'S CHOICE: Arneis Cru San Michele 1992, Deltetto, £14; Malbech del Veneto 'Santa Margherita' 1987, £17.

CHEF/PROPRIETOR: Marco Vessalio OPEN: Tue to Sat; 12.30 to 2, 7 to 10 CLOSED: bank hols MEALS: alc (main courses £11 to £13.50). Set L £14 SERVICE: not inc, card slips closed CARDS: Access, Amex, Diners, Visa DETAILS: 22 seats. Private parties: 12 main room. Vegetarian meals. Children's helpings. Smart dress preferred. No smoking in dining-room. Wheelchair access. No music

St Benedicts Grill

9 St Benedicts Street, Norwich NR2 4PE	COOKING 1
NORWICH (0603) 765377	COST £22–£33

The style is informal bistro, the décor sparse and functional – pews for larger tables – and blackboards list daily specials in addition to the *carte*. Chump of lamb and Thai-style chicken are among the main courses. Dishes do not always match their descriptions, and there have been inaccuracies in the cooking, but good pastry tarts – of smoked salmon with creamy leek and gruyère cheese, and of treacle with a jug of cream, for example – have received plaudits. The wine list is short, sharp and jazzy, with modest mark-ups. House wine is from £6.95 (£1.30 per glass). Pinocchio's next door is under the same ownership.

CHEF: Nigel Raffles PROPRIETORS: Nigel and Jayne Raffles OPEN: Tue to Sat; 12 to 2, 7 to 10 (10.30 Fri and Sat, pre- and post-theatre by arrangement) CLOSED: 25 to L 31 Dec MEALS: alc (main courses £7 to £10.50) SERVICE: not inc CARDS: Access, Amex, Visa DETAILS: 42 seats. Private parties: 42 main room, 24 private room. Vegetarian meals. Children's helpings. No cigars/pipes in dining-room. No music

Not inc *in the details at the end of an entry indicates that no service charge is made and any tipping is at the discretion of the customer.*

map 5

Saagar £

473 Mansfield Road, Sherwood,
Nottingham NG5 2DR
NOTTINGHAM (0602) 622014 and 692860   COOKING 1
on A60, 3m from city centre   COST £14–£37

Since 1984, Mohammed Khizer and chef Amjaid Habib have provided consistently good food at this restaurant near the centre of Nottingham. Their regularly changing menu ranges far and wide across the Indian subcontinent and many items are quite novel. From Punjab and the north come tandooris and tikkas, while the south is represented by kaallan dishes cooked with mango, yogurt and coconut. Kashmiri baltis and Parsee dhansaks also feature. Unusual specialities could include aubergine paneer topped with garlic and cheese, green pepper stuffed with mushrooms, and nizami masala chicken (with nuts, coconut, yogurt and sesame seeds). The price of most main dishes includes rice, poppadum and chutney. Cobra lager is probably the best choice for drinking; otherwise, house wine is £8.50 a litre.

CHEF: Amjaid Habib   PROPRIETOR: Mohammed Khizer   OPEN: all week; 12 to 2.15, 6 to 12.15
CLOSED: 25 Dec   MEALS: alc (main courses £7 to £10.50). Set L £7, Set D £14 (minimum 2)
SERVICE: not inc   CARDS: Access, Amex, Visa   DETAILS: 75 seats. Private parties: 45 main
room. Car park. Vegetarian meals. Children's helpings L, and D before 7. No children under 5.
Smart dress preferred. Wheelchair access (3 steps). Music. Air-conditioned

Sonny's

3 Carlton Street, Hockley,
Nottingham NG1 1NL   COOKING 1
NOTTINGHAM (0602) 473041   COST £14–£39

This lively venue not far from the rejuvenated Lace Market wears two hats. The café area, with its bare, uncovered tables, is a useful spot for snacks and pasta, while the restaurant offers eclectic modern dishes that are similar in style to its Barnes parent (see entry, London). The short *carte* and even shorter set menus are peppered with ideas gleaned from the big boys in London – smoked haddock rarebit with tomato and chive salad (Gary Rhodes), Cantonese salad of braised shin of beef (Alastair Little) – but the kitchen generally knows its stuff and dishes are executed with some skill. Roasted peppers with anchovy and mozzarella, chargrilled salmon with couscous, pork fillet with grapefruit chutney and blackened cod with Cajun sauce have found favour with reporters. Sweets such as sticky toffee pudding and chocolate soufflé cake with prune and armagnac have been impressive. Service is youthful and friendly, the mood is relaxed. The wine list is modern and fairly priced, with a well-chosen stock of halves. House wine is £8.95.

All entries in the Guide *are rewritten every year, not least because restaurant standards fluctuate. Don't trust an out-of-date* Guide.

ENGLAND

CHEF: Graeme Watson   PROPRIETOR: Rebecca Mascarenhas   OPEN: restaurant all week; 12 to
2.30 (2 Sun), 7 to 10.30 (11 Fri and Sat, 10 Sun). Café Mon to Sat L; 11 to 3.30   CLOSED: 25 and
26 Dec, 1 Jan   MEALS: alc (main courses restaurant £7 to £12, café £4 to £5). Set L Mon to Fri
£10.95 (2 courses) to £13.95, Sun £10.95, Set D Mon to Fri £13.95   SERVICE: not inc   CARDS:
Access, Amex, Visa   DETAILS: 80 seats. Private parties: 80 main room. Vegetarian meals.
Children welcome. No-smoking area café. Wheelchair access. Music. Fax: (0602) 507776

Truffles

43 Broad Street, Nottingham NG1 3AP   COOKING 2
NOTTINGHAM (0602) 526116   COST £20–£34

No false glitziness invades the Scotts' intimate restaurant in the centre of
Nottingham. The tables once supported sewing-machines (the Lace Market is
not far away) and the floors are bare boards, but the atmosphere is softened via
the candlelight and murmuring jazz in the background. Understandable despair
is felt by the proprietors when Truffles is characterised as French. To be sure,
pâté de foie gras with a glass of sweet Jurançon followed by magret of duck with
framboise sauce may have you dreaming of old Gascony, but there is little of
France in 'spring rolls' of merguez, Stilton and Camembert on a tomato and
ginger coulis, roast quail with green curry sauce, or a puff-pastry 'pizza' topped
with prawns and goats' cheese.

There is less cross-fertilisation in the main courses, which may be lambs'
kidneys with wild mushrooms, steamed lemon sole with crab sauce or corn-fed
chicken with white wine, garlic, tarragon and cream. The dessert range widens
again to take in orange and Grand Marnier cheesecake, date and ginger pudding,
mango parfait and tiramisù. There have been complaints of overcooking of fish,
but vegetables are usually a 'good selection', coffee is 'excellent – strong without
being bitter', and the ambience is found 'pleasant' even if the floorboards make
for a certain amount of clatter. The compact wine list offers bottles of reasonable
quality at friendly prices. House French is £7.75.

CHEF: Anthony Scott   PROPRIETORS: Anthony and Firooze Scott   OPEN: Tue to Sat, D only; 7 to
10.45   CLOSED: 24 Dec to end Jan   MEALS: alc (main courses £9 to £13). Set D Tue to Fri
£10.95 (2 courses)   SERVICE: not inc   CARDS: Access, Amex, Diners, Visa   DETAILS: 45 seats.
Private parties: 45 main room. Car park. Vegetarian meals with prior notice. Children welcome.
Smart dress preferred. Wheelchair access (1 step; also WC). Music

OLD BURGHCLERE Hampshire   map 2

Dew Pond ⁵✳

Old Burghclere RG15 9LH
BURGHCLERE (0635) 278408   COOKING 2*
off old A34, 3m W of Kingsclere   COST £23–£44

There has been a change to the operation at this family-run restaurant, with a
homely atmosphere and pleasantly country feel: lunch is no more, except for
parties – a casualty of the recession. Dinner now offers a choice of two fixed-price
menus which are changed six times a year to take advantage of what is in season.

422

Dishes such as salad of duck's liver, rillettes of pheasant, and fillet of sea bass on a bed of fennel betray a leaning towards France. Game is a speciality, particularly venison, and lamb is regularly praised. First courses, including sausage of guinea-fowl with caramelised apples, spiced mussel broth with coriander and chilli, and warm smoked salmon, excite most interest. Puddings might include crème brûlée, hot chocolate soufflé, or apple and caramel tart.

Some comments indicate the kitchen's variability – 'sliced breast of duck from which all taste had gone, and it was tough' – but ingredients are good, portions are ample, and basic cooking skills are not in doubt. Service 'couldn't have been bettered; it is attentive yet unobtrusive', and meals end with good coffee and petits fours. The short house selection of wines under £15 is helpful, as are the 30 half-bottles, and pricing is reasonable across the board.

CHEF: Keith Marshall   PROPRIETORS: Keith and Julie Marshall   OPEN: Tue to Sat, D only; 7 to 10   CLOSED: First 2 weeks Jan, 2 weeks mid-Aug   MEALS: Set D £16.50 to £23   SERVICE: not inc   CARDS: Access, Visa   DETAILS: 50 seats. Private parties: 50 main room, 20 and 30 private rooms. Car park. Vegetarian meals. Children's helpings on request. No children under 10. Smart dress preferred. No smoking in dining-room. Wheelchair access (also women's WC). No music

---

OSWESTRY Shropshire   map 4

Sebastian

45 Willow Street, Oswestry SY11 1AQ	COOKING 2
OSWESTRY (0691) 655444	COST £21–£56

A sixteenth-century Grade II listed building is the unlikely setting for the Fishers' patriotically French restaurant. The interior is all log fires and low beams and the place clearly makes 'concessions to the formality which seems to be expected in Shropshire'. Mark is a highly professional cook who cares about quality ingredients, and is prepared personally to collect fish from the North Wales ports. A no-choice 'menu routier' and a slightly more varied and expensive 'menu touristique' are alternatives to the *carte*, which is in the classic French tradition of breast of duck with pear and red wine sauce, sirloin steak béarnaise, and grilled turbot with saffron noodles and basil sauce. Vegetarian visitors have approved of watercress soup with excellent home-baked rolls, a main course of delicate herbed pancakes layered with wild mushrooms and served with an 'exact' chive hollandaise and crisp vegetables, followed by an impressive Gallic version of banoffi pie. Canapés, petits fours and coffee have all been given the seal of approval. The fairly priced wine list pays allegiance to France, although it tips its hat to the New World. House wine is £8.75.

CHEF: Mark Sebastian Fisher   PROPRIETORS: Mark S. Fisher and Michelle A. Fisher   OPEN: Tue to Sat, exc L Tue and Sat; 12 to 2, 6.30 to 10.30   CLOSED: 25 and 26 Dec, 1 Jan   MEALS: alc (main courses £14.50 to £19.95). Set L £14.95, Set D Tue to Fri £14.95 to £16.95 (minimum 6)   SERVICE: not inc, card slips closed   CARDS: Access, Amex, Visa   DETAILS: 40 seats. 4 tables outside. Private parties: 20 main room, 6 private room. Vegetarian meals. Children welcome. Smart dress preferred. Wheelchair access. Music. Fax: (0691) 653452

See the back of the Guide *for a listing of all restaurants in the Main Entries sections.*

Al-Shami £

25 Walton Crescent, Oxford OX1 2JG
OXFORD (0865) 310066

COOKING 1
COST £18–£37

Reporters continue to extol the virtues of this popular Lebanese restaurant near the centre of Oxford. Lunch-time is quiet, but the place buzzes in the evening with a lively, mixed clientele. The strength of the menu is in its wide choice of hot and cold meze: one regular visitor writes: 'Our meal normally consists of chicken livers, fattoush (mixed salad with herbs and toasted Lebanese bread), falafel, tabbouleh, ful medames (broad beans with lemon, olive oil and garlic), cheese and spinach in pastry and sundry other wonderful delicacies.' In addition, there is a good choice of vegetarian options, kebabs and grills: shish taouq (garlicky barbecued chicken) is reckoned to be 'excellent'. A short list of authentic desserts rounds things off. To drink, try strong Lebanese coffee spiked with cardamom seeds or mint tea. The short wine list features Ch. Musar and Arak as well as a handful of French and German bottles from around £7.

CHEF: Mimo Mahfouz   PROPRIETOR: Mimo Catering (Oxford)   OPEN: all week; noon to midnight   MEALS: alc (main courses £6 to £12). Set L £10 to £12, Set D £15 to £20. Cover £1   SERVICE: not inc (10% for 6 or more)   DETAILS: 50 seats. Private parties: 60 main room, 30 private room. Vegetarian meals. Children welcome. Smart dress preferred. Wheelchair access (also WC). Music. Fax: (0865) 311241

▲ Bath Place Hotel ♥ ⅚✱

4–5 Bath Place, Holywell Street,
Oxford OX1 3SU
OXFORD (0865) 791812

COOKING 2*
COST £26–£59

'A new chef has taken over here,' wrote one reporter, 'and if our experience is anything to go by, it augurs well for the future.' Jeremy Blake O'Connor has moved on from Moreteyne Manor and fetched up with the Fawsitts in the middle of Oxford. Bath Place is small, attractive, family-run and hidden down a narrow cobbled alley off Holywell Street, near Blackwell's music shop, in a cluster of seventeenth-century cottages. The style resonates with past O'Connor ventures, from wafts of Mediterranean oil and herbs (with a raviolo of salmon and scallops) to provençale vegetables: ratatouille with fillet of lamb is a classic of its kind. The bold, macho meaty offerings are here in plenty too. Terrine of venison and hare saddle with wild mushrooms comes with a madeira sauce, and roast woodpigeon on braised lentils is served with a game and red wine sauce flavoured with dark chocolate and raspberry vinegar.

Fish soup, or to give it its Sunday name, 'light potage of seafood with Noilly Prat and parsley', was rated as 'one of the best we have tasted' by a well-travelled couple who also enjoyed escalopes of free-range Oxfordshire pork in an apple and armaganac sauce with a purée of swede and potato. The set menus are no-choice but might offer warm salad of red mullet fillets with a basil and tomato butter sauce, followed by fricassee of chicken with mushrooms and onions in a red wine sauce, and then rhubarb bavarois with a confit of ginger and a passion-fruit sauce. The wine list is neatly arranged, with one-line notes to help, and it is good to see Italy and the New World given serious consideration alongside decent French growers. Prices are very fair, as are half-bottles. House wine is £10.50 (£2.50 per glass). CELLARMAN'S CHOICE: Menetou-Salon 1992, Clément, £14.50; Cape Mentelle Cabernet Sauvignon 1987, £19.75.

CHEF: Jeremy Blake O'Connor PROPRIETORS: Kathleen and Yolanda Fawsitt OPEN: Tue to Sun, exc Tue L and Sun D; 12 to 2, 7 to 10 (10.30 Fri and Sat) MEALS: alc (main courses £13 to £18.50). Set L Tue to Sat £12 (2 courses) to £16.50, Sun £14.50 (2 courses) to £19.50 SERVICE: not inc (10% for 6 or more) CARDS: Access, Amex, Visa DETAILS: 30 seats. 3 tables outside. Private parties: 40 main room. Vegetarian meals. Children's helpings. Smart dress preferred. No smoking in dining-room. Music. Air-conditioned ACCOMMODATION: 10 rooms, all with bath/shower. TV. Phone. B&B £50 to £100. Deposit £25. Children welcome. Pets by arrangement. Doors close at 10. Fax: (0865) 791834

Cherwell Boathouse ▮

| Bardwell Road, Oxford OX2 6SR | COOKING 2 |
| OXFORD (0865) 52746 | COST £21–£30 |

'A lovely evening – apart from nearly slipping into the River Cherwell,' commented one reporter. The attractions of this old wooden building are its idyllic riverside setting, cosy intimacy and interestingly 'different' food. Gerard Crowley's short, fixed-price menu has plenty of variety and off-the-wall ideas, such as pepper fritters with a ragoût of mixed beans, and rosemary pasta with caramelised onions and walnuts. Simple things are often given an unusual twist, as in local asparagus with hazelnut sauce or fillet of salmon with orange and green peppercorns. Locally reared, free-range pork and beef are beginning to find their way on to the menu. Sweets are equally enterprising: cranberry or marmalade or coffee and walnut ice-creams, sticky toffee pudding, candied oranges with Cointreau and 'perfect' sherry trifle. Service is exemplary.

The broad scope of the wine list should satisfy most requirements, although the depth is uneven: over a dozen white burgundies from Comte Lafon yet only three Italians, all Chiantis. Quality is high, styles are varied, and prices impressively low. Eighteen house wines from £6.50 to £12 make up for the relatively few half-bottles. CELLARMAN'S CHOICE: Mâcon 'La Roche Vineuse' 1991, Merlin £12; Quinta de la Rosa 1992, £8.

CHEF: Gerard Crowley PROPRIETOR: Anthony Verdin OPEN: Tue to Sun, exc Tue L and Sun D; 12 to 2, 6.30 to 12.30 CLOSED: 24 to 30 Dec MEALS: alc L Wed to Sat (main courses £8 to £9). Set L Sun £16.50, Set D £16.50 SERVICE: not inc (10% for 6 or more) CARDS: Access, Amex, Diners, Visa DETAILS: 60 seats. 3 tables outside. Private parties: 50 main room, 120 private room. Car park. Vegetarian meals. Children's helpings. No smoking before 2 L, 10 D. Wheelchair access (1 step; also WC). No music. Fax: (0865) 391459

15 North Parade

| 15 North Parade, Oxford OX2 6LX | COOKING 1* |
| OXFORD (0865) 513773 | COST £21–£43 |

This Oxford fixture has changed chefs and style. The décor has moved from Laura Ashley to modern minimalist, and the food has jumped on the contemporary Mediterranean-inspired bandwagon. Pasta and pulses, squid and swordfish, chutneys, salsas and splashes of bright colour are now the form, although inspiration is drawn more from the western Med – Spain and Morocco – than is customary, even down to the mint tea. Fish, vegetables and less expensive cuts of meat are to the fore.

The cooking is confident, with flavours mostly bolder than before: a crispy spring roll, for instance, with a moist and tasty filling of crab and rice, and a strong onion salsa. The crisp beetroot and celeriac chips, the spinach, and the sweet-and-sour effect that all came with barbecued spare ribs (rather tough in themselves) were effective both individually and in combination. Likewise the wild rice and lentil risotto that accompanied guinea-fowl was judged a success. Puddings vary from Moroccan rice pudding with tangerine confit through hot chocolate brownie to an individual summer pudding that was 'light in colour and light on fruit', but there was praise for lemon tart with thin pastry, and peach tarte Tatin – 'nicely unsweet with a good bitter caramel'. The wine list is short and bright, although some mark-ups are on the high side. House Mâcon white and Penfold's red are £9.75 (£2.50 per glass).

CHEFS: Sean Wood and Ben Gorman   PROPRIETOR: Georgina Wood   OPEN: Tue to Sun, exc Sun D; 12 to 2, 7 to 11   MEALS: alc (main courses £8.50 to £14.50). Set L Tue to Sat £12, Sun £13.75   SERVICE: not inc   CARDS: Access, Visa   DETAILS: 60 seats. 10 tables outside. Private parties: 60 main room. Vegetarian meals. Children's helpings on request. No-smoking area. Wheelchair access (1 step; also WC). Music. Air-conditioned

---

▲ Old Parsonage Hotel, Parsonage Bar ♥

1 Banbury Road, Oxford OX2 6NN
OXFORD (0865) 310210

COOKING 1*
COST £26–£50

Oscar Wilde once frequented this converted parsonage, built on a site dating back to the Middle Ages. Today, it is an eminently agreeable and informal venue, with a bar for all-day snacks and meals. On sunny days you can while away the time in the walled front garden; otherwise, opt for the comfort of the bar, with its closely packed tables and picture-covered walls. Polite young men in green aprons render impeccable service.

The place works to a brasserie formula, with a menu that reads as if it has travelled easily from London: toasted bagels with smoked salmon and cream cheese, warm salad of scallops and monkfish, salmon fish-cakes, steak with French fries. Balanced flavours, simple and effective cooking (of lamb's liver, for example) and a deft hand with pastry – lemon tart is good – confirm the unfussy directness of the food. First-rate breads and bowls of olives are left on the table, and the cafetière coffee is strong. The wine list is short, sharp and savvy, mostly under £20, with a good selection available by the glass, bringing enjoyable wines within everybody's reach. House wine is from £10.50. CELLARMAN'S CHOICE: Stewart Point Shiraz/Cabernet 1992, £14.95; Pilton Manor Bacchus 1991, £12.30.

All entries in the Guide *are rewritten every year, not least because restaurant standards fluctuate. Don't trust an out-of-date* Guide.

CHEF: Alison Watkins   PROPRIETOR: Jeremy Mogford   OPEN: all week; 12 to 3, 6 to 11   MEALS: alc (main courses £7.50 to £17)   SERVICE: not inc, card slips closed   CARDS: Access, Amex, Diners, Visa   DETAILS: 37 seats. 11 tables outside. Car park. Vegetarian meals. Children's helpings. Smart dress preferred. No cigars/pipes in dining-room. Wheelchair access. Music. Air-conditioned   ACCOMMODATION: 30 rooms, all with bath/shower. TV. Phone. B&B £105 to £190. Rooms for disabled. Children welcome. Pets by arrangement (bedrooms only). Afternoon teas. Garden. Doors close at 12.30am. Confirm by 4. Fax: (0865) 311262 (*The Which? Hotel Guide*)

Restaurant Elizabeth ▼

82 St Aldate's, Oxford OX1 1RA
OXFORD (0865) 242230

COOKING 1
COST £22–£44

This old stager exists in a time warp, with Antonio Lopez and Salvador Rodriguez clinging to the idea of perennial youth, culinarily speaking. On the first floor of the seventeenth-century building, with views over St Aldate's towards Christ Church meadows, is a tiny bar (where you may be dissuaded from loitering by 'rather brusque Spanish staff') and two dining-rooms. Dark varnished tables are close-set, but there is comfort and a clubby feel. A French menu with short explanations in English dates the cooking: escargots bourguignonne and boeuf Stroganov, for example. But the kitchen turns out good shellfish soup with bits of crab in it, and 'four delicious spoonfuls of very fine and smooth salmon mousse, drowned in a sea of thick, rich Nantua sauce made with crayfish'. The creaminess can get a bit much, as in the sauce for a chicken breast, and in the dauphinois potatoes that accompany it, but that's old-fashioned food for you. Service mellows as the meal progresses. Note that 10 per cent service is included in the prices, but credit card slips are left open. House wine is poor, but well-heeled conservative drinkers will find old vintages of classic French wines, a good run of Sauternes and Barsac, and good Rioja. CELLARMAN'S CHOICE: Mâcon Lugny, 'Les Genièvres' 1991, Louis Latour, £15.70; Rioja Imperial Reserva 1986, £20.35.

CHEF: Salvador Rodriguez   PROPRIETOR: Antonio Lopez   OPEN: Tue to Sun; 12.30 to 2.30, 6.30 to 11 (7 to 10.30 Sun)   CLOSED: 24 to 30 Dec, Good Fri   MEALS: alc (main courses £13.50 to £17.50). Set L £15. Cover £1. Minimum £12   SERVICE: net prices   CARDS: Access, Amex, Diners, Visa   DETAILS: 45 seats. Private parties: 40 main room, 20 and 40 private rooms. Vegetarian meals. Children's helpings. Smart dress preferred. No music. Air-conditioned

Whites ▼ ⚡✱

16 Turl Street, Oxford OX1 3DH
OXFORD (0865) 793396

COOKING 2
COST £18–£49

Students coming out of Lincoln College Library may cast longing glances at Whites on their way to the nearest sandwich bar. Eating out in central Oxford continues to show signs of improvement, and this wine merchant and restaurant has been at the forefront of developments. Beneath the dining-room are vaults dating back to the thirteenth century, still stuffed with wine. Upstairs, some increasingly confident cooking is taking place.

A variety of fixed-price menus with pre-selected wines supplements the *carte*. Starters show plenty of bright ideas in dishes such as monkfish with carrot butter sauce and fig tapénade, crab salad with orange and chive mayonnaise, and pigeon breast with pineapple confit and a red lentil salad. Fortifying main courses may include fillet of hare with pink peppercorns, grapes and port, best end of lamb with tomatoes and black olives, and veal fillet with glazed apples and calvados. A party of four taking lunch found nothing to fault, praising clarity of flavour in everything, including 'crisp and perfectly cooked' vegetables and 'good coffee'. Service is variously lauded as 'affable and skilled', 'friendly and efficient'. Good producers abound on the short wine list, which is predominantly French but also finds room for Hollick's Coonawarra Pinot Noir and the glorious Jackson Estate Sauvignon Blanc from New Zealand among non-Europeans. Vintages are generally sound, prices are fair, half-bottles are extensive, and seven interesting choices are offered by the glass. House French is £8.50. CELLARMAN'S CHOICE: Mercurey Blanc 1991, Leflaive, £23.50; Notre-Dame de Landiras 1990, Premières Côtes de Bordeaux, £15.50.

CHEFS: Christopher Bland, David Owens and Bertrand Faucheux   PROPRIETOR: Whites Restaurant (Oxford) Ltd   OPEN: all week; 12.30 to 2, 6.30 to 10   CLOSED: July to Sept Sun
MEALS: alc (main courses £10 to £18). Set L £11.95, Set D £23.95 to £29.95   SERVICE: not inc
CARDS: Access, Amex, Diners, Visa   DETAILS: 45 seats. Private parties: 40 main room. Vegetarian meals. Children welcome. No smoking in 1 dining-room. Wheelchair access (3 steps). Music. Fax: (0865) 200303

PADSTOW Cornwall   map 1

▲ *St Petroc's* ⁑✳   NEW ENTRY

4 New Street, Padstow PL28 8EA   COOKING 1
PADSTOW (0841) 532700   COST £22–£26

This is the budget alternative to the Seafood Restaurant (see entry, opposite). 'We opened St Petroc's partly because we have been looking for extra bedrooms in Padstow for some time and partly because we have long wanted to run a second, simpler and cheaper restaurant to complement the Seafood Restaurant,' writes Rick Stein. The two are only 150 yards apart, and the grub at St Petroc's is indeed very straightforward: currently a choice of three, three and three at each course plus a fixture of grilled goats' cheese salad as an alternative finish. Dishes are individually priced, so there is no need to eat a full meal. Only one main course is fish – 'truly delicious, firm, fresh, baked cod' for one party, 'beautifully cooked haddock' for another – served with potatoes. Otherwise there may be chargrilled steak with salsa, or grilled Tywardreath sausages. Buckets of baguettes are generously supplied to mop up the remains of moules marinière, carrot and green coriander soup or whatever is on offer to start. Gooey lemon-flavoured treacle tart or bread-and-butter pudding make a hearty finish. An utterly sensible and reasonably priced wine list contributes to the pleasure of the package. House wine is £8.50 (£1.80 per glass).

▲ *This symbol means accommodation is available.*

CHEF: Paul Hearn PROPRIETORS: Rick and Jill Stein OPEN: Tue to Sun; 12.30 to 2.15, 7 to 9.15 MEALS: alc (main courses £8). Set L and D £13.95 SERVICE: not inc CARDS: Access, Amex, Visa DETAILS: 38 seats. Private parties: 10 main room. Car park. Vegetarian meals. Children's helpings. No smoking in dining-room. Music ACCOMMODATION: 8 rooms, all with bath/shower. TV. Phone. B&B £20 to £75. Deposit: 25%. Children welcome. Baby facilities. Pets welcome. Garden. Doors close at 11 (*The Which? Hotel Guide*)

▲ *Seafood Restaurant* 🍾

Riverside, Padstow PL28 8BY   COOKING 3*
PADSTOW (0841) 532485   COST £30–£74

Rick Stein has run this place for 20 years, doing for fish what Pavarotti did for 'Nessun dorma'. It has been a Mecca for anybody who wanted to taste really fresh fish, cooked with imagination and few frills. Reporters tell of their considerable detours, and how it was all worthwhile. The freshness of the raw material is outstanding. It has 'the briny, seaweedy freshness of fish straight off the water-front, nothing like we get in London', according to a knowledgeable visitor. No wonder people travel for miles, mull over the day's catch in the conservatory with aperitifs and olives (from a huge preserving jar, with toothpicks and paper napkins) and traipse eagerly into the huge, cool dining-room with white walls and white linen, which buzzes even when not full. The atmosphere is invariably cheerful.

When Rick Stein is firing on all cylinders the plaudits roll in for excellent shellfish soup and rouille, and for lightly steamed scallops – four shells on a large plate, muscle still attached – with a dressing of soy sauce, pungent sesame oil and the odd leaf fragment of shocking coriander that electrifies the dish. Lobster, too, is as fresh as can be, kept in chilled seawater until ordered, and served grilled or steamed. White fish is equally impressive and comes with similar mild or strong options of hollandaise or a spicy salsa: for example, a tomato, coriander and chilli relish with sea bass 'cooked to perfection'. Poaching, grilling, deep-frying of cod (with chips and tartare sauce), boiled crab and a cold platter of fruits de mer add further variety.

Not all reporters, however, have considered their detours worth it, listing overcooking among the faults or food that uncharacteristically fails to arouse enthusiasm. Long-standing supporters have noticed the drop in standards – 'a loss of grip', as one put it. It all seems to coincide with a new baby (see entry for St Petroc's, opposite), which could explain why Rick Stein might have taken his eye off the ball here. Puddings, however, seem impervious to change. Bakewell tart with clotted cream for one reporter was 'the best I can remember', and 'superb' blueberry tart pleased another. Poached pear is soft and gritty, doused with port syrup heavily spiked with cinnamon, and served with a crème brûlée ice-cream full of toffeeish caramelised sugar flavour and tiny shards of caramel. There are gaps in service. 'The young staff give the impression that this is their second job' and are not always as informed as they might be.

White wines naturally predominate, but quality is equally good throughout the list, and thrills and tingles appear on most pages. The range of styles and grape varieties is impressive, half-bottles are moderately well spread, and prices are generously in the drinker's favour. 'Our Selection' of about 10 wines shows off current enthusiasms. House wines start around £9.50, and five are available by the glass from £2.20 to £3.80. CELLARMAN'S CHOICE: Pacherenc du Vic-Bilh 1991, Ch. Bouscassé, £16.20; Rockford Basket Press Shiraz 1990, £23.95.

CHEF: Rick Stein PROPRIETORS: Rick and Jill Stein OPEN: Mon to Sat; 12.30 to 1.15, 7 to 9.30 (10 Sat) MEALS: alc (main courses £17 to £30). Set L £20.25, Set D £27.85 SERVICE: not inc CARDS: Access, Amex, Visa DETAILS: 70 seats. Private parties: 15 main room. Car park. Vegetarian meals. Children's helpings. Wheelchair access (3 steps). Music. Air-conditioned ACCOMMODATION: 10 rooms, all with bath/shower. TV. Phone. B&B £36.30 to £106. Children welcome. Baby facilities. Pets welcome. Fax: (0841) 533344 (The Which? Hotel Guide)

PAULERSPURY Northamptonshire   map 2

▲ Vine House

100 High Street, Paulerspury NN12 7NA
PAULERSPURY (0327) 811267   COOKING 2
off A5, 2m SE of Towcester   COST £22–£40

Considering it is only a few hundred yards from the A5, and three miles from Silverstone, the Vine House is remarkably tranquil. Whoever renovated the seventeenth-century house (built from local limestone) a few years back wisely avoided the tweeness of artificial beams and mock antiques, and produced a modern-looking dining-room that feels both comfortable and fresh. Meals begin with a nibble in the bar, and proceed to an appetiser at table.

Marcus Springett's ideas are good. He makes a terrine of home-smoked cod and butter-beans with a saffron dressing, and a soup of young nettles, potato and lobster. For pudding, battered strawberry jam sandwiches are deep-fried and served with a red fruit sauce and Jersey cream. Ingredients on the whole are fine – although a little longer hanging for the beef might be welcome – and techniques are generally sound. Sometimes a small error of judgement takes the shine off what would otherwise be very good food: overpowering pepper in a crab soup, for example, or the bitter flavour of garlic purée instead of the real thing. Well-flavoured steak and kidney 'sausage', a sort of elongated meatball, has a first-rate madeira sauce, and vegetables come as part of the package. Among other desserts are pears set in honey jelly with home-bottled blackberries, served with warm creamy rice pudding.

Service is pleasantly amateur, 'but the atmosphere is relaxed and easy-going'. Home-made ginger beer is light and refreshing. Wines are interesting, many of them moderately priced. French and Australian house wines are £8.95.

CHEF: Marcus Springett PROPRIETORS: Marcus and Julie Springett OPEN: Mon to Sat, exc L Mon and Sat; 12 to 2.30, 7 to 10.30 MEALS: Set L £13.95, Set D £19.50 (Mon to Thur) to £23.50 (Fri and Sat) SERVICE: not inc CARDS: Access, Visa DETAILS: 45 seats. Private parties: 30 main room, 12 private room. Car park. Vegetarian meals with prior notice. Children's helpings. Smart dress preferred. No cigars/pipes in dining-room. No music ACCOMMODATION: 6 rooms, all with bath/shower. TV. Phone. B&B £39 to £61. Children welcome. Baby facilities. Garden. Doors close at 11.30. Confirm by 6 (The Which? Hotel Guide)

Remember, if you especially want the set menu, that some restaurants restrict availability, particularly at weekends and on public holidays.

PENZANCE Cornwall   map 1

Harris's

NEW ENTRY

46 New Street, Penzance TR18 2LZ   COOKING 2
PENZANCE (0736) 64408   COST £25–£47

Down a narrow alley not far from the impressive Lloyds Bank in the main street
is this white-washed building with red paintwork and window boxes outside.
Pinks, reds and beige are the colours in the dining-room, which has well-spaced
tables, pot plants and pictures of fish on the walls. Appropriately the kitchen
makes good use of the catch from the Newlyn boats, and specials such as grilled
scallops with salad leaves and a herb dressing, and poached John Dory with a
well-judged saffron sauce, augment the short *carte*. The cooking is accurate,
timing is spot-on, and there is no needless embellishment: rack of lamb is
cooked pink as requested, and served on a reduced rosemary jus with a scoop of
crab-apple jelly on the side. Reporters have also commented on the quality of
fresh pasta with tomato and basil sauce, crab florentine and beef Stroganov.
Desserts are normally cold: strawberry tart with clotted cream is often
mentioned; otherwise you might find chilled lemon soufflé, chocolate pot (very
rich, this) and summer pudding. Service is polite and polished. France
dominates the short wine list, which has a good showing of halves at keen
prices. House wine is £8.90.

CHEF: Roger Harris   PROPRIETORS: Roger and Anne Harris   OPEN: Mon to Sat, exc Mon L; 12 to
2, 7 to 9.30   CLOSED: 2 weeks Nov, 25 and 26 Dec, 1 Jan, 1 week Feb, Mon D Oct to May
MEALS: alc (main courses £10.50 to £18.50)   SERVICE: 10%, card slips closed   CARDS: Access,
Amex, Diners, Visa   DETAILS: 40 seats. Private parties: 24 main room. Vegetarian meals with
prior notice. Children welcome. Smart dress preferred. Music

PLUMTREE Nottinghamshire   map 5

Perkins Bar Bistro ⁵✶

Old Railway Station, Plumtree NG12 5NA
PLUMTREE (0602) 373695
off A606, 2m S of Nottingham   COOKING 2
                                                                            COST £21–£33

In that *Brief Encounter* era when a place like Plumtree had a railway station, this
was it. For the past 12 years, however, it has been run as a much-loved bar and
bistro by Tony and Wendy Perkins. The conservatory extension on what was
once the platform affords views of the track, and not much disrupts the bucolic
idyll in which rabbits may safely graze.

Inside, a twin-track approach is evident. On the bar side of the operation,
half-pint beer mugs are filled up with prawns and offered with cocktail sauce for
dipping, while the bistro tries out more florid French fare, so that paupiettes of
pork may be 'napped with sauce Robert'. Pigeon, venison and duck terrine
'tasted satisfyingly of garlic' and was given a runny Cumberland sauce. The
same meal yielded 'firm but juicy' monkfish on a brochette with bacon, red
peppers and mushrooms, with good basmati rice, and a rack of lamb of fine
flavour that was bolstered by creamy onion sauce but was let down by a stock
reduction that 'lacked flavour'. Otherwise, pigeon breast in puff pastry with

431

mushroom duxelles and orange sauce, or roast cod fillet with parsley butter and aubergine fritters, show what can be done. Vegetables are varied and good, but cost extra, and puddings can be 'sensational', as in a lattice tart of mixed fruits and frangipane. The wine list, led by commendable southern French selections, goes for value without sacrificing choice. A smattering of good halves is available. House wines are £7.80.

CHEF: Tony Perkins   PROPRIETORS: Tony and Wendy Perkins   OPEN: Tue to Sat; 12 to 2, 6.30 to 9.45   CLOSED: bank hols, exc Good Fri   MEALS: alc (main courses £7.50 to £10.50) SERVICE: not inc   CARDS: Access, Amex, Diners, Visa   DETAILS: 75 seats. 6 tables outside. Private parties: 24 main room, 30 private room. Car park. Vegetarian meals. Children welcome. Smart dress preferred. No smoking in 1 dining-room. Wheelchair access (1 step). Music. Fax: (0602) 376405

PLYMOUTH Devon   map 1

Chez Nous ♀

13 Frankfort Gate, Plymouth PL1 1QA   COOKING 3*
PLYMOUTH (0752) 266793   COST £39–£48

It is in a pedestrian precinct – a *very* pedestrian precinct – near the market and close to ample parking. It is so discreet you might walk past it: many have. Once inside, do not be put off by the blackboard menu. Just because the dishes are written in chalk, and French prints and menus make it feel like a bistro, does not mean the cooking is casual. Jacques Marchal takes his trade seriously, serving up stylish French food, according to one reporter, in a 'convivial, relaxing atmosphere conducive to happy dining and conversation' – infinitely preferable to hushed tones and reverential whispers. Staff are friendly, efficient and welcoming.

The cooking rests on a firm foundation of classical techniques applied to notably good ingredients, but is not ossified or old-fashioned. Dinner, for example, might begin with a taste of chicken gizzard and Puy lentils in red wine. Jacques Marchal cooks a proper onion soup, croustade of lamb sweetbreads with madeira sauce, and chicken liver mousse with brioche, and makes it look easy – the sure sign of a professional. Steaming – of fish and vegetables – maintains a welcome lightness of touch. French wines with an excellent pedigree dominate the list, but good drinking can be had among less expensive bottles, including the token dozen from around the world; half-bottles are generous but not cheap. Sweet Banyuls wines and eau-de-vie from Alsace add interest. House Chardonnay and Cabernet Sauvignon are around £10 a bottle. CELLARMAN'S CHOICE: St Véran, Dom. de Maillettes 1992, £16.50; Morgon Les Versauds 1992, £14.

CHEF: Jacques Marchal   PROPRIETORS: Suzanne and Jacques Marchal   OPEN: Tue to Sat; 12.30 to 2, 7 to 10.30   CLOSED: 3 weeks Feb, 3 weeks Sept, bank hols   MEALS: Set L and D £28.50   SERVICE: not inc   CARDS: Access, Amex, Diners, Visa   DETAILS: 28 seats. Private parties: 32 main room. Vegetarian meals with prior notice. No children under 8. Smart dress preferred. Wheelchair access (1 step). Music

---

See the back of the Guide *for a listing of all restaurants in the Main Entries sections.*

Yang Cheng £

30A Western Approach, Plymouth PL1 1TQ
PLYMOUTH (0752) 660170

(WEST COUNTRY 1995 DIM-SUM)

COOKING 1
COST £16–£42

'It made our day and the weekend,' commented a couple who sought relief in this easy-going Chinese restaurant after a drab early evening party. This is perhaps the only place in the West Country serving authentic dim-sum (everything from Shanghai dumplings to chicken feet with black-bean sauce), although prices might alarm people used to eating in big-city Chinatowns. One-plate set lunches are available for those with less adventurous tastes. The full menu stays close to its Cantonese roots, with dishes such as roast duck on rice, mixed meat and vegetable chow-mein, and wun-tun with noodles in soup, while also playing to the gallery with more Westernised offerings, including sweet-and-sour chicken and deep-fried king prawns. Seafood from Plymouth's Barbican market is the main strength. 'Faultless within its price and range' was one happy verdict on the cooking. Service is exceedingly attentive. Drink Tsingtao beer, saké or house wine at £6.30.

CHEF: K.Y. Wong PROPRIETORS: K.Y. Wong, Mrs K.S. Ling and Mrs L.Y.K. Wong OPEN: Tue to Sun; 12 to 2.30 (3 Sun), 6 to 11 (6.30 to 10.30 Sun) MEALS: alc (main courses £6 to £10.50). Set L £9 (2 courses), Set D £12.80 (2 courses) to £17 SERVICE: not inc CARDS: Access, Amex, Visa DETAILS: 70 seats. Private parties: 70 main room. Vegetarian meals. Children welcome. Smart dress preferred. Music. Air-conditioned

---

POLPERRO Cornwall

map 1

Kitchen

The Coombes, Polperro PL13 2RQ
POLPERRO (0503) 72780
on A387, 3m SW of Looe

COOKING 1
COST £21–£36

'On the walk between the car park and the harbour' is how the brochure describes the position. Tourism reigns in Polperro, but visitors agree that the Batesons' little pink restaurant is not to be missed. The place was once a fisherman's cottage, and it is 'a miracle of the jigsaw maker's art' that so many tables have been fitted into one tiny room. Ian Bateson works to an extensive menu that relies heavily on the daily catch from the boats. John Dory with a zesty sauce of oranges and lemons, and swordfish with cream and coriander have been enjoyable offerings. Other dishes, including lamb korma and chicken jalfrezi, no doubt please city tourists suffering curry house withdrawal symptoms; desserts such as banoffi pie and hazelnut meringue appeal to those with a sweet tooth. Service is chatty and deft. Fifty-odd wines provide keenly priced and satisfying drinking. House wine is £8.60.

CHEFS/PROPRIETORS: Ian and Vanessa Bateson OPEN: Tue to Sat and bank hols, D only (varies out of season – telephone to check); 7 to 9.30 MEALS: alc (main courses £8.50 to £12). Minimum £8.50 SERVICE: not inc, card slips closed CARDS: Access, Visa DETAILS: 24 seats. Private parties: 6 main room. Vegetarian meals. No children under 10. Smart dress preferred. No cigars/pipes in dining-room. Wheelchair access. Music

POOLE Dorset map 2

▲ *Mansion House*

Thames Street, Poole BH15 1JN COOKING 1
POOLE (0202) 685666 COST £22–£42

This Georgian house in the old part of town operates as a dining club as well as a conventional hotel and restaurant. Members are offered discounts, but all comers are welcome (albeit for a 15 per cent surcharge on meal prices) and many decide to join. The *carte* has been scrapped in favour of less expensive fixed-price menus, plus a daily table d'hôte. Weekday lunches include a short menu with unlimited house wine on offer until the main course is completed, while Sunday lunch brings a couple of roasts. Dinners are more ambitious, taking in duet of venison and pigeon with game sauce and orange-braised chicory, and fillet of salmon in tomato and chive sauce spiked with green peppercorns, as well as more traditional grilled Dover sole and fillet of beef with béarnaise sauce. The wine list divides into 'under £20' and a 'classic selection' for those with fat wallets. France is the main source with a few other bottles added for variety. House wines start at £9.75.

CHEF: Gerry Godden PROPRIETOR: Robert Leonard OPEN: all week, exc Sat L and Sun D; 12.30 to 2, 7.30 to 9.30 MEALS: Set L Mon to Sat £14 (inc wine), Sun £12.95, Set D £12.95 (plus supplements) – 15% surcharge on all meals for non-members SERVICE: not inc CARDS: Access, Amex, Diners, Visa DETAILS: 100 seats. Private parties: 100 main room, 14, 31 and 40 private rooms. Car park. Vegetarian meals. Children's helpings. No children under 5. Smart dress preferred. Music. Air-conditioned ACCOMMODATION: 28 rooms, all with bath/shower. TV. Phone. B&B £50 to £110. Children welcome. Baby facilities. Pets by arrangement (not in public rooms). Afternoon teas. Doors close at midnight. Confirm by 6. Fax: (0202) 665709 (*The Which? Hotel Guide*)

POOL IN WHARFEDALE West Yorkshire map 5

▲ *Pool Court*

Pool Bank, Pool in Wharfedale LS21 1EH
LEEDS (0532) 842288
on A658, 3m N of Leeds/Bradford Airport COST £32–£58

As the *Guide* comes out, this establishment is scheduled to close and transfer to the centre of Leeds. Michael Gill opened Pool Court in 1966 and has been in the *Guide* almost from the beginning. Had we been compiling an entry this year it would certainly have confirmed its position as one of Yorkshire's finest, and while departure from the country spread is sad to see, the logic for a city-centre operation is strong. The new restaurant is planned at 42 The Calls, next door to Brasserie Forty Four (see entry), in which Michael Gill is a partner. Reports, please. (The details following relate to the Pool in Wharfedale premises, and may well change when the restaurant moves to Leeds.)

▲ *This symbol means accommodation is available.*

CHEF: David Watson PROPRIETORS: Michael and Hanni Gill OPEN: Mon to Sat, exc L Mon and Sat; 12 to 2, 7 to 10 CLOSED: 2 weeks from 24 Dec MEALS: alc (main courses L £7.50 to £10, D £7.50 to £14). Set D £25.50 (2 courses) to £33.50 SERVICE: not inc CARDS: Access, Amex, Diners, Visa DETAILS: 75 seats. Private parties: 30 private rooms. Car park. Vegetarian meals. Children's helpings on request. Smart dress preferred. No cigars/pipes in dining-room. Wheelchair access (1 step). Music. Air-conditioned ACCOMMODATION: 6 rooms, all with bath/shower. TV. Phone. B&B £70 to £105. Children welcome. Garden. Confirm by 6. Fax: (0532) 843115

PORTHLEVEN Cornwall   map 1

▲ *Critchards* ✳ £ | NEW ENTRY |

The Harbourside, Porthleven TR13 9JA   COOKING 1
HELSTON (0326) 562407   COST £20–£50

Steve and Jo Critchard are obviously proud of their restaurant: everything, from the china and napkins to the wrapped chocolates served with coffee, has their name on it. The building is a converted granary hard by Porthleven quay, and seafood is the star of the show. What cannot be gleaned from the local boats comes from Newlyn. Jo's regularly changing menu (backed up by a host of daily specials) has a global ring to it and she is prepared to pull in ideas from near and far. Freshness is the key to grilled brill with a 'fantastic light lemony sauce', lemon sole in Muscadet and grape sauce, and salmon and monkfish in herb butter sauce. Seafood chowder ('masses of different fish in chunks') is a regular favourite. Jo also offers a full vegetarian menu and cooks steaks and duck for meat-eaters. Puddings are calorific concoctions such as rich chocolate fudge cake and crème brûlée. Service is local and good-natured. The modest wine list favours whites, and prices are extremely fair. House wine is £7.95.

CHEF: Jo Critchard PROPRIETORS: Steve and Jo Critchard OPEN: Mon to Sat, D only; 6.30 to 10 MEALS: alc (main courses £6 to £23) SERVICE: not inc, card slips closed CARDS: Access, Visa DETAILS: 44 seats. Private parties: 34 main room. Vegetarian meals. Children's helpings. No children under 5. Smart dress preferred. No smoking in dining-room. Wheelchair access (1 step). Music ACCOMMODATION: 1 room, with bath/shower. TV. B&B £42. Deposit: 25%. Children welcome. Afternoon teas. Doors close at 11.30

PORTHOUSTOCK Cornwall   map 1

Volnay

Porthoustock, nr St Keverne TR12 6QW
HELSTON (0326) 280183   COOKING 2
off B3293, 1½m E of St Keverne   COST £17–£37

Porthoustock is a cluster of whitewashed buildings on the east side of the Lizard. Volnay (formerly Café Volnay) is right on the sea-front, opposite an old red telephone box. Inside, it is pleasantly unstuffy, tables have red and white checkered cloths and waiting staff wear the house T-shirt. The menu is recited from table to table by Steven Chapman, mistakes cheerfully acknowledged as he goes: 'We were told that the Emmenthal tart may be off as the custard was having difficulty setting.' Those familiar with the wine regions of France may be led by the restaurant's name to expect Burgundian cooking, but Colin Rye's food looks south to the Mediterranean.

The shortish *carte* may offer grilled Scamorza cheese with roasted red peppers, tomato galette with anchovies and olives, or cassoulet. One couple eating in June found it 'amazing what they can turn out of that small kitchen'. They had scallops on toasted ciabatta with a good garlicky pesto, duck leg confit with sun-dried tomatoes and a tomato vinaigrette (the meat long-cooked to extreme tenderness), and sauté loin of lamb with black olives, its pan juices lifted with a little oregano and lemon. Desserts tend to the Italianate and simple. A pear is poached and split in two, the halves topped with mascarpone and sitting on a dark chocolate sauce. Alternatively, there may be torta delizia (a toasted gâteau of rum and marzipan) or sharp lemon tart served with crème fraîche. The laughing, chattering ambience of Volnay will compensate for the stormiest of Cornish weather. The very terse wine list provides an adequate selection at eminently sensible prices. House wines from Verona are £7.50.

CHEF: Colin Rye   PROPRIETORS: Steven Chapman and Colin Rye   OPEN: Tue to Sun, D only (also bank hol Mons); 11 to 12.30, 7 to 9.30   CLOSED: winter Sun D and Tue D   MEALS: alc (main courses £9.50 to £13)   SERVICE: not inc   DETAILS: 20 seats. Private parties: 18 main room. Vegetarian meals. Children welcome. No cigars in dining-room. Music

---

PORT ISAAC Cornwall   map 1

▲ *Slipway*

Harbour Front, Port Isaac PL29 3RH   COOKING 1
BODMIN (0208) 880264   COST £17–£51

The setting is north Cornwall at its best. The sixteenth-century building opposite the slipway is a former chandler's, locals drink in the bar, and the location is crucial. Crab and lobster are landed daily in season, just yards away, then grilled and served cold in a shellfish platter, or any other way you fancy. White fish gets similar treatment. Freshness is all, and there is certainly no fancy cooking, which is exactly as it should be. In addition to the fish, spicy vegetarian options of chickpea rissoles or bean bakes share equal billing with fillet steak and good roast lamb or pheasant. Wines are serviceable, mark-ups low, and half a dozen are available by the glass from £1.30.

CHEFS: Karen Smith and Eden Osabofu   PROPRIETORS: Simon, Paul and James Bishop   OPEN: all week; 12 to 2.30, 7 to 9.30 (10 summer)   CLOSED: Nov to Dec, Feb to Mar, Mon off-season   MEALS: alc (main courses £9 to £22.50). Set D Apr, May and Oct £17.50. Bar L menu   SERVICE: not inc, card slips closed   CARDS: Access, Amex, Visa   DETAILS: 40 seats. 5 tables outside. Private parties: 70 main room. Car park. Vegetarian meals. Children's helpings on request. No-smoking area. Wheelchair access (1 step). Music   ACCOMMODATION: 10 rooms, 5 with bath/shower. Phone. B&B £19 to £64. Deposit: £15. Older children welcome. Pets welcome (small dogs £3.50 per night). Afternoon teas. Doors close at 1am. Confirm by 6. Fax: (0208) 880264 (*The Which? Hotel Guide*)

Not inc in the details at the end of an entry indicates that no service charge is made and any tipping is at the discretion of the customer.

POULTON-LE-FYLDE Lancashire   map 5

▲ *River House* ♥

Skippool Creek,
Thornton-le-Fylde FY5 5LF   COOKING 2*
POULTON-LE-FYLDE (0253) 883497 and 883307   COST £24–£52

'We went at September high tide and it was exquisite,' commented a couple who thoroughly appreciated the Scotts' long-established restaurant with panoramic views of the Wyre. The house – built in 1830 – has an appealing 'lived-in' feel, Bill Scott's personable presence adds to the experience, and 'the smell of cooking is mouthwatering'. First-rate ingredients are used to telling effect in dishes that range from beef teriyaki to 'bloody young grouse' with game sauce, although the kitchen steers clear of fashionable frippery. Soups of broccoli and Brie, or 'ebullient' carrot and coriander, are perfectly seasoned and based on excellent stock. Chateaubriand and pink loin of lamb with spinach and béarnaise sauce show the virtue of handling prime cuts with care and astute timing. Individual cheese soufflés and impeccable vegetables draw rave reviews. Desserts round things off on a high note: legendary ticky-tacky pudding 'lives up to its reputation', while home-made ice-creams are quite simply 'superb'. Colombian coffee, a fine range of teas, hunks of cheese with home-made biscuits and dainty petits fours are in line with the aspirations of this likeable set-up.

Wines are a pleasing combination of high class, interest and affordability. The list carries a note to the effect that deliveries are erratic and supplies (particularly vintages) are uncertain. The Loire and Alsace seem most at risk here. But the variety and scope of the list is such that most gaps can be covered with a reasonable alternative. House wines vary, but should be around £12.50 (£2.50 per glass). CELLARMAN'S CHOICE: Lark Hill Chardonnay 1991, £20; Bandol Cuvée Migoua 1992, Dom. Tempier, £25.

CHEF: Bill Scott   PROPRIETORS: the Scott family   OPEN: all week, exc Sun D; meal times by appointment   MEALS: alc (main courses £16 to £18). Set L and D £18.50, Set L Sun £12.75
SERVICE: not inc   CARDS: Access, Visa   DETAILS: 40 seats. Private parties: 40 main room, 14 private room. Car park. Vegetarian meals. Children's helpings by arrangement. Smart dress preferred. Music   ACCOMMODATION: 5 rooms, all with bath/shower. TV. Phone. B&B £50 to £180. Children welcome. Pets welcome. Garden. Confirm by 6. Fax: (0253) 892083 (*The Which? Hotel Guide*)

POWBURN Northumberland   map 7

▲ *Breamish House* ⁵⁄✳

Powburn NE66 4LL   COOKING 1
POWBURN (0665) 578266   COST £21–£36

An impressive avenue of trees leads up to this neat Georgian house at the foot of the Cheviot Hills. All around is wild moorland dotted with sheep and gorse. The Johnsons have marked the place with their own stamp, offering comfort and luxury without ostentation. The four-course dinner menu follows suit: the food is not over-ambitious and shows off local ingredients to good effect. Game is

437

from the moors, fish is from the quay at Amble and farmed wild boar attracts much attention. Northumbrian lamb is served the old way with redcurrant jelly and mint sauce, although the meat has not always been as tender as it could be. Reporters have liked pâté of prawns, bacon and cheese, wild mushroom soup and breast of wild duck; vegetables are consistently good and the kitchen can also deliver – on request – vegetarian dishes such as nut roast with coriander sauce that are way above the usual hotel clichés. The dessert trolley has varied in quality, although bread-and-butter pudding and lemon meringue gâteau have been praised. The wine list offers a good range and many reliable names from France and the New World. House wine is £10.90.

CHEFS/PROPRIETORS: Doreen and Alan Johnson OPEN: all week, D only, and Sun L; 12.30 to 1, 7.30 to 8 CLOSED: Jan to 14 Feb MEALS: Set L Sun £13.50, Set D £21.50 SERVICE: not inc, card slips closed CARDS: Access, Visa DETAILS: 30 seats. 1 table outside. Private parties: 40 main room, 12 private room. Car park. Vegetarian meals with prior notice. Children's helpings Sun L. Children under 12 by arrangement. Smart dress preferred. No smoking in dining-room. Wheelchair access (1 step; also WC). No music ACCOMMODATION: 11 rooms, all with bath/shower. TV. Phone. B&B £36 to £102. Deposit: £25. Children under 12 by arrangement. Children's high tea. Pets welcome (not in public rooms). Afternoon teas. Garden. Doors close at 11. Confirm by 6. Fax: (0665) 578500 (*The Which? Hotel Guide*)

POWERSTOCK Dorset   map 2

▲ *Three Horseshoes* ✳ £

Powerstock DT6 3TF
POWERSTOCK (0308) 485328 and 485229   COOKING 1*
off A3066 at Gore Cross, 4m NE of Bridport   COST £18–£45

Set in the prehistoric, almost deserted landscape of deep Dorset, this country pub now feels more like a 'casual restaurant'. The tiny patio 'plastered into the hillside' is wonderful on a warm evening as the local church bells peal out. Inside is a dining-room that reminded one reporter of 'a plush railway carriage', while the bar area is largely given over to blackboards advertising the food on offer. Jason Williams has taken over as chef, although Pat Ferguson's hand remains firmly on the tiller. People come here to eat fish above all else. The catch is from the Weymouth boats and its freshness is never in doubt: chargrilled monkfish with a wreath of ratatouille was, quite simply, 'good clean fun'. Otherwise you might find sea bass steak with garlic cream sauce, grilled plaice or steamed crab with ginger, garlic and soy. Lovers of meat and game are also accommodated with rack of lamb or fiercely marinated escalopes of venison with red wine sauce. Quibbles about prices, poor extras and slip-ups in the kitchen suggest that the set-up sometimes over-reaches itself; amateurish, 'sixth-former' service doesn't help. Draught beer is an alternative to the short wine list, which has several interesting offerings by the glass. House wine is £7.50.

CHEFS: Jason Williams, Martin Lewis and Pat Ferguson PROPRIETORS: Pat and Diana Ferguson OPEN: all week; 12 to 2, 7 to 10 MEALS: alc (main courses £7.50 to £25) SERVICE: not inc CARDS: Access, Amex, Visa DETAILS: 100 seats. 10 tables outside. Private parties: 60 main room, 16 private room. Car park. Vegetarian meals. Children's helpings. Smart dress preferred. No smoking in dining-room. No music ACCOMMODATION: 4 rooms, 2 with bath/shower. TV. B&B £24 to £45. Deposit: 1 night. Children welcome. Pets welcome. Garden. Doors close at midnight. Confirm by 6

PRESTBURY Cheshire   map 5

▲ *White House*

The Village, Prestbury SK10 4DG
PRESTBURY (0625) 829376   COOKING 1
on A538, 4m N of Macclesfield   COST £20–£60

Decked out in 'silk and lace' with sisal flooring and cane furniture, the White House restaurant is a well-heeled fixture of the Cheshire scene. The plant-bedecked conservatory extension is perfect for a sunny evening meal, although the whole place feels 'smartly summery'. Fish from Fleetwood shows up well on a menu which has many 'alluring' starters, fresh pasta and main dishes with a cosmopolitan slant. Much of the output sounds and looks up-to-the-minute: 'fat and juicy' seared scallops with stir-fried vegetables, Chinese cabbage and a soy-based sauce; crispy duckling with lentils and kumquat marmalade; well-timed rack of Welsh lamb with mint pesto and creamed julienne of courgettes; sticky toffee pudding with dates on a duo of vanilla and coffee sauces. Dull bread, vegetables at high prices and average petits fours can let the side down. Eighty wines are split between the New World and the rest. Prices are kept in check: house wine is £10 a litre.

CHEFS: Ryland Wakeham and Mark Cunniffe PROPRIETORS: Ryland and Judith Wakeham OPEN: all week, exc Mon L and Sun D; 12 to 2, 7 to 10 MEALS: alc (main courses £8 to £18.50). Set L £11.95 SERVICE: not inc, card slips closed CARDS: Access, Amex, Diners, Visa DETAILS: 75 seats. 3 tables outside. Private parties: 28 main room, 5, 28 and 40 private rooms. Car park. Vegetarian meals. Healthy eating options. Children's helpings. Smart dress preferred. No cigars/pipes in dining-room. Wheelchair access (also WC). Music ACCOMMODATION: 9 rooms, all with bath/shower. TV. Phone. B&B £70 to £127. Rooms for disabled. Children welcome. Baby facilities. Pets welcome. Garden. Doors close at midnight. Confirm by noon. Fax: (0625) 828627 (*The Which? Hotel Guide*)

PULBOROUGH West Sussex   map 3

Stane Street Hollow ❢

Codmore Hill, Pulborough RH20 1BG
PULBOROUGH (0798) 872819   COOKING 2
on A29, 1½m NE of Pulborough   COST £21–£45

Seen from the outside, this is a pair of delightful old Bargate stone farm cottages. Inside, it is all cow bells and – coming from the bar – oompah-pah music, on account of René Kaiser being Swiss. There are beams, an 'electric coal' fire in the dining-room and a somewhat cheerless bar; one reporter found the atmosphere 'reminiscent of a Tunbridge Wells tea-room'. But the welcome is genuine and warm, from homely ladies with low-cut frilly blouses, gathered skirts and sensible stockings who bustle in with dish after dish. Everything arrives in vast quantities, with enormous amounts of goodwill. Service is quick: 'We were in at 8 o'clock, and it was all over by 9.30.'

It is the French bit of Switzerland that drives the cooking: chicken liver pâté with home-pickled vegetables, rabbit with white wine and thyme, or lamb sweetbreads with sorrel and cream. For eight months of the year, the Kaisers grow and serve their own vegetables, soft fruits and herbs. Hams, chicken and fish are home-smoked. Vegetables are the star turn: best of all, for one visitor, was a dish of light, creamy spinach and nettles for which she was assured, 'chef went out this morning with his rubber gloves on'. Puddings are also praised features, particularly feather-light cheesecake with a rhubarb purée on top, and home-made ice-creams are superb. Wines are mostly French, well selected, and so reasonably marked up that even burgundies look affordable. There are no house wines but a fair selection of half-bottles, and half a dozen dessert wines by the glass. CELLARMAN'S CHOICE: Oeil de Perdrix 1991, £13.50; Pouilly Fumé 1991, Dagueneau, £18.65.

CHEF: René Kaiser PROPRIETORS: René and Ann Kaiser OPEN: Wed to Sun, exc Sat L and Sun D; 12.30 to 1.15, 7.15 to 9.15 CLOSED: 2 weeks Nov, 24 to 27 Dec, 2 weeks June MEALS: alc (main courses £9.50 to £13), Set L £8.25 (2 courses) SERVICE: not inc DETAILS: 32 seats. Private parties: 24 main room, 16 private room. Car park. Vegetarian meals. Children's helpings. Smart dress preferred. Wheelchair access (3 steps). Music in bar

---

RAMSBOTTOM Greater Manchester   map 5

Village Restaurant

16–18 Market Place, Ramsbottom BL0 9HT
RAMSBOTTOM (0706) 825070   COOKING 1
off A56/M66, 4m N of Bury   COST £14–£28

'Paradise found,' gushes one supporter. 'A major disappointment,' writes a senior inspector. The Village Restaurant that used to serve languorous six-course no-choice dinners ending after midnight is no more. But the new bistro, originally called the Supper Room, has now been renamed the Village Restaurant, and serves a fixed-price three-course menu in the evening. Lower prices are one obvious change, as the enterprise struggles with recessionary times.

The food has been simplified accordingly: pared down to essentials, with a laudably green philosophy that relies on organic farming and eschews salt. For the converted, this results in enhanced natural flavours: superb brill with sea urchin sauce, for example. For others, it is nothing short of bland. Unfortunately, Chris Johnson so oversells the food with his wonderfully descriptive lectures that it has a hard time living up to the hype. On top of this are some serious lapses in service. One couple arrived at 7.30, in time to visit the shop and choose their wine, and it was only 'at 9.20, when my wife began to devour her napkin, that the food began to arrive'. Everybody is very pleasant, 'the supply lines have been scrupulously cultivated', but the cooking doesn't always match up. There are still enough supporters, however, who will happily return, and everybody praises the wines, whether by the glass from the short list, or from the shop or cellar (to which the bottle symbol refers): just add £4.95 corkage to the retail price.

CHEF: Ros Hunter PROPRIETORS: Ros Hunter and Chris Johnson OPEN: Wed to Sun, exc Sun D; 12 to 2.30, 7.45 (1 for 1.30 Sun L) MEALS: alc L (main courses £3 to £8). Set L Sun £14.95, Set D £9.95 to £14.95. Minimum £3.95 L, £9.95 D SERVICE: not inc, card slips closed CARDS: Access, Amex, Diners, Visa DETAILS: 32 seats. Private parties: 32 main room. Vegetarian meals. No children under 12. Smart dress preferred. No smoking in dining-room. No music

REIGATE Surrey   map 3

Dining Room ⁵⨯

59A High Street, Reigate RH2 9AE   COOKING 2
REIGATE (0737) 226650   COST £20–£43

The name reflects the wish to create a dining-club atmosphere at this restaurant on the first floor above a shop on Reigate's main thoroughfare. Heavy curtains and window boxes frame the outward view, and the room itself is 'extremely pleasant and relaxing', with very proper table-settings. Anthony Tobin arrived here from South Lodge, Lower Beeding in late June 1994, and has given the cooking something of a lift. A meal eaten just after he took over tapped at least some of the potential. Sauté scallops on a crisp potato cake with chive cream was 'absolutely excellent', the shellfish tender, the potato underlay of the kind of quality that induces white-knuckled envy. Thinly sliced smoked chicken in a salad with asparagus was a first course of agreeable lightness on a ragingly hot evening, while a main course of monkfish roasted in a bandaging of Parma ham 'worked unexpectedly well'. Crispy grilled duck breast with a confit of leg came with a fine accompaniment of lentils and pickled turnips. Caramelised pear tart with vanilla ice-cream and chocolate tart with orange sauce show an aptitude for pastrywork. Espresso could do with livening up a bit. The indicators are that, once he has settled in, Anthony Tobin could be capable of achieving great things here. Wines, from Bibendum, are a sound international collection at keen prices, although totally lacking information on vintages. House wines are from £7.50.

CHEFS: Anthony Tobin, Andrew Tester and Carl Sherman   PROPRIETOR: Paul Montalto   OPEN: Mon to Fri; 12 to 2.30, 7 to 10   CLOSED: 1 week Christmas and Easter   MEALS: alc (main courses £11.50 to £13). Set L £9.95 (2 courses), Set D £13.95 (2 courses)   SERVICE: not inc CARDS: Access, Amex, Diners, Visa   DETAILS: 50 seats. Private parties: 45 main room. Vegetarian meals. Children welcome. Smart dress preferred. No smoking in dining-room. Music

RICHMOND Surrey   map 3

▲ Petersham Hotel, Nightingales

Nightingale Lane, Richmond TW10 6UZ   COOKING 2
081-940 7471   COST £27–£40

Standing proud on Richmond Hill, overlooking a memorable stretch of the River Thames, this impressive mid-Victorian mansion is now a hotel with an equally impressive restaurant. Chef Tim Richardson learned his craft at the Connaught and the Savoy (see entries, London) and his aim is to resurrect 'classical cookery styles which have been left behind', although he is also prepared to be innovative. Fish is a feature of his fixed-price menus. Grilled cod with lime and herb butter, and fish-cakes rub shoulders with chargrilled swordfish with baby fennel and tomato and basil béarnaise. Elsewhere you might find spinach and pumpkin tartlet, sauté breast of chicken with mango purée, apple and calvados, and baron of rabbit casseroled with oyster mushrooms. Desserts are in similar style: a hot English pudding is always on offer, along with more fancy ideas such as bananas en papillote with vanilla and passion-fruit coulis. The wine list is a long run through serious clarets, burgundies and champagnes backed up by some affordable stuff from further afield. House wine is £12.50.

CHEF: Tim Richardson   PROPRIETOR: C.S. Dare   OPEN: all week; 12.30 to 2.15 (2.45 Sun), 7 to 9.45 (8.45 Sun)   CLOSED: 25 and 26 Dec   MEALS: Set L Mon to Sat £16.50 to £22.50, Set D Mon to Sat £22.50, Set L and D Sun £20   SERVICE: not inc   CARDS: Access, Amex, Diners, Visa
DETAILS: 80 seats. Private parties: 14 main room, 20 and 36 private rooms. Vegetarian meals. Children welcome. Smart dress preferred. No-smoking area. Music   ACCOMMODATION: 54 rooms, all with bath/shower. TV. Phone. Lift. B&B £97 to £150. Children welcome. Baby facilities. Afternoon teas. Garden. Confirm by noon. Fax: 081-940 9998

RIDGEWAY Derbyshire   map 5

Old Vicarage ▮ ✶✗

Ridgeway Moor, Ridgeway S12 3XW
SHEFFIELD (0742) 475814
off A616, on B6054 nearly opposite   COOKING 4
village church   COST £43–£53

'Ridgeway is a suburb of Sheffield,' writes Andrew Bramley. 'It is rural, green-belt and a conservation area.' The stone-built Victorian house – with views down the hillside – comforts with lavishly decorated sitting-rooms full of antiques and squashy sofas. Booking is necessary for lunch, and advisable at dinner if only to get up-to-date directions around roadworks caused by construction of the South Yorkshire Supertram network. Tessa Bramley cooks and runs the place, son Andrew is front-of-house. Poultry and game come from the village, and the Old Vicarage's kitchen gardens provide most of the vegetables and herbs.

The food moves with the times, bringing together British favourites such as oxtail soup and sunnier dishes of roast red mullet with fried saffron risotto cake and tapénade. Individual ideas surface too, as in pork fillet which is smoked over sage and served on creamed polenta with broccoli, prunes and pancetta. Roast pork (with apple and thyme stuffing and a light jus in this case) was 'pork as it is seldom found these days – moist and full of piggy flavour,' said one enthusiast. Plus-points are the outstanding quality of meat and vegetables (particularly in summer), and good use of fresh herbs. Pursuit of flavour is an overriding aim. When ingredients lack natural intensity, they are helped along by, for example, roasting (for tomatoes destined for soup or a tart), or the addition of herbs (to polenta, 'which actually made it exciting' – a rare thing in polenta circles).

Modest invention pleases – Barbary duck with black-bean sauce and Cantonese pancakes, or crab-cakes on saffron rice with a 'mind-blowing shellfish sauce' – and puddings get good reports. A trio of strawberry desserts is 'perfect for a summer's evening: a soufflé, a tart (I cannot stress how light) and a parfait'. Or there might be baked chocolate pudding with hot fudge sauce and custard, or woodruff ice-cream. Old Vic cheese savoury, topped by crossed anchovies of good provenance, is a welcome alternative for those without a sweet tooth. A bistro service in the conservatory is more Young Vic, with lower prices. Bread is home-made and first-rate, although not all are happy with some of the incidentals: wine arriving already opened, rather haphazard topping up, the odd credit card slip left open, for example.

Apart from a handful of German, Spanish and a few other wines, the list is entirely French, covering a broad band of flavours, vintages and prices. It largely sticks to the security of classic regions and has built up an enviable stock of impressive names. There is a fair number of half-bottles, and the short list of recommendations is well worth a look. House wine is £12. CELLARMAN'S CHOICE: St-Joseph Blanc, Clos de l'Arbalestrier 1986, Florentin, £29; Vega-Sicilia Valbueña 1986, £35.

CHEF: Tessa Bramley PROPRIETORS: Tessa Bramley and Andrew Bramley OPEN: Tue to Sun, exc Sun D; 12.30 to 2.30, 7 to 10.30 (11 Sat) CLOSED: 1 week after Christmas MEALS: Set L and D £27.50 (2 courses) to £32 SERVICE: not inc, card slips closed CARDS: Access, Amex, Visa DETAILS: 50 seats. 8 tables outside. Private parties: 40 main room, 10 to 30 private rooms. Car park. Vegetarian meals. Children's helpings. No smoking in dining-room. Music. Fax: (0742) 477079

RIPLEY North Yorkshire　　　　　　　　　　　　　　　　map 7

▲ Boar's Head

Ripley HG3 3HY　　　　　　　　　　　　　　　　　COOKING 2
HARROGATE (0423) 771888　　　　　　　　　　　　COST £22–£47

A coaching-inn on the Leeds to Edinburgh run, the Boar's Head was declared an alcohol-free zone on Sundays in 1919 by one of the current owner's antecedents. The embargo was lifted when, in 1991, the Ingilbys reopened the place as a country hotel. Guests may freely wander, by arrangement, in the grounds of nearby Ripley Castle Estate, whence come many of the soft fruits, vegetables and herbs used by chef David Box. His food is not as Olde Worlde as the surroundings might imply.

The à la carte evening menus offer dishes such as a warm langoustine soufflé, duck salad with ginger and coconut, or beef tournedos with salsa verde and crisp polenta. A reporter admired the delicacy of touch in a fillet of salmon, lightly sauté and served with olive-oil marinated vegetables and a rich, lightly spiced tomato sauce. Desserts show an inventive mind in mille-feuille of fried mango with passion-fruit mousse and kumquat ice-cream. The ice-creams – kumquat, real vanilla or gooseberry – are always good. Service is usually 'exceptionally pleasant, natural and forthcoming'. The lengthy and thoughtfully constructed wine list will provide much pleasurable dilemma in choosing. It travels the world intrepidly, offers a good spread of halves, and prices throughout are extremely fair. House wines are £8.95.

CHEF: David Box PROPRIETORS: Sir Thomas and Lady Ingilby OPEN: all week; 12 to 2, 7 to 9.30 MEALS: alc (main courses £11.50 to £18.50). Set L £12.95 SERVICE: not inc CARDS: Access, Amex, Visa DETAILS: 40 seats. Private parties: 16 main room. Car park. Vegetarian meals. Children's helpings. Smart dress preferred. No cigars/pipes in dining-room. Wheelchair access (also WC). Music ACCOMMODATION: 25 rooms, all with bath/shower. TV. Phone. B&B £70 to £85. Rooms for disabled. Children welcome. Baby facilities. Pets welcome in some rooms. Afternoon teas. Garden. Tennis. Fishing. Confirm by 6. Fax: (0423) 771509

See inside the front cover for an explanation of the symbols used at the tops of entries.

Michels'

13 High Street, Ripley GU23 6AQ
GUILDFORD (0483) 224777 and 222940
off A3, 4m SW of Cobham

COOKING 3*
COST £28–£62

The secluded walled garden of this Georgian house is well suited to growing herbs, flowers and vegetables. In warm weather it doubles as a delightful setting for aperitifs. The dining-room is graceful and spacious with 'a good deal of eager design' (the Michels met at art college), and the big window surrounds have been stripped back to the original wood and hung with pinky apricot drapes. The collection of plates and objets d'art continues to grow, and cane chairs are comfortably padded.

The food is ambitious, sophisticated and well crafted, with a pleasing interplay of tastes and textures. There is decoration here to delight the eye, not mindless fiddly arrangement, all done to good purpose to integrate the components of a dish. Slices of well-hung fillet of beef, cooked rare as requested, crisp outside and meltingly tender inside, are flanked by cylinders of oxtail, in a light, clear reduced sauce, with small glazed onions for crunch and sweetness. The freshness of fish is striking: for example, sweet, firm-textured scallops and langoustines in a concentrated consommé the colour of dry sherry, with bite-sized chunks of gurnard. Delicate sea bass is given a crisp skin and served with a generous gang of tiny mushrooms, nutty and fungal in aroma, and a ball of cabbage filled with finely minced carrot, celeriac, fennel and Bayonne ham, moistened and cooked with veal stock. Much is happening in these dishes, but it is all done with confidence and style.

Puddings are a tour de force: a tiramisù gâteau of mascarpone and mocca cheese glazed with Tia Maria, and a light, creamy terrine of three chocolates – white, milk and dark – served with white and dark chocolate ice-creams, for example. The only disappointment at inspection was bread rolls that were 'almost leaden in texture', but this was mitigated by good oily black olives to start, and the provision of sauce spoons ('all the sauces were worth finishing'). Service has again come in for criticism, although not at inspection. Wines are dependable, more affordable outside the classic regions than in, span a reasonable range, and maintain quality throughout. There are 20 half-bottles, and the 10 house wines begin at £8 (£1.20 per glass).

CHEFS: Erik Michel and Paul Warner PROPRIETORS: Erik and Karen Michel OPEN: Tue to Sun, exc Sat L and Sun D; 12.30 to 1.30, 7.30 to 9 (7 to 9.30 Sat) CLOSED: first week Jan MEALS: alc (main courses £15 to £19.50). Set L £19, Set D Tue to Fri £21 to £28 (inc wine) SERVICE: not inc (10% for 6 or more) CARDS: Access, Amex, Visa DETAILS: 50 seats. Private parties: 12 main room, 12 private room. Car park. Vegetarian meals. Children welcome. Smart dress preferred. Wheelchair access (2 steps). No music

The Guide relies on feedback from its readers. Especially welcome are reports on new restaurants appearing in the book for the first time. All letters to the Guide are acknowledged.

RIPON North Yorkshire

map 7

▲ *Old Deanery* ✦✱

Minster Road, Ripon HG4 1QS
RIPON (0765) 603518

COOKING 2
COST £23–£49

The Deanery is old indeed – early seventeenth-century – and sits directly opposite the cathedral. In darkest winter a fire crackles in the grate, and flickering candles illuminate the old paintings – a 'delightfully restful' place in which to down a sherry. The dining-rooms were thought 'slightly tea-roomy' by one visitor, who appreciated the fact that tables were 'not crammed in'.

The cooking offers classic French bistro dishes in the main restaurant, and simpler things in the newer La Brasserie, which is open from Tuesday to Friday. In the evenings, there may be prawns and mushrooms in garlic cream gratinated with smoked applewood Cheddar, spicy chicken sausage on mixed rice with a port, redcurrant and citrus sauce (a starter, that), or Gressingham duck with rösti and an acacia honey and lemon sauce. Fillet of wild boar marinated and served with fried plantain is an enterprising option. La Brasserie has provided fresh mussels with a poached egg and cream sauce, pork à la normande (with Granny Smiths) and fine crème brûlée. Some have thought that the cooking is 'over-complicated', or that too much fruit crops up in main courses. The wine list is a fairly straightforward international selection at mostly agreeable prices. House wines from the Loire are £9.

CHEFS: Daphne Dooley and Jon Dooley PROPRIETORS: Graham Dooley, Daphne Dooley and Jon Dooley OPEN: restaurant Tue to Sun, exc Sat L and Sun D; 12 to 2, 7 to 9.30 (10 Sat). La Brasserie Tue to Fri; 12 to 2, 7 to 9 MEALS: restaurant alc (main courses £12 to £18), Set D Sat £15.95. La Brasserie alc (main courses £7 to £9), Set L and D Tue to Fri £11.95 to £13.95 SERVICE: not inc, card slips closed CARDS: Access, Amex, Diners, Visa DETAILS: 60 seats. 7 tables outside. Private parties: 80 main room, 15, 25 and 35 private rooms. Car park. Vegetarian meals. Children's helpings Sun L only. Smart dress preferred. No smoking in dining-room. Wheelchair access. No music ACCOMMODATION: 2 rooms, both with bath/shower. TV. D,B&B £45 to £60. Children welcome. Baby facilities. Garden. Doors close at midnight. Confirm by 6

ROADE Northamptonshire

map 3

Roadhouse Restaurant

16 High Street, Roade NN7 2NW
ROADE (0604) 863372
off A508, 4m S of Northampton

COOKING 3
COST £20–£37

'Since the Kewleys have enlarged their restaurant, they have been keeping prices low with straightforward good-value dishes while maintaining their high standard of materials and preparation,' reports one knowledgeable regular. The pinks are now deeper and the chairs plusher, but the place retains an informal feel, in keeping with its ambition 'to dispel any notion that restaurants have to do with reverence or solemnity'.

The menu has been smartened up too, with a gentle breeze of change blowing through the kitchen. Casserole of ox cheek with red wine, bacon and mushrooms is 'outstandingly delicious, with a plate-licking sauce', and the Mediterranean adds a few dabs of colour in the form of baked anchovies with a pepper and basil salad, or chickpeas and quail's eggs with a tapénade croûton. This is a slowly but continuously evolving style of cooking, balancing innovation and conservatism, and always carefully considered. 'Christopher Kewley is a chef with harmonious and sympathetic personal tastes, and the skill to share them in an exciting way. More Mozart than Wagner in his work,' reflects one, who is also impressed by the consistent quality. 'Cannot be equalled within a good one hour's motoring of where I live,' adds another. Puddings – brioche of prunes and apricots with honey ice-cream, for example – are as reassuring as the service from Susan Kewley: 'no pretension or flunkiness – first-class'. Her quiet knowledge of food and wine make tasting notes unneccessary on the moderately priced list of £50. House wines are from £9.

CHEF: Christopher Kewley PROPRIETORS: Christopher and Susan Kewley OPEN: Tue to Sun, exc Sat L and Sun D; 12.30 to 1.45, 7 to 9.30 CLOSED: 2 weeks summer, 1 week Christmas MEALS: alc (main courses £11 to £15.50). Set L £14.50, Set L Sun £15.75 SERVICE: net prices, card slips closed CARDS: Access, Amex, Visa DETAILS: 45 seats. Private parties: 45 main room. Car park. Vegetarian meals with prior notice. Children's helpings. Smart dress preferred. No music

---

ROMALDKIRK Co Durham   map 7

▲ Rose and Crown ⁙✕ £

Romaldkirk DL12 9EB
TEESDALE (0833) 650213   COOKING 1
6m NW of Barnard Castle, on B6277   COST £14–£39

Built as a coaching-inn in 1733, the Rose and Crown still serves as a local pub with a creditable reputation for bar meals and real ale. In addition, it offers the comforts of a country hotel. The oak-panelled dining-room has had a facelift and is an agreeable setting for Christopher Davy's cooking. A feeling of well-being pervades the place and service is willing. Dinner is a fixed-price, four-course affair that changes daily. Mr Davy is enterprising enough to offer filo tartlets of salmon and oyster mushrooms alongside steak and kidney pie cooked with Old Peculier ale. The results can be mixed, but reporters have liked rich duck liver parfait ('a poor man's foie gras') with home-made chutney as well as sticky walnut tart with amaretto ice-cream. Home-baked rolls and spot-on vegetables have also been given the thumbs-up. The wine list runs from the New World to Europe, prices are fair and half-bottles show up well. House wine is £8.50.

CHEF: Christopher Davy PROPRIETORS: Christopher and Alison Davy OPEN: restaurant Mon to Sat, D only, and Sun L; 12 to 1.30, 7.30 to 9. Bar all week; 12 to 1.30, 6.30 to 9.30 CLOSED: 25 and 26 Dec MEALS: Set L Sun £10.95, Set D £22 SERVICE: not inc, card slips closed CARDS: Access, Visa DETAILS: 24 seats. 6 tables outside bar. Private parties: 30 main room. Car park. Vegetarian meals with prior notice. Children's helpings Sun L. No children under 6 D. Smart dress preferred. No smoking in dining-room. No music ACCOMMODATION: 12 rooms, all with bath/shower. TV. Phone. B&B £54 to £75. Deposit: £20. Rooms for disabled. Children welcome. Pets welcome (not in public rooms). Afternoon teas. Doors close at 11. Confirm by 4. Fax: (0833) 650828 (The Which? Hotel Guide)

See the back of the Guide *for a listing of all restaurants in the Main Entries sections.*

ROMSEY Hampshire   map 2

Old Manor House ▮

21 Palmerston Street, Romsey SO51 8GF   COOKING 2
ROMSEY (0794) 517353   COST £27–£52

The setting is a Tudor building dating from 1540, complete with beams, large
fireplaces and diamond-paned windows. Mauro Bregoli isn't much of a one for
shopping: 'I shoot all the venison we use. I gather wild mushrooms,' he writes.
The Italian input is strong, balanced by Anglo-French staples. Commendably,
the set price for two or three courses remains the same at dinner as at lunch,
while the *carte* offers a greater choice of dishes. Thin slices of veal in tuna
mayonnaise, and clams in white wine and garlic share the billing with
asparagus in chive sauce, salmon with sorrel sauce, and Lymington lobster.
There has been praise for 'muscular' cotechino sausage with lentils, soft-
textured venison, and roast rack of lamb with garlic and rosemary sauce, cooked
perfectly pink. More and more reporters, however, are questioning the value for
money, when comparing meals today with those had here in the past.

Elderflower cordial makes a good start to a meal, and pear and walnut tart,
very sweet with 'excellent pastry', is a fine way to finish. Service has varied from
'exemplary' to 'lacking interest', but the wines are as good as ever, generous
in scope and spot-on for quality, with France rather than Italy forming the
backbone, and Bordeaux providing much of the flesh. Aristocracy doesn't come
cheap, so there are plenty of three-figure prices. It would be nice to see more than
a token two dozen wines under £20. House French is £9.50. CELLARMAN'S
CHOICE: Côtes du Ventoux, Ch. Valcombe 1993, £13.50; Carignano del Sulcis
Riserva 1990, £16.

CHEF/PROPRIETOR: Mauro Bregoli OPEN: Tue to Sun, exc Sun D; 12 to 2, 7 to 9.30 CLOSED: 24
to 31 Dec MEALS: alc (main courses £12.50 to £19.50). Set L and D £13.50 (2 courses) to
£17.50 SERVICE: not inc CARDS: Access, Amex, Visa DETAILS: 45 seats. Private parties:
22 private room. Car park. Vegetarian meals. Children welcome. Smart dress preferred.
No cigars/pipes in dining-room. No music

ROSS-ON-WYE Hereford & Worcester   map 4

▲ Pheasants ▮

52 Edde Cross Street,
Ross-on-Wye HR9 7BZ   COOKING 2*
ROSS-ON-WYE (0989) 565751   COST £19–£45

Pheasants are not the only fauna you will encounter in Eileen Brunnarius's
out-of-the-way bistro in hilly Ross-on-Wye: hippopotami roam the bathroom
upstairs. The dining-room décor looked almost 'accidental' in the eyes of one
man, but he found himself impressed by the ability of a two-handed restaurant
to cope with a flurry of arrivals with 'pleasantness and no obvious fluster'. Wine
expert Adrian Wells runs the front-of-house, and his impeccable and friendly
advice perfectly counterpoints the cooking, which is thought 'simple and robust'
and not given to sophistication for its own sake. The chattily written menus
celebrate 'honest flavours' in such dishes as smoked duck breast with melon and

447

a honey and lemon dressing, croustade of venison accompanied by mushrooms 'with a hint of anchovy', and chocolate mousse with 'cinnamon thins' and a muscat sauce. Endorsements also come in for spiced lamb kebab with saladings, sliced duck breast on a 'very rich' sauce of blackcurrants and prunes, the stalwart bread-and-butter pudding, and 'enjoyable, fruity' sorbets. Good coffee and fresh black olives with aperitifs complete the happy picture.

The page of fortified wines to go with first courses, including a fine de Bortoli Marsala, will give the earliest signal that this is a list to reckon with. Inexhaustible imagination has brought together an exemplary collection that, in true evangelistic spirit, offers many items by the glass for trial. Prices, for the most part exceptionally kind, open at £7.80 for Hugh Ryman's Hungarian Chardonnay. CELLARMAN'S CHOICE: Millton Vineyards Chardonnay 1993, £17; Barbera 'Narbusto' 1983, Ballabio, £18.30.

CHEF/PROPRIETOR: Eileen Brunnarius   OPEN: Tue to Sat (bookings only L); 12.30 to 1.30, 7 to 10   CLOSED: 25 Dec to 2 Jan   MEALS: alc (main courses L £5 to £8.50, D £11.50 to £16). Set D £18.50   SERVICE: net prices, card slips closed   CARDS: Access, Amex, Diners, Visa   DETAILS: 22 seats. 3 tables outside. Private parties: 30 main room. Vegetarian meals. Wheelchair access. Music   ACCOMMODATION: 2 rooms. D,B&B £24 to £50. Children welcome. Doors close at midnight. Confirm by 6

ROWDE Wiltshire

map 2

George & Dragon

High Street, Rowde SN10 2PN
DEVIZES (0380) 723053

COOKING 3
COST £17–£44

This village pub stands in the heart of landlocked Wiltshire, yet its reputation for fine food rests largely on supplies of fresh fish from Cornwall. Tim Withers is an adventurous cook who has no truck with pub grub clichés. Instead, he ventures out into the world of mussels steamed with lemon grass and coriander, grilled red mullet with orange and anchovy, and roast hake with peppers and pesto. The results draw few complaints and the value for money is exceptional. Reporters have spoken highly of scallops with bacon, and salmon fish-cakes, while those with a taste for meat have endorsed warm duck salad, and fillet steak with balsamic vinegar. Clear tastes and fresh flavours are the key. Desserts are sometimes homely (rhubarb fool), sometimes racy (chocolate and ginger roulade with lemon grass custard), although bread-and-butter pudding has been a let-down on more than one occasion.

The place is still unashamedly a country pub, complete with a fire and a fruit machine in the bar, plates on the dark-panelled walls and Wadworth beers on handpump; formal restaurant manners and trappings do not intrude here. Staff are generally quiet and attentive. The short, sharp wine list has an admirable selection of 14 by the glass; prices rarely creep above £12 for a bottle. House wines start at £7.50.

CHEF: Tim Withers   PROPRIETORS: Mr and Mrs T. Withers   OPEN: Tue to Sat; 12 to 2, 7 to 10 MEALS: alc (main courses £7.50 to £16). Set L £10   SERVICE: not inc, card slips closed   CARDS: Access, Visa   DETAILS: 35 seats. 4 tables outside. Private parties: 30 main room. Car park. Vegetarian meals with prior notice. Children's helpings. No music

RYE East Sussex map 3

Landgate Bistro £

5–6 Landgate, Rye TN31 7LH
RYE (0797) 222829

COOKING 2*
COST £20–£33

Celebrating the fourteenth anniversary of the Landgate in 1994, Nick Parkin allowed himself a wry smile at the 'complete naivety' with which he and chef Toni Ferguson-Lees first stepped into the restaurant world. In a somewhat run-down part of Rye, their straightforward, unpretentious bistro has a white-painted dining area with good photographs on the walls and plastic cloths on the tables.

Reports praise the good value and splendid presentation of the food. A fixed-price midweek dinner menu bolsters the long, handwritten *carte*, and the kitchen makes maximum use of the best of the catch from local boats, lamb and beef from Romney Marsh and organic saladings. Salmon and smoked haddock fish-cakes (one of each, not mixed) with parsley butter are a much-loved starter of precise textural contrasts. Squid is done in a white wine, tomato and garlic braise – 'succulent, aromatic, delicious'. Fish stew has come in for brickbats this year, mostly for being too thin, though no one doubts the quality of the stock. Grilled lamb leg steak with flageolets, and more tomatoes and garlic, is well judged and full of juices. Cherries in a biscuit cup with a bayleaf custard was a bold idea that worked, while home-made ice-creams such as honey and a kulfi-like cardamom version impress for sheer depth of flavour. Nick Parkin describes the approach as unintrusive, 'fresh and unpolished'. The wine list is wide-ranging, succinct and very fairly priced, with house wines from Mommessin at £7.90. CELLARMAN'S CHOICE: Pouilly-Fumé, Dom. des Fines Caillottes 1992, £14; Côtes du Vivarais, 1990, £10.90.

CHEF: Toni Ferguson-Lees PROPRIETORS: Nick Parkin and Toni Ferguson-Lees OPEN: Tue to Sat, D only; 7 to 9.30 (10 Sat) CLOSED: 1 week Christmas, 1 week early summer, 1 week autumn MEALS: alc (main courses £8 to £12). Set D Tue to Thur £14.90 SERVICE: net prices, card slips closed CARDS: Access, Amex, Diners, Visa DETAILS: 30 seats. Private parties: 10 main room. Vegetarian meals. Children's helpings. No cigars/pipes in dining-room. Music

ST IVES Cornwall map 1

Pig'n'Fish

Norway Lane, St Ives TR26 1LZ
ST IVES (0736) 794204

COOKING 2*
COST £25–£44

For those who can throw a stone 300 yards the restaurant is a stone's throw from the Tate Gallery, overlooking the rooftops and the bay. The enterprise is founded on fish, from grilled cod and brill to pot-roast skate, bought daily in small quantities from St Ives and Newlyn boats, and cooked with an eye to France and Italy; hence the sun-dried tomatoes, basil, parsley pesto, roasted red peppers, aïoli, and fish soup with rouille and Parmesan. 'Friendly staff, excellent fish and seafood, relaxed atmosphere' was one reporter's description.

Top-rated dishes have included crisp crab pancakes subtly flavoured with chilli, lemon grass and coriander, oysters with shallot vinegar, hot shellfish with olive oil, smoked sausages, and pork, of course: pot-roast loin served with sweet-and-sour aubergines. The bourride (with red mullet, Dover sole, John Dory and mussels) sells like hot fish-cakes. Meals are backed up by good peripherals – breads, vegetables and coffee – and the hospitality is 'exactly right, friendly but not familiar'. A simple but good wine list with reasonable prices includes house French from £8.

CHEFS: Paul Sellars and Grant Nethercott PROPRIETORS: Paul Sellars and Debby Wilkins OPEN: Tue to Sat; 12.30 to 1.30, 7 to 9.30 CLOSED: Nov to mid-Mar MEALS: alc (main courses £10.50 to £15.50). Set L £14 (2 courses) to £17.50 SERVICE: not inc CARDS: Access, Visa DETAILS: 30 seats. Private parties: 30 main room. Vegetarian meals with prior notice. Children's helpings on request. No cigars/pipes in dining-room. Music

---

ST KEYNE Cornwall   map 1

▲ *Well House*

St Keyne PL14 4RN
LISKEARD (0579) 342001   COOKING 3*
on B3254, 3m S of Liskeard   COST £32–£45

In October 1993, Wayne Pearson took command of the stoves at the Well House, and the already formidable standard of cooking seems, if anything, to have moved up a gear. The backdrop to the place is an engagingly tranquil Cornish house near St Keyne's well, where the water is reputedly very good for the eyes. Nicholas Wainford is a capable host, full of advice but resisting any tendency to excessive joviality. The interiors of the house show restraint in the decoration; the dining-room is a mellow place adorned with foodie pictures and with adequate space between tables.

Menus offer a fixed-price deal, according to the number of courses wanted, inclusive of coffee and petits fours. An inspection dinner occasioned great admiration for a terrine of lamb's sweetbreads and oyster mushrooms, and 'truly stupendous' paupiettes of Dover sole stuffed with white crabmeat with a good fish stock sauce. Hereford duck breast with braised red cabbage converted a red cabbage hater and came with a port reduction that made a refreshing change from the usual fruity accompaniment. Pastrywork is excellent, as evidenced by a warm apple and calvados flan with cinnamon ice-cream, while a lemon parfait 'tasted intensely of lemon' and came with a suitably upstanding raspberry coulis and a lump of 'slightly chewy' oatmeal meringue. All incidentals, from the canapés and good home-made breads to the carefully cooked vegetables and chocolate truffles with coffee, were up to the mark. For the quality available, it feels like 'remarkably good value for money'. House wine is £8.50.

CHEF: Wayne Pearson PROPRIETOR: Nick Wainford OPEN: all week; 12.30 to 1.30, 7 to 9.30 MEALS: Set L and D £19.95 (2 courses) to £29.70 SERVICE: not inc, card slips closed CARDS: Access, Visa DETAILS: 34 seats. 5 tables outside. Private parties: 36 main room. Car park. Vegetarian meals. Children's helpings. No children under 8. Smart dress preferred. No cigars/pipes in dining-room. Wheelchair access (1 step; also WC). No music ACCOMMODATION: 7 rooms, all with bath/shower. TV. Phone. B&B £60 to £105. Children welcome. Baby facilities. Dogs welcome. Garden. Swimming-pool. Tennis. Confirm 1 day ahead. Fax: (0579) 343891 (*The Which? Hotel Guide*)

ST MARGARET'S AT CLIFFE Kent   map 3

▲ Wallett's Court ⭐

West Cliffe,
St Margaret's at Cliffe CT15 6EW
DOVER (0304) 852424
on B2058, off A258 Dover to Deal road,   COOKING 2
3m NE of Dover   COST £28–£41

Chris and Lea Oakley acquired Wallett's Court in 1976 as a rundown farmhouse
and began cooking in 1985. The building's links with figures from Bishop Odo
(of Bayeux tapestry fame) to William Pitt the Younger have endowed it with a
certain historical gravitas. Restoration has been done sensitively and work
continues. There is strong personal and professional involvement from the
dedicated, enthusiastic and friendly Oakleys.

Drinks are taken in the lounge, where a log fire burns on chilly evenings, and
the form is a monthly-changing menu of three courses or a five-course bonanza.
The cooking ploughs a Kentish furrow with game terrine (a house speciality),
jugged hare, locally landed monkfish (in a light curry sauce) and venison in a
port wine sauce, but also runs to Cullen skink, and pork loin 'Normandy-style'
with apples and calvados. Port is a favourite ingredient for sauces, and it works
well with perfectly cooked and seasoned breast of Barbary duck served with
Cumberland jelly. Anything left in the bottle might be used to make damson
preserve, which then adds its piquancy to calf's liver sauté in butter with
madeira sauce. Crisp vegetables, and huge helpings of bread-and-butter
pudding or Eton mess, are followed by unlimited coffee with Belgian chocolates.
The modest wine list is well annotated and reasonably priced. House wine is
from £8.75

CHEF: Chris Oakley   PROPRIETORS: Chris and Lea Oakley   OPEN: Mon to Sat, D only; 7 to 9
(9.30 Sat)   MEALS: Set D £19.50 (Mon to Fri) to £25 (Sat)   SERVICE: not inc, card slips closed
CARDS: Access, Visa   DETAILS: 50 seats. 5 tables outside. Private parties: 40 main room, 30
private room. Car park. Vegetarian meals. Children's helpings (6 to 9pm). Smart dress preferred.
No smoking in dining-room. No music   ACCOMMODATION: 10 rooms, all with bath/shower. TV.
Phone. B&B £35 to £70. Children welcome. Baby facilities. Afternoon teas (summer only).
Garden. Tennis. Snooker. Doors close at midnight. Fax: (0304) 853430 (*The Which? Hotel
Guide*)

ST MICHAEL'S ON WYRE Lancashire   map 5

Mallards

Garstang Road,
St Michael's on Wyre PR3 0TE   COOKING 1
ST MICHAEL'S (0995) 679661   COST £16–£32

John and Ann Steel's converted village smithy makes an agreeably relaxed
setting for leisurely meals 'judiciously offered' and served without fuss. John
works to a fixed-price menu of two, three or four courses that might include Bury
black pudding with Meaux mustard sauce, pasta with salmon and prawns in
vermouth sauce, loin of pork with apricots and calvados, and grilled sirloin steak
with Stilton and mushroom sauce. Mallard and other local game appear in

451

season. Loin of lamb in garlic, redcurrant and red wine sauce has been 'as nearly perfectly cooked as possible'. Reporters also approve of the seasonal vegetables (often including a soufflé), and the home-made sweetmeats served with cafetière coffee. The Steels have set up a dining club, which gathers on the last Friday of each month (four courses for £19.95). Half-bottles figure strongly on the wine list, which is a well-spread selection of sound names from reliable makers. House wine is £8.50.

CHEF: John Steel   PROPRIETORS: John and Ann Steel   OPEN: Mon to Sat, D only, and Sun L; 12 to 2.30, 7 to 9 (9.30 Sat)   CLOSED: 1 week Jan, 2 weeks Aug   MEALS: Set L Sun £9.95, Set D £14.50 (2 courses) to £17.95   SERVICE: not inc, card slips closed   CARDS: Access, Visa DETAILS: 36 seats. Private parties: 36 main room. Car park. Vegetarian meals with prior notice. Children's helpings. Smart dress preferred. No smoking while others eat. Wheelchair access. Music

---

SANDIWAY Cheshire   map 5

▲ *Nunsmere Hall* ⁵⁺

Tarporley Road, Sandiway CW8 2ES
NORTHWICH (0606) 889100   COOKING 3*
off A49, 4m SW of Northwich   COST £26–£51

A luxury hotel has been fashioned from this Edwardian mansion surrounded by a big lake. The Hall was built around 1900 for Sir Aubrey Brocklebank, chairman of the Brocklebank shipping line that later merged with Cunard, and remained in private hands until the 1980s. Despite the inevitable de-humanisation that attends the bolting on of 'conference facilities', it retains a freshness and vigour: dramatic curtains splash across restful wallpaper, elegant carpets are laid on polished wood floors, and there is space to savour in the dining-room.

Paul Kitching's menus echo the panache of the décor, soothing away with smoked salmon, roasted scallops, a pinch of caviare here, a scent of truffle there. But beneath the gloss is serious cooking. Grilled nuggets of Cornish codling sound like something from a fast-food outlet, but are in fact small fillets served on a julienne of vegetables, surmounted by a lobster beignet, and sitting in a concentrated jus. Ultra-fresh ingredients seem to concentrate the flavours, and Cornish sea bass is no less exciting, in an unlikely sauce of beetroot and dill with red wine. Even when combinations appear to trespass near the edge of credibility, they still pull back from the precipice with the adroitness of Indiana Jones: chunks of rare game are bound in a chicken and orange mousse with pistachios and almonds, and served with a confit of apricot, chives and shallots – 'All the tastes came through, and the sweetness of the confit complemented the flavours of the terrine. Entirely delectable.' Desserts are accomplished too: banana is wrapped in a puff-pastry case, popped in the oven, and served with a warm toffee sauce; tiramisù is a superior version.

Service is smooth and efficient, despite the apparent absence of top brass. 'There was no sign of the management,' reported one mystified customer. 'Where is the owner of this place?' asked another. Wine mark-ups are what you might expect of a posh country house; the only saving grace is that the remarkably few wines under £15 are reasonably well chosen. House wines are from £12.25.

CHEF: Paul Kitching   PROPRIETORS: Malcolm and Julie McHardy   OPEN: all week; 12 to 2, 7 to 10   MEALS: Set L £14.95 (2 courses) to £17.50, Set L Sun £17.95, Set D £25 to £32   SERVICE: not inc, card slips closed   CARDS: Access, Amex, Diners, Visa   DETAILS: 60 seats. 6 tables outside. Private parties: 60 main room, 10, 22, 60 private rooms. Car park. Vegetarian meals. Children's helpings. Smart dress preferred. No smoking in dining-room. Wheelchair access (also WC). Music   ACCOMMODATION: 32 rooms, all with bath/shower. TV. Phone. B&B £97 to £235. Rooms for disabled. Lift. Children welcome. Baby facilities. Afternoon teas. Garden. Snooker. Fax: (0606) 889055 (*The Which? Hotel Guide*)

SAXTON North Yorkshire   map 5

Plough Inn £ | NEW ENTRY |

Headwell Lane, Saxton LS24 9PB
BARKSTON ASH (0937) 557242
off A162, between Tadcaster and   COOKING 2
Sherburn in Elmet   COST £15–£30

'The statement in last year's *Guide*, in the county round-up – "pub producing fair food" – must be one of the understatements of the season,' writes a supporter. Saxton is a quiet village, signposted from the Tadcaster direction but not from Sherburn in Elmet, and the pub sits four-square at the crossroads. It is warm and unpretentious, with oak tables and benches, paper napkins and a blackboard menu over the fireplace. You have a drink and place your order in the bar, and are conducted to the dining-room when the food is ready.

Typically there will be around eight first courses and a dozen mains, a third of them fish. The food would not seem out of place in a city brasserie: pigeon salad or confit of duck with balsamic dressing to begin, then roast rump of lamb with lentils, or guinea-fowl and herb sausage with a mustard sauce. Fresh fish arrives daily, producing 'firm, definitively fresh, very flavoursome' king scallops, lightly poached. 'In winter we braise either oxtail or lamb shanks, and in summer we have a lobster festival for one month,' write the Treanors. Meats are properly hung, cooked pink, generously sliced and come with a simple reduced cooking jus full of flavour. Among puddings, lemon tart has a deep filling, well judged for flavour, and reporters praise the value: '£40 or so was seldom better spent on a meal for two,' writes an inspector of long standing. At lunch, £4.95 will buy a one-course special of minute steak with grilled mushrooms and tomatoes, or escalope of salmon with chive sauce, and there are also sandwiches. The short wine list is carefully chosen, full of zip, but rarely tops £15. Southern French house wines are £7.50, and a further half dozen are also available by the glass for around £1.50.

CHEFS: Simon Treanor and Richard Allen   PROPRIETORS: Simon and Nicky Treanor   OPEN: Tue to Sun, exc Sun D; 12 to 2, 6.30 to 10   MEALS: alc Tue to Sat (main courses £6.50 to £9.50). Set L Sun £9.75   SERVICE: not inc   CARDS: Access, Visa   DETAILS: 65 seats. 4 tables outside. Private parties: 65 main room. Car park. Vegetarian meals. Children's helpings. Smart dress preferred. No-smoking area. Wheelchair access (also WC). Music

---

SCARBOROUGH North Yorkshire map 6A

Lanterna

33 Queen Street, Scarborough YO11 1HQ	COOKING 1
SCARBOROUGH (0723) 363616	COST £23–£38

For more than two decades, Gianluigi and Janet Arecco have been serving up good old-school trattoria food to the citizens of Scarborough and beyond. Nothing changes. Visitors come to their bow-windowed listed building to eat minestrone, spaghetti bolognese, pollo principessa topped with asparagus, scampi provençale and veal Marsala followed by cream caramel and zabaglione. Meatballs are a popular daily special, and fresh Scarborough fish appears in season. The wine list is a familar European collection with a bias towards Italy. House wine is £9.50.

CHEFS: Gianluigi Arecco and Tom Kay PROPRIETORS: Gianluigi and Janet Arecco OPEN: Tue to Sat, D only; 7 to 9.30 MEALS: alc (main courses £10 to £13) SERVICE: not inc, card slips closed CARDS: Access, Visa DETAILS: 36 seats. Private parties: 38 main room. Vegetarian meals. Children's helpings. No children under 2. Smart dress preferred. Wheelchair access. Music

---

SEAFORD East Sussex map 3

Quincy's

42 High Street, Seaford BN25 1PL	COOKING 2*
SEAFORD (0323) 895490	COST £29–£36

The setting is a converted shop behind the 'scarred war zone' that is the front at Seaford. The interior has a warm, domestic feel, with prints, posters and an impressive collection of cookery books dotted around the two dining-rooms. At the back are views of the pleasant urban garden. Dawn Dowding and staff run the front-of-house with involved enthusiasm, while Ian works the kitchen. His cooking has improved by leaps and bounds: he knows what he is good at, understands his market and gets everything right. Flavourings are kept in check, and extravagance is avoided for its own sake. The eclectic menus are now free of supplements, and fish from Newhaven is a strong point. Fillet of turbot expertly wrapped in a lattice of pastry with prawn, leek and ginger sauce is typical of the style.

Spot-on execution is also the hallmark of risotto-stuffed squid with ink and red wine sauce, pink medallions of venison with a galette wrapped around a mushroom filling, and duck with spiced red cabbage and lentils. Sweets draw effusive praise: one reporter reckoned the hot lime soufflé with rum ice-cream was the best he had eaten for 35 years. Others have mentioned strawberry and Curaçao crème brûlée, and frangipane with damson and calvados sauce. Cheeses are mostly local. The wine list offers an adequate, well-spread selection and plenty of halves, although a touch more ambition would not go amiss. House wine is from £8.25.

The Good Food Guide *is a registered trade mark of Consumers' Association Ltd.*

CHEF: Ian Dowding PROPRIETORS: Ian and Dawn Dowding OPEN: Tue to Sat, D only, and Sun L; 12 to 2, 7 to 10 MEALS: Set L Sun and D £17.95 (2 courses) to £20.45 SERVICE: not inc CARDS: Access, Amex, Visa DETAILS: 30 seats. Private parties: 30 main room. Vegetarian meals. Children's helpings. Music

---

SEATON BURN Tyne & Wear   map 7

▲ Horton Grange ⁵⁄✗

Seaton Burn NE13 6BU
PONTELAND (0661) 860686
off A1, at Stannington, 3m N of   COOKING 2*
Newcastle upon Tyne   COST £39–£46

The Grange, at the edge of a large, working farm that supplies much of the material used in the kitchen, is a handsome grey-stone building that was once a farmhouse. The renovations undertaken by the Shiltons have been sensitively done: the result is simple elegance and cool colours that are gentle on the eye.

Stephen Martin's dinner menus tend to greater elaboration than might be expected, but he has a sure touch and brings off most things with convincing aplomb. It is a fixed-price, five-course format, with soup or sorbet after the starter and cheeses at the end. First courses are refreshingly light, as in a salad of slivered smoked chicken with baby corn and walnuts, or a 'moist and fresh-tasting, spot-on' timbale of white crab meat topped with a quenelle of the brown meat and an accompaniment of lime mayonnaise. On one occasion, however, an opening dish of 'excellent' red mullet was overcome by a strongly acidulated vinaigrette and much raw onion. Main courses steer clear of wild combinations, opting for the relaxed classicism of steamed salmon with a herb mustard sauce, or rack of lamb, herbed and crumbed, with 'lots of flavour', which came with a thin, crisp spinach and goats' cheese tartlet. Plenty of fruit is used in the substantial desserts; a popular choice is Eton mess, served in a tall glass full of red fruits, smashed meringue and cream lightened with yogurt. Cheeses are of impeccable farmhouse pedigree, and good cafetière coffee arrives with home-made chocolate truffles and shortbread. The wine list is briefer than the cooking merits, does not indicate vintages and has just four half-bottles. House wines in all three colours, from Ochoa in Navarra, are £9.90.

CHEF: Stephen Martin PROPRIETORS: Andrew and Susan Shilton OPEN: Mon to Sat, D only (and Sun D for residents only); 7 to 8.45 CLOSED: 25 and 26 Dec MEALS: Set D £29.90 SERVICE: not inc, card slips closed CARDS: Access, Visa DETAILS: 30 seats. Private parties: 35 main room, 10 private room. Car park. Vegetarian meals with prior notice. Children welcome. Smart dress preferred. No smoking in dining-room. Wheelchair access (also WC). Music ACCOMMODATION: 9 rooms, all with bath/shower. TV. Phone. B&B £59 to £80. Rooms for disabled. Children welcome. Baby facilities. Garden. Confirm by 5. Fax: (0661) 860308

Prices quoted in the Guide *are based on information supplied by restaurateurs. The prices quoted at the top of each entry represent a range, from the lowest meal price to the highest; the latter is inflated by 20 per cent to take account of likely price rises during the year of the* Guide.

SEMINGTON Wiltshire map 2

▲ Highfield House, Edward's Dining Room

NEW ENTRY

High Street, Semington BA14 6JN
DEVIZES (0380) 870554 COOKING 1
on A350, 2m S of Melksham COST £15–£26

If you go down to this elegant Georgian house on the Melksham to Trowbridge road, you're in for a big surprise: 'One has one's aperitif on a sofa flanked by teddy-bears.' Indeed, they are everywhere, including the kitchen, for this is Edward's Dining Room. Edward Street established this idiosyncratic operation in 1991 and appears to have built up a sizeable local following for capable British cooking. His 'Options Menu' is priced for three courses plus coffee, but the courses can be variously permed for the same price, so that if you really want one starter, no main course and three desserts, eyebrows will not be raised.

A reporter who clung resolutely to convention found the quality of a fillet of cod in an 'old-fashioned cheese and chive sauce' particularly good, with plenty of flavour. A main course of honey-glazed Barbary duckling breast with kumquat sauce delivered 'crisp and definitely juicy' meat in a strong stock. Otherwise, try freshly made game sausages with a trio of relishes, or whole baby cauliflower on baked ham with a sauce of sage Derby and smoked Cheddar. Bacon and cheese are used a lot, and the cheese selection to finish may be a better bet than pudding. Service is 'personal and careful' and, although coffee and petits fours show room for improvement, the makings of success are clearly discernible. The wine list is a jumble, but assiduous perusal will turn up some good bottles at eminently fair prices. House wines are £9.25.

CHEF/PROPRIETOR: Edward Street OPEN: all week, exc L Mon and Sat and Sun D; 12 to 2.30, 7 to 9.45 MEALS: Set L Tue to Fri £7.50, Sun £11.50, Set D £15 SERVICE: not inc CARDS: Access, Amex, Diners, Visa DETAILS: 42 seats. 3 tables outside. Private parties: 42 main room. Car park. Vegetarian meals. Children's helpings. Music ACCOMMODATION: 1 room. B&B £20 to £30. Children welcome. Afternoon teas. Doors close at midnight. Confirm by 6

SETTLE North Yorkshire map 7

Blue Goose

Market Place, Settle BD24 9EG
SETTLE (0729) 822901
on B6479, just off A65 Kirkby Lonsdale to COOKING 1*
Skipton road COST £12–£35

In the centre of town, at the back of the old market, is a Victorian town house that has been home to the Goose since 1991. The blue in question is a rich, suave midnight shade, and the signature dish has the braised bird sauced with blueberries. A wine bar and cookery school are also part of the operation, so we may assume that Willi Rehbock has his hands full. His avowed intent is that 'the restaurant is for everybody', although one reader lunching in May noted that only one of the two rooms was open and hungry droves were being turned away.

The simple wine bar menu offers salads, fish-cakes and stir-fries at lunchtime; in the evenings, an ambitious *carte* comes into play, supplemented by a fixed-price menu of three courses plus coffee. Each dish refers by number to a wine from the list that might best accompany it. Recommendations have come in for 'excellent' tagliatelle with a basil, cream and garlic sauce served in ample quantity, a vegetarian dish of marinated aubergine slices with feta, and white chocolate sorbet with caramelised pears and raspberry coulis that was 'improbably delicious'. Home-made breads served with garlic and herb butter are mentioned in dispatches, as is 'decent' coffee with the restaurant's own chocolates. The 'wine menu' is short and serviceable. It lacks some producers' names, but prices are agreeably low, with everything except Mercier champagne under £20. House wines, Cuvée Jean Paul, are £7.95.

CHEF/PROPRIETOR: Willi Rehbock OPEN: Mon to Sat; 12 to 2, 7 to 9.30 (all day July to mid-Sept) MEALS: alc (main courses restaurant £7 to £10.50, wine bar £3.50 to £6). Set L wine bar £5.95, Set D restaurant £14.50 SERVICE: not inc, card slips closed CARDS: Access, Visa DETAILS: 36 seats. 4 tables outside. Private parties: 36 main room, 18 and 22 private rooms. Vegetarian meals. Children's helpings. Music

---

SHAFTESBURY Dorset   map 2

La Fleur de Lys ♥

25 Salisbury Street, Shaftesbury SP7 8EL   COOKING 2
SHAFTESBURY (0747) 853717   COST £26–£47

Climb a flight of steep stairs from the conservatory-style reception area to reach the light, airy first-floor dining-room with good views of Blackmoor Vale. Reporters agree that the young trio who run the place deserve support for offering high-quality cooking in surroundings that have classy touches but no pomposity. This is a kitchen prepared to tackle hot lobster soufflé with sauté shellfish and white crab sauce, and tenderloin of pork wrapped in filo pastry with dried fruit in a date and wine sauce, as well as grilled fillets of Dover sole. The cooking is sharp: turbot is set off admirably by an 'excellent' Pernod sauce, feuilleté of scallops with salmon mousseline is a 'subtly balanced' dish, while lightly cooked liver with mushroom sauce has been 'easily assimilated'. Steamed vegetables may be too daringly al dente for some. Eye-catching sweets have included a 'brilliant' coffee and walnut charlotte mousse, and the cafetière coffee is highly rated. Service is as pleasant as you could wish for. The wine list is classy, extensive, up to date, well annotated and very reasonably priced. House wines (six of them) begin at £7.95 (£1.85 a glass) and wines of the month are well worth exploring. CELLARMAN'S CHOICE: Sauvignon Blanc 1991, Cluver, £12; Nederburg Private Bin R161 1985, £22.

CHEFS: David Shepherd and Marc Preston PROPRIETORS: David Shepherd, Mary Griffin and Marc Preston OPEN: all week, exc Mon L and Sun D; 12 to 3, 7 to 10 CLOSED: Jan weekdays MEALS: alc (main courses L £11 to £12.50, D £14 to £16). Set D Mon to Sat £18.95, Mon to Thur £15.50 (2 courses). Minimum £9 L, £15.50 D SERVICE: not inc CARDS: Access, Amex, Visa DETAILS: 40 seats. 3 tables outside. Private parties: 35 main room, 12 private room. Vegetarian meals. Children's helpings on request. Smart dress preferred. No smoking before 10pm. Music. Air-conditioned (partial)

map 5

Greenhead House 🕏✷

84 Burncross Road, Chapeltown,
Sheffield S30 4SF   COOKING 2
SHEFFIELD (0742) 469004   COST £34–£46

Enter this stone-built detached house in the northern suburbs of Sheffield through a pretty garden, take drinks in the sitting-room before being ushered to the 'lovely' dining-room done up in greens and creams and dark blue velvet. Neil Allen offers a four-course menu, priced according to main-course choice, with soup or melon after the starter. The accent is unmistakably French, with first courses showing most experimentation. Thus quail may be stuffed with a mixture of minced meat, wild mushrooms and pistachios, while smoked duck is given a salad of vegetables and tarragon in balsamic dressing. Entrées are the likes of *cotriade*, a Breton stew of mixed fish and potato under a puff-pastry lid, medallions of pork fillet with fresh tomato sauce, or sauté duck breast with a sauce of garlic, parsley, olive oil and walnuts. Nuts of one sort or another are a favourite flavouring of Neil Allen, and may crop up at any stage of a meal.

Northern France makes its presence felt again in a baked prune pudding from Brittany served with calvados crème fraîche. Otherwise there is very good pine-nut tart with vanilla ice-cream or lemon tart. An inspector who found much to enjoy at Greenhead felt that a lighter touch with sauces, and less reliance on the classical mainstays of cream and butter, would be welcome. Vegetables – enough to feed four – were 'unexciting though competent', bread was 'excellent' and coffee and petits fours up to the mark. Wines are fairly priced, with plenty of choice below £20, but the list could do with a bit more excitement. House wines are from £9.

CHEF: Neil Allen PROPRIETORS: Neil and Anne Allen OPEN: Tue to Sat, D only; 7 to 9 CLOSED: Christmas to New Year, 2 weeks Easter, 2 weeks mid-Aug MEALS: Set D £25.75 to £29.75 SERVICE: not inc, card slips closed CARDS: Access, Visa DETAILS: 34 seats. Private parties: 36 main room. Car park. Vegetarian meals. Children's helpings. Smart dress preferred. No smoking in dining-room. Wheelchair access (also WC). No music

Le Neptune

141 West Street, Sheffield S1 4EW   COOKING 1
SHEFFIELD (0742) 796677   COST £20–£49

Just out of the city centre, five minutes' drive from John Betjeman's favourite Victorian suburb of Broomhill, this swish restaurant is a useful addition to the Sheffield scene. Tiled floors, pastel walls with impressionist pictures, and French-speaking waiters set the Gallic tone of the place, and the cooking follows suit. Fish is the mainstay and the quality of dishes such as fillet of red mullet perched on a whirl of pasta with a red pepper coulis suggests that the kitchen buys shrewdly and knows its stuff. The menu also embraces bouillabaisse, crab and herb quiche, grilled scallops with Roquefort sauce, and sea bass with julienne of vegetables and Pernod sauce. Meat and game are not forgotten: confit of duck with madeira sauce is a typical offering. Desserts centre on pâtisserie, fruit and home-made sorbets. Improving the quality of the bread and vegetables (which are charged separately) would do much to raise the restaurant's standing. Service draws mixed reports. House wine is £8.65.

CHEF: Olivier Delaunoy   PROPRIETORS: Jennie and William Glossop, and Olivier Delaunoy   OPEN: Mon to Sat, exc Sat L; 12.30 to 2, 6.15 to 10.30 (11 Sat)   MEALS: alc (main courses £9 to £17). Set L £12.25, Set D £16.25   SERVICE: not inc, card slips closed   CARDS: Access, Amex, Visa   DETAILS: 70 seats. Private parties: 50 main room, 22 private room. Vegetarian meals. Children's helpings. No pipes in dining-room. Wheelchair access (also WC). Music

---

SHELF West Yorkshire

map 5

Bentley's ⁞✸ £

NEW ENTRY

12 Wade House Road, Shelf HX3 7PB
BRADFORD (0274) 690992

COOKING 1
COST £13–£37

The Bentley family had many years' experience running pub/restaurants before setting up in this converted wine shop. On the ground floor is a pine-furnished bar with bare boards and a stone fireplace. A stone staircase leads down to the basement restaurant – a light, airy room with flagstone floors and rough-cast walls – which feels extremely comfortable and welcoming. Menus are chalked on blackboards and the cooking is 'modern without pretension'. Visitors have been impressed by, among others, an 'elegant' crab mousse, confit of duck with wild mushrooms, tender rack of lamb, and perfectly timed salmon fillet on a bed of spinach with tomato sauce. Sweets are equally good: date and sticky toffee pudding, rum-soaked brûlée and home-made ice-cream have been recommended. The food is satisfying, the value for money is exceptional, and service is invariably pleasant. 'This place is a wonderful find!' exclaimed a reporter. Carefully chosen and very drinkable wines at modest prices – the majority under £15 – add significantly to the pleasure. Six house wines start at £8.50 (£1.75 a glass).

CHEFS: Paul Bentley and Anthony Bickers   PROPRIETOR: Paul Bentley   OPEN: Tue to Sun, exc Sat L and Sun D; 10 to 2, 6.30 to 9 (9.30 Sat)   MEALS: alc (main courses £7.50 to £15). Set L £4.25 (2 courses) to £5.95.   SERVICE: not inc, card slips closed   CARDS: Access, Visa   DETAILS: 44 seats. Private parties: 24 main room. Car park. Vegetarian meals. Children's helpings. Smart dress preferred. No smoking in dining-room. Music

---

SHEPTON MALLET Somerset

map 2

Blostin's

29 Waterloo Road,
Shepton Mallet BA4 5HH
SHEPTON MALLET (0749) 343648

COOKING 2
COST £22–£33

Nick and Lynne Reed's popular, unpretentious restaurant continues to enjoy enthusiastic local support. The mood is happy, and the dining-room is skilfully laid out so that it does not feel cramped even when the place is full. Menus are chalked on blackboards: a short *carte* is backed up by set meals for two or three courses and the cost is reckoned to be 'very fair indeed'. Vegetarians have a separate menu.

Nick Reed's cooking sits comfortably in the bistro mould and he can deliver good versions of fish soup with rouille, medallions of pork in pepper, cream and brandy sauce, and crispy duck with bacon, mushrooms and burgundy sauce, although desserts occasionally let the side down. Regular supplies of Cornish fish are used for specialities such as crab and ginger filo parcels, and fillets of monkfish and sole with mussels and saffron sauce. Many other ingredients are from local sources. The list of around 40 wines is organised around grape varieties; mark-ups are not greedy. House wine is £7.95.

CHEF: Nick Reed   PROPRIETORS: Nick and Lynne Reed   OPEN: Tue to Sat, D only; 7 to 9.30 CLOSED: 2 weeks Jan, 2 weeks June   MEALS: alc (main courses £11 to £12). Set D £13.95 (2 courses) to £14.95   SERVICE: not inc   CARDS: Access, Visa   DETAILS: 30 seats. Private parties: 30 main room. Vegetarian meals. Children's helpings. No cigars/pipes in dining-room. Wheelchair access (1 step). Music

▲ Bowlish House ▼

Wells Road, Shepton Mallet BA4 5JD
SHEPTON MALLET (0749) 342022   COOKING 2*
on A371, ¼m out of town   COST £30–£36

The house has been the focal point of diverse types of business in the 250 years since it was built: the cloth trade, brewing, bricks and tiles. The dignified Palladian façade, flagged entrance hall and understated gilt-edging in the dining-room all give an impression of relaxed civility. That impression is reinforced by Bob Morley, whose unintrusive attention is commended by many. 'It is a place,' remarked a reporter, 'where people dare talk to each other.'

Linda Morley cooks a fixed-price dinner menu of three courses plus coffee, providing considerable choice, and the formula seems to please. The style is English country-house, with Mediterranean and French acknowledgements, as in a chicken and pheasant sausage served with 'fingers of herby polenta'. Vegetarian dishes show real imagination: one night's offering was a spicy pancake filled with megadarra – a Middle Eastern rice, lentil and sweet onion mixture – accompanied by tsatsiki. An early summer meal showed the range of abilities well: asparagus soufflé was timed to the second and came with 'particularly good' béarnaise sauce, local goats' cheese was toasted to bubbling point and served with a salad dressed with raspberry vinegar, and turbot fillet had an admirably delicate saffron and parsley cream sauce. Desserts demonstrate a fondness for the chocolate and caramel end of the spectrum, the quality of the chocolate speaking strongly in a dark mousse pudding and in ice-cream flavoured with mint. Sticky toffee has been called 'superb'. Incidentals, such as the aperitif nibbles and chocolate truffles with coffee, are all done well. The wine list is thoroughly comprehensive, and the selections are unerringly sound. Spanish reds look especially impressive, choice in halves is wide, and there is an intelligent set of house selections at £8.25, all available by the glass. CELLARMAN'S CHOICE: Saumur Blanc 1992, Dom. de la Renière, £9.95; Ch. Musar 1987, £14.95.

▲ *This symbol means accommodation is available.*

CHEF: Linda Morley   PROPRIETORS: Bob and Linda Morley   OPEN: all week, D only (Sun L first Sun of month, other L by arrangement); 7 to 9.30   CLOSED: 1 week spring, 1 week autumn   MEALS: Set D £22.50   SERVICE: not inc, card slips closed   CARDS: Access, Visa   DETAILS: 24 seats. Private parties: 36 main room. Car park. Vegetarian meals. Children's helpings by arrangement. No music   ACCOMMODATION: 3 rooms, all with bath/shower. TV. B&B £48. Children welcome. Baby facilities. Pets welcome (not in public rooms). Garden. Doors close at midnight. Confirm by 6 (*The Which? Hotel Guide*)

SHINFIELD Berkshire   map 2

L'Ortolan

The Old Vicarage, Church Lane,
Shinfield RG2 9BY
READING (0734) 883783   COOKING 4*
off A33, S of M4 junction 11   COST £39–£99

'The atmosphere is just right, not too stuffy.' As old vicarages go, it is delightful, an attractive and mellow brick building with greenery climbing up it. The conservatory extensions are sympathetically done, one a lounge, the other a dining-room. 'Food and service surpassed our expectations,' wrote one. 'We re-booked on the spot,' added another. 'It is as good as we have ever had.' So the plaudits roll in for plump partridge sausage that is meaty, gamey, beautifully spiced and seasoned, skinless, crisp outside, succulent inside, with 'bags of character'. The menu includes a fair bit of pasta, the customary showing of foie gras and truffles, and a reasonable outing for fish – in one case a huge chunk of baked salt cod surrounded by Puy lentils with bacon bits and an onion purée, topped with a characteristic tangle of crisp, hair-like deep-fried vegetables. Another enjoyed 'an interesting combination of lamb cutlets with crab quenelles flavoured with curry that worked surprisingly well'.

But not everybody shares the rosy view. 'It wasn't bad,' wrote one, of a piece of sea bream covering thin strands of vegetables, itself obscured by a handful of angel-hair, 'it just wasn't focused, it didn't have a purpose, it lacked vitality.' In another case, the emulsion surrounding a plump raviolo of snails did not taste of the advertised basil, any more than the filling for a pig's trotter included the advertised sweetbreads, ham and tongue, although the sauce gribiche provided exactly what so many versions of trotter are lacking: some bite to cut through the richness of the wonderfully sticky and gelatinous skin. Likewise, the sauce with pot roast veal kidney was brilliantly reduced, except that the advertised sweet-and-sour effect was undetectable to an inspector. Small lapses are magnified by the price: a shame when the kitchen is as highly skilled as this one. Technical accomplishment and craftsmanship are not at issue, the question is: to what purpose?

A 'chubby hexagon of firm caramel mousse enclosed in a wall of thin crisp caramel' provided an upbeat finish for one reporter: 'quite marvellous to eat'. As for the rest, the green olives are as disappointingly poor as the appetisers and petits fours are spiffingly good. Service is by young people who seem a bit short on style. 'Whenever two or more waiting staff are in the room together, they will, sooner or later, bump into each other.' What a good job Christine Burton-Race is there to manage things properly. High prices (note that the £31.50 menu is not available on Saturday evening) are not helped by occasional shocks. 'I asked for a "small and simple armagnac" – it came and was good. Later I found it had cost £15!' At these prices, to add supplements for some items on the menu seems a bit niggardly. Only the lunch delivers what our reporters consider good value for money – nay, outstanding value. Last year's advice on the wine list remains valid: stick with the first page to find something for less than £20. There are brilliant wines, with good mature vintages, but with exceedingly high mark-ups. House wine is £17.50.

CHEF: John Burton-Race   PROPRIETOR: Burton-Race Restaurants plc   OPEN: Tue to Sun, exc Sun D; 12 to 2.15, 7 to 10   MEALS: Set L £22 to £31.50, Set D £31.50 (Tue to Fri only) to £47 (2 courses)   SERVICE: not inc   CARDS: Access, Amex, Diners, Visa   DETAILS: 65 seats. Private parties: 45 main room, 12 and 25 private rooms. Car park. Vegetarian meals with prior notice. Children's helpings. Smart dress preferred. Wheelchair access (3 steps; also men's WC). Music. Fax: (0734) 885391

SHIPTON GORGE Dorset   map 2

▲ *Innsacre* ▼ ⚹

Shipton Lane, Shipton Gorge DT6 4LJ
BRIDPORT (0308) 456137
2m E of Bridport, 13m W of Dorchester,
take Shipton Gorge/Burton Bradstock turn   COOKING 2
S off A35   COST £24–£44

The restaurant is in a peaceful spot, with Jacob sheep and donkeys in the meadow above the seventeenth-century farmhouse. Rough stone walls and comfortable armchairs give it an air of 'rustic chic'. Sydney Davies is very affable, friendly and helpful, and if the pace of things appears slow, then reporters are prepared to 'make allowances for the tempo of Dorset rural life'.

The three-course menu has five items per course and changes every few weeks, but other dishes, particularly fish, may be added according to availability. There are few thrills, but it is interesting and accessible food that might include ravioli of fresh scallops, or flavoursome pigeon and vegetables with black beans, chilli and ginger, followed by pink and tender venison with cassis and redcurrant sauce, and very rich lemon tart with lime syrup, which managed to be tangy and mellow at the same time. The cooking swings between modern and traditional – four-bean soup with virgin olive oil, and steamed fruit pudding with a suet crust and custard – but with a sound basis in good ingredients. Bread, ice-creams and pastry are made in-house, and nibbles and cheeses are particularly good. The wine list comes commendably to the point, with admirable choice under £20. All reporters praise the selection of half-bottles, and house wines begin at £9.80. CELLARMAN'S CHOICE: Borro della Salla 1992, Antinori, £16.50; Rouge Homme Cabernet/Shiraz 1989, £16.90.

⚹ *indicates that smoking is either banned altogether or that a dining-room is maintained for non-smokers. The symbol does not apply to restaurants that simply have no-smoking areas.*

CHEF: Tim Emberley PROPRIETOR: Sydney Davies OPEN: Tue to Sat, D only (L by arrangement), and bank hols; 7 to 9.30 MEALS: alc (main courses £8.50 to £14). Set D £16.80 to £26 SERVICE: not inc, card slips closed CARDS: Access, Visa DETAILS: 36 seats. 4 tables outside. Private parties: 80 main room. Car park. Vegetarian meals. Children's helpings. No smoking in dining-room. Wheelchair access (1 step; also WC). Music ACCOMMODATION: 6 rooms, all with bath/shower. TV. B&B £40 to £66. Deposit: £25. Children welcome. Baby facilities. Pets welcome (small charge). Garden. Doors close at midnight. Confirm by 6. Fax: (0308) 427277 (*The Which? Hotel Guide*)

SHOTLEY Suffolk   map 3

Old Boot House ✴✻

Main Road, Shotley IP9 1EY
IPSWICH (0473) 787755   COOKING 1
10m SE of Ipswich on B1456   COST £16–£36

'You can only admire the owners for establishing such a restaurant on a peninsula of the Suffolk coast which leads nowhere,' marvels one reader. It is a former pub that now offers 'exceptional value. It deserves to succeed.' The cooking sounds more like swimming, the way the Chamberlains describe it: British Free-Style. But you can see what they mean: avocado fritters are served with a fresh tomato coulis, and potted goose comes with an onion and Campari marmalade. The owners admit to serving some 'London-style food', but the enterprise goes deeper than that. Herbs, rose petals, elderflowers, lavender and pickled samphire, as well as game and seafood, make use of local resources. Crab is made into a sausage; so is duck, served 'in the hole'. Sometimes intentions may go too far in an effort to impress: a croissant seems a bit out of its depth in a bouillabaisse-style seafood soup, and melting Cheddar cheese is added to a fillet of cod that is already covered with a dark mushroom pâté. The flavours already speak eloquently enough, and the cooking has the flair to carry them through. Serve your own vegetables, and pour your own wine. The list is a pick 'n' mix bag that rarely rises above £12 a bottle.

CHEF: Ian Chamberlain PROPRIETORS: Ian and Pamela Chamberlain OPEN: Tue to Sun, exc Sun D; 12 to 1.45, 7 to 9 (10 Sat) MEALS: alc (main courses L £4.50 to £9, D £9 to £15.50). Set L Sun £11.95 SERVICE: not inc, card slips closed CARDS: Access, Visa DETAILS: 40 seats. Private parties: 40 main room. Car park. Vegetarian meals with prior notice. Children welcome. Smart dress preferred. No smoking in dining-room. Wheelchair access (1 step; also WC). No music

---

SHURDINGTON Gloucestershire   map 2

▲ Greenway

Shurdington GL51 5UG
CHELTENHAM (0242) 862352   COOKING 2
on A46, 2½m S of Cheltenham   COST £23–£50

The 'green way' refers to an ancient track that runs beside the large house, a hotel since 1947. It is Cotswold architecture at its classiest and most appealing. Lounges are comfortable, decoration is restrained, and the dining-room, which overlooks the fishpond, has a fine view of trees and surrounding countryside. The feel is 'gracious and spacious', with friendly service that prevents too much formality.

Tony Elliott believes that 'eating out should be fun'. Perhaps that is why he serves his own version of prawn cocktail, steak and chips, or fish and chips with mushy peas, followed by iced Black Forest gâteau parfait. But before you stop reading, consider the rest of the menu: potato and leek soup with crunchy bacon lardons, sea bass with black pasta, and lemon crème brûlée – all off the bargain fixed-price lunch menu. The *carte* goes one better: wild mushroom consommé comes with a ravioli of quail and morels; red mullet roasted with garlic and rosemary is given a lobster and lime butter sauce; steamed chocolate pudding, a nursery winner, is served with toffee, vanilla and chocolate sauces.

A delightfully earthy seam runs through the cooking, too, and includes a dish of braised oxtail filled with caramelised black pudding, served with lentils, and boiled ham hock with mashed potato and parsley sauce. The kitchen makes use of up to 30 herbs growing in the garden, and the *carte* lists three meatless dishes. Meals begin with an appetiser, and might finish with a Bailey's ice-cream (in a chocolate shell with white chocolate sauce) or a plate of apple puddings. Wine mark-ups on the long and interesting list are high. House vin de pays is £11.25.

CHEF: Chris Colmer   PROPRIETOR: Tony Elliott   OPEN: all week, exc Sat L; 12.30 to 2, 7.30 to 9.30 (8.30 Sun)   CLOSED: 2 to 6 Jan, L bank hols   MEALS: alc (main courses £12.50 to £19). Set L £15 (2 courses) to £17, Set D £25   SERVICE: net prices, card slips closed   CARDS: Access, Amex, Diners, Visa   DETAILS: 50 seats. 6 tables outside. Private parties: 14 main room, 14 and 28 private rooms. Car park. Vegetarian meals. No children under 7. Smart dress preferred. No pipes/cigars in dining-room. Wheelchair access (1 step; also WC). Music   ACCOMMODATION: 19 rooms, all with bath/shower. TV. Phone. B&B £77.50 to £160. Rooms for disabled. No children under 7. Garden. Doors close at 11.30. Fax: (0242) 862780 (*The Which? Hotel Guide*)

SISSINGHURST Kent   map 3

Rankins' Restaurant

The Street, Sissinghurst TN17 2JH   COOKING 1*
CRANBROOK (0580) 713964   COST £27–£38

For those eager to learn how he does it, Hugh Rankin now offers cookery classes in this well-established beamed restaurant that one local couple on their first (but not last) visit found 'delightful'. The formula of dinner on four nights a week, plus Sunday lunch, has allowed the Rankins to preserve a distinctive freshness about the operation that some lose through over-production. Around four choices per course are offered on the fixed-price menus, and the cooking treats the best local produce in an essentially simple style. The pedantic may question what a 'winter brassica salad' was doing on a spring menu, but faith is maintained in crab and lentil soup with clementine julienne, in minted haricot bean salad with smoked salmon, red onions and orange, and in roast Lunesdale duck legs with Cumberland sauce. Good notices have been received for a spinach terrine with garlic and nutmeg and a mint vinaigrette, gigot of lamb with French beans and mange-tout, and a summer fruit tart. Incidentals are also well looked after, with breads, unsalted butter and coffee all getting the nod. Portions are 'generous', and the service led by Leonora Rankin is 'helpful and correct'. The wine list is short and to the point, and its prices will not alarm. House wines are £7.80.

CHEF: Hugh Rankin   PROPRIETORS: Hugh and Leonora Rankin   OPEN: Wed to Sat, D only, and Sun L; 12.30 to 1.30, 7.30 to 9   CLOSED: 25 Dec, bank hols   MEALS: Set L £15.95 (2 courses), Set D £18.95 (2 courses)   SERVICE: not inc   CARDS: Access, Visa   DETAILS: 30 seats. Private parties: 24 main room. Vegetarian meals. Children's helpings. Smart dress preferred. No music

---

SLAIDBURN Lancashire   map 5

▲ *Parrock Head Hotel* ⁂✳

NEW ENTRY

Woodhouse Lane, Slaidburn BB7 3AH
CLITHEROE (0200) 446614   COOKING 1
1m NW of Slaidburn   COST £20–£34

Supporters of this small Dales hotel, wounded at its exclusion from last year's *Guide*, fight back this year with tales of warm hospitality, unerring value for money and sound cooking. Parrock Head is a rough-cast, whitewashed, seventeenth-century farmhouse on a hill with a vista of contentedly bleating sheep before it and glowering moorland behind. The dining-room, with low-slung beams and neatly dressed tables, is the former milking shed. Vicky Umbers' menus change daily and are built around a fixed-price, three-course format that can be bolstered by taking soup or cheese and biscuits as an extra stage. Fish comes from Fleetwood, lamb from the Trough of Bowland, duckling from Goosnargh, shrimps from Morecambe Bay and herbs from the back garden. The style is country-house but without the flounce. Fruit may crop up in all courses, from tenderloin of Yorkshire venison en croûte with a blackberry sauce to crumbed and deep-fried Camembert sauced with strawberry. Pork loin with prunes, and chicken breast with spinach and pistachios in a sharp watercress sauce both delivered plenty of flavour. Vegetables, particularly the deep-fried salsify, have received acclaim, as have the poppy-seed rolls and good cafetière coffee. Local farmhouse cheeses are in fine condition. The wine list is a cosmopolitan collection of worthy names; prices are kept well in check. House wines are from £7.50.

CHEFS: Dale Thornber and Vicky Umbers   PROPRIETORS: Richard and Vicky Umbers   OPEN: all week, D only, and Sun L (Mon to Sat bar L on request); 12.30 to 1.30, 7 to 8.30   MEALS: Set L Sun £12.50, Set D £16.50   SERVICE: not inc, card slips closed   CARDS: Access, Amex, Diners, Visa   DETAILS: 35 seats. Private parties: 45 main room. Car park. Vegetarian meals. Children's helpings L. No children under 8 D. Smart dress preferred. No smoking in dining-room. Wheelchair access (1 step). No music   ACCOMMODATION: 9 rooms, all with bath/shower. TV. Phone. D,B&B £56.50 to £98. Deposit: £10. Rooms for disabled. Children welcome (high tea for under-8s). Baby facilities. Pets welcome (garden rooms only). Afternoon teas. Garden. Doors close at 11.30. Confirm by 7. Fax: (0200) 446313 (*The Which? Hotel Guide*)

Prices quoted in the Guide *are based on information supplied by restaurateurs. The prices quoted at the top of each entry represent a range, from the lowest meal price to the highest; the latter is inflated by 20 per cent to take account of likely price rises during the year of the* Guide.

---

map 3

Madhu's Brilliant £

39 South Road, Southall UB1 1SW
081-574 1897 and 571 6380

COOKING 2
COST £14–£26

This is a restaurant that expects and likes families: the owners reckon that it is one of the few places where you can see three generations eating together. The décor might seem like that of a café, with long tables at right angles to the walls, a spiral staircase and 'shrill' Indian film music playing in the background, but the cooking is of a consistently high quality. The style is north Indian and Punjabi. Karahi gosht ('probably one of the best meat curries I've ever eaten') bears all the hallmarks of a kitchen on top form: good-quality raw materials, fresh spicing and clear, distinct flavours. A convert noted that 'what remains in the little black wok at the end is a thick syrupy residue reminiscent of reduced meat stock (i.e. the real thing)'. Mater paneer is an above-average version, and other details such as nan bread and 'colour-free' pilau rice are splendid – although poppadums and chutneys disappointed one visitor. Drink lassi, lager or opt for one of the workaday wines. House French is £7.

CHEFS: Jagdish Kumar Anand, Sanjeev Anand and Satpal Singh Gill PROPRIETORS: Jagdish Kumar Anand, Krishna Kumari Anand, Sanjay Anand and Sanjeev Anand OPEN: Wed to Mon, exc L Sat and Sun; 12.30 to 2.45, 6 to 11.30 (midnight Fri and Sat) MEALS: alc (main courses £3 to £8.50). Set L £8 (2 courses) to £12.50, Set D £10 (2 courses) to £15 SERVICE: 10%, card slips closed CARDS: Access, Amex, Diners, Visa DETAILS: 104 seats. Private parties: 60 main room, 60 private room. Vegetarian meals. Children welcome. Smart dress preferred. Wheelchair access. Music. Air-conditioned. Fax: 081-813 8639

SOUTHAMPTON Hampshire map 2

Brown's 🍴✳

Frobisher House, Nelson Gate,
Southampton SO1 0GX
SOUTHAMPTON (0703) 332615

COOKING 2
COST £23–£64

Patrons of the Mayflower Theatre are well served by this personally run restaurant just off Commercial Road. Richard and Patricia Brown will open at 5.30pm for meals before the show (if you book in advance) and will close late if necessary. Patricia's cooking is lively stuff: boned, marinated oxtail is wrapped in crépinette and served with parsnip purée and rich beef sauce; Aylesbury duck is cooked in three styles – roast breast, the leg 'en confit', and a duck boudin with a sauce of orange and thyme. A choice of extra dishes and a set menu provide useful alternatives to the *carte*: fricassee of rabbit with grapes, baked chicken with tarragon and white wine, rhubarb brown betty and apricot délice with crème anglaise are typical offerings. The short, fair-priced wine list keeps within Europe. House wines are £9.50.

Remember, if you especially want the set menu, that some restaurants restrict availability, particularly at weekends and on public holidays.

CHEF: Patricia Brown   PROPRIETORS: Richard and Patricia Brown   OPEN: all week, exc Sat L; 12 to 2.30, 6.30 (5.30 pre-theatre) to 10.30   CLOSED: 14 to 29 Aug   MEALS: alc (main courses £7.50 to £19). Set L and D £16.50   SERVICE: not inc   CARDS: Access, Amex, Diners, Visa   DETAILS: 24 seats. Private parties: 50 main room. Car park D and weekends. Vegetarian meals. No children under 12. Smart dress preferred. No smoking in dining-room. Music. Fax: (0703) 332615

SOUTH MOLTON Devon   map 1

▲ *Whitechapel Manor* ♀ ⁙

South Molton EX36 3EG
SOUTH MOLTON (0769) 573377
1m off A361 at roundabout 1½m E   COOKING 3
of South Molton   COST £36–£57

This Grade I Elizabethan manor may look drab and grey from outside, but inside the Shaplands have made it feel lived in. The dining-room is light and airy, with primrose walls, tablecloths and fresh flowers, and meals begin with miniature appetisers of salmon eggs on a thin pancake, onion purée on a croûton, and brochette of rare beef with mushrooms and courgettes.

Patricia Shapland has been in charge of the kitchen since August 1993. 'Deft, careful, considered, neat, well executed, but all propelled by real enthusiasm and enjoyment' was the verdict of one reporter on what she does. 'It is unassuming sophistication.' She is helped by Martin Lee, formerly at Summer Lodge (see entry, Evershot), and it is the lightness of touch and the combination of flavours that work to such good effect. Sea bass with mustard seed and dill sauce is 'exemplary', and served with 'unaccountably good potatoes'. The style is contemporary, with well-defined flavours that achieve a balance between simplicity and interest, with saucing based on the meat juices – for example, slices of plum-coloured breast of woodpigeon surrounding a beetroot purée, with a scattering of perfectly timed vegetables in a natural pigeon jus.

Cheeses are mostly from Devon and Somerset and might include Devon Oke, Ticklemore and Beenleigh Blue. Warm apple tart is a three-tiered puff-pastry job served with caramel ice-cream. It is worth staying overnight because the breakfasts are so good: breads, pastries, croissants and brioche are all home-made. Wines are interesting, some are even exciting, and mark-ups are variable but not much above average: roughly half the bottles cost £20 or less. House wine starts at £12.50. CELLARMAN'S CHOICE: Mercurey 1990, Ch. de Chamirey, £25; Cloudy Bay Cabernet Merlot 1991, £21.50.

CHEFS: Patricia Shapland and Martin Lee   PROPRIETORS: John and Patricia Shapland   OPEN: all week; 12 to 1.45, 7 to 8.45   MEALS: Set L £26, Set D £37   SERVICE: not inc, card slips closed   CARDS: Access, Amex, Diners, Visa   DETAILS: 30 seats. Private parties: 40 main room, 8 private room. Car park. Vegetarian meals with prior notice. Children's helpings on request. Smart dress preferred. No smoking in dining-room. No music   ACCOMMODATION: 10 rooms, all with bath/shower. TV. Phone. D,B&B £90 to £205. Deposit £100. Children welcome. Baby facilities. Afternoon teas. Garden. Doors close at 11. Confirm by 5. Fax: (0769) 573797 (*The Which? Hotel Guide*)

SOUTHSEA Hampshire

map 2

Bistro Montparnasse

103 Palmerston Road, Southsea PO5 3PS
PORTSMOUTH (0705) 816754

COOKING 1*
COST £21–£41

'An excellent place to spend a couple of hours before embarking on a ferry to France,' enthused one traveller. The Scotts' admirable bistro is a warm, welcoming place with matching terracotta-coloured walls and bright chintz curtains. Gillian Scott can cook well, and her food is uncompromisingly seasonal ('no tomatoes from October to July'). She works to a regularly changing menu supplemented by a fixed-price special (Tuesday to Friday). Mussel soup with orange and chipotle chillies is a nicely judged, perfectly balanced brew; juicy marinated brochettes of chicken receive an 'antidote' of raw diced vegetables and dollops of minty yogurt; 'beautifully tender' salmon is served with a parsley butter sauce that has a pleasant lemon astringency. A fascinating selection of breads is baked on the premises. The short wine list shows a serious interest in the subject. House wine ('far better than the usual plonk') is £9.90.

CHEF: Gillian Scott   PROPRIETORS: Gillian and Peter Scott   OPEN: Tue to Sat, D only (L for 10 or more by arrangement); 7 to 10   CLOSED: 2 weeks Jan, bank hols, Tue following bank hol Mon   MEALS: alc (main courses £8.50 to £15). Set D Tue to Fri £12.50. Minimum £12.50   SERVICE: not inc   CARDS: Access, Amex, Visa   DETAILS: 50 seats. Private parties: 40 main room, 30 private room. Vegetarian meals. Children's helpings on request. Smart dress preferred. No cigars/pipes in dining-room. Wheelchair access. No music

---

SOUTHWOLD Suffolk

map 6

▲ Crown ▮ ⁵✻ £

90 High Street, Southwold IP18 6DP
SOUTHWOLD (0502) 722275

COOKING 2*
COST £17–£33

'It would be highly prized if it were in France,' commented one who had just demolished cod's roe, turbot, and banana fool one fine June day. But it is greatly valued here too. The Crown is the pub part of Adnams' Southwold empire, which also takes in the Swan Hotel and a wholesale wine outlet of some repute. It is 'most definitely a pub', the eating area separated from 'screaming children and general hustle and bustle' by a big old wooden settle. Bar snacks and suppers are just as enthusiastically commended as restaurant meals. Prices for the latter are fixed for two or three courses, and Andrew Mulliss manages to offer a surprisingly wide choice for the scale of the operation. Fish is used well, as in fillet of turbot steamed and served with scallops and prawns, salmon baked en papillote, or simply grilled plaice with lyonnaise potatoes. Otherwise, celery and Stilton soup, sliced pigeon breast with sauerkraut and apricot sauce, or Malay vegetable curry give an idea of the range to be expected. Puddings offer the comfort of baked Alaska, dark chocolate and Cointreau pot or hot apple and almond tart with custard. Vegetables have been judged 'a bit too al dente'. The unflagging cheer is appreciated by one and all.

Fittingly, the wine list is a magisterial array of the great and the good. Around 300 bins are on offer, with positively charitable prices, evocative tasting notes and enthusiasm at every turn. The list pulls out plums from classic and obscure regions alike, every one tempting and juicy. Look at Italy or the French countryside, and among dessert wines: a disappointment from any bottle would be hard to imagine. Prices open at £6.50. CELLARMAN'S CHOICE: Pouilly-Fumé, Ch. de Tracy 1990, £13.95; Pinot Noir de St Bris 1991, Brocard, £9.50.

CHEF: Andrew Mulliss   PROPRIETOR: Adnams Hotels   OPEN: all week; restaurant 12.30 to 1.30, 7.30 to 9.30; bar 12.15 to 1.45, 7.15 to 9.45   CLOSED: first week Jan   MEALS: Set L £12.75 (2 courses) to £14.75, Set D £17.25 (2 courses) to £19.25. Bar menu (main courses £6 to £11.50)   SERVICE: not inc, card slips closed   CARDS: Access, Amex, Diners, Visa   DETAILS: restaurant 38 seats, bar 34 seats. 3 tables outside. Private parties: 22 main room, 22 private room. Car park. Vegetarian meals. Children's helpings on request. Smart dress preferred. No smoking in dining-room. No music. Air-conditioned   ACCOMMODATION: 12 rooms, all with bath/shower. TV. Phone. B&B £38 to £58. Children welcome. Baby facilities. Doors close at 11.30. Confirm by 6. Fax: (0502) 724805 (*The Which? Hotel Guide*)

SPARK BRIDGE Cumbria   map 7

▲ *Bridgefield House* ♟ ⁵⚹

Spark Bridge LA12 8DA
LOWICK BRIDGE (0229) 885239
4m N of Ulverston, off A5084 on back   COOKING 2
road to Coniston, E of River Crake   COST £27–£34

The Victorian stone house, a former 'gentleman's residence', is 500 yards from Lowick Bridge on a narrow lane off the main road (follow directions from the new sign) with views over fields and hills. A warm welcome and unfussy service by the Glisters endear the place to residents and casual visitors alike. Rooms are warm, comfortable and well decorated. The unchanging pattern is one sitting at dinner, a set soup, main course and sorbet, leaving only the first course and pudding to waylay ditherers.

A typical meal might begin with black pudding and shallots in a grainy mustard and cream sauce, followed by carrot and brown lentil soup with oat biscuits. Main courses, such as roast breast of goose or pheasant, or salmon fillets poached in white wine, come with an interesting array of four vegetables: for example, steamed Jamaican cho cho with coriander, carrot with pumpkin seeds, bobbi beans, and potatoes variously roast, sauté, boiled or served 'as a potato pie with cream'. Simple originality extends to the puddings, of which the all-time favourite must be individual date and butterscotch pudding with nuts and pouring cream. The sixth course is either cheese (with apple or pear) or a savoury, usually lambs' kidneys or sweetbreads in madeira on toast.

The recession has hit the wine list – down from 300 bins to 55. It is an intelligent response to difficult circumstances, and only three bottles now stray over £20. If more restaurants followed suit and jettisoned some of the expensive bottles they list solely in order to impress, concentrating instead on simply good drinking, we would all benefit.

See the inside of the front cover for an explanation of the 1 to 5 rating system for cooking standards.

CHEF: Rosemary Glister   PROPRIETORS: the Glister family   OPEN: all week, D only; 7.30 for 8
CLOSED: D 25 Dec   MEALS: Set D £20   SERVICE: not inc, card slips closed   CARDS: Access,
Visa   DETAILS: 24 seats. Private parties: 24 main room. Car park. Vegetarian meals with prior
notice. Children's helpings. Smart dress preferred. No smoking in dining-room. No music
ACCOMMODATION: 5 rooms, all with bath/shower. Phone. B&B £30 to £60. Deposit: £20. Children
welcome. Baby facilities. Pets welcome (in bedrooms only after 9pm). Afternoon teas Sat and
Sun, Easter to Sept. Garden. Fishing. Doors close at 2am. Confirm by 3. Fax: (0229) 885379
(*The Which? Hotel Guide*)

STADDLEBRIDGE North Yorkshire   map 7

▲ *McCoy's* ♟

The Tontine, Staddlebridge DL6 3JB
EAST HARLSEY (0609) 882671
6m NE of Northallerton, at junction of   COOKING 3
A19 and A172   COST £26–£54

All are agreed that McCoy's is a thoroughly idiosyncratic operation. Run by the
three McCoy brothers, it works on two levels: a basement bistro open all week,
and a ground-floor restaurant doing dinners only. The décor is a touching jumble
of odds and ends with no pretensions to finery – an accurate reflection of the
whole approach. Upstairs is more dimly lit and sedate, but not noticeably
smarter. The menu is a fairly long, scribbly *carte*, founded on classic French bistro
lines, with nods to fashion in the form of Italian vegetables with mozzarella or
fried polenta with asparagus and mushrooms. Choice abounds, though, and a
spring menu was able to offer lamb, venison, chicken, duck, two cuts of steak
and quail, as well as turbot, sole, salmon or sea bass for main courses.

A party of four in June enjoyed themselves immensely: they started with
tomato and pesto soup thickened with potato and full of 'rich, natural flavour',
a pasta dish with langoustines in a creamy shellfish sauce that had great
'intensity', crisped foie gras on brioche accompanied by grapes stewed in
madeira ('perfectly textured') and outstandingly fresh scallops with olive oil,
capers and parsley. 'Chicken Jo-Jo' turns out to be the breast cooked with
mushrooms, crème fraîche and vermouth; other sauces may be simply reduced
cooking juices, as with the lamb that was 'brown crispness' on the outside but
'oozing and pink' within. For those who haven't started worrying about their
arteries, sticky toffee pudding comes with an 'extremely calorific syrupy sauce
and a whole jug of cream'. Coffee is 'good and strong'. The wine list succeeds
admirably in its declared aims of succinctness and quality. Its notes are helpful
and knowingly irreverent: Candida's Villa Fontana is flagged as 'Frascati with
the volume turned up', while a Mâcon Chardonnay occasions the reflection 'so
nice not to have a mouthful of oak chips'. Choice of producers is very sound, and
prices are mostly fair. House French is £9.95.

---

*The text of entries is based on unsolicited reports sent in by readers, backed up by
inspections conducted anonymously. The factual details under the text are from
questionnaires the* Guide *sends to all restaurants that feature in the book.*

CHEF: Tom McCoy   PROPRIETORS: the McCoy brothers   OPEN: restaurant Tue to Sat, D only; 7 to 10. Bistro all week; 12 to 2, 7 to 10   MEALS: alc (main courses restaurant £13 to £17, bistro £11 to £17)   SERVICE: not inc   CARDS: Access, Amex, Diners, Visa   DETAILS: restaurant 50 seats, bistro 70 seats. Private parties: 50 main room, 30 private room. Car park. Vegetarian meals. Children's helpings. Music. Air-conditioned   ACCOMMODATION: 6 rooms, all with bath/shower. TV. Phone. Air-conditioned. B&B £69 to £99. Children welcome. Pets welcome. Garden. Fax: (0609) 882660

STAITHES North Yorkshire   map 6A

▲ *Endeavour*

1 High Street, Staithes TS13 5BH	COOKING 1
WHITBY (0947) 840825	COST £22–£45

'A beacon in a gastronomic desert' was one enthusiastic verdict on Lisa Chapman's friendly little restaurant a few yards from the sea. Many visitors have endured the trek up the steep hill from the nearest car park to sample her admirable food. Fish from the boats is the main talking point: big bowls of mussels, superlative scallops (perhaps served with saffron sauce), fillet of salmon with a pink lobster sauce, Dover sole. Her daily blackboard also features meat and vegetarian dishes with global overtones, as in pork terrine with pickled green tomatoes, grilled halloumi cheese kebabs with salsa, and courgette roulade with Mediterranean filling and garlic sauce. Crème brûlée with fresh raspberries is the house speciality, and it gets plenty of votes. Around 40 wines offer the prospect of pleasing drinking at a fair price. House wine is £7.95.

CHEF/PROPRIETOR: Lisa Chapman   OPEN: Mon to Sat (Sun D July to Sept and bank hols); 12 to 2, 6.45 to 9.15 (10 Sat and July to Sept)   CLOSED: 25 and 26 Dec, mid-Jan to mid-Mar   MEALS: alc (main courses £8 to £19)   SERVICE: not inc   DETAILS: 45 seats. Private parties: 25 main room, 12, 20 and 25 private rooms. Vegetarian meals. Children welcome. No-smoking area. Wheelchair access (1 step). Music   ACCOMMODATION: 3 rooms, 1 with bath/shower. B&B £16.50 to £37.50. Children welcome. Doors close at 11

STAMFORD Lincolnshire   map 6

▲ *George Hotel* 🍷

71 St Martins, Stamford PE9 2LB	COOKING 2
STAMFORD (0780) 55171	COST £25–£55

The old gallows that spans the road indicates that highwaymen are not at all welcome at the George. Honest travellers, however, can expect some of the most warmly courteous treatment to be found in any grand hotel. Lighter meals may be taken in a garden lounge and heavily ivied courtyard, while there is a suitably grand oak-panelled dining-room for the serious business.

In the contemporary manner, lunch is a fixed-price deal with a menu from which any two dishes are chosen as starter and main, with dessert and coffee to follow. In the evening, the *carte* comes into play, offering an eclectic, seasonal choice that may take in smoked sweetbreads in pastry with creamed leeks and Meaux mustard, Parmesan mousse garnished with bresaola and chopped black

471

olives, or 'pink and tender' pigeon breasts, followed by a summer pudding spilling forth redcurrants. Cheeses are in 'excellent condition' and come with 'moist, fresh, nutty' walnut bread.

Service is generally exemplary. Greater love hath no maître d' than to cut up the food of a 3-year-old at the table. And this must be one of the few places in the country where wine service is resolutely non-sexist. The mark-up system favours the classier bottles on what is undoubtedly one of the great lists. Ornellaia from Tuscany, Cornas from Clape, Cameron Pinot Noir from Oregon and Saintsbury Chardonnay from Carneros indicate the intelligence of selection across the board, and prices are humane. House wines – themselves an extravagantly large range – start at £8.45. CELLARMAN'S CHOICE: Vins de Pays d'Oc, Marsanne 1992, Dom. Virginie, £8.95; Barbera d'Asti 1991, Ceppi Storici, £10.95.

CHEF: Chris Pitman PROPRIETOR: Poste Hotels Ltd OPEN: all week; 12.30 to 2.30, 7.15 to 10.30 MEALS: alc (main courses £13 to £18.50). Set L Mon to Sat £15.50 to £18.50 SERVICE: not inc, card slips closed CARDS: Access, Amex, Diners, Visa DETAILS: restaurant 100 seats, Garden Lounge 110 seats. 30 tables outside. Private parties: 100 main room, 12 to 70 private rooms. Car park. Vegetarian meals. Children's helpings. Smart dress preferred. Wheelchair access (also WC). Music ACCOMMODATION: 47 rooms, all with bath/shower. TV. Phone. B&B £66 to £154. Children welcome. Baby facilities. Pets welcome (not in dining-rooms). Afternoon teas. Garden. Fax: (0780) 57070 (*The Which? Hotel Guide*)

STAPLEFORD Leicestershire map 5

▲ *Stapleford Park*

Stapleford, nr Melton Mowbray LE14 2EF
WYMONDHAM (0572) 787522
off B676, 9m W of A1 at Colsterworth, turn left 1m past Saxby

NEW CHEF

COST £33–£62

Bob Payton was a big American with big ideas. His warmth endeared him to people whether they loved his food or not, and his death in a car accident in July 1994 robbed the food industry of one its most flamboyant and iconoclastic characters. Although Chicago Rib Shacks and Pizza Pie Factories formed his business empire, Stapleford Park, restored at great expense, was a more personal enterprise. Here he rode to hounds and became part of the very establishment he had challenged, by decorating the bedrooms brashly and outrageously, by serving chips because he loved them, and by insisting on a relaxed informality, despite the grandeur, that would have made other country-house proprietors blush with embarrassment. He probably did more than anyone in recent years to give the traditional country-house idea a kick in the pants, and will be sorely missed.

As we go to press, Mark Barker is replaced by Malcolm Jessop, hence no cooking score, although we assume that the present organisation will remain: dinner is in the ornately carved Grinling Gibbons dining-room, and lunch in the vaulted, stone-clad sixteenth-century kitchen. Wines aim for up-front flavour and are arranged by grape variety. Although mark-ups are standard, much interesting drinking can be had for less than £20. House wines begin at £12.50

(£3 per glass). CELLARMAN'S CHOICE: Firestone Chardonnay 1992, £20.50; Ridge Fiddletown Zinfandel 1992, £20.50.

CHEF: Malcolm Jessup   PROPRIETOR: Wendy Payton   OPEN: all week; 12 to 2.30, 7 to 9.30 (10.30 Fri and Sat)   MEALS: alc (main courses £12 to £20)   SERVICE: not inc, card slips closed   CARDS: Access, Amex, Diners, Visa   DETAILS: 150 seats. 11 tables outside. Private parties: 70 main room, 16, 30 and 40 private rooms. Car park. Vegetarian meals. Children's helpings. Smart dress preferred. No smoking in dining-room. Wheelchair access (also WC). No music   ACCOMMODATION: 39 rooms, all with bath/shower. TV. Phone. B&B £125 to £195. Deposit: £50. Rooms for disabled. Children welcome. Pets welcome (not in public rooms). Afternoon teas. Garden. Tennis. Fishing. Confirm by 2. Fax: (0572) 787651 (*The Which? Hotel Guide*)

STOKE BRUERNE Northamptonshire   map 3

Bruerne's Lock

5 The Canalside, Stoke Bruerne NN12 7SB
ROADE (0604) 863654   COOKING 1
off A508, 3½m from A5 at Towcester   COST £24–£55

The restaurant is at the top of a flight of seven locks on the Grand Union Canal, next to a canal museum. Tables outside are just big enough for a drink before or coffee afterwards. Gavin Caldwell and Nigel Hollick make a big thing of the personal touch, 'explain' the menu to establish contact, then play out the meal at a gentle pace. Changes in the kitchen since the last *Guide* have meant changes to the menu, but meals still begin with a small copper pan of something salady to nibble on.

New chef Glenn Barrable's first offerings included a tartlet of oyster mushroom and bacon on a sea of dark green spinach purée, and an absolutely cracking deep-fried cheese and onion savoury with a light, crisp skin that contrasted wonderfully with the soft and melting interior. An intermediate course – maybe a simple sorbet, or a Yorkshire pudding with a substantial slice of beef – could be followed by pork tenderloin with leeks and white wine, breast of pigeon or fish of the day: monk and tuna in a creamy sauce, perhaps. Puddings are recited and run to lemon soufflé with a layer of lemon curd at the bottom. The wine list was undergoing a refit at the time of writing, and house wine is £11.50 (£2.50 per glass).

CHEFS: Glenn Barrable and Alun Franklin   PROPRIETORS: Gavin Caldwell and Nigel Hollick   OPEN: Tue to Sun, exc Sat L and Sun D; 12.30 to 2, 7.30 to 9.45   CLOSED: 2 weeks mid-Oct, 1 week after Christmas   MEALS: alc D (main courses £12 to £17.50). Set L £16   SERVICE: not inc   CARDS: Access, Amex, Visa   DETAILS: 30 seats. 4 tables outside. Private parties: 30 main room. Car park. Vegetarian meals. Children's helpings on request. Smart dress preferred. Wheelchair access (2 steps). Music

---

The Guide *always appreciates hearing about changes of chef or owner.*

The Guide *office can quickly spot when a restaurateur is encouraging customers to write recommending inclusion – and sadly, several restaurants have been doing this in 1994. Such reports do not further a restaurant's cause. Please tell us if a restaurateur invites you to write to the* Guide.

map 3

▲ *Angel Inn* £

Stoke-by-Nayland CO6 4SA
COLCHESTER (0206) 263245   COOKING 2
on B1068, 5m SW of Hadleigh   COST £19–£34

Visitors are fond of this sixteenth-century Suffolk inn: they appreciate the
'welcoming fire on a bitterly cold December day', and they are even more pleased
to find 'a pub menu with such an exciting choice'. One constantly changing
'chalkboard' covers both the informal bar (no bookings) and the aptly named
Well Room restaurant, with its 52-foot well and exposed timbers. Mark Johnson
follows the market and rings the changes with superbly tender tournedos of beef
on a potato rösti, guinea-fowl with mushroom mousseline and honey-glazed
rack of lamb. Fish from Billingsgate is a feature; expect anything from first-rate
dressed crab and grilled sardines with oregano to brochette of scallops wrapped
in bacon. Vegetables are reckoned to be 'beyond reproach'. As a finale, try
strawberry vacherin or brandy-snaps with port and chestnut ice-cream.

Staff are generally noted for their warmth and cheerful efficiency amid the
bustle, although one reporter's experience was not a happy one. The wine list
keeps its prices in check, and there is plenty of decent drinking to be had for
under £12. House wine is £7.30.

CHEF: Mark Johnson   PROPRIETORS: Richard Wright and Peter Smith   OPEN: all week; 12 to 2,
6.30 to 9 (7 to 9 Sun)   CLOSED: 25 and 26 Dec   MEALS: alc (main courses £6 to £12.50). Cover
£1   SERVICE: not inc   CARDS: Access, Amex, Diners, Visa   DETAILS: 85 seats. 4 tables outside.
Private parties: 28 main room. Car park. Vegetarian meals. No children under 14. Smart dress
preferred. Wheelchair access (1 step; also WC). No music   ACCOMMODATION: 6 rooms, all with
bath/shower. TV. Phone. B&B £44 to £57.50. No children under 10. Doors close at 11.30.
Confirm by 6. Fax: (0206) 37386 (*The Which? Hotel Guide*)

map 7

▲ *Chapters*

27 High Street, Stokesley TS9 5AD   COOKING 2*
MIDDLESBROUGH (0642) 711888   COST £16–£42

It is a sign of the times that Alan Thompson's restaurant now draws the bulk of
its trade from bistro meals rather than from its formal dining-room. The setting
is a three-storey Georgian coaching-inn which has been stripped bare of its
pebbledash to reveal some fine old brickwork. The bistro is a sparse, high-
ceilinged room with whitewashed walls, oak tables and a blackboard menu of
eclectic dishes from East and West. Bouillabaisse, confit of duck and paella are
best-sellers, but the repertoire also includes linguine with scallops, prawns and
sun-dried tomatoes, chicken satay and blackened sole with vegetable gumbo.
The cooking is impressive, although portions may not satisfy Yorkshire
trenchermen. The restaurant goes in for more adventurous stuff in the shape
of duck foie gras terrine with onion confit, carpaccio of salmon, and fillet of
beef with celeriac purée and madeira. Sauces are 'exceptionally good', as
are home-made desserts such as banana and peach cheesecake. Service is

enthusiastic, but the music can be intrusive. The bistro wine list is modest and peppered with familiar names; a few 'premier' wines are added for the restaurant. House Duboeuf is £8.95 a litre.

CHEFS: Alan Thompson and Richard West   PROPRIETORS: Alan and Catherine Thompson
OPEN: restaurant Mon to Sat, D only; 7 to 9 (9.30 Sat). Bistro all week; 12 to 2, 7 to 9.30 (10 Sat)
CLOSED: 25 Dec, 1 Jan   MEALS: alc (main courses bistro L £4.50 to £8.50, D £9 to £13, restaurant £12 to £15.50)   SERVICE: not inc   CARDS: Access, Amex, Diners, Visa   DETAILS: restaurant 40 seats, bistro 60 seats. Private parties: 60 main room. Vegetarian meals with prior notice. Children's helpings on request. Smart dress preferred. Music. Air-conditioned
ACCOMMODATION: 13 rooms, all with bath/shower. TV. Phone. B&B £35 to £59. Children welcome. Baby facilities. Pets welcome. Afternoon teas. Garden. Doors close at 2am. Fax: (0642) 713387 (*The Which? Hotel Guide*)

STON EASTON Somerset   map 2

▲ *Ston Easton Park* ♥ ✽

Ston Easton BA3 4DF
MENDIP (0761) 241631   COOKING 3*
on A37, 12m S of Bristol   COST £34–£62

'A place of overwhelming grandeur but nice with it' is one view of the Smedleys' magnificent Palladian mansion, set in acres of garden. The inside is opulently decorated, with a formal drawing-room and more relaxed dining-room with light panelling and bamboo chairs. It is an aristocrat of a hotel, 'one of those very grand, very beautiful places that actually dedicates itself to meeting the customers' needs rather than imposing its own formula'. 'It is staggeringly expensive but good value,' claims one.

The cooking is light and the flavours shine. The strengths are prime-quality meat and fish, wonderful salads, fruit and vegetables fresh from the garden in season, and some strikingly successful flavour and texture combinations. An inspector who stayed a few days was impressed by 'the whole quality of buying and preparation across the board'. It all came together for one reporter in a meal that began with precisely roasted scallops paired with a spicy, zestful and very finely diced ratatouille, followed by a rosette of venison 'marinated to far more purpose than usual', on a grated potato pancake with an accompanying sandwich of filo pastry enclosing half a roast peach. Huge plates set everything off to great visual advantage, which may also be the thinking behind modern mannerisms such as birds' nests of deep-fried vegetables, but it is the ability to extract every ounce of flavour from ingredients that excites. A fudge ice-cream 'was truly more fudge-tasting than actual fudge', and banana fritters were 'more intensely banana-tasting than any specimen of the fruit could be'. These were lightly battered, partnered with the fudge ice-cream, and served up with a wonderfully creamy rice pudding with a caramelised top.

Reporters would prefer their salads dressed and the bread improved, but they enjoy the nibbles, amuse-gueules, British cheeses, coffee and petits fours, and they welcome no domes, no smoking, the unsalted butter, the fact that vegetables are integral to the dish, and the unequivocal statement that tips are genuinely not expected. The owners keep a low profile but Christine Smedley is a consummate hostess when the occasion requires, and in any case the staff cope perfectly well.

The wine list is organised along classic lines with plenty of blue-blooded claret and burgundy, but also interest in other countries, albeit at a premium: three or four times the retail price in some cases. This disservice to drinkers has to be set against the excellent choice, and the generous selection of half-bottles. Four house wines are £14.50 (£3.75 per glass). CELLARMAN'S CHOICE: Penfolds Semillon/Chardonnay 1992, £18; Fixin 'Les Chenevières' 1988, Dom. Moncaut, £26.

CHEF: Mark Harrington   PROPRIETORS: Peter and Christine Smedley   OPEN: all week; 12.30 to 2, 7.30 to 9.30 (10 Fri and Sat)   MEALS: Set L £26, Set D £38   SERVICE: card slips closed CARDS: Access, Amex, Diners, Visa   DETAILS: 40 seats. 4 tables outside. Private parties: 8 main room, 24 private room. Car park. Vegetarian meals. No children under 7. Jacket and tie D. No smoking in dining-room. Wheelchair access (2 steps; also WC). No music   ACCOMMODATION: 21 rooms, all with bath/shower. TV. Phone. B&B £85 to £320. Babies by arrangement. Children over 7 welcome. Dogs welcome (not in public rooms). Afternoon teas. Garden. Tennis. Snooker. Doors close at midnight. Confirm by 6. Fax: (0761) 241377 (*The Which? Hotel Guide*)

STONHAM Suffolk   map 3

Mr Underhill's ▾ ✸

Stonham IP14 5DW
STOWMARKET (0449) 711206
on A140, 300 yards S of junction   COOKING 4
with A1120   COST £33–£46

The Bradleys are part of the great amateur movement that is at the heart of so much country cooking in Britain: amateur in the sense that they love food, and great because they steer a course between eager have-a-go types who fluff the basic skills, and the cynical professional chef who puts profit first. In Mr Underhill's we get a splendid amalgam of giftedness and enthusiasm. The house, on a main road near Stowmarket, is run with charm by Judy Bradley, and the pattern is a set no-choice menu, checked with each table first to make sure it suits. They did toy briefly with more choice, but customers didn't seem to want it – part of a relaxing evening, obviously, is not having to make any decisions – so the Bradleys are back on track with the original formula.

Handwritten customised menus detail the batting order, with choice of either cheese or dessert – or both for an extra £4.50. In practice, each table may be eating something different, so this is no soft option for the kitchen. Christopher Bradley looks to the Mediterranean, Provence in particular, in his lighter moments, as much for vegetables as anything. He is a great fan of peppers: roasted, dredged with olive oil, flavoured with thyme and basil, spiked with garlic and anchovy, and served up on grilled Tuscan bread: commonplace bruschetta, perhaps, but a well-flavoured, properly seasoned version that can still please enormously. Likewise, 'A taste of Provence' is no mere sop to Peter Mayle but a layered terrine of black olive pâté, tomato, thyme and creamed egg, dressed with lemon oil.

The repertoire runs to thick fillet of warm smoked salmon with, on one occasion, a light, creamy and chive-flecked sauce, and on another, basil and ginger vinegar. Centrepieces are cooked accurately and simply: rack of lamb consisting of 'four succulent, totally fatless, choice pieces on the bone, served slightly pink in a sauce with cream and the meat juices'. The Aga on which everything is cooked is particularly suitable for roasts, and for slow-cooked dishes such as lamb shank, served with leek polenta. Vegetables are likely to be spaghetti strings of courgette, pepper, celeriac – whatever is available – lightly buttered, as colourful as they are tasty. Among puddings, chocolate tart 'without pastry' and poached pear in a cream custard sauce have been enjoyed, as have the 'wonderful bite-sized' petits fours.

The enthusiasm that drives the kitchen also keeps the wine list bubbling along. Unfortunately for the average Underhill's customer, this will mean some decision-making, but the short 'special selection' reduces brainwork to a minimum. The list affords a reasonable balance between France and the rest of the world, and between penny-pinching and splashing-out prices. Over 30 half-bottles are welcome. House wine is £9.95 and wines by the glass change to suit the menu. CELLARMAN'S CHOICE: Selaks Sauvignon 1993, £14.95; Côtes Roannaises, Cuvée Vieilles Vignes 1992, Sérol, £13.95.

CHEF: Christopher Bradley   PROPRIETORS: Christopher and Judy Bradley   OPEN: Tue to Sat, D only, and Sun L (L Tue to Fri by arrangement); 12.30 to 1.45, 7.30 to 8.45   MEALS: Set L Sun £23, Set D £26.50   SERVICE: not inc   CARDS: Access, Diners, Visa   DETAILS: 24 seats. 6 tables outside. Private parties: 24 main room, 24 private room. Car park. Vegetarian meals with prior notice. Children's helpings with prior notice. Smart dress preferred. No smoking in dining-room. Wheelchair access. No music

---

STONOR Oxfordshire   map 2

▲ *Stonor Arms* ♥

Stonor RG9 6HE
TURVILLE HEATH (0491) 638345   COOKING 1*
on B480, 5m N of Henley-on-Thames   COST £23–£51

This bastion of gentility wears two hats. Blades restaurant, which now occupies two conservatories, works to a menu that straddles pork brawn with mustard dressing, chargrilled tuna with caper relish and pan-fried pigeon breasts with braised lentils. The Stonor Restaurant ('a haven of peace', according to one reporter) is akin to a private, country-house dining-room, with antique furniture, portraits and a display of dried hops in the fireplace. The short, fixed-price dinner menu offers dishes that are robustly rustic but also delicately flavoured. Portions are generous. Terrine of lambs' sweetbreads served with sweet-and-sour sauce and slivers of deep-fried vegetables, 'innovative' mussel and saffron soup, and thickly sliced duck with apple purée in wafers of mille-feuille have received endorsements. To finish, hot chocolate soufflé with white chocolate sorbet is well worth the advertised 20-minute wait. Service is correct, confident and knowledgeable. There is much to enjoy on the wine list under £20, and enough headroom for higher spenders (and concentration on Ch. Batailley and Olivier Leflaive for curiosity), but prices overall are not greedy, even for more mature vintages, and half-bottles are generous. CELLARMAN'S CHOICE: Chardonnay Special Reserve 1992, Vanel, £13.55; Côtes du Rhône, 1989, Dom. de Jas, £16.45.

CHEFS: Stephen Frost and Stuart Morrison   PROPRIETOR: Stonor Hotels Ltd   OPEN: Stonor Restaurant Mon to Sat, D only; Blades all week; 12 to 2, 7 to 9.30 (9 Sun)   MEALS: Blades alc (main courses £8 to £15). Stonor Restaurant Set D £29.50   SERVICE: not inc   CARDS: Access, Amex, Visa   DETAILS: Stonor Restaurant 14 seats, Blades 34 seats. 6 tables outside. Private parties: 24 main room, 12 private room. Car park. Vegetarian meals. Children's helpings. No babies D. Smart dress preferred. No cigars/pipes in dining-room. Wheelchair access (also WC). Music   ACCOMMODATION: 9 rooms, all with bath/shower. TV. Phone. B&B £82.50 to £137.50. Rooms for disabled. Children welcome. Baby facilities. Afternoon teas. Garden. Doors close at midnight. Fax: (0491) 638863 (*The Which? Hotel Guide*)

STORRINGTON West Sussex   map 3

▲ *Manleys* ♟

Manleys Hill, Storrington RH20 4BT   COOKING 3*
STORRINGTON (0903) 742331   COST £29–£40

The two brick and stone cottages, merged into a single building, feel lived-in and well looked after. A tucked-away bar, ample fireplace and white-walled dining-rooms speak of comfort rather than luxury. They are very much of a piece with the gentle maturity of the cooking, and of the owners, who take a reassuringly understated approach to the whole business.

The style is predominantly French, with bits of Austria bolted on, and looks deceptively unremarkable: saddle of lamb with a herb crust and ratatouille garnish, or pan-fried scallops with cream and braised leeks. Where are the flashy ingredients, the fashionable pairings, the dabs of Far Eastern spicing? Nowhere to be seen. 'Some may expect more show and élan,' notes an inspector, 'but what counts is the consistency of result achieved here.' It is sheer skill that impresses. An assembly of scallop and crab is wrapped in a tall parcel of sole and surrounded by a creamy chive sauce, the flavours clean, unassertive, natural. Breast of pheasant is combined with finely sliced cabbage, wrapped in paper-thin potato slices to keep it moist, and baked. Menu descriptions are accurate, so you know what to expect, and execution is spot-on. The lack of flamboyance points to integrity, and quiet confidence carries the day, even with humble profiteroles, filled with orange-flavoured cream and dribbled with a rich dark chocolate sauce.

Bread and canapés are up to scratch. Mrs Löderer, her daughter and other helpers are efficient, calm and friendly, and there is no sense of either rush or delay. There are domes to be lifted, and wine service tends to be formal, but none of it grates or intimidates. Wines are virtually all French, and Jaboulet's Rhônes might, in other circumstances, be referred to the Monopolies and Mergers Commission, but choice elsewhere includes a good selection of vintages. House wine starts at a fairly high £13.80. CELLARMAN'S CHOICE: St-Julien, Ch. St Pierre 1986, £26.50; Pinot Blanc Kabinett 1988, £15.50.

CHEF/PROPRIETOR: Karl Löderer   OPEN: Tue to Sun, exc Sun D; 12 to 2, 7 to 9.15 (10 Sat) CLOSED: first 2 weeks Jan   MEALS: Set L £18.60, Set D £28.50 (2 courses)   SERVICE: not inc CARDS: Access, Amex, Visa   DETAILS: 48 seats. Private parties: 36 main room, 22 private room. Car park. Vegetarian meals. Children's helpings. Smart dress preferred. No cigars/pipes in dining-room. Wheelchair access (also WC). No music   ACCOMMODATION: 1 apartment, with bath/shower. TV. Phone. B&B £50 to £75. Children welcome

Old Forge

Church Street, Storrington RH20 4LA   COOKING 1*
STORRINGTON (0903) 743402   COST £21–£38

In the oldest street in the village, this fifteenth-century building has its full cottage complement of low ceilings, beams and inglenooks. Regulars comment that the place is always 'generously graced' with flowers grown in Cathy Roberts' mother's garden. In all, it makes a homely setting for creative cooking and industrious domestic endeavour. Between them, the Roberts make everything from canapés and petits fours to ice-creams and sorbets. Menus change each month and the range extends to brochette of lambs' sweetbreads, mushroom and pepper, pan-fried scallops with warm marinated fennel and supreme of goose with pink grapefruit and green peppercorn sauce. A dish of boneless lamb cutlets with dried fruit and madeira followed by iced chocolate roulade glazed with crème de cacao sabayon made a splendid lunch for one reporter. Monthly gastronomic events are a special attraction. The wine list is an intelligent, global selection tilted towards the New World; the list of dessert wines is particularly enticing. House Californians are £8.50.

CHEF: Clive Roberts   PROPRIETORS: Cathy and Clive Roberts   OPEN: Tue to Sun, exc L Tue and Sat and Sun D; 12.15 to 1.30, 7.30 to 9   CLOSED: 1 week spring, 3 weeks autumn   MEALS: alc (main courses £10 to £13.50). Set L £12 (2 courses) to £14.50, Set D £16 (2 courses) to £20.50 SERVICE: not inc, card slips closed   CARDS: Access, Amex, Diners, Visa   DETAILS: 24 seats. Private parties: 14 main room. Vegetarian meals. Children's helpings. Smart dress preferred. No smoking while others eat. Music

---

STOW-ON-THE-WOLD Gloucestershire   map 2

▲ Wyck Hill House ⁑

Burford Road,
Stow-on-the-Wold GL54 1HY
COTSWOLD (0451) 831936   COOKING 2
on A424, 2m SE of Stow-on-the-Wold   COST £23–£60

'Everywhere there is a feeling of opulent splendour,' summed up one reporter lost in the maze of lounges, libraries and drawing-rooms. The place is a mass of ornate wood carving, oil paintings, huge silk-flower displays and pink and green furnishings. The dining-room overlooks an expanse of sweeping lawn. This is Cotswold 'virtual reality' at its most engaging.

The food is up to date without being too modish, and handles combinations well: crab and spring onion rösti with asparagus salad, fillet of veal with shallots and broad beans. Menus also offer the flexibility of plainly cooked dishes – fillet steak with béarnaise sauce, for example – or vegetarian dishes such as a warm feuilleté of asparagus, or tortellini of spinach and ricotta. A light *carte* at lunch extends the scope of the fixed-price menu with the likes of a toasted club sandwich or poached salmon salad. The kitchen's good intentions may, however, just miss the mark: potted shrimps and lobster with smoked butter, plus a small pile of salsa made from tomato, lime and avocado, didn't quite deliver at an inspection meal. But Ian Smith's skill produced, on the same occasion, three excellent fillets of John Dory on a bed of oyster mushrooms with a herb potato cake on creamed spinach. It may sound fussy, but tastes and textures are clear.

Vegetables such as deep-fried broccoli or cauliflower florets can seem rich, cheeses are good, and so is coffee. A savoury of smoked finnan haddock with parsley croûtons makes an unusual alternative to dessert. Prices are high, but lunch, 'including free chilled tap water, which is no longer common!' is considered good value. Although some of the French wines are less than exciting, claret is a strength, and the list has taken on a welcome international flavour with some New World additions. Mark-ups are still high. House wine is £11.95 (£2.95 for a large glass).

CHEF: Ian Smith   PROPRIETOR: Lyric Hotels   OPEN: all week; 12 to 2, 7.30 to 9.30   MEALS: alc (main courses £15.50 to £22). Set L £11.95   SERVICE: not inc   CARDS: Access, Amex, Diners, Visa   DETAILS: 70 seats. 5 tables outside. Private parties: 30 main room, 40 private room. Car park. Vegetarian meals. Children's helpings. Smart dress preferred. No smoking in dining-room. Wheelchair access (also WC). Music. Air-conditioned   ACCOMMODATION: 31 rooms, all with bath/shower. TV. Phone. B&B £78 to £140. Children welcome. Baby facilities. Pets welcome (not in public rooms). Afternoon teas. Garden. Fax: (0451) 832243

STRATFORD-UPON-AVON Warwickshire   map 2

Sir Toby's

8 Church Street,
Stratford-upon-Avon CV37 6HB   COOKING 1
STRATFORD-UPON-AVON (0789) 268822   COST £21–£36

Despite its limited opening times, this restaurant in a seventeenth-century malthouse is a godsend for hungry tourists and fans of the Bard. Pre-theatre meals kicking off at 5.30pm are one of its selling points. The décor is cottagey bistro, with bench seats, wooden tables and knick-knacks; the lack of background music is welcomed. Carl Watkins oversees proceedings, while Joanna cooks. A few rough edges have been detected, but the cooking is generally sound and reporters have praised many items from the varied menu. Vegetable pancakes with pistachio sauce, seafood casserole with home-made pasta, perfectly cooked sirloin steak with mustard hollandaise, and hot vegetable niçoise with saffron rice have all pleased. Desserts include first-rate home-made ice-creams and caramelised iced grapes with raspberries; otherwise there are a few savouries such as Scotch woodcock. The wine list is modest and a good showing of bottled beers provides back-up. House wine is £6.90.

CHEF: Joanna Watkins   PROPRIETORS: Carl and Joanna Watkins   OPEN: Wed to Sat, D only; 5.30 to 9.30   CLOSED: mid-May to mid-June   MEALS: alc (main courses £8.50 to £11) SERVICE: not inc, card slips closed   CARDS: Access, Amex, Visa   DETAILS: 36 seats. Private parties: 36 main room, 16 private room. Vegetarian meals. Children's helpings. Smart dress preferred. No pipes in dining-room. Wheelchair access (1 step). No music. Air-conditioned

---

Prices quoted in the Guide *are based on information supplied by restaurateurs. The prices quoted at the top of each entry represent a range, from the lowest meal price to the highest; the latter is inflated by 20 per cent to take account of likely price rises during the year of the* Guide.

STRETE Devon	map 1

Laughing Monk

Strete TQ6 0RN
STOKE FLEMING (0803) 770639
5m from Dartmouth on coast road   COOKING 1
to Kingsbridge   COST £22–£35

History and rustic trappings set the tone of this 'very pleasant' restaurant in a converted Victorian schoolhouse. David and Trudy Rothwell have turned the place into something of a local gastronomic centre, with special evenings and events staged throughout the year. Reporters approve of David's efforts in the kitchen: 'The food convinced us that real interest and care had been shown by the chef.' This was for a dinner that included baked avocado with bacon and hollandaise sauce, then fillet steak filled with mushrooms and bacon, followed by a 'particularly fine' summer pudding. The blackboard menu might also advertise herby pan-fried scallops with a timbale of rice, escalope of veal flamed with Marsala, and herb-crusted rack of lamb. The prospect of sampling several delights from the prodigious sweets trolley is much appreciated. Service is very helpful. A page of half-bottles augments the short, affordable list of European and New World wines. House wine is £7.50.

CHEF: David Rothwell   PROPRIETORS: David and Trudy Rothwell   OPEN: Tue to Sat (Sun and Mon bank hols), D only; 7 to 9.30   CLOSED: Tue Nov to Mar   MEALS: alc (main courses £9 to £13.50)   SERVICE: not inc, card slips closed   CARDS: Access, Visa   DETAILS: 50 seats. Private parties: 50 main room. Car park. Vegetarian meals with prior notice. Children's helpings. Smart dress preferred. No-smoking area. Wheelchair access (2 steps; also WC). Music

STROUD Gloucestershire	map 2

Oakes

169 Slad Road, Stroud GL5 1RG
STROUD (0453) 759950   COOKING 3
on B4070, ½m NE of Stroud   COST £31–£56

The residential location is not special, but the building itself is solid, with thick stone walls and 'the air of a medieval retreat, thanks to an octagonal adjoining tower, and pointed arches and windows'. Pink and green suffuse the linked dining-rooms, floors are highly polished, and the new small bar has been welcomed because it 'makes the old schoolhouse seem warmer'. There have been changes and the fixed-price meals have gone, replaced by a wider *carte* of eight choices per course. But support continues to flow in: 'Christopher Oakes is one of the most talented chefs in the UK, meticulous in preparation, imaginative in composition, with a flair that shows' was one comment. Reporters have enjoyed chilled gazpacho, lean breast of duck with crisp skin, sauté calves' kidneys, and all manner of sausages from venison to lamb and rosemary, to wild boar served with lentils and a rich gravy. This robustness is matched by the lightness and freshness of steamed red mullet or fillet of brill. Varied cooking methods keep interest high and balance the menus. Puddings, too, come in for praise, among them hot hazelnut soufflé, sticky toffee pudding with vanilla sauce, and a bread-and-butter pudding that is 'the best in the west'.

More than one reporter, however, has registered a sense of disappointment that the food did not live up to expectation, that it pleases but does not excite, and is occasionally subject to error. 'Dull,' summed up a senior inspector after a meal of crab ravioli, boned stuffed quail, and a blackcurrant and mint pie that 'most housewives could have improved upon'. Christopher Oakes maintains that his food 'is meant to be enjoyed, not put under a microscope', and he has a point. The important thing about Oakes is that enough reporters enjoy themselves to recommend it enthusiastically. Enjoyment is paramount, in this case helped even more by Caroline Oakes, whose attentions are universally approved, as well as by a neat wine list that packs in diversity, quality, sensible prices and a generous run of half-bottles. Five or six 'everyday' wines are normally available for less than £11.50, or around £2 per glass.

CHEF: Christopher Oakes   PROPRIETORS: Christopher and Caroline Oakes   OPEN: Tue to Sun, exc Sun D; 12.30 to 1.45, 7.30 to 9.30   MEALS: alc (main courses £11 to £19)   SERVICE: not inc, card slips closed   CARDS: Access, Amex, Visa   DETAILS: 34 seats. Private parties: 34 main room. Car park. Vegetarian meals. Children's helpings. Smart dress preferred. Wheelchair access. No music. Fax: (0453) 766441

STUCKTON Hampshire   map 2

Three Lions 🍸

Stuckton Road, Stuckton SP6 2HF
FORDINGBRIDGE (0425) 652489   COOKING 2
1m off A338 at Fordingbridge   COST £24–£49

This red-brick ivy-clad building used to be a pub, and still feels like it, which can confuse reporters. 'Is it,' one wonders, 'an informal restaurant serving reasonable food in pub-like surroundings?' – in which case the prices seem rather high. Or is it 'a serious restaurant with serious prices?' – in which case the food and service don't quite correspond. Among the beer mats and ash trays are close-packed pine tables, cushioned chairs and sturdy wine glasses. As you would in a pub, the best way to begin is by going to the bar and ordering a drink.

The menu is two large blackboards placed on easels in the dining-room announcing duck and beetroot soup, Cheddar cheese soufflé, and other items in a varied repertoire that takes in wiener schnitzel and Thai green curry, as well as chocolate marquise, apfelstrudel, and bread-and-butter pudding with sultanas soaked in brandy. Karl Wadsack makes use of the location on the edge of the New Forest for game and mushrooms, gets his vegetables from local farmers and buys fish from several spots along the south coast. Cooking can upon occasion be approximate, which makes simple Abbotsbury oysters, home-smoked salmon, or wing of skate with black butter good bets; more ambitious treatments include steamed whole sea bass Chinese-style, or fillets of grouper with oriental herbs.

The wine list is one of the few to give Germany a convincing showing and, because they are not flavour of the month, there are some reasonably priced mature wines. But sympathetic pricing is a feature of the list, which is largely French with good dessert wines and an impressive New World section – Australians are particularly extensive. There are no house wines, but 10 or 20 are normally available by the glass at any one time. CELLARMAN'S CHOICE: Hunter Valley Chardonnay 1991, Evans Family, £17.50; Herlstone Vineyard Shiraz 1992, £13.75.

CHEF: Karl Wadsack   PROPRIETORS: Karl and June Wadsack   OPEN: Tue to Sun, exc Sun D; 12.15 to 1.30, 7.15 to 9 (9.30 Sat)   CLOSED: 25 Dec to 3 Jan, Feb, 2 weeks July to Aug (phone to check)   MEALS: alc (main courses £7 to £15)   SERVICE: not inc   CARDS: Access, Visa   DETAILS: 55 seats. Private parties: 50 main room. Car park. Vegetarian meals with prior notice. No children under 14. Smart dress preferred. Wheelchair access (1 step; also men's WC). No music. Air-conditioned. Fax: (0425) 656144

STURMINSTER NEWTON Dorset   map 2

▲ *Plumber Manor*

Hazelbury Bryan Road,
Sturminster Newton DT10 2AF
STURMINISTER NEWTON (0258) 472507
A357 to Sturminster Newton, take first left   COOKING 1
to Hazelbury Bryan, on left-hand side after 2m   COST £23–£36

This has been the Prideaux-Brunes' home since the early seventeenth century. Ancestral portraits look down from the upstairs gallery, and the family dogs have the run of the lounges. Conversion of barns and courtyard in recent years has not diminished the country feel, at its height when sporting types flock in to hack or hunt. Space is at a premium and, despite all the activity, the place can lack atmosphere outside the main dining-room. Two parallel menus are offered at dinner, only £5 apart, with an extra fish course that is well worth taking. Pork with cider and apple, or duck with apricot sauce, is the stuff of main courses, but fish has received most praise: light warm crab mousseline in a creamy sauce, langoustine and white fish lasagne, and John Dory with a delicate Pernod sauce. Puddings of mille-feuille, pavlova and roulade are from the trolley. Wines are mostly classic French, with most of the interest over £20; there is a good selection of half-bottles, and a scattering of mature vintages. House wine is £10 (£2 per glass).

CHEF: Brian Prideaux-Brune   PROPRIETOR: Richard Prideaux-Brune   OPEN: Mon to Sun, D only, and Sun L; 12.30 to 1.45, 7.30 to 9.30   CLOSED: Feb   MEALS: Set L £17.50, Set D £20 to £25   SERVICE: net prices, card slips closed   CARDS: Access, Amex, Diners, Visa   DETAILS: 65 seats. Private parties: 52 main room, 12 and 24 private rooms. Car park. Vegetarian meals. Children's helpings on request. Wheelchair access (also WC). No music   ACCOMMODATION: 16 rooms, all with bath/shower. TV. Phone. B&B £65 to £115. Rooms for disabled. Children by arrangement. Pets by arrangement. Garden. Tennis. Fax: (0258) 473370 (*The Which? Hotel Guide*)

CELLARMAN'S CHOICE: *Wines recommended by the restaurateur, normally more expensive than house wine.*

Restaurateurs justifiably resent no-shows. If you quote a credit card number when booking, you may be liable for the restaurant's lost profit margin if you don't turn up. Always phone to cancel.

SUDBURY Suffolk map 3

Mabey's Brasserie ✱

47 Gainsborough Street,
Sudbury CO10 7SS
SUDBURY (0787) 374298   COOKING 2
next to Gainsborough House Museum   COST £21–£35

Robert Mabey dreamed up an idea and put it into practice: keep prices down, work to a seasonal menu and bring the cooking out into the open. Foodie watercolours adorn the walls of his brasserie, paper napkins deck the tables, and church pews sit in partitioned alcoves. Dishes are prepared behind a high counter at the back of the main room. The blackboard lists an assortment of modern British dishes ingeniously chalked up in different colours (blue for fish, green for vegetarian, white for extras such as garlic bread and vegetables, and so on). Steamed fillet of salmon in a green jacket with nori sauce and stuffed aubergine with coriander crust show the intentions of the kitchen. Fine sauces and powerful, well-balanced flavours are the key – as in calf's liver with Dubonnet and orange sauce ('a masterpiece') and grilled smoked duck breast on a bed of onions with a tart reduction of red wine. Superb home-made ice-creams may share the plate with warm almond tart or pancakes with maple syrup. Service is prompt and helpful. The fairly priced wine list from Lay & Wheeler has a strong antipodean backbone and plenty of halves. House wine is £6.95.

CHEF: Danny McClelland   PROPRIETORS: Robert and Johanna Mabey   OPEN: Tue to Sat; 12 to 2, 7 to 10 (late orders Sat D for large groups)   MEALS: alc (main courses £7.50 to £11.50) SERVICE: not inc   CARDS: Access, Amex, Visa   DETAILS: 60 seats. Private parties: 35 main room, 20 private room. Vegetarian meals. Children's helpings. No smoking in main dining-room. Wheelchair access (2 steps). No music. Air-conditioned

---

SURBITON Surrey map 3

Chez Max

85 Maple Road, Surbiton KT6 4AW   COOKING 2
081-399 2365   COST £28–£40

The aim is 'to serve the locality', say the Markarians, whose restaurant is more sophisticated than you might imagine from the unpromising suburban location. A French pine dresser is stacked with plates, glasses and bread, tables are comfortably arranged, plants trail from the ceiling, while flowers on the tables are made of pink silk. Fish accounts for more than half the main courses on the *carte*, which incidentally is laid out perfectly for French visitors, but confusingly for those in the locality whose first language is English. Although the fish itself is good, the cooking of it is 'a bit messed about', according to one reporter, and meat dishes are generally superior.

Some things hardly change, a result of Max Markarian having established his own style (by adapting generally Continental dishes) over the decade or so he has been cooking here. But there is a lightness to the saucing which shows that time has not exactly stood still, while portions are extremely generous. A neat parcel of crisp filo pastry is 'absolutely packed with masses of spicy duck' and comes with a sweet apricot sauce. Roast English rack of lamb is 'six rosy-pink chops, easily enough for two, of well-flavoured, firm sweet meat, the cooking precise, uncluttered'. Puddings are less distinguished, prices are fair, and Mrs Markarian is very helpful indeed; she knows the menu and wine list inside out, and has a keen sense of humour. The French wine list is long on claret, short on detail and half-bottles, and balanced in favour of those who like to spend over £20 on a bottle. House wine is £12.50.

CHEF: Max Markarian   PROPRIETORS: Max and Margaret Markarian   OPEN: Tue to Sat, exc Sat L; 12.30 to 2, 7.30 to 10   CLOSED: 24 to 30 Dec   MEALS: alc (main courses £9.50 to £14). Set L £15.95 (2 courses), Set D Tue to Fri £12.95, Sat £14.95   SERVICE: 10%, card slips closed CARDS: Access, Amex, Diners, Visa   DETAILS: 50 seats. Private parties: 50 main room. Vegetarian meals with prior notice. Children's helpings. No children under 4. Smart dress preferred. No pipes in dining-room. Wheelchair access. Music. Air-conditioned

---

SUTTON COURTENAY Oxfordshire   map 2

Fish at Sutton Courtenay ✷

Appleford Road,
Sutton Courtenay OX14 4NQ   COOKING 2
ABINGDON (0235) 848242   COST £29–£47

It is as well to be aware of the set-up here. The Fish still operates as a pub for those who just want a pint, and the dining-room is not run along formal restaurant lines by any means. On entering, choose your food from a blackboard in the reception area; if you can't remember what the puddings were, you'll have to get up and have another look. One couple regretted the drab brownness of the room, and found themselves the victims of scything draughts on a chill February evening, but still wrote to praise the food.

Fish is not the only business of the menu, although it is the main feature – brave for such a landlocked location. Black bream on saffron tagliatelle with scallops was judged 'excellent' for the quality of ingredients and timing, and the fresh crab served whole with a mayonnaise that variously contains either sherry or brandy usually elicits praise. Foie gras may crop up in a first-course salad of warm boudin blanc and potato, or cooked with beef fillet for one of the richer main courses. Toffee soufflé with banana ice-cream, terrine of strawberries, and lemon tart with speckled vanilla custard have received endorsements for pudding. If things are not quite right once in a while, it may be that vegetables are thought 'pointless' and unrelated to the main dish, or that service is a touch too perfunctory for comfort, so that the platter of British farmhouse cheeses is set down without identification. The wine list has one or two good names, and also a clutch of négoçiant burgundies and a few ambitious prices. House wines are £8.95.

CHEFS: Bruce Buchan and Jason Fretwell   PROPRIETORS: Bruce and Kay Buchan   OPEN: all week; 12 to 2.15, 7 to 9.30 (10 Fri and Sat)   CLOSED: 4 days between Christmas and New Year MEALS: alc (main courses £11 to £16)   SERVICE: not inc, card slips closed   CARDS: Access, Amex, Diners, Visa   DETAILS: 50 seats. Private parties: 30 main room, 20 and 35 private rooms. Car park. Vegetarian meals. Children's helpings. Smart dress preferred. No smoking in 1 dining-room. Wheelchair access (1 step; also WC). Music. Fax: (0235) 848242

SWAFFHAM Norfolk map 6

▲ Stratton House ⁵⁄⁷ NEW ENTRY

4 Ash Close, Swaffham PE37 7NH COOKING 2
SWAFFHAM (0760) 723845 COST £30–£37

Behind the shop-fronts at the north end of Swaffham's attractive Market Square is this Queen Anne hotel. Anyone who did not already know that the young owners have a background in the arts might guess from the pleated lampshades, swagged curtains and magazine-strewn sitting-room. The wealth of detail builds to give a striking sense of identity. Residents ('I don't think we have ever stayed anywhere so relaxing') get first priority for tables, so there can be long waiting lists for non-residents, especially at weekends.

There is a commitment to local produce: 'We are considered a little eccentric in that we personally shop and pick every day all the produce we prepare,' write the Scotts. The tilt of the set menu, with three or four choices per course, is towards 'sensible' dishes of Jerusalem artichoke soup with herb croûtons, correctly cooked halibut fillet with a butter and chive sauce, and 'brilliant' burnt cream with alpine strawberries and crème fraîche. This is fine domestic cooking writ large. Even when they sound elaborate, flavours and textures all work. The savouriness of soft baked pear and Cashel Blue cheese inside crispy flaky pastry contrasts well with a sweet-and-sour honey dressing. 'Fabulous' Cashel Blue also appears on the seriously good British cheeseboard. The wine list, as much an artistic achievement as a vinous one, offers commendably low prices. Eight wines by the glass begin at £1.95.

CHEF: Vanessa Scott PROPRIETORS: Les and Vanessa Scott OPEN: all week, D only; 7 to 10 CLOSED: 24 to 26 Dec MEALS: Set D £22.50 SERVICE: not inc, card slips closed CARDS: Access, Amex, Visa DETAILS: 20 seats. 2 tables outside. Private parties: 18 main room, 60 private room. Car park. Vegetarian meals. Children's helpings from 5pm. No smoking in dining-room. Music. Air-conditioned ACCOMMODATION: 7 rooms, all with bath/shower. TV. Phone. B&B £55 to £85. Deposit: £20. Children welcome. Baby facilities. Pets welcome. Afternoon teas. Garden. Confirm by noon. Fax: (0760) 720458 (*The Which? Hotel Guide*)

SWANAGE Dorset map 2

Galley

9 High Street, Swanage BH19 2LN COOKING 1
SWANAGE (0929) 427299 COST £22–£30

The setting is a corner site close to the pier and the sea-front, with frou-frou curtains at the windows and a blue ceiling hung with nets. Nick Storer cooks, Mick procures the fish. The fixed-price dinner menu in their bustling seasonal restaurant steers clear of wayward ideas, but offers plenty of variety in dishes such as red mullet fillets with tomato and basil sauce, and roast best end of lamb fillet with whole garlic and madeira sauce. The quality of the ingredients shows in excellent mussels, locally smoked salmon and in specials of mackerel fillets sauté in calvados. The owners recommend that visitors try lightly cooked slices of young venison liver when it is available. To finish, old-style pavlova is given a lift with a sharp apricot coulis; otherwise go for the locally made ice-cream.

The short wine list favours whites and has an interesting New World selection. House wine is £9.50.

CHEF: Nick Storer PROPRIETORS: N.D. and M.G. Storer OPEN: all week, D only; 6.45 to 9.30 (10 Sat) CLOSED: 1 Jan to Easter (exc some weekends – telephone to check) MEALS: Set D £14.50 SERVICE: not inc, card slips closed CARDS: Access, Amex, Diners, Visa DETAILS: 36 seats. Private parties: 36 main room. Vegetarian meals. Children welcome. Music. Air-conditioned

---

TADWORTH Surrey   map 3

Gemini

28 Station Approach Road,
Tadworth KT20 5AH   COOKING 2
TADWORTH (0737) 812179   COST £18–£34

'It has the air of a Tudor tea-room, circa 1930s, with French prints and a slightly wilting yucca plant, and serves generous quantities of extremely well-cooked food,' writes a regular reporter. 'It is excellent value for this part of yuppie Surrey,' adds another enthusiast.

Robert Foster describes his cooking as 'neo-classical French', which is to say it rests on sound technique and revolves around largely familiar themes – calf's liver with sage, duck with orange sauce – without going in for baroque embellishments. Yet it retains the freedom to play with anything from pasta (home-made fettuccine, with chunks of salmon, generous mushrooms and plenty of sauce) to lime leaves, which perk up the mussels in white wine and cream. Fish is widely praised, from 'delightful and plentiful' fillets of red snapper in white wine sauce, to a first-course brochette of salmon, scallops and mackerel served with fresh pasta and tomato chutney. This is, simply, a French-trained cook enjoying himself.

Alcohol, a classic French kitchen standby, is used with moderation. Vegetables are properly cooked, and desserts are good, from warm orange sponge to crème brûlée with sultanas and rum, although the highlight is a milk chocolate parfait with white and dark chocolate sauces. Home-made bread is scoffed with enthusiasm. An intelligent, and not exclusively French, wine list backs up the food, majoring on ripe, rich and fruity styles. Six house wines are well chosen, and start at £8.

CHEF/PROPRIETOR: Robert Foster OPEN: Tue to Sun, exc Sat L and Sun D; 12 to 2, 7 to 9.30 CLOSED: 2 weeks June, 1 week Christmas MEALS: Set L £10.50 (2 courses) to £12.50, Set L Sun £14.50, Set D £17.50 (2 courses, Tue to Thur) to £21.50 SERVICE: not inc, card slips closed CARDS: Access, Visa DETAILS: 40 seats. Private parties: 38 main room. Vegetarian meals. Children's helpings L. No children under 10. Smart dress preferred. No cigars/pipes in dining-room. Wheelchair access (1 step; also WC). Music

---

Card slips closed *in the details at the end of an entry indicates that the total on the slips of credit cards is closed when handed over for signature.*

If a restaurant is new to the Guide *this year (did not appear as a main entry in the last edition),* NEW ENTRY *appears opposite its name.*

TAPLOW Berkshire	map 3

▲ *Cliveden House, Waldo's* ♥ ⁵⃰✳   NEW ENTRY

Taplow SL6 0JF
MAIDENHEAD (0628) 668561   COOKING 3*
on B476, 2m N of Taplow   COST £53–£90

They don't come much grander than this. The mansion, reconstructed during the nineteenth century by Houses of Parliament architect Sir Charles Barry, and set in 376 acres of National Trust gardens and parkland, has been home to various dukes as well as the famous Astors, and has seen all sorts of guests come and go, including Kipling, Bernard Shaw, Lawrence of Arabia and Charlie Chaplin. After negotiating the Berkshire lanes just north of Taplow, enter the main gates opposite the Feathers Inn and drive (or get your chauffeur to do it for you) past the Fountain of Love, designed by Thomas Waldo Story, and up the gravel. Staff come out to open doors and escort you past suits of armour and a fireplace as big as the Ritz. Cliveden is the sort of place where you can lose a grand piano in the entrance hall. All right then, you find it.

Ron Maxfield oversees two restaurants, although we have no reports on the Terrace and so cannot comment on its quality, other than to say it is a magnificent dining-room, and serves rather simpler food. Waldo's, in the basement, is the showcase. Here, drinks, nibbles and (to those not already wearing them) ties, are dispensed in the bar. Wood panelling and books abound, as do flash ingredients on a menu that includes pasta parcels with ceps in an armagnac sauce with fresh truffles, and saffron and langoustine risotto with more fresh truffles. If these items are meant to persuade us that high prices are justified, then there is a strong argument for doing away with some of them and bringing down the price of a meal by £10. Fresh morels and ceps, however, impress mightily in a dish of guinea-fowl – the fat breast cooked pink and sliced, the boned thigh cooked through, and the lower leg served with a piece of bitter burnt-to-a-frazzle skin.

Despite expensive ingredients, the food avoids the bland safety that afflicts many grand hotels on the international circuit. It has a classic quality about it, and draws inspiration from Italy as much as France, does not follow fashion as far east as many now do, and yet tosses in an occasional quirk such as couscous – flavoured with pimento, coriander and lemon to partner steamed fillet of sea bass. The cooking has ambition, and skill is not lacking. Mirabelle soufflé was served perfectly risen in a copper pan, although alcohol (rather than fruit) dominated the flavour, and the two scoops of glorious liquorice ice-cream that were propped against the side of the hot pan soon reverted to cream all over the doily. Service is formal and polite. 'I might have been an exhibit in Madame Tussaud's for all the personal interaction I had with the waiters.' Bread at an inspection meal was 'very poor'; wines, however, are very good. Mark-ups are variable but don't allow much to squeeze in under £20, except half-bottles, of which there is a fair selection. House wine is £15 (£4 per glass). CELLARMAN'S CHOICE: Mâcon Blanc 'La Roche Vineuse' 1992, Merlin, £21; Santa Maria Valley Syrah 1992, Qupé, £27.

▮ *denotes an outstanding wine cellar;* ♥ *denotes a good wine list, worth travelling for.*

CHEF: Ron Maxfield   PROPRIETOR: Cliveden Hotel Ltd   OPEN: Tue to Sat, D only; 7 to 10
MEALS: Set D £40 to £60   SERVICE: not inc, card slips closed   CARDS: Access, Amex, Diners,
Visa   DETAILS: 26 seats. Car park. Vegetarian meals. Children welcome. Jacket and tie.
No smoking in dining-room. Wheelchair access (also WC). Music. Air-conditioned
ACCOMMODATION: 37 rooms, all with bath/shower. TV. Phone. 6 rooms: air-conditioned. Room
only £195 to £620. Rooms for disabled. Children welcome. Pets welcome. Garden. Swimming-
pool. Sauna. Tennis. Fishing. Snooker. Fax: (0628) 661837

TAUNTON Somerset   map 2

Capriccio ⅙✳ £

| 41 Bridge Street, Taunton TA1 1TP | COOKING 1 |
| TAUNTON (0823) 335711 | COST £16–£30 |

Floor tiles from Florence and plates and glasses from Milan help to give Andrea
and Kathy Zunino's cosy restaurant a genuine Italian feel. Andrea changes his
menu every six weeks and his cooking is a notch above trattoria basic. Boneless
chicken with fennel, artichokes and white wine, and venison chop with port
wine sauce are typical specialities; pasta and ice-creams are made on the
premises. Otherwise you might find vegetable terrine with capsicum sauce,
fegato veneziana, steak with dolcelatte sauce, or escalopes of veal with white
wine and capers. The two-page wine list is peppered with well-known Italian
names; prices are mostly below £10. House wine is £6.80 a litre.

CHEF: Andrea Zunino   PROPRIETORS: Andrea and Kathy Zunino   OPEN: Mon to Sat, D only; 7 to
10 (10.30 Sat and post-theatre by arrangement)   CLOSED: Christmas to mid-Jan, bank hols
MEALS: alc (main courses £5.50 to £11). Set D £9.95 to £12.95 (2 courses)   SERVICE: not inc
CARDS: Access, Visa   DETAILS: 48 seats. Private parties: 14 main room. Vegetarian meals.
Children's helpings. Smart dress preferred. No smoking in 1 dining-room. Wheelchair access (1
step). Music

▲ Castle Hotel ♥

| Castle Green, Taunton TA1 1NF | COOKING 4 |
| TAUNTON (0823) 272671 | COST £25–£60 |

History does not weigh heavily here, although the site was once a Norman
fortress. The Castle is an imposing, wistaria-clad city-centre hotel with a degree
of luxury that does not overpower. It pleased one couple for 'excellence at every
level. We shall go again, and again, and again.' The dining-room may be
somewhat lacking in character, which the 'pretty' paintings do little to improve,
but 'for sheer enjoyment and lifting of the spirits this was as good as many of the
country's best restaurants, and a lot cheaper'. A party of five, staying over five
days, found 'not a single unsatisfactory dish'.

Phil Vickery's gift is to make the food endlessly interesting but not
overwhelming. Salmon, quickly seared and full of natural taste, might appear on
top of crisp rösti potatoes, and black bream, spicily soused, on a bed of
home-made pasta surrounded by crisp deep-fried parsley sprigs. Laying fish and
meat on a bed of something and building towers are favourite devices. Braised
spinach underneath a layer of dauphinois potatoes provided the foundation for a

thick tournedos, rare and tender, crowned with deep-fried celeriac 'and the biggest diced truffles I have ever seen'.

Although the Castle retains some of the revivalist Englishness that is Gary Rhodes' legacy here, it is not a mere footstep follower. Vickery is very much his own man, and his invention blows a breeze of freshness and lightness through the repertoire. Puddings, such as apple and ginger crumble, and nutmeg ice-cream, might emphasise the basic 'Englishness' of the spicing, but, given steamed lobster sausage with couscous and lobster and caviare dressing, or steamed sea bass with saffron-creamed potatoes and roast garlic, the cooking is by no means closed to other influences.

Dishes can be visually stunning, soups are excellent, vegetables tasty, and the less expensive menus at both lunch and dinner are considered bargains. Bread includes white caraway rolls, high-rise granary, and moist bacon and onion. Service is kindness itself and benefits from teamwork. The wine list abstracts a helpful short version that covers a multitude of styles, and offers half a dozen house wines by the glass. These are backed up by a prodigious number of bottles, predominantly French, largely from good properties and producers, with some mature vintages where appropriate. Mark-ups are about average. Some countries have only a token presence – Italy fields fewer wines than either South Africa or Somerset – which leaves it a bit short on excitement, and quite a few vintages are split, but the choice is large enough and the quality sound.

CHEF: Phil Vickery PROPRIETORS: the Chapman family OPEN: all week; 12.30 to 2, 7.30 to 9 MEALS: Set L £14.50 (2 courses) to £29.90, Set L Sun £14.90, Set D £18.90 to £29.90 SERVICE: not inc, card slips closed CARDS: Access, Amex, Diners, Visa DETAILS: 65 seats. Private parties: 110 main room, 50 and 110 private rooms. Car park. Vegetarian meals. Children's helpings. Smart dress preferred. Wheelchair access (1 step; also WC). No music ACCOMMODATION: 35 rooms, all with bath/shower. TV. Phone. B&B £65 to £150. Rooms for disabled. Lift. Children welcome. Baby facilities. Dogs welcome (bedrooms only). Garden. Doors close at 11.30. Confirm by 3. Fax: (0823) 336066 (*The Which? Hotel Guide*)

TAVISTOCK Devon   map 1

▲ Horn of Plenty ⅝✴

Gulworthy, Tavistock PL19 8JD
TAVISTOCK (0822) 832528
3m W of Tavistock on A390, turn right   COOKING 3
at Gulworthy Cross   COST £36–£56

The Horn describes itself as a restaurant-with-rooms, and both restaurant and rooms make the most of views across the Tamar Valley. A couple who spent a week here 'really appreciated the well-kept garden and friendly gardener, and sitting outside for drinks and exquisite bits and pieces before dinner'. The fixed-price menu is a popular format, and although there are supplements for terrine of foie gras, or beef fillet with bone marrow and wild mushrooms, these are the exception. Ian Gatehouse reports that the less expensive Pot Luck menu of three courses has livened up otherwise dreary Monday evenings.

The kitchen borrows from around the world, serving up tempura fried sole with a Thai sauce, or sea bass with a sweet-and-sour sauce. Most of the borrowings err on the delicate side, adding texture (pearl barley with chicken breast) or a single spike of flavour (fresh ginger to a nage of shellfish). There is happily no attempt to beat the main ingredient into submission. The gist is 'really good local ingredients cooked in an uncluttered way'. And if the Thai sauce does the rounds, ending up with pan-fried pork on another menu, then nobody is complaining. Well, hardly anybody. 'Is cheffie on commission with Jaffa?' wondered one diner, after breast of duck in orange sauce, orange and mint crème brûlées, and vanilla bavarois with orange sauce. But that couple who spent a week here never ate the same dish twice.

Service is generally good-natured, and the majority of reports speak of its warmth. 'We were welcomed in the car park with an umbrella,' noted one diner. We presume it must have been raining. 'What a joy to see such an interesting variety on the wine list,' remarked another reporter. The list now includes skeletal notes for mid-priced wines and below. Commendable house wines start at £2.30 a glass, £10.50 a bottle.

CHEFS: Peter Gorton and Kevin Bingham PROPRIETORS: Elaine and Ian Gatehouse OPEN: all week, exc Mon L; 12.30 to 2, 7.15 to 9.15 CLOSED: 24 to 26 Dec MEALS: Set L £17.50 to £25.50, Set D £25.50 to £30.50 SERVICE: not inc CARDS: Access, Amex, Visa DETAILS: 50 seats. 6 tables outside. Private parties: 50 main room, 12 private room. Car park. Vegetarian meals. No children under 13. Smart dress preferred. No smoking in dining-room. Wheelchair access (also WC). No music ACCOMMODATION: 7 rooms, 5 with bath/shower. TV. Phone. B&B £58 to £98. Deposit: 20%. Rooms for disabled. No children under 13. Pets welcome (not in public rooms). Garden. Doors close at midnight. Confirm by 6. Fax: (0822) 832528 (*The Which? Hotel Guide*)

Neil's ✷

27 King Street, Tavistock PL19 0DT   COOKING 2
TAVISTOCK (0822) 615550   COST £24–£40

'It is big on service, value and style,' writes one. 'The only thing small about this restaurant is the size.' Others call it 'cosy'. The stone walls and oak beams are sixteenth-century, while the cooking is French, moulded to Janet Neil's tastes. Swiss cheese soufflé tart appeared on a spring menu, followed by roast rack of lamb with rosemary, garlic and redcurrant sauce, with baked orange pudding to finish. 'I can cook food simply, without a lot of back-up, or cover-up,' claims Janet Neil, and this shows in a welcome directness to the food.

Striking flavours are found in dishes such as potted duck on a rich buttery sauté brioche paired with spicy preserved kumquats. At other times goose might get the same treatment, but with apple and sage compote for contrast. Favoured devices including tarts, filo pastry or bruschetta are used interchangeably throughout the year to carry flavours of cheese, mushroom, Mediterranean vegetables or fish. There is some richness from cream and alcohol in sauces but this is balanced by a lighter approach to fish. Salmon comes with lemon aïoli, while fillet of bream is marinated in lemon, thyme, coriander and olive oil. Service is personal and warm. Three dozen wines are sensibly chosen both inside and outside France, briefly annotated and commendably priced. House vins de pays are £9.75, or £1.95 per glass.

CHEF/PROPRIETOR: Janet Neil OPEN: Tue to Sat, D only; 7 to 9.30 MEALS: alc (main courses £12 to £14.50). Set D £16 SERVICE: not inc CARDS: Access, Amex, Visa DETAILS: 20 seats. Private parties: 22 main room. Vegetarian meals. Children welcome. Smart dress preferred. No smoking in dining-room. No music

TEFFONT EVIAS Wiltshire   map 2

▲ Howard's House Hotel ⚡✗

Teffont Evias SP3 5RJ
TEFFONT (0722) 716392   COOKING 2*
off B3089, W of Dinton, signed Chicksgrove   COST £23–£48

The aim for tranquillity is such that Howard's House has no truck with the splash
of swimming-pool, the plonk of tennis balls or the creak of exercise machines,
although it does cater for players of that most violent and ferocious game,
croquet. Set in two acres of gardens in a picturesque Wiltshire village, the house
has been in the same family for over three centuries, and the sitting-room retains
an original fireplace. There is pre-dinner seating for 24, on comfortable sofas and
assorted chairs, while in the dining-room gleaming glass, candles, white linen
and well-spaced tables confirm the luxury.

The food is light, not stodgy. 'You come away feeling filled but not stuffed!'
was how one reporter put it. Dishes are a savvy compilation of items with a
contemporary ring – steamed fillet of whiting with spinach and ricotta ravioli in
a Noilly Prat sauce, for example – which excite interest without stretching
credulity. The five or six choices per course might also include 'fabulous' turbot
dressed in olive oil and sherry vinegar, rather ordinary pan-fried scallops around
a 'niçoise vinaigrette', and upside-down banana and butterscotch pudding with
vanilla ice-cream. 'Excellent' pigeon breasts, and rare saddle of venison served
with prunes in a flavourful sauce, reinforce the confidence with game. Good
vegetables, nibbles before, and coffee and chocolate truffles after, contribute to
the value. Some consider £29.50 for two courses a bit on the steep side, although
there are no hidden extras. Wines are predominantly French, many well chosen –
clarets offer more interest than burgundy – and plenty of bottles are under £20,
including a handful of house wines from £9.75.

CHEFS: Paul Firmin and Michael Fox   PROPRIETORS: Paul Firmin, Jonathan Ford and George
Ford   OPEN: all week, D only, and Sun L; 12 to 2.30, 7 to 10   MEALS: Set L Sun £17.50, Set D
£29.50 (2 courses) to £32.50   SERVICE: net prices, card slips closed   CARDS: Access, Amex,
Diners, Visa   DETAILS: 34 seats. Private parties: 40 main room. Car park. Vegetarian meals with
prior notice. Children's helpings. No smoking in dining-room. Wheelchair access (also men's
WC). Music   ACCOMMODATION: 9 rooms, all with bath/shower. TV. Phone. B&B £87.50 to
£107.50. Children welcome. Pets welcome. Garden. Doors close at 11. Fax: (0722) 716820 (The
Which? Hotel Guide)

TETBURY Gloucestershire   map 2

▲ Calcot Manor ♥ ⚡✗

nr Tetbury GL8 8YJ
TETBURY (0666) 890391   COOKING 2
on A4135, 3½m W of Tetbury   COST £23–£45

Every effort is made at this seventeenth-century farmhouse to ensure that time's
onward march is arrested in a Cotswold idyll of hill and hedgerow, arboretum
and wildfowl trust. In March 1994, Alec Howard (formerly of Sonny's in
London, see entry) was installed in the kitchen with a mission to introduce a
lighter note into the food. First reports suggest that things are generally on target,

and that greater simplicity than has hitherto been the case at Calcot is now on offer. A fixed-price Sunday lunch menu remains, but dinner is now à la carte. A seam of hearty tradition is mined in double-baked goats' cheese soufflé, pressed foie gras terrine with fig relish and brioche, and roast chicken with wild mushrooms and sherry vinegar. The balance between lightness and flavour impact can wobble, but first-course salads – of smoked salmon with lemon and capers, or toasted goats' cheese with cherry tomatoes – are perfectly straightforward, and a main course of grilled sirloin with shallots and red wine works well because the accompaniments allow an excellent piece of organic beef to speak for itself. On the other hand, raspberry soufflé did not quite come alive with fruit. No pre-dinner nibbles may cause sulks in this sort of context, as may the hurried service reported at one meal. Breads, Duchy of Cornwall biscuits with cheese and the cocoa-rolled truffles with coffee help to restore faith.

An imaginative choice of southern French wines heads up the list in fine style. Read on for clarets and burgundies which, while not cheap, represent pretty good value in places. Outside France, the selection is a touch perfunctory, but there are plenty of halves. House wines start at £11.95. CELLARMAN'S CHOICE: Jurançon Sec 1992, Dom. Lapeyre, £19.85; Collioure, Cuvée Les Piloumes 1991, Dom. du Mas Blanc, £22.87.

CHEF: Alec Howard   PROPRIETORS: Mr and Mrs M. Stone   OPEN: all week; 12.30 to 2, 7.30 to 9   MEALS: alc (main courses £8.75 to £14). Set L Sun £15   SERVICE: not inc, card slips closed   CARDS: Access, Amex, Diners, Visa   DETAILS: 50 seats. 5 tables outside. Private parties: 40 main room, 14 private room. Car park. Vegetarian meals. Children's helpings. Smart dress preferred. No smoking in dining-room. Wheelchair access (also WC). No music. Air-conditioned   ACCOMMODATION: 20 rooms, all with bath/shower. TV. Phone. B&B £75 to £125. Rooms for disabled. Children welcome. Baby facilities. Afternoon teas. Garden. Swimming-pool. Doors close at midnight. Fax: (0666) 890394 (*The Which? Hotel Guide*)

THORNBURY Avon   map 2

▲ *Thornbury Castle* ✾

Castle Street, Thornbury BS12 1HH
THORNBURY (0454) 281182   COOKING 1
off B4061, at N end of town   COST £27–£48

With its 'eighteen bedchambers and three dining areas', not to mention castellated walls, manicured gardens and a vineyard, this Tudor castle is nothing if not an experience. Guests sleep in rooms with original fireplaces and oriel windows and eat in baronial style surrounded by panelled walls and heraldic shields. Peter Brazill's fixed-price menus change daily, and he can produce dishes such as smoked duck breast with walnut and celeriac salad; grilled salmon with tomato and coriander butter; and escalope of venison with braised red cabbage. Reports suggest that the kitchen is not always in full control: praise for spinach soup, roast lamb, suprême of pheasant and butterscotch pudding is tempered by complaints of 'disappointing' terrine with onion marmalade, and 'most forgettable' soft meringue roulade. Service is usually willing, although one reporter found it less than satisfactory. There are some highfalutin bottles on the largely French wine list, and some interesting museum pieces, although it does not ignore ordinary drinkers and choice is extensive. House wine starts at £12.

CHEF: Peter Brazill   PROPRIETORS: The Baron and Baroness of Portlethen   OPEN: all week; 12 to 2, 7 to 9.30 (10 Fri and Sat, 9 Sun)   CLOSED: 2 days early Jan   MEALS: Set L £16.50 (2 courses) to £18.50, Set D £31   SERVICE: card slips closed   CARDS: Access, Amex, Diners, Visa   DETAILS: 30 seats. Private parties: 30 main room, 12 and 20 private rooms. Car park. Vegetarian meals. No children under 12. Jacket and tie. No smoking in dining-room. Music   ACCOMMODATION: 18 rooms, all with bath/shower. TV. Phone. B&B £75 to £200. No children under 12. Afternoon teas. Garden. Fax: (0454) 416188 (*The Which? Hotel Guide*)

THORNTON-CLEVELEYS Lancashire　　　　　　　　　　　　　map 5

▲ *Victorian House*

Trunnah Road,
Thornton-Cleveleys FY5 4HF
BLACKPOOL (0253) 860619　　　　　　　　　　　　　　COOKING 1
off A585, 3m N of Blackpool　　　　　　　　　　　　COST £16–£34

Round the corner from Thornton Windmill, just off the Fleetwood Road, is this genuine Victorian house that doubles as hotel and restaurant. The comfortably furnished lounges are 'heavily into Victoriana,' noted one visitor. By contrast, Didier Guérin's cooking is resolutely bourgeois French. He can tackle lambs' kidneys in red wine sauce and salt pork with lentils, as well as more modish ideas such as salad of crispy duck with rice vinegar and sesame oil. Lunch (served in the carpeted conservatory) is good value and reporters have liked generous, satisfying dishes of steamed mussels with curry cream, trout fillets with Cajun spices and sauté chicken breast on a bed of spinach. Crêpes gâteau with fresh fruits and an 'astringent' raspberry sauce has been a highly praised finale. A few 'international' wines top up the fairly priced French list. House wine is £9.50.

CHEF: Didier Guérin   PROPRIETORS: Louise and Didier Guérin   OPEN: Mon to Sat, exc Mon L; 12 to 1.30, 7 to 9.30   CLOSED: first 2 weeks Feb   MEALS: alc L (main courses £4.50 to £5.50). Set D £19.95   SERVICE: not inc, card slips closed   CARDS: Access, Visa   DETAILS: 60 seats. Private parties: 44 main room. Car park. Vegetarian meals with prior notice. No children under 6. Smart dress preferred. Music   ACCOMMODATION: 3 rooms, all with bath/shower. TV. Phone. B&B £47.50 to £75. Deposit: £10. Children welcome. Pets welcome (bedrooms only). Garden. Confirm by 6. Fax: (0253) 865350 (*The Which? Hotel Guide*)

THUNDRIDGE Hertfordshire　　　　　　　　　　　　　map 3

▲ *Hanbury Manor* ♟ ✦

Thundridge SG12 0SD
WARE (0920) 487722　　　　　　　　　　　　　　　　COOKING 3
off A10, 1½m N of Ware　　　　　　　　　　　　　COST £34–£68

This is a bit like Turnberry without the sea: a vast golforama and leisure centre devoted to corporate business. Among it all is the luxury Zodiac dining-room, light and airy with lovely views of the garden. The *carte* is a long one, or maybe just seems that way because it is all written out twice, but ambition is high and dishes are delightfully varied: foie gras terrine with braised oxtail and warm brioche, magret of duck with ceps and grapes, and, that rarity nowadays, gâteau Saint-Honoré. Riches abound, the Med exerts a pull, and fish is a strong suit. Baked Provence tomatoes are stuffed with ratatouille and served with warm pesto, while sea bass is sauté with a confit of aubergines, served with peppercorns and a tarragon sauce. 'Soufflé suissesse Gavroche' is a bit cheaper than the original.

A party in early summer enjoyed a Sunday lunch of 'flavoursome' pasta with pine-kernels and wild mushrooms, 'tender' roast veal with white beans and red pepper in a simple jus, 'light' poached filet of halibut, and 'excellent' tarte au citron. It is good to see decent vegetarian offerings of tomato and mozzarella gâteau with olives and mange-tout in balsamic vinaigrette, and a potato 'mille-feuille' with wild mushrooms, purée of artichoke and tomato butter. The fixed-price menu has little choice but is none the less attractive, serving up corn soup, a duo of sea bass and zander with fennel cream and beurre blanc, and warm apricot mousse.

The menu plumbs new depths of pretension when it converts the 'twenty eight pounds fifty' charged for scallops with celeriac and truffle butter to 'vingt-huit livres cinquante'. 'We never attempt to be exclusive or elite,' writes the food and beverage manager, who seems a little out of touch. On the credit side, however, service charge is included. The wine list is a world-hopper and, despite some staggeringly brazen mark-ups, does offer good drinking under £20 (look for the usual bolt-holes), as well as a lot of advice about vintages. A fair number of half-bottles – though none in single figures – plus half a dozen dry wines by the glass (from £3) helps those looking for variety. House wines start at £13. CELLARMAN'S CHOICE: Puligny-Montrachet 1991, Louis Carillon, £36; Margaux, Ch. d'Angludet 1989, £25.

CHEF: Rory Kennedy   PROPRIETOR: Poles Ltd   OPEN: all week, D only, and Sun L; 12 to 2.30, 7.30 to 9.30 (7 to 9.45 Fri and Sat)   MEALS: alc (main courses £19 to £29). Set L Sun £26, Set D £25 to £45   SERVICE: net prices, card slips closed   CARDS: Access, Amex, Diners, Visa
DETAILS: 40 seats. 10 tables outside. Private parties: 100 main room, 80 to 100 private rooms. Car park. Vegetarian meals. Children's helpings. No children under 8. Jacket and tie. Smart dress preferred. No smoking in dining-room. Wheelchair access (1 step; also WC). No music ACCOMMODATION: 96 rooms, all with bath/shower. TV. Phone. B&B £98 to £225. Deposit: 100%. Rooms for disabled. Children welcome. Baby facilities. Pets welcome (dogs £15 per night). Afternoon teas. Garden. Swimming-pool. Sauna. Tennis. Golf. Snooker. Confirm by 11. Fax: (0920) 487692 (The Which? Hotel Guide)

TORQUAY Devon   map 1

▲ Osborne Hotel, Langtry's ✦✻

Hesketh Crescent, Meadfoot,
Torquay TQ1 2LL   COOKING 2
TORQUAY (0803) 213311   COST £27–£35

The hotel occupies an entire and very grand Victorian terrace, restored to swashbuckling form, and filled with conference centre, apartments, leisure centre and restaurant. The view across Torbay is superb. Danny Burley has come up through the ranks, moving from sous-chef to big cheese on the departure of Colin Liddy to St Olaves Court, Exeter (see entry) shortly after the last *Guide* came out. His style, understandably, maintains some continuity in exploring exotic flavours and spices. Breast of chicken, for instance, is rolled with a basil mousseline, fried in lemon butter and served with jasmine-scented rice, while red bream fillets are pan-fried and served on a purée of onion and parsnips with cumin butter. At the same time, there are some good old-fashioned standbys: in pork cutlet braised in an apple and cider sauce with sage, and among the puddings. Slices of poached apple and rhubarb are glazed with a honey sabayon, and a warm pithiviers of apricot and plum is served with a mango sauce and clotted cream. The wine list is sensibly put together, widely spread and fairly priced, and four local wines from the Yearlstone Vineyard include a rarity: an English oak-matured red. House wine is £9.45. More reports, please.

CHEF: Danny Burley   PROPRIETOR: The Osborne Hotel   OPEN: all week, D only; 7 to 10 (later and some Sun L by arrangement)   MEALS: Set D £19.50 to £21.50   SERVICE: not inc, card slips closed   CARDS: Access, Amex, Visa   DETAILS: 70 seats. Private parties: 110 main room, 24 and 65 private rooms. Vegetarian meals. Children's helpings early evening. No babies or toddlers. Smart dress preferred. No smoking in dining-room. Wheelchair access (3 steps). Music   ACCOMMODATION: 23 rooms, all with bath/shower. TV. Phone. B&B £43 to £164. Deposit: £50. Rooms for disabled. Children welcome. Baby facilities. Afternoon teas. Garden. Swimming-pool. Tennis. Snooker. Fax: (0803) 296788

Table ▾ ⁵⚹

135 Babbacombe Road, Babbacombe,
Torquay TQ1 3SR
TORQUAY (0803) 324292

DEVON
1995
FLAVOUR

COOKING 3*
COST £32–£41

The restaurant is in the front room of an end-of-terrace house: not luxurious but wonderfully welcoming. 'Table remains a high spot on my eating itinerary,' writes a traveller. 'I hope it stays small because I am sure that is a reason for its high quality both front and back of house.' Reporters are certainly impressed, some are amazed, that so much good food comes out of such a small restaurant.

No holds are barred in the cooking. Trevor Brooks is not a purist and has no qualms about the culture clash of wasabi butter and Cajun spices that meet over a seared fillet of wild salmon. Such flavour combinations are well thought out, and what strikes reporters repeatedly is the happy coincidence of tastes and textures in something as simple as a Caesar salad with smoked chicken and avocado, or shredded duck confit on layers of crisp pastry with tomato and pesto in between.

Just enough is going on in the dishes to arouse interest, but never too much, so the flavours and textures remain clear. This is particularly true of fish such as grilled Dart salmon with a light veal jus, lentils and crispy bacon lardons. On another occasion, John Dory was made memorable by a pungent gazpacho sauce that had zip and zing. The same holds for puddings of the likes of 'superbly presented' chocolate and macadamia nut torte with coffee-bean ice-cream, and strawberry mille-feuille with mascarpone and rhubarb. The wine list is laid out by style, from drier whites through softer reds to heavier, more concentrated and aromatic wines – all very helpful. Quality and interest are high and prices are reasonable. Good French house wines at £9 or £11.50 are supplemented by others 'available by the glass and priced accordingly'. CELLARMAN'S CHOICE: Edna Valley Chardonnay 1990, £21; Ridge Vineyards Zinfandel 1990, Paso Robles, £17.

CHEF: Trevor Brooks   PROPRIETORS: Trevor Brooks and Jane Corrigan   OPEN: Tue to Sun, D only; 7.30 to 9.30   CLOSED: 1 to 18 Feb, 1 to 18 Sept   MEALS: Set D £26   SERVICE: card slips closed   CARDS: Access, Visa   DETAILS: 20 seats. Private parties: 20 main room. Vegetarian meals with prior notice. No children under 10. Smart dress preferred. No smoking in dining-room. Wheelchair access. No music

---

TUNBRIDGE WELLS Kent   map 3

Cheevers

56 High Street, Tunbridge Wells TN1 1XF   COOKING 2
TUNBRIDGE WELLS (0892) 545524   COST £26–£39

Nothing much changes here: 'The grey carpet must be the same one we saw seven years ago.' Likewise the cooking, which led one reporter to observe that ideas may not be as fresh as they were. Another enjoyed a generous portion of crisp-skinned roast duckling with spring onion and ginger, then checked up and found that 'it was mentioned in the first *Guide* entry for Cheevers in 1987'. But the kitchen still turns out food that pleases.

Lunchtime regulars stick to lamb (roasted with a mint and almond crust) and duck, which have pleased more than the fish. At dinner, greater skill is in evidence: in wobbly pike quenelle in a dill-flavoured cream sauce, in the duck, and in a steamed chocolate pudding in a small pond of hot chocolate sauce, next to a ball of slowly melting vanilla ice-cream, for example. Vegetables are served canteen-style: scoops of mashed potato and mashed swede. Meals begin with warm cheese straws, and raw vegetables with a mayonnaise dip, and finish with florentines and chocolate truffles. A short selection of varied and interesting wines begins at around £10, and the list is well endowed with half-bottles. House vin de pays is £8.75 (£1.95 per glass).

CHEF: Timothy Cheevers   PROPRIETORS: Timothy Cheevers, Martin J. Miles and P.D. Tambini OPEN: Tue to Sat; 12.30 to 2 (1.45 Sat), 7.30 to 10.30   MEALS: alc (main courses £9.50). Set D £25   SERVICE: not inc, card slips closed   CARDS: Access, Amex, Visa   DETAILS: 32 seats. Private parties: 30 main room. Vegetarian meals with prior notice. Children welcome. Wheelchair access (1 step). No music. Air-conditioned. Fax: (0892) 535956

Sankey's £

39 Mount Ephraim,
Tunbridge Wells TN4 8AA   COOKING 1
TUNBRIDGE WELLS (0892) 511422   COST £17–£47

'A real addition to Tunbridge Wells eating out' was one local's verdict on Guy Sankey's Victorian villa. Refurbishment continues. Fresh fish cooking of the old school is the name of the game: grilled Dover sole, salmon with spinach hollandaise, 'superb' sea bass steamed with spring onion, soy and ginger. Lobsters are from sea-water tanks. Details such as plenty of fresh bread, good salads and exactly cooked vegetables are regularly noted. Downstairs, in the cellar wine bar, there is plenty of gregarious activity and noise. Turnover is fast. The décor is all bare boards, beams and a hotch-potch of furniture, and the food is a mix of baguettes loaded with thick slices of rare beef, plates of charcuterie, terrines and pâtés plus hot items such as spicy Cajun chicken and leeks en croûte. A fine choice of teas and King & Barnes draught beers supplement the good-value, well-spread wine list. House wine is £8.

CHEF: Eluitorio Lizzi PROPRIETOR: Guy Sankey OPEN: all week, exc restaurant Sun; 12 to 2, 7 to 10 CLOSED: 25 Dec MEALS: alc (main courses £4 to £19) SERVICE: not inc, card slips closed CARDS: Access, Amex, Diners, Visa DETAILS: restaurant 60 seats, wine bar 40 seats. 10 tables outside. Private parties: 20 main room. Vegetarian meals. Children's helpings. No-smoking area in restaurant. Music. Fax: (0892) 536097

Thackeray's House ♥

85 London Road,
Tunbridge Wells TN1 1EA
TUNBRIDGE WELLS (0892) 511921

COOKING 3
COST £23–£74

Under the auspices of Bruce Wass, this small detached house that once belonged to the novelist has clocked up a decade's performance. It operates on two levels: downstairs the wine bar does simpler food, while upstairs is the restaurant, where the serious business takes place. A reporter who found the lounge area 'cramped' and too full of clamorous voices will be pleased to hear that a second lounge has been opened.

This year's reports show some dissatisfaction over value for money and curiously inconsistent cooking. The *carte* is certainly not cheap (although some starters can be taken as main courses), and it does not help to have to stump up extra for vegetables; but such complaint can often be stilled when the cooking is on target. It was very much so in a 'smooth, creamy, very successful' soup of smoked haddock and John Dory with excellent fish and textural variation introduced with green beans and mange-tout. Breast of duck with sweet-and-sour shallots was a 'lovely, lively dish' with tender pink meat and 'deliciously sweet yet spiky' flavour in the shallots. A finale of lemon brûlée tart was sharp ('simply, delectably' so) with fine crisp pastry. On the other hand, grilled hake with roasted tomatoes and capers disappointed for lack of substance, veal liver was shaved very thin and overpowered by sage, and vegetables have included charred fennel and carrots that offered resistance to the knife. Despite all this, people appreciate the friendly service and good coffee and petits fours. There are many glorious wines on the list, including some seriously mature clarets and burgundies. A real effort has been made in Italy, but Spain is almost entirely Torres, and Germany is totally ignored. Half-bottles are available in generous profusion. More's the pity, then, that mark-ups are so high. House selections open at £11. CELLARMAN'S CHOICE: Selaks Sauvignon Blanc 1993, £19.90; Côtes du Vivarais 1990, Mas la Bégude, £16.75.

CHEF/PROPRIETOR: Bruce Wass OPEN: Tue to Sun, exc Sun D (no Sun L bistro); 12.30 to 2.30, 7 to 10 CLOSED: 5 days Christmas MEALS: alc (main courses restaurant £12 to £17.50, bistro £7 to £10). Set L Tue to Sat £10 (2 courses) to £14.75, Sun £15.50 (2 courses) to £18.50, Set D Tue to Thur £17.50 (2 courses) to £21.50 SERVICE: not inc, card slips closed CARDS: Access, Visa DETAILS: restaurant 50 seats, bistro 30 seats. 6 tables outside. Private parties: 50 main room, 8, 12 and 20 private rooms. Vegetarian meals. Children's helpings. No cigars/pipes in dining-room. Wheelchair access (1 step). No music. Fax: (0892) 511921

TWICKENHAM Greater London   map 3

McClements Petit Restaurant

| 12 The Green, Twickenham TW2 5AA | COOKING 3 |
| 081-755 0176 | COST £24–£43 |

There are now two versions of McClements. This – the original – is where John McClements himself cooks, in a tiny converted house on two levels connected by a steep staircase. Standards in the kitchen have been maintained through this period of diversification. Fish and shellfish are the main business of the menu, and are cooked imaginatively but sensitively, making unexpected but effective use of offal in many of the dishes. Our inspectors found plenty to admire in grilled scallops with black pudding on cabbage leaves with a cheese sauce ('the combination worked perfectly'), 'beautiful' seafood risotto containing salmon, scallops, prawns and squid topped with shaved Parmesan, and grilled duck breast of 'excellent tenderness' accompanied by caramelised apple and chicory and a 'richly gamey' sauce. Technical flair was evidenced in desserts as well. The hot vanilla soufflé was 'light as a feather', pierced at the table and anointed with creamy calvados sauce, while light-textured crème brûlée was 'the best had for many a moon'. Other intriguing dishes include a 'cassoulet' of langoustines with duck gizzards, leek and potato soup with oysters, and lamb with baked aubergine and roasted garlic. Cafetière coffee is 'excellent'. House wine is £9.

Philip Rickerby is chef at the other branch (McClements Bistro, 2 Whitton Road, Twickenham, Tel: 081-744 9610), where the à la carte menu is constructed on broadly similar lines but offers more meat (chopped pig's trotter wrapped in Parma ham and fried, or lambs' offal served with a baked potato filled with tripe provençale, for example). There is also a £12.95 three-course set-price menu. Recent redecoration has given the Bistro's dining-room a much sunnier appearance, with new pictures on the walls and improved lighting.

CHEF/PROPRIETOR: John McClements   OPEN: Tue to Sat; 12 to 2.30, 7 to 10.30   CLOSED: first 2 weeks Aug   MEALS: alc (main courses £8 to £13.50)   SERVICE: 10%, card slips closed   CARDS: Access, Visa   DETAILS: 30 seats. Private parties: 30 main room, 15 private room. Vegetarian meals. Children's helpings. Smart dress preferred. Wheelchair access. Music

---

UCKFIELD East Sussex   map 3

▲ Horsted Place ⁵✳

Little Horsted, Uckfield TN22 5TS	
UCKFIELD (0825) 750581	COOKING 2*
2m S of Uckfield, on A26	COST £27–£59

The 1850s Gothic revivalist pile – in its own 1100-acre estate – was refurbished during the 1980s and goes in for large pictures in gilt frames, heavy brocade wallpaper (rather garish in the dining-room) and weighty striped curtains. Despite all that, 'it is surprisingly pleasant', according to one convert, with views of gardens, golf courses and the South Downs.

The kitchen observes the broad sweep of the seasons, in both supplies and cooking – braises in winter, lighter and sunnier dishes in summer – and the food is refreshingly unfussy. Spring offerings have included roasted scallops with olives, capers, figs and anchovies, followed by veal wrapped in Parma ham, flavoured with sage and served with noodles, and a winter fruit pudding with clotted cream. Fixed-price menus change daily, and one reporter enjoyed a first course of cured beef on mixed leaves with tapénade on toast, monkfish on a bed of broad-bean pods (à la mange-tout) in a rich tomato-based sauce, and 'light as a feather' hot chocolate pudding with fudge sauce. 'The bread was brilliant,' enthused the same reporter of flower-pot-shaped brown rolls and round white ones.

The menu wording could do with a revamp (it comes at you with 'consommé de queue de boeuf' at 'five pounds and twenty pence') and the wide-ranging wine list needs a spell-check as well as a few noughts knocking off the prices. It does list bottles under £20, however, and a fair selection of halves. House French is £12.50.

CHEF: Allan Garth   PROPRIETOR: Granfel Holdings Ltd   OPEN: all week; 12 to 2, 7.30 to 9.30 MEALS: alc (main courses £14.50 to £19.50). Light L menu (£5.50 to £12). Set L Mon to Fri £14.95, Sat and Sun £18.50, Set D £28.50   SERVICE: not inc, card slips closed   CARDS: Access, Amex, Diners, Visa   DETAILS: 50 seats. 6 tables outside. Private parties: 30 main room, 18, 30 and 50 private rooms. Car park. Vegetarian meals. Children's helpings. No children under 8. Jacket and tie. No smoking in dining-room. Wheelchair access (also WC). No music   ACCOMMODATION: 17 rooms, all with bath/shower. TV. Phone. B&B £130 to £325. Deposit: £50. Rooms for disabled. Lift. No children under 8. Afternoon teas. Garden. Swimming-pool. Tennis. Fishing. Golf. Doors close at midnight. Confirm by 6. Fax: (0825) 750240 (*The Which? Hotel Guide*)

ULLSWATER Cumbria   map 7

▲ *Sharrow Bay* ♟ ⅝✳

Ullswater CA10 2LZ
POOLEY BRIDGE (076 84) 86301 and 86483
2m from Pooley Bridge on E side of lake,   COOKING 3*
signposted Howtown and Martindale   COST £35–£60

Francis Coulson and Brian Sack virtually created the country-house hotel idea, way back in the '50s. They also restored British puddings to their rightful place, and might have invented the feel-good factor. 'I would rather eat here than anywhere else' is typical of the eulogy expressed. 'This was without doubt the most breathtaking experience of our dining-out careers. Sitting by the window overlooking Ullswater, catching sight of Helvellyn in the distance, was relaxation enough. To then be served the best meal of our lives was more than anyone deserves.' The rooms have acquired enough fussy decoration to become a caricature of the genre, but the lake and bobbing boats induce a sense of calm and repose, fostered by attentive staff who make everybody feel special.

There is an awful lot of menu. Lunch is four courses, dinner five, plus a mid-meal sorbet at each, and choice swings from a dozen first courses, about eight mains and ten puddings, to no choice at all for the fish course, which is always served with a cheesey soufflé suissesse. Supporters enjoy the formula and the mix of traditional British food spiked with occasional contemporary items, although the kitchen is hardly the pioneer it once was. Everybody troops past a pudding display on the way into the dining-room, making a mental note of what to choose later. Meals unfold at a well-regulated pace, offering smoked chicken consommé with Célestine pancakes, slices of moist and tasty roast goose with a confit of the leg (plus good gravy and rösti potatoes), then queen of puddings with 'magnificent' strawberry sauce in a jug, or warm chocolate dariole made from strong bitter chocolate, with a pleasantly mild coffee sauce.

Perhaps reporters are seduced by the setting, but the food itself does not always have the expected intensity of flavour. The cooking has evident skill and accomplishment, although it can seem a bit like an orchestra without a conductor, sometimes allowing flavours to coalesce into an indistinct mix. Portions suit anybody who has spent the day fell-walking. The package – and it is one of the best – appeals to more mature customers who are well-off, or were before they went in. Supporters, however, have little sympathy with those who wonder about the cost. It is an indulgence, 'and if you are going to indulge yourself, where better to do it than Sharrow Bay?'

Wines are up to date, delightfully varied (Germany is well represented), and mark-ups are generally reasonable, offering a fair spread of prices across the board. Some sections may lack excitement, but quality is indisputably high. Choice by the glass is extraordinarily good, mostly in the £2 to £4 range. House wine is £11.95. CELLARMAN'S CHOICE: Rueda Sauvignon Blanc, NV, £12; Coteaux d'Aix en Provence, Mas de Gourgonnier 1990, £17.50.

CHEFS: Johnnie Martin, Colin Akrigg, Philip Wilson and Chris Bond PROPRIETORS: Francis Coulson and Brian Sack OPEN: all week; 1 to 1.45, 8 to 8.45 MEALS: Set L £29.75, Set D £39.75 SERVICE: net prices DETAILS: 65 seats. Private parties: 8 main room. Car park. Vegetarian meals with prior notice. No children under 13. Jacket and tie. No smoking in dining-room. Wheelchair access (1 step). No music ACCOMMODATION: 28 rooms, 24 with bath/shower. TV. Phone. D,B&B £90 to £300. No children under 13. Afternoon teas. Garden. Doors close at 11.30. Confirm by 10. Fax: (076 84) 86349 (*The Which? Hotel Guide*)

ULVERSTON Cumbria   map 7

▲ *Bay Horse Inn* ♈ ⅓✳

Canal Foot, Ulverston LA12 9EL
ULVERSTON (0229) 583972
off A590, just before centre of Ulverston,   COOKING 3
follow signs to Canal Foot   COST £19–£42

The Bay Horse is one of the three pillars of John Tovey's Lakeland kingdom, along with Miller Howe at Windermere and Uplands at Cartmel (see entries). It is perhaps the homeliest in feel of the three and often appreciated for precisely that quality. Everything from bread at the outset to the chocolate truffles with coffee is made on the premises. The celebrated Toveyesque complexity of dishes seems slightly more in check here than at his other places, although there is certainly no shortage of ingredients on the plate.

The format is a fixed-price, three-course menu at lunch (with alternative soup choices, then fish or meat, and four desserts or cheese) or a longer *carte*, which is available also at dinner. Some of the dishes are renditions of recipes from Tovey's books; signed copies, of course, are for sale. A spring menu offered pea, mango and lime soup with toasted coconut, sauté medallions of venison with chestnuts, garlic and shallots in a mustard and red wine sauce, and raspberry and Frangelico (hazelnut liqueur) mousse with chocolate butter biscuits. By the time the dish arrives, you may have forgotten its contents. The couple who ate some of the above dishes thought the soup 'very tasty – all three flavours could be distinguished', and the venison 'superb', strongly flavoured meat in a 'formidable' sauce. In the lemon sole dish, however, the various elements 'fought each other to a standstill'. Another reporter who stayed the night thought the setting 'good for the harassed soul', enjoyed all the food (especially the 'superb' Aberdeen Angus beef) and appreciated the 'unobtrusive service'.

The European wine list moves briskly through the main regions with about four or five wines in each (but only two Italians and one Alsace). The separate list of New World wines has some very good selections, such as Dashwood Marlborough Sauvignon Blanc or Ridge Paso Robles Zinfandel, though there are only three half-bottles. Prices of New World wines open at £11.95.

CHEFS: Robert Lyons, Esther Jarvis and Craig Brown PROPRIETORS: John J. Tovey and Robert Lyons OPEN: restaurant all week, exc L Mon and Sun; 12 to 1.30, 7.30 for 8; bar Tue to Sun L; 12 to 2 MEALS: alc (main courses £12.50 to £14.50). Set L £14.50. Bar menu L. Minimum £10 SERVICE: 10%, card slips closed CARDS: Access, Visa DETAILS: 50 seats. Private parties: 50 main room, 20 and 30 private rooms. Vegetarian meals. No children under 12. Smart dress preferred. No smoking in dining-room. Wheelchair access (also WC). Music ACCOMMODATION: 6 rooms, all with bath/shower. TV. Phone. D, B&B £88 to £154. No children under 12. Pets welcome (not in public rooms). Afternoon teas. Doors close at midnight. Confirm by 6. Fax: (0229) 580502

UPPER SLAUGHTER Gloucestershire   map 2

▲ Lords of the Manor ᴥ✻

Upper Slaughter,
nr Bourton-on-the-Water GL54 2JD
COTSWOLD (0451) 820243
turn W off A429, 3m S of   COOKING 3
Stow-on-the-Wold   COST £24–£60

In deepest Cotswold, if there is such a place, the Slaughters escape the worst of coachload tourism by simply not being big enough for car parks, tea-shops, gift emporia, souvenir arcades and the rest. The church dates back to Norman times, Milton is reputed to have written *Paradise Lost* half a mile away, and Reverend Witts, the first Lord of the Manor, wrote his eighteenth-century chronicle, *The Diary of a Cotswold Parson*, in this parsonage fit for a bishop. The house has a bit of the Regency stripe about it, and staff are up to the grandness, even hopping out to valet-park the car.

Despite the inclusion of such dishes as soupe de poisson with rouille and croûtons, Clive Dixon's food is not simply a rendition of Mediterranean favourites. Instead he makes clever use of a wide variety of ingredients, to produce interesting contrasts of flavour and texture, as in a terrine of duck and potato with butter-beans and balsamic dressing. The pairing of fish with either richer or earthier flavours works particularly well. Turbot, for example, is braised with wild mushrooms, ham hock, potato, cabbage and salami, and spiked with garlic and thyme, while rack of lamb is studded with garlic and rosemary and served with mushy peas. These high notes and low notes sound to good effect in a first-course salad of scallops, foie gras and crispy bacon with a

Sauternes dressing. Tortilla of potato and smoked haddock is one of the less successful dishes, but reporters have enjoyed most others, including carrot and coriander cream soup, and penne cooked in garlic and butter with prawns and sun-dried tomatoes with Parmesan. Sweets could include honey nougatine glace on a passion-fruit sauce, or prune and almond tart with cinnamon ice-cream.

The pattern is now a series of fixed-price menus instead of a *carte*, which excites different reactions. 'The bill seemed to gather speed as the evening went on and the final total was a bit of a shock' was the experience of one reporter, while at lunch another party was 'astounded at the incredibly reasonable £30 per head'. The wine list has bags of choice, and despite the overwhelming emphasis on expensive stuff, some sections include at least a token bottle of something good under £20, although mark-ups are greedier than they should be. The couple of pages of house recommendations are useful. Half a dozen house wines begin at £13.95 (£2.65 per glass).

CHEF: Clive Dixon PROPRIETOR: James Gulliver OPEN: all week; 12.30 to 2 (2.30 Sun), 7.30 (7 Fri and Sat) to 9.30 CLOSED: 1 to 15 Jan MEALS: Set L Mon to Sat £10.95 (2 courses) to £12.95, Sun £13.95 (2 courses) to £17.50, Set D £27.50 to £33.50 SERVICE: 12.5% D, not inc L, card slips closed CARDS: Access, Amex, Diners, Visa DETAILS: 60 seats. 4 tables outside. Private parties: 60 main room, 10, 30 and 34 private rooms. Car park. Children's helpings. Smart dress preferred. No smoking in dining-room. Wheelchair access (also WC). No music ACCOMMODATION: 29 rooms, all with bath/shower. TV. Phone. B&B £80 to £185. Rooms for disabled. Children welcome. Baby facilities. Afternoon teas. Garden. Fishing. Fax: (0451) 820696 (*The Which? Hotel Guide*)

VOWCHURCH Hereford & Worcester   map 4

Poston Mill ⅝✶

Vowchurch HR2 0SF
GOLDEN VALLEY (0981) 550151
on B4348, between Vowchurch and
Peterchurch

As the Guide *went to press this establishment closed down.*

▲ Manor House

Northlands, Walkington HU17 8RT
HULL (0482) 881645
off B1230 towards Beverley from
Walkington

COOKING 1*
COST £24–£43

The Baughs' late-Victorian house is set in three acres of grounds on the fringes of the Westwood – the medieval pastures that border the town of Beverley. It is country-house through and through, and the cooking follows suit. A short fixed-price menu offers excellent value, but the real action takes place on what is termed the *carte*: four courses of extensive choice for around £28 plus supplements. This can be an exhausting read, but the results on the plate are accomplished. Derek Baugh's imagination seems to know no bounds. As one diner observed: 'A small guinea-fowl, accurately roasted, was expertly jointed, part-boned, reassembled on an apple bubble and squeak, and coated with an intense, but not overpoweringly sweet, blackberry demi-glaze. In case this was not enough, there was a garnish of red pepper and leek. 'You get the impression of a manic energy at work in the kitchen.' Even so, the sense here is of considerable achievement rather than fruitless over-elaboration. Other impressive dishes have included goujons of beef with mushrooms in a 'fritter basket' with a crushed peppercorn sauce, panache of fish glazed with Chablis and herb sauce, and all manner of unrestrained desserts concocted by Lee Baugh. The wine list strikes a fine balance between good value and quality. House wine is £8.95.

CHEFS: Derek and Lee Baugh, and Andrew Warters PROPRIETORS: Derek and Lee Baugh OPEN: Mon to Sat, D only; 7.30 to 9.15 MEALS: Set D Mon to Fri £15 to £27.50 SERVICE: not inc, card slips closed CARDS: Access, Visa DETAILS: 55 seats. Private parties: 35 main room. Car park. Vegetarian meals. No children under 12. Smart dress preferred. No cigars/pipes in dining-room. Music ACCOMMODATION: 7 rooms, all with bath/shower. TV. Phone. B&B £70 to £100. No children under 12. Pets welcome (not in public rooms). Garden. Doors close at midnight. Confirm by 6. Fax: (0482) 866501

▲ Priory Hotel

Church Green, Wareham BH20 4ND
WAREHAM (0929) 551666

COOKING 1
COST £24–£59

The setting is an early sixteenth-century Benedictine monastery in lushly landscaped gardens on the banks of the River Frome, five miles from Corfe Castle. A reporter who tarried amid pergolas and parasols for afternoon tea here as the summer ebbed, and the yachts on the river bobbed in their moorings, thought it a blissful idyll. In addition to the main dining-room, the old cellars have also been converted for eating. Michael Rust's menus celebrate these surroundings, using local seasonal ingredients to inventive effect. Main courses were well executed in the case of salmon fillet with sauté peppers, 'carefully cooked and fresh' whole fried plaice, and 'sweetly rich and creamy' chicken breast with button mushrooms and leeks in a chive butter sauce. Bread-and-butter pudding came with 'excellent' Dorset cream. In the evenings, the *carte* is supplemented by a good-value *prix fixe* of four courses; on Saturdays, the price is higher, but an extra course is added. People appreciate the personal touch and good cheer the Priory readily dispenses.

The wine list is a towering achievement. Hugely impressive in the classic French areas, particularly Bordeaux, it also includes good Germans, some of the best new-wave Italian makers such as Berardenga and Lungarotti, and pedigree American and Australasian selections. Prices are eminently fair. House French is £10.50. CELLARMAN'S CHOICE: St-Véran, Les Grandes Bruyères 1992, Luquet, £15.50; Médoc, Ch. La Tour St Bonnet 1988, £17.50.

CHEF: Michael Rust   PROPRIETORS: Stuart Turner and John Turner   OPEN: all week; 12.30 to 2, 7.30 to 10   MEALS: alc (main courses £11.50 to £19.50). Set L Mon to Sat £14.95, Sun £16.95, Set D Mon to Fri and Sun £22.50, Sat £26.50   SERVICE: not inc, card slips closed   CARDS: Access, Amex, Diners, Visa   DETAILS: Greenwood Room 44 seats, Abbots Cellar 44 seats. 10 tables outside. Private parties: 44 main room, 22 and 44 private rooms. Car park. Vegetarian meals. Children's helpings on request. Smart dress preferred. Wheelchair access (also WC). Music   ACCOMMODATION: 19 rooms, all with bath/shower. TV. Phone. B&B £70 to £175. Rooms for disabled. Children welcome. Afternoon teas. Garden. Fishing. Fax: (0929) 554519 (*The Which? Hotel Guide*)

WARMINSTER Wiltshire   map 2

▲ *Bishopstrow House* ⁵⁄₄✳

Warminster BA12 9HH
WARMINSTER (0985) 212312   COOKING 2
on B3414, SW of Warminster   COST £24–£60

Set at the end of a long drive, amid imposing grounds complete with a swimming-pool, this gold-stone Georgian country house makes a fine, welcoming retreat. Meals are served in a pleasant dining-room with elegant table settings and a buzzy atmosphere. Chris Suter's cooking is accomplished without becoming mannered or over-embellished. Ingredients speak for themselves. Light lunches of baked Finnan haddock with tomato and chive salad, wild mushroom risotto or bourride of chicken with aoïli are excellent value, as is the daily set lunch menu. Dinner, priced for three or four courses, is more elaborate stuff, taking in ravioli of crab and wild salmon, fillet of Scotch beef with foie gras and celeriac sauce, and rhubarb and strawberry gratin with rhubarb sorbet. Carefully described farmhouse cheeses are from Paxton & Whitfield. Dishes such as local langoustines sauté with asparagus and Longleat chanterelles show a keen eye for sourcing appropriate raw materials. Service is reckoned to be first-rate. The wine list is by no means cheap, but it is peppered with top-notch growers; best value is likely to be found in the New World selection. House wine is £12.50.

The Guide *is totally independent, accepts no free hospitality, and survives on the number of copies sold each year.*

CHEF: Chris Suter   PROPRIETOR: Blandy Brothers & Co Ltd   OPEN: all week; 12 to 2, 7.30 to 9.30   MEALS: Set L £12.50 to £25, Set D £31 to £36. Light L menu   SERVICE: not inc, card slips closed   CARDS: Access, Amex, Diners, Visa   DETAILS: 65 seats. Private parties: 65 main room, 15 to 65 private rooms. Car park. Vegetarian meals. Children's helpings. Jacket and tie. No smoking in dining-room. No music   ACCOMMODATION: 32 rooms, all with bath/shower. TV. Phone. B&B £98 to £256. Deposit: £100. Rooms for disabled. Children welcome. Baby facilities. Pets welcome. Afternoon teas. Garden. Swimming-pool. Sauna. Tennis. Fishing. Confirm by 6. Fax: (0985) 216769 (*The Which? Hotel Guide*)

WATERHOUSES Staffordshire   map 5

▲ *Old Beams* 🍷 ✸

Waterhouses ST10 3HW
LEEK (0538) 308254   COOKING 3
on A523, 7m SE of Leek   COST £28–£53

Waterhouses is a little hamlet on the edge of the Peak District, handy for a number of stately homes and only 10 minutes' drive from Alton Towers, should you wish to take a couple of turns on the Revolution before lunch. The Wallises have been running Old Beams since 1980. It is in the classic mould of a restaurant with rooms, with a comfortingly domestic atmosphere of roaring fires, fresh flowers and – of course – lots of beams. Most visitors take their meals in the conservatory, where a grand piano lurks amid the layers of foliage. The formula is fixed-price for lunch and dinner, taking in an appetiser, three courses and coffee, with an intervening sorbet in the evenings. Note that lunch is very much cheaper, and that two-course meals are available weekdays.

The accent is more French than British, although not exclusively so: an April dinner menu offered lamb ragoût on a bed of couscous with a chilli sauce. Otherwise, moules marinière, sauté foie gras in calvados sauce and calf's sweetbreads with truffles are very much the order of the day. All seem to agree with the reporter who called it 'good classical cooking with commendable attention to detail'. Appetisers have been known to be practically little courses in themselves – for example, a miniature salad of duck breast, lardons and pine-nuts with a tomato vinaigrette. Puddings, such as fruit pithiviers on artfully featured crème anglaise, can be 'sensational', and one reporter found the crème brûlée 'the best I have ever tasted'. 'Well-kept' cheeses take in the likes of Pont l'Evêque, Cornish Yarg, and Cashel Blue from Ireland. Incidentals are not neglected either: bread, coffee and home-made chocolates are all praised.

A very fine wine list has been assembled. As one would expect from the food, its main business is in France, but other regions get more than a look-in. Older vintages will be properly decanted. The only regret is that there is very little under £20; white burgundies offer two, reds one, clarets one, Loire one (Muscadet). Go for Alsace, Spain or Italy, or drink the well-chosen house burgundies – a 1992 Mâcon-Uchizy from Sallet at £15.75 or a 1990 Bourgogne Pinot Noir 1990 from Delaunay at £14.55.

CELLARMAN'S CHOICE: *Wines recommended by the restaurateur, normally more expensive than house wine.*

CHEFS/PROPRIETORS: Nigel and Anne Wallis   OPEN: Tue to Sun, exc Sat L and Sun D; 12 to 2, 7 to 9.30   MEALS: Set L Tue to Fri £10.95 (2 courses) to £17.50, Set D Tue to Fri £18.50 (2 courses) to £32.50   SERVICE: not inc, card slips closed   CARDS: Access, Amex, Diners, Visa   DETAILS: 50 seats. 3 tables outside. Private parties: 30 main room. Car park. Vegetarian meals with prior notice. Children welcome. No smoking in dining-room. Wheelchair access (also WC). Music ACCOMMODATION: 5 rooms, all with bath/shower. TV. Phone. B&B £52 to £87. Rooms for disabled. Children welcome. Garden. Fishing. Fax: (0538) 308157 (*The Which? Hotel Guide*)

WATERMILLOCK Cumbria   map 7

▲ *Rampsbeck Country House Hotel* ♟ ⁑✕

Watermillock CA11 0LP
POOLEY BRIDGE (076 84) 86442 and 86688   COOKING 2*
on A592 Penrith to Windermere road   COST £23–£54

Rampsbeck is an attractive eighteenth-century house with whitewashed frontage set in extensive gardens and meadowland at the northern end of Ullswater. Admire the topiary if you will from a chaise-longue in the lounge, or tramp the quiet roads around to work up an appetite for Andrew McGeorge's supremely competent cooking. The 'pretty' dining-room has a view over the lake, but what turns up on the plate may be quite as diverting. In addition to the main fixed-price dinner menu of four courses, there is a cheaper, no-choice offering and a separate menu for vegetarians.

The style is, not unexpectedly, Lakeland modern British, but it is the true sense of imagination that tends to impress people. One reporter found nothing to fault in a dinner that began with an amuse-gueule of vegetable samosa with barbecue sauce, then proceeded through a 'delicately dressed' scallop salad, rhubarb sorbet, and 'pink and tender' rack of lamb with pommes dauphinois, to finish with a tuile basket of pineapple mousse. Menu descriptions tend to be a little florid but at least have the virtue of accuracy. One diner thought there was a tendency to cook meats slightly more than is good for them, and queried the level of seasoning (not enough) in some dishes, but on the whole reports are positive. Service is refreshingly unpompous – no silver dome flummery here – and the good range of breads is commended. The wine list here has developed well in recent years and offers a confident international range of fine bottles at sane prices. A few more halves wouldn't go amiss. House wines start at £8.75. CELLARMAN'S CHOICE: Hawkes Bay Sauvignon Blanc 1993, Delegats, £11; Châteauneuf-du-Pape 1988, Dom. Chante Cigale, £19.50.

CHEF: Andrew McGeorge   PROPRIETORS: T.I. Gibb, Mrs M.M. Gibb and Mrs M.J. MacDowall OPEN: all week; 12 to 1.30, 7 to 8.30   CLOSED: 2 Jan to mid-Feb   MEALS: Set L £19.95, Set D £25 to £32.50. Bar menu L (main courses £9.50 to £10.50   SERVICE: not inc, card slips closed CARDS: Access, Visa   DETAILS: 40 seats. Private parties: 60 main room, 15 private room. Car park. Vegetarian meals. No children under 5. Smart dress preferred. No smoking in dining-room. Wheelchair access (3 steps). No music   ACCOMMODATION: 20 rooms, all with bath/shower. TV. Phone. B&B £48 to £150. Deposit: £15. Children welcome. Dogs welcome (not in public rooms). Afternoon teas. Garden. Fishing. Doors close at 11. Fax: (076 84) 86688 (*The Which? Hotel Guide*)

▲ *denotes an outstanding wine cellar;* ♟ *denotes a good wine list, worth travelling for.*

WATH-IN-NIDDERDALE North Yorkshire   map 7

▲ Sportsman's Arms ⬤ ✳ £

Wath-in-Nidderdale,
Pateley Bridge HG3 5PP
HARROGATE (0423) 711306
take B6156 or B6265 to Pateley Bridge,
follow signs by village, 2m NW of   COOKING 2
Pateley Bridge   COST £20–£40

'We were looking for somewhere to stay on the way home from the east coast, and found it with the help of the police in Pateley Bridge.' This solid, old stone building, a peaceful retreat without frills, is in a *very* rural location. The Dales offer lamb and Nidderdale trout, while fish such as Scarborough woof and 'incredibly fresh whiting beautifully cooked, firm yet tender', is plentiful and delivered daily. Sauces are exact, portions large and satisfying, and vegetables well cooked. A fondness for nut dressings is apparent: walnut on salads, and hazelnut vinaigrette on fried halloumi cheese with tomatoes, for example. Sharp spicing (with limes, capers and chilli peppers) brightens many of the dishes, but those that do not need it, like asparagus in beurre blanc, or a salad of poached egg, bacon lardons and sippets, are left well alone. Puddings are consistently good. Service is leisurely and the dining-room spacious and welcoming. The wine list is up to date, and as good outside the classic regions as within: Rhônes and Loires provide balance, southern French wines help to keep the bill within reason, and the southern hemisphere is well worth a punt. There are nine house wines at £9.50. CELLARMAN'S CHOICE: Jackson Estate Sauvignon 1993, £17.65; Côte Rotie 1986, Chapoutier, £27.

CHEFS: Ray Carter, Chris Williamson and Penny Sollit   PROPRIETORS: Ray and Jane Carter
OPEN: all week; 12 to 2.30, 7 to 10   CLOSED: 25 Dec   MEALS: alc D (main courses £12 to £14).
Bar menu L and D   SERVICE: not inc, card slips closed   CARDS: Access, Visa   DETAILS: 60
seats. 6 tables outside. Private parties: 60 main room. Car park. Vegetarian meals. Children's
helpings. No smoking in dining-room. Wheelchair access. No music   ACCOMMODATION: 7
rooms, 2 with bath/shower. TV. B&B £28 to £50. Children welcome. Pets by arrangement.
Afternoon teas. Garden. Fishing. Fax: (0423) 712524 (*The Which? Hotel Guide*)

WATLINGTON Oxfordshire   map 2

▲ Well House ✳

34–40 High Street, Watlington OX9 5PY   COOKING 1
WATLINGTON (0491) 613333   COST £22–£45

The narrow village street has its quota of half-timbered buildings, plus a good cheese shop a couple of doors away from the Well House, itself a fifteenth-century brick and flint house. The well wells up in the bar, or used to until an Act of Parliament spirited away the right to use it some time back, and its function is now merely decorative. The *carte* offers a choice of five items per course, including twice-baked crab soufflé, roast monkfish wrapped in bacon on a sweet pepper sauce, and coffee meringue gâteau. One springtime visitor who lunched off the fixed price menu enjoyed thick and sticky oxtail soup, the pastry on a lamb and apricot pie (but not the filling), and lemon roulade. Other dishes are roast monkfish wrapped in bacon on a sweet pepper sauce, or roast guinea-fowl with a lime sauce. Wines are mostly French, very decent, reasonably priced, with 20 half-bottles. House wine is £7.50 or £8 (£1.50 per glass).

CHEFS: Patricia Crawford and John McGeever PROPRIETORS: Patricia and Alan Crawford OPEN: all week, exc Mon and Sat L and Sun D; 12.30 to 2, 7 to 9.15(9.30 Sat) MEALS: alc (main courses £10.50 to £14.50). Set L and D £14.50 to £18.50 SERVICE: not inc, card slips closed CARDS: Access, Amex, Diners, Visa DETAILS: 45 seats. 5 tables outside. Private parties: 50 main room. Car park. Vegetarian meals. Children's helpings. Smart dress preferred. No smoking in dining-room. Wheelchair access. No music ACCOMMODATION: 10 rooms, all with bath/shower. TV. Phone. B&B £40 to £70. Rooms for disabled. Children welcome. Baby facilities. Afternoon teas. Doors close at 11. Confirm by 6. Fax: (0491) 612075

WELLS Somerset   map 2

Ritcher's £

5B Sadler Street, Wells BA5 2RR   COOKING 2
WELLS (0749) 679085   COST £13–£30

This keenly run neighbourhood restaurant is tucked away down a narrow passageway between two shops not far from the cathedral. The ground-floor bistro caters for a hungry young crowd who feed well on the likes of cheese and asparagus tart, sauté chicken with tarragon and braised pork cutlets. Up a spiral staircase is the small, intimate dining-room for special occasions and more ambitious food. Nicholas Hart's cooking is classic French with a modern slant and he works to a fixed-price menu that offers excellent value. Grilled salmon with crabmeat and vermouth cream, loin of pork en croûte, and breast of chicken with smoked salmon mousse and asparagus are typical dishes. Reporters have approved of moules marinière, crispy roast duckling, and expertly cooked rack of lamb with garlic and herb crust. Vegetables are capably handled, while sweets might include light chocolate mousse laced with Cointreau. Kate Ritcher is a chatty, cheerful hostess. The short, sensible wine list offers a catholic choice and very fair mark-ups; the choice of vintage ports is also worth exploring. House wine is £7.95.

CHEF: Nicholas Hart PROPRIETORS: Nicholas Hart and Kate Ritcher OPEN: restaurant Tue to Sat, exc Sat L; bistro all week; 12 to 2, 7 (6.30 bistro summer) to 9 (9.30 Sat) CLOSED: 26 Dec, 1 Jan MEALS: alc bistro (main courses £6 to £10.50). Set L bistro £6.95, restaurant £14.50, Set D bistro £12.50 restaurant £17.50. Minimum £14.50 D restaurant SERVICE: not inc, card slips closed CARDS: Access, Visa DETAILS: restaurant 14 seats, bistro 18 seats. Private parties: 12 and 24 main rooms. Vegetarian meals with prior notice. No children under 10 restaurant. Children welcome bistro. Smart dress preferred restaurant. No pipes in dining-room. No cigars while others eat in restaurant. wheelchair access bistro. Music

---

If a restaurant is new to the Guide *this year (did not appear as a main entry in the last edition),* NEW ENTRY *appears opposite its name.*

The Guide *relies on feedback from its readers. Especially welcome are reports on new restaurants appearing in the book for the first time. All letters to the* Guide *are acknowledged.*

Moorings ▼ ⁵⁄✗

6 Freeman Street,
Wells-next-the-Sea NR23 1BA   COOKING 3
FAKENHAM (0328) 710949   COST £20–£32

'The Moorings is somehow smaller than its reputation suggests, though its owners are definitely larger than life' was an early impression for one reporter. Carla Phillips is 'a large and friendly New Yorker' who comes out to talk to everybody when the cooking is over 'and gives you her recipes when asked'. The most popular are printed on the menu. Just off the quay, Moorings is well placed to catch holiday weekenders – hence the Thursday to Monday opening.

The restaurant celebrates the best of this part of Norfolk, which means a preponderance of seafood and vegetables. Close, small handwriting and 'impenetrable numbered sections' which divide the options into meat, fish and vegetable dishes make the menus difficult to follow. There is so much choice, and flavours are so many and varied, that it can take a while to work out a balanced meal. It is 'Antony Worrall-Thompson country-style', according to one reporter, rendered more opaque by sauced vegetables such as beetroot in soured cream, and leeks spiced with cloves, which can fight rather than complement the main dish. The case for the defence, however, is that 'with customers driving through miles and miles of vegetables, a turned carrot or two on the plate just will not suffice'. Several reporters are apparently willing to die for the creamy mashed potatoes.

Pan-frying has diminished in favour of steaming as a treatment for mullet, brill, sea bass, sea trout, and whatever else the boats bring in. Home preserves and pickles run through everything, and vinaigrettes are a new passion: flavoured with sherry for cockles, blackberry for herring, orange for pork brawn. As for meat dishes, there are good reports of pigeon breast, and venison meatballs. Cheeses are British and plentiful, trifle is 'rich and boozy', and one reporter raved about a 'fab Middle Eastern treat' of stewed hunza apricots with pistachio baklava and delicate halva ice-cream 'wonderfully perfumed' with rosewater and orange flower water. Service is relaxed and efficient. If in doubt, ask for advice on wine: 'We were steered towards an excellent and inexpensive Alsace white which was perfect with our food.' The list is an appealing mix of extremely classy wines, curiosities, recent finds and downright interesting bottles, all at very fair prices. Ten house wines, from £6.95, are also available by the half-bottle and glass.

CHEF: Carla Phillips PROPRIETORS: Bernard and Carla Phillips OPEN: Thur to Mon, exc Thur L; 12.30 to 1.45, 7.30 to 8.45 CLOSED: 2 weeks early Dec, 24 to 26 Dec, 2½ weeks early June MEALS: Set L Mon and Fri £9.95 (2 courses) to £14.45, Set L Sat, Sun and bank hols and Set D £12.95 (2 courses) to £17.45 SERVICE: not inc DETAILS: 35 seats. Private parties: 35 main room. Vegetarian meals. Children's helpings. No smoking in dining-room. Wheelchair access (also WC). No music

'Strangely, the overall effect is not as bad as it sounds, but I wouldn't like to work there.' (On eating in London)

WEST BAY Dorset   map 2

Riverside Restaurant £

West Bay, Bridport DT6 4EZ
BRIDPORT (0308) 422011   COOKING 2*
off A35, 3/4m S of Bridport   COST £16–£55

Perched on an islet and umbilically linked to the post office, the Riverside has
been doing its thing for 30 years now. The theme, of course, is fish and shellfish,
the best of the day's catch served either plain grilled or sauced as elaborately as
you want. Close your eyes and you could be in Brittany. One visitor was
transported further afield: 'It reminded me of a Cape Cod fish restaurant –
skyscapes, water, yachts and off-the-boat fish, cooked simply and generously.'
Her moules marinière arrived in great profusion, while 'sweet and succulent'
brill was baked on the bone in a Greek coating of herbs, onions, garlic and olive
oil, served with 'the best sauté potatoes I've had for years'.

Starters mobilise plenty of textures, as in scallops with a salad of pine-nuts,
bacon and croûtons or warm oysters with spinach, laverbread and hollandaise.
Main course sauce variations include sorrel and spinach, watercress and chives,
or onions, wine and cream. Puddings are of the seaside variety: knickerbocker
glory, banana split, toffee and fudge ice-cream with hot chocolate sauce. Service
was 'flustered' one busy day for a couple who didn't mind a bit, and involved
'protracted waiting' at the coffee stage for another pair whose patience did run
out. On the other hand, you could argue that it takes 'clever, unobtrusive
professionals to run it in such a seemingly casual way'. France, Australia and
New Zealand are the countries best served on the wine list. Prices are admirably
fair, and there is a slate of 'wines of the month' to peruse. House French is £10.50
per litre.

CHEFS: Janet Watson and Natalie Ansell-Green   PROPRIETORS: Janet and Arthur Watson
OPEN: Tue to Sun, exc Sun D, and bank hol Mons; 11.30 to 2.30, 6.30 to 8.30 (9 weekends)
CLOSED: end Nov to early Mar   MEALS: alc (main courses £5 to £25)   SERVICE: not inc, card
slips closed   CARDS: Access, Visa   DETAILS: 80 seats. 8 tables outside. Private parties: 70
main room. Vegetarian meals. Children's helpings. Wheelchair access (also WC). Music

---

WEST MERSEA Essex   map 3

▲ Blackwater Hotel, Le Champenois

20–22 Church Road, West Mersea CO5 8QH
COLCHESTER (0206) 383338 and 383038
just off B1025 from Colchester, turn right at   COOKING 1*
West Mersea church   COST £24–£43

The hotel is a charming creeper-clad Victorian building on an Essex island
famous for oysters. Its restaurant strikes people as a mixture of bistro French and
tea-room English, although the cooking is soundly Gallic. The *carte* inhabits the
conservative world of French onion soup, moules marinière, roast rack of lamb
and steak au poivre, with extras such as beef Stroganov in similar traditional
vein. More adventurous dishes appear on the list of fish specials, which might
include fillet of brill with stir-fried leeks or turbot cooked with spices and red

wine. Sweets are recited by the lady of the house: chocolate mousse and crème caramel have been enjoyed. Excellent coffee and petits fours are served in the lounge. Raclette, a type of cheese fondue, is available Monday to Friday. The wine list looks like a massive scrapbook full of labels advertising a mainly French selection of reasonably priced bottles from most growing regions. House wine is £7.95.

CHEF: R. Roudesli   PROPRIETOR: Mrs M. Chapleo   OPEN: all week, exc Tue L and Sun D; 12 to 2, 7 to 10   CLOSED: first 3 weeks Jan   MEALS: alc (main courses £9 to £14). Set L and D (exc Sat) £14.80 (2 courses) to £17.80   SERVICE: not inc, card slips closed   CARDS: Access, Amex, Visa   DETAILS: 46 seats. 3 tables outside. Private parties: 55 main room, 25 private room. Car park. Vegetarian meals. Children's helpings. Smart dress preferred. No cigars/pipes in dining-room. Wheelchair access (1 step; also WC). No music   ACCOMMODATION: 7 rooms, 4 with bath/shower. TV. B&B £25 to £62. Deposit: £10. Children welcome. Baby facilities. Pets by arrangement. Afternoon teas. Garden. Doors close at 1am. Confirm by 7 (*The Which? Hotel Guide*)

WETHERSFIELD Essex   map 3

Dicken's ♥

The Green, Wethersfield CM7 4BS   COOKING 2
GREAT DUNMOW (0371) 850723   COST £27–£40

The culinary philosophy at John and Maria Dicken's small village restaurant is to be aware of trends elsewhere, while refusing to obey the diktats of fashion for their own sake, retaining a core of tried-and-true English and French dishes that have proved popular. In the evenings, the printed *carte* is augmented by daily specials that are recited at the table, and the choice may offer spiced charcuterie and Parmesan salad, king prawn tempura, Mediterranean fish soup with rouille and croûtons, and duck breast with courgettes and garlic mash.

Eating on a May bank holiday weekend, one couple noted that there did not seem to be much seasonal awareness in a menu that included braised lamb shank with 'winter vegetables'. Turkey tempura comes with French beans and salad leaves, and roasted scallops and cod with potato rösti. Vanilla ice-cream with butterscotch sauce was a 'delicious' dessert, the marriage of textures exactly right, and a slice of lemon tart had a fine filling but rather soggy pastry. Others have reported 'perfectly executed' dishes, so the ability is clearly there. The inconsistency perhaps comes from stretched resources: 'We felt rushed from start to finish,' said the bank holiday couple. The extra charge for bread is sad, though the heated granary version spread with 'good, tasty tapénade' is worth a punt.

The wine list is very good. An obvious effort has been made to keep prices within bounds, there is a sufficient supply of halves, and producers in most countries represented are of the best. House wines start at £8.75. CELLARMAN'S CHOICE: Menetou-Salon 1992, Dom. de Chatenoy, £16.25; Penley Estate Shiraz/Cabernet 1990, £18.95.

CHEF: John Dicken   PROPRIETORS: John and Maria Dicken   OPEN: Wed to Sun, exc Sun D; 12.30 to 2, 7.30 to 9.30   MEALS: alc (main courses £11 to £13)   SERVICE: not inc   CARDS: Access, Visa   DETAILS: 47 seats. 5 tables outside. Private parties: 38 main room, 20 and 38 private rooms. Car park. Vegetarian meals. Children's helpings. Smart dress preferred. Wheelchair access (1 step; also WC). Music

WHIMPLE Devon   map 1

▲ *Woodhayes* ¦✳

Whimple EX5 2TD
WHIMPLE (0404) 822237   COOKING 2
off A30, 9m E of Exeter   COST £22–£39

Set in Devon apple-orchard country, the Rendles' well-maintained Georgian
house continues to please allcomers. 'This is our home-from-home which we
visit as often as time and our bank manager will allow,' was one typical report of
the affection it generates. Much of the pleasure centres on the food, which is neat
but unfussy, clearly flavoured and beautifully presented. Fish is from Brixham;
other supplies are local. Fixed-priced dinners run to six courses but the
cumulative effect is never overwhelming. Soups, such as sorrel or vegetable
consommé, are regularly endorsed, as are the luscious home-made ice-creams.
In between, you might find monkfish with pasta, duck with port and orange or
fillet of beef with polenta and salsa verde. English cheeses are served with
grapes and walnuts. A dozen excellent house wines at £9.20 supplement the full
list, which is an affordable selection from around the world.

CHEFS: Katherine Rendle and Michael Rendle   PROPRIETORS: Katherine and Frank Rendle, and
Michael Rendle   OPEN: all week D (L residents only); 12 to 2, 7.30 to 9   MEALS: Set L £15, Set D
£25   SERVICE: net prices, card slips closed   CARDS: Access, Amex, Diners, Visa   DETAILS: 18
seats. Private parties: 12 main room (residents and guests only). Car park. Vegetarian meals.
Children's helpings. No children under 12. Smart dress preferred. No smoking in dining-room.
Wheelchair access. Music   ACCOMMODATION: 6 rooms, all with bath/shower. TV. Phone. B&B
£70 to £90. No children under 12. Afternoon teas. Garden. Tennis. Doors close at midnight (*The
Which? Hotel Guide*)

WHITBY North Yorkshire   map 6A

Magpie Café ¦✳ £

14 Pier Road, Whitby YO21 3PU   COOKING 2
WHITBY (0947) 602058   COST £13–£31

'Parking is impossible! Come on foot!' advises a devotee of this admirable café.
The queues tell their own story: at weekends they stretch down the steps and out
into the street beside the traffic. The distinctive black-and-white building stands
opposite the quay, with handsome views of the harbour and the abbey from its
windows. Don't expect fancy décor or pretension: the tables are the wipe-down
kind, the napkins are paper, and a bevy of cheery waitresses bustles around
coping efficiently with the crowds. Fish from the boats is the mainstay; it arrives
tasting of the sea, with crisp, 'fluffy' batter and fat, handcut chips. The kitchen
will also grill or poach anything from cod and plaice to salmon and halibut;
meat-eaters and vegetarians are well looked after. Regulars enthuse about the
magnificent choice of around 30 home-made puddings: sticky toffee pudding,
hazelnut meringue, Yorkshire curd tart, 'boozy' banana shortcake and many
more besides. Bread is home-baked, tea is leaf; everything is beyond reproach,
especially the excellent children's facilities. House wine is £5.95.

513

CHEF: Ian Robson   PROPRIETORS: Sheila and Ian McKenzie, and Ian Robson and Alison McKenzie-Robson   OPEN: all week; 11.30 to 6.30   CLOSED: late Nov to mid Mar   MEALS: alc (main courses £3.95 to £8.95). Set L and D £7.95 to £12.95   SERVICE: not inc, card slips closed   CARDS: Access, Visa   DETAILS: 100 seats. Private parties: 50 main room, 50 private room. Vegetarian meals. Healthy eating options. Children's helpings. No-smoking room. No music. Air-conditioned

---

| WHITLEY BAY Tyne & Wear | map 7 |

Le Provençale

| 183 Park View, Whitley Bay NE26 3RE | COOKING 1 |
| 091-251 3567 | COST £13–£49 |

'Nearly everyone was drinking house red wine from carafes and eating fillet of beef in mustard sauce.' That observation from a reporter sums up this popular neighbourhood restaurant. The interior is curiously old-fashioned, with brocade curtains, heavily patterned wallpaper and dark-stained woodwork. Service is from a team of pleasant waitresses. The long menu is dyed-in-the-wool 1970s French: rich and substantial, with lots of stuffing and rolling, heavy alcohol sauces and mousses everywhere. What it offers is hearty fish soup, threateningly large breast of pheasant with 'mousse nappé' and red wine sauce, and navarin of lamb. Slightly more experimental stuff includes tartlet of duck breast and chicken with green peppercorns and cranberry coulis. Desserts are mostly calorific 'blasts from the past' – crêpes soufflé, profiteroles, crème caramel. Lunches are cheap and cheerful. The keenly priced wine list plunders the French regions and takes note of the rest of the world. House wine is £7.90 a litre.

CHEF: Michel Guijarro   PROPRIETORS: Mr and Mrs Michael Guijarro   OPEN: L Thur, Fri and Sun, D Mon and Wed to Sat; 12 to 1.45, 7 to 9.45   CLOSED: 2 weeks June/July   MEALS: alc (main courses L £3 to £6, D £12.50 to £20). Set L £6, Set D £16.95   SERVICE: not inc   CARDS: Access, Amex, Diners, Visa   DETAILS: 50 seats. Private parties: 50 main room. Vegetarian meals with prior notice. Children's helpings. No children under 6 D. Smart dress preferred. Wheelchair access (also WC). Music. Air-conditioned

---

| WHITSTABLE Kent | map 3 |

▲ *Whitstable Oyster Fishery Co*

Royal Native Oyster Stores,	
The Horsebridge, Whitstable CT5 1BU	COOKING 1
CANTERBURY (0227) 276856	COST £24–£40

'If something is good to start off with, why mess with it?' ask the owners. The Whitstable Oyster Fishery Co's restaurant, in a plain Victorian building of whitewashed brick, is quite good at not tinkering. It is not perfect yet, because it masks the flavour of baked haddock with a coating of Gruyère cheese, soured cream and spring onions, but it gets very close to the ultimate with dressed Cornish crab, chargrilled salmon, and all sorts of things in garlic butter, including prawns cooked in their shells. The enterprise is a revival of a way of eating that enjoyed huge popularity a century ago, and fresh native Whitstable oysters, which must have kept the whole of London going in the late nineteenth century, are a highlight. Fresh fish may include gurnard, sprats, herring and all kinds of things that do not appear on other supposedly specialist menus. Wines are few but good, and house Yapp wine is £8.95.

CHEFS: Nikki Billington and Chris Williams   PROPRIETOR: Whitstable Oyster Fishery Co   OPEN: Tue to Sun (and L bank hol Mon), exc Sun D; 12 to 2 (2.30 Sat, 3 Sun), 7 to 9 (9.30 Sat)   MEALS: alc (main courses £9.50 to £15)   SERVICE: not inc   CARDS: Access, Amex, Diners, Visa DETAILS: 140 seats. 6 tables outside. Private parties: 65 main room. Car park. Vegetarian meals. Children's helpings. Wheelchair access (also WC). Music   ACCOMMODATION: 8 self-catering fisherman's huts. £15 to £25 per person. Deposit: 100%. Children welcome. Fax: (0227) 770666

WICKHAM Hampshire   map 2

▲ *Old House*

The Square, Wickham PO17 5JG
FAREHAM (0329) 833049
3m N of Fareham, at junction of   COOKING 2
A32 and B2177   COST £26–£40

Richard and Annie Skipwith have been at the helm of this early Georgian house for more than two decades and have marked it with their personal stamp. Everywhere, you will see fine panelling and beams, pictures and vases of fresh flowers. The restaurant is a light, airy room overlooking the garden in what was once a timber-framed outhouse and stables. Visitors can choose between the full fixed-priced menu (two or three courses) or a cheaper, simpler three-course affair. France is the main inspiration, although the kitchen can graft on ideas from the Mediterranean and the Far East: roast guinea-fowl is glazed with sesame oil, soy and candied ginger; grilled fillets of brill are served on a 'caviare' of aubergine spiked with garlic, sun-dried tomatoes and basil. Sauces are a strong point, as in maize-fed chicken with madeira and mushrooms, and spot-on fillet of beef served with a reduction of veal jus, white wine, brandy, cream and sultanas macerated in Darjeeling tea. Sweets are equally self-assured. Service is personable and professional. The short wine list offers some unusual and interesting bottles from France and beyond. House wine is £11.

CHEF: Nicholas Harman   PROPRIETORS: Richard and Annie Skipwith   OPEN: Mon to Sat, exc L Mon and Sat; 12.30 to 1.45, 7.30 to 9.30   MEALS: Set L and D £17.50 to £25   SERVICE: net prices, card slips closed   CARDS: Access, Amex, Diners, Visa   DETAILS: 40 seats. Private parties: 40 main room, 14 private room. Car park. Vegetarian meals. Children's helpings. Smart dress preferred. No cigars/pipes in dining-room. Wheelchair access (1 step). No music ACCOMMODATION: 12 rooms, all with bath/shower. TV. Phone. B&B £65 to £85. Children welcome. Baby facilities. Garden. Doors close at midnight. Confirm by noon. Fax: (0329) 833672 (*The Which? Hotel Guide*)

The Guide *office can quickly spot when a restaurateur is encouraging customers to write recommending inclusion – and sadly, several restaurants have been doing this in 1994. Such reports do not further a restaurant's cause. Please tell us if a restaurateur invites you to write to the* Guide.

WILLINGTON Co Durham   map 7

Stile ⚡✳

97 High Street, Willington DL15 0PE
BISHOP AUCKLAND (0388) 746615   COOKING 1
on A690, 4m N of Bishop Auckland   COST £21–£36

Mike Boustred's enthusiasm for food and wine continues unabated. His latest venture is a wine-tasting buffet held on the last Sunday of each month, while weekly theme nights provide plenty of variety for his regular customers. The restaurant, with its polished pine floors and plant-filled conservatories, is as popular as ever, and the lively atmosphere generally gets full marks, although the paper cloths and 'rather loud music' disappointed one couple. Jenny James' cooking has no truck with nouvelle trickery, but she rings the changes with dishes such as pigeon breasts with chillies, chicken satay and fillet of roe deer with blueberries. Steaks are a fixture. Recent reports have highlighted vegetables and sweets such as gooseberry and elderflower fool. The food is sound and value for money, and portions are generous. The wine list conjures up many interesting and keenly priced bottles. It is a good opportunity to try something you have never heard of. House wine is £6.75.

CHEF: Jenny James   PROPRIETORS: Mike Boustred and Jenny James   OPEN: Tue to Sat, D only; 7 to 9.30   CLOSED: 2½ weeks Sept   MEALS: alc (main courses £10 to £12.50). Set D £15.75   SERVICE: not inc, card slips closed   CARDS: Access, Visa   DETAILS: 46 seats. Private parties: 35 main room, 18 private room. Car park. Vegetarian meals. Children's helpings. No smoking in dining-room. Music. Fax: (0388) 746331

WILLITON Somerset   map 1

▲ *White House Hotel* ❘

Williton TA4 4QW   COOKING 3
WILLITON (0984) 632306 and 632777   COST £36–£53

Dick and Kay Smith wisely pace themselves so that their hotel is only open for half the year. While this frustrates those who would willingly return off-season, it also helps to explain the high quality of what is on offer in the summer and autumn. On a bright day, the frontage shimmers behind a semi-circular drive and an 'extremely weeping willow'. In the stone-walled dining-room, the ticking clock emphasises the tranquillity of the scene and people appreciate the atmosphere of 'friendly informality'.

The Smiths' cooking is full of fond francophilia, but does not ignore British modes, with even a flicker of metropolitan fashion in the likes of black-baked chicken with mango salsa and sweet potato purée. The menus quote prices for three, four or five courses, depending on whether you are in the mood for soup or cheese as well. A reporter eating in early summer admired the 'interesting, strong, clear-cut flavours and contrasting textures' in a starter of marinated beef fillet with mushroom salad in a sharp vinaigrette and a mustard mayonnaise containing whole grains. Sticking with meat, she then ate a fillet of lamb with roasted red peppers and aubergines and a madeira sauce. The 'pink and juicy' meat was well-timed and derived real support from the 'sweetish and earthy' vegetables. The side-dish of veg included impressively accurate sugar-snap peas and a helping of 'classically perfect' dauphinois. A simple dessert of lemon cheesecake ('very, very light and fluffy') with orange segments and sorbet gained marks for freshness, lightness and clear definition. 'Excellent' coffee comes with home-made caramel fudge. Other reports this year have applauded such dishes as smoked haddock soup, warm pigeon breast and beetroot salad, and pork stuffed with olives and pine-nuts.

The wine list is an enthusiast's manifesto that includes most of the major producing countries in its generous sweep. Almost every section contains bottles to savour, the country wines of Provence and good German Rieslings receiving especially handsome treatment. Half-bottles appear in grand profusion, and prices are not at all outrageous. House wines start at £10.50. CELLARMAN'S CHOICE: Wairau River Sauvignon Blanc 1993, £16.50; Le Volte 1991, Tenuta dell'Ornellaia, £16.50.

CHEFS/PROPRIETORS: Dick and Kay Smith   OPEN: all week, D only; 7 to 8.30   CLOSED: Nov to early May   MEALS: Set D £25 to £31   SERVICE: not inc   DETAILS: 26 seats. Private parties: 12 main room. Car park. Children's helpings. No smoking while others eat. Wheelchair access. No music   ACCOMMODATION: 12 rooms, 9 with bath/shower. TV. Phone. B&B £32 to £78. Deposit: £25. Rooms for disabled. Children welcome. Baby facilities. Dogs by arrangement. Doors close at 11.30. Confirm by 6 (*The Which? Hotel Guide*)

WINCHCOMBE Gloucestershire   map 2

▲ *Wesley House*

High Street, Winchcombe GL54 5LJ
CHELTENHAM (0242) 602366   COOKING 1*
on B4632, Cheltenham to Broadway road   COST £19–£42

The half-timbered house is a merchant's dwelling dating back to 1435, and reporters have been quick to acknowledge its new lease of life. In particular, they appreciate the choice of sitting informally by an open fire in the foyer or in the immaculate little dining-room at the back. Jonathan Lewis's cooking draws warm praise. Dinners are fixed-price for three or four courses, and the repertoire is tilted towards fish of all kinds: pan-fried scallops are served with a spaghetti of vegetables and shellfish sauce, and baked fillet of red snapper comes on creamed celeriac and potato with spring onion sauce. Meat-eaters can opt for roast rib of beef, or fillet of venison with wild mushrooms and port. Light lunches take in everything from club sandwiches to fillet of pork with paprika sauce. A traditional 'Taste of the Cotswolds' is offered on Tuesdays, and cookery demonstrations are a monthly attraction. Service is 'beyond reproach'. The short, well-spread wine list is a sound selection at realistic prices. House wines start at £8.95.

All details are as accurate as possible at the time of going to press, but chefs and owners often change, and it is wise to check by telephone before making a special journey. Many readers have been disappointed when set-price bargain meals are no longer available. Ask when booking.

CHEF: Jonathan Lewis   PROPRIETORS: Matthew Brown and Jonathan Lewis   OPEN: all week, exc Sun D; 12 to 2.30, 7 to 10 (open D Sun before bank hols)   CLOSED: last 2 weeks Jan, first 2 weeks Feb   MEALS: alc L (main courses £6 to £8). Set L £12.50, Set L Sun £14, Set D £22.50 to £26   SERVICE: not inc   CARDS: Access, Amex, Visa   DETAILS: 50 seats. Private parties: 60 main room. Vegetarian meals. Children's helpings. Smart dress preferred. No-smoking area. Wheelchair access. Music   ACCOMMODATION: 6 rooms, all with bath/shower. TV. Phone. B&B £39 to £65. Children welcome. Afternoon teas. Doors close at midnight. Confirm by noon. Fax: (0242) 602405

WINCHESTER Hampshire   map 2

Hunters £

5 Jewry Street, Winchester SO23 8RZ   COOKING 2
WINCHESTER (0962) 860006   COST £18–£44

David Birmingham's airy, well-lit restaurant serves its local community admirably. Light lunches appeal to shoppers and barristers from the nearby courts, while the supper menu is appreciated by those visiting the Theatre Royal. The kitchen is able to deliver impressive modern dishes that aspire to higher things than the bistro-style décor of the place might suggest. Fish shows up well in the shape of pan-fried scallops with crispy leeks and shellfish sauce, and grilled red mullet with creamed potatoes and tapénade, while home-smoked salmon is paired with a warm avocado salad. Confit of duck, Mediterranean vegetables marinated in extra virgin olive oil, and new season's lamb steak and sweetbreads on a bed of cabbage have been heartily endorsed. To finish, hazelnut and ginger parfait with raspberry sauce is recommended. Service is attentive, friendly without being servile and efficient without being hurried. David Birmingham also owns Hunters in New Alresford (see entry) and the wine list is shared by both places. It offers plenty of choice and fair prices; 10 wines are available by the glass. House wine is £8.95.

CHEF: Paul Revill   PROPRIETOR: David Birmingham   OPEN: Mon to Sat; 12 to 2.30, 6 to 10 (10.30 Sat)   CLOSED: 25 to 30 Dec   MEALS: alc (main courses L £5 to £14, D £9 to £16). Set Light D £7.95 (2 courses) to £11.50   SERVICE: not inc   CARDS: Access, Amex, Diners, Visa   DETAILS: 70 seats. Private parties: 20 main room, 28 private room. Vegetarian meals. Children's helpings. No-smoking area. Wheelchair access. Music. Fax: (0962) 877707

▲ Wykeham Arms ⅋✶

75 Kingsgate Street, Winchester SO23 9PE   COOKING 1
WINCHESTER (0962) 853834   COST £16–£34

Sandwiched between the cathedral and the college, the 250-year-old Wykeham Arms is a pub with high aspirations. Real ale and wine by the glass are dispensed in the bar, while the emphasis in the civilised dining-room is firmly on food. The chefs, working in rotation, provide a daily-changing menu that is a mixture of traditional pub grub and more up-market brasserie-style dishes. Typical offerings might include salmon, leek and ginger terrine, beef bourguignonne, pan-fried lamb's liver with potato and apple cakes and Dijon mustard sauce, and fillet of salmon with a basil dressing and tomato and sweet pepper salsa. Puddings include chocolate biscuit cake and amaretto ice-cream.

'Service and presentation are good and the food is excellent,' commented one regular customer. The short wine list changes twice a year and much comes from Eldridge Pope. House wine is £8.25.

CHEFS: Vanessa Booth, Belinda Watson, Nicola Jacques and Helen Brooks   PROPRIETOR: Graeme Jameson   OPEN: Mon to Sat; 12 to 2.30, 6.30 to 8.45   CLOSED: 25 Dec   MEALS: alc (main courses L £4 to £11, D £9 to £11.95)   SERVICE: not inc, card slips closed   CARDS: Access, Amex, Visa   DETAILS: 72 seats. 4 tables outside. Private parties: 8 main room. Car park. Vegetarian meals. No children under 14. Smart dress preferred. No smoking in 3 dining-rooms. No music   ACCOMMODATION: 7 rooms, all with bath/shower. TV. Phone. B&B £62.50 to £75. No children under 14. Pets welcome. Afternoon teas. Sauna. Doors close at midnight. Fax: (0962) 854411 (*The Which? Hotel Guide*)

WINDERMERE Cumbria   map 7

▲ *Gilpin Lodge* ♥ ✻

Crook Road, Windermere LA23 3NE
WINDERMERE (053 94) 88818   COOKING 2
on B5284, 2m SE of Windermere   COST £19–£47

The white-painted, slate-roofed lodge and its 20 private acres are well away from the bustle. The bright colours of lounge and drawing-room are subdued in the calmer dining-room, and the place rates high for ambience. At dinner a basic three-course meal (with quite generous choice) is extended to five stages by slipping in a soup or salad before the main course, and tacking on cheese or a savoury at the end. The modern style of cooking has a firm basis in French technique and shows to good effect in feuilleté of lambs' kidneys with mushrooms and bacon in a garlic cream sauce, chicken breast wrapped in Cumbrian air-dried ham and baked, served on an ale and thyme jus garnished with spätzli, and a shortbread galette filled with strawberries Romanoff on a raspberry coulis. Should plainer food be wanted, the offer is there.

Lunches are light affairs of kipper pâté served with lime and apple chutney, some chunky sandwiches of smoked salmon and prawns or roast beef and horseradish, and a variation on Welsh rarebit done with bacon and pineapple. Opinions of the food have been divided. 'A rating of 2 does not do this establishment justice,' claims one, after enjoying a caramelised onion and black pudding tarte fine on a tomato and olive jus, warm mousseline of sole with a lobster sauce, roast rack of lamb on Mediterranean vegetables, and iced lemon and lime parfait on a citrus fruit crème anglaise. On the other hand, 'We would not give the place a second visit,' says another, who experienced a series of culinary shortcomings not helped by the 'abysmal service'. It underscores the problems of many small restaurants that need to stay open every single mealtime, and yet whose staff need to take a break. Wines are sensibly chosen, and if they aim for safety rather than excitement, then at least quality is more or less assured. A wide spread of prices ensures fair play across the board, half-bottles are not neglected, and half a dozen house wines begin at £9.95 (£2 per glass). CELLARMAN'S CHOICE: Castle Hill Sauvignon Blanc 1992, £16; Brouilly 1992, Dom. Martin, £16.50.

CHEFS: Christine Cunliffe and Christopher Davies PROPRIETORS: Christine and John Cunliffe
OPEN: all week; 12 to 2.30, 7 to 8.45 MEALS: alc L Mon to Sat (main courses £4 to £8). Set L Sun
£14, Set D £26 SERVICE: not inc CARDS: Access, Amex, Diners, Visa DETAILS: 45 seats. 3
tables outside. Private parties: 22 main room, 15 private room. Car park. Vegetarian meals. No
children under 9. Smart dress preferred. No smoking in dining-room. No music
ACCOMMODATION: 9 rooms, all with bath/shower. TV. Phone. B&B £50 to £120. No children
under 9. Afternoon teas. Garden. Fax: (053 94) 88058

▲ *Miller Howe* ♀ ⅝✳

Rayrigg Road, Windermere LA23 1EY
WINDERMERE (053 94) 42536
on A592, between Windermere and   COOKING 2
Bowness   COST £22–£56

Old-stagers tend to plod the same route without ever stopping to think where
they are going or why. Over the last season, however, Miller Howe has taken
time out not just to refurbish the lounges and rejig the kitchen, but also to look at
the map and see where it is heading. This is to be applauded, not only because
reporters reckon they can now prepare some of John Tovey's recipes as well as
his team can, but because cooking needs to be refreshed from time to time. The
new style aims to be lighter. 'Gone are the old heavy cream sauces and large
portions,' writes John Tovey, although there are still five courses, and the
gimmickry of seven elaborate vegetables remains.

A sample meal paints the picture. Marinated chicken livers between layers of
puff pastry with parsley sauce are followed by courgette and fennel soup with
toasted flaked almonds, and then baked fillet of cod on garlic mash with
ratatouille. Next, roast loin of pork is stuffed with a mixture of hazelnuts, onion
and mustard and served on rhubarb chutney with a madeira sauce. Don't forget
the seven vegetables, before the first choice of the evening: bread-and-butter
pudding, perhaps, or white chocolate crème brûlée. Did we say the style was
lighter than before?

One reporter found the whole thing 'surprisingly spotty', with fabulous
breakfasts, an excellent dinner one night but not the next. This might explain the
wild fluctuations in reports we have received. 'Far from having too many
flavours, the cooking had virtually none,' wrote one reporter. 'Crisp and
beautifully flavoured' tomato tart, and 'unexpectedly wonderful' smoked
haddock on black pudding are understandable, but fish-cakes that are 'gutsy in
flavour' on one occasion and not on another are more difficult to explain.

Service is a well-oiled machine and does not overheat, provided everything
goes according to plan. The list of New World wines proves the point that it is
perfectly possible to assemble a good selection, almost entirely under £20, if you
don't mind the fact that most were made during this decade. Fruit and high
flavour are the hallmarks, which suits food and reporters alike. Two wines are
normally available by the glass.

⅝✳ *indicates that smoking is either banned altogether or that a dining-room is maintained*
for non-smokers. The symbol does not apply to restaurants that simply have no-smoking
areas.

CHEF: Chris Blaydes   PROPRIETOR: John J. Tovey   OPEN: all week; 1 and 8.30   CLOSED: early Dec to early Mar   MEALS: Set L £12.50 (2 courses), Set D £32   SERVICE: 12.5%, card slips closed   CARDS: Access, Amex, Visa   DETAILS: 70 seats. Private parties: 30 main room. Car park. Vegetarian meals. No children under 8. Smart dress preferred. No smoking in dining-room. Music. Air-conditioned   ACCOMMODATION: 13 rooms, all with bath/shower. TV. Phone.D,B&B £95 to £250. No children under 8. Pets welcome. Afternoon teas. Garden. Doors close at 11. Confirm by 6. Fax: (053 94) 45664 (*The Which? Hotel Guide*)

Miller Howe Café ✻ £

Lakeland Plastics Ltd, Alexandra Buildings,
Station Precinct, Windermere LA23 1BQ   COOKING 1
WINDERMERE (053 94) 46732   COST £15–£23

This café in the shop of a mail-order company specialising in kitchenware sometimes gets chaotic; service, says one lunchtime visitor, can get 'grotesquely overworked', but remains polite. The Duttons' cut-price version of good food is 'simple, well presented and flavoursome': excellent bread and butter, decent soups, 'very good' pâtés à la Miller Howe (see entry above), and honest versions of Cumberland sausage with apple sauce, lamb's liver in red wine sauce and sticky toffee pudding. An inspector concluded that, despite the crush and the rush, 'this is a good-value café which works well'. House wine is £7.50 a litre.

CHEFS: Ian Dutton, Patrick Dacre and Steven Kirkbride   PROPRIETORS: Ian and Annette Dutton   OPEN: all week, 9am (10am Sun) to 5pm (4pm Sat and Sun)   MEALS: alc (main courses £5 to £6.50)   SERVICE: not inc, card slips closed   CARDS: Access, Visa   DETAILS: 45 seats. 5 tables outside. Private parties: 50 main room, Car park. Vegetarian meals. Children's helpings. No smoking in dining-room. Wheelchair access (also WC). No music. Air-conditioned

Roger's

4 High Street, Windermere LA23 1AF   COOKING 2*
WINDERMERE (053 94) 44954   COST £24–£43

'A very pleasant evening in a comfortable atmosphere with friendly staff. The food is excellent' was how one satisfied reporter summed up a spring visit to the two-roomed restaurant opposite the tourist office. 'Special nights' are devoted to regions of France, so it is no surprise to find some French input to the regular menus. But a rummage through other cooking traditions results in hot mousses (of celeriac, or chicken livers) and gnocchi among first courses, followed by calf's liver with bacon, lamb with a herb crust and madeira gravy, and ending with twin chocolate terrine with Irish coffee cream.

Fish comes highly recommended, cream pops up in a few sauces, and vegetables are resolutely al dente. It is good to see blewits and 'penny bun' mushrooms (ceps) appear in season. The cooking is not fashion-conscious, but sticks to its last with a confidence born of experience. Hot almond and amaretto pudding with butterscotch sauce is praised, while apple and bilberry crumble with custard is more English Lakes. The backbone of the wine list is French, with interesting wines outside the classics, a few from the New World and a good spread of prices. House French is £9.95 per litre.

CHEF/PROPRIETOR: Roger Pergl-Wilson   OPEN: Mon to Sat (Sun bank hols), D only; 7 to 9.30 CLOSED: 1 week winter, 1 week summer   MEALS: alc (main courses £7 to £12.50). Set D £16.50   SERVICE: not inc, card slips closed   CARDS: Access, Amex, Diners, Visa   DETAILS: 44 seats. Private parties: 26 private room. Vegetarian meals. Children's helpings. Wheelchair access (1 step). Music

---

WINKLEIGH Devon   map 1

▲ *London House* 🍴

Winkleigh EX19 8HQ   COOKING 1
WINKLEIGH (0837) 83202   COST £13–£28

The Jamesons describe the character of this 1750s listed property as 'correct but relaxed'. They themselves are 'intelligent, knowledgeable and entertaining', according to a visitor from abroad, who appreciated the antiques, attractive fabrics, and the bill of £35 that covered both food and lodging. Dinner is cooked 'in the English style', and is a generous five courses and coffee that might begin with beef consommé and finish with a hot savoury. In between, at one dinner, were a tartlet of smoked fish and scrambled egg, then either game pie or chicken breast, and a choice of trifle, fruit jellies or wine syllabub. It is a very homely mix, even when, as it often does, the cooking strays to Normandy to pick up a main course of pork with apples, calvados and cream, or a ripe Camembert. There is room to eat outside on warm days, and the brief wine list struggles to go above £10. House wine (Rhône red, local white) is £6 (£1 per glass).

CHEF: Barbara Jameson   PROPRIETOR: Barbara and Peter Jameson   OPEN: all week, exc Sun D; 12 to 2, 7.30 to late   CLOSED: occasional days in winter – please phone to check   MEALS: Set L £8, Set L Sun £10, Set D £18   SERVICE: net prices, card slips closed   CARDS: Access, Visa DETAILS: 16 seats. 2 tables outside. Private parties: 16 main room. Vegetarian meals with prior notice. Children's helpings L. Smart dress preferred. No smoking in dining-room. Wheelchair access (1 step; also WC). Music   ACCOMMODATION: 2 rooms, both with bath. D,B&B £40 to £80. Deposit: 10%. No children under 14

Pophams 🍴 £

Castle Street, Winkleigh EX19 8HQ   COOKING 2*
WINKLEIGH (0837) 83767   COST £13–£26

Pophams is tiny and open-plan. At one end is a little delicatessen, and the rest of the space is taken up with three interchangeable tables. Melvyn Popham cooks for all to see, and Dennis Hawkes ensures that service is – in the words of one devotee – 'absolutely first-class'. The food is at a low price, and the style evolves slowly. Visitors perusing the lunchtime blackboard might choose from avocado salad with hot smoked bacon, breast of chicken with Parmesan 'oven-fried' with curry cream sauce and savoy cabbage, and a favourite speciality of marinated duck breast with plum sauce or madeira. Rounding things off are delights such as sticky toffee pudding, and walnut and Drambuie charlotte with vanilla sauce. The place is unlicensed, but you can bring your own wine with no charge for corkage.

CHEF: Melvyn Popham   PROPRIETORS: Melvyn Popham and Dennis Hawkes   OPEN: Mon to Sat, L only; 12 to 3   CLOSED: Feb   MEALS: alc (main courses £5.50 to £10.50). Unlicensed, but bring your own: no corkage   SERVICE: not inc, card slips closed   CARDS: Access, Visa   DETAILS: 10 seats. Private parties: 10 main room. Vegetarian meals. No children under 14. No smoking. Wheelchair access. Music. Air-conditioned

---

WINSTER Cumbria   map 7

Brown Horse £ |NEW ENTRY|

Winster,
nr Bowness-on-Windermere LA23 1NR   COOKING 1
WINDERMERE (053 94) 43443   COST £15–£25

Winster is a tiny village (more a hamlet) in woodland a few miles from Windermere, and the old whitewashed pub is much extended. The inside has been opened up and a modern wooden bar takes centre stage, among false beams and bare pub tables. Think of it as a pub serving food, and the place may well seem above-average. Think of it as a restaurant, and the prices will appear reasonable. Enough people are convinced to make booking advisable.

The style is breezy – pieces of chicken and mushroom are covered in a thick cheesy sauce on a crusty croûton – but there are some sound techniques behind what appears to be routine fare. Deep-frying is particularly successful, although sauces can be clumsy and copious, and there is a tendency to jazz everything with garlic. The effect is one of heartiness that suits a pub. Celery, garlic, onion and ham appear in the pea soup, and lots of olive oil and assertive balsamic vinegar show up in a gratin of Mediterranean vegetables. Prawns are large and juicy, swamped in tomato, garlic and cream sauce. Cannelloni is two large cylinders of light pasta filled with a light mix of ricotta and parsley. Service is well-informed and solicitous, without frills. 'Order your wine from the short selection of good-value bottles at the bar, carry it to your table, and pour your own.' House French is £6.50 (£1.20 per glass).

CHEF: Steven Doherty   PROPRIETOR: Rudolf Schaefer   OPEN: all week; 12 to 2, 6 to 9   CLOSED: 2 weeks Nov, 25 Dec   MEALS: alc (main courses £5.50 to £6.50)   SERVICE: not inc   DETAILS: 65 seats. 3 tables outside. Private parties: 50 main room. Car park. Vegetarian meals. Children's helpings. Wheelchair access. No music

---

WINTERINGHAM Humberside   map 6

▲ Winteringham Fields ♟ ✳

Winteringham DN15 9PF   COOKING 4*
SCUNTHORPE (0724) 733096   COST £25–£70

The setting heralds the style. This is no imposing country mansion, just a small (but extended) house at the village crossroads – 'It is not where you would expect a restaurant with this ambition to be situated.' There are no big signs, no fanfares, and nobody stands on ceremony; it is all unassuming and as natural as could be, which is the key to its charm. As we were going to press the L-shaped dining-room was being redesigned, but the rest of the house is to retain crooked floors, low beams, Victoriana and the conservatory for drinks. 'The Schwabs are 'outstandingly kind and welcoming hosts' is a comment that could have come from almost any report. If it's raining, staff come out with umbrellas to meet you; if it's not, they come out anyway.

Germain Schwab cooks in classical vein but with a lively and inventive streak that raises the food above the merely very good. It may not sound much on paper – sea bass with braised celery and mousseline sauce in a veal and mustard-seed juice, for instance – but on the plate it can be a knockout. Accurately roasted medallions of monkfish rolled in crushed pink peppercorns were served on a bed of sorrel with wafer-thin discs of celeriac and chopped roasted red pepper: 'an inspired dish, full of intense flavours', in the words of one of our senior inspectors. Fish leads the field, Grimsby is the source, and freshness and quality are exemplary. Fish options can be taken either as an intermediary or main course, and a simple daily menu and six-course 'surprise' add further flexibility to the *carte*.

The combination of sound technique and bright invention, coupled with a fine sense of balance, sets Germain Schwab's cooking apart. Where there is sweetness – a tiny compote of apple or quince with pigeon or rabbit, for instance – acidity will counter it. Complexity is achieved by hitting the main components of salt, sweetness and acidity together. Among dishes that have evoked superlatives are a spiced hotpot of tripe with a boudin blanc, and blini of smoked mackerel served with a confit of apple and lemon that was judged 'an ingenious piece of culinary invention – superb'.

The cheese trolley is as good as you will find, although desserts tempt most. A warm, dark chocolate tart in shortcrust pastry is paired with a small bowl of cool cherry soup, acidity and sweetness once again balancing, and the fruit flavour is a natural with chocolate. Others have enjoyed an 'inspired dessert' of crystallised apple with green apple sorbet, mint syrup and lemon ice-cream, while the hot corn tart with butterscotch and fresh cream could 'rank alongside Sharrow Bay's icky sticky toffee pudding' as a classic of its kind. The wine list improves by the year and has a fair range of prices, a full-house of Beaujolais *crus*, a decent spread of antipodeans and enough Swiss wines to remind Germain Schwab of home. House Pinot Noir and Chardonnay are £11. CELLARMAN'S CHOICE: Selaks Sauvignon Blanc 1992, £18.95; Savigny-lès-Beaune 1990, Bize, £29.

CHEF: Germain Schwab   PROPRIETORS: Germain and Annie Schwab   OPEN: Mon to Sat, exc L Mon and Sat; 12 to 1.30, 7.30 to 9.30 (10 Sat)   MEALS: alc (main courses £18 to £22). Set L £15.75, Set D £27 to £42   SERVICE: not inc, card slips closed   CARDS: Access, Amex, Visa DETAILS: 36 seats. 1 table outside. Private parties: 16 main room, 10 private room. Car park. Vegetarian meals. Smart dress preferred. No smoking in dining-room. Wheelchair access. Music   ACCOMMODATION: 7 rooms, all with bath/shower. TV. Phone. B&B £60 to £95. Rooms for disabled. No children under 8. Doors close at midnight. Confirm by 10. Fax: (0724) 733898 (*The Which? Hotel Guide*)

If a restaurant is new to the Guide *this year (did not appear as a main entry in the last edition),* NEW ENTRY *appears opposite its name.*

Report forms are at the back of the book; write a letter if you prefer.

WITHERSLACK Cumbria   map 7

▲ Old Vicarage ▐ ⅜✳

Church Road, Witherslack LA11 6RS
WITHERSLACK (053 95) 52381
off A590, take first left in village to church   COOKING 2
and continue for ¾m   COST £24–£42

Since 1976, the Burrington-Browns and the Reeves have maintained this
pleasing Victorian vicarage as a bastion of old-style Lakeland cooking and
comfort. The informality of the place is appreciated; service is friendly, quiet and
unobtrusive. Paul Axford now helps Stanley Reeve in the kitchen, and the menu
has been revamped. The centrepiece is generally meat and often a roast – perhaps
glazed rack of lamb or Gressingham duck with wild bramble sauce and an
allotment of vegetables – although fish and vegetarian options can be provided.
A handful of first courses such as vermicelli with pine-kernels and watercress
sauce start proceedings well; a choice of two puddings (steamed orange sponge
with damson sauce has been first-rate) plus a highly rated, impeccably sourced
British cheeseboard complete the picture. Coffee is served with Kendal mint
cake in the lounge. Sunday lunch is good value. Upon occasion, however,
criticisms have surfaced in regard to 'bland' flavours, especially in items such as
soup. Sensible wines by the glass, good half-bottles (including sherry), an
appreciation of Italy and bottled British beers add interest to the short and
well-priced list. CELLARMAN'S CHOICE: Gisborne Chardonnay 1991, £19.50;
Coteaux de Languedoc 1991, £13.80.

CHEFS: Stanley Reeve and Paul Axford   PROPRIETORS: the Burrington-Brown and Reeve
families   OPEN: all week, D only, and Sun L; 12.30 for 1, 7.30 for 8   MEALS: Set L Sun £13.50,
Set D £22.50   SERVICE: not inc, card slips closed   CARDS: Access, Visa   DETAILS: 35 seats.
Private parties: 22 main room, 12 private room. Car park. Vegetarian meals. Children's helpings
on request. Smart dress preferred. No smoking in dining-room. Wheelchair access (3 steps).
Music   ACCOMMODATION: 15 rooms, all with bath/shower. TV. Phone. B&B £59 to £138.
Children welcome. Baby facilities. Pets by arrangement. Afternoon teas. Garden. Tennis. Doors
close at 11.30. Confirm by 6. Fax: (053 95) 52373 (The Which? Hotel Guide)

WOBURN Bedfordshire   map 3

Paris House

Woburn Park, Woburn MK17 9QP
WOBURN (0525) 290692
on A4012, 1¼m E of Woburn in   COOKING 2
Abbey grounds   COST £31–£60

The setting has charm. The black and white mock-Tudor timbered house in the
grounds of Woburn Park, where deer graze gracefully, looks a picture. The
classical French bias of the cooking, so long a feature, has been tempered by
other influences. Bruschetta has found its way into the repertoire, served with
aubergine, mozzarella and Parma ham, and so too has sweet-and-sour pork with
pineapple, not to mention good old calf's liver and bacon. But the thrust is still
on confit of crispy duck with blackcurrants, pig's trotter with béarnaise sauce,
tarte fine aux pommes with honey sauce, and a fair amount of cream throughout.

And there would probably be an outcry if hot raspberry soufflé were ever given the heave-ho. Commendably, dishes are not overworked with extraneous flavours or risky partnerships, so rabbit appears simply with mustard sauce, and breast of chicken with wild mushrooms.

Not all is perfection, however. 'We have been eating here since the place opened,' wrote one couple, 'and have just had our first really disappointing meal', citing an over-cheesy fish soup, and a game terrine that seemed to have more in common with coarsely milled pork. The wine list takes an interesting approach, organised partly on geographical lines, partly stylistic. There are some very good bottles, a few that could be weeded out, and many prices that could be brought closer to reality. House wine is £10.

CHEF/PROPRIETOR: Peter Chandler   OPEN: Tue to Sun, exc Sun D; 12 to 2, 7 to 9.30   CLOSED: Feb   MEALS: Set L £23, Set D £36 to £40   SERVICE: not inc, card slips closed   CARDS: Access, Amex, Diners, Visa   DETAILS: 44 seats. Private parties: 44 main room, 14 private room. Car park. Vegetarian meals. Children's helpings on request. Smart dress preferred. No music. Fax: (0525) 290471

WOODSTOCK Oxfordshire   map 2

▲ *Feathers Hotel*

Market Street, Woodstock OX20 1SX   COOKING 2*
WOODSTOCK (0993) 812291   COST £32–£61

This amalgam of seventeenth-century town houses in leafiest Oxfordshire is many people's idea of what a country-house hotel should be. The interiors are all time-worn panelling and uneven floors, with masses of little passageways to explore and a spacious, brightly decorated dining-room. There is none of the reverential murmuring that irritates elsewhere, but neither is the jollity forced. The whole approach, one quartet agreed, is 'quietly British'.

At one time that might have gone for the food as well, but David Lewis is not a man to ignore prevailing trends, and a distinct Mediterranean tinge has lately come into play. Baked goats' cheese with sun-dried tomato vinaigrette has a fairly familiar ring these days, but how about smoked duck breast crostini with pistachio and balsamic dressing? Other good ideas include marinated scallops with chilli and shallots, roast breast of Norfolk duckling with a confit of the leg flavoured with caramelised garlic and honey, or venison steak with green peppercorns and port. Intensity and confidence of flavour are the norm, and do not flag when it comes to desserts of cappuccino and mocha parfait with black cherries and brandy, apricot and amaretto torte, or ginger pudding with vanilla ice-cream and toffee sauce. Trimmings, such as the good breads, and truffles with coffee, do not let the side down. A 'suggested gratuity' of 15 per cent is still added to bills. The wine list has many worthwhile bottles but at hefty prices. The selection of half-bottles is good, some fine wines are offered by the glass, but when non-vintage Veuve-Clicquot is £53 and even a youngish vintage of Ch. Musar is over £30, it all begins to look rather academic. House wines start at £11.60.

CHEF: David Lewis PROPRIETORS: Andrew Leeman, Simon Lowe and Howard Malin OPEN: all week; 12.30 to 2.15 (2.30 Sun), 7.30 to 9.30 MEALS: alc (main courses £13.50 to £19.50). Set L £18.50, Set D £23.50 SERVICE: 15% CARDS: Access, Amex, Diners, Visa DETAILS: 60 seats. Private parties: 60 main room, 25 private room. Vegetarian meals on request. Children's helpings. No cigars/pipes in dining-room. Wheelchair access (also male WC). Music. Air-conditioned ACCOMMODATION: 17 rooms, all with bath/shower. TV. Phone. B&B £75 to £175. Children welcome. Baby facilities. Pets welcome. Afternoon teas. Garden. Doors close at 11.30. Fax: (0993) 813158 (*The Which? Hotel Guide*)

WOOLTON HILL Hampshire   map 2

▲ *Hollington House Hotel*

Church Road, Woolton Hill RG15 9XR
NEWBURY (0635) 255100   COOKING 3*
off A343, 3m S of Newbury   COST £29–£55

People still marvel at the level of investment evident at every turn in John and Penny Guy's gorgeously restored Edwardian country house just over the Hampshire border from Newbury. The galleried entrance hall, the sitting-room with its soft tones of mint and primrose, the view through mullioned windows from the comfortable dining-room: all are designed to impress, and seem to succeed. Bedrooms, says the leaflet, have 'cuddly duvets'; should you need to make a quick getaway, a helicopter can be laid on.

New chef Mark Willoughby looks set to maintain the formidable standards set by his predecessors. The style is recognisably country-house, with most of the inventive flourishes on the long *carte* appearing among the hors d'oeuvre. A May dinner menu offered panaché of squid and artichoke in tomato, basil and olive oil, salmon and monkfish in a lime and ginger marinade, with main courses of sauté spiced cod on fennel with chicken stock, or beef fillet with red wine and shallot sauce. The only clanger at an inspection meal was rather coarse gravad lax, the sauce going too strong on mustard and lacking the expected sweetness. Otherwise, a terrine of rabbit in bacon was well-nigh 'perfect', and a main course of scallops with carrots in a rich saffron cream was hugely admired. Vegetables, plated separately, tend to be '*very* crisp'. Saffron featured again in a crème brûlée served with a micro-salad of fruits in a small pan – 'couldn't be faulted' – while a thin apple tart with vanilla ice-cream and caramel sauce has been eulogised by more than one. It all works out rather expensively, of course, but look around to see why. At least the quality is there on the plate.

The doorstop of a wine list speaks eloquently of the Guys' former life in Australia. The wines of that country receive the in-depth regional treatment normally reserved for France, although France itself – especially Bordeaux – is exhaustively represented, and Spain, Italy and California are all explored with glee. Prices are not low, but this is an impressive list. House French is £12.75. CELLARMAN'S CHOICE: Margaret River Chardonnay 1993, £26; Petit Chablis 1990, Durup, £17.

An asterisk (*) after the 1 to 5 cooking mark at the top of an entry signifies that the Guide *and its readers think that the restaurant is a particularly fine example within its rating.*

CHEF: Mark Willoughby PROPRIETORS: John and Penny Guy OPEN: all week; 12.30 to 2, 7 to 9.30 MEALS: alc (main courses £14 to £16.50). Set L £13.75 (2 courses) to £16.75, Set D £25 SERVICE: not inc, card slips closed CARDS: Access, Amex, Diners, Visa DETAILS: 50 seats. 6 tables outside. Private parties: 50 main room, 50 private room. Car park. Vegetarian meals. Children's helpings. Smart dress preferred. No cigars/pipes in dining-room. Wheelchair access (also male WC). Music ACCOMMODATION: 20 rooms, all with bath/shower. TV. Phone. B&B £80 to £155. Deposit: 50%. Rooms for disabled. Children welcome. Baby facilities. Afternoon teas. Garden. Swimming-pools. Tennis. Snooker. Doors close at midnight. Confirm by 6. Fax: (0635) 255075 (*The Which? Hotel Guide*)

WORCESTER Hereford & Worcester map 2

Brown's

24 Quay Street, Worcester WR1 2JJ COOKING 2
WORCESTER (0905) 26263 COST £20–£42

What was once a working grain mill – by the River Severn, between the bridge and the cathedral, opposite the county cricket ground – is now an elegant and comfortable restaurant with cream walls and pink furnishings. It was converted by the Tansleys in 1980 and is spacious but not cavernous, feels more country than city, and accommodates all sorts, from evening dress to casuals. 'Perhaps the best compliment I can pay Brown's is that they have the right balance: in the décor, in the warm but not overbearing attitude of the staff, in the menu and food, and the inclusive price with no hidden extras,' writes an enthusiast. The lunch menu is not much different from the one at dinner, and is half the price. Why can't dinner be half the price, too?

A vein of traditional English cooking runs through the repertoire, in dishes such as sirloin of beef with pease pudding and onion gravy, or braised beef with herb dumplings. Herbs are used in a conventional, reassuring way: tarragon and lemon with roast chicken, or thyme and juniper with casserole of rabbit, for instance. The kitchen builds a menu round different techniques – braising, chargrilling and roasting – for variety. There is always a vegetarian dish, and smoked salmon appears on most menus. Puddings often rely on France for inspiration, and soufflés are popular, but rhubarb fool nicely contrasts soft texture with a crisp brandy-snap biscuit and has 'a superb rhubarb sauce'. The francophile wine list has some input from the New World and a reasonable selection of half-bottles. French and Australian house wines are £9.90.

CHEFS: W.R. Tansley and K. Powles PROPRIETORS: W.R. and P.M. Tansley OPEN: all week, exc Sat L and Sun D; 12.30 to 2.45, 7.30 to 9.45 CLOSED: 1 week Christmas, bank hol Mons MEALS: Set L £15, Set D £30 SERVICE: net prices, card slips closed CARDS: Access, Amex, Diners, Visa DETAILS: 120 seats. Private parties: 120 main room. Vegetarian meals. No children under 8. Smart dress preferred. Wheelchair access (also WC). No music

---

The 1996 Guide will be published before Christmas 1995. Reports on meals are most welcome at any time of the year, but are particularly valuable in the spring. Send them to The Good Food Guide, FREEPOST, 2 Marylebone Road, London NW1 1YN. *No stamp is needed if posted in the UK.*

Il Pescatore

34 Sidbury, Worcester WR1 2HZ	COOKING 1
WORCESTER (0905) 21444	COST £18–£43

In the heart of old Worcester, this timber-framed former tea-room has discovered a new lease of life as a better-than-average Italian restaurant. Giuliano Ponzi runs it with flair and imagination; not being one to hide his light under a bushel, he has covered the walls with his own paintings.

The culinary philosophy is fresh fish and home-made pasta. While the menu is buttressed by old-wave Italian standards, inventiveness crops up in the daily-changing specials. Fritto misto is made with properly fresh fish, even if the batter 'could have been crisper'. Beef fillet wrapped in smoked ham with a wild mushroom sauce impressed one reporter. Rave notices for raspberry Romanoff and a technically excellent hot passion-fruit soufflé suggest puddings should not be missed. Grumbles surfaced on one occasion over silly, inedible garnishes and the Muzak machine giving it hell with the Verdi. The wine list waves the flag single-mindedly for Italy (apart from champagnes) but doesn't trouble itself with vintages. House wine is £7.25.

CHEF: Kevin Capper   PROPRIETOR: Giuliano Ponzi   OPEN: Mon to Sat, exc Mon L; 12 to 2, 6.30 to 10   MEALS: alc (main courses £7 to £14.50). Set L £11.50, Set D £16.50   SERVICE: not inc   CARDS: Access, Visa   DETAILS: 40 seats. Private parties: 50 main room. Vegetarian meals. Children welcome. Smart dress preferred. Wheelchair access (1 step). Music. Fax: (0905) 21444

WORFIELD Shropshire   map 5

▲ Old Vicarage Hotel ♥ ⅝✕

Worfield WV15 5JZ	
WORFIELD (0746) 716497	COOKING 2
1m N of A454, 4m E of Bridgnorth	COST £22–£47

Although this converted Edwardian vicarage is not a particularly pretty edifice, unless you arrive at night, the interior decorations are thought to have 'great charm and style'. The two acres of grounds and the conservatory extension used for coffee and the post-prandial tot also afford much cheer. The cooking is in the modern British idiom, drawing heavily on local produce for the daily-changing menus. Breads are produced in-house, the smokehouse is employed for the likes of salmon and pigeon, and John Williams is very proud of his sauces.

Menus are fixed-price, the cost varying in the evening according to whether cheese is taken as well as dessert. A vegetable-based soup is always on offer – beetroot and cider, or celery and pesto, for example – and one man so enjoyed an hors d'oeuvre of smoked salmon with mango and horseradish ('a brilliant combination') that he was inspired to reproduce it at home. Judgement of the first courses may well hinge on whether you like fruity accompaniments: one March menu began with chicken liver parfait with apple chutney, roast pigeon salad with avocado and mango, and canteloupe melon with exotic fruits on warm apple and mint tea dressing. Recommended main courses have included baked fillet of salmon with tarragon and lobster cream sauce, medallions of pork with black pudding and a sauce of red wine and thyme, and sauté lamb's liver with tomato and basil sauce and a provençale vegetable gâteau. The signature dessert is chocolate, fruit and nut tart with pear sabayon. British farmhouse cheeses offer a commendable selection.

An impressive wine list has been assembled. It is truly international in scope, and prices are eminently fair once Bordeaux and Burgundy are left behind. Half-bottles run to four pages. Prices for full bottles open at £11.50. CELLARMAN'S CHOICE: Jackson Estate Sauvignon 1993, £16.75; Côtes du Rhône, Brézème 1988, Lombard, £17.95.

CHEF: John Williams PROPRIETORS: Peter and Christine Iles OPEN: all week, exc Sat L; 12 to 2, 7 to 9 MEALS: Set L Mon to Fri £17.50, Set L Sun £12.50, Set D £21.50 to £26.50 SERVICE: not inc CARDS: Access, Amex, Diners, Visa DETAILS: 45 seats. Private parties: 25 main room, 16 private room. Car park. Vegetarian meals. Children's helpings. No children under 8 D. Smart dress preferred. No smoking in dining-rooms. Wheelchair access (2 steps; also WC). Music ACCOMMODATION: 14 rooms, all with bath/shower. TV. Phone. B&B £63.50 to £100. Deposit: £40. Rooms for disabled. Children welcome. Baby facilities. Pets welcome (not in public rooms). Afternoon teas. Garden. Doors close at 11.30. Fax: (0746) 716552

WRIGHTINGTON Lancashire

map 5

High Moor ⁂✳

High Moor Lane, Wrightington WN6 9QA
APPLEY BRIDGE (0257) 252364
off A5209, between M6 junction 27 and
Parbold, take Robin Hood Lane at
crossroads W of Wrightington Hospital,
then next left

COOKING 2
COST £19–£45

Even on a cold, frosty night, with the lights of Wigan twinkling in the Douglas Valley, this rural restaurant high on the moors is particularly appealing. The bar area, with its low ceiling beams and rough-plastered walls, reminded one visitor of a small country pub. By contrast, the dining-room is spacious, stylish and discreetly lit.

New chef Darren Wynn cooks to an ambitious fixed-price menu that does not shy away from complexity, and reporters have enthused about meals of 'immense character and unusual flavours'. Choose two, three or four courses depending on your wallet and appetite. One commendable dinner kicked off with carpaccio of beef topped with a plethora of ingredients including shaved Parmesan, before poached fillet of sea bass with fettuccine and a tarragon sauce perfumed with lemon grass. Then came rack of lamb coated in a herb crust with plenty of good vegetables, followed by a trolley of cheeses. Others have opted for desserts such as caramelised pears with honey ice-cream. The poise and attentiveness of the service draw effusive praise. Superior Bordeaux and burgundies dominate the 150-strong wine list. House wines start at £8.90.

CHEF: Darren J. Wynn PROPRIETOR: John Nelson OPEN: Tue to Sun, D only, and Sun L; 12 to 2, 7 to 10 MEALS: Set D £20.50 (2 courses) to £28, Set L Sun £12.50 SERVICE: 10% CARDS: Access, Amex, Diners, Visa DETAILS: 90 seats. Private parties: 90 main room. Car park. Vegetarian meals. Children's helpings. Smart dress preferred. No smoking in dining-room. Wheelchair access. Music. Fax: (0257) 255120

WYE Kent   map 3

▲ *Wife of Bath*

4 Upper Bridge Street, Wye TN25 5AW
WYE (0233) 812540 and 812232   COOKING 1*
just off A28, Ashford to Canterbury road   COST £20–£37

'Quintessentially an excellent, good-quality, unpretentious English restaurant' is the knowledgeable verdict on this converted doctor's house. The years pass and little changes: the place continues to bring in crowds of all-comers who eat in a tasteful dining-room bedecked with paintings of fruit and architectural prints. Lunch and dinner menus advertise the likes of warm smoked salmon with green peppercorn vinaigrette and loin of lamb with confit of shallots and thyme, while the day's fish dish might be baked sea bass and red mullet paired with asparagus and a buttery lemon sauce. Reporters have spoken well of gratin of crab and courgettes, baked guinea-fowl stuffed with potato and sun-dried tomatoes, and chocolate terrine with tiny balls of home-made lemon ice-cream. 'Masses of staff' tend the customers, although their knowledge of the menu is not always up to scratch. The wine list is tilted towards France, but it offers plenty of choice and fair value. House wines start at £8.95.

CHEF: Robert Hymers   PROPRIETOR: John Morgan   OPEN: Tue to Sat; 12 to 2.30, 7 to 11 CLOSED: first week Jan, first 2 weeks Sept   MEALS: alc (main courses £10.50 to £14, L only). Set L £11.75, Set D £19.95   SERVICE: not inc   CARDS: Access, Visa   DETAILS: 50 seats. Private parties: 55 main room, 20 private room. Car park. Vegetarian meals. Children's helpings. Smart dress preferred. No pipes in dining-room. Wheelchair access. No music   ACCOMMODATION: 2 rooms, both with bath/shower. TV. Phone. B&B £20 to £40. Rooms for disabled. Children welcome. Garden. Doors close at midnight

---

WYLAM Northumberland   map 7

▲ *Laburnum House*

Wylam NE41 8AJ   COOKING 1*
WYLAM (0661) 852185   COST £24–£48

A lot of thought and effort has gone into this converted house and shop over the years, and it is greatly liked for its pleasant village setting, affordable accommodation and sound cooking. The dining-room occupies the whole of the ground floor and has a pleasantly comforting old-fashioned atmosphere, with large wicker armchairs, mirrors and cupped candles on well-spaced tables. A straightforward fixed-price menu offers good value, but most interest centres on the blackboard. Kenn Elliott changes his dishes regularly: local salmon is served with prawns and cheese, monkfish might appear deep-fried with lime hollandaise or as a brochette with a creamy sauce laced with Pernod. Reporters have been impressed by 'fresh as a daisy' mussels, stir-fried king prawns, and a fine meaty duck breast coated with black peppercorns and served with an alcoholic raspberry sauce. Vegetables are well-timed, and good sweets have included a perfectly judged chocolate truffle. The short list of around 20 wines offers plenty of decent drinking for under £15. House wine is £9.50.

CHEF: Kenn Elliott PROPRIETORS: Kenn Elliott and Rowan Mahon OPEN: Mon to Sat D, 6.30 to 10; L by arrangement MEALS: alc (main courses £14 to £16.50). Set D £15.50 SERVICE: not inc CARDS: Access, Amex, Visa DETAILS: 46 seats. Private parties: 46 main room. Vegetarian meals with prior notice. Children's helpings. Smart dress preferred. Wheelchair access (1 step; also WC). Music ACCOMMODATION: 4 rooms, all with bath/shower. TV. B&B £40 to £50. Children welcome. Baby facilities. Pets welcome (not in public rooms)

YORK North Yorkshire
map 5

Kites £

13 Grape Lane, York YO1 2HU   COOKING 1
YORK (0904) 641750   COST £20–£36

Kites is hidden away down a quiet, cobbled back street in the middle of York and reached by toiling up two flights of steps. It is resolutely and doggedly determined to remain unpretentious and free of sophisticated décor: brickwork is painted red in one room, yellow in the other, and that's it. The cooking is in the same mould: as basic as an aubergine cut in two and steaming, with a dollop of pesto sauce, or two fish-cakes with a Thai sauce; as homely as braised shoulder of lamb, with a sauce that shows the kitchen is capable of good things. Other dishes on the menu may include steamed mussels in a lemon and garlic sauce with pine-nuts, game sausage, and banoffi pie. Service is friendly, knowledgeable and efficient, wines are well chosen and inexpensive. House vin de pays is £8.50.

CHEFS: T. Drew and P. Hornby PROPRIETOR: C. Wright OPEN: Mon to Sat, D only, and Sat L; 12 to 2, 7 (6.30 summer) to 10.30 (11 Sat) CLOSED: Christmas MEALS: alc (main courses £6.50 to £12.50) SERVICE: not inc CARDS: Access, Amex, Visa DETAILS: 46 seats. Private parties: 20 main room. Vegetarian meals. Children's helpings. No-smoking area. Music

Melton's ♥ ⚔✳

7 Scarcroft Road, York YO2 1ND   COOKING 3
YORK (0904) 634341   COST £19–£36

Just off the York ring road, 10 minutes from Cliffords Tower and conveniently close to a free public car park, Melton's operates from a converted Victorian terraced house. 'The décor has been greatly improved since our last visit by an exhibition of pictures.' It is cool and unfussy, with grey walls and wooden tables and chairs. Reporters stress the value for money, as well as the hard work and dedication of which they are on the receiving end. The welcome is warm, the atmosphere pleasant, and there is no sense of rush.

A reporter who eats there once a month notes that 'the standard is consistently high and the dishes unfailingly imaginative', citing blinis with shredded beetroot and soured cream, goats' cheese gnocchi with basil sauce, roast pear with butterscotch and lime sauces, and steamed ginger pudding with sherry custard. It would seem that Michael Hjort's time in the Roux empire has not been wasted. Ingredients are good, and properly treated: 'the lamb was superb in texture and flavour', and even fillet steak is tasty. Vegetarians get a fair deal, especially on Thursdays. Wednesday is for pudding people, and Tuesday for fish-fanciers, when specialities might include roast fillet of red snapper with a cucumber salad, or stir-fry of Dover sole with vegetables, noodles and black-bean sauce. Even if some component parts are on occasion less than perfect, that does not diminish enthusiasm for the whole package. Portions are satisfyingly generous without being excessive. Vegetables are up to standard, and apple and calvados soufflé is highly rated. Excellent cheeses are from the deli next door.

The 5.30pm opening time for dinner is for those prepared to leave by 7.45pm. 'There cannot be many restaurants of this quality which include coffee and mineral water in the price', while 'service is impeccable. It is a real joy to eat here.' The Hjorts go out of their way to be accommodating, not least with the wines, which combine excitement and good value, thanks to the mark-up policy of adding a maximum of £10 to wholesale prices. Wines by the glass (from £2.50 to £3.50) are a cut above average too. CELLARMAN'S CHOICE: Wakefield Cruchen Chardonnay 1989, £12; Swan Zinfandel 1988, £24.

CHEFS: Michael Hjort and Elizabeth Cooper PROPRIETORS: Michael and Lucy Hjort OPEN: all week, ex Mon L and Sun D; 12 to 2, 7 to 10 (early D 5.30 to 6.30, leave 7.45) CLOSED: 3 weeks after Christmas, 1 week end Aug/early Sept MEALS: alc (main courses £9.50 to £14). Set L and early D £13.90 SERVICE: net prices, card slips closed CARDS: Access, Visa DETAILS: 40 seats. Private parties: 30 main room, 15 private room. Vegetarian meals. Children's helpings. No-smoking room. Wheelchair access (1 step). Music. Fax: (0904) 629233

19 Grape Lane ⁙✳

19 Grape Lane, York YO1 2HU   COOKING 2
YORK (0904) 636366   COST £27–£48

A cobbled alley in the heart of York is the setting for the Alexanders' pleasingly intimate, low-ceilinged bistro. When tourists are swarming in search of the Minster, Grape Lane will feel like 'an oasis of calm'. Music murmurs unobtrusively: one expert noted the passage of Bernstein, Satie and Beethoven one winter's evening. The formula that has been worked out is successful, and Michael Fraser's cooking is not given to spasmodic changes of direction. One of the corollaries of having a loyal clientele is that they don't expect things to alter overnight. At lunchtime the menu is light, while a fixed-price menu of three courses plus coffee is offered in the evenings alongside the *carte*.

The food is in the modern British idiom of smoked duck salad with raspberry vinaigrette, steamed lemon sole with mixed peppers in a white wine cream sauce, or medallions of hare with mushrooms and madeira. Simple things, such as smoked salmon with melon, are elegantly presented. Roast saddle of lamb with a timbale of the kidneys plus mushrooms marshalled 'intense' flavours to enhance the 'first-class' meat. Puddings fly the Union Jack (sticky toffee, bread-and-butter), use top-quality chocolate in a two-coloured terrine with crème anglaise, or offer 'a little of everything' as a grand selection. Those with a savoury tooth will enjoy Colston Bassett Stilton. Wines offer welcome breadth of choice, with a more than generous collection of half-bottles. The French wines look the best overall, though prices seem a touch over the odds for the surroundings. House wines from Georges Duboeuf are £8.95.

CHEF: Michael Fraser PROPRIETORS: Gordon and Carolyn Alexander OPEN: Tue to Sat; 12 to 1.45, 7 to 10.30 (may vary weekdays) CLOSED: 25 to 28 Dec, first 2 weeks Feb, last 2 weeks Sept MEALS: alc D (main courses £13 to £15.50). Set D £19.95. Light L menu SERVICE: not inc CARDS: Access, Visa DETAILS: 34 seats. Private parties: 22 main room. Vegetarian meals. No children under 5. No smoking in 1 dining-room. Wheelchair access (1 step). Music. Fax: (0904) 702120

Scotland

ABERDEEN Grampian map 8

Courtyard on the Lane

NEW ENTRY

1 Alford Lane, Aberdeen AB1 1YD
ABERDEEN (0224) 213795

COOKING 1*
COST £20–£44

The Courtyard's move from Elrick has brought a division into two parts. Both Martha's Vineyard Bistro (the louder, more informal and less expensive half) and the restaurant upstairs share the same kitchen. A greeter on the stairs directs traffic with good humour. The bistro runs on a breezy yo-ho diet of venison and pork bangers with mash and onion gravy, carbonade of beef with herb dumplings, and dark chocolate mousse, picked off a short menu and a blackboard.

The small pink and green restaurant, calm and well-ordered, is dimly lit by candles. Meals begin with a bowl of warm nuts, oily and smelling very good. What the kitchen turns out for the restaurant is less casual, but still has a bright quality. Honey-roasted boneless quail is served on a bed of green lentils and bacon with oyster mushrooms, fillet of Aberdeen Angus beef on rösti potato gets an onion confit and red wine sauce, and poached pear with port jelly comes with cardamom ice-cream. Scallops are particularly fresh and juicily sweet, lamb is cooked pink, and some of the accompaniments stand out, especially a pile of roughly chopped tomatoes, courgette, aubergine, cheese and garlic with the lamb. Service is pleasingly personable and natural. The short wine list caters for all pockets and tastes, uses reliable producers, and has a reasonable selection of half-bottles. House wines from £9 are good.

CHEFS: Tony Heath, James Massie and Glen Lawson   PROPRIETORS: Tony Heath, Shona Drysdale and Vic Booth   OPEN: Tue to Sat; 12 to 2 (2.30 bistro), 7 (6.30 bistro) to 9.45   CLOSED: 2 weeks mid-July   MEALS: alc (main courses restaurant L £7.50 to £9, D £11 to £15, bistro £6.50 to £9)   SERVICE: not inc, card slips closed   CARDS: Access, Amex, Visa   DETAILS: restaurant 30 seats, bistro 40 seats. Private parties: 30 main room. Vegetarian meals. Children's helpings. Wheelchair access (bistro only). Music. Fax: (0224) 212961

The 1996 Guide will be published before Christmas 1995. Reports on meals are most welcome at any time of the year, but are particularly valuable in the spring. Send them to **The Good Food Guide,** *FREEPOST, 2 Marylebone Road, London NW1 1YN. No stamp is needed if posted in the UK.*

Faraday's

2–4 Kirk Brae, Cults, Aberdeen AB1 9QS
ABERDEEN (0224) 869666   COOKING 1
on A93, 4m from city centre   COST £18–£41

Even though the restaurant is located in a converted electricity substation, dinners are candle-lit, while lunches are light. The kitchen, rarely static, is switched on to current trends that take in tempura of squid and aubergine with a green chilli and lime dip, and Indian bhajias of green pepper and onion flavoured with coriander. It is also wired up to more homely herring or trout fillets in oatmeal, Arbroath smokies, braised oxtail, and rhubarb and apple crumble, and adapts two favourites to produce a sticky bread and toffee pudding served with brandy cream. Those who like strong flavours are in their element. The wine list is plugged into the European circuit, although there is some resistance to the high prices. House wine is £14.50 a litre.

CHEFS: John Inches and Roger Ross   PROPRIETOR: John Inches   OPEN: Mon to Sat, exc Mon L; 12 to 1.30, 7 to 9.30   CLOSED: 26 Dec to 5 Jan   MEALS: alc D (main courses £11 to £18). Set D Fri and Sat £24.50. Light L menu   SERVICE: net prices, card slips closed   CARDS: Access, Visa   DETAILS: 40 seats. Private parties: 40 main room. Car park. Vegetarian meals. Children welcome. Smart dress preferred. No smoking before 2 L and 10 D. Wheelchair access (also WC). Music. Air-conditioned

Silver Darling

Pocra Quay, North Pier,
Aberdeen AB2 1DQ   COOKING 1*
ABERDEEN (0224) 576229   COST £28–£46

A quayside restaurant named after an old catchphrase for herrings might suggest something patriotically Scottish, but chef Didier Dejean pays allegiance to the French half of the 'auld alliance'. Fish from the boats is the star of the show. Poached monkfish with shellfish sauce and served with pasta, wild mushrooms and stewed red cabbage is a typically successful offering. Chargrilling is a speciality: Dover sole with beurre blanc, sea trout with herbs and lemon mousseline sauce, and duck with green olive sauce for meat-eaters. Strong accompaniments can mar the essential flavour of a dish, as in an over-sharp raspberry vinaigrette with warm salad of scallops, but the cooking generally pleases. Sweets might include mango and papaya sorbet and warm apple tart with calvados. 'Crammed in' tables and laid-back service can seem at odds with the prices, which are by no means cheap. The wine list is a short selection from the major French growing regions. House wine is £9.50.

CHEF: Didier Dejean   PROPRIETORS: Didier Dejean and Catherine Wood   OPEN: Mon to Sat, exc Sat L; 12 to 2, 7 to 10   CLOSED: 2 weeks from 24 Dec   MEALS: alc D (main courses £15.50 to £16.50). Set L £15.70 to £17.35 (2 courses)   SERVICE: not inc   CARDS: Access, Amex, Diners, Visa   DETAILS: 35 seats. Private parties: 35 main room. Vegetarian meals with prior notice. Children welcome. Smart dress preferred. Wheelchair access (1 step; also WC). Music. Fax: (0224) 626558

The Good Food Guide *is a registered trade mark of Consumers' Association Ltd.*

ABERFELDY Tayside   map 8

▲ *Farleyer House* ⅜✳ | NEW ENTRY |

by Aberfeldy PH15 2JE   COOKING 2
ABERFELDY (0887) 820332   COST £21–£48

Farleyer looks beautiful. It has magnificent trees and glorious views, the grounds are well cared for, and the general air of prosperity continues inside the house, where immaculate rooms are finely furnished. Drinks are brought to the drawing-room, and the no-choice menu is fixed at four courses plus coffee. It changes daily, special requirements are dealt with when booking, and dinner begins at 8pm. Anybody who does not like fish will have a lean time, as Richard Lyth seems happiest when preparing scallops, mussels, oysters and turbot, although woodpigeon, venison, free-range duck and Highland beef also bring a smile to his face, as they do to reporters'.

Menus are factual and understated, with no flowery descriptions, and the food follows suit. At one meal, salad of Isle of Skye scampi was followed by wild Tay salmon with asparagus, then rack of Tayside lamb with honey and thyme jus, and either a soup of red fruits with vanilla ice-cream or Scottish cheeses. 'It should be comparatively easy to produce a good meal at a fixed time to a set menu,' wrote one reporter, who enjoyed 'a dreamy trout fillet in a sorrel sauce', before a moist breast of guinea-fowl served on a bed of leeks, peas and broad beans. 'Would that others could do it to this standard,' he concluded, after a delightful orange and chocolate soufflé with a cardamom and bayleaf ice-cream. Wine mark-ups are high and France fields some aristocratic bottles, but Italy and the New World are worth exploring. House French country wine is £8.50.

The bistro's *carte* makes lively use of similar ingredients: oysters at £1.25 each, Thai-style fish soup, pan-fried scallops with truffle mash, and filo-baked figs with white chocolate ice-cream. More reports of this, please.

CHEF: Richard Lyth PROPRIETORS: Mr and Mrs D. Reid OPEN: restaurant all week (Fri and Sat only Nov to Apr), D only; 7.30 for 8. Bistro all week; 12 to 2.30, 6 to 9.30 MEALS: alc bistro (main courses £6.50 to £15). Restaurant Set D £27 to £32 SERVICE: not inc, card slips closed CARDS: Access, Amex, Diners, Visa DETAILS: restaurant 25 seats, bistro 54 seats. 6 tables outside bistro. Private parties: 34 and 20 main rooms, 15 private room. Car park. Vegetarian meals (with prior notice restaurant). Children's helpings. Smart dress preferred restaurant. No smoking in restaurant. Wheelchair access (also WC). Music ACCOMMODATION: 11 rooms, all with bath/shower. TV. Phone. B&B £75 to £120. Children welcome. Baby facilities. Pets by arrangement. Afternoon teas. Garden. Golf. Doors close at midnight. Confirm by noon. Fax: (0887) 829430 (*The Which? Hotel Guide*)

ABERFOYLE Central   map 8

Braeval Old Mill ▮

by Aberfoyle FK8 3UY
ABERFOYLE (0877) 382711   COOKING 4
on A81, 1m from Aberfoyle   COST £27–£46

The grey stone walls (and concrete floor slabs) are now softened by yellow tablecloths, and modern fabrics hang on the walls. The old mill is developing a contemporary and slightly less austere feel. The waitress recites the menu for

537

each table, and descriptions are not always accurate. There is a curious imbalance: no choice for first, second or main courses, then suddenly half a dozen puddings come into earshot. At no stage before the bill arrives is there even a whisper of the cost, but nobody seems to mind.

The Mill, in fact, succeeds pretty well on all counts, although roast fillet of salmon with mashed potato and a champagne and chive sauce, for example, shows a degree of safety. The quality of ingredients has impressed: the best olive oil, freshly made pesto, grade-one capers, all brought together in a first course with tomato flesh, powerful black olives and home-made fettuccine, with a shaving of Parmesan for good measure. This is more than just a sop to Mediterranean ideas; it is a genuinely tasty dish to whet the appetite. Even mundane-sounding fare such as a fish-cake of salmon and cod works well because it is professionally executed, with a crisp crumb coating and a zing of coriander leaf in the creamy red pepper and mussel sauce surrounding it. There is no sense of being sated, just of being intrigued and wanting more, which is just as well because the fish-cake was followed at one meal by fillet of beef, well hung and tender, with an excellent flavour coming from finely chopped smoked bacon, seriously good potatoes sautéd in proper fat, and very good gravy. The bread is slices from a large white loaf, which have the texture of cake and a hard (rather than crisp) exterior. A mill, of all places, should do better than that. For puddings, hot chocolate soufflé, caramelised apple tart, and an armagnac parfait with warm prunes and an evanescent Earl Grey flavour to the syrup, are the kinds of things likely to turn up.

The wine list does not attempt to be comprehensive, but bottles are carefully selected, with good choice under £20. Details are clear, producers largely impeccable and styles varied, although half-bottles err on the expensive side. It is a list from which to choose with confidence. House wines start at £11. CELLARMAN'S CHOICE: Entre-Deux-Mers, Ch. de Castelneau 1991, £16.50; Lirac 'Les Queyrades' 1990, £14.50.

CHEF: Nick Nairn   PROPRIETORS: Nick and Fiona Nairn   OPEN: Tue to Sat, D only, and Sun L; 12.30 to 1.30, 7.30 to 9.30   CLOSED: 1 week Feb, 1 week June, 1 week Nov   MEALS: Set L Sun £18.50, Set D £27.50   SERVICE: not inc, card slips closed   CARDS: Access, Visa   DETAILS: 34 seats. Private parties: 30 main room. Car park. Vegetarian meals with prior notice. No children under 10. Smart dress preferred. No cigars/pipes in dining-room. Wheelchair access (1 step; also WC). No music. Fax: (0877) 382400

ACHILTIBUIE Highland   map 8

▲ *Summer Isles Hotel* ▮ ⁵⁄✳

Achiltibuie IV26 2YG
ACHILTIBUIE (0854) 622282   COOKING 2
off A835 at Drumrunie, 10m N of Ullapool   COST £40–£48

Summer Isles Hotel has been in the *Guide*, and in the same family, for 24 years. It is remote – unless you are a bird, access is by a long, single-track road with passing places – and beautiful. Achiltibuie is a string of houses, spun out along a broad sweep of coast where the moorland meets the sea, and where the islands are what everybody comes to look at. The menu is posted in the hall, along with copies of the wine list and today's faxed weather forecast. Aperitifs are taken in the lounge; dinner, five courses, begins at 8pm, with no choice before the cheese and sweet trolleys are trundled round. Gratuities are not expected; indeed, the Irvines 'believe it [the service charge] should not exist'.

It would be a surprise if the kitchen did not rely on local fish and shellfish, and they are often the centrepiece: from scallops and lobster to salmon and cod. Before that comes a soup, perhaps of spinach, or smoked haddock and potato, then a small fish course if the main is meat or game, and vice versa: savoury crab cake with a sorrel sauce precedes breast of pigeon with braised Savoy cabbage, for example. There are errors of judgement, as on one occasion when broccoli was spread with a dry, pungent paste of pulverised pilchards or sardines, but for the most part the incidentals don't get in the way.

Mark Irvine wheels round an interesting selection of cheeses that might include mature Gouda, blue Wensleydale, Bonchester or Cheddar from Mull, while Geraldine Irvine pushes a tower of puddings that recall highlights from dinner party cookbooks: pineapple and raisin upside-down pudding, banana and toffee pie, hazelnut meringue torte, and apple streusel. Wine orders are expected by 6pm, from a comprehensive list that takes in good Rhônes, Loires and Alsaces (as well as Israel and Canada), although, as with most collectors, Bordeaux and Burgundy dominate. There is a good selection of half-bottles, and a choice by the glass for each course. CELLARMAN'S CHOICE: Mount Edelstone Shiraz 1990, £18.50; Rully Rabourcé premier cru 1992, Leflaive, £16.50.

CHEF: Chris Firth-Bernard PROPRIETORS: Mark and Geraldine Irvine OPEN: all week, D only; 8 CLOSED: mid-Oct to Easter MEALS: Set D £32 DETAILS: 26 seats. Private parties: 8 main room. Car park. Vegetarian meals. Children's helpings. No children under 8. Smart dress preferred. No smoking in dining-room. Wheelchair access. No music ACCOMMODATION: 13 rooms, all with bath/shower. Phone. B&B £43 to £92. Deposit: £50. No children under 8. Pets welcome. Afternoon teas. Fishing. Doors close at 10.30. Confirm by 6. Fax: (0854) 622251 (*The Which? Hotel Guide*)

ALEXANDRIA Strathclyde   map 8

▲ *Cameron House Hotel, Georgian Room* ⁏✳

Loch Lomond, Alexandria G83 8QZ
ALEXANDRIA (0389) 55565
off A82, ½m N of Balloch roundabout, 3½m   COOKING 3
N of Dumbarton   COST £23–£61

The Craigendarroch Group knows its market well. It provides comfortable surroundings, tempts visitors with timeshares, throws in fishing, golf and a swimming-pool for relaxation, adds a gym to remind us that hard work is a virtue, then swings open the dining-room doors as a reward. We might pay a bit over the odds for it, but we generally come away happy to have unwound, to have been treated courteously and to have eaten well. Cameron House lives up to all this. True, it has its share of regulation pictures of Highland cattle and seascapes, but it overlooks Loch Lomond, so diversion is easily come by.

The *carte* may seem pricey, but has many appealing touches, including the scallops and sorrel dumplings that float in a cream of langoustine and lentil soup, or the sweetbread stew that comes with roast fillet of beef on a potato, onion and bacon pancake. Even the set-price market menu, a steal at lunch-time, offers three carefully considered courses: open ravioli of scallops with a leek and black olive stew, then pan-fried fillet of monkfish larded with bacon on a spinach pancake (with fresh mussels and a saffron butter sauce), and finally a warm feuilleté of apple and nuts in a toffee sauce with a honey ice-cream. Menus also commendably state that 'gratuities are not accepted'. All of that is good value by any standards.

The food has aesthetic appeal without being flamboyantly arty. It has clean flavours, well-moderated seasoning, and manages to combine delicacy and intensity of flavour in the same dish, and to set light textures off against rich saucing, both of which are impressive balancing acts. One reporter also welcomed the fact that salmon did not appear once on the menu she chose from, a novelty in these parts. Some of the wine mark-ups are very greedy – one Australian sparkler is nearly four times the retail price – which takes a bit of the shine off things. House French is £11.65.

CHEF: Jeff Bland   PROPRIETOR: Craigendarroch Group   OPEN: all week, exc Sat and Sun L; 12 to 2, 7 to 10   MEALS: alc (main courses £17.50 to £20). Set L £13.95 (2 courses) to £16.50, Set D £32.50 to £38.50   SERVICE: card slips closed   CARDS: Access, Amex, Diners, Visa   DETAILS: 42 seats. Private parties: 50 main room, 30, 120 and 240 private rooms. Car park. Vegetarian meals. Children's helpings. No children under 8. Jacket and tie D. No smoking in dining-room. Wheelchair access (also WC). No music. Air-conditioned   ACCOMMODATION: 68 rooms, all with bath/shower. TV. Phone. B&B £125 to £295. Deposit: £50. Rooms for disabled. Children welcome. Baby facilities. Afternoon teas. Garden. Swimming-pool. Sauna. Tennis. Fishing. Golf. Snooker. Confirm by 6. Fax: (0389) 59522

ALYTH Tayside   map 8

▲ *Drumnacree House Hotel* ᣐ✸

St Ninians Road, Alyth PH11 8AP
ALYTH (08283) 2194   COOKING 2
off A926, Blairgowrie to Kirriemuir road   COST £25–£38

'Being self-taught, I don't follow any particular style of cooking,' writes Allan Cull, which explains the appearance of a warm Arbroath smokie mousse alongside gumbos, blackened chicken and 'dirty rice' on his menus. But he is no mere follower of fashion. 'Taste rather than trend' dictates the menu in this small and warmly welcoming house. Allan Cull shares the enthusiasm of most good amateur cooks. He cures his own fish and meats, producing gravad lax, 'lamb ham', confit of gizzard, and bresaola, and has a smokehouse, fed with whisky-barrel shavings, for cold-smoking whatever he can lay his hands on. If any river pike swims his way, he might cook it with peppercorns in duck fat, with a vinegar, shallot and cream sauce.

Vegetables and herbs are organically produced in the garden, although one reporter gave thanks that there were no individual plates of undercooked vegetables to accompany main courses, registering supreme contentment with 'a dish of mashed potatoes to which had been added cream and a little cheese and then lightly grilled'. Steamed puddings – syrup, or sticky gingerbread, for example – are among the more popular desserts, although the potato reporter also enjoyed tarte Tatin and a first-rate chocolate job that was a cross between a mousse and a gâteau. The basic wine list includes house French and German at £12, or £1.60 per glass.

CHEF: Allan Cull PROPRIETORS: Allan and Eleanor Cull OPEN: Tue to Sat, D only (D Sun and Mon residents only); 7 to 9.30 CLOSED: 23 Dec to 31 Mar MEALS: alc (main courses £8.50 to £12.50). Set D £18.50 SERVICE: not inc CARDS: Access, Visa DETAILS: 50 seats. Private parties: 40 main room, 12 private room. Car park. Vegetarian meals. Children's helpings. Smart dress preferred. No smoking in dining-room. Wheelchair access. Music ACCOMMODATION: 6 rooms, all with bath/shower. TV. B&B £33 to £62. Deposit: £20. Children welcome. Pets welcome. Garden. Doors close at midnight. Confirm by 6

ANSTRUTHER Fife   map 8

Cellar

24 East Green, Anstruther KY10 3AA   COOKING 3*
ANSTRUTHER (0333) 310378   COST £22–£48

Anstruther was once a prosperous fishing village, and the Cellar occupies one of the oldest buildings, formerly a cooperage and smokehouse. Whether fish comes from nearby Pittenweem or from further afield, the principles of impeccable buying and simple treatment combine to produce food of a consistently high standard. It says something about the accomplishment of the whole operation when the only disappointing events at a meal for one reporter were bottled orange juice and a lack of butter with the bread rolls, the latter oversight soon corrected with apologies. It is the package that pleases, time and again. 'Our regular customers do not want change,' writes Peter Jukes, 'and that suits me just fine.'

Main courses revolve around satisfyingly fleshy monkfish, turbot or halibut, simply sauced with garlic butter, with wine and cream, or perhaps just the cooking juices with a twist of lime and a pot of hollandaise on the side. Shellfish and smoked fish permeate first courses, including salmon cured three ways, crab mayonnaise, smoked haddock omelette, or a freshly baked hot quiche of lobster, scampi tails and smoked sea trout. There is meat – fillet of beef, perhaps – for those who want it. One reporter from Australia returned home happy after sweet herring salad, grilled halibut with 'just right' vegetables, and a terrine of chocolate mousses. The eye for quality is as unerring in the Cellar's cellar as it is for fish down by the quay. Whites predominate (Alsace and Burgundy are strong suits) but reds are by no means neglected. The splendid choice from excellent producers is sympathetically marked up, and responds well to developments in the market. CELLARMAN'S CHOICE: Riesling cuvée Frédéric Emile 1985, Trimbach £15; Mâcon-Viré, Dom. de Roally 1989, £17.95.

CHEF/PROPRIETOR: Peter Jukes OPEN: Tue to Sat, exc Sat L; 12.30 to 1.30, 7 to 9.30 CLOSED: 24 to 26 Dec, 1 to 3 Jan MEALS: alc L (main courses £6.50 to £10.50). Set D £28.50 SERVICE: not inc, card slips closed CARDS: Access, Amex, Visa DETAILS: 32 seats. Private parties: 36 main room. Vegetarian meals with prior notice. No children under 5. Smart dress preferred. No smoking in dining-room. Music. Fax: (0333) 312544

'The wine waiter came to our table bearing our wine, a bottle of Chilean Cabernet, with the words "Who ordered this, then?"' (On eating in Wales)

541

▲ *Arisaig House* ⁵⭐

Beasdale, by Arisaig PH39 4NR
ARISAIG (068 75) 622   COOKING 2*
on A830, 3m E of Arisaig village   COST £27–£54

The slightly forbidding granite house is softened by stunning grounds with trees, shrubs and woodland walks leading down to the sea. The Smither family take care of every detail, inside and out, and are assisted by staff who balance respect with friendliness. Meals are served in a spacious dining-room hung with fine watercolours and furnished with antiques. The short, fixed-price dinner menu is bolstered by a list of alternatives, and David Wilkinson is capable of cooking with flair. The results are precise and self-assured without resorting to gimmickry. Dishes such as prawn and mussel risotto, perfectly executed langoustine consommé with pastis, and gleaming white turbot fillet with lemon oil and dill have been highlights. A dish of spot-on pink calf's liver paired surprisingly with capers and red wine sauce shows that the kitchen is prepared also to try out new ideas. Desserts such as mocha mousse with red fruit compote are in the same mould. The carefully annotated wine list is peppered with reliable French shippers and is geared to serious drinking at serious prices. The New World is notable by its absence. House wine is £14.50.

CHEF: David Wilkinson   PROPRIETORS: Ruth, John and Andrew Smither   OPEN: all week; 12.30 to 2, 7 to 9   CLOSED: Dec to Mar   MEALS: alc L (main courses £10 to £11.50). Set D £29.50 to £35   SERVICE: card slips closed   CARDS: Access, Visa   DETAILS: 36 seats. 4 tables outside L. Private parties: 10 main room. Car park. Vegetarian meals. No children under 10. Smart dress preferred. No smoking in dining-room. No music   ACCOMMODATION: 14 rooms, all with bath/shower. TV. Phone. B&B £55 to £195. Deposit: £50. No children under 10. Afternoon teas. Garden. Snooker. Doors close at 11. Confirm by 6. Fax: (068 75) 626 (*The Which? Hotel Guide*)

▲ *Collin House* ⁵⭐

Auchencairn, Castle Douglas DG7 1QN
AUCHENCAIRN (0556) 640292   COOKING 2
off A711, ¼m E of Auchencairn   COST £32–£40

This pink-painted, stone-built house has looked out across peaceful Auchencairn Bay to Cumbria for some 250 years. Conversion to a hotel and restaurant by the present owners came in 1990, and the small, personal, manageable scale appeals. Demure pink continues inside, the immaculately laid tables are polished wood and the pattern is a choice of two first courses, a soup, two mains and three puddings or cheese. 'This is cooking you can understand and appreciate,' writes a reporter who enjoyed fricassee of trout with asparagus, then tomato and leek soup, medallions of roe deer in peppercorn sauce, and sticky toffee pudding.

Other soups – red pepper and orange, spicy chicken or tomato and mint, for instance – follow the same line of providing a clean, fresh interlude between risotto of smoked venison and fillet of Galloway beef with madeira sauce, or between salad of warm duck breast and noisette of lamb with spinach and a port sauce. Fish is praised for freshness, and reporters have particularly enjoyed salmon trout and succulent scallops. Although short, the menus allow a choice between lightness and richness. Puddings, for example, range from refreshing lemon parfait or mango fool to weightier hot coffee fudge pudding or chocolate and whisky parfait. Wines on the compact list are varied in style, sympathetically priced and well annotated. Five house wines begin at £6.25.

CHEF: John Wood   PROPRIETORS: Pam Hall and John Wood   OPEN: all week, D only; 7.30 for 8   CLOSED: 3 weeks Jan and Feb   MEALS: Set D £26   SERVICE: not inc, card slips closed   CARDS: Access, Visa   DETAILS: 20 seats. Car park. Vegetarian meals with prior notice. Children welcome. Smart dress preferred. No smoking in dining-room. No music   ACCOMMODATION: 6 rooms, all with bath/shower. TV. Phone. D,B&B £75 to £136. Deposit: 15%. Children welcome. Pets by arrangement. Garden. Confirm by 6. Fax: (0556) 640276 (*The Which? Hotel Guide*)

AUCHMITHIE Tayside   map 8

But 'n' Ben ⁊✳ £

Auchmithie DD11 5SQ
ARBROATH (0241) 877223   COOKING 1
on coast, 3m NE of Arbroath, off A92   COST £14–£29

'The restaurant is a popular local meeting place, but we also get tourists from all over the world,' write the Horns. It is two gleaming white cottages in an old fishing village, with spectacular clifftop views. To many it is a pilgrimage, for fish and shellfish bought directly off the boats, first-rate baking and extremely modest prices. Lunch is simple: soups, smokies in various guises (kedgeree, in a pancake, with poached egg), rich home-made ice-cream with chocolate sauce, or a light coffee gâteau. Lobster is boiled to order and served with lemon butter sauce or home-made tartare.

Dinner is a little more complicated but retains the basic simplicity and lack of pretension. 'It may look easy,' writes an admirer, 'but it is impossible to imagine how the Horns keep up this standard through lunches, teas, high teas (of dressed crab, more smokies, or Grandma Horn's meat roll salad) and dinners each day.' It is staffed by 'gleaming supergrans' who represent the genuine values and unchanging quality of true home-cooking. Despite being run off their feet, they retain their good humour and pride in what they do. Value extends to the short wine list. House wine is £7.25.

CHEFS: Margaret and Angus Horn   PROPRIETORS: Margaret, Iain and Angus Horn   OPEN: Wed to Mon, exc Sun D; 12 to 2.30, 4 to 5.30, 7 to 9.30   CLOSED: 1 and 2 Jan   MEALS: alc (main courses L £4 to £6, D £6.50 to £10.50)   SERVICE: not inc, card slips closed   CARDS: Access, Visa   DETAILS: 40 seats. Private parties: 40 main room. Vegetarian meals. Children's helpings. No smoking in dining-room. Wheelchair access (also WC). No music

---

Prices quoted in the Guide *are based on information supplied by restaurateurs. The prices quoted at the top of each entry represent a range, from the lowest meal price to the highest; the latter is inflated by 20 per cent to take account of likely price rises during the year of the* Guide.

BALLATER Grampian map 8

▲ *Darroch Learg* ✦✗

NEW ENTRY

Braemar Road, Ballater AB35 5UX
BALLATER (033 97) 55443

COOKING 3*
COST £15–£34

It is best to be on the inside looking out, not the other way round. Architectural additions to this Victorian shooting lodge are less inspiring than the view on to Deeside from the rocky hill on which it stands, on the edge of Ballater. The welcome is diffident, but genuinely warm. Well-spaced tables, soft blues, fine linen and fresh flowers in the dining-room – a conservatory built around a previous extension to the house – are overseen by smartly kilted and efficient waitresses.

The cooking is modern Scottish, using game from local estates and fish from the west coast. Salmon is smoked on the premises, and ice-creams, jams and marmalades, bread and chutneys are made in-house. 'We gather brambles, berries, and chanterelle and cep mushrooms on the hill behind us,' write the lucky owners. Robert MacPherson stews the ceps with artichokes and plum tomatoes, and might serve the chanterelles with a fillet of beef and a potato pancake.

Meals begin when tangy canapés of mussels and venison arrive on crisp pastry. The menu offers three choices per course. Flavourings are clear and confident, but don't try to be too clever. A single herb or spice is usually all that is needed to excite interest. Lovage lifts a mushroom soup, coriander and cardamom spike the cream sauces for salmon and roast monkfish, while steamed marmalade and spice pudding is served with aniseed ice-cream, and warm fromage blanc tart has a cinnamon sauce. Fashionable items such as couscous and flageolet beans lend swagger to a crisp breast of duck, and pearl barley is stuffed into chicken. Vegetables are integral to many dishes. Turnips, roast shallots and sauté parsnips abound, and the earthiness extends to fish: a stew of curly kale and spring onions under steamed turbot, or a casserole of mussels and herring with root vegetables, for example. Quality is not in doubt: 'The fillet steak with red wine and shallots was pronounced the best meat ever, and this from someone who has bred prize steers.' There are no house wines, and only two Australians by the glass, but the list is sensitively priced: most wines are around £10–£12, with very little over £20.

CHEF: Robert MacPherson   PROPRIETORS: the Franks family   OPEN: all week; 12.30 to 2, 7 to 8.30   CLOSED: Jan   MEALS: Light L menu Mon to Sat, Set L Sun £10.50, Set D £19.75 to £22.75   SERVICE: net prices, card slips closed   CARDS: Access, Diners, Visa   DETAILS: 48 seats. Private parties: 48 main room. Car park. Vegetarian meals with prior notice. Children's helpings. Smart dress preferred. No smoking in dining-room. Wheelchair access (2 steps; also WC). No music   ACCOMMODATION: 20 rooms, all with bath/shower. TV. Phone. B&B £40 to £90. Deposit: £40. Rooms for disabled. Children welcome. Baby facilities. Pets welcome (not in public rooms). Afternoon teas. Garden. Doors close at midnight. Confirm by 7. Fax: (033 97) 55443

'When I asked how the duck was served, the waiter looked bemused and said, ''On a plate, sir.''' (On eating in London)

▲ Green Inn ⁙✳

9 Victoria Road, Ballater AB35 5QQ	COOKING 2*
BALLATER (033 97) 55701	COST £20–£42

'A small but excellent establishment,' summarises one reporter, applauding this former pub, now a restaurant-with-rooms, that serves food with a decisive Scottish flavour. Jeff Purves makes the most of his Grampian location: fish and shellfish come from Aberdeen and Peterhead, and game from the forests of Balmoral, while local farms supply fruit and vegetables. What's more, he has the good sense to keep the cooking straightforward, or, as he puts it, 'simple and correct'. If the idea of Scottish food brings thoughts of 101 Things To Do With Oatmeal, then the Green Inn has the antidote. A twice-baked soufflé uses Isle of Gigha goats' milk cheese, while haggis is turned into a mousse to accompany a fillet of Aberdeen Angus beef. Orkney scallops are paired with Ayrshire bacon, and smoked venison from Rannoch Moor is filled with a venison mousse. Cheeses follow suit, with Carra, Crowdie, Lochaber smoked and Inverloch blue as just some examples of the wide choice. Flavours are balanced, vegetables 'inspired', and service from Carol Purves is friendly and helpful. The wine selection is no bigger than it needs to be (note the good Bourgogne Aligoté), and there are two home-made liqueurs. House wine is £9.95.

CHEF: Jeff Purves   PROPRIETORS: Carol and Jeff Purves   OPEN: all week, exc Sat L, 12.30 to 1.45, 7 to 9.30   CLOSED: L and Sun D Oct to Mar   MEALS: alc (main courses L £5.50 to £7, D £11.25 to £14.75)   SERVICE: not inc   CARDS: Access, Visa   DETAILS: 32 seats. Private parties: 32 main room. Vegetarian meals. Children's helpings. Smart dress preferred. No smoking in dining-room. Wheelchair access. Music. Air-conditioned   ACCOMMODATION: 3 rooms, all with bath/shower. TV. B&B £25 to £41.50. Deposit: £20. Children welcome. Pets welcome. Doors close at 1am. Confirm by 6

▲ Tullich Lodge ⁙✳

Ballater AB35 5SB	
BALLATER (033 97) 55406	COOKING 2
off A93, 1½m E of Ballater	COST £12–£34

Hector Macdonald and Neil Bannister run a highly personal enterprise. They pride themselves on being talkative, on the grounds that conversation is part of the enjoyment of a good meal. A Victorian lodge of pink granite, just out of Ballater, Tullich overlooks the Dee, and meals begin in the small oak-panelled bar before progressing to the deep mahogany of the dining-room. The sense of home-cooking is strong. An enjoyable, simple lunch began with a rustic broth of mussels, lentils and beans in a large cup, followed by a lamb chop with no frills (except a paper one to hold it by) and a plate of cheese offering a choice of Bonchester, Lanark blue and an unpasteurised Wensleydale look-alike from Kelso.

Just as the lodge feels like a private house (tipping is discouraged), so the kitchen's strength is that it does not go in for 'restaurant cooking'. The four-course dinner menu allows no choice, but there are 'alternatives' for those who ask. The food appeals for its earthiness and lack of pretence, and because supplies are rooted in rural Scotland. Smoked Deeside salmon and Cullen skink are common enough, roast rib of beef is popular, while chanterelles with garlic, parsley and cream, or blewits with sage, bacon and shallot cream are rare treats. Filo pastry and pesto put in an occasional appearance, though old-fashioned puddings – savarins and frangipanes with pear, nectarine or raspberry – are closer to Tullich's heart. The bar is well stocked with whiskies, and house wine is £10.

CHEF: Neil Bannister PROPRIETORS: Hector Macdonald and Neil Bannister OPEN: all week; 1, 7.30 to 9 CLOSED: Dec to Mar MEALS: light L (around £7), Set D £23 SERVICE: card slips closed CARDS: Access, Amex, Diners, Visa DETAILS: 24 seats. Private parties: 30 main room. Car park. Vegetarian meals with prior notice. Children's helpings. Jacket and tie. No smoking in dining-room. Wheelchair access (2 steps; also WC). No music ACCOMMODATION: 10 rooms, all with bath/shower. Phone. D,B&B £90 to £190. Children welcome. Baby facilities. Pets welcome (not in public rooms). Garden. Doors close at midnight. Confirm by 6. Fax: (033 97) 55397

BLAIRGOWRIE Tayside   map 8

▲ *Kinloch House Hotel* ▼ ✸

by Blairgowrie PH10 6SG
BLAIRGOWRIE (0250) 884237
on A923, 3m W of Blairgowrie towards   COOKING 2
Dunkeld   COST £20–£51

Friendly, efficient service is a theme that runs through reports: 'David and Sarah Shentall and their son Charles could not have been more hospitable, genial and accommodating,' writes an American visitor who has stayed at more country-house hotels in Britain than most of us have had hot dinners. The kitchen revolves around a reliable hub of salmon, steak, lamb, fish and game. Scallops (from Kyle of Lochalsh) may be served with bacon and leeks, or flamed in Pernod. Venison is cooked with garlic and wine. As the Shentalls modestly proclaim, 'Scotland has the finest raw materials in the world' – a fact that has not escaped reporters. 'The Kinloch salmon is a variation on smoked salmon in which the fish is cured in whisky and honey,' explains one. 'It is very good and, when served as a salad with lettuce and prawns, makes an excellent lunch.'

The form at dinner is a soup (sea kale or oxtail, for example), sorbet or other light dish slotted in between first and main courses. Alcohol, butter and cream all feature, but are not overwhelming. Variety comes in the form of chickpea mousse, lamb sweetbreads and good use of herbs. Supplements for some dishes, which can easily add £10 to the bill, may annoy. Vegetables are fresh and crisply cooked. Sweets are from a trolley. The wine list is a long one, running from venerable claret and burgundy to more down-to-earth New World choices, with an impressive display of half-bottles. House wines begin at a little over £10 a bottle, or £1.90 a glass.

CHEF: Bill McNicoll PROPRIETORS: David and Sarah Shentall OPEN: all week; 12.30 to 2, 7 to 9.15 MEALS: Set L £14.50, Set D £25.90 SERVICE: net prices, card slips closed CARDS: Access, Amex, Diners, Visa DETAILS: 55 seats. Private parties: 18 main room, 30 private room. Car park. Vegetarian meals. Children's helpings L and high tea. No children under 7 D. Jacket and tie. No smoking in dining-room. Wheelchair access (also WC). No music ACCOMMODATION: 21 rooms, all with bath/shower. TV. Phone. D,B&B £76.50 to £185.50. Rooms for disabled. Children welcome. Baby facilities. Pets welcome (certain bedrooms only). Afternoon teas. Garden. Fishing. Doors close at midnight. Fax: (0250) 884333 (*The Which? Hotel Guide*)

CAIRNDOW Strathclyde   map 8

Loch Fyne Oyster Bar £

Clachan Farm, Ardkinglas,
Cairndow PA26 8BH
INVERARY (049 96) 236   COOKING 1
on A83, at head of Loch Fyne   COST £20–£45

The formula is hard to beat, and readers love it. 'You can eat your oysters while looking out over the beds that produced them!' 'The shellfish platter (oysters, langoustines, queen scallops, clams and crab) bears comparison with other good fish restaurants, but at a fraction of the price.' Recognition that high-quality seafood needs the minimum of adornment is what keeps Loch Fyne on a roll. A warm welcome and a basket of bread greet new arrivals. The big menu advises that there is no set pattern of starters or main courses to follow. Just choose whatever you fancy, in whatever order you like.

The oysters are wonderfully fresh and delicate in flavour, and whole brown crab is a delight. Salmon cold-smoked out the back is first-class, and hot-smoked salmon is a speciality: brined first, so saltier than some versions. Two thick slices are served warm with a white sauce lapping round the edge, tasting gently of horseradish. Langoustines, scallops, herring, clams and mussels are all fished from Loch Fyne. The bacon wrapped around queen scallops swamps the seafood, so the recommendation is to stay with the plainest and simplest dishes of all. Wines are very reasonably priced, with seven or eight by the glass. House wine is £8.95.

CHEFS: Greta Cameron and Morag Keith   PROPRIETOR: Loch Fyne Oysters Ltd   OPEN: all week; 9am to 9pm (6pm Mon to Thu, Nov to Mar)   CLOSED: 25 Dec, 1 Jan   MEALS: alc (main courses £5 to £16)   SERVICE: not inc, card slips closed   CARDS: Access, Diners, Visa   DETAILS: 85 seats. 8 tables outside. Private parties: 85 main room. Car park. Vegetarian meals with prior notice. Children's helpings. No-smoking area. Wheelchair access (also WC). Music. Fax: (049 96) 234

CANONBIE Dumfries & Galloway   map 8

▲ Riverside Inn ❢ ✳ £

Canonbie DG14 0UX
CANONBIE (038 73) 71512 and 71295   COOKING 2
on A47, just over the border   COST £19–£44

The seventeenth-century timbered Inn, not far from the western end of Hadrian's Wall, overlooks the River Esk and has been home to Robert and Susan Phillips for the past 20 years. People travel unconscionable distances to enjoy its distinctive hospitality and the uncomplicated, honest cooking that centres on in-house products, including Mr Phillips's black treacle and beer bread. Blackboard specials in the bar are supplemented by an inclusive restaurant menu of five courses plus coffee. Second course is soup of the day, and fourth is a platter of usually five British cheeses. An early spring menu offered the likes of roast tomato salad, grilled sardines or salmon in filo with leek sauce to start, then chestnut and sherry soup. This was followed by a choice of young hare casseroled in red wine with bacon, mushrooms and shallots, baked sea bass stuffed with fennel, chargrilled guinea-fowl with béarnaise, and roast best end of lamb with onion and garlic purée. Vegetables come in individually cooked profusion, à la Cumbria, while desserts may include challenging ice-creams such as rhubarb and ginger or gin and orange, or steamed guard's pudding with raspberry sauce. Readers write to praise the 'exemplary' service and warmth of reception. This is a very steady performance.

Wines consist of small but perfectly formed bunches from around the world at prices that make a genuinely wide choice available in the sub-£20 bracket. Vacheron's Sancerre, Lingenfelder's Spätlese Trocken Riesling, Chianti Classico from Castello di Volpaia and Saintsbury Pinot Noir from Carneros are all worth a look. Halves are few but well selected. House French is £7.95. CELLARMAN'S CHOICE: Vin de Pays d'Oc, Ozidoc Sauvignon 1992, £8.95; Graves, Dom. de Gaillot 1985, £14.95.

CHEFS/PROPRIETORS: Robert and Susan Phillips OPEN: Mon to Sat; 12 to 2, 7.30 to 8.30 CLOSED: 2 weeks Nov, 25 and 26 Dec, 1 and 2 Jan, 2 weeks Feb MEALS: bar alc L and D (main courses £6 to £11). Set D restaurant £22.50 SERVICE: not inc, card slips closed CARDS: Access, Visa DETAILS: 24 seats. 4 tables outside. Private parties: 24 main room. Car park. Vegetarian meals. Children's helpings. No children under 10. Smart dress preferred. No smoking in dining-room. No music ACCOMMODATION: 6 rooms, all with bath/shower. TV. B&B £55 to £72. Deposit: £20. Rooms for disabled. Children welcome. Pets welcome by arrangement. Garden. Doors close at midnight (*The Which? Hotel Guide*)

COLBOST Highland   map 8

Three Chimneys ♟ ⁵✳

Colbost, by Dunvegan IV55 8ZT
GLENDALE (0470) 511258   COOKING 2*
on B884, 4½m W of Dunvegan   COST £17–£57

A 'superb setting' of magical sunsets and views of the Outer Hebrides are part of the attraction of this restaurant in converted cottages across the loch from Dunvegan. No executive chef oversees proceedings here: Shirley Spear's motto might be 'local distinctiveness', and her endeavours are single-minded. Help has recently arrived in the form of a local lady with a talent for baking, so the place now offers an open-ended daytime menu of buttery cakes baked in the old Scottish fashion, along with sandwiches and light dishes such as spinach and coconut roulade.

Shirley's fiercesome loyalty to Skye fish, meat and game, 'food for free' and Scottish farmhouse cheeses dictates her culinary activities. 'The best meal I've had in years' was one contented verdict on her four-course dinner menu. Soup with home-baked bread is always the overture; to follow, there might be fresh scallop mousse or peat-smoked salmon. Centrepiece dishes draw inspiration from far and wide: consider roast monkfish in rosemary-scented olive oil with whole garlic cloves and fennel in roast red pepper sauce, or even grilled fillet of Highland lamb with Seville orange sauce served with warm bulgar wheat, currants and pine-nuts. The choice of sweets might take in spiced apple crumble with home-made cinnamon ice-cream as well as white chocolate pavé with raspberry sauce. Wines are a sensible selection, with some interesting finds in both France and the New World, and a fair spread of prices. House wines take advantage of the south of France and begin at £9.95. CELLARMAN'S CHOICE: Entre-Deux-Mers, Ch. de Castleneau 1991, £15.25; Côtes du Roussillon Villages 1990, £16.45.

CHEF: Shirley Spear   PROPRIETORS: Eddie and Shirley Spear   OPEN: Mon to Sat; 12.30 to 2 (2 to 4.30 light meals and afternoon teas), 7 to 9   CLOSED: Nov to Mar   MEALS: alc L (main courses £4 to £21). Set D £25 to £65 (2 people). Light meal menu. Minimum £3.50 L, £25 D   SERVICE: not inc   CARDS: Access, Visa   DETAILS: 30 seats. 2 tables outside. Private parties: 18 main room, 16 and 18 private rooms. Car park. Vegetarian meals. Children's helpings L, D by arrangement. Smart dress preferred. No smoking in dining-room. Music. Fax: (0470) 258

CRINAN Strathclyde   map 8

▲ *Crinan Hotel* ♟

Crinan PA31 8SR
CRINAN (054 683) 261   COOKING 1
off A816, 6m NW of Lochgilphead   COST £36–£56

This family-run hotel is the focal point of the village. Views across to Mull and the Paps of Jura are markedly improved by a good sunset, and fish are landed 50 metres from the kitchen most days. Loch 16, the upstairs restaurant, may not always open, depending on the weather. When it does, seafood from the boats is simply cooked. 'Whole Loch Crinan jumbo prawns Corryvreckan, landed at 3pm,' says the menu. It might also serve Loch Craignish mussels and locally smoked salmon, finishing with cheese, sorbet or apple tart.

Food in the Westward restaurant is similar, but with more choice, including Arbroath smokies, Loch Fyne clams, Islay turbot and rack of Kintyre lamb. Note that the provenance of most items is acknowledged. Meals are four courses and assume you would not be here if you did not like seafood. The quality of the fish (particularly sweet, succulent Crinan prawns), and timing of grilling and steaming, are first-rate, although saucing, vegetables, bread and other appurtenances are not in the same league. Service works on the principle that you will ask if you need anything, or help yourself. Bar lunches are available also. The wine list warns that storage space is limited and some lines may run out, but even if it lost a few bottles, there would still be much good drinking under £20 to balance the fine wines above that. Notes are useful, and house French is £9.95. CELLARMAN'S CHOICE: Savennières Clos St-Yves 1992, Baumard £17.50; Bordeaux Supérieur, Ch. de Sours 1990, £14.50.

CHEFS: Nicolas Ryan (Loch 16), Angela Burns (Westward)   PROPRIETORS: Frances and Nicolas Ryan   OPEN: Loch 16 Tue to Sat, D only; 8. Westward all week, D only; 7 to 9   MEALS: Loch 16 Set D £37.50, Westward Set D £27.50   SERVICE: not inc, card slips closed   CARDS: Access, Amex, Visa   DETAILS: Loch 16, 20 seats; Westward 40 seats. Private parties: 20 and 45 main rooms. Car park. Vegetarian meals. Children's helpings. Jacket and tie Loch 16. No smoking while others eat. Wheelchair access (also WC). Music   ACCOMMODATION: 22 rooms, all with bath/shower. TV. Phone. B&B £75 to £135. Deposit: £50. Rooms for disabled. Lift. Children welcome. Baby facilities. Pets welcome. Garden. Doors close at midnight. Confirm by 6 (*The Which? Hotel Guide*)

▲ *This symbol means accommodation is available.*

▲ *Bayview Hotel* £

57 Seafield Street, Cullen AB56 2SU
CULLEN (0542) 841031

COOKING 1*
COST £18–£33

Cullen is as well known to some for its round church (where the devil cannot hide) as for its revitalised skink, a soup based on smoked fish, including haddock. The Bayview, overlooking the harbour and Moray Firth, naturally serves it, along with salmon (locally smoked over whisky-barrel chippings) and scrambled eggs, plus a range of fish that takes in grilled plaice on the bone and deep-fried rock turbot. Home-made stracciatella, a Roman soup, costs (says the menu) £I.LXXV. Bar and dining-room both serve snacks (steak and mushroom pie or spaghetti carbonara) and full meals, in which alcohol and cheese play a major saucing role – for example, pan-fried fillet of red deer flamed in aquavit with a Gjetöst (Norwegian goats' cheese) and redcurrant sauce. Wines are straightforward and moderately priced; house wines start at £8.15.

CHEF: Stuart Scott   PROPRIETOR: David Evans   OPEN: all week; 12 to 2, 6.30 to 9   CLOSED: Christmas   MEALS: alc (main courses £7.50 to £12.50)   SERVICE: not inc, card slips closed   CARDS: Access, Visa   DETAILS: 30 seats. Private parties: 20 main room. Vegetarian meals. Children's helpings. No children in bar. Smart dress preferred. No music   ACCOMMODATION: 6 rooms, all with bath/shower. TV. Phone. B&B £35 to £60. Children welcome. Doors close at 11. Confirm by 6

Ostlers Close ▼

25 Bonnygate, Cupar KY15 4BU
CUPAR (0334) 655574

COOKING 3
COST £21–£46

The Grahams continue to run a first-class establishment. The room remains tiny, the décor unchanged. 'The only thing to have grown is the restaurant's reputation,' wrote a supporter. 'Mrs Graham claims with some justification to have put Cupar on the map.' Ostlers Close is living proof that if you provide quality food and look after your guests the world will beat a path to your door, even if that door is tucked away in a back alley with little room for the world when it gets there.

The menu is a short *carte*, simpler and less expensive at lunch-time, more elaborate at dinner, when dishes may combine elements such as fillet of turbot landed at Pittenweem with west coast scallops in a herb butter sauce, or roast saddle of venison with breast of woodpigeon in a game sauce. The food is reasonably priced for its dependably high standards, and fish is naturally a strength given the location. Goujons of mullet, haddock, sole and monkfish, deep-fried in a light batter are 'exceptionally good', while the 'rich, fragrant, delicate seafood soup' is highly regarded: 'If I close my eyes I can still smell it.' There may be few surprises, but the cooking achieves a welcome clarity of expression in, for example, roast breast of duck and confit of the leg: tender, with just enough fat and a crisp skin, on a bed of Puy lentils. The Grahams pick and preserve their own wild mushrooms, and might serve them with roast saddle of roe venison. Vegetables are 'exemplary'.

Sweets might include a tart lemon pie served warm with lemon sorbet, or an interesting ice-cream. Meals begin with a nibble of spinach and onion quiche. Coffee is a weak point. Wines are sensibly chosen with an eye for quality at all price levels, much commendably under £20. There is a fair selection of half-bottles, David Wynn Australian Riesling and Shiraz are available by the glass (£2.45), and house burgundy is £7.95. CELLARMAN'S CHOICE: Dalwhinnie Shiraz 1991, £17.50; Gewurztraminer 1989, Rolly Gassmann, £14.95.

CHEF: Jimmy Graham   PROPRIETORS: Amanda and Jimmy Graham   OPEN: Tue to Sat; 12.15 to 2, 7 to 9.30   CLOSED: 25 Dec, first 2 weeks June   MEALS: alc (main courses L £8 to £9.50, D £14 to £16)   SERVICE: not inc, card slips closed   CARDS: Access, Amex, Visa   DETAILS: 26 seats. Private parties: 22 main room. Vegetarian meals with prior notice. Children's helpings. No children under 6 D. Smart dress preferred. No smoking during meals. Wheelchair access (1 step; also WC). No music

---

DRYBRIDGE Grampian   map 8

Old Monastery ¶✸

Drybridge AB56 2JB
BUCKIE (0542) 832660   COOKING 1
2½m S of Buckie, junction of A98 and A942   COST £27–£43

It is important not to turn off into the village of Drybridge, but to keep climbing the hill for some two-and-a-half miles from the main road junction. The rewards are a magnificent view of Spey Bay and the Moray Firth, and a warm welcome from the Grays to their monastic hideaway. 'Mr and Mrs Gray are perfect hosts,' writers one reporter who much appreciated the relaxed, informal service from local staff. The abundance of fish, shellfish and game hereabouts, plus, of course, lamb, Aberdeen Angus beef, and soft fruits in season, underpins a simple but varied menu. Alcohol finds its way into a number of sauces – claret with guinea-fowl, or port with venison – along with nothing more elaborate than mushrooms, mustard, or garlic and herbs: a commendable restraint that wins justifiable praise. Puddings may be refreshing (warm lemon tart) or rich (a trio of chocolate cheesecake, ice-cream and mousse), and there is ample choice on the briefly annotated wine list, which also runs to a couple of dozen half-bottles. House wine starts at £1.75 a glass, or £9 a bottle.

CHEF: Douglas Gray   PROPRIETORS: Douglas and Maureen Gray   OPEN: Tue to Sat; 12 to 1.30, 7 to 9.30   CLOSED: 3 weeks Jan, 2 weeks Nov, bank hols   MEALS: alc (main courses £11 to £15)   SERVICE: not inc, card slips closed   CARDS: Access, Amex, Visa   DETAILS: 45 seats. Private parties: 45 main room. Car park. Vegetarian meals. Children's helpings. No children under 8. Smart dress preferred. No smoking in dining-room. Music

---

The Guide *office can quickly spot when a restaurateur is encouraging customers to write recommending inclusion – and sadly, several restaurants have been doing this in 1994. Such reports do not further a restaurant's cause. Please tell us if a restaurateur invites you to write to the* Guide.

DUNKELD Tayside map 8

▲ *Kinnaird* ✻ ♟

Kinnaird Estate, by Dunkeld PH8 0LB
BALLINLUIG (0796) 482440
2m N of Dunkeld, take B898 signed
Dalguise

COOKING 4
COST £50–£60

Kinnaird is set in its own grounds, all 9000 acres of them. The evening begins in a large room with cedar panels halfway up the walls, a blazing fire, deep settees to fall into, a baby grand piano and all manner of knick-knacks that try in vain to personalise it. From the dining-room is a wonderful view across the Tay. Painted wall panels with swirls and curlicues, straight out of some seventeenth-century French palace, look as fresh as if they were painted yesterday. There are only six tables in a room that most restaurateurs would fill with 20. Nibbles come in waves: curry-flavoured almonds and herbed olives, eggy tartlets and pastry rolls, a tiny beefburger with a fried quail's egg on top and a drop of powerful red wine sauce. Now you are ready to eat.

The menu doesn't change often, but individual items do. John Webber refuses to rely on the stereotypes (lobster and venison) that 'grand tour' visitors might expect, although he does use familiar forms: open ravioli, risotto, a grilled guinea-fowl sausage, and fish-cakes, plus chocolate pithiviers and hot marzipan soufflé. Dishes are set-pieces, crafted, designed and executed with a ritual feel to them, sometimes taking humble ingredients just about as far as they will go. Fish-cakes are made from crab and cod, lifted with the heady aromas of lime and coriander leaf, and moistened with a less than piquant salsa of diced tomato flesh and ripe avocado. What looks like a piece of pork scratching but tastes fishy is in fact a deep-fried cod flake.

This is not the sort of place to make a mess, so things are boned and filleted for us. The origin of oxtail is sanitised by removing the meat from the bone and wrapping it in a Savoy cabbage leaf so it looks like a little green mound. But it tastes gloriously sticky, and the turned vegetables are integrated into the dish – not, as so often, an afterthought. The menu says that each dish is complete in itself, and extra vegetables will only come on request. But they come anyway: squeaky fresh green beans, good fennel, and sliced potatoes in olive oil, sprinkled with fresh thyme and large salt crystals. Puddings are skilful and satisfying without resorting to exotica. Hot lemon soufflé, as rich as lemon curd, benefits from the crunch of a tuile-like basket and good vanilla custard. Staff are on their best behaviour, don't hover and make sure that everything runs like clockwork. The wine list is anxious not to miss out a single vintage or respectable property, whatever the cost. Once beyond the nursery slopes, therefore, prices escalate rapidly. An inspector who stayed in nearby Dunkeld paid less for a night's accommodation than for a bottle of Kinnaird's house vin de pays (£15). CELLARMAN'S CHOICE: Rongopai Chardonnay 1991, £21; Bourgogne, Reserve de l'Oratoire 1991, £16.

The Guide *is totally independent, accepts no free hospitality, and survives on the number of copies sold each year.*

CHEF: John Webber   PROPRIETOR: Constance Ward   OPEN: all week; 12.30 to 1.45, 7.15 to 9.30   CLOSED: Feb   MEALS: Set L £19.50 to £24, Set D £38   SERVICE: not inc, card slips closed   CARDS: Access, Amex, Visa   DETAILS: 35 seats. 3 tables outside. Private parties: 25 main room, 6 and 20 private rooms. Car park. Vegetarian meals. No children under 12. Smart dress preferred. No smoking in dining-room. Wheelchair access (also WC). No music   ACCOMMODATION: 9 rooms, all with bath/shower. TV. Phone. B&B £127 to £250. Rooms for disabled. No children under 12. Pets in kennels only. Garden. Tennis. Fishing. Snooker. Fax: (0796) 482289 (*The Which? Hotel Guide*)

DUNVEGAN Highland map 8

▲ *Harlosh House* ✷

by Dunvegan, Isle of Skye IV55 8ZG
DUNVEGAN (0470) 521367   COOKING 2
off A863, 3m S of Dunvegan   COST £26–£45

A dose of salt spray and fine views give many a west coast restaurant an edge, and Harlosh is no exception. In this case, the views are of the Cuillin Hills. The whitewashed house, dating from around 1750, sits on a small peninsula jutting out into Loch Bracadale. 'To say we are remote is an understatement,' claim the Elfords. The peace attracts not only human visitors but also eagles and seals, which can be spotted with the aid of the lounge telescope. Dunvegan sounds as if it has lapsed from a strict vegetarian regime and rediscovered fish and meat. There is no shortage of either on Peter Elford's menu, which is expanding slowly in scope. 'Soufflés will be making an appearance on the dessert menu soon.'

Fish is often steamed, the simplest way to tackle fresh John Dory or halibut, and lack of heaviness is appreciated in the sauces, which range from star-anise through cream and basil to lemon grass. Avocado and smoked sprats on salad leaves were 'a surprising and delicious combination' for one reporter, although not for another. Venison – collops in port sauce, or fillet with Puy lentils – and braised shoulder of lamb flesh out the main courses, followed by baked custard tart or steamed ginger pudding, and Scottish cheeses. A good spread of wines, the majority under £20, offers sensible drinking. House South African is £8.50.

CHEF: Peter Elford   PROPRIETORS: Peter and Lindsey Elford   OPEN: all week, D only; 7 to 8.30   MEALS: alc (main courses £11 to £18)   SERVICE: not inc, card slips closed   CARDS: Access, Visa   DETAILS: 18 seats. Private parties: 6 main room. Car park. Children's helpings 6 to 7pm. No smoking in dining-room. Wheelchair access (1 step). Music   ACCOMMODATION: 6 rooms, 5 with bath/shower. B&B £86. Deposit: £50. Children welcome. Baby facilities. Afternoon teas. Garden. Doors close at midnight. Confirm by 5 (*The Which? Hotel Guide*)

EDINBURGH Lothian map 8

Atrium **NEW ENTRY**

10 Cambridge Street, EH1 2ED   COOKING 3
031-228 8882   COST £26–£45

'Exciting but intimate décor, good ingredients simply cooked, lots of lovely flavours, pleasant service, menus change twice daily' was one brief but ringing endorsement for Andrew and Lisa Radford's new venture. After working at

Waterloo Place, and before that Handsel's, they have opened their own account with bags of brio and assurance in the new business and theatre complex in the West End, close to the Usher Hall and Traverse Theatre. 'Post-modern Gothic punk' is one attempt to pigeonhole the style. But the small scale, canvas-covered seats and guttering orange oil lamps work to advantage, even against a background of railway sleepers for tables, twisted wire and wrought-iron sculptures.

With all this, plus a bright, crisp, Mediterranean-sounding menu, it could be a soulmate of Stephen Bull (see entry, London). The food is simple, modern and lively: crab-cake with oyster mushroom and chive, pan-fried tuna with leek, basil and tomato, poached pear with cocoa sorbet. There are vegetarian options, although goats' cheese brioche at £13.50 seemed less than a snip to one reporter. And on such a short menu the recurrence of some items in more than one dish – duck with lentils for a first course, pigeon with lentils for a main – can whittle choice down a bit. But there is a refreshing lightness and sureness of touch to chicken liver parfait, salmon with balsamic vinegar, and grilled cod steak with pesto crust that breaks into gleaming flakes when forked. 'This is vibrant cooking with a real kick,' writes an inspector. It is full of confidence, with no tricksy combinations or garnishes, and with all tastes distinct and true. Service has varied from 'stiff, formal and pompous' for one reporter to 'relaxed, confident and helpful' for another. Wines are as upbeat as the food, and sensibly priced. House wines begin at £8.95 and a dozen or more come by the glass, from £2.25.

CHEF: Andrew Radford   PROPRIETORS: Andrew and Lisa Radford   OPEN: Mon to Sat, exc Sat L; 12 to 3, 6 to 10.30   CLOSED: 2 weeks Christmas   MEALS: alc (main courses L £8.50 to £9.50, D £11.50 to £15.50)   SERVICE: not inc   CARDS: Access, Amex, Visa   DETAILS: 70 seats. Private parties: 90 main room. Vegetarian meals. Children's helpings on request. Wheelchair access (also WC). No music. Air-conditioned

---

L'Auberge ♼

56 St Mary Street, EH1 1SX	COOKING 2
031-556 5888	COST £15–£55

The restaurant is long and narrow, on two levels, with close-set tables that tend to involve neighbours in conversation. It is French, although the Frenchness is only as convincing as you want it to be. Certainly the cooking hides a bit of Scotland underneath the franglais menu: smoked and marinated salmon and duck (produced in-house, as are breads and ice-creams), fresh salmon, and 'biscuits d'Orkney' for the cheese. Smooth chicken liver pâté with onion confit, and braised duck leg with a slightly sweet-and-sour sauce of berries and red wine, add a welcome dimension of robust flavour. Rosemary and honey sauce has appeared with both pork and lamb. There is praise for aubergine mousse, grilled and set on a tomato coulis, but vegetables divide readers: disappointing for one, the best part of the meal for another.

Lunches are flexible: one, two or three courses, with or without wine, the price adjusted accordingly. Dinner is a more serious affair, with greater choice. Portions tend to be generous, and, for one reader, 'It is one of the few restaurants where our daughter has had full adult portions for all courses and devoured the lot.' Staff are accomplished and pleasant. Regional French wines, mostly from the south, get the highly personal list off to a good start. It is worth a trawl through the petits châteaux of Bordeaux, and value extends to the short New World section, although these tend to stick to French grape varieties. CELLARMAN'S CHOICE: Jurançon Sec, Blanc de Blancs 1992, £14.45; Premières Côtes de Bordeaux, Ch. de Ricaud 1988, £14.25.

CHEF: Fabrice Bresulier PROPRIETOR: Daniel Wencker OPEN: all week; 12.15 to 2, 6.30 to 9.30 (10 Sat) CLOSED: 25 and 26 Dec, 1 and 2 Jan MEALS: alc (main courses £11 to £19). Set L £8.50 (2 courses) to £13.50, Set D £16.85 (2 courses) to £19.85 SERVICE: not inc CARDS: Access, Amex, Diners, Visa DETAILS: 50 seats. Private parties: 35 main room. Vegetarian meals. Children's helpings L. No children under 3. Smart dress preferred. No smoking during meals. Wheelchair access (1 step). Music. Air-conditioned. Fax: 031-556 2588

Denzlers 121

121 Constitution Street, Leith, EH6 7AE
031-554 3268

COOKING 1
COST £17–£35

The Denzlers' well-liked restaurant is in a converted bank building with an impressive marble-pillared façade. Inside, it is all peach, orange and apricot colour schemes from floor to ceiling. The cooking has a strong Swiss vein layered on to classic French, with a few traditional stalwarts such as Cullen skink, pigeon pie and oxtail for good measure. Air-dried beef and ham are regularly endorsed, and reporters have also approved of fish soufflé, medallions of pork with marsala sauce and veal valaisanne (topped with Gruyère cheese and fried in batter). Spätzli and pommes berrichonne are fine accompaniments. Lunch is a simpler affair spanning everything from 'pub grub' to halibut with orange hollandaise. Service is affable and prompt. Swiss Fendant and Dôle wines top the 100-strong list, which is fairly priced across the range. House wine is £10.35 a litre.

CHEFS: Sami Denzler and Ian Gordon PROPRIETORS: Sami and Pat Denzler OPEN: Tue to Sat, exc Sat L; 12 to 2, 6.30 to 10 CLOSED: 25 and 26 Dec, first week Jan MEALS: alc (main courses L £5.50 to £6.50, D £7.50 to £12). Set L £7.50 (2 courses) SERVICE: net prices, not inc, card slips closed CARDS: Access, Amex, Diners, Visa DETAILS: 70 seats. Private parties: 72 main room. Vegetarian meals with prior notice. Children's helpings. Smart dress preferred. No music

Indian Cavalry Club

3 Atholl Place, EH3 8HP
031-228 3282

COOKING 1
COST £19–£40

The long, cream dining-room, only five minutes from Princes Street, is 'reminiscent of an officers' mess of the Indian Cavalry regiments'. A small army of orderlies moves en masse to deliver the food. Chicken and lamb are the main business, with some worthwhile fish and vegetable dishes including salmon in a mild sauce of yogurt, tamarind and ginger. Main courses come with a suggested side dish: pineapple in lentil and tamarind sauce is recommended for barbecued chicken spiced with cinnamon. Saucing impresses: for example, lentil-based with a vegetable pakora, or mixed vegetable curry to accompany a chickpea and mushroom biriani. Seasoning is hot enough to be interesting without obscuring main ingredients, although an oily richness pervades some dishes.

The menu also suggests a style of wine for each dish: Fleurie with sag paneer, Cabernet-Shiraz with Kashmiri lamb, that sort of thing. The only slight problem is that the wines are not available by the glass, so a three-course meal for two, if you follow the recommendations to the letter, could work out to be schligtly echspenshive. The list is short and reasonably priced. House wine is £8.50. Shahid Chowdhury has gone into the franchise business and opened a fast pakora bar, a sort of Indian bistro, serving snacky pakoras, nan with spicy toppings (like an Indian pizza), and kebabs. Address: 4/6 Glanville Place, Edinburgh, Tel: 031-225 9199 and 6853.

CHEF: Mukhtar Miah   PROPRIETORS: Shahid and Bilquis Chowdhury   OPEN: all week; 12 to 2, 5.30 to 11.30   MEALS: alc (main courses £6 to £12). Set L £6.95 (buffet), Set D £12.95 to £16.95. Minimum £7 D   SERVICE: not inc   CARDS: Access, Amex, Diners, Visa   DETAILS: 120 seats. Private parties: 80 main room, 40 private room. Vegetarian meals. Children welcome. Smart dress preferred. No-smoking area. Wheelchair access (3 steps). No music. Fax: 031-225 1911

Kalpna 🍴✳ £

2–3 St Patrick Square, EH8 9EZ   COOKING 2
031-667 9890   COST £10–£21

This South Indian vegetarian restaurant has been a fixture for over a decade, and in truth does not change much from one year to the next. One reporter from London, however, thought blandness tended to triumph over subtlety in some dishes. If spicing is delicate, that may be because it is restrained by yogurt much of the time, or cream, or cheese. Thalis are as good a way as any to rustle up a variety of tastes and textures. Girnar consists of samosa, two vegetables, dahl, pilau rice, chapati, poppadum and pickles, all for less than £10. In addition to the customary array of lentils, chickpeas, okra and spiced spinach with curd cheese, aubergines are cooked with spinach and tomatoes spiced with fenugreek leaves and asafoetida. Vegetable fritters, and coconut-flavoured basmati rice done with white lentils, lemon and coriander, add interest. Classic desserts include gulab jamun, kulfi, and carrot-based halva with almonds and cardamom. The short wine list is worth a look; there is even an Indian wine made from Laski Riesling grapes blended with spices. House French is £6.80, or £1.80 per glass.

CHEF: Ajay Bhartdwaj   PROPRIETORS: Ajay Bhartdwaj, M. Jogee, E. Mehta and E. Barton OPEN: all week, exc Sat L and Sun; 12 to 2, 5.30 to 10.30   CLOSED: Christmas, New Year. MEALS: alc (main courses £3.50 to £6.50). Buffet L £4. Gourmet D Wed £8.50   SERVICE: 10%, card slips closed   CARDS: Access, Visa   DETAILS: 60 seats. Private parties: 60 main room. Vegetarian meals. Children's helpings. No smoking in dining-room. Wheelchair access. Music

Kelly's

46 West Richmond Street, EH8 9DZ   COOKING 2
031-668 3847   COST £30–£36

The opening of the nearby Festival Theatre has resulted in some changes to opening times, aimed at encouraging customers who are going to the shows. Kelly's continues to flourish. Jeff Kelly sets the tone: he is welcoming and attentive without being intrusive, while the charming interior with its warm pink décor strikes a happy medium between formality and familiarity. The three-course set menu is Anglo-French in style, and Jacquie Kelly's cooking is distinctive and well-tuned. A typical meal might take in warm asparagus with honey, orange and ginger sauce, then loin of lamb in pastry with tarragon pistou accompanied by a delicate pyramid of fried onion perched on a slice of aubergine, followed by fried banana slices with crystallised ginger and caramel sauce. Reporters have also endorsed smoked haddock soup with saffron and pan-fried goujons of calf's liver with shallots wrapped in bacon and a redcurrant coulis. The wine list is an enthusiast's choice, knowledgeably put together by Jeff Kelly. Note the impressive range of 'house selections', all at £10; there is also a cheaper house wine at £9.50.

CHEF: Jacquie Kelly PROPRIETORS: Jacquie Kelly and Jeff Kelly OPEN: Wed to Sat D; 5 to 9.30 (Set L by arrangement for groups of 10 or more, and during the Festival) CLOSED: Oct, first week Jan MEALS: Set D £21 SERVICE: not inc CARDS: Access, Amex, Visa DETAILS: 36 seats. Private parties: 36 main room. Vegetarian meals. Children's helpings. No children under 6. Smart dress preferred. No smoking before 9.30pm. Wheelchair access (1 step; also WC). Music

Loon Fung £

2 Warriston Place, EH3 5LE	COOKING 1
031-556 1781	COST £12–£49

What lifts Loon Fung above the standard Cantonese competition is the quality of its fish, the snappy service and some of the specials. It is two light and airy rooms, simply furnished, offering a *carte* of 120 items. A good spread of fairly priced first courses doubling as dim-sum includes steamed spare ribs in black bean sauce, wafer paper prawn, crisp spring rolls, and excellent mushroom siu mai. The fish varies daily, but is likely to include halibut, crab, mussels and lobster, which are best when they are cooked in either ginger or black bean sauce. Among the specials are fried oyster, slices of chicken coated in almonds with an orange sauce, and duck with nicely contrasting sweet pineapple and sharp pickled ginger. Salt and chilli prawns are crisp and flavoursome, while squid is sharpened by a hot, spicy black bean sauce. Wines are very basic (house French is £8.50 a litre), and tea is better than coffee. There is another branch at 32 Grindlay Street, Edinburgh, Tel: 031-229 5757.

CHEF: Tin Fat Siu PROPRIETOR: Sammy Tam OPEN: all week, exc Sat and Sun L; 12 (2 Sat and Sun) to 11.30 (1.30am Fri and Sat) CLOSED: 25 Dec, Chinese New Year MEALS: alc (main courses £5 to £15). Set L £6, Set D £11.50 (minimum 2) to £18.50 (minimum 8) SERVICE: 10% CARDS: Access, Amex, Visa DETAILS: 100 seats. Private parties: 50 main room, 50 private room. Vegetarian meals. Children welcome. Smart dress preferred. Wheelchair access (also WC). Music

£ *indicates that it is possible to have a three-course meal, including coffee, a half-bottle of house wine and service, at any time the restaurant is open (i.e. at dinner as well as at lunch, unless a place is open only for dinner), for £20 or less per person.*

All entries in the Guide are rewritten every year, not least because restaurant standards fluctuate. Don't trust an out-of-date Guide.

SCOTLAND

Le Marché Noir

2–4 Eyre Place, EH3 5EP   COOKING 2
031-558 1608   COST £19–£48

'Delighted that Edinburgh can sustain a simple honest place like this,' writes
one who knows the scene. The style is pure French 'in a nicely dated way', with
flowers on the table, wooden wine-case ends for decoration and fixed-price
menus that eschew English translations. It is comfortable, friendly and cheap.

The food satisfies and the kitchen cares about presentation. Robust, classic
dishes such as black pudding with red wine sauce and escalope of pork with
wild mushrooms and madeira line up alongside more modern ideas, including
roast fillet of salmon with a forceful sauce of vinegar and shallots. The repertoire
also encompasses smoked chicken and avocado salad, guinea-fowl with raisins,
and venison with ginger and juniper. Sweets tend towards bistro favourites such
as bread-and-butter pudding (almost as light as a soufflé), terrine of white
chocolate and orange, and crème brûlée. A 'man-sized' cafetière of hot, strong
coffee brings proceedings to a close. The wine list encourages drinkers to explore
interesting grape varieties, to try wines they might otherwise skip, and to drink
by the glass (don't be afraid to ask what is available). Mark-ups are fair, and a
varied short list is useful. House wine begins at £8.50 (£1.80 a glass).

CHEFS: Neil Ross and David Connell   PROPRIETOR: Malcolm Duck   OPEN: all week, exc L Sat
and Sun; 12 to 2.30, 7 (6.30 Sun) to 10 (10.30 Fri and Sat, 9.30 Sun)   MEALS: Set L £11.50 to
£16.50, Set D £18.50 to £25.50   SERVICE: not inc (10% for 6 or more)   CARDS: Access, Amex,
Visa   DETAILS: 40 seats. Private parties: 40 main room. Vegetarian meals. Children welcome. No smoking while others eat D. Wheelchair access (1 step; also WC). No music. Fax:
031-556 0798

Martins ▼ ⁙

70 Rose Street North Lane, EH2 3DX   COOKING 2
031-225 3106   COST £23–£46

The alleyway behind Rose Street (parallel to Princes Street) may look a bit
gloomy, but the restaurant is brightly lit and handy for local offices, hotels and
the station. Business people and tourists are among the clientele, greeted
enthusiastically by Martin Irons. Meatier kinds of fish are the mainstay, usually
partnered by a vegetable. Baked turbot and grey mullet are served with fennel,
sea bass comes with peppers and chicory. Alternatives to fish may be
guinea-fowl and saddle of venison, loin of lamb or breast of duck.

On paper the food sounds interesting: feuilleté of langoustine with spinach
and nettle sauce, and pigeon breast stir-fried with artichoke, chilli and smoked
bacon, were two spring starters. Overcooking may be a problem, though,
leading to hard scallops and monkfish at one inspection meal. Vegetables are
organically grown, but a reporter found that 'a boiled potato, a spoonful of cubed
beetroot and a couple of fried leeks on a side plate' were not much to write home
about. Guinea-fowl, on the other hand, has been impressive, the breast cooked
moist, the leg crisp-skinned and stuffed with a mixture of wild rice, smoked
bacon and apricots.

Cheeses are good, accompanied by pictures of the cows that produce the milk,
and puddings might include chocolate marquise and elderflower and basil

558

sorbet. Service can easily be slowed down by unforeseen circumstances, although it tries to make amends – 'A glass of wine was offered free of charge as the first hour passed,' wrote a hungry inspector. The wine list seeks out interesting bottles (a vin de pays made from Malvoisie, for example, and some Bonny Doon wines) and makes them available at prices that encourage experiment: a flat mark-up is added, rather than a percentage. The notes help too. House Italian is £9.95. CELLARMAN'S CHOICE: Alsace Riesling 1985, Rolly-Gassman, £23.15; Seville Estate Cabernet Sauvignon 1988, £19.95.

CHEFS: Forbes Stott and Alan Mathieson PROPRIETORS: Martin and Gay Irons OPEN: Tue to Sat, exc Sat L; 12 to 2, 7 to 10 (11 during Festival) CLOSED: 4 weeks from 24 Dec, 1 week June, 1 week Sept MEALS: alc (main courses £14.50). Set L £10.95 (2 courses) SERVICE: not inc (10% for 6 or more) CARDS: Access, Amex, Diners, Visa DETAILS: 28 seats. Private parties: 28 main room, 8 private room. Vegetarian meals with prior notice. No children under 8. No smoking in dining-room. Wheelchair access (3 steps). No music

Rendezvous

NEW ENTRY

24 Deanhaugh Street, EH4 1LY
031-332 4476

COOKING 1
COST £16–£40

The busy main drag in Stockbridge may not be the first place to look for good eating, but it is worth throwing prejudice aside and diving into this small basement, a 10-minute walk from the Botanic Gardens. It was 'like auntie's drawing room' for one reporter whose aunt must have loved art nouveau, and 'looks more expensive than it is'. The food is freshly cooked, straightforwardly done, served in a congenial setting, and (certainly at lunch-time) extremely good value.

The *carte* changes seasonally, everything else daily, and the cooking offers a good mix of Gaelic and Gallic that includes a fresh artichoke and Parmesan soufflé, Dover sole with caper and lime butter, and marzipan and apricot strudel. The set business lunch of two or three courses is absurdly low-priced for the quality, and one reporter enjoyed Cullen skink, a revivalist Scottish dish if ever there was one, correctly cooked lamb chops with rosemary and redcurrant sauce, and tangy fresh lemon sorbet. Although a service charge is added automatically, service is a strong point. Twenty-odd wines are reasonably priced, with house wine at £8, or £1.50 per glass.

CHEF: Richard Easton PROPRIETOR: C.H. Anderson OPEN: all week; 12 to 2.30, 6.30 to 10.30 MEALS: alc (main courses £8 to £15). Set L £5.95 (2 courses) to £7.80, Set D £18.50 SERVICE: 10%, card slips closed CARDS: Access, Visa DETAILS: 24 seats. Private parties: 34 main room. Vegetarian meals with prior notice. Children's helpings. Smart dress preferred. Music. Air-conditioned

Shamiana ✸ £

14 Brougham Street, Tollcross, EH3 9JH
031-228 2265 and 229 5578

COOKING 1*
COST £19–£37

'We still go every fortnight,' confirm Edinburgh regulars, who note that the décor in the Butt brothers' busy restaurant is becoming more 'Indianified'. The dining-room, with its black-and-white tiled floor and luxuriant greenery, has been embellished with new chairs, chandelier wall fittings and more ornate cutlery. The kitchen works to an intriguing menu that centres on north Indian and Kashmiri cooking, with a few forays into other regions such as Parsee saali boti khumbani (a wedding dish of lamb with dried apricots). Visitors have endorsed malai murgh (chicken in a creamy 'milk sauce'), badami gosht, lamb pasanda and sag dhal. The cooking is consistently good. The wine list has about 30 carefully chosen and keenly priced bottles from around the world. House wine is £7.95.

CHEFS: M.A. Butt and Mahmood Khan PROPRIETORS: M.A. Butt and A.N. Butt OPEN: all week, exc L Sat and Sun; 12 to 2, 6 to 11 CLOSED: 25 Dec, 1 Jan MEALS: alc (main courses £6.50 to £9). SERVICE: 12.5%, card slips closed CARDS: Access, Amex, Diners, Visa DETAILS: 43 seats. Private parties: 36 main room. Vegetarian meals. Children's helpings. Smart dress preferred. No smoking in 1 dining-room. Wheelchair access (1 step). Music. Air-conditioned

Shore 🏠✳ £

3–4 The Shore, Leith, EH6 6QW
031-553 5080
off A199, on Firth of Forth, 2m E of
city centre

COOKING 1*
COST £14–£35

Informality and cheerfulness are the hallmarks of this no-nonsense bar-cum-restaurant facing west over the water of Leith. Décor and trappings are kept to a minimum, but the place feels cosy when the fires are lit, and traditional folk music and jazz lift the mood. Daily menus are chalked on a blackboard, and fresh fish is the star attraction. The kitchen keeps things simple: halibut might be poached and served with lime hollandaise or steamed with coriander; monkfish is roasted with avocado, olives and anchovy; baked seawolf comes with ginger and leeks. Game dominates the scene in winter. Well-made soups, exactly cooked vegetables and generous portions have also been noted. Light lunches are good value. Around two dozen wines offer plenty of decent drinking without emptying the wallet. House wine is £7.90.

CHEFS: Kevin O'Connor, Philippa Crookshank and Innes Gibson PROPRIETORS: Philippa Crookshank and Simon Edington OPEN: all week; 12 (12.30 Sun) to 2.30 (3 Sun), 6.30 to 10.15 CLOSED: 25 and 26 Dec, 1 and 2 Jan MEALS: alc (main courses £6.50 to £12). Set L Mon to Fri £6.50 (2 courses), Set L Sun £9.50 (2 courses) to £11.50 SERVICE: not inc (10% for 8 or more), card slips closed CARDS: Access, Visa DETAILS: restaurant 36 seats, bar 30 seats. 5 tables outside. Private parties: 36 main room. Vegetarian meals. Children's helpings on request. No smoking in dining-room. Wheelchair access. Music

Siam Erawan £

NEW ENTRY

48 Howe Street, EH3 6TH
031-226 3675

COOKING 1*
COST £12–£33

Thai restaurants are catching on in Edinburgh, and not before time. This arched cellar, in a fairly smart part of the New Town, works well, with plain white walls and obligatory Thai decoration. The waitresses' costumes – bizarre silk dresses and ruched satin knickerbockers – are something else, but the waitresses themselves get top marks for enthusiasm, friendliness, good humour and attentiveness, and an efficient manager keeps everything under control.

The menu is better than formula Thai, with some individuality in the cooking, and ingredients are impressive: real fresh green papaya in the raw vegetable dish somtum, tasting attractively sharp and lemony, and jackfruit among the sweets. Tom kah gai, an aromatic coconut-rich soup, is impressive, as are the curries, including one with tofu. Pad thai, a rice-flour noodle with peanuts and serve-yourself lemon juice, kills the heat effectively. One reporter ordered a green vegetable curry with aubergines. But where were the aubergines? 'Oh, the chef forgot to put them in,' improvised the waiter. It was good anyway. Banana fritters come topped with un-Siamese whipped cream (if you let them) and golden syrup; the batter, made from rice flour and fresh ground coconut, is chewier than the conventional kind. The wine list is unremarkable, with much in the £10 to £12 range. House wine is £7.80.

CHEF: Thondchai Tun PROPRIETOR: Miss W. Chinnapong OPEN: all week, exc Sun L; 12 to 2.30, 6 to 11 CLOSED: New Years Day MEALS: alc (main courses £4 to £8.50). Set L £5.95, Set D £16 to £22 SERVICE: 10%, card slips closed CARDS: Access, Visa DETAILS: 44 seats. Private parties: 30 main room. Vegetarian meals. Children welcome. Smart dress preferred. No-smoking area. Music

Spices ✸✲

110 West Bow, Grassmarket, EH1 2HH
031-225 5028

COOKING 1
COST £12–£32

This restaurant on two floors was opened in 1992 by the owners of Kalpna (see entry, Edinburgh), but serves meat. It lays claim to some Charles Rennie Mackintosh chairs which, although they do not marry particularly well with Indian paintings, do their bit for style. Chicken and lamb are the mainstays, either from the tandoor, or with a predominantly Kashmiri input: rogan josh or murgh chaman, for example. But the menu changes periodically to incorporate dishes from further afield. Kuku paka is Zanzibar-style chicken in a blackberry-coloured yogurt flavoured with coconut, ginger and lemon. The sour flavour of deep-fried aubergine comes from mango powder. One unusual first course of fruit chaat converted a sceptic who generally prefers fruit at the end of a meal and was dubious about the success of uncooked spices. The diced fresh fruit, rolled in cinnamon and other spices including salt and pepper, came with a coriander chutney, and worked a treat partly because it was not too sweet, partly because it made a very appetising start. Spices certainly get full marks for noble experiment, and nobody is likely to come away bored. Wines on the short and sensible list are reasonably priced; house wine is £6.95 (80p per glass).

CHEFS: Ajay Bhartdwaj and Afaquir Rawat PROPRIETORS: Ajay Bhartdwaj, Moussa Jogee and Pramod Joshi OPEN: Mon to Sat; 12 to 2, 6 to 11 CLOSED: 25 Dec and 1 Jan MEALS: alc (main courses £6 to £7.50). Buffet L £5.50 SERVICE: 10%, card slips closed CARDS: Access, Visa DETAILS: 60 seats. Private parties: 30 main room, 30 private room. Vegetarian meals. Children's helpings. No smoking in 1 dining-room. Wheelchair access (also WC). Music

'Butter came in a big slab. It always comes in a big slab in Wales.' (On eating in Wales)

Vintners Rooms ♀ ✳

The Vaults, 87 Giles Street, Leith, EH6 6BZ
031-554 8423 and 6767

COOKING 3
COST £19–£48

'Fantastic' is one reporter's description of this historic building, which was once the centre of the Scottish claret trade. The places oozes atmosphere. Light lunches and snacks are served in the spacious wine bar; more formal meals are taken in the splendid dining-room with its auctioneer's recess and seventeenth-century plasterwork.

Tim Cumming is capable of mightily good cooking, and generally the kitchen is firmly on target. The menus are peppered with modern, but not outlandish ideas and some unlikely combinations. What impresses is the way that flavours are balanced: wonderfully juicy scallops might come with an outstandingly delicate sauce pointed up with Pernod and capers or with rhubarb butter; guinea-fowl is served with lime and port or with bacon, lentils and laverbread croquette; fettuccine is dressed up with shiitake mushrooms and Parmesan or with saffron and mussels. Reporters have spoken highly of duck terrine with mixed pickles, halibut with sweet pepper and anise sauce, and white and dark chocolate parfait with minted custard sauce. Occasionally things can go wrong, as when a reporter encountered 'flavourless' beef with 'poor' red wine sauce and a 'very strange' crème brûlée with an odd floury texture. But this place is confident in itself and has the added attraction of a thoughtfully compiled, well-priced wine list with bags of interest, good half-bottles, and nine or ten house wines around £10 (£1.75 a glass).

CHEFS: Tim Cumming and James Baxter   PROPRIETORS: Tim and Susan Cumming   OPEN: Mon to Sat; 12 to 2.30, 7 to 10.30   CLOSED: 2 weeks Christmas   MEALS: alc (main courses £13 to £16). Set wine bar L £8.75 (2 courses) to £11.75   SERVICE: not inc   CARDS: Access, Amex, Visa   DETAILS: 60 seats. Private parties: 36 main room. Vegetarian meals. Children's helpings on request. No smoking in dining-room. Wheelchair access (2 steps). No music

Waterfront Wine Bar ♀ £

1C Dock Place, Leith, EH6 6LU
031-554 7427

COOKING 1
COST £13–£33

The wine bar overlooks Leith docks and generates a relaxed atmosphere, but its popularity brings pressure: 'The conservatory is the place to eat but seems to be booked years in advance.' Otherwise booths and small rooms provide intimate spaces in which to eat. Wines are listed in a blur of chalk on the wall, and a blackboard menu is trundled round for inspection. The food relies heavily on a pleasant Mediterranean mix of fresh fish, the grill and salads, although all of these may vary in quality. At one meal, dry sardines and woody asparagus were followed by good fresh fish with upbeat saucing: silver mullet with piquant salsa verde, and grilled mackerel with horseradish. Among shellfish might be baked crab, or scallops (from Mull) in a lobster bisque, backed up by meat dishes such as chargrilled Aberdeen Angus and pan-fried suprême of chicken stuffed with a mousseline of pigeon and pistachio nuts. Puddings were a let-down for one inspector.

The wine list's net is cast worldwide and, apart from a few unenterprising offerings from négociants, there is plenty of good drinking. It is difficult to pay more than £15 and, thanks to the mark-up policy of adding a fixed amount rather than a percentage, the better wines are a relatively good buy. House wine is £7.90, and a couple of dozen wines are available by the glass (£1.60 upwards). CELLARMAN'S CHOICE: Taltarni fumé blanc 1992, £12.80; Bordeaux Ch. de Sours Rosé 1992, £10.80.

CHEFS: Robin Bowie, Jenny McRae and Allanah Harrower   PROPRIETORS: Ian and Helen Ruthven, Sarah Reid and Robin Bowie   OPEN: all week; 12 to 2.30 (3 Fri to Sun), 6 to 9.30 (10 Fri and Sat)   CLOSED: 2 days Christmas, 2 days New Year   MEALS: alc (main courses £6 to £12), Set L Oct to Apr £6.50   SERVICE: not inc (10% for 6 or more)   CARDS: Access, Visa   DETAILS: 120 seats. 10 tables outside. Private parties: 60 main room, 16 and 60 private rooms. Vegetarian meals. No children under 5. No-smoking area. Wheelchair access. Music. Fax: 031-555 6060

ERISKA Strathclyde   map 8

▲ Isle of Eriska

Ledaig, Eriska PA37 1SD
LEDAIG (063 172) 371   COOKING 2
off A828, 12m N of Oban   COST £43–£53

The island of Eriska is 'virtually a nature reserve of over 100 hectares', with nearly 50 species of bird, as well as seals, otters, deer and badgers. The baronial-style house dates from the late nineteenth century, and the Buchanan-Smith occupation began in the mid-1970s. For those unable to settle with a book in the library, water sports, tennis and walking are on offer. 'We were immediately taken in hand by charming and well-trained staff. Robin Buchanan-Smith tells you how nice it is to have you' was the experience of one reporter.

The six-course set meals are eaten off mahogany tables. Since dessert is followed by a savoury and then three well-chosen Scottish cheeses (with excellent oatcakes), not all reporters are able to stay the course. A meal for two in May began with mushroom pithiviers (which suffered from too much pastry and too little filling) and proceeded to pan-fried scallops (sweet, springy and juicy), which, like the alternative carrot and coriander soup, were on the receiving end of a lot of cream. Roast haunch of venison under a copper dome was wheeled round to be carved on to the plate, while halibut fillet was splendidly fresh and poached to a turn in buttery juices. At this meal, praline ice-cream beat the rhubarb crumble. Coffee is self-service and might be improved. Wines cover a commendably wide range of prices and include some very attractive bottles indeed: staying for a month would be no hardship with such a cellar. House wine is £8.20.

The text of entries is based on unsolicited reports sent in by readers, backed up by inspections conducted anonymously. The factual details under the text are from questionnaires the Guide sends to all restaurants that feature in the book.

CHEFS: Sheena Buchanan-Smith and Alan Clark   PROPRIETORS: the Buchanan-Smith family
OPEN: all week, D only; 8 to 9   CLOSED: Dec to Mar   MEALS: Set D £35   SERVICE: not inc, card
slips closed   CARDS: Access, Visa   DETAILS: 40 seats. Private parties: 40 main room. Car park.
Vegetarian meals. High tea 6pm. No children under 10 D. Jacket and tie. No cigars/pipes in
dining-room. Wheelchair access (also WC). No music   ACCOMMODATION: 17 rooms, all with
bath/shower. TV. Phone. B&B £130 to £185. Deposit: £50. Rooms for disabled. Children
welcome. Baby facilities. Pets welcome (in bedrooms only). Garden. Tennis. Fishing.. Fax: (063
172) 531 (*The Which? Hotel Guide*)

FORT WILLIAM Highland   map 8

Crannog ✥✱

| Town Pier, Fort William PH33 7NG | COOKING 1 |
| FORT WILLIAM (0397) 705589 | COST £16–£40 |

Eating simple seafood, overlooking a loch, is one of the great pleasures of being
in Scotland. This former bait store, easily spotted down by the Town Pier thanks
to much timber and red and white paint, is kind to non-smokers, who sit near the
window and get the views.

Fresh seafood is the reason to eat here. Oysters, langoustines and mussels all
benefit from plain treatment, which usually means garlic butter if hot, or
mayonnaise if cold: a trio of garlic, curry-flavoured and herb-flecked mayonnaise
with langoustines, for example. Other fish – skate with black butter, for instance
– is passable but not, in the view of some, up to the same standard. Daily specials
are chalked on a board, but the advice is to avoid attempts at more ambitious
cooking, like trout with ginger, and stay with the simplest dishes. Do not expect
subtlety: portions can be large. The smoked platter is a generous display of
langoustines, mussels, thick-sliced salmon, and trout. Peripherals such as
chunky bread, basic salad and ordinary puddings are reasonably supportive.
The same food at dinner is slightly more expensive than at lunch-time.
Acceptable house white is £7.95.

The Glasgow Branch (28 Cheapside Street, Tel: 041-221 1727) has similar
natural timber and formula: chunky bread, 'the best gravad lax in the UK', and
whopping langoustines in garlic butter. It needs tight supervision to maintain
Fort William standards, and it seems to be getting it. As we went to press, a new
restaurant and seafood and salad bar venture was about to open in Edinburgh
(14 South St Andrew Street, Tel: 031-557 5589); reports, please.

CHEF: Susan Trowbridge   PROPRIETOR: Crannog Ltd   OPEN: all week; 12 to 2.30, 6 to 10 (9
winter)   CLOSED: 25 Dec, 1 Jan   MEALS: alc (main courses L £5.50 to £9.50, D £7.50 to
£13.50)   SERVICE: not inc, card slips closed   CARDS: Access, Visa   DETAILS: 50 seats. Private
parties: 50 main room, 25 private room. Vegetarian meals. Children's helpings. Smart dress
preferred. No smoking in 1 dining-room. Wheelchair access (also WC). Music. Fax:
(0397) 705026

---

*All details are as accurate as possible at the time of going to press, but chefs and owners
often change, and it is wise to check by telephone before making a special journey. Many
readers have been disappointed when set-price bargain meals are no longer available.
Ask when booking.*

▲ *Inverlochy Castle* 🍷 ✳

Torlundy, Fort William PH33 6SN
FORT WILLIAM (0397) 702177   COOKING 3
3m N of Fort William, on A82   COST £30–£60

'Inverlochy appears to be recession-proof,' writes one who noted the new cars, full dining-rooms, hushed voices and casually expensive clothes. 'Four Americans at a neighbouring table were spending a few nights in Scotland on the first leg of a flight around the world in their own jet.' What a pity the hotel has only a helipad. The restaurant is inordinately grand, utterly Victorian and staffed by people who, by virtue of being courteous, attentive, and taking a genuine interest in guests' well-being, manage to make it all feel quite normal. Moreover, no gratuities are expected for this high level of service.

Simon Haigh is into his stride in the kitchen, with mastery in all departments bolstered by great attention to detail. If the style is conservative, it is because international travellers usually want it that way. What we have here is assurance and confidence applied to everything from scallops to Loch Linnhe prawns to grouse and local venison. Partridge, hare and woodpigeon extend the scope of flavours, appearing in terrines, or with braised lentils and root vegetables. Menus are balanced, buying is good, timing is accurate, and saucing, often with roasting jus as the basis, produces a very satisfying feel. Mediterraneanism is kept to a minimum, while game chips, fried breadcrumbs, steamed chocolate pudding and caramelised rice pudding are allowed free rein.

The lengthy wine list is not one for bargains, although there is good drinking under £20. Those who persevere beyond three-figure clarets will find the rest of France, indeed the rest of the world, more reasonable, especially the Rhône, Chile, Australia and New Zealand. Half-bottles are generously sprinkled throughout.

CHEF: Simon Haigh   PROPRIETOR: Mrs Grete Hobbs   OPEN: all week; 12.30 to 1.45, 7 to 9.30
CLOSED: mid-Dec to Mar   MEALS: Set L £25, Set D £40   SERVICE: card slips closed   CARDS:
Access, Amex, Visa   DETAILS: 50 seats. Private parties: 10 main room, 14 private room. Car park. Vegetarian meals. High tea for children under 12. Jacket and tie. No smoking in dining-room. Wheelchair access (also WC). No music   ACCOMMODATION: 17 rooms, all with bath/shower. TV. Phone. B&B £130 to £260. Children under 12 share parents' room. Baby facilities. Afternoon teas. Garden. Tennis. Fishing. Snooker. Confirm by 10am. Fax: (0397) 702953 (*The Which? Hotel Guide*)

GLASGOW Strathclyde   map 8

Amber Regent

50 West Regent Street, G2 2QZ   COOKING 1
041-331 1655 and 1677   COST £17–£56

'One of the classiest Chinese restaurants I have ever been in,' remarked a visitor to this popular venue not far from Queen Street Station. The deep-green interior, subdued lighting, little booths and paintings reminded him more of a stylish French establishment. Prices are by no means cheap, but the kitchen delivers a consistently good standard of mainly Cantonese food without straying into esoteric, unfamiliar territory. Steamed dim-sum and assorted appetisers such as honeyed chicken wings and deep-fried wun-tun have met with approval, along with aromatic crispy lamb, beef with ho fun noodles and tiger prawns in hot garlic sauce. Venison shows up as satay, or shredded with spring onions. Service copes efficiently with the crowds. The wine list is aimed at those with bulging wallets; alternatively drink tea, beer or saké. House wine is £9.95 a litre.

CHEF: Tommy Ho   PROPRIETOR: Andy Chung   OPEN: Mon to Sat; 12 to 2.15, 5.30 to 11 (11.30 Fri, midnight Sat)   MEALS: alc (main courses £8.50 to £14). Set L £6.95 (2 courses), Set D £21 to £28   SERVICE: not inc   CARDS: Access, Amex, Diners, Visa   DETAILS: 90 seats. Private parties: 100 main room, 15 private room. Vegetarian meals. Children's helpings on request. Smart dress preferred. Wheelchair access (1 step). Music. Air-conditioned. Fax: 041-353 3398

Buttery

652 Argyle Street, G3 8UF   COOKING 2
041-221 8188   COST £21–£48

The motorways and flyovers of modern Glasgow have risen around this turn-of-the-century former pub, but inside the attraction is undimmed. It is 'a beautiful, friendly restaurant', with its share of splendour and opulence. Ideas fizz, and obvious ambition shows in first courses of warm white French sausage with morel on a bed of kale and courgette with raisin marmalade, or of curly endive with sliced duck and a red lentil and kumquat yogurt. A platter of melons and cured ham is rendered more interesting for its accompanying fig vinegar sorbet. Main courses are a more familiar jaunt through roast rack of lamb, baked fillet of salmon, or fillet of beef.

Reporters have enjoyed good-quality fish, including cod and halibut, and rich home-smoked loin of venison with wood pigeon and lentil stuffing, on a creamy mustard sauce. A vocal majority, however, believe that ideas are running ahead of execution, and that simpler food, and perhaps lower prices, might be the way forward. Soups, queenies and mussels in puff pastry, vegetables and some of the puddings lead to this conclusion. Variable timing, the sweetness of some savoury sauces, and a general lack of clarity perhaps indicate that the kitchen is taking its eye off the basics while trying too hard to impress with culinary alarums and excursions. Service is courteous and helpful, a bit on the formal side, and one reporter questioned the automatic 10% service charge on the à la carte menu. More basic food, such as chilli con carne or shark with parsley sauce, is served downstairs in the Belfry. The short wine list is not too heavily marked up and offers a dozen half-bottles. House wines are £10.95, or £2.25 per glass.

CHEF: Stephen Johnson   PROPRIETOR: Alloa Pubs and Restaurants Ltd   OPEN: Mon to Sat, exc Sat L; 12 to 2.30, 7 to 10.30   CLOSED: bank and local hols   MEALS: alc (main courses £12 to £14). Set L £14.75   SERVICE: l0% (net prices Set L), card slips closed   CARDS: Access, Amex, Diners, Visa   DETAILS: 50 seats. Private parties: 50 main room, 8 private room. Car park. Vegetarian meals. Children welcome. Smart dress preferred. No pipes/cigars in dining-room. Music. Air-conditioned. Fax: 041-204 4639

See the inside of the front cover for an explanation of the 1 to 5 rating system for cooking standards.

Café Gandolfi £

64 Albion Street, G1 1NY

041-552 6813

COOKING 1

COST £15–£27

Regulars love the unique Glaswegian atmosphere of this youthful, crowded and jolly place. The furniture is handcrafted by art students, stained-glass flying fish are framed in the windows. Décor and trappings are pared to a minimum: no fresh flowers or napkins; candles in Perrier bottles; and laidback student waitresses in jeans and T-shirts. But be warned: everyone smokes. Colour, variety and invention are the hallmarks of the menu. Plates of cold meats, soups and salads are backed up by items such as choux pastries stuffed with blue cheese, couscous with roasted vegetables and a vegetarian koulibiac. Daily specials provide an even greater choice for those who have worked their way through the repertoire. Home-made ice-creams, good coffee and excellent-value wines by the glass are a bonus. House wine is £8.60.

CHEFS: Maggie Clarence and Alisdair Braidwood   PROPRIETORS: Iain Mackenzie and Seumas MacInnes   OPEN: all week; 9am (noon Sun) to 11.30pm   CLOSED: bank hols   MEALS: alc (main courses £5.20 to £7.80)   SERVICE: not inc (10% for 6 or more), card slips closed   CARDS: Access, Visa   DETAILS: 65 seats. Private parties: 16 main room. Vegetarian meals. Children's helpings. No children under 14 after 8pm. Wheelchair access (2 steps). Music

▲ Forte Crest, Jules' Bar and American Grill

Bothwell Street, G2 7EN

041-248 3010

COOKING 1

COST £22–£43

The design and food are Scottish, but the effect is entirely New York Grill, from Cajun chicken and blackened Angus steak with frizzled leek and mashed potato, to Caesar salad and Bloody Mary, not to mention tobacco onions, shoestring fries and deep-fried soft-shell crab with jalapeño salsa. The place jumps with Big Apple life. Booths for privacy, clever lighting, a casual feel and mid-market pricing ensure it is packed at lunch-times. Most effort goes into savoury dishes, leaving drone-like puddings of Häagen-Dazs ice-cream and frozen yogurt, or gratin of peppered strawberries, but by that stage the food is either under your skin or it isn't. As is customary in American-style food outlets, service is warm, open and charming. Wines are punchy, brief and tasty. House Californian is £8.90 (£1.80 per glass).

CHEF: Frank Boggie   PROPRIETOR: Forte plc   OPEN: all week, exc Sat and Sun L; 12 to 2.30, 6 to 11   CLOSED: bank hols   MEALS: alc (main courses £5.50 to £12.50)   SERVICE: not inc   CARDS: Access, Amex, Diners, Visa   DETAILS: 60 seats. Private parties: 70 main room, 20 private room. Car park. Vegetarian meals. Children's helpings. Smart dress preferred. Wheelchair access. Music. Air-conditioned   ACCOMMODATION: 255 rooms, all with bath/shower. TV. Phone. Air-conditioned. B&B £42 to £84. Rooms for disabled. Children welcome. Baby facilities. Pets welcome. Afternoon teas. Confirm by 4

Several sharp operators have tried to extort money from restaurateurs on the promise of an entry in a guidebook that has never appeared. The Good Food Guide *makes no charge for inclusion and does not offer certificates of any kind.*

Killermont Polo Club £

2022 Maryhill Road, nr Bearsden, G20 0AB
041-946 5412

COOKING 1
COST £14–£38

As themed restaurants go, the Polo Club is pretty single-minded. The converted manse certainly looks the part: very 1920s, with trophies and art deco everywhere. It has its own team too, and feels like a club – one of the oak-panelled rooms looks out on to a mini-pitch – although it is much more fun than stuffy. The owners are from Punjab, hence the tandoori dishes, but the style is Anglo-Indian with input from Goa, Kashmir and South India as well as Malaysia. Scottish ingredients – shellfish from Seil Island near Oban, raspberries from Angus, and their own garden herbs – are well treated. Lamb spiced with cumin and coriander is cooled and refreshed by yogurt and mint. Spicing is often subtle, sauces generally rich, and meats of high quality: chicken tikka is particularly good. Pakoras, rice, nan and dips of chilli and raita are up to standard. Desserts are more Anglo than Indian, but there are gulab jamun and kulfi. Buffet nights are used as testing grounds for new dishes. A modest wine list runs round the world offering most bottles for less than £15. House French is £8.25 (£1.80 per glass).

CHEF: Jas Sagoo   PROPRIETORS: Kal Dhaliwal, Pami Dhaliwal and Jas Sagoo   OPEN: Mon to Sun, exc Sun L; 12 to 2, 5 to 10.30 (11 Sat)   CLOSED: 1 Jan   MEALS: alc (main courses £4.50 to £12). Set L £6.95 to £7.95, Buffet D Sun and Mon £9.95   SERVICE: not inc   CARDS: Access, Amex, Diners, Visa   DETAILS: 90 seats. Private parties: 40 main room, 20 and 30 private rooms. Car park. Vegetarian meals. Children's helpings. Smart dress preferred. No-smoking areas. Wheelchair access (also WC). Music. Fax: 041-429 6327

Mitchell's West End £

NEW ENTRY

31/35 Ashton Lane, off Byres Road, G12 8SJ
041-339 2220

COOKING 1
COST £19–£35

This compact, single-room restaurant opposite the Ubiquitous Chip (see entry, Glasgow) opened in 1993 to immediate local acclaim. Mitchell's has the air of being a place in transition (as we went to press, they had just applied for a licence, but intend to continue the bring-your-own-plus-corkage policy as well). Our inspector was told on a Monday evening that there were 'no puddings tonight'. There was, however, a pretty good starter of venison and pigeon on a bed of pickled red and white cabbage, the salt and vinegar of the underlay mixing nicely with the 'rich, gamey' flavour of the meats. Grilled ribeye tasted properly hung and had an edge of well-crisped fat, although the cream sauce was less good. The accompanying salad was engagingly crisp and colourful. Otherwise, chicken liver pâté with Cumberland sauce, rendezvous of seafood with fresh pasta, or lamb's liver with onions in a chicken stock infused with rosemary are the order of the day. Espresso is 'very good'; service can be a bit glum. Note that tables are turned over at 9pm on Fridays and Saturdays, so those with earlier bookings may need to eat quickly. A sister restaurant, Mitchell's Charing Cross (157 North Street, Glasgow, G3 7DA, Tel: 041-204 4312), is already licensed and does not have the bring-your-own policy.

CHEFS/PROPRIETORS: Angus Boyd and Sean Ward   OPEN: Mon to Sat, D only, and Sat L; 12 to 2.30, 5.30 to 10.30   CLOSED: 25 Dec and 2 Jan   MEALS: alc (main courses £7 to £13). Unlicensed, but bring your own: corkage £1.90   SERVICE: not inc   CARDS: Access, Diners, Visa   DETAILS: 40 seats. Private parties: 40 main room. Vegetarian meals. Children's helpings until 8pm. Smart dress preferred. No pipes/cigars in dining-room. Music

---

▲ *One Devonshire Gardens* ⁵⭑

1 Devonshire Gardens, G12 0UX   COOKING 2
041-339 2001   COST £33–£60

The news here is of a change of chef. Andrew Fleming has moved on and Andrew Fairlie has arrived from Paris – well, from the Grill Room at Euro Disney, to be precise, but it's close enough. The hotel, among the Victorian mansions and graceful terraces of the city's West End, remains as opulent as ever. The rooms preserve the original magnificence, decoration is tasteful, and 'staff know it is a restaurant, not a temple', and so are relaxed, informed and helpful. It all feels jolly and congenial. 'The sommelier for the evening was the magnificently named Johnny Walker. With a name like that, he had to get involved in the drinks business', and is good with advice and service.

The menu 'offers little you won't have seen a million times before', apart perhaps from juicily seared scallops with a mound of bright green basil-flavoured couscous and a dribble of gazpacho round the edge: 'visually stunning'. An inspector felt, however, that attractive presentation did not make up for the lack of flavour in some dishes. Ingredients are 'prime' in that they generally opt for breasts and fillets rather than insides or extremities, and roasting is a preferred technique. Smoked salmon, seafood sausage, poached breast of chicken in tarragon cream sauce, and roast loin of lamb with a tartlet of kidneys show that the kitchen prefers to stay largely with the familiar. As to execution, an inspector found that pastry could be improved and timing for some items had gone awry. Grilling on that occasion swung between under- and overcooking, but tart lemon tart and chocolate terrine have been applauded. Canapés and petits fours are first-rate and bread is good. Wine mark-ups are stiff, although there are some bottles under £20. House wine is £16.

CHEF: Andrew Fairlie   PROPRIETOR: Ken McCulloch   OPEN: all week, exc Sat L; 12.30 to 2.30, 7 to 11   MEALS: Set L £21.50, Set D £37.50   SERVICE: not inc, card slips closed   CARDS: Access, Amex, Diners, Visa   DETAILS: 44 seats. Private parties: 50 main room, 12, 16 and 32 private rooms. Car park. Vegetarian meals. Children's helpings. No smoking in dining-room. Music ACCOMMODATION: 27 rooms, all with bath/shower. TV. Phone. B&B £115 to £145. Children welcome. Baby facilities. Pets welcome (not in public rooms). Afternoon teas. Garden. Fax: 041-337 1663 (*The Which? Hotel Guide*)

---

⁵⭑ *indicates that smoking is either banned altogether or that a dining-room is maintained for non-smokers. The symbol does not apply to restaurants that simply have no-smoking areas.*

Card slips closed *in the details at the end of an entry indicates that the total on the slips of credit cards is closed when handed over for signature.*

La Parmigiana £

447 Great Western Road, G12 8HH   COOKING 1
041-334 0686   COST £13–£40

Coming from town, you will find the restaurant just beyond Kelvinbridge underground station, at the end of the bridge after the fish and chip shop. It is a jolly, convivial and animated Italian. Green floral drapes cover the windows, and tables are set in 'promiscuous proximity'. Service is sharp. The set lunch is mostly soup or salad followed by chicken, a braise or stew of beef, a fish or some pasta, finishing with fresh fruit or ice-cream. It can, in other words, be modest or substantial according to requirements.

The evening *carte* is not so much new-wave as old-hat, but it does put some Scottish ingredients to good use: venison might arrive with polenta, and Loch Etive mussels are cooked with garlic, chilli, white wine and tomato. In fact, the bulk of fish, chicken and veal dishes are cooked in white wine, but there is also chargrilling: of the day's fish, or of quail marinated in olive oil, lemon and rosemary. Vegetables are not a strong point, but pasta with home-made pesto is good. Desserts include almondy cantuccini biscuits to dip in vino santo, and 'egg yoke [*sic*] switched [*sic*] with sugar and Marsala', better known as zabaglione. Espresso is good, and the short, mostly Italian wine list is reasonably priced. House wine is £8.90 a litre (£2.30 per glass).

CHEF: Sandro Giovanazzi   PROPRIETORS: Angelo and Sandro Giovanazzi   OPEN: Mon to Sat; 12 to 2.30, 6 to 11   MEALS: alc (main courses £5 to £13). Set L £6.80   SERVICE: not inc   CARDS: Access, Amex, Diners, Visa   DETAILS: 60 seats. Private parties: 60 main room. Vegetarian meals. Children's helpings. Smart dress preferred. Music. Air-conditioned. Fax: 041-332 3533

Puppet Theatre   `NEW ENTRY`

11 Ruthven Lane, G12 9BG   COOKING 2
041-339 8444   COST £23–£51

The Puppet Theatre is not so much *in* an old puppet theatre as *near* one. This used to be Poachers, and a boat-shaped conservatory extension has been added to the nineteenth-century house, using Catalan architect Gaudí for inspiration. The rest of the building is divided into differently themed rooms, decorated with Chinese puppets, an Italianate bust and greenhouse plants. 'Please put it in the *Guide*,' implored a regular reporter, citing cooking skills, quality of ingredients, ambience, and a team of agreeable waiters as recommendations.

The menu wears a smart contemporary badge, offering smoked salmon pizza, girolles in filo pastry, and Greek yogurt and cinnamon mousse with a fresh fruit compote. The vogue for contrasting rich with poor, ordinary with exalted, achieves a new expression here in a first course of Yorkshire pudding with foie gras. The basics are generally well done and include good buying of salmon and beef, and perfectly timed searing and grilling of the same. But 'the chef deserves full marks for his command of mousselines and purées', which sets him above the pack. One reporter who chose leek soup found it lacking in flavour, but the tiny smoked haddock and chive mousse it contained was 'true to the flavours of both and a miracle of delicacy'. Bread-and-butter pudding, in a 'rich, just-set clotted cream liquid custard', has an abundance of plump sultanas and comes with a tiny pile of freshly diced apple and kiwi fruit. Wines are brief and to the point, with house French at £9.95.

CHEF: Douglas Painter   PROPRIETORS: Ron McCulloch and George Swanson   OPEN: Tue to Sun; 12 to 2.30, 7 to 11   MEALS: alc (main courses £12 to £17). Set L £13.95   SERVICE: not inc   CARDS: Access, Amex, Visa   DETAILS: 72 seats. Private parties: 26 main room. Car park. Vegetarian meals. No children under 12. Smart dress preferred. Music. Air-conditioned

Rogano

11 Exchange Place, G1 3AN	COOKING 1
041-248 4055	COST £22–£67

Between Buchanan Street and Royal Exchange Square, Rogano claims to be the oldest-surviving restaurant in Glasgow, having started life in 1935 – the same year Cunard's *Queen Mary* took shape on the Clyde. Much of the period feel remains, the walnut panelling now golden with age, although the lighting (say old hands) is not what it was. Fish and vegetable dishes account for some two-thirds of the menu, and a modish Japanese influence has cropped up among first courses: oysters, sashimi with pickled ginger and wasabi, and thickly cut gravlax with a good dill cream dressing, for example.

Main courses plough a fairly predictable furrow of lamb with rosemary and mint, grilled or meunière lemon sole, and lobster thermidor (for which proper irons are provided). Portion control is tight and cream can dominate sauces. Some combinations, such as whisky parfait with Earl Grey tea sauce, may not please everybody. Coffee is first-rate. 'Given the ambience, space, professionalism of service and general air of relaxation, it was a very enjoyable evening,' noted one, adding that prices are rather higher than the food merits. Waiting is formal, courteous and helpful. Wines, starting at around £11, are pitched to the middle ground with standard mark-ups. The café downstairs is less expensive and turns out the likes of minted lamb soup, penne with smoked haddock and Gruyère, and steamed gingerbread pudding with toffee ice-cream.

CHEF: James Kerr   PROPRIETOR: Alloa Pubs and Restaurants   OPEN: all week, exc Sun L; restaurant 12 to 2.30, 6.30 to 10.30 (6 to 10 Sun); café noon to 11 (noon to midnight Fri and Sat, 6 to 10 Sun)   CLOSED: bank hols   MEALS: alc (main courses café £7 to £10, restaurant £12 to £28). Set L restaurant £16.50   SERVICE: restaurant 10%, café not inc, card slips closed   CARDS: Access, Amex, Diners, Visa   DETAILS: restaurant 55 seats, café 55 seats. Private parties: 60 main room, 16 private room. Vegetarian meals. Children welcome. No smoking before 2 at L, 9 at D. Wheelchair access. Music. Air-conditioned. Fax: 041-248 2608

Ubiquitous Chip ▮ £

12–26 Ashton Lane, G12 8SJ	COOKING 2*
041-334 5007	COST £13–£50

After more than 20 years at the stove and in the *Guide*, Ronald Clydesdale has had a rethink and 'taken a critical look at things'. Big changes then? The result of all this brainwork is to add 'a bit of zest and lift to the cooking'. Oh, and to invest more heavily in crockery, and perhaps make one or two decorative changes. You are forgiven if the earth hasn't moved. There is, in truth, no need to change such a whizz-bang operation much, apart from keeping an ear to the ground to listen out for the rumbles of fashion. Even then, not much note is taken. The Chip's strengths are good supplies, hearty food, and no nonsense in either cooking or service.

'We liked the attractive green décor and the busy and friendly service,' wrote one. Another was 'greeted cheerily by an eccentrically dressed member of staff and served with a nice bottle of Catalan house wine and a plate of crudités'. Menus are long, the sort that might have been out of favour a while back, but the Chip carries it off as well as any brasserie, rustling up shellfish bisque, creel-caught langoustines with mayonnaise, Aberdeen Angus steak with onion and leek marmalade, venison sausage, blueberry tart with Drambuie cream, and a parfait of honey and whisky. It raids the Scottish larder for Oban-landed squid, Ayrshire mutton, Mull of Kintyre goats' cheese and Perthshire woodpigeon (with a game and chocolate sauce).

Cheeses are listed individually – Tobermory truckle Cheddar, Inverloch goats' milk, Lanark blue (from unpasteurised ewes' milk) – and vegetable rennet is specified where appropriate. 'The Italian bread from a Jewish bakery was excellent.' Upstairs at the Chip is cheaper, with a short sharp wine list that does not wander much above £10. The main list is distinguished by its scope, excitement, ability to pick winners across the board, some mature vintages (from the Rhine as well as Bordeaux) and some unbelievably good prices. It is consideration for customers' pockets that produces as many Italian wines as burgundies. Spirits (whisky in particular) are on a par. House wine is £8.75.

CHEF/PROPRIETOR: Ron Clydesdale   OPEN: all week; 12 to 2.30, 5.30 to 11   CLOSED: 25 and 31 Dec (restaurant only), 1 and 2 Jan   MEALS: alc (main courses downstairs £10.50 to £15, upstairs L £4 to £5.50, D £5 to £10.50)   SERVICE: not inc   CARDS: Access, Amex, Diners, Visa   DETAILS: 140 seats. 12 tables outside. Private parties: 60 main room, 30 private room. Vegetarian meals. Children's helpings. Wheelchair access (also WC). No music. Fax: 041-337 1302

GULLANE Lothian   map 8

▲ *Greywalls* ▾ ⅝✳ £   NEW ENTRY

Muirfield, Gullane EH31 2EG
GULLANE (0620) 842144   COOKING 3
on A198, at W end of Gullane   COST £20–£52

The house is Lutyens, the garden is Gertrude Jekyll, and there are splendid views over Muirfield golf course to the Firth of Forth and the Black Rock. Greywalls has been in the Weaver family since the 1930s, and is run as a very tight ship. Everything, from the raked gravel outside to the whiter-than-white blouses of the waitresses, shows care and attention, although the mood is not one of cloistered hush. A happy 'lived-in' atmosphere prevails, helped along by smooth service and a feeling of unfussed efficiency.

After drinks in the bar or the quiet library, diners proceed to the elegant, low-ceilinged dining-room with its green walls and flower paintings. Dinner is built around a four-course fixed-price menu that changes daily to reflect fresh supplies. 'Lovingly created and skilfully balanced' was one reporter's verdict on Paul Baron's cooking. Starters such as fried foie gras with apple and thyme, or terrine of sea trout and langoustine wrapped in spinach, are followed by a soup or sorbet. Exceptional main courses might include modern ideas (steamed fillet of sea bass set on a compote of tomato, garlic and shallots) as well as hotel classics (medallions of beef with madeira sauce). Finely crafted desserts are the likes of pear parfait with ginger, and coffee comes with superb petit fours. Wines cover a healthy range of styles and prices, and the list keeps up to date with modern tastes as well as delving into the archives. House wines begin at £11.50 (£2.30 per glass). CELLARMAN'S CHOICE: Bordeaux, Notre Dame de Landiras 1992, £13; Fairview Estate Chardonnay 1992, £18.

CHEF: Paul Baron PROPRIETORS: Giles and Ros Weaver OPEN: all week; 12.30 to 1.45, 7.30 to 9.15 CLOSED: Nov to Mar MEALS: alc (main courses Mon to Sat L £4.50 to £10.50). Set L Sun £20, Set D £33 SERVICE: not inc, card slips closed CARDS: Access, Amex, Diners, Visa DETAILS: 50 seats. 4 tables outside. Private parties: 50 main room, 20 private room. Car park. Vegetarian meals with prior notice. Children welcome. Smart dress preferred. No smoking in dining-room. Wheelchair access (1 step; also WC). No music ACCOMMODATION: 22 rooms, all with bath/shower. TV. Phone. B&B £95 to £160. Deposit: £60. Rooms for disabled. Children welcome. Baby facilities. Pets by arrangement (not in public rooms). Afternoon teas. Garden. Tennis. Doors close at 11 (night porter). Confirm by 6. Fax: (0620) 842241 (The Which? Hotel Guide)

La Potinière ▮ ⁵⚹

Main Street, Gullane EH31 2AA
GULLANE (0620) 843214
on A198, 4m SW of North Berwick

COOKING 4
COST £24–£46

Pretty well everything in our mailbag about La Potinière is positive and supportive, and much of it centres favourably on the Browns themselves. This is a highly individual restaurant with a strong view about the way things should be done. Meals are meant to be leisurely. This is not a refuelling stop, but a destination restaurant where food and wine are the draw, the focus, the be-all and end-all. An example of the care taken is the Browns' database of dishes eaten by customers over the years, enabling them to vary the diet of regular visitors. Although reports refer to a relatively small number of dishes, not one of them has disappointed. 'My palate has become slightly jaded by years of enforced restaurant eating throughout Europe. La Potinière has re-awakened my interest in eating out for its own sake,' writes one advocate.

Menus are fixed, no-choice affairs, and the pattern at dinner is soup, fish, main course, salad, cheese and dessert. Nothing is smothered or disguised, and the cooking is careful and precise. Soups – red pepper and orange, or rich-flavoured tomato and basil, for instance – come with 'beautiful home-made bread'. Among fish dishes, mousse of Arbroath smokie is 'a Potinière classic', while 'perfectly cooked salmon, beautifully soft, on a bed of spiced lentils with morels' has been a highlight. Among main courses, pink breast of woodpigeon on a slightly bitter purée of Brussels sprouts, with 'an excellent balance of flavours and contrasts', stands out. Salads also win plaudits: 'Until now I had thought of salad as a culinary poor relation. No longer. Here it amply justified its status as a separate course.' All reports of the Brie claim it to be nothing less than 'super', and the gratin of raspberries – 'beautifully cooked, slightly creamy, slightly crunchy' – provides an upbeat finish. On top of all this, reporters are invariably impressed by the good value.

Service is entirely by David Brown, who expects no gratuity. 'We were instantly put at ease despite our late and slightly flustered arrival,' says one reporter. Another wishes he would employ an assistant: 'The wine was promised "as soon as I have a moment", and eventually arrived after the second course.' Wine is not a matter of life and death to Mr Brown; it is much more important than that. The range is stunning, the value generally dazzling, with four or five wines by the glass ranging from £2 to £4. 'I don't bother with the list,' writes a regular. 'I just ask David for advice. The more you ask, the more information he provides.' House wine is £9.75.

CHEF: Hilary Brown   PROPRIETORS: David and Hilary Brown   OPEN: L Mon, Tue, Thur and Sun, D Fri and Sat; 1, 8   CLOSED: 1 week Jun, Oct   MEALS: Set L £18.75 to £19.50, Set D £29.50 DETAILS: 30 seats. Private parties: 30 main room. Car park. Vegetarian meals with prior notice. Children welcome. Smart dress preferred. No smoking in dining-room. Wheelchair access (1 step). No music

---

HADDINGTON Lothian   map 8

▲ *Browns Hotel* ⁵⋇

1 West Road, Haddington EH41 3RD
HADDINGTON (0620) 822254   COOKING 2
off A1, 16m E of Edinburgh   COST £24–£39

A fine late-Georgian house on the outskirts of Haddington, Browns Hotel is enlivened by an interesting collection of contemporary Scottish art that includes bronzes. It is all run on a pleasing domestic scale, though: 'one of the friendliest restaurants I know, and one of the main reasons we return'. The relaxed style 'effectively hides the skill and energy that the hotel brings to your enjoyment'. Dishes might be simple in appearance but they delight, and the cooking is no more elaborate than it needs to be.

The only choice is for the main course, usually three options, but, says one report, 'we have yet to be disappointed'. Fish often provides the first course: poached salmon, for example, served with home-made black noodles and a tomato and cumin coulis, or monkfish paupiette cooked with lime, ginger, garlic and spring onions. Then comes soup, which reporters have praised for flavour and texture. For the main course, fillet of well-hung beef is a regular, and pheasant has proved more popular with city folk than with locals, according to Colin Brown (perhaps because locals do what they do everywhere and just help themselves from nature's larder). Desserts, despite the lack of choice, 'are one of the highlights of the restaurant'; one reporter enjoyed 'a small vanilla soufflé, beautifully made'. Servings are substantial, and service proceeds at a well-controlled pace. As for wines, claret is a strong suit (in line perhaps with sales of beef fillet), and the remainder of the list is very serviceable indeed. Mark-ups are commendably low, and there is enough choice among half-bottles to spread a variety of tastes throughout a meal. House wine is just under £8, or £1.75 per glass.

See the back of the Guide *for a listing of all restaurants in the Main Entries sections.*

CHEF: Colin Brown   PROPRIETORS: Colin Brown and Alexander McCallum   OPEN: all week, D only, and Sun L; 7.30 to 8, and 12.30 for 1   MEALS: Set L Sun £17.50, Set D £25.50   SERVICE: not inc, card slips closed   CARDS: Access, Amex, Diners, Visa   DETAILS: 30 seats. Private parties: 30 main room. Car park. Vegetarian meals with prior notice. Children's helpings. No children under 8. Smart dress preferred. No smoking in dining-room. Wheelchair access (2 steps; also WC). Music   ACCOMMODATION: 5 rooms, all with bath/shower. TV. Phone. B&B £55 to £78. Deposit: £20. Children welcome. Baby facilities. Garden. Doors close at midnight. Confirm by 6. Fax: (0620) 822254

INVERNESS Highland   map 8

▲ Culloden House

Inverness IV1 2NZ
INVERNESS (0463) 790461
off A96 at Culloden signpost,   COOKING 2
3m E of Inverness   COST £24–£52

The scale is grand: a Georgian mansion in 40 acres of parkland where, as you might expect, Bonnie Prince Charlie spent his last night before the battle. Theatricality is compounded by kilted staff who inhabit the stage setting, but for all that the house provides appealing entertainment. The script runs to four courses at dinner, with a mid-meal sorbet or soup: apple, tomato and celery one winter evening. Fish and game appear regularly. Terrine of pigeon and venison is served with rowan and orange jelly, while fillet of salmon comes with a smoked haddock mousse and a creamed langoustine sauce.

Dishes generally uphold the Scottish country-house feel, aiming for import and significance – for example, by coating saddle of lamb with a veal and herb mousse, wrapping it in puff pastry and serving it on a wine sauce flavoured with mint. Some sauces are fruit-based while the garden supplies herbs for others, notably grilled scallops with onion and herb butter. Puddings might include warm poached pear on a butterscotch sauce, with cheese as an alternative. The wine list is most successful where it tries least to impress, especially in the New World. House wine is from £9.50.

CHEF: Michael Simpson   PROPRIETORS: Ian and Marjory McKenzie   OPEN: all week; 12.30 to 2, 7 to 9   MEALS: Set L £12.99 (2 courses) to £16.50, Set D £32.50   SERVICE: not inc, card slips closed   CARDS: Access, Amex, Diners, Visa   DETAILS: 50 seats. 4 tables outside. Private parties: 50 main room, 30 private room. Car park. Vegetarian meals. Children's helpings. No children under 10. Jacket and tie. No music   ACCOMMODATION: 23 rooms, all with bath/shower. TV. Phone. B&B £125 to £220. Deposit: £165. No children under 10. Pets by arrangement. Afternoon teas. Garden. Sauna. Tennis. Snooker. Fax: (0463) 792181

▲ Dunain Park ✼✳

Inverness IV3 6JN
INVERNESS (0463) 230512   COOKING 1*
on A82, 1m out of Inverness   COST £22–£43

A former shooting lodge, Dunain Park is hidden away in six acres of gardens and woodland. Comfort and relaxation rank high among the Nicolls' aims, and their personal style is much appreciated. The fixed-price lunch (bookings only) begins with soup (cauliflower is offered either plain or with 'a garnish of Stilton') and progresses through intermediate and main courses to sweets and cheese. (Light lunches are also available – no booking necessary). Dinner is along the same lines, with each course priced individually. Fish is a feature, and lightness is achieved in a mousseline of smoked haddock and whiting. At one dinner, cheese soufflé or terrine of chicken and guinea-fowl were the other options on the intermediate course. Novel ideas include salmon baked in sea salt, served plain at lunch, and at dinner with a sauce of white port, lime and ginger. Vegetables are cooked crisp, sweets are from the buffet, and there is usually fresh fruit or cheese. Wines are well chosen, the variety welcome, mark-ups are standard, and the choice under £20 is good. House vin de pays is £10.

CHEF: Ann Nicoll   PROPRIETORS: Ann and Edward Nicoll   OPEN: all week (Set L bookings only); 12.30 to 2, 7 to 9   CLOSED: 3 weeks Jan to Feb   MEALS: alc (main courses £12.95). Set L £16.50. Light L menu   SERVICE: not inc, card slips closed   CARDS: Access, Amex, Diners, Visa   DETAILS: 40 seats. Private parties: 10 main room, 10 private room. Car park. Vegetarian meals. Children's helpings. Smart dress preferred. No smoking in dining-room. Wheelchair access. No music   ACCOMMODATION: 14 rooms, all with bath/shower. TV. Phone. B&B £35 to £140. Deposit: £50. Rooms for disabled. Children welcome. Baby facilities. Pets by arrangement. Afternoon teas. Garden. Swimming-pool. Sauna. Doors close at midnight. Fax: (0463) 224532 (The Which? Hotel Guide)

INVERURIE Grampian   map 8

▲ Thainstone House ⅚✷ | NEW ENTRY |

Inverurie AB51 5NT
INVERURIE (0467) 621643   COOKING 3*
on A96, 2m S of Inverurie   COST £21–£43

This creeper-clad, renovated Palladian mansion sits grandly at the end of a tree-lined drive. Bill Gibb (once at the Craigendarroch Hotel) and his partners have spent £3 million renovating it for the country club and conference trade, which explains a lot of the peripherals, including a health spa, or 'trimnasium'. Thainstone's location, half an hour from Aberdeen airport, bumps up the quota of international visitors, but all kinds of people use it, and there is a welcome bustle of shirt-sleeved informality.

Many of Bill Gibb's dishes are artfully prepared and labour-intensive: tarragon quenelles and vegetables in the oxtail consommé, for instance; and a mousse of smoked salmon and langoustine accompanying a breast of chicken, served together with a capsicum sauce with a three-flavoured rice timbale. An orange flan (with wafer-thin glaze on top, and rather thick pastry underneath) surrounded by de-veined slices of clementine, came with a scoop of ice-cream in a brandy-snap basket surmounted by a lattice of spun sugar. That pudding was part of a £14.50 lunch menu, so there is no question of being short-changed; this menu even gets the dome-lifting treatment.

Sometimes the kitchen falls over itself in its enthusiasm, producing a first-course salad of Continental leaves with quail's eggs, smoked venison, Parma ham, avocado, oranges, roasted pine-nuts and raspberry vinegar. And there are occasional sops to the country-clubbers – lobster thermidor on offer as an extra one lunch-time – but the food is not just for show: it has a sound technical basis. Nuggets of roasted monkfish, springily fresh in a spicy red pepper sauce, surrounded a pastry basket filled with crunchy stir-fry vegetables one lunch-time.

Snack lunches are available in the bar, although since that is where diners go to puff on cigars after a meal, the food may suffer. Wine mark-ups are excessive – would you pay £18.50 for a bottle of Mouton Cadet? – and too many details are missing from the list to allow intelligent choice, but house wines at £12.50 (£2.50 per glass) are significantly better than average.

CHEF: Bill Gibb PROPRIETOR: Thainstone House Hotel Ltd OPEN: all week; 12 to 2, 7 to 9.30
MEALS: Set L £14.50, Set L Sun £16.50, Set D £19.50 to £29 CARDS: Access, Amex, Diners,
Visa DETAILS: 42 seats. Private parties: 200 main room, 24 and 24 private rooms. Car park.
Vegetarian meals. Children's helpings. No children under 9 D. Smart dress preferred. No
smoking in dining-room. Wheelchair access (also WC). Music ACCOMMODATION: 46 rooms, all
with bath/shower. TV. Phone. B&B £54 to £120. Rooms for disabled. Children welcome. Baby
facilities. Afternoon teas. Garden. Swimming-pool. Snooker. Fax: (0467) 625084

KILCHRENAN Strathclyde   map 8

▲ *Taychreggan* 🍴✕   NEW ENTRY

Kilchrenan, by Taynuilt PA35 1HQ   COOKING 2
KILCHRENAN (086 63) 211 and 366   COST £17–£41

The hotel is an old inn on the shores of Loch Awe where the drovers used to lodge before swimming their cattle across to Portsonachan. It boasts 13 Munros (peaks over 3,000 feet) within an hour of its door, not counting the climb, of course. Boswell and Johnson stayed here during their Scottish tour, and although the building dates back 300 years, the new attractive dining-room extension is all brightness and light. The lunchtime blackboard menu is relatively simple, and food is eaten in less formal surroundings, but the choice goes well beyond sandwiches and bar snacks into the realms of crispy duck, steak, or pan-fried chicken breast with a sauce of green peppercorns and cumin seeds.

Dinner is a five-course affair with coffee thrown in. Sorbet (tamarillo perhaps) or soup (asparagus or langoustine bisque, for example) precedes the main course, cheese follows dessert and, while there is little choice, the menu changes daily and the overall balance is good. Main courses explore the likes of lamb, duck or beef, fairly simply treated with a mustard or herb crust or, in the case of Barbary duck, served with gnocchi and a red onion and beetroot marmalade. The first course might be a salad with pan-fried hare, sweetbreads and speck, or Loch Linnhe prawns in garlic butter, and the last could include pavlova, rich bitter chocolate truffle cake on a red fruit coulis, or peach poached in white wine and served with honey and yogurt ice-cream and toasted almonds. Flavours are well judged, vegetables are up to scratch, number-one chef is an authority on local fungi, bread is home-made, and service is well paced, efficient and friendly. Wines are generally dependable rather than exciting, and there is plenty under £20. House Côtes-du-Rhône is sold by the carafe (£6.75), while Domaine Virginie Vin de Pays d'Oc is £7.75 a bottle; dry house wines are £1.85 per glass.

CHEFS: Hugh Cocker and Michael Nicholson PROPRIETORS: Dr and Mrs E.H.M. Paul OPEN: all week; 12.30 to 2, 7.30 to 8.45 MEALS: bar alc L (main courses £5.50 to £8). Set D £26.50 SERVICE: not inc CARDS: Access, Amex, Visa DETAILS: 35 seats. 5 tables outside. Private parties: 50 main room, 50 private room. Car park. Vegetarian meals with prior notice. No children under 12. No smoking in dining-room. Music ACCOMMODATION: 15 rooms, all with bath/shower. Phone. B&B £38.50 to £145. Deposit: £50. Children welcome. Pets welcome. Afternoon teas. Garden. Fishing. Doors close at 1am. Confirm by noon. Fax: (086 63) 244

KILLIECRANKIE Tayside　　　　　　　　　　　　　　　　　　　　map 8

▲ *Killiecrankie Hotel* 🍸✸ £

Killiecrankie PH16 5LG
PITLOCHRY (0796) 473220　　　　　　　　　　　　　　　　COOKING 1
off A9, on B8079, 3m N of Pitlochry　　　　　　　　　　　COST £16–£45

The proprietors of this small, modest hotel are perfectly friendly. 'We have been criticised in the past for being 'too friendly' and then after such criticism for being 'not friendly enough. We are now following our own instincts.' Quite right too. Paul Booth has left, and his sous-chef has taken over the bar meals (sweet-cured herrings, lamb korma with rice and banoffi pie, for example) as well as the more ambitious dinner menu of spicy Malaysian fish curry soup, a fricassee of pigeon with chestnuts, chanterelles and smoked cheese, and queen of puddings. It is the 'good hearty meals at reasonable prices' in the bar that one regular reporter returns for, the kind that warms walkers up and sends them on their way with a spring in their step: try spicy bean soup (particularly welcome on a cold day), followed by sauté potatoes with diced ham and onions with two fried eggs on top. There is a garden where children can let off steam in summer. Wines offer a fair range of styles and prices, and most bottles are under £20. House wines begin at £8.20.

CHEF: John Ramsay PROPRIETORS: Colin and Carole Anderson OPEN: all week; bar 12.30 to 2, 6.30 to 9.30; restaurant 7 to 8.30 CLOSED: Jan and Feb MEALS: alc bar (main courses L £5 to £7, D £7 to £11.50). Set D £25.50 SERVICE: not inc, card slips closed CARDS: Access, Visa DETAILS: restaurant 32 seats, bar 32 seats. Private parties: 10 main room. Car park. Vegetarian meals. Children's helpings. No children under 5 in dining-room. Smart dress preferred. No smoking in dining-room. Wheelchair access (2 steps). No music ACCOMMODATION: 10 rooms, all with bath/shower. TV. Phone. B&B £48 to £92. Deposit: £30. Rooms for disabled. Children welcome. Pets welcome (not in public rooms). Afternoon teas. Garden. Doors close at 11.30. Fax: (0796) 472451 (*The Which? Hotel Guide*)

KINCLAVEN Tayside　　　　　　　　　　　　　　　　　　　　map 8

▲ *Ballathie House* 🍸✸

Kinclaven, by Stanley PH1 4QN
MEIKLEOUR (0250) 883268　　　　　　　　　　　　　　　　COOKING 2
off B9099, take right fork 1m N of Stanley　　　　　　　　COST £19–£42

Ballathie is pure Scottish baronial: big, turreted, tartaned, loud kilts and louder voices, and everything kept in apple-pie order. It is warm, welcoming, with wooden floors and panelling, leather furnishings and heavy curtains. Huntin', shootin' an' fishin' (not to mention walkin' an' golfin') are everyday pursuits here, all in 1500 acres, including a stretch of the Tay. The bag of the day appears on the table as roast loin of venison in a herb crust on a celeriac and apple pancake, or as steamed fillet of salmon with prawns and asparagus. Vegetarians are looked after with the likes of ratatouille and coriander samosas with salad.

Dinner can be three or four courses, starting with melon and soft fruit or tartlet of warm Arbroath smokie, then sorbet or soup: fish chowder maybe, or pumpkin and almond. Roast rack of lamb or steamed halibut with saffron noodles might be main-course options, and interest is cranked up when local and seasonal items appear: chanterelles tossed together with woodpigeon in a warm salad with smoked bacon and sherry vinegar dressing, or a compote of berries with crème fraîche. Lunchtime snacks can be had in the bar. The sensible wine list goes in for friendly prices across the board and spans a good range of claret vintages. House wines start at £8.75.

CHEF: Kevin MacGillvray   PROPRIETOR: Ballathie House Hotel Ltd   OPEN: all week; 12 to 2, 7 to 9   MEALS: Set L £12.95, Set D £22.50 to £25. Light L menu   SERVICE: not inc   CARDS: Access, Amex, Diners, Visa   DETAILS: 80 seats. Private parties: 60 main room, 30 private room. Car park. Vegetarian meals. Children's helpings. Smart dress preferred. No smoking in dining-room. Wheelchair access (also WC). No music   ACCOMMODATION: 27 rooms, all with bath/shower. TV. Phone. B&B £75 to £150. Rooms for disabled. Children welcome. Baby facilities. Pets welcome (not in public rooms). Afternoon teas. Garden. Tennis. Fishing. Fax: (0250) 883396

KINGUSSIE Highland   map 8

▲ *The Cross* ▮ ⅚✳

Tweed Mill Brae, Ardbroilach Road,
Kingussie PH21 1TC   COOKING 3*
KINGUSSIE (0540) 661166   COST £21–£55

The Hadleys have worked wonders with this late nineteenth-century former tweed mill (uphill from the traffic lights on Main Street, then 250 metres along on the left), providing two lounges and extravagantly spaced tables in acres of dining space. The wines are still as big a draw as the food, and there is simplicity in the cooking, integrity in the people, and assurance in the package. 'I have not eaten so consistently over three nights, even in London,' one report concluded.

The menu's limited choice – two or three items per course – bothers no one. Gressingham duck and Aberdeen Angus beef are regular visitors, and an old Hadley favourite, venison 'Francatelli', appears from time to time. The venison is, of course, local, as are pike, hare and wild mushrooms, and the Hadleys are missionaries for Scottish produce in all its forms, particularly halibut, brill and turbot landed at Lochinver, Shetland salmon (fresh or smoked), and dived scallops. Ruth Hadley's style is all her own, barely touched by fashion, resolutely but gently Scottish. A trademark is a light sharpness to counteract richness, as in a first course of hot-smoked salmon with a few thin slivers of dill-pickled cucumber, and a red and green 'relish' of avocado and tomato which, further south, would be called a 'salsa'. Well-roasted duck (leg and breast) has a dark purple sauce of cooking juices, with cubes of beetroot and the acidulation of pickled red cabbage. Flavours do not shout, and the food is satisfying without being over-filling.

The wine list is a monster: 48 pages long and 'more interesting than *War and Peace*. Tony Hadley's approach is completely unstuffy and eminently sensible, taking its cue from the customer: security for those who prefer it, adventure for others. Mark-ups are almost irrelevant. It is a wine lover's approach, not a commercial one, dedicated to changing perceptions: excellence can come from some unlikely sources. Officially, no wines are served by the glass, but after five minutes' conversation with Tony Hadley there might be several. CELLARMAN'S CHOICE: Rully 1986, Dom. Guyot, £16.50; Regnié 1991, Dom. des Braves, £13.90.

CHEF: Ruth Hadley   PROPRIETORS: Tony and Ruth Hadley   OPEN: Wed to Mon, exc Wed L (L summer only – phone to check); 12.30 to 2, 7 to 9   CLOSED: 1 to 26 Dec, 5 Jan to 1 Mar   MEALS: Set L £12.50 (2 courses) to £15, Set D £27.50 to £35   SERVICE: not inc, card slips closed CARDS: Access, Visa   DETAILS: 28 seats. 6 tables outside. Car park. Vegetarian meals with prior notice. No children under 12. No smoking. Wheelchair access (also WC). No music ACCOMMODATION: 9 rooms, all with bath/shower. Phone. D,B&B £75 to £150. Deposit: £50. No children under 12. Afternoon teas. Garden. Fax: (0540) 661080

KINLOCHMOIDART Highland   map 8

Kinacarra ⁑✳ £

Kinlochmoidart, Lochailort PH38 4ND
SALEN (0967) 431238   COOKING 2
on A861, at head of Loch Moidart   COST £20–£32

'Somewhat remote' is the Macleans' description of their little cottage restaurant on the roadside close to Loch Moidart. The location dictates supplies. Shellfish and game, fresh vegetables, home-made bread and calorific puddings are the benchmarks. 'We thought it was a little gem,' commented a travelling couple who called in for a light lunch of soup (full of assorted vegetables), followed by a plate of fresh langoustines ('fresh from the loch that morning and cooked but an hour before'), rounded off with light, crisp coffee meringues and good strong coffee. 'I wish they had rooms so one could stay and enjoy dinner,' they mused.

In the evening, visitors might be tempted by savoury profiteroles filled with crab, breast of duck with bramble sauce, then sticky toffee pudding with pecan toffee sauce, not to mention Stilton and oatcakes. Generosity, uncluttered simplicity and 'outstanding' value for money are what give the place its appeal. Like the menu, the wine list is brief – but exact – and prices are realistic. House wine is £7.50.

CHEF: Frances MacLean   PROPRIETORS: Angus and Frances MacLean   OPEN: Tue to Sun; 12 to 2, 7 to 9   CLOSED: Oct to Easter (exc block bookings Christmas)   MEALS: alc (main courses £8 to £12)   SERVICE: not inc   DETAILS: 24 seats. 1 table outside. Private parties: 30 main room. Car park. Vegetarian meals. Children's helpings. Smart dress preferred. No smoking in dining-room. Wheelchair access (also WC). No music

---

'The kitchen is divided by a counter from complete view, but what one can see is hair-raising enough. One lad constantly fingered the Stilton, even when he wasn't cutting it, and he was the one who smoked behind the counter.' (On eating in London)

KYLESKU Highland   map 8

▲ *Kylesku Hotel* 🍴✳ £

Kylesku, by Lairg IV27 4HW
SCOURIE (0971) 502231 and 502200
on A894, at S side of old ferry crossing, by   COOKING 2*
bridge linking Ullapool and Kylestrome   COST £18–£36

The views over Loch Glendhu to the mountains are fine enough, but this place is
more for people who have been walking the hills all day to work up an appetite,
and who can eat heartily of unspoiled food in a congenial atmosphere at
remarkable prices. The bar bustles most, while the dining-room is 'a less noisy
haven'. Either way, the seafood is as fresh as can be. Langoustines, scallops,
monkfish, haddock, crab and lobster are unloaded from boats less than 20 yards
from the front door, and appear alongside chicken tikka, bangers and mash, or
roast loin of local lamb.

Marcel Klein picked up his skills in Strasbourg and Switzerland and knows
enough not to overdo the saucing and seasoning. His recipes would make a very
slim volume: sizzling hot mussels come with garlic butter, langoustines with
garlic mayonnaise, and skate wing with red wine and capers. He also smokes his
own salmon. Home-made puddings are laid out on a table: almond tart,
bread-and-butter pudding, meringues and gâteaux. The wine list is a curious
mix of oddments from a bald 'Châteauneuf-du-Pape, various vintages', to Ch.
Talbot 1929. House wines from £6.75 are basic.

CHEF/PROPRIETOR: Marcel Klein   OPEN: all week; bar 11.30 to 2.30, 6 to 9.30; restaurant 12 to
2.15, 6.30 to 9.30   MEALS: alc restaurant (main courses £6.50 to £10.50). Set L and D £12.50 to
£19. Bar menu (main courses, £5.50 to £12). Minimum £10   SERVICE: not inc, card slips
closed   CARDS: Access, Visa   DETAILS: restaurant 28 seats, bar 30 seats. Private parties: 18
main room. Car park. Vegetarian meals. Children's helpings. Smart dress preferred. No smoking
in dining-room. Wheelchair access (also WC). Music   ACCOMMODATION: 7 rooms, 6 with
bath/shower. TV. B&B £40 to £48. Deposit: £10. Rooms for disabled. Children welcome. Baby
facilities. Pets welcome. Afternoon teas. Garden. Fishing. Snooker. Doors close at 11.30.
Confirm by 7. Fax: (0971) 502313

LINLITHGOW Lothian   map 8

Champany Inn 🍸

Champany, Linlithgow EH49 7LU
PHILPSTOUN (050 683) 4532 and 4388
2m NE of Linlithgow at junction of A904   COOKING 3*
and A803   COST £39–£68

The Champany does what it does extremely well. Here, where the mechanisms
of restaurant catering are at their most transparent, the lack of reverence in the
approach is appreciated by those who perceive that the focus is well and truly on
ensuring immaculate quality in the food. Aberdeen Angus beef, for example, is
hung on the bone for three weeks and cut as it is ordered, to your own
specification if you like (and you won't phase them by asking for pope's eye).
Once weighed and costed, the cut is charcoal-grilled and served plain as you
please, or with a sauce that may contain heather honey, whisky and Drambuie,

or with some sort of insert – a bit of smoked salmon or an oyster. There is also local salmon, some of it home-smoked, as well as lobsters drifting unsuspectingly around a seawater pool, and a range of classic salads such as niçoise and Caesar. Simple puddings like raspberry meringue use the best of the seasonal fruit. 'Expensive' is a word that sprang to mind for more than one reporter when the bill arrived, but people do seem to go back for more. A simpler, quicker menu is available at lunch-times.

If the wine list were any longer, they would need to bring it to the table by fork-lift truck. Page after page of illustrious classics will delight the connoisseur, confuse the interested amateur and totally alienate the uninitiated. As the Romanée-Contis and Latours flash by, the eye nervously flits down the right-hand margin for a sighting of anything under £20 – such wines do exist, but they need tracking down. House wines from South Africa start at £10.50. CELLARMAN'S CHOICE: Gewurztraminer Reserve Serge Dubs 1988, Trimbach, £21; Stellenbosch Cabernet Franc 1990, £25.

CHEF: Clive Davidson PROPRIETORS: Clive and Anne Davidson OPEN: Mon to Sat, exc Sat L; 12.30 to 2, 7 to 10 CLOSED: 2 days Christmas, 2 days New Year MEALS: alc (main courses £15.50 to £25.50). Set L £13.75 (2 courses), Set D £27.50 to £35. Minimum £14.50 D SERVICE: 10%, card slips closed CARDS: Access, Amex, Diners, Visa DETAILS: 50 seats. 10 tables outside. Private parties: 56 main room. Car park. Vegetarian meals. No children under 8. Smart dress preferred. Wheelchair access (1 step; also WC). No music. Fax: (050 683) 4302

MILNGAVIE Strathclyde   map 8

Gingerhill £

1 Hillhead Street, Milngavie G62 8AS
041-956 6515   COOKING 1
4m N of Glasgow, off A81   COST £14–£41

This is not entirely a meatless restaurant, but it does major on fish and vegetables. It is very small indeed: two rooms of a converted house just off the Milngavie shopping centre, only yards from the railway station. But once diners are seated, there is no pressure on tables: 'We operate a strict "one sitting only" policy and close when our last customer leaves.' Fish and shellfish are mostly from Gigha. Small quantities are bought through a network of suppliers and offered as specials of the day: dived scallops with cream and pink peppercorns, steamed Oban mussels with tomato and garlic, chargrilled squat lobsters. The specials are praised for quality, but it is worth asking the price before choosing since they can send the bill up to the point where, according to one reporter, value for money begins to peter out. Staff are friendly, service efficient and meals informal. The place is unlicensed, and charges no corkage.

CHEF: Heather Andrew PROPRIETOR: Carol Thomson OPEN: Mon to Sat L, Thur to Sat D; 11.30 to 3, 7 MEALS: alc (main courses £7.50 to £17). Unlicensed, but bring your own; no corkage SERVICE: not inc, card slips closed CARDS: Access, Visa DETAILS: 26 seats. 4 tables outside. Private parties: 16 main room. Vegetarian meals. Children's helpings. Music

---

Not inc *in the details at the end of an entry indicates that no service charge is made and any tipping is at the discretion of the customer.*

▲ *Beechwood Country House Hotel* ⅚✳

Moffat Place, Moffat DG10 9RS   COOKING 1
MOFFAT (0683) 20210   COST £18–£32

At the northern end of Moffat turn right at St Mary's church and follow the 'hotel' sign. Jeffrey and Linda Rogers run a friendly outfit, which may not open at lunch if there are no bookings. Dinner is four courses plus a soup or sorbet after the first, which may be shallow-fried fish-cakes with a caper sauce, Welsh rarebit with anchovy or, more unusually, steamed fillet of perch with tomatoes and black olives. Simply cooked fillet steak is a regular main dish, and there is usually a vegetarian option; otherwise, it might be breast of duck, or pork fillet with black pudding. Reporters endorse thickly sliced smoked salmon, lamb cutlets, lemon soufflé and peach cheesecake. The chef brings out the puddings himself and presents them with a flourish. The reasonably priced wines are on the ball. Four house wines begin at £7.50 (£1.50 per glass).

CHEF: Carl Shaw   PROPRIETORS: Jeffrey and Lynda Rogers   OPEN: Thur to Sun L, all week D; 12 to 2, 7.30 to 9   CLOSED: 2 Jan to 16 Feb   MEALS: Set L £12.50, Set D £19.50   SERVICE: not inc, card slips closed   CARDS: Access, Amex, Visa   DETAILS: 26 seats. 2 tables outside. Private parties: 26 main room, 14 private room. Car park. Vegetarian meals. Children's helpings. Smart dress preferred. No smoking in dining-room. Wheelchair access (1 step). Music ACCOMMODATION: 7 rooms, all with bath/shower. TV. Phone. B&B £48 to £68. Children welcome. Baby facilities. Pets welcome. Afternoon teas. Garden. Doors close at midnight. Fax: (0683) 20889 (*The Which? Hotel Guide*)

▲ *Well View* ▼ ⅚✳

Ballplay Road, Moffat DG10 9JU   COOKING 1
MOFFAT (0683) 20184   COST £17–£35

This small and plainly decorated family hotel on the outskirts of town is a converted Victorian house set back from the road, one of many plying a similar trade. Janet and John Schuckardt (former teachers) split the food and drink duties between them. Dinners begin with canapés in the lounge, one of them a tiny haggis coated in breadcrumbs and deep-fried – 'very light and acceptable even to haggis-haters'. A meal might consist of herbed cheese tagliatelle with smoked bacon and mushrooms before a sorbet, and then gigot of lamb with a sweet redcurrant and thyme sauce and 'sensible seasonal vegetables'. Desserts come after cheese, and one couple enjoyed crème brûlée and an apricot tart with good pastry and a proper crème anglaise. Another reporter was less happy about the Sunday lunch three-course no-choice 'menu surprise', although the value was good. The wine list, with one-line annotations, includes some tasty and less usual examples as well as more mainstream bottles. Mark-ups are generally fair, with stacks of choice under £20, plus a couple of dozen half-bottles, and no shortage of advice on hand. House wines begin at £8.20. CELLARMAN'S CHOICE: Haut-Médoc, Ch. Cissac 1988, £24; Sancerre 'Le Chêne' 1992, Lucien Crochet 1992, £16.90.

CHEF: Janet Schuckardt   PROPRIETORS: Janet and John Schuckardt   OPEN: all week, exc Sat L; 12.15 to 1 (24 hours' notice required L), 6.30 to 8.30   CLOSED: 2 weeks Jan, 1 week Nov   MEALS: Set L £11, Set D £22   SERVICE: not inc, card slips closed   CARDS: Access, Amex, Visa   DETAILS: 24 seats. Private parties: 14 main room, 6 private room. Car park. Vegetarian meals with prior notice. Children's helpings. No children under 6 D. Smart dress preferred. No smoking in dining-room. Wheelchair access (2 steps). No music   ACCOMMODATION: 6 rooms, all with bath/shower. TV. B&B £33 to £80. Deposit: £20. Children welcome. Baby facilities. Pets welcome (not in public rooms). Afternoon teas. Garden. Doors close at 11.30. Confirm by 5.30 (*The Which? Hotel Guide*)

MUIR OF ORD Highland
map 8

▲ *Dower House* ♟ ⁵⋇

Highfield, Muir of Ord IV6 7XN
MUIR OF ORD (0463) 870090
on A862, 1m N of Muir of Ord

COOKING 2*
COST £38–£46

The gardens of this unusual eighteenth-century house are extensive, the lawns spacious, and some of the trees are up to 200 years old. Inside, masses of bric-à-brac decorate the rooms, from shelves packed with books through stuffed birds to pictures and oriental rugs. The dining-room is all the more imposing thanks to polished wood tables, heavy silver and fresh flowers. Robyn Aitchison is a self-taught cook with imagination and a passion for fish. Dinners are four courses, with soup after the first. At one meal, langoustine vinaigrette and fillet of halibut with lime sauce appeared either side of a clear turnip and herb soup. Choice is limited but appealing.

Bright flavours owe much to another Aitchison passion, the herb garden (guinea-fowl is braised with fresh herbs and garlic, for instance), and vegetables play a central role in first courses, such as artichokes baked with an egg, or mushroom gâteau with broad-bean salad. The lightness of cooking and the edge gained by clear flavours are not lost in a mass of chocolate or sticky toffee, but upheld by a gratiné of tropical fruit, warm peach soufflé or an Andalusian orange and almond terrine. Wines run to some unusual styles, which adds to the interest, but the foundation is sound, half-bottles are extensive, and prices are kept within reason. House wines are £13.

CHEF: Robyn Aitchison   PROPRIETORS: Mr and Mrs R.G. Aitchison   OPEN: all week, D only; 7.30 to 9 (L by arrangement)   CLOSED: Christmas   MEALS: Set D £28   SERVICE: not inc, card slips closed   CARDS: Access, Visa   DETAILS: 28 seats. 2 tables outside. Private parties: 28 main room. Car park. Vegetarian meals. Children's helpings. No children under 5. Smart dress preferred. No smoking in dining-room. Wheelchair access (also WC). No music   ACCOMMODATION: 5 rooms, all with bath/shower. TV. Phone. B&B £40 to £100. Deposit: 25%. Rooms for disabled. Children welcome. Baby facilities. Dogs by arrangement. Afternoon teas. Garden. Doors close at 11. Confirm by 4. Fax: (0463) 870090 (*The Which? Hotel Guide*)

Restaurateurs justifiably resent no-shows. If you quote a credit card number when booking, you may be liable for the restaurant's lost profit margin if you don't turn up. Always phone to cancel.

An asterisk (*) after the 1 to 5 cooking mark at the top of an entry signifies that the Guide and its readers think that the restaurant is a particularly fine example within its rating.

NAIRN Highland   map 8

▲ *Clifton House* ▮ ✸

Nairn IV12 4HW
NAIRN (0667) 453119   COOKING 2
W of town roundabout on A96   COST £24–£45

This is a one-off, a genuine original. J. Gordon Macintyre has lived here, man
and boy, for over 60 years. The creeper-clad Victorian house built in 1873 is
stuffed full of paintings, drawings, statues and *objets d'art*, not to mention plants,
flowers and antiques. Concerts and theatrical events add more colour to winter
evenings.

Meals begin with olives, crumbly pastry tartlets and a glass of wine in front of
a wood-burning stove. 'We use Scottish raw materials and French provincial
cooking techniques,' explains J. Gordon Macintyre. And, he might have added,
a French pen to write the menu, and a Scottish tongue to translate it. Subtlety and
elegant presentation are eschewed in favour of freshness and strong tastes. Pigs'
kidneys ('rognons de porc Henri IV') are simply cut up, grilled with garlic butter
and served with rashers of bacon and grilled halves of tomato. One night queen
scallops from Loch Fyne were fresh in, taken out of the shell, cleaned, returned,
moistened with garlic butter, and then 'cooked under a very hot grill for 40
seconds, no more, no less'. An inspector found them 'the best queen scallops I
have ever tasted'.

Wines are outstanding in scope, running all the way up from humble Spanish
and South African wines at under £10, via some attractive and inexpensive
German whites, to some of France's greatest at over £100. Only pudding wines
come in half-bottles, though about eight dry wines are normally available by
the glass.

CHEFS: J. Gordon Macintyre and Charles Gordon Macintyre   PROPRIETOR: J. Gordon
Macintyre   OPEN: all week; 12.30 to 1, 7 to 9.30   CLOSED: early Nov to end-Mar   MEALS: alc
(main courses £7.50 to £14)   SERVICE: not inc, card slips closed   CARDS: Access, Amex,
Diners, Visa   DETAILS: main room 40 seats, Green Room 12 seats. Private parties: 30 main
room, 12 Green Room. Car park. Vegetarian meals. Children's helpings by arrangement. Smart
dress preferred. No smoking in Green Room. Music   ACCOMMODATION: 12 rooms, all with
bath/shower. B&B £45 to £96. Children welcome. Pets welcome. Afternoon teas. Garden.
Doors close at midnight. Fax: (0667) 452836 (*The Which? Hotel Guide*)

NEWTONMORE Highland   map 8

▲ *Ard-Na-Coille* ▮ ✸

Kingussie Road, Newtonmore PH20 1AY
NEWTONMORE (0540) 673214   COOKING 3
on A86, at N end of Newtonmore   COST £39–£47

This is a relaxed place, with the accent less on excitement, inspiration and
fireworks than on solid achievement. A scattering of books points up the
reflective, slightly scholarly mood. Reporters get friendly attention from the
proprietors, and unobtrusive and efficient service from everybody else. As so
often in Scotland, there is no lunch. We are expected to be out walking the hills,
or skiing, or otherwise working up an appetite for the five-course dinner, which

might begin with fillet of turbot with a béarnaise sauce, and proceed to carrot, ginger and coriander soup, before roast fillet of pork stuffed with blue cheese and sage. Scottish cheeses are served before desserts such as amaretto torte with strawberry coulis, or warm cherry strudel.

Cooking makes full use of roasting, stir-frying and chargrilling, seasonal game is one of the pillars on which the kitchen is founded, and salmon is in plentiful supply. Vegetables could do with pepping up – 'uninspiring' and 'unimaginative' were two independent comments – but much else appeals: for example, Loch Linnhe scallops or cassoulet of duck in winter, and in summer warm salad of monkfish and chanterelles, and chargrilled salmon with a shellfish and whisky sauce. The style is not elaborate. Breast of either pigeon or duck, cooked rare, might be served simply on a bed of lentils with a herb-infused wine sauce. Portions are generous and flavours can be robust: a leek and lime soup in spring was rich, creamy and attractively sharp.

The wine list is an object lesson to those who simply assemble big names at hefty prices. Clarets (the longest suit) certainly include some top properties, but equal attention is paid to humble wines, and prices are within reason – with a few sold at little more than retail prices. The only imbalance, a self-confessed lacuna, is sweet wine. Half a dozen house wines at around £13 to £14 are also available by the glass for around £3. CELLARMAN'S CHOICE: St-Joseph Blanc 1986, E. Florentin, £19.50; Gigondas 'Cuvée Prestige' 1989, Santa Duc, £18.

CHEF: Barry Cottam   PROPRIETORS: Barry Cottam and Nancy Ferrier   OPEN: all week, D only; 7.45   CLOSED: mid-Nov to end-Dec, 1 week Apr, 1 week Sept   MEALS: Set D £28.50   SERVICE: not inc, card slips closed   CARDS: Access, Visa   DETAILS: 24 seats. Private parties: 18 main room, 6 private room. Car park. Vegetarian meals with prior notice. Children's helpings. No smoking in dining-room. No music   ACCOMMODATION: 7 rooms, all with bath/shower. Phone. DB&B £63 to £150. Deposit: £30 (new customers only). Children welcome. Baby facilities. Dogs welcome (in 2 bedrooms, not in public rooms). Garden. Doors close at 11.30. Confirm by 4. Fax: (0540) 673453 (The Which? Hotel Guide)

OBAN Strathclyde   map 8

▲ Knipoch Hotel 🍷 ✸

Knipoch, by Oban PA34 4QT
KILNINVER (085 26) 251, will change to
(0852) 316251 autumn 1994   COOKING 2
on A816, 6m S of Oban   COST £37–£59

'A delicious smell of baking wholemeal rolls had drifted out during the preceding hour,' mused a couple who found them 'irresistible'. The Craig family have been incumbent here since 1981 and their long, yellow house by the shores of Loch Feochan is a hive of industry. In addition to baking, roasting their own coffee from green beans and producing ice-creams and terrines, they smoke their own salmon and scallops (which are now distributed by mail order). Fish is from local waters, game and beef are from Aberdeenshire, and most vegetables are from the Glasgow markets – although France is also plundered for supplies. The kitchen now offers a fixed-price three-course menu as well as the 'gourmet' five-course affair, and reports are unanimous in praise of the cooking. Soups such as cock-a-leekie and cream of spinach are based on intense stocks, then

comes a light course along the lines of salad of duck breast with pickled
clementines. Admired centrepieces have included loin of lamb with a port sauce
and herb-stuffed poussin, accompanied by a kaleidoscopic array of up to seven
perfectly timed vegetables. Cheese with home-made oatcakes and a dramatically
presented dessert round things off. Service is always pleasant, while attention to
wine is 'impeccable'.

The wine list is not too proud to include nine Bulgarians, all under £10, while
seven of the Beaujolais *cru* villages are here, all under £20 – grand restaurants
please note. The New World gets a good outing, while extensive clarets, with
commendable depth in vintages, include something for all pockets. The value is
stupendous. For services to drinking pleasure Mr Craig deserves a sir-ship. His
recommended wines simplify the choice without sacrificing quality, and house
vins de pays (mostly around £11.50) act as a safety net for those terminally
uninterested in wine lists. CELLARMAN'S CHOICE: Stoneleigh Vineyards
Sauvignon Blanc 1992, £11.70; Côte de Brouilly 1992, Ch. de Thivin, £13.40.

CHEFS: Colin and Jenny Craig PROPRIETORS: the Craig family OPEN: all week, D only; 7.30 to 9
(L by arrangement) CLOSED: mid-Nov to mid-Feb MEALS: Set D £28.50 to £38.50 SERVICE:
not inc, card slips closed CARDS: Access, Amex, Diners, Visa DETAILS: 44 seats. Private
parties: 24 main room, 12 private room. Car park. Vegetarian meals with prior notice. Children's
helpings. Smart dress preferred. No smoking in dining-room. No music ACCOMMODATION: 17
rooms, all with bath/shower. TV. Phone. B&B £62 to £124. Children welcome. Baby facilities.
Afternoon teas. Garden. Doors close at midnight

PEAT INN Fife   map 8

▲ Peat Inn 🍾 ⅝✳

Peat Inn KY15 5LH
PEAT INN (0334) 840206
at Junction of B940 and B941,   COOKING 4
6m SW of St Andrews   COST £30–£65

The first thing that hits you is the aroma from the log fire in the comfortable bar
lounge (it burns even in June). Then the ruched curtains come into focus, and the
scalloped lampshades and bright colours, distancing it pretty effectively from
the old coaching inn it once was.

'We have not wavered in our belief in the restaurant reflecting the area it is in
by using exclusively local main ingredients,' writes David Wilson, who has
been cooking here since 1972. That is certainly the case for scallops, lobster and
venison, which all appear regularly ('you won't find foie gras or Barbary duck').
Ancillaries, however, are another matter. 'Why give us Guatemalan pea pods,
Kenyan beans and Spanish broccoli?' queried one reporter. Perhaps we cannot
expect a kitchen to resist exotica these days; even this one uses Thai spices with
roast salmon. What David Wilson does with those main ingredients is
impressive. Lobster broth is a clear consommé with bits of white fish and lobster
chopped up small, and a wonderful smell and taste that defies the apparent
lightness of the liquid. Venison liver and kidney are pan-fried and served with a
lentil salad, while the saddle – tender and not too gamey – is roasted pink, sliced,
and arrives on a bed of small brown lentils with slivers of tasty smoky bacon.
These are among the signature dishes, only occasionally marred by clumsy

seasoning. Richness is a feature of puddings, which might include a trio of nut (or of caramel) desserts, or a white chocolate ice-cream sandwiched between two crisp biscuits, in a dark chocolate sauce. Portion sizes, always a difficult matter, err on the cautious side, leaving some with the impression that nouvelle cuisine is alive and well, while others feel they have enjoyed a light and perfectly balanced lunch. Indeed, lunch is an amazing bargain, one of the best. Espresso coffee is good.

The wine list benefits from a large dose of common sense: here bottles are served with a minimum of fuss and left within reach. They embrace a stunning range of styles and grape varieties, with interest, excitement and quality at every turn. The list is clearly laid out, well annotated, with good drinking at all price levels, and is generous in scope yet highly selective. There are lots of half-bottles. CELLARMAN'S CHOICE: Carmenet Vineyards Sauvignon Blanc 1989, £14; Bourgogne Pinot Noir 1990, Roulot, £18.

CHEFS: David Wilson and Angus Blacklaws   PROPRIETORS: David and Patricia Wilson   OPEN: Tue to Sat; 12.30 for 1, 7 to 9.30   CLOSED: 25 Dec, 1 Jan   MEALS: alc (main courses £16 to £19). Set L £18.50, Set D £28 to £42   SERVICE: not inc, card slips closed   CARDS: Access, Amex, Diners, Visa   DETAILS: 48 seats. Private parties: 24 main room, 12 and 12 private rooms. Car park. Vegetarian meals with prior notice. Children's helpings. Smart dress preferred. No smoking in dining-room. Wheelchair access (also WC). No music   ACCOMMODATION: 8 rooms, all with bath/shower. TV. Phone. B&B £75 to £140. Rooms for disabled. Children welcome. Pets welcome. Garden. Confirm by 4. Fax: (0334) 840530 (*The Which? Hotel Guide*)

PEEBLES Borders   map 8

▲ *Cringletie House* ⁙⋇

Peebles EH45 8PL
EDDLESTON (0721) 730233   COOKING 2
on A703, 2½m N of Peebles   COST £17–£43

This nineteenth-century red sandstone baronial mansion, in 28 acres of gardens and woodland, is handsomely decorated, with high ceilings, beautiful woodwork, and fresh flowers everywhere. It is a family-run country house which, for all the apparent grandeur, still feels unpretentious. The pattern is a weekday lunchtime *carte*, fixed-price Sunday lunch (three courses plus cheese) and four-course dinners. The choice is normally three or four items per course.

The menu changes frequently to suit long-stay guests, and among the more interesting dishes might be Dijon tart with tomatoes and Gruyère cheese, game terrine with beetroot chutney, and lemon and peanut soup. Fish cooking is assured; sole, salmon and monkfish might be served with sauces as varied as dill, spiced fruit and hollandaise. There is praise for a light and delicately flavoured cheese mousse baked in cream, and for a rich and smooth layered pâté of smoked fish: trout and mackerel wrapped in salmon, the flavour of each quite distinct. Vegetables, many from the two acres of kitchen garden, are particularly impressive. Chocolate and orange profiteroles are 'light, well-filled and perfectly sauced', and good Scottish cheeses include Ettrick and smoked Orkney. Breakfasts are splendid. The New World in particular helps to keep wine prices on an even keel without compromising quality. House Duboeuf is £5.75 a half-litre.

CHEFS: Sheila McKellar, Paul Maguire and Aileen Maguire PROPRIETORS: the Maguire family
OPEN: all week; 1 to 1.45, 7.30 to 8.30 CLOSED: Jan and Feb MEALS: alc L Mon to Sat (main
courses £5.50 to £6.50). Set L Sun £14, Set D £23.50. Minimum £5.50 L SERVICE: not inc, card
slips closed CARDS: Access, Visa DETAILS: 56 seats. Private parties: 27 main room. Car park.
Vegetarian meals. Children's helpings. No smoking in dining-room. · No music
ACCOMMODATION: 13 rooms, all with bath/shower. TV. Phone. B&B £52.50 to £98. Children
welcome. Baby facilities. Pets welcome (not in public rooms). Afternoon teas. Garden. Tennis.
Doors close at 11. Confirm by 5. Fax: (0721) 730244 (*The Which? Hotel Guide*)

PERTH Tayside   map 8

Number Thirty Three

33 George Street, Perth PH1 5LA	COOKING 1
PERTH (0738) 633771	COST £19–£42

Good modern prints and Art Deco trappings, plus a Charles Rennie Mackintosh
chair, combine to lend a sense of elegance and style to this pink-walled,
mirrored, mainly seafood restaurant. The Oyster Bar serves light meals of soup,
oysters and gravlax, with lemon vacherin or Welsh rarebit to finish, while the
restaurant aims for slightly more substantial food. The Billinghursts estimate
that 'only two out of every ten Scots dine out on fish or shellfish', but that doesn't
stop them offering seafood soup, fillets of sole or turbot, poached scallops and
seafood platter. Bourride is a winner, so is elderflower ice-cream. The other eight
Scots can dine on breast of duckling or grilled fillet steak. House wine is £9.60.

CHEF: Mary Billinghurst PROPRIETORS: Gavin and Mary Billinghurst OPEN: Tue to Sat; 12.30 to
2.30, 6.30 to 9.30 CLOSED: 10 days Christmas and New Year MEALS: alc restaurant (main
courses £10 to £13.50). Light menu Oyster Bar (£2.50 to £7) SERVICE: not inc CARDS: Access,
Amex, Visa DETAILS: restaurant 24 seats, Oyster Bar 18 seats. Private parties: 24 main room.
Vegetarian meals. No children under 5. Smart dress preferred. No cigars in dining-room.
Wheelchair access. Music

PORT APPIN Strathclyde   map 8

▲ Airds Hotel ▮ ✳✳

Port Appin PA38 4DF	
APPIN (063 173) 236	
2m off A828, on E shore of Loch Linnhe	COOKING 4
	COST £45–£61

The house faces Loch Linnhe, just a hop, skip and a jump back from the straggle
of houses that leads down to the water's edge. Every available inch of wall is
covered with something: Victorian prints, landscapes in oil, impressionist
reproductions and Toulouse-Lautrec posters. Then there are the tartan carpets,
shiny sateen draperies at the windows, potted plants and bright fresh flowers.
Unity of line, colour or style may be lacking, but, more importantly, warmth and
comfort prevail.

Betty and Graeme Allen have developed an assured line in familiar fish and
cuts of meat, from loin of rabbit or fillet of Aberdeen Angus to monkfish and
brilliantly fresh prawns from the loch. There are some luxury items, as in an
open ravioli of mushrooms and sweetbreads with asparagus and a truffle sauce,

but these are not relied upon for impact. This is sensible cooking that aims at balance, and often hits the bull's-eye: for example, a crab tart with a light, crisp pastry shell and a bouncy, fresh, truly crab-flavoured filling.

Dinners are four courses, including a no-choice soup such as smoked haddock or thick pea and mint. Fish is treated with simplicity; and turbot on 'two delicious slices of honeyed aubergine' showed originality, although its tarragon sauce was light on tarragon and more of a cream than a sauce. At the same meal, a breast of duck was crisply roasted, served with a warm, attractively tart prune and apple purée, but with a port sauce that was lacking in concentration. Sauces could perhaps do with an injection of vitality.

Among puddings, a peerless iced coffee soufflé with pistachios had 'a silky, luscious texture and very pure coffee flavour', and crème brûlée was distinguished by a rich eggy mixture under a properly caramelised top that was penetrated with a satisfying crunch. 'The texture contrast was provocative,' according to the sensuous note of one correspondent. Reports have indicated an unnecessary hauteur in the staff and a lack of expert guidance. Light lunches (soups, sandwiches and desserts) are also available. The wine list, at over 900 bins, is stupendous, as kind to those who want change from £20 as it is generous to those with no financial brake. It does not take risks, quality is a priority at every level, producers are tip-top, older vintages are interesting rather than merely historic, and Italians are good. Unusually, the list does not draw sweet wines together, but anybody who compiles a list like this will be free with advice and suggestions. The choice of half-bottles is extensive. House wines are from £11.

CHEFS: Graeme Allen and Betty Allen PROPRIETORS: Eric, Betty and Graeme Allen OPEN: all week; 8 MEALS: Set D £35 SERVICE: not inc, card slips closed CARDS: Access, Amex, Visa DETAILS: 36 seats. Private parties: 36 main room. Car park. Vegetarian meals. Children's helpings. Smart dress preferred. No smoking in dining-room. No music ACCOMMODATION: 12 rooms, all with bath/shower. TV. Phone. D,B&B £125 to £260. Deposit: £100. Rooms for disabled. Children welcome. Pets by arrangement. Afternoon teas. Garden. Doors close at 11.30. Confirm by 4. Fax: (063 173) 535 (*The Which? Hotel Guide*)

▲ *Pierhouse* ‡※ | NEW ENTRY

Port Appin PA38 4DE
APPIN (063 173) 302
off A828, on E shore of Loch Linnhe, | COOKING 1
opposite Lismore ferry | COST £16–£58

The idea is simple: shellfish are landed at the pier, lobsters and oysters kept in cages until needed, and not much is done to them. Follow the road to the Lismore ferry, signposted from the A828, and keep going until you reach the water's edge opposite the whitewashed stone building with a slate roof. Inside are wooden tables and chairs, a linoleum floor, short laminated menus during the day and a bigger selection in the evening. Dad MacLeod potters, mother cooks, while son Callum jumps around energetically reciting extra dishes, taking orders, delivering food, drinks and rapid-fire advice.

Peeled Loch Linnhe prawns in garlic butter are brilliantly fresh. Plump scallops, coral attached, are dry-cooked then lobbed into a small butter loch. Salads, mayonnaise, butter (lemon or garlic) and Mornay sauce are the usual treatments applied to lobsters, scallops, prawns and salmon. The few token meat dishes (and sandwiches during the day) are overshadowed by fish, especially the giant platter (for two) of lobster, king prawns, scallops, oysters, cockles and mussels. Every loch should have a place like this: Linnhe has two (see Crannog, Fort William). Come on, you other lochs, wake up, get yourself a little place down by the shore, tart it up, and cook what the boats bring in. House Californian is £8.95.

CHEF: Sheila MacLeod   PROPRIETORS: the MacLeod family   OPEN: all week; 12 to 4, 6.30 to 9.30   MEALS: alc (main courses L £5 to £13, D £9 to £17)   SERVICE: not inc, card slips closed   CARDS: Access, Visa   DETAILS: 65 seats. 6 tables outside. Private parties: 40 main room, 18 private room. Car park. Vegetarian meals. Children's helpings. No smoking in 1 dining-room. Wheelchair access (also WC). Music   ACCOMMODATION: 11 rooms, all with bath/shower. TV. Phone. B&B £35 to £70. Deposit: 20%. Rooms for disabled. Children welcome. Baby facilities. Afternoon teas. Garden. Snooker. Doors close at 1am. Fax: (063 173) 521

PORTPATRICK Dumfries & Galloway   map 8

▲ *Knockinaam Lodge* ⅜✳

Portpatrick DG9 9AD
PORTPATRICK (0776) 810471   COOKING 2
off A77, 3m S of Portpatrick   COST £30–£52

The restaurant is remote, 'at the edge of the world', as the owners describe it, overlooking the sea and, on a good day, Ireland. It was ruggedly built in a sheltered cove towards the end of the nineteenth century for the Orr-Ewing family, and the small rooms probably owe their size to the fact that it was intended as a summer-house. The Frichots came from the Seychelles in 1985 and found peace, quiet and a succession of impressive sunsets.

The menu is determinedly French, in modern vein, with three courses offering a choice of two dishes each. Why Marcel Frichot does not write it in English and *then* translate into French remains a mystery. Fish plays a major role, appearing as turbot on the bone with sherry vinegar, or small strips of sole in sesame seeds with a creamy chive sauce. Casseroling is a favoured cooking method, especially in winter: wild pigeon with mushrooms, beef in red wine, spring chicken with smoked bacon, for example. Grilling produces 'pink, succulent and tender lamb', served with ratatouille, mushooms and potatoes. Cheese is an alternative to vanilla bavarois or crème brûlée. The rather conservative wine list has some good bottles, mostly classic French but with a handful of Swiss and New World wines for interest, and a good selection of half-bottles. Half a dozen house wines start at £10.25.

CHEF: Stuart Muir   PROPRIETORS: Marcel and Corinna Frichot   OPEN: all week; 12.30 to 2, 7.30 to 9   CLOSED: 2 Jan to 25 Mar   MEALS: Set L £22.50, Set D £32   SERVICE: not inc, card slips closed   CARDS: Access, Amex, Diners, Visa   DETAILS: 28 seats. Private parties: 40 main room. Car park. Vegetarian meals with prior notice. No children under 8 D. Smart dress preferred. No smoking in dining-room. Wheelchair access (1 step; also WC). No music   ACCOMMODATION: 10 rooms, all with bath/shower. Phone. B&B £70 to £140. Deposit: £100. Children welcome. Baby facilities. Pets welcome (not in public rooms). Afternoon teas. Garden. TV. Fishing. Doors close at 1am. Fax: (0776) 810435 (*The Which? Hotel Guide*)

▲ *The Creel*

Front Road, St Margaret's Hope KW17 2SL
KIRKWALL (085 683) 311, will change to
(0856) 831311 autumn 1994
off A961, 13m S of Kirkwall, on   COOKING 3
South Ronaldsay island   COST £17–£36

Take the A961 across the four Churchill barriers, built to curtail U-boat activity
during the war, and turn off at St Margaret's Hope. The Creel is a plain grey
house on the sea-front. Divers congregate, summer sunsets last all evening, and
Alan Craigie's cooking appeals to Orcadians and visitors alike. This is more than
just a good place to go if you happen to be in Orkney: it is reason enough for
visiting the islands. 'We cannot enthuse too much over this restaurant, and this
meal,' wrote one mainland couple. They ate creamed smoked haddock soup,
seafood terrine with marinated salmon and creamed rock turbot, then wolf-fish,
and salmon in light puff pastry, before an 'over-the-top' pudding of bride's cog
pears, an island speciality of roasted fruit arranged around a honey basket filled
with ice-cream, sitting in a creamy sauce.

The pattern is a choice between five first and main courses, then four sweets or
local cheese. Soups are a barometer of the Craigie approach: wholesome broths
full of flavour, from fresh crab or mutton stock, for example. The cooking is
without pretence or artifice; the mutton stock is not dressed up as lamb stock,
although North Ronaldsay lamb feeds on seaweed and has a special flavour. One
member of every Orcadian family is bound to be a fisherman, so seafood,
naturally, dominates. Salted ling is served lightly grilled on a bed of buttered
cabbage, and queen scallops come with a lentil and ginger sauce. Service is
friendly and helpful to a fault. The wine list is short, with house Australian
Semillon Chardonnay at £7.30, or £1.60 per glass.

CHEF: Alan Craigie   PROPRIETORS: Joyce and Alan Craigie   OPEN: Mon to Sat, D only, and Sun
L April to July; Fri and Sat, D only, and Sun L Aug to Mar; 12.30 to 2, 7 to 9   MEALS: alc (main
courses £8.50 to £18.50). Set Sun L £12, Set D £22   SERVICE: not inc, card slips closed
CARDS: Access, Visa   DETAILS: 38 seats. 11 tables outside. Private parties: 38 main room.
Vegetarian meals with prior notice. Children's helpings. Smart dress preferred. Wheelchair
access (2 steps; also WC). Music   ACCOMMODATION: 3 rooms, all with bath/shower. TV. B&B
£27 to £60. Deposit: 10%. Children welcome. Baby facilities. Afternoon teas. Doors close at
12.30am. Confirm by 4

Prices quoted in the Guide *are based on information supplied by restaurateurs. The prices
quoted at the top of each entry represent a range, from the lowest meal price to the highest;
the latter is inflated by 20 per cent to take account of likely price rises during the year of
the* Guide.

The Guide *relies on feedback from its readers. Especially welcome are reports on new
restaurants appearing in the book for the first time. All letters to the* Guide *are
acknowledged.*

STEIN Highland   map 8

▲ Loch Bay Seafood Restaurant ✳ £   NEW ENTRY

1–2 Macleod Terrace, Stein, Waternish,
Isle of Skye IV55 8GA
WATERNISH (0470) 592235
off B886, 4m from top of Waternish   COOKING 1
Peninsula, on shores of Loch Bay   COST £18–£44

'The Loch Bay has been open for a dozen years under the same management and
has never varied in its policy of providing the best fish and seafood,' writes a
reporter. In 1796 the British Fisheries Society built a row of cottages at Stein, on
the shores of Loch Bay, which was intended to form the nucleus of a fishing
village. Although other villages laid out by the Society, including Ullapool and
Tobermory, flourished, Stein remained a single row of cottages. The restaurant is
little more than the front room of one of these.

The range of food includes soups like Cullen skink, scallops cooked in garlic,
Skye oysters, crab, queenies, squat lobster, mussels and a daily selection of fish
chalked on the blackboard. 'Everything was cooked from raw or live,' noted one
who feasted on shellfish, adding that 'it was the treat of our holidays, exactly
what we go to Scotland for'. Haddock, hake, skate and plaice are simply grilled
and served with a baked potato or good chips. Puddings include clootie
dumpling, and there is a short and useful list of 'fishy wines' beginning with
house French at £6.50.

CHEFS/PROPRIETORS: Margaret and Peter Greenhalgh   OPEN: all week, exc Sat; 12 to 3, 6 to 9
CLOSED: Nov to Mar   MEALS: alc (main courses £9 to £19)   SERVICE: not inc, card slips closed
CARDS: Access, Visa   DETAILS: 26 seats. 2 tables outside. Car park. Vegetarian meals with prior
notice. Children's helpings. No smoking in dining-room. Wheelchair access (also men's WC).
Music   ACCOMMODATION: 3 rooms. B&B £16 to £32. Children welcome. Baby facilities.
Afternoon teas. Garden

STEWARTON Strathclyde   map 8

▲ Chapeltoun House ♟ ✳

Irving Road, Stewarton KA3 3ED
STEWARTON (0560) 482696   COOKING 1
2m from Stewarton on B769 towards Irvine   COST £24–£46

Built in 1900, Chapeltoun is certainly spacious enough for a restaurant, never
mind the private house it once was. Oak panelling, rich colours and big
luxurious armchairs give it a stately-home feel, of the kind that appeals
particularly to 'overseas golfing fanatics', although home-grown and non-
sporting readers enjoy it too. Comfort and good living are its currency. Meals are
sensibly set at three courses, with an optional extra soup or pasta, and the
cooking ranges from straightforward, very good Aberdeen Angus fillet or sirloin
with herb butter, to rather more elaborate breast of chicken filled with smoked
ham and brie, encased in pastry and served with a sherry essence.

Soft fruits are grown locally, which may explain the cherry and cranberry
sauce with deep-fried camembert wedges, the raspberry sauce with galantine of

guinea-fowl, and the redcurrant sauce with roast rack of lamb flavoured with grain mustard. Fish landed at Ayr appears as the chef's special. Half a dozen puddings include raspberry gratin served with shortbread fingers, and chocolate mille-feuilles filled with a white chocolate mousse on a Tia Maria sauce. Although the wine list follows a familiar path, it threads its way carefully between expensive obstacles to deliver good value up to and around the £20 mark, in France as well as the rest of the world. Twenty half-bottles are sensible too, and ten house recommendations begin around £9. CELLARMAN'S CHOICE: Bordeaux, Notre Dame de Landiras 1991, £14.20; Chianti Classico Riserva 1983, Castel in Villa, £19.90.

CHEF: Tom O'Donnell PROPRIETORS: Colin and Graeme McKenzie OPEN: all week; 12 to 2, 7 to 9 (9.30 Sat) CLOSED: first 2 weeks Jan MEALS: Set L £16.50, Set D £25.50 SERVICE: not inc, card slips closed CARDS: Access, Amex, Visa DETAILS: 50 seats. Private parties: 30 main room, 55 private room. Car park. Vegetarian meals. No children under 12. Smart dress preferred. No smoking in dining-room. Wheelchair access (2 steps). No music ACCOMMODATION: 8 rooms, all with bath/shower. TV. Phone. B&B £65 to £129. No children under 12. Pets welcome in certain rooms by arrangement. Afternoon teas. Garden. Fishing. Doors close at midnight. Fax: (0560) 485100 (*The Which? Hotel Guide*)

STRONTIAN Highland   map 8

▲ *Kilcamb Lodge* ⁵✳

Strontian PH36 4HY
STRONTIAN (0967) 402257   COOKING 3
on A861, by N shore of Loch Sunart   COST £31–£38

'This is without doubt one of the most pleasant hotels we have ever stayed in,' writes an inspector. All ages and ranks come here, and the Blakeways are as caring as they are professional. Even the regimen does not feel regimented: choose from the four-course menu by 6pm, turn up at 7.30 for tiny amuse-gueules of prawns, fish mousse, pizza and so on. Soup and sandwiches only are available at lunch.

A light touch throughout makes the most of first-class ingredients, fish in particular. Langoustines from the loch are kept there until the last minute, then cooked, shelled and simply presented with a small mixed-leaf salad and a lightly tangy lemon grass mayonnaise. Textures make an impact, and flavour combinations are well considered. Cream of mushroom soup is 'deeply fungoid', and a mixture of Paris browns, oyster, shiitake and dried Chinese turn up in a thin, light, perfectly textured open ravioli. Main courses make use of year-old lamb, 'so the flavour is excellent', and good Aberdeen Angus beef – a 'thick slice served rare as requested'. Duck is marinated in red wine and juniper berries and cooked confit-syle, the crisp skin glazed with honey. It is served with velvety butter-beans, while endive adds a dimension of bitterness to counteract the sweetness of the honey. Organic vegetables are well timed and full of taste.

Those who tour Scotland welcome the rare beneficence of fresh fruit, in first-course salads or terrine for dessert. 'Every pudding we had was excellent,' reported one couple who stayed a week. Rice pudding is 'the real thing', and the raisins for bread-and-butter pudding are plump and alcoholic after maceration in sherry. 'Splendid pastry' houses a lemon filling that is gentle, creamy, but firm enough to cut without falling apart. For good-value everyday wine drinking, Alsace, the Loire and the New World are out in front. House wine is £8.50.

CHEFS: Ann Blakeway and Peter Blakeway   PROPRIETORS: the Blakeway family   OPEN: all week, D only; 7.30   CLOSED: Dec to Feb   MEALS: Set D £24   SERVICE: not inc, card slips closed   CARDS: Access, Visa   DETAILS: 26 seats. Private parties: 36 main room. Car park. Vegetarian meals with prior notice. Smart dress preferred. No smoking in dining-room. Wheelchair access (1 step). No music   ACCOMMODATION: 10 rooms, all with bath/shower. B&B £40 to £80. Deposit: £35. Children welcome. High tea 6pm. Baby facilities. Pets in 2 rooms. Afternoon teas. Garden. Fishing. Confirm by 4. Fax: (0967) 402041 (*The Which? Hotel Guide*)

SWINTON Borders   map 8

▲ *Wheatsheaf Hotel, Four Seasons* ✳ £

Main Street, Swinton TD11 3JJ
SWINTON (0890) 860257   COOKING 1
on A6112, Coldstream to Duns road   COST £17–£38

The inn opposite the village green extends a warm and smiling welcome. It is modernised Victorian with a bar that is both light and cosy, and a choice of summery conservatory or a more wintry room done out in dark crimson. The *carte* of standard items is supplemented by more interesting dishes posted on the blackboard. The former offers chicken liver pâté, pork fillet in mustard sauce, and passion fruit sorbet; the latter smoked salmon bisque, steamed halibut on a carrot and coriander coulis, and breast of pigeon on a celeriac and potato cake with Puy lentils. Good workaday cooking has produced warm monkfish and prawn salad with 'a lovely flavour', and iced praline soufflé with a dark chocolate sauce. Prawns in a hot baked avocado were overwhelmed on one occasion by a rather salty cheese sauce, and other sauces have erred in the opposite direction. Teviotdale cheese is kept in good condition. The short wine list covers a range of tastes and styles at reasonable prices, with half-bottles and bin ends to match. House Australian is £7.95 (£1.65 per glass).

CHEF: Alan Reid   PROPRIETORS: Alan and Julie Reid   OPEN: Tue to Sun; 12 to 2.15, 6 to 9.30   CLOSED: 1 week Oct, 2 weeks mid-Feb   MEALS: alc (main courses £5.50 to £14.50)   SERVICE: not inc, card slips closed   CARDS: Access, Visa   DETAILS: 50 seats. 6 tables outside. Private parties: 28 main room, 16 private room. Vegetarian meals. Children's helpings. Smart dress preferred. No smoking in dining-room. Wheelchair access (1 step; also WC). No music   ACCOMMODATION: 4 rooms, 3 with bath/shower. B&B £28 to £58. Deposit: 20%. Children welcome. Baby facilities. Pets welcome (not in public areas). Garden. Doors close at midnight. Confirm by 6

£ indicates that it is possible to have a three-course meal, including coffee, a half-bottle of house wine and service, at any time the restaurant is open (i.e. at dinner as well as at lunch, unless a place is open only for dinner), for £20 or less per person.

The 1996 Guide will be published before Christmas 1995. Reports on meals are most welcome at any time of the year, but are particularly valuable in the spring. Send them to **The Good Food Guide**, FREEPOST, 2 Marylebone Road, London NW1 1YN. No stamp is needed if posted in the UK.

map 8

▲ *Tiroran House* 🎉✳

Tiroran, Isle of Mull PA69 6ES
TIRORAN (068 15) 232   COOKING 2*
off B8035, 6m S of Gruline   COST £36–£47

The Blockeys don't like to think of their country house as a hotel, which is fine by
reporters, who would consider it more like their own home were it not so
peaceful, relaxing and comfortable. Furnished with antiques and the family
silver, kept spick and span by spit and polish, it generally provides a haven from
the real world. Staffa and Iona are a short boat trip away. The garden is more than
decorative, supplying herbs and salad ingredients. Chickens and ducks provide
eggs, while beef and lamb are from the estate, and fish is landed on the island.

All this provides a sound basis for Sue Blockey's cooking, which doesn't so
much follow a school as its own nose. Meals might begin with old English
mustard soup with deep-fried pastry croûtons, or Dunsyre blue cheese tartlets,
progress to venison steak and kidney pie (with optional oyster sauce) and finish
with pavlova, grape and claret jelly, or a fruit fool. Main and cheese courses are
set, as is kick-off time, but there is usually a choice of three first courses and
puddings. Bread and gravlax are home-produced. Wines are a sensible and
careful selection, with broad and genuine appeal, all very reasonably priced.
Good *cru bourgeois* claret and Leflaive Bourgogne blanc are the house wines at
£13.75 (£1.75 a glass).

CHEF: Sue Blockey   PROPRIETORS: Robin and Sue Blockey   OPEN: all week, D (L residents
only); 7.45   CLOSED: late Oct to mid-May   MEALS: Set D £28.50   SERVICE: not inc   DETAILS:
22 seats. Private parties: 8 main room. Car park. Vegetarian meals with prior notice. No children
under 10. Smart dress preferred. No smoking in dining-room. No music   ACCOMMODATION: 9
rooms, all with bath/shower. D,B&B £100 to £210. Deposit: £50. No children under 10. Dogs by
arrangement. Garden. Confirm by noon (*The Which? Hotel Guide*)

map 8

▲ *Highgrove House* £

Old Loans Road, Troon KA10 7HL   COOKING 1
TROON (0292) 312511   COST £18–£44

The house, built by a retired sea captain, overlooks the Firth of Clyde, the Isle of
Arran, and beyond that the Mull of Kintyre. Bill Costley cooks a host of dishes on
a variety of menus that take in set-price lunch and dinner, plus a long informal
lunchtime *carte* and a similar brasserie-style list in the evening, both of these
reasonably priced. On top of that is the full *carte*. This is nothing if not flexible,
and covers a lot of ground, from warm mousseline of sole and smoked salmon
with a dill butter sauce, or brie in filo pastry with Cumberland sauce, to diced
lamb with tomatoes and ginger served with pilau rice and poppadums, and
tiramisù. One reporter enjoyed strips of chicken stir-fried with cashew-nuts and
ginger, then an immense seafood casserole with mussels, langoustines, salmon,
haddock and sole, followed by warm apple and almond sponge. The mixed list
of 60 fairly standard wines is enlivened by a few more interesting bottles, such as

Ch. de Landiras white and Ch. de Cabriac red, while four house wines are £9.95, or £1.65 per glass.

CHEF: Bill Costley   PROPRIETOR: Bill and Catherine Costley   OPEN: all week; 12 to 2.30, 6 to 9.30   MEALS: alc (main courses L £5.50 to £10.50, D £6.50 to £14). Set L £12.95, Set D £19.50 to £21.50   SERVICE: not inc, card slips closed   CARDS: Access, Amex, Visa   DETAILS: 110 seats. 6 tables outside. Private parties: 80 main room, 20 private room. Car park. Vegetarian meals. Children's helpings. Smart dress preferred. No cigars/pipes in dining-room. Music ACCOMMODATION: 9 rooms, all with bath/shower. TV. Phone. B&B £55 to £75. Children welcome. Baby facilities. Afternoon teas. Garden. Confirm day before. Fax: (0292) 318228

TURNBERRY Strathclyde   map 8

▲ *Turnberry Hotel*   NEW ENTRY

Turnberry KA26 9LT
TURNBERRY (0655) 31000, changes to   COOKING 2
(0655) 331000 autumn 1994   COST £31–£107

Built in 1906 as the world's first hotel/golf complex, this awesome Edwardian edifice has magnificent views of Ailsa Craig, especially from the vast dining-room. Its grand 'ocean liner' style evokes an air of nostalgia, especially when Cole Porter tunes are being played on the piano. Best value is the fixed-price four-course menu, although prices are far from bargain basement. Stewart Cameron's cooking is in tune with the aspirations of the hotel: his repertoire encompasses lobster thermidor, grilled Dover sole and medallions of beef flamed with madeira as well as more lavish ideas such as 'cassoulette' of halibut, salmon, scampi and scallops with lobster and cognac sauce. One admirable, finely executed meal consisted of venison terrine, then beef consommé with tomato croûtons and chive dumplings, before fillet of beef carved from the trolley and served with red wine sauce and baby turnips. Desserts might include milk chocolate truffle parfait and poached pear with butterscotch ice-cream. Details such as canapés, hot toast and 'exceptionally good' petits fours are those of an enterprise that knows how to cosset its customers. Service is in keeping: it is silky smooth, professional and caringly attentive. Wines are mostly big hotel style, at big hotel prices, heavily French but including half a dozen Swiss. House wine is £17.

CHEFS: Stuart Cameron and Mark Bulle   PROPRIETOR: Nitto World Co Ltd   OPEN: all week, D only, and Sun L; 1 to 2.30, 7.30 to 10   MEALS: alc (main courses £20 to £35). Set L Sun £19.50 to £37.50, Set D £37.50   SERVICE: not inc, card slips closed   CARDS: Access, Amex, Diners, Visa   DETAILS: 200 seats. Private parties: 10 main room, 12 to 120 private rooms. Car park. Vegetarian meals. Children's helpings. Jacket and tie. No pipes in dining-room. Wheelchair access (also WC). Music   ACCOMMODATION: 132 rooms, all with bath/shower. TV. Phone. B&B £170 to £235. Rooms for disabled. Lift. Children welcome. Baby facilities. Pets welcome (not in public rooms). Afternoon teas. Garden. Swimming-pool. Sauna. Tennis. Golf. Snooker. Fax: (0655) 31706, changes to (0655) 331706 autumn 1994 (*The Which? Hotel Guide*)

'We were not told that coffee in the lounge was self-service from a thermos jug hidden away in a hole in the wall, so we sat rather a long time before other [resident] guests let us into the secret.' (On eating in Cumbria)

▲ *Baile-na-Cille* ✦✕

Timsgarry, Uig, Isle of Lewis PA86 9JD
TIMSGARRY (0851 672) 242
B8011 to Uig, then right down track   COOKING 1*
on to shore   COST £27–£32

Richard Gollin is 'a wonderful host' who wears several hats. One visitor
recognised him as her squash instructor from Stornaway. The building is a
converted manse and stables, mostly eighteenth and nineteenth century, down
by the shore. Meals are three courses, five if you count cheese and fruit. There is
no service charge, but you must add VAT to the set-menu price. One reporter's
party began with hot, light smoked haddock soufflé, full of flavour. The main
course, pork en croûte, was paraded for inspection before serving: a large, flat,
beautifully golden brown loaf, 'perfectly cooked inside and out'. The huge
basket of fruit to finish is full of everything from apples, pears and grapes to
mango, passion fruit and pineapple.

'Wonderful bread, carefully cooked vegetables, and herbs from the garden'
helped to make another reporter's visit memorable, and black pudding is a
feature. 'Amateur fisherfolk, such as ourselves, were encouraged to hand in our
brown trout for the freezer, and when they had sufficient we were served them
for starters.' This service is available to residents only. And there is another good
reason for staying. 'Owing to the restrictive nature of licensing laws in Lewis,'
explains a reporter, 'Baile-na-Cille (pronounced Bally na Killy) may not serve
alcohol to non-residents, who should therefore take their own.' Special diets
including vegan and low-fat are catered for, as are dogs, grannies and children.
Wines include Breaky Bottom from Sussex; French and New Zealand house
wines are £8.50.

CHEF: Joanna Gollin   PROPRIETORS: Richard and Joanna Gollin   OPEN: all week, D only; 7.30.
(Mon to Sat L by reservation only; 12.30 to 1.30)   CLOSED: Oct to 1 May   MEALS: Set D
£18 – plus VAT. Unlicensed for non-residents, but bring-your-own: no corkage.   SERVICE: inc
(but VAT added), card slips closed   CARDS: Access, Visa   DETAILS: 24 seats. Private parties: 24
main room. Car park. Vegetarian meals. Healthy eating options. Children's helpings. No
smoking in dining-room. No music   ACCOMMODATION: 14 rooms, 8 with bath/shower. B&B £19
to £60. Deposit: £50. Children welcome. Baby facilities. Dogs welcome (by arrangement).
Afternoon teas. Garden. Fishing. Fax: (0851 672) 241 (*The Which? Hotel Guide*)

ULLAPOOL Highland   map 8

▲ *Altnaharrie Inn* ❙ ✦✕

HIGHLAND
1995
FLING

Ullapool IV26 2SS   COOKING 5
DUNDONNELL (0854) 633230   COST £61–£74

'Wonderful', 'magnificent', 'perfect', say reports, and, even more importantly,
'the place fully came up to expectations'. Park the car in Ullapool, ring for the
ferry and chug across on *Mother Goose* to the south side of the loch, leaving roads
and electricity behind. What an adventure! Some people seem to feel that, if they
went any further, they would fall off the edge of the world. It is probably best to
arrive in the afternoon, walk up the hill to find an appetite, come back for a cup of

tea in one of the lounges, pick over the wine list, go for a shower and wait for eight o'clock to come round. Despite the apparent lack of mod cons, 'creature comforts are not neglected, and beds, bathrooms and heating are all to a very good modern standard'. The generator is switched off when everybody is tucked in, hence the torch beside the bed. Tasteful, simple, clean rooms are testimony to Gunn Eriksen's artistic background; everything is there for a purpose.

Exactly the same applies to the food: freshness and quality of supplies are paramount, and the cooking is versatile, inventive, and modern without being modish. Fred Brown delivers the five-course menu verbally on arrival. With no choice before pudding, diners are asked for a second time (the first when booking) to name whatever they don't like or can't eat. This does not mean, however, that everybody eats the same. Gunn Eriksen keeps a record, and never serves the same dish to the same person twice. The inn has only eight rooms, so the pre-dinner gathering for lightly fishy canapés is small and sociable.

Fish naturally figures prominently: white fish is landed at Lochinver, and shellfish is kept in creels in the loch until needed. One meal began with fillet of baby halibut, springily fresh, 'out of this world', folded over once and steamed, and placed on twisted leaves of spinach. Around it are preserved morels, strands of leek tied in bows, and a butter sauce acidulated with champagne. Lobster soup is really lobster and soup: a small quantity of pale, clear consommé derived from shells and vegetables, with sliced lobster tail to one side and the claw meat (in a single piece) to the other. Although herbs are a passion – dill, chervil and lemony-tasting root ginger in this dish – they are never allowed to get the upper hand. By the main course, flavours and richness begin to mount. Two pieces of boned saddle of pink lamb have the intense flavour 'you think you remember from childhood'. Richness comes from lamb fillet encased in a mixture of foie gras and herbs, and from thinly sliced potatoes that seem to have been cooked in lamb fat. The sauce is slightly thickened lamb juice. After cheese – Cashel blue, unpasteurised Cheddar, and Lochy goats' from Gigha – pudding is a choice from three. Tiny scoops of pear are sandwiched between thin layers of dark chocolate, with a powerful poire William sauce around the edge, and a chocolate cake which has a cake-like exterior but gets softer and squidgier towards the molten centre.

Service is well choreographed and gently paced, and wines are all the more tempting when there are no roads. If money is no object, make for Burgundy. Prices generally do not take advantage of a captive clientele, and there are stacks of half-bottles, as well as a decent selection of house wines from £11.70.

CHEF: Gunn Eriksen PROPRIETORS: Fred Brown and Gunn Eriksen OPEN: all week, D only; 8 CLOSED: late Oct to Easter MEALS: Set D £55 SERVICE: net prices, card slips closed CARDS: Access, Amex, Visa DETAILS: 18 seats. Private parties: 10 main room. Car park. Vegetarian meals with prior notice. No children under 8. Smart dress preferred. No smoking in dining-room. No music ACCOMMODATION: 8 rooms, all with bath/shower. D,B&B £125 to £300. Deposit: £100. No children under 8. Pets welcome by arrangement. Garden. Confirm by 4 (*The Which? Hotel Guide*)

Net prices *in the details at the end of an entry indicates that the prices given on a menu and on a bill are inclusive of VAT and service charge, and that this practice is clearly stated on menu and bill.*

WALLS Shetland   map 8

▲ Burrastow House ¾✗

Burrastow, Walls ZE2 9PB
WALLS (059 571) 307
head N from Lerwick to Hillswick, then W
to Walls, go uphill through Walls, then left   COOKING 1
2½m to Burrastow   COST £18–£36

Diners are not advised to attempt to drive back to Lerwick after a meal here
unless it is summer or they know the roads: sound advice from a traveller who
emphasised the remoteness of this eighteenth-century house approached via a
single track through a landscape of peat bogs. The location is stunning, and you
may glimpse otters and seals at play or watch the fishing boats drifting around
Vaila Sound.

Bo Simmons's cooking is based on judicious use of local produce, especially
fish, and she works to a healthy philosophy of clean flavours without plunging
into puritanism. Her short menus change daily, and there is plenty to satisfy
meat-eaters and vegetarians. Sustaining soups such as curried parsnip or celery
and apple come with home-baked bread; otherwise you might expect fillet of
pork stuffed with spinach and pine-nuts, grilled shark, roast lamb with damson
cheese and wild mushroom brioche. Sweets are the likes of apple and guava
crumble and chocolate torte. The wine list is a carefully chosen selection of good
names, with a serious commitment to organic production. House wine is £8.50.

CHEF/PROPRIETOR: Bo Simmons   OPEN: all week, exc D Mon and Sun; 12.30 to 2.30, 7.30 to 9
CLOSED: Jan and Feb   MEALS: alc L (main courses £6.50 to £8). Set D £22.50   SERVICE: not
inc   DETAILS: 30 seats. Private parties: 20 main room. Car park. Vegetarian meals. Children's
helpings. No smoking in dining-room. No music   ACCOMMODATION: 2 rooms, both with
bath/shower. D,B&B £56 to £112. Children welcome. Baby facilities. Pets welcome. Afternoon
teas. Garden. Fishing. Doors close at midnight. Confirm by 6. Fax: (059 571) 213 (The Which?
Hotel Guide)

Wales

Hive on the Quay £

Cadwgan Place, Aberaeron SA46 0BU   COOKING 1
ABERAERON (0545) 570445   COST £14–£34

An offshoot of the Holgate family's honey business, the café comes complete
with honey exhibition and specialist shop with queues for its honey ice-cream.
Naturally it buzzes: the season is short, with barely enough time to cram all the
visitors in. The Hive occupies the old coal wharf between the two harbours,
serving food with a strong organic bias in a small whitewashed dining-room
with pine tables and a large plant-strewn conservatory.

The café is open all day for teas, sandwiches and bara brith; lunches offer
hearty soups, honey-baked ham, a sausage, apple and onion pie, or Cardigan
Bay prawns, while dinners are barely more elaborate. Cracked crab or half a
lobster with large salad, mayonnaise and bread are regular items, bolstered by
baked cod with leeks and black olives, Welsh lamb kebabs and various exotic
sundaes chalked on the board. The only surprise among drinks is the absence of
mead. Honey was fermented before the Romans arrived, and Metheglin,
flavoured with spices, was a Welsh speciality. But there is organic wine on the
minuscule list. House wines are £7.30 (£1.35 per glass).

CHEFS: Sarah Holgate, Margaret Morgan and Dawn Drummond   PROPRIETORS: Margaret and
Sarah Holgate   OPEN: all week (D July and Aug only); 12 to 2.30, 6 to 9.30   CLOSED: mid-Sept
to end-May   MEALS: alc (main courses £4.50 to £12)   SERVICE: not inc, card slips closed
CARDS: Access, Visa   DETAILS: 60 seats. 2 tables outside. Private parties: 20 main room.
Vegetarian meals. Children's helpings. Wheelchair access. Music

---

▲ *Penhelig Arms Hotel* ▮

Aberdovey LL35 0LT   COOKING 2
ABERDOVEY (0654) 767215   COST £14–£39

In the eighteenth century this was no more than a modest harbourside inn.
Today it continues to serve locals and tourists with good humour, in addition to
functioning as a hotel and restaurant. Monday-to-Saturday lunches are now
confined to the bar, where coq au vin, fish-cakes and beef goulash can be
accompanied by real ale or a glass of top-notch house wine. Sunday lunch and
evening meals in the dining-room are reasonably priced and unpretentious,

with a leaning towards fresh fish and local produce, although they may lack flair and finesse. Duck and pork terrine with Cumberland sauce, steamed halibut, pork steak with mushroom and coriander, Bakewell tart and chocolate pudding have continued to please regular visitors. Robert Hughes is known for his personal warmth and dedication to fine wines. He is an expert and an enthusiast. Keen pricing and sharp buying of tasty bottles, across a wide range, keep the wine list bubbling with interest. It aims for flavour and quality rather than big names or reputations, and is the kind that can only be put together by someone who keeps a finger on the pulse. House wines are from £8. CELLARMAN'S CHOICE: Viña de tavola Bianco 1992, Avignonesi, £12.90; Chinon 1990, Charbonnier, £11.50.

CHEF: Janie Howkins PROPRIETORS: Robert and Sally Hughes OPEN: all week; 12.15 to 2, 7 to 9 CLOSED: restaurant 25 and 26 Dec MEALS: alc bar L (main courses £4 to £9). Set L Sun £11.50, Set D £18.50 SERVICE: not inc, card slips closed CARDS: Access, Visa DETAILS: 34 seats. Private parties: 20 main room. Car park. Vegetarian meals on request. Children's helpings on request. No music ACCOMMODATION: 10 rooms, all with bath/shower. TV. Phone. B&B £38 to £94. Deposit: £40. Children welcome. Pets welcome (in bedrooms only). Afternoon teas. Doors close at midnight. Confirm by 6. Fax: (0654) 767690 (*The Which? Hotel Guide*)

ABERSOCH Gwynedd

map 4

▲ *Porth Tocyn Hotel*

Abersoch LL53 7BU
ABERSOCH (0758) 713303
on minor road 2½m S of Abersoch, drive
through Abersoch, passing Sarn Bach
crossroads, bear left at next fork, then left at
Porth Tocyn sign, follow road to end

COOKING 2*
COST £19–£36

After the Connaught, this is one of the longest-serving entries in the *Guide*, with 38 years under its belt: 'almost as long as I have been alive,' writes Mr Fletcher-Brewer. 'This is very much a happy family hotel with a good relaxed atmosphere,' sums up a reporter. The '30s white pebble-dashed house might be in need of a face-lift, but views the other way are magnificent: across the Lleyn Peninsula, Cardigan Bay and Snowdonia. It is too far from conurbations and expense accounts (and perhaps too close to the tourist trade) to be avant-garde and pursue lofty ambitions. Steady and reliable, it sticks to a set dinner of five courses, or just two if preferred. The repertoire is large enough for the menu to change every day for weeks on end without much repetition.

A meal might begin with kidneys sautéd with a mustard sauce, then celery and Stilton soup, and steamed lemon sole paupiettes stuffed with a red pepper mousseline, before treacle sponge and a plate of Welsh cheeses. More exotic and aromatic ingredients crop up from time to time – a prawn sauce flavoured with coconut and cardamom to accompany brill, or a lime and coriander hollandaise for poached salmon, for example – but puddings are back in traditional mould with rich creamy chocolate and cherry cheesecake, maple syrup and walnut ice-cream, or banana fritters with fudge sauce. Lunches are more casual affairs, buffet-style on Sunday with 'a tempting spread of fishy delights', as well as cold roast beef and chicken. Directions are 'mega important', so guests are asked to ring if uncertain how to find the place. Carefully chosen wines across the board with standard mark-ups make it a sound list. The house selection begins with vin de pays and Corbières at around £11.

CHEF: Mrs Louise Fletcher-Brewer PROPRIETOR: the Fletcher-Brewer family OPEN: all week; 12.30 to 2, 7.30 to 9.30 CLOSED: mid-Nov to week before Easter MEALS: Set L Sun £14.50, Set D £18 (2 courses) to £24. Light L weekdays SERVICE: card slips closed CARDS: Access, Visa DETAILS: 60 seats. 12 tables outside L. Private parties: 60 main room. Car park. Vegetarian meals. No children under 7 D. Smart dress preferred. No pipes in dining-room. Wheelchair access (1 step; also WC). No music ACCOMMODATION: 17 rooms, all with bath/shower. TV. Phone. B&B £41.50 to £99. Deposit: £40. Rooms for disabled. Children welcome. Baby facilities. Pets welcome (not in public rooms). Afternoon teas. Garden. Swimming-pool. Tennis. Doors close at midnight. Fax: (0758) 713538 (*The Which? Hotel Guide*)

▲ *Riverside Hotel*

Abersoch LL53 7HW
ABERSOCH (0758) 712419   COOKING 1*
on A499, 6m SW of Pwllheli   COST £17–£34

Canoe and rowing boat are provided. The hotel sits between the River Soch and the harbour, both handy for messing about in. Two-storey flat-roofed extensions have been bolted on over the years as the Bakewells have responded to growing custom. The Riverside is a family affair, with sensible provision for children who sit down to high tea in the late afternoon, leaving the field clear for grown-ups in the evening. Dinner is served in the basement among imitation beams, tiled floor, raffia-backed chairs, varnished pine tables and crocheted table-mats.

The style has developed over the years from old-fashioned farmhouse grub to more cosmopolitan food. The only things to have remained constant throughout are the Aga and a dedication to serving what one reporter described as 'good, honest, home-cooked food'. Welsh lamb is a staple, while fillets of cod with fennel and leeks, or scallops pan-fried with lime and ginger, make good use of the seaside location. Dishes can be as intriguing as 'a little bread box of curried kidneys' or as simple as tropical fruit ice-cream. Meals of four courses include soup as an intermezzo and cheese for finale (there is also a two-course option), and the Bakewells make great play of vegetables and are happy to cook low-fat dishes. Bread, yogurt, biscuits, jams and ice-creams are home-made, and the orange juice freshly squeezed. There are two wine lists, a straightforward trot round the world from wine merchant Terry Platt, and a short supplementary job from Adnams, both offering good value. House wine is £8.95.

CHEFS/PROPRIETORS: John and Wendy Bakewell OPEN: all week; 12 to 2, 7.30 to 9 CLOSED: mid-Nov to 1 Mar MEALS: alc bar meals L (main courses £3.50 to £9). Set D £15.95 (2 courses) to £21 SERVICE: not inc, card slips closed CARDS: Access, Amex, Diners, Visa DETAILS: 30 seats. Private parties: 30 main room. Car park. Vegetarian meals with prior notice. Children's helpings. No children under 5 D. Smart dress preferred. Music ACCOMMODATION: 12 rooms, all with bath/shower. TV. Phone. B&B £27.50 to £80. Deposit: £30. Children welcome. Baby facilities. Afternoon teas. Garden. Swimming-pool. Fishing. Doors close at 11.30. Confirm by 4. Fax: (0758) 712671

The Guide *always appreciates hearing about changes of chef or owner.*

BEAUMARIS Gwynedd

map 4

▲ *Ye Olde Bulls Head Inn* ♥ ✳

Castle Street, Beaumaris LL58 8AP
BEAUMARIS (0248) 810329

COOKING 2*
COST £15–£43

The Bulls Head is a venerable beast. It lurks in the glowering shadow of Beaumaris Castle and was the operational base for one of Cromwell's generals while the fortress was besieged. Less pugnacious guests in later centuries included Dr Johnson, and Charles Dickens, whose spirit lives on in the naming of bedrooms after characters from his novels. The interior is all low beams and crooked corridors. The lounge is a cheerful, floral-carpeted place with a fire crackling in the stone fireplace when conditions dictate, while the upstairs dining-room has a bare wooden floor and has been thought 'gloomy'.

The style of the cooking is not easy to capture. Some of it is recognisably in the modern British style (as in a ballottine of local game with spiced aubergine relish) and some is '90s Mediterranean (bresaola and carpaccio with a basil and pepper salsa), while a Sunday lunch menu offered stir-fried roast duck with pak choi, garlic and ginger. Moules marinière have been generous and good, and a traditional approach to lamb – 'cooked pink and tender' – was greatly appreciated, although one reporter was disappointed by 'not particularly tasty' stir-fried spiced lamb with peppers on plain boiled rice. Welsh farmhouse cheeses are singled out for praise, while 'excellent, rich, tangy' lemon tart won over one who had grumbled at earlier courses. Coffee comes with rich, home-made chocolate truffles. Bar food is also good, and wines are a joy. The list's geographical spread is wide, but the choices are reliable throughout. No fewer than five of the ten Beaujolais crus are represented, the Loire and Rhône receive concise and impeccable treatment, and the clutch of fine German wines looks good. Outside Europe, the footing is just as secure. Pricing is eminently fair. House wines start at the £11.95 mark. CELLARMAN'S CHOICE: Hawkes Bay Chardonnay 1991, £18.95; St-Aubin premier cru 'Les Frionnes' 1989, Prudhon, £17.95.

CHEFS: Keith Rothwell and Anthony Murphy PROPRIETOR: Rothwell and Robertson Ltd OPEN: all week; bar Mon to Sat L 12 to 2.30; restaurant Sun L 12 to 1.30, D 7.30 to 9.30 (9 Sun) CLOSED: 25 and 26 Dec, 1 Jan MEALS: alc (main courses bar £4.50 to £5.50, restaurant £11.50 to £15). Set L Sun £14.75, Set D Mon to Fri £18.95 SERVICE: not inc CARDS: Access, Visa DETAILS: 70 seats. Private parties: 70 main room. Car park. Vegetarian meals. Children's helpings. No children under 7 restaurant (exc Sun L). Smart dress preferred. No smoking in dining-room. No music ACCOMMODATION: 11 rooms, all with bath/shower. TV. Phone. B&B £43 to £75. Children welcome. Baby facilities. Doors close at midnight. Confirm by 6. Fax: (0248) 811294 (*The Which? Hotel Guide*)

▌ *denotes an outstanding wine cellar;* ♥ *denotes a good wine list, worth travelling for.*

The text of entries is based on unsolicited reports sent in by readers, backed up by inspections conducted anonymously. The factual details under the text are from questionnaires the Guide *sends to all restaurants that feature in the book.*

BRECHFA Dyfed

map 4

▲ Tŷ Mawr ✾

Brechfa SA32 7RA
BRECHFA (0267) 202332
on B4310, 6m N of A40 at Nantgaredig

COOKING 2
COST £18–£32

The setting is West Wales at its tranquil best: a small sixteenth-century stone house beside a bridge overlooking the River Marlais. Inside are beams, quarry-tiled and stone-flagged floors, Welsh oak furniture, and lace cloths on well-spaced tables. The locality furnishes salmon and sewin from the River Towy, Pencarreg and Pen-y-bont cheeses, as well as lamb in the form of kidneys served in a mild mustard sauce with muffin croûtons, and cawl, a dish of cutlets in a winter vegetable broth.

The menu is three courses and coffee, and some of the half-dozen items at each stage have a seasonal slant, although fixtures such as the twice-baked soufflé are particularly popular. Hare cooked in a sweet-and-sour sauce is a rather exotic exception to the generally homely style. Puddings rarely stray into the unusual, and are none the worse for it. Meringue with strawberries and cream is 'well presented, fresh and enjoyable'. Bread is baked on the premises from locally milled flour, coffee is good, and the bar serves Dragon beer. Wines are well chosen, generally in the young and fruity mould, with standard mark-ups. House French is £8.25.

CHEF: Beryl Tudhope   PROPRIETORS: Beryl and Dick Tudhope   OPEN: Wed to Mon, D only (L by arrangement); 7 to 9.30   CLOSED: last week Nov, 25 and 26 Dec   MEALS: Set L £12 to £14, Set D £18 to £20   SERVICE: not inc, card slips closed   CARDS: Access, Amex, Visa   DETAILS: 30 seats. Private parties: 50 main room. Car park. Vegetarian meals. Children by arrangement. Smart dress preferred. No smoking in dining-room. Music   ACCOMMODATION: 5 rooms, all with bath/shower. B&B £48 to £76. Deposit: £10. Children welcome. Baby facilities. Pets welcome. Afternoon teas. Garden. Doors close at 11.30. Confirm by 10am. Fax: (0267) 202437 (The Which? Hotel Guide)

BROAD HAVEN Dyfed

map 4

▲ Druidstone £

Druidstone Haven, Broad Haven,
nr Haverfordwest SA62 3NE
BROAD HAVEN (0437) 781221
from B4341 at Broad Haven turn right at
sea, after 1½m turn left to Druidstone
Haven, hotel ¾m on left

COOKING 1
COST £17–£33

The Pembrokeshire coastal path passes this house, the cliffs are full of wild flowers, and a steepish path leads down to the beach. Druidstone, a nineteenth-century family seaside home with stone walls and slate floors, littered with original paintings, photographs, flowers, dogs, children and other parapher-nalia, is immediately warm and welcoming.

There is lots of fish, and always something for vegetarians. Generous pieces of sewin or sea bass are cooked simply with a buttery sauce, or sometimes 'to an old Pembrokeshire recipe' which involves shredded orange peel, spring onions and spices. Alongside lamb cutlet or breast of duck are non-meat options of spinach and cream cheese flan or spiced chickpeas with brown rice. These, together with apple pie and rhubarb crumble, all add up to good country cooking, entirely appropriate to the surroundings. Plans are afoot to re-create an old family kitchen, so guests can congregate round the Aga, eat off a refectory table and gaze into the garden. This may in turn bring simpler lunches of soup, cheese and cold meats in due course. We await developments, and reports, with interest. Staff are young, willing and friendly. The wine list is short. House French is £6.

CHEFS: Rod and Jane Bell, and Donna Banner PROPRIETORS: Rod and Jane Bell OPEN: all week, exc Sun D; 12.30 to 2.30, 7 to 9.30 CLOSED: Mon to Wed 6 weeks before Christmas and after New Year MEALS: alc (main courses £6 to £12) SERVICE: not inc, card slips closed CARDS: Access, Amex, Visa DETAILS: 40 seats. 6 tables outside. Private parties: 40 main room, 10 private room (winter only). Car park. Vegetarian meals. Children's helpings. No-smoking while others eat. Wheelchair access (also WC). Music (some nights) ACCOMMODATION: 9 rooms and 5 cottages. B&B £24 to £58. Deposit: £20. 2 cottages for disabled. Children welcome. Baby facilities. Pets welcome. Afternoon teas. Garden. Doors close at midnight (*The Which? Hotel Guide*)

CAPEL COCH Gwynedd   map 4

▲ Tre-Ysgawen Hall

Capel Coch, Llangefni, Anglesey LL77 7UR
LLANGEFNI (0248) 750750   COOKING 2
on B5111, between Llangefni and Amlwch   COST £21–£50

The building has been likened in reports to a fortress, a gaol, a nursing home and a mental institution – but only from the outside. The large rooms, with windows running from floor to high ceiling, are quite sumptuous, 'in strong contrast to the forbidding exterior'. So the sooner you get inside, the better.

The cooking is modern and largely French-inspired, but with a classical training somewhere in the background. Chicken liver parfait, for example, is layered with foie gras, and served on a Cumberland sauce with hot brioche toast, while ravioli of lobster and sole are served in a warm sherry vinaigrette with chanterelles. Occasional flourishes add interest. Loin of Welsh lamb, coated in mint mousse and wrapped in spinach, appears on a potato and onion bhajia with a mild curry sauce. Some dishes require a fair degree of skill to accomplish, and the kitchen is up to the job. Half a dozen very good fresh scallops in a light batter are perfectly timed; the stock-based sauce that accompanies an enormous tournedos of first-class Anglesey beef, cooked blue as requested, avoids the mistake of being over-reduced or caramelised. The grated potato cake on which it rests is crisply baked.

Mille-feuilles, warm fruit tarts, steamed sponge puddings and something chocolatey are among typical desserts, and soufflés are confidently turned out. A tip-top rum and banana version had risen beautifully, with an even texture, and had a clear banana flavour with no trace of raw alcohol. It came with two ice-creams – vanilla and caramel – in an almond tuile basket. Given this level of achievement, one inspector found it surprising on one occasion that some of the incidentals – appetiser, bread and coffee – left so much room for improvement.

But service is impressively well-informed and attentive, and enough wines are under £20 on the wide-ranging list to satisfy. House wine is £9.80.

CHEF: Mark Colley PROPRIETORS: Mr and Mrs Ray Craighead OPEN: all week; 12 to 2.30, 7 to 9.30 MEALS: alc (main courses £13 to £18). Set L £14, Set D £19.95 SERVICE: not inc, card slips closed CARDS: Access, Amex, Diners, Visa DETAILS: 64 seats. Private parties: 120 main room, 30 and 120 private rooms. Car park. Vegetarian meals. Children's helpings. Jacket and tie. No cigars/pipes in dining-room. Wheelchair access (2 steps; also WC). Music ACCOMMODATION: 20 rooms, all with bath/shower. Phone. B&B £79.50 to £164. Deposit: 20%. Rooms for disabled. Children welcome. Baby facilities. Pets by arrangement. Afternoon teas. Garden. Doors close at 12.30am. Confirm by 7. Fax: (0248) 750035 (*The Which? Hotel Guide*)

CARDIFF South Glamorgan   map 4

Armless Dragon

97 Wyeverne Road, Cathays,	
Cardiff CF2 4BG	COOKING 2
CARDIFF (0222) 382357	COST £14–£36

David Richards's bistro is the setting for some strikingly individual cooking. His feel for local produce shows in laverballs with mushrooms, home-made duck sausage with pickled samphire, and all kinds of fish cooked in varying ways with different sauces. But the approach is far from parochial: anything, from rabbit boudin and Barbary duck breast with lemon and almond sauce to crab soup with lemon grass and crispy chicken winglets with five spices, is tackled. Vegetarians are more than happy with the range of meatless dishes. Fixed-price lunches (including a drink) are excellent value for items such as squid salad, red pepper stuffed with lamb and bulgar wheat, and strawberry sponge. Service is invariably excellent, even under pressure, and David Richards often takes time out to chat to his customers. The wine list was being expanded as we went to press, but it continues to offer a fair-priced selection pulled from all corners of the globe. House wine is £7.90.

CHEFS: David Richards and Debbie Coleman PROPRIETOR: David Richards OPEN: Tue to Sat, exc Sat L; 12.15 to 2.15, 7.15 to 10.30 (later post-opera) MEALS: alc (main courses £8 to £14). Set L £9.90 SERVICE: not inc CARDS: Access, Amex, Diners, Visa DETAILS: 50 seats. Private parties: 55 main room. Vegetarian meals. Children's helpings. No cigars/pipes in dining-room. Wheelchair access. Music

La Brasserie/Champers/Le Monde £

60 St Mary Street, Cardiff CF1 1FE	COOKING 1*
CARDIFF (0222) 372164/373363/387376	COST £18–£37

This already large affair has spilled over into the Costa Rica building next door and can now accommodate around 425 people. David Legg is the linking thread between the three kitchens, La Brasserie for grills and fish with a French accent, Champers for tapas, Le Monde for fish. Wooden tables, and sawdust on the floor, are not related. Buzz and activity are the currency, and there is a genuine Mediterranean feel, thanks partly to language difficulties, but staff are smiling and pleasant even when rushed.

La Brasserie serves suckling pig, although nobody has reported on it, plus grills of meat and tasty fish: hot shrimps or king prawns with a mopping sauce, for example. Pork satay kebabs, honeyed duck, and quail salad indicate more ambition than La Brasserie's partners show, although 'a tender, tasty steak and quick service' is a more likely scenario, with crêpes suzette to finish. The old Champers is now a bar serving beers and tapas: salmon with olives, tortilla, *croquetas de bacalao*, or *pimientos à la malagueña*, while food in the new expanded Champers remains much the same as before, with fishy starters followed by spicy chicken or rump steak with salad – hardly the stuff to stretch the kitchen, but accurately cooked. Le Monde is more of a pub, with smoke and thump-thump Muzak, doesn't have menus, but displays the food – mostly fish – in cold cabinets. Fish soup is left in a tureen on the table, and some exotic specimens take their place beside grilled sardines, sewin and halibut. Sauce is extra. Wines are well reported throughout; house wines are £7.35.

CHEFS: David Legg (Executive Chef); Carmen Laventure and Kurt Fleming (La Brasserie), Denis Louis (Champers) and Andrew Jones (Le Monde) PROPRIETOR: Benigno Martinez OPEN: all week (exc Sun Le Monde and Sun L Champers); 12 to 2.30 (3 La Brasserie), 7 to 12 MEALS: alc (main courses £6 to £12). Set L La Brasserie £5 (2 courses) SERVICE: not inc, card slips closed CARDS: Access, Amex, Diners, Visa DETAILS: La Brasserie 75 seats, Champers 130 seats, Le Monde 220 seats. Private parties: 70, 75 and 100 main rooms, 70 and 100 private rooms. Vegetarian meals. Children welcome La Brasserie and Champers. Smart dress preferred. Wheelchair access in all (La Brasserie 2 steps; also WC). Music. Air-conditioned. Fax: (0222) 668092

Le Cassoulet

| NEW ENTRY |

5 Romilly Crescent, Canton,
Cardiff CF1 9NP
CARDIFF (0222) 221905

COOKING 2*
COST £27–£44

Le Cassoulet has been a stalwart of Cardiff restauration for a number of years, but was dropped from the *Guide* last year owing to a change of chef as we went to press. This caused some consternation among readers unaware of the reason, but we are happy to see it return as good as ever under a new chef. 'I think this is now the best restaurant in Cardiff,' writes one of several supporters. It is an out-of-context French bistro in a converted corner shop in the Victorian suburbs, the 'bohemian' part of Cardiff as some call it. 'Stepping through the doorway pre-empts the Channel tunnel' and leads to a small room – no space for a bar – with a view of the kitchen at the far end. It is not just the décor and food but also the staff and quality of service – attentive yet discreet – that are French.

The set menu of six or more items at each stage is supplemented with daily specials (including fish) chalked on a board. To get the best out of it, according to one reporter, requires a tolerance of traditional, rich south-western French cooking. The eponymous hearty cassoulet needs advance notice, although boned pig's trotter stuffed with chicken mousseline and morels fulfils a similar role. An inspector, however, considered that the food was now less robust and down to earth than previously, but more enticing. A lighter, subtler hand shows through in an asparagus mousse with a leek and butter sauce. Depth of flavour is not sacrificed though: langoustine soup with lobster ravioli, for example, is 'deeply fishy'. Seasoning and presentation are up to scratch, as are the vegetables. French cheeses from a good selection in perfect condition are cut to order 'with no rationing'. Among puddings, passion-fruit crème brûlée with iced oatmeal parfait is a particularly well-judged contrast of flavours and textures. The reasonably priced French wine list is short but varied, with dessert wines only by the glass. House vin de pays is £8.95.

CHEF: Michael Wignal   PROPRIETORS: Gilbert and Claire Viader   OPEN: Tue to Sat, exc Sat L; 12 to 2, 7 to 10.30 (post-theatre by arrangement)   CLOSED: 2 weeks Christmas, Aug   MEALS: Set L £16 (2 courses) to £18, Set D £19 (2 courses) to £24   SERVICE: not inc   CARDS: Access, Amex, Visa   DETAILS: 40 seats. Private parties: 40 main room. Vegetarian meals. Children's helpings. Smart dress preferred. No music

Chikako's £

10–11 Mill Lane, Cardiff CF1 1FL	COOKING 1
CARDIFF (0222) 665279	COST £18–£32

Look for the sign and menu on the wall, ring the security bell to gain entry and wait for Chikako Cameron to greet you. Cardiff's only Japanese restaurant is in a basement done out in typically austere style with black lacquered tables, a wooden floor and glass-fronted cupboards loaded with crockery. The menu divides between dishes cooked in the kitchen and d-i-y specialities such as teppanyaki that are prepared at the table. Chikako is keen on ingredients and grows Japanese vegetables organically in her garden (Welsh weather permitting); other supplies are flown in from Japan. The kitchen can deliver creditable appetisers such as edamame (boiled soya beans in their pods) and silken tofu with pickled cucumber, as well as deeply flavoured mishoshiru soup, delicately battered tempura and beef teriyaki. Sushi is available with advance warning, and sashimi can be had for a supplement of £5. Drink green tea and saké by the flask. House wine is £7.50.

CHEF/PROPRIETOR: Chikako Cameron   OPEN: all week, D only; 6 to 11 (L by arrangement)   CLOSED: 25 Dec   MEALS: alc (main courses £8 to £18). Set L and D £11.80 to £19.50   SERVICE: 10%, card slips closed   CARDS: Access, Amex, Visa   DETAILS: 72 seats. Private parties: 50 main room, 10 and 10 private rooms. Vegetarian meals. Children's helpings. Smart dress preferred. Separate smoking area. Music. Air-conditioned. Fax: (0222) 665279

CHIRK Clwyd   map 4

▲ Starlings Castle ▼

Bronygarth, nr Chirk SY10 7NU	
OSWESTRY (0691) 718464	
take Weston Rhyn turn from A5 N of	
Oswestry to Selattyn, turn right through	
village, climb for 2½m, turn right at top of	COOKING 3
hill, then follow signs	COST £25–£43

Starlings Castle (not really a castle, but an eighteenth-century farmhouse) 'is not only in the middle of nowhere, it is 1400 feet up', and directions are more help than the postal address in finding the place. The dining-room is as light as the lounge is dark, and a new extension has turned the long grey-stone building, with low ceilings and recessed windows, into an L-shape. The Pitts describe it as 'a restaurant with bedrooms and pottery', and evidence of the potter's art fills the rooms. 'Very '60s,' observed one reporter. Whatever the service may lack in speed – the Pitts do everything themselves – it more than makes up for in friendliness. The atmosphere is relaxed, comfortable and domestic.

The small scale and personal approach explain why last-minute preparation is kept to a minimum. Marinades, soups and terrines to start, plus a long-simmered main course such as local wild rabbit provençale-style, keep the whole affair manageable. That is not to say corners are cut – far from it. A terrine of crab mousse and spinach 'which could so easily have been a cold, lifeless solid slab', in one jaded reporter's view, was in fact 'a really exciting dish – very fresh, roughly textured, creamy and full of flavour'. Seasoning may be generous, but combinations are interesting and well balanced. Pigeon breasts are sautéd pink, the sauce is stock-based, and whole garlic cloves are added. Ideas range from very traditional – smoked gammon cooked in hay, or floating islands – to grilled chicken with avocado and coriander salsa.

Sounds of hand-whisking were heard from the kitchen after one diner had ordered syllabub, while another enjoyed white chocolate and strawberry mousse with whole strawberries embedded in it. Home-made, crusty, springy granary rolls come with salty, deep-yellow Welsh farmhouse butter. Although the list is relatively short, wines are chosen for taste and quality, and passed on at tolerable mark-ups. Four house wines begin at £9.50. CELLARMAN'S CHOICE: Bergerac Ch. la Jaubertie 1992, £13.50; McLaren Vale Shiraz 1990, £17.

CHEF: Antony Pitt   PROPRIETORS: Antony Pitt and Jools Pitt   OPEN: all week, D only, and Sun L (Mon to Sat by arrangement); 12.30 to 2.30, 7.30 to 9.30 (10.30 weekends)   MEALS: alc (main courses £9.50 to £15)   SERVICE: not inc   CARDS: Access, Amex, Diners, Visa   DETAILS: 70 seats. 8 tables outside. Private parties: 50 main room, 15 private room. Car park. Vegetarian meals with prior notice. Children's helpings. Wheelchair access. Music   ACCOMMODATION: 7 rooms. TV. B&B £20 to £40. Deposit: £30. Children welcome. Baby facilities. Pets welcome (not in public rooms). Garden (*The Which? Hotel Guide*)

CLYTHA Gwent   map 4

▲ *Clytha Arms* ✸ £

Clytha, nr Abergavenny NP7 9BW
ABERGAVENNY (0873) 840206
off old Abergavenny to Raglan road, S of   COOKING 1
A40, 6m E of Abergavenny   COST £16–£33

'Truly rural! Set in lawned gardens thick with snowdrops,' commented a reporter who enjoyed a February visit to this converted dower house not far from the River Usk. The Canning family still run it as an exemplary country pub – complete with five real ales and bar snacks – but the core of the place is now its open, solidly furnished dining-room. Menus are chalked on blackboards, and the Cannings bring together Wales and France in a happy alliance: oysters with leeks and Caerphilly, and bacon with laverbread and cockles share the bill with salmon in filo pastry and lamb with flageolet beans. Further afield, they trawl the globe for bresaola with Tuscany bread, sea bass cooked Chinese-style, and Malaysian pineapple. Sunday lunch is a well-reported roast. The mood is congenial, service is 'decidedly youthful', and the food is 'remarkably good value'. The list of around 40 wines offers plenty of decent, affordable drinking. Australian house wine is £7.50.

CHEFS/PROPRIETORS: Andrew and Beverly Canning   OPEN: all week, exc Sun D and Mon L; 12.30 to 2.30, 7.30 to 9.30   MEALS: alc (main courses £7 to £11.50). Set L Sun £8.80   SERVICE: not inc, card slips closed   CARDS: Access, Visa   DETAILS: 50 seats. 10 tables outside. Private parties: 55 main room, 18 private room. Car park. Vegetarian meals. Children's helpings. Smart dress preferred. No smoking in dining-room. Wheelchair access (2 steps). Music ACCOMMODATION: 3 rooms, all with bath/shower. TV. B&B £30 to £60. Children welcome. Baby facilities. Pets welcome (not in dining-rooms). Afternoon teas. Garden. Doors close at midnight. Confirm by 5. Fax: (0873) 840206

COLWYN BAY Clwyd   map 4

Café Niçoise £

124 Abergele Road, Colwyn Bay LL29 7PS   COOKING 2
COLWYN BAY (0492) 531555   COST £20–£42

'Well worth the 140-mile round trip, twice,' confirmed a reporter from Liverpool. This converted Victorian shop has a bistro feel, with candles on the midnight-blue tablecloths and French accordion music playing in the background. Prints of Paris street scenes line the walls, and the cooking is rooted in the provincial tradition of noisettes of lamb with aubergine and rosemary, and tournedos with creamed cabbage and Dijon mustard. Lynne Swift recites the day's dishes from a blackboard. The fixed-price 'menu touristique' is excellent value: a meal of courgette soup, 'well presented' suprême of chicken with mushrooms and tarragon, and an exemplary crème brûlée proved highly enjoyable.

The more elaborate *carte* also draws favourable comments: sea bass baked in Pernod with pumpkin and carrot sauce, and salmis of pheasant with braised shallots and red cabbage in port sauce have been first-rate. The mixed plate of desserts has included 'the best passion fruit creation I have ever tasted', although 'heavy' chocolate mousse and 'unripe strawberries' on one occasion did not meet with approval. The list of some 50 wines looks beyond France to Italy and the New World; prices are realistic. House wines start at £7.50.

CHEF: Carl Swift   PROPRIETORS: Carl and Lynne Swift   OPEN: Thur to Sat L, 12 to 2; Mon to Sat D, 7 to 10   CLOSED: 1 week Jan, 1 week June   MEALS: alc (main courses £7 to £14). Set L and D £13.95 (exc Fri and Sat D)   SERVICE: not inc, card slips closed   CARDS: Access, Amex, Visa DETAILS: 32 seats. Private parties: 34 main room. Vegetarian meals. Children's helpings. Smart dress preferred. Music

---

£ indicates that it is possible to have a three-course meal, including coffee, a half-bottle of house wine and service, at any time the restaurant is open (i.e. at dinner as well as at lunch, unless a place is open only for dinner), for £20 or less per person.

Card slips closed in the details at the end of an entry indicates that the total on the slips of credit cards is closed when handed over for signature.

CRICKHOWELL Powys   map 4

Nantyffin Cider Mill Inn £

Brecon Road, Crickhowell NP8 1SG
CRICKHOWELL (0873) 810775
on junction of A40 and A479, 1½m W of   COOKING 1
Crickhowell   COST £16–£36

The lack of ostentation is a plus for this whitewashed sixteenth-century
stone-built country pub, with its original cider press and wheel. Bare stone
walls and lots of beams keep alive the mill idea, while connection to mains gas
has improved the efficiency of the heating. A loyal local following carries it
through most of the year, topped up by tourists in season, so the cooking aims for
wide appeal. 'We still feel that a pub should offer good old-fashioned food such
as faggots, liver and onions, and fish-cakes,' say the owners, who get through a
lot of mashed potato, onion gravy, mushy peas, steak and kidney pie, and
lasagne. But the net is widely spread, to take in chargrilled red mullet with
Mediterranean vegetables, Moroccan lamb casserole, and chicken tikka with
pilau rice. Some local rabbit, pigeon and pheasant find their way into the
kitchen, and seafood appears on the daily specials board. Puddings can be rich.
Wines major on good value from round the world, with generous offerings
under £20. House wines begin at £8.15 (£1.20 per glass).

CHEFS: S. Gerrard and P. Davies   PROPRIETORS: S. Gerrard and G. Bridgeman   OPEN: all week;
12 to 2.30, 6.45 to 9.45   CLOSED: Mon Oct to Apr, exc Dec; closed 2 weeks Jan   MEALS: alc
(main courses £5 to £13). Set L Sun £10.50   SERVICE: not inc   CARDS: Access, Visa   DETAILS:
65 seats. 10 tables outside. Private parties: 70 main room. Car park. Vegetarian meals.
Children's helpings. Smart dress preferred. No cigars/pipes in lounge bar. Wheelchair access
(also WC). No music

DEGANWY Gwynedd   map 4

Paysanne £

Station Road, Deganwy LL31 9EJ
ABERCONWY (0492) 582079   COOKING 2
off A55, 2m S of Llandudno   COST £14–£31

True to its name, Paysanne is a busy, atmospheric French-style bistro devoted to
the rich seam of French country cooking. Barbara Ross is at the stove and Bob is a
friendly patron out front. The kitchen works to a short *carte* backed up by daily
specials, although from Tuesday to Friday attention often shifts to the 75-, 95-
and 125-franc three-course menus. Soupe de poisson is an authentically Gallic
brew with croûtons and aoïli, black pudding comes with hot mustard sauce and
apples, and asparagus is wrapped in a crêpe with lemon and tarragon butter.
Fish is well handled and the kitchen does a good line in regional casseroles –
daubes, poule au pot and marmite de pêcheurs. A dish of honey-glazed Barbary
duckling with kumquat and ginger sauce was memorable for one seasoned
diner. Sweets are the likes of chocolat St-Emilion and tarte Tatin. Special
evenings of French regional cooking are a feature. Wines continue the

francophilia. Most are imported direct – names may be unfamiliar – but interest is high and prices are keen. House wines are from £7.50.

CHEF: Barbara Ross   PROPRIETORS: Bob and Barbara Ross   OPEN: Tue to Sat, D only; 7 to 9.30   CLOSED: first 2 weeks Jan   MEALS: alc (main courses £8 to £11). Set D Tue to Fri £7.50 to £12.50   SERVICE: not inc, card slips closed   CARDS: Access, Visa   DETAILS: 40 seats. Private parties: 40 main room. Vegetarian meals with prior notice. No children under 7. Smart dress preferred. No smoking before 9.30pm. No pipes in dining-room. No-smoking area. Music. Fax: (0492) 583848

DOLGELLAU Gwynedd   map 4

Dylanwad Da ✳ ♟ £

2 Ffôs-y-Felin, Dolgellau LL40 1BS   COOKING 1*
DOLGELLAU (0341) 422870   COST £19–£30

The name means 'good welcome' in Welsh, which says a great deal about Dylan Rowlands's admirable bistro. Essentially it is a 'great neighbourhood restaurant' that serves the local community well. Meals are eaten in a sunny little dining-room with pine tables and colourful paintings on the custardy-yellow walls. The menu is dotted with some up-to-the-minute ingredients such as sun-dried tomatoes, although the cooking retains its old-style robustness and generosity. Apple, walnut and goats' cheese salad is dressed with walnut oil and balsamic vinegar, haddock is poached with smoked salmon sauce, and steak is paired with horseradish. Lamb is Welsh, as are the cheeses. Vegetables are served in great quantities to be heaped on to the plate. Sweets might include filled pear and almond tart, and lime mousse with orange sauce. The lady of the house is a great asset, and hits just the right note in terms of friendliness and good humour. The short but interesting wine list is extremely well priced: everything apart from champagne is under £15, yet it keeps in touch with developments. House wine is £7.95. CELLARMAN'S CHOICE: Oyster Bay Chardonnay 1993, £11.95; Graves, Ch. Chicane 1990, £11.60.

CHEF/PROPRIETOR: Dylan Rowlands   OPEN: D only; all week Easter and Whitsun, July to Sept; Thur to Sat winter; 7 to 9.30   CLOSED: Feb   MEALS: alc (main courses £7 to £11)   SERVICE: not inc   DETAILS: 30 seats. Private parties: 30 main room. Vegetarian meals. Children's helpings. No smoking in dining-room. Music

---

EGLWYSFACH Powys   map 4

▲ Ynyshir Hall ✳

Eglwysfach SY20 8TA
GLANDYFI (0654) 781209   COOKING 2
off A487, 6m SW of Machynlleth   COST £24–£42

The warm welcome and convivial atmosphere at this country hotel are great attractions, and the place is clearly stamped with the personality of its owners. Guests talk to each other and residents enjoy the pampering. Rob Reen is a keen painter, and his bright, bold work is everywhere. The long, white house stands in 12 acres of landscaped gardens surrounded by a noted RSPB bird sanctuary. Art courses and birdwatching weekends are a feature. New chef Tony Pierce worked his passage in some high-flying venues, including Mallory Court and Inverlochy Castle (see entries – Bishop's Tachbrook and Fort William), and has settled in comfortably. This is elaborate and exact cooking, with an occasional backward glance to the arty, miniature world of nouvelle cuisine. One typically fine fixed-price dinner comprised some excellent dishes: casserole of local mussels with home-made ravioli and saffron; roast loin of Welsh lamb with Puy lentils and confit of shallots; and paupiettes of guinea-fowl with poached apricots, bacon and thyme. Puddings, such as terrine of three chocolates, are visually stunning, and the cheeseboard has a strong Welsh contingent. The wine list from Tanners is well-spread and sensibly chosen, and half-bottles show up well. House wines start at £11.

CHEF: Tony Pierce PROPRIETORS: Rob and Joan Reen OPEN: all week; 12.30 to 1.30, 7 to 8.45 MEALS: Set L £15, Set D £25 SERVICE: not inc, card slips closed CARDS: Access, Amex, Visa DETAILS: 40 seats. Private parties: 26 main room, 16 private room. Car park. Vegetarian meals. No children under 9. Smart dress preferred. No smoking in dining-room. Music ACCOMMODATION: 8 rooms, all with bath/shower. TV. Phone. B&B £75 to £125. Deposit: 20%. No children under 9. Pets welcome by arrangement. Afternoon teas. Garden. Doors close at midnight. Fax: (0654) 781366 (The Which? Hotel Guide)

FISHGUARD Dyfed   map 4

▲ Three Main Street ⁵⚹

3 Main Street, Fishguard SA65 9HG   COOKING 2*
FISHGUARD (0348) 874275   COST £15–£37

As its address implies, this restaurant is in the centre of town, the proverbial stone's throw from the sea, and handy for spectacular clifftop walking to work up an appetite. It is a pleasant Georgian town house, with stripped-pine interiors and vibrantly un-Georgian colour schemes. Marion Evans's cooking is characterised by absorption of a mixture of classic European styles within the framework of a daily-changing *carte* that shortens at lunch-time to offer the likes of pizza with artichokes and peppers, gravlax, and crêpe filled with trout cooked in cheese and cream. Evening starters have included salad of smoked bacon, avocado and croûtons that impressed for textural range, ravioli of walnut pesto with spring onions and Parmesan that was 'perfectly cooked – tastes and textures combining beautifully' – and a bland but 'beautifully cooked and presented' spinach and Gruyère crêpe.

Main courses win praise also: sauté of scallops and monkfish in cream sauce was sensitively cooked and full of flavour, chicken Simla was a 'perfectly balanced' lightly curried dish with 'delicate spices, bloated raisins and sour cream', and roast loin of Welsh lamb with wild garlic was 'beautifully pungent and aromatic'. Welsh cheeses and Stilton have been up to the mark, and desserts such as 'meltingly rich' mascarpone and strawberries, 'delightful' apple tart and an assiette of chocolate impress. All incidentals, from 'rough and yeasty' bread rolls to home-made chocolates with coffee, receive thumping endorsements. The wine list is rather embryonic, with the New World about the best bet. House French is £8.95.

▲ *This symbol means accommodation is available.*

CHEFS: Marion Evans and Andrew Griffith   PROPRIETORS: Marion Evans and Inez Ford   OPEN: Mon to Sat (exc some winter Mons); 2.30, 7 to 9.30   CLOSED: Feb   MEALS: alc (main courses L £3.50 to £5, D £9 to £13)   SERVICE: not inc   DETAILS: 36 seats. Private parties: 24 main room, 12 and 24 private rooms. Vegetarian meals. Children's helpings. No smoking in dining-room. Wheelchair access (1 step). No music   ACCOMMODATION: 3 rooms, all with bath/shower. B&B £30 to £50. Deposit: £20. Children welcome. Doors close at midnight. Confirm by 6 (*The Which? Hotel Guide*)

FORDEN Powys   map 4

▲ *Edderton Hall*

Forden SY21 8RZ
WELSHPOOL (0938) 580339   COOKING 1
off A490, 4m S of Welshpool   COST £22–£40

The bow-fronted house, with stunning views from its bare hilltop location, is personal and quirky rather than posh country house, although there is no stinting on comfort. 'The chairs and sofas aren't easy to get out of once sunk into,' wrote a relaxed reporter. Dinner is a no-choice stretch of four courses, often beginning with fish, which may have a specially flavoured bread to accompany it. Then comes something light and salady, or a soup. Main courses can be as simple as fillet of beef served with batter puddings with fresh oysters inside and a sauce of Guinness and champagne; and lamb with mint and elderflower is something of a speciality. Threesomes involving diferent methods of preparation on the same plate are rather ambitious. Salmon smoked over sugar, marinated in lime, and cooked in a filo swagbag – 'delicious, interesting and presented beautifully' – is nothing compared to what happens to pheasant. It seems a lot of trouble to go to, especially when other aspects of the operation do not always fall into line. 'Evelyn Hawksley is not short of culinary ability, but there is a lack of organisational ability' was one opinion, and lapses in service have been noted. House wine is £8 a litre.

CHEF: Evelyn Hawksley   PROPRIETORS: Evelyn and Warren Hawksley   OPEN: Tue to Sat, exc L Wed and Sat (Sun L on 'special' days and by arrangement for 6 or more); 1 to 2, 7.30 to 9.30   CLOSED: Christmas to New Year   MEALS: Set L £15, Set D £25   SERVICE: not inc, card slips closed   CARDS: Access, Amex, Diners, Visa   DETAILS: 34 seats. 3 tables outside. Private parties: 20 main room, 12 and 45 private rooms. Car park. Vegetarian meals with prior notice. Children's helpings. No children under 8. Smart dress preferred. Wheelchair access (also WC). Music   ACCOMMODATION: 8 rooms, all with bath/shower. TV. Phone. B&B £20 to £85. No children under 8. Pets welcome. Afternoon teas. Garden. Confirm by 1pm. Fax: (0938) 580452 (*The Which? Hotel Guide*)

The Guide office can quickly spot when a restaurateur is encouraging customers to write recommending inclusion – and sadly, several restaurants have been doing this in 1994. Such reports do not further a restaurant's cause. Please tell us if a restaurateur invites you to write to the Guide.

Restaurateurs justifiably resent no-shows. If you quote a credit card number when booking, you may be liable for the restaurant's lost profit margin if you don't turn up. Always phone to cancel.

FREYSTROP Dyfed   map 4

Jemima's ❧✳ £

Freystrop, nr Haverfordwest SA62 4HB
JOHNSTON (0437) 891109   COOKING **2**
on Burton road, 2m SW of Haverfordwest   COST £16–£35

Jemima's now boasts both a restaurant and a new bistro that serves lighter food.
Ann Owston cooks, serves and chats. Seasonal supplies dictate her short,
handwritten menus and she cares about flavour. Above all, her food is honest.
Plundering the globe for ideas, she might come up with sweet-and-sour
aubergines, Thai spiced pork, smoked chicken and sauerkraut or Greek stifado.
Rabbit pâté arrives with home-made fruit 'mostarda' and a few green leaves
from the garden; fillet of salmon trout ('delicate but positive') is poached with
white wine, herbs and cream. Vegetables are simple and good: 'quite the best
roast potatoes apart from my own that I have eaten', admitted one reporter.
Home-baked bread, Welsh cheeses and strong cafetière coffee are impressive
extras. Although the short wine list neglects a few details (e.g. some vintages), it
makes a serious effort to list good wines under £15. The small fixed mark-up –
'no customer is penalised for wanting to drink Bollinger'– is made possible by
quick turnover. House wine is £8.

CHEF: Ann Owston   PROPRIETORS: Ann Owston, Wendy Connelly and April Connelly   OPEN:
restaurant Mon to Sat, D only, and Sun L; bistro all week, exc Sun; 12 to 2, 7 to 9   CLOSED: Tues
and Wed in winter   MEALS: alc (main courses restaurant £8.50 to £11.50, bistro £4 to £5). Set
lunch Sun £10   SERVICE: not inc, card slips closed   CARDS: Access, Amex, Visa   DETAILS:
restaurant 16 seats, bistro 12 seats. Private parties: 16 main room. Car park. Vegetarian meals.
Children's helpings. No smoking in dining-room. No music

GLANWYDDEN Gwynedd   map 4

Queen's Head £

Glanwydden,
nr Llandudno Junction LL31 9JP
ABERCONWY (0492) 546570
just off B5115 Colwyn Bay to   COOKING **1**
Llandudno road   COST £15–£34

It may be difficult to track down (look for the Llanrhos Road between Llandudno
Junction and Colwyn Bay), but this converted wheelwright's cottage remains
one of the most popular country pub/restaurants in North Wales. The building
has been given a facelift, and service from a band of busy women is first-rate. The
kitchen takes account of local produce and ingredients for dishes such as Conwy
salmon wrapped in filo pastry with a sauce made from fennel that grows wild in
lanes near the pub. Loin of Welsh lamb is flavoured with local honey and served
with plum and port sauce. Mussels and crab are firm favourites, and the long list
of sweets is 'magnificent'. Bread-and-butter pudding, chocolate nut fudge pie,
and rum and raisin flan have all pleased. The repertoire takes in everything from
pizzas and simple bar snacks to more elaborate evening dishes such as steamed
lemon sole filled with asparagus mousse. Thirty wines provide appropriate and
good-value drinking. House wine is £8.50.

CHEFS: Neil MacKenzie and Andrew Hadfield   PROPRIETORS: Robert and Sally Cureton   OPEN: all week; 12 to 2.15, 6.30 to 9   CLOSED: 25 Dec   MEALS: alc (main courses L £5 to £8, D £6.50 to £13)   SERVICE: not inc, card slips closed   CARDS: Access, Visa   DETAILS: 120 seats. 12 tables outside. Private parties: 26 main room. Car park. Vegetarian meals. No children under 7. Smart dress preferred. Wheelchair access (1 step). Music. Fax: (0492) 546481

GOODWICK Dyfed   map 4

Tate's Brasserie ▮ ⁵✳ £

Bay View House, Main Street, Goodwick,
nr Fishguard SA64 0BN
FISHGUARD (0348) 874190   COOKING 2
off A40, ¾m NW of Fishguard   COST £12–£40

To find the village of Goodwick, set a course for Fishguard Harbour. Tate's draws its trade from a hard core of locals, some seasonal holiday trade and a few stray customers who turn up after missing the Irish ferry. Catering under such unpredictable conditions can cause problems. Diana Richards's solution is to offer plenty of flexible options through the day, from coffee and snacks, and amazing-value set lunches ('a real winner', noted one traveller), through afternoon teas and snacks, to an early evening bistro menu (6 to 7pm, and afterwards in the bar only), plus a fully-fledged *carte* and set meals from 7pm.

She keeps faith with local produce, but her cooking has lots of distinctive angles and looks far beyond South Wales for inspiration. Laverbread is served with a pie of cockles, bacon and wild garlic; it is also turned into a sauce for Cardigan Bay scallops with pasta. With the net cast wider, you might also be offered pan-fried duck with cardamom and orange sauce, Vietnamese beef stew or spicy aubergines with vegetable pilaff. Plates of anchovy toast with green olives arrive in tandem with the menu, while sweets continue the wide-ranging eclectic theme with lemon posset, gooseberry crumble and gâteau Basque. The modestly priced wine list is arranged by style, keeps up to date, and shows an eye for a bargain and knowledge of quality. It may look scruffy, but its heart is in the right place and is just the sort to encourage exploratory drinking and reward it with clear and interesting flavours. About half a dozen wines are normally available by the glass for under £2. House wine is £7.75. CELLARMAN'S CHOICE: Jackson Estate Sauvignon Blanc 1993, £13.90; Weinert Cabernet Sauvignon 1983, £14.95.

CHEF/PROPRIETOR: Diana Richards   OPEN: all week, exc Tue L (Tue D by arrangement mid-Oct to June, exc 2 weeks Easter and Tue after spring bank hol); noon (11am for snacks) to 9.30 (12 to 2, 7 to 9.30 Sun)   MEALS: alc D (main courses £9 to £17). Set L £5 (2 courses) to £5.95, Set L Sun £8.95, Set D £11.75 (vegetarian) to £14. Bistro menu £11 (inc wine)   SERVICE: not inc   DETAILS: 33 seats. Private parties: 31 main room. Vegetarian meals. Children's helpings before 7.30pm. No smoking in dining-room. Wheelchair access. Music

'On asking for a table for two, we were asked to look at the menu first "as you might not want to eat when you have seen it". This has never happened to us before.'
(On eating in the Isle of Man)

HARLECH Gwynedd   map 4

▲ Castle Cottage 🍴✕

Pen Llech, Harlech LL46 2YL   COOKING 1*
HARLECH (0766) 780479   COST £17–£32

Almost in the shadow of the medieval castle, this is one of the oldest houses in
Harlech, run as a hotel and restaurant by the Roberts family since 1989. It is
small-scale and friendly, with a homely and unfussy menu that brings
traditional food up to date. Eastern flavours and spices might mingle with Italian
on a set menu of five choices at each stage: for example, Chinese spices and
black-bean sauce with a breadcrumbed fillet of pork, or polenta grilled with
assorted mushrooms, tomato and Gruyère cheese. Where would a Welsh
restaurant be without lamb? Here noisettes and kidneys are simply grilled,
served with a port sauce and parsnip purée. Swedish fish soup, and a main
course feuilleté of Conwy salmon and queen scallops in orange butter, exploit
other local resources. Welsh cheeses (Pencarreg and Llanboidy among them)
fight steamed sponge pudding with raspberry jam for attention. Interesting
bottles at modest prices on the 75-strong list make house wines (from £7.95)
virtually redundant.

CHEF: Glyn Roberts PROPRIETORS: Jacqueline and Glyn Roberts OPEN: all week, D only, and
Sun L; 12.30 to 2, 7 to 9.30 MEALS: Set L Sun £11, Set D £15 (2 courses) to £17.50 SERVICE:
not inc CARDS: Access, Amex, Visa DETAILS: 50 seats. Private parties: 50 main room.
Vegetarian meals. Children's helpings. Smart dress preferred. No smoking in dining-room.
Wheelchair access (3 steps). Music ACCOMMODATION: 6 rooms, 4 with bath/shower. B&B £22
to £48. Deposit: £10. Children welcome. Baby facilities. Pets welcome (not in public rooms).
Doors close at midnight. Confirm by 6

LLANBERIS Gwynedd   map 4

Y Bistro 🍴✕

43–45 High Street, Llanberis LL55 4EU
LLANBERIS (0286) 871278   COOKING 1
off A4086, at foot of Mount Snowdon   COST £28–£38

Llanberis, at the foot of Snowdon, is much beloved of walkers, and the Snowdon
railway starts here. It is what visitors might call deepest Wales, and the bistro
reflects this: a little out of touch, perhaps, with national preoccupations, but very
hospitable, and taking on the role of neighbourhood restaurant, packed with
hungry walkers and local families. The food, from a longish menu, is wholesome
fuel. Ham and lentil soup has a spicy kick to it, and chunky pieces of locally
smoked chicken breast combine well with their baked tomatoes and spicy salsa.
Roast lamb is pink, tender and plainly served. Rump steak, lambs' kidney, and
pork loin with apples, sage and cider are alternative main courses. Puddings rely
on heavy or alcohol-based sauces for effect. The wine list is modest in scope and
prices, but perfectly suitable for the job. House wine is £8.50 (£1.65 per glass).

The Good Food Guide *is a registered trade mark of Consumers' Association Ltd.*

CHEF: Nerys Roberts   PROPRIETORS: Danny and Nerys Roberts   OPEN: Mon to Sat, D only; 7.30 to 9.45   MEALS: Set D £21 to £24. Minimum £18 D   SERVICE: not inc, card slips closed   CARDS: Access, Visa   DETAILS: 50 seats. Private parties: 50 main room, 22 private room. Vegetarian meals. Children's helpings. Smart dress preferred. No smoking in dining-room. Wheelchair access (2 steps). Music

---

LLANDDEINIOLEN Gwynedd   map 4

▲ Ty'n Rhos ⅝✳   [NEW ENTRY]

Seion, Llanddeiniolen LL55 3AE
PORT DINORWIC (0248) 670489   COOKING 2
off B4366 on road signposted Seion   COST £24–£32

House in the Vale, as it translates, is a comfortably converted farmhouse with the Straits of Beaumaris and Snowdonia as a backdrop. Cottagey rather than grand (although it has 72 acres of its own), it is filled with antiques, china and a collection of cheese plates, and shows to particularly good effect on long summer evenings. The Kettles are welcoming, and generate an informal and informed impression. The scope for adventurous cooking is limited, given the conservatism that many country restaurants like this are up against, but Ty'n Rhos walks a careful tightrope, operating as riskily as it dare in the circumstances, and offering an attractive and lively blend of the homely and contemporary.

All meals are four courses plus coffee, with one menu offering a no-choice set meal and another listing half a dozen choices at each stage priced according to the main course. Residents may have to ask for the latter. Local supplies, and the Kettles' own vegetable and herb garden, get the kitchen off to a flying start. Welsh lamb may be honey-roasted with a herb-scented jus, and fish is well reported: perhaps five different kinds, notably fresh, in a buttery sauce, or mussel soup, or a salmon mousse surrounded by queen scallops in a sorrel sauce. Mastery of the basics has produced smoked duck consommé that is 'beautifully clear and full of flavour', and tasty chicken in 'perfectly cooked' puff pastry. Puddings come in for particular praise: 'brilliant' tarte Tatin, 'stunning' rhubarb in an almond shortbread basket with rhubarb crumble ice-cream, and 'marvellous' Grand Marnier iced soufflé. Welsh cheeses 'in wonderful condition' follow. The clearly set-out wine list offers plenty of choice, 'but doesn't take a week to read'. As so often in Wales, prices are commendably low. House wine is £8, or £1.50 per glass.

CHEFS: Lynda Kettle and Bill Ashton   PROPRIETORS: Nigel and Lynda Kettle   OPEN: Mon to Sat, D only; 7 to 8.30   CLOSED: Christmas and New Year   MEALS: Set D £17.50 to £19.75   SERVICE: not inc, card slips closed   CARDS: Access, Amex, Visa   DETAILS: 30 seats. Private parties: 27 main room, 15 private room. Car park. Vegetarian meals. Children's helpings. No children under 6. Smart dress preferred. No smoking in dining-room. Wheelchair access (1 step). No music   ACCOMMODATION: 11 rooms, all with bath/shower. TV. Phone. B&B £35 to £70. Deposit: 10%. Rooms for disabled. No children under 6. Pets welcome by arrangement. Afternoon teas. Garden. Doors close at 11.30. Confirm by 4.30. Fax: (0248) 670079 (*The Which? Hotel Guide*)

---

*See the inside of the front cover for an explanation of the 1 to 5 rating system
for cooking standards.*

Walnut Tree Inn |

Llandewi Skirrid NP7 8AW
ABERGAVENNY (0873) 852797   COOKING 4
on B4521, 3m NE of Abergavenny   COST £26–£63

Now into its fourth decade, the Walnut Tree has gone from being a simple restaurant in a pub on a B-road just outside Abergavenny to what it is today: a simple restaurant in a pub on a B road just outside Abergavenny. It is normally bursting at the seams. No bookings are taken for the informal bistro, the dining-room is small, and the entrance bar is tiny. Everybody feels cramped, but it is a happy place, where customers and staff feel they are on an equal footing. Enough reporters are grateful that the Taruschios have not decamped to a grand hotel, as others in their successful circumstances might have done, and have kept prices within reason. For this, people are willing to sacrifice some comfort.

The same vast menu is available throughout, with no obligation to follow the three-course format. The deceptively simple food does not try to impress with expensive ingredients, is not classically French nor hooked on elaborate saucing. Most of all, it spurns fashion, is proudly down to earth and has grown organically over the years, out of the real experiences of the owners. The foundations are Franco's Italian background, an interest in Thai food forged long before anybody else got wind of it, a French input from the beginning, and a Welsh element that sprang up naturally from the location.

In spring, local roast suckling lamb on the bone with hints of rosemary and garlic comes with a simple, unthickened sauce. Lady Llanover's salt duck is 'wafer-thin slices, pink and tender, with an excellent gooseberry pickle and pleasantly spicy pickled damsons, which complemented the meat perfectly'. Fish also comes in for praise. Brodetto, a refined version of a peasant dish from the Italian Marches, combines langoustines, mussels, chunks of skate, monkfish and sole, all fresh and full of flavour, in a robust sauce of fish juices, tomatoes, onion, garlic and white wine. Nevertheless, the food can divide reporters. On the one hand, some individual items may not be particularly distinguished – 'a perfectly ordinary pub meal which did not impress', wrote one. But the fact that the kitchen can turn out a great variety of dishes of consistent quality counts for something. 'The whole is more than the sum of its parts,' maintained an inspector, for whom 'the unpretentiousness of the place belies a subtle and refined culinary excellence'.

Meals might finish with Gorgonzola, mature Cheddar and a smoked ewes' milk cheese served with home-made walnut bread and a salami of ham and figs, or with caramelised apple tart and elderflower ice-cream. Service is generally cheerful, informal and efficient, although it has lapses, leaving one reporter feeling 'forgotten and unloved'. A vigorous Italian section is to be expected on the wine list, which enthusiastically embraces eccentricities of grape variety and style, throws in some very odd names, and generally revels in the glorious variety of Italian wines to which most other restaurants pay only lip service. Good value extends to French and token New World wines. House wine is £9.75.

See the back of the Guide *for a listing of all restaurants in the Main Entries sections.*

CHEF: Franco Taruschio   PROPRIETORS: Franco and Ann Taruschio   OPEN: Tue to Sat; 12.15 to 3.15 (bistro only), 7.15 to 10.15   MEALS: alc (main courses £7 to £23). Cover £1 dining-room SERVICE: not inc   DETAILS: dining-room 46 seats, bistro 56 seats. 5 tables outside. Private parties: 46 main room. Car park. Vegetarian meals. Children's helpings on request. Wheelchair access (also WC). No music. Air-conditioned

LLANDRILLO Clwyd	map 4

▲ *Tyddyn Llan*

Llandrillo LL21 0ST
LLANDRILLO (049 084) 264
changes to (0490) 440264 in autumn 1994   COOKING 3
on B4401, 4½m S of Corwen   COST £19–£40

The elegant Georgian farmhouse has been sympathetically enlarged, and there is a generous feeling of space. It is a quiet spot, with plenty of good walks and a host of other healthy outdoor pursuits. The lounge is full of squashy sofas and interesting magazines. French windows lead from the modern dining-room – done out in soft yellow and grey-blue – to the garden and to mountain views, and the Kindreds have planted an Elizabethan-style herb garden for the kitchen.

Some of Dominic Gilbert's cooking has a boldness about it – in particular a leitmotif of spicy sweetness – that may not please everybody, but we have to applaud its character and individuality. One evening, all three first courses touched on it: scrambled egg with rhubarb and cashew nuts, chicken livers with spicy fruit chutney, hot confit leg of guinea-fowl with pickled kumquats. Whatever else, the flavours make diners sit up and take notice.

But while meals get off to a thumping start, main courses can rein back a little. Chicken breast may be served with tarragon sauce, for example, and tender Welsh lamb with a rosemary jus, or else in a navarin with spring vegetables. There is no doubting the quality of the meat. 'We buy only when we know the animals have been humanely treated and farmed in the traditional way,' writes Bridget Kindred. Roast rib of well-hung Welsh Black beef is 'superb, pink in the middle, thickly sliced, with a rim of crisp fat', enthused one visitor. Vegetables on side plates do not get much support, but there is always a vegetarian dish on the menu: risotto perhaps, or a mille-feuille.

'A cheeseboard of unpronounceable Welsh cheeses' might include Pencarreg, or Hen Sir, a mature Cheddar from Pwllheli, all in good condition. 'This must be good, I've heard of it,' wrote one reporter who enjoyed a bottle of Louis Latour's light but attractive Pinot Noir, the house red burgundy (£15), from the enterprising range of wines with some reasonable prices. Ten house wines from £7.50 introduce the list.

CHEF: Dominic Gilbert   PROPRIETORS: Peter and Bridget Kindred   OPEN: all week; 12.30 to 2, 7 to 9.30   CLOSED: first week Feb   MEALS: Set L £10 (2 courses) to £12.50, Set D £21.50 to £23.50   SERVICE: not inc, card slips closed   CARDS: Access, Visa   DETAILS: 95 seats. 4 tables outside. Private parties: 50 main room, 40 and 50 private rooms. Car park. Vegetarian meals. Children's helpings. Smart dress preferred. No cigars/pipes in dining-room. Wheelchair access (also WC). Music   ACCOMMODATION: 10 rooms, all with bath/shower. Phone. B&B £56.50 to £97. Deposit: £25. Children welcome. Baby facilities. Pets welcome by arrangement (not in public areas). Afternoon teas. Garden. Fishing. Doors close at midnight. Confirm by 6. Fax: (049 084) 414, changes to (0490) 440414 in autumn 1994 (*The Which? Hotel Guide*)

▲ Bodysgallen Hall ▼

Llanrhos, Llandudno LL30 1RS
ABERCONWY (0492) 584466　　　　　　　　　　　NEW CHEF
off A470, 2m SE of Llandudno　　　　　　　　　　COST £22–£50

Bodysgallen is a seventeenth-century house set in magnificent grounds on the outskirts of Llandudno, with views over Snowdonia. It is one of the finest hotels in North Wales, and has been restored to its former glory by Historic House Hotels, with magnificent décor, exquisite antique furniture, great chandeliers, beautiful floral arrangements, a deeply comfortable library, and a grand piano in the dining-room.

In contrast to the hotel, Mair Lewis's cooking has been homely: smoked trout fillet with horseradish mayonnaise, a trio of fish with prawns in white wine sauce, and iced strawberry parfait on a mango coulis, for example. There have been good roasts too, including loin of pork and sirloin of Welsh beef with Yorkshire pudding. As we go to press, however, Mair Lewis is leaving, hence no score for cooking.

Although fine wines are plentiful they do not swamp the field, so good drinking can be had at all levels. A page of wines all at £15 a bottle is handy for anybody who does not want to plough through the entire list, and there is a generous supply of half-bottles. Half a dozen house wines begin at £11.75. CELLARMAN'S CHOICE: Minervois, Ch. la Grave Rouge 1990, £15; Vins de pays des Côtes de Thongue, Marsanne 1992, £15. Reports, please.

PROPRIETOR: Historic House Hotels Ltd　OPEN: all week; 12.30 to 2, 7.30 to 9.30　MEALS: Set L Mon to Sat £13.90 (2 courses) to £15.90, Sun £16.50, Set D £27.50 to £29.95　SERVICE: net prices, card slips closed　CARDS: Access, Amex, Diners, Visa　DETAILS: 80 seats. Private parties: 48 main room, 40 private rooms. Car park. Vegetarian meals. No children under 8. Jacket and tie. No smoking during meals. No cigars/pipes in dining-room. Wheelchair access (2 steps). Music　ACCOMMODATION: 28 rooms, all with bath/shower. TV. Phone. B&B £96 to £179. 1 room for disabled. No children under 8. Pets welcome in some rooms. Afternoon teas. Garden. Tennis. Confirm by 5. Fax: (0492) 582519 (The Which? Hotel Guide)

Martin's　　　　　　　　　　　　　　　　　NEW ENTRY

11 Mostyn Avenue, Craig-y-Don,
Llandudno LL30 1YS　　　　　　　　　　　　　COOKING 1*
ABERCONWY (0492) 870070　　　　　　　　　　COST £22–£36

Martin James opened here early in 1992, his first solo venture, after a stint at Bodysgallen Hall (see entry above). The two dining-rooms, with windows blocked to seal off the outside world, sentimental pictures on the walls, and 'a tub filled with plastic houseplants, with a cuddly toy climbing up the stem of one', seem at odds with what the kitchen can produce.

What appears on the plate can be good: a hot chicken mousse, wrapped in paper-thin slices of asparagus, sits in a sharp lemon butter sauce with asparagus and turned vegetables at quarter-hour intervals around the edge. Not only is timing accurate and technique capable, but ingredients too show an eye for quality. An inspector's roast loin of new-season Welsh lamb was juicy with lots of flavour. It came pink, with cranberry and onion marmalade and a mound of piped mashed potato, the latter somewhat unnecessary in view of the six vegetables (including potatoes) that arrived on a side plate. Puddings can be impressive: a six-inch cartwheel of excellent, very thin, flat puff pastry topped with thin slices of good apple is one example. The perfunctory 20-bottle wine list keeps prices low, with house vin de pays at £7.50 (£1.60 per glass).

CHEF/PROPRIETOR: Martin James   OPEN: Tue to Sat, D Only; 7 to 9.45. Christmas L bookings by arrangement   CLOSED: first 2 weeks Jan   MEALS: alc (main courses £8 to £10.50)   SERVICE: not inc, card slips closed   CARDS: Access, Amex, Visa   DETAILS: 30 seats. Private parties: 30 main room. Vegetarian meals. Children welcome. Smart dress preferred. No music

Richard's £

| 7 Church Walks, Llandudno LL30 2HD | COOKING 1 |
| LLANDUDNO (0492) 877924 and 875315 | COST £17–£33 |

Regular full houses testify to the success of Richard Hendey's bistro in a street of terraced guest-houses. The restaurant is on two levels, and the décor is all stone-tiled floors and closely packed bare wooden tables, with an open kitchen at the rear. Turnover is fast, prices are reasonable and the cooking is generally sound. The printed menu is backed up by a blackboard of specials along the lines of lentil and cheese pâté and chargrilled pigeon breasts with port and redcurrants. Fish is a strong suit: halibut with spinach and champagne sauce, local crab salad, and boneless cod steak au poivre are typical. Vegetables are served in generous portions. Lemon tart, toffee and hazelnut cheesecake, and chocolate truffle terrine feature among the sweets. 'Really good' bottomless cups of coffee round things off. The reasonably priced, workmanlike wine list is supplemented by a regularly changing collection of 'fine' wines. Romanian house wine is £6.95.

CHEFS: Richard Hendey and Mark Roberts   PROPRIETOR: Richard Hendey   OPEN: all week, D only; 6 to 10   MEALS: alc (main courses £8 to £13)   SERVICE: net prices, card slips closed   CARDS: Access, Amex, Visa   DETAILS: 48 seats. Private parties: 20 main room, 20 private room. Vegetarian meals. Children's helpings. No-smoking area. Music

▲ St Tudno Hotel ⁑✳

| Promenade, Llandudno LL30 2LP | COOKING 2 |
| LLANDUDNO (0492) 874411 | COST £21–£43 |

Since the early '70s, the Blands have nurtured this small hotel opposite John Betjeman's favourite pier, and it is now an establishment of some distinction. A feeling of personal pride, care and interest pervades the whole place. Meals are served in a luxuriantly decorated dining-room with 'spring garden green' colour schemes, heavy curtains and white wooden trellises. Dinner runs to five courses, and the kitchen puts great emphasis on local ingredients and seasonal produce. Crab and laverbread tart with chive sauce, and Welsh lamb cutlets with wild mushrooms, are close to home, while grilled goats' cheese with crispy bacon and walnuts, and collops of veal with blue cheese sauce and green noodles show other influences. Vegetables are plentiful and seconds are offered. Desserts draw enthusiastic comments: 'rich, tangy' passion-fruit syllabub, 'light, buttery' bread-and-butter pudding, 'highly desirable' treacle tart. Organically produced

Welsh cheeses round things off. Mrs Bland is an 'effusive', ever-present hostess, although her staff can be more self-effacing. The revamped wine list from Bibendum Wine offers a well-spread choice and an excellent showing of halves. House wines start at £9.50.

CHEFS: David Harding and Ian Watson PROPRIETORS: Martin and Janette Bland OPEN: all week; 12.30 to 2, 7 to 9.30 (9 Sun) MEALS: Set L £14.50, Set D £26 SERVICE: not inc, card slips closed CARDS: Access, Amex, Diners, Visa DETAILS: 55 seats. Private parties: 30 main room. Car park. Vegetarian meals. Children's helpings. No very young children D. Smart dress preferred. No smoking in dining-room. Wheelchair access (3 steps). No music. Air-conditioned ACCOMMODATION: 21 rooms, all with bath/shower. TV. Phone. B&B £65 to £130. Deposit: £25. Lift. Children welcome. Baby facilities. Pets by arrangement. Afternoon teas. Swimming-pool. Doors close at 11.30. Fax: (0492) 860407 (*The Which? Hotel Guide*)

LLANFIHANGEL NANT MELAN Powys   map 4

▲ *Red Lion Inn* ⁵⁄ ✳ £   NEW ENTRY

Llanfihangel nant Melan,
nr New Radnor LD8 2TN
NEW RADNOR (054 421) 220   COOKING 1
on A44, 3m W of New Radnor   COST £12–£28

The pub is right on the A44, but in the middle of nowhere as 'the traffic just goes screaming past'. The Johns family are a godsend to the area. Keith Johns reigns behind the bar, pulling pints and taking food orders. Meals are eaten in the plant-filled conservatory or in a second dining area complete with an upright piano. Daily menus are chalked on blackboards and the emphasis is on local produce: lamb, duck, ice-creams, goats' cheese and first-rate breads. Lunch is simple pub grub, but chef Gareth Johns flexes his culinary muscles for an evening repertoire that might include baked wild sewin with home-pickled samphire or medallions of venison with chanterelles and port. The strength of his cooking is to pair very good cuts of meat or fish with, often, 'a really brilliant sauce', as in Wye salmon with mint and marjoram or duck with walnut and madeira. Sweets include a first-rate truffle cake courtesy of Alastair Little. Service is pleasant and observant, and wine prices – house wine is £4.95, for example – are exceptional.

CHEF: Gareth Johns PROPRIETORS: Keith, Elizabeth and Gareth Johns OPEN: all week; 12 to 2.15, 6.30 to 9.30 (7 to 9 Sun) MEALS: alc (main courses L £3.50 to £5, D £4.25 to £11) SERVICE: not inc, card slips closed CARDS: Access, Visa DETAILS: 60 seats. 4 tables outside. Private parties: 20 main room. Car park. Vegetarian meals. Children's helpings. No smoking in 1 dining-room. Music ACCOMMODATION: 3 rooms, all with bath/shower. B&B £17.50 to £30. Children welcome. Pets by arrangement. Afternoon teas. Garden. Doors close at 11pm. Confirm by 11am

---

Prices quoted in the Guide *are based on information supplied by restaurateurs. The prices quoted at the top of each entry represent a range, from the lowest meal price to the highest; the latter is inflated by 20 per cent to take account of likely price rises during the year of the* Guide.

LLANGAMMARCH WELLS Powys   map 4

▲ *Lake Country House* ▼ ⚒

Llangammarch Wells LD4 4BS
LLANGAMMARCH WELLS (0591) 620202
and 620474   COOKING 1*
off A483 at Garth, 6m W of Builth Wells   COST £20–£44

There is certainly plenty to do in the vicinity of this charmingly decorated
country house. Pony-trekking, golf and shooting clay pigeons are all on offer,
and anglers should know that the rivers teem with trout. The imposing
half-timbered exterior does nothing to prepare visitors for the swathes of floral
flounce within.

Richard Arnold's cooking is in similar vein. Daily-changing menus reflect a
four-course structure, the first always a soup. Layers of ingredients pile up in the
descriptions, raising the stakes of expectation. On a June evening, the soup was
a 'very correctly seasoned' courgette and rosemary that went well with
home-made tomato and olive bread. An intermediate dish of mixed seafood in a
pastry parcel had good textures and a sauce in which butter and lemon
predominated over the advertised ginger and Pernod, while quail with
honey-roast peppers on a salad was 'delicious'. Main courses were galantine of
guinea-fowl stuffed with watercress, which showed intricate technique brought
off 'amazingly well', and local venison done in a roulade with rosemary and
juniper on a bed of rather sweet red cabbage and a port sauce. Cheeses were
good, but puddings let the side down. The formidable wine list runs to well over
300 bins, the exhaustive list of clarets ascending through the classed growths to
the insane majesty of Mouton '70 at £235.50. Burgundies are less great, Alsace is
very cursory, but a good Spanish selection makes amends, and there is even a
Swiss wine. Some mark-ups are high. House French is £9.75.

CHEF: Richard Arnold   PROPRIETORS: Jean-Pierre and Jan Mifsud   OPEN: all week; 12.30 to 2,
7.30 to 9.15   MEALS: Set L £12.50 to £15.50, Set D £24.50   SERVICE: card slips closed
CARDS: Access, Amex, Diners, Visa   DETAILS: 60 seats. Private parties: 70 main room, 20 and 70
private rooms. Car park. Vegetarian meals. No children under 8 D. Smart dress preferred. No
smoking in dining-room. Wheelchair access (also WC). No music   ACCOMMODATION: 19 rooms,
all with bath/shower. TV. Phone. B&B £75 to £120. Deposit: £40. Rooms for disabled. Children
welcome. Pets welcome (not in public rooms). Afternoon teas. Garden. Tennis. Fishing.
Snooker. Fax: (0591) 620457 (*The Which? Hotel Guide*)

LLANGOLLEN Clwyd   map 4

▲ *Gales* ▼ £

18 Bridge Street, Llangollen LL20 8PF   COOKING 1
LLANGOLLEN (0978) 860089   COST £13–£22

'A wine bar with food as well as a wine bar with rooms,' say the owners – Gales
has a great deal going for it. Visitors endorse the informal, relaxed atmosphere
and the appetising platefuls of home-cooked food served up in a setting of
panelling and church pews. Home-made soups, pâté, honeyed chicken wings
and salads built around smoked meat, poultry and fish are the mainstays;
otherwise go for a hot dish such as pork pilaff or chicken casserole. After this,

home-made ice-cream seems an appropriate finale for many regulars. Sensible choice and good prices on the main wine list make it difficult not to drink several bottles. Another mark of the Gales' passion is the fine wine list, which offers mature bottles also at knock-down prices. They are doing what all restaurateurs should: laying down wines for the future and selling them with a modest mark-up rather than at prevailing market prices. House wine is £6.95. CELLARMAN'S CHOICE: Petit Chablis 1992, Bruno Hamelin, £13.95; Rhône 1992, Cuvée André Sándler, £6.95.

CHEFS: Jenny Johnston, Joanne Thomas and John Gosling   PROPRIETORS: Richard and Gillie Gale   OPEN: Mon to Sat; 12 to 2, 6 to 10   MEALS: alc (main courses £4.50 to £6.50)   SERVICE: not inc   CARDS: Access, Visa   DETAILS: 80 seats. Private parties: 20 main room. Car park. Vegetarian meals. Children's helpings. Wheelchair access (1 step). Music   ACCOMMODATION: 14 rooms, all with bath/shower. TV. Phone. B&B £30 to £46.50. Children welcome. Baby facilities. Pets by arrangement. Confirm by 6 (*The Which? Hotel Guide*)

LLANSANFFRAID GLAN CONWY Gwynedd   map 4

▲ *Old Rectory* ⁵✕ ▮

Llanrwst Road, Llansanffraid Glan Conwy,
nr Conwy LL28 5LF
ABERCONWY (0492) 580611   COOKING 3
on A470, ½m S of junction with A55   COST £39–£47

Perched at the top of a short, steep incline, this small Georgian house is stuffed full of wood panelling, pictures, drapes, cushions, fabrics and books. The setting is magnificent, with views of Snowdon and the Conwy estuary (watch the tide come in) across to the castle, floodlit at night. The food looks a picture too, 'and tastes as good as it looks'. The four-course fixed-price menu gives no choice until cheese, when the alternatives are a green salad or a sorbet. Pudding is a choice of two; both are brought to table, and the unwanted dish returned to store. Don't arrange anything else for the evening, because there are long waits between courses and dinner can easily last four hours.

The raw materials are good, and the cooking, which sometimes requires intricate timings, is accomplished. One meal began, after first-rate canapés, with fresh fillet of sole (landed at Conwy) wrapped in thin leaves of courgette and carrot, baked, and served in a pool of beautifully spiced pink sauce, somewhere between rouille and aïoli. The main course was even better, piling sliced duck breast – 'outstanding for its taste and soft texture' – on top of a flat round of potato cake, with crisply baked pastry underneath that, soaking up the stock-based sauce, which was nicely spiked with fresh ginger. Excellent Welsh cheeses preceded a dome of coffee and chocolate marquise, with 'a moat of coffee-bean sauce tasting of real beans'.

Service charms, and the wine list (where everything is underlined, which rather defeats the object) combines interest, reliability and value across the board. This is the place to drink the clarets and burgundies that other lists have rendered expensively untouchable, although all sections are very strong. That goes for house wine too, around £12 a bottle (£2.50 per glass). CELLARMAN'S CHOICE: Franschhoek Dieu Donné Chardonnay 1992, £15.90; Tim Adams Shiraz 1990, £15.90.

CHEF: Wendy Vaughan   PROPRIETORS: Michael and Wendy Vaughan   OPEN: all week, D only; 7.30 for 8   MEALS: Set D £27.50   SERVICE: not inc, card slips closed   CARDS: Access, Amex, Diners, Visa   DETAILS: 16 seats. Private parties: 12 main room. Car park. Vegetarian meals with prior notice. No children under 5. Smart dress preferred. No smoking in dining-room. Wheelchair access (1 step). No music   ACCOMMODATION: 6 rooms, all with bath/shower. TV. Phone. D,B&B £89.50 to £159. No children over 9 months and under 5 years. Pets welcome in Coach House and bedrooms only. Garden. Doors close at 11.30. Fax: (0492) 584555 (*The Which? Hotel Guide*)

LLANWDDYN Powys　　　　　　　　　　　　　　　　　　　　　　　　map 4

▲ *Lake Vyrnwy Hotel* ⅙✳

Lake Vyrnwy, Llanwddyn SY10 0LY
LLANWDDYN (069 173) 692　　　　　　　　　　　　　　　　　　　COOKING 1*
on B4393, at SE end of Lake Vyrnwy　　　　　　　　　　　　　　COST £19–£36

The location is brilliant. Lake Vyrnwy was created when a massive Victorian dam was built, and the hotel is a huge edifice of local stone standing high above the water. All around is dramatic countryside, where birds outnumber humans. Everyone wants to sit in the conservatory and soak up the panoramic views; otherwise, meals are taken in the pink dining-room. Andrew Wood's cooking has improved; techniques are sharper, ideas are less fussy. Game and trout are from the estate, and the kitchen garden is in full swing; everything else is made in-house. The daily-changing menu is fixed-price for three courses, and the results are generally on target. One decent meal began with a good-looking layered terrine of trout and smoked salmon, and twice-baked soufflé of Stilton with vermouth sauce, before 'outstanding' chargrilled sirloin of Welsh black beef with roasted shallots and onion confit, then tangy lemon ice-cream with two-fruit coulis. The wine list from Tanners features some good French country wines and New World bottles at realistic prices. House wine is £8.95.

CHEF: Andrew Wood   PROPRIETOR: Market Glen Ltd   OPEN: all week; 12.15 to 1.45, 7.30 to 9.15   MEALS: Set L Mon to Sat £12.75, Sun £13.75, Set D £22.50   SERVICE: not inc, card slips closed   CARDS: Access, Amex, Diners, Visa   DETAILS: 80 seats. Private parties: 120 main room, 140 and 20 private rooms. Car park. Vegetarian meals D. Children's helpings. Smart dress preferred. No smoking in dining-room. Wheelchair access (also WC). No music   ACCOMMODATION: 37 rooms, all with bath/shower. TV. Phone. B&B £55.50 to £122.50. Children welcome. Baby facilities. Pets welcome (not in public rooms). Afternoon teas. Garden. Tennis. Fishing. Doors close at 11. Fax: (069 173) 259 (*The Which? Hotel Guide*)

All details are as accurate as possible at the time of going to press, but chefs and owners often change, and it is wise to check by telephone before making a special journey. Many readers have been disappointed when set-price bargain meals are no longer available. Ask when booking.

The Guide *relies on feedback from its readers. Especially welcome are reports on new restaurants appearing in the book for the first time. All letters to the* Guide *are acknowledged.*

map 4

Seguendo di Stagioni ♟

Harford, nr Pumpsaint,
Llanwrda SA19 8DT
PUMPSAINT (0558) 650671
on A482 between Llanwrda and Lampeter,   COOKING 1
1½m NW of Pumpsaint   COST £18–£33

For some, this is 'a real find in the middle of nowhere', as one reporter described this remote and beautiful part of Wales. Another adds: 'People should be warned that it is an unusual, if not eccentric, restaurant.' A voice at the end of the telephone announces that it is 'Pigs 'n' Piglets', in which unassuming guise it was once a transport café.

Inside is a single low-ceilinged dining-room with wicker and bamboo chairs, and a serious cooking venture incorporating a wine business. Aldo Steccanella's enthusiasm and imagination move the whole thing along with gusto. He believes in the power of food to unite people, echoing the sentiments that bring extended Italian families together around the table. Here the job is helped by grilled vegetables with balsamic vinegar dressing, ravioli filled with braised beef in a butter, sage and pecorino sauce, and stuffed chicken slices: 'whole chicken boned, stuffed, cooked and sliced. Wonderful'. Fish is usually local, spider crab turned up on the menu one day, and puddings are as traditional as tiramisù and zabaglione. The advice is to 'first read the menu, and then ask him what he recommends'. Ask too for advice on pairing wine and food: Mr Steccanella is genuinely interested. Although short, the list packs in some real gems at genuinely low prices, every bottle a steal. House Merlot and Tocai del Veneto are £7.50 a bottle. CELLARMAN'S CHOICE: Valpolicella Classico Palazzo della Torre 1990, Allegrini, £14.95; Arneis Cru San Michele 1992, Deltetto, £14.95.

CHEF: Aldo Steccanella   PROPRIETOR: Jennifer Taylor   OPEN: Tue to Sat D; 7 to 10.15; and Sun L; 12 to 3.30 (bookings only)   MEALS: alc (main courses £9 to £13.50). Set L Sun £12.50, Set D £8.55   SERVICE: not inc, card slips closed   CARDS: Access, Visa   DETAILS: 40 seats. 4 tables outside. Private parties: 40 main room. Car park. Vegetarian meals. Children welcome. Smart dress preferred. No music. Fax: (0558) 650671

LLANWRTYD WELLS Powys   map 4

▲ *Carlton House* ⁙   POWYS 1995 FLAVOUR | NEW ENTRY |

Dolycoed Road, Llanwrtyd Wells LD5 4SN   COOKING 3*
LLANWRTYD WELLS (0591) 610248   COST £22–£35

'I couldn't get a booking for a Thursday because they were full,' noted a surprised reporter, who was grateful to make it on another evening. The hotel, Edwardian and with the air of a glorified guesthouse, is in a side street that is 'not particularly prepossessing, even for Llanwrtyd Wells'. Big bay windows, however, endow the small lounge and dining-room with some style. The Gilchrists opened here in 1991: she cooks, he does front-of-house.

If there is no obvious pattern to the cooking, that may be because 'it is a bit like the chef's mind: all over the place', according to the chef herself. But that merely reflects her insatiable appetite for ideas, irrespective of provenance. Tagliatelle with wild mushrooms, roasted vegetables with couscous, and chicken Val de Loire give an idea of the range. In addition, an inspector found that 'they have quite a few hoary-sounding dishes on the menu: wiener schnitzel for goodness sake! And then when you actually get the dish – venison with Cumberland sauce, in my case – it is absolutely fantastic.' There is nothing old-fashioned or heavy about the cooking. Raw materials are extremely good, flavours are clear and fine, and flavour combinations can be 'brilliant'. 'The vegetables were the best I've had as far back as I can remember' was the enthusiastic view of intensely flavoured carrot purée, and sautéd and steamed green cabbage was 'simply 10 times as good as any other cabbage I've eaten'.

'It is worth a visit just for the cinnamon ice-cream,' claims one, who enjoyed its contribution to a subtly spiced pear in a brandy-snap basket on a pool of spiced syrup. Flavour contrasts and combinations are well thought out, even down to the nibbles of prawn toasts – a thick layer of very fresh prawns encrusted with sesame seed – and a tiny tartlet with tapénade and half a quail's egg. Bread is good, and the wine list – short, strong on the New World, and with a dozen half-bottles – gives value for money. House Australian is £8.

CHEF: Mary Ann Gilchrist   PROPRIETOR: Dr Alan Gilchrist   OPEN: all week, D only; 7 to 8.30   CLOSED: Christmas, New Year   MEALS: alc (main courses £9.50 to £13). Set D £15   SERVICE: not inc, card slips closed   CARDS: Access, Visa   DETAILS: 12 seats. Private parties: 12 main room. Vegetarian meals. Children welcome. No smoking in dining-room. Music ACCOMMODATION: 6 rooms, 3 with bath/shower. TV. B&B £20 to £46. Deposit: £15. Children welcome. Pets welcome (bedrooms only). Doors close at midnight. Confirm by 6 (*The Which? Hotel Guide*)

LLYSWEN Powys   map 4

▲ *Griffin Inn* 🍴✕

Llyswen LD3 0UR
LLYSWEN (0874) 754241   COOKING 1
on A470 Builth Wells to Brecon road   COST £17–£30

Richard and Dianne Stockton's fifteenth-century 'sporting inn' in the upper Wye Valley is a local food pub *par excellence*. Shooting and fishing are the main attractions, and parties descend on the place year after year. Wye salmon, brook trout and feathered game dominate the menu in season. The owners are now able to oak-smoke some of the catch on the premises, and their cottage garden is a source of vegetables, soft fruit and herbs. The menu, which covers the beamed bar and the neat and tidy dining-room, eschews fireworks in favour of straightforward ideas based on sound ingredients, as in white onion, Llanboidy cheese and Bramley apple soup; poached salmon with a sauce tasting of mustard and cucumber; or roast duckling with apple sauce and wild rabbit stew. Welsh cheeses are an alternative to the list of calorific puddings. Choose from the short, accessible wine list or opt for one of the real ales. House wine is £7.50.

Report forms are at the back of the book; write a letter if you prefer.

CHEF: Eileen Havard PROPRIETORS: Richard and Dianne Stockton OPEN: all week, exc Sun D; 12 to 2, 7 to 9 CLOSED: 25 and 26 Dec MEALS: alc (main courses L £4.50 to £6.50, D £8 to £10.50). Set L Sun £12.50. SERVICE: not inc, card slips closed CARDS: Access, Amex, Diners, Visa DETAILS: 80 seats. 4 tables outside. Private parties: 30 main room, 10 and 30 private rooms. Car park. Vegetarian meals. Children's helpings. Smart dress preferred. No smoking in dining-room. Wheelchair access. No music ACCOMMODATION: 8 rooms, 7 with bath/shower. Phone. B&B £28.50 to £50. Deposit 10%. Children welcome. Pets welcome. Fishing. Doors close at 12.30. Fax: (0874) 754592

MATHRY Dyfed   map 4

Ann FitzGerald's Farmhouse Kitchen ▼

Mabws Fawr, Mathry, SA62 5JB
CROESGOCH (0348) 831347   COOKING 2
off A487, 6m SW of Fishguard   COST £16–£42

The dilapidated buildings that surround this rather plain farmhouse – actually a medieval longhouse – have nothing to do with Ann FitzGerald and her restaurant, which is at the end of a bumpy track, three-quarters of a mile off the A487. The low-ceilinged dining-room, with beams, small-paned windows, Victorian and Oriental china, bright flowers and garish chairs, has 'the sort of charm that appeals more to city-dwellers seeking escape than to a person like myself who was brought up on an actual Welsh hill farm,' notes one. Ann and Lionel FitzGerald are kindly hosts. In the words of one report, 'Their generosity of spirit and relaxed understanding of true hospitality deserve endorsement even without the exemplary culinary ability which is so evident.'

The menu reflects a genuine curiosity about food, and a real wish to find fresh ingredients and cook them in the proper way. Any source from Prunier (for an oyster recipe) to Japan (tempura) is raided, and dishes range from tripe and onions to gnocchi alla romana. The FitzGeralds also see what is under their own noses: for example, scallops from Cardigan Bay are served with Pembrokeshire laverbread. Sometimes two cooking methods are applied to a single dish. Chunks of monkfish are breadcrumbed and deep-fried, and paired with mussels cooked in white wine, saffron, cream and calvados. Alcohol plays a significant role. Madeira, cognac, white wine and orange juice all meet in the sauce that accompanies roast Gressingham duck. Flavours (and seasoning) can be powerful, portions generous: soup is help-yourself from a large tureen. Among vegetables, the dauphinois potatoes stand out, and vegetarians have a whole set dinner menu to themselves. The large selection of cheese might include Nantybwla, Cwmtawe Pecorino, Llangloffan, and Pencarreg. A busy wine list keeps up to date with developments around the world; Italy is mouthwatering. There are no half-bottles, but prices of full ones are so reasonable that they hardly seem necessary. House wines are £8.50. CELLARMAN'S CHOICE: Bourgogne Blanc 1991, £15; Mount Langi Ghiran Shiraz 1990, £16.

CHEFS/PROPRIETORS: Ann and Lionel FitzGerald OPEN: all week; 12 to 2.30, 6 to 9 CLOSED: L Christmas to Easter MEALS: alc (main courses L £4.50 to £12, D £10 to £15). Set L £10, Set L Sun £14, Set D £17 to £21.50 SERVICE: not inc CARDS: Access, Visa DETAILS: 40 seats. 3 tables outside. Private parties: 40 main room. Car park. Vegetarian meals. Children's helpings. No-smoking area. Wheelchair access (also WC). Music

NANTGAREDIG Dyfed   map 4

▲ *Four Seasons*

Cwmtwrch Farm Hotel,
Nantgaredig SA32 7NY
CARMARTHEN (0267) 290238   COOKING 1
on B4310, 1m N of Nantgaredig   COST £19–£34

This family-run restaurant, in converted farm buildings, reflects the bounty of
the Towy Valley. A slate floor and wooden tables set the rustic tone, high ceilings
help the airy feel, and a pleasant, friendly atmosphere pervades. The proprietors
are good hosts. 'Farmhouse is the style of cooking,' observes a reporter who
enjoyed hot smoked haddock tart with tarragon sauce, and civet of local venison
with parsley dumplings. Taste has priority over presentation, and portions are
generous. The menu changes daily, and breads, pâtés, soups and puddings are
all made in the restaurant kitchen, along with gravlax. The bounty includes fresh
Towy sewin, wild rabbit and, of course, Welsh lamb. House wines (£8.50 a
bottle, £1.80 a glass) change from week to week, and there are 50 reasonably
priced wines from around the world, plus 10 half-bottles.

CHEFS/PROPRIETORS: Charlotte Pasetti, and Maryann and Simon Wright   OPEN: Mon to Sat;
12.30 to 2.30, 7.30 to 9.30   MEALS: alc L (main courses £6.50 to £13). Set D £16.50   SERVICE:
not inc   DETAILS: 55 seats. Private parties: 45 main room. Car park. Vegetarian meals.
Children's helpings. Music   ACCOMMODATION: 6 rooms, all with bath/shower. B&B £32 to £44.
Deposit: £10. Rooms for disabled. Children welcome. Pets welcome in certain rooms. Garden.
Swimming-pool. Golf. Doors close at midnight. Confirm by 7

NEWPORT Dyfed   map 4

▲ *Cnapan* ⁝✳

East Street, Newport SA42 0SY   COOKING 1*
NEWPORT (0239) 820575   COST £12–£32

The Lloyds and the Coopers take pride in their Welshness ('cnapan' is the name
of an old ball game once popular in South Wales), and their pink-washed
restaurant-with-rooms is cluttered with local books and maps. Knick-knacks
are everywhere, and the place has the 'warm, feminine feel' of a lovingly tended
family home.

Eluned Lloyd and her daughter run the kitchen, and their cooking is
wholesome without being self-righteous. Wholefoods and vegetarian dishes
share the stage with a wide mix of specialities plundered from the cuisines of the
world. Sprigs of lovage and cicely point up dishes ranging from rough pâté to
chicken satay; a leaf of lemon balm is the final flourish for exotically marinated
duck breast with a piquant orange and cherry sauce; while poached salmon
comes with a mussel and laverbread sauce. Soups are served with home-made
hot, garlicky soda bread, vegetables are generous, and Welsh cheeses are kept in
good order. Light meals are available at lunch-time. The short wine list is
described in fond detail; look for the Monnow Valley wine from a tiny vineyard
in Gwent. House wine is £7.35.

631

CHEFS: Eluned Lloyd and Judith Cooper   PROPRIETORS: John and Eluned Lloyd, Michael and Judith Cooper   OPEN: Wed to Mon, exc Sun D (residents only); 12 to 2, 7 to 9   CLOSED: 25 and 26 Dec, Feb, midweek Nov to Mar   MEALS: alc D (main courses £8 to £12.50). Set L Sun £8.75. Light L, exc Sun   SERVICE: not inc, card slips closed   CARDS: Access, Visa   DETAILS: 36 seats. 6 tables outside. Private parties: 30 main room. Car park. Vegetarian meals. Children's helpings. Smart dress preferred. No smoking in dining-room. Wheelchair access (2 steps; also WC). Music   ACCOMMODATION: 5 rooms, all with bath/shower. TV. B&B £38 to £76. Deposit 20%. Children welcome. Baby facilities. Garden. Doors close at midnight. Confirm by 6 (*The Which? Hotel Guide*)

NORTHOP Clwyd   map 4

▲ *Soughton Hall* ⁵⁺✳

Northop CH7 6AB
NORTHOP (0352) 840811   COOKING 2
off A5119, 1m S of Northop   COST £23–£51

The Hall is stunningly beautiful. Built as a bishop's palace in 1714, in a generous 150 acres of parkland, it is approached by a long drive bordered by lime trees, and faces a walled garden with fat, squat yews, formal lawns and flowerbeds. The lounge and dining-room are on the first floor, furnished with fine wooden panelling, good copies of old French tapestries, baroque fireplaces in white marble, and bare wooden floors and tables. Perhaps in an effort to match the surroundings, the ambitious cooking sometimes tries too hard to impress. Certainly some dishes are awash with ingredients: consider pan-fried breast of duckling basted in lavender honey, on an onion and lime marmalade, perfumed with grenadine, finished with a hoisin sauce with liquorice.

At inspection, a terrine of wild mushrooms and supple, tasty, corn-fed chicken with a truffle and walnut vinaigrette looked very attractive, although it probably could have managed without the baked cloves of garlic and tiny dice of madeira jelly. An enormous beef tournedos, accurately cooked, came with a well-reduced sauce of stock, wine and bone marrow, which was stickily sweet and highly seasoned, with truffles and other bits and bobs in it. That same inspector, noting a lack of colour and warmth about the operation, wished they had spent less time on elaborate nibbles and petits fours, and more on improving basics of bread, vegetables and coffee. Yet, when it hits home, the kitchen's potential is evident. A silky smooth, fragrant lemon tart, with an intensely flavoured filling and excellent pastry, is served beautifully simply with a raspberry coulis. House wine is £10.50.

CHEF: Christopher Plummer   PROPRIETORS: John and Rosemary Rodenhurst   OPEN: Mon to Sat; 12 to 2, 7.30 to 9.30   CLOSED: first 2 weeks Jan   MEALS: alc (main courses £10.50 to £18). Set L £14.95, Set D £21.50   SERVICE: not inc   CARDS: Access, Amex, Visa   DETAILS: 45 seats. Private parties: 120 main room, 24 private room. Car park. Vegetarian meals. Children's helpings on request. Jacket and tie. No smoking in dining-room. Music. Air-conditioned ACCOMMODATION: 14 rooms, all with bath/shower. TV. Phone. Air-conditioned. B&B £70 to £119. Deposit 25%. Children welcome by arrangement. Baby facilities. Pets welcome; kennel and run available. Afternoon teas. Garden. Tennis. Fax: (0352) 840382 (*The Which? Hotel Guide*)

See inside the front cover for an explanation of the symbols used at the tops of entries.

PENMAENPOOL Gwynedd

▲ *Penmaenuchaf Hall* ¶ ✺

map 4

Penmaenpool LL40 1YB
DOLGELLAU (0341) 422129
off A493, 2m W of Dolgellau

COOKING 2*
COST £22–£39

Gerard Manley Hopkins, in Welsh Tourist Board mode, hymned the 'treats of Penmaenpool' in the last century. The Hall went up in 1860, a monument to the cotton fortune of one James Taylor of Bolton, whose family crest can still be seen above the front door. It is a handsome pile, situated above the Mawddach Estuary, not that far from the sea. The small dining-room, with its dark oak panelling, may seem a trifle severe initially, but as the nights draw in, the fire crackles and the chandeliers twinkle, and the menu has much to entice.

Lee Jones took over as head chef in the spring, after a short period as sous-chef, and with the plaudit of having been Young Welsh Chef of the Year. It is a four-course, fixed-price format, with soup or sorbet after the opener. An early-spring dinner offered leek and bacon tartlet with oregano hollandaise, halibut ravioli on deep-fried fennel, veal and wild mushroom roulade with cabbage and a pink grapefruit sauce, and loin of Welsh lamb with minted ratatouille and port. This is the modern British idiom at its most unabashed. Most things went well at an inspection meal, although a lighter hand with the salt for some dishes would have been appreciated. Warm oysters with spinach and watercress worked beautifully, and even the sorbet – that solecism of '80s country-house style – was better than expected, a 'piquant and unusual' gazpacho version with asparagus. A crustacean expert could not fault the lobster with green ginger and garlic, and a dessert of mixed fruits on a sabayon with a tuile basket of mead ice-cream provoked raptures. Details like the home-made sesame and cardamom rolls also impress.

The wine list sets out to furnish drinkers with short but intelligent choices from around the world, and largely succeeds. The upward curve in price is a little abrupt, and the request for six hours' notice for decanting presumes an unnatural prescience on the part of diners, but it is a commendable effort none the less. House wines start at £9.85. CELLARMAN'S CHOICE: Rioja Blanco Reserva 1988, Marques de Murrieta, £15.95; Fronsac, Ch. de Carles 1989, £15.50.

CHEF: Lee Jones PROPRIETORS: Mark Watson and Lorraine Fielding OPEN: all week; 12 to 2.30, 7 to 9.30 (9 Sun) MEALS: alc L (main courses £6.75 to £8.50). Set L Sun £13.95, Set D £21.50 SERVICE: not inc, card slips closed CARDS: Access, Amex, Visa DETAILS: 30 seats. Private parties: 75, 18 private rooms. Car park. Vegetarian meals. Children's helpings (not after 8). Smart dress preferred. No smoking in dining-room. Wheelchair access (also WC). Music ACCOMMODATION: 14 rooms, all with bath/shower. TV. Phone. B&B £47.50 to £140. Deposit: £15. Children welcome. Baby facilities. Pets welcome (to stay in gun room only). Afternoon teas. Garden. Fishing. Snooker. Doors close at 11.30. Confirm by 6. Fax: (0341) 422129 (*The Which? Hotel Guide*)

Several sharp operators have tried to extort money from restaurateurs on the promise of an entry in a guidebook that has never appeared. The Good Food Guide *makes no charge for inclusion and does not offer certificates of any kind.*

PONTFAEN Dyfed   map 4

▲ *Tregynon Country Farmhouse Hotel* ✳

Gwaun Valley, Pontfaen SA65 9TU
NEWPORT (0239) 820531
B4313 towards Fishguard, first right, and   COOKING 1
right again for ½m   COST £22–£32

Visitors on their way to this low-ceilinged, stone-walled sixteenth-century farmhouse on the edge of the spectacular Gwaun Valley 'may wonder where they are going as they disappear down winding single-track lanes', but the welcome once they are there is warm. The Heards put a lot of work into the running of the hotel, oak-smoking bacon and gammon themselves and changing the vegetables on a 14-day cycle. Choose your main course in the morning; non-residents may very well pick up the phone at 10am and be given a recitation. Vegetarian dishes are a speciality, but the choice goes beyond that. Rack of lamb with a rosehip, rosemary and elderberry sauce, and breast of duck, left slightly fatty, cooked pink and benefiting from a sauce of Welsh honey, raspberries and calvados were enjoyed at one inspection. A reporter found the Pembrokeshire fish pie too bland (though with 'excellent' pastry), and felt that dishes dominated by sweet sauces were more successful. As for puddings, raspberry meringues were 'excellent' and banoffi pie 'lived up to its reputation'. The wine list globetrots briskly and gathers up many good bottles on its travels, with nearly everything well under £20. With the exception of a sweet Recioto di Soave, it shuns all thought of halves. House French is £7.60.

CHEFS: Peter and Jane Heard, and Sian Phillips   PROPRIETORS: Peter and Jane Heard   OPEN: all week, D only; 7.30 to 8.30 (prior bookings only)   MEALS: Set D £15.50 to £20.50   SERVICE: not inc, card slips closed   CARDS: Access, Visa   DETAILS: 28 seats. Private parties: 16 main room, 12 private room. Car park. Vegetarian meals. Smart dress preferred. No smoking in dining-room. Music   ACCOMMODATION: 8 rooms, all with bath/shower. TV. Phone. B&B £46 to £64 per room. Deposit: 25%. Rooms for disabled. Children welcome. Baby facilities. Afternoon teas. Garden. Fax: (0239) 820808 (*The Which? Hotel Guide*)

PORTHGAIN Dyfed   map 4

Harbour Lights

Porthgain, nr St David's SA62 5BW
CROESGOCH (0348) 831549   COOKING 2*
off A487 at Croesgoch, 4m W of Mathry   COST £18–£33

Porthgain is one of a number of narrow inlets on the south-west Wales coast between St David's and Fishguard. It has a little harbour, single-storey cottages and the expansive ruins of a nineteenth-century stone-crushing works. Harbour Lights, occupying one of the old cottages, has been sensitively modified to suit its current purpose and is very much a family concern. Anne Marie Davies cooks, her husband and mother-in-law run the front-of-house, her sister shuttles between, and her son washes up.

A frequently changing, fixed-price dinner menu and simpler lunch *carte* make enthusiastic use of local meat, fish and crustacea, and it is not unusual for 25lb of laverbread to be got through in the course of a summer week, some of it gratinated with smoked bacon and garlic under a bubbling layer of Welsh cheese. Fresh herbs from the garden are widely used. Reporters have been impressed by the 'deft, pleasant and unobtrusive' approach and precision of flavour in the food, as in a courgette parcel filled with red and yellow peppers on a tomato and basil coulis that 'tasted of all its ingredients'. Herb-encrusted rack of local lamb with roast garlic was 'sweet and tender', while properly matured sirloin was cooked exactly as desired. Copious vegetables included cabbage with lemon and sesame seeds. The cheeseboard hoists the dragon standard high with Llanboidy and Pencarreg in prime condition, while thin apple crêpes with Jersey cream and caramel can be 'delectable'. French house wine is £8.50.

CHEF/PROPRIETOR: Anne Marie Davies   OPEN: Tue to Sat; 12 to 1.45, 6.30 to 9   CLOSED: Dec to 10 Feb   MEALS: Light L (courses £3 to £9.50). Set D £16.50 (2 courses) to £19.50   SERVICE: not inc, card slips closed   CARDS: Access, Visa   DETAILS: 30 seats. 5 tables outside. Private parties: 20 main room. Vegetarian meals. Children welcome L. Smart dress preferred. No smoking during D. Wheelchair access (1 step). Music

---

PORTMEIRION Gwynedd   map 4

▲ *Hotel Portmeirion* ♥ ⁙✳

Portmeirion LL48 6ET
PENRHYNDEUDRAETH (0766) 770228   COOKING 1*
off A487, signposted from Minffordd   COST £20–£40

'The setting is quite magical, beside the water in a village which may be a cliché, but is a pretty one,' writes a reporter, succumbing to the glorious eccentricity of this early example of theme-parkery. Architect Sir Clough Williams-Ellis did it here long before Euro-Disney, and far better. Herons fish beside the quay, tranquillity pervades the 70 acres of subtropical gardens, and the food in the light, conservatory-like dining-room lives up to expectations.

Craig Hindley's cooking does not aim to be as exuberant as the village, but it does apply Mediterranean ideas to good-quality game from local sportsmen, whatever the fishermen catch, and fruit and vegetables from Anglesey farms. First-class loin of Welsh lamb is partnered by a tagliatelle of creamed leeks and garlic, while tomatoes, courgettes and fennel are the sort of things that turn up with white fish. This is a happy convergence. Saucing is light enough to add interest without obscuring other tastes, and applies equally to puddings: the aniseed flavour in the vanilla cream that surrounds summer fruits, for example.

Service comes in for high praise, steering a course between tight control and youthful enthusiasm that charms the socks off most people. Wines are very reasonably priced, with many well-chosen bottles; the special house selection of wines under £13 is particularly helpful. CELLARMAN'S CHOICE: St-Estèphe, Ch. Calon-Ségur 1985, £27.50; Pant Teg, Cyfuniad Sych 1993, £12.50.

CELLARMAN'S CHOICE: *Wines recommended by the restaurateur, normally more expensive than house wine.*

CHEF: Craig Hindley   PROPRIETOR: Portmeirion Ltd   OPEN: all week, exc Mon L; 12.30 to 2.30, 7 to 9.30   CLOSED: 8 Jan to 3 Feb   MEALS: Set L £13.50, Set L Sun £16, Set D £20 (2 courses) to £25   SERVICE: not inc, card slips closed   CARDS: Access, Amex, Diners, Visa   DETAILS: 100 seats. 4 tables outside. Private parties: 16 main room, 16 and 35 private rooms. Car park. Vegetarian meals. Children's helpings. Jacket and tie. No smoking in dining-room. No music ACCOMMODATION: 34 rooms, all with bath/shower. TV. Phone. B&B £56.50 to £132. Children welcome. Pets welcome. Afternoon teas. Garden. Swimming-pool. Tennis. Fax: (0766) 771331 (*The Which? Hotel Guide*)

PWLLHELI Gwynedd   map 4

▲ *Plas Bodegroes* 🍷 ✳️

Nefyn Road, Pwllheli LL53 5TH
PWLLHELI (0758) 612363   COOKING 4
on A497, 1½m W of Pwllheli   COST £35–£46

Christopher Chown has his plate full these days (see entry, Hole-in-the-Wall, Bath), but his second chef now runs the kitchen of this secluded Georgian manor house. As one reporter observed, 'It would worry me to think my deputy was doing it so well.' The garden is hidden from the outside world, contributing to the restful atmosphere, and the view from the verandah is of an ancient avenue of tall beech trees, carpeted with bluebells in spring. Art-lined walls and carefully designed lighting in the dining-room add to the sense of sophistication.

The pattern for dinner is five courses, with a choice of four or five items per course; the value and service are regularly praised, and a light hand with saucing and portion size renders the whole meal undaunting. The repertoire is remarkably stable, which suggests a lack of development, but the kitchen's forte is not so much experiment and innovation as quiet accomplishment. A ballottine of guinea-fowl with finely chopped apricot, garnished with juliennes of cooked beetroot and bright green pistachios, catches it in classical vein. At the same time, the kitchen is not above small lamb kebabs or light smoked haddock fish-cakes with tartare sauce. Proximity to the coast brings excellent fish, usually the focus of second courses. The conservatism of roast fillet of salmon with spinach and chive sauce is balanced by the more upbeat flavours of a hotpot of mussels and scallops with lemon grass and chillies. A warm salad of monkfish was 'out of this world', partly because the thick chunk was so fresh, and partly because of the thin strips of smoked Carmarthen ham scattered around it. The balance of flavours, remarked upon regularly, lifts Plas Bodegroes above any constrictive pigeon-holing of style. Not all, however, is quite hunky-dory. A thick tournedos, cut in two, draped over a mound of 'the most perfect gratin dauphinois imaginable' and cooked rare, had a thin sauce with little flavour, and immature beef is no substitute for the real well-hung thing. An inspector noted also virtually the same salad underlay (with similar dressings) in three out of the five courses.

'It is not often that one can spend £90 on wine and think that you have had a bargain, but that was what we undoubtedly had,' wrote a reporter, in a fairly steady hand, after two-and-a-half bottles of tip-top stuff. The list revels in the excitement of Italian grape varieties, New World fruit, powerful Syrah, classic Bordeaux, heady Burgundy, wonderful Alsace, a good spread of half-bottles and sensationally fair prices. The house selection starts at £10. CELLARMAN'S CHOICE: Gewurtztraminer Herrenweg 1990, Zind-Humbrecht, £20.50; Savigny-lès-Beaune 1988, Les Marconnets, £18.50.

CHEFS: Andrew Price and Christopher Chown PROPRIETORS: Christopher Chown and Gunna à Trødni OPEN: Tue to Sun, D only; 7 to 9.30 CLOSED: Nov to end Feb MEALS: Set D £30 SERVICE: net prices, card slips closed CARDS: Access, Amex, Visa DETAILS: 40 seats. Private parties: 50 main room, 16 private room. Car park. Vegetarian meals with prior notice. Children welcome. No smoking in dining-room. Wheelchair access (1 step; also WC). Music ACCOMMODATION: 8 rooms, all with bath/shower. TV. Phone. B&B £40 to £110. Deposit: £50. Children welcome. Pets by arrangement. Garden. Confirm by 6. Fax: (0758) 701247 (*The Which? Hotel Guide*)

REYNOLDSTON West Glamorgan   map 4

▲ *Fairyhill* ⚲ | NEW ENTRY |

Reynoldston SA3 1BS
GOWER (0792) 390139
from M4 Junction 47 follow signs to
Gower/Gowerton, in Gowerton turn right   COOKING 1
on B4295, turn left to Fairyhill after 10m   COST £20–£44

This early-eighteenth-century house on the Gower Peninsula, with 24 acres of park and woodland, has been a hotel for a decade. At the end of 1993, Paul Davies and Andrew Hetherington (from PA's wine bar in the Mumbles) took over and gave it a lick of paint. They now run it, together with the Camms, as an all-year hotel serving afternoon teas, lunch and dinner in the two dining-rooms and conservatory.

'Modern Welsh' is a fair description of the cooking, which combines Penclawdd cockles with scrambled egg and roasted peppers, and serves laverbread tart with crispy smoked bacon, or Welsh smoked salmon with a lime dressing. Gower lamb and seafood, and local or garden herbs and vegetables, together produce attractive-sounding three-course menus, although execution is not yet a match for the ideas. Puddings might include chocolate mousse with orange sauce or a version of tarte Tatin. The wine list is long (especially in Bordeaux), with producers in Alsace and Beaujolais who are not run-of-the-mill. Italy and the New World are well represented, and mark-ups are about average. There is good drinking under £20, and a fair selection of half-bottles. House French is £8.95. CELLARMAN'S CHOICE: Crozes-Hermitage 1989, Jaboulet, £15.50; St-Helena Pinot Blanc 1991, £15.50.

CHEF: Paul Davies PROPRIETORS: Andrew Hetherington, Paul Davies, Jane and Peter Camm OPEN: all week; 12.30 to 2.15, 7.30 to 9.15 MEALS: Set L Mon to Sat £10.95 (2 courses) to £13.95, Sun £17.50, Set D £22.50 SERVICE: not inc, card slips closed CARDS: Access, Amex, Visa DETAILS: 68 seats. 3 tables outside. Private parties: 45 main room. Car park. Vegetarian meals. Children's helpings. Smart dress preferred. No cigars/pipes in dining-rooms. Wheelchair access (1 step; also WC). Music ACCOMMODATION: 11 rooms, all with bath/shower. TV. Phone. B&B £65 to £95. No children under 8. Pets welcome (not in public rooms). Afternoon teas. Garden. Fax: (0792) 391358 (*The Which? Hotel Guide*)

▲ *This symbol means accommodation is available.*

ROSSETT Clwyd   map 4

Churtons £

Machine House, Chester Road,
Rossett LL12 0HW
ROSSETT (0244) 570163
on B5445, off A483, between Chester   COOKING 1
and Wrexham   COST £18–£38

The setting is a converted barn: 'We crossed the cobbled yard, entered the darkened space, and went straight to the heavy wood bar and looked at the long blackboard menu at the foot of the stairs.' The wooden tables are large enough to seat half a dozen, so people share when it gets busy. Steak is a constant, but there is enough experiment to give regulars a chance to try something different, such as lambs' kidneys in red wine sauce topped with Cheddar cheese. Fish are simply grilled, whether lemon sole with flavoured butter or more exotic barracuda steak with kumquat and caper sauce. Vegetables are praised for simplicity, flavour and accurate cooking. Fish-based pâtés or terrines – prawn and broccoli, for example – share first-course billing with soused herrings and grilled goats' cheese with basil sauce, while blackcurrant tart and lemon cheesecake bring up the rear.

A second branch at Tarporley in Cheshire is run along the same lines. An associate company ships the wines: a fair spread with ample choice under £20. In a reversal of the Bring Your Own idea, these can be taken away at rather advantageous prices, singly or by the case. House wines begin at £7.90.

CHEFS: Ade Garratt, Jackie Lloyd and Louise MacDougall   PROPRIETORS: Nicholas Churton, James Churton and Richard Bowen-Jones   OPEN: Mon to Sat; 12 to 2.15, 7 to 10   CLOSED: 24 Dec to 3 Jan, bank hol Mons   MEALS: alc (main courses £6 to £15)   SERVICE: not inc   CARDS: Access, Amex, Visa   DETAILS: 55 seats. 2 tables outside. Private parties: 20 main room, 12 private room. Car park. Vegetarian meals. Children's helpings on request. No children under 12 (exc Sat L). Wheelchair access (1 step). Music. Air-conditioned. Fax: (0244) 570099

SWANSEA West Glamorgan   map 4

Annie's

---

56 St Helen's Road, Swansea SA1 4BE   COOKING 1
SWANSEA (0792) 655603   COST £24–£29

'I thought I was in heaven, then realised I was on terra firma...in Annie's' was the ecstatic comment from one visitor to this eminently likeable converted schoolhouse. Customers become regulars and few have any complaints about the informal, friendly atmosphere or Ann Gwilym's cooking. Her monthly set menu has a distinct French accent, although local ingredients appear centre stage in unexpected guises: laverbread and cockle tart comes with an orange beurre blanc; mussels are served with coriander, curry sauce and fresh pasta. In summer are the light dishes, often with a Mediterranean slant; in winter the menu is peppered with cassoulets, rillettes and ragoûts. Recent successes have included warm salad of provençale vegetables with Parmesan, roast duck breast with plums and ginger, 'a perfect marriage' of monkfish and cockles with chicory and lettuce sauce, and mango sorbet. The modest French wine list is topped up with a few bottles from Australia. House wine is £8.80.

CHEF/PROPRIETOR: Ann Gwilym OPEN: Tues to Sat, D only (and Mon D summer); 7 to 9.30 (10.30 Fri and Sat) MEALS: Set D £17.50 SERVICE: net prices, card slips closed CARDS: Access, Visa DETAILS: 34 seats. Private parties: 34 main room, 22 private room. Vegetarian meals. Children's helpings. Music

La Braseria

28 Wind Street, Swansea SA1 1DZ
SWANSEA (0792) 469683

COOKING 2
COST £14–£35

Meat is downstairs, fish upstairs in this busy Spanish bodega-style restaurant: 'a happy, noisy place without pretension, similar to the Brasserie trio in Cardiff' (see entry). It certainly pulls in the crowds, especially at lunch-time, when the formula is a set two-course meal for £5. This 'incredible bargain' might begin with garlic mushrooms, oysters, spare ribs or thick slices of tasty gravlax and a fresh, crisp, help-yourself salad with a mustard dressing. 'You choose your food before it is cooked, from a display.' The bulk of it is charcoal-grilled, fried or baked (some in rock salt). Rump steak and chargrilled salmon have impressed for their taste and succulence. Jacket potatoes, French fries, garlic bread and salads are the accompaniments. Wines from Rioja and Penedès are a strength, helped by a string of good clarets. House Rioja is £7.85.

CHEFS: M. Tercero and I. Wing PROPRIETOR: Iceimp Ltd OPEN: Mon to Sat; 12 to 2.30, 7 to 12 CLOSED: 25 Dec MEALS: alc (main courses £6 to £12). Set L £5 (2 courses) SERVICE: not inc, card slips closed CARDS: Access, Amex, Diners, Visa DETAILS: 160 seats. Private parties: 100 main room. No children under 6. Smart dress preferred. Wheelchair access (1 step; also WC). Music

Number One Wind Street

1 Wind Street, Swansea SA1 1DE
SWANSEA (0792) 456996

COOKING 2
COST £18–£33

Kate Taylor has 'consistently provided the best food in Swansea', in the opinion of one reporter, who has followed her career at this restaurant in the centre of town. The bright, modern décor is in restrained good taste, and people find both that and the food 'delightful'. The cooking idiom is described by Kate Taylor herself as a mixture of 'classical and French provincial', though there are nuances of modern Britain in smoked duck breast with a celeriac and walnut salad, veal with lemon and capers, or roast haunch of venison with poached pear and a port sauce. French notes sound in provençale fish soup with aïoli, rillettes of duck, roast woodpigeon with Puy lentils and ham, and steak en croûte. Laverbread is used in a starter with bacon and cockles, and crops up in a sauce with baked sea bass. Desserts offer a classic choice of tarte Tatin, tarte au citron, oeufs à la neige and 'light, delicately flavoured' crème brûlée. Coffee is 'ad lib', and service 'attentive' and friendly. The wine list does an efficient job in seeking out the best value in each of the regions it covers, though it confines itself to France, Spain and Germany, plus one Welsh white. House wines are £6.95.

CHEF: Kate Taylor   PROPRIETORS: Peter Gillen and Kate Taylor   OPEN: Mon to Sat L, Wed to Sat D; 12 to 2.30, 7 to 9.30   CLOSED: bank hols   MEALS: alc (main courses £9 to £12.50). Set L £9.50 (2 courses) to £11.95   SERVICE: not inc   CARDS: Access, Amex, Visa   DETAILS: 40 seats. Private parties: 40 main room. Vegetarian meals. Children's helpings. No pipes in dining-room. Wheelchair access. Music

---

TALSARNAU Gwynedd   map 4

▲ Maes-y-Neuadd ⚡✳

Talsarnau LL47 6YA
HARLECH (0766) 780200   COOKING 2
off B4573, 1m S of Talsarnau   COST £17–£43

The old manor house on a wooded hillside has views across Snowdonia National Park, and plenty of good walks for the energetic. It was built less than a century after Harlech Castle, and sympathetic renovation has turned it into something of a haven for the traveller, with a welcome that is warm and genuine.

When it latches on to a good thing, the kitchen certainly makes the most of it. 'The breads are as good as you say,' wrote one visitor: brown may be baked with mushrooms, or with dates and walnuts, and is sliced at table. The links with local shoots, and with suppliers of fish, lamb, beef and cheese, make an impact on the plate, largely because Peter Jackson's light touch allows them to. He steams brill, salmon and turbot, pot-roasts guinea-fowl, and applies a creamy tarragon sauce to escalope of pork, which he serves with an apple gâteau. Then comes the 'Grand Finale', a selection of three Welsh cheeses – Merlin, perhaps, or Pencarreg or Caerphilly – followed by no fewer than three puddings, not a choice but the whole lot: dessert of the day such as nougatine gâteau, plus a fruity pud like banana mousse on a cinnamon cream sauce, and finally an ice-cream. What with a nibble of warm quail and scallop salad, or terrine of leeks and laverbread to start with, then soup, then a fish course, and sweetmeats with the coffee, it all adds up to a belly-filling nine courses. Few make it to the finishing post.

The kitchen has also diversified over the past year, converting surplus herbs, fruits and vegetables into a range of oils, vinegars, jams, jellies, pickles and chutneys, and providing meals on the Ffestiniog Railway. Wines are predominantly French, priced slightly higher than you might like, but with some interesting bottles. House wines begin at £2.10 a glass.

CHEFS: Peter Jackson   PROPRIETORS: Michael and June Slatter, and Malcolm and Olive Horsfall   OPEN: all week; 12.15 to 1.45, 7 to 9.15   MEALS: Set L £8.75 (2 courses) to £10.75, Set L Sun £13.50, Set D £19.95 to £26.50   SERVICE: not inc, card slips closed   CARDS: Access, Amex, Diners, Visa   DETAILS: 50 seats. Private parties: 50 main room, 16 private room. Car park. Vegetarian meals. Children's helpings. No children under 8. Smart dress preferred. No smoking in dining-room. Wheelchair access (1 step; also WC). Music   ACCOMMODATION: 16 rooms, all with bath/shower. TV. Phone. D,B&B £59 to £192. Deposit: £25. Rooms for disabled. Children welcome. Baby facilities. Pets welcome by arrangement (not in public rooms). Afternoon teas. Garden. Doors close at 11.30. Confirm by 5. Fax: (0766) 780211 (*The Which? Hotel Guide*)

'The only menu shown outside the front door was the starters; maybe they thought the price of the mains might frighten people away.' (On eating in Essex)

TALYLLYN Gwynedd   map 4

▲ Minffordd Hotel §*

Talyllyn LL36 9AJ
CORRIS (0654) 761665
at junction of A487 and B4405,   COOKING 1
8m SW of Dolgellau   COST £23–£27

Jonathan Pickles now runs the show at this converted drover's inn sitting snugly
in the shadow of Cader Idris. Regulars confirm that 'ostensibly nothing has
changed'. The house is still delightfully cosy, the welcome is as warm as ever,
and the easy peacefulness of the place is irresistible. The food is the kind of stuff
that country cooks have been producing for years with the help of trusty Agas;
the repertoire may not evolve, but the results are comforting. Mushroom soup or
egg cocotte with herbs might start things off. A couple of alternative main
courses could take in rainbow trout with Pernod or 'perfectly cooked' chicken
supreme with orange and ginger sauce. Vegetables are done to a turn, and sweets
are 'superb' offerings such as queen of puddings and crème caramel. The Welsh
cheeseboard is 'excellent', as is the coffee. The short, enterprising wine list is
from Tanners. House wine is £7.75.

CHEF: Jonathan Pickles   PROPRIETOR: Jessica Gibbs   OPEN: Mon to Sat D; 7.30 to 8.30
CLOSED: Nov to Mar   MEALS: Set D £18.50   SERVICE: net prices, card slips closed   CARDS:
Access, Visa   DETAILS: 24 seats. Private parties: 24 main room. Car park. Vegetarian meals with
prior notice. Children's helpings. No children under 3. Smart dress preferred. No smoking in
dining-room. Wheelchair access. No music   ACCOMMODATION: 7 rooms, all with bath/shower.
D,B&B £65 to £118. Deposit: 10%. No children under 3. Afternoon teas. Garden. Doors close at
11. Confirm by 6. Fax: (0654) 761517 (The Which? Hotel Guide)

THREE COCKS Powys   map 4

▲ Three Cocks Hotel

Three Cocks LD3 0SL
GLASBURY (0497) 847215   COOKING 2
on A438, between Brecon and Hay-on-Wye   COST £28–£47

The hotel – a fifteenth-century, stone-clad house built around an oak tree –
appears quintessentially British. Inside, however, it has the flavour of old
Belgium. Michael Winstone and his wife once ran a hotel in the Ardennes and
have succeeded in grafting Continental ideas on to a bedrock of Welsh
ingredients. He cooks, she serves. The short menu advertises mussel soup with
finely sliced vegetables, Ardennes ham – of course – with onions pickled in
honey ('a perfect accompaniment', noted one satisfied customer), loin of Welsh
lamb in pastry with duxelles and blue cheese, and breast of duck with sherry and
honey sauce. Wild boar with apples, cranberries and pears cooked in red wine is
reckoned to be well worth the price supplement. Meals finish enticingly with an
array of alluring sweets: 'My policy of trying not to eat puddings has been truly
scuppered,' confessed one convert, who could have chosen between cold apple
mousse with cinnamon sauce or iced nougatine with fruit sauce. A fascinating

range of Belgian beers bolsters the keenly priced, mainly French wine list. House wine is £8.

CHEF: Michael Winstone   PROPRIETORS: Mr and Mrs Michael Winstone   OPEN: Wed to Mon, exc Sun L; 12 to 1.30, 7 to 9   CLOSED: Dec and Jan   MEALS: alc (main courses £13 to £16.50). Set L and D £23   SERVICE: not inc   DETAILS: 30 seats. Private parties: 25 main room. Car park. Vegetarian meals. Children's helpings on request. Smart dress preferred. Music ACCOMMODATION: 7 rooms, all with bath/shower. B&B £60. Children welcome. Baby facilities. Garden. Doors close at midnight. Confirm by 5 (*The Which? Hotel Guide*)

TREFRIW Gwynedd   map 4

Chandler's ✻*

Trefriw LL27 0JH
LLANRWST (0492) 640991   COOKING 1
off B5106, NW of Llanrwst   COST £22–£36

The tag 'brasserie' fits comfortably around this friendly neighbourhood eating place, where décor and trappings matter less than atmosphere. Most of the customers are local and so is much of the produce. Welsh lamb is a permanent fixture, game appears in season, and a strong showing of fish might include anything from Lleyn Peninsula sea bass to Conwy turbot. For one reporter, a salad of warm chicken livers 'couldn't have been executed better'. On one occasion, however, both breast of pheasant and pear and almond tart failed to impress. Vegetarians have approved of hot goats' cheese; other meatless options that should please include the Indian platter, or stuffed buckwheat pancakes with sherry and mushroom sauce. The wine list is a racy, maverick selection with plenty from the New World and a useful scattering of halves. House wines are £8.25.

CHEFS/PROPRIETORS: Adam and Penny Rattenbury, and Tim Kirton   OPEN: Tue to Sat, D only; 7 to 10   CLOSED: 3 weeks Jan to Feb, 3 weeks Oct   MEALS: alc (main courses £8.50 to £13) SERVICE: not inc, card slips closed   CARDS: Access, Visa   DETAILS: 36 seats. Private parties: 30 main room. Car park. Vegetarian meals. Children welcome. No smoking in dining-room. Wheelchair access (2 steps). Music

---

WELSH HOOK Dyfed   map 4

▲ Stone Hall

Welsh Hook, Wolf's Castle SA62 5NS
LETTERSTON (0348) 840212
1½m off A40, between Letterston and   COOKING 1
Wolf's Castle, W of Welsh Hook   COST £22–£35

The restaurant and homely accommodation is set in 10 acres of gardens and woodland, with unusual trees and hybrid rhododendrons and azaleas. The oldest part of the house, with slate floors and rough wooden beams, has survived 600 years well, while the more recent (seventeenth-century) extension is notable for its wood panelling. The Watsons converted it to a hotel in 1984, adopting a traditional French approach to the cooking: snails in garlic butter, duck leg confit with baked apple, or breast with green peppercorns, and scallops in a cream and vermouth sauce. Some of the treatments are more individual: red cabbage chutney, for example, or coconut sauce and beetroot crisps served with grilled monkfish. The *carte* changes three or four times a year, and the four-course set menu daily in order to take advantage of game birds that drop on the mat, or landings of sea bass and langoustines at nearby ports. Bread and cured and smoked fish and meats are prepared on the premises. Meals might finish with crème brûlée, or choux pastry with coffee ice-cream and hot chocolate. Wines are almost entirely French and sympathetically priced, with much under £15. House Gamay and Sauvignon de Touraine are £9.50 (£1.60 per glass).

CHEFS: Christophe Caron and Martine Watson PROPRIETORS: Alan and Martine Watson
OPEN: Tue to Sun, D only; 7 to 9.30 (L by arrangement) CLOSED: 2 weeks Nov MEALS: alc
(main courses £9 to £12). Set D £15.50 SERVICE: not inc CARDS: Access, Amex, Visa
DETAILS: 34 seats. Private parties: 45 main room, 30 private room. Car park. Vegetarian meals.
Children's helpings. Smart dress preferred. No cigars/pipes in dining-room. Wheelchair access
(1 step; also WC). No music ACCOMMODATION: 5 rooms, all with bath/shower. TV. B&B £46 to
£63. Deposit: £20. Children welcome. Baby facilities. Garden. Doors close at 12.30am (*The Which? Hotel Guide*)

WHITEBROOK Gwent   map 4

▲ *Crown at Whitebrook* ❦ ⚒

Whitebrook NP5 4TX
MONMOUTH (0600) 860254
5m S of Monmouth, between   COOKING 2
A466 and B4293   COST £17–£38

Roger and Sandra Bates run their restaurant-with-rooms along French lines. Any reader who hankers after the sort of food they remember eating in some out-of-the-way French village will find sympathetic resonance here: 'Having spent much time in the south of France, I have not had better' was one verdict.

The location, on an unclassified road on the edge of Tintern Forest, a mile from the River Wye, whence comes salmon in season, is the biggest strength and the biggest weakness, admit the Bateses. There is no passing trade, but as much tranquillity as you can handle – a haven from the high prices and pretence of the 'gourmet mafia'. The cooking does not follow any particular school or fancy, but is a personal adaptation with a pleasingly country feel. It plays with guinea-fowl, local rabbit (served with croûtons, onions and lardons), or pork fillet with a sage and onion crust and butter-beans. Tarte aux pommes is a natural for dessert, as are pancakes flamed with the liqueur of your choice. Snacks, the lunchtime alternative, are a snip, and might include venison sausages in puff pastry with onion marmalade for not much more than a fiver.

The seventeenth-century inn has been an ale house, a cider house and a traditional pub in its time, and drink continues to play its part. Wines run the gamut of styles and prices, with some notably less expensive than in many other restaurants; half-bottles are good. House wine is £7.50. CELLARMAN'S CHOICE: Margaux Private Reserve 1987, Schroder et Schyler, £16.95; Lenton Brae Chardonnay 1991, £13.95.

The Guide *always appreciates hearing about changes of chef or owner.*

CHEF: Sandra Bates PROPRIETORS: Roger and Sandra Bates OPEN: all week, exc Mon L and Sun D; 12 to 2, 7 to 9 CLOSED: 2 weeks Jan, 2 weeks Aug MEALS: alc Tue to Sat light L (main courses £5 to £7). Set L £14.95, Set D £24.95 SERVICE: card slips closed CARDS: Access, Amex, Diners, Visa DETAILS: 36 seats. 6 tables outside. Private parties: 24 main room, 12 and 12 private rooms. Car park. Vegetarian meals. Children's helpings. Smart dress preferred. No smoking in dining-room. No music ACCOMMODATION: 12 rooms, all with bath/shower. TV. Phone. B&B £35 to £70. Children welcome. Baby facilities. Pets welcome (bedrooms only). Garden. Fax: (0600) 860607 (*The Which? Hotel Guide*)

Isle of Man

La Rosette

Main Road, Ballasalla IM9 2DA   COOKING 2
CASTLETOWN (0624) 822940   COST £25–£51

La Rosette is a 'restaurant français' now expanded into a joint operation with a 'café-bistro' just up the road. There seems to be intriguingly little difference between the various fixed-price menus offered, save that the dinner menu has a few more dishes on it. The raw materials, such as the fresh fish, are good: Manx queenies are cooked with bacon in white wine, while other fish may be grilled, baked with garlic or served with a champagne cream sauce. Meat dishes are mainly beef, but the range runs from steak au poivre and Stroganov to beef curry with banana and poppadums, and strips of fillet with mango in sweet-and-sour sauce. Lemon terrine with lime sauce is a bracing way to finish. Coffee is from a bottomless cafetière, and service is usually found 'excellent'. The short wine list has stiffish prices and does not always list producers. House French is £9.

CHEFS/PROPRIETORS: Bob and Rosa Phillips OPEN: Tue to Sat; 12 to 2.30, 7.30 to 9.30 MEALS: Set L £16, Set D £30 SERVICE: not inc CARDS: Access, Visa DETAILS: 45 seats. Private parties: 27 main room, 6, 8 and 16 private rooms. Vegetarian meals. Children's helpings. Music. Fax: (0624) 822702

Silverburn Lodge

Ballasalla IM9 3DA   COOKING 2
CASTLETOWN (0624) 822343   COST £16–£46

Set in seven acres of parkland, this sprawling single-storey building is described by its owners as an 'old coach-house-style restaurant'. Bistro meals are served in the Saddle Lounge, and the menu promises beef pudding with chips and mushy peas, ham shank with parsley sauce, steak butties and other trencherman's grub. Food in the restaurant revolves around classics of the old school of catering: nantaise salad, poached halibut steak with prawn and cucumber butter sauce, roast duckling with orange sauce and trimmings, crumbed pork cutlet baked with Stilton and served on a pineapple glaze. Sweets are from the trolley; the cheeseboard is a mix of English, French and Manx. The wine list is a well-spread selection of reasonably priced bottles from around the globe. House wine is £9.50.

CHEF: David Kennish   PROPRIETOR: Bernie Hamer   OPEN: Tue to Sun, exc Sat L (restaurant) and Sun D; 12 to 1.45, 7.30 to 9.15   MEALS: alc (main courses restaurant £11.50 to £17, bistro £4 to £12). Set L £8.50 (2 courses) to £11.50, Set D £20   SERVICE: not inc   CARDS: Access, Visa   DETAILS: 70 seats. Private parties: 75 main room. Car park. Vegetarian meals. Children welcome. Smart dress preferred. Wheelchair access (also WC). Music

---

DOUGLAS Isle of Man   map 4

▲ *Boncompte's*

Admiral House, Loch Promenade,
Douglas IM1 2LX   COOKING 2
DOUGLAS (0624) 629551   COST £17–£43

Admiral House is a Victorian hotel on the promenade, just five minutes' walk from the centre of Douglas. It attempts to create an aura of 'country-house past', with shelves of books, portraits and antique furniture filling much of the ground floor. Boncompte's restaurant is on the first floor and boasts fine views of Douglas Bay from big windows framed with drapes. Locally caught fish figures strongly on the handwritten menu in the shape of pan-fried queenies with garlic and bacon, grilled Dover sole, and poached fillet of brill with a sauce of green peppers and mango. Other dishes are a similar blend of old-school and exotic: eggs florentine and duckling à l'orange sit alongside home-smoked duck breast with grapefruit and sauté chicken on a bed of puréed banana with a light peppercorn sauce. Vegetarians are offered a meatless Stroganov or curried pineapple. Around 70 wines offer plenty of decent drinking for under £15. House wine is £9.50.

CHEF: Michael Ashe   PROPRIETORS: Jaime and Jill Boncompte   OPEN: Mon to Sat, exc Sat L; 12.30 to 2, 7.30 to 10   CLOSED: 25 and 26 Dec   MEALS: alc (main courses £8.50 to £17). Set L £10.50, Set D £15.95   SERVICE: not inc, card slips closed   CARDS: Access, Amex, Diners, Visa   DETAILS: 85 seats. Private parties: 85 main room, 25 and 25 private rooms. Car park. Vegetarian meals. Children's helpings. Smart dress preferred. No cigars/pipes in dining-room. Wheelchair access (also WC). Music   ACCOMMODATION: 12 rooms, all with bath/shower. TV. Phone. B&B £40 to £110. Rooms for disabled. Lift. Children welcome. Baby facilities. Confirm 1 day ahead. Fax: (0624) 675021

Channel Islands

Apple Cottage £

Rozel Bay, St Martin JE3 6AN   COOKING 1
JERSEY (0534) 861002   COST £15–£46

Fresh local seafood steals the show in this quaint eighteenth-century granite cottage by the bay. Simple things like mussels, oysters, plaice and skate are backed up by luxury items in the shape of lobster thermidor, baked sea bass with garlic and fennel, and salmon trout with cream and almonds. Prices are very fair, although an ounce of Beluga caviare will set you back £24. The carnivorous tendency is represented by tournedos Rossini, calf's liver with bacon, grilled lamb cutlets and other staples. Salads are also available at lunch-time. Home-made apple pie with Jersey cream is an appropriate finale. The wine list is surprisingly wide ranging for such a set-up, with big clarets and burgundies to the fore. House wine is £6.

CHEF: S.C. Pozzi PROPRIETORS: Mr and Mrs S.C. Pozzi OPEN: Tue to Sun, exc Sun D; 12 to 2.30, 7 to 9.30 CLOSED: late Dec to early Feb MEALS: alc (main courses £6 to £18). Set L £9.75 to £10.50, Set D Tue to Fri £15.75 SERVICE: not inc (10% for 10 or more), card slips closed CARDS: Access, Visa DETAILS: 65 seats. 15 tables outside. Private parties: 60 main room. Car park. Vegetarian meals. Children's helpings. Smart dress preferred. No cigars/pipes in dining-room. Wheelchair access (1 step; also WC). Music

---

Café du Moulin

Rue du Quanteraine, St Peters GY7 9DP   COOKING 1
GUERNSEY (0481) 65944   COST £16–£39

David and Gina Mann's restaurant is in a converted granary set in a lovely quiet valley. They have deliberately eschewed the flashy trappings adopted by most other establishments on the island: no place here for silver service, wine pouring and flambéeing. Instead, they put their faith in local ingredients and have built up a network of growers and fishermen who can deliver anything from 'dived' scallops to pink fir apple potatoes. Suppliers from further afield are able to offer Shetland salmon, Scottish farmhouse cheeses and tiny boudins for cassoulets. Fish dominates in summer; game figures strongly in winter. High points from recent meals have included warm salad of pigeon breast with mustard seed and balsamic vinegar dressing, Gressingham duck with orange liqueur sauce and a tartlet of onion confit, hot seafood grill with garlic butter, and desserts such as the assiette du chocolat. A vegetarian menu and light lunches are also available. The wine list shows a liking for up-to-date names from the New World. House wine is £7.25.

CHEFS: David Mann and Guy Moinan   PROPRIETORS: David and Gina Mann   OPEN: Tue to Sun, exc Sun D; 12.15 to 1.15, 7.15 to 9.15   CLOSED: 4 weeks Feb to March   MEALS: alc (main courses £12 to £13). Set L £13.95. Light L menu.   SERVICE: not inc   CARDS: Access, Visa   DETAILS: 50 seats. 10 tables outside. Private parties: 50 main room. Car park. Vegetarian meals. Children's helpings. No children under 7 D. Smart dress preferred. No smoking while others eat. No cigars/pipes in dining-room. Wheelchair access (also WC). Music

---

ST SAVIOUR Jersey   map 1

▲ *Longueville Manor* ⁵⁄✴

St Saviour JE2 7SA   COOKING 2*
JERSEY (0534) 25501   COST £23–£65

The manor has stood since the 1200s, as parts of its gnarled stone façade will confirm. It has been under the same family ownership since conversion just after the Second World War. The imposing interiors, full of dark wood panelling and fireplaces 'big enough to spit-roast a whole Jersey cow in', are lightened by curtained flounce, good antiques and paintings. A trim kitchen garden keeps Andrew Baird supplied with plentiful provender.

The *carte* is bolstered by fixed-price menus at lunch and dinner, a separate vegetarian menu and an eight-course 'tasting' menu. Plenty goes on in most dishes: globe artichoke filled with wild mushrooms and poached quail's eggs with hollandaise, steamed sea bass with a crab soufflé and a shellfish cream sauce, and grilled beef fillet topped with celeriac and foie gras give some idea of what to expect. One reporter enjoyed an 'absolutely enormous' plate of sauté scallops with a 'wonderful' sauce that seemed to be not much more than pan juices with a squeeze of lemon – 'the scallops were cooked so quickly that they had caramelised on one side but were succulent in the middle'. Hot soufflés, perhaps banana or praline served with chocolate ice-cream, crop up at the dessert stage, or there may be pear charlotte with pink champagne sorbet, or gratin of fruits with Grand Marnier sabayon. Service is 'very courteous and friendly'. The predominantly French wine list is good, though prices can be high: the sole California wine is 1985 Mondavi/Rothschild Opus One at over £80. House burgundy is £8.

CHEF: Andrew Baird   PROPRIETORS: the Lewis and Dufty families   OPEN: all week; 12.30 to 2, 7.30 to 9.30   MEALS: alc (main courses £17.50 to £19.75). Set L £16 (2 courses) to £18.50, Set D £28.50 to £50   SERVICE: net prices, card slips closed   CARDS: Access, Amex, Diners, Visa   DETAILS: 65 seats. 10 tables outside L. Private parties: 70 main room, 16 and 24 private rooms. Car park. Vegetarian meals. Children welcome. Smart dress preferred. No smoking in 1 dining-room. Wheelchair access (also WC). No music. Air-conditioned   ACCOMMODATION: 32 rooms, all with bath/shower. TV. Phone. B&B £125 to £300. Deposit: £55. Rooms for disabled. Lift. No children under 7. Dogs welcome (not in public rooms). Afternoon teas. Garden. Swimming-pool. Tennis. Confirm by 6. Fax: (0534) 31613 (*The Which? Hotel Guide*)

Northern Ireland

---

                                                      map 9

Ginger Tree

29 Ballyrobert Road, Ballyclare BT36 8TL   COOKING 1
BELFAST (0232) 848176   COST £12–£44

This Japanese restaurant has been established over 10 years now, and it seems that all the locals know how to find it: follow the signs to Larne, rather than Ballyclare, seems to be the hot tip. Traditional set menus – tempura, teriyaki, sukiyaki – are accompanied by an elaborate *carte* that offers fine sashimi at the weekends, grilled Lough Neagh eel, beef or pork yakinikufu (cooked with garlic, ginger, saké and soya), and a couple of vegetarian dishes. Desserts have included sculpted fruits, and banana Osaka (banana in pastry stuffed with soya bean paste, almonds and hazelnuts, with a sauce of orange and mandarin). The mainly European wine list provides an unexpectedly wide choice, all the way up to Ch. Gruaud-Larose 1970, for those who don't want saké. House French is £7.95.

CHEF: Shotaro Obana   PROPRIETORS: Elizabeth English and Shotaro Obana   OPEN: Mon to Sat, exc Sat L; 12 to 2.30, 7 to 9.30   CLOSED: 12 and 13 July, 24 to 26 Dec   MEALS: alc (main courses £7.50 to £13.50). Set L £5.95 to £10.25, Set D £13.50 to £25.70   SERVICE: not inc CARDS: Access, Amex, Diners, Visa   DETAILS: 50 seats. Private parties: 80 main room, 20 private room. Car park. Vegetarian meals. Children welcome. Wheelchair access (also WC). Music. Air-conditioned

---

                                                        map 9

La Belle Epoque

61–63 Dublin Road, Belfast BT2 7RS   COOKING 2
BELFAST (0232) 323244   COST £12–£35

French by name and French by inclination, this bubbly restaurant serves the city well. It offers classic cuisine – augmented by a few modern flourishes – to a mixed bag of customers, including visitors to the nearby Opera House. Menus change regularly and the repertoire continues to evolve. Couscous (both meat and vegetarian) is a current favourite, but the kitchen also creates dishes such as tartare of salmon with cucumber salad, baked turbot in puff pastry with a langoustine sauce, and roast Barbary duck with plum and lime sauce. Vegetables take in everything from an oriental stir-fry of carrots, courgettes, peppers and bean sprouts flavoured with star-anise and hoisin sauce to a full market-garden 'bouquetière'. Desserts are hot and cold classics: tarte au citron, crème brûlée, assiette de sorbets. The wine list tips its hat to the New World, although its heart is in France; halves show up well. House wines start at £7.50.

CHEF: A. Rousse   PROPRIETORS: J. Delbart, G. Sanchez, C. Fitzgerald and A. Rousse   OPEN: Mon to Sat, exc Sat L; noon to 11   MEALS: alc (main courses £6.50 to £11.50). Set L (2 courses) £5 to £10, Set D £15   SERVICE: not inc   CARDS: Access, Amex, Diners, Visa   DETAILS: 84 seats. Private parties: 20 main room. Vegetarian meals. Children welcome. Wheelchair access (also WC). Music. Fax: (0232) 240040

Nick's Warehouse

35–39 Hill Street, Belfast BT1 2LB   COOKING 1*
BELFAST (0232) 439690   COST £13–£32

Firmly established as part of the Belfast eating scene, Nick and Kathy Price's converted warehouse continues to offer imaginative bistro-style food at keen prices. Visitors can choose light lunches or evening snacks in the downstairs wine bar, or plump for a full meal in the restaurant. The cooking is modern, and ingredients are thoughtfully chosen. Chinese spiced squid with chilli dressing, breast of chicken with sun-dried tomato pesto, and duck breast with blackberry sauce are some things you will find. Carrot and rosemary soup, guacamole with crudités, or warm salad of black pudding, mushrooms and potatoes might suit those looking for speedy sustenance. The wine list is a good slate of drinkable stuff with a modern bias. House wines start at £5.95.

CHEFS: Nick Price and Simon Toye   PROPRIETORS: Nick and Kathy Price   OPEN: Mon to Sat, exc Mon D and Sat L; 12 to 2.30 (3 wine bar), 6 to 9   CLOSED: 25 and 26 Dec, 12 July, bank hol Mons   MEALS: alc L (main courses wine bar £4 to £5, restaurant £6 to £12). Set D £13.50 (2 courses) to £16.50. Minimum £7.50 restaurant   SERVICE: not inc (10% for 6 or more)   CARDS: Access, Amex, Diners, Visa   DETAILS: restaurant 45 seats, wine bar 45 seats. Private parties: 45 main room. Vegetarian meals. Children's helpings on request restaurant. No children wine bar. Wheelchair access (1 step; also WC). Music. Air-conditioned

Roscoff ♥

7 Lesley House, Shaftesbury Square,
Belfast BT2 7DB   COOKING 3*
BELFAST (0232) 331532   COST £21–£52

Paul Rankin's career has taken him from an initial training at Le Gavroche, through stints in North America, to the opening of this former Indian restaurant in the heart of Belfast. It is not the easiest place in the world in which to succeed with ambitious modern cooking, but a reputation has been forged, and Roscoff is now for many the best restaurant in Northern Ireland. The 'self-consciously modern' décor bears more than a passing resemblance to an expanded version of Alastair Little (see entry, London), and the food too is in the same transcontinental vein.

The fixed-price lunch and dinner menus, of three courses plus coffee, offer undoubted value for such dishes as asparagus and wild mushroom risotto, hake fillet with mussels and a basil and saffron cream, or crisp duck confit with haricot beans and red onions, with perhaps orange and caramel cake or chocolate pâté with a red berry coulis to finish. Although one reporter thought the portions a trifle nouvelle, others have enjoyed 'wonderful' lobster and prawn tagliatelle, 'tasty, tender' chargrilled rump steak with mustard butter sauce, and 'the best apple pie ever'. Service is 'efficient and friendly'. Any wine list that includes Louis Michel's Chablis, Schlumberger's grand cru Alsace Riesling, Frescobaldi's Chianti Rufina and Montes Alpha Cabernet Sauvignon from Chile has to have something going for it. House wines start at £8.95. CELLERMAN'S CHOICE: Riesling grand cru Saering Dom. Schlumberger, £17.95; Pommard 1985, Jadot, £28.

CHEFS/PROPRIETORS: Paul and Jeanne Rankin   OPEN: Mon to Sat, exc Sat L; 12.15 to 2.15, 6.30 to 10.30   CLOSED: 25 and 26 Dec, Easter Mon, 12 July   MEALS: alc (main courses £9.50 to £15.50). Set L £14.50, Set D Mon to Thur £19.50   SERVICE: not inc (10% for 6 or more)   CARDS: Access, Amex, Diners, Visa   DETAILS: 75 seats. Private parties: 20 main room. Vegetarian meals. Children's helpings. No-smoking area. Wheelchair access (also WC). Music. Air-conditioned. Fax: (0232) 312093

Strand £

12 Stranmillis Road, Belfast BT9 5AA   COOKING 1
BELFAST (0232) 682266   COST £13–£28

Although you may feel cosy in your curtained-off, brass-railed booth at the Strand, the bustle and buzz will leave you in no doubt that this is true brasserie eating in the classic manner. One-plate meals such as a peanut cheeseburger, meatballs bourguignonne, or lightly battered cod and chips are served all day from noon to 11.30 at night. The *carte* presents plenty of choice, with enough for vegetarians not to feel unloved. Leek tart, smoked chicken salad, pork fillets in Gorgonzola, and curried lamb steak with minted yogurt are among dishes offered at almost surrealistically low prices. Finish with zuccotto, banoffi or pears in grenadine. Most regions are covered on the wine list, though many are represented by only one producer. House French is £5.95.

CHEFS: Michael McAuley and Donna Donaldson   PROPRIETOR: Anne Turkington   OPEN: all week; noon to 11.30   CLOSED: 25 and 26 Dec, 12 and 13 July   MEALS: alc (main courses £4 to £9). Sun brunch £5.95   SERVICE: not inc   CARDS: Access, Amex, Diners, Visa   DETAILS: 100 seats. Private parties: 30 main room, 30 private room. Vegetarian meals. Children's helpings. Smart dress preferred. Music. Air-conditioned. Fax: (0232) 663189

BELLANALECK Co Fermanagh   map 9

Sheelin £

Bellanaleck, nr Enniskillen BT92 2BA   COOKING 1
ENNISKILLEN (0365) 348232   COST £14–£30

Arthur and Marion Cathcart's beguiling thatched house doubles as a home bakery and country restaurant. The fixed-price menus take few risks with modern fashion, although they steer clear of homespun clichés. Starters such as avocado seafood salad or melon with strawberry vinaigrette are followed by a choice of soup or sorbet. Centrepieces include fresh salmon hollandaise, scampi provençale or Caribbean chicken, all served with fresh vegetables. Home-made sweets are chosen from the serving counter. Around 40 wines are mostly priced below £10. House French is £6.45 or £6.80.

CHEFS: Marion Cathcart and Jacqueline Owens   PROPRIETOR: Arthur Cathcart   OPEN: Mon to Sat (Sun June to Aug), exc L Mon and Tue; 12.30 to 2.30, 7 to 9.30   MEALS: alc (main courses £8.50 to £11.50). Set L £9, Set D £15 to £19   SERVICE: not inc, card slips closed   CARDS: Access, Amex, Visa   DETAILS: 30 seats. Private parties: 30 main room. Car park. Vegetarian meals. Children's helpings. Smart dress preferred. Wheelchair access (also WC). Music. Fax: (0365) 348190

BUSHMILLS Co Antrim   map 9

▲ *Auberge de Seneirl* 🍴

28 Ballyclough Road, Bushmills BT57 8UZ
DERVOCK (026 57) 41536   COOKING 2
off B17 Coleraine road   COST £24–£40

The Defreses' converted schoolhouse near the Giant's Causeway is a restaurant-with-rooms dedicated to French provincial cooking and warm hospitality. The short menu is a classic run through paupiettes of salmon and sole, fillet of pork dijonnaise, duck Montmorency and chicken breast poached in Gewurztraminer, augmented by a few unexpected starters such as a salad of chicken and oysters in ginger sauce. On the first Saturday of each month a multi-course 'menu de dégustation' is available, when the kitchen moves up a gear for fillets of John Dory and red gurnard in lime sauce and braised saddle of wild boar with red cabbage and red wine sauce. The all-French wine list has a handful of personal selections from M. Defres (cheapest bottles are £8.35).

CHEF: Mrs B. Defres   PROPRIETORS: J. and B. Defres   OPEN: Wed to Sat, D only; 7 to 9.30   MEALS: Set D £16.50 to £25   SERVICE: not inc   CARDS: Amex, Diners   DETAILS: 30 seats. Private parties: 30 main room. Car park. Vegetarian meals with prior notice. Children's helpings. No smoking in dining-room. Smart dress preferred. Wheelchair access. Music   ACCOMMODATION: 5 rooms, all with bath/shower. TV. B&B £21.50 to £74. Deposit: £20. Children welcome. Baby facilities. Pets welcome (in bedrooms only). Garden. Swimming-pool. Sauna

---

LONDONDERRY Co Londonderry   map 9

▲ *Beech Hill Country House Hotel*

32 Ardmore Road, Londonderry BT47 3QP
LONDONDERRY (0504) 49279
off A6 Londonderry to Belfast road at   COOKING 2
Faughan Bridge, opposite Ardmore Chapel   COST £17–£40

Gushing waterfalls are the only signs of turbulence at Beech Hill, an eighteenth-century manor house in impressive grounds opposite the chapel at Ardmore. Noel McMeel continues his inventive train of culinary thought, offering a fixed-price menu of three courses plus coffee as well as a short *carte*. A keen calligrapher has inscribed the titles of dishes on the latter in painstaking Gothic. They may include guinea-fowl and fig terrine with grape and redcurrant jelly, smoked duck with sauté potatoes as a starter with walnut oil and balsamic vinaigrette, and venison with orange and tarragon beurre blanc and deep-fried celeriac. Home-made pasta is used well, and creativity is maintained into the dessert stage with, for example, chocolate cannelloni filled with a cream liqueur mousse. The Irish farmhouse cheeses are also good. Wines are a brisk international selection, with house French wines at £7.95.

CHEF: Noel McMeel   PROPRIETORS: Leo and Seamus Donnelly   OPEN: all week; 12 to 2.30, 6 to 9.45   CLOSED: 25 Dec   MEALS: alc (main courses £12.50 to £14). Set L £11.50, Set D £17.95   SERVICE: not inc, card slips closed   CARDS: Access, Amex, Visa   DETAILS: 40 seats. 3 tables outside. Private parties: 80 main room, 15 and 30 private rooms. Car park. Vegetarian meals. Children's helpings. No children under 10. Smart dress preferred. No-smoking area. Wheelchair access (also WC). Music   ACCOMMODATION: 17 rooms, all with bath/shower. TV. Phone. B&B £50 to £100. Children welcome. Baby facilities. Afternoon teas. Garden. Tennis. Fishing. Doors close at 11. Confirm 1 day ahead. Fax: (0504) 45366

PORTRUSH Co Antrim   map 9

Ramore £

The Harbour, Portrush BT56 8BN   COOKING 2
PORTRUSH (0265) 824313   COST £19–£38

In a coastal resort on the northern tip of County Antrim, this lively restaurant offers cooking that plunders the globe, throws ideas into the melting pot and puts the emphasis on style and value for money. George McAlpin's short _carte_ tells its own story: asparagus hotpot is packed with leeks, morels and white truffles; fillet of Irish spring lamb comes with grilled vegetable antipasto; marinated lemon chicken is embellished with fettuccine, shiitake mushrooms and served with a lemon and basil dressing. Fresh pasta and fish vary from day to day. A handful of one-dish meals are a novel feature: Panang chicken with pilau rice and Thai coconut curry sauce is a typical offering. The wine list follows suit: most major producing countries are represented and prices are kept in check. Australian house wine is £7.50.

CHEF: George McAlpin   PROPRIETORS: John and Joy Caithness, and George and Jane McAlpin   OPEN: Tue to Sat, D only; 6.30 to 10.30   MEALS: alc (main courses £7 to £11)   SERVICE: not inc   CARDS: Access, Visa   DETAILS: 85 seats. Private parties: 85 main room. Car park. Vegetarian meals. Children welcome. Wheelchair access (1 step). Music. Air-conditioned

Republic of Ireland

We have not given marks for cooking for the Republic of Ireland entries because of a shortage of reports; please do give us feedback should you visit. To telephone the Republic from mainland Britain, dial 010 353 (00 353 from April 1995) followed by the number listed, but dropping the initial 0. Prices are quoted in Irish punts.

ADARE Co Limerick   map 9

▲ *Adare Manor*

Adare
LIMERICK (061) 396566   COST £26–£83

A vast Gothic pile in 840 acres of parkland may sound imposing but, once within its walls, you will find yourself wrapped in comfort and attention. The music heard distantly in the dining-room may be Beethoven or Gershwin, and the cooking is in similarly diverse mode. Brutus salad is obviously an associate of Caesar, or there are home-made ravioli with oyster mushrooms and chervil, beef consommé with soft-boiled quail's eggs, cod on mashed potato with chickpeas, courgette and yellow pepper, or breast of local pheasant with a rillette of the leg meat in a rich armagnac sauce. Fruits are used to good advantage at dessert stage. House French is £15.

CHEF: Gerard Costelloe PROPRIETORS: Tom and Judy Kane OPEN: all week, D only, and Sun L; 7 to 9.30 MEALS: alc (main courses £16.50 to £27). Set L Sun £14.95, Set D £32 SERVICE: 15%, card slips closed CARDS: Access, Amex, Diners, Visa DETAILS: 70 seats. Private parties: 60 main room, 25 and 200 private rooms. Car park. Vegetarian meals. Children's helpings. Jacket and tie. Wheelchair access (1 step; also WC). Music ACCOMMODATION: 64 rooms, all with bath/shower. TV. Phone. B&B £107 to £285. Rooms for disabled. Lift. Children welcome. Baby facilities by arrangement. Afternoon teas. Garden. Swimming-pool. Sauna. Fishing. Golf. Snooker. Fax: (061) 396124

AHAKISTA Co Cork   map 9

Shiro ✳

Ahakista
BANTRY (027) 67030
on coast road from Durrus towards
Sheep's Head   COST £41–£50

A 'Japanese dinner house' is how Werner and Kei Pilz describe their restaurant in a former priest's dwelling overlooking Dunmanus Bay. The day's menu starts with zensai appetisers, followed by a bowl of suimono soup. The choice of centrepiece dishes runs through sashimi, tempura, yakitori and teriyaki, but it's worth noticing masu yaki (a less common speciality from Sapporo, consisting of roast wild sea trout which is then boiled in ginger and lemon) and saké mushi (steamed salmon with capers and a garlic mayonnaise dip). Home-made ice-cream rounds things off refreshingly. A full vegetarian menu is also available. Drink saké, Japanese tea or something appropriate from the creditable wine list (prices start at £11).

CHEF: Kei Pilz PROPRIETORS: Kei and Werner Pilz OPEN: all week, D only; 7 to 9.30 CLOSED: Christmas and New Year MEALS: Set D £33 SERVICE: net prices CARDS: Access, Amex, Diners, Visa (5% surcharge) DETAILS: 14 seats. 3 tables outside. Private parties: 12 main room. Car park. Vegetarian meals. No children under 14. Smart dress preferred. No smoking in 1 dining-room. Wheelchair access (1 step). No music. Air-conditioned. Fax: (027) 67206

BALLINA Co Mayo   map 9

▲ *Mount Falcon Castle*

Ballina
BALLINA (096) 70811
on N57 between Foxford and Ballina   COST £18–£36

Built as a country mansion in 1876, this neo-Gothic stone edifice stands in a 100-acre estate with grounds running down to the River Moy. Salmon and trout fishing are major attractions. The kitchen works in tandem with the river, the garden and the farm, and dinner is a model of country house restraint. One day it might be smoked salmon salad, carrot and orange soup, and baked gammon with parsley sauce, the next it could be spinach and fish mousse, duck soup and roast sirloin of beef. Home-made sweets and Irish cheeses round things off. House wine is £8.50.

CHEF: Michael ffrench Davis PROPRIETOR: Constance Aldridge OPEN: all week, D only, and Sun L; 1 and 8 CLOSED: Christmas, Feb MEALS: Set L Sun £12, Set D £22 SERVICE: 10% (not inc from Mar 1995), card slips closed CARDS: Access, Amex, Diners, Visa DETAILS: 28 seats. Car park. Vegetarian meals. Children's helpings. Smart dress preferred. Wheelchair access (also WC). No music ACCOMMODATION: 10 rooms, all with bath/shower. Phone. B&B £45 to £90. Deposit: £10. Children welcome. Baby facilities. Pets by arrangement. Garden. Tennis. Fishing. Fax: (093) 71517

BALLYDEHOB Co Cork   map 9

Annie's

Main Street, Ballydehob
BALLYDEHOB (028) 37292   COST £24–£37

Some sadness will be occasioned by the news that Annie is no longer doing lunches in her little west Cork restaurant. However, she has opened a coffee-shop further up the street, which serves midday meals. Diners, however, may still pop over to the pub just across the road to look at the menu, and enjoy a pint of the black stuff before claiming their table for dinner. That may consist of lambs' kidneys in filo, mussels grilled with garlic breadcrumbs, baked wild salmon with lemon and herbs, or 'superb' chicken Kiev. Everything is as fresh as can be, and the welcome could not be friendlier. The wine list has gone on developing and now offers some enterprising selections, starting from £11.

CHEFS/PROPRIETORS: Anne and Dano Barry   OPEN: Tue to Sat, D only; 6.30 to 9.30 (times may differ in winter)   CLOSED: 1 to 21 Nov   MEALS: alc (main courses £11 to £14). Set D £20   SERVICE: 10% (on food only), card slips closed   CARDS: Access, Visa   DETAILS: 24 seats. Private parties: 20 main room. Vegetarian meals. Children's helpings. No cigars/pipes in dining-room. Wheelchair access. Music

---

BALLYVAUGHAN Co Clare   map 9

▲ Gregans Castle Hotel

Ballyvaughan
ENNIS (065) 77005
on N67, 3m S of Ballyvaughan   COST £16–£65

On the edge of the Burren – 100 square miles of craggy limestone that subsides into Galway Bay – this hotel offers views of the water from its comfortable dining-room. Margaret Cronin cooks a daily-changing, fixed-price menu as well as an ambitious *carte*, making use of the shellfish that are right on the doorstep. Supporting the traditionalism of gravlax, oysters and poached lobster are the likes of grilled Irish goats' cheese with pesto, Dublin Bay prawns dressed with chilli and coriander, and steamed John Dory with buttered tagliatelle and cucumber. Meats, too, receive imaginative treatment. The forward-looking wine list majors on non-European bottles: try Hua Dong Riesling from China. House wines start at £11.95.

CHEF: Margaret Cronin   PROPRIETORS: the Haden family   OPEN: all week; 12 to 3, 7 to 8.30   CLOSED: Nov to Feb   MEALS: alc D (main courses £10 to £26). Set D £27. Bar L (main courses £3.50 to £17). Minimum £10 D   SERVICE: 12.5%, card slips closed   CARDS: Access, Visa   DETAILS: 50 seats. Car park. Vegetarian meals. Children's helpings on request. Smart dress preferred. No-smoking area. Wheelchair access (also WC). No music   ACCOMMODATION: 22 rooms, all with bath/shower. Phone. B&B £76 to £160. Rooms for disabled. Children welcome. Baby facilities. Afternoon teas. Garden. Doors close at 11.30. Fax: (065) 77111

BRAY Co Wicklow   map 9

Tree of Idleness

Seafront, Bray
DUBLIN (01) 2863498 and 2828183   COST £24–£50

Just down the coast from Dun Laoghaire, this sea-front restaurant feels a long way from its Mediterranean home, but the good Greek Cypriot cooking convinces many of its authenticity. Grilled halloumi with tahini, thalassina melitzanes (mixed seafood in prawn and wine sauce served on grilled aubergine), guinea-fowl stuffed with apples and sultanas, and the house speciality of roast suckling pig stuffed with apple and apricot are all competently handled. Finish with a tot of 20-year-old Mavrodaphne. The wine list is wide-ranging and house wines start at £10.

The Good Food Guide *is a registered trade mark of Consumers' Association Ltd.*

CHEF: Ismail Basaran   PROPRIETOR: Susan Courtellas   OPEN: Tue to Sun, D only; 7.30 to 11 (10 Sun)   CLOSED: Christmas, first 2 weeks Sept   MEALS: alc (main courses £10 to £16.50). Set D £16 to £19   SERVICE: 10%, card slips closed   CARDS: Access, Amex, Diners, Visa   DETAILS: 50 seats. Private parties: 28 main room. Vegetarian meals. Children welcome. Smart dress preferred. No-smoking area. No pipes in dining-room. Wheelchair access (1 step; also WC). Music

---

CASHEL Co Tipperary   map 9

Chez Hans

Rockside, Cashel
CASHEL (062) 61177
at foot of Rock of Cashel   COST £30–£49

Hans-Peter Matthiä has been running this converted Wesleyan chapel below the Rock of Cashel for nearly 30 years, and his style remains true to old-world generosity ('gigantic' portions) but absorbs modern ideas as well. Dishes include spinach tagliatelle with smoked salmon and Parmesan, Rossmore mussel gratin, and herb-crusted rack of Tipperary lamb with rosemary jus. The fine local cheese, Cashel Blue, is used with leeks in a sabayon to accompany chicken breast. Some excellent producers have been assembled on the wine list, which kicks off with house Côtes du Roussillon at £10.50 and a pair of Rieslings from the Matthiä family vineyard in the Nahe.

CHEF/PROPRIETOR: Hans-Peter Matthiä   OPEN: Tue to Sat, D only; 6.30 to 9.30 (10.30 Sat)   CLOSED: 4 days Christmas   MEALS: alc (main courses £14.50 to £19.50). Minimum £14.50   SERVICE: not inc, card slips closed   CARDS: Access, Visa   DETAILS: 70 seats. Private parties: 80 main room. Car park. Vegetarian meals with prior notice. Children's helpings. Smart dress preferred. No-smoking area. Wheelchair access (also WC). Music

---

CASTLEBALDWIN Co Sligo   map 9

▲ Cromleach Lodge ⁵⅄ | NEW ENTRY |

Ballindoon, Castlebaldwin
SLIGO (071) 65155   COST £39–£47

'The quality of the cooking is out of this world,' reports an awestruck visitor to this hillside hotel, which enjoys splendid views from dining-room tables and guest rooms. Moira Tighe cooks a daily-changing five-course menu that includes a soup or salad after the first course, and then a sorbet before the main. 'Brilliant sauces and delightful presentation' crop up in such dishes as tartlet of quail breasts on armagnac cream, a seafood plate of turbot, salmon and monkfish with lemon butter, or venison on a sauce of vintage port. 'Tonight's delights' to finish may take in strawberry shortcake tartlet with apple cream, or home-made ice-creams on rum and butterscotch sauce. Service is adjudged 'first-class'. A preliminary list of wines under £15 will afford some respite from the premium prices commanded by the thoroughbreds. House Bordeaux is £11.95.

Report forms are at the back of the book; write a letter if you prefer.

CHEF: Moira Tighe PROPRIETORS: Christy and Moira Tighe OPEN: all week, D only; 7 to 9 (6.30 to 8 Sun) CLOSED: 18 Dec to 28 Jan MEALS: Set D £29.50 SERVICE: not inc, card slips closed CARDS: Access, Amex, Diners, Visa DETAILS: 40 seats. Private parties: 20 main room, 6 and 20 private rooms. Car park. Vegetarian meals. Children's helpings. No children under 7. Smart dress preferred. No smoking in dining-room. Wheelchair access (2 steps; also WC). Music ACCOMMODATION: 10 rooms, all with bath/shower. TV. Phone. B&B £69 to £118. Deposit: 10%. Rooms for disabled. Children welcome. Garden. Doors close at 1am. Confirm by 6. Fax: (071) 65455

CLIFDEN Co Galway   map 9

O'Grady's

Market Street, Clifden
CLIFDEN (095) 21450   COST £25–£40

'A taste of Connemara,' promises Michael O'Grady at this seafood restaurant in the west of Ireland that has also caught today's prevalent mood of culinary internationalism. Smoked shellfish salad with a soy dressing, gratinated gingered crab with pink grapefruit, blackened scallops with angel-hair pasta and coriander, and best end of veal with salsify on an apricot and cherry sauce give the range of references to be expected. The wine list is equally wide-ranging. House French is £10, Australian £11.

CHEF: P.J. Heffernan PROPRIETOR: Michael O'Grady OPEN: all week; 12.30 to 2.30, 6.30 to 10 (late closing July to Aug) CLOSED: Nov to 31 Dec, 12 Jan to Mar MEALS: alc (main courses £8 to £12.50) SERVICE: not inc, card slips closed CARDS: Access, Amex, Visa DETAILS: 60 seats. Private parties: 20 main room, 12 private room. Vegetarian meals. No children under 6. No pipes in dining-room. Wheelchair access (2 steps). Music. Fax: (095) 21994

CLONAKILTY Co Cork   map 9

Dunworley Cottage ⅌✳

Butlerstown, Clonakilty
BANDON (023) 40314
signposted from Timoleague, S of Bandon   COST £17–£41

A Swiss pair on the golfing circuit of Ireland hiked up the hill to Dunworley and were astonished at 'how small it was'. They none the less enjoyed Asa Helmersson's Scandinavian-inspired dishes: smoked mussels, a seafood casserole based on the day's catch, fillet steak with garlic butter and a green peppercorn sauce, and Apfelstrudel with ice-cream all went down very nicely. The friendly and expeditious service was also appreciated. Symbols on the menu cater for most of today's dietary observances. The short, unspectacular wine list starts at £9.75.

CHEF: Asa Helmersson PROPRIETOR: Katherine Norén OPEN: Wed to Sun (L summer only); 1 to 3, 6.30 to 9 (last orders vary) CLOSED: Nov, Jan to Mar MEALS: alc (main courses £7.50 to £14). Set L Sun £10 SERVICE: not inc CARDS: Access, Amex, Diners, Visa DETAILS: 55 seats. Private parties: 20 main room, 20 private room. Car park. Vegetarian meals. Healthy eating options. Children's helpings. No smoking in 1 dining-room. Wheelchair access (also WC). No music

CORK Co Cork   map 9

▲ *Arbutus Lodge*

Montenotte, Cork
CORK (021) 501237   COST £18–£51

Arbutus, an eighteenth-century town house full of antiques and paintings and warm good cheer, looks down from its hill on to the gentle city of Cork. An amusingly ungentle portrait on the menu shows a woman reading a little light Samuel Beckett as she gnaws on a trotter. Despite a niggle or two about treatment of fish and overseasoning, many 'memorable' dishes have been enjoyed, including mussels in saffron sauce, fine wild salmon, orange and cardamom ice-cream, and pear and almond tart. A family from England appreciated the generosity that allowed everybody a little taste of all the Irish cheeses on the board. The encyclopaedic wine list must still be one of the best in Ireland. House wines are from around £10.

CHEFS: Declan Ryan, Helen Ward and John O'Leary   PROPRIETORS: Declan and Patsy Ryan   OPEN: Mon to Sat; 1 to 2.15 (12 to 2.30 bar), 7 to 9.30   CLOSED: 1 week Christmas   MEALS: alc (main courses £14 to £15). Set L £12.50, Set D £21.50. Bar L (main courses £5.50 to £6.50)   SERVICE: not inc   CARDS: Access, Amex, Diners, Visa   DETAILS: 70 seats. 10 tables outside. Private parties: 20 and 100 private rooms. Car park. Vegetarian meals. Children's helpings. No cigars/pipes in dining-room. No music. Air-conditioned   ACCOMMODATION: 20 rooms, all with bath/shower. TV. Phone. B&B £42 to £110. Deposit: 50%. Children welcome. Baby facilities. Garden. Tennis. Doors close at midnight. Confirm by 5. Fax: (021) 502893

Clifford's

18 Dyke Parade, Cork
CORK (021) 275333   COST £22–£47

Michael Clifford's cooking attracts eulogies ('I could not criticise it on any front'), as does his willingness to please. A family of regulars from England phoned in advance to ask him to whip up some home-made tagliatelle and a lemon sorbet, and had their requests seen to without a blink. His inventive flair produces such dishes as a savoury crêpe filled with scrambled eggs and Clonakilty black pudding, sauté chicken and mushrooms with a sauce of cream and Irish whiskey, lamb's liver with apple and onion compote, and grilled pork served with cinnamon-scented plums. Coffee and rum bavarois will round off a meal successfully. House wines from an international list start at £12.50. A new venture next door, Michael's Bistro, has its own kitchen offering simpler fare.

CHEF: Michael Clifford   PROPRIETORS: Michael and Deirdre Clifford   OPEN: Mon to Sat, exc L Mon and Sat; 12.30 to 2.30, 7 to 10.30   MEALS: Set L £12.95, Set D £28   SERVICE: not inc   CARDS: Access, Amex, Diners, Visa   DETAILS: 50 seats. Private parties: 60 main room, 30 private room. Vegetarian meals with prior notice. Children's helpings. Smart dress preferred. No music. Air-conditioned

---

The text of entries is based on unsolicited reports sent in by readers, backed up by inspections conducted anonymously. The factual details under the text are from questionnaires the Guide *sends to all restaurants that feature in the book.*

Crawford Gallery Café £

Emmet Place, Cork
CORK (021) 257714   COST £15–£25

The Allens of Ballymaloe (see entry, Shanagarry) have the concession in the ground-floor lunchtime café of Cork's municipal art gallery, next door to the Opera House. A sceptic thought it had 'better paintings than in the gallery upstairs', but admired the 'good home-cooking – a boon in Cork'. Salads use vegetables grown at Ballymaloe and may come with an avocado dip; fish is landed at Ballycotton pier (baked cod receives praise); and cheeses are Ireland's finest. Superb breads, and house wines from Georges Duboeuf at £10, add lustre. Breakfasts are also served.

CHEF: Rory O'Connell   PROPRIETOR: Ballymaloe House Hotel   OPEN: Mon to Sat, daytime only; 12.30 to 5   CLOSED: 25 Dec, bank hols   MEALS: alc (main courses £4 to £7)   SERVICE: not inc   CARDS: Access, Visa   DETAILS: 80 seats. Private parties: 90 main room. Vegetarian meals. Children's helpings. No cigars/pipes in dining-room. Wheelchair access (3 steps; also WC). Music

---

DINGLE Co Kerry   map 9

▲ *Doyle's*

4 John Street, Dingle
TRALEE (066) 51174   COST £25–£43

This 'businesslike' restaurant is worth a trip into the west of Kerry, and seafood is the business. Mille-feuille of warm oysters with a Guinness sauce demonstrates a willingness to invent, or there are garlic-stuffed mussels, mackerel with apples and cider, turbot with sauce ravigote and maybe raspberry meringue cake to finish. The wines are mainly white, of course, and include some fine German selections. House wines start at £10.80.

CHEF: Stella Doyle   PROPRIETORS: John and Stella Doyle   OPEN: Mon to Sat, D only; 6 to 9   CLOSED: mid-Nov to mid-Mar   MEALS: alc (main courses £11 to £16)   SERVICE: 10%, card slips closed   CARDS: Access, Diners, Visa   DETAILS: 50 seats. Private parties: 20 main room. Vegetarian meals with prior notice. Children's helpings. No-smoking area. Wheelchair access (1 step; also WC). No music   ACCOMMODATION: 8 rooms, all with bath/shower. TV. Phone. B&B £39 to £62. Deposit: £20. Rooms for disabled. Children welcome. Doors close at midnight. Fax: (066) 51816

Half Door

John Street, Dingle
TRALEE (066) 51600   COST £17–£48

The seafood-lovers of Dingle are spoilt for choice. At this 'very friendly' restaurant, Denis O'Connor smokes his own salmon and offers some fairly intricate dishes that register high approval. These may be sauté oysters on toasted brioche with chive sauce, baked herb-crusted plaice with mustard, or paupiettes of sole wrapped around smoked salmon mousse. 'Delicious' desserts may include vanilla cheesecake with orange sauce. House Australian is £10.75.

CHEF: Denis O'Connor   PROPRIETORS: Denis and Teresa O'Connor   OPEN: Wed to Mon; 12.30 to 2.30, 6 to 10   CLOSED: 15 Nov to 15 Dec, 15 Jan to 2 Apr/Easter   MEALS: alc (main courses L £4.50 to £20, D £11 to £20)   SERVICE: not inc   CARDS: Access, Amex, Diners, Visa   DETAILS: 52 seats. Private parties: 20 main room, 18 and 20 private rooms. Vegetarian meals. Children's helpings L, 6 to 8 D. No babies after 8. No-smoking area. Wheelchair access. Music. Air-conditioned

---

DOUGLAS Co Cork   map 9

Lovetts

Churchyard Lane, Well Road, Douglas
CORK (021) 294909   COST £22–£45

'Our fish translation facility (in five languages) has prevented many an international incident,' notes Dermod Lovett. His restaurant and bar on the ground floor of a Georgian house makes admirable use of the Southern Irish catch (oysters, mussels, scallops, monkfish kebabs, grilled black sole), with much more besides. Local beef and lamb, free-range chickens and ducks, and seasonal game all appear in different guises, and vegetarians are given plenty of choice. Breads, biscuits and pasta are made on the premises. Herbs are home-grown and the cheeseboard flies the flag for Irish farmhouse producers. House wine is £11.

CHEF: Marie Harding   PROPRIETORS: Dermod and Margaret Lovett   OPEN: Mon to Sat, exc Sat L; 12.30 to 2, 7 to 9.45   CLOSED: 1 week Christmas, bank hols   MEALS: alc (main courses £9 to £16). Set L £14.50, Set D £21   SERVICE: not inc, card slips closed   CARDS: Access, Amex, Diners, Visa   DETAILS: 35 seats. Private parties: 50 main room, 26 private room. Car park. Vegetarian meals. Healthy eating options. Children's helpings. Smart dress preferred. No-smoking area. Wheelchair access (also WC). Music. Fax: (021) 508568

DUBLIN Co Dublin   map 9

Commons

Newman House,
85–86 St Stephen's Green, Dublin 2
DUBLIN (01) 4752597, 4780530 and
4780531   COST £28–£62

Newman House, the original home of University College, Dublin, is now the glorious setting for this very fancy restaurant. Modern flamboyance sums up Michael Bolster's cooking, witnessed in dishes such as foie gras and black pudding with warm pear dressing, pan-fried John Dory with mange-tout, tomato and olive vinaigrette, and roast cannon of lamb with spinach, celeriac and oregano jus. It promises a great deal, although the outcome has not impressed everyone, especially as prices are high and service has not always been up to the mark. House wine is £14.

The Guide *is totally independent, accepts no free hospitality, and survives on the number of copies sold each year.*

CHEF: Michael Bolster   PROPRIETOR: Michael Fitzgerald   OPEN: Mon to Sat, exc Sat L; 12.30 to 2.15, 7 to 10.15   CLOSED: 1 week Christmas, public hols   MEALS: alc (main courses £16 to £19). Set L £17, Set D £27.50   SERVICE: 15%   CARDS: Access, Amex, Diners, Visa   DETAILS: 60 seats. Private parties: 12 main room, 20 and 50 private rooms. Vegetarian meals. Children welcome. Smart dress preferred. No-smoking area. No music. Air-conditioned. Fax: (01) 4780557

Le Coq Hardi

35 Pembroke Road, Ballsbridge, Dublin
DUBLIN (01) 6689070   COST £26–£79

A magnificent cellar and a gargantuan wine list set the tone for this bastion of haute cuisine in Dublin. The décor is splendid and John Howard's cooking follows suit. Lunch menus are in English, while the full *carte* reverts to French with translations. The style is defined by dishes such as consommé of guinea-fowl with ravioli of wild mushrooms, Irish stew, skate wing with brown butter and hazelnuts, and breast of free-range duckling with confit, green cabbage and madeira sauce. Twenty wines are offered as daily selections and house wines start at £14.

CHEFS: John Howard and James O'Sullivan   PROPRIETORS: John and Catherine Howard   OPEN: Mon to Sat, exc Sat L; 12.30 to 3, 7 to 11   CLOSED: Christmas, 2 weeks Aug, bank hols   MEALS: alc (main courses £13 to £22.50). Set L £16, Set D £28   SERVICE: 12.5%   CARDS: Access, Amex, Diners, Visa   DETAILS: 45 seats. Private parties: 50 main room, 2 to 35 private rooms. Car park. Vegetarian meals. Children welcome. Smart dress preferred. No-smoking area. Music. Air-conditioned. Fax: (01) 6689887

Eastern Tandoori

34–35 South William Street, Dublin 2
DUBLIN (01) 6710428 and 6710506   COST £15–£53

Sitar and tabla provide the live accompaniment to eating at this 'authentic with a capital A' Indian restaurant that also has branches in Blackrock and Malahide. One reporter quite liked the tandoori mackerel to start, but was less impressed with the vegetable biriani. Otherwise the range spans the familiar dishes of most of India's regions, and there is a determination to please. Roses are presented to women on arrival; hot towels appear after each course. House French from an acceptable list is £11.50.

CHEFS: Henry Paul, Olli Ullah and Iqbal Ahmed   PROPRIETORS: Mr and Mrs Feroze Khan   OPEN: all week, exc Sun L; 12 to 2.30, 6 to 11.30   CLOSED: 25 and 26 Dec, Good Fri   MEALS: alc (main courses £7.50 to £14). Set L £7.50, Set D £14.95 to £19.95. Minimum £8.50   SERVICE: 12.5%, card slips closed   CARDS: Access, Amex, Diners, Visa   DETAILS: 64 seats. Private parties: 80 main room. Vegetarian meals. Children welcome. Smart dress preferred. Wheelchair access (2 steps). Music. Air-conditioned. Fax: (01) 6779232

Restaurateurs justifiably resent no-shows. If you quote a credit card number when booking, you may be liable for the restaurant's lost profit margin if you don't turn up. Always phone to cancel.

Les Frères Jacques ✼

74 Dame Street, Dublin 2
DUBLIN (01) 6794555   COST £21–£58

Just opposite Dublin Castle is this wholeheartedly French family restaurant that makes a virtue of tradition. The backbone of the menu is composed of classics such as snails with garlic butter, game pâté on brioche with port sauce, saddle of lamb provençale, and beef fillet with wild mushrooms and red wine. There is also space, though, for chicken breast in a curry sauce with mango, and Irish-inspired strawberry pound cake with lemon sauce. A fine selection of fish and seafood, including lobster, turbot and oysters, is always available. The extensive wine list is largely French but allows in a few Spanish, Australian and South African bottles as well. House wines are £10.50.

CHEFS: Brian Porteus and David Robinson   PROPRIETORS: Jean-Jacques Caillabet and Suzy Caillabet   OPEN: Mon to Sat, exc Sat L; 12.30 to 2.30, 7.30 to 10.30 (11 Fri and Sat)   CLOSED: 25 to 30 Dec, some bank hols   MEALS: alc (main courses £16.50 to £20). Set L £13, Set D £20   SERVICE: 12.5%   CARDS: Access, Amex, Visa   DETAILS: 70 seats. Private parties: 40 main room, 16 and 40 private rooms. Vegetarian meals. Children's helpings. No smoking in 1 dining-room (no pipes in either dining-room). Music. Fax: (01) 6794725

Kapriol

45 Lower Camden Street, Dublin 2
DUBLIN (01) 4751235 and 2985496   COST £29–£53

'Our dishes are two centuries old,' boast the Peruzzis from their Italian restaurant, which is appealingly off the Dublin tourist track. There are good pasta and seafood specialities, as well as more familiar trattoria dishes and steaks. 'Sea melody' is prawns, scallops, turbot and salmon done in garlic, cream and brandy. Pheasant in season is marinated for several days in red wine and spices, and then casseroled. The Italian wines include many new-wave names. Carafes of house wine are £10.80.

CHEF: Egidia Peruzzi   PROPRIETORS: Egidia and Giuseppe Peruzzi   OPEN: Mon to Sat, D only (L by special arrangement); 7.30 to 12   CLOSED: 3 weeks Aug, bank hols   MEALS: alc (main courses £11 to £16)   SERVICE: 12.5%   CARDS: Access, Amex, Diners, Visa   DETAILS: 30 seats. Private parties: 36 main room. Vegetarian meals. Children's helpings. Smart dress preferred. Wheelchair access (1 step). Music

Locks

1 Windsor Terrace, Portobello, Dublin 8
DUBLIN (01) 543391 and 538352   COST £22–£56

Locks, not surprisingly, is by the canal, and a fiercely loyal clientele supports Brian Buckley's innovative cooking. A first course of black pudding with a sauce based on duck fat and onions has become something of a signature dish. Fish is intelligently cooked, and sauces are matched to meats with distinct aplomb: balsamic vinegar with calf's liver, orange and ginger with chargrilled chicken, port and thyme with venison, for instance. Crêpes suzette end a meal with panache. Duboeuf house wines at £10.95 head up a sound list.

CHEF: Brian Buckley   PROPRIETOR: Claire Douglas   OPEN: Mon to Sat, exc Sat L; 12.30 to 2, 7.15 to 11   CLOSED: 1 week Christmas, bank hols   MEALS: alc (main courses £13 to £18). Set L £13.95, Set D £21   SERVICE: 12.5%, card slips closed   CARDS: Access, Amex, Diners, Visa   DETAILS: 50 seats. Private parties: 50 main room, 10 and 30 private rooms. Vegetarian meals. Children's helpings. Smart dress preferred. Wheelchair access. No music. Fax: (01) 538352

Patrick Guilbaud

46 James Place, Dublin 2
DUBLIN (01) 6764192   COST £29–£76

Roast Challan duck with Seville orange and ginger sauce, and wild Irish salmon wrapped in potato shells served with red wine sauce and deep-fried herbs, show the thrust of Guillaume Lebrun's cooking in this elegant city-centre restaurant. Grand modern French is the idiom, and no expense is spared with the foie gras and black truffles, although fixed-price lunch and dinner menus offer financial relief from the *carte* and the 'menu surprise'. A sommelier advises diners about the choice of wine from the French list. House wines start at £13.

CHEF: Guillaume Lebrun   PROPRIETOR: Patrick Guilbaud   OPEN: Tue to Sat; 12.30 to 2, 7.30 to 10.15   CLOSED: bank hols   MEALS: alc (main courses £17 to £19). Set L £18.50, Set D £25. 'Menu surprise' £45   SERVICE: 15%   CARDS: Access, Amex, Diners, Visa   DETAILS: 80 seats. Private parties: 90 main room, 28 private room. Car park. Vegetarian meals with prior notice. Children's helpings on request. Smart dress preferred. No-smoking area. No music. Air-conditioned. Fax: (01) 6601546

La Stampa   [NEW ENTRY]

35 Dawson Street, Dublin 2
DUBLIN (01) 6778611   COST £20–£46

The ballroom of the Engineers' Institute became, in 1990, a mirrored, candlelit pleasure-dome, neatly anticipating the revamped brasserie school in London by a couple of years. In 1993, Paul Flynn – one of Nico Ladenis's brightest stars – came to cook here, and tongues have been set wagging. Modern modes fill out a menu that takes in chilled crab gazpacho with aïoli, a salad of grilled field mushrooms on rocket with white truffle oil and Parmesan, braised ham hock in its own bouillon with peas and chervil, and confit of Bresse pigeon on mashed potato with broad beans, cabbage and port. Trend-setters will be kept happy at dessert stage by strawberry crème brûlée and chocolate tart. The four-course set lunch looks an absolute bargain. House wines are £10.

CHEFS: Paul Flynn and Martin Lynch   PROPRIETOR: Louis Murray   OPEN: all week, exc L Sat and Sun; 12.30 to 2.30, 6.30 to 11.30 (11.45 Fri and Sat)   CLOSED: 25 Dec, St Stephen's Day, Good Fri   MEALS: alc (main courses £10 to £16). Set L £12.50   SERVICE: not inc (10% for 6 or more)   CARDS: Access, Amex, Diners, Visa   DETAILS: 200 seats. Private parties: 55 private room. No small children D. No pipes in dining-room. Music. Air-conditioned. Fax: (01) 6773336

All entries in the Guide *are rewritten every year, not least because restaurant standards fluctuate. Don't trust an out-of-date* Guide.

DUN LAOGHAIRE Co Dublin   map 9

Restaurant Na Mara

1 Harbour Road, Dun Laoghaire
DUBLIN (01) 2800509 and 2806767   COST £22–£70

The national railway's catering department running a restaurant in the converted booking-hall of an old commuter station – imagine how that would go down in Britain. 'Linen and table appointments are exceptionally good,' writes a reporter, and fish habitually arrives only 15 minutes before the place opens. Recommended dishes from a January menu were warm avocado and bacon salad, shellfish terrine, sea trout baked en croûte, corn-fed chicken with mushrooms and hot apple frangipane tart. Fine wines dominate the comprehensive list. House French is £10.

CHEFS: Derek Dunne and Stephane Magaud PROPRIETOR: Irish Rail Catering Services OPEN: Mon to Sat; 12.30 to 2.30, 7 to 10.30 CLOSED: 1 week Christmas, bank hols MEALS: alc (main courses £15.50 to £29.50). Set L £11 (2 courses) to £13.50, Set D £23 SERVICE: 15%, card slips closed CARDS: Access, Amex, Diners, Visa DETAILS: 75 seats. Private parties: 75 main room, 30 private room. Vegetarian meals. Children welcome. Smart dress preferred. No-smoking area. Wheelchair access (1 step). Music. Fax: (01) 2844649

DURRUS Co Cork   map 9

Blairs Cove

Durrus, nr Bantry
BANTRY (027) 61127
1m out of Durrus on Barleycove
to Goleen road   COST £34–£41

It couldn't be simpler. A cold buffet table is arrayed with seafood, cooked meats and enterprising salads; main courses revolve around the grill – rib of beef, rack of lamb, Greek-style chicken breast, for example – but also take in lambs' kidneys in mustard sauce and spicy vegetable sambar. Fish is to the fore: bouillabaisse, John Dory with ginger, lemon and shoyu (Japanese soy), baked salmon with horseradish crust. Puddings are home-made, cheeses are mainly from West Cork. House wines are £11.

CHEFS/PROPRIETORS: Philippe and Sabine De Mey OPEN: Tue (Mon July and Aug) to Sat, D only; 7.30 to 9.30 CLOSED: Nov to end Mar MEALS: Set D £24 SERVICE: 10%, card slips closed CARDS: Access, Amex, Diners, Visa DETAILS: 59 seats. Private parties: 35 main room. Car park. Vegetarian meals. Children's helpings. No-smoking area. No cigars/pipes in dining-room. Music

---

Prices quoted in the Guide *are based on information supplied by restaurateurs. The prices quoted at the top of each entry represent a range, from the lowest meal price to the highest; the latter is inflated by 20 per cent to take account of likely price rises during the year of the* Guide.

The Guide *always appreciates hearing about changes of chef or owner.*

GOREY Co Wexford   map 9

▲ *Marlfield House* ⁵✷

Courtown Road, Gorey
GOREY (055) 21124   COST £23–£46

Even if you don't sit in the conservatory to eat, the dining-room is the next best thing, as its walls are awash with painted ferns and foliage. The interiors of this Georgian sandstone house near Arklow are quite stunning, and many find the food is as good. Warm salad of cod, turbot and monkfish with balsamic vinegar, croustade of lambs' kidneys and oyster mushrooms with port sauce, and passion-fruit crème brûlée announce the style. Set-price menus include both soup and sorbet. The extensive wine list contains many classic bottles, as well as a rundown of recent vintages. House wines are £13.

CHEFS: Keith Arundel and Mary Bowe PROPRIETORS: Mary and Raymond Bowe OPEN: all week; 12.30 to 1.45, 7.15 to 9.30 MEALS: Set L £17.50, Set D £28. 'Library snack menu' L (main courses £5.50 to £14) SERVICE: 10%, card slips closed CARDS: Access, Amex, Diners, Visa DETAILS: 60 seats. Private parties: 60 main room, 25 private room. Car park. Vegetarian meals. Children's helpings. No children under 6 D. Smart dress preferred. No smoking in dining-room. Wheelchair access (also WC). No music ACCOMMODATION: 19 rooms, all with bath/shower. TV. Phone. B&B £60 to £383. Deposit: 1 night. Rooms for disabled. Children welcome. Baby facilities. Pets by arrangement. Afternoon teas. Garden. Sauna. Tennis. Doors close at 11.30. Confirm by 5. Fax: (055) 21572

HOWTH Co Dublin   map 9

King Sitric

East Pier, Howth
DUBLIN (01) 8325235 and 8326729   COST £21–£55

A Viking monarch gives his name to this green-painted fish restaurant overlooking Balscadden Bay. Traditional dishes form the backbone of the menu – gravlax, fish-cake with parsley sauce, poached skate with capers and black butter, for example – but there are also modernist moves afoot in queen scallops with nectarine in spicy sauce, or grilled plaice in a sauce of Cashel Blue. As at many another outwardly humble place in Ireland, an extraordinary wine list is harboured. House wines are £11.50.

CHEF: Aidan MacManus PROPRIETORS: Aidan and Joan MacManus OPEN: Mon to Sat (L May to Sept only); 12 to 3 (seafood bar), 6.30 to 11 CLOSED: first week Jan, week before Easter, bank hols MEALS: alc (main courses L £5 to £15.50, D £12.50 to £17.50). Set D £22 SERVICE: not inc, card slips closed CARDS: Access, Amex, Diners, Visa DETAILS: 70 seats. Private parties: 46 main room, 22 private room. Vegetarian meals. Children's helpings. Smart dress preferred. No-smoking area. Wheelchair access (also WC). No music. Fax: (01) 8392442

The Guide *office can quickly spot when a restaurateur is encouraging customers to write recommending inclusion – and sadly, several restaurants have been doing this in 1994. Such reports do not further a restaurant's cause. Please tell us if a restaurateur invites you to write to the* Guide.

▲ Assolas Country House

Kanturk
KANTURK (029) 50015
signposted from N72, NE of Kanturk,
8m W of Mallow   COST £33–£41

'An excellent family atmosphere in a most peaceful country setting,' summed up an English couple who stayed three nights at Assolas. The elegantly manicured gardens, well-furnished interiors and the achievement of Hazel Bourke's good domestic cooking will cause many to echo their sentiments. Choices include the likes of baked crab-cakes, roast chicken with a sauce of Ardrahan cheese (produced just up the road), venison with red wine and juniper, and great home-made ice-creams. 'Tipping is not encouraged,' say the proprietors. Joe Bourke knows his wines, and the list is a fine, predominantly French one. House wines – Guigal's red and white Côtes du Rhône – are £14.

CHEF: Hazel Bourke   PROPRIETORS: the Bourke family   OPEN: all week, D only; 7 to 8.30
CLOSED: 1 Nov to 1 Apr   MEALS: Set D £27   SERVICE: card slips closed   CARDS: Access, Amex, Diners, Visa   DETAILS: 30 seats. Private parties: 20 main room, 20 private room. Car park. Vegetarian meals. No children under 7. Smart dress preferred. No cigars in dining-room. No music   ACCOMMODATION: 9 rooms, all with bath/shower. Phone. B&B £50 to £144. Deposit: 1 night. Children welcome. Garden. Tennis. Fishing. Doors close at 11. Fax: (029) 50795

▲ Park Hotel Kenmare

Kenmare
KILLARNEY (064) 41200   COST £28–£73

Antiques abound at the Park, and chef Brian Cleere did some collecting of his own during a stint in Melbourne, so the out-of-the-ordinary is not restricted to the décor, but also extends to the repertoire. Sea trout marinated in oriental spices with a soy butter sauce, grilled monkfish in olive oil and herbs with garlic flowers, and poached chicken breast with lemon grass bouillon and coconut rice will provide plenty of food for thought as well as digestion. For those with room, there is the 'grand selection' of puddings. The wine list is gargantuan, and real effort has been made to offer a democratic spread of prices. House French is £15.25.

CHEF: Brian Cleere   PROPRIETOR: Francis Brennan   OPEN: all week; 1 to 1.45, 7 to 8.45
CLOSED: 6 Nov to 23 Dec, 2 Jan to 15 Apr   MEALS: alc (main courses £20 to £22.50). Set L £17.50, Set D £36   SERVICE: not inc   CARDS: Access, Amex, Diners, Visa   DETAILS: 80 seats. Private parties: 30 main room, 15 private room. Car park. Vegetarian meals with prior notice. Healthy eating options. Children's helpings. No children under 5 D. Jacket and tie. No-smoking area. Music   ACCOMMODATION: 50 rooms, 45 with bath/shower. TV. Phone. B&B £110 to £264. Deposit: £200. Rooms for disabled. Lift. Children welcome. Baby facilities. Afternoon teas. Garden. Tennis. Golf. Snooker. Doors close at midnight. Fax: (064) 41402

▲ Sheen Falls Lodge, La Cascade

Kenmare
KILLARNEY (064) 41600   COST £28–£57

Bent Hoyer's hotel stands a mile outside Kenmare, off the Glengarriff road. It is an appropriately stylish setting for cooking described to us as 'modern Irish'. Seafood is a strong suit and the hotel has its own smoke room for salmon. Dinner is fixed-price and chef Fergus Moore shows his flair with dishes such as oven-roast breast of pigeon with grilled polenta croûtons, truffle and madeira essence, and langoustines on a tomato and shallot concassé with sea urchin rouille. Visitors have described the wine list as 'outstanding' and the cellar as 'unique'. House wine is £15.95.

CHEF: Fergus Moore   PROPRIETOR: Bent Hoyer   OPEN: all week, D only, and Sun L; 1 to 2, 7.30 to 9.30   CLOSED: first 2 weeks Dec, Jan, first 2 weeks Feb   MEALS: Set L Sun £17.50, Set D £27.50 (2 courses) to £35   SERVICE: not inc, card slips closed   CARDS: Access, Amex, Diners, Visa   DETAILS: 120 seats. Private parties: 120 main room, 20 and 20 private rooms. Car park. Vegetarian meals. Children's helpings. Smart dress preferred. Wheelchair access (also WC). Music   ACCOMMODATION: 40 rooms, all with bath/shower. TV. Phone. B&B £125 to £230. Deposit: £100. Rooms for disabled. Lift. Children welcome. Baby facilities. Pets welcome (in kennels). Afternoon teas. Garden. Sauna. Tennis. Fishing. Snooker. Fax: (064) 41386

KILKENNY Co Kilkenny   map 9

▲ Lacken House

Dublin Road, Kilkenny
KILKENNY (056) 61085   COST £27–£42

Clonakilty black pudding, wild Wicklow venison, Callan bacon and Kilkenny Rooster potatoes are some of the local materials and products that define Eugene McSweeney's cooking. He also smokes his own salmon, trout and chicken, serves organic vegetables and is a staunch supporter of Irish cheesemakers. His cooking is serious, his style direct. The result on the plate might be boxty potato with marinated salmon, fillet of beef stuffed with Cashel Blue cheese, and chestnut leaves with home-made ice-cream and orange sauce. House wine, from a good list, is £12.

CHEF: Eugene McSweeney   PROPRIETORS: Eugene and Breda McSweeney   OPEN: Tue to Sat, D only; 6.30 to 10.30   CLOSED: 1 week Christmas   MEALS: alc (main courses £12 to £16.50). Set D £22   SERVICE: net prices, card slips closed   CARDS: Access, Amex, Diners, Visa   DETAILS: 30 seats. Private parties: 35 main room, 10 private room. Car park. Vegetarian meals. Children's helpings. Smart dress preferred. No-smoking area. No music. Air-conditioned   ACCOMMODATION: 8 rooms, all with bath/shower. TV. Phone. B&B £31 to £56. Deposit: 10%. Children welcome. Baby facilities. Garden. Doors close at midnight. Confirm by 6. Fax: (056) 62435

Net prices *in the details at the end of an entry indicates that the prices given on a menu and on a bill are inclusive of VAT and service charge, and that this practice is clearly stated on menu and bill.*

KINSALE Co Cork

map 9

▲ Blue Haven £

3 Pearse Street, Kinsale
CORK (021) 772209

COST £16–£48

Kinsale is a harbour town and the Cronins take full advantage of the local catch for their hotel/restaurant. Two kitchens are at work here: one for the bar/conservatory, the other for the main dining-room. Those wanting a snack might go for a bowl of seafood chowder, half a dozen Rossmore oysters, a plate of smoked salmon or some pasta. More substantial offerings are the likes of roast duckling from Mrs Cronin's farmyard, brill and scallop bake, or vegetables provençale in filo pastry. The wine list is a good read: look for the choice of intriguing French country wines procured personally by the owners. House wine is from £10.50.

CHEF: Stanley Matthews PROPRIETORS: Brian and Anne Cronin OPEN: all week; 12.30 to 3, 7 to 10.30 CLOSED: 25 Dec MEALS: alc (main courses £9 to £18.50). Bar menu (main courses £4.50 to £12.50) SERVICE: 10% restaurant, not inc bar, card slips closed CARDS: Access, Amex, Diners, Visa DETAILS: restaurant 50 seats, bar 112 seats. 8 tables outside. Private parties: 50 main room. Vegetarian meals. Children's helpings. Smart dress preferred. No-smoking area. Wheelchair access. Music. Air-conditioned ACCOMMODATION: 19 rooms, all with bath/shower. TV. Phone. B&B £45 to £130. Deposit: 1 night. Rooms for disabled. Children welcome. Baby facilities. Afternoon teas. Doors close at 11.30. Confirm by 7. Fax: (01) 774268

LETTERFRACK Co Galway

map 9

▲ Rosleague Manor ⁵⧣

Letterfrack
CLIFDEN (095) 41101
on N59 to Westport, 7m NW of Clifden

COST £25–£50

'The hotel is still our favourite place to stay,' write a pair of Londoners for whom summer without a trip to Rosleague would be unthinkable. They have noticed a Chinese tone creeping into some of Nigel Rush's thoughtful cooking: deep-fried king prawns in sesame-seed batter, and a ginger and spring onion vinaigrette with melon both cropped up among starters in June. 'Accomplished' sauces come with fish (vermouth cream with black sole, tomato and basil with turbot), while beef, lamb and 'excellent' lamb's liver with orange all impress. Vegetables and desserts have not always been as successful. The wine list offers a fair choice, with house wines from the Pays d'Oc at £11. Light lunches are available in the bar.

CHEF: Nigel Rush PROPRIETORS: Anne Foyle and Patrick Foyle OPEN: all week; 1 to 2.30, 8 to 9.30 CLOSED: Nov to Easter MEALS: alc (main courses £8.50 to £14.50). Set D £25 SERVICE: not inc, card slips closed CARDS: Access, Amex, Visa DETAILS: 65 seats. Private parties: 65 main room. Car park. Vegetarian meals. Children's helpings. Smart dress preferred. No smoking in dining-room. Wheelchair access (2 steps). No music ACCOMMODATION: 20 rooms, all with bath/shower. Phone. B&B £35 to £120. Rooms for disabled. Children welcome. Dogs by arrangement (not in public rooms). Afternoon teas. Garden. Sauna. Tennis. Snooker. Doors close at 11.30. Confirm by 6. Fax: (095) 41168

MALLOW Co Cork   map 9

▲ *Longueville House* ✦

Mallow
MALLOW (022) 47156
3m W of Mallow on N72 Killarney road   COST £23–£59

Built on the grand scale in 1720, Longueville nevertheless retains an unmistakably domestic air, thanks to the warm hospitality of Michael and Jane
O'Callaghan. Their son William is one of the most talented chefs in the Republic
and, although you will eat his food under the stern gaze of Eamonn de Valera and
others among the paintings in the Presidents' Dining Room, there is plenty to
raise the spirits. The style successfully maximises flavours in dishes such as
chicken and bacon roulade on bean sprouts, medallions of monkfish and salmon
in lime sauce, and beef sirloin with celeriac purée and a red wine sauce. Desserts,
of the likes of gratinated apples with honey and almond ice-cream or a grand
selection, should not be missed. The fairly priced wine list offers many French
classics and includes a generous slate of Spanish bottles. House wines are £12.

CHEF: William O'Callaghan   PROPRIETORS: Michael and Jane O'Callaghan   OPEN: all week, D
only, and Sun L; 12.30 to 2, 7.30 to 9   CLOSED: mid-Dec to mid-Mar   MEALS: Set L Sun £15, Set
D £25 to £38   SERVICE: not inc, card slips closed   CARDS: Access, Amex, Diners, Visa
DETAILS: 55 seats. Private parties: 40 main room, 20 private room. Car park. Vegetarian meals.
Children's helpings. No children under 8. Smart dress preferred. No smoking in dining-room.
Wheelchair access (2 steps; also WC). No music   ACCOMMODATION: 16 rooms, all with
bath/shower. TV. Phone. B&B £51 to £102. Children welcome. Afternoon teas. Garden. Fishing.
Snooker. Doors close at midnight. Confirm by 6. Fax: (022) 47459

MIDLETON Co Cork   map 9

Farmgate

Coolbawn, Midleton
MIDLETON (021) 632771   COST £14–£37

'Local produce, freshness and lack of disguise' underpin Máróg O'Brien's
culinary philosophy at this unpretentious restaurant in the centre of town. That
translates as scallops in a Pernod sauce, moules marinière, bowls of tripe,
salmon fillet in lemon and cream, and sliced fillet of beef in a sauce of Jameson's
whiskey. Prices, at lunch-times especially, are low: £3.95 for roast pork with red
cabbage, for instance. The short, handwritten wine list leaves you to guess the
vintages. Weekly-changing house wines are £9.50.

CHEFS: Máróg O'Brien and Angela Collins   PROPRIETOR: Máróg O'Brien   OPEN: Mon to Sat L,
Fri and Sat D; 12 to 4, 7.30 to 9.45   MEALS: alc (main courses L £4 to £7, D £9 to £14)   SERVICE:
not inc   CARDS: Access, Visa   DETAILS: 75 seats. 5 tables outside. Private parties: 60 main
room, 20 private room. Vegetarian meals. Children's helpings. No-smoking area. Wheelchair
access (1 step; also WC). Music. Air-conditioned

Not inc *in the details at the end of an entry indicates that no service charge is made and
any tipping is at the discretion of the customer.*

MOYCULLEN Co Galway   map 9

Drimcong House

Moycullen
GALWAY (091) 85115 and 85585   COST £25–£49

Gerry Galvin is a collector of recipes, recollections and poems; he is also a
talented chef who is bold enough to go his own way. He holds cookery courses
for young enthusiasts in this lakeland house not far from Galway, but feeds all
comers from a repertoire that is traditional (roast rack of mutton with caper
sauce), eclectic (grilled oysters with polenta and red pepper mayonnaise) and
idiosyncratic (salad of melon and Jerusalem artichokes). Children and
vegetarians have their own menus. House wine is £9.50.

CHEF: Gerry Galvin   PROPRIETORS: Gerry and Marie Galvin   OPEN: Tue to Sat, D only; 7 (6.30
summer) to 10.30   CLOSED: Christmas to Mar   MEALS: alc (main courses £16 to £17.50). Set D
£15.95 to £18.95   SERVICE: 10%, card slips closed   CARDS: Access, Amex, Diners, Visa
DETAILS: 60 seats. Private parties: 60 main room, 12 private room. Car park. Vegetarian meals.
Children's helpings. Wheelchair access (3 steps; also WC). Music

NEWPORT Co Mayo   map 9

▲ Newport House ⁵⁄ₓ

Newport
NEWPORT (098) 41222   COST £33–£41

Overlooking the tidal river and quay, between Achill Island and the mountains
of Mayo, this Georgian-style house has countless attractions and comforts.
Produce is gleaned from the fishery, the walled kitchen garden and the farm;
salmon is home-smoked. Dinner might begin with gravlax or carpaccio, before
carrot and coriander soup and a handful of main courses such as beef Stroganov
or scallops with leeks and Noilly Prat. Desserts range from fresh fruit and home
made ice-creams to strawberry mille-feuille. Kieran Thompson's classy wine list
is worth a serious perusal. House wines are from £10.

CHEF: John Gavin   PROPRIETORS: Kieran and Thelma Thompson   OPEN: all week D (light L also
available); 7.30 to 9.30   CLOSED: 1 Oct to 18 Mar   MEALS: Set D £28   SERVICE: not inc, card
slips closed   CARDS: Access, Amex, Diners, Visa   DETAILS: 36 seats. Private parties: 12 main
room. Car park. Vegetarian meals with prior notice. Children's helpings on request. Smart
dress preferred. No smoking in dining-room. Wheelchair access (3 steps). No music
ACCOMMODATION: 18 rooms, all with bath/shower. Phone. B&B £58 to £120. Rooms for
disabled. Children welcome. Baby facilities. Pets welcome (annexe only). Afternoon teas.
Garden. Fishing. Snooker. Doors close at 11.30. Confirm by 6. Fax: (098) 41613

▲ *This symbol means accommodation is available.*

*The 1996 Guide will be published before Christmas 1995. Reports on meals are most
welcome at any time of the year, but are particularly valuable in the spring. Send them to*
The Good Food Guide, *FREEPOST, 2 Marylebone Road, London NW1 1YN. No stamp
is needed if posted in the UK.*

OUGHTERARD Co Galway	map 9

▲ *Currarevagh House* ⁵⭑

Oughterard, Connemara
GALWAY (091) 82312 and 82313
4m NW of Oughterard on Hill of Doon
Lakeshore road   COST £25–£30

'A time warp. A brilliantly eccentric Edwardian country-house hotel,' enthused one visitor to this superbly situated retreat overlooking Lough Corrib with gardens sweeping down to the water's edge. It caters mainly for residents, although passers-by can book for dinner if there is room. Set five-course meals, along the lines of crab bisque, lettuce and parsley mousse, roast lamb, meringue baskets of strawberries plus Irish cheese, are served by an army of waitresses with massive trays. Second helpings are encouraged and great hospitality abounds. House wines start at £8.20.

CHEF: June Hodgson   PROPRIETORS: Harry and June Hodgson   OPEN: all week, D only; 8 CLOSED: Nov to Mar   MEALS: Set D £18   SERVICE: 10%   DETAILS: 30 seats. Private parties: 12 main room. Car park. Vegetarian meals with prior notice. Children's helpings with prior notice. Smart dress preferred. No smoking in dining-room. No music   ACCOMMODATION: 15 rooms, all with bath/shower. B&B £42.50 to £90. Deposit: £40. Children by arrangement. Dogs by arrangement (not in public rooms). Garden. Tennis. Fishing. Doors close at midnight. Confirm by 4. Fax: (091) 82731

SHANAGARRY Co Cork	map 9

▲ *Ballymaloe House* ⁵⭑

Shanagarry, nr Midleton
MIDLETON (021) 652531
2m outside Cloyne on Ballycotton road   COST £21–£49

Staying the distance for 30 years means that people will look for signs of flagging in your performance. Some niggles have surfaced, but by and large reports on Ballymaloe are positive, precisely because long practice has to confer some sureness of touch. The 'deservedly legendary hospitality' at this comfortable country-house hotel never seems to weary: playmates are found for the kids, for whom chips on demand ensure tranquillity at mealtimes. The post-chip generation will enjoy shrimp tartlet, warm salad of sweetbreads, monkfish with red pepper sauce and sea kale, and the eighteenth-century-sounding braised hogget with wild garlic, buttered scallions and thyme leaves. Home-made ice-creams, chocolate fudge cake or rhubarb tart will send diners away contented. The wine list also contains much to delight. House wines from Georges Duboeuf are £13.

---

⁵⭑ *indicates that smoking is either banned altogether or that a dining-room is maintained for non-smokers. The symbol does not apply to restaurants that simply have no-smoking areas.*

CHEFS: Myrtle Allen and Paddy Cullinane   PROPRIETORS: Ivan and Myrtle Allen   OPEN: all week; 12.45 to 2, 7 to 9.30   MEALS: alc L (main courses £6 to £12). Buffet L Sun £16.50, Set D £30   SERVICE: not inc, card slips closed   CARDS: Access, Amex, Diners, Visa   DETAILS: 90 seats. Private parties: 60 main room, 25 private room. Car park. Vegetarian meals. Children's helpings. Smart dress preferred. No smoking in 1 dining-room. No cigars/pipes in dining-rooms. Wheelchair access (also WC). No music   ACCOMMODATION: 30 rooms, all with bath/shower. Phone. B&B £67 to £120. Deposit: £50. Rooms for disabled. Children welcome. Pets by arrangement. Garden. Swimming-pool. Tennis. Golf. Doors close at 1am. Confirm by 2. Fax: (021) 652021

WATERFORD Co Waterford   map 9

Dwyers ✸

8 Mary Street, Waterford
WATERFORD (051) 77478   COST £20–£37

The scale of this intimate restaurant down a Waterford side-street may be small, but the culinary span is broad. There is classic French inspiration in fillets of John Dory à la niçoise, Russian in mushroom and blue cheese pirozhki, and modern rootlessness in chicken livers in filo with Dubonnet and orange, or marinated smoked salmon with lemon and fennel sabayon. The lamb noisettes en croûte with minted hollandaise prompted one man to reproduce the dish at home. A concise, well-chosen wine list (from £10.20) completes the picture.

CHEF: Martin Dwyer   PROPRIETORS: Martin and Sile Dwyer   OPEN: Mon to Sat, D only; 6 to 10   CLOSED: 1 week Christmas, 2 weeks July   MEALS: alc (main courses £10.50 to £13). Set D (6 to 7.30) £13   SERVICE: not inc   CARDS: Access, Amex, Diners, Visa   DETAILS: 32 seats. Private parties: 30 main room, 8 private room. Vegetarian meals. Children's helpings. No smoking in 1 dining-room. Wheelchair access (also WC). Music

---

WEXFORD Co Wexford   map 9

Granary

Westgate, Wexford
WEXFORD (053) 23935   COST £20–£42

A converted grain store on the Wexford coast, the Granary offers a menu that manages to please both traditionalists and the avant-garde. Mussels baked with tomato and garlic, peppered sirloin, and profiteroles with chocolate sauce share the menu with grilled salmon with carrot and lime, chicken breast stuffed with blue cheese and walnuts, and fruit compote poached in geranium syrup. The ambience is bustly, the wines are well chosen. House Duboeuf is £9.95.

CHEFS: Mary Hatton and Vincent Whitmore   PROPRIETORS: Paddy and Mary Hatton   OPEN: Mon to Sat (Sun bank hols and Wexford Festival) D only; 6 to 10   CLOSED: 3 days Christmas   MEALS: alc (main courses £10.50 to £15.50). Set D £12.95 (6 to 7/7.30) to £18.95   SERVICE: not inc   CARDS: Access, Amex, Diners, Visa   DETAILS: 45 seats. Private parties: 20 main room, 20 private room. Vegetarian meals. Children's helpings 6 to 7.30. Wheelchair access. Music

---

See the back of the Guide *for a listing of all restaurants in the Main Entries sections.*

WICKLOW Co Wicklow   map 9

▲ *Old Rectory* ꭥ❊

Wicklow Town
WICKLOW (0404) 67048   COST £31–£44

'No fuss, no pressure, no false airs and graces' might sum up a score of places in Ireland, but was written in this instance about the Saunders' charming peach-fronted house on the edge of town. Linda Saunders is fond of edible flowers – the tendency reaches its apogee during the County Gardens Festival when a 10-course floral menu is devised – and there is an enveloping sense of the pastoral to her dishes. These have included bean and parsnip soup with wild garlic flowers, Irish mist egg nog with frosted primrose cinnamon biscuits, 'farmer's delight' (pot-roasted beef with smoked pheasant sausage in damson wine), and fruit medley with apricot coulis and a rose-petal tartlet. Home-made bread is described as 'excellent'. The wine list is notably strong in Spain, including two house wines at £11.

CHEF: Linda Saunders   PROPRIETORS: Paul and Linda Saunders   OPEN: all week, D only; 8 (7.30 to 9 Fri and Sat)   CLOSED: 1 Nov to 30 Mar   MEALS: alc (main courses £16 to £18). Set D £25   SERVICE: card slips closed   CARDS: Access, Amex, Diners, Visa   DETAILS: 20 seats. Private parties: 20 main room. Car park. Vegetarian meals. Children's helpings. Smart dress preferred. No smoking in dining-room. Wheelchair access (3 steps). Music   ACCOMMODATION: 5 rooms, all with bath/shower. TV. Phone. B&B £64 to £88. Deposit: £30. Children welcome. Baby facilities. Garden. Doors close at 12.30am. Confirm by 6. Fax: (0404) 69181

Round-ups

Good restaurants are not evenly distributed across the country. If we find ourselves in a black spot and really must eat, how can we get a reasonable meal? If we want a decent pub lunch, which one do we choose? The round-ups are a mixed bag of places that take in bars, cafés, bistros and the like. Some are 'useful in the area', some were in the *Guide* last year but have new chefs. These are places on which we may need more reports, or for which reports may have been contradictory, or where standards over the year may have fluctuated. But they are all worth a visit, and if we get some more feedback from you, the readers of the *Guide*, some of them could become main entries in the future. In response to numerous requests, we have kept all the round-up entries outside London together, and have arranged them alphabetically by location within England, Scotland, Wales and the Channel Islands, as with the main entries.

England

● **ALTRINCHAM** (Greater Manchester)
Franc's 2 Goose Green, 061-941 3954. Pleasant French bistro that's good for an informal meal at fairly modest prices. Lots of choice on the menu.
Smart Orders 4 Kings Court, Railway Street, 061-928 6983. Courtyard restaurant off a shopping street. Well-presented meals along the lines of cheese filo parcels and Cajun salmon.

● **AMBLESIDE** (Cumbria)
Sheila's Cottage The Slack, (053 94) 33079. Long-established cottage and converted barn restaurant that's best for simple things such as potted shrimps, home-baked breads and cakes, and fresh coffee.

● **ASHFORD** (Derbyshire)
Riverside Country House Hotel Fennel Street, (062 981) 4275. The river in question provides a peaceful backdrop to the brasserie-style dining-room, as do the established gardens. Fair results.

● **ASKRIGG** (North Yorkshire)
King's Arms Hotel Market Place, (0969) 650258. Although it shot to fame as The Drovers Arms in the TV series *All Creatures Great and Small*, this coaching-inn has a deserved reputation as a comfortable place to stay and for its food.

● **ATHERSTONE** (Warwickshire)
Chapel House Friar's Gate, (0827)

718949. Attractive Georgian property with comfortable accommodation, serving fair meals.

● **BARNARD CASTLE**
(County Durham)
Market Place Teashop 29 Market Place, (0833) 690110. Restful stone-flagged tea-rooms open till late afternoon. Hot lunch dishes, puddings, prices and service have all received a favourable response.

● **BASLOW** (Derbyshire)
Cavendish Hotel (0246) 582311. This old stone place occupies an attractive corner of the Chatsworth Estate and, inside, all is comfortable. Two restaurants offer lots of choice between them, and standards are upheld.

● **BATH** (Avon)
Beaujolais 5A Chapel Row, Queen Square, (0225) 423417. Long-running French restaurant for reasonably priced bistro-style food. Still popular, but recent reports have had a few niggles.
Moon and Sixpence 6A Broad Street, (0225) 460962. Courtyard bistro that's pleasantly decorated and particularly relaxed. Roast pigeon breast with cherries and red wine sauce, and lemon and lime tart are representative.
Priory Hotel Weston Road, (0225) 331922. Country-house hotel in the suburbs. The kitchen employs a lighter

style while retaining traditional French and English cuisines. More reports, please.

● **BERWICK-UPON-TWEED** (Northumberland)

Rob Roy Dock Road, Tweedmouth, (0289) 306428. Cosy place for a bar meal of Lindisfarne oysters, mussel chowder or fish dishes. These are fine, but some things are more successful than others.

● **BEVERLEY** (Humberside)

Cerutti 2 Beverley Station, Station Square, (0482) 866700. Converted railway station with a pleasant atmosphere and a predominantly fish menu (although there is more meat here than at its sister establishment, Cerutti's, in Hull). Generally mild flavours and decent ancillaries.

● **BICKLEY MOSS** (Cheshire)

Cholmondeley Arms Cholmondeley, nr Bickley Moss, (0829) 720300. Converted schoolhouse operating as a pub and brasserie with good accommodation. An eclectic menu has lots to offer.

● **BIRMINGHAM** (West Midlands)

Café des Artistes Lakeside, The Custard Factory, Gibb Street, 021-608 7878. The Custard Factory is billed as 'Birmingham's revolutionary new arts and media quarter' (it is the old Bird's Custard works). This modern café has a menu of salads, risottos, pastas, etc., and baguettes and savoury croissants are always available.

Punjab Paradise 377 Ladypool Road, 021-449 4110. Balti house with a civilised atmosphere and accommodating staff. Fresh ingredients, forthright flavours and decent breads. Only open evenings, and Sunday lunch. Cheap.

San Carlo 4 Temple Street, 021-633 0251. Ristorante/pizzeria five minutes' walk from New Street Station. Modern décor and old-style trattoria cooking, plus a blackboard listing fresh fish.

Taipan 2A Wrottesley Street, 021-622 3883. Interesting Korean restaurant where diners can barbecue their own pre-marinated meats and seafood.

● **BLEWBURY** (Oxfordshire)

Blewbury Inn London Road, (0235) 850496. Restaurant and bar seats for those choosing from the interesting menu in this unspoilt pub. Starters and puddings are the best things; country pâté with apple chutney, lambs' kidneys with mustard sauce, and iced coconut parfait have brought favourable response.

● **BOOTLE** (Merseyside)

Rui's 13 Aintree Road, 051-922 1212. Colourful trattoria run by helpful staff and offering value for money. Fresh fish, pastas and seafood risotto are recommended.

● **BOURNEMOUTH** (Dorset)

Helvetia 61 Charminster Road, (0202) 555447. Swiss restaurant and wine bar serving more than just fondues, and to good effect.

● **BRADFORD-ON-AVON** (Wiltshire)

Dandy Lion 35 Market Street, (0225) 863433. Potentially useful pub/restaurant; starters and puddings have been much more successful than mains.

● **BRANSCOMBE** (Devon)

Masons Arms (029 780) 300. Spruce fourteenth-century pub with food that's a cut above the average, and with well-equipped accommodation, both in cottages and the main building.

● **BRIGHTON** (East Sussex)

Terre à Terre 7 Pool Valley, (0273) 729051. Vegetarian restaurant that, while simple and unflashy, avoids the sandals and wholemeal approach, instead drawing inspiration from Italy. Firm flavours, large portions, interesting desserts, decent espresso.

Topps Hotel 17 Regency Square, (0273) 729334. Bottoms Restaurant is in the basement and, thanks to its own entrance, is just as popular with outsiders as it is with residents. Competent production of basically English food.

● **BRIGHTWELL BALDWIN** (Oxfordshire)

Lord Nelson Inn (0491) 612497. Lovely place with a pretty garden and seats under willow trees. Good variety of food changing according to what's in season.

● **Bristol** (Avon)
Bistro Twenty One 21 Cotham Road South, Kingsdown, (0272) 421744. French bistro with an easy atmosphere and competent cooking. Desserts have on occasion been better than main-course offerings.

Michael's 129 Hotwell Road, Clifton, (0272) 276190. Attractive, Victorian-style surroundings, a comfortable bar and glamorous menus; though, apart from desserts, results upon occasion have not lived up to expectations.

● **Broadstairs** (Kent)
Marchesi Bros. 18 Albion Street, (0843) 862481. Friendly, family-run restaurant that remains popular for traditional seaside favourites such as moules marinière, coq au vin, and shallow-fried wing of local skate with prawns, croûtons and lemon butter.

● **Brockenhurst** (Hampshire)
Le Blaireau Lyndhurst Road, (0590) 23032. Unusual roadhouse restaurant (often packed-out) that's useful for New Forest visitors wanting outside tables and French-inspired food.

● **Burgh le Marsh** (Lincolnshire)
Windmill 46 High Street, (0754) 810281. Restaurant in the mill yard that, appropriately, bakes its own fresh bread. The set-price menu is competitively priced, the food enjoyable. Expect such items as deep-fried beignets, apricot and walnut chicken, and innovative vegetables.

● **Bury St Edmunds** (Suffolk)
Ravenwood Hall Rougham Green, nr Bury St Edmunds, (0359) 70345. Lovely old house and grounds that makes a relaxing place for a short stay, with competent cooking and keen service.

● **Cambridge** (Cambridgeshire)
Browns 23 Trumpington Street, (0223) 461655. Buzzing, youthful all-day restaurant (other branches in Brighton, Bristol and Oxford) serving up decent burgers, pies, ribs and pastas. Children's menu available.

● **Canterbury** (Kent)
George's Brasserie 71–72 Castle Street, (0227) 765658. Lively, centrally situated brasserie where some dishes are better than others: main courses and coffee have scored higher than starters or sweets.

● **Chalfont St Peter** (Buckinghamshire)
Water Hall Amersham Road, (0494) 873430. Promising French cooking from chef David Mutter and a warm welcome from staff. The set-price dinner menu and Sunday lunch menu offer reasonable value.

● **Chester** (Cheshire)
Abbey Green and Garden House 1 Rufus Court, Northgate Street, (0244) 313251 and 320004. A change of ownership at these two restaurants on the same site. Abbey Green is vegetarian and the Garden House offers, in addition, meat and fish. Reports, please.

Franc's 14A Cuppin Street, (0244) 317952. Useful French brasserie attracting a happy crowd. Often busy, although there are plenty of tables. Ideal for reasonably priced plats du jour and interesting, mostly unpasteurised French cheeses.

● **Chichester** (West Sussex)
Comme Ça 67 Broyle Road, (0243) 788724. Popular French place that welcomes pre- and post-theatre bookings, does a special family lunch on Sundays (with a children's menu) and is useful for familiar choices.

Little London 38–39 Little London, (0243) 537550. Mediterranean-style menu in the heart of Chichester. Some successful flavours, others less so; on occasion let down by over-casual service.

● **Clacton-on-Sea** (Essex)
Wendle's 3 Rosemary Road, (0255) 426316. Charmingly run restaurant specialising in every conceivable type of fish, including tropical, together with game and steaks. More reports, please.

● **Clitheroe** (Lancashire)
Brown's Bistro 10 York Street, (0200) 26928. Good-value bistro producing familiar food for a local clientele.

● **Coggeshall** (Essex)
White Hart Market End, (0376) 561654. Old but comfortable inn with accommodation and fair Italian food.

● **COLTISHALL** (Norfolk)
Norfolk Place Point House, High Street, (0603) 738991. Nick Gill (ex-Hambleton Hall) has now opened his own restaurant and is cooking five courses (an unusually formal fixed-price menu) using quality ingredients; foie gras, white truffles, lobster and Cromer crab often feature. Open only for dinner. Reports, please.

● **COMBE HAY** (Avon)
Wheatsheaf Combe Hay, nr Bath, (0225) 833504. Attractive hillside pub with good bar food and a garden with seating.

● **COTHERSTONE** (County Durham)
Fox and Hounds (0833) 500241. Small pub in pretty countryside serving reliable bar food (the same menu is also available in the restaurant) and traditional Sunday lunch. The three tastefully furnished *en suite* bedrooms make this a pleasant place to stay.

● **CRANBORNE** (Dorset)
La Fosse London House, The Square, (0725) 517604. Fair cooking from a reasonably priced set menu. There is also accommodation.

● **CROYDON** (Surrey)
Siamese 164 Cherry Orchard Road, East Croydon, 081-681 3402. Thai restaurant with welcoming staff and a long menu. Freshly cooked, well-prepared dishes and bought-in ice-creams.

● **CUMNOR** (Oxfordshire)
The Vine 11 Abingdon Road, (0865) 862567. Busy pub with a long blackboard menu of freshly made things, competitively priced. Good choices have been smoked salmon tart, moules marinière, chicken satay, and lamb stir-fry. Garden with children's play area.

● **DARLEY ABBEY** (Derbyshire)
Darleys on the River Darley Abbey Mill, (0332) 364987. Well-run riverside restaurant utilising good ingredients. Sunday lunch has received favourable mention.

● **DARTMOUTH** (Devon)
Taylor's 8 The Quay, (0803) 832748. Husband-and-wife team cooking a 'marvellous range' of fresh fish and choice puddings. Super location overlooking the river.

● **DODDINGTON** (Lincolnshire)
Littlehouse Restaurant Doddington Hall, (0522) 690980. Period piece adjunct to Doddington Hall that's open for teas as well as lunch, dinner and Sunday lunch. Informal, open-plan surroundings and reasonable execution of mostly English recipes, although results have been known to vary.

● **DODDISCOMBSLEIGH** (Devon)
Nobody Inn (0647) 52394. Cosy, friendly pub that's big on wines and British farmhouse cheeses. Traditional bar food of the best kind.

● **DORCHESTER-ON-THAMES** (Oxfordshire)
George Hotel High Street, (0865) 340404. Comfortable coaching-inn offering a range of options foodwise and an interesting selection of wines.

● **DULVERTON** (Somerset)
Ashwick House nr Dulverton, (0398) 23868. Edwardian country house delightfully situated overlooking a valley; fine views from some bedrooms. Short set menus and good ingredients carefully cooked.

● **EASTON ON THE HILL** (Northamptonshire)
Exeter Arms Stamford Road, (0780) 57503. Pub and restaurant majoring in steaks and Sunday lunch. Incidentals such as salads and coffee have not always satisfied.

● **EAST WITTON** (North Yorkshire)
Blue Lion (0969) 24273. Unspoilt estate village with a honey-stone old coaching-inn. An impressive range of modern bar meals and an extensive wine list.

● **ELSTOW** (Bedfordshire)
St Helena High Street, (0234) 344848. Elegant house with conservatory addition just two miles out from Bedford. Reliable execution from a contemporary menu, and attentive staff. More reports, please.

● **ELTON** (Cambridgeshire)
Loch Fyne Oyster Bar The Old Dairy, (0832) 280298. Fresh and smoked seafood and fish served with the minimum of frills. A refreshingly wide range of choices, although presentation

and service have been less wonderful for some.

● **EMSWORTH** (Hampshire)
36 on the Quay 47 South Street, (0243) 375592 and 372257. Smart restaurant with views of the quay, a pleasant ambience and attentive service. Good for fish.

● **EPPING** (Essex)
Neil's 142 High Street, (0992) 576767. Charming place with a regularly changing menu. Fish is a feature (barracuda in a grapefruit and lime sauce), as are dessert soufflés: baked Alaska, and raspberry soufflé with a hot fruit and vodka sauce have been enjoyed. More reports, please.

● **EVESHAM** (Hereford & Worcester)
Riverside The Parks, Offenham Road, (0386) 446200. Pleasant hotel for reliable cooking and imaginative flavours.

● **EXETER** (Devon)
Royal Clarence Hotel Raleigh's Restaurant, Cathedral Yard, (0392) 58464. Old hostelry (now owned by Queens Moat Houses) frequented by those on weekend breaks. Stay with the straightforward dishes for best results.

● **FAWLEY** (Buckinghamshire)
Walnut Tree (049 163) 8360. Charming country inn convenient for Henley, popular for bar food and, in the restaurant and conservatory addition, full meals. Service has been known to vary; accommodation is comfortable.

● **FLETCHING** (East Sussex)
Griffin Inn (0825) 722890. Highly popular sixteenth-century inn listing good bar meals on the blackboard. A wide choice of standard fare alongside modern dishes such as Mediterranean fish pie and king prawns in filo pastry. Well-kept real ales; separate restaurant menu.

● **FOSSEBRIDGE** (Gloucestershire)
Fossebridge Inn (0285) 720721. Ivy-clad Tudor pub in a picturesque Cotswold setting. Comprehensive wine list and real ales, but food has received variable reports.

● **FOULSHAM** (Norfolk)
Gamp Claypit Lane, (036 284) 4114. Friendly restaurant in an out-of-the-way village. Worth a detour for fair British

cooking; spinach soup, fresh fish, and bread-and-butter pudding are typical choices.

● **GATESHEAD** (Tyne & Wear)
Fumi 248 Durham Road, 091-477 1152. Japanese restaurant with Formica tables that's only open for dinner Tuesday to Sunday. Lowish prices compared with most of this type; one of a very few in the North-east.

● **GLOOSTON** (Leicestershire)
Old Barn Inn Andrews Lane, (0858) 545215. Delightful old inn where bar food is taken seriously, as are real ales.

● **GOOSNARGH** (Lancashire)
Solo Goosnargh Lane, (0772) 865206. Pleasant restaurant where reassuring food is featured on the set-price menu. The wine list has a good selection of half-bottles.

● **GOSFIELD** (Essex)
Green Man The Street, (0787) 472746. Well-frequented pub producing sound English food, and different cuisines promoted on special evenings. Game soup with sherry, roast shoulder of wild boar, home-made chips, and syrup pudding are the type of thing to expect.

● **GRANGE IN BORROWDALE** (Cumbria)
Borrowdale Gates Hotel Grange in Borrowdale, nr Keswick, (076 87) 77204. Hotel just below Derwent Water that has the benefit of excellent views. The table d'hôte dinners have met with approval; coffee and truffles are included.

● **GREAT YARMOUTH** (Norfolk)
Seafood Restaurant 85 North Quay, (0493) 856009. Small family restaurant specialising in fresh fish from Lowestoft, and with fresh lobster from the tank. Some rather nice wines at reasonable prices.

● **GUISELEY** (West Yorkshire)
Harry Ramsden's White Cross, (0943) 874641. Friendly, fast-moving fish-and-chips restaurant (queues likely) with daily specials and first-class desserts such as steamed ginger sponge and bread-and-butter pudding. Cheap.

● **HALIFAX** (West Yorkshire)
Holdsworth House Holdsworth, nr Halifax, (0422) 240024. Jacobean house,

now a comfortable hotel with some atmosphere. First-class service and fair cooking.

● **HARROGATE** (North Yorkshire)
Bettys 1 Parliament Street, (0423) 502746. Constantly packed, splendid tea-room where service is a strong point, as is the provision of separate smoking and no-smoking rooms. Light lunches are served too, although it would be a shame to miss the cakes.

● **HAWKSHEAD** (Cumbria)
Room with a View 1st Floor, Laburnum House, Hawkshead, nr Ambleside, (053 94) 36751. This vegetarian, no-smoking restaurant describes itself as a 'natural food café', and has freshly baked bread and cakes, also successful soups, nut pâté, aubergine charlotte, broccoli strudel, etc.

● **HESWALL** (Merseyside)
Crispin's 106 Telegraph Road, 051-342 8750. Small place run by a husband-and-wife team. Fair cooking; if it's on the menu, finish with bread-and-butter pudding.

● **HIGH WYCOMBE** (Buckinghamshire)
Blue Flag Cadmore End, (0494) 881183. Pub producing tried-and-tested dishes; good for home-smoked salmon, roast duck and treacle tart.

● **HOCKLEY HEATH** (West Midlands)
Nuthurst Grange Nuthurst Grange Lane, (0564) 783972. Country-house-style cooking with prices to match. Best end of English lamb with rosemary and onion mousse, stuffed quails with wild mushroom and truffle sauce, and decent coffee and petits fours are typical.

● **HOPTON WAFERS** (Shropshire)
Crown Inn (0299) 270372. Creeper-clad country inn dating from the sixteenth century. The blackboard daily specials are more intriguing than the standard bar food menu. Other pluses are good wines and a garden sloping down to a stream.

● **ILKLEY** (West Yorkshire)
Bettys 32–34 The Grove, (0943) 608029. Branch of the well-known Yorkshire tea-room that also serves light meals. Don't leave without sampling the cakes.

● **IPSWICH** (Suffolk)
Orwell House 4A Orwell Place, (0473) 230254. Pleasing cooking, good presentation, welcoming atmosphere.
Singing Chef 200 St Helen's Street, (0473) 255236. Long-established French bistro. Variable results but desserts are good, as are grilled goats' cheese and ragoût of beef. Prices are low (especially if you stay with the fixed-price menu).

● **IVY HATCH** (Kent)
Plough Coach Road, (0732) 810268. Traditional tile-hung Kentish pub with brasserie-style food and a conservatory and garden.

● **KENILWORTH** (Warwickshire)
Simpson's 101 Warwick Road, (0926) 864567. New place attracting a smart crowd and offering well-conceived food from a set menu (two or three courses). Duck leg confit, Lyon sausage salad, Tuscan red peppers, Normandy apple flan, and bread-and-butter pudding are fashionable examples. More reports, please.

● **KESWICK** (Cumbria)
Brundholme Hotel Brundholme Road, (076 87) 74495. Quietly located country-house hotel with fine fell views and an ambitious kitchen. Although short, the menu is appealing and dishes are quite involved; vegetables maintain standards.
Dale Head Hotel Lake Thirlmere, Keswick, (076 87) 72478. Small family-run hotel producing good standard meals.

● **KINGSTEIGNTON** (Devon)
Old Rydon Inn Rydon Road, (0626) 54626. Comfortable old pub half hidden by a housing estate. Sit in the conservatory for freshly made bar meals, including seafood dishes, and excellent wines. A separate children's menu is available.

● **KIRDFORD** (West Sussex)
Half Moon Inn (0403) 820223. Archetypal village inn with a well-tended garden and a reputation for fresh fish. Drinkable house wines, decent coffee.

● **KNUTSFORD** (Cheshire)
Dick Willett's The Toft, Toft Road, (0565) 632603. Enthusiastic, jovially run vegetarian restaurant and B&B housed in

a rustic barn conversion. Fair results from the set menu of savoury toasts, crêpes, strudels and traditional desserts: comforting rather than innovative food.
La Belle Epoque 60 King Street, (0565) 633060. A beautiful building both outside and in – period drapes and lots of Art Nouveau – and a recent conversion from restaurant to brasserie (still with accommodation). First reports are not discouraging; the atmosphere is a plus.

● **LACOCK** (Wiltshire)
At the Sign of the Angel Church Street, (0249) 730230. Ancient merchant's house in a National Trust village that's appropriately furnished and has accommodation. From the blackboard menu, Dover sole, kidneys in madeira sauce, salads, and raspberry meringue have pleased.

● **LAMBERHURST** (Kent)
Brown Trout The Down, (0892) 890312. Appealing village pub with a garden that's crowded at weekends. Fresh fish, Sunday roasts, and blackcurrant cheesecake are worth sampling.

● **LAVENHAM** (Suffolk)
Angel Market Place, (0787) 247388. First licensed in 1420, this pub has three lounge bars, a no-smoking area, piano and board-games. Reliable bar meals have included game terrine and Cumberland sauce, partridge braised in cider with pears, and Austrian coffee cake.

● **LEEDS** (West Yorkshire)
La Grillade 31–33 East Parade, (0532) 459707. Bright, stylish surroundings for fair French food: watercress soup, moules marinière, chateaubriand, and chocolate mousse have pleased.
Olive Tree Oaklands, 55 Rodley Lane, (0532) 569283. Pleasant Greek restaurant just out of the city centre. Reporters have noted a few inconsistencies in preparation, although starters and the house dessert have been praised. Tuesdays are bouzouki nights.

● **LEICESTER** (Leicestershire)
Bobby's 154 Belgrave Road, (0533) 660106 and 662448. Indian vegetarian restaurant in the heart of the city's Asian community. Open nearly 20 years, it continues to serve Gujerati, Punjabi and South Indian dishes to regulars. Bring your own wine.

● **LICHFIELD** (Staffordshire)
Swinfen Hall Hotel Swinfen, nr Lichfield, (0543) 481494. Listed eighteenth-century manor house with restaurant and accommodation. A new chef as we went to press. Reports, please.

● **LITTLEBURY** (Essex)
Queens Head Inn High Street, (0799) 522251. Pleasant, unpretentious place with enterprising ideas. The set-lunch menu is good value.

● **LIVERPOOL** (Merseyside)
La Grande Bouffe 48A Castle Street, 051-236 3375. Arguably the best bistro in Liverpool, this basement room has a self-service area and, for those taking the set menu, table service. Adequate cooking from a very straightforward selection.

● **LODERS** (Dorset)
Loders Arms (0308) 22431. Very popular pub serving innovative bar meals such as warm salad of pigeon breasts, duck breast with peaches, and lamb chops in a soy and ginger sauce.

● **LONG MELFORD** (Suffolk)
Chimneys Hall Street, (0787) 379806. A well-run restaurant in a half-timbered Tudor house, with enjoyable cooking and an agreeable atmosphere.

● **LOWER ODDINGTON** (Gloucestershire)
Fox Inn (0451) 870888. Tardis-like pub with flagstone floor, open fire, lots of eating areas and a garden. Ambitious menu and mostly good cooking; well-kept draught beers, interesting wines by the glass and a fair mix of visitors.

● **LYNMOUTH** (Devon)
Rising Sun Hotel Harbourside, (0598) 53223. Ancient oak-panelled thatched inn that's a good bet for a D,B&B break overlooking the sea. Reliable English food including notable puddings: for example, summer pudding with clotted cream.

● **MADINGLEY** (Cambridgeshire)
Three Horseshoes 1 High Street, (0954) 210221. Smart pub within easy driving distance from Cambridge and worth the detour for good, brasserie-style bar food (or eat in the conservatory restaurant).

● **MANCHESTER** (Greater Manchester)
Café Alto 9–11 Wilmslow Road, 061-225 7108. Fashionable modern décor and fashionable Mediterranean food. Find pastas, duckling with raspberry sauce, pan-fried calf's liver and excellent cappuccino.

Café Istanbul 79 Bridge Street, 061-833 9942. Recent expansion has afforded semi-open-air dining in warm weather; the pleasant atmosphere remains unchanged. Start with meze, move on to swordfish or mixed grills, and finish with syrupy pastries and Turkish coffee.

Café Primavera 48 Beech Road, Chorlton, 061-862 9934. Twin establishment of Manchester's Café Alto (see above), this restaurant has a similarly modern menu that's handled well.

Granada Hotel, El-Meson 404 Wilmslow Road, Withington, 061-434 3480. Formerly the Armenian Restaurant, now a Spanish tapas bar and restaurant but with the same chef. Reports, please.

Market Restaurant Edge Street/104 High Street, 061-834 3743. Charming bistro tucked away in a centrally located backwater. Chic-sounding, eclectic menus, but the cooking is less slick; fine for big portions and interesting beers.

Sanam 145–151 Wilmslow Road, 061-224 8824. Well-known Indian not lost among a long strip of sweet centres and curry houses. Fairly basic surroundings but vivid spicing, fresh ingredients and useful late opening hours.

Sonarga 269–271 Barlowmoor Road, Chorlton cum Hardy, 061-861 0334 and 860 6363. While the location is unprepossessing, the food at this Indian restaurant is rather better. A few interesting items on the menu, and breads are recommended.

● **MARTINHOE** (Devon)
Old Rectory Martinhoe, nr Lynton, (059 83) 368. Stylishly renovated Georgian rectory hotel in a peaceful setting. Short set menus and good delivery of such things as smoked quail, baked sole and chocolate torte. Individually designed bedrooms for sleeping off dinner.

● **MELBOURN** (Cambridgeshire)
Sheen Mill Station Road, (0763) 261393. Inviting waterside setting, well-thought-out menus, good service.

● **MELLOR** (Greater Manchester)
Devonshire Arms Longhurst Lane, 061-427 2563. Spruce, stone-built pub with a good line in bar snacks; home-made gravlax is a winner.

● **MIDDLEHAM** (North Yorkshire)
Waterford House Kirkgate, (0969) 22090. Sparkling guest house with some style that attracts a horse-racing crowd. Well-presented meals, wonderful wine list; essential to book.

● **MORETONHAMPSTEAD** (Devon)
Reverend Woodforde 11A Cross Street, (0647) 40691. Restaurant with a short set menu and a competent kitchen. Successes have included watercress soup, home-baked bread, lambs' sweetbreads with Dartmoor chanterelles and summer pudding.

● **MORPETH** (Northumberland)
La Brasserie 59 Bridge Street, (0670) 516200. Relaxing and comfortable bistro providing reliable food at reasonable prices.

● **NANCENOY** (Cornwall)
Trengilly Wartha Inn (0326) 40332. Picturesque spot that serves a purpose for bar meals (choose from the blackboard), but incidentals have, on occasion, disappointed. Difficult to find.

● **NEWCASTLE UPON TYNE** (Tyne & Wear)
Café Procope 35 The Side, Quayside, 091-232 3848. A curious selection of 'radical chic' ethnic dishes (including some vegetarian) on offer round the clock. Although décor is almost non-existent, the location is a vibrant part of town and items like Malaysian lamb curry, tarragon chicken, and Kurdish apple tart are good.

● **NIDD** (North Yorkshire)
Nidd Hall Nidd, nr Harrogate, (0423) 771598. Large hotel in 45 acres a short distance from Harrogate. The rooms, some say, are more impressive than the restaurant, where the à la carte prices are possibly more suited to delegates on expenses.

● **NORTHALLERTON** (North Yorkshire)
Bettys 188 High Street, (0609) 775154. Smaller offshoot of this well-known chain of tea-rooms serving snacks and afternoon teas, with professional service.

● **NORTHAMPTON** (Northamptonshire)
Ristorante Ca' d'Oro 334 Wellingborough Road, (0604) 32660. Useful trattoria for all things Italian.

● **NORTH BOVEY** (Devon)
Blackaller Hotel (0647) 40322. Quiet, comfortable hotel with a reliable restaurant and a warm welcome. Open to non-residents.

● **NORTH PERROTT** (Somerset)
Manor Arms (0460) 72901. Old country inn with a local reputation and a small garden and children's play area at the rear. Good pub grub; go for the blackboard specials.

● **NORTON** (Shropshire)
Hundred House Hotel Bridgenorth Road, Norton, nr Shifnal, (095 271) 353. Characterful, slightly eccentric inn with a pretty garden and accommodation. Fresh ingredients and fair cooking.

● **NORWICH** (Norfolk)
Thailand 9 Ring Road, Thorpe St Andrew, (0603) 700444. Elegant dining-room and friendly waiting-on, plus fair Thai flavours cooked to order, and some bought-in sweets.

● **NOTTINGHAM** (Nottinghamshire)
Higoi 57 Lenton Boulevard, (0602) 423379. Japanese restaurant with an extensive menu, especially the hors d'oeuvre. More reports, please.
Hotel des Clos Old Lenton Lane, (0602) 866566. An unlikely location on the southern edge of the city (ask for directions) for a farm-conversion, now a hotel and restaurant. Good food including excellent desserts and cheeses, and a wine list dominated by Chablis.

● **OLDBURY** (West Midlands)
Jonathans Hotel 16–24 Wolverhampton Road, 021-429 3757. There is a main restaurant, but it is the bistro that has received recent acclaim for dishes such as warm onion tart, black pudding and apple, and cheese soufflé.

● **ORFORD** (Suffolk)
Butley-Orford Oysterage Market Hill, (0394) 450277. Basic but charming place that's terrific for oysters, smoked mackerel or smoked salmon.
King's Head Inn Front Street, (0394) 450271. Atmospheric old pub, once a smugglers' haunt, with open fire and beams. Food is taken seriously here and ingredients are good; both bar snacks and restaurant meals are served.

● **OXFORD** (Oxfordshire)
Bangkok House 42A Hythe Bridge Street, (0865) 200705. Consistent Thai cooking; drink South-east Asian beers.
Browns 5–11 Woodstock Road, (0865) 511995. Large, long-established restaurant and bar eternally popular with students and families. Fair cooking of favourite dishes, reasonable wines, decent cappuccino and clued-up service. A strong cocktail in the bar removes the pain of waiting for a table (no bookings).
Gee's Brasserie 61A Banbury Road, (0865) 53540. Delightful conservatory restaurant, agreeably crammed with tables and potted palms and home to dependable cooking of the French/Mediterranean mould.
Ma Cuisine 21 Cowley Road, (0865) 201316. Despite an unpromising location, this French restaurant can be considered a find by those seeking authentic food at fair prices.
Opium Den 79 George Street, (0865) 248680. Better-than-average Chinese with polite service. The deep-fried garlic prawns are described as 'wonderful'.

● **PADSTOW** (Cornwall)
Bistro Margot Thomas 11 Duke Street, (0841) 533441. Small bistro with fair-value set menus. Things enjoyed have included Thai fish soup, crab-cakes, and poussin with lime and coriander.

● **PINNER** (Greater London)
La Giralda 66 Rickmansworth Road, 081-868 3429. An excellent Spanish wine list and straightforward cooking of simple ideas: rack of lamb roasted in honey, and poached pears with vanilla ice and hot chocolate sauce. A new espresso machine is being put to good use.

● **PITTON** (Wiltshire)
Silver Plough (0722) 712266. Pub food and a decent choice of house wines in a beamed dining-room. A new chef as we went to press. Reports, please.

● **PORT ISAAC** (Cornwall)
Old School House Hotel (0208) 880721. With its fishing village location, it is no surprise to find this menu concentrating on all things aquatic. Chocolate fudge cake, toffee pie or treacle tart (plus clotted cream) round off a meal.

● **PORTSMOUTH** (Hampshire)
Seagull 13 Broad Street, (0705) 824866. Enthusiastically run seafood spot with daily-changing menus and a log fire. Highlights have been seafood brochette, red bream baked with peppers, spatchcock poussin, hazelnut meringue cake, and chocolate roulade.

● **PRIORS HARDWICK** (Warwickshire)
Butcher's Arms Priors Hardwick, nr Southam, (0327) 60504 and 60597. Open 365 days a year, this country pub with gazebo and gardens is nearly always busy. Serves restaurant meals and Portuguese wines (the nationality of the owners).

● **REDE** (Suffolk)
Plough (028 489) 208. Thatched pub in the heart of the countryside continuing to provide well-cooked food.

● **REDMILE** (Leicestershire)
Peacock Inn Church Corner, (0949) 42554. Different eating areas, two bars and a garden add to the enjoyment of chef Jean-Louis David's cooking. French bread, seafood with mushrooms on spaghetti, calf's liver with shallots and apple, and raisin tart are representative.

● **REETH** (North Yorkshire)
Burgoyne Hotel (0748) 884292. Handsome, well-furnished house that provides comfortable accommodation – with exceptional views – and consistent cooking.

● **REIGATE** (Surrey)
La Barbe 71 Bell Street, (0737) 241966. French restaurant where tables are separated into cubicles by wooden partitions. An imaginative menu, well-chosen wines and creditable cooking; fish is particularly well-handled.

● **RICHMOND** (Surrey)
Burnt Chair 5 Duke Street, 081-940 9488. Great attention to detail in presentation of dishes, and a warm welcome, add to the enjoyment of the reliable cooking here.

Cantina 32 The Quadrant, 081-332 6262. Worthy Mexican restaurant using organic meat and clearly labelling dishes for hotness of chillies. Fairly child-friendly; ice-cream confections to end a meal.

● **ROCHDALE** (Greater Manchester)
French Connection Edenfield Road, Cheesden, nr Rochdale, (0706) 50167. An out-of-the-way, moorland location for this tastefully converted ex-pub, now offering enjoyable French food at a modest outlay. Run with enthusiasm. More reports, please.

● **ROCHFORD** (Essex)
Renoufs Bradley Way, (0702) 544393. Smoothly run hotel and French restaurant providing sound meals.

● **ROSS-ON-WYE** (Hereford & Worcester)
Peterstow Country House Peterstow, (0989) 562826. Relaxing, attractively furnished hotel offering three- and four-course set menus and traditional Sunday lunch. Puddings such as lemon tart and figs baked in filo have been particularly praised.

● **ROYDHOUSE** (West Yorkshire)
Three Acres Inn (0484) 602606. Eighteenth-century coaching-inn run by the Truelove family for over 20 years. Reliable bar food; real ales on handpump.

● **SAFFRON WALDEN** (Essex)
Old Hoops 15 King Street, (0799) 522813. Oak-beamed restaurant above a former coaching-inn featuring an Anglo-French bistro-style menu. Stay with the simpler dishes for the most success.

● **ST HELENS** (Isle of Wight)
St Helens Restaurant Lower Green Road, (0983) 872303. Enthusiastically run village spot that may be a little short on space but compensates with fair cooking, encompassing notable desserts.

● **ST MARTIN'S** (Isles of Scilly)
St Martin's Lowertown, (0720) 422092. Beautifully situated and well-run modern

hotel that has a relaxing ambience and some tables with sunset views. Pleasing cooking; careful presentation.

● **SALCOMBE** (Devon)
Schooners 71 Fore Street, (0548) 843568. Open-all-day spot with oil-cloth-covered tables, offering every meal including breakfast. The evening menu has fish straight from the boats, organic meat and home-made terrines and patés. More reports, please.

● **SALISBURY** (Wiltshire)
Harper's 6–7 Ox Row, The Market Square, (0722) 333118. Informal restaurant overlooking the old market-place that is popular with shoppers at lunch but quieter in the evenings (when occasional live music may intrude). Variable cooking but useful for the area.

● **SCARISBRICK** (Lancashire)
Master McGraths 535 Southport Road, (0704) 880050. If you can ignore the background music, you will enjoy choosing from an appealing menu with some fashionable things. Food from the bar has on occasion been less successful.

● **SEAVIEW** (Isle of Wight)
Seaview Hotel High Street, (0983) 612711. Smart seaside hotel with an immaculate dining-room that's home to best island produce, resulting in sound cooking. Lots of lobster and flat fish; desserts are also praised.

● **SHEFFIELD** (South Yorkshire)
Mediterranean 271 Sharrowvale Road, (0742) 661069. Deservedly popular Sheffield restaurant; some Spanish ideas and friendly, first-class service.

● **SHERBORNE** (Dorset)
Pheasants 24 Greenhill, (0935) 815252. Pleasing English food at this restaurant-with-rooms. Bread-and-butter pudding has pleased.

● **SHERE** (Surrey)
Kinghams Gomshall Lane, (0483) 202168. Seventeenth-century cottage restaurant with a reasonably eclectic menu. Sound cooking and service. Also does cream teas.

● **SHIPTON-UNDER-WYCHWOOD** (Oxfordshire)
Lamb Inn (0993) 830465. Ancient inn

with accommodation and an interesting cold buffet available from April to October. In addition, a set-price menu operates in the dining-room.

● **SOUTHALL** (Greater London)
Brilliant 72–74 Western Road, 081-574 1928. This Indian is related to Madhu's Brilliant, also in Southall (see main entry), and the menu has some variations. Breads are excellent, and recommended dishes are prawn masala, karahi gosht (made with lamb) and aloo chollay.

● **SPEEN** (Buckinghamshire)
Old Plow Inn Flowers Bottom Lane, Flowers Bottom, (0494) 488300. Beautiful pub/restaurant with an attractive atmosphere and service. Stay with the straightforward things for best results.

● **STOCKSFIELD** (Northumberland)
Branches Branch House, Branch End, (0661) 844264. Small restaurant that's been open about a year, and is gathering a regular clientele. Table d'hôte and à la carte menus list dishes like terrine of wild game, galantine of baby chicken, and medallions of monkfish. Also does morning coffee and weekend afternoon teas.

● **STOKE-ON-TRENT** (Staffordshire)
Ria 61–67 Piccadilly, Hanley, (0782) 264411. Typical Thai restaurant with a long menu and some unusual options. Food cooked to order includes volcano chicken, chilli fish, clay pot crab claws, and authentic desserts.

● **STORRINGTON** (West Sussex)
Abingworth Hall Thakeham Road, (0798) 813636. Well-decorated 1930s country house with an able team. Straightforward food in a peaceful dining-room; choice of menus. Men are requested to wear jacket and tie.

● **STOW-ON-THE-WOLD** (Gloucestershire)
Grapevine Hotel Sheep Street, (0451) 830344. Takes its name from the antique living vine overhanging the conservatory dining-room. Both restaurant and bar meals; attractive surroundings.

● **Stratford-upon-Avon**
(Warwickshire)
Le Bonaparte Caterham House Hotel,
58–59 Rother Street, (0789) 267309.
Very useful spot for a pre-theatre set
dinner. Sound French production of
dishes such as mussels terrine with basil
sauce, and apple tart.

● **Stretton** (Leicestershire)
Ram Jam Inn Great North Road, (0780)
410776. Indispensable for A1 travellers,
this roadside inn with rooms has a good-
value, all-day menu, plus more complex
dishes in the main restaurant. Decent
coffee and newspapers provided.

● **Sutton Gault** (Cambridgeshire)
Anchor Inn Bury Lane, Sutton Gault, nr
Ely, (0353) 778537. Miles from anywhere
but popular as an eating place with a
pleasant atmosphere. A frequently
changing menu and successful
production of pâtés, soups, main courses
and home-made puddings.

● **Tewkesbury** (Gloucestershire)
Le Bistrot André 78 Church Street,
(0684) 290357. Compact bistro with a
large mural and a friendly welcome.
French onion soup, mussels, tarte Tatin
and well-kept cheeses are typical. Open
evenings only.
New World 61 High Street, (0684)
292225. Reliable Vietnamese restaurant
which also does take-aways. Good
service.

● **Tideford** (Cornwall)
Heskyn Mill (0752) 851481. Wonderful
old flint watermill that is now a
restaurant. Watercress soup, game pie
and crème brûlée are typical choices.

● **Tiverton** (Devon)
Lowman 45 Gold Street, (0884) 257311.
Relaxed restaurant that remains popular.
Successes have been bangers and mash,
satay chicken, Grand Marnier soufflé, and
sticky toffee pudding.

● **Tregony** (Cornwall)
Kea House 69 Fore Street, (0872)
530642. Small, tastefully decorated
restaurant specialising in fresh local fish
and seafood, plus several Scottish recipes.
In summer it also opens for light lunches
and cream teas.

● **Tresco** (Isles of Scilly)
Island Hotel (0720) 22883. Magical
surroundings and a conservatory-style
setting, although food results this year
have been mixed. Individual spinach and
nutmeg mousse, sauté fillet of black
bream with ribbon vegetables, and pan-
fried marinated venison have been
praised.

● **Troutbeck** (Cumbria)
Mortal Man Hotel Troutbeck, nr
Windermere, (053 94) 33193. Genuine
country pub with comfortable bedrooms
and pleasing food. Dinner is a set-price
affair.

● **Tuckenhay** (Devon)
Floyd's Inn Maltsters Arms, Bow Creek,
(0803) 732350. Keith Floyd's hostelry
provides large open sandwiches through
to full-blown restaurant meals. Not
cheap.

● **Uppingham** (Leicestershire)
Lake Isle 16 High Street East, (0572)
822951. Restaurant-with-rooms with a
weekly-changing menu and well-drilled
staff. Sauces have come in for some
criticism though bread, wines and cheeses
have been praised.

● **Upton Bishop** (Hereford &
Worcester)
Moody Cow (0989) 780470. Village pub a
short distance from Ross-on-Wye, with a
short bar menu of such things as
mushroom pancakes, 'exquisite' deep
lemon tart, and good cafetière coffee.

● **Veryan** (Cornwall)
Nare Hotel Carne Beach, (0872) 501279.
Super sea views from this relaxing,
traditional spot south of Tregony. Reliable
cooking of fresh ingredients; portions
have been found generous and the sweet
trolley 'tempting'.

● **Wansford** (Cambridgeshire)
Haycock Hotel London Road, Wansford,
nr Peterborough, (0780) 782223. Old
coaching-inn set around a courtyard and
attractive garden. Two restaurants cater
for most requirements, and residents are
made comfortable.

● **Warenford** (Northumberland)
Warenford Lodge (0668) 213453. Spruce
inn complete with an open log fire. Only
bar food is available weekend lunch-

times and Tuesday to Sunday dinner, but choices such as prawn fritters with an Oriental sauce, marinated herrings, and hazelnut mousse are fine.

● **WARWICK** (Warwickshire)
Fanshawe's 22 Market Place, (0926) 410590. Husband-and-wife team providing a warm reception and creditable food. Two set menus offer fair value; portions are generous.

● **WATTON-AT-STONE** (Hertfordshire)
George & Dragon High Street, (0920) 830285. Deservedly popular pub, first licensed in 1603, that has a blackboard menu with dishes of the day, plus a printed menu. Fresh fish, pâtés, pies and desserts are the strengths; all home-made.

● **WELLINGTON** (Somerset)
Orchards Dipford Road, Angersleigh, nr Wellington, (0823) 275440. Old farmhouse restaurant with a relaxed atmosphere, pleasant service and reasonable cooking.

● **WENTBRIDGE** (West Yorkshire)
Wentbridge House (0977) 620444. Creeper-clad hotel and restaurant with ambitious menus and a comprehensive wine list with detailed tasting notes. More reports, please.

● **WESTCLIFF-ON-SEA** (Essex)
Paris 719 London Road, (0702) 344077. Uninspiring surroundings, yet sound cooking of a daily-changing set menu, and a seafood menu. Items that have pleased include fish-cakes in coriander sauce, chicken breast with chorizo, and raspberry shortbread.

● **WEST HOATHLY** (West Sussex)
Cat Inn North Lane, (0342) 810369. Well-known pub with various seating areas and a terrace. Creditable bar meals may be pâté with fresh French bread and salad, good prawns, and home-made puddings.

● **WEST KIRBY** (Merseyside)
Banks Bistro 95 Banks Road, 051-625 6767. Lively haunt with a friendly welcome and a good list of well-received dishes on the blackboard. More reports, please.

● **WETHERAL** (Cumbria)
Fantails The Green, (0228) 560239. Traditional, family-run English restaurant that's open Tuesday to Sunday dinner. There is increased attention to vegetarian dishes. More reports, please.

● **WEYBRIDGE** (Surrey)
Casa Romana 2 Temple Hall, Monument Hill, (0932) 843470. Traditional Italian with a happy local reputation; a nice spot for Sunday lunch.
Colony 3 Balfour Road, (0932) 842766. Respectable Chinese that, although smartly decorated, offers fair value. Finish with toffee bananas and jasmine tea.

● **WEYMOUTH** (Dorset)
Perry's 4 Trinity Road, The Old Harbour, (0305) 785799. Harbourside place for local seafood, where the specials are chalked up on a blackboard every day (there is also a short à la carte menu). Desserts are good, but fish flavours have, for some, been a little bland.

● **WHITEWELL** (Lancashire)
Inn at Whitewell Forest of Bowland, (0200) 448222. Wonderful, isolated forest location complete with fishing rights on the River Hodder. Although there is accommodation, an art gallery and a wine merchant, the traditional bar food is not ignored and the pub gets busy at weekends.

● **WHITTLESFORD** (Cambridgeshire)
Tickell Arms (0223) 833128. Pretty pub with an even prettier conservatory and garden providing tasty bar lunches and pleasing wines by the glass. Admits smartly dressed, no-smoking adults only.

● **WIGMORE** (Hereford & Worcester)
Queen's House Wigmore, nr Ludlow, (056 886) 451. Beamed house with a comfortable cellar restaurant and a husband-and-wife team cooking straightforward meals from fresh ingredients.

● **WILMINGTON** (East Sussex)
Crossways Lewes Road, (0323) 482455. Cheery hotel and restaurant open for dinner Tuesday to Saturday. A monthly-changing menu and reliable cooking of local produce: game terrine with apricot

relish, pigeon breast with lentils, home-made plum ice-cream.

● **WINCHESTER** (Hampshire)
Nine the Square 9 Great Minster Street, The Square, (0962) 864004. Wine bar and restaurant with plenty on offer and fair cooking, especially of fish.

Old Chesil Rectory 1 Chesil Street, (0962) 851555. Reputedly Winchester's oldest house, but a comparatively new venture for the present owners. Bistro-esque menus may include shellfish bisque, chicken liver parfait with toasted brioche, and casserole of pheasant, partridge and venison. More reports, please.

● **WINDERMERE** (Cumbria)
Holbeck Ghyll Holbeck Lane, (053 94) 32375. Intelligently run country-house hotel, once a hunting-lodge, now home to peaceful accommodation and fair cooking.

● **WINDSOR** (Berkshire)
Cody's 4 Church Street, (0753) 858331. Wine bar and restaurant with relaxed atmosphere, cheerful staff and lots on the menu, from snacks to full meals. Useful for visitors to Windsor Great Park and handy enough for Heathrow.

● **WINFORTON** (Hereford & Worcester)
Sun Inn (0544) 327677. Whitewashed inn that's home to real ales and innovative food. Piggy in the orchard (a dish of pork, fruit and oxtail braised in cider) was a favourite with one reporter, as were accompanying vegetables.

● **WITHAM** (Essex)
Lian High House, 5 Newland Street, (0376) 510684. Reliable Chinese with a variety of set menus; crispy roast duck was 'as good as ever'. Occasional lapses have been noted.

● **WOBURN** (Bedfordshire)
Black Horse 1 Bedford Street, (0525) 290210. Well-run pub that has no menu; ingredients chosen are charged by the ounce and cooked in full view of diners.

Good steaks, shellfish and exotic fish feature.

● **WOODBRIDGE** (Suffolk)
Wine Bar 17 Thoroughfare, (0394) 382557. First-floor premises with a long list of interesting wines and an eclectic menu. Useful for a casual meal.

● **WOOLHOPE** (Hereford & Worcester)
Butchers Arms Woolhope, nr Fownhope, (0432) 860281. Charming rural pub complete with half-timbers, garden and stream. Good bar food includes soups, pâtés and pies alongside the more exotic.

● **WORTHING** (West Sussex)
Paragon 9–10 Brunswick Road, (0903) 233367. English restaurant offering good-value mid-week set dinners. Fair ingredients and cooking; pleasant service.

● **YATTENDON** (Berkshire)
Royal Oak The Square, (0635) 201325. A few changes at this pub and restaurant with accommodation. The set meals of English dishes are quite expensive, but there is a bar menu worthy of investigation.

● **YEALAND CONYERS** (Lancashire)
New Inn 40 Yealand Road, (0524) 732938. Old ivy-clad pub under new management presenting an interesting menu. First signs are encouraging, and wines and coffee are very drinkable.

● **YORK** (North Yorkshire)
Bettys 6–8 St Helen's Square, (0904) 659142. Prime place for tea and traditional scones and cakes, or more modern lunches and early-evening suppers.

Grange Hotel, Ivy Restaurant Clifton, (0904) 644744. Sympathetically decorated Regency building that's well placed for seeing York. Dishes enjoyed in the main restaurant have been gravlax with grapefruit and lime dressing, lemon sole roulade, and chocolate and rum torte. Casual meals are also available in the brasserie.

Scotland

● **ABERLOUR** (Grampian)
Archiestown Hotel (0340) 810218.
Compact hotel several have found ideal
for a fishing party, with a restaurant open
to non-residents. Set dinners offer fair
value, and the kitchen makes use of
home-grown and local supplies and
produces 'delicious' ice-creams and
puddings.

● **ACHNASHEEN** (Highland)
Loch Torridon Hotel By Achnasheen,
Wester-Ross, nr Inverness, (0445)
791242. Refurbished, comfortable hotel
surrounded by Highland scenery. Well-
presented food interesting enough for a
short stay; ditto drinkable wines.

● **AYR** (Strathclyde)
Fouter's Bistro 2A Academy Street,
(0292) 261391. The fixed-price bistro
menu offers the best value in this
basement (although only a few tables are
given over to customers choosing this);
otherwise there is an à la carte menu.
Seafood dishes are recommended, as are
cheeses. Don't let the lack of space put
you off.

● **BALLATER** (Grampian)
Craigendarroch Hotel, The Oaks
Braemar Road, (033 97) 55858. Large
hotel, restaurant and time-share complex
with extensive country-club facilities. A
change of chef as we went to press;
reports, please.

● **BALQUHIDDER** (Central)
Monachyle Mhor Balquhidder, nr
Lochearnhead, (0877) 384622. A few
miles off the main road overlooking two
lochs, this small hotel manages splendid
breakfasts and enjoyable set dinners;
puddings are especially good.

● **BIGGAR** (Strathclyde)
Culter Mill Coulter, nr Biggar, (0899)
20950. Sensitively converted old water
mill housing a bistro and, upstairs, a
restaurant. Downstairs, dishes enjoyed
have included moules à la crème,
bouillabaisse, game pie and strawberry
meringue nests.

● **CALLANDER** (Central)
Roman Camp Hotel off Main Street,
(0877) 330003. Very attractive old
hunting lodge set in 20 acres, where a
daily four-course menu with no choice is
offered at dinner – lunches are cheaper
and varied.

● **EDINBURGH** (Lothian)
Ann Purna 45 St Patrick's Square, 031-
662 1807. Indian vegetarian specialising
in Gujerati dishes. The thalis are
especially good value and service is keen.
Bombay Bicycle Club 6 Brougham Place,
031-229 3839. Comfortable Indian
restaurant with an interesting menu and
a good vegetarian section. First-class side
orders include tarka dhal and paratha.
Cosmo Ristorante 58A North Castle
Street, 031-226 6743. Continues to be
good for mussels, prawns 'generally
larger and more succulent than most',
grilled halibut and chocolate mousse
cake.
Grain Store 30 Victoria Street, 031-225
7635. Modest enterprise promoting a
good-value two-course-plus-coffee
menu.
Paradores 26 William Street, 031-225
2973. Spanish restaurant with a tapas bar
that's useful for its selection of 30-odd
dishes. The reasonable prices extend to
wines.
Les Partisans 144 High Street, Royal
Mile, 031-225 5144. Big, simply
decorated and relaxed first-floor bar/
restaurant with an adventurous wine list
that includes some bargains. Reliable
French-style cooking at fair prices. More
reports, please.
Pierre Victoire 10 Victoria Street, 031-
225 1721. Pierre Levicky's original,
cramped, budget French venue that is
popular because at these prices people are
prepared to forgive a few inconsistencies.
Another company-owned branch (as
opposed to franchise) is at 6–8 Union
Street, Edinburgh, 031-557 8451.
Suruchi 14A Nicolson Street, 031-556
6583. Indian with a wide range of

vegetarian dishes, also chicken and fish items available. There is an inexpensive set Sunday lunch menu, and the restaurant also does take-aways.

● **GLASGOW** (Strathclyde)

Cabin 996 Dumbarton Road, Whiteinch, 041-954 7102. Genuine enthusiasm for ingredients – game and fish especially – cooked freshly to order. Avert eyes from décor to concentrate on groups of Glaswegians having fun. No credit cards; unlicensed, but bring your own.

Mata Hari 17 West Princes Street, 041-332 9789. Basement Malaysian restaurant that's colourfully decorated and staffed by a friendly team. However, spicing can be approximate and desserts are mostly ice-creams.

● **KELSO** (Borders)

Sunlaws House Hotel Heiton, nr Kelso, (0573) 450331. Ancient house and estate with a historic past and Jacobite connections. The cooking has less substance than this, although items such as poached salmon, loin of Border lamb, and accompanying vegetables are fine.

● **KENTALLEN** (Highland)

Ardsheal House (063 174) 227. Owners changed at this relaxed country-house hotel beside Loch Linnhe as we went to press. Chef George Kelso remains. The wine list is fairly priced and has a good range of clarets.

● **KINLOCH RANNOCH** (Tayside)

Cuilmore Cottage (0882) 632218. Tiny, whitewashed croft with two bedrooms and a small dining-room that can cater for up to eight non-residents. Sound cooking using organically home-grown fruit and vegetables wherever possible, and home-baked bread.

● **KINROSS** (Tayside)

Grouse & Claret Heatheryford, (0577) 864212. Appealing restaurant and accommodation in a natural and relaxing setting. Fair cooking using generally local produce; desserts less imaginative.

● **LOCHINVER** (Highland)

Lochinver Larder Main Street, (0571) 844356. Riverside bistro and deli serving basic snacks all day. Useful in the area.

● **MARKINCH** (Fife)

Balbirnie House Balbirnie Park, (0592) 610066. Supremely elegant house in landscaped grounds run by a topnotch team. The set dinner menu of four courses is fairly executed.

● **NEWTON STEWART** (Dumfries & Galloway)

Kirroughtree Hotel (0671) 402141. Lovely place to stay standing in eight acres of gardens with distant bay views. Choice of dining-rooms (smoking or no-smoking), short four-course dinner menu and sound cooking of such things as game, seafood and Scottish cheeses.

● **ST ANDREWS** (Fife)

Vine Leaf 131 South Street, (0334) 477497. Tucked away down an alley, this tiny restaurant is popular enough to be frequently full. Fair cooking of crab soup, mussels, monkfish and white chocolate mousse, although, on occasion, the kitchen is overstretched.

● **STONEHAVEN** (Grampian)

Tolbooth Old Pier, (0569) 762287. Quayside fish restaurant with an à la carte menu of local and far-flung varieties accompanied by good sauces (and sometimes followed by a good bread pudding). Antipodean wines get a showing.

Wales

● **BARMOUTH** (Gwynedd)
Llwyndu Farmhouse Llanaber, nr Barmouth, (0341) 280144. Old dining-room that's currently for B&B residents only (open to everyone very soon), serving traditional food, including vegetarian options.

● **CARDIFF** (South Glamorgan)
Quayles 6–8 Romilly Crescent, Canton, (0222) 341264. The 'early bird' menus and the desserts are what's popular here, though the modern cooking shows signs of losing its way, and some have found service slow.

● **CARMARTHEN** (Dyfed)
Old Curiosity 20A King Street, (0267) 232384. Modest, long-standing town centre restaurant-cum-coffee shop. Although the menu is dated, everything is freshly prepared and chips are excellent.

● **CLYDACH** (Gwent)
Drum & Monkey Blackrock, (0873) 831980. Low-rise stone building with a small bar and a split-level dining-room. Freshly made offerings might include smoked bacon and lentil soup, roasts, home-made ice-creams.

● **CRICKHOWELL** (Powys)
Bear Hotel High Street, (0873) 810408. Black-and-white country pub with an attractive interior, interesting bar food, real ales and notable wines. Ingredients are mostly local but recipes can be global.

● **HAWARDEN** (Clwyd)
Swiss Restaurant Imfeld 68 The Highway, (0244) 534523. Swiss-style, evenings-only operation currently looking for larger, more comfortable premises. Food is familiar rather than daring, and fondues are available Friday and Sunday nights.

● **HAY-ON-WYE** (Powys)
Old Black Lion 26 Lion Street, (0497) 820841. Ancient, cosy inn with accommodation and fishing rights on the Wye. Order meals in the bar (with the option of eating in the restaurant) and enjoy tasty results from fresh ingredients.

Gets very busy with both bibliophiles and walkers.

● **LALESTON** (Mid Glamorgan)
Great House High Street, (0656) 657644. Attractive Grade II listed house with a high, half-timbered ceiling and open fireplace. Fair cooking, friendly service.

● **LLANDEILO** (Dyfed)
Fanny's 3 King Street, (0558) 822908. Victorian-style licensed (no-smoking) tearooms open for morning coffee, lunch and afternoon tea Tuesday to Saturday. Find red dragon pie, toffee pudding and Perigord walnut tart.

● **LLYSWEN** (Powys)
Llangoed Hall (0874) 754525. Sir Bernard Ashley's handsome country-house hotel designed by architect Clough Williams-Ellis has had a change of chef and management since last year's main entry. Early reports suggest a falling-off in standards, though prices are still high.

● **MOLD** (Clwyd)
Chez Colette 56 High Street, (0352) 759225. Small, simply furnished French bistro with a really good-value three- or four-course fixed-price menu. Pleasing production of garlic mussels, paté maison, boeuf bourgignon, gratin dauphinois, chocolate fudge cake, etc.

● **PONTFAEN** (Dyfed)
Gelli Fawr Country House (0239) 820343. Old stone farmhouse surrounded by hills in a remote part of Dyfed. Good for daytime bar meals or dinner (non-residents welcome). Very informally run – doesn't feel like a hotel.

● **PWLLHELI** (Gwynedd)
Glynllifon Country House Llanbedrog, (0758) 740147. Not the usual country-house cooking, but authentic Indian food that has variety and is reasonably priced.

● **ST CLEARS** (Dyfed)
Butchers Arms High Street, (0994) 231069. Small, jolly pub that's handy for a straightforward bar snack (also has a restaurant). Try Felinfoel beer straight from the cask.

● **SWANSEA** (West Glamorgan)
P.A.'s 95 Newton Road, Mumbles, (0792) 367723. A wine bar that's ideal for simple dishes such as smoked salmon, spinach and ricotta mille-feuille, and Dover sole.

● **TENBY** (Dyfed)
Plantagenet Quay Hill, Tudor Square, (0834) 842350. Atmospheric building in one of this resort's oldest streets; acts as a magnet to visitors anxious to avoid fish and chips. Fair cooking includes fried Lampeter Pencarreg cheese, steaks, fresh fish.

Channel Islands

● **GOREY** (Jersey)
Jersey Pottery Restaurant (0534) 851119. Modern building housing the Pottery workshops and shop, as well as the self-service café and formal restaurant. The latter is conservatory-styled and turns out quality seafood and fish dishes, and tempting patisserie.

● **ST AUBIN** (Jersey)
Old Court House Inn (0534) 46433. Cheerful bistro and restaurant that fills up fast at weekends and in season. Good-value, mostly fish dishes such as crab claws in a ginger and soy sauce, and grilled fillets of sea bass. End with espresso.

● **ST BRELADE** (Jersey)
Sea Crest Hotel Petit Port, (0534) 46353. Overlooking a small cove, this is hard to find and essentially for holidaymakers, though fair renditions of Anglo-French food and smart service make this a useful venue.

● **ST PETER PORT** (Guernsey)
La Frégate Les Cotils, (0481) 724624. Lovely views overlooking the harbour and competent French cooking. The Sunday lunch menu is competitively priced.
Le Nautique Quay Steps, (0481) 721714. Converted wine cellar decorated with fishing nets and paraphernalia; satisfying cooking and good cappuccino.

Your rights in restaurants

This feature remains unchanged in each new edition of the Guide, *unless the law changes. It explains your rights in restaurants, and your obligations.*

This is the nasty bit of the *Guide*. No one wants to go out for a meal only to end up in court. No one wants to start a soufflé, then progress to a bout of fisticuffs with the waiting staff. That sort of behaviour ruins an appetite, and is certainly fatal to digestion. However, we should not be coy about money, or the goods and services that money buys. If restaurants manifestly fail to deliver, we should expect reasonable recompense. But it's not all one way. A restaurant has rights too. When you make a booking or you start to order food in a restaurant, you enter into a legally binding contract with the restaurant.

A restaurant is in the business of providing food to customers who consume it on the premises. It must therefore offer satisfactory food, safe practices of cooking and preparation, the equipment and hardware with which to eat it, and a place in which to eat it. The restaurant must also generally deliver things from the spot where they were prepared to the customer who is going to eat it. For food, read also wine and beverages. There is a lot of potential trouble in that short definition.

Satisfactory food means broadly that the dishes are as described on the menu and are prepared with reasonable skill and care. Food must be prepared in a way that does not endanger health and conforms to whatever standards are generally accepted. If a chef says that a bullet-hard potato is 'cooked', he may be expressing a new-wave theory about potatoes. It would be difficult to get him for endangering health, but you can easily claim the food has not been prepared properly.

Satisfactory equipment and furnishings for preparation and eating are rather easier to assess. This is not a matter of taste, more a question of potential injury. You can call on any number of experts to help determine whether these aspects of the restaurant's obligations conform to the law. If you can't abide eating in a blue room, and the owner has painted it cerulean – hard chips. That's just likes and dislikes.

Serving the food is integral to the restaurant's function. Bad service is often a cause of complaint, perhaps dispute. While the restaurant should always provide reasonable service, it is never easy to determine when it passes from adequate to bad. This depends on the type of restaurant and the price you are asked to pay for the meal. If the service is not of a reasonable standard you are entitled to withold a charge for service.

But hold hard! You, the customer, have to conform to certain standards as well. A customer must behave reasonably, and may have to dress in an acceptable fashion (the rules for this are made up by the management); he or she must turn up to a reserved table at the time agreed; he or she must pay the bill if the meal and service are satisfactory. The restaurateur does have rights and these are often ignored by the public at large who think that restaurants are there to serve them 24 hours a day every day of the year. A restaurant may open and close when it chooses. A restaurant may refuse admission to whomever it wishes, unless it be on grounds of gender, colour or race. A restaurant may charge what it likes, provided it tells you first. And finally, a restaurant may cook what it chooses, so long as it has a menu displaying details in the correct places. If it wants to have a 'potato day' it can do an utterly tuberous menu.

All these rights can collide with wishes; all these obligations can turn to trouble if not performed. A superstructure of regulation has arisen to set out rights. Hence criminal laws such as the Consumer Protection Act 1987 (to prevent misleading price indications), the Trades Descriptions Act 1968 (to ensure that statements in menus and other promotional literature are accurate), the Food Safety Act 1990 (covering hygiene in places where the public eats).

A chapter of accidents

Rodney and Samantha are celebrating their fifth wedding anniversary and decide the Pasty Diamond is the place at which to retie the knot. It has an entry in The Good Food Guide; *their friends speak highly of the food; everyone, it seems, has a good time there. Samantha says she will book a table for Wednesday night and rings up accordingly.*

A booking made is a contract between two parties. The intending customer must turn up at the time agreed. Any delay (for instance, because the car breaks down), should be notified to the restaurant. It is within its rights to refuse to re-arrange the time, and to re-let the table. If Rodney and Samantha don't turn up at all, then they are liable for the restaurant's loss of profit (not the entire cost) if the table cannot be re-let. It sometimes happens that people arrive at the Pasty Diamond and George the manager has no record of their booking. This can be very embarrassing. If George cannot give them a table and they really did make that booking, they can claim recompense for travel expenses, possibly even for inconvenience. If the transaction was not in writing, it can be difficult to prove your case. Many's the restaurateur who has people lying through their teeth that they made a booking; just as many's the customer who has found his or her reservation lost when in fact the place is a shambles that could never keep a diary straight. So keep a record of when you telephoned and to whom you spoke.

Actually, Rodney and Samantha make it on time and George's welcome is impeccable. Sitting on plump sofas with a glass of sherry each, they are handed the menu. Rodney's face falls. His friend Bill had assured him, '£30 a head'. But it is plain as a pikestaff that it's going to be more than that. 'Wonderful French food,' Samantha's workmate had told her. In fact, what she is reading is a menu full of Italian specialities.

The proper display of menus and charges is a pool of clarity in the fog surrounding 'trouble at table'. A restaurant must show a menu at or near its entrance. The prices should include VAT. Any extra costs should be displayed in as equally prominent type as the rest of the contents. Hence any cover charge, charge for bread and butter or additional levy for service should be clearly mentioned. A Code of Practice under the Consumer Protection Act 1987 suggests various ways of including 'extras' as inclusive prices with the food. The Code is very influential when deciding if a restaurant has broken the law with misleading prices, but it is neither compulsory, nor has everyone heeded it. 'Discretionary' service charges, for instance, exist in many places even though the Code frowns on them. If the restaurant has conformed to regulations pertaining to display, there is nothing Rodney or Samantha can do about their misapprehensions. They can leave straight away but are breaking their contract. Otherwise, they are liable for what they should have found out about in the first place.

Another problem is that Samantha is none too hungry. What she really fancies are two light first courses, not a substantial meat or fish main course. George the manager slides up to take the order and points out that the chef will not enjoy doing this. His attitude is 'I've bought all this food, now I'm going to sell it.' Actually, what he says is 'I fear there is a minimum charge, madam, and that means you will have to order a main course.'

A minimum charge must be stated prominently on the menu. However, no customer is under any obligation to eat either prescribed dishes or in a prescribed order so long as he or she is willing to pay what is requested. Chef must curb any urge to say what the customer should eat. Similarly, if a customer asks for his or her meat well done, chef has to do it – unless something is declared on the menu along the lines of 'our meat is cooked medium or rare'.

That little problem over, George leaves the wine list to Samantha as he pops off to the kitchen. She chooses a Sancerre 1990. This comes from a maker other than the one who makes the wine she gets at the off-licence, for which she pays about £7. The Pasty Diamond has it on the list at £25. No sooner is the order taken than George leads Rodney and Samanatha to their table. He returns with the wine and offers it to Rodney for tasting – typical! Rodney passes it to Samantha, who gives it a good nose and careful tasting. It's off! George rushes round as if his tail's on fire, slurps some out of a glass and firmly disagrees.

The wine list is governed by the same rules as the menu. However, a restaurant need not display the whole list at its door, just a few representative entries. If the cellar is in chaos and 1989 is served instead of 1990, or the maker is different, then the customer is entitled to demand the correct vintage, or a replacement bottle (which doesn't mean it comes free). If you feel, as the customer, that £25 is much too much to pay, choose something cheaper. George can charge whatever he likes. Remember, however, that when you make these simplistic comparisons with supermarket prices the producer may make a considerable difference, so may the year, so may any variation between your benchmark and what is actually offered for sale. There is much difficulty about disputes over a wine's condition. How do you canvass opinion against George's denial? Do you approach other tables? You must hope to settle amicably. It is in George's interest to agree with you. The one sanction would be to pay for the wine under protest, put it in your shopping bag and take it to an accepted expert: a vivid illustration of how uneasily legal disputes sit with the experience of dining out.

Our couple's dinner is fraught with disaster at every turn. Waits between courses are interminable, and the staff cannot even get the order right. When the waitress arrives with Samantha's monkfish and Rodney's medium-to-well-done entrecôte it turns out that George has told chef best end of lamb, not steak. Rodney sends the lamb back. The waitress doesn't know what to do. She leaves Samantha with her fish dish and rushes off to ask for a steak. By the time it appears, Samantha's fish and vegetables are cold. Starting to tremble every time she comes near the table, the waitress spills wine over Rodney's shirt. Already, the first courses have been fairly poor: the warm salad of calf's liver that Samantha had ordered was stone cold, and the liver like leather; she is convinced that Rodney's prawns were off-colour well before they were bathed in sauce.

Rodney is getting a case for 'bad service', even though it may not have been the waitress's fault, but due entirely to delays and confusions in the kitchen. However, it's still bad service in the eyes of the customer. The cold salad when the menu said 'warm' is a case of misrepresentation; the shoe-like liver is a matter of opinion, clear though it may seem to the hapless eater. If the prawns really do seem off, it is suicidal to eat them. This is the time to complain. Don't let things slide just because you wish to avoid a fuss. Actually, disregarding the trouble with the wine, Rodney and Samantha wanted to have a good time. Unfortunately, if you want to get your rights, you may have to sacrifice enjoyment. The wrong order is another self-evident fault that has to be rectified for the customer to be satisfied. However, the waitress went about it in the wrong way. People really do like to eat together. The only answer is to start the whole main course again. Spilling wine down Rodney's front will entitle him to be paid for dry cleaning or laundry, or even a replacement.

It's pudding time and the couple order brown sugar meringues with bananas and cream. What turns up? Peaches instead of bananas. (Bananas were forgotten from the greengrocer's order.)

A restaurant may not vary the menu without warning. Mistakes can and do happen, but they need to be admitted before, not after, the dish arrives at table. Our man can't insist on bananas if there are none, but he could refuse the dish and try something else.

The consequences of real incompetence can sometimes be greater than restaurants realise. Rodney asks for the bill and notices that there is a 15 per cent service charge. He removes this from the total and says he will pay only a proportion of the bill. For George, this is the last straw. He reckons they have been fussing on purpose. He loses his temper and threatens to call the police. He also shows signs of becoming violent. So Rodney pays, but under protest. George won't take his cheque, and insists on cash.

A restaurant can refuse payment by cheque. Similarly, restaurants have to accept credit cards only if they have agreed to do so before you order, or there is a sign on the door indicating acceptance. Rodney is within his rights to deduct service, whether it be 'discretionary' or not, if he thinks the service has been truly bad. If service is included in the prices displayed on the menu, then he may deduct a proportion. He is also entitled to refuse payment for any dishes that are not what he ordered, or do not meet the description on the menu, or do not seem to be of a reasonable standard. However, if George cuts up rough, he may think it politic to leave the money. To protect any future action, he should make it clear that he is paying under protest – either write a note there and then, or write later (but not too late) and keep a copy. The police will not usually involve themselves in such disputes unless a breach of the peace, say, is in question. If George thinks the whole affair was engineered, for some reason, he may be right to insist on payment. It is not easy to enforce this, but if he decides not to pay, Rodney has to leave his name and address.

When the couple are about to leave, Samantha's coat can't be found.

A restaurant must take reasonable care of your belongings, yet most places have notices disclaiming liability. These are valid if your clothes are not left in a cloakroom and the notices are displayed prominently, and the loss is not caused by the restaurant's negligence. If there is no cloakroom, you need to ask staff to put your coat in a safe place otherwise you may lose your right to compensation.

During the night, Rodney falls ill. It's those prawns.

Well, is it? Not every case of sickness after a meal in a restaurant is down to food poisoning. It may be drunkenness, unfamiliarity with rich cooking, coincidental illness. It is never easy to prove food poisoning, or to point with confidence at the source. The only answer is to see a doctor, who will identify the symptoms and their possible cause. Then you need to call the Environmental Health Officer so that he or she may visit the restaurant and perhaps identify the source of danger – either in kitchen practice or in unsound foodstuffs. The ideal is that you should have samples of the foods consumed, but that is another development of the surreal premise that every meal in a restaurant is a case for lawyers, not a reason for enjoyment.

Rodney's and Samantha's anniversary celebration has been disastrous. What could they do about it? In the beginning, they need to complain. No anger necessary, merely a quiet word about what they were expecting. Restaurants prefer that complaints come on the spot, not in letters three weeks later. If it gets beyond this, then tinkering with the bill is one way to solve the problem – small comfort though this usually gives. All parties should work towards compromise from the word go. When Rodney rushes home vowing legal action, he would have to go to a solicitor, or get advice free from a Citizens Advice Bureau, Law Centre or Consumer Advice Centre. The Trading Standards departments or the Environmental Health Officers of the local council may be able to help him without his having recourse to legal advice. Or he could join *Which? Personal Service*, which gives help to individuals – ring (0992) 587773 for details.

Rodney could then, probably, write to the restaurant itself, stating his reasons for complaint and claiming a refund of his bill. If no satisfactory result is achieved, then a solicitor's letter could be the next step, or action under the small claims procedure in the county court (sheriff court in Scotland) – which can be undertaken without a solicitor. The financial limits to small claims cases (£1,000 in England, Wales and Northern Ireland; £750 in Scotland) are rarely going to be exceeded in a dispute with a restaurant.

General lists

New entries

These restaurants are new to the *Guide* this year, although some may have appeared in previous years, or in the round-ups last year.

London

L'Altro, W11
Arcadia, W8
Aubergine, SW10
Belvedere, W8
Blakes, SW7
Butlers Wharf Chop House, SE1
Chez Max, SW10
Chueng Cheng Ku, W1
Conrad London, Brasserie, SW10
Del Buongustaio, SW15
Fire Station, SE1
Fulham Road, SW3
Halcyon Hotel, W11
Hyde Park Hotel, The Restaurant, SW1
Isohama, SW1
Lahore Kebab House, E1
London Hilton, Windows Rooftop Restaurant, W1
Mas Café, W11
Mirabelle, W1
Nosh Brothers, SW6
Orsino, W11
The Peasant, EC1
Quincy's, NW2
Saga, W1
St Quentin, SW3
Shaw's, SW7
Tatsuso, EC2
Tokyo Diner, WC2

England

Barnard Castle, Blagraves House
Bath, Clos du Roy
Bath, Hole in the Wall
Bibury, Swan Hotel
Carlton, Foresters Arms
Castle Cary, Bond's
Frome, Croft's
Harrogate, Grundy's
Harrow, Percy's
Honley, Mustards & Punch
Horsham, Cole's
Huddersfield, Bradley's
Linton, Wood Hall
Little Shelford, Sycamore House
Little Walsingham, Old Bakehouse
Lockington, Rockingham Arms
Lymington, Gordleton Mill Hotel, Provence
Minchinhampton, Markey's
Minster Lovell, Lovells at Windrush Farm
Norwich, Brasted's
Norwich, Green's Seafood
Padstow, St Petroc's
Penzance, Harris's
Porthleven, Critchards
Reigate, Dining Room
Saxton, Plough Inn
Semington, Highfield House, Edward's Dining Room
Shelf, Bentley's
Slaidburn, Parrock Head Hotel
Swaffham, Stratton House
Taplow, Cliveden House, Waldo's
Winster, Brown Horse

Scotland

Aberdeen, Courtyard on the Lane
Aberfeldy, Farleyer House
Ballater, Darroch Learg
Edinburgh, Atrium
Edinburgh, Rendezvous
Edinburgh, Siam Erawan
Glasgow, Mitchell's West End
Glasgow, Puppet Theatre
Gullane, Greywalls
Inverurie, Thainstone House
Kilchrenan, Taychreggan
Port Appin, Pierhouse
Stein, Loch Bay Seafood Restaurant
Turnberry, Turnberry Hotel

Wales

Cardiff, Le Cassoulet
Llanddeiniolen, Ty'n Rhos
Llandudno, Martin's
Llanfihangel nant Melan, Red Lion Inn
Llanwrtyd Wells, Carlton House
Reynoldston, Fairyhill
Republic of Ireland
Castlebaldwin, Cromleach Lodge
Dublin, La Stampa

Closures

Whatever happened to that restaurant? Those listed below have closed since the last edition of the *Guide*.

London

Brasserie Faubourg, SW8
Buzkash, SW15
Chanterelle, SW7
Connolly's, SW15
Gavvers, SW1
Le Sémillante, W1
Tageen, WC2

England

Castle Hedingham,
  Rumbles Castle

Cleeve Hill, Redmond's
Louth, Alfred's
Lower Brailes, Feldon
  House
Marston Moretaine,
  Moreteyne Manor
Newark, Le Gourmet
Richmond, Howe Villa
  (closed for 1 year)
Walton-on-Thames, Le
  Pecheur

Scotland

Inverness, Whitecross
North Berwick, Harding's
Perth, Timothy's

Wales

Harlech, Cemlyn

Northern Ireland

Ballynahinch, Woodlands

London restaurants by cuisine

Boundaries between some national cuisines – British, French and Italian particularly – are not as marked as they used to be. Thus the restaurants listed below are classified by the predominant influence, although there may be some crossover.

American

Christopher's, WC2

Belgian

Belgo, NW1

British

Brady's, SW18
Buchan's, SW11
Butlers Wharf Chop House,
  SE1
Connaught, W1
Dorchester, W1
English Garden, SW3
Faulkner's, E8
Greenhouse, W1
Ivy, WC2
Quality Chop House, EC1
Rules, WC2
The Savoy (Grill), WC2
Two Brothers, N3
Upper Street Fish Shop, N1
Wiltons, SW1

Chinese

Cheng-du, NW1
Chuen Cheng Ku, W1
Dorchester (Oriental), W1

Fung Shing, WC2
Imperial City, EC3
Jade Garden, W1
Mandarin Kitchen, W2
Mayflower, W1
Mr Kong, WC2
New Loon Fung, W1
Panda Si Chuen, W1
Pearl of Knightsbridge,
  SW1
Poons, WC2
Royal China, W2
Vegetarian Cottage, NW3
Zen Central, W1

French

Alexandra, SW20
Les Associés, N8
Aubergine, SW10
Au Jardin des Gourmets,
  W1
L'Aventure, NW8
Bibendum, SW3
Bistrot Bruno, W1
Le Cadre, N8
Chez Max, SW10
Chez Moi, W11
Chez Nico at Ninety Park
  Lane, W1

La Dordogne, W4
L'Estaminet, WC2
Four Seasons Hotel, W1
Le Gavroche, W1
Grill St Quentin, SW3
Hyde Park Hotel, The
  Restaurant, SW1
Inter-Continental Hotel, Le
  Soufflé, W1
Lobster Pot, SE11
London Hilton, Windows
  Rooftop Restaurant, W1
Lou Pescadou, SW5
Magno's Brasserie, WC2
Le Meridien Hotel, Oak
  Room, W1
Le Mesurier, EC1
Mirabelle, W1
Le P'tit Normand, SW18
Pied-à-Terre, W1
St Quentin, SW3
Les Saveurs, W1
The Savoy (River
  Restaurant), WC2
Soho Soho, W1
Le Suquet, SW3
Surinder's, W2
La Tante Claire, SW3
La Truffe Noire, SE1

Greek
Daphne, NW1
Greek Valley, NW8
Kalamaras, W2

Hungarian
Gay Hussar, W1

Indian
Bombay Brasserie, SW7
Gopal's of Soho, W1
Great Nepalese, NW1
Lahore Kebab House, E1
Malabar, W8
Ragam, W1
Salloos, SW1

Indian vegetarian
Kastoori, SW17
Rani, N3
Sabras, NW10
Sree Krishna, SW17

Indonesian/ Straits
Melati, W1
Singapore Garden
    Restaurant, NW6

Italian
Alba, EC1
Al San Vincenzo, W2
L'Altro, W11
Bertorelli's, WC2

Billboard Café, NW6
Cantina del Ponte, SE1
Casale Franco, N1
Condotti, W1
Daphne's, SW3
Del Buongustaio, SW15
Eagle, EC1
Granita, N1
The Halkin, SW1
L'Incontro, SW1
Neal Street Restaurant,
    WC2
Olivo, SW1
Orsino, W11
Orso, WC2
Osteria Antica Bologna,
    SW11
Osteria Basilico, W11
The Peasant, EC1
Pizzeria Castello, SE1
Riva, SW13
River Café, W6

Japanese
Ajimura, WC2
Arisugawa, W1
Inaho, W2
Isohama, SW1
Mirabelle (tatami room and
    teppanyaki bar), W1
Mitsukoshi, SW1
Miyama, W1
Saga, W1
Shogun, W1
Suntory, SW1
Tatsuso, EC2
Tokyo Diner, WC2
Wagamama, WC1

Korean
Bu San, N7

Kosher
Grahame's Seafare, W1

Mauritian
Chez Liline, N4
La Gaulette, W1

North African/ Middle Eastern
Adams Café, W12
Al Bustan, SW1
Al Hamra, W1
Efes Kebab House, W1
Iznik, N5
Laurent, NW2

Spanish
Albero & Grana, SW3

Swedish
Anna's Place, N1

Thai
Bahn Thai, W1
Bedlington Café, W4
Blue Elephant, SW6
Phuket, SW11
Sri Siam, W1
Sri Siam City, EC2
Thai Garden, E2
Thailand, SE14

London restaurants open after midnight
These restaurants take last orders after midnight. Check the entry for details.

Billboard Café, NW6 (Fri
    and Sat)
Bistrot 190, SW7 (Mon to
    Sat)
Blue Elephant, SW6 (Mon
    to Sat)
dell'Ugo, W1

Langan's Brasserie, W1
    (Sat)
London Hilton, Windows
    Rooftop Restaurant (Fri
    and Sat)
Mayflower, W1
Melati, W1 (Fri and Sat)

Mr Kong, WC2
Quaglinos, SW1 (Fri and
    Sat)
Soho Soho, W1 (rotisserie
    only)

London budget eating

At these restaurants it should be possible to have a three-course meal, including coffee, a half-bottle of house wine and service, at *any* time the restaurant is open, for £20 or less per person. Meals may often cost much more than this, but, by choosing carefully, it should be possible to keep to a £20 budget. These restaurants are marked in the *Guide* with the pound sign symbol.

Adams Café, W12
Bedlington Café, W4
Belgo, NW1
Billboard Café, NW6
Bistrot 190, SW7
Brady's, SW18
Bu San, N7
Cheng-du, NW1
Chuen Cheng Ku, W1
Condotti, W1
Cork & Bottle, WC2
Daphne, NW1
Eagle, EC1
Efes Kebab House, W1
Faulkner's, E8
Fire Station, SE1
Fung Shing, WC2
Grahame's Seafare, W1
Great Nepalese, NW1

Greek Valley, NW8
Isohama, SW1
Iznik, N5
Jade Garden, W1
Kalamaras, W2
Kastoori, SW17
Lahore Kebab House, E1
Lansdowne, NW1
Laurent, NW2
Mandarin Kitchen, W2
Melati, W1
Mr Kong, WC2
New Loon Fung, W1
O'Keefe's, W1
Osteria Antica Bologna,
    SW11
Osteria Basilico, W11
Panda Si Chuen, W1
Phuket, SW11

Pizzeria Castello, SE1
Poons, WC2
Ragam, W1
Rani, N3
RSJ, SE1
Sabras, NW10
Singapore Garden
    Restaurant, NW6
Soho Soho, W1
Sree Krishna, SW17
Thai Garden, E2
Thistells, SE22
Tokyo Diner, WC2
Two Brothers, N3
Upper Street Fish Shop, N1
Vegetarian Cottage, NW3
Wagamama, WC1
Zoe, W1

London restaurants open for Sunday lunch

Albero & Grana, SW3
Al Bustan, SW1
Alexandra, SW20
Al Hamra, W1
All Saints, W11
L'Altro, W11
L'Aventure, NW8
Bahn Thai, W1
Bedlington Café, W4
Belgo, NW1
Belvedere, W8
Bibendum, SW3
Billboard Café, NW6
Bistrot 190, SW7
Blakes, SW7
Blue Elephant, SW6
Blueprint Café, SE1
Bombay Brasserie, SW7
Brackenbury, W6
Buchan's, SW11
Butlers Wharf Chop House,
    SE1
Café des Arts, NW3

Café Royal, W1 (Brasserie
    only)
Canteen, SW10
Cantina del Ponte, SE1
The Capital, SW3
Le Caprice, SW1
Casale Franco, N1
Cheng-du, NW1
Christopher's, WC2
Chuen Cheng Ku, W1
Claridge's, W1
Connaught, W1
Conrad London, Brasserie,
    SW10
Cork & Bottle, WC2
Criterion Brasserie, W1
Daphne's, SW3
Del Buongustaio, SW15
Dorchester, W1
English Garden, SW3
Faulkner's, E8
First Floor, W11
Four Seasons Hotel, W1

French House Dining
    Room, W1
Fulham Road, SW3
Fung Shing, WC2
La Gaulette, W1
Gopal's of Soho, W1
Granita, N1
Great Nepalese, NW1
Greenhouse, W1
Grill St Quentin, SW3
Halcyon Hotel, W11
Harveys, SW17
Inter-Continental Hotel, Le
    Soufflé, W1
Ivy, WC2
Iznik, N5
Jade Garden, W1
Joe's Cafe, SW3
Kastoori, SW17
Kensington Place, W8
Lahore Kebab House, E1
Lanesborough, SW1
Lansdowne, NW1
Launceston Place, W8

London Hilton, Windows Rooftop Restaurant, W1
Lou Pescadou, SW5
Malabar, W8
Mandarin Kitchen, W2
Mas Café, W11
Melati, W1
Mr Kong, WC2
New Loon Fung, W1
Noughts'n'Crosses, W5
Odettes, NW1
192, W11
Orsino, W11
Orso, WC2
Osteria Antica Bologna, SW11
Osteria Basilico, W11

Pearl of Knightsbridge, SW1
The Peasant, EC1
Le P'tit Normand, SW18
Le Pont de la Tour, SE1
Poons, WC2
Quaglino's, SW1
Quality Chop House, EC1
Ragam, W1
Rani, N3
Ransome's Dock, SW11
The Regent London, NW1
Riva, SW13
River Café, W6
Royal China, W2
Rules, WC2
Sabras, NW10

Saga, W1
St Quentin, SW3
The Savoy, WC2
Shaw's, SW7
Singapore Garden Restaurant, NW6
Snows on the Green, W6
Sonny's, SW13
Sree Krishna, SW17
Le Suquet, SW3
Thistells, SE22
Tokyo Diner, WC2
Turner's, SW3
Vegetarian Cottage, NW3
Waltons, SW3
Wiltons, SW1
Zen Central, W1

London restaurants open for Sunday dinner

Albero & Grana, SW3 (tapas in bar only)
Al Bustan, SW1
Al Hamra, W1
Arcadia, W8
L'Aventure, NW8
Bahn Thai, W1
Bedlington Café, W4
Belgo, NW1
Bibendum, SW3
Bistrot 190, SW7
Blakes, SW7
Blue Elephant, SW6
Bombay Brasserie, SW7
Buchan's, SW11
Bu San, N7
Café des Arts, NW3
Canteen, SW10
The Capital, SW3
Le Caprice, SW1
Casale Franco, N1
Cheng-du, NW1
Chuen Cheng Ku, W1
Claridge's, W1
Connaught, W1
Conrad London, Brasserie, SW10
Cork & Bottle, WC2
Daphne's, SW3
Dorchester, W1
La Dordogne, W4
English Garden, SW3
Faulkner's, E8
First Floor, W11
Four Seasons Hotel, W1

French House Dining Room, W1
Fulham Road, SW3
Fung Shing, WC2
Gopal's of Soho, W1
Granita, N1
Great Nepalese, NW1
Greenhouse, W1
Grill St Quentin, SW3
Halcyon Hotel, W1
The Halkin, SW1
Harveys, SW17
Ivy, WC2
Iznik, N5
Jade Garden, W1
Kastoori, SW17
Kensington Place, W8
Lahore Kebab House, E1
Lanesborough, SW1
Lansdowne, NW1
Leith's, W11
Lou Pescadou, SW5
Malabar, W8
Mandarin Kitchen, W2
Manzi's, WC2
Mas Café, W11
Mayflower, W1
Melati, W1
Mr Kong, WC2
Miyama, W1
New Loon Fung, W1
192, W11
Orsino, W11
Orso, WC2

Osteria Antica Bologna, SW11
Osteria Basilico, W11
Pearl of Knightsbridge, SW1
Le P'tit Normand, SW18
Phuket, SW11
Le Pont de la Tour, SE1
Poons, WC2
Quaglino's, SW1
Quality Chop House, EC1
Ragam, W1
Rani, N3
The Regent London, NW1
Riva, SW13
Rotisserie, W12
Royal China, W2
Rules, WC2
Sabras, NW10
Saga, W1
St Quentin, SW3
The Savoy, WC2
Shogun, W1
Singapore Garden Restaurant, NW6
The Square, SW1
Sree Krishna, SW17
Sri Siam, W1
Le Suquet, SW3
Tokyo Diner, WC2
Turner's, SW3
Vegetarian Cottage, NW3
Waltons, SW3
Wiltons, SW1
Zen Central, W1

The Good Food Club 1994

Many thanks to all the following people who contributed to this year's *Guide* ...

N. Abercrombie
Dr Sidney
 Abrahams
Sir John Acland
Robert Adams
Peter Adcock
William Adolph
Dr J.B. Ainscough
John Aird
N.S. Alcock
Mr and Mrs H.
 Aldersey-
 Williams
Mrs D. Aldridge
Minda and Stanley
 Alexander
Simon Alexander
Dr and Mrs A.A.
 Alibhai
Mrs J. Alker
Julian Allason
Mrs Angela
 Allaway
C.D. Allen
R.C. Allen
T.R. Allen
Sir Anthony
 Alment
Walter Almond
R.J. Ames
Mrs Jane Amherst
Paul Amos
Ms F. Anderson
Keith Anderson
Gwen and Peter
 Andrews
Steve Angel
Mr and Mrs Kurt
 Angelrath
Sir Michael Angus
Nick Antill
T. Appleton
Mrs Cynthia Archer
S.R. Arnes

M.E. Arnold
Ms Sue Arnold
Brian Ashby
Mrs E. Ashford
Mrs J.A. Ashton
Mr and Mrs F.W.
 Aspinall
Mrs Hazel Astley
Dr P.L. Aston
Craig Atkin
W. Atkinson
J.E. Attas
Ms K. Austin
Andrew Averill
Mrs Jean Aviss
Ms Claire Ayling
Mrs J. Baber
Dr J.R. Backhurst
Keith Bacon
Joseph Bailey
R. Bailiff
Alan and Margot
 Baker
Eddie Baker
Howard Baker
Mr and Mrs I.
 Balaam
Ms Amanda Ball
W. Ballmann
C. Banfield
Mr and Mrs A.
 Banks
Ronald Banks
Edward Bannon
H.F.H. Barclay
John Barker
Lt Col K.A.S.
 Barker
David Barlow
Tim Barlow
K.J. Barmes
Colin Barnes
David Russell
 Barnes

R.J. Barnes
Alan Barnett
Mr and Mrs R.
 Barnett
Jeanne and George
 Barnwell
Ms Charlotte
 Barraclough
Geoff Barratt
R.G. Barrett
Mrs B.J. Barry
M.J. Barry
Matthew Bartlett
L. Basham
David Baty
K. Baxter
K. Baxter
Conrad Bayliss
Ms Sarah Beards
Ms Sarah Beattie
Mr and Mrs Richard
 Bebb
Mrs J.M. Beck
Ms E. Becker
F.R. Beckett
Ian Bedford
Robert Beebe
M.J. Beech
Mr and Mrs R.
 Beech
Prof M.E. Beesley
Mrs C.D. Bell
Ms Catherine Bell
M. Bell
N. Bell
Russell Bennet
G.G. Bennett
F.W.P. Bentley
Mrs Katy Bentley
Suzanne and Philip
 Bentley
William Bentsen
B. Beresford
Stephen Beresford

Mr and Mrs H.I.
 Berkeley
Mrs Ann Berne
Mrs Gabriele
 Berneck
J.P. Bernie
D. Berry
Mr and Mrs E.
 Berry
P.E. Berry
W.J. Best
Ms Karen Bibby
Dr D.R. Bickerton
Stephen Bickford-
 Smith
Mr and Mrs
 Norman Bidgood
J.D. Bidwell
Russell Birch
C.A.K. Bird
R.G. Birt
Mr and Mrs Julian
 Bishop
T.J.M. Bishop
Mrs Blackburn
Robert Blackmore
Richard Blades
C.J. Blake
Fiona M. Blake
R.S. Blake
Robin Blanche
Mrs J.A. Blanks
Edward Blincoe
Mr and Mrs S. Bliss
Mr and Mrs Jay
 Bluck
Dr S.M. Blunden
Dr P.L. Boardman
Mr and Mrs Neil
 Boggon
Heather Bogle
K.W. Bogle
Julian Boles
J. Bolt

L.A. Bolton
Mr and Mrs Richard
  Bone
M.T. Bonney
John Borland
Ms Lindsay
  Boswell
J.A. Boucher
Canon M.A.
  Bourdeaux
Peter Bourne
R. Bourne
Patrick Bowden
Richard Bowden
Paul Bowdler
A.J. Bowen
Dr Philip Bowens
Dr K.M. Bowkett
Michael Bowyer
Dr J.M. Boyce
S. Boyd
Lorraine Boyle
Anthony Bradbury
Dr P.G. Bradley
Mr and Mrs J.G.
  Bradshaw
Peter Bradshaw
Dr and Mrs Donald
  Braid
Mrs M. Bramble
Roger Bramble
Miss Anne Branch
Mr and Mrs Frank
  Branney
N.P. Bray
M.J. Brett
Donald Breuner
Edwin Brew
Mrs Jonica Bridge
Mr and Mrs John
  Brierley
K.H. Brining
Mrs L. Britnell
Mrs R. Brittle
B.J. Britton
Mr and Mrs Julian
  Britton
Geoff Brodie
Dr O.G. Brooke
Mr and Mrs J.
  Brooker
Mr and Mrs John
  Brookes
R. Brooking
Douglas Brooks
W.L. Brooks
Mrs Kathleen
  Broom
Chris Brown
Mrs Clement
  Brown

Colin and Shirley
  Brown
Dr and Mrs D.G.
  Brown
Ms Jane Brown
Ms Kaye Brown
Mrs Louisa Brown
R.D. Brown
Mr and Mrs Max
  Bryan
V.C. Bryan
Ian Bryant
Nicholas Buck
R.W. Buckle
Mrs Daphne
  Bullock
R.M. Burbeck
Mrs Daphne
  Burgess
Mrs Maureen
  Burgess
Paul Burgess
E.B. Burns
M.H. Burr
His Honour Judge
  Michael Burr
Derek Burrell
J.R. Burrows
Ms Sandra Burrows
Khan Busby
Mrs K.B. Bushen
P. Busman
Lindsay Butcher
J. Butler
Sarah Butler
Peter Byworth
J. Cadbury
Ms C. Cadwell
David Calder
Mrs W.N. Calder
Robert Caldicott
Mrs M.V. Callaghan
M.J. Calvert
A.R.H. Cameron
Mrs Janet Capel
Ms Louise Capeling
Anthony Capo-
  Bianco
J.R. Carder
Betty Carey
The Earl and
  Countess of
  Carlisle
Mr and Mrs Carlisle
Mrs Patricia Carr
Ms Jane Carroll
J.M. Carson
N. Carter
Mrs P.E. Carter
P.E. Carter
Kim Cartledge
R. Carty

M. Carwithen
John Cass
Mr and Mrs Paul
  Cassidy
C.J. Castledine
J.P. Catcheside
R.E. Catlow
Paul Catmur
J. Cavalla
Ian Cawley
J. Cawley
George Cernoch
Keith Chadwick
P.H. Chamberlain
Mrs V. Chandley
Mrs Ann Chapman
Clive Chapman
D.I. Chapman
J.A. Chard
Mr and Mrs Barry
  Charles
S. Charles
Ms Jane Charlton
Alan Cheetham
G.D. Child
Ms Stephanie
  Chinn
W.R. Chrisp
E.W. Christie
M.J. Clapham
Lesley Clare
Dr M.G. Clark
J.W. Clarke
Ms Maggie Clarke
Nick Clarke
Paul Clarke
Mr and Mrs
  Clarkson
Mrs Constance
  Clasper
R.S. Clayton
Kenneth Cleveland
Jennifer Clickner
E. Clifford White
Mrs P.A. Clough
Adam Cochrane
Mrs H.R. Cockeram
Roger Cockhill
W.F. Coghill
Dr A. Cohen
D. Cohen
J.D. Cohen
Dr John Coker
Mrs S.J. Cole
B.M. Collins
Mr and Mrs Barry
  Collins
Mrs D. Collins
John Colton
Dr R.G Compton
Bernard Conn
William Connon

Peter Constable
Andy Cook
Dr and Mrs R.C.
  Cooke
Barry Coombs
Miss C. Cooper
Derek Cooper
Dr G.C. Cooper
P.J. Cooper
J. Corbluth
P.M.A. Corke
Mrs Hannah Corton
Ms J. Cottrell
Mr and Mrs Robert
  Courtneidge
Max Coventry
H. Cowan
A. Cowell
Teresa Cowherd
Tim Cowling
Dr Andrew Cox
J.L. Cox
R.D. Cramond
Mr and Mrs S.
  Crampton
Dr K.W.E. Craven
T.J. Craven
Mrs J. Crawford
Denis Creighton
Mrs J.M. Cresswell
J. Crewe
Stewart Crichton
Andrew M.
  Critchley
Mrs Paula Critchley
J. Crocker
D. Crockett
T.E. Crompton
Ms Helen
  Crookston
A.D. Cross
M.J. Cross
Dr W.G. Cross
Barbara Crossley
Mrs A. Crowhurst
Ms Alison
  Crowther
T. Crum
Dr S.N. Crutchley
Drs Paul and Kathy
  Cullen
M.P. Cullinan
Frank Cummins
Mark Cunniffe
Steve Currid
Steven Curson
Jill Cutting
Mr and Mrs Brian
  Dale
Dr M.A.R. Dale
K.W. Daley
J. Dalmon

Mr and Mrs J.C. Damron
M. Daneshvar
Ms H.J. Daniell
Mr and Mrs C. Daniels
N.A. Daniels
Ms Sue Daniels
Mrs H. Dannatt
Peter Danny
L, and P. Darby
B. Davey
David Davey
Mr and Mrs P. Davey
Mr and Mrs R. David
I.D. Davidson
W.H. Davidson
Andrew Davies
Ms Anne Davies
Dr C.H. Davies
C.V. Davies
Dr C.W. Davies
Mrs Elisabeth Davies
J.E. Davies
K.B. Davies
R.F. Bryn Davies
Dr and Mrs R.J. Davies
R.P. Davies
R.W. Davies
Mrs V. Davies
Andrew Davis
Elizabeth Davis
Roger Davis
Dr and Mrs R.P.R. Dawber
Mrs Katie Dawson
Ms J.A. Day
Mrs June Day
P.T. Day
Nigel Deacon
J.B. Dean
N.C. Dee
Mrs G.M. Deering
Mr and Mrs A.E. Demby
Michael Dempsey
Mr and Mrs Jonathan Denby
John Denison
George Denton
John Derbyshire
I.C. Dewey
Ms B. Sella di Monteluce
Dr D.O. Dickie
Ms Mertel Dickinson
Phillip Dignan

J. Dillon
Mr and Mrs Robert Dillon
Colin Divval
George Dobbie
Mr and Mrs Dobson
Mrs Maureen Dodshon
Rev and Mrs Donaghy
Ms Susan Dorey
James and Mary Douglas
J.N. Douney
Dr and Mrs J.R. Dove
Mrs Ann Downes
Colin Dowse
Mrs Heather Doyle
K.B. Drapkin
John Drayson
R.C. Drew
Ms Annabelle Drinkell
Dr M.H. Drucquer
Mr and Mrs Mark Dubbins
Mr and Mrs Adam Duff
Rev James Duncan
Dr O.J. Dunmore
David Durbin
Denis Durno
Paul Dwyer
R.S. Dyson
Mr and Mrs W.A. Eaglesham
Mrs Judith Earl
Mr and Mrs C. Easthaugh
Dr and Mrs Lindsay Easton
C.H. Eckert
Neville Eckley
Dr S. Eden
John Edington
Neil Edkins
B.J.S. Edmond
Dr Roger Edmonds
Mrs Edwards
Caroline Edwards
J.G. Edwards
Dr John Eggleton
John Elder
Dr and Mrs P.D. Elderfield
Steven Elief
D. Ellery
L.C. Elliott
Mrs A. Ellis
D.R. Ellis
Mr and Mrs G. Ellis

Martin Ellis
R.C. Ellis
Ms Karen Elmer
Bernard Elsey
N. and V. Elton
John Elvidge
Mr and Mrs O. Elwood
Mrs P. Emlyn-Williams
Roger Emm
Michael and Anita Emmott
Prof and Mrs C.E. Engel
Mr and Mrs Stephen Engel
Adam England
Ms Caroline England
Robert Entwistle
David Erskine
Mrs Elizabeth Esteve-Coll
Mrs H. Etherington
Paul Etherington
H. Evaham
W. Graham Evans
P.Evans
E.G. Eyre
P.M. Eyre
Mrs R.N. Eyre
John Fahy
Adrian Faiers
Ms M.C. Fairlie
Jed Falby
Ms Melissa Farguilo
A.G. Farkas
M. Farmer
T. Farrell
Ms Melissa Farrin-Thorne
Ms Ann Farrow
D. Farrow
Nick Farrow
Mr and Mrs D.R. Farthing
J. Faulkner
Elizabeth Fay
Roger Feakins
C.J. Feeters
G.A. Fenn
A.B.X. Fenwick
Stephen and Susan Ferguson
Mr and Mrs N. Fergusson
M.A. Ferrero
S.J. Few
Eric Fiddian
Lady Ann Fielding

Mr and Mrs Alan Figg
Ms Mary Filby
Mrs P.S. Fincher
Mrs G.C. Findeisen
A. Firth
James Fish
Mr and Mrs J. Fitton
Mr and Mrs T. Fitzgerald
T.C. Flanagan
Dr Ron Fletcher
I.H.K. Flinter
Ms N. Foley
M.R.D. Foot
Dr David Forbes
Mr and Mrs Alan Ford
Mrs Fiona Forder
Mrs A.D. Forrest
P.E.A. Forrest
E. Forrester
Brian Forsyth
S.E. Foster
J. Foulston
P.N. Fowkes
Mrs Anne Fowler
J.A. Fowler
Ms Clare Fox
Mohammed Foysol
Richard Francis
Miss Marion Frank
R. Frankland
Dr N.P. Franks
C. Fraser
Jane Fraser
G.M. Freakes
A. Freeman
Dr and Mrs Anthony Freeman
Alan Freemantle
Andrew Frey
Mrs Caroline Friend
David Frise
Mr and Mrs P.J. Frogley
Mrs B.J.R. Fuchs
Mr and Mrs A. Fuer
Mrs Emma Gabbertas
K.F. Gabbertas
John Gagg
Audrey and Adrian Gale
Tom Gallagher
Iain Garner
Courtney Garnsworthy
I. Garrett

Michael Garrison
Ms Caroline Garthwaite
Mrs P.J. Garvey
Dr Ian Gavin
Donald M. Gay
J. Gazdak
Mrs Pauline Geake
Sqn Ldr M.S. Geddes
Mrs Ann Geen
Mrs Vera George
Ms Christine Gerezdi
Mr and Mrs G.P. Ghedrych
Hunter Gholson
Mr and Mrs Austin Gibbons
Ms Gibson
Mr and Mrs David Gibson
Mrs Ken Gibson
Richard Gibson
T.J. Gibson
Dominic Gilbert
G.R. Gilbey
Dr A.C. Gilby
Mr and Mrs Peter Gillett
Peter Gillings
Miss H. Gillmore
Albert Gillotti
Dr Alan Gilston
Mr and Mrs Bud Glickman
Mrs Joy Glover
Roger Glover
Christopher Godber
Peter and Sue Godber
Mrs Marion Godfrey
Mrs Carol Godsmark
Basil Golding
Mr and Mrs Raymond Goldman
D.C. Goldrei
B.J. Goldthorpe
Tom Gondris
R.P Good
Mrs Ann Goodburn
D. Goodger
Sir Philip Goodhart
Mrs Pamela Goodman
M. Gordon-Russell
Dr S.M. Gore
Mrs V. Gorst
D.M. Gostyn

Mr and Mrs A. Gough
P. Gould
G.K. Gouldman
C.H.C. Graham
Hugh Graham
Dr C.L. Grandage
R.L. Grant
Stephen Grant
Dr Travers Grant
Keith Granville
K.C. Gray
Dr Alan Green
Mr and Mrs Frank Green
Hylton Green
Mrs Rita Green
C. Greenhow
Andrew Greenwood
B.V. Greenwood
Mr and Mrs K. Greenwood
Ian Gregg
Conal R. Gregory
Mr and Mrs Peter Gregory
Tony Gregson
R.F. Grieve
E.F. Griffin
J.R. Griffin
J.G. Griffiths
William Griffiths
R.F.B Grimble
J.W. Grimes
Nigel Grimshaw
N.M. Grimwood
Don Grisbrook
R. Grover
Rosalind Gunning
A.B. Guy
Dr Fatima Habib
Mr and Mrs R. Haest-Ruys
Mrs A.L. Haines
Mrs Sara Halewood
C.J. Hall
Charles Hall
Sir John Hall
W.J. Hallett
Mrs G. Hallsworth
G.B.T. Hammond
P. Hancock
A. Hanney
Dr Denis Hardwick
Jonathan Harfield
Christopher Harlowe
Mr Harper
Mr and Mrs Harris
Alan and Sue Harris
David Harris

Katy Harris
Malcolm Harris
Naomi Harris
Philip J. Harris
Raymond Harris
Mrs Rita Harris
Ms Rosemary Harris
Ms Sue Harris
Mrs Isabelle Harrison
M. Harrison
C.P. Harrold
Mrs S.J. Harry
Miss W. Hart
Andrew Hartley
J.V. Hartley
Mr and Mrs J. Harvey
Miss M. Harvey
Arthur Hasler
J.P. Hastings
D. Hattersley Smith
Mr and Mrs Hatton
Maurice Hawker
Mrs P.D. Hawker
David Hawkes
Frank Hawkins
Dr and Mrs David Hawkridge
Richard Hayes
E.F. Hayward
Roger Heading
Vincent Healy
Mrs R.V. Hebdon
Mr and Mrs Terence Hedley
Mrs A.M. Heitman
Mrs P.L. Hemfrey
Ms Jenny Henderson
Paul Henderson
N.F. Henshaw
Lord Herschell
Ms Sara Hertz
Andrew Herxheimer
Gad Heuman
Perry Hewitt
Mr and Mrs D. Heywood
D.A Hickling
Mary Hickman
Mr and Mrs Charles Hickox
Mrs F. Higgin
F.R. Hilborne
Mrs C.L. Hill
J.M.M. Hill
Rupert Hill
Simon Hill
Wendy Hillary

Mr and Mrs D.W. Hills
G. Hilton
Mr and Mrs G. Hilton
Ms Janet Hinckley
K. Hindle
Dr K.L. Hindle
Mr and Mrs R. Hinds
B. Hippsley
C. Hitchings
Elizabeth Hjort
Mr and Mrs P.A. Hoare
Dr Stephen Hoare
J.M. Hodgson
David Holbrook
Roger Hole
L. Holford-Strevens
John Holland
Mr and Mrs C. Holles
Ms S.D. Holliday
Mrs A.E. Hollingworth
Keith Holmes
Ruth and David Honour
Ms Flora Hood
J.A. Hope
Derek Hopes
Ms E. Hopkins
Kelvin Hopkins
Ralph Hopton
Mr and Mrs R.H. Horncastle
Mrs Victoria Horrocks
Mr and Mrs R. Hotopf
Dr Keith Hotten
P. Houlton-Jones
David House
Mrs Meg Howard
Mrs A. Howard-Jones
Michael Howarth
Zelda and Ian Howarth
Derek Howell
Geoffrey Howell
Mr and Mrs J. Howell
Mrs L. Howell
Dr and Mrs S. Howlett
David Hudd
Mr and Mrs C.H.F. Hudson
Max and Cordelia Hudson

Jon Hughes
Sir Alan Hume
Mrs Darwin Hunt
Karen Hunt
Dr Tim Hunt
C.J. Hurd
J.D.W. Hurd
D.T. Hussey
J.D. Hussey
Michael Hutton
R.J. Hyatt
Mr and Mrs David Hyman
Mrs Ann Hynes
T.J. Hypher
Dr Ibbotson
Miss Dale Idiens
Peter and Christine Iles
David Ing
Mrs Rosemary Inge
J.E.K. Ingram
Mr and Mrs N.C. Ireland
Miss J.P. Irving
William Israel
June and Del Ivory
Mr and Mrs Jack
Dr H.R.S. Jack
James McG Jackson
Ms Mrs Jackson
P.H. Jacobsen
Eric Jaffe
Mrs B. James
Nigel James
Alastair Jamieson
Ms Sarah Jane
M.D. Janson
Moira Jarrett
Ms Claire Jauffret
G. Jeffries
Ms Kate Jeffries
M. Jeffries
David Jervois
Dr Elizabeth Jewell
James E. Jewell
B.M. Joce
D. Johansen
P.E. John
Mr and Mrs Mike Johnson
Nick Johnson
Miss R.I. Johnson
V.H. Johnson
Ms Zoe Johnson
Dr I.H.D. Johnston
Ms Janet Johnstone
Mrs Jan Jolivet
J. Joll
Audrey Jones
Gary Jones
Ian Jones

Sarah Jones
Ms Sharon Jones
Mr and Mrs Nathan Joseph
Ms Sarah Joseph
Mr and Mrs M. Joyce
M.R. Judd
Dr S.R. Juliard
G. Just
Ms Fiona Kameen
Ms J. Kaminski
Drs Leon and Dina Kaufman
W.B. Keates
Anthony Kedros
D. Keel
Dr D.V. Keen
Mrs Ann Keene
Ms Sheila Keene
Mrs Ann Kefalas
Duncan Keith
Peter and Maria Kellner
Dr C. Kelly
Mr and Mrs Jack Kennedy
Ms Kenny
Dr F.M. Kerawala
W.C. Kerrod
David and Sally Kibble
J.H. Kilby
Mrs Maureen Killi
Derek King
Rev A.B. King
Charles King
Ms Fiona King
Jean King
Capt R.E.H. King
Sarah King
C.R. and T. King-Farlow
R. Kingsley-Smith
W.M. Kingston
James Kingston-Stewart
Mrs Jean Kirk
Mr and Mrs James Kirkman
Dr Paul Kitchener
Ms Janet Kite
Alan Kleiner
Mrs Sylvia Knapp
Ms Liz Kneale
Mr and Mrs Matthew Kneale
Mrs M. Knight
P.D. Kudelka
Steve and Carole Kuhlmann
Mrs B. Kutner

P.J. Kyte
Mrs P. Laidler
N.M. Laird
Susan Laithwaite
D.W. Lancaster
Mr and Mrs Lane
Alan Lane
D. Lane
R.C. Lang
Richard Larkinson
Dr R.D. Last
Joel Latner
D. Laverty
Ms M. Lavery
David Lawrence
Mrs M.E. Lawrence
Susanne Lawrence
Edward Lawson
Dr Susan Lea
V. Leach
D.R. Leathley
George Leckie
Kate Lee
M.J. Leese
Mme Lege-Germain
V.J. Legg
Miss C.J. Leighfield
Yang Put Leng
P.L. Leonard
Ms Patricia Lesslie
Felix Letterese
A.S. Levitt
B.P. Levitt
Judge D.M. Levy
David Lewis
Mr and Mrs Jimmie Lewis
Ms Leila Lewis
Mrs Maggie Lewis
Mrs A. Lewis-Smith
B.N. Liddiard
Mr and Mrs D. Liebeck
D.W. Light
Mrs Pat Lilley
Miss Kit Wan Lim
Ms L. Lim
Prof D.V. Lindley
Gordon Lindsay
Jenny Linford
D.R. and A.J. Linnell
Mr and Mrs S. Linney
Jeff Lisle
Ms S Littleboy
James Lloyd
Anne Llewellyn
Andrew Lobbenberg
Mrs Brigitta Lock

David Lock
Paul Lock
S. Locke
Ms Janet Lockett
Ms Victoria Logue
N. Lomas
David Long
Mrs J. Long
Mrs M. Losse
Mrs Shirley Loudon
C. Love
Andrew Low
P.A. and J.B. Lowater
Mrs F. Lowe
Mrs Maureen Lucas
David Luke
K. Lyall
Alan Lynch
Mrs C. Lynn
T.C.H. Macafee
Rev R.B. Maccarthy
Mr and Mrs D.I. Macdonald
Donald Macdonald
Ms Sarah Mace
J.S. Macfarlane
R.B. MacGeachy
J.B. MacGill
Mrs Margaret Macgregor
Dr D.C Macinnes
S.A. Mackenzie
C.E.S. Mackirdy
Prof H. Maclean
A. MacLennan
K. Macleod
Ms A. Macrae
George Maddock
Mr and Mrs Nick Maddock
Mr and Mrs Madigan
Sean Magee
Mr and Mrs Peter Maguire
Peter Mahaffey
Miss S.O. Mahoney
Peter Mair
Mrs J.W. Makinson
Mrs Penelope Makower
John Maltby
The Duke of Manchester
Mr and Mrs Tim Manderson
Trevor Manhire
Mr and Mrs D.C. Mann
Brian Manning
Michael Manser

S.A. Manwaring-White
Lt.Col. & Mrs J.P. Margarson
Laurence Marks
Mr and Mrs R. Marks
Eric Marquis
Graeme Marrs
D.S. Marshall
Leslie Marshall
Mr and Mrs R.D. Marshall
R.F.D. Marshall
Mr and Mrs T.F. Marshall
Mrs Rosamond Marshall-Smith
St John Marston
Mrs Anne Martin
Mrs J. Martin
Mrs K. Martin
Tony and Heather Martin
V.R. Martin
E.A. Mason
Christopher Mason-Watts
Adam Mather
Paul Mather
Richard Mathers
J.A. Matheson
Mr and Mrs Roy Mathias
Mrs Jean Mathieson
A. Matthew
A.L. Matthew
P.J. Matthison
Mr and Mrs Robert Maudling
Ian May
David Maynard
Andrew McAlpine
Cullum McAlpine
Ms Joyce McAvoy
Ms Margaret McBrien
Mrs M. McCanch
Ms Jane McCarten
Mr and Mrs G.A. McConnell
E.S. McConway
Sir Robert McCrindle
Mr and Mrs I. McCutcheon
Dr and Mrs G. McDade
Ms Jacky McDonald
Kate McDowall

Dr M.J. McEwen
Colin McFadyean
Mr Robert McFarland
Prof and Dr I.D. McFarlane
C.J. McFeeters
Colin and Lilian McGhee
Ronald McKellar
John McKenzie
Ms C. McLachlan
Dr & Mrs J.G. McLaggan
Ian McLaren
Peter McLeod
Ian McMillan
Finlay McNaughtan
Richard Meacock
H.C. Medcalf
Mrs Robin Mellers
Ms Diane Mercer
Mrs Felicity Meshoulam
Mrs J. Messenger
Ms Hilary Meth
A. Metherell
Derek Mickel
Mrs Linda Middleton
Mrs S.P. Middleton
Ms Caroline Midmore
Paul Milican
William Millar
Mrs M.E. Miller
Mrs Mary Miller
C.K. Millman
Mrs Jose Mills
O.S. Mills
Sue Mills
H.G. Millward
Mrs S.B. Milne
Dr R.S.W. Milnes
A.J. Milton
Mrs Anne Mitchell
I.W. Mitchell
Arthur Mole
Mrs J. Mole
G. Monet
Dr Barry Monk
Miss E. Moody
R. Moon
Ms Traci Moon
Mrs C.M. Moore
Colin Moore
Mrs Michael Moore
T.J. Moorey
Mr and Mrs Moreton
F.V Morgan
J.R. Morgan

P.A. Morgan
R.C. Morgan
Michael Morlan
Mr and Mrs Peter Morrill
Ms Anne Morris
R.P. Morris
Dr J.B. Morrison
Leslie Morse
Mrs Mary Mortimer
Ms C.M. Morton
Brian Moss
Mr and Mrs W.A. Moxon
Mrs Jane Moyle
Ms Lois Mulligan
Mrs M.A. Munro Glass
M. Murgatroyd
David Murray
Dr Douglas Murray
Mrs G.M. Murray
G.R. Murray
Mr and Mrs J.A. Murray
F. Myand
Mrs Patricia Mylan
Richard Nagle
A.M. Neale
Mrs J.I. Needham
Capt John Nelmes
R.H. Nelson
Dr Richard Neville
Dr J. Newbery
G.C. Newell
Stephen Newell
Ms Amy Ney
David Nicholls
Dudley Nicholls
Peter Nicklin
John Nisbet
B.J. Norman
M.C. Norman
J.G. Norris
Mrs Gillian North
Graham Norwood
A.D. Nunn
W.O. Nunn
David Nutt
John Nuttall
Ms Mary O'Connor
Patrick O'Connor
W.B. O'Neill
H.D. O'Reilly
P.W. O'Sullivan
A.P. Oakley
Charles Oatwig-Thain
John Oddey
Charles Odenweller
R.A.L. Ogston
H.N. Olden

Dr R.B. Olding
Jane Oliphant
J.S. Oliver
Mrs M. Olley
Ms Janet Orchard
S.J. Orford
O.R. Orlinski
Mrs E. Orme
Mr and Mrs R.E. Osborne
D.W. Owen
Mr and Mrs S. Owen
Dr H. Owen-Reece
Mr Owner
Ms Jenny Oxley
Mrs Brenda Packman
Michael Page
Dr S.D. Page
Mrs S. Palmer
Mrs S.R. Palmer
Mr and Mrs Panton
Stephen Parish
Andy Park
Mrs Miles Park
Mrs Susan Park
Raj Parkash
Prof E.H. Parker
G. Parker
J.M. Parker
Jim Parker
Dr R.B. Parker
Mrs R.D. Parker
W.E. Parker
D.J. Parkes
Mr and Mrs J.E. Parsons
Ms Linda Passy
Mrs S.J. Pate
Mark Patiky
James Patrick
Adrian Patterson
Akash Paul
Mr and Mrs A. Peace
A.J. Pearce
Ms Janet Pearce
Mrs P. Pearce
C.J. Pearson
David and Tina Pease
Mr and Mrs Oliver Peck
Stephen Pegler
Mr and Mrs Marcus Pembrey
M.C. Pendered
Mr and Mrs P.C. Penrose
N. Pepperell

Mr and Mrs A.J. Percy
John Peters
Miss Thelma Petrie
Peter Petts
Michael Phelan
Drs Anne and Andrew Phellas
Chris Phillips
J.J. Phillips
Dr and Mrs D. Pickering
Dr A.D. Picton
Dr R.M. Pigache
R.I.K. Pipe
Mr and Mrs J. Pitcairn
J.H. Pitman
Hugh Pitt
R.N. Pittman
Gerard Platt
Mr and Mrs R. Polack
Dr and Mrs A.F. Polmear
Adrian Poole
David Poole
Miss Lucy Portch
Keith P. Wood
A. Portman
Jeremy Posnansky
David Potter
Mr and Mrs D.E. Powell
Mr and Mrs James Powell
A. Pownall
Dr and Mrs S.R. da Prato
M. Preston
Mrs V. Prifti
Peter Prior
J.F. Pritchard
Mrs E. Prosser
William Pryce
Mrs A. Pulfer
Robert Purcell
D.L. Purdy
Howard Pursey
B. Quilliam
Dudley Quirk
M.J. Radcliffe
Ms Ingrid Radford
Iain L. Rae
Mr and Mrs Andrew Rafferty
Dr and Mrs Rampton
Mr and Mrs Kevin Ramshaw
Mr and Mrs Graham Ransome

Mrs Caroline Raphael
Mr Peter Ratzer
Marc Rawcliffe
Mrs Mary Rayner
Peter Rea
Mrs G.J. Reddish
Mr and Mrs Andrew Reeves
Judith Reichert
A.S. Reid
Dr and Mrs W. Reith
Ms Claire Reubens
Prof and Dr E.O.R. Reynolds
Peter Reynolds
George M. Rich
Mrs H. Richards
Simon Richards
Mr and Mrs Richardson
C.J. Richardson
Ms Celia Richardson
David Richardson
Mr and Mrs Patrick Richardson
Mr and Mrs Pierre Richterich
Carol Riddick
Lloyd Ridgwell
Gordon Ringrose
Ms Charlotte Rix
Scott Robbins
A.G. Roberts
Mrs Clare Roberts
Mrs Colette Roberts
Derek Roberts
Mrs E.J. Roberts
L. Roberts
Mr and Mrs John Robertson
Sheelagh Robertson
Mrs A. Robinson
D.R. Robinson
Mr and Mrs Ivor Robinson
Miss Katheryn Robinson
Mrs P.N. Robinson
R.N. Robinson
Mrs Zelda Robinson
E.A. Robotham
Mrs Sheila Robson
Mr and Mrs J. Roche
Mr and Mrs K. Rockett
Simon Rodway
Mrs M. Roe

Paul Roebuck
Neil L. Rogall
Mrs J. Rogers
Jean Rogers
Dr John Rogers
Mrs Lesley Rogers
P. Roitt
Daniel Rose
Mr and Mrs Jeffery Rose
Alan Ross
Mrs Cicely Ross
Nicholas Ross
Ms Sarah Ross
John Rosser
Mrs Daphne Roth
B. Rough
Mrs Virginia Routh
Michael Rowland
Mrs Jill Rowley
Miss G.M. Roy
Angela Royle
Peter Rozee
Miss M.J. Ruddick
A.J. Rugg
Mrs E.M. Runnacles
Mrs P.E. Rush
K. Russam
Alexander Russell
Dr J.G.B. Russell
Susan Russell-Flint
J.S. Rutter
George Ryan
Ms Ilse Ryder
V. Sakal
Sarah Sapper
Miss Louise Sargent
Donald Sartain
Dr C.J.P. Saunders
Mrs C. Sausman
Mrs L. Savvides
Canon Michael Saward
David de Saxe
Mrs Eithne Scallan
Tony Schneider
K.W. Schofield
Michael Schofield
I. Schwaiger
R. Schwarz
Dr G.L. Scott
Mr and Mrs John Scott
P.D. Scott
Mr and Mrs W.P. Scott
C.G.P. Scott-Malden
Private Brian Scott-McCarthy

Mr and Mrs James Scott-Smith
Dr J.W.F. Scrimgeour
Simon Scrutton
Marc Seale
Philip Seaman
A.G. Searle
A.V. Seaton
J.R.E. Sedgwick
Ms Gillian Seel
A. de Segundo
Mrs Penelope Self
A. Sellar
M.P. Sellwood
Giles Semper
Mr and Mrs B. Shadrack
Dr E.S Shaffer
Mrs D.M. Shalit
Dr C.W. Sharp
D. and S. Shaw
K.L. Shaw
Peter Shaw
Very Rev D.J. Shearlock
Dr Martin Shepherd
S. Sherwood
Dr Annette M. Shiels
Peter Shier
James Shorrocks
Mr and Mrs E. Short
Mr and Mrs G. Short
N. Shroeder
Dr and Mrs T.E. Sicks
Brian Silverstone
Daniel Silverstone
George Sim
Ms Sheila Simison
M. Simonow
Hugh Simons
R.J. Simons
Ms Helen Simpson
Ms Anne Sinclair
Joseph Sinclair
R. Sinclair-Taylor
Ms Nicola Singh
Mrs D.M. Sivewright
P.E. Skerrett
Dr S. Skevington
D. Skimmer
Dr C.M. Skinner
Dr M.S. Sladden
D.A. Slade
Ms Jane Sladen
Ms Lysbeth Sleath

Dr and Mrs J.
  Sluglett
Jennifer Smart
N.S.L. Smart
D.C. Smith
Ms E. Smith
Ms F.M.K. Smith
J.H.B. Smith
Mrs Jan Smith
Kenneth Smith
Mark Smith
Michael Smith
N.H. Smith
Mrs Pat Smith
Paul Smith
Mr and Mrs Ray
  Smith
Miss S. Smith
S.E. Smith
Ms Sheila Smith
S.L. Smith
Ms Zoe Smith
F. Smithies
Miss P.M. Snell
Mrs Pauline Snoad
Mr and Mrs
  Jonathan
  Snowden
J.B. Solandt
Mr and Mrs S.
  Solley
Mrs A. Sommerville
Ms Suzanne Sontar
Mrs A. Southall
Mrs W.S. Soutter
Wg Cdr R.M.
  Sparkes
Dr M.E. Speechly-
  Dick
Dr C.J. Spencer-
  Jones
Christopher Spivey
Robin Spon-Smith
Jill Springbett
Dr and Mrs W.B.
  Spry
Ms L. Squire
W.I.St.G. Light
Miss M. Stacey
Ms Gertrude
  Stafford
T.J. Stanford
J. Stanley-Smith
J.C Stapleton
Marc Starling
Simon Starr
A.J. Stead
P.J. Steadman
Mr and Mrs Richard
  Stear
Lesley Stears
Mrs G.M. Stein

F.M. Steiner
Dr and Mrs C.J.
  Stephens
Mrs J.C.
  Stephenson
Robin Stephenson
Mrs Gladys E.
  Stevens
John Stevens
Mrs Alexander
  Stevenson
John Stevenson
Mrs Sara Stevenson
Mrs Angela Stewart
Capt and Mrs
  Stewart
Dr and Mrs J.
  Stewart
Mrs Joan Stewart
L. Stewart
Mr Stirling
Lord Stodart of
  Leaston
Robert Stoker
R.G. Storer
Richard Storey
Mr and Mrs J.
  Stoumann
Leonard Strange
Terence H. Stubbins
Mike Sturgeon
Ms Helen Style
Michael Sugden
Barry Sullivan
Miss Tunstall
Major L.A.
  Summersell
Dr P. Swan
Mrs Rita Swatridge
Ms Brenda Symes
Cdr Patrick
  Tailyour
Ms Anne Tait
James Taljaard
G.D. Tan
Ms Sarah Tanburn
Dr and Mrs J.
  Tanner
J.A. Tarrant
Robin Tassell
D.W. Tate
Ms D. Tattersall
Mrs Ann Taurins
A. Taylor
Mrs A.C. Taylor
Mrs Jean Taylor
Mr and Mrs John
  Taylor
Paul Taylor
S. Taylor
Simon Taylor
T.W. Taylor

Prof D. Taylor-
  Smith
B.G. Terry
Ms Valerie Thaler
A.W. Thomas
Alan Thomas
Mrs B. Thomas
Mrs Barbara
  Thomas
J.R. Thomas
Owen Thomas
R.E. Thomas
Mrs V. Thomas
David Thompson
J.G. Thompson
Ms Jacqueline
  Thompson
Mrs D.M. Thomson
Mrs Sheila
  Thomson
R.J. Thorne
Mr and Mrs A.R.
  Thornhill
Dr A.G. Thornton
Peter Throssell
Michael Thrusfield
Prof. B.A. Thrush
Louise Thynne
Don Tibbenham
R.B.S. Timpson
P.M. Tindall
Henry Tinsley
H. Tint
Mrs Marjorie
  Tipton
Mrs Jan Todd
Mrs Norma
  Tolmach
Michael Tomlinson
C.G. Toomer
Richard Topping
Erik Tornvall
Stephen Tosswill
Zafer Tosunlar
J.P.S. Tottman
Richard Totty
L. Toulekki
Tim Townshend
Ms Sylvia Trench
Ms Carol Trewin
Ms Teresa Trimble
Mr and Mrs L.
  Trimm
Ms Victoria
  Trombetta
Nick Tsatsas
Ian Tunnacliffe
J.R. Tunnadine
L.A. Turnberg
Miss Tunstall
Ms Celia Turner
Charles Turner

D.R. Turner
Mrs Helen Turner
Stuart Turner
J.S. Turpin
D.R. Tyler
Mrs J.A. Tymms
C.P. Ulitzner
Adrian Underwood
Mr and Mrs Paul
  Underwood
Dr G. Undrill
I.M.W. Ure
K.A. Uttley
Thomas Vacara
Ms Patricia
  Valentine
Mrs Sarah Vance
Mrs C. Van der Wallis
Pamela Vandyke
  Price
Mr and Mrs Varley
Prof M.G.R. Varma
Mrs S. Vaughan
A.C. Verdie
Lt Col and Mrs
  Vere-Laurie
G.W. Verspyck
Mr and Mrs A.
  Vickers
Ms Suzanne Viner
Gerald Vinestock
P.J. le Voir
Mrs N.A. Waddell
Dr M.H.G.
  Waddington
P.H. Wainman
Mrs J. Wainwright
Mrs A.M. Walden
Adam Walford
Miss C.J. Walker
Dr Clive Walker
Mr and Mrs John
  Walker
Mrs K. Walker
Mrs Val Walker-
  Dendle
Dr M.V. Wallbank
Dr Robert Waller
D.J. Wallington
M.C. Wallis
Mrs Virginia Wallis
Barry Wallwork
Ms Joyce Walter
Mrs A. Warburton
Dr C.C. Ward
Mr and Mrs David
  Ward
Mr and Mrs T.E.
  Ward-Hall
A.J. Wardrop
Mr and Mrs J.
  Wareham

Mr W. Waring
Mrs D.S. Warland
Mrs Angela Warren
Major E.M. Warrick
Stephen Warshaw
R.A. Wartnaby
John Warwicker
Derek and Maggie Washington
Toshio Watanabe
J.S and F. Waters
F.R. Waterstone
D. Watkins
J.H. Watkins
David Watson
G.O. Watson
Stephen Watson
Mr and Mrs E.K. Watts
Dr Mary-Clare Waugh
M.K. Webster
D.R. Wells
Dr Frank Wells
Prof S.W. Wells
Ms Barbara Wensworth
J.F.M. West
M.J. West
Philip West
Mr and Mrs Richard West
Mark Westaway
Brian Weyland
Paul Wharton
Miss C.M. Whatham
Mr and Mrs John Wheeler
Mrs S.H. Wheeler
B. Whitaker
G.T. Whitaker

Dr D.R. Whitbread
I. Whitby
Mr and Mrs Bob White
Mr and Mrs Colin White
J.W. White
J.R. White
James White
M.J. White
N.H. White
Dr and Mrs Michael Whitehead
R.J. Whitelam
C. Whittaker
Paul Whittaker
Stephen and Susan Whittle
Mrs L.S. Whitworth
D.N. Whyte
Jasper Wight
Lord Wigoder
E.J. Wilde
R.C. Wiles
Dr and Mrs B.R. Wilkey
Mr and Mrs B.M. Wilkins
Dr M.P. Wilkins
Clive Wilkinson
Lloyd Wilkinson
Mark Wilkinson
P. Willer
A.J. Williams
Dr A.J. Williams
Alan Williams
Mrs Alma Williams
Ms Ann Williams
B.J. Williams
Glendon Williams
Dr J. Williams
J.M. Williams

Rev J.R. Williams
J.R. Williams
Philip Williams
Dr and Mrs R. Williams
Dr R.T. Williams
Mr and Mrs R.W. Williams
B.J. Williamson
Stephen Williamson
Mr and Mrs M.J. Williets
Peter Willis
Michael Wills
Mrs C. Wilson
Mrs E. Wilson
John D. Wilson
Kevin Wilson
Nicholas Wilson
Prof P.N. Wilson
Peter Wilson
Peter and Shirley Wilson
Mrs S.J. Wilson
Mrs Sandra Wilson
T.M. Wilson
Prof J. Wilson-Barnett
E.P. Wiltshire
Dr A.J. Winbow
Mr and Mrs Winstanley
L.D. Winward
Mr and Mrs Paul Withers
D.E. Witts
Richard Wolf
David and Jennie Wolff
C.H. Wood
Ms I. Wood

John Wood
Prof T.V. Wood
Dr F. Peter Woodford
G.J. Woodward
Ms P. Woodward
Dr Philip Woodward
Mrs Anne Woolhouse
Ms Vivien Woolls
Alan Worsdale
J.P. Worsley-Cox
Nicholas Wraight
Mr and Mrs P. Wraight
Mrs A. Wright
Mr and Mrs A. Wright
Andrew Wright
Dr Harold Wright
J. Wright
Mrs Olive Wright
Dr R. Wright
Mr and Mrs John Wyatt
K.C. Wyatt
Sally Wyllie
R.J. Wyndham
Mrs S.J. Wynn
T.J. Wynn-Williams
J.L.A. Wyteham-Hurford
Mrs M.J. Yates
Michael York-Palmer
Yasuko Yoshida
Dr Peter Zacharias
D. Zackheim
Ms Yasmeen Zafar
Barry Ziff
Mrs Sybella Zisman

Alphabetical list of main entries

Adams Café, London W12
Adare Manor, Adare, Co Limerick
Adlard's, Norwich, Norfolk
Airds Hotel, Port Appin, Strathclyde
Ajimura, London WC2
Alastair Little, London W1
Alba, London EC1
Albero & Grana, London SW3
Al Bustan, London SW1
Alexandra, London SW20
Alfonso's, Cookham, Berkshire
Al Hamra, London W1
All Saints, London W11
Al San Vincenzo, London W2
Al-Shami, Oxford, Oxfordshire
Altnaharrie Inn, Ullapool, Highland
L'Altro, London W11
Amberley Castle, Queen's Room, Amberley, West Sussex
Amber Regent, Glasgow, Strathclyde
Angel Hotel, Midhurst, West Sussex
Angel Inn, Hetton, North Yorkshire
Angel Inn, Long Crendon, Buckinghamshire
Angel Inn, Stoke-by-Nayland, Suffolk
Anna's Place, London N1
Ann FitzGerald's Farmhouse Kitchen, Mathry, Dyfed
Annie's, Ballydehob, Co Cork
Annie's, Moreton-in-Marsh, Gloucestershire
Annie's, Swansea, West Glamorgan

Apple Cottage, Rozel, Jersey
Arbutus Lodge, Cork, Co Cork
Arcadia, London W8
Ard-Na-Coille, Newtonmore, Highland
Argyll, London SW3
Arisaig House, Arisaig, Highland
Arisugawa, London W1
Ark, Erpingham, Norfolk
Arkle, Chester Grosvenor Hotel, Chester, Cheshire
Armadillo, Liverpool, Merseyside
Armless Dragon, Cardiff, South Glamorgan
Armstrongs, Barnsley, South Yorkshire
Arundell Arms, Lifton, Devon
Les Associés, London N8
Assolas Country House, Kanturk, Co Cork
Atrium, Edinburgh, Lothian
L'Auberge, Edinburgh, Lothian
Auberge de Seneirl, Bushmills, Co Antrim
Aubergine, London SW10
Auctioneer, Clitheroe, Lancashire
Au Jardin des Gourmets, London W1
Austins, Aldeburgh, Suffolk
L'Aventure, London NW8
Ayudhya, Kingston upon Thames, Surrey
Bahn Thai, London W1
Baile-na-Cille, Uig, Highland
Ballathie House, Kinclaven, Tayside
Ballymaloe House, Shanagarry, Co Cork

La Barbe Encore, Cranleigh, Surrey
Barnaby's Restaurant, Exmouth, Devon
Barnards, Denmead, Hampshire
Barton Cross, Huxham, Devon
Bath Place Hotel, Oxford, Oxfordshire
Bath Spa Hotel, Vellore Restaurant, Bath, Avon
Baumann's Brasserie, Coggeshall, Essex
Bay Horse, Ulverston, Cumbria
Bayview Hotel, Cullen, Grampian
Beadles, Birkenhead, Merseyside
Bedlington Café, London W4
Beech Hill Country House Hotel, Londonderry, Co Londonderry
Beechwood Country House Hotel, Moffat, Dumfries & Galloway
Beetle & Wedge, Moulsford, Oxfordshire
Belgo, London NW1
La Belle Alliance, Blandford Forum, Dorset
Belle Epoque, Belfast, Co Antrim
Bell Inn, Aston Clinton, Buckinghamshire
Bell's Diner, Bristol, Avon
Belvedere, London W8
Bentley's, Shelf, West Yorkshire
La Bergerie, Harrogate, North Yorkshire
Bertorelli's, London WC2
Bibendum, London SW3
Billboard Café, London NW6

Dundas Arms, Kintbury, Berkshire

Dunworley Cottage, Clonakilty, Co Cork

Dusty Miller, Low Laithe, North Yorkshire

Dwyers, Waterford, Co Waterford

Dylanwad Da, Dolgellau, Gwynedd

Eagle, London EC1

Eastern Promise, Grampound, Cornwall

Eastern Tandoori, Dublin, Co Dublin

Eastwell Manor, Boughton Lees, Kent

L'Ecluse, New Haw, Surrey

Edderton Hall, Forden, Powys

Ees Wyke, Near Sawrey, Cumbria

Efes Kebab House, London W1

Elio's, Barton-upon-Humber, Humberside

Elms Hotel, Brooke Room, Abberley, Hereford & Worcester

El Nido, Forton, Lancashire

Endeavour, Staithes, North Yorkshire

English Garden, London SW3

Epicurean, Cheltenham, Gloucestershire

Epworth Tap, Epworth, Humberside

L'Escargot, London W1

Eslington Villa Hotel, Gateshead, Tyne & Wear

Esseborne Manor, Hurstbourne Tarrant, Hampshire

L'Estaminet, London WC2

Evesham Hotel, Cedar Restaurant, Evesham, Hereford & Worcester

Fairyhill, Reynoldston, West Glamorgan

Faraday's, Aberdeen, Grampian

Farlam Hall, Brampton, Cumbria

Farleyer House, Aberfeldy, Tayside

Farmgate, Midleton, Co Cork

Faulkner's, London E8

Feathers Hotel, Woodstock, Oxfordshire

Fifehead Manor, Middle Wallop, Hampshire

15 North Parade, Oxford, Oxfordshire

Fifth Floor, London SW1

Fire Station, London SE1

First Floor, London W11

Fischer's Baslow Hall, Baslow, Derbyshire

Fish at Sutton Courtenay, Sutton Courtenay, Oxfordshire

Fisherman's Lodge, Newcastle upon Tyne, Tyne & Wear

Fishes', Burnham Market, Norfolk

La Fleur de Lys, Shaftesbury, Dorset

Flitwick Manor, Flitwick, Bedfordshire

Floodlite, Masham, North Yorkshire

Food for Thought, Fowey, Cornwall

Foresters Arms, Carlton, North Yorkshire

Forsters, East Boldon, Tyne & Wear

Forte Crest, Jules' Bar and American Grill, Glasgow, Strathclyde

Fountain House, Dedham, Essex

Four Seasons, Nantgaredig, Dyfed

Four Seasons, Wheatsheaf Hotel, Swinton, Borders

Four Seasons Hotel, London W1

Fox and Goose, Fressingfield, Suffolk

French House Dining Room, London W1

French Partridge, Horton, Northamptonshire

Les Frères Jacques, Dublin, Co Dublin

Fulham Road, London SW3

Fung Shing, London WC2

Funnywayt'mekalivin, Berwick-upon-Tweed, Northumberland

Gales, Llangollen, Clwyd

Galley, Swanage, Dorset

Gannets Bistrot, Newark, Nottinghamshire

Garlands, Bath, Avon

La Gaulette, London W1

Le Gavroche, London W1

Gay Hussar, London W1

Gaylord, Manchester, Greater Manchester

Gemini, Tadworth, Surrey

General Havelock Inn, Haydon Bridge, Northumberland

George and Dragon, Burpham, West Sussex

George & Dragon, Rowde, Wiltshire

George Hotel, Stamford, Lincolnshire

Georgian Room, Cameron House Hotel, Alexandria, Strathclyde

Gidleigh Park, Chagford, Devon

Gilbert's, London SW7

Gilpin Lodge, Windermere, Cumbria

Gingerhill, Milngavie, Strathclyde

Ginger Tree, Ballyclare, Co Antrim

Gopal's of Soho, London W1

Gordleton Mill Hotel, Provence, Lymington, Hampshire

Grafton Manor, Bromsgrove, Hereford & Worcester

Grahame's Seafare, London W1

Granary, Wexford, Co Wexford

Grand Hotel, Mirabelle, Eastbourne, East Sussex

Granita, London N1

Gravetye Manor, East Grinstead, West Sussex

Great House, Lavenham, Suffolk

Great Nepalese, London NW1

Greek Valley, London NW8

Greenhead House, Sheffield, South Yorkshire

Greenhouse, London W1

Green Inn, Ballater, Grampian

Green's Seafood, Norwich, Norfolk

Lake Vyrnwy Hotel, Llanwddyn, Powys

Lamb Inn, Burford, Oxfordshire

Lamb's, Exeter, Devon

Landgate Bistro, Rye, East Sussex

Lanesborough, London SW1

Langan's Bistro, Brighton, East Sussex

Langan's Brasserie, London W1

Langar Hall, Langar, Nottinghamshire

Langley House Hotel, Langley Marsh, Somerset

Langtry's, Osborne Hotel, Torquay, Devon

Lansdowne, London NW1

Lanterna, Scarborough, North Yorkshire

Laughing Monk, Strete, Devon

Launceston Place, London W8

Laurent, London NW2

Leatherne Bottel, Goring, Oxfordshire

Leela's, Newcastle upon Tyne, Tyne & Wear

Leith's, London W11

Leodis, Leeds, West Yorkshire

Lettonie, Bristol, Avon

Lewtrenchard Manor, Lewdown, Devon

Lillibet's, Liversedge, West Yorkshire

Lime Tree, Manchester, Greater Manchester

Little Barwick House, Barwick, Somerset

Little Yang Sing, Manchester, Greater Manchester

Lobster Pot, London SE11

Loch Bay Seafood Restaurant, Stein, Highland

Loch Fyne Oyster Bar, Cairndow, Strathclyde

Locks, Dublin, Co Dublin

Lodge Hotel, Huddersfield, West Yorkshire

London Hilton, Windows Rooftop Restaurant, London W1

London House, Winkleigh, Devon

Longueville House, Mallow, Co Cork

Longueville Manor, St Saviour, Jersey

Loon Fung, Edinburgh, Lothian

Lords of the Manor, Upper Slaughter, Gloucestershire

Lou Pescadou, London SW5

Lovells at Windrush Farm, Minster Lovell, Oxfordshire

Lovetts, Douglas, Co Cork

Lower Pitt, East Buckland, Devon

Lower Slaughter Manor, Lower Slaughter, Gloucestershire

Lucknam Park, Colerne, Wiltshire

Lychgates, Bexhill, East Sussex

Lygon Arms, Broadway, Hereford & Worcester

Lynton House, Holdenby, Northamptonshire

Lynwood House, Barnstaple, Devon

Mabey's Brasserie, Sudbury, Suffolk

McClements Petit Restaurant, Twickenham, Greater London

McCoy's Restaurant, Staddlebridge, North Yorkshire

Madhu's Brilliant, Southall, Greater London

Maes-y-Neuadd, Talsarnau, Gwynedd

Magno's, London WC2

Magpie Café, Whitby, North Yorkshire

Magpies, Horncastle, Lincolnshire

Maharaja, Birmingham, West Midlands

Malabar, London W8

Mallards, St Michael's on Wyre, Lancashire

Mallory Court, Bishop's Tachbrook, Warwickshire

Mandarin Kitchen, London W2

Manleys, Storrington, West Sussex

Le Manoir aux Quat'Saisons, Great Milton, Oxfordshire

Manor, Chadlington, Oxfordshire

Manor House, Walkington, Humberside

Manor House Hotel, Castle Combe, Wiltshire

Manor House Inn, Carterway Heads, Northumberland

Mansion House, Poole, Dorset

Manzi's, London WC2

Le Marché Noir, Edinburgh, Lothian

Marco's, Norwich, Norfolk

Markey's Restaurant, Minchinhampton, Gloucestershire

Markwicks, Bristol, Avon

Marlfield House, Gorey, Co Wexford

Marryat Restaurant, Chewton Glen, New Milton, Hants

Marsh, Eyton, Hereford & Worcester

Marsh Goose, Moreton-in-Marsh, Gloucestershire

Martha's Vineyard, Nayland, Suffolk

Martins, Edinburgh, Lothian

Martin's, Llandudno, Gwynedd

Mas Café, London W11

Mauro's, Bollington, Cheshire

Maxine's, Midhurst, West Sussex

Mayflower, Cheltenham, Gloucestershire

Mayflower, London W1

Melati, London W1

Melbournes, Bristol, Avon

Melton's, York, North Yorkshire

Le Meridien Hotel, Oak Room, London W1

Le Mesurier, London EC1

Michael's Nook, Grasmere, Cumbria

Michels', Ripley, Surrey

Midsummer House, Cambridge, Cambridgeshire

Mijanou, London SW1

Riverside Restaurant, West Bay, Dorset

Roadhouse Restaurant, Roade, Northamptonshire

Rocher's, Milford on Sea, Hampshire

Rocinante's, Bristol, Avon

Rockingham Arms, Lockington, Humberside

Rococo, King's Lynn, Norfolk

Rogano, Glasgow, Strathclyde

Roger's, Windermere, Cumbria

Roscoff, Belfast, Co Antrim

Rose & Crown, Romaldkirk, Co Durham

Röser's, Hastings, East Sussex

La Rosette, Ballasalla, Isle of Man

Rosleague Manor, Letterfrack, Co Galway

Rothay Manor, Ambleside, Cumbria

Rotisserie, London W12

Royal China, London W2

Royal Crescent Hotel, Dower House, Bath, Avon

RSJ, London SE1

Rules, London WC2

Rumbles Cottage, Felsted, Essex

Saagar, Nottingham, Nottinghamshire

Sabras, London NW10

Saga, London W1

St Benedicts Grill, Norwich, Norfolk

St Olaves Court Hotel, Exeter, Devon

St Petroc's, Padstow, Cornwall

St Quentin, London SW3

St Tudno Hotel, Llandudno, Gwynedd

Salisbury House, Diss, Norfolk

Salloos, London SW1

Sankey's, Tunbridge Wells, Kent

Saverys, Frampton on Severn, Gloucestershire

Les Saveurs, London W1

The Savoy, London WC2

Scutchers Bistro, Long Melford, Suffolk

Seafood Restaurant, Padstow, Cornwall

Sebastian, Oswestry, Shropshire

Seguendo di Stagioni, Llanwrda, Dyfed

September Brasserie, Blackpool, Lancashire

Shamiana, Edinburgh, Lothian

Sharrow Bay, Ullswater, Cumbria

Shaw's, London SW7

Sheelin, Bellanaleck, Co Fermanagh

Sheen Falls Lodge, La Cascade, Kenmare, Co Kerry

Shiro, Ahakista, Co Cork

The Shoes, High Ongar, Essex

Shogun, London W1

Shore, Edinburgh, Lothian

Siam Erawan, Edinburgh, Lothian

Siam Orchid, Manchester, Greater Manchester

Silverburn Lodge, Ballasalla, Isle of Man

Silver Darling, Aberdeen, Grampian

Simply Nico, London SW1

Singapore Garden Restaurant, London NW6

Sir Charles Napier Inn, Chinnor, Oxfordshire

Sir Toby's, Stratford-upon-Avon, Warwickshire

Slipway Hotel, Port Isaac, Cornwall

Sloans, Birmingham, West Midlands

Snows on the Green, London W6

Soho Soho, London W1

Sonny's, London SW13

Sonny's, Nottingham, Nottinghamshire

Sophisticats, Bournemouth, Dorset

Le Soufflé, Inter-Continental Hotel, London W1

Soughton Hall, Northop, Clwyd

Sous le Nez en Ville, Leeds, West Yorkshire

South Lodge, Lower Beeding, West Sussex

Spencers, Emsworth, Hampshire

Spices, Edinburgh, Lothian

Splinters, Christchurch, Dorset

Sportsman's Arms, Wath-in-Nidderdale, North Yorkshire

The Square, London SW1

Sree Krishna, London SW17

Sri Siam, London W1

Sri Siam City, London EC2

Staithes Restaurant, Cheltenham, Gloucestershire

La Stampa, Dublin, Co Dublin

Stane Street Hollow, Pulborough, West Sussex

Stannary, Mary Tavy, Devon

Stapleford Park, Stapleford, Leicestershire

Starlings Castle, Chirk, Clwyd

The Starr, Great Dunmow, Essex

Stephen Bull, London W1

Stephen Bull's Bistro and Bar, London EC1

Stile, Willington, Co Durham

Stock Hill, Gillingham, Dorset

Ston Easton Park, Ston Easton, Somerset

Stone Close, Dent, Cumbria

Stone Hall, Welsh Hook, Dyfed

Stonor Arms, Stonor, Oxfordshire

Stour Bay Café, Manningtree, Essex

Strand, Belfast, Co Antrim

Stratton House, Swaffham, Norfolk

Sully's, Canterbury, Kent

Summer Isles Hotel, Achiltibuie, Highland

Summer Lodge, Evershot, Dorset

Sundial, Herstmonceux, East Sussex

Suntory, London SW1

Le Suquet, London SW3

Surinder's, London W2

Swan Hotel, Bibury, Gloucestershire

LIST OF MAIN ENTRIES

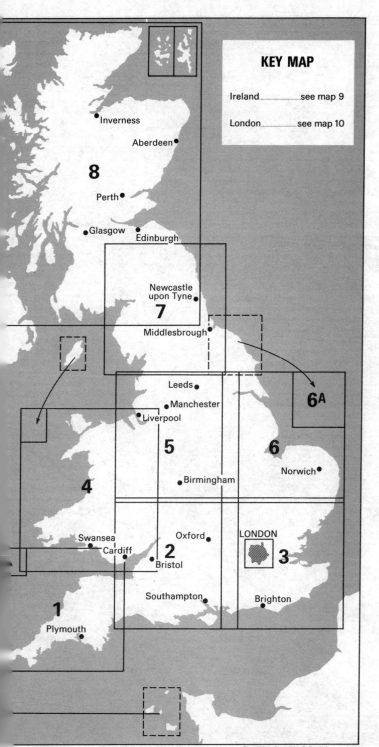

KEY MAP

Ireland............see map 9

London............see map 10

Inverness

Aberdeen

8

Perth

Glasgow
Edinburgh

Newcastle
upon Tyne

7

Middlesbrough

Leeds
Manchester
Liverpool

6^A

5

4

Birmingham

6

Norwich

Swansea
Cardiff

Oxford

2

Bristol

LONDON

3

Southampton

Brighton

1

Plymouth

Base Map Copyright © Bartholomew 1994

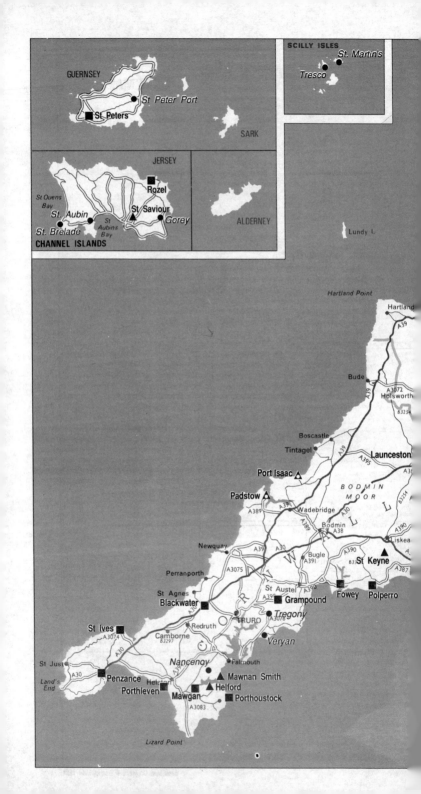

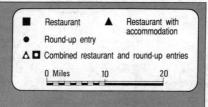

1

DEVON and CORNWALL

CHANNEL ISLANDS

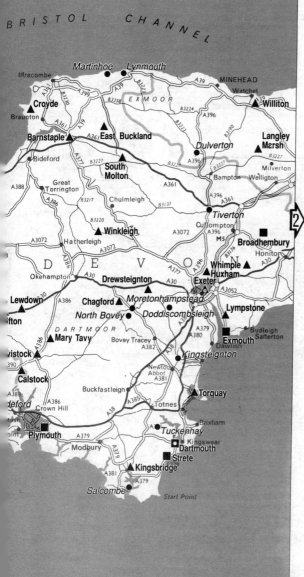

Restaurant ■ Restaurant with accommodation ▲

Round-up entry ●

Combined restaurant and round-up entries △ ▫

0 Miles   10   20

BRISTOL CHANNEL

Ilfracombe
Martinhoe Lynmouth
MINEHEAD
Watchet
Croyde
EXMOOR Williton
Braunton
Barnstaple East Buckland
Langley Marsh
Bideford
Dulverton Milverton
South Molton Bampton Welligton
Great Torrington
Chulmleigh
Tiverton
Cullompton
Winkleigh M5
Hatherleigh Broadhembury
D E V O N Honiton
Okehampton Drewsteignton Whimple
Lewdown Exeter Huxham
Chagford Moretonhampstead
ifton North Bovey Doddiscombsleigh Lympstone
DARTMOOR Budleigh Salterton
Mary Tavy Bovey Tracey Exmouth
vistock Dawlish
Calstock Kingsteignton
Buckfastleigh Newton Abbot
leford Crown Hill Totnes Torquay
Plymouth Brixham
Modbury Tuckenhay
Kingswear
Dartmouth
Kingsbridge Strete
Salcombe Start Point

Base Map Copyright © Bartholomew 1994

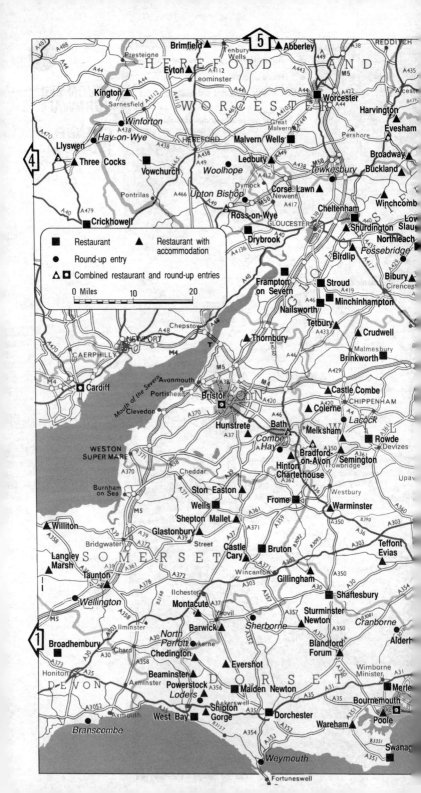

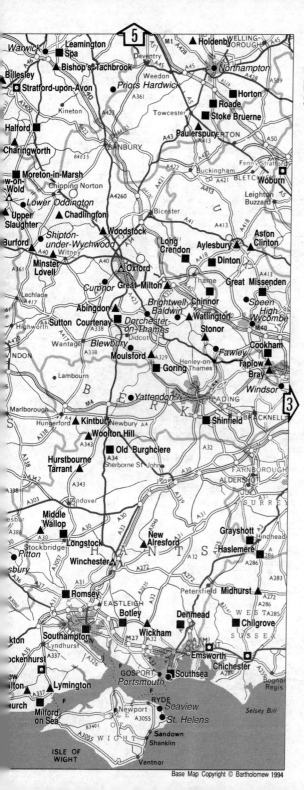

Warwick
Leamington
Spa
Bishop's Tachbrook
Billesley
Stratford-upon-Avon
Priors Hardwick
Daventry
Holdenby
WELLING-
BOROUGH
M1
Weedon
Northampton
Horton
Roade
Stoke Bruerne
Towcester
Paulerspury
ERTON
Halford
Charingworth
Kineton
BANBURY
Buckingham
Fenny Stratford
BLETCH
Wōburn
Moreton-in-Marsh
w-on-
Wold
Chipping Norton
Bicester
Leighton
Buzzard
Lower Oddington
Upper
Slaughter
Chadlington
Woodstock
Long
Crendon
Aylesbury
Aston
Clinton
Burford
Shipton-
under-Wychwood
Witney
Dinton
Great Missenden
Minster
Lovell
Lechlade
Oxford
Cumnor
Great Milton
Speen
High-
Wycombe
Highworth
Abingdon
Brightwell
Baldwin
Chinnor
Watlington
Stonor
Cookham
Sutton Courtenay
Dorchester-
on-Thames
Didcot
Blewbury
Wantage
Fawley
Taplow
Bray
Moulsford
Goring
Henley-on-
Thames
Windsor
Lambourn
Yattendon
READING
BRACKNELL
Marlborough
Hungerford
Kintbury
Newbury
Woolton Hill
Shinfield
Old Burghclere
Sherborne St John
Hurstbourne
Tarrant
Andover
FARNBOROUGH
ALDERSHOT
SURREY
Middle
Wallop
Stockbridge
Longstock
Pitton
Winchester
New
Alresford
Grayshott
Hindhead
Haslemere
Romsey
EASTLEIGH
Botley
Denmead
Midhurst
Petersfield
WEST
SUSSEX
Chilgrove
Southampton
Lyndhurst
Wickham
Emsworth
Chichester
ckton
ckenhurst
ew
ilton
Lymington
GOSPORT
Portsmouth
Southsea
RYDE
Seaview
St. Helens
Selsey Bill
Bognor
Regis
Milford
on Sea
Newport
ISLE OF WIGHT
Sandown
Shanklin
ISLE OF
WIGHT
Ventnor

Base Map Copyright © Bartholomew 1994

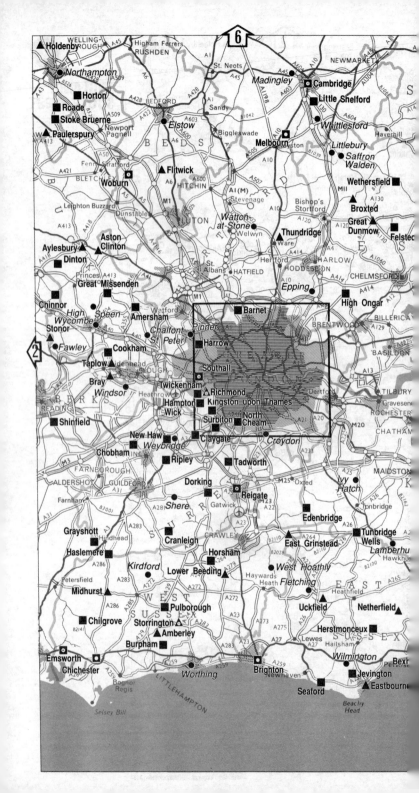

3

ENGLAND:
SOUTH EAST

■ Restaurant	▲ Restaurant with accommodation
● Round-up entry	
△ ◻ Combined restaurant and round-up entries	

0 Miles 10 20

Base Map Copyright © Bartholomew 1994

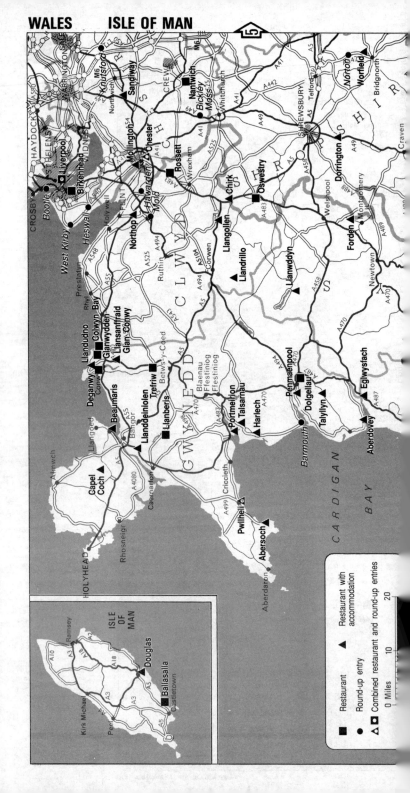

WALES   ISLE OF MAN

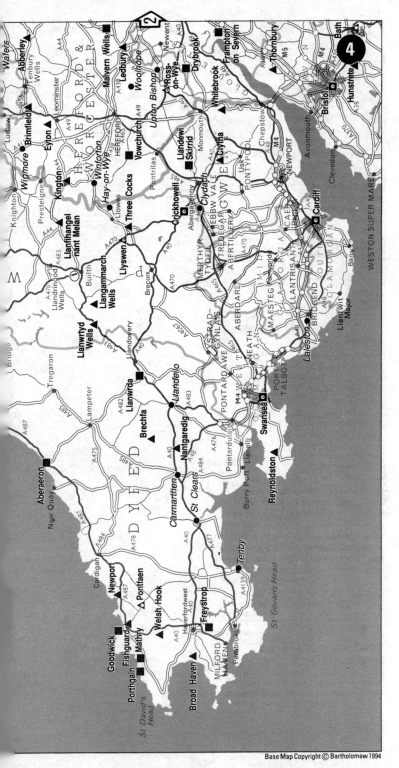

Base Map Copyright © Bartholomew 1994

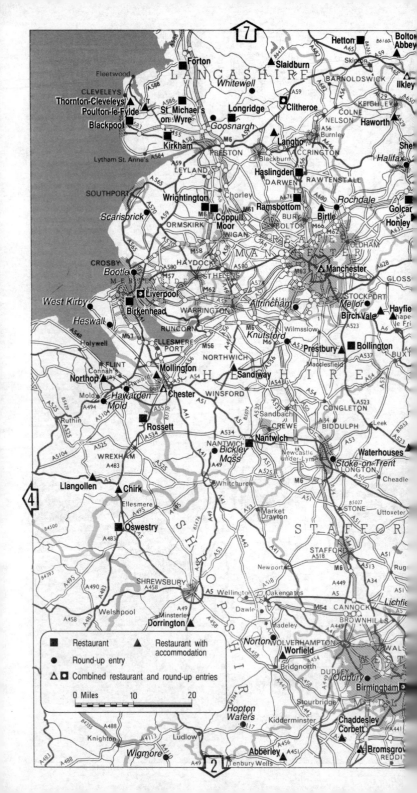

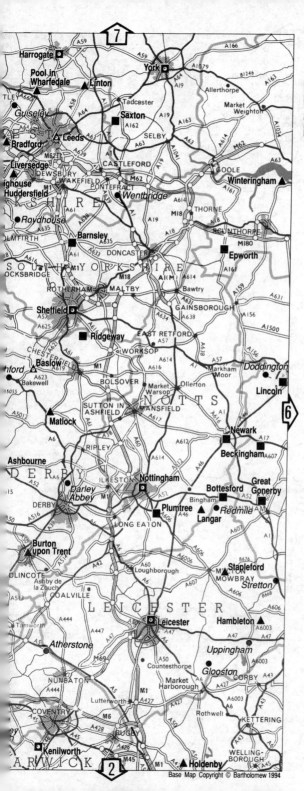

Base Map Copyright © Bartholomew 1994

ENGLAND: EAST

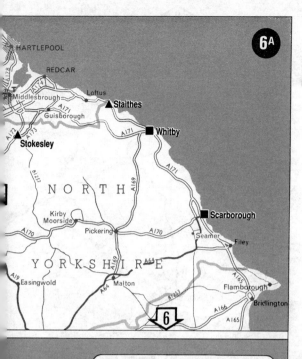

Legend:

■ Restaurant   ▲ Restaurant with accommodation
● Round-up entry
△▢ Combined restaurant and round-up entries

0 Miles   10   20

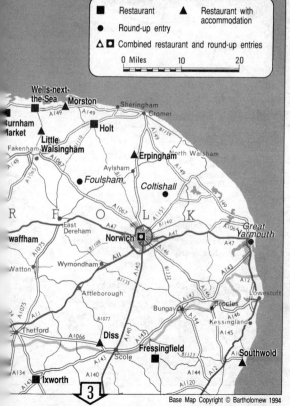

Base Map Copyright © Bartholomew 1994

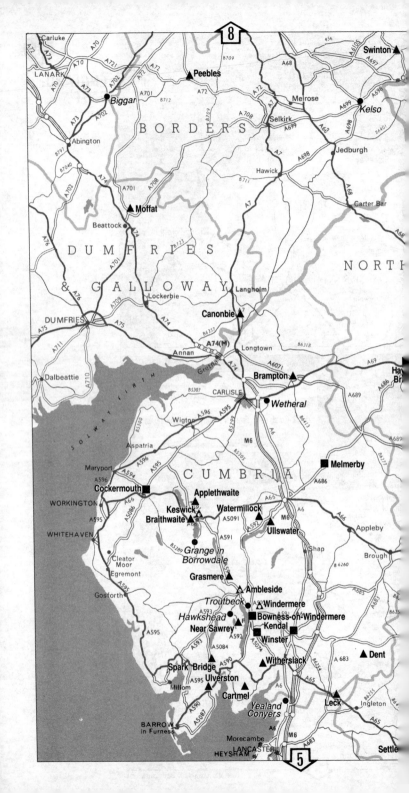

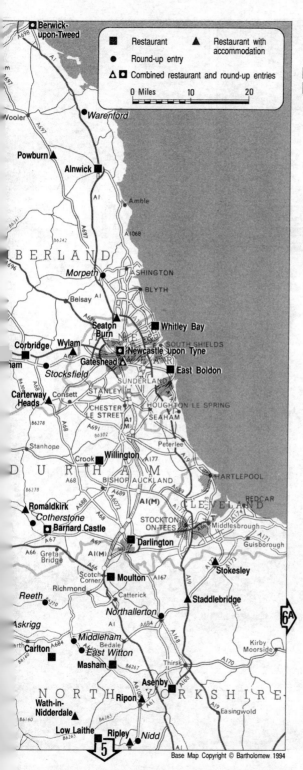

ENGLAND: NORTH

7

SCOTLAND

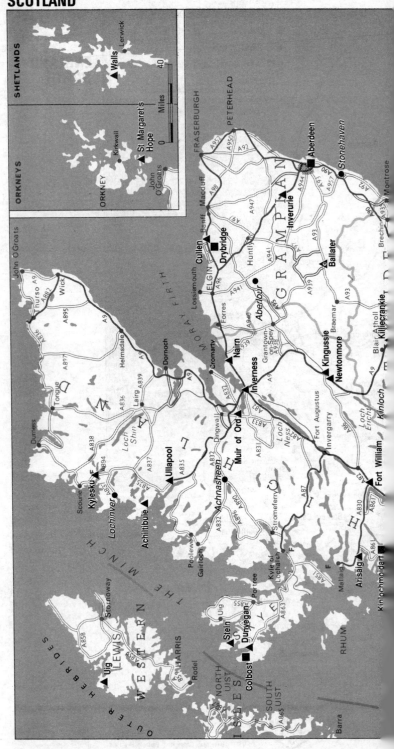

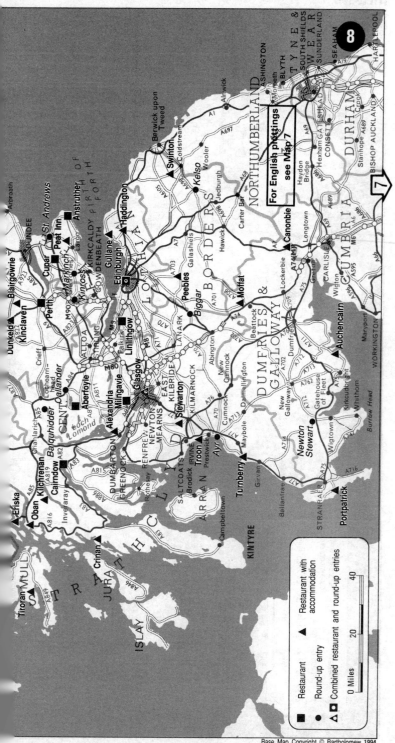

8

For English plottings
see Map 7

7

Base Map Copyright © Bartholomew 1994

▲ Restaurant

■ Round-up entry

▲ ■ Combined restaurant and round-up entries

▲ Restaurant with
accommodation

0 Miles   20   40

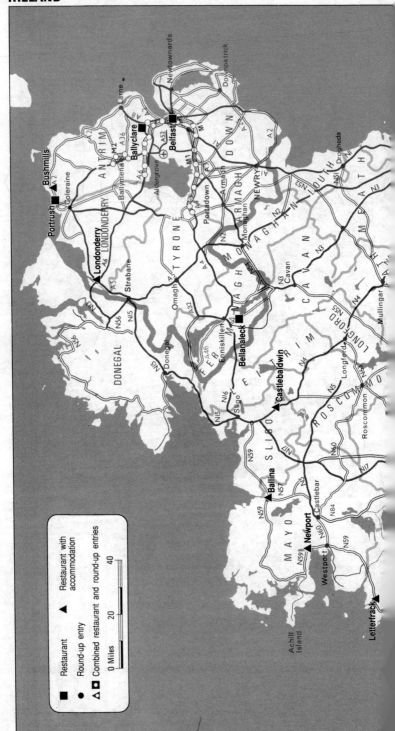

9

Dun Laoghaire
Bray
Wicklow
Arklow
Gorey
N11
N80
WICKLOW
Wexford
Enniscorthy
N11
N25
Dunmore East
Naas
N7
Curragh
Port-Laoise
6N
Carlow
CARLOW
KILKENNY
New Ross
N9
Waterford
N25
Tullamore
N80
OFFALY
N7
LEIX
Kilkenny
N10
WATERFORD
N25
N62
Birr
N52
Roscrea
8N
TIPPERARY
Cashel
N24
Clonmel
N72
Shanagarry
N6
N18
Nenagh
N7
Limerick
N8
Midleton
N25
GALWAY
CLARE
Shannon Airport
N18
Adare
N20
LIMERICK
N73
N72
Cobh
Kinsale
N20
Cork
Douglas
Ballyvaughan
N9
Ennis
N68
Mallow
KANTURK
N20
N22
N71
Clonakilty
Kilkee
N72
Killarney
KERRY
Tralee
N21
Kenmare
Bantry
Durrus
Ballydehob
N70
N71
Killorglin
N70
N22
Ahakista
Dingle

Base Map Copyright © Bartholomew 1994

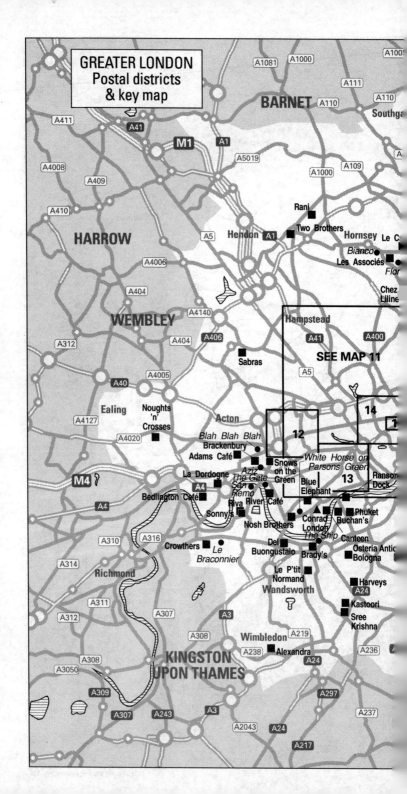

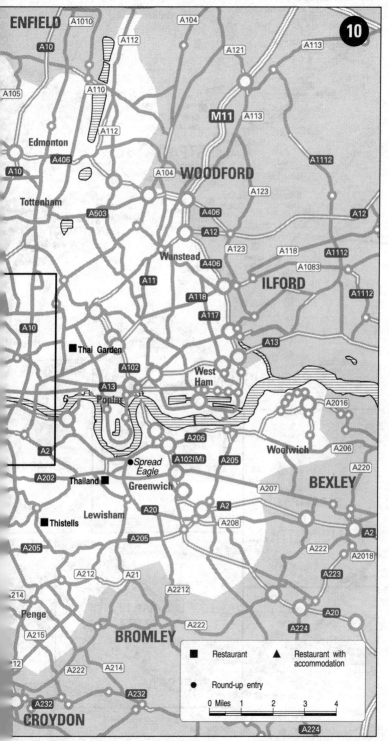

Base Map Copyright © Bartholomew 1994

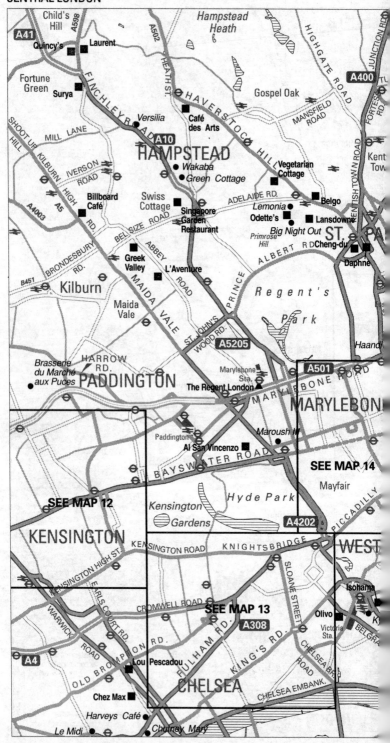

CENTRAL LONDON

A41

Child's Hill A598 A502 Hampstead Heath HIGHGATE ROAD JUNCTION RD.

Quincy's ■ Laurent

Fortune Green

Surya ■

FINCHLEY ROAD

Gospel Oak A400 FORTESS RD.

Kent Tow

MILL LANE

IVERSON ROAD

KILBURN HIGH RD. SHOOT UP HILL

A4003 A5

B451 BRONDESBURY RD.

Kilburn

Versilia Café des Arts

HEATH ST. HAVERSTOCK HILL

A10

HAMPSTEAD

● Wakaba
● Green Cottage

Vegetarian Cottage

Billboard Café ■

Swiss Cottage

BELSIZE ROAD

ADELAIDE RD. ■ Belgo

Lemonia ●

Odette's ■ ● Lansdowne

Big Night Out ST. PA

Singapore Garden Restaurant

Greek Valley ■

L'Aventure

ABBEY ROAD

MAIDA VALE

Maida Vale

Primrose Hill

Cheng-du
● Daphne

ALBERT R D

Regent's

Park

PRINCE ALBERT

Brasserie du Marché aux Puces ●

HARROW RD.

PADDINGTON

ST. JOHN'S WOOD RD.

A5205

Marylebone Sta.

A501

The Regent London ▲

MARYLEBONE ROAD

MARYLEBON

Haandi

Paddington

Al San Vincenzo ■

BAYSWATER ROAD

Maroush I ●

SEE MAP 14

Mayfair

PICCADILLY

SEE MAP 12

KENSINGTON

Kensington Gardens

Hyde Park

A4202

WEST

KENSINGTON ROAD KNIGHTSBRIDGE

KENSINGTON HIGH ST. EARLS COURT RD.

CROMWELL ROAD

SEE MAP 13

A308

SLOANE STREET

Victoria Sta.

Isohama

Olivo ■

BELGRA

A4 WARWICK ROAD OLD BROMPTON RD.

Lou Pescadou ●

Chez Max ■

FULHAM RD. KING'S RD.

CHELSEA BR.

CHELSEA

CHELSEA EMBANK.

Harveys Café ●

Le Midi ●

Chutney Mary ●

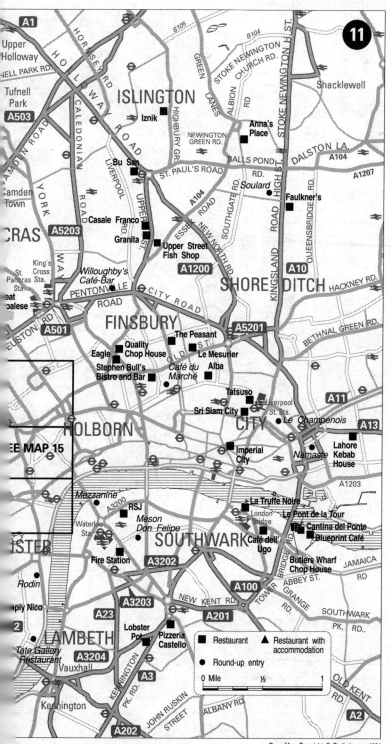

Base Map Copyright © Bartholomew 1994

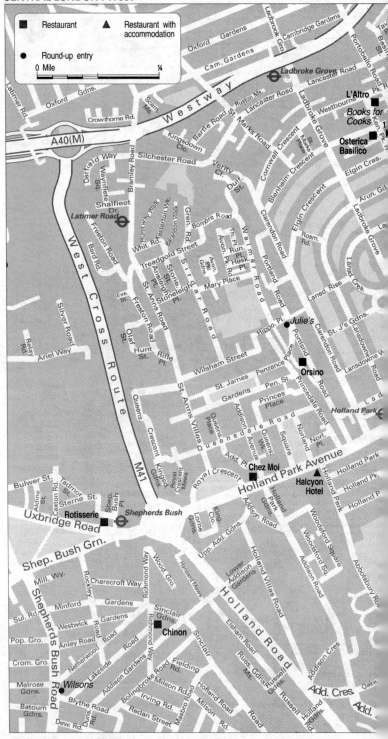

CENTRAL LONDON : West

12

McGregor St. · St. Luke's Rd.
All Saints
Mas Café
Surinder's
West. Pk. Rd.
Westbourne Park Road
Westbourne Park Rd.
Lancs. Rd.
Learn. Rd.
St. Steph. Gdns.
Dart. Cla.
Ledbury Rd.
Talbot Road
Northum. Pl.
Talbot Road
Chepstow Road
Hereford Road
Kild. Terr.
Kild. Terr. Gs.
Alexander St.
Durham Terrace
West. Gdns.
Porchester Road
Porch. Sq.
Bish. Br. Rd.
Clyde.
Gdns.
Powis Terr.
Powis Sq.
rst Floor
oot Rd.
Col.
Colville Terrace
Ledbury Rd.
Courtnell St.
Moor Rd.
Suthern. Pl.
Bridstow Pl-e
Hereford Road
Mono Rd.
Garway Road
New. Rd.
Sun. Terr.
Hath. Gro.
Queensway
Inverness
Lonsdale
Colville Road
Westbourne Grove
Artesian Road
Westbourne Grove
Ken. Gdns. Sq.
Ilch. Gdns.
Redan Place
Porchester Gdns.
Inaho
Leins. Sq.
Hereford Road
Princes
Princes Sq.
Four Seasons
Terr.
Portobello Road
Den. Sq.
Den. Cla.
Pembridge Villas
Chepstow Place
Square
Kalamaras
Sal. Gdns.
Bayswater
Leith's
Stanley Cres.
Kensington Pk. Gdns.
Kensington Pk. Gdns.
Chepstow Villas
Pembridge Cres.
Dawson Place
Moscow Road
St. Petersburg Pl.
St. Pet.
Bark Pl.
Poplar Place
Can.
Place
Queensway
Kens. Pk. Rd.
Portobello Road
Pembridge Road
Pembridge Square
Pembridge
Chapel Side
Ossington St.
Orme
Mandarin Kitchen
Lane
Ladbroke Square
Ladbroke Road
Pembridge Gdns.
Linden Gardens
Clanricarde Gdns.
Palace Court
Royal China
Queensway
Ladbroke Gdns.
Vic. Gdns.
Bulmer Place
Notting Hill Gate
Bayswater Road
The Broad Walk
ke Road
Ladbroke Terrace
Notting Hill Gate
Uxbridge St.
Ken. Mall
Palace Gdns.
Kensington Palace Gardens
KENSINGTON GARDENS
Malabar
Avenue West Eleven
Hillgate Pl.
Kensington Place
Kensington Place
Clarke's
Boyd's
Kensington Church Street
Palace Gdns. Ms.
Cam. Hill Gdns.
Camp. Hill Rd.
Aubrey Road
Holland Walk
Aubrey Walk
Cam. Hill Sq.
Peel Street
Campden Street
Bedford Gardens
Sheffield Terrace
Tor Gdns.
Hornton Street
Campden Gro.
Vic. Gdns.
Vic. Gate
Kensington Palace
Palace Green
Palace Ave.
Camp. Hill
King's College
Sheldrake Place
Glou. Wk.
Obser. Gdns.
Gord. Pl.
Pitt St.
Dukes La.
York House Place
Café Rouge
LAND K
vedere
Duchess of Bedford's Walk
Holland Street
Campden Hill Rd.
Hornton St.
Drayson Ms.
Old Court Pl.
Ken. Ch. St.
Ken. Rd.
Arcadia
Kensington Ct.
Ken. Ct.
Young Street
Holland Walk
Upp. Philli. Gdns.
Philli. Pl.
Essex Vs.
Argyll Road
Staff. Terr.
Campden Hill Rd.
Phillimore Gardens
Phillimore Walk
Holland Walk
High Street Kensington
Derry St.
Kens. Square
Thack. St.
S.E. Row
Ans. St.
Ken. Ct.
Ken. Pl.
St. Alb. Gro.
chester Place
Road
Commonwealth Institute
Melbury C.
H. Pk. Rd.
Phillimore Walk
Adam & Eve Mews
Iver Ct.
Wrights Lane
Allen Street
Abing. Rd.
Iverna Gdns.
Chen. Gdns.
Kelso Pl.
Cottes. Gdns.
Kensington High Street

Base Map Copyright © Bartholomew 1994

Restaurant ■ Restaurant with accommodation ▲

Round-up entry ●

0 Mile   ¼

HYDE

Kensington Rd.

Kensington Gore

Kensington Road

The Flower Walk

Royal College of Art

Royal Albert Hall

Princes Gate

Montrose Court

Exhibition

Kensington Rd.

Rutland Gate

Victoria Road

De Vere Gardens

Palace Gate

Hyde Park Gate

Prince's Gdns.

Ennismore Gardens

Ennismore

Ennis. Ms.

Ennis. St.

■ Bistrot 190

Brem. Rd.

Prince Consort Road

Cullen. Road

Prince's Road

Ennismore Gdns. Ms.

Cottage Place

Bron.

Square

Wódka ●

Cann. Pl.

Kensington Gate

Royal College of Music

Imperial College

■ Launceston Place

Queen's Gate Ms.

Queen's Gate

Ayrton Road

Unwin Rd.

Holy Trinity Church

Launceston Pl. Rd.

Vic. Gro.

Queen's Gt. Terr.

Gore St.

Elvaston Ms.

Wells Way

Arm.

Imperial College Road

Princes Gate Mews

South Kensington ⊖

Brompton Oratory

Gloucester Rd.

Peters. Pl.

Elvaston Pl.

Petersham La.

Elv. Ms.

Queen's Gate Pl.

Science Museum

Exhibition Rd.

Victoria & Albert Museum

■ St Que

Kynance Mews

Peters. Ms.

Queen's Gate Pl.

Geological Museum

South Kensington ⊖

Cornwall Gdns.

Queen's Gt. Gdns.

Queen's Gate Pl. Ms.

Natural History Museum

Crom. Gdns.

Alexander

Grenville Place

South. Gdns.

Queen's Gt. Gdns.

Queen's Gt. Gdns.

Ath. Ms.

Cromwell Road

Crom. Rd.

Ex. Rd.

Thurloe Pl.

Thurloe

South Terrace

Emb. Gt.

Gilbert's ■

Cromwell Rd.

Cromwell Road

Gloucester Road ⊖

Stan. Ms. W.

Stan. Ms. E.

Queen's Pl.

Queens. Pl.

Crom. Pl.

Thurloe St.

Thurloe Sq.

Ashburn Gs.

Ashburn Place

Courtfield Road

Gloucester

Stanhope Gardens

Gate

Manson Pl.

Harrington

Road

South Kensington ⊖

Pelham Street

Joe's C

Pel. Pl.

■ Bombay Brasserie

Stanhope Gardens

Stanhope Pl.

Onslow Sq.

Onslow Sq.

Sydney Pl.

Pelham Cres.

Bibendum ■

Harrington Gardens

Wetherby Pl.

Hereford Sq.

Clareville Gro.

Hilaire ■

Cranley Pl.

Onslow Gardens

Foulis Terrace

Summer Place

Sydney Street

Eli

Wetherby Gardens

Rosary Gdns.

Dove Ms.

Clareville Street

Cranley Gdns.

Onslow Gardens

Neville St.

Onslow Square

Pond Place

Bury Walk

Bina Gdns.

Gledhow Gdns.

Roland Gdns.

Cranley Mews

Shaw's ■

Eagle Pl.

Neville Terr.

Selw. Pl.

Royal Marsden Hospital

Stewart's Grove

Sydney Street

Ixworth

The Boltons

Drayton Gardens

Roland Gardens

Evelyn Gdns.

Evelyn Gdns.

Elm Pl.

South Parade

Chelsea

Royal Brompton & National Heart Hospital

Dovehouse Street

Britte

▲ Blakes

Priory Wk.

Roland Gs.

Elm Park Rd.

■ Fulham Road

Elm Park Gardens

E. Pk. Gs.

Chelsea Square

Old Church Street

Manresa Road

Cresswell Place

Gilston Road

Fulham Road

Carlyle Sq.

Carlyle

King'

Tregunter Rd.

Cathcart Road

Redcliffe Rd.

Seymour Walk

Callow St.

Elm Park Gardens

Beaufort Street

The Vale

Mulberry Wk.

Mallord St.

Argyll ■

Oak

Formula Veneta ●

Hollywood Road

Aubergine ■

Limerston Street

Chelsea Pk. Gardens

Paultons Square

Old Church Street

Bramerton St.

Glebe Pl.

Fawcett Street

Redcliffe Pl.

Netherton Gro.

Chelsea & Westminster Hospital

B. St.

Paul. St.

Upper Che

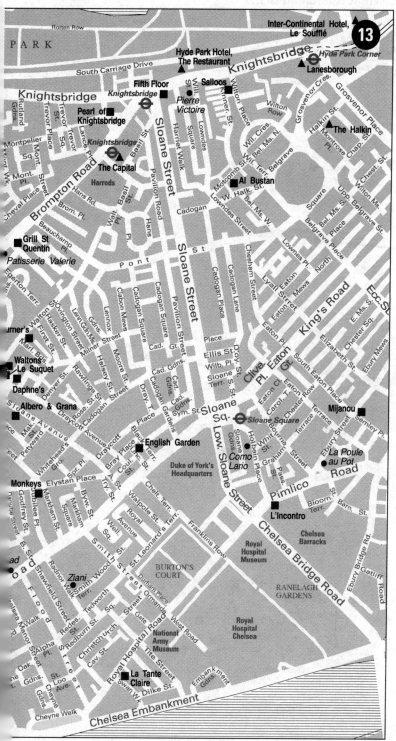

Rotten Row

PARK

South Carriage Drive

Knightsbridge

Inter-Continental Hotel,
Le Soufflé

13

Knightsbridge

Hyde Park Corner
Lanesborough

Hyde Park Hotel,
The Restaurant

Fifth Floor

Salloos

Knightsbridge

*Pierre
Victoire*

Grosvenor Cres.

Grosvenor Place

Pearl of
Knightsbridge

Harriet Walk

Lowndes
Square

Wilton Row

Wilton Place

Halkin St.

The Halkin

Montrose Chap.

Knightsbridge

Lance Pl.

Trevor Place

Trevor Sq.

Trevor St.

Montpelier
Sq.

Rutland
Gdns.

Mont.
Pl.

Cheval Place

Montpelier St.

Brompton Road

Hans Rd.

Brom. Pl.

Hans Pl.

The Capital

Harrods

Basil St.

Sloane Street

Wil. Cres.

Wil. Bel. Ms. N.

Wil. Terr.

Motcomb St.

W. Halk. St.

Lowndes Street

Belgrave

Al Bustan

Bel. Ms. S.

Upp. Belgrave St.

Belgrave Place

Chesham St.

Square

Wilton Ms.

Chest. St.

Cadogan

Pavilion Road

Hans

St.

Beauchamp Pl.

**Grill St
Quentin**

Patisserie Valerie

Egerton Terr.

Pont

Walt. Basil

Pl.

St.

Street

Cadogan Place

Cadogan Lane

Cheshire Street

Lyall Street

Eaton Mews

North

Lownes

King's Road

Belgrave Place

Ecc. St.

E. Ms. S.

Chester Sq.

urner's

Walton St.

Ovington Street

Hasker St.

First St.

Marl. Bs.

Clabon Mews

Lennox
Gdns.

Cadogan Square

Pavilion Street

Cadogan Gate

Place

Ellis St.

Wilb. Pl.

Eaton Pl.

Clive.

Pl. Eaton

Gt.

South Eaton Place

Elizabeth Street

Chester Row

Chester Sq.

Ebury Mews

Waltons

Le Suquet

Daphne's

Albero & Grana

Ovington Street

Halsey Street

Milner Street

Moore St.

Cad.
Gt.

Cad. Gdns.

Cad.
Gdns.

Sloane
Terr.

Sym. St.

Droy. T.

Eaton Cl.

Eaton Terrace

Carol. T.

Eaton
Mews
S.

Terrace

Mijanou

Sloane
Avenue

Mak. St.

Denyer St.

Rawlings St.

Rose St.

Draycott Cadogan

Avenue

Place

Dray. T.

Cad.
Gdns.

Sloane
Sq.

Whitehead's
Gro.

Pet. yard

Draycott

Bray Place

Blac. Terr.

Coull. St.

Sloane Square

Sloane
Gdns.

Holbein Place

Bourne
St.

Whittaker
St.

Graham Terrace

La Poule
au Pot

Ebury Street

Semley Pl.

English Garden

Monkeys

Elystan Place

Jubilee Pl.

Markham
Square

Godfrey St.

Markham St.

Byw. St.

Trv. Sq.

A. Sq.

Chelt. Terr.

Duke of York's
Headquarters

*Como
Lario*

Pimlico

L'Incontro

Graham
St.

Pass.

Bloom.
Terr.

Bam.
St.

Road

Danube Street

Smith Street

Walpole St.

Royal
Avenue

Well.
Sq.

St. Leonard's Terr.

Franklins Row

Chelsea Bridge Road

**Chelsea
Barracks**

ad

Oad

Flood

Redhor Walk

Shawfield Street

Smith Terr.

Tedworth
Sq.

Wood St.

Ormonde

Gate

West Road

Durham Place

Royal
Hospital
Museum

BURTON'S
COURT

**RANELAGH
GARDENS**

Ebury Bridge Road

Gatliff
Road

Ziani

Redes.
St.

Redburn St.

Christchurch

Tite Street

Cav. St.

National
Army
Museum

Royal
Hospital
Chelsea

Chelsea Manor Walk

Oakley

Gdns.

Alpha
Pl.

St.

Loo
Ave.

Royal Hospital Road

Dilke St.

Emb'km't
Gdns.

**La Tante
Claire**

Swan W. Dilke St.

Cheyne Walk

Chelsea Embankment

Base Map Copyright © Bartholomew 1994

CENTRAL LONDON : West End

Outer Circle
York Terr. E.
York Terr. W.
York Gr.
Royal Academy of Music
Regent's Park
Great Portland Street
Eust. Rd.
St Kanishka
Warren
Conway
Clifton Mews
Griffon
Whitfield
Madame Tussaud's
Marylebone Road
Park Crescent
Fitz. Sq.
Cleveland Street
Luxborough St.
Nottingham Pl.
Devonshire Pl.
Devonshire St.
Portland Place
Hallam Street
Great Portland Street
Carburton St.
Bolsover
Green.
Grt.
G.W.
Conway
Clipstone St.
Howland St.
Cleveland
Chit. St.
Notting. St.
Odin's
Paddington St.
Beaumont St.
Upper Wimpole Street
Weymouth Street
Weymouth Mews
Weymouth Street
Hanson St.
Clipstone St.
Telecom Tower
Le Muscadet
Dor. St.
Villandry Dining Room
Moxon St.
Cramer St.
Marylebone H.S.
Wimpole Street
New Cavendish Street
Duchess St.
Duchess Street
Mansfield St.
Broadcasting House
Langham
Foley Street
Riding Ho. St.
Ragam
La Gaulette
Middlesex Hospital
Manchester St.
Aybrook St.
Marylebone St.
Harley Place
Harley St.
Mandeville Pl.
All Souls Church
Rid.
Hse. St.
Efes Kebab House
Blandford St.
George Street
Stephen Bull Street
Buls. St.
Queen Anne Street
Chandos Pl.
Lang Pl.
L Titch. St.
Street
Wells
Robert Adam St.
Thayer
Bent. Ms.
Bentinck Street
Hinde
Marylebone La.
Wel.
Wi.
Wel.
Wimn. Pl.
Cavend.
Cav. Pl.
Mortimer
Lt. Port. St.
Eastcastle
Bake
Street
Port. Fitz. St.
Seymour Ms.
Duke's Ms.
Square
Wigmore
Hall
Wigmore Street
Sq.
Margaret Street
Nico Central
Square
Edwards Ms.
Pic. St.
Zoe
Stratford Pl.
Marylebone La.
Old Cav.
Henrietta Place
Vere St.
Holles St.
J. Princes
Gt. Castle St.
Oxford Str
Grahame's Seafare
Port. Ms. St.
Orchard St.
Barr. St.
James Street
Gilb. St.
Woods
O'Keefe's
Darling
Oxford Circus
Tent.
Han. Princes St.
Argll. St.
Gt. Marlborough S
Oxford Street
North Row
Balderton Street
Duke Street
Bond Street
Sth. Molton Street
New Bond Street
Hanover St.
Hanover Sq.
Gt. Marlborough St.
Regent Street
Carnaby Street
North Row
Prov. Ct.
Green St.
Gilb. St.
Weighouse St.
Saga
Maddox
Geo. St.
George Street
Condotti
W. Ms.
Grosvenor Yd.
Claridge's
Brock's Mews
Avery Row
Grosvenor Street
Conduit St.
Saville Row
Upper Brook St.
Le Gavroche
Culross St.
Brook St.
Square
Carlos Pl.
Mount Row
Grosvenor Hill
Kaspia
Bourdon Street
Bruton Street
Bruton La.
Clifford St.
Old Burlington St.
Cork St.
Café de Colombia
Shogun
Adams Row
Connaught
Mount St.
Berkeley Square
Bruton Pl.
Graft. St.
Old Bond Street
Albemarle Street
Royal Academy of Arts
Chez Nico at Ninety Park Lane
Mount Street
Farm Street
Hay's Ms.
Dover Street
Bice
Mount
Aldford St.
South Street
Greenhouse
Hay's Street
Charles Street
Chesterfield Hill
Charles Street
Berkeley St.
Wiltons
Park Lane
Dorchester
Deanery St.
Tilney St.
Mirabelle
Zen Central
Queen St.
Curzon Street
Clarg's
Bolton St.
Stratton St.
May Fair
Quaglino's
Les Saveurs
Al Hamra
Half Moon St.
Miyama
Green Park
Ritz Hotel
Le Caprice
St James's
London Hilton
Hertford Street
Shepherd St.
Pitts H.
Whitehorse St.
Langan's Brasserie
Suntory
HYDE PARK
Four Seasons Hotel
Old Park Lane
Brick Street
Down St.
Piccadilly
GREEN PARK
Serpentine Road

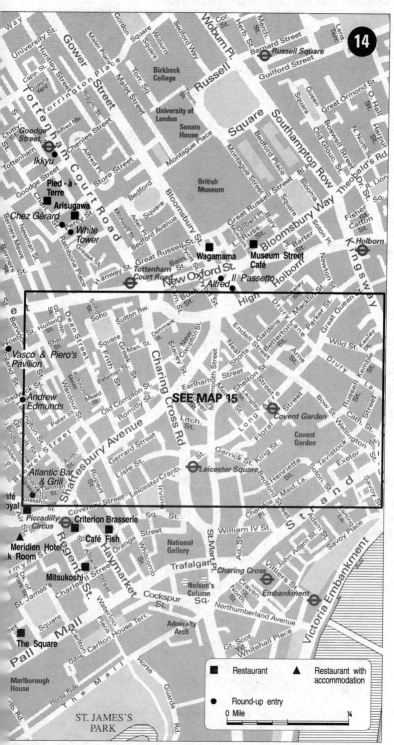

14

Way
University St.
Gower Street
Cor. St.
March. St.
Herb St.
Gordon Square
Woburn Pl.
Wobum Square
Bedford Way
Bernard Street
Russell Square
Guilford Street

Huntley Street
Torrington Place
Maler Place
Maler St.
Torr. Sq.
Birkbeck College
Russell
Queen Square
Great Ormond St.
S.O. Hall St.
Lans. Terr.

Capp. St.
Queens Yard
Tottenham Court Road
Rudum. St.
University of London
Square
Boswell Street
Old Glouc. St.
N. North St.
Harpur St.

Goodge Street
Alfred Me.
Chenies Street
Senate House
Montague Place
Southampton Row
Bl. Russ.
Theobald's Rd.
R. Lion St.
Fisher St.
Catton St.

Ikkyu
Goodge Street
Store Street
Bedford Square
British Museum
Montague Street
Bedford Place
Blooms.
Barter
Soton Pl.
Holborn

Pied-à-Terre
Arisugawa
Chez Gérard
White Tower
Bedford Avenue
Great Russell Street
Bury Place
Gilbert Pl.
Museum St.
Bloomsbury Way
Newton St.
Kingsway

Great Russell St.
Wagamama
Museum Street Café
Holborn

Hanway St.
Tottenham Court Road
New Oxford St.
Alfred
Il Passetto
High

Vasco & Piero's Pavilion
Soho Square
Denmark St.
New Compton St.
Shorts Gardens
Endell Street
Betterton St.
Macklin St.
Great Queen St.
Wild St.
Kemble St.

Andrew Edmunds
Earlham Street
Shelton St.
Langley Street
Drury
Russell St.
Bow St.
Cath. Street
Wellington

SEE MAP 15
Long Acre
Covent Garden
Covent Garden
Tavistock

Atlantic Bar & Grill
Shaftesbury Avenue
Gerrard Street
Lisle St.
Garrick St.
King St.
Leicester Square
Henrietta St.
Maid. La.
Exeter St.

Café Royal
Piccadilly Circus
Criterion Brasserie
Coventry Street
Leicester Square
Irving St.
Charing Cross
St. Adam's St.
Strand
Savoy

Café Fish
Regent St.
Haymarket
National Gallery
St. Martin's Pl.
William IV St.
John Adam St.
Savoy Place

Meridien Hotel
k Room
Charles Street
Orange Street
Trafalgar
Charing Cross
Villiers St.
Embankment
Victoria Embankment

Mitsukoshi
St. James's
Waterloo Place
Cockspur St.
Nelson's Column
Trafalgar Sq.
Craven St.
Northumberland Avenue

The Square
Pall Mall
Carlton House Terr.
Admiralty Arch
Horse Guards
Gt. Scot. Yd.
Whitehall Place

Marlborough House
The Mall
Horse Ride
ST. JAMES'S PARK

■ Restaurant		▲ Restaurant with accommodation
● Round-up entry		
0 Mile		¼

Base Map Copyright © Bartholomew 1994

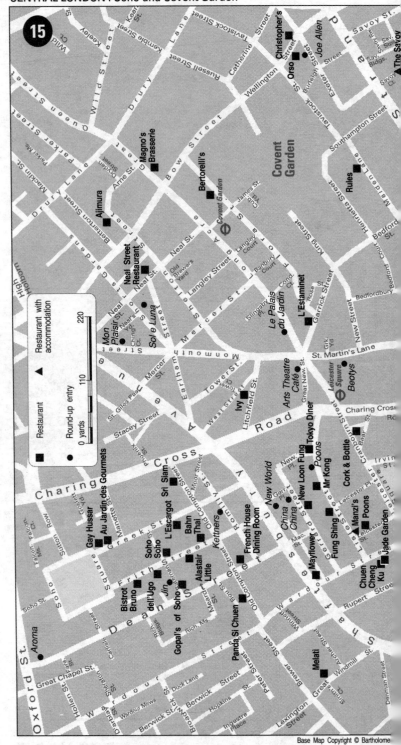

15

Christopher's

Joe Allen

Orso

The Savoy

Magno's Brasserie

Covent Garden

Bertorelli's

Ajimura

Rules

Neal Street Restaurant

Mon Plaisir

Sol e Luna

Le Palais du Jardin

L'Estaminet

Restaurant

Restaurant with accommodation

Round-up entry

0 yards   110   220

Arts Theatre Café

Beotys

Ivy

Charing Cross Road

Tokyo Diner

Gay Hussar

Au Jardin des Gourmets

Sri Siam

New World

China China

New Loon Fung

Poons

Mr Kong

Cork & Bottle

Poons

L'Escargot

Bahn Thai

Soho Soho

Alastair Little

French House Dining Room

Mayflower

Manzi's

Fung Shing

Bistrot Bruno

dell'Ugo

Jin

Gopal's of Soho

Panda Si Chuen

Chuen Cheng Ku

Jade Garden

Aroma

Melati

Base Map Copyright © Bartholome

To the Editor *The Good Food Guide*
FREEPOST, 2 Marylebone Road, London NW1 1YN

From my personal experience the following establishment should/should not be included in the *Guide*.

_____

_____

                                    Telephone_____

I had lunch/dinner/stayed there on _____ 19____

I would rate this establishment _____ out of five.

please continue overleaf

My meal for _____ people cost £ _____ *attach bill where possible*

☐ Please tick if you would like more report forms

All reporters to the *Guide* automatically become members of the Good Food Club. If you *do not* wish your name to be included in the list in next year's *Guide,* please tick the box below.

☐ I do not wish my name to be included in the Good Food Club list

I am not connected in any way with management or proprietors.
Name and address (BLOCK CAPITALS)

_____

_____

Signed _____

To the Editor *The Good Food Guide*
FREEPOST, 2 Marylebone Road, London NW1 1YN

From my personal experience the following establishment should/should not be included in the *Guide*.

_____

_____

Telephone_____

I had lunch/dinner/stayed there on _____ 19____

I would rate this establishment ____ out of five.

please continue overleaf

My meal for ___ people cost £ _____ *attach bill where possible*

☐ Please tick if you would like more report forms

All reporters to the *Guide* automatically become members of the Good Food Club. If you *do not* wish your name to be included in the list in next year's *Guide*, please tick the box below.

☐ I do not wish my name to be included in the Good Food Club list

I am not connected in any way with management or proprietors.
Name and address (BLOCK CAPITALS)

_____

_____

Signed _____

To the Editor *The Good Food Guide*
FREEPOST, 2 Marylebone Road, London NW1 1YN

From my personal experience the following establishment should/should not be included in the *Guide*.

_____

_____

Telephone_____

I had lunch/dinner/stayed there on _____ 19___

I would rate this establishment ___ out of five.

please continue overleaf

My meal for ____ people cost £ _____ *attach bill where possible*

☐ Please tick if you would like more report forms

All reporters to the *Guide* automatically become members of the Good Food Club. If you *do not* wish your name to be included in the list in next year's *Guide*, please tick the box below.

☐ I do not wish my name to be included in the Good Food Club list

I am not connected in any way with management or proprietors.
Name and address (BLOCK CAPITALS)

_____

_____

Signed _____

To the Editor *The Good Food Guide*
FREEPOST, 2 Marylebone Road, London NW1 1YN

From my personal experience the following establishment should/should not be included in the *Guide*.

Telephone_____

I had lunch/dinner/stayed there on _____ 19____

I would rate this establishment _____ out of five.

please continue overleaf

My meal for ＿＿ people cost £ ＿＿＿＿＿＿＿ *attach bill where possible*

☐ Please tick if you would like more report forms

All reporters to the *Guide* automatically become members of the Good Food Club. If you *do not* wish your name to be included in the list in next year's *Guide,* please tick the box below.

☐ I do not wish my name to be included in the Good Food Club list

I am not connected in any way with management or proprietors.
Name and address (BLOCK CAPITALS)

＿＿

＿＿

Signed ＿＿＿＿＿＿＿＿＿＿＿＿＿＿＿＿＿＿＿＿＿＿＿＿＿＿＿＿＿＿＿＿＿＿＿＿

To the Editor *The Good Food Guide*
FREEPOST, 2 Marylebone Road, London NW1 1YN

From my personal experience the following establishment should/should not be included in the *Guide*.

Telephone_____

I had lunch/dinner/stayed there on _____ 19____

I would rate this establishment _____ out of five.

please continue overleaf

My meal for _____ people cost £ _____ *attach bill where possible*

☐ Please tick if you would like more report forms

All reporters to the *Guide* automatically become members of the Good
Food Club. If you *do not* wish your name to be included in the list in
next year's *Guide*, please tick the box below.

☐ I do not wish my name to be included in the Good Food Club list

I am not connected in any way with management or proprietors.
Name and address (BLOCK CAPITALS)

_____

_____

Signed _____

To the Editor *The Good Food Guide*
FREEPOST, 2 Marylebone Road, London NW1 1YN

From my personal experience the following establishment should/should not be included in the *Guide*.

_____

_____

Telephone_____

I had lunch/dinner/stayed there on _____ 19____

I would rate this establishment _____ out of five.

please continue overleaf

My meal for _____ people cost £ _____ *attach bill where possible*

☐ Please tick if you would like more report forms

All reporters to the *Guide* automatically become members of the Good Food Club. If you *do not* wish your name to be included in the list in next year's *Guide,* please tick the box below.

☐ I do not wish my name to be included in the Good Food Club list

I am not connected in any way with management or proprietors.
Name and address (BLOCK CAPITALS)

_____

_____

Signed _____